ENCYCLOPEDIA OF CONTEMPORARY GERMAN CULTURE

ENCYCLOPEDIA OF CONTEMPORARY GERMAN CULTURE

Edited by
John Sandford

London and New York

First published 1999
by Routledge
11 New Fetter Lane, London EC4P 4EE

Simultaneously published in the USA and Canada
by Routledge
29 West 35th Street, New York, NY 10001

First published in paperback 2002

Routledge is an imprint of the Taylor & Francis Group

Typeset in Baskerville by Routledge
Printed and bound in Great Britain by TJ International Ltd,
Padstow, Cornwall

British Library Cataloguing in Publication Data
A catalogue record for this book is available from the British Library

Library of Congress Cataloging-in-Publication Data
Encyclopedia of contemporary German culture /
edited by John Sandford.
p.   cm.
Includes bibliographical references and index.
(alk. paper)
1. Germany—Intellectual life—20th century—Encyclopedias. 2. Austria—
Intellectual life—20th century—Encyclopedias. 3. Switzerland—
Intellectual life—20th century—Encyclopedias. 4. Germany—
Civilization—20th century—Encyclopedias. 5. Austria—Civilization—
20th century—Encyclopedias. 6. Switzerland—Civilization—20th
century—Encyclopedias. 7. Europe, German-speaking—Intellectual life—
20th century—Encyclopedias.
I. Sandford, John.
DD290.26.E53   1999   98-41725
943—dc21   CIP
ISBN 0–415–12448–4 (Hbk)
ISBN 0–415–26352–2 (Pbk)

Contents

Editorial team

General editor

John Sandford
University of Reading, UK

Consultant editors

Russell A. Berman
Stanford University, USA

Rob Burns
University of Warwick, UK

Patricia Herminghouse
University of Rochester, USA

Lothar Probst
University of Bremen, Germany

Dennis Tate
University of Bath, UK

List of contributors

Seán Allan
University of Reading

Martina S. Anderson
University of Minnesota

Petra M. Bagley
University of Central Lancashire

Stephen Barbour
Middlesex University

Peter Barker
University of Reading

Graham Bartram
University of Lancaster

Matthias Bauhuf
University of Sheffield

Shulamith Behr
Courtauld Institute of Art,
University of London

Henk de Berg
University of Sheffield

Russell A. Berman
Stanford University

Brenda L. Bethman
University of Massachusetts, Amherst

Annette Blühdorn
University of Bath

Ingolfur Blühdorn
University of Bath

Anne Blume
Cambridge

Elizabeth Boa
University of Nottingham

Martin Brady
London

Holger Briel
University of Surrey

Bettina Brockerhoff-Macdonald
Laurentian University

Stephen Brown
World Council of Churches, Geneva

Aminia Brueggemann
Old Dominion University

Rob Burns
University of Warwick

Anthony Bushell
University of Wales, Bangor

Michael Butler
University of Birmingham

Barton Byg
University of Massachusetts, Amherst

Godfrey Carr
University of Warwick

Jefferson S. Chase
University of Nottingham

Horst Claus
University of the West of England

Alex Cooke
Norwich, UK

Carol Anne Costabile-Heming
Southwest Missouri State University

Mike Dennis
University of Wolverhampton

Sabine von Dirke
University of Pittsburgh

Sydney Donald
University of Leeds

Beverley Driver Eddy
Dickinson College

Anke Finger
Texas A&M University

Sabine Fischer
University of Sheffield

Clare Flanagan
University of Bristol

Christopher H. Flockton
University of Surrey

Margrit Frölich
Herder-Institut,
Universität Leipzig

Mary Fulbrook
University College London

Mila Ganeva
University of Chicago

Jeffrey Garrett
Northwestern University Library

Michael E. Geisler
Middlebury College

Hans-Johann Glock
University of Reading

Axel Goodbody
University of Bath

Ernst Grabovszki
University of Vienna

Matthew T. Grant
MacTemps, Inc., Boston

Hans-Joachim Hahn
Oxford Brookes University

Brigid Haines
University of Wales, Swansea

Randall Halle
University of Rochester

Jennifer Ham
University of Wisconsin, Green Bay

Michael Hänel
Germany

Beatrice Harper
South Bank University, London

Glyn Hatherall
formerly Thames Valley University, UK

Milan L. Hauner
Universität Leipzig

Richard A. Hawkins
University of Wolverhampton

Michael R. Hayse
The Richard Stockton College of New Jersey

Joel S.A. Hayward
Massey University, New Zealand

David Head
University of Northumbria at Newcastle

Georg Hellmayr
University of Vienna

Astrid Herhoffer
Staffordshire University

Patricia Herminghouse
University of Rochester

Robin B. Hodess
Carnegie Council on Ethics and International
Affairs, USA

Burkard Hornung
Munich

Helen Hughes
University of Surrey

Noah Isenberg
Wesleyan University

Jutta Ittner
Case Western Reserve University

Graham Jackman
University of Reading

Helen Jones
University of Central Lancashire

Rolf Jucker
University of Wales, Swansea

James Keller
St John's University, New York City

Sylvia Klötzer
Zentrum für Zeithistorische Forschung, Potsdam

Karl Koch
South Bank University

Daniel Koep
Courtauld Institute of Art,
University of London

Eva Kolinsky
Keele University

Frederic M. Kopp
Columbia College, Chicago

Karen Ruoff Kramer
Stanford University Program, Berlin

Martin Kudlek
Cologne

Joanne Leal
Birkbeck College,
University of London

David D. Lee
UCLA and University of Groningen

Lisa Yun Lee
Duke University

Judith Leeb
University of Chicago

Jonathan Legg
University of Southampton

Mark Lindsay
University of Western Australia

Ute Lischke-McNab
University of Toronto

Jonathan Long
University of Durham

Derek McCulloch
University of Surrey

Moray McGowan
University of Sheffield

Jonathan McHaffie
University of Sheffield

Peter M. McIsaac
Tufts University

Joanna McKay
University of Central Lancashire

Marianna McKim
Yale University Library

Reinhild Steingröver McRae
State University of New York, Buffalo

Tara Magdalinski
Sunshine Coast University College

Harold Marcuse
University of California, Santa Barbara

Charles W. Martin
Droitwich, UK

Graham Martin
University of Strathclyde

Charlotte Melin
University of Minnesota

Gabriele Metzler
Seminar für Zeitgeschichte, Tübingen

Kerstin Mey
Duncan of Jordanstone College, University of Dundee

Kitty Millet
California State University, Long Beach

Günter Minnerup
University of Birmingham

Gordon R. Mork
Purdue University

Magda Mueller
California State University, Chico

Adrian Murdoch
UK

Brian Murdoch
University of Stirling

Harriet Murphy
University of Warwick

Gerald Newton
University of Sheffield

Kalliopi Nikolopoulou
University of Rochester

Thomas Nolden
Wellesley College

Cecilia Novero
Vassar College, New York

Rachel Palfreyman
University of Nottingham

Stuart Parkes
University of Sunderland

Douglas Peifer
University of North Carolina, Chapel Hill

Malcolm Pender
University of Strathclyde

Berthold Pesch
Stephan Braunfels Architekten, Berlin

Anthony Phelan
University of Warwick

Alison Phipps
University of Glasgow

John Preston
University of Reading

Angharad Price
University of Wales, Swansea

Lothar Probst
University of Bremen

Peter Prochnik
Royal Holloway College,
University of London

Monika Prützel-Thomas
University of the West of England

Mark W. Rectanus
Iowa State University

J.H. Reid
University of Nottingham

Rondall R. Rice
United States Air Force Academy

Michael Richardson
Ithaca College

David Rock
University of Keele

Birgit Röder
University of Reading

Christian Rogowski
Amherst College

Eva Rueschmann
Hampshire College

Richard J. Rundell
New Mexico State University

John B. Rutledge
Davis Library,
University of North Carolina, Chapel Hill

John Sandford
University of Reading

Maggie Sargeant
University of Stirling

Boria Sax
Mercy College, USA

Ines Schlenker
King's College,
University of London

Sabine Schmidt
Rhodes College

Christiane Schönfeld
University of Wales, Lampeter

Hinrich C. Seeba
University of California, Berkeley

Gabriela Steinke
University of Wolverhampton

Janet Stewart
University of Aberdeen

Ulf Strohmayer
University of Wales, Lampeter

Arrigo Subiotto
University of Birmingham

Stuart Taberner
University of Bristol

Dennis Tate
University of Bath

Victor E. Taylor
York College of Pennsylvania

Chris Thornhill
King's College London,
University of London

Penny J. Underwood
University of Tennessee

Margaret Vallance
Imperial College,
University of London

Gert Vonhoff
Institut für Deutsche Philologie II,
Universität Münster

Julia H. Wagner
Cornell University

Ian Wallace
University of Bath

Jenifer K. Ward
Gustavus Adolphus College

Roderick H. Watt
University of Glasgow

Jonathan West
University of Newcastle upon Tyne

Brett R. Wheeler
University of California, Berkeley

John J. White
King's College London,
University of London

John Wieczorek
University of Reading

Wilfried van der Will
University of Birmingham

James Young
University of Wisconsin

Christopher Young
Pembroke College, Cambridge

Introduction

The *Encyclopedia of Contemporary German Culture* reflects the broadening of perspectives and approaches in German Studies that has occurred in the English-speaking world in recent years. It is also a response to the growing interdisciplinarity of academic work, and the consequent needs of teachers and students in other fields who require information and orientation in the area of contemporary German culture. It has thus been written as a tool that can be used not only by those who understand German, but also by those who approach the language and its contexts from outside.

Both 'German' and 'culture' are understood here in the broadest sense: the intention has not been to intervene in any programmatic way in the perennial debates about the applicability of those terms, but simply to provide readers with the widest possible palette of information. As far as 'German' is concerned, a pragmatic approach has been taken in drawing up the list of entries. German Studies scholarship and syllabuses have long reflected a consensus that the primary object of their attention is Germany itself, with the main focus, as far as the post-war decades through to 1990 are concerned, being West Germany. Although this consensus has certainly informed the overall make-up of this encyclopedia, the intention from the outset has also been to embrace the German-speaking world as a whole. Thus, the GDR, Austria and German-speaking Switzerland are all given substantial coverage, while the fact that there are further German-speaking communities outside these territories, as well as minority groups within them, has not been overlooked.

'Culture' is understood here in both its traditional sense and in the broader senses in which it is used in contemporary Cultural Studies. Here too it is recognized that taxonomic debates are rife and the boundaries of the field of enquiry singularly ill-defined. The aim in this encyclopedia has been essentially twofold: to give due coverage to areas of 'high' or 'canonical' culture, and at the same time to extend the purview to 'popular' culture and other manifestations of symbolic practice and production that give identity to the German-speaking peoples. Comprehensiveness rather than caution has been a guiding principle, and, in order to provide essential contextual information, topics have therefore been included (from, for instance, the political or economic spheres) that exceed even the more generous normal definitions of 'culture'.

'Contemporary', the third key term in the title, here means 'post-1945', with particular weighting on more recent decades. Clearly, there are continuities that do not respect the convenient watershed of the 'Year Zero', and reference is accordingly made to the pre-war period where this is necessary to an understanding of the contemporary topics under discussion.

The decisions that have been made in the attempt to do justice to the implications of the terms 'contemporary', 'German', and 'culture' will be particularly apparent from the thematic entry list on pp. xvii–xxx. The question of the extent to which literary topics should be covered in a work of this kind was recognized from the outset as especially problematic. Literature has always played the central role in all the modern language disciplines (and, indeed, even in new syllabuses that proclaim a 'Cultural Studies' approach it still often continues to do so). The fact that there are therefore more books in English on this aspect of German Studies than on any other might provide an argument for downplaying (or even largely omitting) the literary component in an encyclopedia that seeks to broaden the subject's horizons. However, this would be to give an extraordinarily distorted view of German culture, and represent a disservice to that large number of readers who will legitimately approach the encyclopedia precisely because they expect information on literary topics. Literature, using language as its medium, is, after all, the form of cultural expression that links the German-speaking countries more than any other, and at the same time the one whose wider cultural resonances have been most widely appreciated and explored. It was therefore accepted that literary entries would be more numerous than any other category, and they have been divided into two broad fields: on the one hand writers (including novelists, dramatists and poets), and on the other such manifestations of the literary world as movements, genres, journals, theory and criticism. The latter group includes several longer entries; as far as the writers are concerned, some longer essays have also been provided on those of commonly acknowledged status, but the majority of entries in this group have been kept short, the aim being to provide the bare minimum of essential biographical details and a few lines characterizing the work and significance of the individual concerned. There are any number of excellent sources that can then be followed up by readers seeking more detailed information on particular writers. (Those who read German could, for instance, consult the regularly updated loose-leaf *Kritisches Lexikon zur deutschsprachigen Gegenwartsliteratur* [*KLG*, edited by H.L. Arnold [Munich 1978 *et seq.*: Edition Text & Kritik]; D.-R. Moser's *Neues Handbuch der deutschsprachigen Gegenwartsliteratur seit 1945* [Munich 1992: Nymphenburger Verlag]; or Manfred Brauneck's concise *Autorenlexikon deutschsprachiger Literatur des 20. Jahrhunderts* [5th edition, Reinbek 1995: Rowohlt]. Reference sources in English include *The Oxford Companion to German Literature*, by Mary Garland and Henry Garland [3rd edition, Oxford 1997: OUP], and *A Companion to Twentieth-Century German Literature*, by Raymond Furness and Malcolm Humble [London 1991: Routledge].)

A total of 161 scholars have contributed to the *Encyclopedia of Contemporary German Culture*, each of them a specialist in the field concerned. Between them, they have written more than 1,100 entries, ranging in size from thumbnail sketches of a hundred words or so to overview essays of around two thousand words. Many of the former are biographical entries, and these provide the full date of birth and place of birth – and, where appropriate, date and place of death – of the person in question. Cross-referencing has been used extensively, to enable readers to follow up links and contexts that may not always be self-evident, and also in order to obviate as far as possible overlap and repetition. Other navigational tools are the index and the list of headwords grouped by area on pp. xvii–xx. Readers are urged to use the former if they do not find what they are looking for under a particular headword, and to ensure that they have exhausted the references to a particular topic, while the latter is designed to help those who wish to look extensively at a particular field of study to see just what is on offer. Suggestions for further reading are attached to many of the entries – especially the longer ones – and many of these are accompanied by a brief note indicating their relevance where this may not be obvious from the title. Some of the biographical entries include brief bibliographies, and references have been made, where appropriate, to sources in other media (recordings, web sites). As far as possible, preference has been given in the suggestions for further reading to works in English.

I would like to thank the many people who have helped me over the four years that this project has been underway. They are far too numerous for all to be mentioned by name, but I owe a particular debt of gratitude to my five Editorial Consultants – Russell Berman, Rob Burns, Patricia Herminghouse, Lothar Probst and Dennis Tate – not only for the entries that they themselves have written and their ready responses to my numerous queries, but more particularly for their invaluable advice and assistance in the earlier stages when the headword lists were being drawn up and matched with the names of potential contributors, and again in the final stages when decisions were made on as-yet uncommissioned entries. Thanks for similar assistance are also due to my colleagues at the University of Reading – not least Seán Allan, Peter Barker, Graham Jackman, Ian Roe and John

Wieczorek. Many contributors were located by messages posted on the Internet, and I am especially grateful to the organizers of the 'Women in German' and 'H-German' discussion lists for enabling this project to be brought to the attention of their subscribers. Clearly, this work would never have been written without its many contributors: I am indebted to them all. Some took on especially large numbers of entries and/or offered invaluable comments and suggestions about appropriate coverage and other potential contributors in their fields of expertise: they include in particular Shulamith Behr, Martin Brady and Helen Hughes, Stephen Brown, Beatrice Harper, Georg Hellmayr, Martin Kudlek, Derek McCulloch and John B.

Rutledge. The final decision on the choice and length of entries was my own, and I am responsible for omissions, oddities, and oversights.

Finally, thanks are due to my editors and other staff at Routledge for their patience and practical assistance: not least, in the final stages, to Tarquin Acevedo, Denise Rea and Ben Swift; to Samantha Parkinson and Lia Zografou for their involvement in the long haul in the middle; and, from beginning to end, to Fiona Cairns, who conceived the series of which this encyclopedia forms a part.

JOHN SANDFORD

How to use this book

Structure

The *Encyclopedia* contains more than a thousand entries, individually attributed and arranged in alphabetical order. A thematic contents list on pp. xvii–xxx helps readers with a particular interest, e.g. in music or the visual arts, to find the entries relevant to them.

Acronyms have been used in entry headwords, except where the full version is more popularly recognizable. Biographical entries provide dates and places of birth (b.), and death (d.) if appropriate, followed by the entrant's profession. Significant cross-references, leading to other relevant articles, are indicated in bold type at their first appearance in an entry. 'See also' references at the end of entries also lead to related topics.

Please note that where entry names include a vowel with an umlaut, they are alphabetized as though the umlauted letter was: ae, oe, ue, e.g. Karl Böhm appears before Bärbel Bohley. The 'German double-"s"' (ß) has been used throughout in accordance with the traditional spelling rules.

Names including 'von' have been entered under their second element: thus Herbert von Karajan appears under 'Karajan'.

The index will also point the reader to relevant articles, and includes listings under alternative names.

Bibliographic items

Within the text bibliographic items are referred to as follows: if a book has been translated into English and published then the title of the English translation appears first with the original German title in parentheses afterwards. If the book has not been translated into English then the German title appears first with a literal translation of the German words into English in parentheses afterwards. Dates of publication refer to the original version. A similar principle applies to film releases.

In the bibliography following the article published translations are provided where possible; no literal translations are given.

Thematic entry list

Architecture

architecture
Atelier 5
Auer & Weber
Bartning, Otto
Behnisch, Günther
Berlin building boom
Bienefeld, Heinz
Bill, Max
Böhm, Dominikus
Böhm, Gottfried
Coop Himmelblau
Czech, Hermann
Diener & Diener
Döllgast, Hans
Döring, Wolfgang
Domenig, Günther
Eiermann, Egon
Fehling & Gogel
Gisel, Ernst
gmp
Gropius, Walter
Haesler, Otto
Haller, Fritz
Henselmann, Hermann
Herzog & de Meuron
Herzog, Thomas
Hilmer & Sattler
Hollein, Hans
Holzbauer, Wilhelm
HPP
IBA
Kleihues, Josef Paul
Kollhoff, Hans
Krier, Rob
Kulka, Peter

Luckhardt, Hans and Wassili
May, Ernst
Mies van der Rohe, Ludwig
Otto, Frei
Peichl, Gustav
Rainer, Roland
reconstruction
Reichlin/Reinhart
Scharoun, Hans
Schattner, Karljosef
Schürmann, Joachim
Schultes, Axel
Schwarz, Rudolf
Steffann, Emil
Steidle, Otto
Taut, Max
Thut, Doris
town planning
Ungers, Oswald Mathias

Austria

(for Austrian writers and other cultural figures see
other relevant sections)
Arbeiterzeitung
Bacher, Gerd
cultural policy and institutions: Austria
Dichand, Hans
education system: Austria
film: Austria
FPÖ
German language: Austria
Grazer Gruppe
Haider, Jörg
Kleine Zeitung
Kreisky, Bruno
Kurier
Lauda, Niki

Food and drink

food
wine

History

Auschwitz
Berlin
Berlin Wall
Bitburg
Broszat, Martin
currency reform
Dahrendorf, Ralf
denazification
Economic Miracle
Eichmann, (Karl) Adolf
Engelberg, Ernst
European Union
Fest, Joachim
Fischer, Fritz
German Question
'Germany'
Hallstein Doctrine
Hauptstadtfrage
Hillgruber, Andreas
Historikerstreit
historiography
history teaching
Holocaust
Irving, David
Kamnitzer, Heinz
Kocka, Jürgen
memorials
Mitteleuropa
Mommsen, Hans
Nolte, Ernst
occupation
Oder-Neisse line
Potsdam Agreement
re-education
street names
Stunde Null
Stürmer, Michael
Tendenzwende
Trümmerfrauen
Vergangenheitsbewältigung
Wiesenthal, Simon

Intellectual life

Adorno, Theodor W.
Anders, Günther

Arendt, Hannah
Aufklärung
Benjamin, Walter
Bloch, Ernst
Blumenberg, Hans
Buhr, Manfred
Critical Theory
cultural studies
Dahrendorf, Ralf
Elias, Norbert
existentialism
Feyerabend, Paul
Frankfurt School
Fromm, Erich
Gadamer, Hans-Georg
Gehlen, Arnold
Habermas, Jürgen
Heidegger, Martin
Honneth, Axel
Horkheimer, Max
Husserl, Edmund
intellectuals
Jaspers, Karl
Jungk, Robert
Löwith, Karl
Lorenz, Konrad
Lübbe, Hermann
Luhmann, Niklas
Maaz, Hans-Joachim
Marcuse, Herbert
Marcuse, Ludwig
Marxism
Mitscherlich, Alexander
Mitscherlich (-Nielson), Margarete
Paradigmawechsel
philosophy
Popper, Karl Raimund
psychology
Schmidt, Siegfried J.
Sloterdijk, Peter
Weizsäcker, Carl-Friedrich von
Wittgenstein, Ludwig

Language and national identity

Abgrenzung
Abwicklung
asylum, political
Ausländer
Berlin Wall

Music

Performing Arts

Political life: GDR

Schumacher, Emil
sculpture
Sitte, Willi
Staeck, Klaus
Steinert, Otto
Trockel, Rosemarie
Tübke, Werner
Uecker, Günther
visual arts: Austria
visual arts: Switzerland
Vostell, Wolf
Winter, Fritz
Womacka, Walter
Wotruba, Fritz
Zero Group

Writers

Achternbusch, Herbert
Aichinger, Ilse
Amery, Carl
Améry, Jean
Andersch, Alfred
Anderson, Sascha
Andres, Stefan
Artmann, Hans Carl
Ausländer, Rose
Ayim, May
Bachmann, Ingeborg
Becher, Johannes R.
Becker, Jürgen
Becker, Jurek
Behrens, Katja
Benn, Gottfried
Bense, Max
Bergengruen, Werner
Berkéwicz, Ulla
Bernhard, Thomas
Bichsel, Peter
Bieler, Manfred
Bienek, Horst
Biermann, Wolf
Biondi, Franco
Bobrowski, Johannes
Böll, Heinrich
Borchers, Elisabeth
Borchert, Wolfgang
Born, Nicolas
Brasch, Thomas
Braun, Volker

Brechbühl, Beat
Brecht, Bertolt
Brězan, Jurij
Brinkmann, Rolf Dieter
Broch, Hermann
Brussig, Thomas
Bruyn, Günter de
Buch, Hans Christoph
Burmeister, Brigitte
Busta, Christine
Canetti, Elias
Celan, Paul
Chotjewitz, Peter O.
Czechowski, Heinz
Delius, Friedrich Christian
Demski, Eva
Döblin, Alfred
Doderer, Heimito von
Domin, Hilde
Dorst, Tankred
Drewitz, Ingeborg
Duden, Anne
Dürrenmatt, Friedrich
Eich, Günter
Elsner, Gisela
Endler, Adolf
Engelmann, Bernt
Enzensberger, Hans Magnus
Erb, Elke
Erlenberger, Maria
Fassbinder, Rainer Werner
Fels, Ludwig
Feuchtwanger, Lion
Fichte, Hubert
Fleißer, Marieluise
Franke, Manfred
Fried, Erich
Fries, Fritz Rudolf
Frisch, Max
Frischmuth, Barbara
Fritz, Marianne
Fuchs, Jürgen
Fühmann, Franz
Fussenegger, Gertrud
Gaiser, Gerd
Goes, Albrecht
Gomringer, Eugen
Grass, Günter
Gregor-Dellin, Martin

Abgrenzung

This key term – translated variously as 'separation', 'differentiation' or 'demarcation', implying above all 'drawing a clear boundary' – was used by the GDR from 1970 onwards to assert its social, political and cultural differences from the FRG. It was designed to counter any impression that the arrival of an SPD-led government in Bonn and improvements in East–West relations might lead to an eventual merger of the two German states. Although socialism and capitalism might be able to coexist, they remained – in a phrase repeated by Erich **Honecker** – as irreconcilable as 'fire and water'.

See also: German Question; *Ostpolitik*

JOHN SANDFORD

Abitur

This 'leaving certificate' (from the Latin '*abire*', to depart) is granted to pupils on passing an examination at the end of their thirteenth school-year, nine of which must be at the *Gymnasium*. Introduced in Prussia in 1788, the *Abitur* soon became the entry qualification for university and was associated, until 1919, with special privileges (*Berechtigungswesen*), primarily in military service. The *Abitur* is also known as *Reifeprüfung*, indicating that its holder has reached *Hochschulreife*, i.e. a particular level of intellectual maturity.

During the 1960s, rapid expansion in secondary education overtook higher education development, so that the *Abitur* no longer guarantees access to every university course, and special aptitude tests or high grades may be demanded by individual universities for specific subjects such as medicine or dentistry. A Central Admissions Board at Dortmund (*Zentralstelle zur Vergabe von Studienplätzen, ZVS*) was introduced in 1972 to regulate university entrance procedures. By the mid-1960s some 4 to 7 percent of an age group took the *Abitur*, by 1989 this had risen to 24 percent and since unification this figure has increased to slightly over 30 percent. Shortage of university places in some subjects and diminished career prospects for academics, together with a growing demand for *Abitur* candidates in business and management, have resulted in a decline in university entrants from 90 percent of *Abitur* holders in the early 1970s to just over 60 percent by the late 1980s.

Since the 1972 reform, modified further in 1988, the nature of the *Abitur* has changed markedly: whilst still upholding the traditional German concept of general education, it seeks to promote greater flexibility and increased individual choice in curricula studies, allowing for more specialization. Final classification is arrived at via a combination of course-work and examination, with practical projects in subjects such as physical education, music and fine art. The actual examination concentrates on four subjects, one of which must be German, mathematics or a foreign language. One of these four subjects is examined orally. The qualification itself is based on single weighting for twenty-two basic courses, double weighting for six specialized courses of the student's choice, and quadruple weighting for the four subjects examined. Assessment is on a points scale, with at least 280 points out of a possible 840 needed for a pass. As a result of the Republic's federal structure, variations in assessment occur between individual *Länder*. This is taken into account by awarding candidates from different states special 'malus' or 'bonus' points. Since unification, the *Abitur* awarded in the former GDR has been adjusted to the requirements of the FRG.

The Austrian equivalent of the *Abitur* is the *Matura* and in Switzerland the *Maturität*, both words deriving from the Latin '*maturus*'. In both countries this qualification can be gained after twelve years of schooling. All three qualifications are recognized within the member countries of the European Union, just as equivalent diplomas are accepted in the FRG, provided the necessary standard of German is achieved.

Further reading

Neather, E.J. (1993) 'The Abitur Examination', *Language Learning Journal* 70, 4: 19–21.

HANS J. HAHN

ABM

The *Arbeitsbeschaffungsmaßnahmen* (ABM) job creation scheme was established as an instrument of 'active' labour market policy by the Work Promotion Law of 1969 and by subsequent legal revisions, notably in 1986. Grants and subsidies can be provided for employment creation in situations where, for reasons of structural change, regional decline or the business cycle, substantial unemployment would otherwise occur. Difficult-to-place workers may also benefit. Normally, local authorities bear the cost of ABM, although in East Germany, where the scheme has played a vital role in the restructuring of the economy after **unification**, the Federal Labour Office pays. The young and long-term unemployed can benefit from the wage subsidies and rebates of social insurance and corporation tax paid to employers as an incentive to recruit these categories of worker.

CHRISTOPHER H. FLOCKTON

abortion law

Since June 1995 abortion in the FRG has been ruled by a law that allows the termination of a pregnancy within the first twelve weeks (the so-called *Fristenlösung*), but requires a previous consultation. The law (paragraphs 218–19b of the criminal code) somewhat ambiguously states that abortion within this time span is 'exempt from punishment', though it remains 'illegal'. As a result, health care benefits (with certain exceptions) are no longer provided. After the obligatory consultation, the decision is left to the woman. However, since the setting-up of the lawful health centres providing counselling is the responsibility of each individual **Land**, the actual availability of these services differs from one region to another (with more restricted services in Bavaria and Baden-Württemberg).

After 1945, abortion in West Germany was illegal and generally punished with a prison sentence of up to five years (for the woman) and up to ten years (for the person performing the abortion). It was only in 1972 that a legal reform of abortion no longer made it a punishable offence. Preceded by a vehement public controversy, a law permitting an abortion performed by a medical doctor during the first three months of pregnancy (and after a prior consultation) became effective on 18 June 1974. However, due to the petition of two *Länder*, Bavaria and Baden-Württemberg, the Federal Constitutional Court dismissed the law in a verdict on 25 February 1975, arguing that it conflicted with the right to life of the unborn. A revised version took effect on 18 May 1976, legalizing abortion only on the basis of medical, eugenic, ethical or social grounds: (1) when the life of the pregnant woman was in jeopardy; (2) in case of damage to the child's health; (3) if the pregnancy was the result of a rape; or (4) in case of substantial social or economic straits. In order to qualify for a legal abortion, the case had to be approved by a health centre or another doctor at least three days before it was performed. No doctor or medical staff could be required to perform an abortion.

In East Germany, abortion during the first three months of pregnancy was legalized in 1972. Unlike in West Germany, there was no mandatory counselling. The differences of the abortion laws in East and West Germany made it necessary after unification for a new legal basis to be developed. In June 1992 the parliament opted for a concept of legal abortion during the first three months of pregnancy combined with a mandatory consultation. As a result of a petition by **CDU/CSU** politicians, however, the Federal Constitutional Court dismissed the concept before it became law.

In Austria, abortion is legal during the first three months of pregnancy, whereas in Switzerland, abortion is generally a punishable offence except in cases of a proven medical condition.

Further reading

Staupe, G. and Vieth, L. (eds) (1996) *Unter anderen Umständen*, Dortmund: Ebersbach (on the history of abortion in Germany).

MARGRIT FRÖLICH

Abwicklung

Originally a term used in the economic field to denote the 'winding-up' or liquidation of a company, it was applied from 1990 to describe the process of restructuring GDR companies and other institutions after **unification**. This process in the economic field was presided over by the **Treuhand**, which had been given the task in the Unification Treaty of preparing East German firms for privatization. The term came to be used as one of abuse, especially in the eastern *Länder*, because in many cases restructuring meant either the complete closure of a company or institution or a radical reduction in the workforce.

PETER BARKER

academies

Evolving from Plato's academic grove, where Athenian philosophers would meet to discuss their ideas, the academy as a concept or institution has undergone several changes during its long history. During the Enlightenment academies became important institutions for scholarly tuition, specializing in one or two subjects. With the development

of the Humboldtian university concept, they became marginalized as research institutions and meeting places for leading academics.

As a consequence of Germany's particularist history, a great number of academies developed, usually situated in the capital cities of the more progressive German states. Today such academies can be divided into bodies for the promotion of **science** or scholarship in general, for the cultivation of German language and literature, and for the arts. Academies for specific disciplines such as architecture or medicine and others which pursue a broader political, ethical or religious interest also exist.

Historically the most prestigious academy was the Berlin Academy of Science, founded in 1700 as the Preußische Akademie der Wissenschaft, under the influence of the philosopher G.W. Leibniz. In 1946, in accordance with Soviet principles, it was reformed into an association of scholars and undertook the role of co-ordinating GDR research programmes, in association with some fifty-five institutions and laboratories, chiefly dedicated to the promotion of the natural sciences but also charged with specific projects in industry. By the mid-1980s almost half of the Academy's work was geared towards such projects. In ideological terms the Academy was integrated into the GDR's scientific and socialist revolution, working in close association with the **SED** in its anticipation of new research demands, in offering advice on specific research programmes, and in co-ordinating research nationwide. The Akademie der Wissenschaften der DDR, its title after 1972, acquired an international reputation, particularly as far as basic research was concerned. The increasing isolation of the GDR after 1961 and a growing emphasis on specific government-generated projects in the 1980s caused the Academy to lose some of its prestige. With German unification it became the main victim of *Abwicklung*, a controversial programme to disestablish most East German non-university institutes and to attempt their integration into other research organizations and universities. By December 1992, this policy affected some 2,000 academics who were either transferred to universities, assigned to the *Max-Planck-Gesellschaft* or lost their jobs.

The Berlin-Brandenburg Akademie der Künste (Academy of Arts) celebrated its 300th anniversary in 1996. Under the presidency of Walter **Jens**, it is one of Germany's most renowned academies for the fine arts and literature, dedicated to the free expression of ideas. It has become an important link in reconciling the two former Germanys.

Scholarly academies in the FRG have followed a more traditional role than those of the GDR, serving as learned associations, independent of government policy, but charged with the promotion of basic and interdisciplinary research. Most of these academies divide into different specialisms, concentrating on research in science, language and literature, philosophy, geography, the fine arts, architecture and music. In general, each has a membership of approximately thirty chiefly distinguished scholars, artists or writers who elect their president from amongst their number. Most of their findings appear in special yearbooks. Occasionally, and usually at the behest of the membership, special research projects are sponsored, but most of these function outside the scope of the academy. This type of academy is usually financed by the individual **Land** government, with central government funding only in exceptional circumstances.

Since 1945 the term *Akademie* has also been used to define other institutions which seek to influence public opinion and government policy through the organization of conferences, political seminars and briefings. The two main churches, in particular, have sought to encourage dialogue, partly in order to foster the debate on Germany's **Vergangenheitsbewältigung**, but also as a forum for the discussion of current ethical, social and religious themes (see **churches and religion**). The Protestant church founded its first academy in Bad Boll, followed by Tutzing and sixteen other towns. These *Evangelische Akademien*, open to everyone, are financed by the individual *Landeskirche* and aim to provide a third place, outside of work and home, for political, educational and religious groups. Following the Second Vatican Council, the Catholic church also established academies designed to bridge the gulf between catholic dogma and contemporary intellectual, cultural and economic issues. With financial control and the nomination of members in the hands of individual episcopacies, their influence and scope seem more limited.

The various political parties have also organized their own academies as centres for dialogue and forums for public relations. The Politische Akademie Eichholz is run by the Konrad Adenauer Foundation (**CDU**), while the Theodor-Heuß-Akademie comes under the Friedrich Naumann Foundation (**F.D.P.**). The Akademie für politische Bildung (political education) in Tutzing is not associated with an individual political party, but caters for all those in regular contact with politics on a non-partisan level.

Yet another form of academy is related to the concept of life-long learning, focusing in particular on specific professions such as medicine, education, and executive management. The Akademie der Arbeit (labour) in Frankfurt am Main is financed jointly by the DGB and by the state of Hesse; it trains trade-unionists, civil servants and public sector employees in the legal and socio-political fields, whilst the Akademie für Führungskräfte der Wirtschaft (economic management) is specifically geared towards training executives in new management techniques. Some very specialized academies are found within the higher education sector, e.g. the Städtische Akademie für Tonkunst (music) in Darmstadt and the academies for fine arts in Nürnberg, Munich and Hamburg. Academies of this type also existed in the GDR, some of which are still in existence, e.g. the famous Bergakademie Freiberg (mining academy).

Further reading

Langenbucher, W.R. *et al.* (1988) *Handbuch zur deutsch-deutschen Wirklichkeit Bundesrepublik Deutschland/Deutsche Demokratische Republik im Kulturvergleich*, Stuttgart: Metzler, pp. 16–19 (a good general introduction, but not covering developments since unification).

HANS J. HAHN

Achternbusch, Herbert

b. 23 November 1938, Munich

Filmmaker, writer and artist

A maverick writer and filmmaker in the tradition of Karl **Valentin**, Achternbusch's anarchic novels, plays and films have found a small but devoted following in his native Bavaria and provoked considerable political controversy. From his earliest poems and prose texts, written following his move to Munich in 1962, his work has been dominated by three related themes: a volatile love–hate relationship with Bavaria, dreams of escape to far-off shores, and an almost narcissistic obsession with his own life history, resulting in plays such as *Mein Herbert* (My Herbert) (1982), about his mother, and *Weg* (Away) (1985), about his grandmother. The titles of his early films, *Bye-Bye Bavaria* (*Servus Bayern*, 1977) and *The Comanche* (*Der Komantsche*, 1979), reflect these themes. Before being encouraged by Werner **Herzog** to take up filmmaking he published his most ambitious prose work, *Die Alexanderschlacht* (The Battle of Alexander) (1971), a dense collage of memories, fantasies and daydreams. Part fictionalized autobiography and part experimental novel, containing extensive passages in Bavarian dialect, this seminal text provided material for his films (from 1974) and plays (from 1978).

Achternbusch has consistently stylized himself as a hybrid of the anarchic Bavarian comedian and filmmaker Karl Valentin and an eastern guru. An outspoken critic of his native country, it was in his performance as a spurned Bavarian messiah in his 1982 film *Das Gespenst* (The Ghost) that he provoked the most hostile reactions from both church and state. The film was temporarily banned, and Minister of the Interior Friedrich Zimmermann spoke out vehemently against it. The film became a recognized symbol for a turning-point in cultural policy in the FRG and forced its director to produce his subsequent films on a shoe-string budget.

Given his enormous productivity – over thirty volumes of prose, film scripts, plays and poems, twenty-five films, and innumerable paintings and drawings – individual works have been of variable quality, and critics have been cleanly divided into ardent supporters and vociferous detractors. Out-side Bavaria his films have not received the acclaim they deserve due to their linguistic demands, occasional opacity and idiosyncratic humour. At their best – in the film *The Last Hole* (*Das letzte Loch*) (1981), *The Idiot* (*Der Depp*) (1982) and the silent *I Know the Way to the Hofbräuhaus* (1991), as well as the prose collections, *Das Haus am Nil* (The House on the Nile) (1981), and 1982, *Die Olympiasiegerin* (The Olympic Champion) (1982) – they are lyrical, surreal and politically engaged, shot through with a uniquely Bavarian brand of nonsense humour and melancholic defiance summed up in his motto '*Du hast keine Chance, aber nutze sie*' ('you've no prospects, so make the most of them').

See also: New German Cinema

Further reading

Drews, J. (ed.) (1982) *Herbert Achternbusch*, Frankfurt am Main: Suhrkamp (a substantial volume of essays on the literature and films with an extensive bibliography).

Jacobsen, W. *et al.* (ed.) (1984) *Herbert Achternbusch*, Munich and Vienna: Carl Hanser (a comprehensive survey of his films with a substantial interview and bibliography).

MARTIN BRADY

ADAC

The Allgemeiner deutscher Automobilclub (ADAC) was founded in Stuttgart in 1903 as the Deutsche Motorradfahrer-Vereinigung (German Motorcyclists' Association). It moved to Munich in 1905 and was renamed ADAC in 1911. It serves and protects the interests of automobile drivers and supports and furthers the interests of motor sports. A powerful lobbying force, it (together with motor manufacturers) has ensured that Germany's **Autobahn**s remain the last highways in Europe without an overall speed-limit. The membership numbers 13 million and is serviced by about 6,000 staff, among them 1,600 *Gelbe Engel* (yellow angels) who make service calls. The ADAC employs traffic engineers, experts trained in environmental issues, lawyers and medical doctors. Through the ADAC-Reise GmbH the club promotes tourism and travel both within and outside Germany. Its monthly membership magazine *ADAC Motorwelt* has a circulation of close on 12 million, by far the highest in the country.

See also: motor car; vacations and tourism

UTE LISCHKE-MCNAB

Adenauer, Konrad

b. 5 January 1876 Cologne; d. 19 April
   1967 Rhöndorf (near Bonn)

Politician; German Federal Chancellor
   1949–63

As the first chancellor of the Federal Republic, Adenauer set his stamp on the new state and his party, the **CDU**, more than any other post-war politician. President of the commission that drew up the West German constitution (see also **constitution: FRG**), he was instrumental in the decision to locate the federal capital in Bonn. A Catholic Rhinelander, Adenauer was determined to give the Federal Republic a westward-looking orientation in its politics, economics and culture, even if this meant prolonging the German division.

JOHN SANDFORD

Adlon, Percy

b. 1 June 1935, Munich

Filmmaker

Adlon is best known for the film comedies *Sugarbaby* (*Zuckerbaby*) of 1985, *Bagdad Café* (*Out of Rosenheim*) of 1987 and *Rosalie Goes Shopping* of 1989, sometimes referred to collectively as the 'Marianne Trilogy' after the star of all three films, the Bavarian actress Marianne Sägebrecht. The latter two films derive comedy from a German woman's experiences of America (*Bagdad Café* was later made into an American sitcom starring Whoopi Goldberg). The more sombre 1991 production *Salmonberries* features another female émigré who returns to

Germany from Alaska after the fall of the Berlin Wall.

JONATHAN LEGG

ADN

Founded in 1946 and nationalized in 1953, the Allgemeiner Deutscher Nachrichtendienst (ADN) (General German News Service) was the sole news agency for all media in the GDR. Under government control, it was required by its statute to disseminate the perspective of the **SED**. ADN received its news from its correspondents at home and abroad (in over sixty countries) and from other news agencies, whose material it 'filtered' and reformulated in accordance with Marxist–Leninist principles. After the **Wende**, it was privatized, becoming a general news agency with particular strengths in reporting on East Germany and the former Soviet Union.

See also: propaganda

JOHN SANDFORD

Adorno, Theodor W.

b. 11 September 1903, Frankfurt am
   Main; d. 12 August 1969, Visp (Switzerland)

Sociologist, philosopher and musicologist

Theodor Ludwig Wiesengrund Adorno was a member of the Frankfurt Institute for Social Research (the **Frankfurt School**) and its Director after 1958. His concept of the culture industry rejects commercialized mass culture as manipulative and locates the emancipatory potential of art in autonomous, avant-gardist works such as the new music of **Schönberg**.

Further reading

Jay, M. (1984) *Adorno*, London: Fontana (concise overview of life and work).
Petazzi, C. (1977) 'Kommentierte Bibliographie zu Th. W. Adorno', in H.L. Arnold (ed.), *Theodor W.*

Adorno, Munich: edition text + kritik (bibliographical starting point for further research).

GÜNTER MINNERUP

advertising

By the beginning of the 1980s, the FRG had established itself as one of the largest advertising markets in the world. Only the economies of the United States and Japan were estimated to be spending more on advertising than the economy of West Germany. However, restrictions on advertising in the almost exclusively public **broadcasting** system meant that the full potential of advertising in the FRG was not being realized. The development of commercial broadcasting in the late 1980s, together with a far laxer framework of advertising controls for the new commercial channels, therefore represented a highly significant development. Soon afterwards, the **unification** of Germany and, at the beginning of 1993, the completion of the Single European Market provided an additional boost to the FRG advertising market. Adspend figures for the ten-year period from 1985 speak volumes for the impact of the changing environment for German advertising. In 1985, total advertising expenditure in the FRG amounted to DM 31.09 billion. In 1987, the year in which an inter-*Land* treaty (the *Staatsvertrag zur Neuordnung des Rundfunkwesens*) paved the way for expansion of commercial broadcasting and laid down advertising ground rules favourable to commercial broadcasters, the total spent on advertising in the FRG was DM 33.62 billion. Just prior to German unification, in 1989, the level of expenditure on advertising in the FRG reached DM 37.0 billion. The figures (in billion DM, billion being equated with a milliard) for ensuing years are: 39.3 in 1990, 42.3 in 1991, 47.0 in 1992, 48.8 in 1993, 50.8 in 1994 and an all-time high of 53.6 in 1995. The German advertising industry has a very powerful lobbying organization, the Central Association of the Advertising Industry (*Zentralverband der Werbewirtschaft* – ZAW). The industry also performs an important self-regulatory role through the German Advertising Council (*Deutscher Werberat*), which among other things deals with complaints about advertisements and is responsible for upholding standards.

The media which deliver the advertisements themselves (*Werbemittel*) are known in German as *Werbemedien* or *Werbeträger*. Media which exclusively carry advertising (*Werbung*), such as the advertising column (*Litfaßsäule*) which is a feature of many German streets, are *Nur-Werbeträger*. **Newspapers** and **television**, in which advertisements are located within a larger non-advertising framework, are *Auch-Werbeträger*. In the period 1985–95, television increased its share of the advertising market from 8 percent to 17 percent. Daily newspapers maintained their dominant position, with a market share of 30 percent in 1995, and the print media as a whole had a market share of 56 percent. However, back in 1984, when commercial broadcasting made a tentative start in the FRG, this market share was 70 percent. The equivalent figure for the broadcast media as a whole was then 11 percent. By 1995, it had risen to 20 percent. As ownership of commercial broadcasting companies is largely in the hands of major newspaper and magazine publishing groups, it could be argued that the advertising revenue balance remains largely unchanged. The move into advertising-funded broadcasting fulfils a long-stated aim on the part of press owners that was voiced as early as 1967 in evidence given to the commission of enquiry (the so-called *Michel-Kommission*) which reported to the federal government on the economic impact of television advertising on the mass media (the commission rejected the newspaper owners' claim that television was having a negative effect on press advertising revenue). German advertising's heavy dependence on the print media has tended to distinguish it from other national advertising markets in Europe. Another characteristic of German advertising is the early evening advertising zone (*Werberahmenprogramm*) which applies to public-service television and within which the permitted maximum of twenty minutes of commercials per day are broadcast (private broadcasting stations are allowed to broadcast advertising not exceeding 20 percent of daily broadcasting time). This zone is associated with audience-generating and therefore advertising-friendly (*werbefreundlich*) programmes (see also **soap operas**). Both public-service television and commercial broadcasting are required to ensure that broadcast advertisements are clearly separated from the programmes around them and do not influence programme content. This has led to the concept of block advertising (*Werbeblock*), whereby several commercials are broadcast as a group usually linked by short cartoons. Germans have borrowed the term *Zapping* to describe the way viewers use their remote control devices (*Zapper*) to seek refuge from advertising blocks. In the 1980s, advertising began to chase the zapping viewer by means of subtle integration into some programmes (*Product Placement* or *Schleichwerbung*).

A company or industry which uses the media as vehicles for advertising its products and services is a *Werbungtreibender*. In the 1990s, the FRG industrial sector which has consistently spent most on advertising is the car industry, a clear indication of the way in which advertising is able to project the cultural importance of a product, for the **motor car** has a perhaps unique status within Germany. Until 1994, the mass media themselves were the third largest advertisers in the FRG (see **mass media: FRG**). But in 1994 they moved into second place. The reasons for this high level of self-advertising (*Eigenwerbung*) by the FRG media are ever-increasing competition and the continual arrival of new magazines and programmes on the market, factors which have also helped make German advertising more innovative and sophisticated.

Further reading

Gries, R., Ilgen, V. and Schindelbeck, D. (eds) (1995) '*Ins Gehirn der Masse kriechen!*'. *Werbung und Mentalitätsgeschichte*, Darmstadt: Wissenschaftliche Buchgesellschaft (analyses the 'mental code' of German advertising).

Head, D. (1988) 'Advertising and the Media in West Germany', in M. McGowan and M. Pender (eds), *The Media and Society in Contemporary Germany*, Glasgow: University of Strathclyde (examines the FRG media from the perspective of advertising and focuses on the expansion of commercial television and its impact).

Kellner, J., Kurth, U. and Lippert, W. (eds) (1995) *1945 bis 1995: 50 Jahre Werbung in Deutschland*, Ingelheim am Rhein: Westermann Kommuni-kation (shows the changing character of FRG advertising; also available is a companion videocassette).

Kriegeskorte, M. (1992) *Werbung in Deutschland 1945–1965. Die Nachkriegszeit im Spiegel ihrer Anzeigen*, Cologne: DuMont Buchverlag (discusses the advertising of the **Economic Miracle**).

DAVID HEAD

AG

The joint stock company, *Aktiengesellschaft* (AG), is the favoured organizational form for large companies, having substantial capital requirements. There are approximately 2,000 AG in Germany, of which 700 are stock exchange quoted. The legal minimum for paid-up capital is DM 100,000 and the smallest share is DM 50. The shareholders' meeting, the management board and the supervisory board are required by law. The management board is nominated by the supervisory board for a five-year, extendable, period. The supervisory board of twenty members comprises equal numbers of shareholders and employee representatives under parity worker participation agreements.

See also: industrial relations

CHRISTOPHER H. FLOCKTON

agriculture

Farming contributes only 0.9 percent of German gross domestic product and provides less than 3 percent of employment. Agricultural productivity is only two-thirds that of non-farm productivity per head. Small farm size, part-time farming and natural conditions help explain the poorer performance. From 1970–90, the western labour force more than halved to 675,000 and the numbers of holdings fell by 2.7 percent annually, primarily with generation change. Almost one-half of western farms are very small and worked part-time. Radical restructuring in the east has broken up many co-operative farms, leading to a polarized structure and a 70 percent drop in the labour force.

CHRISTOPHER H. FLOCKTON

Aichinger, Ilse

b. 1 November 1921, Vienna

Writer

A post-war Austrian writer, Aichinger produced a slim but dense and poetic œuvre covering all the major literary genres. Influenced by **modernism**, Aichinger's work always challenged literary traditions in its openness and linguistic experimentation, but became increasingly esoteric as it exploited to the full the gap between language and reality.

A member of the **Gruppe 47**, Aichinger first came to prominence with her 1948 novel *Herod's Children* (*Die größere Hoffnung*), which deals with the taboo subject of the **Holocaust** from the perspective of a part-Jewish child caught up in the events; it makes much use of fantasy and dreams. In *Aufruf zum Mißtrauen* (A Call for Mistrust) (1946), Aichinger exhorts her readers to guard against the re-emergence of totalitarianism in the self and in interpersonal relations. The stories in the 1953 volume *The Bound Man* (*Der Gefesselte*) deal with the relations between individuals and an oppressive society. The most famous, *Spiegelgeschichte* (Mirror Story), narrates a woman's life backwards from the moment of her funeral (she died from the effects of a backstreet abortion) to her birth. The later stories in *Eliza, Eliza* (1965) demonstrate Aichinger's increasing rejection of the constricting conventions of narrative and her mistrust of language as a medium capable of organizing and conveying experience. These ideas were articulated in the 1976 volume of poetological essays *Schlechte Wörter* (Bad Words), and further explored in a 1969 volume of radio plays, *Auckland*. *Verschenkter Rat* (A Piece of Advice), published in 1978, contains poems written over the previous two decades. *Kleist, Moos, Fasane* (Kleist, Moss, Pheasants) of 1987 consists of autobiographical sketches, aphorisms, and essays on the works of other writers, including Stifter, Conrad, Trakl and Kafka.

In its mistrust of language as a medium of truth Aichinger's work is part of an Austrian tradition dating back to Hofmannsthal and drawing also on **Wittgenstein**; in its structural openness and deliberate exploitation of multiple and shifting meanings produced in and by language it also has much in common with **postmodernism**. It is also political, however: totalizing discourses are to be undermined and resisted because Nazism showed how they could be misused.

Aichinger was married to the poet Günter **Eich** from 1953 until his death in 1972.

Further reading

Alldridge, J.C. (1969) *Ilse Aichinger*, Chester Springs: Dufour Editions (introduction to her life and works, and English translation of selected stories, dialogues and poems).

Bartsch, K. and Melzer, G. (1993) *Ilse Aichinger*, Graz: Droschl (interview, essays, reviews, biographical sketch and bibliography).

Moser, S. (ed.) (1990) *Ilse Aichinger*, Frankfurt am Main: Fischer (essays on Aichinger's life and works, reviews, photographs, bibliography; also includes three pieces by the author).

Reiter, A. (1996) 'Ilse Aichinger: The Poetics of Silence', in A. Williams, S. Parkes and J. Preece (eds), *Contemporary German Writers, Their Aesthetics and Their Language*, Bern: Lang (overview of the theme of silence in Aichinger's works, detailed reading of a story from *Schlechte Wörter*).

Weigel, S. (1987) 'Schreibarbeit und Phantasie: Ilse Aichinger', in I. Stephan, R. Venske and S. Weigel (eds), *Frauenliteratur ohne Tradition?*, Frankfurt am Main: Fischer (critical reappraisal of Aichinger from a feminist perspective).

BRIGID HAINES

AIDS

It is impossible to determine when HIV arrived in Germany, but it surely reached West Germany before crossing the Wall into East Germany, given the dramatic difference in case numbers at the **Wende** and in the records of first occurrence. In West Germany, first occurrences were diagnosed among gay men in 1982. East Germany denied the existence of HIV and AIDS within its borders until the end of 1986, though the few cases then publicized had certainly been known for some time.

For communist East Germany, AIDS remained a 'capitalist export' whose transmission was to be furtively tracked and halted. Authorities relied on registration, questioning, visitation and safer sex directives. As of 9 November 1989, East Germany had recorded fewer than twenty cases of AIDS and just under ninety cases of HIV infection. West Germany had almost 5,000 cases of AIDS and 36,000 cases of HIV infection at that historic juncture. For both Germanies, an average of 70 percent of those affected to that time had been gay men. Low incidence in East Germany resulted from its geopolitical isolation ('The Wall was the GDR's condom') and from the perpetually closeted status of homosexuality there.

In West Germany, AIDS began its career as a potent cultural metaphor with a cover story by *Der Spiegel* in 1983 (see **Spiegel, Der**). Following *Der Spiegel*'s lead, the conservative popular press quickly christened the new disease *Schwulenpest* (gay plague) and *Homoseuche* (homo-epidemic). Three years of discursive, profitable gay-bashing followed in the Christianized heterosexist establishment media. The demonization (re)awakened anti-gay prejudice in a largely sympathetic, frightened populace. Exclusions in politics, health care, employment, housing and family relations resulted. Until early 1986, the federal government budgeted little or no money to combat a disease that was seen to threaten only homosexuals and intravenous drug users.

In late 1985, a statistically significant increase in heterosexual infections dramatically shifted media focus, which then sensationalized a threat to the mainstream. For two years, a climate of hysteria and panic prevailed, leading to moralistic demands for state protection from groups seen to endanger the mainstream. Bavaria led the reactionary backlash and passed repressive laws that enabled the forced testing of 'suspicious' persons, the prosecution and imprisonment of 'sexually reckless' HIV persons, the closing of 'unsanitary' (gay) establishments and the prohibition of sex for some persons. After a landmark 1987 trial in Nürnberg, in which a gay black HIV American ex-soldier was sentenced to two years in prison for purportedly having unsafe sex, an emboldened Munich announced plans to broaden its AIDS laws.

Joined in a 'Coalition of Reason' with West Germany's remaining states, Bonn rejected the 'Bavarian Course' as a national option, in no small part because it opposed any policy that would resemble Nazi persecution of minorities. Instead, Bonn promoted education, prevention and voluntary, anonymous HIV testing. However, conventional family values still suffused its (**CDU**) policy. For example, Bonn's negligible AIDS education budget skyrocketed in 1986 as the press sensationalized mainstream vulnerability. Federal spending peaked in 1987, then fell precipitously as the mainstream threat failed to materialize and the collapse of communist Europe grabbed headlines. AIDS regained its standing as the disease of homosexuals and other forgettable outsiders.

JAMES YOUNG

Alemann, Claudia von

b. 23 March 1943, Seebach (Thuringia)

Filmmaker and journalist

Having studied at the *Institut für Filmgestaltung* in Ulm (1964–8) Alemann became known as a feminist activist, writing for *Frauen und Film* (Women and Film) and *Brigitte*. Together with Helke **Sander**, she organized the first International Seminar on Women's Film in 1973. Her documentaries and fiction films focus on women living in a male world, and are characterized by slow pace, formal rigour and introspection. Her most famous film, *Blind Spot* (*Die Reise nach Lyon*) of 1978–80, explores the life of the French socialist and feminist Flora Tristan.

See also: film festivals; film: FRG

HELEN HUGHES

Alexander, Peter

b. 30 June 1926, Vienna

Singer, actor and entertainer (real name
Peter Alexander Neumeyer)

Peter Alexander trained as an actor in Vienna
(Max-Reinhardt Drama School) and started his
career performing in various theatres there. From
1952 he acted in musicals and operettas. Since the
mid-1950s he was increasingly popular as a singer
in the genre of the traditional German **Schlager**,
and until the early 1980s was regularly in the
German pop-charts, with several number-one hits.
During the 1970s and 1980s he also became highly
successful as a presenter of entertainment shows for
a middlebrow television audience. He has won
several film and music prizes in Austria and
Germany.

ANNETTE BLÜHDORN

Alt, Franz

b. 17 July 1938, Untergrombach (Baden)

Writer and journalist

Through many books and newspaper publications,
and as the editor of television and radio shows, Alt
has established himself as an important public voice
in Germany on issues ranging from nuclear
disarmament to environmental activism and alternative energies. His moderately conservative,
Christian background has made his call for
ecological awareness more appealing to the mainstream. The argument against the stationing of
American nuclear weapons in Germany in his 1983
book *Peace is Possible* (*Frieden ist möglich*) for example is
based on a reading of the Sermon on the Mount.

See also: environmentalism; nuclear power

REINHILD STEINGRÖVER McRAE

alternative culture

The term 'alternative culture' (synonymous with
'alternative movement') refers primarily to the
highly heterogenous post-1968 counterculture in
West Germany, although a small counterculture
developed in East Germany during the 1980s (see
also **Prenzlauer Berg**). 'Alternative' became a
political signifier for an anti-institutional, leftist-
ecological position. The majority of people involved in alternative projects (like eco-stores selling
organic produce, alternative bookstores and cultural centres, and dentists', lawyers' or craftsmen's
co-operatives) had identified with this position
since the mid-1970s. Referring to oneself as
'alternative' was meant to express a fundamental
opposition to mainstream society and commitment
to developing a comprehensive alternative to the
existing socio-economic system. Post-materialist
values such as self-actualization, ecology, multiculturalism, the grass-roots principle, and an
aesthetic of the hand-made or self-made characterize the alternative culture. The women's movement, the ecology movement (see also
environmentalism) and its party, *Die Grünen*,
the undogmatic left such as the Spontis and the
squatters, the New Age movement and groups
supporting developing countries (Third World
Movement) constituted the alternative culture. All
of these movements permeated each other to
various degrees regarding ideas, attitudes and
individual members. The alternative culture represented a loosely structured network and never a
hierarchical organization, because it emphatically
embraced diversity and thus also supported the
concept of **multiculturalism**.

Historical development

While the alternative culture grew out of the
counterculture of the 1960s, it was nevertheless
critical of the **student movement**. The alternative culture rejected the later student movement's orthodox Marxism which subjugated
everything to the categories of class and objectivity
at the expense of the subjective dimension of
human life. Following the principle that the
personal is the political – voiced first by the
women's movement – the alternative culture set
out to reclaim this lost subjectivity and develop
alternative lifestyles in order to overcome the
individual's alienation from him-/herself, his/her
fellow human beings and – very importantly – from
nature. The alternative culture peaked between the

late 1970s and the mid-1980s. Although the alternative culture has not totally ceased to exist, the borders between mainstream and alternative culture had become diffused by the 1990s. Today, many ideas articulated first by the alternative culture such as environmentalism have become mainstream, and many alternative projects are publicly recognized and funded.

Self-actualization, ecology and the grass-roots principle

The alternative culture denounced mainstream society's focus on material gratification because it fosters consumerism, passivity and alienation. The alternative culture emphasized the individual's right of self-actualization which it perceived to be impossible in the hierarchical organization of work in mainstream society. Alternative projects therefore organized work in an egalitarian manner. If possible, everyone did the same work and received the same base salary, with profits being shared equally. The alternative culture also broadened the idea of exploitation to encompass the exploitation of nature by humankind. The ecology party, *Die Grünen* – a child of the alternative culture – advocated the preservation of nature not only for pragmatic reasons but in order to overcome humanity's spiritual alienation from nature. The idea of non-exploitative relationships further led to alternative concepts of politics and aesthetic culture based on participation rather than representation.

The idea of a grass-roots democracy dominant within the alternative culture aimed at diffusing power and dissolving traditional structures of representative democracy. Grass-roots democracy means that the decision-making process should occur at the lowest possible level. Those affected should be involved in the decision-making process, which would ultimately decentralize the entire political process. Futhermore, grass-roots democracy follows a consensus model and not the majority principle of traditional representative democracy. Not only *Die Grünen* but all alternative projects championed the grass-roots principle, such as the alternative daily, *taz* (*die tageszeitung*), which started publishing in 1979. Instead of having reports, commentaries or editorials written by professional journalists, the *taz* wanted those

affected and/or concerned by an issue to write about it. At the core of grass-roots journalism is the rejection of the mainstream media's claim to objectivity. The grass-roots report articulates instead the immediate experience of those affected, allowing the writer to consciously work through and express his/her concerns. It also allows the reader to appropriate this unmediated experience for his or her own political struggle. With this principle, the *taz* sought to break down the boundary between the writer/journalist and the reader in order to constitute an authentic counter-public sphere.

Art and culture

The alternative culture adhered to this participatory or grass-roots model also regarding its aesthetic concepts and artistic practices. The alternative culture favoured a 'Do-It-Yourself' concept of art over mainstream society's 'Coca-Cola-Karajan-Culture', which condemns the consumer of both 'low' entertainment culture (Coca-Cola) and 'high' culture (Herbert von **Karajan**) to utter passivity. Instead, the alternative culture aimed at turning everyone into a cultural practitioner, rendering mainstream culture's favoured art forms obsolete because they require a high degree of training and professionalism. Folk culture was attractive for the alternative culture because folk art was designed by and for the layperson. The alternative culture therefore developed an aesthetic of the hand-made or self-made product and the body, in opposition to both the industrial ready-made and the abstract and logo-centric aesthetic of high culture. The **circus**, the figure of the fool – a fusion of the circus clown and the court jester – as well as mime and dance theatre emerged as favourite cultural activities of the alternative culture, because these art forms privileged physical over verbal expression. Folk music drawn from an earlier democratic tradition as well as contemporary song writers (see also **Degenhardt, Franz Josef; Wecker, Konstantin**) enjoyed wide popularity. All of these artistic forms are characterized by their roots in a pre-industrial time, though the alternative culture did make an exception for **rock music**, still highly appreciated for both its rebel image and for generational reasons. While the alternative culture – in particular in the ecology and peace movement – found support in all age groups, it was by and large carried by a younger generation of West Germans in their late teens, twenties or thirties in the 1970s and 1980s (see also **peace movement: FRG**).

Further reading

Brand, K.-W., Büsser, D. and Rucht, D. (1986) *Aufbruch in eine andere Gesellschaft. Neue soziale Bewegungen in der Bundesrepublik*, Frankfurt am Main and New York: Campus (historical-descriptive analysis in the context of new social movements).

Brückner, P. *et al.* (1978) *Autonomie oder Getto? Kontroversen über die Alternativbewegung*, Frankfurt am Main: Neue Kritik (anthology of critical essays).

Dirke, S. von (1997) *All Power to the Imagination! The West German Counterculture from the Student Movement to the Greens*, Lincoln, NB and London: University of Nebraska Press (cultural history focusing on correlation of alternative politics and alternative aesthetics).

Die Grünen (1985) *Programme of the German Green Party*, London: Heretic Books (1980 foundational platform of the Green Party; definition of principles: ecology, social welfare, grass-roots democracy, non-violence).

Sarkar, S. (1993) *Green-Alternative Politics in West Germany*, Tokyo and New York: United Nations University Press (descriptive historical survey from a social science perspective).

SABINE VON DIRKE

Amery, Carl

b. 9 April 1922, Munich

Writer and *Dramaturg* (real name Christian Mayer)

A founding member of Gustav Heinemann's *Gesamtdeutsche Volkspartei*, Amery was critically engaged in the politically decisive early phase of the FRG. Sharply critical of the Catholic church (see *Die Kapitulation oder Deutscher Katholizismus heute* (Capitulation, or German Catholicism Today), 1963), he was also a major proponent of **environmentalism**, attacking the Biblical notion of domination over the earth. He also wrote **satire** and **science fiction**.

See also: Gruppe 47; PEN: Verband deutscher Schriftsteller

MICHAEL RICHARDSON

Améry, Jean

b. 31 October 1912, Vienna; d. 17 October 1978, Salzburg

Writer (real name Hanns Maier)

Améry studied philosophy and literature in Vienna in the 1930s. A Jew and an active member of resistance organizations in France and Belgium during the war, he survived incarceration in **Auschwitz** and Bergen-Belsen, and settled in Belgium after the liberation. His post-war works include autobiographical texts, and philosophical essays which display the influence of Sartrean existentialism. His last major work was an essay on suicide. Améry took his own life two years after its publication.

Further reading

Arnold, H.L. (ed.) (1988) *Jean Améry*, Munich: edition text + kritik.

JONATHAN LONG

Anders, Günther

b. 12 July 1902, Breslau (now Wrocław, Poland); d. 17 December 1992, Vienna

Philosopher and essayist (real name Günther Stern)

Anders attained notoriety since the early 1960s as an activist and philosopher of the anti-nuclear movement. An assimilated German Jew, he studied under Martin **Heidegger** and Edmund Husserl, completing his dissertation in 1923. After the University of Frankfurt rejected his habilitation, he began work as a cultural critic. When a Berlin editor with too many writers named Stern on his staff suggested he name himself 'something different', he responded 'then call me "different"' (*anders*). The name is characteristic of Anders's unsparing bluntness. He emigrated to Paris in 1933 and the United States in 1936, divorcing Hannah **Arendt**, who found his pessimism 'hard to bear', as he later put it.

In the United States Anders worked at menial jobs, but also wrote for *Der Aufbau* and later lectured at the New School for Social Research. His first published diary, *The Writing on the Wall: Diaries 1941–1966* (1967), begins with his musings as a labourer in a Hollywood warehouse of historical costumes. Auschwitz and Hiroshima mark turning points in his consciousness. He returned to Europe in 1950 and began work on *Die Antiquiertheit des Menschen* (The Outdatedness of Human Beings), published in 1956. In addition to analysing human feelings of inadequacy in comparison with machines, and to a philosophical settling of accounts with Heidegger, Anders lays out the principles of 'blindness to the apocalypse', the hallmark of his later work. Pressured to categorize his ideas, he later coined the term *Diskrepanzphilosophie* (philosophy of discrepancy) to describe his focus on the increasing divergence between what has become technically feasible (e.g. the atomic holocaust of the entire globe), and what the human mind is capable of imagining.

With Robert **Jungk**, Anders co-founded the anti-nuclear movement in 1954. In 1959 he published his philosophical diary of an international conference in Hiroshima, *Der Mann auf der Brücke* (The Man on the Bridge) and in 1962 his correspondence with a pilot in the Hiroshima squadron, *Burning Conscience*. His politically acerbic books from the 1960s include an open letter to the son of Adolf Eichmann, a speech about the victims of the three world wars, and a primer of American 'warspeak' in Vietnam. In 1967 he served as a juror on the Russell tribunal publicizing atrocities in Vietnam. Anders' œuvre encompasses numerous literary and philosophical works, including books on Kafka (1951, English 1960) and **Brecht** (1962), essays on the atomic age, including *Endzeit und Zeitenende* (Last Days and the End of Time) (1972)

and *Die atomare Drohung* (The Atomic Threat) (1981), reflections from his diaries, including *Ketzereien* (Heresies) (1982), and a second volume of *Die Antiquiertheit des Menschen* (1980).

Anders won numerous awards and honours for his work from 1936 to 1983, some of which he rejected for political reasons. His unsparingly critical pessimism may explain why his pathbreaking works have seldom sparked sustained public discussion, with the major exception of his 'Theses on Violence' during the peace movement of the 1980s (see also **peace movement: FRG; peace movement: GDR**). The renaissance of interest in his works in the 1990s indicates that his uncompromising moralism may have been ahead of its time.

Further reading

Liessmann, K. (1992) 'Moralist und Ketzer: Zu Günther Anders und seiner Philosophie des Monströsen', *Text und Kritik* 115 (July): 3–19 (the introductory article in a special issue devoted to Anders and his work).

Strümpel, J. (1992) 'Vita, Bibliographie', *Text und Kritik* 115 (July): 86–101 (exhaustive bibliography includes secondary works).

HAROLD MARCUSE

Andersch, Alfred

b. 4 February 1914, Munich; d. 21 February 1980, Berzona (Switzerland)

Writer and critic

One of the foremost social and literary critics of his generation, Andersch is known primarily for his early novels which reflect his own experiences of unemployment and political activity under the Nazi dictatorship in the 1930s.

Having trained as a bookseller, he was unemployed from 1931–3 during which time he joined the Communist Party, becoming organizational leader of the Bavarian Communist Youth in 1932. Twice arrested by the Gestapo, he spent three months in Dachau concentration camp after which he gave up his political activities. He was twice called up to serve in the German army, first to serve in the occupation of France, and later at the Italian front. He deserted to the Americans on 6 June 1944.

When he returned to Germany after the war he became Erich **Kästner**'s editorial assistant producing the *Neue Zeitung* in Munich, and then publishing the periodical *Der Ruf* (The Call) with Hans Werner **Richter**, which a group of prisoners of war, including Andersch, had started in America in 1944. In his contributions he rejected the theory of collective guilt and urged the Germans themselves to undertake the task of their own political re-education rather than have it imposed upon them. Andersch was a founding member of the **Gruppe 47**, and his theories concerning the current state of German literature represent an important contribution to the development of literary life in Germany. His enthusiasm for **existentialism** and his belief in man's ability to change inspired his concept of art as an embodiment of freedom. Andersch withdrew from active involvement in the *Gruppe 47* in the early 1950s as its political character became more pluralist.

During this period he produced a number of programmes for West German radio whilst working on his autobiographical work of 1952, *Die Kirschen der Freiheit. Ein Bericht* (The Cherries of Freedom. A Report), which depicts his desertion in the war. The theme of escape is one which features in many of his subsequent works. His first novel, *Flight to Afar* (*Sansibar oder Der letzte Grund*), which appeared in 1957, depicts personal and political conflicts within a group of individuals in the context of a Jewish girl's flight to freedom from Nazi Germany. A further question which concerns Andersch is whether it is possible for an individual to make a free decision while living in a totalitarian state. In 1958 he moved to Switzerland where he lived as a freelance writer, becoming a Swiss citizen in 1972. The 1960 novel *The Redhead* (*Die Rote*, filmed 1962), which describes a woman's escape to Italy from a loveless marriage, and his third novel, *Efraim's Book* (*Efraim*) of 1967, are both critical of the materialism of West German society. His most important work, *Winterspelt* (1974), concerns the plan of a German major to surrender to the Americans in the Ardennes in 1944. The plan comes to nought, allowing Andersch to explore the theme of personal motivation and moral responsibility. Andersch also published several collections of critical essays, short stories and radio plays.

Further reading

Heidelberger-Leonard, I. and Wehdeking, V. (eds) (1994) *Alfred Andersch. Perspektiven zu Leben und Werk*, Opladen: Westdeutscher Verlag.

Littler, M. (1991) 'A Reassessment of the Portrayal of Women in the Work of Alfred Andersch', *German Life and Letters* 44, 5: 443–58.

Williams, R. (ed.) (1992) *German Writers and the Cold War*, Manchester: Manchester University Press (includes a discussion of Andersch's political ideas and how they affect his literary work).

MARGARET VALLANCE

Anderson, Sascha

b. 24 August 1953, Weimar

Writer

Anderson began a career in film, later turning to music and literature, where he investigated the relationship between word and image. He is also well known as an editor of small, private, alternative presses in the **Prenzlauer Berg** district of East Berlin. In 1984 he emigrated to West Berlin. During his Büchner Prize Speech (October 1991), Wolf **Biermann** accused Anderson of complicity with the **Stasi** from 1975 to 1989, using the code names of David Menzer, Fritz Müller and Peters. Because of Anderson's position within the Prenzlauer Berg alternative culture, this Stasi activity called the dissident nature of GDR literature into question.

CAROL ANNE COSTABILE-HEMING

Andres, Stefan

b. 26 June 1906, Breitweis bei Trier; d. 29 June 1970, Rome

Writer and dramatist

A one-time candidate for priesthood, Andres wrote

works characterized by what he called 'Christian humanism': an amalgamation of a not-uncritical Catholic spirituality and the humanism of the ancient Greeks. His writing focused on themes such as the hidden divine order of the world, guilt and reconciliation, and political resistance, for instance in *El Greco malt den Großinquisitor* (El Greco Paints the Grand Inquisitor) (1936) and *Wir sind Utopia* (We are Utopia) (1943). He also wrote plays and poetry.

MICHAEL RICHARDSON

APO

The term *Außerparlamentarische Opposition* (extra-parliamentary opposition) has acquired a special significance in the political history of the Federal Republic, for in the mid-1960s this label attached itself to a movement that came to be known by the acronym APO. Although it only existed for a few years and was essentially preoccupied with one issue, the introduction of emergency legislation, the APO nevertheless marked a caesura in the development of Germany's political culture, for it helped kindle a spirit of anti-authoritarianism that continued to resurface at different sites of protest throughout the 1970s and 1980s.

The APO basically constituted a loose alliance of disparate forces, which embraced Germany's critical intelligentsia as well as sections of the trade union movement. However, the twin pillars of its support were the socialist student organization, **SDS**, and the Campaign for Disarmament (as the peace movement was then known (see also **peace movement: FRG**)). While the latter was a key player on the organizational front, the SDS took the lead with regard to strategy and theoretical analysis. The immediate catalyst for the growth of the APO was the formation of the Grand Coalition in 1966, which left merely the tiny F.D.P. as a vestigial opposition in the Bundestag. For the SPD entrance into this government was made conditional on the party's willingness to support the introduction of Emergency Laws which, in the event of acute national crisis or internal unrest, provided the government with substantially expanded executive power. The chief theoretical perspective which the SDS wished to see established within the APO was that these laws were but a stepping-stone on the path to a right-wing dictatorship. This interpretation, with which the SDS sought to push the APO further along the road towards a doctrinally united protest movement, was given credence by two acts of homicidal violence, namely the killing of the student Benno Ohnesorg by a policeman during a demonstration in West Berlin on 2 June 1967, and the attempted assassination of the SDS leader Rudi **Dutschke** on 11 April 1968. Curiously, the mass demonstrations that followed in the wake of this attack marked both the climax and the end of the APO. For all the thousands of protesters it mobilized, the APO could not prevent the passage of the Emergency Laws through parliament in June 1968. Moreover, the violence that attended some of these demonstrations, particularly those directed against the press empire of Axel **Springer**, exacerbated the rift between those who conceived of the APO as an instrument of radical resistance to a quasi-fascist state, and others who saw extra-parliamentary opposition more as a vital complement to the formal institutions of liberal democracy. With the dissolution of the APO the former tendency was sustained within the sectarian enclave of the *K-Gruppen* (Communist groups), while the latter perspective informed the spectacular growth of citizens' initiatives in the 1970s (see **citizens' initiatives: FRG**).

See also: student movement

Further reading

Otto, K.A. (1977) *Vom Ostermarsch zur APO: Geschichte der außerparlamentarischen Opposition in der Bundesrepublik 1960–70*, Frankfurt am Main: Campus Verlag (an account of the APO from the perspective of the peace movement).

ROB BURNS

Arbeiterzeitung

This Austrian daily paper, published in Vienna, was founded in 1889 by the Social Democratic Party (**SPÖ**). In the wake of the right-wing coup in

1934, it was banned. Publication was resumed in August 1945 by the joint owners, the SPÖ and various local sub-organizations of the party. After the war it made a promising start, but subsequently its readership declined in numbers. By the 1980s the strong party political viewpoint and its traditional and widely respected (but commercially unsuccessful) set-up turned it into a loss-making enterprise. Under private ownership since 1990, the paper was liquidated in October 1991.

GEORG HELLMAYR

architecture

The path towards modernism in Germany was set with the foundation of the Deutscher Werkbund by industrialists and designers in 1907, dedicated to improving the standard of German industrial design and production, which had formerly been known for its low quality. The Werkbund's aesthetic programme came to reflect Hermann Muthesius's proposals to abandon all superficial decoration in favour of strict *Sachlichkeit* (objectivity). Its goals were exemplified by the relationship between Peter Behrens and the AEG company, whose artistic adviser he became in 1907, responsible for all its designs from posters and products to assembly halls and factory buildings. His turbine factory in Berlin Moabit (1909) represents a milestone in early Modernist architecture while still retaining some historical references. The future core of 'High Modernism's' most influential representatives were employed by Behrens in his studio in Berlin Neu-Babelsberg between 1908 and 1913 – Walter **Gropius**, Adolf Mayer, Ludwig **Mies van der Rohe** and Le Corbusier.

Gropius believed that all new forms would necessarily derive from the spirit of the age, of which technology was an important aspect to him (but nevertheless still stressing handcraft). His steel and glass Fagus factory (with Mayer, 1910–14) illustrates his ideas – abandoning historical references, it represents a prototype of Functionalist architecture.

Although the seed of Functionalism had already begun to sprout, the majority of German architects were not to follow pure engineering solutions. Even

within the Werkbund a row blew up at its annual meeting in 1914 concerning merely mechanistic solutions and artistic freedom. The standard or typical solution proposed by Muthesius was attacked by a radical faction around van der Velde, which included **Gropius**, along with Hermann Obrist and Bruno Taut, to whom architecture still embraced further dimensions.

The first expressionist building, Taut's Glashaus for the Cologne Werkbund Exhibition of 1914, reflects the utopian belief that architecture (in association with the other arts) could lead society on an egalitarian and humane path simply by means of its grandeur and beauty. The fourteen-sided glass temple was also decorated with verses by Scheebart, one of which read 'Buntes Glas zerstört den Haß' (Coloured glass destroys hate). The outbreak of war in August 1914 put an abrupt end to expressionist building activity but this credo was to inspire visionary architects and artists between 1914 and 1920 to draw up plans advocating a new architecture of glass, light and colour. Against the background of the horrors of the WWI, pacifism, utopian socialism and brotherly love were to be inspired by such visions exemplified by Bruno Taut's *Alpine Architektur*, published in 1919. His 'Gläserne Kette' (Crystal chain) group which included Max **Taut**, Hans and Wassili **Luckhardt**, Hans **Scharoun** and Gropius, was to influence the course of German architecture, not only by elevating architecture to the paramount position amongst the visual arts and the architect to a kind of social engineer and leader, but also by stressing the importance of craft training and the reforming qualities of new materials and building techniques.

Walter Gropius founded the *Bauhaus* school at Weimar in line with these ideas in April 1919. The almost mystical conviction of the totality of the arts was further stimulated by teachers like Johannes Itten and Wassily Kandinsky who also acted as 'spiritual leaders', encouraging cults such as Zoroastrianism and Theosophy amongst the students.

By the mid-1920s the architectural avant-garde turned to a similarly mystical belief in new technology and the machine. The impulse was not only generated from within Germany but also originated from the Dutch De Stijl movement,

Soviet Constructivism, Le Corbusier's passion for technology and American examples. The cry for 'objective clarity', industrial production, and rationalization of materials and building techniques now embraced the typical solution as opposed to the unique. Gropius subsequently not only changed the Bauhaus policy and replaced Itten with Moholy-Nagy, but also designed a new school building in Dessau (1925–6) echoing the new direction.

The two- and three-storey housing block represent the modernists' greatest architectural achievements. Martin Wagner, Berlin's city architect, Ernst **May**, Bruno Taut and Gropius were responsible for the most important housing schemes of the Weimar period. Nevertheless great diversity can be detected amongst Modernism's architects. In Siemensstadt Gropius' austere repetitive blocks are contrasted by playful and organisist designs by Hugo Häring and Hans **Scharoun**, who defined functionalism on a more individualistic basis.

The *Weißenhofsiedlung* in Stuttgart (1927), designed by fourteen leading avant-garde architects under the direction of Ludwig Mies van der Rohe, also shows a broad spectrum of the modernist canon and of building types, ranging from studio flats to small houses. The location was seen as a provocation to traditionalist architects in Stuttgart such as Paul Schmitthenner, Paul Bonatz and Friedrich Scholer, who were closely connected to the traditionalist *Technische Hochschule* in the same town. These three were amongst the architects who built a rival estate, the *Kochenhof-Siedlung*, employing conventional construction methods and materials. The battle between the two factions was still raging in the late 1920s, with Modernism gaining many enemies. The world economic crisis of 1929–31 put an end to Germany's mass housing programmes, which were closely linked to modernist architecture. The development of Modernism and the debate between the avant-garde and traditionalists represent an important background against which post-WWII architecture developed. The debate continued after the war with Modernism slowly gaining the upper hand.

The Nazi era did not represent a total halt in architectural continuity in Germany, especially concerning town planning. It did, however, result in the emigration of Germany's most prominent modernist architects and planners (Mies van der Rohe, Martin Wagner, Walter Gropius, Erich Mendelson and Bruno Taut, who either died during this period or remained abroad) and, after the Third Reich's downfall, a massive reaction against the soulless monumental classicism along the lines of Paul Ludwig Troost and Albert Speer.

The housing of the people presented the most urgent architectural task in Germany after WWII. The lack of housing units in the West alone measured 6.5 million in 1948. The solutions erected in the 1950s were most likely to be low-rise structures, hastily designed and built. Some of the few distinguished exceptions were the eleven-storey block at Kottbusser Tor, Berlin, (1952–5) designed by the **Luckhardt** brothers, Alvar Aalto's Neue Vahr apartment block in Bremen (1957–62), and many buildings built for the Interbau building exhibition (1957) in the Hansaviertel in West Berlin. Here many well-known German and foreign architects designed model housing schemes in complete denial of Berlin's traditional block building pattern. In the East, Hermann **Henselmann** and his planning collective addressed the problem of urban housing by orientating themselves towards 1930s Soviet precedents while also focusing back on Schinkelesque Prussian architecture. Large characterless and inhumane housing estates dominate housing schemes in both East and West in the 1960s and 1970s. Berlin again houses the most horrific examples – the Märkisches Viertel in West Berlin (1963–74) provides accommodation for 60,000 people, and on the other side of Berlin this was mirrored by the second phase of the Stalinallee (renamed Karl-Marx-Allee, and part of it now the Frankfurter Allee), and ultimately by Marzahn, designed to accommodate 150,000 inhabitants.

Church architecture flourished after the war due to a generous fiscal system. New spatial and structural concepts and modern building materials often produced the most exciting buildings in the 1950s. **Bartning**'s timber emergency churches of the late 1940s were followed by designs by **Schwarz** (e.g. St Anna in Düren, 1951–6, or St Joseph in Cologne, 1954, with Josef Bernhard), Dominikus **Böhm** (e.g. St Maria Königin, Cologne, 1954), Emil **Steffann** (e.g. St Bonifatius,

Dortmund, 1953–8), and Paul Baumgarten (Evangelical church at Litzsee, Berlin, 1956–9).

The (re-)construction of communal buildings such as **theatres** and **concert halls** in order to restore shattered communities was given priority after the war's destructions. In the forefront of the architectural debate, these buildings were constructed in a wide variety of styles. Among the best-known examples are Gottfried **Böhm**'s neo-expressionist town hall in Bensburg (1962–7), **Schwarz**' reconstructed Gürzenich, **Döllgast**'s reconstructed *Alte Pinakothek* in Munich, Hämer and Hämer's monolithic, New Brutalist concrete Municipal Theatre in Ingolstadt (1960–6), and **Scharoun**'s organic *Philharmonie* (1956–63) in Berlin. Here the cascading seats totally surround the stage, creating a new relationship between audience and performer. In contrast, situated next to this, the émigré Mies van der Rohe built the clear-cut, strictly geometric steel and glass *Neue Nationalgalerie* (1962–8). The East Berlin *Palast der Republik* by the collective Graffunder, Prasser, Aust (1973–6) appears conventional and dull in contrast.

While Modernism had suppressed traditional styles, the former debate was refashioned in the 1960s with one side arguing for Misian formalist purity and the other gathering around **Scharoun**, who was concerned with functional disposition in connection with formal freedom.

The large-scale commercial architecture made possible by the **Economic Miracle** was largely fashioned on North American models which in turn were often developed by German émigrés, especially Mies. The Thyssen skyscraper in Düsseldorf by HPP (1957–60) is a direct descendent of Mies van der Rohe's high-rise towers (e.g. South Shore Drive Apartments, Chicago, 1949). Egon **Eiermann** designed his office and administration buildings with a similar rectilinear discipline. His *Abgeordnetenhaus* (Bundestag offices) in Bonn (1965–8) is a good example for the quality of his detailing and convincing sense of massing. Again **Scharoun** offered alternative solutions. His apartment blocks in Stuttgart Zuffenhausen (1954–9) avoid the predominance of the right angle in their plans. **Scharoun**'s challenge to the set-square and box-like structures continued throughout his career (National Library, Berlin, 1966–78) and was taken further by such architects as Günther **Behnisch**

and Otto **Steidle**. Together with Frei **Otto**, **Behnisch** was part of a team of designers in charge of the Olympic Stadium complex in Munich (1965–72), of which the suspended tent roof represents one of the most celebrated and influential structures of post-war Germany. This synthesis of organic forms and high-technology materials and structures is an often-repeated theme in his later work, more recently taken further by introducing deconstructivist elements into his designs. **Steidle**'s buildings also shun predetermined formal solutions although he encourages the use of prefabricated materials. He never allows these to determine the design though, which he always develops from a building's function, closely focusing on its occupants. The spontaneous, often improvised quality of his designs and his superb circulation and spatial planning have broadened the possibilities of social interaction.

The 1980s saw the International Building Exhibition in Berlin with its motto 'the inner city as a residential area'. This entailed both the renovation of domestic quarters in parts of Kreuzberg under the direction of Hardt Walther Hämer and, under the direction of Josef Paul **Kleihues**, the repair of holes torn into the urban fabric by WWII and more recent planning (see also **IBA**).

The 1980s also saw a boom in innovative museum building in West Germany. James Stirling and Michael Wilford built the highly influential Staatsgalerie in Stuttgart (1977–82), full of postmodernist citations. The **postmodernism** debate had by now reached Germany, bringing with it new stylistic impulses. Oswald Mathias **Ungers**' Architecture Museum in Frankfurt (Fritz Geldmacher, 1912–13 and **Ungers** 1979–84) is often seen as his postmodern masterpiece. The Schaumainkai district in Frankfurt also houses the Museum of Arts and Crafts by Richard Meier (1979–85), the German Post Museum designed by Günther **Behnisch**, and the Museum of Modern Art by Hans **Hollein** (1985–91), who had already built the highly acclaimed Mönchengladbach Municipal Museum, which stands in vigorous dialogue with its surrounding landscape (1972–82).

With German unification in 1990, the architectural landscape changed radically. Many western firms are now active in the rebuilding of the new federal states in the east. **gmp** for instance, who were responsible for many large projects before the wall came down (Post Office building, Brunswick 1982–9, Stuttgart Airport 1980–9), have designed such major schemes as the *Neue Messe* in Leipzig (1992–6) and the *Lehrter Bahnhof* (1993–), the future main train station in Berlin. The rebuilding programme has focused on the centre of Berlin, formerly in the eastern part of the city. The idea of radical reconstruction proposals was soon abandoned by the city authorities in favour of conservative voices wishing to maintain the historical city block grid and a twenty-two-metre cornice height. The three blocks erected along Friedrichstraße (1991–5) by Jean Nouvel, Pei, Cob and Freed and **Ungers**, are early results of this decision. Other major redevelopments have been started in order to erect new ministerial quarters at the Spreebogen and a commercial centre at Potsdamer Platz (see also **Berlin building boom**).

Outside Berlin, the International Building Exhibition Emscher Park (1987–97) is the largest and most interesting single project of the recent past, where new usage schemes have been developed to restructure the Ruhrgebiet's abandoned industrial sites. This consists of over fifty separate projects, including housing and commercial building schemes, the regaining and de-polluting of natural environments and the development of a wide range of leisure facilities. The IBA Emscher Park has since become a convincing example for similar plans in the former German Democratic Republic, especially for the industrial landscapes around Bitterfeld and Dessau.

See also: town planning

Further reading

Burchard, J. (1966) *The Voice of the Phoenix: Postwar Architecture in Germany*, Cambridge, MA: MIT Press.

Feldmayer, G. (1993) *The New German Architecture*, New York: Rizzoli.

Pehnt, W. (1970) *German Architecture 1960–1970*, London: London Architectural Press.

MARTIN KUDLEK

ARD

The Arbeitsgemeinschaft der öffentlich-rechtlichen Rundfunkanstalten der Bundesrepublik Deutschland (Association of German Public Broadcasters) was founded in West Germany in 1950 to represent the common interests of the new post-war **broadcasting** services. Today the ARD – as the umbrella body for all of Germany's public-service broadcasting (except for the 'second' television channel, which is produced by the **ZDF**) – has become one of the biggest **television** and radio broadcasting organizations in the whole of Europe (see also **radio: cultural role**) More than fifty regional and local radio channels, the national radio services *DeutschlandRadio* and the overseas service *Deutsche Welle*, the worldwide television service *Deutsche Welle TV*, the nationwide television 'First' service (*Das Erste*) and the eight regional television 'Third' programmes (*Die Dritten*) can be received by practically all households throughout Germany: over thirty-one million homes with one or more television sets.

The allied victors were determined that German radio after the war would not show the same faults as the pre-war *Reichsrundfunk*. A federal structure (see also **federalism**), the renunciation of state influence, and the avoidance of economic dependence were to be the key of the radio and television institutions under public law (*öffentlich-rechtliche Rundfunk- und Fernsehanstalten*). In 1947 the US military governor Lucius D. Clay declared diversity of public opinion as the main aim of post-war media policy.

After the creation of the German federal state's institutions these principles were further consolidated by *Land* broadcasting laws, verdicts of the Federal Constitutional Court (Bundesverfassungsgericht), and state treaties between the *Länder*. ARD services are thus free of government influence, and rely for only a small part of their income on advertising (1995: 10 percent), the bulk coming mainly from licence fees paid monthly by owners of radio and television equipment. The proclaimed aim of the ARD corporations is not only to inform and to entertain, but also to encourage the integration of various parts of society, and let minorities have a say in the programming.

In the 1950s the ARD radio services became the

major factor in the mass media system in West Germany (see **mass media: FRG**). As early as 1952 the ARD radio stations had ten million listeners. However, the radio stations operated at the regional level, and it was only the development of a television umbrella that helped the ARD to establish itself countrywide. The broadcasting of a countrywide television service was the goal of the ARD from the outset, and the go-ahead for this was given at the end of 1952. The first daily news feature, the *Tagesschau*, went on the air from Hamburg in 1956. The eight o'clock announcement of the *Tagesschau* newsreader: '*Hier ist das Erste Deutsche Fernsehen mit der Tagesschau*' (This is German television's Channel One with the *Tagesschau*) continues to be the ARD's trade mark, currently attracting eight million viewers every day. Starting as a two-hour evening programme, in colour since 1967, television became generally accepted during the 1960s. Without competition from private television companies the ARD stations made considerable progress in becoming modern and respected broadcasters in the 1970s, and have been a significant force in German politics. Investigative news magazines (for example *Monitor, Panorama*) reached million of viewers every Tuesday evening. The environmental movement of the 1980s increased in popularity not least as a result of the disclosures made by the ARD. During the 1980s most of the ARD radio channels changed either to a mixed schedule of information and entertainment, to music-dominated background listening, or to programmes for special interest listeners, becoming more or less like the programmes offered by commercial broadcasters.

Since 1989 the 'First' television channel has been broadcasting a twenty-hour full schedule, clearly structured into breakfast television and morning programme, afternoon talk shows, pre-prime-time daily soap and the prime-time information programmes, entertainment, sport, and television movies, produced on a proportional basis by the separate ARD corporations. Information programmes on television and the orientation of *Deutschlandfunk* (the pre-unification all-German radio service) programmes towards the GDR were of crucial importance for the eventual collapse of the GDR. Established in 1974, the ARD bureau in East Berlin made ARD television the most important source of information for GDR citizens (80 percent of them could watch what they referred to as '*Westfernsehen*'). Notwithstanding obstruction on the part of the GDR authorities and the repeated expulsion of their correspondents, the ARD-*Tagesschau* and *Deutschlandfunk* broadcast reports about the Leipzig Monday demonstrations as early as September 1989. After unification and the closure of the GDR television service two new corporations – *Mitteldeutscher Rundfunk* and *Ostdeutscher Rundfunk* – were established in the East, becoming associate members of the ARD in 1992. Some thirty offices in foreign countries (from Mexico City to Tokyo) are a symbol of the ARD's world-wide status, rivalling that of many other international news services, such as CNN or the BBC. ARD and most of the regional broadcasters are also represented on the World Wide Web.

Further reading

ARD-Jahrbuch (annual) Baden-Baden: Nomos (informative year-book with articles, annual accounts, and address list).

Benz, W. (1989) *Die Geschichte der Bundesrepublik Deutschland*, vol. 4, *Kultur*, Frankfurt am Main: Fischer (history of radio and television to the end of the 1980s).

Humphreys, P. (1994) *Media and Media Policy in Germany*, Oxford and Providence, RI: Berg (detailed coverage of history of broadcasting in the FRG).

Meyn, H. (1994) *Massenmedien in der Bundesrepublik Deutschland*, Berlin: Colloquium Verlag (introduction to the mass media system).

MICHAEL HÄNEL

Arendt, Hannah

b. 14 October 1906, Linden (Hanover); d. 4 December 1975, New York

Philosopher and political theorist

Arendt's philosophical training was influenced by Martin **Heidegger**, Rudolf **Bultmann** and Karl **Jaspers**. Her biography of Rahel Varnhagen (1958) discusses the status of Jews as pariahs in society, while her *Origins of Totalitarianism* (1951) analyses the roots of Nazi anti-Semitism and totalitarianism. Her report on the Jerusalem trial of Adolf **Eichmann** (1963) was received controversially. Arendt emigrated to the US in 1941, served as the director of Jewish Cultural Reconstruction (1949–52) and held several teaching positions. Her works *The Human Condition* (1958), *On Revolution* (1963), *Men in Dark Times* (1968), and *On Violence* (1969) address political phenomena such as modern mass society, freedom, individualism, institutionalization of liberal thought, and societies' responses to crisis.

Further reading

Young-Bruehl, E. (1982) *Hannah Arendt: For Love of the World*, New Haven, CT: Yale University Press.

THOMAS NOLDEN

art collections

Without the passion of private collectors no sizeable museum in the world would possess its present status. The collections that have found their way from obscurity to the public have enriched and even defined the character of museums and exemplify the fruitful interaction of private and public patronage. Private collections are determined by the personality of the collector, expressed in focal points within the collection, rather than the comprehensive overview of a museum. In Germany, most post-war collections concentrate on modern and contemporary art. Trying to re-establish what the Nazis branded as 'degenerate', modern art was collected when it was still not widely understood.

The foundations for many German collections were laid by industrialists, of whom Thyssen-Bornemisza is the most outstanding. Located in Lugano, the Thyssen-Bornemisza Collection is one of the world's finest private collections with a wide range of possessions. Still added to today, it was formed by two generations of Thyssen-Bornemiszas. While the elder Baron Heinrich, whose father was a prominent figure in the German steel

industry, devoted himself to fourteenth- to eighteenth-century European masters, his son, Baron Hans Heinrich, from the early 1960s shifted the focus to art from the impressionists onward, his first modern purchase being a watercolour by Emil Nolde. Therefore, there are now two distinct parts of the collection: the father's historical and the son's modern, ranging from Corot and Manet as forerunners, impressionism and post-impressionism, fauvism, Russian avant-garde, the pioneers of abstract art, German expressionism, and surrealism to post-war American paintings, thus unfolding the history of modern painting from the late nineteenth century. In 1992 a major part of the collection, mainly old master paintings, was moved to the Fundación Colección Thyssen-Bornemisza in Madrid.

Like Thyssen-Bornemisza, Hermann F. Reemtsma was an industrial magnate, ruling over the Hamburg cigarette empire. He never intended to form a big private collection, but rather incorporate favourite works in his home. Yet, Reemtsma became a famous collector of nineteenth- and twentieth-century art, and also of Dutch seventeenth-century paintings. Thirty years of interest in the sculptor Ernst Barlach led to the setting-up of a foundation and to the subsequent opening of the Ernst Barlach Haus in Hamburg in 1962, which houses Reemtsma's collection of Barlach's works. A selection of works from the entire collection was shown in Hamburg in 1992.

The more recent Sprengel Museum in Hanover was opened in 1979, with an extension finished in 1992. Its history began in 1969, when the industrialist Bernhard Sprengel offered his collection to his home city of Hanover. After long negotiations, the city of Hanover and the state of Niedersachsen agreed to share the costs for building and maintenance of the museum. The Sprengel Museum combines three different collections: the Sprengel Collection, the collection of the state of Niedersachsen, and the collection of city of Hanover, all of which harmoniously complement each other. The Sprengel Collection concentrates on several focal points within the art of the twentieth century: the internationally unique collection of installations by Kurt Schwitters, El Lissitzky, and James Turrell, classical modern art, German expressionism, Neue Sachlichkeit, Max

Beckmann, Max Ernst, Paul Klee, and art after 1945.

Founded in 1976 as Cologne's newest museum, the Museum Ludwig is now one of the most important collections of modern art in the world. The museum acquired its new profile through a spectacular donation negotiated in a contract between Peter and Irene Ludwig, chocolate manufacturers from Aachen, and the city of Cologne. Cologne promised to build a new museum, the Ludwigs would give more than 300 works of art (mainly European and American avant-garde from the 1960s, including the famous collection of Pop Art) to the new Ludwig Foundation. The Ludwig Collection had been on permanent loan to the Wallraf-Richartz-Museum since 1969 and, growing steadily, had become too big for the old building. The new museum was opened on 6 September 1986 and established Cologne as one of the centres of the art world. Ludwig's interest in modern contemporary art was worldwide, and he tirelessly founded museums in numerous places which he furnished with his collections (e.g. Aachen, Basel, Budapest, Havana, St Petersburg and Vienna). Ludwig began to amass a large collection of GDR art in the 1970s which eventually led to the establishment of the *Ludwig-Institut für Kunst der DDR* in Oberhausen in 1984. Before his death in 1996 he was interested in communist art.

Thanks to Oskar Reinhart, a member of a wealthy merchant family, the Swiss town of Winterthur now possesses two significant collections, the Oskar Reinhart Collection, housed in Reinhart's former residence above the town, and the Oskar Reinhart Foundation, located in the centre of the town. Reinhart started collecting at an early age. When, in 1924, he withdrew from the family business, he devoted himself entirely to art. He bought the villa 'Am Römerholz' and was able to realize his dream of building a gallery of his own. Over the following years the collection was enriched and can now bear comparison with the finest museums in the world. Later it was divided into two parts, the 'Am Römerholz' Collection (private until Reinhart's death and opened to the public in 1970), which encompasses a great variety of masterpieces, mainly old masters and French nineteenth-century works, and the Oskar Reinhart

Foundation, which had been a public gallery from its inception in 1951. The collection of works by Swiss, German and Austrian artists from the eighteenth to the twentieth century can be regarded as a Swiss-German national gallery on a smaller scale.

Two of the youngest outstanding collectors in south-west Germany are Reinhold Würth and Rolf Deyhle. For the industrialist Reinhold Würth, art is a hobby and not his whole life. He understands the passion for collecting as a counterpole to the rationality of a businessman and aims at reducing the distance between his company and the public and creating a harmonious symbiosis of the working environment and art. Thus works of art are displayed in the offices at Künzelsau, Baden-Württemberg. The new administration building, opened in 1991, was planned to house two museums, one for the products of the company – screws and threads – the other for changing exhibitions from his collection. The Würth Collection started with a watercolour by Nolde, bought in the late 1960s. Until 1985, most works were added sporadically to the collection by Würth himself, following his wish to possess a specific work of art. Gaps in the collection were slowly closed with the help of experts, and in the late 1980s a concept was developed that emphasizes the main areas of the collection: classical modern art, contemporary Austrian and German art and fantastic realists like Rudolf Hausner.

Unlike Würth, the Swabian industrialist Rolf Deyhle started his collection in the mid-1950s with gothic madonnas, but soon turned to concentrate on artists living or working in south-west Germany of the last hundred years. Deyhle specialized in members of the Berlin Secession and their pupils who originated in the south-west, plein-air painting, abstract art, and Berlin contemporary art. The collection, one of the biggest German private collections, is not housed in a permanent museum, but could be seen in a travelling exhibition in 1992–3.

Apart from rich industrialists, gallery owners played a crucial role in introducing modern art after WWII. With the founding of a gallery in Munich in 1947, Etta and Otto Stangl started the long process of helping to re-anchor the long defamed avant-garde in the public's mind (mainly

Blauer Reiter, expressionism, classical modern art). The gallery soon became, commercially, extremely successful and renowned. Apart from loans to the Staatsgalerie moderner Kunst in Munich, granted from 1984, which determined the high standard of the display there, the Stangls endeavoured to found the Franz Marc Museum in Kochel. In 1990, after the death of Etta and Otto, the whole estate (circa 2,000 objects) went to the Staatsgalerie moderner Kunst in Munich.

Heinz Berggruen settled in Paris after the war where he founded his art gallery and slowly started collecting. On retiring in 1980, he became a collector wholeheartedly, focusing on Cézanne, Seurat, Matisse, Giacometti, Picasso (Berggruen's Picasso collection is one of the most important in private hands) and Klee. Twelve works by Klee were given to the Centre Pompidou, Paris, in 1972, and ninety to the Metropolitan Museum of Art, New York, in 1984. Lent to the National Gallery in London for several years, the Berggruen Collection was moved to another temporary home, a newly refurbished part of the Antikenmuseum in Berlin, in 1996, where it will be displayed for ten years.

The most eminent Swiss gallery is the Galerie Beyeler. Established in Basel in 1949, it was to become one of the crucial forces in the international modern art market. From his fund of art works, with which he supplied museums and private collections across the globe, Beyeler kept masterpieces back for his own collection, mainly classical modern art. In contrast to the sold works, the collection is more personal, selective and inconsistent. In 1982, the domestic art possessions were turned into a collection with a public claim with the establishment of the Beyeler Foundation that has since been responsible for the Collection Ernst and Hildy Beyeler. Parts of the collection could be seen in an exhibition in Madrid in 1989, and Beyeler opened his own museum for a permanent display in Riehen near Basel in 1997.

Quite an exception among the collectors is Lothar-Günther Buchheim, painter, publisher and author, who started to collect German expressionism straight after the war and has written and published several books on the subject since. The extraordinary collection is now the most extensive private collection of its kind. The works by *Die Brücke* are especially famous and were shown in the international travelling exhibition *Expressionisten: Sammlung Buchheim* (Expressionists: Collection Buchheim). Negotiations with Munich and Feldafing about a museum to accommodate his collections failed. The museum will now be built in Bernried near Munich, next to Buchheim's place of residence.

Over the last two decades, big firms have taken over the role of patrons. Corporate collecting may not purely be motivated by the passion for art, but instead follow mercantile and monetary aspects, complying with a marketing strategy or employed to improve the image of the firm. Yet, activities in the field of culture now being part of the conception of many companies, remarkable results have been achieved. The best example is Daimler-Benz who started its collection, dedicated to twentieth-century art of south-west Germany, in the late 1970s. Nevertheless, the regional emphasis is no dogma. At the new offices in Stuttgart, Andy Warhol featured prominently. Young and unknown artists are often contacted directly and employed in the activities of cultural sponsoring that Daimler-Benz has used since 1987. At the Deutsche Bank, only portraits of the directors hung in the offices at first. A concept, developed in 1980, was to put emphasis on works on paper by young comtemporary artists from the German-speaking regions. Purchases decorate the offices in order to enable staff and public to engage with art. On the occasion of its 125th anniversary in 1995, the Deutsche Bank organized an exhibition of works from the collection and set up the Cultural Foundation of the Deutsche Bank in Berlin. The Hypo-Bank, taking a slightly different approach, has never started its own collection. Already in the 1960s and 1970s the Hypo-Bank financed acquisitions by the Alte Pinakothek, Munich, to close gaps in their collection of eighteenth-century works. The Hypo Cultural Foundation was set up in 1983 with the purpose of supporting culture in general and running the Kunsthalle in Munich, where exhibitions of a high standard and international reputation take place. The attention given to such exhibitions shows that the individual collector will be pushed into the background in the future. It is initiatives like these that will put a different complexion on the structure of collections and museums in Germany.

See also: art exhibitions; museums; visual arts: Austria; visual arts: Switzerland

Further reading

The following catalogues give a good overview of the respective collections.

Auf Papier: Kunst des 20. Jahrhunderts aus der Deutschen Bank (1995) exhibition catalogue, Schirn Kunsthalle, Frankfurt am Main.
Colección Beyeler (1989) exhibition catalogue, Centro de Arte Reina Sofia, Madrid.
Modern Masters from the Thyssen-Bornemisza Collection (1984) exhibition catalogue-National Museum of Modern Art, Tokyo.
Museum Ludwig (ed.) (1996) *Kunst des 20. Jahrhunderts: Museum Ludwig Köln*, Cologne: Taschen.

INES SCHLENKER

art colleges

In a broad sense the term *Kunsthochschulen* (art colleges) comprises colleges or academies of visual arts, music and performing art, in a narrow sense only visual arts. Usually named Akademie der Bildenden Künste, Hochschule für Bildende Künste or Kunstakademie, these are federal institutions aimed at teaching the fine arts in the traditional disciplines of painting, sculpture, and architecture. In some German states, *Gesamthochschulen* or **universities** offer an equivalent course of study (e.g. Kassel, Mainz or Münster). The amendment to the *Hochschulrahmengesetz* (the federal university framework law) of 1985 clarified the status of art colleges as corporations having legal capacity, guaranteeing greater autonomy. The particular form and the finances of art colleges are regulated by individual laws of the federal states.

Art colleges are dedicated to the education of the rising artistic generation and the art teachers for schools. The range of subjects offered includes photography, video, visual communication, interior decoration, product, industrial, graphic, stage, and book design, fashion, textiles, and ceramics. Entrance examinations have to be taken, the ***Abitur*** is required for future art teachers, though not necessarily for art students. Numbers of students vary considerably from *c.* 120 at the Städelschule in Frankfurt am Main to *c.* 5,100 at the Hochschule der Künste in Berlin.

The FRG has had the following art colleges: Berlin (Hochschule der Künste, founded in 1696), Brunswick (Hochschule für Bildende Künste, 1963), Bremen (Hochschule für Gestaltende Kunst und Musik, 1988), Düsseldorf (Staatliche Kunstakademie – Hochschule für Bildende Künste, 1767), Frankfurt am Main (Staatliche Hochschule für Bildende Künste – Städelschule, 1815), Hamburg (Hochschule für Bildende Künste, 1767), Karlsruhe (Staatliche Akademie der Bildenden Künste, 1854), Munich (Akademie der Bildenden Künste, 1808), Nürnberg (Akademie der Bildenden Künste, 1940), Offenbach am Main (Hochschule für Gestaltung, 1970), Saarbrücken (Hochschule der Bildenden Künste, 1989), and Stuttgart (Staatliche Akademie der Bildenden Künste, 1761).

Four art colleges, which have undergone staff and structural renewals after unification, existed in the GDR: Berlin (Kunsthochschule, 1947), Dresden (Hochschule für Bildende Künste, 1764), Halle (Burg Giebichenstein, Hochschule für Kunst und Design, 1958), and Leipzig (Hochschule für Grafik und Buchkunst, 1764).

The workings of the three art colleges in Austria are regulated by the Kunsthochschul-Organisations-Gesetz (law on the organization of art colleges) of 21 January 1970. The art colleges in Vienna (Hochschule für angewandte Kunst, founded in 1867) and Linz (Hochschule für künstlerische und industrielle Gestaltung, 1947) accordingly have carried the title Kunsthochschule since 1970. Only Austria's oldest art college, the Akademie der Bildenden Künste in Vienna, founded as a private school in 1692, possesses its own statute and is allowed to keep the title of 1872 for reasons of tradition.

Switzerland has two higher federal art colleges in Geneva (Ecole supérieure d'Art visuel) and St Gallen (Kantonale Kunstschule) as well as two higher arts and crafts colleges in Geneva (Ecole des arts décoratifs) and Zürich (Höhere Schule für Gestaltung). Zürich also has the Freie Kunstschule and the Neue Kunstschule.

See also: education system; *Hochschule für Gestaltung*

Further reading

Deutscher Hochschulführer (1992) Stuttgart: Raabe.
Kunsthochschulführer (1987) Hamburg, Frankfurt am
   Main: Campus, Dölling und Galitz.

INES SCHLENKER

art exhibitions

Art exhibitions have strong cultural importance in
Germany. The first exhibitions in the post-war
period were begun already in 1947 with a showing of
abstract artists. This gesture had a particular
relevance for Germany, since it had been by means
of a special art exhibition, the *Entartete Kunst*
(Decadent Art) exhibit that toured Germany in the
mid-1930s, that the Nazis had solidified their control
on the cultural sphere. Public taste lagged behind the
attempt to rebuild links with Germany's pre-Nazi
cultural heritage. The years of Nazi rule had left
people with little or no experience with abstract
representation, and the exhibit met with little
success. It was not until the 1950s that Germans
began to widely appreciate expressionist art.

Since the mid-1980s theme-oriented, 'blockbuster' exhibitions have enjoyed incredible popularity.
While this phemonenon is of course not unique to
Germany, Germans show particular interest in
these types of exhibits. Shows that have held
particular interest for Germans are often oriented
along historical lines, such as the 'Europe and the
Orient' exhibit of 1989 and the 'Jewish Life' exhibit
of 1991. Of late particular enthusiasm has emerged
for art from non-European countries. Topics like
'Women of Ancient Egypt', 'Forgotten Cities of the
Indus', 'Old China' and 'Mongolia' drew large
numbers of visitors. Exhibits on specific modernist
artists are also common and highly popular. In
1991 a well-attended exhibition was held on
Modigliani in Düsseldorf, while Tübingen's
Kunsthalle hosted a huge Cézanne exhibit in
1993. In 1996 exhibits were held on Max
Liebermann and Renoir. A notable and highly
commercial component of these art exhibitions are
in-depth catalogues that provide an introduction to
historical framework, artists and reproductions of
the objects displayed at the exhibitions.

As in other countries, art exhibitions in

Germany have changed in recent years due to
innovations such as video, film and computer
technologies. There has also been a tendency with
performance art to blur the boundaries between
art exhibition and theatre. Every five years the city
of Kassel hosts **documenta**, the largest gala of
contemporary art in the world; in 1992 it attracted
over 600,000 visitors. Private collectors like Peter
Ludwig also play a huge role in determining the
direction contemporary art will take and providing
exposure to new artists. The gallery scenes in
Cologne and Berlin, while they can hardly compete
in scale with the blockbuster exhibitions, are
among the most active in the world.

Most recently German history has become a
particular exhibition draw. 1996 saw Germans
from both East and West examining GDR culture
with a touring exhibition that displayed Socialist
art, consumer products and advertising. This
exhibition marks the beginning of a reassessment
of East Germany's heritage and a greater curiosity
for a culture that was suddenly wiped off the map
in 1990.

See also: art collections; museums

Further reading

Federal Press Office of the Federal Republic of
   Germany, *Museums, Exhibitions and Collections*
   (general information on the importance of
   museums in German culture).

PETER M. McISAAC

Artmann, Hans Carl

b. 12 June 1921, Vienna

Writer and translator

A founding member of the **Wiener Gruppe**
(Vienna Group), Artmann was a key figure in
Austrian post-war avant-garde literature. His first
collection of poems, *med ana schwoazzn dintn* (in
black ink, 1958), pioneered the use of dialect as a
means of deconstructing standard language. It
triggered a wave of dialect poetry. His writing
mimics and juxtaposes different literary epochs,
styles and genres, thereby creating peculiar surrea-

listic effects. Artmann has translated poetry from many languages including Yiddish and Gaelic. He has been awarded the Austrian Prize for Literature (1974) and the Literary Prize of Vienna (1977).

See also: literature: Austria

ANNETTE BLÜHDORN

asylum, political

The West German Basic Law of 1949 granted the unqualified right of asylum to all foreigners who could prove that they had been politically persecuted. Under the pressure of steeply rising numbers of refugees coming to West Germany in the 1980s and claiming political asylum, a campaign to change the law started, which led to its amendment in 1993.

The background to the decision to include an unqualified right to political asylum in Article 16 of the Basic Law was formed by the political persecution of the Nazi period. The Parliamentary Council, which was charged with the task of formulating the Basic Law, decided that in the light of this background any qualification of the right to asylum would be wrong. During the early years of the Federal Republic the numbers of people claiming asylum remained small; 4,379 in 1966, rising to 9,627 in 1975. Many of these claims were from eastern bloc countries in Europe and were treated sympathetically. In the late 1970s, however, the numbers rose dramatically as a result of a number of conflicts, such as the civil war in Afghanistan. In 1980 the number of claims reached 107,818, and the reaction of the West German government was to sharpen the rules governing asylum. It introduced compulsory visas before entry, a ban on the right to work and a reduction in the benefits which could be claimed. Although numbers went down in the middle of the 1980s, they rose again sharply, reaching 121,318 (1989), 256,112 (1991) and 438,191 in 1992. The increase was due largely to the political changes in eastern Europe, and in particular to the civil war in Yugoslavia.

The increase in numbers caused a rise in fears that Germany would be overwhelmed by foreigners which led to increased support for such right-wing parties as the **Republikaner** which exploited these fears, and to a rise in attacks on foreigners. The government tried to reduce the waiting times for claims to be processed since many of the fears were caused by the concentration of a large number of foreigners in camps and hostels. Also there was a general public perception that many of the claimants were not genuine, but economic refugees. This perception was heightened by the fact that the proportion of claims which were recognized had fallen to below 5 percent (4.4 percent in 1990). As a result, the political pressure to change Article 16 grew. After intense debate the new Article 16a was passed in the Bundestag on 1 July 1993 with the support of the opposition Social Democrats. The original sentence guaranteeing the right to asylum is maintained, but it is qualified by a number of conditions. A list of 'safe' countries of origin was established, including all countries in eastern Europe; entry via 'safe' third countries, which include all the countries surrounding Germany, cannot be granted to those seeking asylum. The result of the changes was a steep drop in claims for asylum, by over 70 percent in the following year. But this drop has been accompanied by a steep rise in illegal entries, especially via Poland and the Czech Republic.

PETER BARKER

Atelier 5

Established in Bern in 1955 by E. Fritz, S. Grieber, R. Hesterberg, H. Hostettler and A. Pini, the architectural partnership Atelier 5 regards Le Corbusier as its mentor, his formal language and working method characterizing large parts of the group's work. It gained international recognition with the Halen housing estate in 1961. Densely constructed, yet clearly defined spaces, combined with ecologically and economically sound planning, form the foundation for its high conceptual and formal quality. The group is also known for the development of innovative typologies, from hospital rooms to mixed usage areas (e.g. the Fischergarten in Solothurn 1989–94).

MARTIN KUDLEK AND BERTHOLD PESCH

Auer & Weber

This architectural partnership was established by Fritz Auer and Karlheinz Weber with offices in Stuttgart and Munich. The former **Behnisch** employees' first independent projects are located around Stuttgart and Munich. They became known outside Germany with their award-winning competition-design for the EXPO Pavilion in Seville (1990; in collaboration with the sculptor Albert Hien) which was scandalously left unbuilt. This unusually successful fusion of art and architecture represented a '*Deutschlandschaft*' (Deutsch-landscape) penetrated by a Zeppelin.

Their architecture's characteristic 'southern German lightness' is exemplified in such buildings as the Airport administration building in Erding (1993) and the Pentling service-station (1988 and 1992–4).

MARTIN KUDLEK AND BERTHOLD PESCH

Aufbau Verlag

Established in 1945 in Berlin by the **Kulturbund**, Aufbau rapidly developed an international reputation as the GDR's most prestigious publishing house. Initially committed to making the cultural heritage suppressed by Nazism (the bourgeois tradition of Heinrich and Thomas **Mann** as much as the work of socialist contemporaries like Bertolt **Brecht** and Anna **Seghers**) accessible to a wide readership, Aufbau later attracted leading representatives of the new generation of GDR authors (Christa **Wolf**, Christoph **Hein**, and Helga **Königsdorf**) to its ranks. Strengthened by a new paperback series, it retains a significant publishing presence in unified Germany.

See also: publishing: GDR

DENNIS TATE

Aufklärung

Originally associated with the eighteenth-century 'Age of Reason', *Aufklärung* (or 'enlightenment'), with its emphasis on human autonomy through the power of rationality, has a distinctive tradition in

Germany, and has been an essential component in forming the basis of modern society. However, in an effort to understand the rise of Nazism, Theodor W. **Adorno** and Max **Horkheimer**, as well as other philosophers and social theorists of the **Frankfurt School**, developed a critical understanding of *Aufklärung* that saw human reason being increasingly used as an agent of social control. The term has, none the less, retained positive associations for many radical thinkers in Germany.

See also: Benjamin, Walter; Bloch, Ernst; Habermas, Jürgen; Lukács, Georg; Marcuse, Herbert; Marxism

Further reading

Adorno, T. and Horkheimer, M. (1972) *The Dialectic of Enlightenment*, trans. J. Cumming, New York: Continuum.

VICTOR E. TAYLOR

Augstein, Rudolf

b. 5 November 1923, Hanover

Publisher and writer

Founder and general editor of the influential news magazine *Der Spiegel*, Augstein has frequently been at the centre of political controversies (see also **Spiegel, Der**). He was unjustly jailed during the 1962 scandal known as the **Spiegel Affair**, but released after a short time. Throughout his career as journalist, author and political commentator he has often taken highly controversial positions concerning such subjects as the *Historikerstreit*, **terrorism** and **unification**. These positions have earned him both praise and criticism from influential representatives of the political left and right.

See also: journalism; magazines; mass media

MICHAEL R. HAYSE

Auschwitz

Auschwitz, near the town of Oswieczim in Poland, has come to symbolize the **Holocaust** and the entire process of Nazi genocide. Set up in 1940 as a 'concentration camp' for Soviet prisoners of war, Auschwitz began to function as a death camp in March 1942, one of six such camps in occupied Poland (Belzec, Chelmo, Majdanek, Sobibor and Treblinka). Victims included Poles, Gypsies, Soviet prisoners and others and, above all, Jews from Nazi-occupied Europe. In Auschwitz alone, an estimated four million people were killed, more than half of them Jews.

The Auschwitz complex included the mass-murder installations in Auschwitz-Birkenau and a slave labour camp linked to a synthetic oil and rubber plant (IG Farben) in Monovitz. In October 1941 Himmler ordered Rudolf Hoeß, the first commandant, to enlarge Auschwitz-Birkenau and transform it into a death camp. This entailed the construction of five crematoria by the Erfurt firm of Topf with a capacity of burning up to 10,000 bodies within twenty-four hours, and the construction of 'shower-rooms' where 2,000 victims could be herded together and poisoned by Zyklon-B (supplied by IG Farben). In June 1942 the installations were in place to receive mass 'transports' and effect 'selection'. Between 18 May and 7 July 1944, for instance, over 200,000 Hungarian Jews were murdered.

Having forced the Jews into ghettos, the Nazis deported them in cattle trucks. The railway line ended at Auschwitz-Birkenau. 'Selection' took place directly on the *Rampe*: those young and strong enough were marched off to serve as slave labour in Monovitz; the old and frail, children and women with children went directly to their death. On entering the 'shower' everyone had to strip naked. Death by Zyklon-B was neither immediate nor painless but could take several minutes. *Sonderkommandos*, concentration camp prisoners guarded by the SS, dragged the bodies to the crematoria after removing gold teeth and cutting off their hair for commercial use. Shoes, clothing and belongings of the victims were sent to Germany, including the Nazi *Winterhilfswerk* (Winter Assistance Organization). Those not immediately murdered survived only as long as their function was required by the SS in a *Sonderkommando*, as slave labour or for medical experiments in the 'hospital'.

Bombing the crematoria or the railway line might have saved many lives. It was rejected, although the Americans and the British bombed Monovitz between August and December 1944. *Sonderkommandos* helped by women prisoners succeeded on 7 October 1944 in blowing up one crematorium and damaging another, but the revolt was crushed by the SS. Gassings continued until 26 November 1944 when Himmler ordered the dismantling of the remaining crematoria and the move of prisoners away from the advance of the Soviet troops. Many died on death marches and cattle trains from Auschwitz or, as Anne Frank, in the disease-infested concentration camp Bergen Belsen. On 18 January 1945, the SS ordered the evacuation of Auschwitz and the last thousands of prisoners were marched westwards. Of those too sick to move, several hundred were shot. It was not until 27 January 1945 that the camp was liberated by the Soviet troops. They found the despoils of the victims, including rows of prams and mountains of human hair, and 7,500 survivors.

See also: *Historikerstreit*; *Vergangenheitsbewältigung*

EVA KOLINSKY

Ausländer

This term – usually translated as 'foreigner' – designates people of non-German nationality. Some seven million residents of Germany are *Ausländer*, over half of whom have lived there for more than ten years. Many – especially the large Turkish community – came to Germany as **Gastarbeiter**; others – particularly in the 1990s – came as asylum-seekers (see also **asylum, political**). The official policy that Germany is not a 'country of immigration', coupled with restrictive citizenship laws (which accord citizenship on the basis of descent, *ius sanguini*, rather than birthplace, *ius soli*), means that the descendants of *Ausländer* also retain the status of 'aliens' despite linguistic and cultural assimilation into German life. An easing of naturalization procedures for these subsequent generations of *Ausländer* was promised by the new **Schröder** government in 1998, but the whole issue remains highly contentious: the political establishment is divided on the question of dual nationality, and Germans consistently rank 'the *Ausländer* problem' near the top of their list of worries in opinion polls.

See also: migrant literature; minorities, non-German; multiculturalism; refugees

JOHN SANDFORD

Ausländer, Rose

b. 11 May 1901, Czernowitz (then Romania); d. 3 January 1988, Düsseldorf

Poet

Like her compatriot Paul **Celan**, Ausländer was shaped by the rich pre-war German-Jewish culture of Czernowitz. Much of her poetry deals with irrevocable loss: '*Du suchst das verlorne Eden / stolperst über Grabhügel*' (You seek the lost Eden, stumble over graves). She finds consolation in her 'preferred words: dreams, stars, word, breath, air'. She wrote a number of vibrant New York poems during her American exile.

Further reading

Braun, H. (ed.) (1991) *Rose Ausländer. Materialien zu Leben und Werk*, Frankfurt am Main: Fischer Taschenbuch Verlag (includes documentation, photos, essays and bibliography).

BEVERLEY DRIVER EDDY

Autobahn

An efficient transport net with a strong emphasis on motorways is seen as vital for economic and private mobility, and also, since their inauguration in the Third Reich, as a national symbol of German affluence and freedom (celebrated rather coyly, for instance, in music by the group **Kraftwerk**). Thirty percent of traffic volume occurs on the 11,200 km of motorways, with an ever-increasing traffic volume (increasingly to and

from eastern Europe). There is no speed limit. Concern over the ecological and health problems associated with large volumes of high-speed traffic resulted in proposals for a speed limit, but catalytic converters were opted for instead.

JUDITH LEEB

Autonome

Emerging in the early 1980s, as politically motivated leftist groups without any apparent central organization, the *Autonome* have been involved in agitprop, riots and violent clashes with neo-nazis (see also **neo-nazism**). Total membership estimates range between 2,700 and 6,500 (1992), recruited mostly from the eighteen to twenty-eight age group, with over 1,000 members in Berlin alone. Since their reorganization in 1990–1 they have also been known as *Autonome Antifa*, focusing primarily on anti-fascist activities. Due to their masked militant wing *Schwarzer Block* (Black Bloc), the *Autonome* are widely regarded as left-wing extremists and have been investigated as a terrorist and criminal organization.

See also: neo-nazism; terrorism

FREDERIC M. KOPP

Autumn, German

The traumatic '*Deutscher Herbst*' of 1977 saw the culmination of **terrorism** in the Federal Republic. In retrospect it can be perceived as a turning-point at which the democratic state stood the test of blackmail from armed extremists. At the time many on the left feared the potential consequences of the highly-charged atmosphere of the moment. Their concerns were famously reflected in the film *Deutschland im Herbst*, a joint episodic work to which nine different directors (including **Fassbinder**, **Kluge** and **Schlöndorff**) contributed their individual responses to the 'German Autumn'.

See also: *Tendenzwende*

JOHN SANDFORD

Axen, Hermann

b. 6 March 1916, Leipzig; d. 15 February 1992, Berlin

GDR functionary

After release from a concentration camp, Axen became a founder member of the **FDJ** in 1946. He then became a leading functionary responsible for propaganda and agitation in the **SED** hierarchy, and then editor of the SED newspaper ***Neues Deutschland*** (1956–66). In December 1970 he became a full member of the **Politbüro** with particular responsibility for external relations. From 1984 he led the attempt to establish a dialogue with the West German SPD. After unification he was accused of misappropriation of funds, but was deemed to be too ill to stand trial.

PETER BARKER

Ayim, May

b. 3 May 1960, Hamburg; d. 9 August 1996, Berlin

Writer

Poet, essayist, teacher and social activist May Ayim – known as May Opitz until 1992 – was a key figure in the emergence of contemporary Afro-German consciousness. Of Ghanaian-German origins, she was initially raised in a home for children, then by a foster family. Trained as a teacher and speech therapist, in 1985 she co-founded the Initiative Schwarze Deutsche und Schwarze in Deutschland (Movement of Black Germans and Blacks in Germany) and co-edited two influential books: *Showing Our Colors: Afro-German Women Speak Out* (*Farbe bekennen: Afro-Deutsche Frauen auf den Spuren ihrer Geschichte*, 1986), and *Entfernte Verbindungen: Rassismus, Antisemitismus, Klassenunterdrückung* (Distant Connections: Racism, Anti-Semitism, Class Oppression) (1993). Ayim's first volume of poetry, *blues in schwarz weiss* (Blues in Black and White), appeared to high praise in 1995; the second, *Nachtgesang* (Nocturne), in 1997 after she had taken her own life.

PATRICIA HERMINGHOUSE

B

Baader, Andreas

b. 6 May 1943, Munich; d. 18 October 1977, Stuttgart-Stammheim

Terrorist

A leading figure in West German left-wing **terrorism**, Baader gave his name to the Baader–Meinhof Group or Red Army Faction (RAF). In contrast to the other highly educated group members who had been part of the **student movement**, Baader was an educational drop-out without qualifications. In 1968, together with Gudrun **Ensslin**, he was convicted for an arson attack on a department store in Frankfurt am Main, but was freed by force in 1970 by, amongst others, Ulrike **Meinhof**. Rearrested in 1972, and convicted in April 1977 of murder, bank robbery and other crimes, he committed suicide in prison.

MONIKA PRÜTZEL-THOMAS

Babelsberg

Babelsberg is Germany's most important film studio, named after its location between Berlin and Potsdam (until 1938 'Neubabelsberg'). Before 1945 it was the production centre of Ufa (Universum Film AG), afterwards until 1992 of **DEFA**.

The original glass-house studio was designed and built from 1911 to 1912 for Deutsche Bioscop Gesellschaft under the supervision of its chief cameraman and technical director Guido Seeber. Important productions of the early years included films starring Asta Nielsen and a number of *Autorenfilme* (films based on scripts by renowned authors), amongst them Paul Wegener's *The Student of Prague* (*Der Student von Prag*) in 1913 and his first *Golem* in 1914.

Following a period of economic uncertainty after WWI Deutsche Bioscop merged with Erich Pommer's French-German Decla Film Gesellschaft to become Decla-Bioscop (1920). A year later it was taken over by Ufa, Germany's largest film concern set up in 1917 by the state, big banks and large industrial concerns for the purpose of countering anti-German film propaganda.

Many of the films produced in Babelsberg under Pommer, as executive producer of Decla-Biosop and Ufa, contributed substantially towards the 1920s becoming the 'Golden Age of German Cinema': Fritz Lang's *Mabuse* films (1921–2), his *Nibelungen* (1922) and *Metropolis* (1925), F.W. Murnau's *Phantom* (1922) and *The Last Laugh* (*Der letzte Mann*, 1924). Other directors working at Babelsberg included E.A. Dupont, Ludwig Berger, Alexander Korda, Reinhold Schünzel and G.W. Pabst.

During the 1920s Babelsberg became Europe's largest film studio and Ufa the only serious challenge to Hollywood hegemony. It also faced severe financial and organizational difficulties due to mismanagement, lack of financial control and attempts to compete with expensive Hollywood epics. For a brief period financially dependent on the American companies Paramount and Metro-Goldwyn-Meyer, Ufa was acquired by the right-wing newspaper tycoon Alfred Hugenberg in 1927. The new management under the directorship of

Ludwig Klitzsch appointed Ernst Hugo Correll as chief of production and introduced strict controls along Hollywood production-line methods.

After the advent of sound, Ufa built Europe's most modern sound studio and scored a number of successes, amongst them Josef von Sternberg's *The Blue Angel (Der blaue Engel*, 1930) and a series of big budget musicals such as Eric Charell's *Congress Dances (Der Kongress tanzt*, 1932). Despite being responsible for *Hitler Youth Quex* (1933), Ufa did not become the main producer of Nazi propaganda feature films after the take-over of power by the National Socialists. Instead, it pursued a policy of safeguarding its commercial interests while producing occasional nationalist films. Propaganda minister Goebbels did not manage to get a tight control over Ufa until 1939 when he finally succeeded in removing Correll from his post and, in 1942, integrated the company into the state concern UFI (Ufa Film GmbH).

After WWII Babelsberg became the home of the GDR state film company **DEFA** and, following unification, the property of the **Treuhand**. In 1992, it was sold to a French property investment company; filmmaker Volker **Schlöndorff** became one of its two managing directors.

See also: film: GDR

Further reading

Bock, H.-M. and Töteberg, M. (1992) *Das Ufa-Buch*, Frankfurt am Main: Zweitausendeins (standard work on Ufa).

Jacobsen, W. (ed.) (1992) *Babelsberg. Das Filmstudio*, Berlin: Argon (collection of essays covering the entire history of Babelsberg; includes bibliography and filmography).

HORST CLAUS

Bacher, Gerd

b. 18 November 1925, Salzburg

Journalist

Originally a newspaper journalist in Salzburg, from 1954–61 Bacher was chief editor of various papers in Vienna. He was director-general of the

Austrian broadcasting corporation **ORF** from 1967–74, 1978–87 and 1990–4, and worked as a media adviser to German Chancellor **Kohl** (1974) and as managing director of a Salzburg publisher. From 1989–90 he was editor of the Austrian daily *Die Presse*, and was at times consultant to various large German publishing houses (see **Presse, Die**).

He is regarded as one of the most controversial and most powerful Austrian journalists of the post-war era.

GEORG HELLMAYR

Bachmann, Ingeborg

b. 25 June 1926, Klagenfurt; d. 17 October 1973, Rome

Writer

Austrian poet and novelist Ingeborg Bachmann first came to prominence through her association with the **Gruppe 47** and, after her death, was a major influence on the **Frauenliteratur** of the 1970s and 1980s. The modernist poems in the post-war volume *Die gestundete Zeit* (Mortgaged Time) of 1953 contain a call for moral engagement but were interpreted apolitically and praised in purely aesthetic terms, as were those in the subsequent 1956 volume, *Anrufung des großen Bären* (Invocation of the Great Bear), which reflect Bachmann's experiences in Italy and seek escape from the darkness of the present day in myth and utopian visions. Bachmann's turn to prose and to gender-related themes with the two volumes of short stories, *The Thirtieth Year (Das dreißigste Jahr)* of 1961 and *Three Paths to the Lake (Simultan)* of 1972, signalled the path she was to take in her seminal novel *Malina* (1971) and the other novels in the planned *Todesarten* (Ways of Death) cycle, *Der Fall Franza* (1979) and *Requiem für Fanny Goldmann* (1979). The cycle, presenting variations on the theme of the murderous effects of a patriarchal society on women, remained unfinished at the time of her accidental death in 1972. Bachmann also wrote three radio plays, including *The Good God of Manhattan (Der gute Gott von Manhattan)*, published 1958, which was strongly influenced by Bertolt

Brecht, and three librettos for the composer H.W. **Henze**. She was the first writer to deliver the Frankfurt Lectures on Poetics (1959–60). *Der Fall Franza* was filmed in 1987, and *Malina* (with a screenplay by Elfriede **Jelinek**) in 1991.

An intellectual by training, Bachmann wrote her Ph.D. on **Heidegger**'s existentialist philosophy, which, together with **Wittgenstein**'s theories of the limits of language, profoundly influenced her writing. Her most insistently recurring theme is the continuation of fascistic ways of thinking in postwar Austria and Germany. She frequently sought ways to express the inexpressible, to avoid despair and to think beyond the crisis of the modern subject by means of dream, myth and the adoption of musical structures, particularly in the highly complex and intertextual *Malina*. Bachmann's attempt to show how subjectivity is constructed by the forces of history and through language was met with incomprehension by contemporary critics, but led after her death to a reappraisal of her work by feminists, and in particular by Christa **Wolf**. Recent critics have stressed the links between her **modernism** and her understanding of the deadly workings of patriarchy.

Further reading

Achberger, K.R. (1995) *Understanding Ingeborg Bachmann*, Columbia, SC: University of South Carolina Press (overview of works; bibliography).

Arnold, H.L. (ed.) (1984) *Ingeborg Bachmann*, Munich: edition text + kritik (essays).

Bartsch, K. (1988) *Ingeborg Bachmann*, Stuttgart: Metzler (overview of works; bibliography).

Boa, E. (1996) 'Reading Ingeborg Bachmann', in C. Weedon (ed.), *Postwar Women's Writing in German*, Providence, RI: Berghahn Books (contextualizing essay which seeks to reconcile the modernist poet with the feminist novelist).

Lennox, S. (1993) 'The Feminist Reception of Ingeborg Bachmann', in J. Clausen and S. Friedrichsmeyer (eds) *Women in German Yearbook* 8: 73–111 (includes bibliography).

BRIGID HAINES

BAföG

Introduced in 1971, the *Bundesausbildungsförderungsgesetz* (Federal Training Assistance Act) awards means-tested financial assistance, a combination of grant and interest-free loan, to **students** in further and higher education. From the fifth semester, assistance is contingent on academic performance and its duration based on a standard period of study. Repayment begins five years after graduation, consisting of monthly instalments over a twenty-year period. Students who graduate early or achieve exceptionally good results can have their repayments waived. In 1991 nearly 90 percent of students in the new *Länder* received BAföG, compared to a quarter in the old *Länder*.

HANS J. HAHN

Bahro, Rudolf

b. 18 November 1935, Bad Flinsberg (Silesia; now Swiedarow Zdroj, Poland); d. 5 December 1997, Berlin

Marxist dissident in the GDR, later green fundamentalist philosopher

Previously unknown, Bahro emerged as a Marxist critic of the GDR regime when he appeared on West German television in August 1977 to introduce his book *The Alternative in Eastern Europe (Die Alternative. Zur Kritik des real existierenden Sozialismus)*. Arrested the next day and sentenced to eight years imprisonment for 'espionage', an international campaign for his freedom forced his release to West Germany in 1978 where he became a left-wing activist and co-founder of the Green Party. He broke with the **Greens** in the early 1980s over what he considered their excessive political realism and went on to preach an increasingly radical, 'New Age' ecological philosophy centred around rural communities and small-scale, local production, in order to stop what he called the 'modern industrial megamachine'. He also taught philosophy at the University of Bremen and, after unification, the Humboldt University in Berlin.

As an East German dissident, Bahro was unusual in that he had no association with the established dissident circles around Robert **Have-**

mann and Wolf **Biermann**. Having joined the ruling SED in 1954, Bahro graduated in philosophy in 1959 and worked as a journalist on various party journals until 1966, when differences over editorial policy led to his dismissal as deputy editor of the student magazine *Forum* and redeployment as a technical manager in a Berlin rubber factory. Rather than getting involved in political protests, he translated his disillusionment with the **SED**, after the suppression of the Prague Spring in 1968, into a long-term project of a theoretical critique of Soviet-style communism. In his book, he argued that the deformations of Soviet communism had had their origins in the pre-capitalist, 'Asiatic' mode of production prevalent in Russia at the time of the Bolshevik Revolution, and that while Stalinism had served a progressive historical function in bringing Russia and eastern Europe into industrial modernity, the bureaucratic 'socialism as it actually exists' was now an anachronism. Bahro advocated a 'cultural revolution' led by a 'League of Communists' recruited from the most enlightened sections of the ruling communist parties and the intelligentsia, with the aim of overcoming the traditional division into manual and intellectual labour and returning to the original communism of Karl Marx. Bahro's ideas were widely debated among the western left but made little significant impact in the GDR and eastern Europe. His later radical-ecologist writings have had little influence beyond a small band of followers.

See also: dissent and opposition: GDR

Major works

Bahro, R. (1981) *The Alternative in Eastern Europe*, London: Verso (English translation of the 1977 critique of communism).
—— (1984) *From Red to Green: Interviews with New Left Review*, London: Verso (accounts for his development from Marxist dissident to radical ecologist).
—— (1994) *Avoiding Social and Ecological Disaster: The Politics of World Transformation*, Bath: Gateway (introduction to his more recent, radical-ecologist philosophy).

GÜNTER MINNERUP

ballet

Ignored under National Socialism, ballet dominated the early post-war dance scene. The feeling that there was no fascist taint to overcome allowed companies to concentrate on the search for a German identity within the classical vocabulary. In the early 1960s, the Stuttgart Ballet under John Cranko introduced a tacit self-criticism via radical left-wing themes. A vibrant, experimental climate developed known as the 'ballet-boom'. By 1968, the desire to create a visibly German ballet led to rapprochement with the movement vocabulary of the modern dance. A hybrid genre arose that has characterized the German ballet ever since.

See also: dance

JULIA H. WAGNER

Ballhaus, Michael

b. 5 August 1935, Berlin

Cinematographer

After several years as cameraman with Südwestfunk television Baden-Baden, Ballhaus collaborated with R.W. **Fassbinder** on fourteen films, including *The Marriage of Maria Braun* (*Die Ehe der Maria Braun*) of 1979. His cinematography for other German directors, such as Peter **Lilienthal**, Margarethe von **Trotta**, Hans W. **Geissendörfer** and Volker **Schlöndorff** (*Death of a Salesman*, 1985), is equally distinguished for its sophistication and professional polish. Later he became highly sought-after in Hollywood, working with Martin Scorsese, Robert Redford and Wolfgang **Petersen** (*Outbreak*, 1995). He has also achieved success in music videos (for Prince, Bruce Springsteen).

CHRISTIAN ROGOWSKI

banana

Much loved by West German consumers, but unavailable to ordinary GDR citizens, the humble banana became an icon of the East German revolution of 1989. With the opening of inner-German borders in November, this eye-catching fruit was a popular purchase among East Germans visiting the overflowing shops of the West for the first time, and came to symbolize their rejection of an economic and political system which failed to deliver in material terms in favour of the apparent affluence of West German capitalism. The FRG remains the largest market for bananas in Europe.

JOANNA MCKAY

banks

There is more diversity in German banking than is commonly assumed, when only the 'big three' private banks, the Dresdner, Commerz and Deutsche, are under consideration. There are three forms of ownership in the banking system – private, public and co-operative. Typically all take the form of universal banks, offering a full range of services. The exceptions are the specialized mortgage banks, postal giro banks and, finally, the Kreditanstalt für Wiederaufbau, which has played a strategic role in post-war reconstruction, latterly lending to the *Mittelstand* (middle-class) medium-sized firms and for regional development. All of the three main types of bank are affiliated to their national associations and to the umbrella body, the Bundesverband deutscher Banken eV, which has 252 German affiliates and 58 branches of foreign banks affiliated. All these credit institutions are subject to official supervision by the Federal Banking Supervisory Authority, the Bundesaufsichtsamt für das Kreditwesen (BAK).

The private sector commercial banks tended to grow in the phase of rapid industrialization in the late nineteenth century as house banks to industrial firms, financing their capital needs and liquidity, while assuming a commensurate role in their supervisory boards. In this, the banks substituted for poorly-developed German capital markets and they themselves offered brokers' services to companies. In the post-war period, the failure of the allies' deconcentration policy is evident in the reconstitution of the 'big three' banks, facilitated by legislation in 1952 and 1957. The 'big three' each have capital of between DM 5 billion and DM 10 billion, while the Bayerische Hypobank and Bayerische Vereinsbank each have DM 3.5 billion in own capital.

The origins of the co-operative banks are found in the self-help movements among peasants and artisans, namely, the Raffeisen agricultural credit institutions and the Volksbanken in the urban areas. By the end of the nineteenth century, they had a local, regional and national structure, and in the 1990s, the Deutsche Genossenschaftsbank, which manages the liquidity of the sector, is Germany's fourth largest bank. Also part of the co-operative banking sector are Schwäbisch Hall, the largest home loan association, and R&V Versicherungen, the eighth largest insurance company. The trade-union-owned Bank für Gemeinwirtschaft was brought down in the early 1980s by the Co-op's financial difficulties and by the failure of the Neue Heimat property and construction group.

The savings banks and *Landesbanken*, which make up public sector banking, have origins in the nineteenth century, when local authorities sought to encourage small savers. The *Landesbanken* operated a giro cheque system between local savings banks, and came to operate as regional central banks in the *Länder*, housebank to *Land* governments and subsidiaries of the **Bundesbank**. Having begun by attracting savings deposits and lending long-term, the savings banks also now attract short-term deposits and lend to the *Mittelstand* and the self-employed. The three largest *Landesbanken* have seen spectacular balance sheet growth and rank among the ten largest German banks. The power of the banks in their direct shareholdings and their proxy voting on behalf of their depositors has been the subject of a series of Monopoly Commission inquiries, because of fears of insider knowledge. The prevalence of cross-shareholdings increases their power.

Further reading

Owen Smith, E. (1994) *The German Economy*, London: Routledge (exhaustive survey of German economy).

CHRISTOPHER H. FLOCKTON

BAP

BAP (which means 'father'), founded in 1979 by lead singer Wolfgang Niedecken, are a Cologne-based rock group who made their mark by singing in 'kölsch', the local dialect (their immediate precursors in this were the 'kölschrock' band Bläck Fööss). Singing an earnest brand of folk rock, BAP first achieved notoriety in 1982 with their immensely popular album 'Für Usszeschnigge' (To Cut Out) which featured the hit single 'Verdamp lang her' (A Damn Long Time Ago). An uncompromising disdain for fashion trends, as well as a commitment to socially oriented rock music, have been the hallmarks of their long career.

MATTHEW T. GRANT

Barth, Karl

b. 10 May 1886, Basel; d. 10 December 1968, Basel

Protestant theologian

Barth was one of the twentieth century's most influential Protestant theologians. The 1919 publication of his *The Epistle to the Romans* (*Der Römerbrief*) marked a radical break with Protestant liberal theology and the beginning of dialectical theology. Extraordinary Professor at Göttingen (1921), then Professor at Münster (1925) and Bonn (1930), Barth (a Swiss citizen) played a leading role after 1933 in the Confessing Church opposing Nazi church policies. Forced from Germany in 1935, he became in 1935 professor at Basel until his official retirement in 1961. His life's work was the *Church Dogmatics* (*Die kirchliche Dogmatik*), thirteen volumes published between 1932 and 1967.

Further reading

Busch, E. (1976) *Karl Barth (Karl Barths Lebenslaut)*, 2nd edn, trans. J. Bowden, London: SCM Press (a biography by Barth's last assistant, it includes a bibliography).

STEPHEN BROWN

Bartning, Otto

b. 12 April 1883, Karlsruhe; d. 20 February 1959, Darmstadt

Architect

Having studied in Karlsruhe and Berlin, Bartning established a private practice in Berlin in 1908. He was Director of the Staatliche Bauhochschule in Weimar from 1926 to 1930, chairman of the Deutscher Werkbund in 1946, and President of the Bund Deutscher Architekten (Association of German Architects) from 1950 to 1959.

Bartning collaborated with Gropius on the original plans for setting up the Bauhaus which later proceeded without him. He became internationally known with his steel church for the Pressa exhibition in Cologne in 1928. After the war he was in charge of planning an experimental pressed-earth housing estate in Neckarsteinbach (1946) and he also built forty-nine make-shift churches using prefabricated parts (1948–50).

MARTIN KUDLEK

Baselitz, Georg

b. 23 January 1938, Deutschbaselitz

Painter, sculptor and graphic artist

Georg Baselitz is a leading figure of **neo-expressionism**, which has gained international acclaim as a specifically German art since the late 1970s. Baselitz critically explores aspects of Germany's past and present. The 'German motives' are transformed into provocative events of ferocious colours and expressive forms explicitly referring to the tradition of expressionism. By turning his paintings upside down he lends them an additional degree of abstraction. His sculptures are the result of violent forces and great physical effort.

See also: documenta; Kiefer, Anselm; painting; sculpture

KERSTIN MEY

Baser, Tevfik

b. 12 January 1951, Cankiri (Turkey)

Filmmaker

As a director of fiction films, Baser addresses the emotional and cultural problems facing Turkish **Gastarbeiter** and their dependants in Germany. In *40 Square Metres of Germany (40 m² Deutschland)* of 1986 and *Farewell to a False Paradise (Abschied vom falschen Paradies)* of 1988, he focuses on the privations of Turkish women whose lives are restricted to their own four walls. His 1990 film *Farewell Foreign Parts (Lebewohl, Fremde)* is the story of two lovers who do not share a common language, and the theme is broadened to the more general issue of intercultural communication.

See also: film: FRG

HELEN HUGHES

Baumeister, Willi

b. 22 January 1889, Stuttgart; d. 31 August 1955, Stuttgart

Painter and art-theorist

Baumeister devoted his entire œuvre to pictorial abstraction. His early, constructivist style reflected a belief in progress. After 1933, it was replaced by a darker, prehistoric primitivism, treating mythic subject matter. In 1947 his influential treatise *Das Unbekannte in der Kunst* (The Unknown in Art) propounded abstract art as expressive of the spiritual and metaphysical. When abstraction began to dominate art in Cold-War West Germany, Baumeister emerged as one of its leading figures. To the German public, he provided a surviving link to modernism; internationally his art represented the new, democratic Germany.

DANIEL KOEP

Bausch, Pina

b. 27 March 1940, Solingen

Dancer and choreographer

Since 1973 Bausch has been director of the Wuppertaler Tanztheater, a dance collective which has profoundly influenced both modern dance and feminist and postmodern theatre with its often plotless collages of movement, often drawn from everyday gestures and poses (the traumas of childhood, relationships and failed communication are recurrent themes), and integrating the spoken word and a huge range of music: classical, operetta, jazz, evergreens and folk. Despite formal parallels with Brechtian *Verfremdung*, Bausch's aesthetic distancing of the familiar is primarily emotional rather than analytical.

Further reading

Hoghe, R. (1986) *Pina Bausch. Tanztheatergeschichten*, Frankfurt am Main: Suhrkamp

MORAY McGOWAN

Bayreuth Festival

Founded in 1876 by Richard Wagner for the exclusive performance of his music dramas, the Bayreuth Festival had by the 1920s became a stale repository of outmoded tradition, and by the 1930s a centre of Nazi pilgrimage. Its post-war reopening was delayed by conflict between the generations of the Wagner family, who continue to run it. When in 1951 it opened with *Parsifal* and *The Ring*, its stylized and simplified approach to the visual presentation of Wagner's work broke decisively with tradition. In the productions of the composer's grandsons, Wieland and Wolfgang **Wagner**, the new Bayreuth style came to represent the continual re-examination of these mammoth, labyrinthine works. Wieland died in 1966, leaving his brother in sole charge. He has opened out Bayreuth's policy, inviting other distinguished producers, such as Götz **Friedrich**, Harry Kupfer and Patrice Chereau.

BEATRICE HARPER

Becher, Johannes R.

b. 22 May 1891, Munich; d. 11 October 1958, (East) Berlin

Poet and politician

An expressionist poet in his youth, Becher, a revolutionary Marxist, ended his days deeply at odds with his own moral and aesthetic principles as GDR Minister of Culture.

The son of a high court judge, Becher was attracted to the revolutionary idealism of the expressionist movement (see also **neo-expressionism**). By 1912 he was already contributing to the periodical *Die Aktion* and in 1913 he became co-editor of the periodical *Die neue Kunst*. His 1919 volume of poetry *An alle* (To Everyone) expressed his enthusiasm for the Russian Revolution. He joined the newly formed German Communist Party and later served as a Communist member of the Reichstag. In the 1925 collections of poems *Der Leichnam auf dem Thron* (The Corpse on the Throne) and a 1926 novel *Levisite oder der einzig gerechte Krieg* (Levisite or The Only Just War) Becher expressed sympathy with the revolutionary proletariat. He fled from Nazi Germany to the Soviet Union after his books were burned on 10 May 1933 and he was deprived of his German citizenship.

In the Soviet Union Becher edited the antifascist periodical *Internationale Literatur – Deutsche Blätter* from 1935 to 1945. From 1943 Becher was also a member of the *Nationalkomitee Freies Deutschland* (National Free Germany Committee), an organization dedicated to the political re-education of German prisoners of war.

Becher was amongst the first to return to Germany after the war in June 1945 where he founded and became president of the **Kulturbund** zur demokratischen Erneuerung Deutschlands (Cultural Association for the Democratic Renewal of Germany). He played an important part in establishing cultural life in the Soviet occupation zone with the founding in 1945 of the **Aufbau Verlag**, the periodical *Sonntag*, and in 1949 the literary periodical **Sinn und Form**. In 1950 he and Hanns **Eisler** were awarded the National Prize for their composition of the GDR's national anthem, *Auferstanden aus Ruinen* (Risen from the Ruins). In 1954 he became Minister of Culture and played a leading role as exponent of the cultural principles of **socialist realism**. In this capacity Becher was involved in an attempt initiated by Anna **Seghers** to save the writer and critic Georg **Lukács** during the Hungarian uprising in October 1956. He subsequently denied all involvement and refused to help his friend Walter **Janka**, editor of the Aufbau publishing house, who was arrested and accused of treason at a show trial in July 1957. There is little doubt that Becher's physical and mental health suffered as a consequence of his divided loyalties and his betrayal of friends in the interests of political expediency. Although he published a number of works of poetry and literary criticism during the 1940s and 1950s Becher never regained the originality of his earlier expressionist poetry. His 1940 semi-autobiographical novel *Farewell (Abschied)* was filmed in a controversial version by the director Egon **Günther** in 1968.

Further reading

Richter, H. (1991) ' "Vollendung träumend..." Johannes R. Becher's Later Writing', in M. Kane (ed.), *Socialism and the Literary Imagination: Essays on East German Writers*, Oxford: Berg (a discussion of Becher's poetry and literary aspirations).

Tate, D. (1984) 'An Exemplary Failure' in D. Tate, *The East German Novel*, Bath: Bath University Press (a survey of Becher's development as a prose writer).

MARGARET VALLANCE

Beckenbauer, Franz

b. 11 September 1965, Munich

Soccer player

An elegant and innovative libero, Beckenbauer was awarded 103 caps for West Germany between 1965 and 1977 and led his country to the European Championship in 1972 and the World Championship two years later. He also captained his club, FC Bayern München, to three consecutive European Cup final victories from 1974 to 1976.

After playing for New York Cosmos for several years, he retired in 1984 when he was appointed manager of West Germany. Under his guidance the team finished runners-up in the 1986 World Cup and champions four years later.

MIKE DENNIS

Becker, Boris

b. 22 November 1967, Leinen

Tennis player

In 1985 Becker became the first German, the first unseeded and the youngest-ever player to win the Wimbledon men's singles title. This and his many subsequent successes together with an exuberant style boosted popular interest in tennis in Germany. He won the Wimbledon title again in 1986 and 1989, the Australian Open in 1991 and 1996, and the US Open in 1989. He has an outstanding record for Germany in the Davis Cup and was voted West German sportsman of the year in 1985, 1986 and 1989. In mid-1996 his career prize money stood at £13 million. He is an articulate critic of racism in society.

MIKE DENNIS

Becker, Jürgen

b. 10 July 1932, Cologne

Writer

Poet, author of radio plays (*Hörspiele*) and fiction, Becker began as an experimentalist in both poetry, in 1971's *Schnee* (Snow), and prose, in 1968's *Ränder* (Margins), breaking with orthographic and typographic conventions and cultivating a free-associative style similar to concrete poets such as Ernst **Jandl** (see also **Hörspiel: FRG**; **Hörspiel: GDR**). Later works such as 1986's *Odenthals Küste* (The Odenthal Coast) mix real and imaginary details to capture the threatened natural balance and beauty of Becker's own homeland, the increasingly citified hill regions around Cologne. Lyricism and literary iconoclasm also characterize

Becker's numerous radio plays, for instance *Gegend mit Spuren* (Countryside with Traces) of 1996.

JEFFREY GARRETT

Becker, Jurek

b. 30 September 1937, Łódź (Poland); d. 14 March 1997, Berlin

Writer

Confined with his parents to the Łódź ghetto at the age of two, Becker spent much of his childhood in the Ravensbrück and Sachsenhausen concentration camps, during which period he lost his mother. Reunited with his father in Berlin after the war, an experience which is related in his 1976 novel *Der Boxer* (The Boxer), Becker began as an eight-year-old schoolboy to learn the German language, in which he has written ever since. His career as a politically committed writer began when his study of philosophy in East Berlin was ended for political reasons. Writing for cabaret, television and film, in 1969 Becker initially crafted his first and most famous novel, *Jacob the Liar* (*Jakob der Lügner*) as a screenplay, although it was not produced until 1974.

Jacob the Liar, set in a Polish ghetto under the Nazi terror, is Becker's finest work. Translated into a dozen languages, it is unique among novels of the Holocaust in its ability to relate the story of a man in a situation as desperate as that of the 'liar' Jakob Heym with touches of humour and a narrative style which derives from the oral tradition of Jewish writers, such as Scholem Aleichem and Isaac Bashevis Singer. Jakob's lie – his claim to possess a forbidden radio from which he receives reports of the approach of the Russian troops who will liberate him and his fellow Jews from imminent death – is a survival strategy, the attempt to maintain his own credibility and to sustain hope in the ultimately hopeless situation of the ghetto.

In 1973 Becker's next novel, *Irreführung der Behörden* (Misleading the Authorities), tested the limits of an announced relaxation of censorship in the GDR by describing the ruse – in this case a hypocritical role as a law student – in which a talented individual engages to fool the authorities in order to pursue fulfilment as a creative writer. In the wake of his protest against the expulsion of the political singer and poet Wolf **Biermann** from the GDR in 1976, Becker – having himself been expelled from the party and resigned from the **Writers' Union of the GDR** – was allowed to move to West Berlin on a visa that enabled him to maintain his East German citizenship and to publish his work in both countries, at least to the extent that it could pass censorship in the GDR.

After his move to West Berlin in 1977, Becker also emerged as a prolific essayist and outspoken commentator on German and political events. His subsequent works, a 1980 collection of short stories, *Nach der ersten Zukunft* (After the First Future), and the novels of 1978, *Sleepless Days* (*Schlaflose Tage*), 1982, *Aller Welt Freund* (Everyone's Friend), 1986, *Bronstein's Children* (*Bronsteins Kinder*) and 1992, *Amanda herzlos* (Heartless Amanda) met with less success than his early works or his very popular West German television series, *Liebling Kreuzberg*. Becker's literary and film work has been honoured with major awards, including election to the Darmstadt Academy (1983), the Frankfurt University Chair in Poetics (1989), and the German Film Prize in gold for his screenplay *Neuner* (1991).

Major works

Becker, J. (1969) *Jakob der Lügner*, Berlin: Aufbau; trans. M. Kornfeld, *Jacob the Liar*, New York: Harcourt Brace Jovanovich, 1975; also trans. L. Vennewitz, *Jacob the Liar*, New York: Plume, 1997.
—— (1973) *Irreführung der Behörden*, Rostock: Hinstorff.
—— (1976) *Der Boxer*, Rostock: Hinstorff.
—— (1978) *Schlaflose Tage*, Frankfurt am Main: Suhrkamp; trans. L. Vennewitz, *Sleepless Days*, New York: Harcourt Brace Jovanovich, 1979.
—— (1980) *Nach der ersten Zukunft. Erzählungen*, Frankfurt am Main: Suhrkamp.
—— (1983) *Aller Welt Freund*, Frankfurt am Main: Suhrkamp.
—— (1986) *Bronsteins Kinder*, Frankfurt am Main: Suhrkamp; trans. L. Vennewitz, *Bronsteins Children*, New York: Harcourt Brace Jovanovich, 1988.
—— (1986) *Erzählungen*, Rostock: Hinstorff.

—— (1990) *Warnung vor dem Schriftsteller: Drei Vorlesungen in Frankfurt*, Frankfurt am Main: Suhrkamp.
—— (1992) *Amanda Herzlos*, Frankfurt am Main: Suhrkamp.
—— (1992) *Die beliebteste Familiengeschichte und andere Erzählungen*, Frankfurt am Main and Leipzig: Insel.
—— (1996) *Das Ende des Größenwahns*, Frankfurt am Main: Suhrkamp.

Further reading

Heidelberger-Leonard, I. (ed.) (1992) *Jurek Becker*, Frankfurt am Main: Suhrkamp.
Johnson, S.M. (1984) *The Works of Jurek Becker: A Thematic Analysis*, New York: Peter Lang.

PATRICIA HERMINGHOUSE

beer

Beer is associated with the German national character perhaps more than any other beverage. There is some justification for this. Germans consume more than 150 litres of beer per person per year, more than any other nationality on earth, and Germany likewise has the greatest number of breweries, with over 1,400. But as important as beer is to German social pastimes and German cuisine, it should be stressed that other beverages, especially **wine**, occupy nearly as important a place in the national economy and culture. It also bears keeping in mind that despite the quantities involved Germany is hardly one big *Oktoberfest*: most beer drinking is deeply ingrained in daily life and not intended solely to induce drunkenness. The everyday valorization of beer emerges from the countless sayings devoted to the beverage (consider: '*Treue gibt Bier und Brot, Untreue Angst und Not*', literally 'Loyalty gives us beer and bread, disloyalty anxiety and distress', or: '*Das ist die größte Kunst auf Erden, ohne Bier im Leben alt zu werden*', literally, 'It is the greatest art in the world, without beer to grow old'). Finally, beer is not a monolithic concept to Germans. Beers differ by region, style and season in the German-speaking countries, making some beers appropriate for some social events and not others.

While there are some national styles and brands, such as Beck's, Jever, Bitburger and Warsteiner, the large number of breweries in Germany is a reflection of the tendency for beer to be produced and consumed locally. Many small towns and villages will have their own brewery that will often have its own tavern or restaurant. Often these breweries will specialize in a regional style that is unavailable in other parts of the country. Even the city with the largest number of breweries, Cologne, produces a distinctive style (*Kölsch*) that is difficult to find outside of the city. Given a preference, Germans will tend to stick with a smaller local brew, assuming that establishments run by brewers (and not accountants and marketing specialists) must produce better beer. Part of the local beer identity are beer glasses and other paraphernalia specific to a particular style of beer and even brand. The proper glass remains important etiquette, although deviating from this practice is no longer the sacrilege it once was.

As with so many aspects of German culture, beer variations can be roughly split on a north-south line. In the north, top-fermented ales (including styles like *Kölsch*) and wheat beers are predominant, although elegant bottom-fermented Pilsner-style beers such as Jever, Warsteiner and Bitburger are also common. A style of beer known as *Weißbier* is particular to Berlin. This style, which is generally low in alcohol content and light in colour, is often served with a dash of raspberry syrup in the incarnation known as *Berliner Weiße*. Wheat beers are most often drunk in the summer, while ales and Pilsners are enjoyed year-round. Few local northern styles are dark, although this does not mean a low alcohol content.

The south produces predominantly bottom-fermented types of beer (known as 'lager' or 'Pilsner' beers outside Germany), although Bavaria's *Hefeweizen* beers are top-fermented. In Bavaria especially the range is impressive, and also varies widely by season. The reason for the seasonal variation has to do with the nature of yeast. The designation *Märzenbier* (literally 'March beer'), for example, arises from the month it was brewed, the last point before the summer made it difficult to handle yeasts reliably. Traditionally, *Märzenbier* is stored in cool places over the summer and drunk in the fall.

Bock beer (literally, 'billy goat' beer), in contrast, uses a stronger malt and is designed to be a warming drink when consumed in the winter. A particular variation of the *Bock*, *Maibock*, is drunk during the May festivals in villages when they celebrate the arrival of spring and dance around the maypole. In order to last the many months between brewing and consumption, Bock beers have high alcohol contents (at least 6.7 percent by volume) that protect the beer from bacteria and enable it to be transported. Other prominent kinds of beer in Bavaria are *Hefeweizen* (wheat beer) and *Rauchbier* (smoked beer). Smoked beer is produced in a small region of Franconia in a number of ways, either by overroasting the malt or by inserting red-hot stones into the beer during production. In the 1980s wheat beer became particularly popular, especially in an unfiltered form that left the yeast suspended in the beer. These beers are most typically enjoyed in the summer, sometimes with a wedge of lemon. In addition to these seasonal beers, many types of lager beers are produced throughout Bavaria and are consumed year-round.

Despite the regional variations, some commonalities can be identified. One often-cited feature of German beer culture is the *Reinheitsgebot* (Beer Purity Law), a 1516 Bavarian law specifically stating that beer may only contain malt, hops, yeast and water. The only other accepted ingredient is wheat. While the law was originally intended to promote the brewing industry as a means of collecting tax revenues, the law has most recently been invoked as a means of protecting German interests from having to compete with beers from other countries in the **European Union** made with other ingredients. While this claim was being discussed by the European Court it was discovered that some German brewers were themselves violating the law, and the law was struck down as protectionist in 1987. The hardening of the attitudes of German consumers since that decision, and their insistence that beer be made according to the *Reinheitsgebot*, has turned beer into a quasi-national symbol, even though 'impure' brews can be imported without penalty.

Perhaps due to their geographic location, beers in Austria and Switzerland have greater similarity to Bavarian beers. Beers in these countries also exhibit strong regional variation, and local breweries dominate.

Further reading

Das überschäumende Sprüchefäßchen (1986) Jena (small collection of rhymes, sayings and verse having to do with beer).

Jackson, M. (1988) *The New World Guide to Beer*, Philadelphia (an excellent treatment of German beer, although it uses technical brewer's terms).

Seidl, C. (1994) *Noch ein Bier! Reisen zu den Stätten europäischer Braukunst*, Vienna (good guide to specific sites and descriptions of cultural oddities that contribute to the making of certain beers).

PETER M. McISAAC

Behnisch, Günter

b. 12 June 1992, Lochwitz (near Dresden)

Architect

Behnisch worked for Rolf Gutbrod until he set up his own practice in Stuttgart in 1952 and later in Munich. From 1967 to 1987 he was Professor for Design and Director of the Institute for Building Standardization, at TH (Technical University) Darmstadt.

Behnisch displays a variety of architectural approaches in the course of his extensive career. His buildings of the 1960s demonstrate an interest in prefabricated construction methods, while his later work combines this with organic forms (for instance Olympic Park, Munich 1967–72, with Frei **Otto**). His most recent buildings have been labelled deconstructivist, although Behnisch rejects this view. His New Parliament Building in Bonn was completed in 1992.

MARTIN KUDLEK AND BERTHOLD PESCH

Behrens, Katja

b. 18 December 1942, Berlin

Writer and translator

Behrens' translations introduced the American 'Beat' artists to the German audience, while her anthologies, *Frauenbriefe der Romantik* of 1981 and *Das Insel-Buch der Frau* of 1985, lent a historical dimension to **Frauenliteratur**. Her stories and novels, often autobiographically influenced, portray the life of women in different historical settings. The novel *Die dreizehnte Fee* (1983) traces how three generations of assimilated women respond to the societal pressures and historical shifts of the twentieth century. The problems of contemporary Jewish identity, the struggle with anti-Semitism and the failure of **Vergangenheitsbewältigung** are addressed in *Salomo und die anderen. Jüdische Geschichten* (1993).

THOMAS NOLDEN

Benjamin, Walter

b. 15 July 1892, Berlin; d. 26 September 1940, Port-Bou (France)

Literary critic and philosopher of culture

Loosely associated with the **Frankfurt School**, but also influenced by **Brecht** and **Lukács**, Benjamin's wide-ranging writings continue to influence modern cultural studies from theatre to film. His best-known essay, 'The Work of Art in the Era of Mechanical Reproduction', argues that industrial mass culture contains the possibility of revolutionary art. Benjamin's later work is marked by increasing historical pessimism, and he committed suicide while trying to escape the Nazis.

Further reading

Roberts, J. (1982) *Walter Benjamin*, London: Macmillan (the most accessible general introduction to life and work).

Witte, B. (1985) *Walter Benjamin*, Reinbeck: Rowohlt

(concise overview, includes detailed bibliography).

GÜNTER MINNERUP

Benn, Gottfried

b. 2 May 1886, Mansfeld; d. 7 July 1956, (West) Berlin

Writer

Despite the esoteric nature of much of his thinking and his disregard for fashionable literary trends, Benn acquired a reputation as one of the foremost German poets of the century. Trained as a military doctor, he served through WWI and then practised privately in Berlin from 1917 to 1935, specializing in skin and venereal diseases. Benn established his credentials as a modernist in 1912 with a short cycle of poems, *Morgue und andere Gedichte* (Morgue and Other Poems), ruthlessly brutal descriptions of corpses and human decay. He rubbed shoulders with the young expressionist poets in Berlin, but went on to pursue his own idiosyncratic vision of the endurance of poetic form in an ephemeral world.

Benn briefly succumbed to the beguiling promises of Nazi ideas in essays like *Kunst und Macht* (Art and Power) of 1934, but soon became hostile to the new regime. He re-entered the army in 1935 as the 'aristocratic form of emigration', was subsequently expelled from the Reichsschrifttumskammer (Reich Writers' Guild) and forbidden to publish. The authorities regarded him as a nihilistic modernist with affinities to cosmopolitan thinking. His initial enthusiasm for Nazi ideas then earned him a publishing ban from the Allied authorities in 1945.

Statische Gedichte (Static Poems), written over the previous ten years, appeared in 1948 when Benn was cleared of political accusations. It ushered in the fruitful late phase of his writing, which laid stress on the isolation of the poet seeking to express personal, often pessimistic views on the nature of life, history and progress. Benn's poetry struck a chord in the dominant apolitical culture of the time, representing as it did the value-free claims of aesthetic creation against the subservience of

literature to a real socio-political context. Benn at this time exemplified the West German canon of art for art's sake, in contrast to the East German model of Brecht's politically anchored writings.

The bulk of Benn's work was permeated with sometimes esoteric scientific and cultural vocabulary – not unlike W.H. Auden – through which he conveyed a sense of twentieth-century civilization. At the same time he voiced an existentialist weariness with the concept of progress and often yearned for the simplicity of uncomplicated manifestations of being ('a blob of slime in a warm swamp'). The sole justification for writing at all was the absolute independence of the poem, its sense entirely within itself; and the sole meaning of a human life and all its endeavour was that nothing remained but 'the void and the mark of the ego'. The 1951 essay *Probleme der Lyrik* (Problems of Lyric Poetry) spelled out Benn's belief that poetry was 'the monological art of our time'; the poet is essentially an inward-looking loner wrapped in his own aesthetic self. Like Rilke, Benn created no 'school', yet he exerted a formative influence on a whole generation of younger poets after 1945.

Further reading

Ritchie, J.M. (1972) *Gottfried Benn: The Unreconstructed Expressionist*, London: Wolff (introductory monograph with selection of work, in English).

ARRIGO SUBIOTTO

Bennent, David

b. 9 September 1966, Lausanne

Actor

Bennent is best known as the diminutive star of the 1979 film adaptation by Volker **Schlöndorff** of *The Tin Drum* (*Die Blechtrommel*) by Günter **Grass**, in which he played the role of Oskar Matzerath, who threw himself down the stairs at the age of three to halt his physical growth in response to his aversion to the adult world of Danzig at the advent of the Third Reich. The son of Heinz **Bennent**, also an actor, David Bennent has appeared in several other films and on the stage.

See also: film: FRG; New German Cinema

JENIFER K. WARD

Bennent, Heinz

b. 18 July 1921, Atsch (Aachen)

Actor

After starting his career in the theatre in 1947, Heinz Bennent became a leading television actor in the 1950s, working in particular with the director Hans W. **Geissendörfer**, and appearing in such popular series as *Tatort*, *Der Kommissar*, and *Derrick*. From the 1960s onwards he began playing leading roles in cinema films, including Bergman's *The Serpent's Egg* and Truffaut's *Le dernier métro*, and – together with his son David – **Schlöndorff**'s *The Tin Drum*. Much of his work since the early 1980s has been in French-language productions.

See also: Bennent, David

JOHN SANDFORD

Bense, Max

b. 7 February 1910, Strasbourg; d. 24 April 1990, Stuttgart

Scientist, mathematician and poet

Max Bense was a prolific and sometimes controversial writer. In Germany, he achieved fame not only through his experimental poetry, but also for his insistence on a semiotically informed aesthetic. He was a politically committed author and in his dual role as scientist and poet was better able than most to incorporate technological thought into his texts. Bense had a strong interest in the juncture of semiotics, computers and aesthetics and was the editor of the influential journal *Aesthetica*.

HOLGER BRIEL

Bergengruen, Werner

b. 16 September 1892, Riga; d. 4 September 1964, Baden-Baden

Writer

While his early work was influenced by German Romanticism, the underlying basis of Bergengruen's writing is the religious notion of a character's fate in a divinely-ordered universe. Best known for his 1935 novel about the dangers of authority, *A Matter of Conscience* (*Der Großtyrann und das Gericht*), for which the National Socialists ejected him from the Reichsschrifttumskammer, he was a prolific writer of novels, novellas, and, in his middle and later years, of lyric poetry.

See also: poetry

MICHAEL RICHARDSON

Berghaus, Ruth

b. 2 July 1927, Dresden; d. 25 January 1996, Zeuthen (near Berlin)

Producer and choreographer

Though more recently renowned as the most controversial and imitated opera producer in Germany, Berghaus trained as a dancer and choreographer. She succeeded Helene **Weigel**, Brecht's widow, as Artistic Director of the **Berliner Ensemble** (1971–7). After her departure she gradually consolidated an eminent position in opera; by the late 1980s few German houses called themselves up-to-date without one of her stagings in their repertory. Regularly working at the German State Opera (East Berlin) her violently anti-naturalistic concepts also made their mark at the Frankfurt Opera during the artistic reign of Michael **Gielen**, notably in exceptional stagings of *The Ring* and Berlioz' *Trojans*. The last years were marked by her growing discontent at the artistic and moral results of German unification.

BEATRICE HARPER

Berkéwicz, Ulla

b. 5 November 1951, Gießen

Writer (also Ursula Schmidt)

Berkéwicz studied drama and music in Frankfurt am Main from 1966 to 1969, after which she wrote for several different German theatre companies. She began writing prose in the late 1970s. Written in easily understandable language, her first novel *Josef stirbt* (Joseph Dies), published 1982, addresses issues of dying and death. *Michel, sag ich* (Michel, I Say), of 1984, is cast in an apocalyptic dream world, and focuses on events within the **student movement**. *Adam* (1987) draws on her experiences in the theatre.

MARTINA S. ANDERSON

Berlin

As the largest and arguably most important city in Germany, Berlin is like most European capitals in being both representative of and rather exceptional to the nation as a whole. Political division and eventual unification, however, have radicalized Berlin's situation so that the name, not only metaphorically, encompasses multiple cities. This entry will introduce Berlin as a geographical entity, summarize its history, discuss social developments in both East and West, offer a sketch of the post-unification period and analyse its cultural importance.

Berlin has no definitive founding date. Covering 883 square kilometres, the city has only gradually coalesced out of previously autonomous municipalities such as Charlottenburg and Neu-Kölln, forerunners of Berlin's persistently individual, village-like districts. For a capital, it is neither central nor especially large: although its population comprised some 4.7 million by 1943, it had sunk to barely 3 million in 1987. It is not primarily industrial: the economy has historically centred upon supplying the needs of residents, not producing exports. Moreover, even its status as Germany's capital has not been constant. After WWII, with the city lying in ruins, East Berlin became capital of the GDR, while the FRG based its government in Bonn. The physical division of the city began with the post-war breakdown in relations between the western Allies and the Soviet Union. Itself divided into four sectors, and located in Soviet-occupied Germany, the western part of the city was blockaded in 1948 and 1949 by Soviet troops and had to be supplied by plane in what become known as the Berlin airlift. In 1961, responding to crippling waves of emigration, the GDR government constructed a barrier along the entire border between East and West Germany, including the internal borders within Berlin. The 103 mile, 10–13 foot high **Berlin Wall** turned busy streets into culs-de-sac, disrupted districts and kept the populace of the two sides in geographically proximate isolation until 1989. At that point of widespread civil unrest and further mass emigration to the FRG, the GDR government's repeal of restrictions on travel and the countermanding of the shoot-to-kill order for attempted fugitives effectively led to the Wall's gradual dismantlement – the first act in German unification.

The effects of Cold War division on social development in both East and West were mixed. Certainly few on either side would want the Wall back. Populations fell throughout the city. In the East, economic conditions did not allow for the expenditure necessary to repair and rebuild the war-damaged city, so that numerous buildings and parts of the infrastructure fell into dilapidation. In the West, largely because of Berlin's precarious position as a political island, restarting the economy also proved difficult: standards of living fell below the FRG average, and life in the city was essentially subsidized by special benefits from Bonn to the municipal government. Thus unification has faced extraordinary material obstacles: in 1994 Potsdamer Platz at the heart of the city became Europe's largest construction site. Perhaps more problematic still had been the personal legacy of forty-odd years of separation, causing major difficulties and even open hostility between former West and East Berliners.

None the less, the positive aspects of Berlin's development during the Wall's twenty-eight-year history should not be ignored. Both East and West developed into cultural meccas, attracting many of the most creative among their own citizens, as well as an enriching influx of foreigners. The cafés of East German districts like **Prenzlauer Berg** and

Mitte emerged as the focal point for a literary renaissance, while the low rents and decadent possibilities of West Berlin made it one of the most fashionable European addresses for **punks**, squatters and other acolytes of **alternative culture**. Berlin in this time also became Germany's first truly multicultural city (see **multiculturalism**), a development largely due to the massive settlement of Turks in western districts like Kreuzberg and Wedding. By 1982, 12.5 percent of West Berlin's population was made up of non-German minorities (see **minorities, non-German**), and Berlin had become the centre of Germany's small Jewish community. Accompanying these trends, the city's post-unification population has once more begun to expand.

Nowhere is the positive side of Berlin's strange history more apparent than in its cultural life. It has three universities and numerous art galleries, **museums**, **libraries**, newspapers, publishing houses and clubs. It is home to the world-renowned Berlin Philharmonic Orchestra as well as several other **orchestras** and three major opera companies. Its **theatres**, including the Volksbühne, **Deutsches Theater** and **Berliner Ensemble**, have seen the premieres of dramas by Peter **Weiss** and Heiner **Müller**. In the tradition of **Döblin**'s *Berlin Alexanderplatz*, Berlin has provided subject matter for generations of German authors, especially in the former GDR, from official dissidents like Christa **Wolf** and Stefan **Heym** to outsiders like Jurek **Becker** and Wolfgang **Hilbig** and 1990s iconoclasts like Thomas **Brussig** and Ingo Schramm. The cinematic importance of the Berlin of the Weimar Republic was largely a casualty of the division, as the famed **Babelsberg** studios were taken over by the East German **DEFA** group. None the less the city has continued to serve as backdrop for filmmakers as varied as Billy **Wilder** and Wim **Wenders**. All in all, despite some weak points, Berlin is the cultural capital of Germany.

See also: Hauptstadtfrage; Judaism; Ossi/Wessi; *taz*

Further reading

Bornemann, J. (1991) *After the Wall: East Meets West in the New Berlin*, New York: Basic Books (sociological account of unification).

Langguth, G. (ed.) (1990) *Berlin: Vom Brennpunkt der Teilung zur Brücke der Einheit*, Bonn: Bundeszentrale für politische Bildung (omnibus written by German historians, foreign analysts and prominent politicans).

Smith, K. (1990) *Berlin: Coming-in from the Cold*, London: Hamish Hamilton (journalistic portrait of pre- and post-Wall Berlin).

Wallace, I. (1993) *Berlin*, Oxford: Clio (annotated bibliography of books about Berlin).

JEFFERSON S. CHASE

Berlin building boom

An unprecedented boom in the building sector swept over Berlin after German unification in 1990, especially triggered by the government's decision to move the capital city from Bonn to Berlin. Previously, West Berlin had been an isolated enclave with an economic and social structure hollowed out by the exodus of investment, while East Berlin was the capital of a socialist state that by the end of its forty-year existence was bankrupt, providing a standard of life comparable to that of West Germany in the 1960s. With Berlin being placed on the front line of the cold war, the majority of building projects of the 1950s and 1960s also served as political propaganda or were closely linked to political functions.

Henselmann's Stalinallee (first phase 1952–9), (subsequently Karl-Marx-Allee and Frankfurter Allee) borrows Schinkelesque motifs as well as emulating much of the then-current representative Soviet architecture. Ironically, this 'first socialist boulevard' was the starting point of the **June Uprising** of 1953 which was forcefully put down with the help of Soviet tanks. In West Berlin the Interbau building exhibition of 1957 produced the Hansaviertel where international western architects realized an estate based on block housing in an open-plan arrangement. Major parts of East Berlin were subject to the international competition '*Hauptstadt Berlin*' (capital Berlin) of the same year. Soon prefabricated and standardized open housing complexes became the creed in the GDR due to economic restrictions. Central East Berlin is reconstructed to suit the (exaggerated) requirements of motorized traffic and mass rallies. A conservation programme along the main tourist sites was set up in the 1970s and 1980s, resulting in modest renewal in the nineteenth-century districts.

With almost the same lack of consideration for older structures during the 1960s and 1970s, western parts of the city (as in all West Germany) were reconstructed by means of the so-called *Kahlschlagsanierung* (renewal by complete demolition). The Internationale Bauausstellung Berlin (**IBA**) was then set up to counter this trend.

With unification the aims, speed and economic structures of planning have changed drastically. The estimated growth, the geographical situation and the city's future importance seemed to necessitate a rapid development of the service sector. The German government has commissioned (often by competition) an array of architects and planners, largely of international reputation, to build new governmental quarters. Many private investors have also moved into the city, taking advantage of the possibility to write off 50 percent of building development costs as large parts of eastern Berlin were declared a *Förderungsgebiet* (subsidized area). This measure, now abolished, was fiercely criticized as an estimated one million square metres of office space subsidized by tax payers' money was still waiting to be let in Berlin in 1995 while the demand for cheap housing is still great.

Another fierce debate, known as the *Berlindebatte*, blew up concerning building-models for the future city. The traditional *Lochfassade* (limited window area for the façades), the cornice height of 22 metres, and the historical city block grid, laid down by the city, stood at the centre of this.

In his controversial essay 'Die Provokation des Alltäglichen' (*Der Spiegel* 51, 1993) Vittorio Magnago Lampugnani, director of the Architekturmuseum in Frankfurt am Main, rejects the democratic and individualistic claim of postmodern thinking and architecture, proposing a 'convention of building' based on a new aesthetics of simplicity (meaning a kind of neo-rationalism). By arguing that small-scale individualism cannot solve the problems of mass housing and stands in the way of a successful reconstruction of Berlin, he promotes a quiet and solid tradition-conscious uniformity. His suggestions that the layman cannot comprehend

modern architectural processes anyway and the consequences of his proposals mark him as a follower of modernist ideas of overall validity. He also seems to believe that the idea of urbanism does not have to be reinvestigated, that adequate living and working conditions can be realized on the grounds of existing structures and traditions.

A radically different stance in the battle that follows is taken by Daniel Libeskind, who completely rejects the idea of order and conformity in urban design in favour of a pluralistic architecture and a pluralistic society that is driven by respect for the individual and for the manifestations of history in an urban context ('Die Forderung nach dem Handwerklichen führt in eine Sackgasse', *Frankfurter Rundschau*, 9 March 1994). He believes that a uniform appearance is not only the expression of unreflected adherence to existing power structures but also helps to level individuality, to create the 'one-dimensional man'. Libeskind's design proposals (e.g. the Jewish Museum in Berlin) are consistent with these ideas in their comprehensive search for individual solutions based on references to social structure, location and history.

Architectural historian and critic Wolfgang Pehnt represents a more dialectical view. In his article 'Das Proletarierhemd kommt vom Herrnschneider' (*Frankfurter Allgemeine Zeitung*, 10 January 1994) he differentiates between tradition, typology and variation. Attacking neo-rationalist theories, he concludes that type is not reality and a typology does not constitute a city. The individual solution must not necessarily contradict a 'typical' appearance. Linking the application of uniform architecture to the actual size of building sites, Pehnt predicts monotonous results.

Although other voices partook in the debate it did not reach a wider level of public interest and has now died down. Thus in a sense it mirrors the restricted quality of the building boom's designs that triggered it off.

Meanwhile the overheated Berlin real estate market has cooled down considerably. Berlin's bid for the Olympic games in 2000 has been lost and the government's transfer is taking its time – where possible, existing buildings will be used. The conservative political decision to give priority to the return of East German property to its former owners ('restitution before compensation'), and the resulting problems of ownership as well as administrative friction, have put an end to the boom before any of the major projects could be finished. While some of the vast Berlin Wall sites that were sold cheaply to private investors will stay undeveloped in the near future, the areas that have been neglected so far will get the chance of considerate planning and slow but steady development.

Of the building projects triggered by Germany's unification the Friedrichstraße (see **architecture**), Potsdamer Platz, Reichstag, Spreebogen, and Alexanderplatz developments have generated the most interest. Following the 1992 urban design competition won by the architects **Hilmer & Sattler**, Potsdamer Platz and the adjacent Leipziger Platz have changed from derelict strips of land (formerly the border between West and East) into Europe's largest building site. A purpose-built 'infobox' gives details of the cluster of office buildings interspersed with retail uses, cinemas and a token portion of housing designed by an international élite of architects, based on a master plan that lifted cornice heights to 35 metres, the largest individual schemes being Renzo Piano's Mercedes-Benz building and Murphy & Jahn's designs. A painted panorama of the future Potsdamer Platz exhibited on-site in a tent in 1996 made obvious the tragic neglect of public space in favour of self-righteous representation of company images and massive traffic arteries. And although Jahn's Sony building does incorporate a football-pitch-sized 'plaza', this is only public to a certain extent.

Axel **Schultes**' scheme for the new government district in the Spreebogen area of the Tiergarten borough is characterized by a 'federal belt' that links eastern and western parts of the city. His design for the chancellery will be complemented by offices and facilities for MPs for which the Munich architect Stephan Braunfels is responsible. The section between the two buildings, envisaged as a 'public forum', still awaits further steps towards realization.

Close by, the former Reichstag building is being reconstructed to house the new federal parliament. Norman Foster's winning design is dominated by a glass cupola which underwent frequent changes after fierce attacks by conservative politicians. Its design is now based on the dimensions of Wallot's original structure (1884–94) that had not been reconstructed after WWII.

Owing its mythical image to Döblin's famous novel set in the 1920s social milieu of an overcrowded and underprivileged quarter, the Alexanderplatz in East Berlin was redesigned as a modern open-plan forum, incorporating a hotel tower block, a television tower and extremely wide road sections to suit the requirements of mass rallies. Today this space stands as a monument to 1960s East German town planning and building. Except for Behrens' two early modern office and retail blocks lining the elevated railway (*S-Bahn*), none of the pre-war structures have survived. The square's commercial attractiveness has faded with the construction of new shopping malls on the periphery. Surrounded by the large housing estates along Karl-Marx-Allee, it serves as a major traffic junction. The urban design competition of 1992, leaving most existing structures at the disposal of eight participants, highlighted three positions for the redevelopment of the Alexanderplatz. While the eastern planners Weber & Kny promoted the reintroduction of five-storey perimeter blocks in a carefully linked street grid, Daniel Libeskind proposed several individually designed volumes largely given up to public uses. **Kollhoff**'s winning scheme features a cluster of high-rise office blocks that allow for public spaces on the ground level. The city administration's strategy to attract investment to the eastern boroughs by laying down advantageous planning parameters for future clients is obvious. Planning risks, such as the missing traffic concept, the complicated question of land ownership, and wrong predictions of future demands for office space, have reversed the project of a skyscraping downtown to a vacuum of building activity. Ignoring the absence of economic pressure generated by the shortage of building land, the speculative character of the competition's parameters has positioned Alexanderplatz at the centre of a 'tower-block debate' that draws on Manhattan as an example for the balance between private and public space.

Further reading

Burg, A. (1995) *Downtown Berlin: Die Entstehung einer urbanen Architektur*, Berlin: Birkhäuser Verlag.

Ladd, B. (1990) *The Ghosts of Berlin*, Cambridge, MA: Harvard University Press.

MARTIN KUDLEK AND BERTHOLD PESCH

Berlin Wall

Erected in 1961, the fortified boundary between the two halves of the former German capital quickly became the most familiar symbol of the division of Europe and Germany after WWII. The night of 9 November 1989, when the Berlin Wall was stormed by thousands of western revellers and opened to East Germans by their own bemused authorities, signalled the historic moment when the collapse of the GDR and the advent of German **unification** became inevitable.

Although the GDR had sealed off its borders with the Federal Republic in 1952, the sector boundary between East and West **Berlin** remained open. This presented a serious problem for the East German economy as, in the years up to 1961, some two million (out of a total of three million) refugees availed themselves of this opportunity to abandon the GDR and move to the West. In the late 1950s the exodus increased steeply in the wake of Soviet threats to end the four-power status of the divided city, and by the summer of 1961 it had risen to between one and two thousand people a day.

In the early hours of 13 August 1961 armed East German workers and soldiers began sealing off the sector boundary with barbed wire and concrete blocks. The GDR, which designated these measures as the erection of an 'anti-fascist protective rampart', insisted that it had lowered the temperature of East–West conflict and even prevented a third world war. The West, which took no action to remove the fortifications, seemed grudgingly to concur.

Over the second half of the 1960s the original barriers were replaced with the familiar 4-metre-high wall which ran for a distance of 43 kilometres between the two halves of the city and also along substantial sections of the sealed 112 kilometre border between West Berlin and the surrounding GDR. The wall itself was backed on the eastern side by a 50-metre-deep strip of further traps and obstructions, the whole illuminated at night and guarded by foot and vehicle patrols and dogs, and overlooked by 300 sentry towers. The wall cut off more than sixty streets between East and West Berlin. Seven tightly controlled crossing points for vehicles and pedestrians were opened, including the famous 'Checkpoint Charlie' on the Friedrichstraße.

Though the wall was inaccessible from the eastern side, the western side became a major attraction both for tourists and graffiti artists. When it was eventually demolished in the course of 1990, enterprising street-traders sold thousands of brightly coloured fragments to souvenir hunters, while whole sections of the wall were sold to art collectors by the GDR government. Today only a few short sections remain standing, preserved as memorials to the division of the city and to the hundred or so East Germans killed when attempting to cross it. The bulk of the wall has been turned into hard-core for construction projects.

Further reading

Schürer, E., Keune, M. and Jenkins, P. (eds) *The Berlin Wall: Representations and Perspectives*, New York and Bern: Lang (essays from a range of disciplines).

JOHN SANDFORD

Berliner Ensemble

The term refers both to the theatre company created by Bertolt **Brecht** and Helene **Weigel** in 1949 after their return to East Germany, and to the theatre they were given by the GDR cultural authorities for the performance of their productions. The theatre, situated off Friedrichstraße in what was the cultural heart of 1920s Berlin, was previously known as the Theater am Schiffbauerdamm. It was the place where Brecht had enjoyed his first major stage success with *The Threepenny Opera* (*Die Dreigroschenoper*) in 1928, produced in collaboration with the composer Kurt Weill. Until they were able to take formal possession of the building in 1954, Brecht's company was housed in the nearby **Deutsches Theater**.

In the years up to Brecht's death the company concentrated on producing 'model' performances of the plays he had written during his years of exile, such as *Mother Courage* (*Mutter Courage*) in 1949 and *The Caucasian Chalk Circle* (*Der kaukasische Kreidekreis*) in 1954, which were subsequently performed in Paris and London. The Berliner Ensemble also produced radical adaptations of works from the classical repertoire, like Goethe's *Faust* (in its original form *Urfaust*, 1952), Molière's *Don Juan* (1954) and Synge's *Playboy of the Western World* (1956), and promoted work by new GDR playwrights, notably Erwin **Strittmatter**'s *Katzgraben* in 1953.

After 1956 the company dedicated itself to continuing Brecht's unfinished work. His assistant directors Benno **Besson**, Peter **Palitzsch** and Manfred **Wekwerth** enjoyed considerable success with their respective productions of *The Good Person of Szechwan* (*Der gute Mensch von Sezuan*) in 1957, *Arturo Ui* in 1959 and *Coriolanus* (*Coriolan*) in 1964. The team-spirit gradually began to disintegrate, however, through a drain of talent to the FRG and growing disquiet that the theatre was being turned into a Brecht 'museum' under the control of Weigel and Wekwerth. Only after Weigel's death did its new manager Ruth **Berghaus** begin to explore fresh dramatic territory with performances of Wedekind's *Spring Awakening* (*Frühlings Erwachen*) in 1974 and Strindberg's *Miss Julie* in 1975. The appointment of Wekwerth as her successor in 1977 marked a return to conservatism which prevailed – apart from occasional innovative performances of Volker **Braun**'s plays – up to the collapse of the GDR.

In 1992 the fortunes of the now struggling theatre were placed in the hands of a five-person management team which included famous names like Heiner **Müller**, Peter Zadek and Palitzsch but found itself unable to reach agreement on the way forward. Its performance of Rolf **Hochhuth**'s *Wessis in Weimar* in 1993, which took a provocatively negative line on the effects of unification on the ex-GDR, was a factor behind Zadek's resignation in 1995. The death of Müller has ushered in a further period of uncertainty regarding the future of post-war Germany's best-known theatre.

See also: drama: GDR; theatres

Further reading

Kleber, P. and Visser, C. (eds) (1990) *Reinterpreting Brecht: His Influence on Contemporary Drama and Film*, Cambridge: Cambridge University Press (includes a chapter on the Berliner Ensemble).
Subiotto, A. (1975) *Bertolt Brecht's Adaptations for the Berliner Ensemble*, London: Modern Humanities Research Association (full account of the early years of the Ensemble).

DENNIS TATE

Bernhard, Thomas

b. 9 February 1931, Heerlen (The Netherlands); d. 12 February 1989, Gmunden (Austria)

Writer

The illegitimate son of a carpenter and a housemaid, Bernhard grew up in Vienna, Salzburg and Bavaria. The dominant figure in his childhood was his maternal grandfather, the unsuccessful novelist Johannes Freumbichler. After grammar school Bernhard became a grocer's apprentice. During the 1950s he studied music and drama, worked as a reporter and wrote lyric poetry. In 1963 Bernhard settled in Ohlsdorf, Upper Austria, where he poured forth a constant stream of novels, short stories, autobiographical works (1975–82), and plays (from 1970). The uncompromising bleakness of his artistic vision, his manically insistent, almost musical prose style, and the vividness and humour of his depiction of Austrian settings, combined to make Bernhard the most influential author of post-war Austria. His repeated excoriations of Austrian society have had a permanent effect on Austria's image, at home and abroad.

Early fiction (1963–75)

In Bernhard's early texts isolated individuals generate ornate visions of madness, decay and death against a background of primitive rural delinquency and degeneracy. Their sense of the absurdity of human existence derives from Bernhard's awareness of the dichotomy between the ideal, which can only be imagined, and reality, which must be experienced. In *The Lime Works* (*Das Kalkwerk*) of 1973 a narrator haphazardly assembles scraps of material, gathered from a wide range of sources of varying reliability, relating to the mental state of Konrad, who has ended his terrible marriage by killing his wife. Like many of Bernhard's characters, Konrad has set up an academic project as a refuge from the world. It becomes apparent that his essay on the sense of hearing is an impossibility; the perfect work of scholarship which Konrad envisages cannot be produced within the real world. This failure compounds the meaninglessness of the world as experienced by Konrad.

In *Correction* (*Korrektur*) of 1991 Roithamer devotes himself to the task of designing and building a cone-shaped house which will correspond absolutely to the personality of his sister and guarantee her total happiness. As an exercise in abstract thought taken to its farthest limits, the cone represents an attempt to subdue all of reality, and contain it within a total rational framework; at the same time, it is the apotheosis of Roithamer's life. The point of the cone represents the point at which the ideal and the real coincide, total intellectual clarity is reached – and existence ceases. Roithamer is the heir to a great country estate, Altensam; this is depicted as a grotesque anachronism, but it also provides a focus for a sense of nostalgia for a pastoral Austria of bygone days.

Autobiography and later fiction

In Bernhard's autobiography *Gathering Evidence*, the traumas of his emotionally and materially deprived childhood are laid bare, including his disturbed relationships with his mother and grandfather, and his year-long battle with the tuberculosis which nearly killed him at eighteen, and from which he never fully recovered. At one point he is banished to a boarding school for difficult children. It becomes apparent from the parallels between autobiography and fiction that the existential problems which confront Bernhard's fictional protagonists are a rationalization of problems in the author's own life, and that the characters are

reflections of himself. His grandfather, who bore the main responsibility for bringing him up, sought to inculcate his own anarchist and nihilist views into the young boy, thereby turning him into a misfit. Ironically, Bernhard then rationalized his otherness by embracing the same nihilist tenets. Bernhard's early fiction can be interpreted as a vast exercise in self-justification designed to create for him an identity which his traumatic childhood would otherwise have denied him. Present throughout the autobiography is an awareness of the atrocities of the Nazi era, which spanned Bernhard's childhood.

The process of writing the autobiography enabled Bernhard to come to terms with his difficult childhood. In his later fiction he emerges from solipsism and engages the real world; tone and imagery are lighter and the prose style is more controlled. The lurid evocations of rural decadence are replaced by rabid denunciations of the Austrian nation, its people, traditions and leading political and cultural figures. The texts tend to refer back to the autobiography, or to aspects of the early fiction, in self-parody. In *Concrete* (*Beton*) of 1989, a self-absorbed aesthete is briefly jolted out of solipsistic withdrawal by an encounter with a young widow whom he meets on holiday. It becomes apparent that contemporary Austrian social reality is for Bernhard scarcely less harrowing than the more purely personal problems which first motivated his writing. The narrator of his final novel, *Extinction* (*Auslöschung*) of 1995, considers the crimes against humanity committed under the Nazis, and the singular readiness of post-war Austrian society to forget them. The contemporary Austrian is, he repeatedly alleges, an inveterate Nazi. The novel vilifies the Austrian people, their stupidity, complacency and deceitfulness.

Plays

Bernhard's plays are effectively an extension of his prose fiction. Characters, situations and style are all familiar from the prose, as is the increasing tendency towards self-parody. In *Eve of Retirement* (*Vor dem Ruhestand*) Bernhard uses the figure of a former concentration camp commandant to argue that virulent Nazi beliefs are still widespread in the 1970s. *Heldenplatz* (*Heroes' Square*), written to mark the 50th anniversary of the *Anschluß*, claims that there are more Nazis in Vienna in 1988 than there were in 1938. Bernhard's uncompromising, if vague, allegations were designed to trap the Austrian public into revealing its reactionary attitudes, and the uproar which greeted the play's performance bore ample witness to the success of his provocative attacks.

Major works

Bernhard, T. (1973) *The Lime Works* (*Das Kalkwerk*), trans. S. Wilkins, New York: Knopf.
—— (1986) *Gathering Evidence*, trans. D. McLintock, New York: Knopf (autobiography).
—— (1989) *Concrete* (*Beton*), trans. D. McLintock, London: Quartet.
—— (1991) *Correction* (*Korrektur*), trans. S. Wilkins, London: Vintage.
—— (1995) *Extinction* (*Auslöschung*), trans. D. McLintock, London: Quartet.

Further reading

Martin, C.W. (1995) *The Nihilism of Thomas Bernhard*, Amsterdam and Atlanta, GA: Rodopi (general survey of Bernhard's prose).

CHARLES MARTIN

Bertelsmann

The Bertelsmann Corporation, a privately-owned German-based media company founded in 1835 by Carl Bertelsmann (1791–1850), attained a leading position in the worldwide media business during the latter half of the 1980s and is now – after the – Disney Corporation – the second-largest media corporation worldwide. The group has more than 300 companies and offices spread across 40 countries. Its acquisition of Random House in 1998 made it the biggest publishing group in the English-speaking world.

Bertelsmann is structured along major product lines: books, entertainment, press, and new media. It publishes and distributes books, magazines and newspapers, owns record labels (Bertelsmann Music Group), and operates record and film companies. Bertelsmann is also very active in German multimedia and online services, and has interests in commercial radio and television (including RTL, Germany's most successful channel).

BETTINA BROCKERHOFF-MACDONALD

Berufsverbot

In the history of the FRG few government measures have stimulated greater controversy than the practice which was dubbed *Berufsverbot* (exclusion from professional employment) by its detractors. While at one level part of a long-standing debate in Germany about the limits of political tolerance, the *Radikalenerlaß* (Decree on Radicals) of January 1972, concerning 'extremists' employed in the public sector, was the first in a series of actions undertaken by the state to protect itself not only against the guerrilla tactics of urban **terrorism** but also against the threat posed by the **student movement**'s strategy of the 'long march through the institutions'.

Originally entitled 'Basic Principles on the Question of Anti-Constitutional Personnel in the Public Service', the *Radikalenerlaß* was in fact a statement of policy, agreed by the prime ministers of the *Länder* and endorsed by the **Brandt** government, aiming to regularize the implementation of the 1957 Civil Service Law. While the latter stated that only those persons could be employed in the public service who pledged to uphold the 'free democratic basic order', the new decree specified that each case should be investigated in its own right and not be decided merely on the basis of blanket proscriptions. Consequently some 3.5 million individuals were subjected to this test of ideological suitability, with 2,250 applicants actually being rejected on political grounds and a further 2,000 already in state employment undergoing disciplinary proceedings.

It was precisely because the size of the public sector affected by the decree was so extensive – as well as departments of government at federal, regional and local level it included virtually the entire education system, the postal service and the railways – that the term *Berufsverbot* quickly gained currency among its opponents. Not only, they argued, was the *Radikalenerlaß* itself fundamentally unconstitutional (since Article 3(3) of the Basic Law prohibits political discrimination), but the principle of individual evaluation licensed a system of ideological screening which, in its scale, methods and intimidatory effects, was all too redolent of the apparatus fashioned by National Socialism to weed out undesirables from the state service. Precisely this parallel was drawn by Alfred **Andersch** in a highly controversial poem of 1976 entitled 'Artikel 3(3)', which refers to the mental 'torture' inflicted on civil servants and concludes

> a smell is spreading
> the smell of a machine
> which produces gas.

In the wake of concerted criticism from intellectuals, sustained legal action by citizens' initiatives (see **citizens' initiatives: FRG**), and powerful international protests, a number of SPD-governed *Länder* – beginning with the Saarland in June 1985 – formally renounced the guidelines authorized by the decree (while states under the control of the CDU and CSU, if anything, stepped up their practice of ideological scrutiny).

Further reading

Braunthal, G. (1990) *Political Loyalty and Public Service in West Germany*, Amherst, MA: University of Massachusetts Press (detailed account of the *Radikalenerlaß* and its consequences).

Schneider, P. (1974) ... *schon bist du ein Verfassungsfeind*, Berlin: Rotbuch (a fictional prose-work, with both autobiographical and documentary elements, portraying the case of a teacher in Baden-Württemberg).

ROB BURNS

Besson, Benno

b. 4 November 1928, Yverdon (Switzerland)

Actor, director and theatre manager

After an assistantship at the Zürich playhouse (1943) Besson went to Paris to become a scholar of

Roger Blin. In 1949 he became an assistant and actor at the **Berliner Ensemble**, which he left in 1958 to become a freelance director. In 1969 he worked at the **Deutsches Theater** in Berlin where he perfected his style of intentional exaggeration and over-obviousness. At the Volksbühne Berlin he held positions of first artistic director (1969–74) and general director (1974–8). Since 1982 he has been director at the Geneva Comedy, directing also at the Zürich Schauspielhaus.

Further reading

Kranz, D. (1990) *Berliner Theater. 100 Aufführungen aus drei Jahrzehnten*, Berlin: Henschel Verlag.

MATTHIAS BAUHUF

Beuys, Joseph

b. 12 May 1921, Krefeld; d. 23 January 1986, Düsseldorf

Painter, sculptor and performance artist

Popularly known as the 'fat and felt artist', his reputation rested as much on his charismatic personality, political involvement with the **Greens**, and philosophy that 'Everyone is an artist' ('*Jeder Mensch ist ein Künstler*') as on his vast œuvre of paintings, drawings, sculptures and performances. A modernist with artistic roots in Celtic mythology, romanticism, Dada and expressionism, he advanced complex sociopolitical theories based on the writings of Rudolf Steiner and Karl Marx, which he elucidated in his artistic production as '*soziale Plastik*' (social sculpture).

Following a Catholic upbringing and early interest in botany, he became a pilot and was shot down in the Crimea in 1943, where locals swathed him in fat and felt to protect him against the cold. A pupil of sculptor Ewald Mattaré, his early work (1946–61) consists of delicate drawings, oils and watercolours of plants, animals and female figures. These elaborate key concepts in a vocabulary of natural symbolism in which, for example, the hare represents movement and rebirth, and the beehive unites reason (a solid, crystalline comb) and intuition (fluid, organic and amorphous honey). His striking 1952 sculpture *Bienenkönigin III* (Queen Bee), for example, compounds insect and human forms. In Beuys' scheme, fat, which he used from around 1952, represents the evolutionary principle of warmth, signifying spiritual vitality. Felt is an insulator and conserver of warmth, and copper a conductor or communicator of energy. Numerous *Fettecken* (fat corners) and sculptures – including his *Filz-Fettplastik* (Felt and Fat Sculpture) of 1963 – demonstrate how these everyday materials could symbolically suggest ways of bringing about evolutionary social change in the living organism of society.

In 1963 Beuys embarked on a series of performances – initially within the framework of the Fluxus movement – translating his theory of materials into ritualistic actions, which echo the anti-art stance of neo-Dada whilst rejecting its nihilism. An example of this was his 1965 performance *Wie man dem toten Hasen die Bilder erklärt* (How to Explain the Pictures to a Dead Hare). During the 1960s his fame as an artist and teacher spread rapidly at home and abroad and he became increasingly involved in political activities, initially at the Düsseldorf Academy of Arts where he was professor for sculpture, and subsequently in the public arena. Major contributions to the **documenta** in 1972, when for 100 days he patiently answered questions about direct democracy, art and ecology, and 1973, with the installation *Honigpumpe am Arbeitsplatz* (Honey Pump at the Work Place) and founding of the Free International University, confirmed his reputation as the leading German artist of his generation. His last major environmental project, the huge tree-planting scheme *7000 Eichen* (7000 Oaks), was completed after his death in 1987.

See also: sculpture

Further reading

Adriani, G. *et al.* (1984) *Joseph Beuys: Leben und Werk*, Cologne: DuMont (the standard chronological account of his life and work; detailed and well illustrated).

Temkin, A. and Rose, B. (1993) *Thinking is Form: The Drawings of Joseph Beuys*, London: Thames & Hudson (contains an introductory essay and is excellently illustrated).

MARTIN BRADY

Beyer, Frank

b. 26 May 1932, Nobitz (Saxony)

Filmmaker

Educated at the Prague Film School, Beyer was assistant to, amongst others, Kurt **Maetzig** before directing his first film in 1957. Recurring subjects are ***Vergangenheitsbewältigung*** and the moral and social responsibility of fellow travellers. Beyer was repeatedly blacklisted for his critical stance towards GDR society. On its revival in 1991, *Trail of Stones* (*Spur der Steine*) of 1966 became the most successful of the films banned in the aftermath of the **Eleventh Plenum**. *Jacob the Liar* (*Jakob der Lügner*) of 1974, based on the novel by Jurek **Becker**, was the only GDR film to be nominated for an Oscar as 'Best Foreign Film'.

See also: film: GDR

HORST CLAUS

Bezirk (GDR)

The Bezirke were the fifteen administrative districts created in the GDR in 1952 (including East Berlin) – officially as a move to greater 'democratization', in practice to provide greater centralization of power. At the same time the five eastern *Länder* were abolished. The process was reversed in 1990 so that the reconstituted *Länder* could vote to adopt the West German constitution (see **constitution: FRG**) and thereby bring about German **unification**. The term is also used in the Federal Republic for local administrative districts.

JOHN SANDFORD

BGB

The *Bürgerliches Gesetzbuch*, the German civil code, is made up of five books covering general concepts of civil law, the law of obligations (contract and tort), property law, family law and the law of succession. It first came into force in the year 1900, which meant that many statutes were written in the spirit of laissez-faire liberalism, whilst others showed nineteenth-century patriarchal-authoritarian traits (family law). Nevertheless, the general concepts proved flexible enough to be adapted to changing social and economic circumstances and since 1949 to the requirements of the Basic Law.

See also: constitution: FRG; Federal Constitutional Court; legal system: FRG

MONIKA PRÜTZEL-THOMAS

Bialas, Günter

b. 19 July 1907, Bielschowitz (Upper Silesia)

Composer

A varied career saw Bialas in a range of teaching posts: Breslau (now Wrocław) (1940), Weimar (1947), Detmold (1950) and Munich (1959). Although primarily remembered as an outstanding teacher, his own individual output under various influences, including Stravinsky, twelve-note technique and traditional forms, includes substantial contributions to opera, music for theatre and film, choral works, and orchestral and chamber music.

DEREK McCULLOCH

Bichsel, Peter

b. 24 March 1935, Luzern

Writer

Peter Bichsel's work is not extensive, but his unique style expresses itself with great charm in a collection of short stories and miniatures in which he executes variations on basic human conditions that pinpoint the moral complexities of life. He trained as a teacher and for thirteen years taught in a small Swiss community until 1970 when he devoted himself fully to writing and journalism. The recipient of numerous literary awards including the prize of the **Gruppe 47** in 1965, he was also invited to give the prestigious Frankfurt University lectures. A long-time social democrat, Bichsel was politically active and was a close friend and advisor to Willi Ritschard, a member of the Swiss government.

Opinion about him is divided in Switzerland where some have called him a '*Nestbeschmutzer*' (a nest soiler), on account of his critical statements about his homeland, while others see him as an important writer. His literary reputation was secured with his first collection of miniatures (*And Really Frau Blum Would Very Much Like to Meet the Milkman*) (*Eigentlich möchte Frau Blum den Milchmann kennenlernen*) in 1964 with their sympathetic portrayal of ordinary individuals in their petit-bourgeois environment. The deceptive simplicity of the pieces hides the profoundly disturbing nature of his characters. They have simple desires and wish to escape from the bleakness of their lives into more meaningful existences, but ultimately are resigned to the hopelessness of their situation.

His first and only novel *Die Jahreszeiten* (Seasons) (1967) is an 'anti-novel', that questions the traditional values of fiction and received a lukewarm reception, but he was back to form with *Stories for Children* (*Kindergeschichten*) (1969), which was an immediate sensation. Ironically his children's stories actually have nothing to do with children, but are about old men who, through their strange behaviour, separate themselves from society. A fallow period followed until 1979 when a collection of his journalism appeared. In later works he returned to his earlier style, but has not enjoyed quite the same success.

Bichsel is a gifted writer, often funny and light-hearted, who writes plain, unadorned sentences in a quiet melancholy tone. He brings small, seemingly unimportant events to light, yet behind the surface simplicity there is a highly conscious and skilled craftsman at work.

Bichsel has a sharp eye for social circumstances and has never fought shy of addressing some of Switzerland's social problems and the attitudes of some of his bourgeois fellow citizens. He attacks, reveals and adopts standpoints. A trenchant example is 'Das Ende der Schweizer Unschuld' (The End of Swiss Innocence) which first appeared in *Der Spiegel* (a further cause of controversy) and dealt with the unrest of the young in Switzerland (see **Spiegel, Der**). Bichsel has always identified with ordinary people and his scepticism, as evinced in broadcasts, has often endeared him to the man in the street.

Further reading

Bänziger, H. (1984) *Peter Bichsel. Weg und Werk*, Bern: Benteli (a valuable introduction).

Hove, H. (ed.) (1984) *Peter Bichsel: Auskunft für Leser*, Darmstadt: Luchterhand (a useful collection of pieces on and by Bichsel).

PETER PROCHNIK

Bickhardt, Stephan

b. 3 September 1959, Dresden

Priest and human rights activist

Bickhardt became involved in opposition groups in the GDR during his theological studies in the early 1980s. From 1986 he was in contact with the citizens' group, *Initiative Frieden und Menschenrechte* (Initiative for Peace and Human Rights), and in early 1989 he was co-author of the *Aufruf Neues Handeln* (Call for New Action) which called for the right to put forward independent candidates in the local elections in the GDR in May 1989. In September 1989 he was a co-founder of the citizens' group, *Demokratie Jetzt* (Democracy Now), and in 1990 he became its secretary.

See also: citizens' movements: GDR

PETER BARKER

Bieler, Manfred

b. 3 July 1934, Zerbst (Anhalt)

Writer

Bieler's parodies of GDR society in numerous radio plays and the picaresque novel *Bonifaz oder der Matrose in der Flasche* (Boniface or the Sailor in the Bottle) (1963) led to the banning of his second novel (1963), filmed by Kurt **Maetzig** for **DEFA** in 1965, but only published in 1969 under the title *Maria Morzeck oder Das Kaninchen bin ich* (Maria Morzeck or I am the Rabbit) after Bieler left the GDR in 1964. The film was shown for the first

time in 1989. He lived in Czechoslovakia until the Soviet invasion in 1968, moving to West Germany where he published several best-selling novels and radio plays including *Der Mädchenkrieg* (The War of the Girls) (1975), filmed in 1977.

MARGARET VALLANCE

Bienefeld, Heinz

b. 8 July 1926, Krefeld; d. 28 April 1995, Swisttal (near Bonn)

Architect

Studied at Kölner Werkschule under D. **Böhm** whose assistant he became. Worked with G. **Böhm** from 1955 and with Emil **Steffann** 1958–63. Set up his own office in Krefeld in 1963.

W. Strodthof called Bienefeld one of the very quiet but great German architects. Private houses, inspired by classical proportion and tradition represent the largest part of his œuvre. His ascetic spaces demonstrate unusual sensibility towards material and detail. Externally barely opened brick walls dominate his designs while the 'Roman' atrium is the prominent feature on the inside, around which the house and life is organized.

MARTIN KUDLEK

Bienek, Horst

b. 7 May 1930, Gleiwitz (now Gliwice, Poland); d. 30 November 1990, Munich

Writer and filmmaker

After expulsion from his native Gleiwitz, Horst Bienek settled in the Soviet zone during the years immediately following the end of WWII, first in Köthen (Anhalt), then near Berlin, where he became a pupil of Bertolt **Brecht**. In 1951 he was arrested for distributing anti-Stalinist propaganda and sentenced to twenty-five years hard labour in the Soviet Union. After four years in the Gulag Archipelago, Bienek was amnestied. Until 1961 he worked as literary editor for the Hessischer Rundfunk in Frankfurt am Main and subsequently as a publisher's reader in Munich before becoming a freelance writer. Although Bienek first made his mark as editor of the influential *Werkstattgespräche mit Schriftstellern* (Workshop Talks with Writers) (1962), it was as a poet and novelist of incarceration and as the sympathetic chronicler of the recent history of Upper Silesia that he was to become a major writer of fiction in the 1970s and 1980s.

Bienek's 1968 début novel *Die Zelle* (The Cell, filmed, script by Bienek, in 1971) is a powerfully claustrophobic evocation of the day-to-day indignities and personal triumphs of prison-life, told in an experimental manner indebted to the chosisme of the French new novelists. Bienek also explored his experiences in the Soviet Union in poetry, in *Traumbuch eines Gefangenen* (A Prisoner's Dream Diary) (1957) and in essays on Solzhenitsyn and the Gulag-apparatus. But it was eventually as a novelist of his home region of Upper Silesia that he was to give a voice to the non-revanchist strain of dispossessed Germans.

The year 1975 saw the publication of *Die erste Polka* (The First Polka), part one of Bienek's *magnum opus*: the 'Gleiwitz tetralogy', also including the novels *Septemberlicht* (September Light) (1977), *Zeit ohne Glocken* (Time without Bells) (1979), and *Erde und Feuer* (Earth and Fire) (1982). *Die erste Polka*, set in Gleiwitz on the eve of WWII, gives a detailed picture of a world on the brink of catastrophic change, and yet presented without hindsight knowledge. The central event, a raid on the Gleiwitz radio-station staged by National Socialists as a pretext for reprisals, is set alongside scenes of '*Alltagsfaschismus*' (daily fascism), largely presented from the perspective of a group of adolescents on the margins of history. All four Gleiwitz novels document the clash between Catholicism and National Socialism, Aryanization and Polish allegiances, Germans and Jews, widening in *Erde und Feuer* to a panorama of the 1945 débâcle, encompassing the bombing of Dresden and the fate of Upper Silesian Jews at Auschwitz. The cycle is permeated with a sense of the region's fatalism and irrationality and a nostalgic recognition of a lost world too ethnically mixed to belong either to Germany or Poland. In a companion volume, *Beschreibung einer Provinz* (Description of a Province) (1983), Bienek describes the project as a 'requiem' for Upper Silesia, a description that applies equally well to his various later evocations of the lost territories of the Third Reich.

JOHN J. WHITE

Biermann Affair

On 16 November 1976 the Politbüro of the **SED** revoked the citizenship of Wolf **Biermann**, the dissident singer and poet who had just begun a series of concerts in the FRG. The shock waves produced by this measure, with its uncomfortable reminder of practices previously associated with the Nazis, were all the greater because Biermann's father was a Jewish communist who had perished in Auschwitz. Despite protests by Biermann himself and by his supporters both in the GDR and elsewhere, he was not allowed to return to the GDR until after the fall of the Berlin Wall. The affair greatly exacerbated the divisive mistrust which already characterized the relationship between the state's political leadership and its leading intellectuals, many of whom subsequently left the GDR for the West. This impoverishment of the country's cultural life marked, in Biermann's view, the beginning of the end of the GDR.

Biermann had been banned in 1965 from performing or publishing in the GDR. In September 1976, however, there was no official protest when he performed in a church in Prenzlau and, only a few weeks later, he was able to undertake a concert tour in the FRG. It is often suspected but not yet finally proven that these events were a calculated trick by a political leadership which, having already had Reiner **Kunze** thrown out of the **Writers' Union of the GDR** on 29 October, was encouraged now to remove an even greater source of irritation. There is documentary evidence from as early as 1973 showing that the authorities had previously considered the kind of measures to be taken if Biermann were to leave the GDR. However, leading members of the Politbüro, the cultural bureaucracy, and the Writers' Union all claim that the expatriation took them completely by surprise. The most likely explanation currently is therefore that Erich **Honecker** (possibly in consultation with Erich Mielke, head of the **Stasi**) was solely responsible. Whether the decision was premeditated or spontaneous is still open to question. The official justification was that, at a concert given in Cologne on 13 November before an audience of 7,000 people and transmitted in North-Rhine Westphalia by WDR radio, Biermann had made hostile remarks about the GDR, thereby seriously breaching his duties as a citizen. To make matters worse, on 17 November WDR transmitted televised excerpts from the concert and two days later the ARD network broadcast the entire concert.

Twelve leading writers (including Christa **Wolf**, Volker **Braun**, Stephan **Hermlin** and Stefan **Heym**) and the sculptor Fritz **Cremer** published a letter of carefully-worded protest respectfully requesting that the Politbüro reconsider its decision. The petition gained the public support of over 150 other intellectuals, but *Neues Deutschland* responded by publishing a collection of statements in which party loyalists as well as widely respected intellectuals such as Anna Seghers and Konrad Wolf distanced themselves from Biermann with varying degrees of emphasis.

Those petitionists who were members of the SED quickly found themselves called to account for their breach of party discipline and above all for the fact that, instead of being discreetly addressed to and dealt with by the party, their letter had been published in western newspapers (it never appeared in the GDR media despite being made available). Cremer withdrew his name, others received punishments ranging from official censure to removal from the party and the party's records. Surveillance of critical intellectuals by the *Stasi* was intensified, and leading writers became aware with increasing sharpness that the Writers' Union did not reflect their views or interests. Over two hundred took advantage of the party's decision to allow troublesome writers and other intellectuals to leave the GDR for the West. The resultant damage to the country's cultural fabric was only made worse when a misguided attempt to use the law to discipline Stefan Heym provided a controversy which led to the exclusion of nine critical writers from the Union, including Heym himself.

According to Biermann, Honecker admitted to a group of Swiss socialists a few years after 1976 that the expatriation had been misconceived, but it was not until the fall of the Berlin Wall made possible his return to the GDR on 1 December 1989 that the Minister of Culture, Dietmar Keller, admitted publicly that 'The expatriation was a mistake. We who now bear the responsibility make a commitment that this will not happen again in this country.' On the same day in Leipzig Biermann gave his first concert in the GDR for twenty-five years.

See also: cultural policy: GDR; dissent and opposition: GDR

Further reading

Berbig, R. *et al.* (eds) (1994) *In Sachen Biermann. Protokolle, Berichte und Briefe zu den Folgen einer Ausbürgerung*, Forschungen zur DDR-Geschichte, vol. 2, Berlin: Ch. Links (comprehensive documentation, with three introductory essays).

Chotjewitz, R. *et al.* (eds) (1994) *Die Biermann-Ausbürgerung und die Schriftsteller. Ein deutsch-deutscher Fall*, Bibliothek Wissenschaft und Politik, vol. 52, Cologne: Verlag Wissenschaft und Politik (verbatim record of hearings into the Biermann Affair held in 1992 under the auspices of the Historical Commission of the German Writers' Union).

Heym, S. (1996) *Der Winter unsers Mißvergnügens. Aus den Aufzeichnungen des OV Diversant*, Munich: Goldmann (a diary of the affair by one of the signatories of the original letter of protest).

Jäger, A. (1995) *Schriftsteller aus der DDR. Ausbürgerungen und Übersiedlungen von 1961 bis 1989*, 2 vols, Frankfurt am Main: Peter Lang (Schriften zur Europa- und Deutschlandforschung, vols 1 and 2) (volume 1 contains biographies of 97 writers who left the GDR between 1961 and 1989, with full bibliographies; volume 2 presents a critical evaluation of representative examples of their work).

Keller, D. and Kirchner, M. (eds) (1991) *Biermann und kein Ende. Eine Dokumentation zur DDR-Kulturpolitik*, Berlin: Dietz (documentation, with helpful commentary by the GDR's last-but-one Minister of Culture, Dietmar Keller).

Krug, M. (1996) *Abgehauen. Ein Mitschnitt und Tagebuch*, Düsseldorf: Econ (revealing account in diary form by one of Biermann's strongest supporters).

Roos, P. (ed.) (1977) *Die Ausbürgerung Wolf Biermanns aus der DDR. Eine Dokumentation*, Cologne: Kiepenheuer & Witsch (full documentation of the immediate reaction, in Germany and abroad, to Biermann's expatriation; useful commentary).

IAN WALLACE

Biermann, Wolf

b. 15 November 1936, Hamburg

Singer and composer of political ballads

Born to working-class, communist parents, Biermann moved at the age of seventeen to East Germany. He studied mathematics and philosophy at the Humboldt University in East Berlin, but interrupted his studies to work as an assistant producer at the **Berliner Ensemble** from 1957 to 1959. His early songs conformed to the communist party line, but in the 1960s he started to write critical songs which led to a performance ban in 1965. Together with his friend Robert **Havemann** he became a focus for opposition to Stalinist socialism in the GDR. When he undertook a concert tour in West Germany in 1976, his GDR citizenship was revoked and he was forced to stay in West Germany. Since unification he has been strongly critical of those intellectuals and writers who stayed in the GDR and collaborated with the authorities.

Biermann's life and work have been dominated by the legacy of Nazism and the division of Germany. His father, a Jewish communist, was arrested for anti-fascist activities and died in Auschwitz in 1943. Wolf followed in his father's political footsteps, and shortly after the **June Uprising** in the GDR he went in the opposite direction to most inner-German émigrés by moving to East Berlin in search of a socialist society. Whilst working at the Berliner Ensemble he was deeply influenced by **Brecht**'s iconoclastic approach to art and politics. As a student Biermann began writing poems and ballads, at first conforming to the aims of socialist realism adopting the *agitprop* style, and inspired in his musical composition by Hanns **Eisler**. But he soon started to display a provocative

tone in his treatment of political and erotic themes, with an impudence which endeared him to young people and intellectuals suffering from heavy-handed restrictions imposed by a Stalinist government. As he himself became subject to these restrictions – a play he had written for a students' and workers' theatre was banned after its dress rehearsal, and the theatre closed in 1962 – Biermann soon acquired his credentials as the *enfant terrible* of the GDR and was banned from performing for a whole year until June 1963. His songs became angrier, more provocative and strident in tone. His satirical barbs were mainly directed at the hypocrisy and narrow-mindedness of party and state functionaries. Half clown, half troubadour, he claimed kinship with the French mediaeval troubadour poet, François Villon, and the exiled nineteenth-century German Jewish poet, Heinrich Heine. In 1965, following a highly successful concert tour in West Germany which culminated in a joint performance in West Berlin with the political cabaret artist, Wolfgang **Neuss**, he was banned from performing or publishing in the GDR. The record of this concert and his first published collection of ballads and poems, *Die Drahtharfe* (*The Wire Harp*), both of which appeared only in West Germany in 1965, made his name in both Germanys. In the GDR he became the main focus of a sustained attack by the SED leadership on 'cultural decadence' at the **Eleventh Plenum** in December 1965, and he was banned from performing indefinitely. He continued, however, to smuggle his songs to the West and a series of collections appeared in a left-wing publishing house in West Berlin in the 1960s and 1970s.

In November 1976 he was unexpectedly granted permission to give a concert tour in West Germany. After his first performance in Cologne, broadcast live on West German television, the GDR authorities declared that he had forfeited his right to GDR citizenship, thus resorting to a measure which had been widely used in the Third Reich. This action provoked public protests to the GDR government by many artists and writers, but to no avail. The '**Biermann Affair**' proved to be a watershed in relations between the cultural intelligentsia and the state, and the ensuing conflict led to an exodus of artists and writers on a scale hitherto unknown.

In the years following his expatriation Biermann, living once more in Hamburg, and for a time in Paris, began to address himself to political themes in the West, for instance the treatment of Turkish guest workers. The stridency of some of his early work mellowed into melancholic scepticism, but never resignation. The dream of a non-Stalinist form of socialism would not die. His audiences remained loyal, but were largely confined to a left-wing minority. Cut off from GDR society, which had been his true inspiration, Biermann, in common with most other exiled GDR writers, remained isolated.

This position changed with the political upheavals of 1989/90 in the GDR. His response to the collapse of SED rule was to compose a ballad to the corrupt old men of the SED leadership which he was able to sing at a triumphant concert to an audience of 5,000 in Leipzig on 1 December 1989, his first performance in the GDR for twenty-five years. However, as the atmosphere in the post-unification period became more acrimonious, Biermann found himself at the centre of a number of public debates, most notably that concerning the use to which the archives of the GDR secret police should be put when the files were opened to victims of persecution in January 1992. Even before the files were opened, Biermann caused a sensation on 19 October 1991 when he denounced the poet, Sascha **Anderson**, as a **Stasi** spy in the speech that he gave on receiving one of the most prestigious literary prizes in Germany, the Georg Büchner prize. Biermann's talent for being controversial was further demonstrated by his strong support for the actions of the western allies against Iraq in the Gulf War in 1991 and his linking of the supply of chemical weapons from West Germany to Iraq with Nazi atrocities against the Jews.

See also: cultural policy: GDR; dissent and opposition: GDR

Major works

Biermann, W. (1965) *Die Drahtharfe*, Berlin: Klaus Wagenbach (ballads, songs and poems).
—— (1968) *Mit Marx-und Engelszungen*, Berlin: Klaus Wagenbach (ballads, songs and poems).

—— (1972) *Für meine Genossen*, Berlin: Klaus Wagenbach (songs, poems and ballads).
—— (1977) *Poems and Ballads*, trans. S. Gooch, with introductions by S. Hood and J. Zipes, London: Pluto Press (the only large collection in English).
—— (1978) *Preußischer Ikarus*, Cologne: Kiepenheuer & Witsch (poems, songs and prose).
—— (1986) *Affenfels und Barrikade*, Cologne: Kiepenheuer & Witsch (poems, songs and prose).
—— (1990) *Klartexte im Getümmel*, Cologne: Kiepenheuer & Witsch (a collection of essays written since 1976).

Recordings

Biermann, W. (1965) *Wolf Biermann (Ost) bei Wolfgang Neuss (West)*, Philips 838, 349–1.
—— (1969) *Chausseestraße 131*, re-released in 1975 on CBS 80 798.
—— (1973) *Warte nicht auf beßre Zeiten*, CBS 65 753.
—— (1988) *VE (Volkseigener) Biermann* EMI Electrola 066 791258 1.
—— (1991) *Nur wer sich ändert*, EMI Electrola 066 7982221.

Further reading

Chotjewitz, R. *et al.* (eds) (1995) *Die Biermann-Ausbürgerung und die Schriftsteller. Ein deutsch-deutscher Fall*, Cologne: Verlag Wissenschaft und Politik (recent collection of essays on Biermann's expatriation).
Graves, P. (ed.) (1985) *Three Contemporary German Poets: Wolf Biermann, Sarah Kirsch, Reiner Kunze*, Leicester: Leicester University Press (collection of poems with introductions).
In Sachen Biermann. Protokolle, Berichte und Briefe zu den Folgen einer Ausbürgerung (1995) Berlin: Ch. Links Verlag (collection of documents on Biermann's expatriation).
New German Critique (1977) 10 (contains an editorial and documentation on Biermann's expatriation.
Roos, P. (ed.) (1977) *Nachlaß I, 1977: Exil*, Cologne: Kiepenheuer & Witsch (a documentation of Biermann's forced expatriation from the GDR).
Rosellini, J. (1992) *Wolf Biermann*, Munich: Beck (general survey of life and work).

PETER BARKER

Bild

The daily paper *Bild* (or *Bild-Zeitung*) has long been seen not only as the epitome of sensationalist popular journalism in Germany, but also as the newspaper most detested by the country's intelligentsia. Founded in 1952 by Axel **Springer**, it was initially – true to its title – conceived as a picture newspaper, but the formula did not catch on, and was soon replaced by the aggressively garish layout of bold headlines and brief stories that has been its hallmark ever since. Sales rose steeply throughout the 1950s and well into the 1960s to make *Bild* not only by far the biggest-selling daily paper in Germany, but in the whole of western Europe. Already 2 million copies a day were being sold in 1955, 3 million by 1956, 4 million by 1962, and a peak of around 5 million by 1966. Since unification, the paper's sales have settled down to around 4.4 million. The Sunday edition, *Bild am Sonntag*, sells around 2.5 million copies.

The *Bild-Zeitung* is in many ways the exception to the normal patterns of German newspaper publishing. Not only is its circulation untypically high in a country where figures of less than a hundred thousand are much more the norm, but its more or less even distribution across the country (albeit in a number of regional editions) contrasts sharply with the regional structure characteristic of other daily **newspapers**. Its brash and vulgar manner is also untypical of the staidness that characterizes most other German dailies.

Bild has been at the centre of fierce debates about the power of the press in Germany. These first came to a head in the 1960s when Springer gave his papers a more overtly right-wing hue. *Bild*'s vitriolic attacks on the **student movement** led to accusations that Springer was abusing the freedom of the press in order to manipulate public consciousness, and to demands for his expropriation. In the early 1970s *Bild* further alienated the country's intellectuals with its accusations of sympathy for the **terrorism** of the Baader–Meinhof gang. The most prominent victim of the paper's attacks, Heinrich **Böll**, responded with the best-selling novel *The Lost Honour of Katharina Blum* (see also **Blum, Katharina**), a critique of the destructive power of the gutter press that was quite unambiguously aimed at the *Bild-Zeitung*. The third phase of *Bild* criticism came with the appearance of a series of books by the investigative writer Günter **Wallraff**, who managed in 1977 to work incognito for four months as a journalist for the paper's Hanover edition.

Since Springer's death in 1985 *Bild* has shaken off some of the negative images of the previous decades. Attempts have been made to deal with the unsavoury journalistic practices revealed by Wallraff, and the paper has won admiration for a number of major news scoops.

Further reading

Müller, H.D. (1969) *Press Power: A Study of Axel Springer*, London: Macdonald (still the best account of the early years of the *Bild-Zeitung*; the German original – *Der Springer-Konzern: Eine kritische Studie*, Munich: Piper Verlag, 1968 – contains slightly more material).

Wallraff, G. (1990) *Der Aufmacher: Der Mann, der bei BILD Hans Esser war*, ed. J. Sandford, Manchester and New York: Manchester University Press (annotated edition, with detailed English introduction, of Wallraff's 1977 account of his experiences as a *Bild* journalist).

JOHN SANDFORD

Bill, Max

b. 22 December 1908, Winterthur

Architect, sculptor, painter and writer

From 1927 to 1929 Bill was a student at the Bauhaus. Amongst numerous occupations he co-founded and designed the **Hochschule für Gestaltung** in Ulm from 1953–5 and held a Professorship for Environmental Design at the State Institute of Fine Arts in Hamburg 1967–74. In the post-war period Bill was active at many architectural conferences, CIAM (Congrés Internationaux d'Architecture Moderne) most importantly, to improve the poor conditions architects found themselves in. He edited the third volume of *Le Corbusier: Œuvre Complète* in 1939 and wrote a wide variety of books, e.g. *Der Wiederaufbau* of 1945, and *Mies van der Rohe* of 1955.

MARTIN KUDLEK

Biondi, Franco

b. 8 August 1947, Forli (Italy)

Writer

Franco Biondi is one of the most important representatives of current **migrant literature** in West Germany. Through his literary texts, his theoretical essays, and his activities as a publisher he has had a significant influence on the development of this literary phenomenon.

As he travelled with his parents through the north of Italy and worked on fair grounds Biondi experienced homelessness and discrimination as typical aspects of a migrant existence even before he arrived in Germany. In spite of his vocational training he was unable to settle down in his home country and followed his father into emigration. He worked for ten years as a **Gastarbeiter**, studied psychology and today works as a family-therapist.

Biondi started his literary career at the beginning of the 1970s. After some attempts in the Italian language, he soon began to write in German. Initially regarding his writing as a part of a European workers' literature he soon joined the *Werkkreis Literatur der Arbeitswelt*. As he did not feel that the interests of the labour immigrants were fully represented there, he became involved in the first organization of migrant writers and artists in West Germany, formed by Italians. In 1980 he distanced himself from this group and founded the *Polynationale Literatur- und Kunstverein (PoLiKunst)*, alongside writers and artists from twelve different countries. He also co-founded the multinational publishing group *Südwind*. Within the framework of these cultural and political activities, in co-operation with Rafik **Schami** he formulated the *Literatur der Betroffenheit* (Literature of Emotional Involvement) in 1981. This was the first programme of a multinational literature movement set up by members of ethnic minorities in West Germany.

In his early poems Biondi looks closely at the diverse forms of discrimination which face labour immigrants in West Germany, not least the disparagement of *Gastarbeiterdeutsch* (the German spoken by foreign workers) by the Germans. As a countermove Biondi raised this language to an art form in his 1979 poetry collection *Nicht nur Gastarbeiterdeutsch* (Not Just *Gastarbeiter* German). In his narrative texts from the 1980s Biondi highlights the different phases of the immigration process. Whilst his 1982 volume of short stories *Passavantis Rückkehr* (Passavanti's Return) focuses on some of the typical problems facing the first generation of immigrant workers, such as the pain of separation and gradual alienation from the homeland, the 1984 novel *Abschied der zerschellten Jahre* (Farewell to the Broken Years) describes the despair of a second-generation immigrant who is threatend by extradition and fights for his right to stay in Germany.

In the course of his literary development Biondi turns away from representing the fates of labour immigrants and concentrates on the existential experience of uprootedness and its effect on the process of writing (see *Die Unversöhnlichen. Im Labyrinth der Herkunft* (The Unreconciled. In the Labyrinth of Origin), of 1991).

Further reading

Krechel, R. and Reeg, U. (eds) (1989) *Franco Biondi. Werkheft Literatur*, Munich: iudicium verlag.

Tantow, L. (1986) 'Franco Biondi', in H.L. Arnold (ed.) *Kritisches Lexikon der deutschsprachigen Gegenwartsliteratur, Band 1*, Munich: edition text + kritik.

SABINE FISCHER

Bisky, Lothar

b. 17 August 1941, Zollbrück (eastern Pomerania)

Academic and politician

From 1979 to 1986 a professor of cultural sciences at the Humboldt University in East Berlin, in November 1986 Bisky became rector of the Film and Television Institute in Potsdam-**Babelsberg**.

From 1963 a member of the **SED** in the GDR, he became a leading figure in the transformation of the party into the **PDS** (Party of Democratic Socialism) from 1989–90. From 1991 to 1993 he was leader of the PDS in Brandenburg and 1993 to 2000 he was national party leader. Together with Gregor **Gysi** he became one of the most prominent advocates of a clear break with the party's Stalinist history.

PETER BARKER

Bitburg

A town in the Rhineland-Palatinate that has given its name to a widely-sold brand of beer, Bitburg is also the location of a military cemetery including graves of *Waffen-SS* and German *Wehrmacht* soldiers. On 5 May 1985 the American president Ronald Reagan and the German chancellor Helmut Kohl commemorated the fortieth anniversary of the end of WWII in a double ceremony at the Bitburg cemetery and at the Nazi concentration camp at Bergen-Belsen. A highly controversial symbolic event, it aimed at reshaping public memory, relativizing the singularity of the Nazi crimes by equating victims of the Holocaust and dead German soldiers as 'victims of the war'.

See also: *Historikerstreit*

MARGRIT FRÖLICH

Bitterfelder Weg

A state-led movement in literature and the arts in the GDR which sought to bridge the gap between culture and the ordinary working people, the 'Bitterfeld Path' became a by-word for conventionally affirmative depiction of industrial life and the political instrumentalization of culture.

In 1957 Walter **Ulbricht** called for a new socialist content in literature and art, which should document the country's industrial and economic progress, and exhorted class-conscious workers to 'storm the heights of culture'. He was, however, motivated less by a desire to foster genuine working-class culture than by a wish to tighten the Party's control over literature and theatre, art

and film. The initiative was taken a step further when the **Mitteldeutscher Verlag** invited 150 professional writers and 300 'worker writers' to a conference in the industrial town of Bitterfeld in April 1959, under the slogan 'Reach for your pen, mate!'. Circles of writers, artists and musicians were established in factories and offices. At the same time professional writers and artists were sent to building sites, factories and collective farms to experience industrial life and make this the subject of their work.

The fundamental problems the movement shared with comparable efforts in the Weimar Republic and West Germany (see also **Gruppe 61**) were that creative writing cannot simply be taught, and that prescribing artistic themes and forms is rarely successful. The conflict between authentic portrayal of industrial life and the state's demands for glorification of the status quo also soon became apparent. A flood of reportage articles, poems and shorter prose pieces appeared in print, but aesthetic innovation and individual self-expression were stifled by the requirement of positive role models and an optimistic perspective.

The Bitterfeld aims were redefined in 1960 and 1964, when, in line with the New Economic System, new emphasis was placed on depicting executives and managers, rather than ordinary workers. The movement was, however, tacitly conceded to have failed soon after. Its most significant achievements came in a second wave of substantial prose works by professional writers who had spent periods in industry (e.g. Franz **Fühmann**, Brigitte **Reimann**, Christa **Wolf**). At best, for instance in Wolf's *Divided Heaven* (*Der geteilte Himmel*) (1963), these reflect the complexity of the situation, and draw attention to fundamental moral and political problems without offering oversimplified answers.

See also: censorship: GDR; cultural policy: GDR; prose fiction: GDR

Further reading

Jäger, M. (1995) 'Die Windungen des Bitterfelder Weges und der Streit um die ideologische Koexistenz 1958–1964', in *Kultur und Politik in der DDR 1945–1990*, Cologne: Edition Deutschland Archiv, pp. 87–117 (a critical account including extracts from key documents).

Silberman, M. (1976) *Literature of the Working World: A Study of the Industrial Novel in East Germany*, Bern and Frankfurt am Main: Herbert Lang (examines novels by Fühmann, Strittmatter, Neutsch and others).

Tate, D. (1984) 'Continuity and Conflict in the GDR's Development', in *The East German Novel: Identity, Community, Continuity*, Bath: Bath University Press, pp. 90–134 (focuses on thematic and formal innovation in novels emerging from the movement).

AXEL GOODBODY

Blacher, Boris

b. 19 January 1903, Niu-chang (China); d. 30 January 1975, (West) Berlin

Composer

Blacher came to music after initially studying architecture and mathematics. His first teaching appointment was in Dresden, but he fell foul of the authorities for his anti-Nazi views. These manifest themselves in his post-war scores for films on the concentration camp at Sachsenhausen and on the Weimar Republic politician Gustav Stresemann. Other scores centre round Bismarck (silent film), various Shakespeare plays, Tolstoy's *War and Peace*, and a satirical operetta on Zuckmayer's *Der Hauptmann von Köpenick*, published in 1949 under the title *Preußisches Märchen*. In his instrumental music he combined virtuosity with jazz elements and his later chamber works after 1962 included electronic inputs. Among his pupils are Gottfried von **Einem** (whom he assisted over the score of Kafka's *Der Prozeß*) and Aribert **Reimann**.

DEREK McCULLOCH

Blick

Founded in 1959 by the Ringier publishing conglomerate as the first Swiss popular newspaper along the lines of the German *Bild-Zeitung*, *Blick* had by the mid-1960s, despite initial difficulties because of its sensational material, achieved the highest circulation of any Swiss newspaper, a position which it has maintained (circulation in 1995 was approximately 355,000 daily). Two-thirds of sales are at kiosks and one-third from readers' subscriptions. *Blick* is the first German-Swiss daily to aim, not at a locality, but at the whole of German-speaking Switzerland. In 1969, a Sunday edition, *Sonntags-Blick*, was started (circulation in 1995 was approximately 350,000).

MALCOLM PENDER

Bloch, Ernst

b. 8 July 1885, Ludwigshafen; d. 4 August 1977, Tübingen

Marxist philosopher

Exiled in Czechoslovakia (from 1933), then the US (from 1938), Bloch was Professor of **Philosophy** at the University of Leipzig (1949–57), until he found himself in conflict with the **SED**. From 1961 until his death, he was Professor of Philosophy at the University of Tübingen. Research interests included: utopian thought in poetry and art; the relationship between aesthetics and politics; and hope of a concrete utopia, still to be attained. He was a friend of Walter **Benjamin**.

See also: dissent and opposition: GDR; Marxism; Moltmann, Jürgen

Further reading

Geoghegan, V. (1996) *Ernst Bloch*, London: Routledge (Bloch's life and work, includes bibliography).

JANET STEWART

Blum, Katharina

Protagonist of Heinrich **Böll**'s 1974 novel *The Lost Honour of Katharina Blum* (*Die verlorene Ehre der Katharina Blum*). A film version, directed by Volker **Schlöndorff** and Margarethe von **Trotta**, and starring Angela **Winkler**, appeared the following year.

See also: *Bild*; terrorism

JOHN SANDFORD

Blumenberg, Hans

b. 13 July 1920, Lübeck; d. 28 March
1996, Altenbergen

Philosopher

Blumenberg's thought is an elaborate critique of
anti-rationalism and theological absolutism. His
major work is *The Legitimacy of the Modern Age* (*Die
Legitimität der Neuzeit*, 1966), in which he takes
Descartes as the paradigm of modern rationality,
and defines the key attributes of the modern age as
'self-assertion' and 'theoretical curiosity'. Blumenberg's thought is also opposed to ontological and
phenomenological truth-concepts, indeed to all
philosophy which defends its certainties as fixed.
He understands human thought and endeavour as
a process of self-production through transfigurative
labour on reality. In this, his ideas strongly recall
nineteenth-century historicism. *Labour on Myth*
(*Arbeit am Mythos*, 1979) is the rubric for this
endeavour.

CHRIS THORNHILL

Bobrowski, Johannes

b. 9 April 1917, Tilsit; d. 2 September
1965, (East) Berlin

Writer

Johannes Bobrowski was one of the leading poets
and prose writers of the GDR. The impetus for his
writing came from a number of sources: his
Christian beliefs; his childhood enthusiasm for the
Old Prussians (the 'Pruzzi' – indigenous inhabitants of East Prussia); the experiences of visits to
relatives and friends in the Memelland; and above
all his experiences during the German invasion of
the Soviet Union in 1941, when he was stationed
near Novgorod on Lake Ilmen. Out of this
complex of interests arose what Bobrowski later
called his 'Theme', the long and unfortunate

history of relations between the Germans and their
eastern neighbours.

Bobrowski saw the start of his poetry proper in
works written about Novgorod between 1941 and
1943, some of which were published during the
war. The poems that made his reputation were,
however, written between 1952 and 1961 and
published in the two volumes *Sarmatische Zeit*
(Sarmatian Time) (1961) and *Schattenland Ströme*
(Shadowland Streams) (1962). In these he developed the tradition of German nature poetry to
create poetic cycles in which the landscape, history,
peoples, myths and customs of 'Sarmatia' (the
name used by Ptolemy to describe much of eastern
Europe) are presented to the modern reader in the
full awareness of their passing, and especially of the
German part in their destruction, but without
sentimentality or self-pity. Characteristic is the
extent to which this landscape is infused with
history, the geographical including the historical
and the prehistoric.

In the 1960s Bobrowski turned increasingly to
prose, but his final volume of poetry, *Wetterzeichen*
(Weather-Signs), published posthumously, showed
new developments: poems turned increasingly to
themes and subjects related to his immediate
present, but also developing a personal esotericism
in which elements of linguistic mysticism coexisted
with the presentation of epiphanic experiences.
While lacking the coherence of the earlier volumes,
Wetterzeichen also contains many of Bobrowski's
most impressive individual poems.

Bobrowski's prose works helped introduce a
new, more colloquial, hesitant narrative tone in
East Germany. Of his two novels, *Levins Mühle*
(Levin's Mill) (1964) is set in West Prussia in 1874,
while *Litauische Claviere* (Lithuanian Pianos) (1965) is
set in the Memelland in 1936. Both works
combined detailed local and historical knowledge
with surprisingly direct involvement in some of the
East German literary debates of the time, as
Bobrowski defended himself against increasing
political criticism in the run-up to the **Eleventh
Plenum** of December 1965. His shorter prose
works dealt frequently with the fraught relations
between historical intellectuals and the established
power of the state, here too reflecting Bobrowski's
own experiences.

See also: cultural policy: GDR

Further reading

Scrase, D. (1995) *Understanding Johannes Bobrowski*, Columbia, SC: University of South Carolina (most recent monograph in English, general introduction, good bibliography).

Tgahrt, R. (ed.) (1993) *Johannes Bobrowski oder Landschaft mit Leuten*, Marbach am Neckar: Deutsche Schillergesellschaft (useful source of material on Bobrowski's life and works).

Wolf, G. (1971) *Beschreibung eines Zimmers: 15 Kapitel über Johannes Bobrowski*, (East) Berlin: Union Verlag (sensitive introduction to Bobrowski's life and aspects of his works).

JOHN WIECZOREK

Böhm, Dominikus

b. 23 October 1880, Jettingen; d. 6
   August 1955, Cologne

Architect

Having studied under Theodor Fischer at the TH (Technical University) Stuttgart, Böhm went into private practice in Cologne in 1903, and was in partnership with his son Gottfried **Böhm** from 1952. He held professorships at the Kunstgewerbeschule (School of Arts and Crafts) Offenbach (1914–26) and the Cologne Werkschule (1926–35 and 1945–50).

Böhm is foremost a church architect, exclusively Roman Catholic. His building style is of conservative-modern nature with expressionistic tendencies. His best known post-war building is St Maria Königin in Cologne of 1954.

MARTIN KUDLEK

Böhm, Gottfried

b. 23 January 1920, Offenbach am Main

Architect

Having studied at the TH (Technical University) Munich from 1942 to 1947 under Hans **Döllgast**,

Böhm worked for his father, Dominikus **Böhm** (1948–50), for Rudolf **Schwarz** (1950) and C. Baumann (New York 1951). He went into partnership with his father (1952–5), taking over the office at his death. He was Professor of Town Planning at the RWTH (Technical University), Aachen (1963–85).

Gottfried's work follows on from his father's although his approach is more organic and site-related and his œuvre is far more varied. His earlier buildings are most often executed in concrete for which he finds highly original and expressive forms (e.g. Wallfahrtskirche, Nieviges 1963–8). In the 1970s he moved towards a postmodern style. He has been in partnership with his sons since 1989.

MARTIN KUDLEK

Böhm, Karl

b. 28 August 1894, Graz; d. 14 August
   1981, Salzburg

Conductor

Music Director of the Dresden Staatsoper (1935–44) and of the Vienna Staatsoper (1943–5 and 1954–6), he inaugurated the reconstructed Staatsoper in 1955 with Beethoven's *Fidelio*. Thereafter Böhm became a highly valued guest conductor of the Vienna and Berlin Philharmonics and a leading protagonist of the **Salzburg Festival** and **Bayreuth Festival**. His principal specialities were Mozart and Richard Strauß, with whom he enjoyed a close personal collaboration; Strauß's opera *Daphne* is dedicated to him and he gave its premiere in 1938.

BEATRICE HARPER

Böll, Heinrich

b. 21 December 1917, Cologne; d. 16 July
   1985, Bornheim-Merten

Writer

Known as the 'advocate of the little man', Böll is widely regarded as representing the moral conscience of the German people after the war. His work revolves around five central themes: the experience of war, morality in politics and society, the role of the Catholic church and religious faith, the function of art, and his deep identification with his native Rhineland.

Böll grew up in a Catholic environment, the son of a craftsman. He trained as a bookseller, began studying German literature and classics in the summer of 1939, but was called up to join the German army with the outbreak of war. Wounded several times, he spent periods in hospital and in French and British prisoner-of-war camps. After his release in December 1945 he returned to Cologne where he resumed his studies and supported himself and his family with part-time work. His first short stories appeared in 1947 and his first longer work, *The Train was on Time* (*Der Zug war pünktlich*) was published in 1949. Böll's narrative skill, the clarity of his language, and his mastery of the short story form led to his growing popularity.

The experience of war, its futility, and the suffering it inflicted on the lives of ordinary men and women is the central theme of much of his early work. The collection of short stories *Traveller, If You Come to Spa ... (Wanderer, kommst du nach Spa...)* published in 1950 is a testimony to the suffering endured by those involved. In May 1951 Böll read his story *Die schwarzen Schafe* (The Black Sheep) to the eighth meeting of the **Gruppe 47** and in that year was awarded the group's prize. Böll's first full-length novel *And Where Were You, Adam?* (*Wo warst du, Adam?*) was published later that year, a powerful and sober account of a young man who survives the horrors of the war, only to be killed on the threshold of his home.

The policy of German rearmament favoured by Konrad Adenauer in 1950 horrified Böll, as did the support for this policy expressed by the Catholic church. This sense that the Catholic church had betrayed its moral principles became a theme which was to dominate Böll's mature fiction.

In the 1950s Böll criticized the growing materialism of post-war West German society and questioned the role of the Catholic church in his 1953 novel *Acquainted with the Night* (*Und sagte kein einziges Wort*). In *The Unguarded House* (*Haus ohne Hüter*, 1954) Böll contrasts the parallel lives of two war widows, one from a bourgeois background and one from the working class, to reveal the loss of

moral integrity and the emergence of 'restorative tendencies' in middle-class German society. The aesthetic and ethical principles that Böll developed during the 1950s found expression in his 1959 novel *Billiards at Half-Past Nine* (*Billard um halbzehn*) in which he questions the inability of the German bourgeoisie to confront the past and face up to its moral failure. The religious symbols of the buffalo and the lamb represent the author's view of the destructive nature of society and those who become its victims.

In the 1960s Böll made one more attempt to challenge the innovative power and the humanity of Christian faith by founding the periodical *Das Labyrinth*, but was forced to realize the fruitlessness of the venture. These experiences are reflected in those of the clown protagonist in the 1963 novel *The Clown* (*Ansichten eines Clowns*) in which Böll expresses bitter criticism of the heartlessness of bourgeois society and lack of humanity shown by the Catholic hierarchy. His growing resignation in view of what he perceived as the increasing materialism of German society and the ensuing loss in human values are articulated in much of his work published in the 1960s. In the 1966 satire *End of a Mission* (*Ende einer Dienstfahrt*) Böll questions the opportunity for ordinary people to defend themselves and their way of life against the encroachments of the state. In his *Frankfurter Vorlesungen* (Frankfurt Lectures) of 1964 he defended his view of the artist's role in society, and of the essential link between moral and aesthetic values. The writer, he believed, seeks the fundamental source of his art in the lives of ordinary men and women.

During the student unrest in 1968 and in the 1970s Böll sympathized with the ideals of the *Außerparlamentarische Opposition* (**APO**) but urged the use of non-violent methods of political opposition. The protagonists of his 1972 novel *Group Portrait with Lady* (*Gruppenbild mit Dame*) reflect his belief in a non-profit-orientated and classless society. Here Böll draws on forty years of German history, relating memories of the Nazi past to the xenophobia of the 1970s. In the same year Böll was awarded the Nobel prize for literature. Böll's most outspoken criticism, this time directed at the role of the tabloid press, exemplified by the *Bild-Zeitung*, was expressed in the 1974 story *The Lost Honour of Katharina Blum* (*Die verlorene Ehre der Katharina Blum*) (see also **Blum, Katharina**). Böll himself was victimized by the right-wing press who attempted to identify him with terrorists such as Ulrike **Meinhof** and Andreas **Baader**. Böll's contention that civil rights were becoming increasingly endangered in the Federal Republic was taken further in works such as *Berichte zur Gesinnungslage der Nation* (Reports on the Mood of the Nation) (1975). His last novel, *Women in a River Landscape (Frauen vor Flußlandschaft)*, was published posthumously in 1985.

Further reading

Butler, M. (ed.) (1994) *The Narrative Fiction of Heinrich Böll*, Cambridge: Cambridge University Press.

Reid, J.H. (1987) 'Heinrich Böll: From Modernism to Post-Modernism and Beyond', in *The Modern German Novel*, Oxford: Berg.

—— (1988) *Heinrich Böll. A German for his time*, Oxford: Berg.

—— (1989) 'The End of Urbanity: Heinrich Böll in the 1970s', in K. Bullivant (ed.) *After the 'Death' of Literature. West German Writing of the 1970s*, Oxford: Berg.

MARGARET VALLANCE

Böttcher, Jürgen

b. 1931, Frankenberg (Saxony)

Documentary filmmaker, painter and writer

Böttcher studied at the Academy of Fine Arts in Dresden (1949–53), and was a freelance artist and art teacher before entering **Babelsberg** Film School (1955–60). He joined the **DEFA** Studio for Newsreels and Documentaries in 1960, but after his first (and only) feature film *Jahrgang 45* (Born in '45) (1966) was shelved before completion in the wake of the **Eleventh Plenum** for supposedly being 'degenerate', he was assigned to routine documentaries. Through subtle observations utilizing cinéma vérité techniques he managed to break out of the conventional documentary mode imposed to emerge as one of the most important and influential GDR documentarists.

See also: film: GDR

HORST CLAUS

Bohley, Bärbel

b. 24 May 1945, Berlin

Painter and political activist

Bohley co-founded the independent network Frauen für den Frieden (Women for Peace), 1982, in East Berlin. Imprisoned in 1983 because of her peace activities, she was released after international protests. From 1985 to 1986 she was involved in the foundation of the Initiative für Frieden und Menschenrechte (Initiative for Peace and Civil Rights). After a public protest against the SED dictatorship during the official Rosa Luxemburg demonstration in East Berlin in 1987, she was arrested and expelled to England; she returned to the GDR in summer 1988. One year later Bohley initiated the foundation of the citizens' movement organization **Neues Forum** (see also **citizens' movements: GDR**), and became a prominent figure in the politics of the ***Wende***.

See also: dissent and opposition: GDR; peace movement: GDR

LOTHAR PROBST

Bohm, Hark

b. 18 May 1939, Hamburg

Filmmaker and actor

Bohm is a respected actor who played important supporting roles in films of the **New German Cinema** by Rainer Werner **Fassbinder**, Alexander **Kluge**, Helke **Sander** and others. He has directed fiction and documentary films for young people, often dealing with ecological and social themes. *Tschetan, the Indian Boy (Tschetan, der Indianerjunge*, 1972), his first feature film, set a new gritty tone for youth films in West Germany, whilst *Yasemin* (1988) focused on the conflicting pressures facing a Turkish girl who falls in love with a young German.

HELEN HUGHES

Bonhoeffer, Dietrich

b. 4 February 1906, Breslau (now Wroc-ław, Poland); d. 9 April 1945, Flössen-bürg concentration camp

Protestant theologian

Lutheran theologian and opponent of National Socialism, Bonhoeffer was arrested in 1943 and executed in 1945. He was significant in the ecumenical movement in the inter-war years, but his greatest influence came after the posthumous publication of his *Letters and Papers from Prison* (*Widerstand und Ergebung*) with its reference to 'religionless Christianity'. The GDR Protestant churches (see also **Kirche im Sozialismus**) drew on Bonhoeffer's heritage. His vision of an ecumenical peace council speaking with the authority of all Christian churches influenced the peace movement of the 1980s, particularly in Germany.

See also: churches and religion

Further reading

Bethge, E. (1970) *Dietrich Bonhoeffer*, trans. E. Robertson *et al.*, London: Collins (a biography by Bonhoeffer's student and friend, includes bibliography).

Krötke, W. (1993) 'Dietrich Bonhoeffer als Theo-loge der DDR' in T. Rendtorff (ed.), *Protestantische Revolution? Kirche und Theologie in der DDR*, Göttingen: Vandenhoeck & Ruprecht (a discus-sion of the reception of Bonhoeffer's theology in the GDR).

STEPHEN BROWN

book clubs

The **Bertelsmann** Group dominates both the German book-club market (Bertelsmann Leserring, Deutsche Buch-Gemeinschaft, Europäische Bil-dungsgemeinschaft (EBG), Buch + Musik, Deutscher Bücherbund) and international markets (including 25 million members in 18 countries). Many Bertelsmann clubs retain their core member-ship by offering multimedia products (e.g. compact discs, videos and software) which represent a large percentage of sales. 'Club-Centers' also provide a variety of leisure services (e.g. tickets to concerts and special events).

Further reading

Kollmansberger, M. (1995) *Buchgemeinschaften im deutschen Buchmarkt*, Wiesbaden: Harrassowitz (a good overview of the development and function of book clubs).

MARK W. RECTANUS

Borchers, Elisabeth

b. 27 February 1926, Homberg (Nieder-rhein)

Writer

Borchers grew up in Alsace and lived and studied in France and the US for extended periods. In 1959 she began teaching in Ulm, then worked for the publishing houses **Luchterhand Verlag** (1960–71) and **Suhrkamp** and Insel (starting in 1971). Her poem 'eia wasser regnet schlaf' (hush, water rains sleep), published in the ***Frankfurter Allgemeine Zeitung*** in 1960, sparked a furious debate among readers about modern poetry. A translator and editor of numerous anthologies, she writes poetry and short stories, as well as children's books and internationally popular *Hörspiele* (radio plays) (see also ***Hörspiel:*** **FRG**; ***Hörspiel:*** **GDR**).

MARTINA S. ANDERSON

Borchert, Wolfgang

b. 20 May 1921, Hamburg; d. 20 November 1947, Basel

Writer and dramatist

One of the most promising writers of his generation, Borchert achieved world fame with his 1947 radio play *The Man Outside* (*Draußen vor der Tür*) filmed as *Liebe 47* in 1949.

Apprenticed as a bookseller and briefly engaged as an actor in the Lüneburger Landesbühne theatre, Borchert was called up to serve in the German army in 1941. Seriously wounded, he was arrested and imprisoned several times for anti-Nazi remarks and satirical sketches. His health already damaged by his ill-treatment, Borchert was sent to the Russian front at the end of 1942. By early 1943 he was in hospital with jaundice and typhus. Allowed home to recover he was once again arrested, this time for telling political jokes. He spent a year and a half in prison. Once more released to fight at the front, he was taken prisoner by the French. He escaped to Hamburg where, although gravely ill, he worked as assistant producer and director of cabaret in the Hamburg Schauspielhaus theatre. At the end of 1945 he was admitted to hospital but discharged as incurable. Friends enabled him to travel to a sanatorium in Switzerland, but he died shortly before the first theatre performance of *The Man Outside*, although a radio version had already been broadcast earlier in the year.

Borchert's work represents the so-called **Kahlschlag** literature, produced by writers confronted by the physical and moral devastation of their country at the end of WWII. He was also inspired by the literature of expressionism (see also **neo-expressionism**), as can be seen in his rhetorical devices, his delight in unexpected linguistic contrasts, his staccato language, his use of alliteration and his addiction to puns.

The Man Outside expresses the tragedy of the returning soldier. The protagonist, Bachmann, comes home from the war after three years in a Soviet prisoner-of-war camp to find that he is forgotten by his wife and unwanted by society. Haunted by guilt and despair Bachmann poses the question of who the guilty are, who bears the ultimate responsibility for the catastrophe. The play struck a powerful chord with the generation of those who had been involved in the war. Experiences of the war and the immediate post-war period, vivid portrayals of poverty and hardship provide the central elements in his 1947 volume of short stories *Die Hundeblume* (The Dandelion). They represent the cry of despair of the young genera-

tion, deceived and disillusioned and yet hoping for a new beginning.

His 1946 volume of verse, *Laterne, Nacht und Sterne* (Lantern, Night and Stars), melancholic and satirical, is a prelude to the staccato urgency of his prose style. His strong points were his sensitivity to human values and to the significance of the unimportant, his ability to express the chaos and suffering of his time in genuinely poetic symbols, his feeling for prose rhythm and his creativity in the use of language.

A collection of his work, *Das Gesamtwerk*, was published in 1949 and some hitherto unpublished stories, *The Sad Geraniums* (*Die traurigen Geranien*), in 1962.

Further reading

Poppe, R. (1992) *Erläuterungen zu Wolfgang Borchert: Draußen vor der Tür, Die drei Könige, An diesem Dienstag, Die Küchenuhr, Nachts schlafen die Ratten doch* (German commentary on Borchert's principal works).

Rühmkorf, P. (1961) *Wolfgang Borchert*, Reinbek bei Hamburg: Rowohlt (standard documentation of Borchert's life and work).

MARGARET VALLANCE

Born, Nicolas

b. 31 December 1937, Duisburg; d. 7 December 1979, Hamburg

Writer

Born's poetic and fictional work at times reflected, and at others contributed to the development of diverse literary trends in the 1960s and 1970s. Originally trained in chemigraphy, he worked in the printing industry before becoming involved in the mid-1960s in Walter **Höllerer**'s Berlin Literary Colloquium where he worked with fifteen other writers, on the *Gemeinschaftsroman* (Collectively Written Novel), *Das Gästehaus* (The Guesthouse). His own first novel, *Der zweite Tag* (The Second Day) (1965), is indebted to the new realism of the Cologne School and the theoretical influence of Dieter **Wellershoff**. From 1966 to 1972 he published a number of radio plays and three collections of poetry – *Marktlage* (Market Conditions) (1967), *Wo mir der Kopf steht* (I've Got My Head Screwed On) (1970) and *Das Auge des Entdeckers* (The Eye of the Discoverer) (1972) – which reveal an increasing emancipation from earlier influences. In the first two collections, Born focuses largely on reproducing everyday social reality as it was reflected in over-formulaic linguistic clichés behind which the individual disappeared (in this he has much in common with the early **Handke**). Although only a few of his poems are directly political, Born's avoidance of overtly poetical effects reflects the anti-literary mood of the late 1960s. In his third collection the focus shifts to the individual subject and to the search for a space where it can experience itself outside the constraints of contemporary social reality. The new direction marks the collection as an early, and influential, example of the trend which dominated the 1970s, **New Subjectivity**, of which Born's final two novels are also representative examples. Both *Die erdabgewandte Seite der Geschichte* (The Far Side of History) (1976) and *The Deception* (*Die Fälschung*) (1979), filmed by Volker **Schlöndorff**, focus on the existential disorientation of protagonists who have lost faith in the relationships and constructs which gave meaning to their lives. The former depicts the disintegration of the narrator's relationship to his girlfriend against the backcloth of an increasingly half-hearted participation in the Berlin student movement. *The Deception* portrays the crisis of a journalist in war-torn Beirut who, faced with his inability to report the reality of a senseless war, begins to interpret his former life as a series of self-delusions. Born set out many of the ideas informing his literary work in a series of essays, collected in the posthumous 1980 volume *Die Welt der Maschine. Aufsätze und Reden* (The World of the Machine. Essays and Speeches).

Further reading

Grzimek, M. and Rohowski, W. (1978) 'Nicolas Born', in H.L. Arnold (ed.), *Kritisches Lexikon zur deutschsprachigen Gegenwartsliteratur*, Munich: edition text + kritik (a comprehensive survey of Born's work with a useful bibliography).
Stegers, R. (1981) ' "Aber eines Tages werden alle Bilder wahr". Über Nicolas Born und seine Romane', *Literaturmagazin* 21: 147–64 (combines a biographical sketch with analyses of the novels).

JOANNE LEAL

Bornkamm, Günther

b. 8 October 1905, Görlitz; d. 18 February 1990, Heidelberg

Protestant theologian

During the Nazi regime Bornkamm taught at the universities of Königsberg (1934) and Heidelberg (1936) and worked as a minister in Bethel (1937–9) and in Münster (1940–5) after his *venia legendi* was revoked. In 1946 Bornkamm resumed his duties as a university professor in Göttingen (until 1947) and in Heidelberg (after 1949), where he continued his critical interpretation of the New Testament by insisting on the pretext of the biblical word. He is internationally known for his scholarly work on the New Testament and early Christianity.

MAGDA MUELLER

Boskovsky, Willi

b. 16 June 1909, Vienna; d. 21 April 1991, Visp (Switzerland)

Violinist and conductor

An infant prodigy on the violin, Boskovsky studied at the Vienna Academy at the age of nine and was awarded the Kreisler Prize when only seventeen. His first appointment was to the Vienna Philharmonic Orchestra in 1932, becoming one of the leaders in 1939, as well as leading the orchestra of the Staatsoper in Vienna. Ultimately it was in the field of lighter Viennese classics, notably Johann Strauß father and son, that he made his reputation, after directing the famous New Year's Day Concert in Vienna from 1954 onwards. His recording of *Die Fledermaus* with the Staatsoper in 1973 remains his most memorable achievement.

DEREK McCULLOCH

Boulevardzeitung

Unlike their more serious counterparts – which are often bought on subscription – German tabloids (for example *Bild*, *Berliner Kurier*, Cologne's *Express* and Munich's *Abendzeitung*) are typically sold on the street by vendors and **kiosks**. The term *Boulevardzeitung* has a negative ring to it because of the dubious journalistic practices sometimes associated with these papers.

MICHAEL HÄNEL

Brandauer, Klaus Maria

b. 22 June 1944, Bad Aussee (Austria)

Actor, film and theatre director (real name Klaus Georg Steng)

Initially acting in the theatre (e.g. the **Burgtheater** in Vienna), Brandauer gained international recognition with the film *Mephisto* (1981), based on the life of Gustav **Gründgens**. This film was part of a trilogy, with *Colonel Redl* (*Oberst Redl*) (1984) and *Hanussen* (1987), directed by István Szabó and set in the fading Austro-Hungarian Empire and its aftermath, in which Brandauer portrayed the main character, entangled in a web of power, intrigue and ruthless ambition. In his characterizations he embodies a quintessentially Austrian persona: sensitive, unstable, yet smoothly charismatic.

JUDITH LEEB

Brandenburg Gate

The Brandenburg Gate more than any other building has become the symbol of the united **Berlin**. When the GDR opened the **Berlin Wall** on the night of 9 November 1989, pictures of celebrating Germans in front of the Brandenburg Gate were broadcast around the world. The Gate itself was officially reopened on 22 December 1989 and the wall in front of it was taken down in the first half of 1990. Since May 1992 public transport, taxis, and bicycles may pass through again.

The Brandenburg Gate was built between 1789 and 1791 by Carl Gotthard Langhans as the first example of classicist architecture in Berlin. It is the only remaining gate of the last city wall, which had been build by Friedrich Wilhelm I in the 1730s. It replaced an older, smaller structure and was inspired by the Propylaeum on the Acropolis in Athens. The monument was intended to celebrate peace after a series of wars and was supposed to be called the 'peace gate'. The Quadriga on top of the gate, designed by Gottfried Schadow, was added to the structure in 1794 and depicts the goddess of Peace riding in a wagon. Napoleon, who led his victorious troops through the Brandenburg Gate into Berlin in 1806 had the bronze Quadriga taken down and transported to Paris, from where it was returned after Napoleon's defeat in 1814. Berlin's famous architect Schinkel designed the iron cross, which was added to the sculpture, making it known as the goddess of victory.

The Brandenburg Gate itself consists of twelve massive columns that measure 14 metres in height and 1.73 metres diameter on the bottom. Five passageways allow traffic to pass from the Pariser Platz at the foot of the Gate to the 'via thriumphalis', the elegant boulevard Unter den Linden. Until 1918 the widest passage in the middle was reserved for members of the royal family only. The Gate reaches an imposing height of 20 metres, a width of 65.5 metres and a depth of 11 metres. Pedestrians may walk through special passages on the side of the gate. The two side buildings were originally used to house the gate keepers and the customs office.

The National Socialists held the infamous march with torches through the gate on 30 January 1933 to celebrate Hitler's takeover of power. The Brandenburg Gate was heavily damaged in WWII and renovated by the East Berlin city authorities in 1956. A new Quadriga was made from the old casts in West Berlin and left at the Gate on 1 September 1958 where East German workers picked it up the following night. From 1961 to 1990, with the Berlin Wall running along its western side, the Brandenburg Gate became inacessible to all but Soviet and East German military personnel.

See also: unification

Further reading

Berlin Handbuch (1993) Berlin: FAB Verlag (contains a succinct summary of the history and significance of the Brandenburg Gate).

Laabs, R. (1990) *Das Brandenburger Tor: Brennpunkt deutscher Geschichte*, Berlin: Ullstein (richly illustrated history of the Brandenburg Gate from its initial planning to its role in Germany's unification; text in German and English).

Schache, W. (1995) 'Zur Geschichte und stadträumlichen Bedeutung des Pariser Platzes', in *Bauwelt* 86, 11: 520–5 (introductory essay on historic buildings around the Pariser Platz, including the Brandenburg Gate).

REINHILD STEINGRÖVER McRAE

Brandt, Willy

b. 18 December 1913, Lübeck; d. 9 October 1992, Unkel (near Bonn)

Politician; German Federal Chancellor 1969–74 (real name Karl Herbert Frahm)

A member of the **SPD** from the age of 17, Brandt escaped to Norway when Hitler came to power (adopting Norwegian nationality and the name 'Willy Brandt' as a cover) and then to Sweden, where he worked as an anti-Nazi journalist. A member of the Bundestag from 1949 to 1957, he became prominent as mayor of West Berlin from 1957 to 1966. He took the SPD into coalition with the CDU in 1966, and was then elected head of the country's first SPD-led government in 1969. His ground-breaking ***Ostpolitik*** brought him the Nobel Prize for Peace in 1971. He was forced to resign in 1974 when it transpired that one of his aides had been an East German spy. Brandt headed the 'Brandt Commission' on development issues from 1977 to 1983. His vision of a peacefully united Germany was finally realized two years before his death.

JOHN SANDFORD

Brasch, Thomas

b. 19 February 1945, Westow (Yorkshire)

Writer

A spiritual heir of **Brecht** and Heiner **Müller**, Brasch's anarchistic talents and critical views angered the GDR establishment in the 1960s and 1970s as did his disregard for the official cultural policy.

Son of the high-ranking **SED** functionary Horst Brasch, Thomas was born in English exile and attended a GDR military academy from the ages of eleven to fifteen. After completing his schooling in 1963 he trained as a printer and studied journalism at the University of Leipzig, from which he was expelled after one year for making derogatory remarks about leading political figures and for holding existentialist views. He worked as a packer, a waiter and a road worker before being accepted by the Film Institute in Potsdam in 1967. Arrested and imprisoned in 1968 for distributing pamphlets protesting against the invasion of Czechoslovakia by the Warsaw Pact countries, he was released on probation in 1969. A few of Brasch's poems were published in the GDR by Bernd Jentsch in his *Poesiealbum* series; most were eventually published in West Germany under the title *Der schöne September* (Beautiful September) in 1980.

The play *Das beispielhafte Leben und Tod des Peter Göring* (The Exemplary Life and Death of Peter Göring), based on the life of an East German border guard, was banned in the GDR after its first performance in 1972, but published in 1976.

His jazz oratorio *Hahnenkopf* (Cock's Head) on the Peasants' War of 1525, a montage of dialogues, songs and description, was performed in the *Kramladen*, a youth centre in East Berlin, and recorded for radio, but was never broadcast. The rehearsals for his play *Lovely Rita* at the **Berliner Ensemble** were broken off after three weeks. Brasch later published the play in the West and it was performed at the Schiller-Theater in West Berlin. His play, *Pabst Urban VIII – Galileo Galilei, ein Kampf* (Pope Urban VIII – Galileo Galilei, a Struggle) was performed only once in the GDR.

In December 1976, three weeks after **Biermann**'s expulsion from the GDR, Brasch was allowed to leave the country. Since then he has lived as a freelance writer in West Berlin.

His collections of prose fragments, *Vor den Vätern sterben die Söhne* (The Sons Die Before the Fathers), and *Kargo* (Cargo), both published in 1977, express the spirit of rebellious GDR youth and led to Brasch being lionized in the West as a dissident. Much of his work portrays rebellion, for example that of the poet Georg Heym in the play *Lieber Georg* (1980), Lackner in *Rotter* (1977) and Rita in *Lovely Rita* (1977), though the rebellion is existentially rather than politically motivated. Much of his work features the role of violence in human relations, as in *Frauenkrieg* (Women – War) (1988) and *Mercedes*, performed in Zürich in 1983. In the 1980s Brasch concentrated on adaptations (Shakespeare, Chekhov) and films, *Engel aus Eisen* (Iron Angel) (1981), *Domino* (1982) and *Welcome to Germany* (*Der Passagier*) (1988).

Further reading

Davis, G.V. (1985) '*Gegenbilder*: Order and Anarchy in the Work of Thomas Brasch', *Studies in GDR Culture and Society* 5: 153–71.

Fehervary, H. (1977) 'Thomas Brasch: A Storyteller after Kafka', *New German Critique* 12: 125–68 (an introduction to Brasch's work written in the GDR, including a translation of the story 'Flies on My Face' from *Vor den Vätern sterben die Söhne* and an interview with the author).

MARGARET VALLANCE

Braun, Volker

b. 7 May 1939, Dresden

Writer

Braun has distinguished himself through his versatility as a writer, producing literary works in all genres. In 1948, under the auspices of the Red Cross, he fled to Switzerland with his mother and four brothers. He returned to the Soviet occupied zone with his family and completed his *Abitur* in 1957. After graduation, he worked for the *Sächsische Zeitung*. He was unable to finish this practical year because he was thrown out for political contra-

dictions. This also delayed his matriculation at a university. From 1957 to 1960 he held various jobs in industry including printer, excavator and machinist. In 1960 he began his study of philosophy, receiving the degree of *Diplom* in 1964. Thereafter he moved to Berlin where he began to work in the theatre, first at the **Berliner Ensemble** and later at the **Deutsches Theater**. While Braun's earliest texts are illustrative of his excitement at the potential for socialist society, his optimism eventually wanes. The utopian euphoria of early works is eventually replaced with disillusionment. Following the unification of Germany, Braun's texts have taken on a lamenting tone.

Braun's life and works have been dominated by his struggle to reconcile social contradictions with his belief in communism. His early works contained a youthful optimism aimed at exciting his readers about the newly developing society. His literary debut exemplifies the ideology espoused by the Bitterfeld Conference (1959): this report 'Der Schlamm' (The Slime) (1959) reflects the experiences Braun gained working as an excavator for the Kombinat Schwarze Pumpe in 1958–9. His early poetry, including *Provokation für mich* (Provocation for Me) (1965) and *Wir und nicht sie* (We and Not They) (1970), contains provocations designed to motivate the masses. Similarly, early theatrical texts concern themselves with workers' problems and production themes: *Die Kipper* (The Dumpers) (1962–72), *Hinze und Kunze* (Hinze and Kunze) (1968–73), *Tinka* (1972–3), *Schmitten* (1978).

During the 1970s, writers hoped for a liberalization of cultural politics. In 1971, Erich Honecker proclaimed an end to aesthetic taboos in the GDR, as long as artists approached their topics from the fortified position of socialism. Yet, censoring organs grew more watchful of critical literature following Honecker's proclamation. Braun's narrative *Unvollendete Geschichte* (Incomplete Story) was published in **Sinn und Form** in 1975, but thirteen years passed before the narrative appeared in book form in the GDR (1988). This story portrayed the presence of the State critically, as the protagonist is forced to sacrifice her personal life for the sake of her family and the State. Braun leaves the narrative open-ended, a sign that he sought the possibility of dialogue with the State and a hopeful vision of the future.

The expatriation of the oppositional East German singer, Wolf **Biermann**, in 1976 produced a crisis for GDR writers; twelve signed an original letter of protest that *Neues Deutschland*, the official Party newspaper, refused to print. The letter subsequently appeared in the West. Braun was one of the original twelve signatories, but considerable controversy surrounded his participation. He did not condone the publication of the letter in the West and asserted that western media used the protest as a propagandistic means to criticize literary life in the GDR. This reaction prompted critics to accuse him of distancing himself from the entire affair. Braun has refuted these accusations. Because the controversy intensified, Braun tried to tone down his criticism. In a follow-up letter he addressed to *Neues Deutschland* (25 November 1976) he claimed that he was attempting to justify the writers' actions.

In his theatrical texts, Braun moved away from GDR-specific themes, opting for historical portrayals. In *Guevara* (1977) Braun grappled with socialist ideology, examining the concept of revolution. Guevara's life serves as a parable, exposing society's inability to attain the goals of the revolution. In *Großer Frieden* (The Great Peace) (1976), Braun turned to ancient Chinese history to show the roots of his desired utopia. His criticism proposes that GDR society has not progressed far beyond this beginning stage. In *Dmitri* (1980) Braun turns to Polish-Russian power struggles eerily reminiscent of the power structures of the Warsaw Pact.

Throughout the 1980s Braun's disillusionment with GDR society grew more apparent. While earlier plays such as *Großer Frieden* depicted society in transition, Braun grew tired of this transitional period. Plays such as *Transit Europa* (1986) and *Die Übergangsgesellschaft* (The Transition Society) (1984) criticized the paralysis of GDR society. In the *Hinze-Kunze-Roman* (Hinze-Kunze-Novel) (1985), Braun re-introduced two characters from his earlier play, once again illustrating the extreme discrepancies in GDR society. Kunze (Party functionary) and Hinze (Kunze's chauffeur) demonstrate the arbitrariness of the haves and the have-nots.

In his pre-unification texts, Braun had constantly promoted reform. Though highly critical, Braun's literary and essayistic texts clearly indicate that he never really envisioned a 'Germany' without socialism. Braun's dream was of a better society, one that was humane, just and free from oppression and hierarchy. While Braun held fast to the belief that this utopia was attainable, a desire for freedom superseded these utopian philosophical ideals among the people of the GDR. The post-unification texts depict a man who is severely troubled, deeply disillusioned, and very bitter. His poetry, prose, essays, and theatrical works have a plaintive undertone and they read like laments – Braun mourns his old society. Despite his lofty ambitions, he was unable to find a place for himself within the new social construct. In fact, as the poems in *Die Zickzackbrücke* (The Zigzag Bridge) (1992) clearly demonstrate, Braun had gone from promoting utopian visions to signalling the death of utopia.

Two post-unification plays, *Böhmen am Meer* (Bohemia by the Sea) (written 1989–93) and *Iphigenie in Freiheit* (Iphigenia in Freedom) (written 1987–91), confront recent history. In *Böhmen am Meer*, the struggle between the superpowers to attain ideological supremacy is clearly over. The idealist, Pavel, forced to leave Prague in 1968, lives in exile on an island, where he held the middle ground between his American and Russian friend. While Braun highlights the mistakes of socialism and capitalism, he gives no insight as to how these contradictions may be conquered. Indeed, while both the American and the Russian conclude that Pavel's idealism in exile was an appropriate, even correct, life choice, his ultimate death precludes this as an alternative. *Iphigenie in Freiheit* is a revision of Goethe's classic play, in which Braun removes the humanity inherent in Goethe's character, portraying Iphigenia's freedom not as something earned, but as something granted from an outside power.

Major works

Braun, V. (1976) *Es genügt nicht die einfache Wahrheit. Notate*, Frankfurt am Main: Suhrkamp (essays).

—— (1988) *Verheerende Folgen mangelnden Anscheins innerbetrieblicher Demokratie. Schriften*, Leipzig: Reclam (essays).

—— (1989–93) *Texte in zeitlicher Folge 1–10*, Halle: Mitteldeutscher Verlag (collected works).
—— (1992) *Böhmen am Meer*, Frankfurt am Main: Suhrkamp (theatrical work).
—— (1995) *Der Wendehals*, Frankfurt am Main: Suhrkamp (theatrical work).

Further reading

Costabile-Heming, C.A. (1997) *Intertextual Exile: Volker Braun's Dramatic Re-Vision of GDR Society*, Hildesheim: Georg Olms Verlag (general survey of life and dramatic works).
Grauert, W. (1995) *Ästhetische Modernisierung bei Volker Braun. Studien zu Texten aus den achtziger Jahren*, Würzburg: Königshausen & Neumann (examination of texts from the 1980s from various genres).
Jucker, R. (ed.) (1995) *Volker Braun*, Cardiff: University of Wales Press (essays on Braun's later works and comprehensive biobliography from 1986 to 1994).
Rosellini, J. (1983) *Volker Braun*, Munich: Beck (general survey of life and work).
Wallace, I. (1986) *Volker Braun Forschungsbericht*, Amsterdam: Rodopi (general overview of Braun's works and secondary literature with a comprehensive bibliography).

CAROL ANNE COSTABILE-HEMING

Brechbühl, Beat

b. 28 July 1939, Opplingen (Switzerland)

Writer and artist

Brechbühl grew up in Niederwichtrach in the canton of Bern. After studying typesetting, he worked for five years in various book-related fields in Geneva, Egnach (canton Thurgau) and Berlin. After spending several years travelling throughout Europe he worked for a Zürich publisher. Since 1973, he has worked as a freelance writer and artist in Pfyn (canton Thurgau). Known for his poetry, novels and collages, he also writes children's books. He became well-known for *Kneuss* (1970), a critique of society in the form of a detective novel.

MARTINA S. ANDERSON

Brecht, Bertolt

b. 10 February 1898, Augsburg; d. 14 August 1956, East Berlin

Dramatist, poet and theatre director

World-famous as a playwright, Bertolt Brecht, with his theory of **epic theatre**, had a profound influence on the development of twentieth-century drama. His poetry is also regarded as some of the best in German in the twentieth century.

Born of middle-class parents, Brecht wrote a number of plays in the 1920s which rejected the sentimental idealism of expressionist drama. In 1928 he achieved popular success in Berlin with the *Threepenny Opera* (*Die Dreigroschenoper*), based on the *Beggar's Opera* (1728) by John Gay, with songs by Kurt **Weill**. It was the most successful demonstration of 'epic theatre' put forward by Brecht and expounded by him in many of his theoretical works on the theatre, for instance *Small Organon for the Theatre* (*Kleines Organon für das Theater*) (1949).

When the Nazis came to power in 1933 Brecht went into exile, spending time in several European countries before travelling across the Soviet Union to the United States in 1941. In exile he wrote plays warning the world about the nature of fascism: *The Round-Heads and the Pointed-Heads* (*Die Rundköpfe und die Spitzköpfe*) (1933, first performed 1936); *Fear and Misery of the Third Reich* (*Furcht und Elend des dritten Reiches*) (1938); and *The Resistible Rise of Arturo Ui* (*Der aufhaltsame Aufstieg des Arturo Ui*) (1941, first performed 1958). The world-famous *The Good Woman of Setzuan* (*Der gute Mensch von Sezuan*) (written 1938–42, first performed in Zürich in 1943 with music by Paul **Dessau**) demonstrates the impossibility of behaving as a decent human being under inhuman conditions; *The Life of Galileo* (*Das Leben des Galilei*), written in 1938, first performed in Zürich (1943), was conceived by Brecht after he had heard the news of the splitting of the atom. The condemnation in the play of the betrayal by the scientist of his responsibility towards humanity was intensified by the dropping of the atom bomb on Hiroshima in 1945 and resulted in a second version which was performed in Hollywood in July 1947 with Charles Laughton in the title role; *Mother Courage and her Children* (*Mutter Courage und ihre Kinder*) (1938–9) provides one of Brecht's strongest statements against war; and *The Caucasian Chalk Circle* (*Der kaukasiche Kreidekreis*) (first performed in America in 1948 in English, in Germany in 1954), with music by Dessau sets the victory of the good person, Gruscha, against the idiosyncratic verdicts of the judge, Asdak, a reminder of the questionable values on which most societies are based.

After the end of hostilities in 1945 Brecht became anxious to return to Germany, especially in the light of the increasingly anti-communist mood in America. He left for Europe on 31 October 1947, the day after being interrogated by the Committee on Un-American Activities. He did not immediately return to the Soviet zone of Germany but spent almost a year in Switzerland before visiting East Berlin in October 1948 at the invitation of the *Kulturbund* to discuss the creation of a theatre ensemble. In January 1949 *Mutter Courage* was performed there in the **Deutsches Theater**. In May he finally settled in East Berlin with his wife, Helene Weigel, and in November the first production of the **Berliner Ensemble**, *Herr Puntila and his Man Matti* (*Herr Puntila und sein Knecht Matti*) (1940–1), was staged.

Brecht's hesitations about an immediate return to Berlin concerned not only fears about restrictions on his own personal freedom which he guarded against by obtaining an Austrian passport and opening a Swiss bank account, but also worries about how his theatre would be received in a cultural atmosphere dominated by the Soviet theory of **socialist realism**. During the campaign in the GDR in the early 1950s against 'formalist and decadent' art, Brecht's theatre was frequently criticized for its coldness and intellectualism. The **SED** was suspicious of the experimental nature of Brecht's theatre, and his distance from the officially approved theatre styles. In March 1951 his opera, *The Trial of Lucullus* (*Das Verhör des Lukullus*), with music by Dessau, was taken off after several closed performances. Dessau's music was strongly criticized for its 'formalism', and Brecht's libretto was accused of pacifism. Brecht rewrote parts of the text, and the revised version, *The Condemnation of Lucullus* (*Die Verurteilung des Lukullus*) was performed in October. Brecht's reaction to criticism was typical of his ambivalent attitude towards the authorities in the GDR. Although a

Marxist, he was never a member of the **KPD**, nor of the **SED**, but there was no doubt that his sympathies lay with the ruling ideology of the GDR. Even when this ideology was directly confronted in the **June Uprising** in 1953, Brecht's criticism of certain functionaries and of the SED was tempered by expressions of continuing support for the political system. Perhaps the deciding factor was his desire to have his own theatre. In March 1954 the Berliner Ensemble moved into the *Theater am Schiffbauerdamm*. By now Brecht was famous for his productions of his earlier plays and for adaptations, such as *The Tutor* (*Der Hofmeister*) by J.M.R. Lenz, in 1950. The Berliner Ensemble also gave guest performances in Amsterdam and Paris in 1954 and 1955. Brecht died shortly before the visit of the Ensemble to London in the autumn of 1956. One of the most important features of the last period of Brecht's life was the influence that his work had on a younger generation of dramatists and poets in the GDR, such as Heiner **Müller**, Wolf **Biermann** and Volker **Braun**, and on other German dramatists, such as Max **Frisch**, Friedrich **Dürrenmatt** and Peter **Weiss**.

Further reading

Esslin, M. (1959) *Brecht. A Choice of Evils*, London: Methuen (an early standard work on Brecht).

Fuegi, J. (1994) *The Life and Lies of Bertolt Brecht*, London: HarperCollins (a controversial account of Brecht's life and work).

Thomson, P. and Sacks, G. (eds) (1994) *The Cambridge Companion to Brecht*, Cambridge: Cambridge University Press (a useful reference work).

Willett, J. (ed.) (1959) *The Theatre of Bertolt Brecht*, London: Methuen (the definitive early work on Brecht).

—— (1964) *Brecht on Theatre*, London: Methuen (a collection of Brecht's theoretical texts on theatre).

MARGARET VALLANCE

Breker, Arno

b. 19 July 1900, Eberfeld; d. 13 February 1991, Düsseldorf

Sculptor and architect

One of the most representative sculptors of the Third Reich, Breker's state commissions included glorifying monumental statues for the Olympic stadium and Hitler's *Reichskanzlei* in Berlin, and numerous portrait busts in a neoclassicist style. After the war he continued to work as a sculptor and architect in the FRG. His artistic reputation grew through portraits commisisoned by industrialists and artists such as Cocteau and Dali. The bust of the art collector Peter Ludwig provoked fierce debates about the legacy of Third Reich art and artists.

KERSTIN MEY

Brendel, Alfred

b. 5 January 1931, Wiesenberg (Austria)

Pianist

At the age of six Brendel started serious study of the piano in Zagreb and then from 1937–43 in Graz. His debut recital was in Graz in 1948, and he later received an award at the Concorso Busoni in Bolzano (South Tyrol). While in the 1950s he enjoyed great esteem in Austria it was the many recordings he made in the following decade that secured his international reputation, especially in the field of late eighteenth- and early nineteenth-century music. His publications include Beethoven editions, cadenzas for Mozart concertos and a 1976 collection of essays *Musical Thoughts and Afterthoughts*.

DEREK McCULLOCH

Brězan, Jurij

b. 9 June 1916, Räckelwitz (Saxony)

Writer

A member of the Sorbian ethnic minority in Lusatia (see also **minorities, non-German**), Brězan became the most important bilingual writer of prose works in German and Sorbian from the 1950s onwards. His most successful novel, *Krabat oder die Verwandlung der Welt* (Krabat or the Transformation of the World) (1976), was strongly influenced by Sorbian myths. He also writes short stories, plays and childrens' books. From 1969 Brězan was a vice-president of the Writers' Union of the GDR.

PETER BARKER

Brinkmann, Rolf Dieter

b. 16 April 1940, Vechta (near Oldenburg); d. 23 April 1975, London

Writer

Brinkmann's life, tragically cut short in a traffic accident in London, was characterized by much controversy and notoriety on account of his experimental literary work and radical life style. His early work was influenced by the French 'nouveau roman', but basically he belonged to the 1960s pop and sub-culture influenced by American Beat and underground poetry, which he brought to the attention of a sceptical German public which rejected him.

Brinkmann had published some verse with small publishers in the late 1950s, and made his prose debut in 1962, but it was with his translations of American poetry in two representative volumes, *ACID* and *Silver Screen* (both 1969), that he aroused the wrath of both sides of the political spectrum as well as being rejected by literary critics who considered the books culturally and socially subversive, totally failing to understand their true significance. Their form was unconventional, consisting of poetry, short stories, essays and illustrations from underground publications with sexually explicit photographs.

Charged with conveying pornography, he was really aiming to combine high and low culture in a different art form as he searched for new concepts that would separate the distinction between reality and art as they dissolved into each other. In a remarkable radio play (*Auf der Schwelle*) (On the

Threshold) Brinkmann created a collage of voices that actually 'assaulted' the listeners' hearing by acts of pure aural violence and which are incredibly disturbing.

Having aligned himself to the **student movement** in Germany, Brinkmann was seized by depression at its failure to achieve its goals and by the subsequent commercialization of the subculture itself. Brinkmann's pessimism led to his quarrelling with nearly all his friends and colleagues and he became increasingly isolated. A book of text collages, with its ambiguous title *Gras* (Grass), appeared in 1970 reflecting his own drug use which had been condemned by the literary establishment.

An intriguing work dealing with the decline of western civilization in a series of horrifying stages is *Westwärts 1 & 2* (Westwards 1 & 2) (1975). Part 1 focuses on America and part 2 on Cologne, a city with which he had always had an uneasy relationship. This multi-layered picture of mankind's history is seen intertextually, the two sections being held together visually by two series of photographs, although there is no logical sequence of texts or rational order.

Brinkmann's work repeats motifs and themes endlessly, but what is new and innovative is his experiment with form. New typography and photographs and cut-outs from comic books fill his texts, most of which are autobiographical and relate almost exclusively to himself. A major theme running through his work is that of sexual hedonism, equated with freedom for the individual without constraints.

Rom, Blicke (Rome, Viewpoints), which appeared posthumously (1979), is perhaps Brinkmann's most significant work, comprising a montage of disparate elements including letters to his wife, picture postcards and city plans, all reflecting his desperate search for identity in a collapsing world. Rome is a dead landscape, the past having no relevance for contemporary man.

Further reading

Späth, S. (1989) *Rolf Dieter Brinkmann*, Stuttgart: Metzler (a sympathetic and informative analysis of the works).

PETER PROCHNIK

broadcasting

The broadcasting system established in West Germany after the war was made up of regional public-service corporations, responsible initially for radio and then, from the 1950s onwards, for television as well (see also **radio: cultural role (FRG)**). This pattern remained intact until the 1980s, when the advent of commercial radio and television led to the present 'dual system' of public and private provision. Today the ten public-service corporations each provide a range of (typically four) radio services for their particular region, and contribute programmes to the national 'first' television channel, **ARD**, as well as producing their own regional 'third' channels. The 'second' public-service television channel, the **ZDF**, is organized nationally rather than regionally. Two national radio services are provided under the joint umbrella of ARD and ZDF by DeutschlandRadio, and overseas services in both German and various foreign languages are provided by the Deutsche Welle. In the commercial sector there are numerous mainly local radio stations, and some twenty nationally available television channels, of which two in particular – RTL and SAT.1 – have achieved an audience share on a par with that of ARD and ZDF. The number of channels on both radio and television is set to increase steeply with the advent of digital broadcasting.

The admissability and function of commercial broadcasting has been the subject of a series of important rulings of the **Federal Constitutional Court**, while debate about the power of commercial interests in the media has grown more urgent as the new broadcasters have consolidated their positions. In the GDR, broadcasting was much more centrally organized, and firmly in the hands of the state and the **SED**, whose heavy-handed attempts to use it as an instrument of **propaganda** were constantly undermined by the fact that, over much of the country, western programmes could be – and were – received by the majority of listeners and viewers.

While the public-service principle behind post-war West German broadcasting was inspired by the BBC, its regional structure is partly an echo of the way radio was organized in the Weimar Republic, partly a reaction to the centralized system of the Third Reich, but above all a reflection of the German federal principle of *Land* responsibility for cultural matters. The commonly-applied term *Landesrundfunkanstalten* ('*Land* broadcasting corporations') is, however, somewhat misleading, as the principle of 'one *Land*: one broadcasting service' applies in only seven *Länder*. Thus, Bavaria is served by the Bayerischer Rundfunk (BR), Berlin by the Sender Freies Berlin (SFB), Bremen by Radio Bremen (RB), Brandenburg by the Ostdeutscher Rundfunk Brandenburg (ORB), Hessen by the Hessischer Rundfunk (HR), North Rhine-Westphalia by the Westdeutscher Rundfunk (WDR), and the Saarland by the Saarländischer Rundfunk (SR). In the rest of the country, however, three *Länder* (Saxony, Saxony-Anhalt and Thuringia) are served by the Mittel-deutscher Rundfunk (MDR), four (Hamburg, Mecklenburg-West Pomerania, Lower Saxony and Schleswig-Holstein) by the Norddeutscher Rundfunk (NDR), and two (Rhineland-Palatinate and Baden-Württemberg) by the Südwestrundfunk (SWR). (Indeed, until 1998, the situation in the southwest was even more complicated, with Rhineland-Palatinate and the southern part of Baden-Württemberg being served by one corporation, the Südwestfunk (SWF), and the rest of Baden-Württemberg by the Süddeutscher Rundfunk (SDR).) The peculiar anomalies in this structure derive in large part from the differing approaches to the re-establishment of broadcasting taken by the three western Allies during the post-war occupation.

Although each corporation is subject to the Broadcasting Law of the *Land* (or State Treaty between the *Länder*) it serves, the principles behind these ten laws are very similar, with each corporation ultimately beholden to its Broadcasting Council (*Rundfunkrat*), whose members represent a range of interest groups from within the region concerned as well as the political parties of the relevant *Land* parliaments. Although the system is designed to keep the State at arm's length, it does not guarantee total political neutrality, with Broadcasting Councils – and hence the broadcasting corporations themselves – frequently regarded as recognizably 'red' or 'black' in their leanings, depending on the political hue of the region in question. Public-service broadcasting in Germany is financed by a mixture of advertising revenue and licence dues levied from listeners and viewers.

Commercial broadcasting came to West Germany later than to many other European countries, not least because of serious reservations raised by the Federal Constitutional Court, in its landmark 'First Television Verdict' of 1961, about commercial television's compatibility with the guarantee of freedom of expression contained in Article 5 of the Basic Law. The Court ruled that comparisons with the commercially-organized free press were inapposite since the variety of competing opinions accessible across the range of the country's many newspapers could not be guaranteed in the field of television, given the far more limited number of available channels. By the 1980s, new cable and satellite technologies had begun to render these premises obsolete, whilst in the political sphere the new CDU-led government that came to power in 1982 was determined – unlike its much more sceptical SPD-led predecessor – to exploit to the full these new technologies.

Although commercial broadcasting was provided initially via satellite and cable, terrestrial frequencies were increasingly provided during the course of the 1980s. The pace of this development depended largely on the political complexion of the *Land* in question, with the SPD adopting a much more cautious approach than the CDU and CSU. The prospect that this might lead to the establishment of two quite different patterns of media provision in Germany was averted after lengthy negotiations by a 1987 agreement between the *Länder*, which recognized the legitimacy of a mixed public-service and commercial system, and which was in its turn succeeded after unification by the 'State Treaty on Broadcasting in the United Germany' of 1992. By now each *Land* had introduced its own 'Media Law' to govern the licensing and operation of commercial services and a 'Land Media Authority' (*Landesmedienanstalt*), organized on a representative basis like the

Broadcasting Councils, to supervise their activities. These various enactments were all underpinned by the successive Broadcasting Verdicts of the Federal Constitutional Court, which, in the course of the 1980s, set a series of markers for the new landscape of German radio and television, and established and refined the terminology of the debate about commercialization.

Terms introduced by the Court have included such notions as 'internal' and 'external pluralism' (*Binnen- und Außenpluralismus*), both of which are now recognized as acceptable ways of meeting the requirements of Article 5 of the Basic Law: the former is exemplified in the public-service corporations, where the Broadcasting Councils are designed to ensure a range of views *within* the organization, whilst 'external pluralism' is a characteristic of the press and, as the number of stations grows, increasingly of the new commercial broadcasting services, where the multiplicity of outlets is deemed to ensure variety of opinion *between* the different providers. In its 1986 Broadcasting Verdict the Court stated that in the 'dual order' of public and private provision the public corporations were now entrusted with the 'essential basic provision' (*die unerläßliche Grundversorgung*) – the breadth, variety, and quality of programming that could not automatically be expected of the commercial services. This crucial point – which made the continuing existence of public broadcasting a precondition of the admissability of commercial services, and implied that the former could never be replaced by the latter – was further elaborated in a 1987 verdict that required a 'guarantee of continued existence and development' (*Bestands- und Entwicklungsgarantie*) for the public corporations, implying in particular that they must be adequately funded to keep up with technical and other developments that might affect their competitiveness.

The establishment of commercial broadcasting in Germany has renewed and intensified the debate about concentration of media ownership. There have been criticisms that the *Land* media authorities have been too lax in this area, though the sheer complexity of the patterns of cross-ownership and influence between the press, radio and television has made the policing of developments a singularly problematic task. Attention has focused in particular on the activities of the Leo **Kirch** group and the emergence of multimedia conglomerates such as the **Bertelsmann** organization.

Broadcasting in the GDR

Like the press, radio and television in the GDR were seen primarily as instruments of state and party **propaganda**. The controlling bodies – the State Radio Committee and the State Television Committee, which in 1968 replaced the original single State Broadcasting Committee – were organs of the government, and programme content – especially in the area of news and current affairs – was closely determined by the SED's Department of Agitation and Propaganda. The three main domestic radio services and the two television channels were all Berlin-based, and, with the exception of early-morning programmes on Radio DDR I and a special summer service for holiday-makers on the Baltic, provided little in the way of regional programming. The authorities' attempts to seal the citizens of the GDR in an ideologically pure cocoon failed more in broadcasting than in any other sphere, as the majority of the population were avid consumers of West German programmes. Only the far northeast of the country and the Dresden area (the so-called '*Tal der Ahnungslosen*' or 'Valley of the Clueless') were out of reach of western television transmitters. Early attempts at discouragement – through intimidation and the dismantling of roof-top aerials – had minimal impact, and were replaced in the **Honecker** years by open acknowledgement of the population's viewing habits.

The GDR's broadcasters made speedy use of the new freedoms that came with the fall of Honecker in October 1989, and, with their new openness and liberality, soon won unprecedentedly high viewing figures for GDR television. However, widespread popular feeling that at least a partial eastern service (such as the interim 'New *Länder* Network' of 1991) should remain intact was not reflected in the Unification Treaty, on the basis of which, after a contentious period of re-structuring, the new *Länder* came fully into line with the West German broadcasting system at the beginning of 1992.

Broadcasting in Austria

The Austrian constitution, unlike the German Basic Law, places competence for broadcasting in the hands of the federation rather than of the *Länder*, and consequently both radio and television are provided nationally by the public-service corporation **ORF** (Österreichischer Rundfunk, the umlaut having been removed from the abbreviation in order to render it more internationally user-friendly). The ORF produces three national radio services plus a regional service in each of the nine *Länder*, as well as a shortwave overseas service, and two national television channels. Austrian governments have long resisted the introduction of commercial television, but commercial radio (initially one station per *Land*, with two for Vienna) was finally introduced in the mid-1990s. German television, both public and commercial, is widely watched – off-air from terrestrial transmitters where reception permits, and via satellite and cable elsewhere.

Broadcasting in Switzerland

The main radio and television services are provided by the **SRG** (Schweizerische Radio- und Fernsehgesellschaft, which, in English, calls itself the Swiss Broadcasting Corporation), with three component divisions for the three main language areas: RTSR (French), CORSI (Italian), and for German (and also Romansh) Switzerland, RDRS (Radio- und Fernsehgesellschaft der deutschen und der rätoromanischen Schweiz). Three radio services and one television service are provided for each of the regions; the second and third television channels in each region are used to carry the programmes of the other two languages. A fourth television channel, S Plus, was introduced in 1993, partly to complement the existing German-language service, and partly to provide a national service in such areas as sports coverage. The overseas service, Swiss Radio International, broadcasts in seven languages. German, French and Italian television are widely watched, both off-air as well as via cable and satellite. There are also numerous local commercial radio stations.

Further reading

Bausch, H. (ed.) (1980) *Rundfunk in Deutschland*, Munich: dtv (the standard, five-volume history of German broadcasting up to 1980; volumes three and four cover the post-war period).

Holzweißig, G. (1989) *Massenmedien in der DDR*, Berlin: Verlag Gebr. Holzapfel (standard concise survey of GDR media).

Humphreys, P.J. (1994) *Media and Media Policy in Germany: The Press and Broadcasting since 1945*, 2nd edn, Oxford and Providence, RI: Berg (detailed account of media organization and policy issues through to the post-unification period).

Meyn, H. (1996) *Massenmedien in der Bundesrepublik Deutschland*, Berlin: Colloquium Verlag (introduction to structure of the media and problems of press and broadcasting freedom; regularly updated).

Porter, V. and Hasselbach, S. (1991) *Pluralism, Politics and the Marketplace: The Regulation of German Broadcasting*, London: Routledge (on the development of the 'dual system' of public and commercial broadcasting).

Sandford, J. (1976) *The Mass Media of the German-Speaking Countries*, London and Ames, IA: Oswald Wolff and Iowa State Univeristy Press (covers the history of German broadcasting up to the mid-1970s, with separate chapters on Austria, Switzerland and the GDR).

The monthly journal *Media Perspektiven* and the annual *ARD-Jahrbuch* are invaluable sources of analyses and documentation relating to broadcasting.

JOHN SANDFORD

Broch, Hermann

b. 1 November 1886, Vienna; d. 30 May 1951, New Haven, Connecticut

Writer

Broch studied mathematics, philosophy and psychology, and from 1950 was a professor at Yale University. Beside Robert Musil and Franz Kafka, Broch is the third writer to renew the modern German novel by using the inner monologue to illuminate all spheres of the human psyche. His works deal with the corruption of contemporary morals and values. In his major work, *Der Tod des Vergil* (1946), Broch depicts the disintegration of personality and of modern culture.

ERNST GRABOVSZKI

Brockhaus

The name F.A. Brockhaus stands for authoritative **encyclopedias**; in German cultural areas 'the Brockhaus' carries much the same weight and significance as the *Encyclopaedia Britannica* in English-speaking nations. Founded by Friedrich Arnold Brockhaus in 1805, the firm came to define the word encyclopedia in Germany. For almost two centuries the firm has developed and produced a family of encyclopedias and specialized dictionaries. It also influenced lexicographical developments in northern and eastern Europe. In 1984 Brockhaus merged with the Bibliographisches Institut, a rival firm which had produced the various Meyer reference works and the authoritative **Duden** series.

JOHN B. RUTLEDGE

Broszat, Martin

b. 14 August 1926, Leipzig; d. 14 October 1989, Munich

Historian

Best known for his work as Director of the Munich Institute of Contemporary History, Broszat was an outstanding interpreter of the Third Reich. His work ranged from analyses of Nazi atrocities and concentration camps in eastern Europe, through the structure of the Nazi state (in *The Hitler State*, 1981), to patterns of popular opinion, resistance and opposition, explored with particular theoretical sensitivity and local detail in the Bavaria project. He opened up new approaches to the study of Nazi Germany with his concept of the 'historicization' of the Third Reich.

See also: *Historikerstreit*; historiography

MARY FULBROOK

Brückner, Jutta

b. 25 June 1941, Düsseldorf

Filmmaker

Brückner first explored her principal theme of emancipation and female identity in a documentary film about her mother, *Do Right and Fear No-one* (*Tue recht und scheue Niemand!*, 1975). *Hungry Years* (*Hungerjahre*, 1979), a realist, semi-autobiographical portrait of youth in the 1950s, also focuses on a mother–daughter relationship. Her later work is more formally experimental, incorporating performance and multimedia elements, as in *One Glance and Love Breaks Out* (*Ein Blick und die Liebe bricht aus*, 1986). She began to experiment with video in the mid-1980s.

See also: feminism and the women's movement; film: FRG

HELEN HUGHES

Brus, Günter

b. 27 September 1938, Ardning (Austria)

Painter, performance artist, graphic artist and writer

Emerging around 1960 as an action painter before turning to performance (*Selbstbemalung 1*, 1964), Brus became one of the most notorious of the Viennese Actionists, his performances increasingly focused on his own body, its functions and fluids, culminating in acts of self-mutilation, for instance in *The Total Madness* (*Der helle Wahnsinn*, 1968) and *Endurance Test* (*Zerreißprobe*, 1970). He abandoned performance in 1970 to concentrate on drawing and writing. His prose, poetry and drawings (often illustrating his own texts) fuse ecstatic romanticism with violent and pornographic imagery.

See also: Mühl, Otto; Nitsch, Hermann

MARTIN BRADY

Brussig, Thomas

b. 19 December 1965, East Berlin

Writer

Presented as the autobiography of the ineffectual but boastful Klaus Uhlzscht, Thomas Brussig's best-selling 1995 comic novel *Helden wie wir* (Heroes Like Us) satirizes the history of the GDR since 1968, the year of Uhlzscht's birth and of the Prague Spring, and dismantles the 'heroic' version of the 1989 revolution. The prudery characteristic of much GDR literature is swept aside by the hero's obsession with his penis and its alleged role in the fall of the Berlin Wall. Brussig's first novel *Wasserfarben* (Watercolours) appeared in 1991 under the pseudonym Cordt Berneburger.

IAN WALLACE

Bruyn, Günter de

b. 1 November 1926, Berlin

Writer

As a member of the generation of unwilling young soldiers fortunate to survive WWII, de Bruyn became a citizen of the GDR, more out of a personal determination to atone for the crimes of fascism than through ideological commitment to state socialism. After embarking on a career as a librarian in East Berlin he became a freelance writer in 1961. Temperamentally inclined to avoid the glare of state-sponsored publicity, he rose slowly to prominence in the 1970s both as an ironical observer of everyday life and as a cultural historian. His disenchantment with the Honecker regime became fully apparent in the 1980s, when he aligned himself with the international peace movement and exposed the workings of the previously taboo subject of censorship (see also **censorship: FRG**; **censorship: GDR**). His judicious interventions in the often acrimonious East–West German cultural debate which followed the collapse of the GDR earned him widespread respect. He was also the first major author of the ex-GDR to enjoy acclaim throughout Germany for a post-unification publication, *Zwischenbilanz* (Interim Report) (1992),

the first part of his autobiography, dealing with his life up to 1949.

De Bruyn made his literary breakthrough in 1968 with the novel *Buridan's Ass* (*Buridans Esel*), which established the parameters of his fictional world: the everyday conflicts faced by unexceptional members of the professional classes such as librarians and teachers; problematic male–female relationships in a society whose claims to have fostered gender equality were now being put to the test; the tension between career-conformism and being true to oneself; and the contrast between life in the would-be socialist metropolis of East Berlin and the surrounding countryside of the province of Brandenburg. His biography of the author Jean Paul Richter, published in 1975, demonstrated his gift for making cultural history accessible while using it as a vehicle for drawing attention to the cultural and political stagnation of the contemporary GDR. Its success gave him the creative confidence to confront one of the main causes of that stagnation, the corruption of the new ideological élite, in his two major works of fiction, *Märkische Forschungen* (Researches in the (Brandenburg) Marches) (1979) and *Neue Herrlichkeit* (New Glory) (1984). The delayed publication of the latter in the GDR reflected the cultural paralysis of the final years of the Honecker regime, and de Bruyn embarked on his autobiography in 1986 knowing that it would not be publishable in the GDR. The second volume, *Vierzig Jahre* (Forty Years) (1996), confirms the literary significance of his memoirs while providing a coherent overview of cultural life in the GDR.

See also: prose fiction: GDR

Further reading

Arnold, H.L. (ed.) (1995), *Günter de Bruyn*, Munich: edition text + kritik (collection of critical essays with a full bibliography).

Bruyn, G. de (1990) *Märkische Forschungen*, ed. D. Tate, Manchester: Manchester University Press (includes introduction and notes in English).

Wittstock, U. (ed.) (1991) *Günter de Bruyn: Materialien zu Leben und Werk*, Frankfurt am Main: Fischer (documents the reception of de Bruyn's work inside and outside the GDR).

DENNIS TATE

Buber, Martin

b. 8 February 1878, Vienna; d. 13 June 1965, Jerusalem

Philosopher and theologian

Brought up in Lvov, Buber studied in Vienna, Leipzig, Berlin and Zürich. An active member and leader in the Zionist movement, he advocated Jewish cultural renewal; turning to Hasidism at the beginning of the century, he published his early works on Hasidic lore. He lectured on Judaism in Prague, edited his acclaimed journal *Der Jude*, and in 1921 moved to work at the Freies Jüdisches Lehrhaus in Frankfurt am Main, where he later taught as a professor of religion at the university. Together with Franz Rosenzweig, he began his translation of the Bible in the 1920s and in 1923 his most renowned work, *I and Thou* (*Ich und Du*), appeared. Buber migrated in 1938 to Jerusalem, where he taught at the Hebrew University and worked for peace between Jews and Arabs. In 1960 he became the first president of the Israel Academy of Sciences and Humanities.

NOAH ISENBERG

Buch, Hans Christoph

b. 13 April 1944, Wetzlar

Writer

After early essays on Marxism, culture, and colonialism, Buch found his main subject-matter on a visit to Haiti in 1968. The novels *Die Hochzeit von Port-au-Prince* (The Wedding at Port-au-Prince) (1984) and *Haiti Chérie* (1992) chronicle Haiti's turbulent history from the slave uprising against the Napoleonic occupiers to the Duvaliers' dictatorship in a flamboyant collage of documentary and surreal styles. Although his literary interest in the exploited Third World continues, Buch's more recent fiction has been concerned with war, oppression and injustice in a European context.

JOHN J. WHITE

Buck, Detlev

b. 1 December 1962, Bad Segeberg

Filmmaker and actor

Buck's films are marked by dry humour and a strong regional identity: many of them are set in Schleswig-Holstein, where he grew up. His early short films, especially *Erst die Arbeit und dann...?* (First Work – And then...?) (1984), attracted a cult following. Buck's fame then spread with his début feature, the 1991 police satire *Little Rabbits* (*Karniggels*), and the 1993 road movie *No More Mr Nice Guy* (*Wir können auch anders*), while the 1995 prison comedy *Jailbirds* (*Männerpension*) brought him mainstream commercial success.

JONATHAN LEGG

Bündnis 90

Bündnis 90 was founded as an amalgamation of different GDR citizens' movements (see also **citizens' movements: GDR**) in Potsdam in September 1991. After German unification in October 1990 these movements had to adapt their organizational structure to the Parties Law of the Federal Republic within a year. In addition to this the citizens' movements were forced to co-ordinate their work because of their political marginalization. Therefore Bündnis 90 (Alliance 90) was constituted as a common political association by three of the citizens' movements organizations: **Demokratie Jetzt** (Democracy Now), Initiative für Frieden und Menschenrechte (Initiative for Peace and Human Rights), and part of **Neues Forum** (New Forum). The Green Party in East Germany and other citizens' movements such as the Vereinigte Linke (United Left) and the Unabhängiger Frauenverband (Independent Women's Association), however, did not join.

According to the self-perception of the members of Demokratie Jetzt, Initiative für Frieden und Menschenrechte and Neues Forum, the amalgamation of the three organizations was formally to adapt to the requirements of the Parties Law of the Federal Republic but remain in essence a citizens' movement. The founding statement says in this respect, 'The citizens' movement Bündnis 90 is an open, electable political association. It is part of a general citizens' movement, representing an informal network of political organizations, non-profit-making organizations, citizens' initiatives, working and discussion groups'. As leading members of Bündnis 90 conceded in a process of self-reflection, however, this decision supported the development of party-like structures. Participation in elected bodies on different levels (East German local councils and *Land* parliaments, the Bundestag) after unification had a great impact on the internal structures, too. On the one hand many people left the citizens' movements, on the other hand more and more members were involved in parliamentary work. Against this background the organizations themselves were reduced to a small number of activists.

To survive as an all-German political organization and to get enough votes (according to the German Electoral Law only parties with more than 5 percent of the votes or three direct mandates obtain seats in the Bundestag and the *Land* parliaments; the separate counting of votes in East and West was an exception for the first all-German elections in 1990) Bündnis 90 and the Green Party (East and West) started to draw up a treaty for the amalgamation of both political organizations in 1992. This treaty was confirmed by a majority of delegates from both organizations in spring 1993. Since this time Bündnis 90 and Die Grünen have operated as one party, obtaining 6.7 percent of the votes and forty-seven seats in the Bundestag elections of September 1998. The merger has not been unproblematic, with factions developing and a feeling among some West German **Greens** that their East German partners have been too accommodating towards their new capitalist environment.

Further reading

Wielgohs, J., Schulz, M. and Müller-Enbergs, H. (eds) (1992) *Bündnis 90: Entstehung, Entwicklung, Perspektiven*, Berlin: Gesellschaft für sozialwissenschaftliche Forschung und Publizistik mbH (fundamental analysis of the evolution and programme of Bündnis 90).

LOTHAR PROBST

Buhr, Manfred

b. 22 February 1927, Kamenz

Philosopher

After a doctorate with Ernst **Bloch** in the early 1950s Buhr worked (1969–90) as the head of the GDR Academy of Science's Institute of Philosophy. His contentious involvement with the censorship policies of the state was accompanied by widespread respect for his research on Kant and Marx.

MICHAEL HÄNEL

Bultmann, Rudolf Karl

b. 20 August 1884, Wiefelstede (near Oldenburg); d. 30 July 1976, Marburg

Protestant theologian

Bultmann, a leading twentieth-century New Testament scholar, believed that the expression of the biblical message in mythological terms was a barrier to its contemporary understanding. In 1941, he coined the term 'demythologising' (*Entmythologisierung*) to refer to the need to reveal the existential significance underlying the mythological accounts of the biblical narratives. Bultmann's understanding of the biblical message was influenced by the existentialist philosophy of Martin **Heidegger**.

Further reading

Morgan, R. (1997) 'Rudolf Bultmann' in D. Ford (ed.), *The Modern Theologians*, 2nd edn. Oxford: Blackwell, pp. 68–86 (includes bibliography).

Schmithals, W. (1968) *An Introduction to the Theology of Rudolf Bultmann (Die Theologie Rudolf Bultmanns, Eine Einführung)* trans. J. Bowden, London: SCM Press (includes bibliography).

STEPHEN BROWN

Bundesbank

The antecedents of the German central bank can be found in the Bank deutscher Länder established by the Allies in 1948. The Bundesbank, which was established by law in 1957, had even greater independence, and its seventeen-member Central Bank Council has exclusive responsibility for monetary policy, free from government direction, although ministers may attend its meetings. Pursuing monetary targeting since 1974, it controls bank liquidity by the use of minimum reserves, rediscount quotas and open market operations, in this last case by the 'quick tender' of Treasury bills or by repurchase agreements, its favoured instrument. Its Discount and Lombard rates directly influence European interest rates.

CHRISTOPHER H. FLOCKTON

Bundesgartenschau

German enthusiasm for gardens and gardening finds its ultimate expression in the biannual Bundesgartenschau (BUGA), a federal horticultural display. The Bundesgartenschau was inaugurated in Hanover in 1951. Large tracts of arid land are turned into a park with numerous displays. Allotment gardens, including small cottages, are also exhibited. The legacy of the Bundesgartenschau is that the display is turned over to the municipality which continues to maintain it as a public park. Every ten years, beginning with Hamburg in 1953, the Internationale Gartenbauausstellung (IGA), an international horticultural exhibit, takes place. Some *Länder* also host their own regional shows.

See also: *Schrebergarten*

UTE LISCHKE-McNAB

Bundesrat

Representative body of the *Länder*, mainly concerned with participation in the legislative process, forming the upper house on the federal level in Bonn. The sixty-nine members of the Bundesrat are appointed, recalled, and vote on instruction by their respective *Land* governments. Depending on the number of its inhabitants, each *Land* has either three, four, five or six representatives. Since the 1970s the parliamentary opposition parties have

frequently held the majority in the *Bundesrat*, leading to a situation where the government can only pass legislation by seeking an all-party compromise.

See also: Bundestag; Bundesversammlung; federalism; *Hauptstadtfrage*; *Land*

MONIKA PRÜTZEL-THOMAS

Bundestag

Since 1949 the Bundestag has been the parliament (lower house) of the FRG. Every four years 656 representatives (before unification 518) are directly elected in 328 constituencies through a mixture of proportional representation and majority vote. Main functions are legislation, budget approval, control of government and election of the Federal Chancellor. It can withdraw support from the government by casting a vote of no confidence, which, however, only takes effect if an absolute majority for an alternative candidate is found ('constructive vote of no confidence'). Currently seated in Bonn, the Bundestag will meet in the renovated Reichstag building in Berlin from the year 2000.

See also: elections: FRG; *Hauptstadtfrage*

MONIKA PRÜTZEL-THOMAS

Bundesversammlung

This is an *ad hoc* federal convention, whose sole purpose is the election of the Federal President, the formal head of the German state, for a five-year period in office. The Bundesversammlung consists of all members of the **Bundestag** (parliament) and the same number of representatives sent by the *Land* parliaments, altogether over 1,300 members after unification.

MONIKA PRÜTZEL-THOMAS

Bundeswehr

The Bundeswehr comprises the armed forces and civilian administration which constitute the FRG's military establishment. International and domestic concerns during the 1950s resulted in a West German military completely integrated into the NATO alliance; lacking chemical, biological, or nuclear weapons; organized to ensure civilian control; and committed to the concept of the 'citizen in uniform' guided by *Innere Führung* (inner guidance). Protest movements and debate focusing on the Bundeswehr and security issues include the 'Ohne mich!' (count me out!) movement of the 1950s, the cruise and Pershing missile protests of the 1980s, and post-unification deployments of Bundeswehr personnel to Somalia and Bosnia.

The catastrophic role of the German military in modern history meant that the establishment of the Bundeswehr in 1955 and the introduction of conscription in 1956 met initially with widespread popular opposition. Although young men become liable to conscription at the age of nineteen, there are various possibilities for exemption and delay, and Germany's conscientious objection provisions are among the most generous in the world. Around a quarter of conscripts currently opt for *Zivildienst* ('civilian service', which lasts a third longer than the ten months of basic military service), playing a major role in the country's health service and care for the elderly and disabled, and in a wide range of other fields such as environmental and development-aid projects.

DOUGLAS PEIFER

Bunte

Published by **Burda** publications, *Bunte Illustrierte* is a weekly periodical dealing with glamorous society stories and photographs of German and foreign jet-setters and their hot-spots. The literal English translation meaning 'colourfully illustrated', its name is its motto: picture spreads and 'exciting' stories about the rich and famous. Modelled on the American *Life* magazine, its stories move it closer to the tabloids than its model had ever been. It has a circulation of about one million.

See also: magazines; mass media: FRG; publishing: FRG

HOLGER BRIEL

Burda

Burda is one of the largest publishers in Germany, with over thirty magazines. Its titles include *Bunte*, *Freundin*, *Bild+Funk* and *Elle*. In 1993, Burda launched the news magazine ***Focus***, whose success in an already competitive market niche surprised many. Burda Publishers was set up in 1927 in Offenburg by Franz Burda. His children, who have retained full ownership of the company, were involved in the controversy that surrounded the fate of the Axel Springer Verlag after **Springer**'s death in 1985. Today, Burda is run by Dr Hubert Burda, and has diversified into several new media areas. The firm has a yearly turnover of more than DM 1.7 billion.

See also: magazines

ROBIN B. HODESS

Burgtheater

This Viennese theatre was founded in 1741 and declared national theatre in 1776. In its present form it was designed by Gottfried Semper (1803–79) and Carl von Hasenauer (1833–94) as part of the Ringstraße (1874–88; damaged in 1945; restored 1953–5). Smaller productions are played at various venues including the Akademietheater.

The Burgtheater is regarded as the most important theatre in Austria at which classical as well as modern plays are produced. The language and the pronunciation cultivated by the company represent the highest standard of German in its Austrian variety.

GEORG HELLMAYR

Burmeister, Brigitte

b. 25 September 1940, Posen (now Poznán, Poland)

Writer

First known in the GDR as an academic expert on French literary theory, including structuralist and feminist approaches, Brigitte Burmeister came to prominence as a novelist in 1987. Her first novel

Anders oder Vom Aufenthalt in der Fremde (Anders or Living Among Strangers) (1987), composed of reports by its protagonist David Anders, who appears to be a **Stasi** agent in East Berlin, is a complex work often compared to the French 'Nouveau Roman'. Burmeister's second novel, *Unter dem Namen Norma* (Under the Name of Norma) of 1994, reflects a similar concern for the possibility of individual identity, this time amid the tensions both among East Germans and between East and West Germany following unification. Burmeister also published a volume of stories, *Herbstfeste* (Autumn Festivals), in 1995.

Further reading

Cosentino, C. (1996) 'Ostdeutsche Autoren Mitte der neunziger Jahre: Volker Braun, Brigitte Burmeister und Reinhard Jirgl', *New German Critique* 68 (spring–summer 1996): 177–94.

Grant, C.B. (1995) *Literary Communication from Consensus to Rupture: Theory and Practice in Honecker's GDR*, Amsterdam and Atlanta, GA: Editions Rodopi.

GRAHAM JACKMAN

Busch, Ernst

b. 22 January 1900, Kiel; d. 8 June 1980, Berlin

Actor and singer

Busch has given acclaimed performances in **Brecht** productions at the **Berliner Ensemble** and in *Kuhle Wampe* (a Brecht/Dudow film, 1932). His renditions of *Solidaritätslied* (Song of Solidarity) and *Spaniens Himmel* (Spanish Sky) are famous. A communist who fought in the Spanish Civil War, Busch was incarcerated by the Nazis; late effects of his imprisonment (partial facial paralysis) shortened his acting career. The East Berlin acting school carries his name (Schauspielschule Ernst Busch).

Further reading

Siebig, K. (1980) *Ich gehe mit dem Jahrhundert mit*, Reinbek bei Hamburg: Rowohlt.

KAREN RUOFF KRAMER

Busta, Christine

b. 23 April 1915, Vienna; d. 3 December 1987, Vienna

Poet (real name Christine Dimt)

One of a number of female Austrian poets, including Ingeborg **Bachmann**, Christine **Lavant** and Friederike **Mayröcker**, who have given a distinctive tone to post-1945 German poetry. Busta's poetry is decidedly unexperimental in her earlier volumes. A simple, intense religious preoccupation informs both her imagery and her vocabulary and, as in the work of Marie Luise **Kaschnitz**, her later work betrays the struggle to capture in verse the unresolved polarity of faith and the disappointment of individual experience.

ANTHONY BUSHELL

C

cabaret

The German term *Kabarett* refers both to the socially critical yet entertaining form of artistic expression, and to the venue (*Kleinkunstbühne*) for the performance of satirical (and sometimes erotic) sketches, songs, mimes and one-act plays. Successful cabaret depends crucially on the informal atmosphere and close rapport between stage and auditorium characteristic of small club-like establishments.

The development of German cabaret goes back to the beginning of the twentieth century when, modelled on the Parisian cabaret Chat Noir, the first cabarets were founded in Berlin and Munich. During the 1920s literary, satirical, and political cabaret reached its peak with artists and authors like Walter **Mehring**, Kurt Tucholsky and Karl **Valentin**. The more entertainment-oriented genres of revue and **variety theatre** developed parallel to the literary cabaret; the boundaries are fluid. The Nazi dictatorship suppressed the critical cabaret culture in Germany, but it survived in exile in the neighbouring countries.

After 1945 German cabaret re-established itself, providing a platform for cautious attempts to initiate a debate on the National Socialist past as well as on the experience of post-war reconstruction. The most famous West German post-war cabarets are the Kom(m)ödchen in Düsseldorf (founded 1947), the Stachelschweine in Berlin (1949) and the Münchner Lach- und Schießgesellschaft (1956). In the GDR, cabarets like the Distel in Berlin (1953) and the Pfeffermühle in Leipzig (1954) were restricted by state censor-ship. In Austria cabaret was revived by artists like Georg Kreisler and Helmut **Qualtinger** (see also **Distel, Die**).

With the spread of television during the 1960s, live performance generally began to lose its appeal, but political cabaret continued to thrive. Individual cabaret artists like Hans Dieter Hüsch and Wolfgang **Neuss** came to the fore with their *Einmannkabarett* (one-man-cabaret). Within the context of the general politicization of West German society in the latter half of the 1960s (see **APO** and **student movement**), cabaret became a medium for increasingly radical left-wing criticism. New forms of cabaret and criticism were established: **Floh de Cologne** introduced elements of rock music into their cabaret programme. Singer-songwriters like Franz Josef **Degenhardt** and Dieter Süverkrüp eventually made the combination of critical protest and music work outside the sphere of the cabaret. In the GDR, Wolf **Biermann** established the political protest song (see also **protest songs**). At the same time individual humorists like **Loriot** and Otto developed the light entertainment dimension of the traditional cabaret.

Since the 1970s the significance of live cabaret as a form of artistic expression has been in constant decline. It continues to exist in the cultural centres of Hamburg, Berlin and Munich, but television cabaret and entertainment programmes like Dieter **Hildebrandt**'s *Scheibenwischer* have emerged as its popular successors. The element of entertainment has largely displaced the once crucial political message.

Further reading

Budzinski, K. and Hippen, R. (1996) *Metzler-Kabarett-Lexikon*, Stuttgart: Metzler (covers all aspects of cabaret).

Greul, H. (1971) *Bretter, die die Zeit bedeuten*, 2 vols, Munich: dtv (history of the German-speaking cabaret from its beginning up to 1970).

Jelavich, P. (1993) *Berlin Cabaret*, London: Harvard University Press (cabaret in Berlin from 1901–44).

ANNETTE BLÜHDORN

Canetti, Elias

b. 25 July 1905, Rustschuk (Bulgaria); d. 14 August 1994, Zürich

Writer, anthropologist and sociologist

The three volumes of Canetti's autobiography (published 1977–85) provide a highly dramatic and intense narrative of his early home life and intellectual development from his birth in 1905 to the emigration from Vienna to London in 1937, where he settled in Hampstead. The popular success of the autobiography suggests there is still a strong market in the contemporary German-speaking world and beyond for epic narratives which emphasize the values of survival, belated professional success, understated personal happiness and general intellectual and emotional coherence. This humanism has made Canetti internationally famous, and resulted in the award of the Nobel Prize for Literature in 1981. The autobiographical account begins with an insight into the life of an upper-middle-class Jewish family on the Danube in Bulgaria in the twilight years of the Austro-Hungarian Empire. It contains a brilliant account of a precociously bright and eager student, who learns German for the first time at the age of eight with his mother on the shores of Lake Geneva and who loves Stendhal, Kafka, Büchner and Kraus, but hates Brecht and anything to do with *fin de siècle* Vienna. It is useful as a historical testimonial because Canetti goes on to witness riots and inflation in Frankfurt am Main between 1921 and 1924, which lead to his first brilliant novel, *Auto de fé (Die Blendung)*(1935), and a survey of crowds and power, published as *Crowds and Power (Masse und Macht)* in 1960. Whilst the former has been the subject of any number of highly ambitious, systematic interpretations since its belated recognition as a masterpiece of world literature, many of which credit it with an acute understanding of the horrors of fascism, capitalism, modernism and secularism, the latter is much more ambiguous. It makes an idiosyncratic contribution to the disciplines of psychology, psycho-pathology, sociology and anthropology, wandering aimlessly across cultures in ways which are often trivialising, and always problematic. It has always been attractive to professional intellectuals because it contains any number of pithy aphorisms, many of which retain an appearance of charisma and mystique, even when they are intellectually impenetrable or incoherent. The same complaints cannot be levelled against the three early plays, which are still on the repertory (*Hochzeit, Komödie der Eitelkeit* and *Die Befristeten*), *The Voices of Marrakesh* (*Die Stimmen von Marrakesch*), the notes after a trip to Marrakesh, which even his arch-critic Marcel Reich-Ranicki dubbed 'Dichtung' (fiction), and *Ear-Witness (Der Ohrenzeuge)*, a work in the tradition of Theophrastus and La Bruyère.

Further reading

Krüger, M. (1995) *Einladung zur Verwandlung: Essays zu Elias Canettis Masse und Macht*, Munich: Hanser (gives best overall view of the huge range of responses to the most difficult of Canetti's works).

Murphy, H. (1997) *Canetti and Nietzsche: Theories of Humor in Die Blendung*, Albany, NY: State University of New York Press (develops the unconventional idea that the quality of the novel's seriousness is expressed in its facetiousness, which is Nietzschean in origin and implication).

HARRIET MURPHY

caricature

Caricature may be described as a form of primarily visual, but also literary, representation of either prominent public figures, or a particular type of person, event, or idea submitted with the intention of making a political statement, offering critical commentary, or exposing contradictory or hypo-critical circumstances. Caricature utilizes exaggera-tion, minimalization, or distortion of distinctive external characteristics. Within the visual arts it primarily encompasses sketches and graphic arts in the public press, and constitutes an essential element in satirical magazines. Within drama and literature caricature functions in **satire** and parody as one of the cruder, more direct and shrill forms of representation.

Within the public press caricature is closely linked to contemporary topics and responds to current affairs through graphics that are sometimes accompanied by text. In particular, the personal caricature (*Porträtkarikatur*) depends on an audience familiar which the respective public figure. As the product of an aesthetic abstraction or abstract idea, the caricature imparts a clearly comprehensible visual concept at a glance by seizing upon isolated traits or habits and either mocking, criticizing or denouncing these.

The moment of surprise or the ironic twist plays an important role, often offering support or contrast to the accompanying text. The caricature may exhibit either strongly satirical or humorous qualities according to whether the object is to be condemned or ridiculed. Within the latter instance it is the severity of ridicule or critique which determines whether the category of *Witzzeichnung* (humorous drawing) or of caricature is more pertinent. In German, the English word 'cartoon' is used alongside the native word *Karikatur* as a designation for (satirical) cartoons.

Given the close supervision of all GDR mass media (see **mass media: GDR**), which only published political caricature with great hesitation, most GDR caricaturists sought refuge in the 'weekly for satire and humour', *Eulenspiegel* founded in 1954. Caricatures attacked and were supposed to attack the so-called 'class enemy', the capitalist west. However, they increasingly commented on shortfalls in GDR society, substituting for sup-pressed criticism an open and direct public criticism. The founding generation of East German caricaturists comprise primarily artists of an anti-fascist background, such as Karl Holz; Alfred

Baier-Red who had worked for the proletarian satirical paper *Der Knüppel* (The Truncheon); Herbert Sandberg who began his career in the Weimar Republic's *Roter Pfeffer* (Red Pepper); and Ernst Jazdzewski. The following generation was the first to come of age in the GDR, and includes Heinz Behling, Barbara Henniger, Peter Dittrich and Karl Schrader.

Important caricaturists in the former West Germany are Mirko Szewczuk who, until his death in 1957 at the age of 38, had worked for *Die Zeit* and *Die Welt* and was one of the few German caricaturists acknowledged and reprinted outside of the FRG; Fritz Meinhard, who worked for the *Stuttgarter Zeitung*; the Austrians Manfred Deix and Gerhard Haderer; Michael Sowa (Berlin), Ernst Kahl (Hamburg); and Robert Gernhardt (Frankfurt am Main). Leading caricaturists of the satirical journal *Titanic* (founded in 1979 in the FRG) are Friedrich Karl Waechter, Chlodwig Poth, Rat-telscheck, and Hans Traxler.

Further reading

Lammel, G. (1995) *Deutsche Karikaturen vom Mittelalter bis heute*, Stuttgart: Metzler (survey of the art of caricature in Germany from the Middle Ages on to the present).

Lettkemann, G. and Scholz, M.F. (1994) '*Schuldig ist schließlich jeder... der Comics besitzt, verbreitet oder nicht einziehen läßt*'. Comics in der DDR – Die Geschichte eines ungeliebten Mediums (1945/49–90), Berlin: Mosaik (concentrates on *Mosaik*, an East German comic strip journal, examining the difficult position of comic and caricature in the GDR).

SYLVIA KLÖTZER

Carow, Heiner

b. 19 September 1929, Rostock; d. 31 January 1997, Berlin

Filmmaker

Carow founded a youth theatre before joining **DEFA**'s trainee director scheme (1951–2); he acquired his professional skills partly in DEFA's Documentary Film Unit, partly under the tutelage of Gerhard Klein and veteran director Slatan Dudow. Considered a specialist in films for children and young people, he also addressed such 'adult subjects' as the breakdown of marriage under pressure of everyday life, and the coming-out of a homosexual teacher. His *The Legend of Paul and Paula* (*Die Legende von Paul und Paula*, 1973; script: Ulrich **Plenzdorf**) became one of DEFA's biggest hits.

See also: film: GDR

HORST CLAUS

Carrell, Rudi

b. 19 December 1934, Alkmaar (The Netherlands)

Television personality, singer and comedian

Carrell enjoys one of the most durable careers in German entertainment. He began as a *Schlager* singer in his home country, where he won a national award in 1960. Since the 1960s he has hosted major game and comedy shows such as *Am laufenden Band* and the *Rudi Carrell Show*. He has had several hit singles and continues to be a household name with the progamme *Rudis Tiershow*. Carrell's reputation as a charming, non-controversial entertainer is rooted in his amiable personality.

SABINE SCHMIDT

CDU

The Christlich Demokratische Union Deutschlands (CDU) (Christian Democratic Union) was founded after WWII. Its equivalent in Bavaria is the Christian Social Union (**CSU**), which has retained a distinctive name and a separate organization though the two parties act as one *Fraktion* (grouping) in the **Bundestag**.

Although the CDU has significant roots in the Weimar Republic – primarily in the Catholic Zentrum Party – it essentially represents a postwar phenomenon. It had inherited little ideological baggage and therefore had the chance to create a recognizable policy profile; this was mainly based on the right to private property and the proclaimed

necessity for a welfare state as a general commitment to a social market economy within the framework of democratic and Catholic social thought. The CDU's commitment to an interconfessional alliance attracted support from a wide social and religious spectrum and secured the party's first electoral victory in 1949. During the ensuing term of office of Konrad **Adenauer**, the first Chancellor of the FRG, Ludwig Erhard's successful economic policy led to the *Wirtschaftswunder-Jahre* (years of the **Economic Miracle**) which still play a vital part in the self-definition of today's party and the pragmatic approach to social and political issues which is so highly valued amongst its electorate. This seems to be one of the main reasons why the party has been the dominant political force during most of the Federal Republic's history.

Because of Cold War tensions, the CDU in the Soviet zone became more and more isolated from the rest of the party in the western zones. After 1949 it became totally integrated into the East German party system which eventually meant complete marginalization under the leadership of the **SED**. Almost immediately after the **Wende** the East German CDU, which had been a conformist bloc-party for forty years and was therefore associated with old-style thinking, presented itself to the voters as a conservative 'popular party of the centre' with policies based mainly on ethical values under the leadership of Lothar **de Maizière**. After some initial hesitation in view of the eastern party's conformist past, the CDU in the Federal Republic decided to support its counterpart in the East. The GDR's first free elections in March 1990 showed clearly that a majority of East German voters supported the CDU and this surprise victory subsequently yielded sharp gains for the CDU in West German polls. Election results of the first national elections in December 1990 illustrated the success of the the CDU's politics under Chancellor Helmut **Kohl** with regard to the unification of the country, having promised what most East Germans wanted: security, freedom and a share in the prosperity of the West – and what most West Germans hoped for: to achieve these goals without any sacrifices on their part.

However, in the next elections (1994) the party succeeded by only a tiny margin over the **SPD**

(Social Democrats), which can be attributed to the problems the CDU as the governing party had to face in the aftermath of unification as well as to structural and organizational problems within the party itself. In the 1998 elections the Kohl era finally came to an end and the CDU lost power to the SPD.

Further reading

Dalton, R.J. (1993) *The New Germany Votes. Unification and the Creation of the New German Party System*, Oxford: Berg (includes information on CDU politics throughout, but especially in the very informative chapter 'The Christian Democrats and in 1990: Saved by Unification?').

Merkl, P.H. (1989) *The Federal Republic Of Germany At Forty*, New York: New York University Press (contains a chapter on the evolution of the party system with detailed information about the Christian Democrats).

Pridham, G. (1977) *Christian Democracy in Western Germany. The CDU/CSU in Government and Opposition*, London: Croom Helm (provides a detailed account of developments within the party between 1945 and 1976).

ASTRID HERHOFFER

Celan, Paul

b. 23 November 1920, Czernowitz (then Romania); d. 20 April 1970, Paris

Poet

Acclaimed as the modern successor of Hölderlin and one of the foremost post-war poets of the German language, Paul Celan is a figure who defies the strict categories of a national canon. Born to a German-speaking, eastern European Jewish family and raised in the multicultural region of the Bukovina, Celan's background combined different intellectual, cultural, and linguistic traditions. Although his father insisted on a Judaic education, Celan's mother provided him with his earliest interests in German language and literature. In 1938 Celan left Czernowitz to study medicine in France, but he returned in 1939 to continue his studies in Romance philology. During the 1940 German invasion Celan went into hiding, but his parents were deported to the Ukraine, where they died in concentration camps. In 1948, after failed attempts to settle in his native Czernowitz and in Vienna, Celan moved to Paris in self-exile, where he taught at the École Normale Supérieure, and wrote and translated poetry until his suicide by drowning in the Seine in 1970.

Celan's poetry ranges from the surrealist influences of the 1940s to the idiosyncratic poems of the later collections such as *Force of Light* (*Lichtzwang*), *Snow-Part* (*Schneepart*) and *Farmstead of Time* (*Zeitgehöft*). However, 'Death Fugue' ('Todesfuge') remains his most celebrated poem because it expresses the suffering of the Jews in a more accessible language.

The city of Bremen honoured Celan in 1958, and in 1960 he was awarded the prestigious Georg Büchner Prize. At a reading in Freiburg in 1964 he met the philosopher Martin **Heidegger**, whose theories Celan respected, but who disappointed Celan in his refusal to recant his National Socialist past. Celan visited Israel in 1969 and addressed the Hebrew Writers Association. Yet none of these places could alone claim Celan's legacy and none succeeded in providing him with the security and warmth of a home. Isolated in Paris, Celan lived with depression, guilt at his survival, and the constant fear of persecution.

The experience of persecution along with the devastation at his parents' loss marked Celan's life and distinguished his work as a compelling meditation on the role of poetry after the **Holocaust**. Celan's concerns about post-war poetry link him to the philosopher Theodor **Adorno**, who – after reading Celan – softened his claim on the impossibility of poetry after Auschwitz. While in France and despite his multilingual abilities, Celan continued to write in German, since he deemed that only the mother tongue can truly express the poetic experience. Celan's choice reflects his wish to reinvent the German language after its abuse by the Nazis. By inserting neologisms and foreign words into his poems and composing in an elliptical syntax, Celan problematized the alleged purity of German and furnished it with linguistic and cultural aspects that the Nazis had expunged. In spite of these formal difficulties, which limit the reader's access, Celan insisted that his work intends to communicate the horror of the Holocaust.

Further reading

Colin, A. (1991) *Paul Celan: Holograms of Darkness*, Bloomington, IA: Indiana University Press (introduction to Celan's reception and interpretations of his less discussed early work).

Felstiner, J. (1995) *Paul Celan: Poet, Survivor, Jew*, New Haven, CT: Yale University Press (best biography linked with readings of poems).

Fioretos, A. (ed.) (1994) *Word Traces: Readings of Paul Celan*, Baltimore, MD: Johns Hopkins University Press (philosophical essays on Celan's work).

Szondi, P. (1972) *Celan-Studien*, Frankfurt am Main: Suhrkamp Verlag (historical and textual analysis which incited much of Celan criticism)

KALLIOPI NIKOLOPOULOU

censorship: FRG

The first section of Article 5 of the German constitution (see also **constitution: FRG**) – the article which guarantees freedom of expression – concludes with the sentence 'There shall be no censorship' (*Eine Zensur findet nicht statt*). Freedom of expression is not, however, absolute: Article 5 goes on to indicate limitations in the shape of 'the provisions of the general laws, the legal provisions for the protection of young people, and the right to inviolability of personal honour'.

Legal prohibitions may thus be brought to bear against certain kinds of expression (whether in speech, writing or picture) which could do damage to other constitutional rights, or to the democratic order itself. Such laws may proscribe incitement to violence against groups, individuals or property, or threats against public order or the security of the state. Restrictions on the availability of **pornography**, and laws against slander and libel are also deemed to be compatible with Article 5. The basic principle of free speech remains, however, that of 'publish and be damned': i.e. the state cannot *pre*-censor the expression of any individual opinion, but the law may be brought to bear after the event

against those who have overstepped the mark in expressing it.

In the cultural sphere, state intervention comes closest to a form of censorship in the shape of the 'Law on the dissemination of material representing a danger to young people'. This is administered by a 'Federal Inspectorate' (*Bundesprüfstelle*) within the Ministry for Women and Young People, with powers to limit the display and availability (including by mail-order) of books, magazines, videos and other material that it deems to be a 'threat to the moral well-being of young people'. Indexable material includes pornography and materials 'glorifying crime, war, and racial hatred'.

Film censorship is administered not by the state but by the industry itself through its voluntary self-control board, the Freiwillige Selbstkontrolle der Filmwirtschaft (FSK), which classifies all films and videos destined for public exhibition; membership of the FSK includes representatives of the film industry, the state and recognized interest groups within society. Radio, television and the press are subject to *Land* jurisdiction, and operate under the **broadcasting**, media, and press laws of the *Länder* in which they are based. These laws are also formulated in keeping with the constitutional prohibition of state censorship.

The manner and extent of state intervention in public expression has changed with political and social attitudes over the history of the Federal Republic. Thus in the Cold War era of the 1950s and 1960s the distribution of films and other materials from communist countries was subject to control by the Office for the Protection of the Constitution. The most marked changes can be seen in the area of sexually explicit materials: from the late 1960s onwards depictions and discussions of a kind that would earlier have incurred public opprobrium and legal proscription have extended increasingly into the mainstream media.

See also: censorship: GDR; computers; sex shops

JOHN SANDFORD

censorship: GDR

The apparatus of censorship was established in the GDR in response to the belief – widely held in the aftermath of the Third Reich – that some degree of control over the mass media and cultural production was necessary. In 1946 few intellectuals in the Soviet zone of occupation objected to the setting up of a 'Cultural Advisory Board' charged with identifying works of a fascist or militarist nature and 'removing them from circulation'. The new culture which was to replace them was given a specific educational function (initially of the broadest 'anti-fascist' kind). This not only placed pressures on the producers of culture to exercise self-censorship throughout the creative process; it also led political leaders to overestimate the power of individual works to influence public opinion and thus to overreact to criticism expressed in them. Both of these factors gradually came to distort the course of cultural life in the GDR. Although the term 'censorship' was never officially used – the emphasis was always on promoting the right kind of culture within each year's carefully worked out cultural plan – a distinctive GDR variant on a centuries-old practice was soon recognizable.

The Cold War provided the justification for a tightening of the screw, and by 1951 even artists with impeccable socialist credentials were suffering its effects. A network of new bureaucracies under the direct control of the SED Central Committee ensured that no sphere of cultural life escaped scrutiny: an opera by Bertolt **Brecht** and Paul **Dessau**, the film-version of a novel by Arnold **Zweig**, Hanns **Eisler**'s libretto of the Faust legend and a commemorative exhibition of drawings and sculptures by the expressionist Ernst Barlach were amongst the first victims. Widespread disillusionment had set in by the time of the **June Uprising** of 1953, but the SED tried to make amends the following year by establishing a Ministry of Culture, with an author, Johannes R. **Becher**, at its head, to mediate between artists and the Party leadership.

By the 1960s the structures of a less dogmatic, but nevertheless inescapable censorship process had been put in place, in a form which was to change little over the rest of the GDR's lifetime. Outsiders, however, only gradually gained a clear picture of its hierarchical workings, and it was not until 1984 that a newly exiled author, Erich **Loest**, took the trouble to provide, under the title *Der vierte Zensor* (The Fourth Censor), a case-study which offered a very helpful overview. The four levels to which Loest referred (and which existed in a broadly similar form for all spheres of culture) extended from the self-censorship of the politically committed artist, through the protracted negotiations with his or her publisher, before the main hurdle of the appropriate division of the Ministry of Culture (in this case the 'Central Administration for Publishing and the Book-Trade') was faced. And even if the Deputy Minister responsible, Klaus **Höpcke**, could finally be persuaded to give his seal of approval to a challenging work of literature – Loest's 1978 novel *Es geht seinen Gang* (Things Take Their Course) – there was still the risk of an arbitrary veto from the fourth level of authority, whether in the form of the Politburo's ideological secretary Kurt **Hager**, or a regional boss of the SED, or even the Soviet military high-command, which could undo years of painstaking progress. Getting a work published was still not the end of the process, however, since its impact could be severely restricted by keeping the print-run absurdly low, ensuring that it received minimal discussion in the cultural media or banning subsequent editions (the breaking-point in Loest's case).

The most disheartening periods in the history of GDR censorship were the mid-1960s, when the banning of a whole year's production of **DEFA** films was the most spectacular aspect of the comprehensive clampdown on culture by the SED Central Committee at its **Eleventh Plenum**, and the late 1970s (after the **Biermann Affair**), when Erich Honecker's promise of a socialist culture 'without taboos' disintegrated in a succession of bitter battles between artists and a Ministry of Culture which continued to claim it was doing its best on their behalf. In general, GDR drama suffered disproportionately from the effects of censorship (see also **drama: GDR**). Stage performances of many challenging works by outstanding playwrights such as Heiner **Müller**, Volker **Braun** and Christoph **Hein** were banned, often for years after the same works had appeared in the GDR in printed form or been widely performed in the West. As in the case of film, the

'Central Administration' appeared particularly intent on eliminating the kind of opportunity for collective disapproval of the regime which public performances could have provided.

The final straw for many artists who remained in the GDR right up to end was the regime's indifference to the cultural revolution proclaimed by Michail Gorbachev in the Soviet Union under the slogan of glasnost in 1985. At the Writers' Congress of 1987, following courageous speeches by Günter de **Bruyn** and Christoph Hein, the easing of censorship was at last placed on the political agenda, but the concessions which followed were, as ever, too few and too late.

Further reading

Agde, G. (ed.) (1991) *Kahlschlag: Das 11. Plenum des ZK der SED 1965. Studien und Dokumente*, Berlin: Aufbau (a good example of the growing number of case-studies published since unification).

Darnton, R. (1991) 'The Viewpoint of the Censor', in his *Berlin Diary 1989–90*, New York: Norton, pp. 202–17 (an admirably concise account arising from discussions with two ex-censors).

Loest, E. (1990) *Der Zorn des Schafes*, Künzelsau-Leipzig: Linden (a full account of an author's struggles with censorship and the Stasi, incorporating most of the material from *Der vierte Zensor*, mentioned above).

Wichner, E. and Wiesner, H. (eds) (1993) *'Literaturentwicklungsprozesse': Die Zensur der Literatur in der DDR*, Frankfurt am Main: Suhrkamp (a good collection of essays by authors and literary critics, edited by the organizers of the first major exhibition in post-unification Berlin of the workings of censorship).

DENNIS TATE

Central Committee

The Zentralkomitee (ZK) of the **SED** in the GDR was formally its highest body between the party conferences (*Parteitage*); in practice the **Politbüro**, chosen by the ZK, represented the most powerful body in the party, and the day-to-day running of the party apparatus was supervised and controlled by the *Sekretariat* of the ZK. The first ZK voted in by the third *Parteitag* in July 1950 reflected the adaptation of the party structure to that of the Soviet Union. The size of the ZK was not laid down and it was only required to meet at least once every six months. Membership of the ZK indicated the high status of individuals in the SED, and the institutions they represented.

PETER BARKER

charities

Charitable activity is most evident in the numerous foundations and in voluntary welfare services (the *Freie Wohlfahrtspflege*). These stretch back to the religious and charitable welfare foundations of the early Middle Ages. The *Freie Wohlfahrtspflege* has particular German characteristics in that the voluntary welfare associations (of which there are six main groups) are legally given precedence in the provision of caring and advice services according to the subsidiarity principle. The six include the German Red Cross, *Caritasverband* and *Arbeiterwohlfahrt*, and have 62,000 centres.

Foundations for education, research and the arts include the large political party foundations as well as those established by industrial benefactors.

CHRISTOPHER H. FLOCKTON

childhood

Childhood has been influenced by politics, church and culture. Unchanged, however, is the close connection of mothers to their children. Women, in their biological function as the bearer of children, remain as primary caretakers.

In pre-industrial German society families had many children. A cheap source of labour, they guaranteed parents' security in old age. *Kinderreichtum* (having many children) sustained a three-generation family usually living under one roof. At the turn of the twentieth century, children had few rights or privileges. Children were treated like 'small' adults with the same rights and responsibilities. The high death rate of infants and children, and mothers who died in childbirth, meant that many children were raised by stepmothers and had no status within the family.

In the Weimar Republic educators became concerned with child pedagogy and children's developmental stages, and emphasis was placed on child-specific concerns such as language development, the role of play, emotional security and physical development. These changes were annihilated under Nazi ideology. Children were considered an asset to the state. Mothers who had at least four children were decorated.

After 1945, the German birth rate began to decline. *Kinderfeindlichkeit* (antipathy towards children) became a social problem. The war was blamed for creating an atmosphere in which the generations no longer got along. Children were subjected to stringent parental and state control. For example, no children were allowed to play outside during the strictly adhered to afternoon quiet time. Fruitlessly, the government undertook advertising campaigns to encourage couples to have children. Today the German birth rate is still the lowest in the world.

Many German children continued to struggle against an authoritarian upbringing. It has been said that Germans suffer from a collective pathology brought on by child-rearing techniques that were both arbitrary and violent. The Economic Miracle that had brought wealth to Germans had a devastating impact on the emotional development of German children.

Most recently, the relationship of parents to children has changed as has the position of the child within the family. The traditional strict authority of parents, widely challenged in the generational revolts of the late 1960s, is no longer the norm. Equality, a liberal parenting style and *elterliche Sorge* (parental care) have replaced *elterliche Gewalt* (parental force) in a new partnership between parents and children. Nowadays, a child often takes the central position in a family around which parents organize their lives. Nevertheless, parents who centre their lives exclusively around an only child are in danger of making that child into an object of their own wish-fulfilment.

Schools have implemented programmes that instil a *Gemeinschaftsgefühl* (community feeling), where the child progresses through school with the same group, much like an extended family.

Children today are materially well-off and medical advances and cultural influences have expanded their opportunities. Notwithstanding these advances and government-sponsored publicity campaigns, child poverty is prevalent in families with more than three children, and the children of **Gastarbeiter** as well as those children who are physically and mentally challenged continue to experience problems in German society.

Further reading

Brückner, J. (1980) *Hungerjahre* (Years of Hunger) (this film is an autobiographical account of growing up in Germany in the 1950s).

Evans, R. (1981) *The German Family: Essays on the Social History of the Family in Nineteenth- and Twentieth-Century Germany*, London: Croom Helm (a collection of essays on the history of the German family in the nineteenth and twentieth centuries).

Parkes, S. (1997) *Understanding Contemporary Germany*, London: Routledge (a survey of German society focusing on the post-unification situation).

Schneider, N. (1994) *Familie und private Lebensführung in West- und Ostdeutschland. Eine vergleichende Analyse des Familienlebens 1970–92*, Stuttgart: Enke (a study of the position of the family in contemporary German society).

UTE LISCHKE-McNAB

Chotjewitz, Peter O.

b. 14 June 1934, Berlin

Writer

The author of socio-critical, generally realistic novels, Chotjewitz was controversial in the 1970s. The 1978 *Die Herren des Morgengrauens* (The Gentlemen of the Dawn) evoked Kafka in its portrayal of anti-terrorist surveillance and led to the end of co-operation between the **Bertelsmann** publishing corporation and the self-managed AutorenEdition. A major interest of his work has been the fate of German Jewry (as in *Saumlos*, 1979). The 1968 novel *Die Insel* (The Island) uses collage techniques to portray life in West Berlin during the student movement. Chotjewitz was also a lawyer and acted as defence counsel to the terrorist Andreas **Baader**.

STUART PARKES

church tax

Church tax (*Kirchensteuer*) is levied as a surcharge on the income tax of church members and amounts to between 8 and 9 percent of income tax depending on the *Land*. Church taxes are administered and collected by the tax office and passed on to the churches, which are charged a fee for the service (approximately DM 500 million per annum). The main Protestant (EKD) and Roman Catholic churches each receive approximately DM 8,000 million per annum in church tax. Since unification, this system has also been applied to churches from the former GDR. However, the economic recession in the 1990s, and the decline in influence of the churches has led to a significant number of people leaving the church and thus ceasing to pay church tax.

See also: churches and religion

STEPHEN BROWN

churches and religion

The main Protestant churches had 27.7 million, and the Roman Catholic church 27.5 million members in Germany in 1996. Both the main Protestant churches and the Catholic church describe themselves as *Volkskirchen*. Regular church attendance is much lower than these figures suggest. There are no clear geographical dividing lines between the two main confessions, but in general Catholicism predominates in the south and west of Germany, and Protestantism in the north and east. There are 2.4 million Muslims in Germany (see also **Islam in Germany**), and Jewish congregations have about 61,000 members (see also **Judaism**).

There is a separation of church and state and the state is committed to neutrality in all matters of religion and to the protection of the right to worship, provided by Articles 4 and 140 of the Basic Law). But the Basic Law follows the 1919 Weimar constitution in giving the main Protestant

and Roman Catholic churches – and certain other religious communities – a special status as 'corporate bodies under public law' (*Körperschaften des Öffentlichen Rechts*). **Church tax** provides a substantial part of the income of the main Protestant and Roman Catholic churches.

Religious education is guaranteed in state schools, although parents can decide whether or not children take part (Article 7 of the Basic Law). Professors at the nineteen Protestant and twelve Catholic theological faculties at state universities are paid by the state, but appointed only after approval by the relevant church authorities. Pastoral care in the armed forces – except in the new federal states – is provided by chaplains who have the status of civil servants, and are attached to the defence ministry. The main churches have guaranteed broadcasting time on the publicly-owned **broadcasting** stations, and, as 'socially-significant groups', they are members of their monitoring committees (*Rundfunkräte*); they also support news agencies – the evangelischer Pressedienst (epd) and the Katholische Nachrichten-Agentur (KNA).

Church-sponsored associations such as *Caritas* (Roman Catholic) and Diakonisches Werk (Protestant) – together having over 700,000 employees – play a significant role as independent welfare agencies (*freie Träger*) in the provision of welfare services. The state also provides financial support for church-sponsored development agencies Misereor (Catholic) and Brot für die Welt (Protestant).

Protestantism

Despite its name, the *Evangelische Kirche in Deutschland* (Evangelical Church in Germany), is a federation of twenty-four independent *Landeskirchen* (territorial churches) – ten Lutheran, two Reformed (Calvinist) and twelve United (Lutheran and Reformed) – which together account for the overwhelming majority of German Protestants. In large part, the *Landeskirchen* correspond to the territorial states that made up the 1871 German Reich rather than today's Federal *Länder*. The EKD was officially founded on 31 August 1945 in Treysa but its *Grundordnung* (constitution) was adopted on 13 July 1948 in Eisenach only after three years of protracted negotiations. Among the EKD's prominent founders were Otto **Dibelius** and Martin **Niemöller**, but also Gustav Heinemann, the later Federal President.

The EKD represents its member churches *vis-à-vis* the public authorities and the worldwide church, but it possesses no doctrinal or theological authority over them. The EKD and its member churches play a significant role in international church bodies, such as the World Council of Churches (WCC), the Lutheran World Federation (LWF), the World Alliance of Reformed Churches (WARC) and the Conference of European Churches (CEC), all based in Geneva.

Women are ordained as pastors by the EKD's member churches. In 1992, Maria Jepsen became the world's first female Lutheran bishop when she was elected bishop in Hamburg. The Protestant churches have a wide political spectrum within their own ranks, with prominent politicians from the main parties also belonging to the synods or other institutions of the EKD.

Alongside its official character, German Protestantism has also spawned a remarkable lay movement, concentrated particularly around the Evangelical Academies and the *Deutscher Evangelischer Kirchentag* (DEKT) (German Protestant Church Convention), which gathers tens of thousands every two years. The EKD has been involved in all the major political controversies of the postwar era. The *Stuttgarter Schulderklärung* (Stuttgart Declaration of Guilt), made by the EKD's provisional council at a meeting in October 1945 with international church representatives, caused controversy by appearing to suggest that there was a collective guilt by Germans for the crimes of the Third Reich, but opened the way for German Protestantism, and through it Germany, to become again part of the international community.

The 1957 *Militärseelsorgevertrag* (agreement on military chaplaincy) between the federal government and the EKD was strongly criticized by the GDR authorities, which described it as support for West German rearmament. As a result, the GDR broke off contacts with the EKD, setting in process the events that led to the founding of a separate church federation in the GDR in 1969.

The EKD's 1965 *Ostdenkschrift* (Memorandum on relations with the East) created consternation in the conservative camp because of its suggestion that the FRG should forgo its claims to the eastern territories, but it prepared the way for the later **Ostpolitik** of Willy Brandt's SPD/FDP coalition.

In the late 1970s and in the first half of the 1980s, the EKD was strongly affected by the peace movement (see also **peace movement: FRG**; **peace movement: GDR**), with the meetings of the *Kirchentage* (particularly in Hamburg 1981, Hanover 1983 and Düsseldorf 1985) providing a forum for the Christian-influenced peace movement.

Roman Catholic church

The Catholic church in Germany is comprised, as of 1995, of 20 dioceses and 7 archdioceses, grouped into seven church provinces (Bamberg, Berlin, Hamburg, Freiburg, Cologne, Munich-Freising and Paderborn). The German Bishops' Conference, located in Bonn, serves as the co-ordinating headquarters for the church. The Zentralkomitee der deutschen Katholiken (founded in its present structure in 1952), organizes the *Katholikentage* (normally taking place every two years, alternating with the Protestant *Kirchentage*), acts as an umbrella for various lay bodies and represents Catholics in the public arena.

After 1945, the Catholic church desisted from supporting an exclusively Catholic political party, instead supporting the foundation of the Christian Democratic Union (**CDU**) and the Christian Social Union (**CSU**) (in Bavaria) as inter-confessional political parties. The Catholic church in Germany made no declaration analogous to that of the Stuttgart Declaration of Guilt, but on 5 December 1965, following the EKD's *Ostdenkschrift*, the Roman Catholic bishops in both the FRG and GDR asked for 'forgiveness' from Polish Catholics.

The church was strongly affected by the Second Vatican Council (1962–5), convened by Pope John XXIII, which started a process of reassessment within Roman Catholicism. At about the same time, the opening in 1963 in Berlin of *Der Stellvetreter* (The Representative), Rolf **Hochhuth**'s controversial play about the alleged silence of Pope Pius XII on the persecution of the Jews, started a process of ***Vergangenheitsbewältigung*** that has continued to the 1990s.

Humanae Vitae, Pope Paul VI's 1968 encyclical prohibiting artificial birth control, led to public demonstrations, and demands for the Pope's resignation, at the 1968 Essen *Katholikentag*. Shortly afterwards, the Königstein Declaration of the German Bishops' Conference stressed the need to respect the conscientious decision of a married couple. The Catholic church opposed attempts to revise Article 218 of the penal code, which governed **abortion law**, after the coming to power in 1969 of Brandt's SPD/FDP coalition.

Pope John Paul II visited the Federal Republic in 1980, 1988 and 1996.

Other Christian churches

Alongside the EKD (and its *Landeskirchen*) and the Roman Catholic church, the following Christian churches are members of the Arbeitsgemeinschaft Christlicher Kirchen in Deutschland (officially translated as Council of Churches in Germany): Greek Orthodox Metropolitinate of Germany (450,000 members); Bund Evangelisch-Freikirhlicher Gemeinden in Deutschland (Baptists) (87,000 members); Evangelisch-Methodistische Kirche (Methodists) (68,000 members); Selbständige Evangelisch-Lutherische Kirche (SELK) (39,750 members); Syrian Orthodox church (37,000 members); Old Catholic church (25,000 members); Moravians (7,200 members); Evangelisch altreformierte Kirche (7,000); Mennonites (6,875); the Salvation Army (2,000), the Russian Orthodox church (50,000) and the Armenian Apostolic Church (35,000).

East Germany

The territory making up the GDR in 1949 was overwhelmingly Protestant, and until 1969 the EKD covered the whole of Germany, having eight member churches in the GDR. Although the GDR's 1949 constitution gave churches a status as 'corporate bodies under public law', including the right to levy church tax and to provide religious education, these provisions were abrogated in the course of the 1950s.

In 1952–3, the authorities launched a campaign against church youth and student groups, which they halted on 10 June 1953 following a high-level church-state meeting. Both the Protestant and

Roman Catholic churches denounced the introduction of the *Jugendweihe* as a secular alternative to confirmation but were unable to prevent most church members acquiescing. However, after conscription was introduced in the GDR in 1962, the churches were able to persuade the authorities to introduce an unarmed service undertaken by *Bausoldaten*, soldiers in construction units, as an alternative to full military service.

The building of the **Berlin Wall** in 1961 prevented almost all joint meetings and most contacts between the churches in East and West. The status of churches as 'corporate bodies under public law' was removed in the 1968 GDR constitution. Its stipulation that churches should regulate their affairs in accordance with the provisions and the laws of the GDR was taken as prohibiting all-German church bodies. As a result, the eight member churches of the EKD on the territory of the GDR annulled their membership of the EKD and on 10 June 1969 founded a separate Federation of Evangelical Churches in the GDR, which, from 1971, described itself as a *Kirche im Sozialismus* (Church within Socialism).

At the end of the 1970s and start of the 1980s, the Protestant churches in the GDR became a focus for an independent – and largely decentralized – peace movement, which in the course of the 1980s embraced other aspects of alternative culture, including ecological, human rights groups, and gay and lesbian groups, which later formed the nucleus of many of the **citizens' movements** of the *Wende*.

Whereas the borders of the Protestant churches generally followed the border between the FRG and the GDR, the borders of the Roman Catholic dioceses in Germany crossed between East and West Germany and also over to post-war Poland. Although the Vatican responded pragmatically by appointing apostolic administrators, this state of affairs remained in existence *de jure* until after the treaties between the FRG and its eastern neighbours of 1972. The Berlin Bishops' Conference was placed directly under the Holy See in 1976.

There was no equivalent either to *Kirche im Sozialismus* or to the autonomous groups which gathered under the umbrella of the Protestant churches. The Roman Catholic church in the GDR concentrated on maintaining its own identity, and played down any political role, whether supporting or opposing the state.

In 1988 and 1989, the Protestant churches, the Free churches, and the Roman Catholic church jointly sponsored an Ecumenical Assembly gathering both representatives of the groups and of church governing bodies.

The *Wende* and German unification

In the immediate run-up to the *Wende*, churches increasingly became the scenes of protest demonstrations, in particular, the *Montagsdemonstrationen* in Leipzig began after peace prayers in the Nikolaikirche. Moreover, Protestant pastors and church workers played a prominent role in many of the new political movements founded in autumn 1989 (such as **Bickhardt**, Eppelmann, **Schorlemmer** and **Meckel**), leading some observers to characterize the *Wende* as a 'Protestant revolution'. Not least because of their role in the Ecumenical Assembly, the Protestant churches, Free churches and Catholic church acted as moderators of the **Round Table**.

A meeting of Protestant church leaders from the FRG and the GDR in Loccum in January 1990 issued the Loccum Declaration which called for the speedy re-unification of German Protestantism. In June 1991, the BEK was dissolved and the eight territorial churches in the former GDR re-joined the EKD. Following German unification, there was a process of restructuring the Roman Catholic dioceses in Germany, which was completed in 1995.

New challenges

The situation after unification presents new challenges for the main churches in Germany. The effects of forty years of socialist government in the GDR have meant that the population of the new *Bundesländer* are overwhelmingly non-religious. The increase in taxes following unification has led many – not least in West Germany – to leave the church to avoid paying church taxes. Moreover, the majority of the *Länder* abolished *Buß- und Bettag* (a Protestant public holiday) in the face of church opposition, as part of an effort to increase productivity and taxes. Further signs of an erosion

in the traditional position of the churches in German public life were the 1995 'crucifix verdict' in which the Federal Constitutional Court prohibited a crucifix automatically being displayed in Bavarian state schools, and the determination of the SPD in Berlin-Brandenburg (ironically under Premier Manfred **Stolpe**, a former prominent Protestant official in the GDR) to introduce LER (lifestyle, ethics and religion) rather than religious education.

Further reading

Helmreich, E.C. (1975) *The German Churches under Hitler: Background, Struggle and Epilogue*, Detroit, MI: Wayne State University Press (despite its title, the book includes much valuable information on the history of the churches in Germany, and its final chapters on the churches in post-war Germany offer a very clear and comprehensive account of developments until the early 1970s).

Helwig G., and Urban D. (eds) (1987) *Kirchen und Gesellschaften in beiden deutschen Staaten*, Cologne: Edition Deutschland Archiv im Verlag Wissenschaft und Politik (a useful comparative overview of the churches in both the FRG and the GDR until the mid-1980s).

STEPHEN BROWN

circus

The modern circus evolved from Roman hippodromes, renaissance fairs, and the equestrian dressage shows of eighteenth-century riding schools, expanded to include acrobatics and clowning. Many nineteenth-century circuses, such as the Cirque Olympique and Cirque d'Hiver in Paris, and later the Schumann Circus, Circus Busch, and the Ernst Renz Circuses in Berlin, Breslau, Bremen and Hamburg, moved indoors into enclosed circus arenas. These later distinctively German forms included not only equestrian acts of French and British origin, and impressive pantomime re-enactments of historical battles and holiday spectacles modelled after those in London, but also sensational stunts and exotic animal acts. Hagenbeck, Sarrasani and Krone imitated the success of the American three-ring circus, championed by P.T. Barnum, and established Germany's first travelling tent circuses. The Sarrasani and Krone circuses still count among Germany's largest financially secure circuses today, a list including the Althoff, Busch, Renz, Hein, Probst and Roncalli Circuses, all of which provide contemporary audiences with entertainment and the vicarious experience of dramatized risk.

JENNIFER HAM

citizens' initiatives: FRG

The early 1970s in the Federal Republic witnessed the spectacular growth of what came to be known as *Bürgerinitiativen* (citizens' initiatives). This was the term applied to:

> spontaneous, loosely organized associations of citizens, normally in existence for a limited period of time only, who, directly affected by a specific issue, intercede outside the traditional institutions and participatory forms of representative party democracy in order to prompt action by the authorities.
>
> (Guggenberger 1980: 18)

Such was their proliferation that by the mid-1970s *Bürgerinitiativen* had become an established feature of the West German political culture (see also **political culture: FRG**), preparing the ground both for the emergence of the new social movements later in the decade and for the electoral success of *Die Grünen* in the 1980s.

Although in part a legacy of the 1960s **student movement** (sections of which subsequently turned to local politics as a site for political consciousness-raising) *Bürgerinitiativen* drew their membership solidly from the ranks of the educated middle class. Broadly opposed to the technocratic thinking of the state and local authorities and ever more disenchanted with the remoteness of established parliamentary politics, Germany's affluent middle class increasingly looked to non-party forms of association as a conduit for their political energies and to their locality as an environment in which it might be possible – in Willy **Brandt**'s celebrated words of 1969 – 'to dare to have more democracy'. Hence a survey of over 2,000 *Bürgerinitiativen*,

conducted in 1975, found that more than 60 percent of the sample could be located in that whole complex of issues connected with education, child-care and problems of the inner cities such as traffic, housing and urban planning. From 1975 onwards, however, the issue which more than any other established the political status of citizens' initiatives and at the same time gave direction to the emergent ecology movement in the Federal Republic was the campaign against the civil use of **nuclear power**. In particular, two epic struggles against plans to build a nuclear reactor at Wyhl (in Baden-Württemberg) and at Brokdorf (in Schleswig-Holstein) proved to be such a powerful catalyst for protest that thereafter virtually every projected atomic energy plant became a centre of controversy.

Another reason for the increasing dominance of environmental themes within the *Bürgerinitiativen* movement was the role played by the Bundesverband Bürgerinitiativen Umweltschutz (BBU). Founded in June 1972 the BBU had by 1977 become the most important umbrella organization for environmental groups, and at its peak in 1982 it could boast over 1,000 *Bürgerinitiativen* with an estimated membership of between 300,000 and 500,000. By that stage, however, the BBU had long ceased to be a merely co-ordinating body: not only was it crucially involved in the renaissance of the peace movement in the early 1980s (see also **peace movement: FRG**), but it was also advancing an elaborate vision of ecological politics which, in many respects, prefigured the political platform of *Die Grünen*.

See also: Greens

Further reading

Burns, R. and Will, W. van der (1988) *Protest and Democracy in West Germany*, Basingstoke: Macmillan, pp. 164–204 (chapter 5 deals with citizens' initiatives).

Guggenberger, B. (1980) *Bürgerinitiativen in der Parteiendemokratie*, Stuttgart: Kohlhammer Verlag.

Mayer-Tasch, P. (1985) *Die Bürgerinitiativenbewegung*, 5th edn, Reinbek bei Hamburg: Rowohlt (a pioneering study when first published in 1976, subsequently revised and expanded).

ROB BURNS

citizens' initiatives: GDR

At the end of the 1970s independent and unofficial citizens' initiatives (*Burgerinitiativen*) emerged in the GDR, mainly under the roof of the Protestant church. Most of them dealt with issues concerning protection of the environment, peace, solidarity with the Third World, gender and civil rights. In the 1980s there were about 500 action groups in the GDR, not only in big cities like East Berlin, Leipzig and Dresden, but also in smaller towns and communities. According to estimates more than 10,000 people were organized in these groups. To improve their communication and infrastructure the groups created network organizations like *Frieden Konkret* (Practical Peace), *Grünes Netzwerk Arche* (Green Network Ark), and *Kirche von unten* (Church from Below), and published *samisdat* booklets. The citizens' initiatives are regarded as the forerunners of the citizens' movements founded in fall 1989 (see also **citizens' movements: GDR**).

Political scientists explain the emergence of citizens' initiatives in the GDR as a reaction to international conflicts (e.g. the arms race) and specific GDR problems like the destructive effects of the real-socialist form of industrialization and the lack of democracy under the **SED** dictatorship. Because of the SED's control of the public sphere the action groups were forced to work under the roof and protection of the Evangelical church, the only major organization independent of the state in the GDR (Catholics were a minority in the GDR). The activities of these groups caused not only conflicts with the state authorities and the **Stasi** but also with more conservative leaders of the Protestant church who were arguing for co-existence between state and church. Therefore some of the groups tried to loosen their ties to the church. During the reform period in the Soviet Union under Gorbachev, however, the action groups and part of the authorities of the Evangelical church improved their co-operation. In the

Ökumenische Versammlung für Frieden, Gerechtigkeit und Bewahrung der Schöpfung (Ecumenical Council for Peace, Justice and the Preservation of Creation) action groups and church authorities together called for fundamental reforms in the official politics of the GDR. According to theories about the peaceful revolution in 1989 the activities of citizens' initiatives were one important factor in the collapse of the SED dictatorship.

See also: peace movement: GDR; *Wende*

Further reading

Knabe, H. (1988) 'Neue soziale Bewegungen im Sozialismus: Zur Genesis alternativer politischer Orientierung in der DDR', *Kölner Zeitschrift für Soziologie und Sozialpsychologie* 40, 3: 551–69 (theoretical explanation of the evolution of citizens' initiatives in the GDR).

Pollack, D. (ed.) (1990) *Die Legitimität der Freiheit: Zur Rolle der politisch-alternativen Gruppen in der DDR*, Frankfurt am Main, Bern, New York and Paris: Peter Lang Verlag (basic essays for the study of citizens' initiatives in the GDR).

Woods, R. (1986) *Opposition in the GDR under Honecker 1971–85*, Houndmills, Basingstoke, Hampshire and London: Macmillan (description and documents of citizens' initiatives in the GDR).

LOTHAR PROBST

citizens' movements: GDR

Citizens' movements (*Bürgerbewegungen*) were founded throughout the summer and autumn of 1989 by groups of GDR citizens demanding democratic rights for the population including free elections. Most founding members came from the oppositional peace, environmental, and human rights movements that existed in the GDR despite the fact that opposition was not countenanced within a socialist state. Several groups had been sheltered by the Protestant church which lent them meeting rooms and the use of its printing facilities.

One of the main reasons for the emergence of the citizens' movements was the growing discontent with the leading role of the *Sozialistische*

Einheitspartei Deutschlands (**SED**); the last straw was the overt falsification of the local election results in May 1989. GDR citizens also wanted the right to travel freely; after the Hungarians opened their borders with Austria in September 1989 the flood of East Germans thus escaping to the West reached crisis proportions. At this, the ***Neues Forum*** (NF) published its founding paper, calling for dialogue between the people and the state to provide an alternative to mass emigration; this broad-based statement attracted more than 200,000 signatories in the first months – a scale of support unrivalled by any of the other movements.

The Initiative für Frieden und Menschenrechte (IFM), and **Demokratie Jetzt** (DJ) had their origins in the GDR human rights and church discussion groups. Other citizens' movements were the Sozialdemokratische Partei (SDP), **Demokratischer Aufbruch** (DA), the Vereinigte Linke (VL), the Unabhängiger Frauenverband (UFV), and the Grüne Partei der DDR (GP). Initially, all were agreed on democratizing and reforming the GDR, but, from December 1989, because of diverging views concerning unification, their unity began to crumble. All but the SDP and DA were against a quick unification, fearing that this would result in the effective annexation of their state.

Other subjects prompted diverging views, such as the transition towards a market economy, and the approach to organizational structure. For example, DA and DJ supported the former, rejected by the VL with its Marxist orientation; the disagreement on organizational structure revolved around the movement versus party debate. The SDP and the GP were clear from the outset, choosing the party structure and eventual fusion with their West German counterparts. DA, having started as a movement, soon constituted itself as a party, and was ultimately absorbed into the West German **CDU**. The IFM, the NF, and DJ formed the electoral alliance, **Bündnis** 90, in January 1990, prior to the March elections to the **Volkskammer**; the party Bündnis 90 was founded in September 1991, and merged with the Green Party in January 1993, creating Bündnis 90/Die Grünen. The rest remained loyal to their original ethos and continue to exist in their own right.

See also: dissent and opposition: GDR; *Wende*

Further reading

Dennis, M. (1993) 'The Vanishing Opposition; the Decline of the East German Citizens' Movements', in S. Padgett (ed.), *Parties and Party Systems in the New Germany*, Aldershot: Dartmouth Press.

Müller-Enbergs, H., Schulz, M. and Wielgohs, J. (1992) *Von der Illegalität ins Parlament: Werdegang und Konzept der neuen Bürgerbewegungen*, Berlin: Christoph Links Verlag (literature on the subject is mainly in German).

BEATRICE HARPER

civil rights

The first nineteen Articles of the constitution of the FRG contain an explicit catalogue of basic rights (*Grundrechte*) (see also **constitution: FRG**), some of which, like the protection of human dignity, equality before the law, and freedom of expression, are general human rights; others, like the freedom to choose an occupation or the freedom of association, are exclusive to German citizens. Fierce debate in recent years has focused around restriction of the right to asylum (see also **asylum, political**), introduced in 1993, and the view of the **Federal Constitutional Court** that the right to life must extend to the unborn child, thus impeding a liberalization of the **abortion law**.

MONIKA PRÜTZEL-THOMAS

class

Class is no longer the social marker that it was in the past in Germany. The levelling effect of WWII and the wealth created by the **'Economic Miracle'**, together with the importation of foreign labour to service the more menial jobs, has led to claims that Germany is now a *nivellierte Gesellschaft* (a classless or semi-classless society) and that there is such a degree of free-and-easy mixing between the classes that it is now virtually impossible to use the marker of class as a distinguishing feature of contemporary German society. Certainly in socio-economic terms the quantitative statistics suggest that wealth is reasonably evenly distributed among Germans and that the majority belong to an affluent middle class. There is certainly no real 'establishment' in German society servicing the wealthy members of the élite in the way that Oxford, Cambridge and the schools of the 'independent' sector are seen to do in Britain. Social distinctions are created along lines of education rather than necessarily along the lines of class. The education system (FRG) encourages the streaming of pupils and only some schools feed into the universities thus creating a significant educated class (see also **education system: FRG**), with the capital of education to spend both in their quest for professional employment and in their leisure time. The training given in apprenticeships also creates a skilled and educated workforce.

However, although the class system appears to have levelled itself out in Germany in socio-economic terms this is not necessarily the case in terms of attitude. Skilled workers, although middle class in terms of their income and their standing in society, still behave along the conservative lines which distinguish them from the middle classes. There is still a degree of suspicion of those with university education expressed in groups dominated by non-university educated people. The homogenization of gender roles in the younger middle classes is not as far developed in this group. Space among this artisan class is also defined along gender lines. Racism and sexism are further features of the differing class attitudes, although these attitudes are also more prevalent among the older generation. None of these aspects suggest quite the 'free-and-easy' mixing of a classless society. The struggle for hegemony, for power and authority, is another feature found particularly in *Vereine* dominated by the artisan class which does not suggest the achievement of classlessness in Germany.

The outward appearance of the classes may have changed, but the values still appear to be intact. This is also demonstrated in the strong sense of community, loyalty and a sense of place expressed by the artisan classes. These are characteristics of the working and artisan classes, more than of the middle classes. The fragmentation of society and the rapid changes brought about by advances in technology have changed the face of society but also served to strengthen bonds of community through the very threat imposed. The disintegration of the class structures and the homogenization of society are not, therefore, perhaps as far progressed as socio-economic research may suggest.

See also: sociology; *Verein*

Further reading

Claessens, D., Klönne, A. and Tschoepe, A. (1978) *Sozialkunde der Bundesrepublik*, Düsseldorf and Cologne: Diederichs (an introduction to the notion of Germany as a classless society).

ALISON PHIPPS

Clever, Edith

b. 13 December 1940, Wuppertal

Actress

Engaged by theatres across Germany, and a member of the Berlin Schaubühne since 1970, Edith Clever has played leading roles in productions directed by Peter **Stein**, Peter Zadek and Claus **Peymann**. Renowned for her elegant detachment and emotional intensity, she has starred on screen in Eric Rohmer's adaptation of Kleist's *The Marquise of O* (*Die Marquise von O*) and *The Left-handed Woman* (*Die linkshändige Frau*) by Peter **Handke**. She began a long collaboration with filmmaker Hans Jürgen **Syberberg** through playing Kundry in *Parsifal*, and became the sole actress in his stage productions and film monologues from 1984 to 1995.

HELEN HUGHES

Cohn-Bendit, Daniel

b. 4 April 1945, Montauban (France)

Politician

A son of German-Jewish parents who emigrated to France during the Third Reich, Cohn-Bendit attended school in Germany, and then returned to France in 1965 in order to study Sociology at the University of Nanterre. He became a leader of the student revolt in France (May 1968), and was then expelled from the country. Continuing his political activities in the anarcho-Marxist *Sponti* scene in Frankfurt, he joined the **Greens** in 1984, supporting their 'Realo'-wing. Cohn-Bendit is editor of the leftist intellectual magazine *Pflasterstrand*, and has been spokesperson for multicultural issues in the Frankfurt City Council since 1989 and Green member of the European Parliament since 1994.

INGOLFUR BLÜHDORN

comics

Comic strips and comic books have become an established sector of mass communication and a significant component of everyday culture. While several publishers (e.g. Ehapa, Carlsen and Moewig) license and print many of the well-known international characters in Germany, a limited number of medium-sized (e.g Alpha and Krüger) and small presses also contribute to a lively and constantly-changing regional scene in urban areas. Despite the similar historical traditions of **caricatures, satires** and comic genres, the social acceptance of comics only evolved gradually during the post-war decades.

The cultural debate over comics was particularly pronounced during the 1950s. Critics dismissed them as *Schmutz- und Schundliteratur* (trashy or filthy literature), claiming that they lacked any link to 'serious' narrative literature. At best, they begrudgingly recognized series such as *Fix und Foxi* (by Rolf Kauka) – a modernized version of Wilhelm Busch's *Max und Moritz*. However comic proponents (primarily children and young adults) rejected the repetition of the same old stories and characters disguised in new clothes. They wanted new heroes from a new world of comics: *Micky Mouse, Superman* and *Batman*.

By the 1960s comics achieved greater legitimacy as they gained popularity among adults. This success was largely due to series such as the French best-seller *Asterix und Obelix* by Réne Goscinny and Albert Uderzo and was also a result of comics' reception among young intellectuals who empha-sized the ideological contents of comics – particularly Disney's *Donald Duck* and his 'capitalist' relative *Uncle Scrooge McDuck*. Meanwhile, underground cartoonists expanded the spectrum for sophisticated, adult comics through erotic, artistic and experimental treatments. The visual and political provocations of 1960s music and pop art (e.g. Heinz Edelmann's art for The Beatles' *Yellow Submarine*) reinforced the aesthetic and social impact of comics.

The commercial success of comics in the 1970s represented a growth market for both large and small publishers. German newspapers and magazines recognized the power of syndicated strips, like *Hägar, Familie Feuerstein* (*The Flintstones*), and *Die Peanuts*, to 'hook' readers. Comic book publishers also relied on the popularity of international characters (e.g. *Superman*). The 1980s marked a further diversification of comic formats and audiences. Book stores sold expensive, glossy hardcover editions, characters were marketed for German television series and animated films, comic exhibits appeared in museums, and universities offered comics seminars.

Contemporary comics function simultaneously as a mass medium and a specialized medium for youth subcultures. Although many publishers rely on well-known international comics, some have been successful in niche markets (erotic, humour, science fiction and fantasy) and in promoting the rare best-selling German cartoonist (e.g. Rötger Feldmann 'Brösel', Ralf König and Mathias Schultheiß). Merchandising comic characters (e.g. toys, caps, T-shirts, mugs) is a significant economic factor in the German market and has contributed to a further commercialization of comics.

Further reading

Dolle-Weinkauff, B. (1990) *Comics. Geschichte einer populären Literaturform in Deutschland seit 1945*, Weinheim: Beltz (good historical survey of German comics).

BURKARD HORNUNG AND MARK W. RECTANUS

computers

In the early 1980s computers began to appear in the German shops, mostly as high-tech substitutes for typewriters. This limited usage changed very quickly, and it was especially the young who began to use them as game machines. After the success of Atari games and consoles, computers offered newer and more interactive facilities. With that, the dual role of computers, as buttoned-down business tools and entertainment instruments, had been established. Furthermore, by 1990 a frequently embittered discussion, continuing from the 1980s and dealing with the belief that computers invariably take jobs away from humans, had been laid to rest. It had become accepted fact that they had probably helped to create many more new jobs than they had destroyed. These jobs can be found in many areas, be they computer aided design, manufacturing or distribution, the writing of software, hardware manufacturing, or the translation of programs into and from German.

It took until the early 1990s for the German public to discover the Internet. Just as had been the case with the early history of computing, a limiting factor for computers in Germany was their almost complete reliance on English as program(ming) language. At first it was therefore the young, who had had the most exposure to English at school, who 'surfed' the Internet. But following other examples, such as France (which had already gained experience with the Minitel network) and The Netherlands, many started to realize that the Internet had the capacity to revolutionize German communicative practices. Internet computers began to appear in clubs as well as in schools, Internet cafes opened, and chat-rooms and MUDs (multi-user dungeons) were established.

While the dominant language in computing and on the Internet continues to be English, other languages have begun to make headway; German is certainly among them. And the ever wider distribution of German web-sites has fuelled the appearance of well-accepted and popular local web-pages, sometimes sponsored by local mass media, but more often put together by individuals. Cities began to create their own web-page networks, and it is now possible to read many local newspapers on the Internet, to find out what's on television in the evening, what kind of gigs are on offer for a region, when what films are showing, and to make a date with friends from a chat-room for later on in the day.

Other information is also available. The German government has created many web-pages, and universities and their researchers, who had been the original addressees of the Internet, are making productive and extensive use of the medium.

But Germany has also been in the forefront of more contentious issues, and here especially the attempt to censor Internet content. In 1995 the Bavarian government forced CompuServe, the American Internet provider, to block access to some of its members' pages, because of what was deemed to be pornographic content. While the fight against pornography on the Internet is a worldwide concern, it was the heavy-handed approach of a conservative German state government which produced a global outcry of 'censorship!' on the Internet.

But it was not only some of the recreational usage of the Internet that worried some German politicians. In 1996 yet another provider was threatened with legal action if it did not close a web-page containing pro-*RAF* (*Rote Armee Fraktion*, the largest German terrorist organization in the 1970s) statements in the periodical *Radikal*. Fearing prosecution, the provider complied. However, the international Internet community was quick to act, and within days mirror sites carrying these statements had been established outside of Germany and German jurisdiction. Similar altercations have also taken place in regard to neo-Nazi material on the Internet.

These examples of attempted Internet censorship serve to demonstrate some very important points regarding the Internet. The first, and most obvious, is that the Internet is a global, decentralized network, which refuses to be regulated by national interests. Hence, it questions the nation state and its powers. While the notion of a 'German' Internet has validity in regard to the language used on particular web-pages, this notion does not extend into actual locations. And, indeed, many 'German' web-sites are maintained in America or the UK, locations where German jurisdiction is weak at best or completely non-existent. Of course, this is not only a German problem, but one which addresses all governments.

Second, the Internet has begun to fulfil the multimedia promise made by television. Being a digital technology, all information produced, distributed, and received is in the same code, irrespective of what that information is: picture, sound, text. This has repercussions for these individual media. Just as radio to some extent took over from newspapers, and was itself superseded by television, the computer is a new media plateau, but with the difference that it can combine and simultaneously display all media functions and also add a few others, such as e-mail. What remains to be seen is how the other, older media will arrange themselves with and on the computer. Already in television, the visual had overtaken the written text as the main mode of 'infotainment' and this development might continue with computers. In any case, in Germany the sale of computers is growing at a staggering rate and computers are poised to outsell televisions in the near future.

Last, while in America the right to free speech is the leading argument against censorship, Germany, due to its recent history, is loathe to follow this argument all the way. What is of more concern to many Germans, and perhaps this is still one of the greatest worries in regard to computers, is the possible loss of privacy. The computer's ability to gather information about people's private lives, (shopping) preferences and official records has created a potentially dangerous situation. It is already becoming clear that the fight for secure 'inter-faces' will probably define and dominate many of the technological discussions and developments of the next decades, not only in Germany but worldwide.

See also: censorship: FRG; mass media: FRG

Further reading

Faulstisch, W. (1994) *Grundwissen Medien*, Munich: Fink (overview of media history and the development of single media with a chapter on computers).

Mersch, D. (ed.) (1989) *Computer, Kultur, Geschichte. Beiträge zur Philosophie des Informationszeitalters*, Vienna: Passagen (essays presenting an overview

of historic media modalities and their philosophies with the computer in mind).

HOLGER BRIEL

concert halls

In Germany today there are approximately 121 government-subsidized opera houses and concert halls and 146 professional orchestras, as well as more than 700 music schools, hundreds of **music festivals**, music libraries, music councils and other musical organizations. Promotion of music occurs in the context of foreign cultural policy, public music archives, museums and musical memorials, and at resorts, colleges of music, and training centres for musical professions. The infrastructure of musical culture is therefore generally very impressive, especially in comparison with foreign countries. The concert hall and **opera** house has traditionally been associated with the classical music tradition and with world renowned **orchestras** such as the Berlin Philharmonic, the Munich Philharmonic and the Leipzig Gewandhaus Orchestras, and several radio symphony orchestras. The concert hall and opera house have gradually evolved from private institutions of courtly life to public cultural buildings.

In the years immediately following 1945, there were at first few intact theatres, concert halls, teaching institutions or other public buildings, as a result of wartime destruction. But very soon the individual German *Länder*, communities, and private patrons began to convert their concepts of music and the transmission of music into architectural form. The modern concert hall, in architectual terms, usually has a rectangular outline, but often a trapezoid, or calculated curves are used around the podium. The audience is usually seated in rising circles. The sound is directed with movable reflectors and the ceilings and walls are usually covered with special acoustically designed materials. Nevertheless, the reconstruction of historic buildings is still very prominent, as the chance for a fundamentally new design drawing on different social conditions or new acoustic discoveries is scarcely ever exploited. Therefore the proscenium stages once again appeared with tiers of box and balcony seats in the auditorium. Only the technical facilities on and behind the stage, as well as building materials, colour schemes, and formal decor were modernized to meet contemporary standards. The few German exceptions to the traditional, modernized concert hall are the Neues Gewandhaus in Leipzig, which includes both large and small concert halls, and the circular tiers of the new Philharmonie in the Berlin Tiergarten, designed by Hans **Scharoun**.

With the recent architectural trend of building cultural centres, which combine spaces given to theatre, orchestras, opera and ballet, the concert hall has been incorporated into massive structures such as the concert and congress centre Alte Oper in Frankfurt am Main, the Philharmonie in Cologne and the Gasteig in Munich.

BETTINA BROCKERHOFF-MACDONALD

constitution: FRG

In May 1949 the parliaments of the *Länder* in the western parts of Germany accepted the Basic Law (*Grundgesetz*) as a provisional constitutional framework for the Federal Republic of Germany, founded on 23 May 1949. This document was to lose its validity on the day that a unified German people could freely determine a new constitution. However, despite its transitory name, the Basic Law came to be a widely respected constitution, an important symbol of national pride (*Verfassungspatriotismus*) in a state with an otherwise underdeveloped sense of national identity. Therefore, when, after forty-one years, unification finally happened on 3 October 1990, only a few articles were changed to accommodate the merger of the two Germanies; the name *Grundgesetz* was kept.

The Basic Law was drafted by 65 representatives of the *Länder*, the so-called Parliamentary Council (Parlamentarischer Rat), between September 1948 and May 1949 and accepted in its final version on 8 May 1949; only Bavaria voted against it.

The Basic Law provides two sets of rights: a bill of **civil rights** (Articles 1–19, 103 and 104) protecting the individual from arbitrary encroachment by the state, and, second, the organizational framework for the state, regulating the rights of the various governmental organs and their relationship to each other. It is highest ranking in the hierarchy of German statutes and its rules are binding for all ensuing legislation and government and court decisions. The main irrevocable principles on which the state is built are laid down in Article 20. It requires the FRG to be a democratic and federal state with social commitment (*Sozialstaat*) whose institutions are bound by and respect the rule of law (*Rechtsstaat*). A further requirement is the separation of powers into the legislature, the executive and the judiciary.

As laid down in Article 79,3, the principles in the first twenty Articles of the Basic Law are exempt from substantive changes even by act of parliament. Changes to the remaining articles are possible but require a difficult-to-achieve two-thirds majority in both legislative chambers. The explanation for this inflexible set of rules lies in the experience of the Nazi dictatorship. The Basic Law was a conscious attempt to avoid the perceived shortcomings of the Weimar constitution, which had allowed Hitler's rise to power, and to establish once and for all a stable democracy in West Germany, where individual citizens would be safe from state persecution.

The ensuing representative, liberal democracy allows virtually no direct involvement of the people in the process of political decision-making. Unlike in most western democracies there are no provisions for a referendum on federal level. Calls for more direct democracy, mainly from the left, regained momentum during the unification process through demands for a completely new constitution sanctioned by the German people or, failing that, far-reaching constitutional reform; but neither happened.

See also: civil rights; Federal Constitutional Court; legal system: FRG

Further reading

Foster, N. (1996) *German Legal System and Laws*, London: Blackstone (a concise account).
Starck, C. (ed.) (1991) *New Challenges to the German*

Basic Law, Baden-Baden: Nomos Verlag (an in-depth treatment).

MONIKA PRÜTZEL-THOMAS

constitutions: GDR

The GDR's first constitution was adopted in 1949 when the state was founded. It combined the **SED**'s socialist aspirations with features of the Weimar Constitution of 1919. Germany was still envisaged as a unitary and democratic republic when the constitution was first drafted in September 1946. It defined the limits of state authority and contained a catalogue of liberal democratic basic rights including the right to strike and to emigrate. This constitution was a compromise which potentially allowed development either towards a socialist state or a western-type, all-German republic. However, the absence of an independent constitutional court limited the real legislative power of this constitution quite significantly.

During the following two decades some developments took place: the traditional five *Länder* (states) were replaced in 1952 by a system of fifteen regional *Bezirke* (administrative units) (see also **Bezirk (GDR)**); military service was introduced in 1955 and made compulsory seven years later; in 1960 – on the death of Wilhelm **Pieck** – the office of president was abolished in favour of a Council of State; and a new law on a separate GDR citizenship clashed with the 1949 constitution's proclamation of a common German citizenship. Thus, changes in society and politics made constitutional changes necessary.

After intense public discussions a new constitution came into force in April 1968. Greater emphasis was now placed on the notion of the GDR as a 'socialist state of the German nation'. The political hegemony of the ruling party was laid down, as well as the main principles of 'socialist democracy' – such as the right to work, democratic centralism, a planned economy and equality between men and women. The right to strike and the right to emigrate both disappeared; and although basic rights like freedom of speech and assembly, as well as freedom of conscience and belief, could be found in the constitution, they were heavily circumscribed and the granting of these rights was to a large extent a matter of interpretation.

Following the consolidation of the GDR as a separate East German state in the early 1970s – during which period the Basic Treaty with the Federal Republic was signed and the relationship between the two parts of Germany changed fundamentally – Erich **Honecker** announced in September 1974 that it was necessary to amend the constitution. Hostile references to West Germany were eradicated from the constitution, and those identifying the GDR as a German nation state were also removed. The ties with the Soviet Union were tightened with the GDR now described as a 'socialist state of workers and peasants' under 'the leadership of the working class and its Marxist–Leninist party'.

The latter phrase was removed in December 1989, even before the eventual total collapse of the GDR. Other changes – which would allow private investment and foster joint ventures with the West – were introduced by the *Volkskammer* (GDR parliament). However, it soon became obvious that these modest improvements to the existing constitution would not be enough to keep up with the impetus of democratic change. Therefore the newly established **Round Table** agreed to draft a new constitution for the GDR which simultaneously was intended to provide a template for a future all-German constitution or an improved Basic Law. Yet the pace of unification defeated this process, and the two states became one under the West German Basic Law.

See also: constitution: FRG

Further reading

Childs, D. (1985) *Honecker's Germany,* London: Allen & Unwin (includes a comprehensive chapter on the East German constitution).

Glaessner, G.-J. (1992) *The Unification Process in Germany. From Dictatorship to Democracy,* London: Pinter (contains a detailed account of the controversies surrounding the post-*Wende* constitution of East Germany).

ASTRID HERHOFFER

Coop Himmelblau

This architectural partnership was established in Vienna in 1968 by Wolfgang D. Prix, Helmut Swiczinsky and R.M. Holzer (who left in 1971).

Under **Hollein**'s influence, Coop Himmelblau created inflatable pneumatic apparatuses, designed to lead away from what Alexander **Mitscherlich** titled 'the unreality of cities' (see also **town planning**). In the 1970s they became known through performances, creating burning objects in reaction against the ordered postmodern style. They became one of the most prominent European exponents of deconstructivist architecture, developing new designing methods (often coincidental, e.g. with half-closed eyes). The best known construction amongst their small building œuvre is the roof extension in Falkenstraße, Vienna (1984–9).

MARTIN KUDLEK

Costard, Hellmuth

b. 1 November 1940, Holzhausen

Filmmaker and inventor

Costard began filmmaking in 1964 whilst studying psychology in Hamburg. His early short films combining formal experimentation and comic elements owe a debt to the *nouvelle vague* and, after 1967, New American Cinema. *Of Special Merit* (*Besonders wertvoll*, 1968), a savage attack on film funding, became a *cause célèbre* and was banned at the Oberhausen Short Film Festival. During the 1970s and 1980s he developed unorthodox cinematographic techniques employing multiple cameras, Super-8 systems and time-coding. *Real Time* (*Echtzeit*, 1983), co-directed by Jürgen Ebert, is an innovative 'docu-fiction' essay on computer technology.

See also: film, experimental

MARTIN BRADY

Cremer, Fritz

b. 22 October 1906, Arnsberg (Ruhr); d. 1 September 1993, Berlin

Sculptor and graphic artist

After captivity Cremer worked in Austria and then settled in the GDR in 1950. His artistic work was influenced by his political position as a former member of the Communist Party. He was commissioned for public monuments such as the Buchenwald memorial (1952–8). His work comprised portraits, statues, reliefs, drawings and prints. With his symbolic realism he substantially contributed to the development of GDR **sculpture**. He also illustrated books. From 1974 onwards, he was the Vice-President of the Academy of Arts of the GDR (see also **academies**).

KERSTIN MEY

Critical Theory

According to its founder, Max **Horkheimer**, Critical Theory, with its emphasis on social change and individual self-determination, should be understood as a variant on traditional theories. Within German **philosophy** the **Frankfurt School**, with which Critical Theory is to all intents and purposes synonymous, represents the most thorough critique of **modernism**. Concerned with general human emancipation, its desire is to define man as a self-reflective subject, ready to change an apparently unalterable objective world whilst still adhering to inalienable truth concepts. Interdisciplinary in nature, it has its base in philosophy and, having Marxist origins, is primarily concerned with sociological issues, while also being indebted to Freudian psychology, art, music and the natural sciences.

Horkheimer defined his 'social philosophy' as covering all aspects of human life: state, law, economics, religion and the totality of man's intellectual and material civilization (see also **churches and religion**). The individual is perceived as a rational subject to whom 'the facts, as they emerge from the activity of society, are not extrinsic' (Horkheimer 1937: 264) but can be altered to correct the abuses of capitalism. It shares with **Marxism** a search for 'the right kind of society' which can overcome the categories of class, exploitation, surplus value, profit, etc. Despite their aim of transforming the present unjust capitalist society into a just one, representatives of Critical Theory are less optimistic than Marxists. In particular, they refute the revolutionary potential as the key to such a transformation and remain sceptical of the role of a proletariat, which is the victim of false continuities, corrupted by capitalist ideology. Never developing a homogeneous system or intrinsic methodology, their predominant form of publication was the essay or some other open form of communication. Whilst striving to avoid an exclusively theoretical and speculative approach through empirical studies and factual data, Horkheimer was, in the last analysis, opposed to positivist methods or purely empirical analysis 'as though it were grounded in the nature of knowledge as such or justified in some other ahistorical way' (Horkheimer 1972: 194). Along with many representatives of modernity, they took a normative approach in their search for basic values and some new metaphysical totality which might serve to reconcile Hegelian and Schopenhauerian ideas. Wary of liberalist individualism, they advocated a rational society where the critical individual would recognize the historically and socially conditioned state of present-day society.

Horkheimer was influenced by German philosophy, especially Kant, Hegel, Schopenhauer and Kierkegaard. Contemporary influences came in the work of Karl Mannheim, the new sociological school of Max Weber, and the new discipline of psychoanalysis. Almost inextricably associated with Horkheimer is **Adorno**, though more orientated towards philosophy and aesthetics than sociology. Herbert **Marcuse**, the third representative, and slightly more of an optimist, emphasized a new revolutionary capability which might release man's libidinous potential from one-dimensional repression. **Benjamin** is sometimes associated with Critical Theory, but this rests on little more than a common Jewish background, Nazi persecution, and an interest in aesthetics. Apart from Marcuse, who adapted more easily to American exile, and Adorno's aesthetics, Critical Theory failed to penetrate intellectual circles outside Germany, despite a brief spell of popularity during the late

1960s. With the school's demise in the early 1970s, its influence began to wane and only **Habermas** and possibly Albrecht Wellmer continue aspects of its work.

The school's development falls into an early formative period during the 1930s, American exile during the 1940s, and the return to Germany in the late 1950s. During its formative stage its main thrust was directed against late capitalism, seen from a modified, intellectual Marxist viewpoint. A decisive change occurred with the triumph of National Socialism and the contamination of Marxist philosophy by Soviet Bolshevism. Fascism was perceived as the natural and logical continuation of capitalism in a state of permanent crisis, its totalitarian order representing an even more inhuman system. The roots of fascism were located in the authoritarian features of German society, particularly its family structure. *The Authoritarian Personality* (1950) was the response of Adorno and Horkheimer to the threat of international fascism.

Critical Theory's middle period began with the *Dialectic of Enlightenment* (1947), a critique of the modern search for knowledge which, while promising enlightenment and freedom, failed to recognize the dialectical downside: domination, barbarism and the transformation of reason into myth. Hope for the development of a 'rational society' was abandoned in despair over an irredeemable western civilization that had descended into a new form of barbarism: 'The course of irresistible progress is irresistible regression' (Horkheimer and Adorno 1947: 8). The dialectic progression proclaimed by Hegel and Marx is rendered in negative terms as the reversal of enlightened rationality into myth. The vision of a totally managed society is understood as the continuation of fascism in a *de facto* post-fascist world. Modern mass media are just one example of such a comprehensive deception of the masses, exemplifying the all-pervasive authoritarian character.

Returning to Germany, a final phase began with the major input from Adorno. Philosophical totality became a central concept, developing a mystical and mythological faculty, abandoning Marxism altogether and rejecting any form of positivism and academic compartmentalization. Their negative dialectics no longer accepted Hegelian reconciliation. Similarly, totality is no longer conceived in positive terms as an affirmative category. Capitalism is seen as self-perpetuating, demonstrating immense technical and scientific potential, with the total *Vergesellschaftung* (instrumental socialization) of the individual. The reality of the **Holocaust** and the collapse of Marxism turned history into a 'progress towards hell': the just society failed to develop. Adorno withdrew into aesthetics and Horkheimer into religious mysticism, while the Theory became increasingly more pessimistic and escapist.

Major works

Adorno, T.W. (1961) *Minima Moralia. Reflexionen aus dem beschädigten Leben*, Frankfurt am Main: Suhrkamp.

Horkheimer, M. (1937) 'Traditionelle und kritische Theorie', *Zeitschrift für Sozialforschung* 6, 2: 264.

—— (1972) *Critical Theory*, New York: Herder & Herder.

—— (1981) *Sozialphilosophische Studien*, Frankfurt am Main: Fischer.

Horkheimer, M. and Adorno, T.W. (1947) *Dialektik der Aufklärung*, Amsterdam: Querido Verlag.

Further reading

Arato, A. and Gebhardt, E. (eds) (1978) *The Essential Frankfurt School Reader*, New York and Oxford: Urizen Books and Basil Blackwell (English versions of representative texts).

Couzens Hoy, D. and McCarthy, T. (1994) *Critical Theory*, Oxford: Blackwell (a postmodern assessment).

Jay, M. (1973) *The Dialectical Imagination. A History of the Frankfurt School and the Institute of Social Research 1923–50*, London: Heinemann (detailed history).

Zoltán, T. (1977) *The Frankfurt School. The Critical Theories of Max Horkheimer and Theodor W. Adorno*, New York: John Wiley & Sons (an excellent survey).

HANS J. HAHN

CSU

The Christlich Soziale Union (CSU) was founded in 1945 as a regional party for Bavaria, linked with but distinctly separated from the **CDU**. The special relationship entailed that the CDU did not set up a regional organization in Bavaria while the CSU confined itself to Bavaria. It also meant that CDU and CSU co-operated in the Bundestag as members of the same parliamentary party (although the CSU also maintained a so called *Landesgruppe*, a regional representation of its own), and several ministers in CDU-led governments have always come from the CSU. The CSU enjoys the unique position of a political party with an established political role at the national and government level, but an exclusively regional electoral and organizational base.

The exceptional role of the CSU as a regional party with a national role depends on the collaboration with the CDU, but would not have developed without some specifically Bavarian factors. When it was founded in 1945, the CSU faced a dual challenge: on the one hand, the party needed to secure the support of a predominantly Catholic, agrarian electorate with traditional leanings towards Bavarian separatism; on the other hand the party needed to spearhead social and economic modernization and secure a voice in the emergent Federal Republic. Until 1948, the CSU seemed set for regional dominance; after 1948, it lost half its electorate to the Bavarian Party (BHE) which pursued a stridently Catholic and Bavarian course and even helped displace the CSU from the Bavarian government in 1954 in a four-party coalition with SPD, FDP, and the expellees' party BHE.

By the mid-1950s however, Bavaria had begun to undergo a rapid transformation from an agrarian to an industrial society, eroding traditional political milieus and creating new patterns of mobility. The CSU managed to reap the political benefit of economic and social modernization through developing an extensive organizational net and through a dual focus on tradition and progress (*Tradition und Fortschritt*), a blend of farming interest, Bavarian culture, and hi-tech and intensive industrialization. From 1957 to 1998, the CSU enjoyed an absolute majority among the Bavarian electorate and constituted the Bavarian regional government, while the **SPD** remained below 30 percent.

CSU conservatism has been more distinctly right-wing (and Catholic) than that of the CDU. During his time as party leader, F.J. Strauß in particular was vilified by the far left and revered by the far right for his politics; some credited the CSU with integrating the extreme right into mainstream politics while their opponents accused the CSU of giving **neo-nazi**-style ideas parliamentary respectability and of shifting the German party system itself towards the right. The right-wing profile of the CSU appears to render the party largely unelectable outside Bavaria but constitutes its special strength in the region. Until unification, the CSU absolute majority in Bavaria translated into over 10 percent of the West German vote; after unification, the CSU absolute majority amounted to no more than 7 percent. The enlargement of Germany reduced the weight of the region and with it the potential role of the CSU outside Bavaria in German politics and political culture.

EVA KOLINSKY

cultural policy: FRG

The effects of cultural policy in Germany

Patronage of the arts was historically significant in Germany and continues to have a high value in contemporary German culture. Cultural policy is one of the many aspects of the federal system of government in Germany where power is devolved to the individual states. Each state is therefore responsible for the administration and implementation of cultural policy and education. Each town is also in possession of a degree of civic freedom which enables it to administer the finances for specific cultural events or for specific local festivals. For example, the city of Cologne spends at least a million DM of its cultural budget on the Cologne *Karneval*. In 1990 Baden-Württemberg had a DM 400 million budget to spend on culture. Consequently there is a fairly even spread of cultural institutions across Germany, giving rela-

tively easy access to an opera house, civic theatre or well-endowed museum. The funding of cultural institutions, has, however, also been a contentious issue and, whereas policy broadly supported the provision of 'high' culture for many years, this policy has been called into question and there has consequently been a policy shift in many states, embodying a more inclusive understanding of culture, and allowing for greater support of lay cultural activity, and an increased partnership between amateurs and professionals.

Subsidies are divided between the cultural institutions in each town: the theatres, museums, orchestras and concerts, dance and opera, music schools, adult education, local organizations (see also *Verein*), libraries and other cultural activities such as the Christmas lights and local festivals. According to statistics produced by **Inter Nationes** there are over 150 publicly funded theatres in Germany producing approximately 57,000 performances annually and attracting audiences totalling roughly 20 million, including the figures for the particularly popular spectacles of opera, ballet and musicals.

The depth of public support for the cultural policy and thus for German cultural institutions may be seen in the example of the planned closure of Berlin's Schillertheater in 1993 and the public outcry which led to a debate about the role of 'high' culture in German society. A clear link between crime and the arts was made by commentators and artists alike. Dennis Staunton, writing in *The Guardian* at the time of the closure of the Schillertheater wrote that if you wish to see what kind of society you will get if you stop subsidizing the arts you should look at Britain. Culture, in Germany, is seen as bringing both economic benefits in making a town attractive and social benefits in that it feeds the so-called cultural needs of capitalist society.

Public financing of culture and the arts in Germany is generous in comparison with Britain. Large cultural institutions such as theatres, opera houses, orchestras, museums etc., are financed by the federal state or by the town or city, or by both. Some of the independent theatres which are privately owned such as the Schaubühne in Berlin or the Lindenhof Theater in Melchingen and the **Naturtheater** in southern Germany are also dependent upon subsidy from the local town or from the state for their survival.

In spite of the high levels of subsidy for culture and the arts there is still a good deal of debate as to what constitutes worthwhile cultural activity. Lothar Schmidt-Mühlisch, a broadsheet journalist and noted theatre commentator, has questioned the continued high subsidies of the state theatres when their audiences have declined so substantially in recent years leaving the independent and lay theatres to absorb their audiences, producing high quality, often experimental theatre but theatre which does not alienate the audiences because it cannot afford to do so.

The debate over subsidies for the arts and the fact that much of the funding is seen to go to élite institutions and not therefore to benefit others directly has led both to some interesting experiments such as the pub theatres and bread-and-soup theatres of the 1970s designed to draw working-class people into the theatre. However, these experiments have for the most part been abandoned, and instead the focus has switched to projects aimed at initiating the young, in particular school children and youth groups into the arts.

In 1990 the total of museums in Germany was estimated to be approximately 3,900. The majority of these are heavily subsidized by the state. Some, however, are private initiatives, perhaps attached to a tourist attraction such as a large brewery and therefore serving commercial needs, or established by a history society keen to promote their local town. The number of visitors to museums in Germany has been estimated at 90 million; however, numbers are steadily in decline. Particularly popular are the *Freilichtmuseen* (open-air working museums) such as the Black Forest museum in Gutach. This is a large open-air, working museum attracting tourists in particular. It consists of several thatched buildings belonging to a typical Black Forest farmstead and it is laid out to represent the daily life of a rich farming family. On working days these open-air museums will be run by staff in traditional costume and involve working the water wheels and baking in the bread ovens, for example. The purpose of such a museum is broadly educational, but it also feeds into nostalgic desires and perceptions of a rural idyll in the past. The cultural policy also allows for the provision of live,

classical music, both in terms of the subsidy of around fifty orchestras, over 8,000 professional musicians and numerous concert halls, and in terms of the promotion of music education through school initiatives and through the funding of music schools of which there are over 1,000 in the whole of Germany. The network of music schools enables school children to take extra-curricular music lessons, and especially talented pupils may attend a music academy.

Further beneficiaries of cultural policy are the *Volkshochschulen*. These adult education institutions provide a variety of courses ranging from foreign languages and computing courses to pottery and woodwork. In 1993 it was estimated that 6.4 million people attended adult education courses in Germany and over 483,000 courses were run. The subsidies provided from the cultural budget are used to maintain the cost of these courses at a relatively low level. Town libraries benefit in a similar manner as do local *Vereine*. The *Vereine* enjoy tax benefits designed to help promote their activities and they therefore function in a similar way to registered charities in Britain, in terms of their economic status.

It can be seen from the extensive range of institutions affected by cultural policy and by the relative generous cultural budgets that the role of culture is of great significance in the ideological development of cultural citizenship in contemporary Germany.

Ideology and development of cultural policy

The formulation of cultural policy, as with any politically and economically motivated deliberations, is affected by the competing ideologies of the state apparatus and by the societal and cultural changes which affect policy decisions. Paradigmatic changes in German society have influenced cultural policy as much as power shifts between the dominant political parties. Influence on policy may be exerted from the grassroots, as in the case of the *Straßentheater* (street theatre) artists of the late 1960s and the 1970s, as well as from those with significant cultural power, such as the politicians and the intellectual 'élite'. The early twentieth century saw the rise of cultural institutions serving the working classes, the *Arbeitervereine* and *Arbei-*

tertheater (workers' clubs and theatres), for example, designed to educate working-class people in the works of literature. Culture began to be seen as politically necessary in feeding minds and spirits drained by the monotony of factory work and mass production practices. As machines replaced the hard, physical labour of the past the belief in the need to provide a balance with intellectual stimulation and entertainment became a significant part of the motivations behind the formulation of cultural policy. Culture was no longer a preserve of the élite, with indigenous folk culture and diverse **festivals and customs** serving a large rural population. The rise of mass literacy and mass education as well as the development of radio and later television networks and the mass media necessarily influenced the ideology of cultural policy. During the 1920s and 1930s the fear that mass popular culture would produce passive consumption and a disregard for the 'real' cultural institutions of the élite (see also **Frankfurt School**) resulted in cultural institutions becoming less of a preserve of the élite and more readily available to the middle and even lower classes, a process which has continued throughout the twentieth century. The ideology of cultural policy became inextricably bound up with a clear belief in the intrinsic value of 'high' culture against the evils of 'popular' culture and mass entertainment. Subsidies were available for the 'high' arts and not for other forms of cultural activity. In this way the desire to stimulate those bored by the monotony of mass production processes failed in its aim to reach working-class audiences.

In spite of a thriving alternative arts scene and the questioning of the ideology behind cultural policy (see also **alternative culture**), indeed the questioning of the whole concept of 'normal', 'élite', 'canonical' cultural provision as a desired end to cultural policy, the impulse for further changes to the regional cultural policies has been motivated essentially by changing working practices, which have seen a shift away from mass production and towards the development of service industry supporting the production and sale of goods within the capitalist system. Cultural policy in Germany now seeks to address the new working patterns and to provide culture which unashamedly serves the need, under the current technolo-gical consumer society, of business and industry for a highly motivated, well-trained interactive work force, capable of creative, contextual thought, team spirit, good communication and flexibility, and able to take responsibility for their own continued training and development. Mental stimulation is no longer seen as something provided solely by leisure activities but, for an increasing proportion of the work force, it is also a prerequisite of the work environment. At the same time the amount of leisure time available for cultural recreation has increased threefold in one generation and the population of Germany is ageing to such an extent that a policy of cultural provision for the third generation has also had to be formulated.

The aim of cultural and education policy is therefore one of enabling the development of balanced and well-rounded individuals who will interact responsibly, critically and creatively with their cultural environment and thus further serve the needs of a changing capitalist system. The *Kunstkonzeption des Landes Baden-Württemberg* (the cultural policy blueprint for Baden-Württemberg) written in partnership with several political ministries is introduced by the *Staatsrat für Kunst* (the state advisor for art) who states 'Wir brauchen Menschen mit kreativer Fantasie, die den Problemen der Gegenwart mit Zukunftsgerichteten Ideen begegnen' ('We need people with creative imaginations, who are able to confront the problems of the present with ideas focused on the future').

Contemporary cultural policy is based on plurality, subsidiarity, decentralization and freedom of expression designed to move away gradually from traditional concepts of art and culture and the provision of 'élite' culture for an 'élite' audience. A partnership between lay and professional cultural groups is deemed highly desirable, and the furtherance of the *Verein* structure in particular is seen as one of the best ways of creating differential, pluralistic cultural activity which responds both to the needs of the grassroots whilst continuing to support alternative and provocative art forms and their interaction with the political present. The failure of projects in the 1970s designed to bring art to the masses is to be addressed with a policy shift towards funding local community groups in their individual enterprises, with the aim of strengthening the links between art and community. Within this project the protection of monuments plays a significant role, in that it allows for the development of space for the purpose of cultural recreation.

Built into the rubric of current cultural policy is the principle of sponsorship by business, lottery revenue and the requirement of matched funding. This policy is designed to make cultural institutions more accountable and to further the skills through leisure activity which will be of benefit in the business world. However, it is seen as of primary importance in the formulation of cultural policy that art and culture (*Kunst und Kultur*) should in no way be instrumental either to business or to politics, and the criticism of both must be tolerated as a necessary and desirable function of art in society.

The value placed upon culture in an ever broader sense is reflected in the German constitution and in the aim of creating a *Kulturstaat*, a cultural state, as this further indicates the overall significance of cultural policy in contemporary German culture.

Further reading

Rettich, J. (1990) *Kunstkonzeption des Landes Baden Württemberg*, Freudenstadt: Verlag und Druck (a clear outline of cultural policy both in the FRG and in the federal state).

Schmidt-Mühlisch, L. (1992) *Affentheater:Bühnenkrise ohne Ende*, Frankfurt am Main: Ullstein Sachbuch (a scathing attack on the current policy of funding the state theatres).

ALISON PHIPPS

cultural policy: GDR

The **SED** regarded culture as an essential component of the GDR's socialist revolution, requiring like politics and the economy the party's firm control. Cultural policy was underpinned by a belief that the inevitable progress of human history towards communism is significantly influenced by what human beings themselves achieve in changing their own social conditions. Its major task was therefore that of nurturing a socialist consciousness among the population. However, the rapid disintegration of the GDR after the fall of the **Berlin Wall** in 1989 demonstrated the clear failure of cultural policy to achieve this central purpose.

In practice, culture was usually taken to refer to literature and the arts in general, which were perceived to have enormous political significance. For example, the statutes of the **Writers' Union of the GDR** (as revised in 1973) referred to writers as 'active co-shapers' of socialist society and echoed the fundamental purpose of all cultural policy: 'The members of the Writers' Union of the GDR take an active part in shaping the socialist present. Their art helps to form the thoughts, feelings and actions of the people constructing and completing socialism.' This helps to explain the heavy subsidization of culture in the GDR, as reflected in the remarkably low cost of books and records and of tickets to the theatre, opera, cinema, concerts and other cultural events. A cultural fund was built up by means of a modest levy on the charge for such goods. This was used to finance selected cultural projects and to improve the living and working conditions of writers and others in the arts. The same concern to guarantee the material security of creative intellectuals is reflected in the number of prizes available to them and in other ways too (e.g. generally large editions of books, generous royalties, and relatively high levels of payment for work in television, radio, and film). This has led to the charge that creative intellectuals were privileged and therefore corruptible. While this may be true of some, a significant number refused to harness their work to the requirements of ideology, and this led to a series of conflicts which punctuated the history of cultural policy in the GDR.

In the immediate post-war period, cultural policy emphasized the lessons to be learned from the Nazi period and sought to involve all intellectuals in the process of reconstruction while ensuring that communists occupied the key positions in the cultural sphere. Following the Soviet example, however, the SED took a firm grip on cultural policy in 1951 by setting up the Bureau for Literature and Publishing and the State Commission for Artistic Matters, followed one year later by the State Committee for Film and the State Committee for Radio. These organizations sought to mould the arts to the needs of the Five Year Plan and the increasingly confrontational Cold War with the West, promoting in the process the doctrine of **socialist realism** at the expense of modernism and attacking formalism, i.e. a perceived preoccupation with questions of form rather than socialist content. Inevitably, this dogmatic approach led to controversy. The first such case, in 1951, involved the opera *The Trial of Lucullus* (*Das Verhör des Lukullus*: music by Paul Dessau, text by Bertolt Brecht). Similarly, the libretto of Hanns Eisler's opera *Johann Faustus* provoked so much official opposition that the work was never completed. The DEFA film based on Arnold Zweig's novel *The Axe of Wandsbek* (*Das Beil von Wandsbek*) was withdrawn after its premiere, and an exhibition of Ernst Barlach's sculptures was prematurely terminated because of their alleged lack of optimism.

Such were the protests against the repressive policy associated with these organizations that (with the exception of the State Committee for Radio) they were soon closed down. Their functions were taken over by a new Ministry of Culture, founded on 7 January 1954 and headed until 1958 by the poet Johannes R. **Becher**. The dominant personality in cultural matters for over thirty years, however, was without doubt Kurt **Hager**, a leading member of the Politbüro and the Secretary for Science and Culture in the Central Committee of the SED (1955–November 1989). Among the organizations whose function was to promote the cultural policy for which the Ministry bore the major responsibility were the Academy of Arts (presided over by Arnold **Zweig** from 1950–2, Johannes R. Becher 1952–6, Otto Nagel 1956–62, Willi Bredel 1962–4, Konrad **Wolf** 1965–82, and Manfred **Wekwerth** 1982–9), and professional organizations such as the **Writers' Union of the GDR** (its presidents were Bodo Uhse from 1950–2, Anna **Seghers** 1952–78 and Hermann **Kant** 1978–89). A number of bodies were entrusted with the task of realizing the goals of cultural policy at local level. These included the Cultural Alliance for German Democratic Renewal (founded in 1945 and represented at all levels of government) and the Union of Free German Trade Unions with approximately 250,000 officials responsible for cultural activities at the shop-floor level.

Like other countries in the eastern bloc, the GDR experienced a cultural 'thaw' in the mid-1950s following Stalin's death, but after the Hungarian revolution in 1956 the Party quickly re-established tight controls. Initiated in 1959, the **Bitterfelder Weg** was intended to be a major turning-point in cultural policy. Its principal innovation was the determined attempt to give workers a creative role in the development of socialist culture: 'In state and economy the working class of the GDR is already master. Now it must also storm the heights of culture and take possession of them' (Walter Ulbricht). This was reflected in the oft-repeated motto of the conference: 'Reach for your pen, mate, the socialist national culture needs you!' Groups known as 'circles of writing workers' were set up at the workplace, often under the guidance of a full-time writer. Underlying this development, however, was the wish to strengthen the workers' ideological commitment and their contribution to economic efficiency. Their most characteristic products were documentary reports and diaries kept by small teams of workers, known as 'brigade diaries'. These were generally colourless and predictable, with workers presented either as heroes of labour or as individuals rescued from their inadequacies by the intervention of the collective. While the movement did promote an appreciation of literature among workers, it was recognized by the 1970s to have been a failure.

Although the building of the Berlin Wall in 1961 was followed by some relaxation of state control over culture, the **Eleventh Plenum** of the SED's Central Committee in December 1965 represented a renewed attempt to insist that culture's role was to reinforce a positive ideological message about socialism's inexorable progress. On this occasion public intimidation was used, with disastrous results. Countless writers, dramatists, filmmakers and beat musicians, as well as many in positions of responsibility in the Ministry of Culture, radio, and the Writers' Union, were accused of nihilism, anarchy, scepticism and pornography. Wolf **Biermann** and Stefan **Heym** were among those singled out for particular abuse, and films representing a year's work by **DEFA** were suppressed. The inevitable outcome of such heavy-handed tactics was a deep loss of faith in the party leadership among leading cultural figures.

A much-quoted announcement by Erich **Honecker**, Walter **Ulbricht**'s replacement as First Secretary of the SED in 1971, held out promise, at last, of a more enlightened cultural policy:

> If the starting point is the firm position of socialism, there can, in my opinion, be no taboos in the field of art and literature. This applies to questions both of content presentation and of style – in short: to the questions of what is called artistic excellence.

Texts which had previously been suppressed were now able to appear, including Volker **Braun**'s controversial work *Unfinished Story* (*Unvollendete Geschichte*), and above all Ulrich **Plenzdorf**'s *The New Sufferings of Young W.* (*Die neuen Leiden des jungen W.*), which enjoyed enormous public success both in the theatre and as a prose text. But in 1976 the party reverted to the use of force. Reiner **Kunze** was thrown out of the Writers' Union following publication in the West of his critical prose texts *The Wonderful Years* (*Die wunderbaren Jahre*), and Wolf Biermann was deprived of his citizenship and refused permission to return from a concert tour in the West. For a number of years cultural policy now became a war of attrition between the party and those cultural figures who remained in the GDR when so many of their colleagues were forced or chose to leave. In 1979, attempts to use the law as a means of discrediting Heym's unauthorized publications in the West led only to a defiant letter of protest from eight writers: 'We are against the arbitrary use of laws: problems in our cultural policy cannot be solved through criminal proceedings'. Nine members of the Berlin branch of the Writers' Union, including Heym, were subsequently deprived of their membership for what was seen as their defamation of the party's cultural policy. Despite the fact that over sixty members voted against this measure, changes were made to the Criminal Code which made it a prisonable offence to disseminate any information which might 'damage the interests of the German Democratic Republic'. This served only to increase the number of those writers leaving for the west, since 'to write in a state of fear is unacceptable' (Jurek Becker).

The impression of a failed cultural policy was confirmed by the party's seeming inability to act against the rise of an autonomous cultural scene in **Prenzlauer Berg** which openly declared its independence of official cultural policy. The discovery since the fall of the Berlin Wall that leading members of the scene were in fact agents of the *Stasi* suggested that the threat represented by Prenzlauer Berg had been more apparent than real. The same could not be said, in the mid-1980s, of Gorbachev's policy of 'new thinking', which encouraged an increasingly open challenge to the party's control mechanisms, a notable example being in 1987 Christoph Hein's courageous attack on censorship.

The destruction of the Berlin Wall led to the rapid abandonment of a discredited cultural policy. Works previously suppressed now appeared as a matter of urgency. The twelve feature films banned in 1965 were retrieved from the archives and made available for public showing. Those once forced to leave were now able to return, though they usually chose not to make the move permanent.

The Unification Treaty of 1990 stipulated in Article 35 (section 2) that, as part of post-unification cultural policy, no damage should be inflicted on 'the cultural substance' of the GDR. However, the disappearance of generous state subsidies and of the GDR's familiar cultural institutions as well as the sudden exposure to market forces led to fears, subsequently justified, that little of GDR culture would survive the demise of the state.

See also: censorship: GDR; dissent and opposition: GDR; film: GDR; Kulturbund

Further reading

Berger, M. *et al.* (eds) (1978) *Kulturpolitisches Wörterbuch*, 2nd edn, East Berlin: Dietz (a dictionary which reflects the official view of cultural policy).

Goodbody, A. *et al.* (1995) 'The Failed Socialist Experiment: Culture in the GDR', in R. Burns (ed.), *German Cultural Studies: An Introduction*, Oxford: Oxford University Press, pp. 147–207 (discusses the GDR's attempt to nurture a socialist culture, referring to the part played in this by cultural policy).

Jäger, M. (1995) *Kultur und Politik in der DDR 1945–90*, Cologne: Edition Deutschland Archiv (detailed account of the fraught relationship between culture and politics in the GDR).

Lübbe, P. (ed.) (1984) *Dokumente zur Kunst-, Literatur- und Kulturpolitik der SED 1975–80*, Stuttgart: Seewald (comprehensive collection of major documents from the GDR relating to cultural policy. Indispensable, like Rüß and Schubbe below).

Rüß, G. (ed.) (1976) *Dokumente zur Kunst-, Literatur- und Kulturpolitik der SED 1971–4*, Stuttgart: Seewald.

Schubbe, E. (ed.) (1972) *Dokumente zur Kunst-, Literatur- und Kulturpolitik der DDR*, Stuttgart: Seewald.

Wallace, I. (1992) 'The Failure of GDR Cultural Policy under Honecker', in G.-J. Glaeßner and I. Wallace (eds), *The German Revolution of 1989. Causes and Consequences*, Oxford and Providence, RI: Berg, pp. 100–23 (concentrates on the period 1971–90).

IAN WALLACE

cultural policy and institutions: Austria

Cultural policy and cultural institutions play a prominent role in Austria and they are often regarded as vehicles for supporting the identity of the country and for promoting tourism. Even though there is no separate Ministry of Culture the political responsibility for cultural affairs lies with a federal minister, thus giving high priority to cultural matters and the arts. Local authorities on various levels also pride themselves on cultural activities.

The situation of Austria in 1945 was marked by the tremendous difficulties the country had with its own past. It had lost the war and even though it was clear that the future would only lie in an independent Austrian state, the world still had to be convinced that Austria and Germany were to be differentiated from each other. The political strategy was to create a cultural identity on the basis of the achievements of the pre-war era in order to build a friendly image of Austria abroad and to convince the people at home of their identity. Austrian culture was vaguely defined as the German-speaking element of the former Hapsburg Empire. With the course of time this broad concept was narrowed down to the small state of Austria. Since the 1980s Austrian cultural policy has attempted to promote the concept of central Europe, which comprises the area and the cultures of the former Austro-Hungarian Empire (see also **Mitteleuropa**).

In the first few years after the war, hardly any new cultural initiatives were undertaken on a national basis. It took until 1950 before the first prizes and competitions were set up and became a pillar of cultural policy. Until today prizes of various categories (for young as well as for established artists) are regarded as an important source of income for creative artists. In addition, subsidies for specific projects, for travel expenses, for health insurance contributions and for scholarships provide artists with some financial support. Until the end of the 1960s a rather conservative strategy was in place, mainly funding those who were already well-known and well-established. With the shift of power from the conservative People's Party to the Social Democrats in 1970 a more modern view took over. Since then artists are also among the jurors who shortlist nominees and projects that are to be subsidized.

The major museums in the country are also funded and administered by the state. The federal museums, most of which are situated in Vienna, reflect the rich past of the Hapsburg Empire as well as that of today's Austria. Thus they have a much wider scope than the mere size of the present state suggests. Apart from famous collections of fine art, like the Museum of Fine Arts or the Albertina graphic arts collection, the imperial palaces in Vienna, Schönbrunn Castle and the Hofburg, are important showpieces of traditional cultural values.

Private funding and sponsoring schemes are less important than in other European countries. However, important private art collections like the Ludwig Collection of modern art, the Leopold Collection, which specializes in *Jugendstil* paintings, or the Essl Collection of contemporary Austrian art have gained wide acclaim.

Whereas the state runs the main theatres and opera houses in Vienna by means of the Bundestheaterverband (Federal Theatre Association) and thus dominates the **Burgtheater**, the Akademietheater, the Vienna Staatsoper, and the Volksoper, the theatres in the various *Bundesländer* are funded by local authorities. Among the well-established privately run theatres are the Theater in der Josefstadt (Vienna, founded in 1788), a theatre associated with Max Reinhardt, which retains a traditional approach to drama, and the Volkstheater (Vienna, established 1889 as a counterpart to the Burgtheater).

A few fringe theatres like the Schauspielhaus (Vienna, founded in 1979) or the Serapions Theater (Vienna, founded in 1972 as the Pupo-Drom) provide a lively alternative to the established traditions.

The Vienna Philharmonic Orchestra and the Vienna Boys' Choir are the musical symbols of Austria and are consequently often employed for tourist promotion schemes, especially in the Far East.

During the summer months various festivals dominate the scene, the most important of which are the Salzburg Festival, with internationally renowned concerts, opera performances and also theatrical productions, the Bregenz Festival, and the Mörbisch Festival of operettas. The Viennale, an international film festival, and the Vienna Festival (mainly international theatre, dance and opera productions) take place in the capital and underline the cultural importance of Vienna. The most important avant-garde events are the *steirischer herbst* (Styrian autumn) festival in Graz and the high-tech *Ars Electronica* in Linz.

Over the years the importance of culture as a means for achieving national identity has receded and at the same time cultural activities have become increasingly relevant as a selling point for tourism. A considerable number of local festivals mainly serve the purposes of the tourist industry.

It is a major pillar of the regulations which govern the state-run radio and television company **ORF** that cultural events are regularly represented in the programming schedules. In addition, the ORF produces and broadcasts educational pro-

grammes, which have proved to be an important element in teaching.

As a consequence of state influence, cultural matters play a major role in public life and it is the general view of the population that it is everybody's right to comment on and to have a pronounced view of cultural affairs. Ultimately, public interest, which is partly reinforced and sometimes directed by the media, creates pressures which very often undermine and jeopardize innovative developments.

Further reading

Bushell, A. (ed.) (1996) *Austria 1945–1955: Studies in Political and Cultural Re-emergence*, Cardiff: University of Wales Press.

Lauber, V. (ed.) (1996) *Contemporary Austrian Politics*, Boulder, CO and Oxford: Westview.

Sully, M.A. (1990) *A Contemporary History of Austria*, London: Routledge.

Wimmer, M. (1995) *Kulturpolitik in Österreich, Darstellung und Analyse, Innsbruck*, Vienna: Österreichischer Studien Verlag.

GEORG HELLMAYR

cultural policy and institutions: Switzerland

The complexity of the Swiss federal structure is nowhere more manifest than in the manner in which all forms of popular and formal culture are supported. Broadly speaking, there are four main sources from which patronage and financial support come: private individuals and organizations, the cantons, the communes, and the Confederation. Their contributions and competences interlock to sustain a rich variety of activity. Since 1992, it has been government policy that culture should be funded in the first instance by the private sector with support from the public sector, with the communes and the cantons having an obligation to fund prior to the Confederation.

The best-known private sponsor is the cultural section of the Migros food and services co-operative, which, since 1957, has devoted 1 percent of its turnover to supporting cultural matters. The huge funds thus made available – equal to the amount spent by the city of Zürich – support a wide range of activities. Approximately 40 percent of expenditure, for example, goes towards adult education. Clearly, Migros is in a special class because of the size of its income, but there are many banks, firms and family trusts which are well-known for their contributions towards culture. Landis & Gyr, for example, the electronics firm in Zug, owns property in Switzerland and abroad (as do many other similar institutions) for which those working in the creative arts can apply for a period of subsidized residence. Amongst the philanthropic trading and industrial families are the Reinhart family and the Bührle family who maintain world-class art galleries in Winterthur and Zürich respectively. There are many institutions which are not well-known and which refuse to disclose how they operate, but it was estimated in 1990 that the private sector accounted for one-sixth of the total amount spent on culture.

The Swiss constitution provides for a *Kulturhoheit der Kantone*, which means that the cantons are independent in cultural matters, including education. It is effectively the sub-divisions of the cantons, the communes – there are in total over 3,000, themselves enjoying a large degree of autonomy – which support culture in all its manifestations. More specifically in the matter of formal culture, the important cities in their capacity as communes bear more than half the cost of theatres, opera, ballet, etc., although they account for only about a quarter of the population of the country as a whole. They can also, by their size, sustain less permanent cultural manifestations and forms. Of the expenditure from the public purse on culture, just over 50 percent is accounted for by the communes and just under 40 percent by the cantons.

There is no provision in the Swiss constitution requiring the Confederation to support culture. In a country suspicious of central government, a referendum on 29 September 1986 and another on 12 June 1994, both seeking to oblige the government to spend 1 percent of its expediture on culture, were defeated. In fact, the Confederation supports culture mainly in two ways. First, there is, in the Swiss Interior Ministry, the *Bundesamt für Kultur* (the Federal Office of Culture), which was established in 1975 as part of a wide-ranging review of Swiss cultural policy. The office has a broad remit, and provides subventions for literature, the theatre, music, the plastic arts, film (for which, since 1963, the Confederation exercises a constitutional responsibility) (see also **film: Switzerland**), and the preservation of monuments. Since 1989, the office has been responsible for the Schweizerisches Landesmuseum (National Museum) in Zürich (founded 1898) and for the Schweizerische Landesbibliothek (National Library) in Bern (founded 1900).

The Confederation also provides the funds for *Pro Helvetia*, the Arts Council of Switzerland (founded 1939). The general aims of the council are to maintain the Swiss cultural heritage, to support creative work in all fields of the arts, to further cultural links between the language areas of Switzerland, and to promote Swiss culture abroad. Specifically, *Pro Helvetia* provides financial support for writers working on projects, grants towards the publication of books, support for art exhibitions and for dance and theatrical performances, for the showing of films, for a variety of Swiss cultural events abroad, and for translations (since 1976 *Pro Helvetia* helps to support the *CH-Reihe*, translations of Swiss works of literature into the other languages of Switzerland). The Confederation, through *Pro Helvetia* and the *Bundesamt für Kultur*, accounts for over 10 percent of the money spent from the public purse on culture.

See also: culture: Switzerland

Further reading

Kessler, F. (1993) *Die Schweizerische Kulturstiftung 'Pro Helvetia'*, Zürich: Schulthess (an absorbing and exhaustive history and assessment of the contemporary functions of *Pro Helvetia*).

Tätigkeitsbericht (published annually) Zürich: Pro Helvetia (annual report of the activities and subsidies of the Arts Council of Switzerland).

Tschäni, H. (1990) *Profil der Schweiz*, Zürich: Werd (the best guide in German for the lay reader of the political structures which shape the culture of Switzerland).

MALCOLM PENDER

cultural studies

Cultural studies designates the redefinition of the project of scholarship in some humanities and social science fields which took place during the 1980s and which mainly concerned efforts to transfer theories, methods and specific knowledge between disciplines. It is therefore closely associated with notions of 'interdisciplinarity'. However, cultural studies does not represent an addition of several existing disciplines, entailing instead transformations and sometimes radical breaks with existing practices. This results particularly from an implicit insistence on culture as a uniform field of texts, all of which are equally available to examination and none of which can claim priority on the basis of innate value. This textual egalitarianism, reflecting an ethnographic definition of culture, breaks with aesthetic traditions of evaluation and canonic quality, and it is therefore in the literary realm that cultural studies has had its strongest impact. Rather than studying the great works of national canons, cultural studies eschews normative judgement and hierarchies of taste, examining, for example, traditional poetry, popular entertainment and the objects of everyday life side by side and asking how such texts betray the discourses that are deemed to construct collective identity. Since however identity is assumed to emerge through a history of contestation (rather than some pure or 'essentialist' substance), cultural studies focuses on conflicts inhering in texts, especially those having to do with issues of gender, class and ethnicity. Cultural studies, which has impacted much of the humanities and some of the social sciences, has played a role in the Anglo-American study of Germany, as evidenced by the proliferation of the term '**German studies**', as opposed to the traditional project of studying major works of literature.

Cultural studies borrows from several intellectual traditions, which co-exist, often with some discomfort, within this wave of scholarship. The tradition of the Birmingham School, especially the work of Richard Hoggart and Raymond Williams, contributed to the interest in popular culture and in the relationship between canonic literature and social life. The **Frankfurt School** legacy is evident in concerns with commercialization and the critical potential of autonomous art. Post-structuralism, especially the discourse theory of Michel Foucault, has also nuanced cultural studies, just as have feminism and a wider interest in gender politics. However, these several impulses are not fully compatible, and cultural studies has not yet achieved a systematic articulation of its central assumptions. Consequently the term tends towards an eclectic accumulation of various methods and cannot yet lay claim to internal rigour.

The major accomplishment of cultural studies is the expansion of the field of study, which, ironically, echoes the beginnings of nineteenth-century ***Germanistik***, which included the study of literature along with legal codes and other historical evidence of national life. The attention which cultural studies pays to the wider context contrasts sharply with the neo-formalism of literary study associated with deconstruction. However, theoretical inconsistencies, a sometimes pronounced anti-aesthetic bias, and the weaknesses of interdisciplinarity have flawed the project.

See also: modernism

Further reading

Berman, R.A. (1993) *Cultural Studies of Modern Germany: History, Representation, and Nationhood*, Madison, WI: University of Wisconsin Press (a collection of essays examining national identity and aesthetic forms from Heine's poetry of the early nineteenth century through to the debate on the Gulf War of 1991).

Burns, R. (ed.) (1995) *German Cultural Studies: An Introduction*, Oxford: Oxford University Press (a survey of German cultural history from the imperial era through to the present, focusing on literature and the arts in their socio-political context).

Denham, S., Kacandes, I. and Petropoulos, J. (eds) (1997) *A User's Guide to German Cultural Studies*, Ann Arbor, MI: University of Michigan Press (a wide-ranging anthology).

During, S. (ed.) (1993) *The Cultural Studies Reader*, London: Routledge (an extensive anthology of accounts of cultural studies).

Grossberg, L., Nelson, C. and Treichler, P.A. (eds)

(1992) *Cultural Studies*, New York: Routledge (a foundational anthology for the American discussion on cultural studies).

RUSSELL A. BERMAN

culture: Austria

Cultural affairs are an issue of vital importance for the state and the political establishment, even more so as culture is often exploited for other purposes, most prominently for tourist promotion. Artists are seen as important ambassadors for the country, especially as the political importance of Austria dwindled after WWI when, from being the largest central European state, it shrank to a comparatively small area with a population of about 6.3 million people.

The year 1945 marks a crucial moment in Austrian history. After the Nazi years, Austria was divided into four zones which were under the control of the Allied Powers. Consequently, the end of Nazi rule in Austria was regarded as the beginning of ten years of Allied occupation rather than the liberation from dictatorship. As it was common before 1938 to doubt whether Austria could exist on its own, the newly established Second Republic, which was re-created within the borders of 1937 and with the former constitution, had to develop a new identity in order to sever all possible links – historical or other – with Germany. In the grim post-war years, there was a strong tendency not to address Austria's involvement with the Third Reich. It was a general policy to blame the Germans alone for the war and all the atrocities that were an integral part of the Nazi state.

For at least three decades the country's identity was based on traditional cultural values and on a clear anti-German concept of culture in spite of the fact that the distinction between German and Austrian artists was very often unclear. The re-emergence of Austria as a fully independent state was reflected in the re-opening of the **Burg-theater** with *König Ottokars Glück und Ende* – a play by Franz Grillparzer (1791–1872) which is closely associated with the traditional concept of Austrian identity – and of the Vienna Staatsoper with

Ludwig van Beethoven's *Fidelio* in 1955. In the same year St Stephen's Cathedral, burnt out after Allied bombing in 1945, was opened for religious services again and became a symbol of post-war reconstruction and of the spirit of a new-born Austrian state.

The cultural heritage of the Hapsburg Empire, and not the inter-war period of the First Republic (1918–38), was widely regarded as a firm basis for the new era. During the inter-war years the main political groups, namely the Social Democrats, the Conservatives, and the German Nationalists, had drifted apart and had increased the problems of the country. Cultural life, especially in the 1930s, was heavily influenced by these partisan conflicts. Even though the political traditions of the Hapsburg Empire were widely rejected in the aftermath of WWI as they were associated with inflexible bureaucracy and uninspiring conservatism, people nostalgically longed for the seemingly hedonistic way of life and the stability of the past. It is still common to use the term Austrian culture for the whole of the Hapsburg Empire as well as for the much smaller Austrian state that remained when the Austro-Hungarian Empire ceased to exist in 1918. The concept of **Mitteleuropa** (Central Europe) which was introduced in the 1980s tries to revive the spirit of the traditions of the Hapsburg era. Before WWI Austria regarded itself as the leading nation of central and southeast Europe, now it is seen by many of these nations as a gate to western Europe. However, there is no real two-way cultural exchange between mainstream Austria and the nations of the former Hapsburg Empire, because the common languages are still German or English, but not the other languages of the former Empire.

Apart from mainstream Austrian culture, which is German-based, there are lively activities by the various ethnic minorities in Austria, notably the Slovenes in Southern Styria and in Carinthia, and the Croat population in parts of the Burgenland. Whereas the Croats, a minority which speaks a dialect four hundred years old, tend to assimilate strongly and have, apart from their language, retained primarily folklore as their cultural heritage, the Slovenes are far more active in their attempts to preserve their cultural identity, which results mainly in literary activities and their desire to gain political recognition.

An important influence on cultural life in Austria is exerted by the Christian traditions of the country, mainly the Roman Catholic church. The vast majority of the population receives religious education at school, and consequently the values which are promoted by the church are important elements of the cultural background. Religious themes are often referred to in all forms of art – sometimes favourably, sometimes critically – and it can well be expected by artists that these references are easily understood by the majority of the people. Controversial topics are also discussed by church leaders in public, so the position of the church is always known. In addition the church owns numerous cultural sites (churches, monasteries, schools, etc.) and has to pay for their upkeep as well as for necessary renovations. The state subsidizes these undertakings with considerable sums of money.

Baroque traditions, as epitomized in Austrian architecture, in literature and in well-preserved customs, are still highly influential. Many works of art oscillate between the Baroque themes of death on the one hand and worldly pleasures on the other. Balls are held all over the country mainly between New Year's Eve and the beginning of Lent, a tradition that started in the seventeenth century and is still so popular that the Viennese Opera Ball, which takes place in the building of the Vienna Staatsoper, has become a meeting point for celebrities not only from Austria, but from all over the world.

The theatrical tradition in Austria and in Vienna is especially strong and often the contents of plays or individual productions take centre stage in public discussions. Immediately after the war, traditional plays by German and Austrian writers were put on stage, but since the late 1950s the works of modern authors from all over the world have been produced and have been favourably received, thus opening up the country to international modern literature. Increasingly contemporary Austrian texts have been performed on stage by major theatres.

State subsidies are common in nearly all fields of culture, with the performing arts as their major recipient. The most important theatres and opera houses in Vienna and elsewhere are run by the state, by local authorities or by municipalities, and consequently it is of public interest how and what these companies perform. The management of these theatres as well as of the Vienna Staatsoper are under public scrutiny and are very often targets of fierce criticism.

Musical life in Austria relies on the traditional repertoire played by excellent orchestras, such as the renowned Vienna Philharmonic Orchestra, in famous concert halls like the Wiener Musikverein and the Wiener Konzerthaus. The internationally orientated Vienna Staatsoper is widely regarded as a centrepiece of Austria's cultural identity. The conductor Herbert von **Karajan** (1908–89) exerted a commanding influence not only on the development of the Vienna Staatsoper, but also on the **Salzburg Festival**.

Egon Wellesz (1885–1974), Ernst **Křenek** (1900–91), Gottfried von **Einem** (1918–96) and Friedrich Cerha (1926–) became the leading composers of the post-war era. Among others the Hungarian composer György Ligeti (1923–) found a new home in Austria. Apart from the traditional Viennese operettas, musicals (mainly British and American) have been produced in Vienna since the 1960s and have become an important aspect of musical life.

Post-war literature had to reposition itself after the 1945 turning point with authors like Heimito von **Doderer** (1896–1966) of the older generation, and Ilse **Aichinger** (1921–), Paul **Celan** (1920–70), and Ingeborg **Bachmann** (1926–73) of the younger generation as the protagonists. The lively literary scene of the 1950s is best reflected in the works of the **Wiener Gruppe** of poets who were devoted to language experiments and the use of the Viennese dialect. In the 1960s Graz established itself as a literary centre alongside Vienna with the **Grazer Gruppe**, a free association of authors, which set the tone. In 1973 the Grazer Autorenversammlung (Graz Association of Writers) was founded, but failed to gain recognition by the **PEN** Federation as a second Austrian PEN centre. Peter **Handke** (1942–), one of the protagonists of the Graz group, became the outstanding literary figure of the late 1960s and 1970s. Apart from language experiments and the reflection on the literary process in general,

Austria's identity was a predominant literary theme. Often the traditional form of the *Volksstück*, a form of popular theatre, is freely interpreted to show the limits of expression and identity and to rebel against theatrical traditions. Authors like Thomas **Bernhard** (1931–89), the dominant author of the 1970s and 1980s, tried to confront Austria with its own past and the way in which the people dealt with it.

The impact of Austrian painting and visual arts was comparatively small with the exception of the Viennese School of Fantastic Realism, which favoured traditional painting techniques and new mythological and fantastic themes. In the 1960s the Wiener Aktionismus, a performance-orientated movement, emerged and culminated in the Orgien Mysterien Theater of Hermann **Nitsch** (1938–). Die neuen Wilden (New Savages), a group of young painters, dominated the scene in the 1980s with large, highly expressive paintings which reflected international trends. Fritz **Wotruba** (1907–75), father figure of many Austrian artists, and Alfred **Hrdlicka** (1928–) became the most influential Austrian sculptors of the post-war era.

Austrian film production was taken up again immediately after the war, but could not develop into a successful commercial enterprise. It was the romantic clichés of the *Heimatfilm* that dominated the 1950s and helped present the Austrian landscape as a pleasant backdrop for tourism. The favoured themes of the cinema were predominantly the distant past, notably the Hapsburg Empire, and rural idylls rather than the immediate historical experience of WWII. Especially since the 1970s highly critical treatment of the Nazi years has become increasingly important. Since then literary subjects have often been turned into film scripts and achieved considerable success.

Post-1945 Austrian architecture has achieved international acclaim through Clemens Holzmeister (1886–1983), Roland Rainer (1910–), Gustav Peichl (1928–) and Hans Hollein (1934–). These architects are often regarded as important ambassadors of Austrian culture abroad. Painters like Friedensreich **Hundertwasser** (1928–) developed their own architectural style and left their mark with unusual buildings that are reminiscent of their paintings.

Owing to Austria's historical development and the centuries-long Hapsburg tradition the museums of the country have much larger collections than one might expect given the size of the country. Alongside the traditional Museums of Fine Art, of Natural History, and the Albertina, all of which are to be found in Vienna, new museums were founded, among them the Museum of Modern Art (which includes the Museum of the Twentieth Century) in Vienna and art galleries around the country, in order to communicate modern art. A forthcoming Museum of *Jugendstil*, whose emphasis is on artists like Egon Schiele (1890–1918) and Gustav Klimt (1862–1918), has led to plans to reorganize the museum structure of Vienna and to create a newly designed museum district in the city centre.

Folk traditions (e.g. folk music, dancing and local customs) are still widespread, but most of them have reverted from indigenous customs to vehicles of tourist promotion. With the help of the media, especially radio and television, commercialized folk music is the most popular form of music in Austria. At the same time there is another strand of music which goes back to the roots of folklore and tries to revive explicitly non-commercialized musical traditions.

The legal situation of the broadcasting industry favours the **ORF**, the nationalized provider, whose commanding position is challenged by satellite television and cable networks, which have become increasingly important. The ORF, which is required by law to report on cultural events, is not only the main source of information and the dominant medium, but also one of the most important sponsors of cultural activities.

In general cultural affairs are seen as a major constituent of the country's identity, because they provide the opportunity to link the past of the Hapsburg Empire with the modern era and because they help to underpin the concept of an independent Austrian state. It is only there that the country – comparatively small as it is – can gain international importance and consequently the authorities provide financial support on a large scale.

See also: cultural policy and institutions:

Austria; education system: Austria; film: Austria; literature: Austria; Vienna; visual arts: Austria

Further reading

Breicha, O. and Urbach R. (eds) (1982) *Österreich zum Beispiel. Literatur, Bildende Kunst, Film und Musik seit 1968*, Salzburg and Vienna: Residenz-Verlag.

Bushell, A. (ed.) (1996) *Austria 1945–1955: Studies in Political and Cultural Re-emergence*, Cardiff: University of Wales Press.

Günther, B. (1998) *Lexikon zeitgenössischer Musik aus Österreich: Komponisten und Komponistinnen des 20. Jahrhunderts*, Vienna: mica (music information centre Austria).

Müll, E. (ed.) (1988) *Österreich, Kultur und Gesellschaft: 1945 – 1955 – 2000*, Vienna: Bundespressedienst.

GEORG HELLMAYR

culture: Switzerland

The historical formation of the Confederation of Switzerland has imparted to its constituent elements, the cantons, the large degree of autonomy which they retain today. Thus the individual German-Swiss identifies in the first instance with his or her locality, in the second instance with Switzerland, a national structure characterized by its linguistic and cultural diversity and by its neutrality. The German-Swiss speaks a dialect of German but normally writes in standard German (see also **German language: Switzerland**), although in the 1970s and 1980s an upsurge in the use of dialect put the acquisition of standard German at risk. Local popular culture, in the form of the observance of customs, is strong, and extends to the celebration of the Swiss national day on 1 August. In 1991 the 700th anniversary of the founding of Switzerland saw differences in the attitudes of groups and generations towards the country, and 1992 marked differing views on integration with Europe. Constitutionally, the promotion of culture in its widest sense is mainly a matter for the cantons and communes, and the large cities, as communes, are effectively the centres of formal culture such as music, theatre

and art. Through the *Bundesamt für Kultur* (Federal Office of Culture), the Confederation maintains the National Museum in Zürich and the National Library in Bern, and promotes the production of films and other cultural activities. The Confederation also funds *Pro Helvetia*, the Arts Council of Switzerland, which supports Swiss culture at home and abroad (see also **cultural policy and institutions: Switzerland**). The number of Swiss-owned publishing houses has, since the 1980s, been sharply reduced by economic pressures which are also eliminating the diversity of the German-language press. Ecological damage manifests itself visibly in the restricted area of the country: the trees are badly diseased and, since the mid-1980s, restrictions have been placed on transit road traffic from European Union countries.

The present composition of Switzerland, a federal state of 26 cantons with four language regions (French, German, Italian and Romansch), reflects the way in which Switzerland came together over the centuries: around a small nucleus of three geographical areas in what is today central Switzerland, other independent areas gradually gathering for mutual protection. Even after the creation of the modern federation in 1848, these areas, or cantons, retained a large measure of autonomy within the federal structure, and the cantons continue today to be a central feature of Swiss democracy, exercising direct control over, for example, education and social services. Thus every Swiss acquires an awareness of identity with a limited area. A sense of national identity, which relates to more abstract concepts such as diversity and neutrality, is inevitably secondary. There is no Swiss national culture, but rather a variety of cultures, so that most Swiss belong to a local culture which is part of one of three major European cultures, French, German or Italian.

Awareness of common national history and traditions is, however, still a potent factor, as the referendum of 16 March 1986, which rejected membership of the United Nations, shows. But the pressures created by the speed of technological development allied with radical political change in Europe since 1989 produce severe tensions in a political system whose chief characteristics are stability, change based on carefully negotiated compromise, and neutrality in a world of rapidly increasing international co-operation. The referendum of 6 December 1992 rejecting the proposal by the Confederation for closer alliance with Europe illustrated the increasing dilemma of Swiss political traditions in the geographical heart of Europe. That the twenty German-speaking cantons, with one exception, all rejected the proposal, whilst the five French-speaking cantons all accepted it, indicates differences between constituent parts of Switzerland.

For the approximately 70 percent of the native Swiss population who speak German, one of the main cultural features which differentiates them, even one from another, is that their normal mode of communication is the dialect of their locality. During WWII, the use of dialects affirmed political difference from Nazi Germany. Yet in German-speaking Switzerland standard German was, and largely still is, the mode of formal usage in the public domain, and for newspapers and formal culture. Thus German-Swiss literature, for example, is accessible to all German speakers, the largest language group in western Europe. In the early 1970s, however, a *Mundartwelle* (wave of dialect) occurred. Driven partly by an increased sense of regional variety throughout Europe, and chiefly by a hugely increased use of dialect on Swiss radio and television, this wave pushed back the accepted frontiers so far that by the mid-1980s fears were being voiced that the younger generation was becoming incapable of using standard German, that the many local dialects were being endangered by the creation in the broadcast media of a debased, all-purpose dialect, and that communication with other parts of Switzerland was being impaired because other language groups learn standard German, not dialect. There were signs at the beginning of the 1990s that the wave was retreating somewhat.

The celebration of local customs and the commemoration of historical events thrive and testify to a strongly maintained sense of the past. Many of these customs reflect a pre-industrial Alpine culture, or the readiness of the community to defend itself or to take its own decisions (for example, at the remaining *Landsgemeinden*, open cantonal parliaments in public places). Awareness of special characteristics also extends to the wider manifestations of the Swiss national day of 1

August, which is celebrated with a unique sense of dedication. Yet here, too, change is apparent. 1988 and 1989 saw financial and political scandals in the wake of which extensive secret surveillance of its own citizens by the Swiss state was uncovered. Additionally, generational differences in the perception of Switzerland made themselves felt at the ballot box for the first time, when, at the referendum of 26 November 1989, an astonishing 35.6 percent of voters – mainly the younger people – opted for the abolition of the Swiss army, a central feature of Swiss political life and one of the few obvious unifying factors in a diverse country. The celebrations of 1991, the 700th anniversary year of the founding of Switzerland, were thus perceived as the backward-looking project of an establishment which was not only tainted, but also out of touch. A boycott was organized, and although it was largely confined to those involved in formal culture, it none the less highlighted change in perceptions in a society where conservative views are sustained by the customs which are such a feature of German-Swiss life.

Under the Swiss constitution, there exists a *Kulturhoheit der Kantone*, which means that the cantons are independent in cultural matters, including education. In practice, the sub-divisions of the cantons, the communes, carry by far the larger cost of everything which can be understood by culture. In contrast with Germany, there was no tradition in Switzerland of royal patronage of formal culture. The important cities in their capacity as communes bear more than half the cost of cultural life although they account for only about a quarter of the population of the country as a whole. Thus the formal culture of German-speaking Switzerland – its theatre, literature, music and art – has, because it is predominantly middle-class and city-based, more affinities with the formal culture of other countries in western Europe than does its popular culture. Basel, Bern and above all Zürich, which is the focus of the richest agglomeration in Switzerland, provide centres which have the resources and the buildings necessary for theatre, opera and art galleries, for example, and which, by their size, can also sustain less permanent cultural manifestations and forms. The Schauspielhaus in Zürich and the Stadttheater in Basel are acknowledged as major contributors to the

German-speaking theatre, and the Kunsthaus in Zürich and the Kunsthalle in Basel house important European collections of paintings. All forms of art are supported at the level of canton and commune by cash prizes and grants enabling work to be completed, and many of the innumerable semi-public and private foundations in German-speaking Switzerland make similar subsidies.

The constitution grants the Confederation relatively little formal competence in cultural matters, and traditional Swiss distrust of central government ensures that the role of the Confederation continues to be circumscribed: a referendum on 29 September 1986 and one on 12 June 1994, which sought to commit the Confederation to spending 1 percent of its income on culture, were both defeated. In practice, the Confederation funds *Pro Helvetia* (founded 1939), which disburses support for writers, musicians, artists and for associated events (such as, since 1979, the annual gathering for writers at Solothurn), for publications, and for the promotion of contacts at home and abroad. The Confederation also maintains the *Nationalfonds* (National Fund) (set up 1952), which supports research projects in all branches of science and learning. In 1975, the *Bundesamt für Kultur* (the Federal Office of Culture) was set up as a division of the Swiss Interior Ministry; its responsibilities include providing financial help for Swiss films (see also **film: Switzerland**), for the protection of the national heritage, for the preservation of works of art and national monuments (for all of which the Confederation has constitutional responsibility), and for the maintenance of the Landesmuseum (National Museum) in Zürich (founded 1898) and the Landesbibliothek (National Library) in Bern (founded 1900).

The only German-Swiss publishing house with a firmly established profile in Germany, where it has 80 percent of its sales, is Diogenes of Zürich. For writers, the problem has always been to reach the German market by being taken on by a German publisher. Yet, paradoxically, normally four-fifths of the sales of a German-Swiss novel published in Germany are in Switzerland. The German-Swiss publishing houses set up in the 1970s – Limmat, Ammann, Nagel + Kimche – have survived in a situation where many long-established German-Swiss houses have gone under, because they are small and have clear and limited aims. Economic pressures have also, since the 1980s, been eliminating the diversity of the local press, formerly particularly strong in German-speaking Switzerland where many small newspapers have disappeared. The Ringier conglomerate, one of whose publications is the popular daily ***Blick***, and TA-Media, publishers of *Tages-Anzeiger*, the serious German-language daily with the highest circulation, increasingly dominate the market.

Ecological pollution and impoverishment have manifested themselves drastically on the restricted terrain of the country. The German-Swiss have a particularly strong relationship to the countryside, and since 1962 there has been an article in the constitution pledging the Confederation to the preservation of animal and plant life. As early as the mid-1980s, every second tree was discovered to be diseased, a crucial factor in a country where trees have a vital role as snowbreaks etc. The Swiss themselves have been responsible for much damage by creating ski-slopes, tourist complexes and the like. At the cross-roads of Europe, Switzerland is affected by increased vehicular traffic within the European Union. The German-Swiss central cantons, who suffer most, have led the fight conducted by the Swiss to restrict, for ecological reasons, the transit traffic which its geographical position attracts and which, in earlier centuries, was an important source of livelihood.

Further reading

Bonjour, E., Offler, H.S. and Potter, G.R. (1952) *A Short History of Switzerland*, Oxford: Clarendon (still the best account in English of the evolution of Switzerland, invaluable for the understanding of Swiss attitudes).

Luck, J.M. (1985) *A History of Switzerland*, Palo Alto: SPOSS Inc (a vast and very useful compendium).

Schwander, M. (1991) *Schweiz*, Munich: C.H. Beck (a very readable account of the diversity and difficulties of contemporary Switzerland).

Switzerland (published annually) Bern: Kümmerly + Frey (the English version of a handy reference booklet on Switzerland which is published in several languages).

Switzerland – Culture (published occasionally) Pro

Helvetia: Zürich (an information sheet available free from Pro Helvetia, Hirschengraben 22, 8024 Zürich).

Tschäni, H. (1990) *Das neue Profil der Schweiz*, Zürich: Werd (the best guide in German for the lay reader of the political structures which shape the culture of Switzerland).

MALCOLM PENDER

currency reform

The *Währungsreform* of 1948 helped re-establish the market economy by engendering confidence in a new and relatively price-stable currency: hitherto hoarded goods were now released onto the market, with a collapse overnight in black-market prices. A draconian measure, it eliminated the vast excess holdings of *Reichsmark* by exchanging cash and bank deposits at a rate of 10:1 for the new deutschmark, though finally, for money supply reasons, only 6.5 percent (not 10 percent) was paid. Individuals exchanged their first RM 60 at parity. Debtors, who stood to gain, paid a windfall profits tax into the War Damage Payments Fund, and banks received compensatory claims to restore their assets.

See also: Economic Miracle

Further reading

Wallich, G. (1955) *Mainsprings of the German Revival*, New Haven, CT: Yale University Press (standard account of early post-war period).

CHRISTOPHER H. FLOCKTON

Czech, Hermann

b. 10 November 1936, Vienna

Architect

Czech studied at the Technical University Vienna

under Konrad Wachsmann and as E.A. Plischke's master student. He has held various teaching positions and is now in private practice in Vienna.

Without dispensing with the demands of design and function, Czech's work evolves around the irregular and the absurd, and does not shy away from violating rules. For Czech architecture represents a background against which to act, rendering all eye-catching meanings obsolete. The Wunderbar in Vienna (1975–6), Haus S. in Vienna (1980–3) and the Rosa-Jochmann-Schule (1991–4) are well-known designs amongst his small œuvre.

MARTIN KUDLEK

Czechowski, Heinz

b. 7 February 1935, Dresden

Poet and essayist

Czechowski was one of a generation of young poets which emerged in the GDR in the early 1960s, expressing support for socialism but calling for political liberalization. His loosely-structured philosophical poems reveal growing political disillusionment, melancholy detachment, and fundamental doubts about the development of modern industrial society.

Further reading

Hilton, I. (1991) 'Heinz Czechowski: The Darkened Face of Nature', in A. Williams *et al.* (eds) *German Literature at a Time of Change 1989–90*, Bern: Peter Lang, pp. 401–12 (illustrates the central themes in Czechowski's poetry).

AXEL GOODBODY

D

DAAD

The Deutscher Akademischer Austauschdienst (German Academic Exchange Service) (DAAD) is a private, self-governing organization of the higher education institutions in Germany. Founded in 1925 and re-established in 1950, its principal aim is to promote relations with higher education institutions in other nations. Through a variety of funding schemes and scholarships, the DAAD encourages academic exchange of staff, researchers, and students in all academic disciplines, although the promotion of the German language and German Studies is particularly emphasized. The Head Office is located in Bonn; the London Office is also the liaison office for the **Humboldt Foundation**.

GABRIELA STEINKE

Dahrendorf, Ralf

b. 1 May 1929, Hamburg

Sociologist and politician

As an eminent neo-liberal, opposed from the 1950s onwards to the reigning functionalist views of Talcott Parsons, Dahrendorf espoused a 'constraint' approach within **sociology** that understands social norms as the outcome of social exchange between power and resistance. Social structures and institutions are thus viewed as dynamic historical products of continual conflict between the interest and goals of those in power and their opposition. His groundbreaking survey of German political culture, *Gesellschaft und Demokratie in Deutschland*, appeared in 1965 (*Society and Democracy in Germany*, 1966). As a member of **F.D.P.** in the late 1960s and early 1970s, he was a member of parliament, the federal government and the European Commission. Instrumental in the foundation of the University of Konstanz in the 1960s, he served as Director of the London School of Economics from 1974 to 1984, and as Warden of St Antony's College, Oxford, from 1987 to 1997. Knighted in 1982 and made a Life Peer in 1993, he adopted British nationality in 1988.

BRETT R. WHEELER

dance

One set of determinants affected both modern dance and **ballet** post-1945. Both were separated into subsidized, state-sponsored companies, and the 'free' or unsubsidized, independent companies of the 'Off'-scene. Ideologically, all those involved were implicated in a fundamental contradiction: while anxious to transcend the National Socialist aesthetic, ballet and modern dance separately strove to acquire a style that set each apart from the British, the French, the Americans, etc., but also avoided the trap of a fascist essentialism. Finally, both ballet and modern dance continued to pursue the cultural-political goal already sought by expressionist dance in the Weimar period, aspiring to raise the status of dance to one of equality with the other arts.

Unlike ballet, modern dance in its post-war incarnation proved more thoroughly willing to engage in self-criticism. By all accounts, 1968 was a turning point. The demand for reforms raised by a new generation of students quickly infiltrated the dance scene. With the tumultuous residency of John Cranko in Bremen ballet began to change; a new seriousness arose, carried primarily by themes questioning social givens. Ballet, however, could stretch only so far without losing its identity. Its aesthetics and choreography remained wedded to a long tradition of transcendence, and a strictly hierarchical (and, too frequently, patriarchal) organizational structure. Modern dance, through the expressionist dance, was similarly rooted in hierarchical modes of practice and organization. However, this tradition was a weaker one, born of and carried by criticism. High seriousness drove its themes from the beginning; its immanent, material choreography began to emphasize the individual's attachment to quotidian reality. Trained by Kurt Jooss at the Folkwang School in Essen, and by Mary Wigman in her studio in Berlin, a new generation of choreographers and dancers could finally continue this deconstructive work: Gerhard Bohner, Pina **Bausch**, Johann Kresnik, Reinhild Hoffmann, Susanne Linke and Rosamund Gilmore.

Tanztheater was the term chosen to characterize a heterogeneity of styles. What unites these diverse tendencies is an interest in incorporating dramatic devices, most notably speech, into dance. Since 1973, when she stepped into lead the Wuppertal *Ballettensemble,* Pina Bausch's aesthetic vision has proven paradigmatic. The style she created is subjective and psychological, using speech to complete and complement movements in order to invite spectators into a reciprocal dialogue. She attempts to avoid the ideological dangers associated with a transcendent aesthetic by nurturing an intimate connection with mundane reality during dance-making and performance. *Blaubart* (1977) signalled this new direction, one rooted in a conversational approach to choreographic praxis and organization, in themes often drawn from immediate experience, and in the fragmentation of visual narrative.

Since then, a dearth of creativity has become evident, attributed primarily to the conservatism of the subsidy system. As a potential counterbalance, the first dance lobby, Gesellschaft für zeitgenössischen Tanz (GZT), was founded in 1993.

Further reading

Gesellschaft für zeitgenössischen Tanz e.V. (1995) *Tanz – Tradition und Zukunft. Dokumentation zum ersten Tanzsymposion Nordrhein-Westfalen 1993,* Cologne: Kallmeyerische Verlagsbuchhandlung (documents, transcripts and newspaper articles associated with the first German symposium on dance that led to the formation of the 'GZT').

Regitz, H. (ed.) (1984) *Tanz in Deutschland,* Berlin: Quadriga Verlag (standard anthology of essays on the post-1945 dance scene).

Schmidt, J. and Dyroff, H-D. (ed.) (1990) *Tanzkultur in der Bundesrepublik Deutschland,* Bonn: Deutsche UNESCO-Kommission (another anthology that surveys the contemporary dance-scene and updates information from Regitz 1984).

JULIA H. WAGNER

Darboven, Hanne

b. 29 April 1941, Munich

Conceptual artist and sculptor

Darboven became internationally famous in the context of concept art. Her early work consisted of spatial arrangements of regular and repetitive patterns made of sophisticated series of numbers or letters, which did not signify anything else beyond themselves. She has continuously expanded her art to multimedia projects where the visual is interwoven with texts, music and new media based on scientific order or categories, thus building up complex spaces for communication. Like Hans **Haacke** she now lives in New York.

See also: documenta; sculpture

KERSTIN MEY

Darmstadt Festival

The *Internationale Ferienkurse für Neue Musik* (International Holiday Courses for New Music) were founded at Darmstadt in 1946 by Wolfgang

Steinecke. More than any other festival, this didactic and educational event shaped the German, and European, post-war musical aesthetic. Rejecting the conservative, late Romantic ideals of Nazism, young composers like **Stockhausen** and Boulez met each summer, in an attempt to forge a new technique. Their models were previously banned composers, notably the serialists Arnold Schoenberg and Anton von Webern. The resulting avant-garde movement developed into a strong magnet for new talent; in the 1950s and 1960s most new European musical developments passed through Darmstadt.

BEATRICE HARPER

'Death of Literature'

This was the name given to a debate that took place in the Federal Republic in the late 1960s at a time when a number of intellectuals, influenced by the **student movement**, considered that priority should be given to political agitation and that literature had little social relevance.

As early as 1965 Peter **Schneider** had suggested that there were conditions under which writers might have to neglect the aesthetic in favour of writing manifestoes. The debate, however, only came to a head three years later, principally in the pages of the magazine ***Kursbuch***, co-edited at that time by Hans Magnus **Enzensberger**. It was Enzensberger's own comment in the essay 'Gemeinplätze die Neueste Literatur betreffend' (Commonplaces Regarding the Latest Literature) that literature lacked an essential social function that attracted most attention. In fact, this statement was much less radical than that of his co-editor Klaus Markus Michel who claimed that literature, however critical, diverted attention away from necessary political concerns. Moreover, Enzensberger himself never stopped his own literary activity, whilst in his essay he conceded that talk of the death of literature had been prevalent for 150 years.

The kind of writing that was championed during the debate was documentary reportage, as exemplified in the work of Günter **Wallraff**, and, in the case of Enzensberger, the political columns of Ulrike **Meinhof**. Another name that became prominent at the time was that of Erika **Runge**, who sought to capture the authentic voices of ordinary people, for instance in the 1968 volume *Bottroper Protokolle* (Bottrop Transcripts) in which citizens of the Ruhr town give an account of their lives. Despite such publications Hans Christoph **Buch** criticized those who saw no function for literature for ignoring the needs of the working class, whose true voice was still not being heard. In keeping with this view, a number of books appeared in which 'non-authors' gave an account of their lives. Two such 'social reports', *Vorleben* (Earlier Life) by Ursula Trauberg and *Vom Waisenhaus ins Zuchthaus* (From Orphanage to Prison) by Wolfgang Werner, were published in 1968 and 1969 respectively with the support of Martin **Walser**, who nevertheless tried to play down his editorial role.

Not surprisingly talk of the death of literature did not go unchallenged. Conservative critics such as Marcel **Reich-Ranicki** were supported by Dieter **Wellershoff**, who accused Enzensberger of applying the crude criteria of success to literature. Indeed, it was not long before a reaction set in. As works associated with **New Subjectivity** began to appear in the 1970s, the relieved cry went up 'Jetzt dichten sie wieder' (Now they're writing poetry again).

Further reading

Enzensberger, H.M. (ed.) (no date), *Kursbuch*, 2 vols, Frankfurt am Main: Zweitausendeins (these two volumes are a reprint of the first twenty editions of *Kursbuch* that appeared between 1965 and 1970, containing most of the essays referred to here; the most relevant issue is number 15).

Parkes, K.S. (1986), *Writers and Politics in West Germany*, Beckenham: Croom Helm (chapter 4 deals with the relevant period).

STUART PARKES

DEFA

Abbreviation of Deutsche Film Aktiengesellschaft, the first German film production company licensed after WWII (in May 1946 by the Soviet Military Administration). Founded by a group of communist filmmakers, it became a state monopoly consisting of several nationally-owned companies. The most important of these were the DEFA Studios for Feature Film Production, for Popular Scientific Films (both located in the former Ufa film studios at **Babelsberg**), for Newsreels and Documentaries (East Berlin), and for Animation Films (Dresden). Prior to German unification DEFA employed almost 2,500 people and produced approximately 15 to 18 feature films, as well as 30 to 35 television films, per year.

See also: film: GDR

HORST CLAUS

Degenhardt, Franz Josef

b. 3 December 1931, Schwelm (Westphalia)

Singer-songwriter and novelist

A civil servant's son, Degenhardt studied law in Freiburg, Cologne and Saarbrücken, completing his *Doktor Jura* in 1966, and practising briefly as an attorney after 1969. He now lives in Quickborn, near Hamburg. Degenhardt began writing and performing songs in the *chanson* style of Georges Brassens. His debut on Radio Bremen and his first public concert appearance in Göttingen were both in 1963. He appeared at the definitive song festivals at Burg Waldeck (Eifel) in the mid-1960s and is one of the founding fathers of the *Liedermacher* (singer-songwriter) scene of the 1960s, with the nickname 'Väterchen Franz' (Papa Franz). He accompanies his singing playing guitar, with harmonica and guitar backup, since the early 1990s with his son Kai Degenhardt. He has toured with concerts since the 1970s.

Degenhardt's early songs reflected an individualistic cabaret tone (*Spiel nicht mit den Schmuddelkindern*). Since 1965, he has sung about contemporary political issues (Easter Marches, protests against Emergency Laws, the Vietnam War, imperialism, neo-fascism, unemployment and prejudice against foreigners, Eurocommunism, the nuclear freeze and problems of German unifica-

tion). He was an active member of the **SPD** until his expulsion in 1971, then joined the **DKP**. The socialist standpoint is often clear in Degenhardt's songs, particularly their emphasis on international class solidarity. He was elected to the **PEN** Club in 1971. Particularly effective are Degenhardt's numerous *Rollenlieder* (role songs), in which he sings from the standpoint of unrepentant Nazis and ultra-conservative politicians.

His first LP *Rumpelstilzchen* of 1963 was followed by twenty-four more through to 1996, including *Spiel nicht mit den Schmuddelkindern* (Don't Play with the Filthy Kids) (1965), *Wenn der Senator erzählt* (When the Senator Tells His Tales) (1968), *Mutter Mathilde* (Mother Matilda) (1972), *Wildledermantelmann* (Suede Jacket Man) (1977), *Lullaby zwischen den Kriegen* (Lullaby between the Wars) (1983), *Wer jetzt nicht tanzt* (Those Who Don't Dance Now) (1990), *Aus dem Tiefland* (From the Lowlands) (1994), and *Weiter im Text* (Farther Along in the Text) (1996). Degenhardt also recorded his translations of several Georges Brassens songs in *Junge Paare auf Bänken* (Young Couples on Park Benches) (1986).

He has written six novels since 1973, including *Die Mißhandlung* (The Mistreatment) (1979), *Der Liedermacher* (The Singer-Songwriter) (1982), *Die Abholzung* (Clearing the Forest) (1985), and the biographical novel *August Heinrich Hoffmann, genannt von Fallersleben* (August Heinrich Hoffmann, called von Fallersleben) (1991). His first two novels *Zündschnüre* (Fuses) (1973) and *Brandstellen* (Fire Sites) (1975) were both filmed for television. Almost none of Degenhardt's work has been translated into English. All of Degenhardt's song texts are included in anthologies or CD liners (after 1990).

Major works

Degenhardt, F.J. (1972) *Väterchen Franz: Franz Josef Degenhardt und seine politischen Lieder* (Papa Franz: F.J.D. and His Political Songs), Munich: edition text + kritik.

—— (1986) *Kommt an den Tisch unter Pflaumenbäumen: Alle Lieder mit Noten bis 1975* (Come to the Table Beneath the Plum Trees: All Songs with Music up to 1975) Reinbek bei Hamburg: Rowohlt.

—— (1987) *Reiter wieder an der schwarzen Mauer: 53*

Lieder mit Noten (Riders Again at the Black Wall: 53 Songs with Music), Munich: Bertelsmann.

RICHARD J. RUNDELL

Delius, Friedrich Christian

b. 13 February 1943, Rome

Writer

Delius has established himself as an important socio-critical writer within the literature of the Federal Republic. He has written a series of novels which relate to the theme of terrorism, whilst more recently he has been concerned with German unity. His prose writing, although remaining largely within the parameters of realism, contains a variety of carefully crafted styles, whilst his poetry is marked by its lack of unnecessary linguistic adornment. He was brought up as the son of a pastor in provincial Hessen, a way of life described in the 1994 autobiographical story *Der Sonntag, an dem ich Weltmeister wurde* (The Sunday on which I Became World Champion) in which the youthful hero experiences a moment of liberation from his strict upbringing as West Germany triumphs over Hungary in the 1954 football world cup.

Along with other young intellectuals such as Hermann Peter Piwitt and Hans Christoph **Buch**, Delius worked for the SPD in Berlin writing slogans and speeches during the 1965 election campaign. When a year later the party joined the Grand Coalition with the CDU, his poem 'Abschied von Willy' (Farewell to Willy) beginning 'Brandt: es ist aus' (Brandt, it is over) encapsulated the disappointment of a generation. The controversial nature of his political views was underlined with the appearance in 1972 of *Unsere Siemens-Welt* (Our Siemens World), an attack on the past and present policies of the company that was the subject of protracted litigation.

Using official company documents, Delius wrote his critique of Siemens in the form of a spoof *laudatio*. The ability to take on a variety of personas is one of Delius' major accomplishments. His novels, even when written in the third person, are frequently narrated from the point of view of an individual protagonist whose character and experiences are far removed from his own. This is the case in the 1981 work *Ein Held der inneren Sicherheit* (A Hero of Internal Security), which portrays events following the kidnap and murder of a leading industrialist, a figure based on the victim of Baader-Meinhof **terrorism** Hanns Martin Schleyer, from the standpoint of a careerist who has worked as his ghostwriter. Particularly striking is the use of interior monologue in the 1991 story *Die Birnen von Ribbeck* (The Pears of Ribbeck), although in this case the figure of the narrator remains less clearcut. Consisting of a single sentence, a device that underlines the continuity of exploitation, this work shows how the inhabitants of Ribbeck have suffered at the hands of their rulers from the Prussian aristocrat of Fontane's hagiographic ballad down to the GDR leadership. With unification, there is a new threat in the form of western property speculators approaching from the easterly direction of West Berlin.

Further reading

Durzak, M. and Steinecke, H. (eds) (1997) *F.C. Delius: Studien über sein literarisches Werk*, Tübingen: Stauffenburg.

Graf, K. and Schmidjell, A. (eds) (1990) *Friedrich Christian Delius*, Munich: iudicium verlag (contains a variety of useful material, including analysis of selected texts).

STUART PARKES

Demokratie Jetzt

The East German citizens' movement Demokratie Jetzt (DJ) was founded in September 1989 (see also **citizens' movements: GDR**. Its origins lay in a church working group established in 1986: 'Absage an Praxis und Prinzip der **Abgrenzung** ('Say No to the Practice and Principle of *Abgrenzung*'). DJ concentrated on civil rights and the democratic process; its members played a central role in establishing the **Round Table** and preparing a new GDR Constitution (see also **constitutions: GDR**). Having initially supported a reformed GDR, it later proposed a staged unification process, accepting market economic principles. It joined the electoral alliance **Bündnis 90** in February 1990, together with the Initiative für Frieden und Menschenrechte and parts of **Neues Forum**, which became the political party Bündnis 90 in September 1991; this merged with the **Greens** in 1993.

BEATRICE HARPER

Demokratischer Aufbruch

The East German citizens' movement Demokratischer Aufbruch (DA) was founded in October 1989 (see also **citizens' movements: GDR**), following the setting up of a working group in June, with the descriptive label *sozial, ökologisch*. It differed from most other citizens' movements in that it soon embraced the formal constitution as a political party rather than remain a movement; this followed the marginalization of the majority of its socially liberally oriented founding members in December 1989. In March 1990 DA joined the conservative Allianz für Deutschland that won the majority in the **Volkskammer** elections. In August 1990 DA officially entered the **CDU**.

BEATRICE HARPER

Demski, Eva

b. 12 May 1944, Regensburg

Writer (née Küfner)

A student of German literature, art history and philosophy in Mainz and Freiburg, Demski was an active member of the socialist student organization **SDS** (Sozialistischer Deutscher Studentenbund). She worked as a *Dramaturg*'s assistant and as a reader for various publishers. From 1969 to 1977 she worked for the Hessischer Rundfunk writing television features. Since 1977, she has worked in Frankfurt am Main as a freelance journalist and author. She won critical acclaim in 1981 for her second novel *Karneval* (Carnival), a satirical caricature of life in the FRG.

MARTINA S. ANDERSON

denazification

Following German surrender in WWII, the victorious Allies instituted 'denazification' policies to eliminate Nazis from positions of influence. The most prominent Allied attempts to punish top National Socialists were the Nürnberg Trials and related war crimes trials conducted by the victorious Allies. Other trials took place in countries occupied by Germany during the war, with the result that thousands of perpetrators were executed or sentenced to prison terms. In the western zones of occupation, 668 of the 5,133 persons brought before military tribunals were sentenced to death. The purge of the mid- and low-level Nazi activists from positions of responsibility proved a much more daunting task than the punishment of the highest-ranking Nazi officials. The process was severely hampered by chaotic post-war conditions, lack of policy co-ordination among the Allied occupation authorities, and the practical difficulties involved in such a massive and unprecedented undertaking.

As demonstrated by the Potsdam Accords of August 1945 and guidelines issued by the four-power Allied Control Council between 1945 and 1947, the four Allied governments (the United States, the Soviet Union, Britain and France) agreed that 'denazification' was a primary goal of the military occupation. In light of the fact that well over one tenth of the population (eight million out of eighty million) had belonged to the Nazi Party or one of its main affiliate organizations, this was a tall order to fill. In practice, each power pursued its own form of denazification in its respective zone of occupation, further complicating the process. The Soviet Military Administration (SMAD), which officially viewed Nazism as an outgrowth of high monopoly capitalism, placed as much emphasis on structural and social reforms such as the 1946 land reform as it did on the removal of individuals from their posts. SMAD removed, arrested, interned, and in many cases deported as slave labourers former NSDAP members from key institutions. The purge was greatest in education, the civil service, the judiciary, and big business. In other sectors, the purge was less systematic and thorough, and in any case the mass of 'small fry' and technical specialists were left in their posts. As early as August 1947, former Nazis who were not highly tainted by activities in the Third Reich were restored full citizenship rights. A lack of concern for legalistic niceties enabled the SMAD to declare denazification completed in their occupation zone in February 1948. French authorities conducted a less thorough but highly arbitrary purge in their zone of occupation in southwest Germany.

By contrast, the American Military Government, and to a lesser extent the British, attempted a more sweeping and systematic review of the population in their zones of occupation. American and British military governments were overwhelmed by the challenge of assessing individual levels of responsibility on a case-by-case basis. The British instituted special denazification courts (*Spruchgerichte*) to try the more heavily implicated former Nazis. The American solution was to place the denazification machinery in the hand of state (*Land*) governments. In March 1946 the American-zone states of Bavaria, Hesse, Württemberg-Baden and Bremen passed the 'Law for the Liberation from National Socialism and Militarism' in nearly identical form. The law established questionnaires submitted by the vast majority of the population: individuals who demonstrated a 'nominal' association with National Socialism were subjected to closer scrutiny by the tribunals, resulting in a classifications of 'major offender', 'offender', 'minor offender', 'fellow traveller' (*Mitläufer*) or 'exonerated'. American officials retained ultimate authority and the right to review and veto German tribunal decisions. In addition, the accused could appeal decisions to a higher body of review. The vast majority of those coming before the tribunals were either amnestied or sentenced as 'fellow travellers' and considered 'denazified' after paying a monetary fine. All of those sentenced to internment were released by the early 1950s. In all zones of occupation, denazification generated criticism among the German public, and therefore proved a liability in the competition for public opinion in the emerging Cold War.

See also: *Vergangenheitsbewältigung*

MICHAEL R. HAYSE

design

Design in Germany, unlike British and US design with their empiricism or Latin design with its cultural orientation, has been governed by social and educational intentions. In the immediate post-war period the need for regeneration dominated design, and despite the slight hangover of art deco, it took up the theme of pre-war formalism, espousing an ideology of simplicity and utilitarianism that could be manufactured throughout the country.

In Konrad **Adenauer**'s 1950s there was little of the culture of the modern age, compared to the US and Britain. The Braun gadgets that have come to typify the era express the sense of style of the few. There remained considerable resistance to the work of the German Design Council (see below), hence the rise of **kitsch** in the German living room and the attitude that design was no substitute for technological progress and hence the domain of the engineer.

The 1970s began with pop culture and minimalism and ended with miniaturized technology and a sense of neo-Baroque. The decade developed the ideas of the Ulm **Hochschule für Gestaltung**, and discovered its technological field of design in ergonomics, which has continued throughout the 1980s and 1990s with the microchip.

The Munich Olympics of 1972 stand out as a landmark as they were the first presentation of a comprehensive design system, co-ordinated from the village itself through to the programmes: a throwback to the Ulm school's idea of designing all aspects of life.

Design was not ignored in the GDR either. Most notable was the Wartburg 353 car, the successor to the **Trabant**, which went into production in 1967. Despite criticism from East German design magazines, it succeeded in reflecting the aims of the state by being a functional car without status and this idea of designed functionalism was followed closely by designers at the Ulm school.

Since 1980 German designers have begun to throw off the shackles of functionalism. The relatively limited colours of the 1960s have been replaced by exuberance. Instead of competing for design awards, the watchword became 'change'.

The trend was exacerbated by technology,

which made the functions themselves invisible. Therefore, the surface and how objects were portrayed became important, rather than their use. A typical example is the Swatch watch, which instead of emphasizing accuracy or durability, is now a seasonal and fashion item.

Although the influence of the Ulm Hochschule für Gestaltung remains, little has become collectable. (Typical assignments were, for instance, vending machines). The items which stand out are the Ulm stool designed by Max **Bill**, Paul Hildinger and Hans Gugelot; and Walter Zeischegg's ashtray which has been in continuous production since 1967.

Hans Gugelot, who taught in Ulm from the beginning, has emerged as the hero of the school for his contribution to the products which have become known as Ulm Functionalism. He helped develop the Kodak carousel slide projector, the Pfaff sewing machine and the Braun Sixtant electric shaver, which, through its black casing, became central to Braun AG's corporate design and a symbol of high-quality technical gadgets until well into the 1990s.

German Design Council and Dieter Rams

In 1949 the Social Democrats introduced a bill proposing a Rat für Formebung, a German 'Design Council'. Inspired by members of the Werkbund, it focused discussion on form. Ratified in 1953, a foundation was established to ensure the good form of German products, which took on the role of an agency of good taste. Again the economic element of form was a social objective, although West German design swiftly recognized the existence of corporate identity and culture.

Work that the Council did was typified in the work of Dieter Rams, executive director of corporate identity affairs of Braun AG, and a president of the council in 1988. Dieter Rams' activities for Braun and Vitsoe are Germany's most important contribution to the design of the 1960s and Braun's corporate identity was, along with Olivetti's pluralist company image, repeatedly cited as exemplary.

Rams was the architect of the Braun Audio 1 receiver. What makes it stand out is not just the technology – although it was designed from the

inside-out – but that the design was functional, clean, simple and transparent. At the time few companies were seriously trying to achieve functional design bringing together all aspects of the product. This was followed soon afterwards by kitchen appliances, electric shavers, and the Vitsoe 606 shelving system still used today.

Throughout the 1960s as manufacturers of electronic goods reached comparable levels of technical expertise, companies found themselves forced to examine consumer behaviour to find a differentiating factor. The importance of design to the sales success of a product became critical. As an offshoot of this, 1965 saw the launch of the Stiftung Warentest consumer foundation which carried out tests in similar products – just as *Which?* magazine has done in Britain – with the results published in *Test* magazine.

ADRIAN MURDOCH

Dessau, Paul

b. 10 December 1894, Hamburg; d. 28 June 1979, (East) Berlin

Composer and conductor

Dessau's first public performance as a solo violinist was in 1905, but in adolescence he decided that conducting was his first interest, and studied in Hamburg, where, at the age of 18, he became répétiteur at the Stadttheater, moving two years later to Bremen, where he conducted light operas at the Tivoli Theatre, before returning towards the end of the war to Hamburg as composer to the Kammerspiele. By now famous conductors had taken cognizance of his talents, and Klemperer called him to Cologne as répétiteur and associate conductor in 1919. In 1925, after two years in Mainz, he was appointed principal conductor of the Städtische Oper in Berlin by Bruno Walter.

In the 1920s Dessau took an increasing profile as a composer, with important works premiered in Donaueschingen and Prague. As the grandson of a Jewish cantor Dessau took refuge in Paris in 1933 and in the US in 1939. Here he met **Brecht** in 1942, collaborating with him over the next decade and a half till the playwright's death in 1956, which

Dessau marked with his moving orchestral work *In Memoriam Bertolt Brecht* (1957). Dessau was an intensely political figure, and his collaborations with Brecht comprised among others the musical settings for *Furcht und Elend des Dritten Reiches*, *Deutsches Miserere*, *Mutter Courage* and *Die Verurteilung des Lukullus* (1951). The two returned together to Germany in 1948 and settled in East Berlin. Dessau remained a committed socialist and a proud citizen of the GDR. In 1968 he resigned from the West Berlin Academy of the Arts, and continued to receive national prizes from the GDR, to whom earlier he had dedicated all his compositions, 'for without her they would have been quite unthinkable'.

His Jewishness is manifested in the titles of many of his works: *Jüdische Chronik* (with **Blacher**, **Henze**, *inter alia*); *Hawel Hawalim*; *Hebräische Melodie*; *Jewish Dance*; *11 Jüdische Volkstänze*, etc., as well as various Psalm settings. These are juxtaposed with works of an overtly political nature: *Appell der Arbeiterklasse*; *Grabschrift für Rosa Luxemburg*; *Orchestermusik Nr 3, 'Lenin'*; *Requiem für Lumumba*, etc.

Dessau's opera *Einstein* (1971–3) pursues the theme of the social responsibility of the scientist. The music is strikingly and effectively eclectic, with elements of jazz, improvisatory interludes, twelve-note technique, pop, taped music and quotations from the works of J.S. Bach, all symbolizing his achievement in marrying political ideology to his highly individual creative inventiveness.

DEREK McCULLOCH

Deutsche Forschungsgemeinschaft

Founded in 1951, the DFG (German Association for Research) provides financial assistance for higher education research projects in some 180 disciplines, supporting both individual projects and special programmes, mainly in basic research. In addition, it sponsors postgraduate research projects at centres abroad, and also advises the German federal and regional governments. With a membership drawn from **universities**, **academies**, the **Max-Planck-Gesellschaft** and other research institutions, it receives two-thirds of its income from federal sources, most of the remainder from the *Länder*, and some additional funding from donations and earned income.

Further reading

InterNationes (1993) *Bildung und Wissenschaft* 3, 4.

HANS J. HAHN

Deutsches Theater

For the fifty years after its establishment in 1883 the Deutsches Theater had been renowned for the quality of its performances. In the 1890s its director Otto Brahm pointed the way forward with his productions of Hauptmann, Ibsen and Schnitzler, while his successor Max Reinhardt, who controlled the theatre's fortunes between 1904 and 1933, gained international recognition for his productions of Shakespeare, Shaw, Wedekind and Hofmannsthal. Located close to Berlin's Friedrichstraße, it was at the centre of the city's thriving theatre-life during the years of the Weimar Republic.

It was thus no surprise that it was one of the first German theatres to be reopened in 1945, with a version of Lessing's *Nathan the Wise* (*Nathan der Weise*) which was intended to mark the dawning of a new era of tolerance and reconciliation. It benefited during the years which followed from the strong financial support provided by a Soviet administration seeking to harness established cultural institutions to its programme of anti-fascist re-education. Under the management of Wolfgang Langhoff (1946–62) it regained something of its earlier status. As the **Berliner Ensemble** was based there until it was able to take possession of its own theatre in 1954, its first five productions were premièred in the Deutsches Theater. Langhoff's focus was otherwise directed towards popularizing the classical repertoire. When he took a risk with a more controversial contemporary work exploring industrial conflicts, Peter **Hacks**'s *Die Sorgen und die Macht* (Concerns and Power) (1962), it cost him his job.

Langhoff's successor, Wolfgang Heinz, enjoyed similar mixed fortunes. After attracting Benno **Besson** from the Berliner Ensemble the theatre broke new ground with his productions of adaptations from Greek drama, Hacks' version of Aristophanes' *Peace* (1962) and Heiner **Müller**'s version of Sophocles' *Oedipus the Tyrant* (1967). Then Heinz too was deposed (following ideological objections to Adolf Dresen's production of *Faust* in 1968), and Besson moved on to the Volksbühne. Hanns Anselm Perten took over as manager in 1970 and only slowly developed the confidence to introduce challenging new productions into his repertoire. His most respected director was Alexander Lang, whose productions of Büchner's *Danton's Death* (*Dantons Tod*, 1981) and Christoph **Hein**'s *Ah Q* (1983) attracted international interest. Yet he too, together with Perten, was forced to leave by ideological pressures in the period from 1986 to 1987.

In the GDR's final years the Deutsches Theater enjoyed a new lease of life when it became the centre for new productions of Müller's plays, with Müller celebrating his absurdly belated official recognition in the GDR by directing memorable performances of *Der Lohndrücker* (The Scab) (1988) and *Hamletmaschine* (Hamlet Machine), which was staged together with Shakespeare's *Hamlet* in 1990. Müller's move to the Berliner Ensemble in 1992 to become part of its experimental collective management was another severe loss to the Deutsches Theater as it faced the new competitive pressures of cultural life in unified Berlin.

See also: drama: GDR; theatres

Further reading

Kuschnia, M. (ed.) (1983) *100 Jahre Deutsches Theater Berlin*, Berlin: Henschel (a celebratory volume marking the theatre's centenary).

DENNIS TATE

DFD

The Demokratischer Frauenbund Deutschlands (DFD) was a mass women's organization in the GDR, founded on 8 March 1947 in Berlin. Its original mandate was as a non-partisan, non-denominational, democratic organization, but it soon developed into a mass organization totally controlled by the Sozialistische Einheitspartei Deutschlands (**SED**). It had voting rights in the **Volkskammer**, also advising on women's legislation. Since 1964 it increased its activities, and its membership, from *c*.1.3 million in 1970 to 1.5 million in 1989. Losing the vast majority of its members in 1990, the DFD continues to exist as a marginal organization, the *Demokratischer Frauenbund e.V.*

BEATRICE HARPER

dialect

German is arguably the most diverse language in Europe, with many of its speakers using dialects which are often so different from each other (and from the standard language) as to be scarcely mutually intelligible. When discussing German, the term 'dialect' refers to varieties of the language quite clearly distinct from the standard, and from each other, in grammar, vocabulary and pronunciation. The differences between German dialects are often greater than the differences between distinct languages elsewhere in the world. Why then are these different varieties described as dialects of a single language? One answer lies in the existence, alongside the dialects, of a reasonably uniform standard **language**, understood by virtually all, and used by many, particularly those with formal education, and felt by most to be 'the same language' as their local dialects.

Standard languages, where they exist at all, are generally a modern phenomenon, dating back about 500 years at the most; until this century the vast majority of people used highly localized varieties for most of their communication. Standard German arose around the end of the fifteenth century and has slowly been supplanting dialects ever since. Its adoption in writing occurred much earlier than its acceptance as a spoken medium.

There are large regional differences in the degree of use of standard German. In German-speaking Switzerland it is the most common written medium, but is generally restricted in speech to highly formal utterances, or to conversation with non-Swiss, all other spoken exchanges being in Swiss dialects. In Austria, and in southern

Germany, traditional dialects were used roughly until WWII by all social groups in everyday speech, the standard language being used in more formal settings. Now, particularly in towns and among educated people, it is probably true to say that various forms of colloquial speech predominate, intermediate between dialect and standard, but the situation is not well investigated. In northern Germany traditional dialect is now rare and clearly rural, the vast majority using colloquial speech or the standard language. Central Germany shows patterns of language use intermediate between those found in the north and south.

In writing, and in formal public speaking, most German-speakers use exclusively the standard language, but church services, plays, folk song and poetry in dialect are found in many regions. There is much broadcasting and some film in Swiss dialect, and some broadcasting in others. There have been notable German dialect writers, and other writers may have extensive quotations of (often untranslated) dialect speech in their writings, notably Thomas **Mann** and Siegfried **Lenz**.

In all discussions of German dialects it is useful to distinguish three regions: the north (roughly north of Cologne, Kassel and Halle); the south (roughly south of Frankfurt am Main and including Austria and Switzerland); and the centre. Northern dialects are described as Low German (*Niederdeutsch, Plattdeutsch*), southern dialects are Upper German (*Oberdeutsch*), and central dialects are Middle German (*Mitteldeutsch* – often referred to locally as *Platt*). The latter two groups may be grouped together as High German (*Hochdeutsch*), but this term is best avoided, since it is also the popular label for the standard language. The standard language arose chiefly from central and southern dialects, East Middle German being strongly represented, but it is today substantially different from most of these dialects.

German dialects differ from each other and from the standard language in manifold ways. It is common for different dialects of any language to differ in vowel sounds, and German is no exception here, with a wide variety of different vowels occurring in many words; for example the word 'know': *weeß* and *woaß* occurring as alternatives to *weiß* (spellings here can give no more than a rough guide to pronunciation differences). Less common

are radical differences in consonants between dialects, but these are found abundantly in German; Low German and southern Upper German dialects usually distinguish clearly between the consonant pairs p-b, t-d, and k-g, but other dialects have often reduced or lost these distinctions, with, for example, *Karten* (cards, maps) and *Garten* (garden) sounding very similar or identical. There is a whole range of consonant differences between Low German, Middle German and Upper German dialects; for example the standard German words *ich, machen, Dorf, das, Wasser, Apfel, Pfund, hoffen* and *Kind* (I, make, village, that, water, apple, pound, hope and child respectively) correspond to forms such as *ick, maken, Dorp, dat, Water, Appel, Pund, hopen, Kind* in Low German dialects, to forms such as *ich, machen/maken, Dorp/Dorf, dat/das, Wasser, Appel, Pund/Fund, hoffen* and *Kind* in Middle German dialects, and *ich, machen, Dorf, das, Wasser, Apfel, Pfund, hoffen* and *Kind/Chind* in Upper German dialects.

In vocabulary, many words, even common ones, have quite different variants in different dialects. For example, for *sprechen* (speak), there are at least the following alternatives: *reden, schreien, schnacken, küren, kallen, schwatzen, schwätzen, schmatzen, plaudern, brachten*. Even pronouns may differ: *er* (he) is replaced by forms like *he* and *hei* in Low German and some Middle German dialects. Grammatical differences are many; the dialects have fewer distinct grammatical forms of nouns, verbs and adjectives. For example genitive cases, like *des Mannes* (of the man, the man's) are virtually absent, and preterite tenses, like *ich sang, ich kaufte* (I sang, I bought) are rare, being almost entirely absent in Upper German dialects.

The radical differences between Low German dialects and the standard language are one of the reasons why their speakers, and some linguists, regard them as constituting a distinct Low German language. The European Union has accorded Low German the status of a regional language.

Language is highly significant in German-speakers' sense of identity, and dialects still play a part in regional identity; along with regionalism they experienced a notable revival in the 1960s and 1970s. Given the continued strength of regionalism it is impossible to obtain a complete picture of contemporary German politics and culture without some insight into the nature of and the role of dialects.

See also: German language: Austria; German language: Switzerland; language; Luxembourg

Further reading

Barbour, S. and Stevenson, P. (1990) *Variation in German*, Cambridge: Cambridge University Press.

König, W. (1994) *dtv-Atlas zur deutschen Sprache*, Munich: dtv.

Russ, C.V.J. (1989) *The Dialects of Modern German*, London: Routledge.

STEPHEN BARBOUR

Dibelius, (Friedrich Karl) Otto

b. 15 May 1880, Berlin; d. 31 January 1967, (West) Berlin

Protestant church leader

Bishop of Berlin from 1945 to 1966, Dibelius was a major influence on the post-war formation and development of the Evangelical church in Germany (EKD), of which he was Chairman (*Ratsvorsitzender*) from 1949 to 1961. A staunch anti-communist, Dibelius played a major role in the conclusion of the 1957 *Militärseelsorgevertrag* (agreement on military chaplaincy) between the EKD and the federal government, which the GDR attacked as supporting West German re-armament and prohibited him from entering the GDR. Dibelius was the first German to be a president of the World Council of Churches (1954–61).

See also: churches and religion

Further reading

Dibelius, O. (1964) *In the Service of the Lord* (*Ein Christ ist immer in Dienst*), trans. M. Ilford, London: Faber & Faber (Dibelius' autobiography).

Stupperich, R. (1989) *Otto Dibelius: ein evangelischer Bischof im Umbruch der Zeiten*, Göttingen: Vanden-hoeck und Ruprecht (a comprehensive biography that includes a full bibliography).

STEPHEN BROWN

Dichand, Hans

b. 29 January 1921, Graz

Journalist, author, newspaper owner and art collector

Starting his career as a journalist in Styria, Dichand became chief editor of the daily **Kleine Zeitung** in Graz (1949–55) and of the Viennese paper **Kurier** (1955–8). With Kurt Falk he founded the largest Austrian daily, the tabloid **Neue Kronen Zeitung**, in 1959. In 1987 he bought out Falk and then sold a 50 percent share of the paper to the German media group *Westdeutsche Allgemeine Zeitung*. Their company is the largest press conglomerate in Austria, occupying a dominating market share.

GEORG HELLMAYR

dictionaries

A German dictionary will usually have *Wörterbuch* in its title but often be referred to colloquially as a *Lexikon*. Works of reference with *Lexikon* in their titles are more likely to be **encyclopedias** but could include for instance dictionaries of quotations. Sometimes the term **Duden** is loosely used to designate any one-volume monolingual German language dictionary.

Depending on historical context, a monolingual dictionary can be seen by its speech community as handy, like money, to help users 'get around', or also be perceived, like a currency, as a declaration of cultural identity. The 'dictionary landscape' of the German-speaking world is complex, wherein both a strong tradition of scholarship (historical linguistics has a distinguished German-language pedigree) and political history have played a major part. The most prestigious and least handy general German dictionary by far, that of the brothers Grimm, has been called a 'national monument', a description reflecting both its ultimate scale and initial intent. Projected in the 1840s to document a language seen by most progressives as defining the 'cultural space' of a nation needing to emerge politically from reactionary particularism, by the time the dictionary was actually complete (in thirty-two volumes, and more than a century after its inception) the equation 'German language = German nation' was inconceivable and political unity in *Deutschland* (however defined) had come and gone.

Another much-delayed multi-volume dictionary, the *Deutsches Fremdwörterbuch*, published in seven volumes from 1913 to 1988, was triggered by the fact that the Grimms had sought to exclude **Fremdwörter** (foreign words) from their own idealistically *Deutsches Wörterbuch*. *Trübners Deutsches Wörterbuch*, appearing in eight volumes from 1939 to 1957, and named after a publisher – as the preface puts it '*im deutschen Straßburg*' – set out to describe, in flowing prose and in greater detail than Grimm, the histories of a limited selection of words described as '*linguistisch anziehend*' (linguistically attractive) und '*kulturgeschichtlich interessant*' (interesting from the perspective of cultural history). It is to be consulted with caution: the earlier volumes are a very clear product of their time, but for students of linguistic, cultural and political change (who can also read *Fraktur*, the 'Gothic' script in which even the final volumes were printed) it has insights to offer.

The first multi-volume German dictionary to be conceived and completed exclusively post-war was the *Wörterbuch der deutschen Gegenwartssprache* (Klappenbach *et al.*, 1964–77). It was compiled in the GDR. Predictably, perhaps, but unfortunately for German lexicography, it too acquired a role in defining would-be nation- (or at least state-)hood. Fulfilling its early promise as an important advance in the documentation of current, everyday German, it became a *cause-célèbre* when seen to have succumbed to political pressure and regurgitated a number of wishful definitions – in accordance with a claim made in the preface to volume four (1974) that '*Veränderung der Bedeutungen*' (change in meanings) had taken place now that the '*sich weiter entwickelnde gesellschaftlich-politische Wortschatz*' (constantly developing vocabulary of society and politics) had become '*mehr und mehr... festen Besitz des Staatsvolkes der DDR*' (ever more decisively the

property of the people of the GDR). (See Hausmann 1986 and also Müller 1994 on German dictionaries and twentieth-century politics.)

The popular market for single-volume German dictionaries had been catered for pre-war mainly by the *Sprach-Brockhaus* and the ever-present *Duden Rechtschreibung*. These were strongly challenged in post-war West Germany when general 'defining' dictionaries reflecting English- and French-language lexicographical traditions began to appear: '*Mackensen*' in 1952, '*Wahrig*' in 1967 (rigorously structured and highly influential), and the *Duden Universalwörterbuch* in 1983 – each of them subsequently updated. In 1993 a first substantial monolingual German dictionary aimed specifically at foreign learners of German also appeared (Götz *et al.* 1993).

What the Grimms failed to achieve – the creation of a full and eminently usable record of everyday, modern German – the innovative post-war East German *Wörterbuch* (above) was at least instrumental in stimulating. Between 1976 and 1981, a six-volume *Großwörterbuch der deutschen Sprache* emerged from the Dudenverlag, with subsequent competition from a six-volume *Brockhaus-Wahrig Deutsches Wörterbuch* (1980–4). A revised East German 'Klappenbach' appeared as a *Handwörterbuch* (Kempcke) in two-volume form in 1984 and a second edition of the 'big' Duden (now *Das große Wörterbuch der deutschen Sprache*) appeared in eight volumes from 1993 to 1995.

Aware that 'standard German' can be far too tightly defined, major German dictionary compilers all acknowledge broad geographical language variation by listing 'standard regional' lexical variants. But German-language dictionaries are mainly produced in Germany, the largest of the German-speaking markets, and so there is a natural tendency for such dictionaries to under-represent, for instance, Austrian or Swiss linguistic features. The Austrian Ministry for Education has therefore long sponsored a compact general German-language dictionary entitled *Österreichisches Wörterbuch* (in many ways similar to the *Duden Rechtschreibung*). 'Standard' dictionaries are usefully complemented by the *Wie sagt man in...?* series (see below). Information on narrower geographical language variation is to be found in dialect (*Dialekt* or *Mundart*) dictionaries.

References

Hausmann, F.J. (1986) 'Wörterbuch und Wahrheit. Zur Rezeption des Wörterbuchs der deutschen Gegenwartssprache in der Bundesrepublik', in H. Malige-Klappenbach (ed.), *Das 'Wörterbuch der Deutschen Gegenwartssprache': Bericht, Dokumentation und Diskussion*, Tübingen: Niemeyer.

Müller, S. (1994) *Sprachwörterbücher im Nationalsozialismus. Die ideologische Beeinflussung von Duden, Sprach-Brockhaus und anderen Nachschlagewerken während des 'Dritten Reiches'*, Stuttgart: M & P.

General dictionaries

Drosdowski, G. *et al.* (1989) *Duden. Deutsches Universalwörterbuch*, Mannheim, Leipzig, Vienna and Zürich: Dudenverlag.

—— (1993–5) *Duden. Das große Wörterbuch der deutschen Sprache*, 8 vols, Mannheim, Leipzig, Vienna and Zürich: Dudenverlag.

Götz, D., Haensch, G. and Wellman, H. (1993) *Langenscheidts Großwörterbuch Deutsch als Fremdsprache*, Berlin and Munich: Langenscheidt.

Grimm, J. and Grimm, W. *et al.* (1995) *Deutsches Wörterbuch*, 33 vols, Munich: dtv (compiled from 1852–1960, originally in 32 vols, the 1995 edition includes an index of sources).

Kempcke, G. (1984) *Handwörterbuch der deutschen Gegenwartssprache*, 2 vols, Berlin: Akademie-Verlag.

Klappenbach, R. and Steinitz, W. *et al.* (1964–77) *Wörterbuch der deutschen Gegenwartssprache*, 6 vols, Berlin: Akademie-Verlag.

Mackensen, L. (1952) *Deutsches Wörterbuch*, Munich: Südwest.

Wahrig, G. *et al.* (1967) *Das große deutsche Wörterbuch*, Gütersloh: Bertelsmann.

Wahrig, G., Krämer, H. and Zimmermann, H. (1980–4) *Brockhaus–Wahrig. Deutsches Wörterbuch*, 6 vols, Stuttgart: Deutsche Verlags-Anstalt.

Historical and etymological dictionaries

Drosdowski, G. (1989) *Duden Etymologie. Herkunftswörterbuch der deutschen Sprache*, Mannheim, Leipzig, Vienna and Zürich: Dudenverlag.

Götze, A. *et al.* (1939–57) *Trübners Deutsches Wörterbuch*, Berlin: de Gruyter.

Henne, H. and Objartel, G. (1992) *Hermann Paul, Deutsches Wörterbuch*, Tübingen: Niemeyer.

Kirkness, A. *et al.* (1913–88) *Deutsches Fremdwörterbuch*, Berlin: de Gruyter.

Pfeifer, W. *et al.* (1993) *Etymologisches Wörterbuch des Deutschen*, Berlin: Akademie-Verlag.

Seebold, E. *et al.* (1995) *Friedrich Kluge, Etymologie der deutschen Sprache*, Berlin: de Gruyter.

Thesauri

Dornseiff, F. (1970) *Der deutsche Wortschatz nach Sachgruppen*, Berlin: de Gruyter.

Wehrle, H. and Eggers, H. (1993) *Deutscher Wortschatz. Ein Wegweiser zum treffenden Ausdruck*, Stuttgart: Klett (follows the structure of *Roget's Thesaurus*).

Weiß, J., Clark, M. *et al.* (1994) *The Oxford Duden Pictorial Dictionary* Oxford: Oxford University Press (word listings are bilingual).

Contextual dictionaries

Agricola, E. (1992) *Wörter und Wendungen. Wörterbuch zum deutschen Sprachgebrauch*, Mannheim: Bibliographisches Institut.

Drosdowski, G. *et al.* (1988) *Duden Stilwörterbuch. Die Verwendung der Wörter in Satz*, Mannheim, Leipzig, Vienna and Zürich: Dudenverlag.

Dictionaries of pronunciation

de Boor, H. *et al.* (1969) *Siebs, Deutsche Aussprache. Reine und gemäßigte Hochlautung mit Aussprachewörterbuch*, Berlin: de Gruyter.

Mangold, M. *et al.* (1974) *Duden Aussprachewörterbuch*, Mannheim, Vienna and Zürich: Dudenverlag.

Other dictionaries

Back, O. *et al.* (1990) *Österreichisches Wörterbuch*, Vienna: ÖBV.

Baer, D. *et al.* (1986) *Der Große Duden Rechtschreibung*, Leipzig: VEB Bibliographisches Institut (the last GDR *Duden* to appear).

Bridgham, F. (1996) *The Friendly German–English Dictionary. A Guide to German, Language, Culture and Society through Faux Amis, Literary Illustration and Other Diversions*, London: Libris.

Ebner, J. (1980) *Wie sagt man in Österreich? Wörterbuch der österreichischen Besonderheiten*, Mannheim, Vienna and Zürich: Dudenverlag.

Küpper, H. (1987) *PONS Wörterbuch der deutschen Umgangssprache*, Stuttgart: Klett (a dictionary of 'colloquialisms').

Meyer, K. (1989) *Wie sagt man in der Schweiz? Wörterbuch der schweizerischen Besonderheiten*, Mannheim, Vienna and Zürich: Dudenverlag.

Seibicke, W. (1983) *Wie sagt man anderswo? Landschaftliche Unterschiede im deutschen Sprachgebrauch*, Mannheim, Vienna and Zürich: Dudenverlag.

Strauß, G. *et al.* (1989) *Brisante Wörter von Agitation bis Zeitgeist*, Berlin: de Gruyter.

GLYN HATHERALL

Diener & Diener

This architectural partnership was established by Roger and Markus Diener in Basel.

Diener & Diener's buildings are characterized by the purest form of plainness found in new German-Swiss architecture. The reduction of forms, colours, materials and details does not stand in the way of an astonishing variety of expression, though. Their office buildings are mostly clad in natural stone (Picassoplatz, Basel, 1992–3) while the Gallery Gmurzynska in Cologne (1990–1) surprises by its bold façades.

MARTIN KUDLEK

Dietrich, Marlene

b. 27 December 1901, Berlin; d. 6 May 1992, Paris

Actress and *chanteuse*

A world-famous icon through her seductive portrayal of Lola-Lola, the night-club singer in von Sternberg's *The Blue Angel* (*Der blaue Engel*, 1930), Dietrich left Germany in 1930 and through clever lighting and sophisticated sexuality became the embodiment of Hollywood glamour despite the varied quality of her films. Major films include *Morocco* (1930), *Shanghai Express* (1932), *Destry Rides Again* (1939) and *A Foreign Affair* (1948). A staunch anti-Nazi, she subsequently extended her career as a *chanteuse* into the 1970s before living out her old age as a recluse in Paris.

HELEN HUGHES

Dietz Verlag

Dietz Verlag, the Berlin-based publishing house of the **SED**, was charged with making the entire ideological canon of Marxism–Leninism available to a GDR readership. This included not just the work of Marx, Engels and Lenin, in a range of complete and selected editions, but virtually every public utterance of leading SED figures. As there was no scope in these reverential publications for critical editorial comment, their appearance tended to be greeted with indifference by all but the Party faithful. Dietz Verlag has survived unification mainly as the publisher of work by **PDS** members.

See also: publishing: GDR

DENNIS TATE

DIN

The Deutsches Institut für Normung (DIN) is an autonomous body supported wholly by German industry. It develops product norms so as to simplify and make more transparent the supply of goods and components, to promote the saving of energy and materials and to ease the technical production process and component compatibility problems of firms. Quality standards offer a guarantee to the purchaser. Norms are prepared and revised by 600 DIN employees and 40,000 associates employed by member firms. The federal government and consumer representatives have consultation rights. There are 20,000 DIN norms, including such internationally-familiar standards as the A4 paper sheet, with approximately 2,000 new additions or revisions annually.

CHRISTOPHER H. FLOCKTON

Dinner for One

Dinner for One was filmed in Hamburg in 1963 and has become an institution in German cultural life. Every New Year's Eve this black and white cabaret piece is shown to millions of viewers in its English original. The author of the sketch is unknown. The film stars May Warden as Miss Sophie, celebrating her ninetieth birthday with a dinner party for absent friends – Mr Winterbottom, Admiral von Schneider, Sir Toby and Mr Pommeroy – and Freddy Frinton as James the Butler. Lines from the sketch such as 'Cheerio Miss Sophie' and 'same procedure as every year' have become part of German folklore.

Further reading

Dinner for One: Freddy Frinton, Miss Sophie und der 90. Geburtstag (1985) Edition Nautilus, Hamburg: Verlag Lutz Schulenburg (includes English and German transcripts of the sketch, stills from the film and an overview of its reception).

ALISON PHIPPS

disability

The nature of disabilities in all parts of Germany after 1945 was profoundly affected by the experiences of the Third Reich. The structure of the disabled population was unusual compared with other European countries for two major reasons: first, there was only a small number of mentally disabled people as a result of the Nazi euthanasia programme; second, a very high proportion of physically disabled people were suffering from injuries sustained during the war. Until the mid-1950s more than half the disabled population was in this category, and a high proportion was male. The carers of the disabled, especially those looking after mentally disabled people, were also psychologically scarred by the Nazi period. As a result, there was a reluctance in the immediate post-war period to allow the state to take responsibility for the disabled. Also, the legal duty of parents, doctors and social workers to register the disabled officially was not introduced in the Federal Republic; the German Democratic Republic did reimpose this

duty in 1954. For all these reasons, provision for the disabled in both parts of Germany was slow to develop in the 1950s and 1960s. There was no specific clause in either the West or East German constitutions specifically giving rights or protection to people with disabilities.

Schools for the physically disabled have existed in Germany since the latter part of the nineteenth century, but the idea of educating the mentally disabled is relatively new. Both German states had highly differentiated systems. In West Germany the *Empfehlung zur Ordnung des Sonderschulwesens* (Recommendation on the Structure of the Special School system) of 1972 established a system of ten types of special school (*Sonderschulen*) for those children who could not cope with normal schools. They range from schools for the blind and deaf to two kinds of school for the mentally disabled; for children with mild learning difficulties, and for those with severe learning difficulties. All schools for children with a physical disabilty lead to a leaving qualification. In some states provision for mentally disabled children is in day centres.

In the GDR there was also a highly differentiated system. Children were assessed as being educable or ineducable. For those in the first category who could not attend the ten-year polytechnical high school, there was a system of special schools for children with physical disabilities and special schools for children with mental disabilities (*Hilfsschulen*) which came under the Ministry of Education. For those children who were regarded as ineducable, there were day centres which were administered by the Ministry of Health, and residential homes which were largely run by the churches. Provision in the 1950s and 1960s was inadequate in the GDR, but improved in the 1970s, especially in the area of special crèches and kindergartens where the provision was much more extensive than in the Federal Republic. After unification the West German system of special schools was introduced into the new *Länder*.

Both states had systems of vocational training after schooling. But in West Germany employment for disabled people was difficult, especially after the mid-1970s. Employers of more than fifteen people were required by the 1974 *Schwerbehindertengesetz* (Law concerning the Severely Disabled) to offer employment to the disabled, but they could opt out of the system by paying DM 200 a month. As a result, these quota places fell below what was intended, and the majority of disabled people moved on from the Work Training Centres to Workshops for the Disabled. In the state-run economy, of the GDR each organization was required to provide protected workshops. This system collapsed after unification. In West Germany disabled people only had a right to a pension under certain circumstances, for example war disabled; the majority depended on the social benefit system (*Sozialhilfe*). In the GDR all disabled people received a pension. In the amendment to the *Schwerbehindertengesetz* of 1 July 1990 disabled people in the former GDR were granted a pension of DM 495 a month for an interim period. Since the end of 1995 the West German system applies.

After unification there was pressure to change Article 3 of the Basic Law to ensure the rights of the disabled. Although a general clause on minorities in Germany did not obtain the necessary two-thirds majority in the Bundestag on 30 June 1994, the clause relating to disability was approved. The following sentence: 'Nobody may be discriminated against because of his disability' was added to Article 3(3) of the Basic Law in October 1994.

PETER BARKER

dissent and opposition: GDR

The history of dissent and opposition in the GDR can be divided into three major phases. During the first, in the late 1940s and 1950s, opposition in the population to Soviet occupation and radical changes in the political and economic structure of the GDR caused mass emigration to West Germany, and within the political structures opposition to the imposition of the Soviet model caused a series of challenges to the leadership of the **SED**. In the second phase, the 1960s and 1970s saw opposition centred on specific individuals, such as Rudolf **Bahro**, Wolf **Biermann** and Robert **Havemann**, who expressed dissenting, if still Marxist, criticism of the SED and the GDR state. The third phase, in the late 1970s and 1980s, saw the development of oppositional groups for the first

time, and the re-emergence of large numbers of GDR citizens who made formal applications to emigrate to West Germany, some of whom then forced a mass exodus from the GDR via third countries in the summer of 1989, thus provoking the final crisis which led to the collapse of the GDR.

The 1940s and 1950s

Traditional forms of opposition common to a democratic system were steadily eroded during the period of Soviet occupation from 1945 to 1949. Political parties other than the **KPD** found their independence gradually reduced and then destroyed, either by being forced to operate in a block with the communists from July 1945, as in the case of the Christian Democrats (**CDU**) and the Liberals (LDPD), or by being coerced into an amalgamation with the KPD, as happened to the Social Democrats (**SPD**) in April 1946. The only elections in which parties competed against each other took place at local and state level in the autumn of 1946, but even here the backing and resources of the Soviet military administration were firmly behind the **SED**. After the creation of the GDR in October 1949 parties other than the SED lost all independence when they were forced into the National Front which put up single lists of candidates for elections. As a result the **Volkskammer**, the parliament of the GDR, did not operate as a body in which parties representing different interests came to democratic decisions. On only one occasion before the **Wende**, in March 1972, did a group of deputies in parliament vote against a bill, when fourteen CDU members voted against the introduction of abortion on demand.

Opposition and dissent in the GDR therefore took place either outside the political system, or in the form of power struggles in the upper echelons of the SED. From the SED's point of view opposition could not objectively exist since the party regarded itself as the representative of the will of the people. Any form of opposition would logically be directed against the people itself. In fact, throughout the history of the GDR, manifestations of opposition and dissent recurred. The initial battles within the SED were between the social democratic and the communist wings and concentrated on the question of a 'German road to socialism'. This concept had been put forward by Anton Ackerman, a leading KPD member, in February 1946 as part of a strategy to make a merger seem more attractive to social democrats, but was then refuted in autumn 1948 after the SED had moved decisively towards the Soviet party model. In the initial agreement governing the structures of the SED the principle of parity between communists and social democrats was established, but by 1948 this principle had been eroded in practice and social democrats pushed aside or forced to accept the new party model. After the show trials in Hungary and Bulgaria in 1949 against 'nationalist' communists in the wake of Tito's rejection of Soviet influence in Yugoslavia, the SED carried through a purge of members suspected of ideological or nationalist tendencies. In 1950–1 more than 150,000 SED members were expelled from the party, including one member of the **Politbüro**, Paul Merker. The major impetus behind these purges was to remove social democratic tendencies in the SED during the period when major changes in the economic and political structures of the GDR were planned.

These changes were announced at the Second Party Congress of the SED in July 1952 when the programme of 'socialist construction' was put forward, including further socialization of the means of production, the creation of agricultural co-operatives and further centralization of the political structures through the abolition of the federal states. These radical changes and increased political repression led directly to the **June Uprising** in 1953. Although the immediate cause was a general increase in work norms which affected the natural supporters of the SED, the working class, and the withdrawal of measures directed against the middle class and the churches, the June revolt, which spread from East Berlin throughout the GDR, quickly turned into an expression of political opposition to the SED, the Sovietization of the GDR and the division of Germany, and had to be put down by Soviet military force. The failure of this revolt and the clear reluctance of western countries to become involved meant that this was the last and only expression of general opposition to communist rule in the GDR. Its suppression was followed by a

sharp increase in emigration to West Germany. Within the SED Walter **Ulbricht** used the situation to remove from their functions a group within the Politbüro and the **Central Committee**, led by Wilhelm **Zaisser** and Rudolf **Herrnstadt**, which had challenged his position. Further opposition within the SED to Ulbricht's uncompromising political line came after Krushchev's speech in 1956 criticizing Stalin's rule. It was led by a group of intellectuals, the leading figures of which, the philosopher, Wolfgang **Harich**, and the head of the **Aufbau Verlag**, Walter **Janka**, were sentenced to long terms of imprisonment in 1957. The following year Ulbricht moved against another group, this time within the top ranks of the SED, which was threatening his position. At the thirty-fifth plenary session of the Central Committee in February 1958, Karl **Schirdewan**, a member of the Politbüro, and Ernst Wollweber, head of the Ministry for State Security, were removed from their functions. After 1958 there were no further serious attempts to remove Ulbricht or to force a change in the SED's strict adherence to Soviet policy until his replacement by Erich **Honecker** in 1971.

The 1960s and 1970s

After the building of the **Berlin Wall** in 1961 and the introduction of a more flexible economic policy in the early 1960s the bulk of the population resigned itself to the fact that it was now extremely difficult to leave the GDR and it therefore had to come to terms with its situation, however unwillingly. Open opposition was confined to a small number of intellectuals, mostly from within the SED. Robert Havemann, a scientist at the Humboldt University in East Berlin, and a leading member of the SED in the 1950s, started in the early 1960s to criticize what he regarded as the 'Stalinist deformations' of the GDR. He was expelled from the SED in March 1964 and removed from his university post after delivering a series of controversial lectures at the Humboldt University. In the late 1960s he became attracted to the reformist ideas of Alexander Dubcek in the 'Prague Spring', but within the GDR he remained an isolated figure, especially after the forced emigration of his close friend and fellow dissident,

Wolf Biermann, in 1976, after which Havemann was put under house-arrest. His ideas were mostly known from a number of works published in West Germany, which had been smuggled out of the GDR. In the latter part of his life he became associated with the development of an independent peace movement; his collaboration with a young priest, Rainer Eppelmann, resulted in the publication shortly before his death in 1982 of the *Berliner Appell* (Berlin Appeal) which called for disarmament in both German states.

The other major oppositional figure in this period was Rudolf Bahro. He was also significant for having worked at the heart of the establishment of the GDR, as an economist. He published a critique of socialism in the GDR in 1977 in West Germany, called *Die Alternative* (The Alternative). He was immediately arrested, put on trial and sentenced to eight years' imprisonment. He was, however, given an amnesty a year later and deported to West Berlin. Bahro and Havemann were isolated figures during a period when West Germany and other western countries had granted the GDR a limited recognition, and the GDR seemed more stable both internally and in its external relations.

The development of opposition groups

The signing by the GDR of the Final Helsinki Agreement on human rights in 1975 marked a turning point in the development of an opposition. In particular, groups which wanted to emigrate used the fact that the GDR had signed international agreements on human rights as the basis for protest. These groups tended to operate separately from the peace groups which started to appear towards the end of the 1970s in response to the introduction of military-type training in schools in 1978. The latter groups, operating largely under the wing of the Protestant churches, contained people who believed that the GDR was still reformable in a socialist way and they tended to concentrate on particular issues such as the environment, policy towards women, as well as peace issues, where they thought there was a possibility of influencing changes in policy in the GDR. Despite repressive measures against them, these groups continued to exist through the 1980s

and formed the basis for the citizens' movements which came into existence during the autumn of 1989.

They remained at odds with the large groups of GDR citizens who from the mid-1980s onwards made formal applications to leave the GDR; there were over two million applications in 1988. These would-be émigrés found themselves subject to a campaign of discrimination and harassment by the GDR authorities, starting with the loss of their jobs. They found themselves relegated to the edge of GDR society, and although some were allowed to emigrate, there were many more who were not, or who had to wait for substantial periods. They tried to gain support from opposition groups, but were met with extreme distrust because their motivations were totally different. In the end, however, it was the pressure to emigrate leading to the mass exodus from the GDR via Hungary in the summer of 1989 after the dismantling of the Hungarian border with Austria in May, and the occupations of the West German embassies in Prague and Warsaw, which brought the greatest pressure on the GDR and started the process of collapse. The GDR had proved to be unreformable by the intellectual opposition presented by the citizens' groups or by pressure from reformers from within the SED who wanted to follow the example of Gorbachev in the Soviet Union. After the *Wende* in 1989 attention soon shifted from attempts to reform the GDR to negotiating the path to **unification** with West Germany.

See also: citizens' initiatives: GDR; citizens' movements: GDR; parties and mass organizations: GDR; peace movement: GDR

Further reading

Bahro, R. (1978) *The Alternative in Eastern Europe*, London: New Left Books (a translation of Bahro's most important work).

Fricke, K.W. (1984) *Opposition und Widerstand in der DDR*, Cologne: Verlag Wissenschaft und Politik.

Havemann, R. (1990) *Dialektik ohne Dogma?*, Berlin: Deutscher Verlag der Wissenschaften (a reissue of Havemann's lectures from 1963–4 with accompanying essays).

Neubert, E. (1997) *Geschichte der Opposition in der*

DDR 1949–1989, Berlin: Ch. Links Verlag (detailed and comprehensive history).

Poppe, U., Eckert, R. and Kowalczuk, I.-S. (eds) (1996) *Zwischen Selbstbehauptung und Anpassung. Formen des Widerstandes und der Opposition in der DDR*, Berlin: Ch. Links Verlag (collection of essays by historians and participants in the opposition in the GDR).

Woods, R. (1986) *Opposition in the GDR under Honecker, 1975–1985*, New York: St Martin's Press (standard work in English on opposition in the later years of the GDR).

PETER BARKER

Distel, Die

Opened in 1953 in Berlin's Friedrichstraße, a street steeped in the cultural history of the Weimar Republic, *Die Distel* (The Thistle) was the first professional **cabaret** to be permitted in the GDR. As it was expected to produce 'positive' **satire** broadly supportive of the socialist cause and to submit its programmes for approval in advance, it was no more than a pale reflection of the city's world-famous political cabarets of the 1920s. Its shows were nevertheless invariably sold out to audiences eager to experience even a whiff of controversy. It remains a popular location in post-unification Berlin.

DENNIS TATE

DKP

Founded in 1969 as the de-facto successor to the banned **KPD**, the Deutsche Kommunistische Partei (DKP) escaped proscription partly by keeping its programme free of the Leninist turns of phrase that had been the downfall of its predecessor in 1956, and partly thanks to the relaxation in West Germany of former Cold-War attitudes. The DKP did little to disguise its support for the GDR, from which it received generous funding. Its membership figures and electoral support remained minimal, and, unlike communist parties in some other western European countries, it had little following among

intellectuals. (The handful of exceptions included the writers Franz Xaver **Kroetz**, and, for a while, Martin **Walser**.) The DKP's prominent involvement in the peace movement (especially in the guise of the 'German Peace Union' (DFU)) was an embarrassment to many non-communist activists. After the collapse of the GDR the party's membership shrank to only a few thousand.

See also: Verband deutscher Schriftsteller

JOHN SANDFORD

documenta

This periodical exhibition of international contemporary art in Kassel was first held in 1956 as a survey of the last fifty years of western modernism. Due to its success a repeat was organized in 1959. Since then, it has become a regular event. During its forty-year history the concept of the show has undergone considerable change reflecting the prevailing ideological and socio-cultural climate in Germany and beyond. The first shows sought to demonstrate the successful reintegration of West German art into the continuum of western modernism, and, as such, played a significant part in the process of cultural and political dissociation from the GDR and the eastern block. Thematizing art after 1945, the documenta 2 celebrated abstraction as the art of the day. And so did the third show in 1962, although, by then, new figurative forms had gained momentum on the international scene. Post-painterly abstraction and pop art figured prominently at the documenta 4 in 1968. As in the previous shows the cultural dominance of the US shaped the selection of artists. Against the background of the **student movement**, the private view saw protests by art students and artists against the undemocratic structures of its selection process in the form of the absolute power exerted by an appointed curator – an arrangement that has remained unchanged to the present day. The Vietnam war and the Watergate affair put an end to the idealized image of the US, and with the documenta 5, held in 1972, the selection of artists and styles became more pluralistic. The focus on '*individuelle Mythologien*' (individual mythologies) mirrored the retreat of art into the private sphere. The documenta 6 in 1977 saw the first appearance of artists from the GDR. In general, it presented styles such as photo-realism and pop art within a broader concept of new media such as performance and video. The exhibition of neo-expressive figurations (see also **neo-expressionism**) at the documenta 7 in 1982 paved the way for the international recognition of artists such as **Baselitz**, Lüpertz and **Kiefer** as representatives of a new German figurative imagery. The documenta 8 carried all the signs of 1980s enterprise culture, aiming at and depending on an increasing number of visitors; their number rose from 355,000 in 1977 to 476,000 in 1987. Art, now increasingly commodified, referred to the familiar every-day and to art history with slants of parody, mockery and pastiche. The documenta in 1992 followed the trends established by its predecessor: a superlative show centred around images and their presentation that appealed to a wide public.

Further reading

Catalogues of the documenta 1–9 (various publishers) (essential for the documentation of participating artists and exhibition concepts).

Damus, M. (1995) *Kunst in der BRD 1945–1990*, Reinbek bei Hamburg: Rowohlt (comprehensive survey of FRG art).

Schneckenburger, M. (ed.) (1983) *documenta. Idee und Institution. Tendenzen – Konzepte – Materialien*, Munich: Prestel (useful compilation and analysis of material on the documenta until 1982).

KERSTIN MEY

documentary film

Kurt **Maetzig**'s weekly newsreel *The Eyewitness* (*Der Augenzeuge*), founded in the Soviet sector of Berlin in 1946, marks the starting point of documentary cinema in post-war Germany, and it was to be the GDR which would dominate non-fiction filmmaking until the 1960s. State-funded **DEFA** documentaries of the 1950s confronted National Socialism, ideological conflicts with the West, and the achievements of socialism. Leading documentarists of the period include the director and producer Karl Gass, and Andrew and Annelie **Thorndike**. The Thorndikes pioneered the compilation film using archive material to portray the progress of humankind towards socialism. Walter Heynowski and Gerhard Scheumann – who ran their own independent studio – continued this party-line work into the 1960s in a spirited, agitational style, attacking West German policy towards the GDR, as in *Brothers and Sisters* (*Brüder und Schwestern*, 1962), and the American involvement in Vietnam. A younger generation of documentarists was to turn away from propaganda during the 1960s towards a more sober observation of the contradictions inherent in GDR society. A reflective, stark and compelling DEFA style was developed by Jürgen **Böttcher**, Volker Koepp and Winfried Junge. In 1988 Helke Misselwitz' landmark *Winter adé* broke through state censorship to present a shockingly frank picture of the everyday struggles of GDR women.

Bereft of funding and audiences, documentary film languished in the FRG during the 1950s, and it was not until the mid-1960s that a new wave of documentary filmmaking emerged out of television journalism. Despite important impulses from the *Autorenfilm*, documentary filmmaking remained relatively independent of the **New German Cinema**, and very few documentaries made it into the cinema. Whilst Rolf Strobel and Heinrich Tichawsky's *Notizen aus dem Altmühltal* (Evidence From the Altmühltal) caused a scandal as early as 1961 with its portrayal of poverty and feudal injustice in Bavaria, it was Klaus Wildenhahn, Peter Nestler (*Mülheim*, 1964) and Harun **Farocki** who pioneered the political documentary in the late 1960s alongside agitational films produced by and for the **student movement**. Wildenhahn's *Far From Home* (*In der Fremde*, 1967) began a series of films about the workplace, all produced for the television service of Norddeutscher Rundfunk (NDR), characterized by a narrative 'dramatization of the everyday'. Whilst Farocki and Hartmut Bitomsky developed hybrid forms under the influence of *cinéma vérité*, many *Autorenfilmer* of the New German Cinema, including Hans Jürgen **Syberberg**, Werner **Herzog**, Ulrike **Ottinger**,

Helke **Sander**, and Rosa von **Praunheim** also made outstanding documentaries. The productive encounter of fiction and documentary filmmaking in the New German Cinema resulted in a fertile tradition of 'essay filmmaking' – pioneered by Alexander **Kluge** and Farocki – which critically and self-reflexively investigated both the mendacity of fiction and the pseudo-objectivity of documentary.

The **Wende** heralded a short-lived renaissance of documentary, as filmmakers from East and West Germany tackled the tumultuous changes with a sure eye for the contradictions and human suffering behind the political slogans and media euphoria.

See also: film: FRG; film: GDR

Further reading

Jordan, G. and Schenk, R. (eds) (1996) *Schwarzweiß und Farbe: DEFA-Dokumentarfilme 1946–92*, Berlin: Jovis (a comprehensive study of DEFA documentaries).

MARTIN BRADY AND HELEN HUGHES

Doderer, Heimito von

b. 5 September 1896, Weidlingau (near Vienna); d. 23 December 1966, Vienna

Writer

Heimito von Doderer's reputation as one of the most distinguished writers of the Second Austrian Republic, the state re-established after the defeat of the Third Reich in 1945, rests on two works of epic proportions published after WWII, when the author was well into his middle age: *Die Strudelhofstiege oder Melzer und die Tiefe der Jahre* (The Strudelhof Stairs) (1951) and *The Demons* (*Die Dämonen. Nach der Chronik des Sektionsrates Geyrenhoff*, 1956). A number of works predate these novels but Doderer's pre-war achievements received little attention at the time of their publication.

Critical assessment of Doderer's work has been coloured, however, by his political allegiances before the war. In 1933 he had joined the banned Austrian Nazi party, only to renounce his membership during the war. (He had become a Catholic

convert in 1940.) Much of Doderer's subsequent writing has been seen as an act of evasion of personal responsibilities because of his tenet that Austria's embracing of fascism was no more than an aberration, a period to be pushed aside to allow contemporary Austria to renew contact with its own imperial history, a strategy which the Doderer scholar Andrew Barker sees as the 'avoidance of recent history'.

Both *Die Strudelhofstiege* and *Die Dämonen* are so multifaceted, brimming with characters and involved plots, and underpinned by detailed descriptions of, for instance, place and smell, that they almost defy summary. Both novels are set in the Vienna of the inter-war years, yet it would be a mistake, one often made, to see Doderer as simply the chronicler of his times or as a local historian in fiction of Vienna. Despite his fascination for detail and for history, Doderer's concerns lie elsewhere, as Bruno Hannemann has commented in *Major Figures of Modern Austrian Literature* (ed. D.G. Davian, 1988, p. 190):

> Leaving contemporary history to the historian and sociologist, Doderer is primarily concerned with probing the ahistorical realm of memory and perception. Writing for him is first and foremost a tool in the personal struggle against his own subjective mind and the disorders associated with it.

Doderer's elaborate notebooks reveal the urge to make sense and give order to a world in which characters initially fail to see the path that fate has ordained for them. In giving an ultimate order to his characters' lives, Doderer's works are not entirely free from contrivance, and despite his stature in modern Austrian writing, and his considerable service as a champion of younger, more experimentally-minded writers, it cannot be said that Doderer re-defined the novel form.

See also: literature: Austria

ANTHONY BUSHELL

Döblin, Alfred

b. 10 August 1878, Stettin; d. 26 June 1957, Emmendingen

Novelist

Prominent in left-wing intellectual circles of the Weimar Republic, Döblin was acclaimed for the inventive, filmic technique of his 1929 novel *Alexanderplatz, Berlin* (*Berlin Alexanderplatz*), often compared with Joyce's *Ulysses*, which attempts to encompass the kaleidoscopic complexity and vibrant energy of the teeming modern metropolis. Among his other writings was the semi-autobiographical *Men Without Mercy* (*Pardon wird nicht gegeben*, 1935). In 1933 Döblin emigrated to France, then to New York, returning in 1945 as cultural officer with the French Miltary Government in occupied Germany.

Further reading

Kort, W. (1974) *Alfred Döblin*, New York: Twayne (critical study of work, in English).

ARRIGO SUBIOTTO

Döllgast, Hans

b. 1 April 1891, Bergheim; d. 18 March 1974, Munich

Architect

Döllgast studied at the TH (Technical University) Munich (1910–14), worked for Richard Riemerschmid in Pasing (1919–22), and was assistant to Peter Behrens (see also **architecture**) in Vienna, Berlin and Frankfurt am Main (1922–6). He established his own practice in 1927, and taught at the TH Munich from 1929 where he became Professor for Architectural Drawing (1939–56).

The historian W. Nerdinger calls Döllgast 'the outsider of modern architecture'. His most celebrated work after the war is the (critical) reconstruction of St Bonifaz and the Alte Pinakothek in Munich. In his teaching, he develops *gebundenes*

Zeichnen, a much-copied drawing method characterized by loose pencil-strokes.

MARTIN KUDLEK AND BERTHOLD PESCH

Dönhoff, Marion Gräfin

b. 2 December 1909, Friedrichstein (East Prussia; now Russia near Kaliningrad)

Publisher, editor and writer

A leading voice in post-1945 publishing, Dönhoff is best known as the publisher (since 1973) and chief editor (since 1968) of the weekly newspaper, *Die Zeit* (see **Zeit, Die**). Her social–liberal political views remain the weekly's hallmark. She joined the editorial staff shortly after the paper's founding in 1946. Born into an aristocratic East Prussian family in 1909, Dönhoff earned a doctorate in economics at the University of Basel. After returning to administer the family estate, she became involved in the anti-Nazi resistance and the 20 July 1944 plot to assassinate Hitler. She survived, but many central figures with whom she was associated were executed.

Further reading

Dönhoff, M. (1990) *Before the Storm: Memories of My Youth in Old Prussia*, trans. J. Steinberg, New York: Knopf.

Schwarzer, A. (1996) *Marion Dönhoff: Ein widerständiges Leben*, Cologne: Kiepenheuer & Witsch.

MICHAEL R. HAYSE

Döring, Wolfgang

b. 31 March 1934, Berlin

Architect

Studied at the TH (Technical University) Munich and the TH Karsruhe from 1954 to 1959, Döring worked for Egon **Eiermann**, Max **Bill** and Paul Schneider-Esleben until establishing his own practice in Düsseldorf in 1964. He is Professor for Design and Building Construction at the RWTH (Technical University) Aachen since 1973.

Döring's early projects demonstrate an interest in prefabricated, sculptural design-elements. His later architectural language moves from a modernist to a more postmodern style. His most innovative work is from the 1960s and 1970s, for instance Haus Wabbel, Düsseldorf (1973).

MARTIN KUDLEK

Dörrie, Doris

b. 26 May 1955, Hanover

Filmmaker and author

Dörrie specializes in witty film comedies, many of which are based on her own short stories. Her romantic comedy *Men* (*Männer*) was a surprise domestic and international hit in 1985, and helped pave the way for a wave of films of this genre in Germany. Her attempt to break into Hollywood with the 1988 black comedy *Me and Him* (*Ich und er*) failed, and she subsequently returned to Germany, making socially critical comedies such as *Happy Birthday* (*Happy Birthday, Türke!*, 1991) and *Nobody Loves Me* (*Keiner liebt mich*, 1995).

JONATHAN LEGG

Domenig, Günther

b. 6 July 1934, Klagenfurt

Architect

Having studied at the TH (Technical University) Graz until 1958, Domenig's partnership with Eilfried Huth followed from 1960 to 1975.

Reacting against steel and glass architecture in the tradition of **Mies**, Domenig develops a formal language characterized by expressive, organically sculptural forms. His *Steinhaus* in Kärnten (begun 1986), was at the centre of a celebrated art performance when a Viennese Gallery transmitted twenty-four hours of live building site work. Other important works are his *Mensa der Schulschwestern* in Graz (1973–7) and the *Zentralsparkasse* in Vienna (1975–9).

MARTIN KUDLEK AND BERTHOLD PESCH

Domin, Hilde

b. 27 July 1912, Cologne

Writer (née Löwenstein)

Born into a prominent secular Jewish family, Domin studied law, political science, sociology and philosophy in Cologne, Heidelberg and Berlin (with Karl **Jaspers**, Karl Mannheim, and Max Weber), earning her doctorate (with a dissertation on Pontanus as a precursor to Machiavelli) in 1935 in Florence. In 1932, she travelled to Italy with her future husband, Erwin Palm, who was studying classical archaeology. With the onset of the war, this trip became an emigration. Domin married Palm in 1936, stayed in Italy from 1932 to 1939, then moved to England for six months before leaving for the Dominican Republic, where she lived from 1940 to 1952 (and from which she derived her pseudonym). While in exile, she earned her living by teaching (including teaching German at the University of Santo Domingo starting in 1948), translating, and working as a photographer. After a brief stay in the United States (1953–4), she returned to Germany, spent years moving frequently (including four years in Spain), and then moved to Heidelberg in 1961, where Palm had earned a position in 1960 at the university. Finally in a permanent home, Domin could have her 10,000-book library sent to her from the Dominican Republic. She has lectured widely both within Germany and all over the world. In the 1987 to 1988 winter semester she lectured at the University of Frankfurt, a series which became the book *Das Gedicht als Augenblick von Freiheit* (The Poem as a Moment of Freedom) (1988).

Domin began writing poetry in 1951, a time she describes as a second birth. Written in German (and later translated into Spanish), her first poem returned her to active participation in her native culture, although her writing is also influenced by Spanish surrealism. She has written numerous volumes of poetry, starting with *Nur eine Rose als Stütze* (Only a Rose for Support) (1959); academic commentary on poetry; a novel, *Das zweite Paradies* (The Second Paradise) (1968); and the non-fiction work *Aber die Hoffnung. Autobiographisches: Berichte aus und über Deutschland* (Still Hope: Autobiographical Reports Out of and About Germany) (1982), about several writers whose fates were similar to hers: Else Laske-Schüler, Nelly **Sachs**, Paul **Celan** and Jean **Améry**.

Hans-Georg **Gadamer** dubbed Domin 'the writer of return'. Much of her work focuses on the experience of exile and return, exploring the ways in which politics intersect with people's personal lives. Within the literature of exile, Domin's work stands out as more hopeful and forgiving than that of her fellow exiled writers. Domin sees poetry as an intense encounter with the self and the poet as a truthteller who uses poetry to establish the foundation for relationships with others. Her work has been described as a poetic justification for humankind.

Further reading

Koßman, B. and Giesen, W. (eds) (1988) *Hilde Domin*, Frankfurt am Main: Stadt-und Universitätsbibliothek (collection of documents assembled for Domin's lecture series at the University of Frankfurt).

MARTINA S. ANDERSON

Domowina

Founded in 1912 as the umbrella organization for Sorbian cultural groups in Lusatia with its headquarters in Bautzen, and banned by the Nazis in 1937, the *Domowina* (Homeland) was refounded in May 1945. It was purged of 'nationalist' elements in the 1950s, brought under communist control and used by the **SED** to oversee the implementation of the nationalities policy which gave the Sorbs a degree of cultural autonomy in the GDR. During the political changes of 1989 to 1990 it was criticized for its role in the GDR, but has survived since unification as the main representive of Sorbian interests in a united Germany.

See also: minorities, non-German

PETER BARKER

Domröse, Angelica

b. 4 April 1941, Berlin

Actress

Discovered by Slatan Dudow for his film *Verwirrung der Liebe* (Confused Love) (1958) the former shorthand typist trained with the Babelsberg Film Academy before joining the **Berliner Ensemble** (1961–6) and the Volksbühne (1967–79). Her good looks and professionalism made her a GDR film and television star. Though always committed to the ideals of a socialist state she left the GDR, together with her second husband Hilmar **Thate**, after the '**Biermann Affair**'. Best known for her role as Paula in Heiner **Carow**'s 1972 film *The Legend of Paul and Paula (Die Legende von Paul und Paula)*.

HORST CLAUS

Donaueschingen Festival

The first festival (1913) in this small Black Forest town was founded by Prince Max Egon zu Fürstenberg, who dedicated it to contemporary music. Since 1950 the Festival has actively collaborated with South West German Radio, Baden-Baden, using its orchestra and its distinguished music directors (Hans **Rosbaud**, Ernest Bour and Michael **Gielen**) to present a remarkable array of commissions and premieres by such distinguished composers as Hartmann, **Stockhausen**, Boulez, **Henze**, Nono and Messiaen.

BEATRICE HARPER

Dorst, Tankred

b. 19 December 1925, Sonneberg (Thuringia)

Dramatist

Dorst first became widely known for his play *Toller* (1968) based on the revolutionary events which took place in Munich from 1918 to 1919. A soldier in the German army at the age of seventeen, Dorst was a PoW in the US and Britain. His first plays were written for the student **puppet theatre** in Munich where he lived as a freelance writer. He wrote about his experiences with this form of theatre and examined its influences on his writing, for example the use of the grotesque and ironic foreshortening, in *Auf kleiner Bühne* (On the Small Stage) (1959). His play *Gesellschaft im Herbst* (Society in the Autumn), performed in 1960 and published in 1961, won the Mannheim National Theatre drama competition. Dorst's early work shows the influence of the commedia dell'arte, of Beckett, Ionesco and Giraudoux. In the one-act play *Die Kurve* (The Curve), also performed in 1960 and published in 1961, Dorst uses bitter satire to expose the hypocrisy behind bourgeois morality.

In plays such as *Große Schmährede an der Stadtmauer* (Great Invective at the City Wall) (1961), *Die Mohrin* (The Mooress) (1964), *Graf Grün und die Notwendigkeit der Räuber* (Count Green and the Necessity of Robbers) (1965) and the documentary play *Dem Gegner den Daumen ins Auge und das Knie auf die Brust* (Stick Your Thumb in Your Opponent's Eye and Knee Him in the Chest) (1969) Dorst uses the methods of **Brecht** and **Piscator** – film clips, protest songs and political slogans – to arouse critical awareness in his audience. He collaborated with the director Peter Zadek on the television film, *Rotmord* (Red Murder) (1969) of *Toller*, and on the revue *Kleiner Mann – was nun?* (1972) based on the novel by Hans Fallada.

In the 1970s and 1980s Dorst's work is occupied with historical-political themes, as in the radio play *Eiszeit* (Ice-age) (1973) about an old man who bears a close resemblance to the Norwegian Nazi sympathizer Knut Hamsun, and the Merz cycle, an extensive chronicle, using various media, of a middle-class family from the late 1920s, consisting of *Auf dem Chimborazo* (On Mount Chimborazo) (1975, play, radio play and television film), *Dorothea Merz* (1976, novel and television film), *Klaras Mutter* (Klara's Mother) (1978, story and television film), *Die Villa* (The Villa) (1980, play), *Mosch* (1980, film), *Fragment einer Reise nach Stettin* (Fragment of a Journey to Stettin) (1981, radio play) and *Heinrich oder die Schmerzen der Phantasie* (Heinrich or the Pain of Imagination) (1985, play and radio play).

Other themes which Dorst investigates are the consequences of misguided idealism, as in the dramatization of parts of the Arthurian cycle, including *Merlin* (1980) and the story *Der nackte Mann* (The Naked Man) (1986), about Parsifal's search for God, and the theme of the artist-intellectual in times of political upheaval.

Further reading

Erken, G. (1989) *Tankred Dorst. Materialien*, Frankfurt am Main: Suhrkamp (collection of essays).

McGowan, M. (1990) 'Past, Present and Future: Myth in Three West German dramas of the 1980s', *German Life and Letters* 43, 3: 267–79 (sets *Merlin* in the context of European literature).

Sheppard, R. (1989) *Tankred Dorst's Toller: a Case Study in Reception*, New Alyth: Lochee.

MARGARET VALLANCE

dpa

As the leading news agency in the Federal Republic, the Deutsche Presse-Agentur (dpa) (established 1949) covers both domestic and international news. Based in Hamburg, dpa receives some 200,000 words of raw material daily from its network of correspondents, editing and producing more than 50,000 words for its subscribers. dpa material is accessed by almost every German newspaper and broadcast outlet, as well as by the press offices of leading political organs. The agency is a publicly-traded company (**GmbH**) owned primarily by the news media organizations that use it. However, the share of ownership is strictly limited so as to protect dpa from acquiring a particular political orientation.

ROBIN B. HODESS

Drake, Heinrich

b. 15 February 1903, Ratsiek, Berlin

Sculptor

Drake was educated in the archaic-classical figurative tradition of early twentieth-century German sculpture, and his harmonious, self-contained depictions, particularly of women and animals, were influential for a younger generation of figurative sculptors in the GDR during the 1950s and 1960s. He belonged to the founders of the Art School in Berlin-Weißensee and worked as a professor there until 1976. He was commissioned for a number of public art works including portrait busts of Goethe and Heine.

See also: sculpture

KERSTIN MEY

drama: FRG

German-language dramatic writing since 1945 comprises an impressive array of playwrights: Bertolt **Brecht**, Thomas **Bernhard**, Peter **Handke**, Ernst **Jandl**, Max **Frisch**, Friedrich **Dürrenmatt**, Heiner **Müller**, Volker **Braun** and Peter **Hacks**. Although indisputably of great import for the theatre scene of West Germany, none of these writers can be included in an account of West German drama: they were (or are) East German, Austrian or Swiss. And Peter **Weiss**, one of the foremost German-language dramatists of the period, was a citizen and resident of Sweden. West German drama of the post-war period will be remembered not for great playwrights but rather for having, in the 1950s, assimilated international trends from which it had been cut off during the Third Reich, and, in subsequent decades, for having contributed in aesthetically innovative and politically controversial ways to the socio-political culture, most importantly the discourses of *Vergangenheitsbewältigung* (coping with the National Socialist past), the left-politicization of the 1960s and early 1970s, and so-called *Neue Subjektivität* (new subjectivity).

German theatre had been largely cut off from international impulses for over a decade when the war ended. The Nazis had instrumentalized the theatres and, in 1944, closed them down; countless playwrights and theatre professionals had gone into exile. The division of the country in 1949 split the renascent theatre scene into two disparate institutional networks. With a few notable exceptions, dramatic writing of the 1950s provided escape from, rather than confrontation with, the moral, psychological and physical devastations of the Nazi period; the greatest hit was Carl **Zuckmayer**'s

The Devil's General (*Des Teufels General*, 1946), which offered retreat to a less conflict-riven, illusionary space. A few playwrights attempted, in the first few years after the war, to confront the recent past directly (Wolfgang **Borchert**, Günther **Weisenborn** and Stefan **Andres**), but dramatic writing of the 1950s reflected instead the absurdist or existentialist influence of an international scene from which Germany had been cut off during the Third Reich.

It was not until the radical political dramas of the mid-1960s and early 1970s that German drama effectively re-entered the international arena. The most acclaimed of these were Rolf **Hochhuth**'s *The Deputy* (*Der Stellvertreter*, 1963, on complicity of the Catholic church in the Third Reich), Peter Weiss's *Marat/Sade* (1964, on the problematic dialectics of revolution), and the documentary dramas: Heinar **Kipphardt**'s *In the Matter of J. Robert Oppenheimer* (*In der Sache J. Robert Oppenheimer*, 1964) on the moral and political responsibility of science, Peter Weiss's *The Investigation* (*Die Ermittlung*, 1965), an 'oratorio' based on Weiss's memory protocols of the Auschwitz hearings), and Hans Magnus **Enzensberger**'s *Havana Hearing* (*Das Verhör von Habana*, 1970). Documentary drama was defined less by a coherent aesthetic than by its indictment of the establishment in the light of historical legacies and/or systemic contradictions.

The political theatre of the mid-1960s was a precursor to a decade of radical movements in politics and politicization of the arts. The West German **student movement**, consisting as it did of the children of Nazi-era parents, went beyond the agenda of the international youth- and anti-Vietnam War movements by demanding also an investigation of systemic continuities between the Third Reich and the post-war corporate, governmental and military establishment; it spanned the left-political spectrum from anti-authoritarianism to countless socialist or communist variants and the **terrorism** of the Red Army Faction. In keeping with an agitated rejection of 'art for art's sake' (e.g. the **'Death of Literature'** controversy launched in the Journal *Kursbuch*), innovative drama of the 1960s and 1970s was characterized by an overt, left-wing political stance. The most influential dramas to arise in the context of the student movement were the socially critical children's plays of Volker Ludwig, house playwright of the **GRIPS-Theater** ensemble in West Berlin; GRIPS productions were to the pre-schoolers of the *Kinderläden* (anti-authoritarian, co-operative nursery schools established by the '68ers') what the 1 May demonstrations were to their parents. But the politicization of theatre was not limited to institutions close to the movement itself. The ensemble of the *Schaubühne am Halleschen Ufer* in Berlin (organized on principles of co-determination under the direction of Peter **Stein** in 1970) opened with a production of Brecht's pro-communist play *Die Mutter*. The emergence of radical playwrights like Werner Rainer **Fassbinder**, Franz Xaver **Kroetz** and Martin **Walser** (the latter two of whom joined, but later left, the German Communist Party) reflected the political climate of the period.

The broad (if internally conflicted) left-consensus of intellectual life began to break down in the mid-1970s; *Feuilleton* critics propounded a *Neue Subjektivität* (**New Subjectivity**), contending (not entirely accurately) that leading left-wing writers had abandoned politics for the concerns of private life and the eternal themes of art (e.g. novelist and student-leader Peter **Schneider**); many of the writers themselves rejected this reading of their work, countering that the personal sphere was the real locus of the political. However one chooses to assess that dispute, political culture in Germany was indeed changing. The West German playwright most closely associated with New Subjectivity is Botho **Strauß**, currently one of the most-produced playwrights in Germany (and a figure of some controversy due to recent flirtation with positions of the neo-right). Although he emerged from the co-operative, socially critical *Schaubühne am Halleschen Ufer*, where he was *Dramaturg* for Peter Stein, Strauß's work is often likened to that of the Austrian Peter Handke; both playwrights thematize the diffuse socio-psychological malaise of contemporary life, isolation as the modern condition, the improbability of connection. Further contemporary FRG playwrights of note are Tankred **Dorst**, Gerlind **Reinshagen**, and Thomas **Brasch**.

Further reading

Calandra, D. (1983) *New German Dramatists*, New York: Grove Press (comparative analysis of the plays of Handke, Kroetz, Fassbinder, Müller, Brasch, Bernhard and Strauß).

Innes, C. (1979) *Modern German Drama*, Cambridge: Cambridge University Press (useful, wide-range analysis of major tendencies of German-language drama 1945–77)

KAREN RUOFF KRAMER

drama: GDR

Within weeks of the end of WWII the cultural policy-makers of Germany's new socialist regime displayed their belief in the potential of drama as an educational force by the priority they gave to reopening theatres right across their territory. From the outset theatre productions were heavily subsidized by the state, ticket prices were kept low, and special performances were regularly organized for factory groups, youth organizations and the like. The Theatre Department in what later became the GDR Ministry of Culture was proud of the sixty-eight nominally independent **theatres** which it supported, believing that they catered for the full range of the population's tastes, from serious opera and operetta to variety and puppet shows. Some of the GDR's best-known theatres – the **Berliner Ensemble**, the **Deutsches Theater**, the Volksbühne and the Maxim Gorki-Theater – were located in East Berlin, but there was also a strong network of serious regional theatres, notably those in Dresden, Leipzig, Karl-Marx-Stadt (now Chemnitz), Weimar, Potsdam and Schwerin. In 1955 the number of recorded theatre-visits was 17.4 million from amongst a population of under 20 million, a remarkably high figure by western European standards. Even when the figure fell to almost half that level, to 9.9 million in 1982, as the counter-attractions of television made their impact, it was still considerably above equivalent western levels. There was one publishing house responsible for the majority of editions of plays, the Henschel Verlag, and a good-quality illustrated monthly journal, *Theater der Zeit*.

The rosy impression these statistics create of the GDR as a state committed to fostering the creative potential of its dramatists was, however, not confirmed in practice. Precisely because such high expectations had been placed on the theatre as a forum for generating group experiences which would help to make audiences more sympathetic to the regime, there was less tolerance than in the more private sphere of prose fiction of authors whose work focused on the fundamental conflicts which state socialism had failed to resolve, even where these problems were being considered from a utopian Marxist perspective. The three GDR dramatists of undisputed international significance who followed in the footsteps of Bertolt **Brecht** – Heiner **Müller**, Volker **Braun** and Christoph **Hein** – all had to battle constantly against a censorship process which led to much of their best work being banned from the stage for long periods (see also **censorship: GDR**). Although almost all of it appeared eventually, often in regional theatres which had somehow managed to find more room for manœuvre than their metropolitan counterparts, it was generally too late to stimulate the critical debate intended by the playwrights on the key issues of the original time of writing.

The essence of this conflict between dramatists and the state lay in the hostility of socialist realist theorists (see **socialist realism**) to Brecht's open-ended presentation of issues, to his view of the theatre-audience as partners in working out answers rather than pupils to be provided with the fruits of the playwright's wisdom. This led Brecht himself, after his return to the GDR, to shy away from the contemporary issues of socio-economic change which the SED wished to be treated in a propagandist manner and to concentrate on productions of his exile works. Müller began his career more provocatively by tackling one of the subjects Brecht had dropped, the personality of the worker-hero behind the ideological façade, in *Der Lohndrücker* (The Scab, 1958), placing himself on a collision course which made it virtually impossible for him to have his work performed in the 1960s, even though he was effectively fulfilling the demands of the **Bitterfelder Weg** for industrially based literature in subsequent plays like *Die Umsiedlerin* (The Resettler) (1961) and *Der Bau* (Construction) (1965). Braun's career as a dramatist, starting a decade later, took a similar course: training with the Berliner Ensemble, problems with the industrial subject-matter of his

early work (heightened in his case by the emphasis on discrimination against working women in *Schmitten* (1969) and *Tinka* (1972)), followed by a move into historical and mythical themes which – less explicitly perhaps, but no less radically – showed that the contemporary GDR was still only part of the 'prehistory' of human development.

Hein is part of the third generation of GDR dramatists who started with a solid grounding in stagecraft (in his case alongside Benno **Besson**, mainly at the Volksbühne) but now without political illusions. Some of his equally talented contemporaries, such as Stefan **Schütz** and Thomas **Brasch**, were forced into West German exile after the **Biermann Affair**, while Hein – whose successes with historical and parable plays such as *Cromwell* (1980) and *Ah Q* (1983) only came after years of frustration – eventually turned to prose-writing as the basis of a more fulfilling career. The only time during these years when a significant new work was given the full public exposure it deserved came in 1972 and 1973, when fourteen different productions of Ulrich **Plenzdorf**'s *Die neuen Leiden des jungen W.* (The New Sorrows of Young W.) ran virtually simultaneously to packed houses. This underlines the exent of Plenzdorf's good fortune in having such a genuinely accessible work to hand when **Honecker** made his deceptive promise of an end to cultural taboos. Otherwise only unthreatening comedy-writers like Rudi Strahl could hope to have their work performed so widely across the GDR. It is hardly coincidental that the GDR's final years were marked by (rarely performed) depictions of revolutionary failure, such as Müller's cycle *Die Wolokolamsker Chaussee* (The Road to Volokolamsk) (1985–8) or of a world in chaotic transition, such as Braun's *Transit Europa* and Hein's *Passage* (both 1987).

Further reading

Emmerich, W. (1996) *Kleine Literaturgeschichte der DDR*, Leipzig: Kiepenheuer (includes a concise overview of each phase in the development of GDR drama).

Fiebach, J. *et al.* (1994) *Theater in der DDR: Chronik und Positionen*, Berlin: Henschel (post-*Wende* stock-taking).

Flood, J.L. (ed.) (1990) *Kurz bevor der Vorhang fiel: Zum*

Theater der DDR, Amsterdam: Rodopi (mainly UK perspectives).

Profitlich, U. (ed.) (1987) *Dramatik der DDR*, Frankfurt am Main: Suhrkamp (reliable collection of essays).

DENNIS TATE

Dramaturg

Dramaturg denotes a theatre-professional specific to the German-speaking world. Based on the Greek word for 'play maker', the term originated in the eighteenth century, designating the combined functions of playwright and director (Lessing became *Dramaturg* of the Hamburg Nationaltheater in 1767). The contemporary *Dramaturg* is literary advisor to the theatrical production; advises director, set and costume designers on appropriate rendering of the dramatic text; participates in selection of plays for production, collects editions and adaptations of the text; and designs programme documentation. Many playwrights and directors have entered theatrical practice in the role of *Dramaturg* (e.g. Peter **Stein** and Botho **Strauß**).

KAREN RUOFF KRAMER

Drechsler, Heike

b. 16 December 1964, Gera

Athlete

A member of SC Jena since 1972 and a winner at the 1979 children's and youth Spartakiad, Drechsler made a major contribution to the GDR's medal factory, gaining a silver medal in the long jump and a bronze in the women's 100 m and 200 m at the 1988 Olympic Games. She was world champion in the long jump in 1983 and has set several world records in this event. After German unification she continued to perform at a high level, becoming Olympic and world champion in the long jump in 1992 and 1993 respectively.

MIKE DENNIS

Drewermann, Eugen

b. 20 June 1940, Bergkamen

Catholic theologian and psychotherapist

Ordained a priest in 1972, Drewermann worked as a therapist and developed a theological hermeneutic that is informed by his analysis that *angst* remains the focus of human existence. His widely and passionately discussed publications merge psychoanalysis with theology. In 1987–8 the German bishops compiled a dossier concerning his theological disagreements with the Catholic tradition. In *Kleriker. Psychogramm eines Ideals* (1989) Drewermann radically criticized the self-understanding of the church. Because of his controversial views, his canonical mission to teach (1991) and his right to preach (1992) were revoked. These disciplinary actions have not diminished his passion for scholarly activity, and he became a popular media figure.

MAGDA MUELLER

Drewitz, Ingeborg

b. 10 January 1923, Berlin; d. 26 November 1986, (West) Berlin

Writer

Ingeborg Drewitz grew up in Berlin during the reign of fascism. Forced to work for the war effort she none the less managed to continue her studies and obtained a Ph.D. in philosophy in 1945. Her 1951 novel *Alle Tore waren bewacht* (All Gates Were Guarded) was one of the first German novels to tackle the topic of the concentration camps. In this work, as in many other of her novels, Drewitz' themes are political. Her works are the works of an 'engaged' writer, treating topics such as history, its impact on contemporary society, and other social issues.

As a feminist author Drewitz is important because most of her characters who explore these themes are women. In novels as varied as *Eis auf der Elbe* (Ice on the Elbe) (1984), *Gestern war heute. Hundert Jahre Gegenwart* (Yesterday Was Today. 100 Years of the Present) (1978) and *Wer verteidigt Katrin Lambert?* (Who is Defending Katrin Lambert?)

(1974), Drewitz created female characters who are confronted with issues such as WWII and its aftermath, motherhood, the ghettos of Turkish workers and employment struggles. Exploding the myth that it is men who determine and are determined by history, Drewitz created female characters who are not just affected by the events around them, but who are active agents and participators in those events.

Drewitz was not only a writer of fiction, however. She also wrote important political pieces and was instrumental in rediscovering the work of many 'lost' German women writers, such as Bettina von Arnim.

Major works

Drewitz, I. (1969) *Bettina von Arnim. Romantik, Revolution, Utopie*, Düsseldorf and Cologne: Diederichs (one of the first scholarly works by a woman to systematically address von Arnim and her work).
—— (1974) *Wer verteidigt Katrin Lambert?* Stuttgart: Gebühr (a short novel about a female reporter who becomes intrigued by a former acquaintance's death. Her investigation eventually leads to the narrator replacing the dead woman).
—— (1978) *Gestern war heute. Hundert Jahre Gegenwart*, Düsseldorf: Claassen (in this novel Drewitz tells the story of Gabriele M., a story which spans the years 1923–77 and many major historical events, such as the depression, WWII, reconstruction and the social unrest of the 1960s).

Further reading

Häussermann, T. (ed.) (1988) *Ingeborg Drewitz: Materialien zu Werk und Wirken*, Stuttgart: Radius (the most comprehensive work on Drewitz currently available; includes biographical information, critical texts, and a comprehensive bibliography).

BRENDA L. BETHMAN

drugs

Until the late 1960s, drugs and drug abuse had never been a serious social or political issue in postwar Germany. However, influenced by their American counterparts, the hippies, and by psychedelic music, many German youths began experimenting with cannabis products and LSD for the first time during the student protests of 1968. In countercultural circles, drugs quickly gained acceptance as a new form of expression, as a symbol of generational protest, and as a means of realizing alternative lifestyles.

As the initial drug euphoria gradually wore off, however, drugs became increasingly used as a way of escaping the grim reality of the 1970s. Harder drugs, particularly heroin (which was first marketed by Bayer in 1890 as a cough suppressant!), saw widespread use in Germany's inner cities and housing project wastelands by the middle of the decade. Heroin addiction also spread to young teenagers, and along with it the problems of procurement criminality and **prostitution**. The German public was made aware of these problems by the steadily rising number of drug related deaths and documentaries of individual cases, such as the 1979 book by Christiane F., *Wir Kinder vom Bahnhof Zoo* (The Children of Zoo Station), which director Uli Edel turned into the successful motion picture of the same name (1981).

The spread of **AIDS** among heroin addicts and the rise of drug-related crime in the 1980s eventually caused many federal states and local communities to modify their approach to the drug problem. Cities like Frankfurt am Main successfully implemented needle exchange and methadon programmes, while Schleswig-Holstein led the way in a movement to decriminalize the use of so-called soft drugs (i.e. marijuana). The Federal Government still maintains a zero-tolerance policy towards drugs, but the possession of small amounts of certain substances for personal use is no longer subject to criminal prosecution in virtually all states (although definition of 'small amounts' varies greatly).

Despite some moderate successes in drug prevention and rehabilitation, about 5 percent of Germany's population are considered to be drug addicts in need of treatment. The number of drug overdoses has been fluctuating greatly, reaching a peak in 1991, with 2,125 deaths; however, on the whole, drug related crime is declining. It is estimated that at least 16 percent of all Germans between the ages of 12 and 39 have consumed illegal substances in their lifetimes. Furthermore, over 2.5 million Germans are alcoholics, and even though cigarette consumption was down by 10 percent in 1992, 40 percent of adult males, and 30 percent of adult females, are still smokers.

Beginning in the early 1990s, a new wave of psychedelic drugs swept through Germany's burgeoning techno, rave and hip-hop scene, rekindling LSD use and introducing the synthetic party drug Ecstasy (MDMA or MDEA) to masses of hedonistic youngsters at DJ performances or events such as Berlin's annual **Love Parade**.

See also: alternative culture; Neuss, Wolfgang; student movement

FREDERIC M. KOPP

dtv

Founded in 1960 by a group of publishers to issue paperback editions of previously published works, the first Deutscher Taschenbuch Verlag (dtv) editions appeared in 1961. Initially the house focused on novels, short stories and non-fiction, but the scope of publication has since been greatly enlarged. A successful programme of reference works, such as an atlas of world history, broadened the publishing programme even further. In recent years dtv has issued inexpensive reprints of the Grimm brothers' dictionary and of the authoritative edition of Goethe's works (the *Sophienausgabe*). The Munich-based firm has produced millions of widely-used books.

JOHN B. RUTLEDGE

Duden

The name *Duden* has four familiar referents, listed here in chronological order: (a) Dr Konrad Duden, 1829–1911, a high-school teacher of German and author of (b) the 'spelling dictionary' edited by Duden himself in its first eight editions, first published in 1880 as *Vollständiges Orthographisches Wörterbuch der deutschen Sprache. Nach den neuen preußischen und bayerischen Regeln*, and since 1915 called the *Duden Rechtschreibung* or similar; (c) the publishing house, *Dudenverlag*, which is now responsible not only for the *Rechtschreibung* but also for a range of **dictionaries** and other works of reference; (d) Anne **Duden**.

The *Duden* of sense (b) is a product of the perceived need to move towards the standardization of a German language in the mid-nineteenth century and particularly after the founding of the German Empire in 1871. The Duden spelling dictionary in effect acquired a national role which the various education ministries in the founding states, some of whom had been issuing less detailed guidelines on spelling for their own limited areas of jurisdiction, had not been able to assume. In 1902, Duden's *Orthographisches Wörterbuch der deutschen Sprache*, incorporating spelling reforms put forward at a Spelling Conference held the previous year in Berlin, was able to declare that it conformed to the official rules pertaining in Germany, Austria and Switzerland. While being perceived generally as authoritative on matters of spelling, *Duden* is not in any sense an official publication.

In the English-speaking world, 'standard' desk dictionaries invariably define the words they list. The *Duden Rechtschreibung*, the best-seller among German **dictionaries**, provides definitions – and then briefly – only when the compilers consider this to be particularly useful (e.g. in 1991 *Buch* is not defined, *Buffo* – '*Sänger komischer Rollen*' – is), the primary focus being very much on spelling and core grammatical information such as gender and inflexions. This willingness to forgo exhaustive coverage of meaning has meant that Duden has always managed to contain an exceptionally large number of entries within a conveniently small format.

Because of its longevity but also the fact that its publishing house split into two separate organizations during the Cold War era (one 'exiled' in Mannheim, FRG, and a state-controlled enterprise in the GDR at the original home in Leipzig), there have probably been more different editions of the *Duden Rechtschreibung* than of any other dictionary worldwide. These various editions, each being a product of its time and place, provide a useful source of information about linguistic and social developments over more than a century; in particular the many separate FRG and GDR editions have been analysed for their divergences. Since 1991 there has again been a single edition of the *Duden Rechtschreibung* and this has generated observations on, for instance, how political unity expresses itself in a lexicographical context.

See also: spelling reform

Further reading

Hatherall, G. (1986). 'The Duden Rechtschreibung 1880–1986: development and function of a popular dictionary', in R.R.K. Hartmann (ed.), *The History of Lexicography*, Amsterdam and Philadelphia, PA: J.J. Benjamins.

Sauer, W.W. (1988). *Der 'Duden'. Geschichte und Aktualität eines 'Volkswörterbuches'*, Stuttgart: J.B. Metzler.

Schaeder, B. (1994) 'Wir sind ein Wörterbuch! – Wir sind das Wörterbuch! Duden-Ost + Duden-West = Einheitsduden?', in *Zeitschrift für germanistische Linguistik* 22, 1: 59–86.

GLYN HATHERALL

Duden, Anne

b. 1 January 1942, Oldenburg

Writer

Duden trained as a bookseller in West Berlin, worked at **Wagenbach Verlag**, and in 1973 co-founded the left-wing publishing house Rotbuch Verlag. She lives in Berlin and London. Duden employs a precise, matter-of-fact style to explore concepts of the body, identity, memory and language in her innovative short stories (e.g. the collections *Übergang*, 1982, and *Steinschlag*, 1993) and longer narratives (e.g. *Das Judasschaf*, 1985).

Further reading

Adelson, L.A. (1993) *Making Bodies, Making History: Feminism and German Identity*, Lincoln, NB: University of Nebraska Press (includes discussion of *Übergang*).

Duden, A. (1985) *Opening of the Mouth*, trans. D. Couling, London: Pluto (translation of *Übergang*).

SABINE SCHMIDT

Dürrenmatt, Friedrich

b. 5 January 1921, Konolfingen (Canton Bern); d. 14 December 1990, Neuchâtel

Dramatist, novelist and artist

Along with his compatriot Max **Frisch**, who was ten years his senior, Friedrich Dürrenmatt achieved major international status and dominated the theatrical and literary scene in Switzerland from the 1950s onwards. Although his work for the theatre centred around Zürich, Dürrenmatt settled in French-speaking Neuchâtel in 1952 and remained there for the rest of his life. He married the actress Lotti Geissler in 1943; they had three children. After Lotti's death in 1983, Dürrenmatt married the actress and filmmaker Charlotte Kerr. Often a controversial figure in cultural and political matters, Dürrenmatt soon earned the epithet 'uncomfortable' (*unbequem*), and indeed much of his appeal derived from his critical stance towards his nation and its hallowed institutions. His creative work was characterized by black humour, while his theoretical and philosophical writing was informed by an acute and rigorous intellect. If writing was his profession, his lifelong passion was drawing and painting, and he has left behind him an extensive and accomplished œuvre. Shortly before his death, Dürrenmatt persuaded the Swiss Federation to establish a national literary archive and undertook to bequeath his entire literary estate to it. The Swiss Literary Archive (*Schweizerisches Literaturarchiv*) in Bern was officially opened in 1991, a month after his death.

Friedrich Dürrenmatt's stage debut, *It is Written* (*Es steht geschrieben*, 1947) made him instantly notorious in Switzerland. Zürich theatre-goers, misled by the biblical title into expecting a devotional work from this son of the manse, were deeply shocked by the scurrilous tone of the play, and the first night ended in uproar. A fertile imagination, an infectious sense of humour, a taste for the outrageous and an impish delight in springing surprises on his audiences remained the hallmarks of a score of plays over the next four decades. The leading position of the Zürich Schauspielhaus as the world's foremost German-language theatre throughout WWII and in the immediate post-war years gave Dürrenmatt's newly-launched career a vital boost, and with only a few exceptions (notably a brief flirtation with Basel in the late 1960s) he remained faithful to the Schauspielhaus, where thirteen of his plays were premièred. In 1952 Dürrenmatt began to establish an international reputation with his first German première, *The Marriage of Mr Mississippi* (*Die Ehe des Herrn Mississippi*), in Munich, and the first performance of one of his works in a foreign language, *Les fous de dieu* (It is Written) in Paris. Four years later in 1956, the real breakthrough came with *The Visit* (*Der Besuch der alten Dame*), his masterpiece. This disturbing indictment of consumer society is a textbook example of Dürrenmatt's preferred genre, tragi-comedy: the audience, lured by the bait of comic entertainment, are caught in the 'mousetrap' of serious engagement and confronted with their own tragedy through that of the hero, the mediocre 'man of courage' who rises to something approaching tragic stature. Besides *The Visit*, Dürrenmatt's reputation outside the German-speaking world rests principally on *The Physicists* (*Die Physiker*, 1962), a wry commentary on the moral obligations incumbent on scientists in times when advances in knowledge have the capacity to destroy civilization. Dürrenmatt also wrote eight radio plays, mostly during the 1950s.

Although Dürrenmatt continued to write and direct plays until shortly before his death, he never again enjoyed the same level of success as in the 1960s, not least because his later drama took on an increasingly experimental character, most evident in successive versions of his bewildering study of madness and sanity explored through a series of multi-layered characters in *Achterloo* (four versions, 1983–8).

Dürrenmatt's first published work was *The Old Man* (*Der Alte*, 1945), one of a series of apocalyptic short stories written in the last years of the war. In *The Sausage* (*Die Wurst*, 1943), a man murders his wife and turns her into sausages. Brought to trial and condemned to death, he begs one final request:

to eat the last-remaining, succulent sausage. But the judge, it seems, has already eaten it. The story provides a neat introduction to Dürrenmatt as a writer of the grotesque, and to one of his major preoccupations, the fragile nature of human justice. In *The City* (*Die Stadt*, 1943, subsequently revised), the longest of these early tales, Dürrenmatt depicted Bern, his home from the age of fourteen, as an austere, bewildering, menacing city built over a vast cave system. Drawing on the myth of the minotaur and the labyrinth, Dürrenmatt explores the relationship of each individual (we are all unique minotaurs) with other individuals and his environment. The minotaur theme is further developed in the sequel to *The City*, *The Winter War in Tibet* (*Der Winterkrieg in Tibet*, 1981) and in the poignant prose-poem, illustrated by the author, *Minotaur: A Ballad* (*Minotaurus: Eine Ballade*, 1985). Although he published ten novels and many important theoretical essays, notably *Problems of the Theatre* (*Theaterprobleme*, 1954), as a prose writer Dürrenmatt is best known for his detective novels, *The Judge and his Hangman* (*Der Richter und sein Henker*, 1950), *The Quarry* (*Der Verdacht*, 1951) and *The Pledge* (*Das Versprechen*, 1957).

Dürrenmatt's relationship with his pastor father was always fraught, and generated an antipathy towards authority and religion which informs much of his writing, for instance *The Son* (*Der Sohn*, 1943) and *The Rebel* (*Der Rebell*, written 1950, first published 1951). Five years of sporadic university studies in Bern and Zürich ended in 1946 with his decision to become a professional writer, but his contempt for the literary canon and its guardians remained, and re-emerged in 1966–7 in the *Zürich Literary Dispute* (*Zürcher Literaturstreit*). Frusch and Dürrenmatt were denounced as decadent by the latter's erstwhile professor of literature, Emil **Staiger**, and a bitter exchange ensued. Controversial to the end, on 22 November, 1990 Dürrenmatt delivered a rousing speech in honour of Václav Havel, *Switzerland: a Prison* (*Die Schweiz ein Gefängnis*, 1990), culminating in a scathing attack on the complacency and paranoia of his fellow-Swiss, who live, not in a 'bastion of freedom', but in a self-imposed prison where they spend their days in fear of one another and the rest of the world, anxiously guarding their mostly illusory democracy. Just three weeks later, he suffered a fatal heart attack at his home in Neuchâtel.

Major works

Dürrenmatt, F. (1998) *Werkausgabe*, 37 vols, Zürich: Diogenes (standard edition).
—— (1984) *Stoffe I-III*, Zürich: Diogenes.
—— (1990) *Turmbau. Stoffe IV-IX*, Zürich: Diogenes.

Further reading

Bolliger, L. and Buchmüller, E. (eds) (1996), *Play Dürrenmatt: Ein Lese- und Bilderbuch*, Zürich: Diogenes (rich and varied range of contributions, issued on the occasion of major television retrospective on Dürrenmatt).
Jenny, U. (1978) *Dürrenmatt: A Study of his Plays*, London: Eyre Methuen (succinct discussions of the major plays).
Spycher, P. (1972) *Friedrich Dürrenmatt: Das erzählerische Werk*, Frauenfeld: Huber (standard work on his narrative prose).
Tiusanen, T. (1977) *Dürrenmatt: A Study in Plays, Prose, Theory*, Princeton, NJ: Princeton University Press (extensive analysis of the plays).
Whitton, K.S. (1990) *Dürrenmatt. Reinterpretation in Retrospect*, New York, Oxford and Munich: Wolff (comprehensive study of his œuvre).

SYDNEY G. DONALD

Dutschke, Rudolf

b. 7 March 1940, Schönefeld (Kreis Luckenwalde, Mark Brandenburg); d. 24 December 1979, Aarhus (Denmark)

Leading figure in the West German student movement (popularly known as Rudi Dutschke)

The son of a post office worker, Rudi Dutschke grew up in East Germany. Although a member of the communist youth organization **FDJ**, he was deeply committed to Christian values. At school in Luckenwalde, he publicly criticized the 'voluntary' service in the armed police that awaited most young men. As a result of this 'anti-social

conduct' his *Abitur* (equivalent to A-levels) was marked down, spoiling all hope for a place at university in the GDR. He went to West Berlin, successfully retaking his exams in 1961, then enrolling as a university student to read sociology. He was deeply influenced by the texts of Marx, Lenin, **Lukács**, **Marcuse**, Fanon and Ernst **Bloch**. From 1963 he became a member of Subversive Aktion, a radical political group which merged with the **SDS**. Under Dutschke's and Bernd Rabehl's leadership, the SDS became a much more radical, socialist organization, breaking away from the parent organization, the Social Democratic Party (**SPD**). In his writings Dutschke was critical of existing socialist states like the GDR or the Soviet Union, claiming that 'real socialism' had yet to be achieved. Despite his socialist convictions, he never broke with his Christian past; in 1964 he met his later wife Gretchen, a theology student.

Dutschke's charisma made him the leading figure in the Berlin **student movement** and as such he hit the headlines in the national press. On 11 April 1968, probably as a result of the continued press attention, Dutschke was shot and severely wounded by a young Bavarian right-wing extremist, Josef Bachmann. Mass student protests and violent demonstrations, particularly against the reporting of the **Springer** press, followed that incident.

After a slow and never complete recovery from his head wounds, Dutschke moved to Cambridge to work on a Ph.D. but had his British residence permit revoked in 1971, because of 'political activities'. He was offered work at the University of Aarhus in Denmark, where he finished his doctorate about Lenin in 1974. A deep friendship with Ernst Bloch developed from 1971. Although Dutschke had some contacts with the terrorists of the Baader–Meinhof group from his student days in Berlin, he always denounced terrorist activity as a means to further the class struggle. He was also very critical of all communist groupings loyal to Moscow or Peking. In the late 1970s he played with the idea of founding a socialist party to the left of the SPD in West Germany, but then, more realistically, joined the green movement. In December 1979 he had been elected to represent green groups in Bremen at the founding conference of the Green Party (January 1980); however, he died unexpectedly from an epileptic fit, a late consequence of his headwounds, on Christmas Eve 1979.

Major works

Dutschke, R. (1974) *Versuch, Lenin auf die Füße zu stellen. Über den halbasiatischen und den westeuropäischen Weg zum Sozialismus* (his Ph.D).
—— (1980) *Mein langer Marsch*, Reinbek bei Hamburg: Rowohlt.
—— (1980) *Die Revolte*, Reinbek bei Hamburg: Rowohlt.
—— (1980) *Geschichte ist machbar*, Berlin: Wagenbach.

Further reading

Miermeister, J. (1986) *Rudi Dutschke*, Reinbek bei Hamburg: Rowohlt.

MONIKA PRÜTZEL-THOMAS

E

Ebstein, Katja

b. 9 March 1945, Königshütte (Silesia)

Singer and actress (real name Karin Witkiewicz)

Katja Ebstein grew up in Berlin, and took a university degree in archaeology and French. She did voluntary work and training at the radio station Sender Freies Berlin, and also undertook professional training in singing and acting. Since the late 1960s a singer of folk songs, **Schlager** and *chansons*, she came third in the Eurovision Song Contest in 1970 and 1971, and second in 1980. Although she had a formative influence on the German popular music of her time, she is largely forgotten today. Since the mid-1980s she has pursued a career as a theatre actress and done occasional work as a television presenter.

ANNETTE BLÜHDORN

Economic Miracle

This term (*Wirtschaftswunder* in German) is applied to the rapid recovery of the West German economy after the destruction of WWII. The period from 1949 to 1959 saw the high point of German economic achievement, when annual real growth rates were double those of 1871 to 1913. High export demand and investment surplus, and an ample, trained labour force fostered the long, non-inflationary boom. European Recovery Programme (Marshall Aid) counterpart funds were channelled to eliminate bottlenecks, promoting the reconstruction. After the war destruction, the high growth allowed 11 million refugees and expellees to be absorbed, such that by 1960, there was an unemployment rate of 0.8 percent and West Germany was again Europe's largest economy.

See also: currency reform

CHRISTOPHER H. FLOCKTON

economic and monetary union

After the fall of the Berlin Wall on 9 November 1989, and the election of a Christian Democrat-led government in the East on 18 May 1990, the State Treaty establishing economic, monetary and social union between the two Germanys was passed in mid-May and came into effect on 1 July 1990. Overnight, the barely-reformed centrally-planned economy, with its administered prices and elaborate system of subsidies, its 126 centrally-administered giant industrial combines, collectivized agriculture and its state-trading monopoly, was absorbed into the West German economic order. Exposed immediately to international competition, it had to adopt deutschmark (DM) pricing at world prices, in addition to the full assumption of West German economic and social legislation. This latter involved the monetary and banking order, competition policy, pensions, social security and employment protection. The State Treaty specified the exchange rate terms which underpinned the monetary union, and provided six main funds which would support the transformation of East Germany into a market economy, while alleviating the associated distress in the labour market. Among these was the Treuhandanstalt (Trustee Institution) which, in acting as a holding company for all the East German state's productive assets, had become the world's largest property company. The relevant State Treaty clauses duplicated the legislation passed earlier by the **Volkskammer**, which set as the Treuhand's objectives 'privatization, restructuring, and lastly, closure of wholly unprofitable enterprises'.

The political imperative of shoring up a collapsing eastern state, which was suffering a haemorrhage of key personnel and purchasing power, dictated the rapid pace. On the 6 and 7 February 1990, the federal cabinet decided hurriedly to pursue rapid **unification**, despite warnings of the dangers of a slump in the uncompetitive eastern economy. The terms of the exchange of GDR marks for deutschmarks imposed a fourfold overvaluation on the East German tradeable goods sector, but other factors, notably wage harmonization and the collapse of Comecon, also played substantial roles in the deep slump which ensued.

West German interests, and particularly the **Bundesbank**, appeared most concerned not to offer a too generous rate of exchange which would lead to a large expansion of DM liquidity in the hands of eastern consumers, with its inflationary risk. The terms agreed exchanged the stock of GDR mark assets in aggregate at 1.81:1, although savings by children, adults and pensioners were translated at parity to ceilings of 2,000, 4,000 and 6,000 GDR marks respectively. Enterprise debt was translated at 2:1. All current prices, wages, pensions and transfers were exchanged at 1:1. This led to an expansion of the DM money supply of DM 15.2 billion, or 10 percent, which did not prove inflationary. Even the translation of wages at parity did not appear wholly inappropriate, given the relativities of wage levels and productivity between East and West. It was the subsequent wage harmonization agreements, raising the tariff wage of the lower productivity workers to western levels, which guaranteed mass unemployment. The switch to trading in dollars at world prices by Comecon countries on 1 January 1991 then led to the loss of 75 percent of East Germany's export markets.

Further reading

Owen Smith, E. (1994) *The German Economy*, London: Routledge (exhaustive survey of the German economy).

CHRISTOPHER H. FLOCKTON

education system: Austria

Equality is the overriding principle of the Austrian educational system. Every child should have the same educational opportunities irrespective of social or regional origin, sex, religion or personal wealth. Education is broadly based with an emphasis on general and wide-ranging knowledge. Nine years of schooling are compulsory. Major changes in the traditional educational system that went back to the last century started in the 1960s and have led to a series of improvements in the Austrian educational system.

Pre-school and primary education

Pre-school education, *Kindergarten*, is only optional from three to six years of age and in most cases parents have to pay fees. Primary school, *Volksschule*, from six to ten should provide the basic skills needed for secondary education. Special schools provide specific support for children with special needs.

Secondary education

Between ten and fourteen there are two main options to choose from: the less demanding basic secondary school, *Hauptschule*, and the junior section of general secondary school with an emphasis on general knowledge, *Unterstufe AHS* (*Allgemeinbildende Höhere Schule*). An additional year of general pre-vocational training (*Polytechnischer Lehrgang*) completes the requirements of compulsory school education.

In rural areas, the basic secondary school is the more popular type of school whereas in towns many more pupils would attend general secondary school.

At the age of fourteen pupils can enter the senior section of general secondary school, *Oberstufe AHS* –

a course of four years leading to the *Matura*, the Austrian school leaving exam that gives access to university education.

There is a large variety of secondary school types that take care of specific interests, the most popular ones being grammar schools (*Gymnasium*) with an emphasis on Latin and other foreign languages, and grammar schools for students especially interested in mathematics and science (*Realgymnasium*).

Vocational training and education

Students who want to undergo a specific vocational training in addition to their general education can attend an advanced-level vocational secondary school from fifteen to nineteen. A number of highly specialized schools cater for these educational needs, for instance schools for trade and commerce, engineering, tourism, farming and forestry. In addition to their vocational qualification these students also have to sit the school-leaving exam, the *Matura*.

Intermediate level vocational schools (*Berufsbildende Mittlere Schulen*) do not lead up to the *Matura*, but provide a three- to four-year course in a number of professional fields.

Pupils who prefer to take up a trade have to finish nine years of compulsory schooling, and then they have to undergo an apprenticeship as well as a compulsory course of basic vocational training (*Berufsschule*).

In general, it is the aim of the Austrian educational system to provide a sound and wide-ranging academic training as well as social and communicative skills. A national curriculum for all schools (with a considerable number of variations according to the various school types) provides the basis for a nationwide standard of education.

Students are tested regularly by their teachers throughout the whole school year and their marks determine whether they can go on to the next level. They have to repeat a year if they do not meet the requirements for a certain level.

Most schools are run by the state, with a certain number of privately run schools (mainly church schools).

According to the principle of equal access for everyone state education as well as university courses are free of charge and expenses like travel cards and textbooks are largely met by the state.

Since 1974 parents and pupils have had the explicit right to participate in all decisions that affect school life apart from purely pedagogical matters.

Teacher training

Prospective teachers at *Volksschule* and *Hauptschule* receive their professional training at specific colleges that specialize in educational theory, methodology and subject-orientated courses. Secondary school teachers have to complete a university course in their respective subjects as well as a university training course in pedagogy.

Colleges of further education (*Fachhochschulen*)

In 1994 a new system of mostly decentralized colleges of further education was created. The basic entrance requirements are the *Matura* or entrance examinations for students without *Matura*. These colleges can be run by private organizations and only need state approval. The range of courses is limited to certain fields of advanced professional training (e.g. software engineering, construction management and industrial design). They offer fixed-term courses and also lead to degrees, *Magister* (FH) or *Diplomingenieur* (FH).

University education

The twelve highly independent Austrian universities and six colleges of art, mostly situated in provincial towns and the capital Vienna and funded by the state, provide free university education in the form of more than 600 course options.

Apart from the *Matura* neither entrance examinations nor entrance restrictions based on student numbers or grades exist. However, certain additional qualifications may be required for specific courses.

University courses take a certain minimum number of semesters, but there is no upper limit, and many students take much longer than the minimum requirement to complete their studies.

Owing to high student numbers and also high staff-student ratios students have a lot of independence, as well as no effective guidance. Student support in the form of a tutorial system does not exist. These factors lead to long and often open-ended courses and high drop-out rates.

A degree is only awarded at the end of a course if all its individual sections have been successfully completed. There is neither an overall mark for a university course nor are 'first' class degrees awarded. The degree titles *Magister* (for the humanities and law school, etc.) or *Diplomingenieur* (for technical studies) are the equivalent to about five or more years of study. Ph.D. students receive the title *Doktor*.

In general, Austrian universities are devoted to research as well as higher education. Owing to the small size of the country and consequently to the restricted funding opportunities, research can only be carried out on a limited scale. However, Austria has always tried to take part in and contribute to international research projects.

Further reading

Plank, F.H. (1993) *Education in Austria. A Concise Presentation*, Vienna: Federal Ministry of Education and the Arts.

GEORG HELLMAYR

education system: FRG

German education has traditionally been state-controlled and despite the perversion of power by the National Socialists, state control was re-established by the various **Land** governments soon after 1945. In general, education is the responsibility of each individual *Land* and central government has only limited power in educational matters, restricted to such fundamental issues as guaranteeing the freedom of scholarship, the provision of religious education, and the establishment of private schools. Some additional control came in the wake of the 1969 educational reforms, with the recognition that some form of harmonization was necessary to provide central funding and rationalization in vocational training, higher edu-

cation and research. Co-ordination between individual *Länder* was first established in 1948 with the *Ständige Konferenz der Kultusminister* (Standing Conference of *Länder* Ministers of Education and Cultural Affairs). Teachers at state schools and universities normally enjoy civil service status. Most schools are half-day schools with only a minimum of extra-curricular provision for pupils. Private education has a very minor role: some 5 percent of pupils attend private schools. Since the Weimar Republic's abolition of private preparatory schools on the grounds of social divisiveness, private education in the FRG does not cater for privileged social groups but instead ministers to specially perceived needs, either in vocational or other pedagogic areas or to religious groups. Fees are minimal and most private schools are church-maintained, the majority belonging to the Catholic church. In addition to these are *Rudolf Steiner* or *Waldorf* schools, and schools for vocational training and for the handicapped. The *Länder* provide up to 90 percent of the funding for these schools.

In 1945 the comprehensive re-education programme imposed by the Allies met with considerable resistance from the West German educators and politicians who favoured a return to the pre-fascist education patterns of the Weimar Republic, ignoring international developments in pedagogical studies and oblivious to the undemocratic, authoritarian and paternalistic nature of the traditional German system. Despite the importance often attributed to economic factors, the debate on education reforms, continuing at various levels of intensity since the end of WWII has, in fact, been a debate on the degree of modernity to be embraced by German society. The churches and the *Philologenverband* (grammar school association) were amongst the more conservative forces and as a result of their reactionary policies (see also **churches and religion**), supported by the **CDU/CSU**, the new FRG returned to a tripartite system with pupil selection at the age of ten. Pupil ratios in different types of school remained virtually unchanged until the mid-1960s with about 70 percent attending the *Hauptschule* (secondary modern school) and only 16 percent entering the *Gymnasium*. Since then, enrolment at the *Hauptschule* has fallen by 50 percent, with a corresponding increase for *Gymnasien* of 66 percent and for *Realschulen* of over 120 percent.

First signs of public interest in education reforms emerged in response to economic forecasts: in 1961 an OECD report sought to establish a causal relationship between investment in higher education and economic growth, and a comparison of the FRG with countries such as France and Sweden revealed a dramatic, almost fifty-fold imbalance in **students** entering higher education. In 1964, Georg Picht employed these figures in an article entitled 'Die deutsche Bildungskatastrophe' (The German Education Catastrophe). His thesis was that student numbers are indicative of a nation's intellectual potential and decisive for its economic competitiveness, general standard of living and political status (Picht 1964: 17). Whole sections of society, the *Begabungsreserven* (educational reserves), were being excluded from higher education: in particular women, pupils from working class and rural backgrounds, and Catholics. Picht's article caused a sensation and made education reform the most important political issue for nearly a decade. His thesis was amended by Ralf **Dahrendorf**, applying a more socio-political slant with his formula '*Bildung ist Bürgerrecht*' (education is a citizen's right) (Dahrendorf 1965). The impact of such claims was the greater since a latent interest in education had already emerged, particularly amongst the middle-class, whose children increasingly found conditions at overcrowded universities unacceptable. A period of reformist optimism and euphoria coincided with the Grand Coalition (1966–9), followed by the SPD government of Willy Brandt (1969–74). Educational co-operation between federal and *Land* governments was facilitated by large government majorities and a general desire for internal reform. In addition to constitutional changes previously mentioned, there was agreement on widening access to the *Gymnasium* and to the *Realschule*. By the late 1960s these reforms ensured that the 'educational reserves' were being exploited, leading to a more than fourfold increase in university students.

More ambitious plans failed to take root: the elimination of Germany's tripartite school system and its replacement by a *Gesamtschule* (1969) (comprehensive school) was unsuccessful. The introduction of the *Gesamthochschule* (1972) (comprehensive university) was never accepted by a majority of *Länder*, the experiment collapsing in the mid-1970s. The role of the 1968 **student movement** has often been exaggerated in this respect. Whilst doing much to publicize and politicize the debate, it had not initiated the reform movement. A political compromise emerged in 1973 in the form of the *Bildungsgesamtplan* (comprehensive education plan) which outlined educational policy until 1985. The plan endorsed a general opening up of education with greater flexibility, allowing transfer from one system to another whilst retaining the tripartite structure. In the meantime, however, the reformist zeal had begun to wane and the international economic slump, precipitated by the oil crisis of 1973, ushered in a general shift in politics and a retreat from modernist education policies. New priorities in the 1970s also rendered some of the plan's objectives obsolete: the expansion in *Gymnasium* pupils was to cause serious university overcrowding, whilst apprenticeships often remained unfilled, leading to skill shortages in crafts and industry.

When the GDR collapsed in 1989, the FRG missed the opportunity of adopting some of the GDR's more enlightened features, such as better provision for pre-school children, a positive approach to comprehensive education, and the award of the ***Abitur*** after twelve years. The unification itself, in constitutional terms a treaty of accession, illustrates this clearly. Virtually all changes affected the former GDR: education came under the auspices of the five newly formed *Länder*, and federal structures such as the Standing Commission and the *Wissenschaftsrat* (Science Council) extended their competence across former GDR territory. Some transitional exceptions apply for most of the new *Länder*, for instance gaining the *Abitur* after twelve years at school. Religious education, however, became compulsory, though parents (and pupils from the age of fourteen) have the right of withdrawal from these classes. The tripartite system has generally been adopted, though a greater provision of comprehensive schools is retained.

A definitive description of the existing education system is problematic, as several *Länder* have special regulations which cannot be encompassed here. At nursery level, the largely church-owned *Kindergärten* accept children from the age of three, attended by 75 percent of three-year-olds and over 80 percent of five-year-olds. Attendance is voluntary and parents are charged fees, varying in amount and often income-related. The *Grundschule* (primary school) is compulsory for children from the age of six to ten. The weekly timetable covers between twenty to thirty lessons and children attend school in the mornings only. Teaching methods have become more pupil-centred with specialist subjects introduced in the final year only. Hesse retains some English lessons in Year Four, but other *Länder* have abandoned experimental classes at this level and have returned to a more traditional curriculum. Children of foreign workers (**Gastarbeiter**) are expected to integrate into the German school environment but help with extra lessons is provided. In some urban areas they have lessons in the mother tongue.

Transition to the secondary level has been made easier, but some form of assessment remains. An *Orientierungsstufe* (orientation stage) has been introduced in most *Länder* in years five and six where a co-ordinated syllabus exists for all types of school, effectively postponing a final decision by two years. The *Hauptschule*, intended to cater for the majority of students, has suffered a severe decline, since an increasing number of parents now seek a higher educational standard for their children. It has become a '*Restschule*' (school for left-overs), a typical development in a system which distinguishes between different intellectual levels (Etzold 1996: 33). The *Hauptschule* concentrates on practical subjects and vocational studies which are designed to facilitate the transition from school to work. It has introduced a special core curriculum for German and mathematics and offers English as a foreign language. In general, more pupils in southern Germany and in rural areas attend this type of school but, on leaving, find increasing difficulty in gaining employment.

The *Realschule* has expanded more than any other type of school and is now the major school at secondary level. It prepares for employment in the middle ranks of administration, industry and crafts and tends to have a vocational orientation. It also affords access to the upper level of the *Gymnasium*. The *Gymnasium*, catering for students with an aptitude for higher education, normally extends over nine years. Following its expansion in the 1970s, it is no longer élitist, with an intake of approximately 27 percent of an age group. The traditional distinction between *Gymnasium* oriented towards humanism, modern languages, and mathematical science has largely disappeared. The first foreign language tends to be English, with French or Latin offered in Class Seven. Minority languages, economics, arts and other distinctive subjects are offered in some special *Gymnasien*. Basic training in information technology is the rule. The upper level of the *Gymnasium* (years eleven to thirteen) has seen radical changes, leading to a reduction of subjects in favour of a core syllabus, leading to the *Abitur*, calculated on a points system. The situation with regards to the remaining *Gesamtschulen* is complicated, as a distinction exists between co-operative and integrated types. The former consist of different school types under one roof and the latter rely on streaming, much as with British comprehensives.

The tertiary level of education has widened enormously, offering many different options other than university education, amongst them the specialized *Fachoberschule*. An often underrated area is Germany's system of vocational training, standardized by the *Berufsbildungsgesetz* (vocational training law) in 1969. All youngsters have to follow some kind of education programme until the age of eighteen and those not in full-time education have to attend the *Berufsschule* (vocational college) or a similar college. The most common form of training involves the dual system, training on the job as an apprentice with either day- or block-release attendance at the *Berufsschule*. College provides the apprentice with basic general education, a subject-related foundation course and particular craft- or trade-related skills. Unemployed youngsters also have to attend college in order to obtain some form of basic training. Students are recruited in equal measure from *Haupt-* and *Realschule*, with an additional 15 percent from the *Gymnasium*.

In short, although the German education system has been rather reluctant to introduce reforms, it has become much more flexible, transparent, and permeable, and provides excellence in vocational training. Secondary and higher education has been opened up to a wide range of the population and, with its many different pathways, it might be seen to have the edge over the comprehensive system which cannot offer the same degree of flexibility.

Further reading

Dahrendorf, R. (1965) *Bildung ist Bürgerrecht*, Hamburg: Nannen.

Etzold, S. (1996) 'Die Hauptschule. Ein Nachruf', *Die Zeit* 6: 33.

Führ, C. (1989) *Schools and Institutions of Higher Education in the Federal Republic of Germany*, Bonn: Inter Nationes (a detailed survey of reforms and individual types of school).

—— (1992) *On the Education System in the Five New Länder of the Federal Republic of Germany*, Bonn: Inter Nationes (provides a detailed follow-up to the above).

Phillips, D. (ed.) (1995) *Education in Germany: Tradition and Reform in Historical Context*, London and New York: Routledge (indispensable for further study with parts 1, 3 and 4 offering a detailed insight into the subject-matter).

Picht, G. (1964) *Die deutsche Bildungskatastrophe*, Olten: Walter.

HANS J. HAHN

education system: GDR

The GDR education system, based on Marxist–Leninist principles of the unity of politics and pedagogics, and emphasizing the development of an 'all-round socialist individual', was generally considered the model for an industrialized socialist society. Organized in accordance with the principle of democratic centralism, it sought to achieve an optimal unity of education and work through a process of life-long learning.

GDR education began with pre-school provision which eased labour shortages by providing free child care: 80 percent of children were attending crèche or *Kindergärten* in 1989. Compulsory schooling began at age six with the Polytechnical School, offering lower level general education and providing daycare (*Schulhort*) to some 85 percent of pupils with supervision of homework, sport and leisure activities. From age ten, sciences, social sciences and modern languages were introduced, with Russian as first language and a second choice of English, French, Polish or Czech. Three years later technical subjects followed, underpinned by ideological instruction in *Einführung in die sozialistische Produktion* (introduction to socialist production methods) and the *Unterrichtstag in der Produktion* (day of instruction in socialist industry and agriculture). Still affiliated to the Polytechnical School, the *Erweiterte Oberschule* specifically prepared students for higher education, producing 65 percent of all university entrants. A distinctive feature of GDR education was its special schools, catering for exceptional children in sports, arts, Russian, maths and science. Vocational training followed the traditional German pattern of dual training in vocational schools and the workplace, compulsory for those leaving school at sixteen and divided into a foundation course, followed by specialist subjects and always reenforced by political and ideological instruction. Higher education was available in fifty-four institutions, including six universities and eighteen technical universities with an overall staff-student ratio of 1:5.3. A two-year basic studies programme, followed by three years specialist studies, led to the award of a diploma. Instruction in Marxism–Leninism, Russian, sport, and military training were compulsory. Limited to the most talented 6 percent of the student population, postgraduate studies were regulated in accordance with the demands of industry.

The development of the education system underwent five stages. With the collapse of the Third Reich, the Soviet Military Government, together with German communist and anti-fascist groups, implemented de-militarization and democratization as laid down by the **Potsdam Agreement**. The *Gesetz zur Demokratisierung der deutschen Schule* (Law on the Democratization of German Schools), introduced in May to June 1946, enforced strict **denazification** of teachers and introduced an eight-year *Einheitsschule* (integrated school system), replacing the traditional German selective tripartite system. Strict separation of church and state was observed. Several of these measures reintroduced programmes suppressed by conservative forces during the Weimar Republic (e.g. the abolition of private schools and the promotion of education in rural areas). The establishment of the

GDR (October 1949) introduced a more socialist education system, closely following Soviet patterns. A further strengthening of the integrated school, an expansion of vocational training, and progress towards the implementation of a Marxist–Leninist ideology were its chief aims, the latter becoming a working principle from 1952 onwards. A third stage began in 1959 with the *Gesetz über die sozialistische Entwicklung des Schulwesens* (Law on the Socialist Development of the School System) which introduced the *Zehnklassige allgemeinbildende polytechnische Oberschule* (ten year polytechnical school for general education), based on similar developments in the USSR. Linking education and training with productive work, it established the compulsory *Unterrichtstag in der Produktion*. This new strictly comprehensive school replaced the old system. Remaining at least partly outside was the *Erweiterte Oberschule* (extended secondary school) which prepared students from the eigth class of the polytechnical school for an academic career, selecting according to achievement, social background, and ideological commitment, with a catchment of approximately 10 percent of an age group. Its students followed a more academic curriculum and were awarded the **Abitur** after two years, as opposed to a three-year vocational training *Abitur* at the polytechnical school. In 1965 a fourth phase was initiated with the *Gesetz über das einheitliche sozialistische Bildungssystem* (Law on the Integrated Socialist Education System). This sought to underpin and integrate the existing system according to strict scientific and ideological principles. New curricula and revised study and teaching programmes were introduced and teacher-training was standardized. The reforms not only aimed to reconcile the needs of an industrialized society with those of the individual and of socialism, but also attempted to broaden access for people already at work. The final stage came with **Honecker**'s accession in 1971 and in response to the need for greater co-operation among Comecon countries. With the actual framework in place, a period of stability and continuity began. Educational policies were fully integrated into a five-year economic plan, seeking to adjust education to the needs of industry. Student numbers at university declined slightly after 1976 whilst enrolment at technical and vocational colleges saw a correspond-

ing rise. Despite continuing ideological differences, friction between the two German states began to decline during the late 1970s and 1980s. The needs of technology and industry came to outweigh ideological objectives, preparing the ground for a cultural agreement between the two Germanies (1986). Nevertheless, two further changes gave the GDR a distinctive direction: the introduction of *sozialistische Wehrerziehung* (socialist military training) in 1978 and the transformation from socialist to communist pedagogics in 1976. Both measures signalled further progress towards the fulfilment of the Marxist aim, while in reality the system became more relaxed, conforming to the '*real existierender Sozialismus*' (the reality of existing socialism).

See also: education system: FRG; education system: GDR

Further reading

Anweiler, O. (1988) *Schulpolitik und Schulsystem in der DDR*, Opladen: Leske und Budrich (the definitive study of the GDR education system).

Günther, K.-H. and Uhlig, G. (1973) *History of the Schools in the German Democratic Republic 1945–68*, Berlin: Volk & Wissen (a thorough, but pro-GDR, account).

Wolter, W. (1984) 'Educational Policy alongside Technological Development in the German Democratic Republic', *Quarterly Review of Education* 14, 4: 497–507 (examines scientific-technological developments in relation to educational planning).

HANS J. HAHN

education system: Switzerland

One of the difficulties in getting a clear picture of the Swiss education system is that each of the cantons and half-cantons has its own system. This means that there are twenty-six systems in all; even leaving aside the purely French and Italian-speaking cantons, there are still twenty-two fully or partly German-speaking ones. The differences from canton to canton are mostly slight, and there are many common denominators between all cantons. The following refers only to the German-speaking cantons and will concentrate on features common to most of them.

Pre-school education (*Kindergarten*), though fairly commonly available, falls largely outside the formal educational system and is provided by various organizations. The length of the course is usually two years.

Compulsory education starts at the age of six or seven. The first level of schooling, which mostly lasts for six years, is known in all parts as *Primarschule*.

The types of school, and their nomenclature, are considerably more complicated in the realm of secondary schooling. Most cantons offer two grades of lower secondary schooling, known as *Realschule* and *Sekundarschule*, both normally lasting three years. (It must be noted that in most of German-speaking Switzerland the term *Sekundarschule* refers specifically to a type of intermediate secondary school.) The higher secondary school is invariably known as *Gymnasium* (the course lasts either seven years after a *Primarschule* or four years on top of a *Sekundarschule*), though it often forms part of a multilateral *Kantonsschule* (cantonal school), which may embrace other specialized forms of secondary school. The leaving certificate – equivalent to the German *Reifeprüfung* (**Abitur**) – is called *Maturität* (commonly known as *Matura*); this exam has several types, based on different combinations of subjects; the syllabuses follow strict federal guidelines.

There are German-language universities at Basel, Zürich, and Bern, as well as the bilingual one at Fribourg; all of these institutions are run by the cantons in which they are situated. The Eidgenössische Technische Hochschule at Zürich is a large university of technology run by the Federal authorities, while the University 'Hochschule' at St Gallen is oriented towards economics and social sciences. The basic degree offered by most of the German-speaking universities is the *Lizentiat*, which involves examinations and submission of a substantial dissertation.

Vocational education in Switzerland is based on a well-organized network, following for most occupations the pattern of the 'dual system': young people are apprenticed to a firm or organization, where they are occupied for most of the time, attending a *Berufsschule* (vocational school) for two days in the week. The highest form of vocational education is traditionally known in German-speaking Switzerland as *Technikum* (for technological subjects).

Teacher training for the primary school is carried out in institutions at secondary-school level, which are mostly called *Lehrerseminar*. To teach at secondary schools, students attend university courses of varying durations.

See also: education system: Austria; education system: FRG; education system: GDR

Further reading

Schule und Elternhaus (1994) *Schulsysteme der Schweiz. Eine tabellarische Übersicht*, Basel: Schule und Elternhaus Schweiz.

GRAHAM MARTIN

Egk, Werner

b. 17 May 1901, Donauwörth; d. 10 July 1983, Inning (Bavaria)

Composer

After secondary schooling in Augsburg, Egk studied music in Frankfurt am Main in 1919, moving to Munich and Carl **Orff**. Here he wrote his first scores for the theatre. From 1925 to 1927 he lived in Italy, before returning to Munich via Berlin. His first major works came in the 1930s with the oratorio *Furchtlosigkeit und Wohlwollen* (1931), the radio opera *Columbus* (1932) and the stage opera *Die Zaubergeige* in 1935. His specially commissioned work for the Berlin Olympics in 1936 was rewarded by Hitler with a gold medal. Egk remained in Germany throughout the war, for most of the time as conductor of the Staatsoper. His first work after the war, the ballet *Abraxas* (1948) was banned after five performances by the Bavarian authorities for its alleged obscenity. Shortly after he moved to West Berlin.

Although he composed in all genres, it is his stage music that has nearest approached durability. His other vocal works owe much to French influences, as their titles indicate: *Drei Chansons d'Orleéans* (1940), *La Tentation de St Antoine* (1947) and *Chanson et Romance* (1953). Egk also published various essays, such as *Musik, Wort, Bild* (Music, Word, Picture) (1960), and was a contributor to the major German and Austrian music journals.

DEREK McCULLOCH

Eich, Günter

b. 1 February 1907, Lebus an der Oder; d. 20 December 1972, Großgmain (Salzburg)

Writer (also wrote as Erich Günter)

Eich, whose works include approximately thirty radio plays and six volumes of poetry, was one of the most remarkable poets after 1945 and the creator of the poetic radio play. As a student of Chinese at the university of Berlin, Eich 'wanted to do something which could not be of much use to anyone'. This gesture of refusal remained typical of the author and his work. In his most famous radio play *Träume* (Dreams) (1950) he wrote: '*Seid unnütz'* (Be useless). Eich first published a number of poems under the pseudonym Erich Günter in the *Anthologie jüngster Lyrik* (edited by Klaus **Mann** and Willi Fehse) in 1927. His first radio play, *Das Leben und Sterben des Sängers Caruso* (The Life and Death of Caruso) appeared in 1929, and a year later his first book of poems, *Gedichte*, was published. From 1930 he studied economics, but decided to become a writer in 1932 – for him, this was not only a profession, but a decision to see the world as language. In 1939, he was conscripted to serve in the war, and was taken prisoner by the Americans (1945–6). During his imprisonment, he started to write poetry again, and his matter-of-fact poem 'Inventur' (Stocktaking) became the epitome of the German literary renewal or *Kahlschlag* (clean sweep) after 1945. Its verses of dry, sparse reality, desperate irony and yet hope offered language once again new possibility. Yet he was not interested in describing reality but in experiencing it through poetry.

From 1946 to 1947 he contributed to the journal *Der Ruf* (The Call) edited by Alfred **Andersch** and Hans Werner **Richter**, and became one of the founding members of *Gruppe 47*. His most important radio plays, such as *Die Mädchen aus Viterbo* (see *Journeys: Two Radio Plays*) (1968), and poems (see *Valuable Nail: Selected Poems*, 1981) were written in the 1950s. He married the Austrian writer Ilse **Aichinger** in 1953, and received a number of literary prizes, among them the Büchner Prize (1959). In the last years of his life, Eich published a form of short prose, which he called *Maulwürfe* (Moles). In the three volumes of nonsense miniatures, political slogans, and aphorisms entitled *Maulwürfe* (1968), *Ein Tibeter in meinem Büro* (A Tibetan in My Office) (1970) and *49 Maulwürfe* (1970) (see *Pigeons and Moles: Selected Writings of Günter Eich*, 1991) he once more gives evidence of his mistrust of unambiguity, his awareness of the power of language, and his belief in the necessity of refusal.

See also: Gruppe 47; *Hörspiel: FRG*; *Hörspiel: GDR*; *Vergangenheitsbewältigung*

Further reading

Foot, R. (1982) *The Phenomenon of Speechlessness in the Poetry of Marie Luise Kaschnitz, Günter Eich, Nelly Sachs and Paul Celan*, Bonn: Bouvier.

Fowler, F.M. (1966) 'Günter Eich', in B. Keith-Smith (ed.) *Essays on Contemporary German Literature*, Philadelphia, PA: Dufour.

Steiner, P. (1971) 'The World of Günter Eich's Radio Plays', *Germanic Review* 46: 210–27.

CHRISTIANE SCHÖNFELD

Eichmann, (Karl) Adolf

b. 19 March 1906, Solingen; d. 31 May 1962, Tel Aviv

Nazi bureaucrat and war criminal

During the last of his thirteen years in the SS, Eichmann organized anti-Semitic operations, including the transportation of Jews in the 'final solution'. He escaped from American custody in 1946, later settling, incognito, in Argentina. In 1960, the Israeli Secret Service finally located and captured him, smuggling him to Israel. He stood trial for war crimes in 1961, received a guilty verdict and died by hanging six months later. Prominently reported in the media, the Eichmann trial was a defining moment in the discussion about the **Holocaust**, focusing for the first time on the culpability of 'behind-the-scenes' bureaucrats ('*Schreibtischtäter*'). Neo-Nazis inside and outside Germany still proclaim Eichmann's execution unjust and proof of Jewish hatred of Germans. Yet they consider Eichmann no martyr; his confession and defence of 'acting under orders' disgust those nostalgic for Hitler's regime.

JOEL S.A. HAYWARD

Eiermann, Egon

b. 29 September 1904, Neuendorf (Berlin); d. 19 July 1970, Baden-Baden

Architect

Having studied at the TH (Technical University) Charlottenburg, Berlin, from 1923 to 1927 (under Hans Poelzig), Eiermann worked for Rudolf Karstadt Company, Hamburg (1927–8) and BE-WAG, Berlin (1928–30). He established a private practice in Berlin (1931–1945) and in Karlsruhe (1947–70). He also held the post of Dean of Faculty of Architecture, University of Karlsruhe (1947–70).

Eiermann is a modernist architect who nevertheless stresses the human denominator in his designs, especially in his later buildings. His work demonstrates great adaptability and variety and a formidable attention to detail. His Olivetti building (1968–72) in Frankfurt am Main marks one of the high points in post-war architecture.

MARTIN KUDLEK

Einem, Gottfried von

b. 24 January 1918, Bern

Composer

The son of a military attaché, von Einem's early years were spent in a variety of places, including Plön in Schleswig-Holstein, Ratzeburg and England. His first appointments were as répétiteur both at the Staatsoper in Berlin and at the Festspielhaus in Bayreuth. He was arrested and interrogated by the Gestapo, an experience redolent of Kafka's *Der*

Progeß, the subject matter of his second opera. He became a friend and pupil of **Blacher**, who collaborated with him as librettist for various of von Einem's operas. These were mostly adaptations of works of literary merit: Nestroy's *Der Zerrissene*, Büchner's *Dantons Tod*, **Dürrenmatt**'s *Besuch der alten Dame* and Schiller's *Kabale und Liebe*, in addition to the above Kafka novel. Though indubitably 'conservative' his operas continue to hold their own in the repertoire of the German-language opera houses.

DEREK McCULLOCH

Eisler, Georg

b. 20 April 1928, Vienna; d. 14 January 1998, Vienna

Painter and graphic artist

The son of the composer Hanns **Eisler**, Georg Eisler left Vienna for Prague in 1938 with his mother and thereafter settled near Manchester in England. He trained at the Salford School of Art and, by 1944, became acquainted with Oskar Kokoschka. His œuvre links with an expressive painterly tradition but his figural works – portraiture, studio interiors and city scenes – are invested with a compelling sense of contemporaneity. So, too, his politically-inspired paintings of the 1970s and 1980s that are enriched by his concurrent interest in graphic techniques and caricature.

SHULAMITH BEHR

Eisler, Hanns

b. 6 July 1898, Leipzig; d. 6 September 1962, (East) Berlin

Composer

The son of a Viennese philosopher, Eisler moved to Vienna in 1901, attending the Staatsgymnasium and teaching himself the rudiments of music. After the war he was accepted as a pupil by Schoenberg (who waived his fee), and on occasion had lessons with Webern. His early compositions were much influenced by Schoenberg, and in 1924 his first Piano Sonata won the Vienna Arts Prize. In 1925 he moved to Berlin. A year later he joined the Communist Party; at this time he became disaffected with much modern music, and fell out with Schoenberg. His own compositions displayed an increasingly political dimension, and in 1930 he began his long association with **Brecht**. His music was banned after 1933, allowing him the opportunity to travel and have his works performed abroad (including the première of his *Kleine Sinfonie* in London in 1935). Like **Blacher** he took refuge in the US where he continued to collaborate with Brecht. In 1947 he fell foul of the Committee on Un-American Activities, but with the support of the international artistic community he was released and extradited in 1948, returning via Vienna and Prague to Berlin and a professorship at the Hochschule für Musik, where he dedicated himself to *angewandte Musik* (applied music), music written for performance other than in the formal concert hall. For a while his commitment to the communist ideals of the GDR (he composed the **national anthem**) obscured for many western commentators the merits of his music, but the picture of a truly original talent is emerging from the process of re-appraisal.

DEREK McCULLOCH

elections: FRG

National elections are held in the Federal Republic of Germany every four years. As mandated by the constitution, elections for all parliaments are general, direct, free, equal and secret, and every German citizen aged eighteen or above can vote and can stand as a candidate for the **Bundestag**.

The distribution of seats is decided by a modified type of proportional representation where half of the seats are allocated by direct majority representation, the other half by proportional representation. Thus, every voter has two votes. The first vote is cast for a specific candidate of a particular constituency who – if successful – will represent his or her constituency in the Bundestag. The second vote is cast for a party. Parties in each federal state draw up a list with candidates

containing the names of eligible politicians with the most important politicians topping the list (making it virtually certain that key figures placed at the top of the list will enter the Bundestag). A party's total nationwide share of second votes determines its total number of seats in the Bundestag, which in the final count combines the seats won by individual candidates in the first vote with candidates chosen from the *Land* lists. In some cases a party can win more direct seats in the constituencies than its proportion of the votes would justify. These seats – known as 'overhang' (*Überhangmandate*) are kept by the party. As a result the overall number of MPs will increase for the session. This system of proportional representation benefits smaller parties and allows them to have a say in the legislative process.

However, in order to prevent splinter parties from entering parliament and to permit larger parties to obtain workable majorities, there is a provision that a party must obtain at least 5 percent of all second votes cast or win in at least three constituencies to qualify for proportional representation in the Bundestag. This rule also helps to avoid unstable coalition governments – a lesson learnt from the Weimar Republic. This 5 percent hurdle does not apply in the case of national minorities (in particular the Danish speakers of Schleswig-Holstein) and was temporarily modified for the first national elections after unification in 1990 in order to make it easier for small parties in the former GDR – such as *PDS* (the reformed East German Communist Party) and *Bündnis 90/ Grüne* (the Green Party in coalition with an alliance of some East German citizens' movements) – to gain representation in the Bundestag.

Once the elections have determined how many seats each party will have, the Bundestag chooses the federal Chancellor, who is proposed by the party or the coalition of parties commanding a majority of seats.

Special off-year elections for a new Bundestag can be called if the regular election has not resulted in a parliamentary majority for any party or coalition of parties or if an incumbent chancellor loses a vote of confidence in parliament and asks the Federal President to dissolve the Bundestag. Such a situation has arisen only twice – in 1972 and in 1983 – when Willy **Brandt** and Helmut

Kohl respectively engineered failed votes of confidence in order to precipitate early elections.

Regional elections in the *Länder* follow the same principles as the national elections for the Bundestag. Their outcome ultimately decides not only the distribution of seats in the regional parliament (Landtag) but indirectly also the distribution of seats in the **Bundesrat** (the second chamber) as members of the Bundesrat are delegates from the regional parliaments and not directly elected representatives.

See also: constitution: FRG; elections: GDR; *Land*

Further reading

Kappler, A. and Grevel, A. (eds) (1995 *et seq*) *Facts About Germany*, Frankfurt am Main: Societäts-Verlag (the yearly up-dated editions are a valuable source of information which provides a survey of the country and current developments; it can be obtained from the German embassy or consulate).

Padgett S. and Burkett T. (1986) *Political Parties and Elections in West Germany. The Search for a New Stability*, London: C. Hurst & Company.

ASTRID HERHOFFER

elections: GDR

Although elections at all levels were held at five-yearly intervals in the GDR (four-yearly prior to 1974), the voters had no choice between parties or programmes, as the question of power was deemed to have been decided once and for all. The procedure – the main function of which was mobilization of the populace – was more akin to a referendum: under the leadership of the **SED**, the parties and mass organizations drew up a single set of proposals which the voters could accept or reject. Elections also had no effect on the distribution of seats, as these were pre-allocated. Voters came under much pressure to vote 'yes', and normally more than 99 percent were recorded as having done so. However, accusations of vote-rigging were a factor in the events of 1989 that led to the collapse of communist rule. The first (and last) free election to the **Volkskammer** was held on 18 March 1990, in which the **CDU**-led Allianz für Deutschland unexpectedly won nearly half the votes.

JOHN SANDFORD

Eleventh Plenum

The infamous eleventh plenary meeting of the **Central Committee** of the **SED**, held 16–18 December 1965, was the most spectacular instance of political intervention in art and intellectual debate in the history of the GDR. Economic difficulties and social unrest, which followed the brief phase of consolidation after the closing of the state borders in 1961, led the Party to react by clamping down in the cultural sphere, terminating a five-year period of relative liberalization with a reinstatement of Stalinist cultural policy.

Since the early 1960s a new mood of self-confidence had prevailed in the arts. Writers had come to feel entitled to a degree of independence of judgement where the balance should be struck between criticism and affirmation of the state's potential, as well as in questions of artistic quality. However, the dismissal of Peter **Huchel** as editor of the literary journal *Sinn und Form*, the closing of an exhibition of modern art, and outbursts of official criticism of youth culture indicated the continuing influence of ideological hard-liners and the possibility of a return to a more restrictive cultural regime. Faced with mounting political pressures, Walter **Ulbricht** prepared a concerted move against works seen to focus unduly on the discrepancy between socialist ideals and everyday reality.

At the Plenum Erich **Honecker** led the carefully orchestrated attack on 'cultural decadence', supported by Alexander Abusch, Kurt **Hager** and others. Writers, theatre directors, filmmakers and rock bands, and those cultural functionaries who had supported them, were accused of 'modernism', 'scepticism', 'anarchism' and 'nihilism', and their demoralizing influence was made directly responsible for declining standards of discipline at work, lack of respect for authority, and sexual promiscuity. Manfred **Bieler**, Wolf **Biermann**, Werner

Bräunig, Volker **Braun**, Peter **Hacks**, Stefan **Heym**, Günter **Kunert**, and Heiner **Müller** were singled out for censure, and subsequently subjected to repressive measures, Biermann being banned from publishing and performing in the GDR indefinitely. Christa **Wolf** was almost alone in speaking out in their defence, and championing the right to say the truth about GDR society. Film was the medium hardest hit: a year's work in the **DEFA** studios was broken off, a dozen films being relegated to the archives. These banned films, many of them by leading directors, attracted international attention when they were released after the *Wende*.

Though the political and cultural debates interrupted by the Eleventh Plenum were revived in the 1970s, the intimidatory tactics of the Party leadership had effectively shattered the illusions of many writers and artists as to the possibility of reforming socialism.

See also: censorship: GDR; cultural policy: GDR; dissent and opposition: GDR; film: GDR

Further reading

Agde, G. (ed.) (1991) *Kahlschlag: Das 11. Plenum des ZK der SED 1965. Studien und Dokumente*, Berlin: Aufbau Verlag (contains papers on aspects of the Plenum from a colloquium held in the Academy of Arts in 1990, together with the recollections of persons involved, documents and key speeches).

AXEL GOODBODY

Elias, Norbert

b. 22 June 1897, Breslau (now Wrocław); d. 1 August 1990, Amsterdam

Sociologist

Exiled in Switzerland, then England (1933), Elias taught **sociology** at the Universities of Leicester (1954–62) and Ghana (1962–4). He held the position of Professor Emeritus at the University of Frankfurt, and was Visiting Professor at the Centre for Interdisciplinary Research, Bielefeld. Research interests included social conflict in Germany in comparison to England and France, focusing on the relationship between *Kultur* (culture) and

Zivilisation (civilization); the nature of sociology; process sociology; and the sociology of sport.

Further reading

Mennell, S. (1989) *Norbert Elias: An Introduction*, Oxford: Blackwell (introduction to Elias' life and work: includes bibliography).

JANET STEWART

Elsner, Gisela

b. 2 May 1937, Nürnberg; d. 13 May 1992, Munich

Writer

Having studied philosophy, German literature, and drama in Vienna (did not graduate), Elsner lived in London, Rome, Paris, Hamburg, and then Munich where she works as a freelance writer. In 1961, she participated in the **Gruppe 61**, and in 1962–3 joined **Gruppe 47**. She became widely known in 1964 with the publication of *Der Riesenzwerge* (*The Giant Dwarfs*), a biting social critique satirizing the petty bourgeoisie, written from the perspective of a young boy. Known for her novels and **Hörspiele** (radio plays), she has also written a libretto for an opera by Christof Herzog.

MARTINA S. ANDERSON

Emigholz, Heinz

b. 22 January 1948, Achim (near Bremen)

Filmmaker, graphic artist and writer

Emigholz, who trained as a draughtsman, began filmmaking at college. During the 1970s he became the FRG's foremost structural filmmaker, experimenting with framing, duration and perception, first in a series of landscape films shot frame by frame (*Schenec-Tady I–III*, 1973–5). *Hotel* (1976), made in New York, explores causality, simultaneity and spatial interaction. He writes and illustrates numerous striking notebooks which are sometimes integrated into his films (such as in *The Basis of Make-Up*, 1983). Emigholz has gradually integrated narrative, literary and philosphical material into feature-length experimental films, including *The Cynical Body* (*Der Zynische Korper*, 1992).

See also: film, experimental

MARTIN BRADY

Emma

Beginning publication in January 1977, both this feminist women's monthly and its founder Alice **Schwarzer** quickly became synonymous with women's rights and *Emanzipation*. Now appearing bimonthly, the magazine profiles women artists, politicians and activists; discusses political issues, and informs about cultural events of interest to women. Often derided by opponents as extremist and partisan, *Emma* is in fact much more influential in German political and cultural life than the number of sold copies might indicate (the magazine initiated the public debate on **pornography**). Its readers identify strongly with the magazine; however, it has experienced difficulties in attracting young women to its readership.

SABINE SCHMIDT

encyclopedias

The German contribution to encyclopedia-making has been distinctive and influential, for the advancement of book production technology, for the development of the genre, and for the spread of knowledge. Several noteworthy historic encyclopedias have played a significant role in German culture and may still be used with profit today and, indeed, have been reprinted. Johann Heinrich Zedler's *Großes vollständiges Universal-Lexicon aller Wissenschaften und Künste* in 64 folio volumes preserves the knowledge of the seventeenth and eighteenth centuries. *Zedler* (1732–50) was the most important of the new type of alphabetically (as opposed to systematically) organized encyclopedias in Germany. In its time it was the largest printed 'Universallexikon' of the western world. Johann Georg Krünitz' 242-volume *Oekonomisch-technologische Enzyklopädie* (1773–1858) contains a wealth of technological information about the Age of Goethe.

Ersch and Gruber's *Allgemeine Enzyklopädie der Wissenschaften und Künste* stands as a monument to nineteenth-century German scholarship. It is one of the most significant reference works of the nineteenth century and the most extensive European encyclopedia. This is an encyclopedia of almost unimaginable detail – the entry for Great Britain alone occupies about 700 pages. Begun in 1818, the project remained incomplete in 167 volumes when it ended in 1889. Although Ersch-Gruber was acquired by **Brockhaus** in 1831, even Brockhaus could not bring so enormous an undertaking to completion.

Many German encyclopedias can be characterized as *Konversationslexica*, a term suggesting the type of knowledge that would enable one to function well in polite society. Self-improvement is an unstated goal. The *Konversationslexikon* is more popular in orientation and came about as a result of the efforts to popularize the sciences as the end of the eighteenth century. The alphabetically listed entries are narrow in compass, heavily illustrated, tersely written, and brief. Entries are linked by a thorough system of cross-referencing. The first significant *Konversationslexikon* was produced by Friedrich Arnold Brockhaus and dates from 1808, although the term occurs earlier.

The name Brockhaus occupies a place in German culture similar to the *Encyclopedia Britannica* in English-speaking countries. As the *Britannica* became the model encyclopedia for English-speaking countries, so the *Brockhaus* provided a model for northern and eastern European countries in the nineteenth century. Brockhaus is actually a family of encyclopedia makers. In terms of the organization of knowledge, Brockhaus stands for extensive and intensive information with a thorough system of cross-references. The information contained is extremely compact; zealous use of abbreviations saves space. In contradistinction to the *Encyclopaedia Britannica*, the Brockhaus tradition prefers shorter entries in dictionary style.

German encyclopedias tend to be typographically conservative: the first Brockhaus in a Roman typeface rather than gothic or blackletter dates from 1949. The fifteenth edition of the Brockhaus (1928–35), an edition noted for its high book production values, featured small colour plates mounted at the correct site in the text. This encyclopedia claimed to represent the 'highest standard of encyclopedia-making ever attempted'. National encyclopedias naturally concentrate on their own cultural area, and German encyclopedias follow this pattern.

In the early 1950s Germany saw a renaissance of encyclopedia production. In 1952 Brockhaus, Herder, and **Bertelsmann** all began new '*Großlexika*' (major encyclopedias). Another strong period for the publishing of encyclopedias began in the mid-1960s. In addition to the relatively expensive encyclopedias in twenty volumes or more, the German book market has usually offered smaller sets of encyclopedias ('*mittlegroße Lexika*'), typically in four to five volumes. These medium-sized lexica sometimes confine their purview to a single science or field such as zoology or music.

Three large modern encyclopedias now serve as the workhorses of basic information gathering: the highly reliable *Brockhaus Enklopädie* in 24 volumes (1986–95) and the slightly older *Meyers enzyklopädisches Lexikon* in 25 volumes (1971–81). The ninth edition of Meyer was the first complete new edition produced after WWII. Articles are similar to those in the Brockhaus, as are size and format. Both have slightly more than 200,000 entries. The most widespread encyclopedia in Germany is probably *Die Grosse Bertelsmann Lexikothek*, with approximately fourteen million copies sold. This is a work in 25 volumes, but not the standard alphabetical organization. Rather, it consists of 10 alphabetical volumes covering basic information, plus 14 thematic volumes. The smaller *Herder* provides an encyclopedia with a Catholic perspective.

Germans typically acquire large-scale reference works through door-to-door sales or through mail-order services rather than through bookstores. Publishers tend to issue the volumes of a set over several years rather than all at once. Later volumes may therefore be more up-to-date than earlier ones. Several medium-sized encyclopedias on CD-ROM were marketed in the mid-1990s. None seem to rival the earlier *Britannica On-line* or *Encarta*. Meyer was the first German firm to offer an on-line encyclopedia on the Internet. The electronic version, *Meyers Lexikon – Das Wissen A–Z*, is a joint project of F.A. Brockhaus, the *Institut für Informationsverarbeitung und Computergestützte Neue Medien*, and *B.I.-Taschenbuchverlag Bibliographisches Institut*. The electronic version stores some 44,000 articles and 12,000 links.

Further reading

Collison, R. (1964) *Encyclopaedias: Their History Throughout the Ages*, New York: Hafner.
Kister, Kenneth F. (1994) *Kister's Best Encyclopedias*, Phoenix, AZ: Oryx Press.

JOHN B. RUTLEDGE

Ende, Michael

b. 12 November 1929, Garmisch-Partenkirchen; d. 31 August 1995, Stuttgart

Writer

A highly successful author of children's fantasy tales, but much appreciated by adults too, Ende first attracted attention in the early 1960s with his two 'Jim Knopf' stories. His two best-known books are *Momo* (1973), about a little girl's battle against the bandits who steal our time, and, on the theme of the redeeming power of the imagination, *The Neverending Story* (*Die unendliche Geschichte*, 1979). The equally successful film version of the latter (1984, directed in English by Wolfgang **Petersen**) was dismissed by Ende as a 'kitschy commercial melodrama'. His books have been translated into over thirty languages, with sales of over seventeen million copies.

JOHN SANDFORD

Endler, Adolf

b. 10 September 1930, Düsseldorf

Writer

Endler moved from West Germany, where he had worked for several newspapers, to the GDR in 1955 because of an accusation of being 'a threat to the security of the state', and studied from 1955 to 1957 at the Johannes R. Becher Literary Institute in Leipzig. His collection of poetry entitled *Das*

Sandkorn (The Grain of Sand) (1974) is regarded as one of the most important contributions to the GDR lyric of the 1970s. His poems contain, among other themes, sharp denunciations directed towards poetic trivialities, conventional scribblings and the lower middle-class and petit bourgeois mentality.

BETTINA BROCKERHOFF-MACDONALD

Engelberg, Ernst

b. 5 April 1909, Haslach

Historian

The GDR historian Ernst Engelberg's two-volume biography of Bismarck (1989, 1990) was received to widespread acclaim in both West and East. A member of the **KPD** from 1930, Engelberg emigrated from Germany in 1935, returning after the war. Following appointment as Professor at Leipzig University in 1949, Engelberg held a succession of leading positions in the GDR historical profession, including first President of the Deutsche Historiker-Gesellschaft (1958–65), Director of the Institut für Geschichte of the Deutsche Akademie der Wissenschaften (1960–9), and President of the Nationalkomitee der Historiker (1960–80). Other publications include *Theorie, Empirie und Methode in der Geschichtswissenschaft* (1980).

See also: historiography

MARY FULBROOK

Engelmann, Bernt

b. 20 January 1921, Berlin; d. 14 April 1994, Munich

Novelist, journalist, and historian

After serving as a soldier, Engelmann spent the last part of the war in concentration camps. Once he established himself as a freelance writer in 1961, his fictional and non-fictional writing was dominated by his abhorrence of all forms of nationalistic excess and by his critical attitude towards many social developments in the Federal Republic.

Accordingly, he was a controversial figure in literary life, especially in the 1970s and 1980s.

His first works were mainly documentary reports on aspects of life in the Federal Republic. In the 1970s he embarked on his project of writing 'Ein deutsches Antigeschichtsbuch' (A German Antihistory), of which three parts appeared. The first *Wir Untertanen* (We Subjects) dealt with German history before 1918, the second *Einig gegen Recht und Freiheit* (United Against Justice and Liberty) with the Weimar Republic and the Third Reich, and the third *Trotz alledem. Deutsche Radikale 1777–1977* (Despite All That. German Radicals 1777–1977) with the tradition of protest in Germany. These works, which are characterized by their political commitment, are popular histories rather than traditional academic studies. That they achieved bestseller status is a tribute to their readability.

For his less extensive fictional work Engelmann favoured the form of the *Tatsachenroman* (the novel of fact). In these works he deliberately uses the techniques of the popular novelist of the Frederick Forsyth type to put over his political message, which is substantiated by reference to real people and events. The 1974 novel *Großes Bundesverdienstkreuz* (Federal Order of Merit with Bar) typically deals with the right-wing activities of former Nazis who subsequently embarked on successful business careers. As in his historical writing, Engelmann is keen to expose links between capitalism and Nazism.

From 1977 to 1983 Engelmann was chair of the Verband deutscher Schriftsteller (VS). He used this office and that of a vice-president of the West German **PEN** to initiate discussions on nuclear disarmament between writers from eastern and western Europe. His good working relationship with Hermann **Kant**, with whom he initiated a 'peace appeal of European writers', also led to meetings between East and West German writers on the same topic in Berlin in 1981 and 1983. These meetings, although not dominated by a single viewpoint, led to criticism of the VS in general and Engelmann in particular, who was accused of having too close a relationship with official GDR bodies. It was this issue that led to his resignation in 1983.

Recently his reputation has suffered from the discovery that he used **Stasi** materials for his researches. His work has also been criticized for its formulaic use of the techniques that guaranteed success in the market place. Nevertheless, it should be stressed that he was a democratic socialist rather than a communist. Moreover his historical writing undoubtedly contributed to a new wider interest in German history.

STUART PARKES

Ensslin, Gudrun

b. 15 August 1940, Bartholomä, Württemberg; d. 18 October 1977, Stuttgart-Stammheim

Terrorist

A member of the Baader–Meinhof group, the pastor's daughter and postgraduate literature student Gudrun Ensslin was a leading figure of West German left-wing **terrorism**. Together with her boyfriend Andreas **Baader**, she was convicted in 1968 for an arson attack on a department store in Frankfurt am Main. Ensslin and Ulrike **Meinhof** were the intellectual driving force in justifying the group's terrorist actions ('You can't talk to people who made Auschwitz'). After two years of bank robberies, shootings and bomb attacks, she was rearrested in 1972, and in April 1977 sentenced to life imprisonment. She committed suicide, hanging herself in prison.

MONIKA PRÜTZEL-THOMAS

environmental literature

The term 'environmental literature' has been used with increasing frequency since the late 1970s, but it is not yet a clearly defined or universally recognized genre. It refers to literature, most especially prose, that explores the interactions of living beings in environments. The tradition of environmental literature begins with the writers of natural theology such as the poet Barthold Heinrich Brockes in the seventeenth century, who attempted to understand the wisdom of God through close observation of the natural world. It has affinities with the work of Goethe, Hölderlin

and the romantics, who celebrated the natural world. Environmental literature, however, differs from that of German classicism and romanticism in that it does not focus primarily on the subjective responses of the observer to the natural world. Instead, it attempts to describe the interactions of all creatures, including human beings, in an ecosystem. Environmental literature has further affinities with the 'blood-and-soil' literature of the early twentieth century such as the work of Hans Grimm and Hermann Löns, but it does not generally share their intense nationalism.

As an aesthetic tradition, environmental literature has been influenced by the American authors such as Henry David Thoreau and John Muir, who developed a style based on the combination of observation of nature and speculative philosophy. Their work, however, centres on communion with a relatively pristine wilderness, something that is not possible in a country settled as long or as densely as Germany. As a social and political movement, however, **environmentalism** has had a greater impact in Germany than in the United States or perhaps any other western country.

The latter 1970s and the 1980s, especially, saw a great proliferation in Germany, both West and East, of manifestos, novels and other writings on environmental themes. This period was also marked by dramatic electorial successes of the German **Greens**. Among the many noteworthy works of environmental literature since the end of WWII are the novel *Der Tanz mit dem Teufel* (The Dance with the Devil) by the Austrian Günter Schwab (1958), the political thesis *Natur als Politik: Die ökologische Chance der Menschen* (Nature as Politics: the Ecological Chances of Humanity) by the philosopher Carl **Amery** (1976) and the collection of essays *Um Hoffnung kämpfen. Gewaltfrei in eine grüne Zukunft* (Fighting for Hope. Peace in a Green Future) by the political figure Petra **Kelly** (1983).

Environmental literature in Germany, however, remains unusually difficult to circumscribe. It is perhaps less a cohesive movement in literature than a range of concerns which pervades much of German society across political and social lines. Other figures who have often emphasized environmental themes include the philosopher Hans Jonas, the physicist Robert **Havemann**, the novelist

Heinrich **Böll**, and the journalist Günter **Wall-raff**.

Further reading

Hermand, J. (1991). *Grüne Utopien in Deutschland: Zur Geschichte des ökologischen Bewußtseins*, Frankfurt am Main, Fischer Taschenbuch (a study of environmental themes in German literature).

BORIA SAX

environmentalism

This term refers in the most general way to the social and political changes brought about by the interplay between public environmental awareness and official environmental policy since the early 1970s. Environmentalism is the expression of a new perception of **nature** that seeks to take account of external constrictions to socio-economic development, in particular the rapid growth of the global population, the finiteness of natural resources and the limited capacity of the natural environment to absorb the emissions of mass production and consumption. These three parameters constitute what is experienced as the 'ecological crisis', which raises concerns regarding the future of humanity, the diversity of natural species and the preservation of nature as an aesthetic value. Environmentalism strives to make the existing civilizatory model compatible with ecological requirements by implementing a wider concept of growth. Qualitative growth (as opposed to quantitative growth) goes beyond the accumulation of material wealth and focuses attention on 'post-material' needs like a secure future or a healthy and pleasant living environment. Within the environmental debate there are several different strands ranging from purely anthropocentric to radically ecocentric positions. Hence, the concept of environmentalism has been supplemented by a number of other terms (conservationism, ecologism, deep ecology, etc.) aiming to conceptualize these differences. As a new stage in the process of social and economic modernization, environmentalism's struggle for 'ecological sustainability' is comparable to earlier phases of the twentieth

century when the 'social question' was solved through the introduction of the social market economy.

Within the European Union Germany enjoys the reputation of being particularly environmentally progressive. Since the 1970s Germany has developed and implemented strict environmental standards for its industry. Germany is known for its environmentally sensitive public, its strong and politically active environmental organizations, its successful Green Party and, more recently, its role as a leading provider of advanced environmental technology.

Environmentalism and government policy

Whilst environmentalism is normally associated with political pressure from the grass-roots of society, German environmentalism was initiated 'from above' by the social democratic-liberal coalition government under Chancellor Willy **Brandt** (1969–74). Stimulated by legislative advances in the US, the Brandt government presented its first environmental programme in 1971 and, following the example of the 'US Council of Environmental Quality', a 'Council of Experts on Environmental Issues' (Sachverständigenrat für Umweltfragen) was established in the same year. As part of his comprehensive programme of social reforms Brandt aimed to develop the environmental awareness of the public, which was in its infancy at the time. A number of environmental laws were passed and central principles were established, like the principle of precaution and the polluter-pays principle. In 1974, once again following the US example, the 'Federal Environmental Agency' (Umweltbundesamt) was founded to provide technical, scientific and administrative assistance to the government. However, when Chancellor Brandt was succeeded by Helmut **Schmidt** (1974), the phase of pro-active environmental policy by the government came to a halt. Against the background of the mid-1970s economic recession, industrial leaders were assured that economic growth would once again become the top priority (1975 Gymnich Conference). The conflict between economic and ecological interests obstructed significant environmental progress until the first half of the 1980s, when the new conservative government under Chancellor Helmut **Kohl** sought to increase its popularity by passing new legislation (SO_2-filters for coal-fired power stations and catalytic converters for private motor cars). Following the 1986 catastrophe of the nuclear reactor in Chernobyl (USSR), the Kohl government established the 'Federal Ministry for the Environment and Reactor Safety' (Ministerium für Umwelt, Naturschutz und Reaktorsicherheit) thus recognizing officially that environmentalism had become a major issue in German politics. Following German unification, however, Chancellor Kohl replaced his internationally renowned minister for the environment, Klaus Töpfer, with an inexperienced new-comer, thus signalling a further shift of political priorities.

The environmental movement – origins

The starting point of the German environmental movement is normally located in 1972, when the Club of Rome published its report on the *Limits to Growth*. This report, and the 1973–4 oil crisis, put an abrupt end to the belief fostered by the **Economic Miracle** in the unlimited accumulation of material wealth. The public was alerted to the ecological unsustainability of the dominant civilizatory model. Particularly those social strata whose material needs were largely satisfied and educational standards unprecedentedly high responded by showing a high level of commitment to protecting the natural environment.

To some extent, the new environmentalism of the early 1970s had been anticipated by the youth movement around the turn of the twentieth century. At that time, the rapid progress of industrialization and urbanization had given rise to a feeling of cultural uprootedness and alienation from nature. New ramblers' associations, conservation societies, vegetarian groups and life reformers sought to protect the national and cultural heritage (**Heimat**) against the disruptive process of modernization, to resuscitate disappearing traditional values and to establish a new relationship with nature. National Socialism was able to exploit this feeling of cultural uprootedness and harness it to serve its perverted nationalism. In the 1970s, however, the ecological crisis could be conceptualized in an entirely new and untainted language.

Unlike its precursors, the new environmental movement was fundamentally progressive. Post-1970 environmentalism was inseparably connected to the emancipatory ideals of radical democratization, global solidarity, social justice, human rights, feminism, peace, etc. In the new citizens' initiatives these individual strands of environmentalism were given expression (see also **citizens' initiatives: FRG**; **citizens' initiatives: GDR**).

The organization of environmental concerns

Citizens' initiatives soon started to establish regional co-operative networks which were formalized and expanded when, in 1972, the 'Federal Association of Environmental Citizens' Initiatives' (Bundesverband Bürgerinitiativen Umweltschutz, BBU) was founded as a national umbrella organization. One of the central issues of the BBU, and a catalyst for the formation of an influential political protest scene in Germany, was the government's plan to develop **nuclear power**. The issue amalgamated currents of conservative or even anti-modernist critique of social and economic progress with leftist currents emerging from the **student movement**. Their new forms of political activity indicated a widespread loss of confidence in the government's ability to offer appropriate solutions to a new set of problems. Man-made catastrophes like the 1976 spillage of dioxin in Seveso (Italy) or the 1979 nuclear accident in Harrisburg (US) resulted in waves of new mobilization and kept the public alert to the unmanageable risks of modern high-tech civilization. While official environmental politics was in a phase of stagnation, a widely shared optimism developed that if the politicians could not, then direct democratic participation and political pressure from the grass-roots of society would bring about the fundamental changes required to solve the environmental problem.

The organizational and communicative structures developed by the BBU provided the basis for the establishment of regional Green electoral lists towards the end of the 1970s and the national party Die Grünen (**Greens**) in 1980. The party continued to make a close connection between the ideas of environmentalism, pacifism, feminism and democracy. Against the background of the Cold War, nuclear war and ecological collapse appeared equally threatening to the future of mankind as two varieties of the global apocalypse. The electoral success of the Greens in 1983 was a clear signal of public discontent with official environmental politics. It forced the established parties to include environmental aspects in their programmes and policies.

As the political energies of the Green party began to be absorbed by the day-to-day business of parliamentary politics, the still increasing environmental concern of the public found a new expression in the rapid growth of non-parliamentary organizations, most notably Greenpeace and the 'German Alliance for Environment and Nature Conservation' (Bund für Umwelt- und Naturschutz Deutschland, BUND). The German section of Greenpeace was only founded in 1980 but by the early 1990s it could already boast over 500,000 supporters. BUND raised its membership from under 89,000 in 1983 to about 230,000 in the mid-1990s. These organizations have contributed to the shaping of environmental policy in Germany by constantly reminding the public and its parliamentary representatives of pressing issues like the dangers of nuclear energy, the decline of the forests (**Waldsterben**), the management of industrial and domestic waste (see also **recycling**), the continuous increase of road traffic and innumerable less spectacular concerns. Beyond their campaigning activities, these organizations developed networks of scientific expertise which can be drawn upon for the development of environmentally more compatible alternatives to untenable social and economic practices.

Success and limitations of environmentalism

Since the latter half of the 1980s political scientists have spoken of the 'institutionalization' of the German environmental movement. The term refers to the lasting success of green parliamentary and extra-parliamentary organizations and the concomitant decline of street protests. Environmental organizations, including the Green Party, have become less ideological, their confrontational style of campaigning has given way to more cooperative approaches. The organizations now prefer to see themselves as environmental advisors working constructively towards the 'greening' of

industry and commerce. Despite such signs of general appeasement, the 1995 controversy surrounding the disposal of Shell's disused oil-platform 'Brent Spar' demonstrated the undiminished confrontational potential of the movement and the political effectiveness of direct protests.

The success of the movement is difficult to quantify. At the local as well as the national level, environmental organizations exert a formal and an informal influence on political and economic decision-making. The fact that several nuclear installations in Germany were never completed or commissioned, despite substantial initial investments, and that energy providers are, in fact, considering scenarios for the phasing-out of nuclear energy, is at least partly due to the eco-movement. Germany's strict standards for pollution control would not have been implemented if it had not been for the environmentally sensitized public. Throughout Europe Germany's achievements regarding SO_2 emissions, catalytic converters and the recycling of packaging waste are considered as exemplary. Green consumerism is further developed in Germany than in other countries, and ecological products continue to increase their market shares. Organic farming may be quoted as an example: the number of alternative farms increased from 2,330 in 1990 (cultivating a total of 42,400 hectares) to 5,275 (185,000 hectares) in 1995.

Since the early 1990s, however, various factors have contributed to a relative crisis of environmentalism itself. The globalization of markets and economic strains in the aftermath of German unification have focused attention on problems of unemployment and the modernization of the welfare state. Environmentalists are finding it increasingly difficult to identify political enemies, sketch out convincing utopias and formulate political strategies. The high expectations arising from environmental activism remain largely unfulfilled. Environmental awareness does not automatically mean that alternative forms of behaviour are possible or convenient. Against the background of a general crisis of values and the fragmentation of the social consensus, the ideas of nature and naturalness enjoy unprecedented popularity in the social and political debate. The triad of problems constituting the environmental crisis is more pressing than ever. At the same time however, it is becoming ever more difficult to define what is to be protected, for whom, and for what reasons. This dilemma is a focal point of the contemporary environmental debate in Germany. It is paralysing the movement and shows the need for a fundamental reformulation of the environmental question as the twenty-first century approaches.

Further reading

Blühdorn, I., Krause, F. and Scharf, T. (eds) (1995) *The Green Agenda: Environmental Politics and Policy in Germany*, Keele University Press (includes contributions by the major actors shaping contemporary environmental politics and offers academic analyses).

Dominick, R.H. (1992) *The Environmental Movement in Germany*, Bloomington and Indianapolis, IN: Indiana University Press (on the history of environmentalism since the ninteenth century).

Haan, G.D. and Kuckartz, U. (1996) *Umweltbewußtsein. Denken und Handeln in Umweltkrisen*, Opladen: Westdeutscher Verlag (on the concept of environmental awareness and its empirical quantification).

Rucht, D. (1994) *Modernisierung und neue soziale Bewegungen*, Frankfurt am Main: Campus (views political protest movements, including the environmental movement, as phenomena of social modernization).

Sieferle, R.P. (1984) *Fortschrittsfeinde? Opposition gegen Technik und Industrie von der Romantik bis zur Gegenwart*, Munich: Beck (on the genealogy of the ideas of nature and its conservation).

Wey, K.-G. (1982) *Kurze Geschichte des Umweltschutzes in Deutschland seit 1900*, Opladen: Westdeutscher Verlag (A history of official pollution control).

INGOLFUR BLÜHDORN

Enzensberger, Hans Magnus

b. 11 November 1929, Kaufbeuren

Writer

From the time he began writing in the 1950s Enzensberger reflected dominant intellectual and political currents in Germany, contributing combative and reasoned argument to public discussion. His conviction that it was the writer's task to criticize the forms of society he lives in generated polemical assessments of economic, political and social structures in the industrialized world and kept him in the eye of public controversy in Germany. Initially he propounded an acute analysis of the cultural condition of the late 1950s, targeting in particular the manipulation of consciousness by the media designed to sustain existing power structures. His literary assaults then focused on the ruling establishment itself, first in alliance with radical thinking in the 1960s, later highlighting the excesses and neuroses of the consumer society and warning of the inherent dangers in an overhasty German unification.

Born and brought up in Bavaria, Enzensberger came to prominence through the **Gruppe 47** after obtaining his doctorate with a dissertation on the romantic poet Brentano. The iconoclasm of his first poems, *verteidigung der wölfe* (in defence of wolves) (1957), aligned him with Günter **Grass** and Heinrich **Böll**, who also exposed the hypocrisy of the FRG trying to ignore rather than face up to its Nazi past. Gross affluence and moral apathy in an economically resurgent Germany, the political dangers of power in the hands of incompetent, self-seeking decision-makers, the threat of global destruction through the misuse of contemporary technology – these themes permeated his writing in the 1960s. Enzensberger was not introspective, he aimed to analyse the world and influence his fellow-citizens, proudly regarding his poetry as '*Gebrauchslyrik*' (poetry for practical use).

Enzensberger's seminal work, *The Industrialization of the Mind* (*Bewußtseins-Industrie*, 1962), and related essays attacked the insidious distorting of language in the media and advertising as a means of brainwashing and exploiting the public. With the founding of his journal **Kursbuch** in 1965 Enzensberger became the guru of the burgeoning student revolution. *Kursbuch* became a focal point for the **APO** (extra-parliamentary opposition), highlighting the negative aspects of German success.

In the notorious 1968 essay, *Commonplaces on the Newest Literature* (*Gemeinplätze, die neueste Literatur betreffend*), Enzensberger was thought to have pronounced the **'Death of Literature'**; what he actually suggested was that literature could be neither rejected nor justified, but in the right conditions it possessed 'a Utopian impetus, a critical potential'. His contribution to the need for a 'massive education in basic politics' of the German people was to devise an informative documentary genre – he called it 'factography' – such as *The Havana Inquiry* (*Das Verhör von Habana*, 1970) about Castro's Cuban revolution, and *Der kurze Sommer der Anarchie* (The Short Summer of Anarchy) (1972), which analysed the struggle of Buenaventura Durruti in the Spanish Civil War.

The 1970s also saw an expansion of Enzensberger's originality in lyric poetry. He had already been characterized as a 'poeta doctus' for his readiness to engage poetically with learned, sometimes recondite themes and the paraphernalia of modern living – science, technology, politics – as well as his skill in incorporating ordinary language and recalcitrant technical jargon into the poetic discourse. In *Mausoleum. 37 Ballads from the History of Progress* (*Mausoleum. 37 Balladen aus der Geschichte des Fortschritts*, 1975) Enzensberger breathed fresh life into the out-of-fashion ballad form, surveying the achievements of famous and obscure men across the centuries to demonstrate the contradictory nature of progress. Two years later he again caught the gloomy, chastened mood of Germany, with its scourge of **terrorism** and visions of nuclear catastrophe, in a long meditative 'comedy', *The Sinking of the Titanic* (*Der Untergang der Titanic*, 1977). Its thirty-three cantos deliberately evoked Dante's grandiose *Divine Comedy*, injecting into the epic form the dominant concerns of our century, summed up in the brash concept of progress so vividly negated by the fate of the *Titanic*.

In his later poetry Enzensberger avoided the majestic metaphor and became more personal, questioning and elegiac. The underlying indictment of a society that engenders anxiety, neurosis, alienation and boredom in its citizens was still plainly to the fore, and all the more telling for the muted tones of utterance. Understatement in *Die Furie des Verschwindens* (The Avenging Goddess of Disappearance, 1980), *Zukunftsmusik* (Pipe Dreams, 1991) and *Kiosk* (1995) only served to strengthen the impact of his wry assessments. The perception of Enzensberger as 'conscience of the nation' was confirmed by the continuing flow of hard-hitting, idiosyncratic essays on a variety of topical debates – immigration and asylum, racism and xenophobia, genocide, environmental pollution, cultural imperialism, unification – that exercised his fellow-citizens and demanded solutions.

Enzensberger's credentials as a European writer of wide perspectives have been enhanced by his command of several languages, frequent periods of travel and residence outside Germany, and numerous translations and editions of foreign authors.

Major works

Enzensberger, H.M. (1968) *Poems for People Who Don't Read Poems*, trans. M. Hamburger, J. Rothenberg and H.M. Enzensberger, London: Secker & Warburg (selection in German and English).

—— (1974) *The Consciousness Industry. On Literature, Politics and the Media*, trans. M. Roloff, New York: Seabury Press (selected essays with afterword).

—— (1976) *Mausoleum. 37 Ballads from the History of Progress*, trans. J. Neugröschel, New York: Urizen Books.

—— (1980) *The Sinking of the Titanic* trans. H.M. Enzenzberger, Boston, MA: Houghton Mifflin.

—— (1982) *Critical Essays*, ed. R. Grimm, B. Armstrong, New York: Continuum (some of these essays appeared in *The Consciousness Industry*).

—— (1983) *Die Gedichte*, Frankfurt am Main: Suhrkamp (the lyric poems up to date of publication).

—— (1988) *Mittelmaß und Wahn*, Frankfurt am Main: Suhrkamp (selected essays written before the fall of the Berlin Wall).

Further reading

Dietschreit, F. and Dietschreit, B. (1986) *Hans Magnus Enzensberger*, Stuttgart: Metzler (a study of Enzensberger's writings).

Grimm, R. (ed.) (1984) *Hans Magnus Enzensberger*, Franfurt: Suhrkamp (contains a broad selection of critical essays on Enzensberger).

Siefken, H. (ed.) (1990) '*Lektüre – ein anarchischer Akt*', Nottingham: University of Nottingham Monographs in the Humanities VI (proceedings of a symposium held with Enzensberger, in English).

Subiotto, A. (ed.) (1985) *Hans Magnus Enzensberger*, Leicester: Leicester University Press (selection of poems, in German, annotated with introduction).

ARRIGO SUBIOTTO

epic theatre

Term used by Bertolt **Brecht** to characterize his theatre praxis (understood to include both his dramas and his style of production), conceived in opposition to the theatrical conventions of his time, which Brecht variously described as 'Aristotelian' or 'dramatic'. Epic theatre abandons the theatre of illusion and psychological identification, striving to awaken the critical faculties of the audience; rather than suspending disbelief, it integrates techniques of self-referentiality which draw attention to the constructedness of the theatrical event. The most systematized exposé of epic theatre is Brecht's *Short Organum for the Theatre* (*Kleines Organon für das Theater*).

The fundamental aesthetic paradigm of epic theatre is *Verfremdung* (translated variously as 'alienation' or, more accurately, 'defamiliarization'): the process of rendering the familiar strange, of awakening awareness of the changeability of human and class relations. Characteristic components include a truncated, episodic structure; actors' stepping out of the action to address or sing to the audience; narrative headlines which underscore contexts, foreshadow action, and inhibit psychological identification and the forward thrust of expectation; and an acting style in which actor and role are not fully fused.

Whereas epic theatre is correctly associated with the formal innovations of Brecht's work, it is more than a sum of techniques or methods, and an understanding of it should not be based solely on the expository texts in which Brecht elaborated his aesthetics and praxis. The dramas themselves – the text-base of his theatrical praxis – are richer and more nuanced than his aesthetic principles. Finally, epic theatre cannot be abstracted from the project of social transformation which it sought to further. Brecht's theatre was grounded in a Marxist analysis of class society and was inextricable from the process of social transformation to which he hoped to contribute.

Errors of reception finally led Brecht to distance himself from the term 'epic theatre'. He substituted various terms, including 'dialectical theatre' and 'theatre for a scientific age' – the latter in the context of arguing that entertainment in an age characterized by human mastery of natural processes must facilitate commensurate intervention into social processes; he later abandoned this term as well, however, finding it to be soiled by colloquial usage.

The theatre and troupe most renowned for epic theatre is the **Berliner Ensemble**, established by Brecht in 1949. Here Brecht was able, despite difficulties with orthodox party officials, to develop and refine the theatre practice he had long advocated in renowned workshop productions and highly acclaimed world premieres of many of his greatest plays.

Further reading

Willett, J. (ed. and trans.) (1978) *Brecht on Theatre*, London: Methuen (an excellent annotated, English-language collection of Brecht's writings on theatre).

KAREN RUOFF KRAMER

Erb, Elke

b. 18 February 1938, Scherbach (Eifel)

Writer

Erb emigrated from West Germany to the GDR in 1949. She made her poetic debut in the 1960s with a type of 'pure poetry' (Volker Braun) that appeared in journals and anthologies. Her first independent publication (1975) was a collection of poetry and prose entitled *Gutachten* (Opinions). Characteristic of all of her texts is her attempt to find new possibilities for expression. Both her poetry and prose are experimental in nature. Despite an apparent generation difference, Erb played an active role in the alternative culture of the **Prenzlauer Berg** district of East Berlin, helping to foster and nurture new talent.

CAROL ANNE COSTABILE-HEMING

Erlenberger, Maria

Writer

Maria Erlenberger is a pen-name. There is no information on the writer's real name or biography. It is assumed that she is Austrian. Between 1977 and 1982, Erlenberger authored four novels as well as other prose texts, including the highly acclaimed *Der Hunger nach Wahnsinn* (The Hunger for Madness) (1977), which details the female protagonist's treatment in a psychiatric hospital. Critics have praised especially her early works as an important contribution to the demystification of women and illness in literature.

See also: *Frauenliteratur*; literature: Austria

REINHILD STEINGRÖVER McRAE

European Union

The European Union (EU) has been at the heart of the FRG's, and now united Germany's, foreign policy emphasis on western integration. It consists of three pillars: the European Community (EC), Common Foreign and Security Policy (CFSP), and Co-operation in Justice and Home Affairs (JHA). The EU has also taken on responsibilities in the cultural sphere in such areas as student mobility, film production, and harmonization of broadcasting regulations. The central element of the EC, the most important pillar, is the Common Market, which eliminates tariff and other trade barriers between member states while establishing a common external trade policy. Germany, along with France, is one of the two key members.

The EU, whose main institutions are located in Brussels, is the latest incarnation of the supranational association of western European countries that began with the European Coal and Steel Community in 1951. The original concept, devised by French statesman Jean Monnet, was in large part an attempt to deal with the post-war **German Question**, and tied willing nation-states into a common community that would gradually work towards the economic goal of a common market and political integration. The key innovative element, incorporated into the later European Economic Community (EEC), was member states' ceding of political sovereignty to 'supranational' organizations, above all a European Commission, responsible for day-to-day implementation. An intergovernmental European Council sets common policy. Spurred by the success of the ECSC, the founding countries (Germany, France, Italy and the Benelux countries) signed and ratified the Treaty of Rome in 1958, establishing the EEC and a common nuclear regulatory agency, Euratom.

The European Community has since 'widened' to include fifteen members. The six founding nations were joined by the United Kingdom, Ireland and Denmark in 1973, Greece in 1981, Spain and Portugal in 1986, and Sweden, Austria and Finland in 1995. In June 1997, the European Commission agreed to open negotiations with six new applicant countries: Poland, the Czech Republic, Hungary, Slovenia, Estonia and Cyprus.

The community has also undergone considerable 'deepening' of its responsibilities. The ECSC, EEC and Euratom merged in 1967. The European Parliament, created as a weak consultative institution which meets in Strasbourg, was transformed in 1979 into a body elected by popular vote. None the less, the parliament's role remains restricted to reviewing Commission decisions and approving the Commission budget. In 1986 the European Council approved the Single European Act, which set a deadline of 1992 for the completion of the internal market and streamlined some of the EC's cumbersome decision-making procedures. The Maastricht Treaty, signed in 1991 and ratified by member countries, launched the most ambitious phase of 'deepening' since the Treaty of Rome. The renaming of the community as the European Union (EU) reflects the greater integration sought by the treaty. It called for the simplification of decision-making in the Community, the development of a Common Foreign and Security Policy, and the creation of a European Monetary Union (EMU), with a target completion date of 1999. None of these goals has yet been fully realized. In particular, the war in the former Yugoslavia

(1992–5) called into question member countries' ability to co-ordinate foreign and military policies. The EMU, which involves the establishment of a common currency (the 'euro') and a European central bank, has been hampered by members' difficulties in meeting strict economic criteria to join in the first round of economic union.

Despite benefits for member states, the Maastricht Treaty's closer union has been criticized on many fronts, and in Germany official enthusiasm for the European project encounters increased public scepticism. Some labour leaders contend that the union offers unfair advantages to multinational corporations at the expense of unions and the environment. A significant portion of the German public worries that the euro will not offer stability comparable to the deutschmark.

MICHAEL R. HAYSE

exhibition and congress centres

The privilege to hold fairs in German cities stems back to the early Middle Ages, when Emperor Friedrich II granted the right to Frankfurt am Main in 1240, with all travellers to the fair enjoying the emperor's protection. Leipzig was granted the privilege by Emperor Maximilian in 1507. In the present day, Germany shows great international strength in mounting exhibitions, whether universal or specialist in nature, whether international, national or regional. Of the world's leading fairs, two-thirds are German, with nine million visitors annually, of whom 18 percent are foreign. Among exhibitors at Germany's international fairs, more than 40 percent are non-German. There are 118 national fairs and 130 regional fairs.

Germany's largest cities all tend to be important exhibition centres, but the world's largest industrial fair is that of Hanover, founded in 1947. Its strengths lie in investment and consumer goods and its display area covers half a million square metres. Frankfurt am Main is the second most important exhibition centre, with fairs in spring and autumn, covering an array of consumer goods, and a book fair. Cologne and Berlin both show greater specialization. In the GDR, the Leipzig universal fair was a showcase for all East Germany's manufactures, particularly machinery and electrical goods, and its book fair came to be rivalled by Frankfurt am Main after 1949. Since unification, the book exhibition has been lost to Frankfurt am Main: Leipzig, with its poorer infrastructure and facilities, must specialize while upgrading its services. The Leipzig traditional Spring Fair will now show greater focus as a grouping of specialist fairs, in particular oriented to central and east European neighbours.

Ten exhibition centres of more national or regional importance, such as Dortmund, Hamburg and Karlsruhe, are grouped in the IDFA (Interessengemeinschaft Deutscher Fachmessen und Ausstellungsstätten) and tend to mount specialist fairs. Highly specialized exhibitions contribute as much as the large universal fairs, since they tend to offer quality of information, contact and service for the visitor. The strength of these specialist branch fairs is in the concentration of specialist suppliers. In the case of regional fairs, it is generally the regional agents of companies who exhibit, and so offer high quality information and advice. Second-rank exhibition centres in Germany have built on these advantages.

The conference business in Germany is highly developed and generated a turnover of DM 43 billion or 1 percent of GDP in 1994 alone. This accounts for one-fifth of the total turnover of the tourism and hotels sector. Fifty million participants (5 percent of whom were foreign) attended 610,000 conferences and symposia. The diversity is such that there are approximately 350 congress halls in Germany, and 160 universities also offer conference provision. The larger-scale conferences of more than 50 participants account for two-thirds of the turnover and the largest naturally place great demands on the hotel trade. Though 6,300 hotels offer conference facilities, only those in principal centres receive large conferences. In an international comparison, Germany lies in fourth place behind the US, UK and France as a conference location.

See also: exhibitions

CHRISTOPHER H. FLOCKTON

exhibitions

Trade fairs, art and antiquities fairs and art exhibitions all have considerable prominence in German life, with such events ranking among the largest of their kind. The Stuttgart Antiques Fair and the 'Art Cologne' Fair (which specializes in twentieth-century and contemporary art) both date from the early 1960s and are the largest in the world, attracting both art dealers and collectors alike. As trade exhibitions, they have much in common organizationally with the trade fairs, which are such a part of German economic life, as showcases for regional and national manufactures.

The six largest German exhibition centres – Düsseldorf, Hanover, Frankfurt am Main, Cologne, Berlin and Leipzig – account for the greater share of turnover and visitors, with Düsseldorf having the highest turnover, and Hanover the largest number of visitors. Sometimes at biennial intervals, these cities host the world's largest specialist fairs, such as the automobile fair and book fair in Frankfurt am Main, the consumer electronics fair in Berlin and the plastics fair in Düsseldorf. Hanover mounts the Expo 2000 at the end of the century. Typically, these exhibition centres are owned jointly by the municipality and the state, who bear the cost of the property. This relieves fair organizers from the necessity of maximizing ticket revenues, since the main official objective is to stimulate the local and regional economy. Heavy investments in new infrastructures, including the relocation of the Leipzig fair site, are designed to maintain Germany's foremost position, although the concerns over potential overcapacity exist, particularly in view of the possibilities for sales and marketing offered by electronic media.

Public exhibitions of art and cultural artefacts are mounted by Germany's 4,800 **museums** and exhibition halls. In 1992, 7,800 exhibitions were visited by 93 million people. Most numerous are the local cultural and local history museums, but the larger German cities compete for prestige by new museum-building, where the museum design itself becomes an art work. At the beginning of the 1980s, in particular, a wave of striking public buildings was opened, such as the Neue Staatsgalerie in Stuttgart, the Neue Pinakothek in Munich and the collection on the Rhein-Main-Ufer in Frankfurt am Main. The buildings of the German Film Museum and German Architecture Museum in Frankfurt am Main both attract considerable acclaim as art objects in their own right.

See also: exhibition and congress centres

CHRISTOPHER H. FLOCKTON

existentialism

Existentialism is a literary and philosophical phenomenon of the twentieth century and a response to a sense of crisis triggered by two world wars. It is also a fascinating example of the flow of ideas and influence between Gemany and France. The basic premise is Jean-Paul Sartre's assertion that in human beings existence precedes essence, a reversal of the traditional view of philosophers. According to existentialists individual human beings constantly define their essence in the process of existing. Only by accepting this radical freedom is it possible to lead an authentic existence. Sartre was much influenced by two German philosophers in the inter-war period, Karl **Jaspers** and Martin **Heidegger**, whose lectures he attended. Committed to re-founding philosophy after the moral and spiritual crisis left by WWI they struggled to save the notion of the free individual from the alienating forces of anonymity and distractions in modern mass society.

Jaspers and Heidegger and the later existentialists accept Kant's argument that philosophical truths are not necessary truths, but descriptions of ways in which we structure the world. Existentialist works thus stress the primacy of the problem of being over the problem of knowledge. It is for this reason that Kierkegaard and Nietzsche in the nineteenth century may be considered precursors of existentialism. Both objected violently to Hegel's claim that reality could be entirely comprehended by reason.

The anti-religious, humanist existentialism of post-war France was born of WWII. As a result of their work for the French Resistance Sartre and Camus experienced new extremes of human isolation and solidarity. Consequently they present the situation of the free individual in a much more radical way than Jaspers or Heidegger, emphasizing the fundamental absurdity of existence. In addition the French writers call for a new understanding of the role of the writer and of literature. Both must now be fully 'engaged' in the struggle for freedom. To Germans totally disillusioned with ideological thinking and looking for a literature based on ruthless honesty these ideas proved immensely appealing. Sartre's *Les Mouches*, *Huis Clos* and *Les Mains Sales*, and Camus' *Caligula*, were performed repeatedly on German stages immediately after the war and prose works such as Sartre's *La Nausée* and Camus's *L'Étranger*, *La Peste* and *La Chute* were devoured by young Germans. Alfred **Andersch** and Hans Werner **Richter**, key figures in the German post-war literary scene, affirmed that the French writers articulated the concerns and attitudes of their generation. Certainly existentialism encouraged political commitment and may well have provided a standpoint from which to question the attitude of the older generation to National Socialism. The influence of existentialist thought may be seen in many writers and a clear example is the importance given to the decision to be free in the early works of Andersch. Karl Jaspers's late work *Wohin treibt die Bundesrepublik?* (Where is the Federal Republic Heading?) (1965) is a fierce political critique inspired by an existentialist's sense of the threat to individual freedom.

See also: philosophy

Further reading

Blackham, H.J. (1967) *Six Existentialist Thinkers*, London.

Shrader Jr., George Alfred (ed.) (1967) *Existential Philosophers: Kierkegaard to Merleau-Ponty*, New York, St. Louis, San Francisco, Toronto, London, Sydney.

Solomon, Robert C. (1972) *From Rationalism to Existentialism*, New York.

Sprigge, T.L.S. (1984) *Theories of Existence*, Harmondsworth.

GODFREY CARR

Export, Valie

b. 17 May 1940, Linz

Performance artist, photographer and filmmaker (real name Waltraud Lehner)

Valie Export is most widely known for her taboo-breaking performance art pieces in the late 1960s and the 1976 feminist **science fiction** film *Invisible Adversaries* (*Unsichtbare Gegner*), in which some of her own ground-breaking work since the late 1960s in performance art, video installation and expanded film is used or depicted. She was one of the first artists to employ multimedia techniques to focus on the body as the site of oppression and self-expression. As a teacher she has also exerted a considerable influence on younger artists and filmmakers.

See also: feminism and the women's movement; film: Austria

HELEN HUGHES

F

family

Only recently has the history of the family in Germany become an acceptable subject for scholars there. The abuse of racial and eugenic studies during the Third Reich rendered it taboo for a whole generation of German historians during the 1950s and 1960s. But Germany is an exceptionally valuable field for the study of social change within the family because of the phenomenon of rapid and intense industrialization and urbanization. The effects of two world wars brought their share of stress and strain on family life both in the countryside and in cities.

Until the twentieth century the extended family living under one roof was the norm. Children grew up in this *Großfamilie* being cared for by the older generation while the younger generation worked. The *du* form (informal 'you') of address was a sign of belonging to a family unit. When a son- or daughter-in-law was given permission to use the *du*-form, they were truly accepted into the family.

Patriarchal tradition

The German family has a strong patriarchal tradition which goes back to the times of the *Zünfte*, or guilds, where the house was connected to the place of work. The head of the family was also the boss. Servants and hired help lived under one roof. The man ruled the workplace and the woman ruled the household and oversaw all the work within the home. She had *Schlüsselgewalt*, control over all areas of the home.

In the late nineteenth century there was a movement to the larger cities where apartments were small and there was no room for servants. During this period men became extremely authoritarian. They made all the decisions, and were catered to, often receiving better and larger meals than the rest of the family. Some of these men, subjected to a lot of pressure at their workplace, became tyrants in their homes. The first German Women's Movement, *Die Frauenfrage*, was founded in 1865 partly as a reaction against patriarchy.

After 1919, family life changed only gradually. Influenced by the youth movement, an ideal marriage was viewed as one that was based on friendship and partnership of two people, not just on the authority of the husband. But men still had the final say both legally and practically.

National Socialism

The National Socialists proclaimed that women belonged in the home and in the kitchen and brought back the cliché of *Kinder, Kirche, Küche* (children, church and kitchen) prevalent in the nineteenth century. Women were encouraged to have children since the state wanted families to settle in eastern Europe. Child allowances were given and mothers who had four or more children were decorated. But more women than ever joined the workforce and WWII only accelerated these numbers.

Modern German Society

Both wars had caused turmoil in German families and brought great losses. Husbands and fathers died. Young women were unable to find partners. The young generation grew increasingly sceptical and was unable to communicate with their parents; nor were their parents able to divulge their war experiences. But despite the collapse of social and political structures in 1945, the family remained as a stable unit, helping each other stay together and survive. But there have been changes.

Grandparents usually no longer live close by, apartments are too small for the larger family unit to be accommodated. The desire to live independently has ensured that the generations now live separately. German families today live in an industrial and television society.

The roles of German women within the family have also been transformed. The government has enacted legislation giving women equal rights at the workplace and better rights within the home. For example, it regards work in a family as equal to other employment. It introduced legislation providing for child-raising allowances and leave with pension protection. The average family is now much smaller, usually with one or two children. More than half of all women work outside the home. In the GDR it was over 90 percent before the **Wende** – the highest proportion in the world.

Under German law of 1949 men and women were equal, but in reality, they were not. Men still made the decisions. It was not until 1977 that women received full legal equality. Now both partners have to agree on whose name to assume and who will do the housework. (Until 1994 married women were prohibited from retaining their maiden names.) Women are entering professional careers, but most work only until they have their first child. Contemporary industrial society has also brought stress on families. High unemployment among the general population, but especially among young people, has brought different problems to families. Many young people, afraid to be alone, have attached themselves to groups. Living in communes or *Wohngemeinschaften* has become one alternative. The typical family size has shrunk dramatically since 1945. Families are not prepared to make the sacrifice to support children. Today, members of the family readily go their own ways and leave the tightly knit nuclear family unit.

But the German family has survived in times of crisis and, although marriages have decreased, families remain strong. The roles of mother and father are in a state of flux and it will be interesting to observe where this will lead. Nevertheless, families come together on special occasions to show their strength. The German family remains as an integral part of German culture and society.

See also: childhood; feminism and the women's movement; weddings

Further reading

Evans, R. (1981) *The German Family: Essays on the Social History of the Family in Nineteenth- and Twentieth-Century Germany*, London: Croom Helm (a collection of essays on the history of the German family in the nineteenth and twentieth centuries).

Parkes, S. (1997) *Understanding Contemporary Germany*, London: Routledge (a survey of German society focusing on the post-unification situation).

Schneider, N. (1994) *Familie und private Lebensführung in West- und Ostdeutschland. Eine vergleichende Analyse des Familienlebens 1970–92*, Stuttgart: Enke (a study of the position of the family in contemporary German society).

UTE LISCHKE-McNAB

Farocki, Harun

b. 9 January 1944, Neutitschein (now Nový Jičín, Czech Republic)

Filmmaker and journalist

Having studied at the Berlin Film and Television Academy and made agitational shorts about Vietnam, Farocki developed a Marxist-inspired, essayistic style which combines fictional narratives, documentary and archive footage in a manner reminiscent of Alexander **Kluge**. *Between Two Wars* (*Zwischen zwei Kriegen*, 1978), an examination of German industry's involvement in the run-up to WWII, and *Before Your Eyes: Vietnam* (*Etwas wird sichtbar*, 1981), a study of love, war and Vietnam, combine philosophical aperçus, nonsense, and Godardian alienation into challenging, self-reflexive montages of diverse textual and visual material.

See also: New German Cinema

MARTIN BRADY

fashion

Although the term 'German fashion' is traditionally considered an oxymoron, fashion has always been a constitutive part of serious political and cultural debates in Germany as well as of consumerist culture. From the eighteenth century on, philosophers and politicians have regarded fashion as a manifestation of the nation's contested identity (initially in relation to France, later to America), or a sign of Germany's contribution to the global process of modernization. Fashion has figured prominently in contentious public discussions centred on issues such as nationalism, capitalism, gender equality, ecology. In the first two decades after 1945, the fashion industry in West Germany became one of the glittering facets of the **Economic Miracle**. In the 1950s, it reproduced to a certain extent the structure and organization of the fashion business from the 1920s and 1930s: some of the old *Modellhäuser* (designer houses) were promptly re-established and new businesses were set up, whose owners had started their careers in the 1930s as employees at Jewish-owned businesses. The collections of Staebe-Seger, Schulze-Varell, Gehringer & Glupp, Heinz Oestergaard and Hermann Schwichtenberg were clearly influenced by French Haute Couture, most notably by the models of Christian Dior and Jacques Fath. German as well as international fashion was presented in a number of illustrated magazines. Some of these magazines – *Elegante Welt* and *Blatt der Hausfrau* (later *Brigitte*) – were capitalizing on their prewar popularity with the female public, while others – *Film und Frau*, *Constanze* and *Burda* – were founded in the first post-war years. As the economy in the FRG stabilized and the buying power of the population increased, fashion became a highly profitable business especially for the mail-order companies as well as for the department stores. In the late 1960s and 1970s the trend towards democratization of fashion and widespread preferences for less formal clothing undermined the dominance of the older designer houses, and their fame began to fade. In the 1980s and 1990s, fashionable apparel with the labels of Margaretha Ley and Hugo Boss, Jil **Sander** and Joop!, Helmut **Lang** and Wolff triumphantly conquered the domestic and international markets. In the GDR, the government undertook a sustained effort to hold in check the consumerist impulses of East Germans, and incorporated the business of fashion into a centralized institutional framework with the task of cultivating a 'harmoniously developed socialist personality'. However, after 1968 and especially in matters of youth fashion, the government adopted more liberal policies.

Immediately after the war, the businesses related to fashion (fashion shows, fashion magazines, clothes manufacturing companies, mail-order houses and department stores) were among the first to recover surprisingly fast amidst destruction, human grief and material shortages. As a 1946 Berlin daily newspaper reported, 43 out of 210 businesses in the main shopping area belonged to fashion companies. Despite the poor quality of print and paper, more than thirty fashion and women's periodicals were in circulation around 1947. In 1953, West Berlin fashion designers exported over 20,000 model dresses, a fact which demonstrates how fashion became one of the main industrial strongholds of the still undivided city. The speedy ascendance to international recognition of Berlin-based companies such as Claussen, Staebe-Seger and Gehringer & Glupp is often given as an example of the German Economic Miracle in general and, specifically, of the post-war 'Berlin Miracle' in the sphere of fashion. However, many of those designers of Haute Couture as well as of *Konfektion* (off-the-peg clothing) who were often publicly celebrated as the 'founding fathers' of German fashion, started their careers in the 1930s as employees of renowned Berlin-based Jewish companies (Gerson, Hansenbang, Strohbach). As the Jewish owners were forced to leave Nazi Germany, chief designers Hans Seger, Gerd Staebe, Hans Gehringer and Hermann Schwichtenberg took over these businesses. After the war, their fashion companies achieved fame and prosperity, partly because of the widespread perception that they were the legitimate heirs of a tradition that had been systematically eradicated and 'Aryanized' in the years between 1933 and 1943.

After 1945, the institutions and industries of fashion in West Germany were much more decentralized in comparison with the Weimar period, when Berlin was practically the only centre of exuberant metropolitan fashions, and in comparison with the Nazi period when the German Fashion Office (*Das Deutsche Modeamt*), founded in 1933 and presided over by Magda Goebbels, provided guidelines for women's clothing. Munich and Hamburg as well as other cities retained the tradition of vocational schools for fashion design and sewing (*Meisterschulen für Mode*) and attracted more attention with former Berlin designers settling down there: Heinz Schulze-Varell in Munich, Irmgard Bibernell and Hilda Romatzki in Hamburg, Elise Topell in Wiesbaden. Düsseldorf became the host of the biggest annual fashion show for women's clothing, while men's fashion was presented at the fair in Cologne.

In the 1950s, fashion in West Germany failed to develop its own distinctive style and was strongly influenced by the triumphant 'New Look' designs created by Christian Dior. These designs emphasized the 'ladylike', expressively feminine appearance of women. The business of fashion envisioned women as the dominant consumer group in prospering West German society – eager to forget their war experience, to return to their traditional roles as wives and mothers, to 'catch up' with the pleasures of life, and to emulate and exude distinctly feminine elegance. This was the feminine ideal promoted also by the growing fashion media. Numerous fashion magazines entertained the women's public in West Germany: *Constanze*, *Brigitte*, *Film und Frau*, *Burda*, *Elegante Welt* and *Madame*. Glossy pages (some issues of *Film und Frau* even used golden print for their fashion section) were bringing home to the German housewife Parisian models of high fashion as well as variations created by German designers. In addition, every issue included a considerable number of patterns for readers to cut out and sew their own dresses, as well as directions for knitting. This practice both reflected and catered to the proverbial pragmatism, thrift and prudence of German middle-class women.

Every day practices of fashion were also shaped by what was perceived as 'the American way of life'. These influences were mediated not only by Hollywood films, but also by American troops present in the FRG. From the lucrative black-market deals with coveted nylon stockings in the first post-war years up to the later mass obsession with rolled-up blue jeans, loose-fitted sweaters and T-shirts, objects of American consumerism rapidly and irreversibly entered German mass culture. Although jeans, for example, were worn initially only by younger people and were perceived as a rebellious statement of anti-fashion, they were quickly incorporated into the mainstream patterns of production and distribution of fashion. In 1954, **Neckermann** (founded 1948) was the first mail-order house to offer different jeans styles in its catalogues, and the other two major mail-order companies Quelle (founded 1927) and Otto Versand GmbH & Co (founded 1949) as well as department stores such as Hertie and Karstadt followed suit. In response to an increased demand for cheap and attractive synthetic materials used in the production of fashionable clothing and stockings, West German industry launched into the market of the 1950s a number of newly developed materials such as Perlon, Dralon and Trevira.

In the late 1960s, the trend towards luxurious elegance and élitist exclusivity was reversed, which forced older designer houses such as Claussen, Detlev Albers, Staebe-Seger and Schulze-Varell out of the fashion market. In the FRG, as well as in France (the leading country in matters of clothes, hairstyle, and jewellery) new consumerist practices began to emerge. Fashion followed the impulses coming from youth culture. The youth movement's critique against the hypocrisy, excessive consumerism and conservatism of western societies crystallized in radical disregard for traditional *Kleiderordnung* (class norms governing dress). The various branches of the fashion industry quickly adapted to the changes of taste and transformed the popularity of jeans, mini and maxi skirts, hot pants and women's pants in general into high profits. Designer houses hired trend-scouts with cameras to collect new styles and provocative ideas directly from the street and from the various strata of subculture. Department stores made floor space for profitable Beat Shops, Fashion Corners and Twin Boutiques and offered a variety of youth collections. Uli Richter, a designer who enjoyed a stellar presence in the main-stream fashion media, was the first in Germany to offer a prêt-à-porter line along with his Haute Couture collection. Heinz Oestergaard, the doyen of the post-war generation of German designers, left the scene of high fashion in 1967 in order to become a consultant with Quelle and to pursue his own ideas of 'fashion for the masses'.

By the mid-1970s, high fashion gradually absorbed various elements of earlier anti-establishment fashion, for example highly controversial unisex designs for pants. The most durable silhouette that survived well into the 1980s was the 'Oversize Look', which concealed rather than emphasized bodily shapes. It became popular with German women who did not want to be viewed exclusively as sexual objects.

In the 1980s, when heightened awareness of acute ecological problems and rising anxiety for the peace of the planet precipitated a re-ordering of public preferences, fashion assumed a new political tint. It was the Green Party which carried out the political message of the new, informal clothing style. Their politicians appeared publicly in jeans, woollen jackets and sweaters, and gym shoes, presenting a stark contrast to traditional politicians wearing dark suits, ties and white shirts. Female politicians of the Greens preferred not to use make-up and wore in public house pants (*Wohnhosen*) and self-knit sweaters of pure wool.

Since the mid-1980s, the German fashion industry has gained unprecedented international recognition. Between 1986 and 1991, clothing exports increased by 45 percent, and in 1991 Germany became the second largest exporter of apparel in the world. Among the companies that have contributed most to this achievement are Escada (founded by Margaretha and Wolfgang Ley in 1975 as a knit house, two decades later with stores in over thirty countries), Rena Lange (started by Renate and Peter Gunthert as a small family-owned business, later with stores in Japan and showrooms in New York), Joop! (founded by Wolfgang Joop, who moved from art school to fashion journalism and finally made a break-through in 1987 as a fashion designer), Jill **Sander** (the Hamburg-based business of Jil Sander, which started small in the 1970s only to expand to an international empire for upscale, impeccably crafted minimalist designs), Hugo Boss (manufacturer of men's clothing with over 300 stores in Germany), as well as other growing businesses such as Mondi and Winsor. The worldwide success of these fashion houses has been attributed to the high quality and reliability of their products as well as to their ability to identify quickly trends developed in Paris and Milan and turn them into wearable outfits.

Austrian fashion

For the first time in the 1990s, an Austrian designer of womenswear, Helmut **Lang**, gained international recognition. He debuted in 1986 and quickly made a name with his distinctive preference for synthetic fabrics and minimalist style. Another well-known name in international fashion is Austria's Wolff – an upscale knitwear company.

Swiss fashion

A Swiss designer of the 1980s and 1990s who is well known in Switzerland is Ernst Walder. He became popular with his models representing a pot-pourri of traditional Swiss costume and classical cuts.

Fashion in the GDR

In the early 1950s, the government of the GDR recognized that a specific type of consumerism was beginning to emerge in the country and at its centre was the coveting of attractive West German products, among them clothing and shoes. In 1952 a Fashion Institute (*Deutsches Modeinstitut*) was founded in Berlin with the task of stimulating the development of the GDR's own, progressive, socialist culture of clothing. It interpreted the trends of international fashion and prepared styles suited for industrial production. The Fashion Institute organized fashion shows, designed new colours and patterns, and was officially assigned the task of developing the outfits for GDR representatives at prominent international forums, for example the outfits for the Olympic team and the Leipzig Gewandhaus Orchestra.

In 1969, an additional institution was founded –

VHB Exquisit (*Vereinigte Handelsbetriebe der Bekleidung*, a centrally managed chain of manufacturing businesses and stores) – which targeted consumers of fashionable apparel in the higher price range. VHB Exquisit employed over thirty fashion and textile designers for the design of 2,500 new items every season. The production was distributed in stores named 'Exquisit'. The most prominent designers were Artur Winter, Thea Melis, Ursula Stefke, Rotraud Hornig, and Gerhard Golz.

The main fashion magazines in the GDR were *Sybille* and *Pramo*, which featured styles of the domestic ready-to-wear production, and Exquisit styles as well as fashion from the other socialist countries.

Further reading

Gundlach, F.C. and Richter, U. (eds) (1993) *Berlin en vogue*, Berlin: Wasmuth (detailed historical accounts as well as articles on the development of the media of fashion – photography and film).

Loschek, I. (1995) *Mode im 20. Jahrhundert. Eine Kulturgeschichte unserer Zeit*, 5th edn, Munich: Bruckmann (detailed account of fashion as well of relevant styles of art, political and social developments and economic conditions).

Lott-Almstadt, S. (1986) *Brigitte 1886–1986. Die ersten hundert Jahre. Geschichte einer Frauenzeitschift*, Hamburg: Gruner + Jahr (the last three chapters provide a good overview and analysis of fashion magazines distributed in the FRG, Austria and Switzerland).

Strate, U. (ed.) (1994) *Déjà vu. Moden 1950–90*, Heidelberg: Edition Braus (concise survey of fashion trends accompanied by rich pictorial section).

MILA GANEVA

Fassbinder, Rainer Werner

b. 31 May 1945, Bad Wörishofen (Bavaria); d. 10 June 1982, Munich

Filmmaker, dramatist and actor

Fassbinder was the most dynamic and prolific filmmaker of the **New German Cinema**, who in thirteen turbulent years directed forty-two films for cinema and television in an enormous range of styles and genres – gangster pastiches, thrillers, melodramas, literary adaptations, kitchen-sink dramas, polished international co-productions, frenzied political allegories and historical costume dramas – making him, both at home and abroad, the most celebrated post-war German director. From 1966 to 1977 he was also active as a dramatist for the stage, television and radio, writing around fifteen plays. Renowned both as an artist and public figure for his feverish productivity, unorthodox life style, homosexuality, and outspoken criticism of post-war German materialism and social injustice, his death in 1982 has become synonymous with the end of the second great flowering of German cinema. Fassbinder's colleague Peter Märthesheimer, co-author of his most famous film, *The Marriage of Maria Braun* (*Die Ehe der Maria Braun*, 1978), has subsequently characterized his political goal as a 'radically naïve, almost biblically simple utopia of a future society free of exploitation and subordination, free of all kinds of fear – everyone's fear of everyone else and in particular every individual's fear of himself'.

An autodidact, Fassbinder joined the experimental Action Theater in Munich in 1967, first as an actor and subsequently as a director and author. In the following year he founded his own group, the 'antiteater', together with actors Kurt Raab and Hanna **Schygulla**, and the composer Peer Raben. Antiteater productions included adaptations by Fassbinder of Büchner, Peter **Weiss**, Jarry, Goethe, and Sophocles alongside his own plays, including *Pre-Paradise Sorry Now* and *Anarchy in Bavaria* (*Anarchie in Bayern*), both of 1969. Before it disbanded in 1971, the *antiteater* also produced Fassbinder's first ten feature films, all of which grew organically out of his theatre work.

Fassbinder himself divided his early films into 'bourgeois films, which are all set in a fairly well-defined bourgeois environment' – stylized social dramas including his first **Gastarbeiter** film, *Katzelmacher* (1969) – and 'cinema films', genre exercises influenced by the French New Wave and the Hollywood cinema of Raoul Walsh and Irving Lerner. The second catagory embraces a brooding gangster trilogy begun with *Love is Colder Than Death* (*Liebe ist kälter als der Tod*, 1969), an astonishingly assured debut owing a conspicuous and acknowledged debt to the Brechtian films of Jean-Marie **Straub** and Danièle **Huillet**. With hindsight, however, Fassbinder claimed that his *antiteater* films, despite their inventiveness and energy, had been 'too élitist and too private, just made for myself and a few friends', adding that 'you must respect your audience more than I did'.

The melodrama *The Merchant of Four Seasons* (*Der Händler der vier Jahreszeiten*, 1970), the tragic story of a Munich street trader exploited by family and friends, marked a radical departure from the more experimental early work and a deliberate attempt to orientate his films towards a mass audience. Heralded by the **Süddeutsche Zeitung** as 'the best German film since the war', it is a sensitive, emotionally-charged study of one of Fassbinder's favourite character types, the unloved outcast. Cast in very much the same mould, *Fear Eats the Soul* (*Angst essen Seele auf*, 1973), a 'politicized weepie' about the xenophobia and rejection encountered by a lonely middle-aged German cleaning woman (Brigitte **Mira**) who marries a Moroccan immigrant worker, became one of the first international successes of the New German Cinema, winning the International Critics' Prize at Cannes. It has remained one of his most popular films.

Alongside semi-autobiographical outsider figures in search of love – including Fox, played by Fassbinder himself, in *Fox and his Friends* (*Faustrecht der Freiheit*, 1974) and Hermann Hermann (Dirk Bogarde) in *Despair* (*Eine Reise ins Licht*, 1977) – it is women protagonists who dominate his films and often give them their titles – *The Bitter Tears of Petra von Kant* (*Die bitteren Tränen der Petra von Kant*, 1972), *Martha* (1973), *Effi Briest* (*Fontane Effi Briest*, 1975). According to Fassbinder, women are less conformist than men, they 'have a role, but can break out of it much more easily or can deviate a step or two from the path'. In simultaneously shaping and being shaped by their age they become – in his celebrated 'FRG trilogy' *The Marriage of Maria Braun*, *Lola* (1981) and *Veronika Voss* (*Die Sehnsucht der Veronika Voss*, 1981) – mirrors for examining private and public history.

The final years of his brief career are marked by a balance of films aimed at a mass audience, often with international stars (including Jeanne Moreau in his last film, *Querelle*, 1982) and more personal,

experimental projects such as *The Third Generation* (*Die dritte Generation*, 1978), a violent, hysterical study of **terrorism** without a cause made in the wake of the 'German Autumn', and *In a Year of Thirteen Moons* (*In einem Jahr mit dreizehn Monden*, 1979), a frank, hard-hitting portrait of the tragic demise of a transvestite in a bigoted postmodern society tyrannized by high finance. Together with his celebrated thirteen-part television adaptation of Alfred **Döblin**'s novel *Berlin Alexanderplatz* (1980), a long-cherished project seen by many commentators as the crowning achievement of his career, these strikingly radical films demonstrate that despite his standing as an international art-house director, Fassbinder remained faithful to his *antiteater* roots.

See also: film: FRG; New German Cinema; Schlingensief, Christoph

Further reading

Fassbinder, R.W. (1992) *The Anarchy of the Imagination: Interview, Essays, Notes*, Baltimore, MD and London: Johns Hopkins University Press (a useful collection subdivided into sections including autobiography, social criticism, fellow filmmakers, controversies and literary adaptations).

Jansen, P.W. and Schütte, W. (1995) *Rainer Werner Fassbinder*, Frankfurt am Main: Fischer (the standard work in German with essays, interviews, annotated filmography and extensive bibliography).

McCormick, R. (1981) *Fassbinder*, New York: Tanam Press (a translation of an earlier edition of P.W. Jansen and W. Schütte, with additional essays).

Watson, W.S. (1996) *Understanding Rainer Werner Fassbinder: Film as Private and Public Art*, Columbia, SC: University of South Carolina Press (a detailed chronological survey).

MARTIN BRADY

Fastnacht

Fastnacht, also known as *Fasnet*, is the south German celebration of shrovetide which coincides with the Rhineland celebrations of **Karneval**. Fastnacht begins on the night of the Wednesday preceding Shrove Tuesday and is followed by Dirty Thursday (*Gombiger Donnerstag*), also often known as Women's Fastnacht (*Weiberfasnacht*), and a weekend of processions in traditional *Fastnacht* costumes, such as witches' and fools' masks usually specially commissioned for each town or village (and thus communicating a particular identity), culminates on the eve of Shrove Tuesday (*Rosenmontag*) and order is restored at midnight on Shrove Tuesday itself.

ALISON PHIPPS

FDGB

The Freier Deutscher Gewerkschaftsbund (Free German Trades Union) was the central trade union organization in the GDR and the largest mass organization (see also **parties and mass organizations: GDR**). It had a central role in the political, economic and cultural life of the GDR as is underlined by the devotion of Articles 44 and 45 of the GDR constitution (1968) to the trade unions, and its position as the largest mass organization in the *Volkskammer*.

Permission for the foundation of the FDGB in the Soviet zone of occupation was given by decree number 2 of the Soviet Administration in Germany (SMAD) on 10 June 1945, and in February 1946 the foundation process was completed by a delegates' conference. At first sight, the founding of the FDGB brought together communist and social democrat trade unionists on an equal basis; after the fusion of the **KPD** and **SPD** in April 1946 it became clear that the FDGB was dominated by former KPD members, and the influence of former SPD members was further undermined by the transformation of the FDGB into a trade union organization run along communist lines. Other representatives from the Christian unions in the Weimar Republic were pushed into a minority position from the outset. In 1948 Works Councils (*Betriebsräte*) were abolished and the transfer of workers' representation rights to the Works Trade Union organizations (*Betriebsgewerkschaftsorganisationen*) increased the role of the FDGB. At the Third FDGB Congress in 1950 the leading role of the

SED was recognized which provided a further decisive step in the development of the FDGB's subservient role to the overall political and economic programme of the **SED**, above all the acceptance of the organizational principle of democratic centralism.

The FDGB was organized into twenty unions based on the principle of one union for each plant, but the individual unions lacked the independence of free trade unions, despite the rubric in Article 44(1) of the 1968 constitution which upheld the principle of independence. In the 1968 constitution unions lost the right to strike contained in Article 14 of the 1949 constitution. From the introduction of the first central economic plan in 1949 the main task of the FDGB was to ensure the attainment of planning targets at plant level. There was some slight revision to this role of the FDGB as a 'conveyor belt' for SED policy after the introduction of the New Economic Policy in 1963, when greater emphasis was given to the unions' role in representing worker interests. But this was again restricted in the 1970s, and the scope of FDGB functionaries to have a decisive influence on the running of individual enterprises remained limited to the end. It did however have an important role in the provision of certain social benefits, such as the organization of child-care and the allocation of holiday places in FDGB-run holiday centres. It also had a central role in the provision of a wide range of cultural activities, such as the organization of music, painting and writing groups. In this respect it continued the cultural traditions of the *Arbeitervereine* (Workers' Associations) from the nineteenth century.

After the political changes of late 1989 the FDGB came under strong pressure as a result of its role as an extension of the SED. Its chairman, Harry Tisch, was removed from office in November 1989, and the first discussions with the West German trades union organization (DGB) started. But despite an agreement in March 1990 between the FDGB and the DGB to co-operate, the FDGB collapsed in the rush to unification and was dissolved on 30 September 1990.

PETER BARKER

FDJ

The Freie Deutsche Jugend (Free German Youth) was the only officially sanctioned youth movement in the GDR and played an important role in its political and social life as one of the major mass organizations (see also **parties and mass organizations: GDR**). As such it was allocated thirty-two seats in the People's Chamber. It acknowledged the leading role of the **SED** and acted as the major instrument in the education of young people between the ages of fourteen and twenty-four to an acceptance of the principles and policies of the SED. It was also responsible for the organization of the Young Pioneer groups for children between the ages of six and fourteen.

The FDJ had its foundations in the communist youth movement of the Weimar Republic, especially the KJVD (*Kommunistischer Jugendverband Deutschlands*). It was formally founded on 7 March 1946 in the Soviet zone under the chairmanship of Erich **Honecker**. At the First Parliament of the FDJ in June 1946 any direct association with the SED and socialist principles was avoided; instead emphasis was put on the development of democratic attitudes and greater consideration in political life for the needs of young people. It was not until the third parliament in June 1949 that a new constitution was passed which adopted the aims of the SED. On 6 June 1950 the FDJ became a member of the democratic block of parties, therefore formally a mass organization. The recognition of the leading role of the SED and the adoption of the organizational principle of democratic centralism then followed in the new constitution of the FDJ passed at the Fourth Parliament in May 1952, thus cementing the position of the FDJ as the youth wing of the SED, responsible above all for ensuring a flow of young people loyal to the East German state into the ranks of the SED. A number of leading SED members made their careers initially as functionaries in the FDJ, such as Egon **Krenz**, who was First Secretary from 1974 to 1983.

The organization of the FDJ resembled that of the SED. The Central Council (Zentralrat) was chosen by delegates of the parliament which was nominally the highest body of the FDJ. But the actual political leadership was in the hands of the Office of the Central Council (Büro des Zentralrats) led by a First Secretary who was automatically a member of the **Central Committee** of the SED. There were then regional organizations for each *Bezirk* (county) and *Kreis* (district) in the GDR (see also **Bezirk (GDR)**), and local organizations in each institution where there were at least three members, primarily in schools, colleges, universities, enterprises and **LPGs**. The FDJ had its own daily national newspaper, *Junge Welt*.

Membership was in theory voluntary, but there was strong political and social pressure to join, since many activities for young people, both within institutions and in society in general, were organized by the FDJ. Membership rose steadily from 1.4 million in 1967 to 2.3 million in 1985, more than 70 percent of the age group. Pupils and students in schools, colleges and universities, as well as apprentices, were almost all in the FDJ, but only about a third of the young workforces in factories and agricultural co-operatives belonged. The FDJ in educational institutions was responsible for the active organization of its members, especially in relation to ideological work and extra-curricular activities. It also had an important role in any disciplinary proceedings which involved its members. In enterprises, it had a similar function to the **FDGB** concerning the fulfilling of planned targets and the presentation of SED policy to its members in the workforce.

The FDJ was dissolved at the end of January 1990 and renamed the fdj.

PETER BARKER

F.D.P.

The German liberal party *Freie Demokratische Partei* (F.D.P.), although rarely attracting more than 10 percent of the vote in federal elections, has played a crucial role as 'kingmaker', providing the essential coalition partner that the major parties have needed to form a government. Only during the **Brandt** and **Schmidt** years (1969–82) did it support the **SPD**; otherwise it has been in coalition with the **CDU/CSU**. The party has swung uneasily between the two traditions it embodies: left-of-centre social liberalism and (especially since the 1980s) right-wing market liberalism. Its supporters are predominantly better-off members of the middle classes. The rise of the **Greens** has undermined the F.D.P.'s role as sole potential 'kingmaker' for the two big parties.

JOHN SANDFORD

Fechner, Eberhard

b. 21 October 1926, Liegnitz (Silesia); d. 7 August 1992, Hamburg

Actor and filmmaker

Influenced by the tragedies of the Third Reich, Fechner produced 'film stories', as opposed to documentaries, to chronicle life in Germany and to unravel historical truth. *Nachrede auf Klara Heydebreck* (Klara Heydebreck's Epilogue) (1969) reconstructed the life of an ordinary 72-year-old woman living in West Berlin who committed suicide in 1969. *Die Comedian Harmonists* (The Harmonists Comedians) (1976) recorded the life of three remaining members of the Jewish Ensemble, excluded from the entertainment industry after Jews received *Berufsverbot* (disqualification from jobs) in 1935. *Der Prozess* (The Trial) (1984) was based on the actual Majdanek court case.

UTE LISCHKE-McNAB

Federal Constitutional Court

Both highest appeal court and guardian of the constitution (see also **constitution: FRG**), with its seat in Karlsruhe, the Bundesverfassungsgericht has far-reaching powers, unparalleled in other democracies. Its political role can be inferred directly from its main functions: to rule on cases brought by individuals alleging infringements of **civil rights**; referrals of constitutional issues arising out of pending cases in lower courts; reviews of the constitutional validity of laws or treaties which can overrule legislation passed by parliament. The court has been frequently criticized as a 'side-parliament' meddling in the democratic process.

MONIKA PRÜTZEL-THOMAS

federalism

The federal structure of the FRG, its political division into self-governing *Länder*, has a long historical tradition in Germany, encroached on only briefly in the 1930s by the centralizing efforts of the National Socialists. After WWII, the Americans made a federal structure a precondition for the new republic. Federalism was seen as providing an efficient system of checks and balances. However, all this fitted in well with the strong regional identification of Germans.

Federalism was therefore written into the constitution of the FRG (see also **constitution: FRG**), heightened in importance as a 'structural principle' – one of the cornerstones of West German democracy that must not be removed. Compared with other political systems, the FRG takes a middle position between the looser confederation of states of the US and the more centralized state of Britain. However, as the years went by, more legislative powers have accrued to the federal government in Bonn. This process was spurred on by the desire of many Germans to harmonize, at least roughly, the standard of living in the different *Länder*. Generally, federal law takes priority over *Länder* law. In theory the *Länder* have the power to pass legislation in all spheres that have not explicitly been assigned to federal government; in practice, virtually all that is left to them is education and culture (*Kulturhoheit*), the police (there is no federal police force), and the organization of local government. Since the 1970s, even in these domains, federal government has seized some legislative competence and provided frameworks within which the *Länder* then operate. An example is education: by the late 1960s the education systems in the north and the south of the FRG had grown so far apart that it seriously hindered geographical mobility (see also **education system: FRG**). To combat this situation, the Standing Conference of Education Ministers (*Kultusministerkonferenz*) was created, which now meets at regular intervals in order to harmonize educational structures to some degree and arrange mutual recognition of exams.

Another example of this 'co-operative federalism' is the redistribution of income (*Finanzausgleich*) between the richer and the poorer states, in which tax revenue is channelled between the *Länder* and also between federal government and the poorer *Länder*. With unification this financial system had to have a complete overhaul.

Although the various mechanisms of co-operative federalism have eroded the powers of the *Länder* over the years, the latter have gained influence over federal legislation through their representation in the **Bundesrat**, the upper house. Whilst in the 1950s only some 10 percent of all laws were deemed to affect the interests of the *Länder*, and thus needed the agreement of the Bundesrat, today this is true of more than 60 percent. Also, in exchange for their acceptance of the Maastricht Treaty, the *Länder* were able to strengthen their position at EU level: subsidiarity was made an explicit goal, and any transfer of sovereignty needs the explicit approval of the *Länder*.

Further reading

Jeffery, C. and Sturm, R. (1992) *Federalism, Unification and European Integration*, London: F. Cass.

Laufer, H. (1985) *Das föderative System der Bundesrepublik Deutschland*, Munich.

MONIKA PRÜTZEL-THOMAS

Fehling & Gogel

This architectural partnership was established in Berlin in 1953 by Hermann Fehling and Daniel Gogel. Fehling & Gogel became internationally known with their European Southern Observarory near Munich (1976–80). They demonstrate a highly original treatment of space, deriving from a sure handling of their organic-functionalist style. Their sculptural spaces (surprisingly always developed from the ground plan) are often multifunctional with cleverly thought-out lighting systems. One of their more recent buildings is the

meteorological institute for the FU (Free University) Berlin, which was completed in 1990.

MARTIN KUDLEK

Fels, Ludwig

b. 27 November 1946, Treuchtlingen (Bavaria)

Writer

Fels's depictions of lower-class marginalized characters, who can be found in his novels *Ein Unding der Liebe* (An Absurdity of Love) (1981), *Rosen für Afrika* (Roses for Africa) (1987) and *Bleeding Heart* (1993), are drawn from his own experiences in low-prestige jobs before becoming a writer. Rather than writing in the realist tradition of workers' literature, such as **Gruppe 61**, which focuses on the workplace, Fels concentrates in his prose, drama and poetry on the after-effects of exhausting work, reaching into the more intimate domains of soccer field, living room, bar and bed. His descriptions combine vivid imagery with a fusion of street language and a delicate lyricism.

JUDITH LEEB

Felsenstein, Walter

b. 30 May 1901, Vienna; d. 8 October 1975, West Berlin

Actor and opera producer

Felsenstein's early stage training came at the **Burgtheater** in Vienna from 1921 to 1923, followed by appointments and acting engagements in Lübeck, Mannheim, Beuthen (Silesia) and Basel. In 1929 he went to Freiburg, where he acted and produced until 1932. His first major opera post came with the Cologne Opera in 1932 followed by Frankfurt am Main two years later. Progressively he formed a more realistic approach towards opera productions, an approach that was clearly more suited to some operas than others. In recent times his theories have again attracted attention and recognition.

DEREK McCULLOCH

feminism and the women's movement

The political struggle for women's equal rights began in the mid-nineteenth century and has been successful, but the realization of these rights in everyday life continues to lag behind. The West German constitution (*Grundgesetz*) of 1949 declared men and women equal (see also **constitution: FRG**). While women can now rely on a considerable degree of legal protection of their rights, they still face discrimination in the workplace and in public life. The sociologist and law expert Ute Gerhard writes that 'women's equal rights are no longer in dispute, even among conservatives. But as soon as the right to self-determination is put into practice and the other sex has to give up privileges and rights of disposal, the question of power comes into play' (Helwig and Nickel 1993: 72). A period of activism and change in the late 1960s and 1970s centred on the issues of abortion, physical self-determination and equal participation in public life. Today, the women's movement is still active at a grassroots level but lacks a larger political impact. Many challenges posed by unification were not met, and as a result East German women lost a number of social advantages the GDR system had previously offered them. As in other western societies, the term feminism is often negatively connotated and the continuing need for change deprecated.

Women initially were responsible for the physical reconstruction of Germany after WWII. With such a proportion of men in prison camps, missing or dead, the task of clearing the rubble fell to women, who outnumbered men at a rate of 160 to 100. These *Trümmerfrauen* worked for little or no pay. Their jobs as well as their independence were temporary. The stabilization of the German economy and society sent women back to the domestic sphere.

In 1949, the new Federal Republic and the new Democratic Republic both included equal rights articles in the Basic Law (FRG) and the Constitution (GDR). In West Germany, women had to protest and remind politicians of their contributions to the reconstruction before lawmakers agreed to write unconditional equality into the Basic Law. In the same year, the West German Women's Council was founded to co-ordinate activities of various political and social women's groups and work towards a realization of the new equal rights statement. However, Article 3 of the Basic Law contained no more than a recommendation, and the Civil Code was not changed until 1957. Under the new Equal Rights Law, a husband could no longer prevent his wife from taking a job or end her employment contract for her. But as late as 1972, the Civil Law stated that women's main responsibilities were marriage and family. A woman's right to take up employment depended on her ability to balance her job with her duties as a wife and a mother.

As members of political opposition groups in the 1960s, women realized that their participation in those organizations, especially the **SDS**, was often limited to making coffee and typing up flyers. Stuck in patriarchal traditions, many male activists failed to see that political and social changes would remain incomplete if they excluded women and perpetuated the distribution of power according to gender. In her seminal 1975 narrative *Shedding* (*Häutungen*), one of the first works of modern feminist literature, Verena **Stefan** asserts that sexism runs deeper than racism and class struggle. Her protagonist Veruschka endeavours to separate herself from patriarchal society; her final embrace of lesbianism is a decision of sexuality as well as politics. Concluding that the private sphere is inseparable from the public sphere and that the personal is always political, SDS women started the *Aktionsrat zur Befreiung der Frau* (Action Committee for the Liberation of Women) in 1968. Numerous other organizations followed, including women's health groups, shelters for battered women and children, but also cultural enterprises such as women's bookstores, magazines, theatres, cinemas, libraries, archives and museums for women's history, art galleries, coffee shops, bars and clubs, many of which still exist. The relationship between sexuality and power also was crucial in the anti-pornography debate led by journalist Alice **Schwarzer** and her women's magazine *Emma*.

A main concern of this second women's movement was the decriminalization of abortion; the right to terminate a pregnancy has been called 'the women's rights question of the century' (Helwig and Nickel, 1993: 117). *Paragraph 218* (Section 218 of the Criminal Code), introduced in 1871, allowed abortion only for medical reasons. During the Third Reich, the procedure became punishable by death. The Allied Control Council revoked that part of the law, but abortion remained illegal. In a 1971 cover story of the weekly magazine *Stern*, over 300 women admitted to having had an abortion. The public debate led to a change of the law: abortion was to remain unpunished if performed during the first three months of pregnancy. The law continued to be challenged and tightened. As late as 1989, the so-called 'Memmingen witch trials', which involved more than 350 women, resulted in a thirty-month jail sentence and a temporary suspension of his licence for the gynaecologist Horst Theissen. In 1972, East Germany legalized abortions during the first twelve weeks of pregnancy. After unification, the government failed to reconcile the East and West German laws in a timely fashion despite pressure from individuals and women's groups. A new law was finally passed in 1995, permitting unpunished first trimester abortions after mandatory counselling. The compromise did not change the fact that *Paragraph 218* remains an unenforced statute that considers abortion an offence.

A reform of marital and family laws came into effect in 1977. Couples could now choose either the husband's or the wife's last name as the family name. If they were unable to decide, the man's automatically became the family name. The legal dominance of the husband over his wife was abolished, allowing for individual, gender-neutral designs of partnerships. No-fault divorces were introduced, which generally made the spouse with the higher income responsible for alimony. A law guaranteeing equality in the workplace was passed in 1980. This included equal pay as well as the wording of job ads, which could no longer favour one gender over the other.

Despite the considerable legal progress, reality still differs from the law books. In 1990, the average monthly income for men was DM 5,037, for women it was only DM 3,265. Many job offers are still only directed at men (for management positions) or women (for secretarial positions), even though the second Equal Rights Law of 1994 states once again that no position may be advertised for women or men only, and in fact must encourage

women to apply. This law also introduced a legal defence against sexual harassment in the workplace. A second liberalization of the regulations for family names was passed the same year, allowing both spouses to keep their names. About 90 percent of all couples still choose the man's last name as the family name, indicating that social changes indeed take much longer than legal reforms. This is also reflected in the low acceptance of the *Erziehungsurlaub*, a three-year, partly remunerated sabbatical for staying home with a new baby. Although available to both parents, only 1 percent of new fathers take advantage of this opportunity.

Despite the efforts of the second women's movement as well as many individuals, the traditional West German view of women's biologically-determined main role as mothers still affects all areas of society. The necessity of promoting women's social, personal and political equality was written into East Germany's 1968 revision of the Constitution (while burdening women with the sole responsibilty for household and children). Consequently, 78 percent of all women of working age were employed, making up half the workforce (1989). At the same time, only 55 percent of the women in West Germany worked, and their share of the workforce remained below 39 percent. For East German women, unification resulted in massive loss of employment, childcare facilities, and general recognition of their achievements. The birth rate plummeted, and in the early 1990s some women underwent sterilization in the hope that this would raise their chances of finding employment.

Job-sharing is rare, and part-time employment usually offers limited opportunities for career advancement. In an effort to raise the notoriously low German birth rate, the abortion law reform included a governmental commitment to guarantee child care for every three-year old by 1996. Most states failed to keep this promise, which would have facilitated women's return to the workplace.

In public life, women hold a fraction of the positions they are entitled to, considering that they make up over half of the population. Only a fifth of the members of the federal parliament are female. Although girls account for half of the completed

Abitur exams, they make up only 40 percent of students at post-secondary institutions. Twenty-eight percent of Ph.D. candidates are female, and academic lecturers and professors are 94 percent male.

In the light of the remaining obstacles to true gender equality, it is surprising that the women's movement lacks widespread support. Initiatives that often started in the 1970s continue their work. Many, like the magazine **Emma**, the publishing company Argument (with its Ariadne feminist crime fiction series), or the feminist film publication *Frauen und Film*, are recognized beyond their original feminist scope. In many cities, women's groups have created spaces for cultural, social and educational activies for women but often cannot attract a large variety of women, such as members of the working class and of ethnic minorities. At the same time that many achievements of the women's movement are being taken for granted in everyday life, a backlash against feminist ideas has developed. A young author's statement like 'The generation of the daughters is unwilling to play victim for another century' (Zerrahn, 1995: 13) illustrates the generational change in attitude. It is also visible in the commercialization and trivialization of feminism through humorous women's novels by authors like Eva **Heller** and Hera Lind; pseudo-feminist pop stars like Lucilectric and Tic Tac Toe; and film comedies whose feminist analysis is limited to the female protagonist getting back at men. There are indications, however, that a third women's movement is developing consisting of well-educated young women who simply expect to be taken seriously as professionals, parents and members of society.

See also: abortion law; *Frauenliteratur*; weddings

Further reading

Helwig, G. and Nickel, H.M. (eds) (1993) *Frauen in Deutschland 1945–92*, Bonn: Bundeszentrale für politische Bildung (collection of essays on various aspects of the situation of women in East and West Germany; extensive statistical information).

Sommerhoff, B. (1995) *Frauenbewegung*, Reinbek bei Hamburg: Rowohlt (brief and informative survey of the German women's movement since the nineteenth century, with an emphasis on the post-war period).

Stefan, V. (1994) *Shedding and Literary Dreaming*, New York: Feminist Press (new translation of *Häutungen*, including additional writings and a critical essay by Tobe Levin).

Zerrahn, V. (1995) *Entmannt. Wider den Trivialfeminismus*, Hamburg: Rotbuch (a polemic against the second-wave generation of feminists and controversial call for a pragmatic women's agenda).

SABINE SCHMIDT

Fest, Joachim

b. 8 April 1926, Berlin

Journalist, newspaper editor and historian

Joachim Fest, an influential opinion shaper in West Germany, was Joint Editor of the highbrow daily newspaper, the ***Frankfurter Allgemeine Zeitung*** from 1973 to 1993, and chief editor of television for NDR in Hamburg from 1963 to 1968. His massive biography *Hitler* (1973) narrated Hitler's background, life and psychology in some depth, presaging the West German 'Hitler-wave' of the 1970s. Other publications include *Thomas und Heinrich Mann* (1985), *Der tanzende Tod* (1986), *Im Gegenlicht* (1988) and *Staatsstreich* (1994). In the ***Historikerstreit*** of 1986 to 1987, Fest, a member of the **CDU**, defended Ernst **Nolte** with a bitter attack on Jürgen **Habermas**.

MARY FULBROOK

festivals and customs

The prominent function and significance of festivals and customs in Germany is undeniable. Community, family, regional and national life are punctuated by a rhythm of ritual behaviour, much of which revolves around the legacy of both Catholic and Protestant festivals but which has come to be more broadly accepted in secular circles. Festivals and customs are part of the fabric of tradition which is disseminated as part of the heritage and roots of a cultural identity. Festivals and customs therefore function as both relics of past behaviour and as a restatement of identity, be it national – a relatively new construction in the Germany of post-war Europe – regional or familial. Festivals and customs act as markers strengthening through ritual behaviour the structures of a culture, celebrating the corporate agreements made about what constitutes cultural identity and allowing for its clear manifestation.

The religious function and continued symbolism of festivals and customs allows their rehearsal to be imbued with what Walter **Benjamin** terms an 'aura'. This links them directly to the religiosity in which they have their roots, in spite of their transformation in the culture of late twentieth-century Germany where the festivals and traditions increasingly constitute an opportunity for cultural consumption. The cycle of cultural life in contemporary Germany is therefore expressed in festivals and customs which are at once both traditional and creative, responding to changing paradigms in society and celebrating in the present a perception of past behaviour.

Many of the festivals which are celebrated seasonally in contemporary Germany have their roots both in the religious calendar and also in rural patterns of life from previous centuries. Some, however, are festivals and traditions which have been reactivated since WWII as a statement of regional as opposed to national identity. They have the appearance of being 'traditional' medieval celebrations but are to all intents and purposes relatively recent constructions based on perceptions of past festivals and traditions. Theories as to the reason for the development of relatively new festivals and customs since WWII are numerous. Bausinger, for example, sees the development of customs as a response to the technologization of contemporary society. Dorson labels such customs 'fakelore' as opposed to 'folklore' and sees them as a manifestation of a culture which is otherwise ill at ease with its own identity. The regional, town or village specificity of the celebration of certain customs and festivals may also be viewed as either evidence for the increased desire for collective consumption of cultural experience or as a way of creating cultural distance from the excessive

national folklore abuses under the Nazis. Through small, regional or local celebrations it is possible to make a clear statement of identity which does not evoke the spectre of nationalism.

In view of the diversity and plurality of festivals and customs within contemporary Germany, particularly at a local and regional level, it is impossible to give a full inventory here, or to examine each region's particular celebrations. Instead what follows will contain a descriptive discussion of key festivals and customs celebrated nationally and one or two specific examples of regional festivals.

As many of the national festivals have their roots in the Church calendar, even in the former GDR, the beginning of the church year may be taken as a starting point for this discussion.

Advent, the first Sunday in December, is celebrated in German homes usually with the making of an advent crown from evergreen fir branches and five candles. One candle is lit every Sunday until Christmas Eve (*Heligabend*). This tradition represents a privatization of the symbolic advent crown housed in churches. During the period of Advent (*Adventszeit*) the commercial business of Christmas preparation begins. Christmas goods do not usually appear in the shops until this period, although exceptions to this rule are becoming more widespread with the increasing commercialization of Christmas. Christmas markets with stalls selling mulled wine, Christmas biscuits, hot food and many craft goods such as carved crib figures, often made by people from the local area and sold in a good cause, are a popular feature of the festive season. The markets are invariably set up in the market square or around the central church or cathedral, in the heart of the most symbolic, public space.

December 6 is St Nicholas' Day (*Nikolaus*) and on St Nicholas' Eve children all over Germany put empty shoes outside their bedroom doors which, if they have been good, they wake up to find full of sweets, nuts and fruit and other small gifts. The bringer of Christmas presents is not the same throughout Germany. In the more Protestant north Father Christmas (*Weihnachtsmann*) brings presents. Traditionally this was a figure dressed in a blue cape and representing St Nicholas, but the associations of the figure with Coca Cola advertisements in the 1920s have seen him increasingly clad in a globalizing red. In the Catholic south the Christ Child (*Christkindl*) is the bearer of presents. The traditional Dresden *Stollen*, a seasonal cake made of raisons and candied peel and butter, representing the manger in which Christ was born, and the *Lebkuchen*, a spiced ginger bread, originally from Ulm, have a rice paper base (*Oblaten*) which, like communion wafers, symbolizes the body of Christ and reinforces the festival as a major feast day in the Catholic church. Other Christmas fare also comes with stories and traditions attached, such as the story of the pepper nuts (*Pfeffernüsse*), supposedly baked by a princess. In the small medieval town of Biberach an der Riß in southern Germany the whole town gathers on the market square at dusk on Christmas Eve and watches the letting down of the Christ Child from a window under the church tower (*das Christkindl runterlassen*). All the lights in the town square are turned off and a doll in a small cradle covered in lights is lowered from the lighted window. The lights are then switched on again, the town band plays *Silent Night* and people wish each other a happy Christmas. When they return home they find that the tree is decked with home-made decorations, wooden figures, straw stars and with candles rather than fairy lights, and that the Christ Child has brought the presents and placed them under the tree ready for them to be exchanged. Not only does this particular custom add an individuality to the celebrations in this particular town, as do other individual events in other towns, such as the presentation of a two-metre-long *Stollen* to the mayor of Dresden and its subsequent sale to the people of the town, but it also has the function of making the celebrations a community affair occupying the public space and allowing an easy, clearly defined dialectic between the continuity and the changing paradigms within German society.

The Christmas season is punctuated by New Year (*Silvester*) celebrated with firework displays which, again, due to the privatized nature of this custom, leaves the streets littered with burnt-out cartridges on New Years' Day. *Silvester* is the party for the Christmas period and contrasts with the quietness and peaceful cosiness of the Christmas celebrations. The end of the Christmas period is marked by Epiphany (*Drei Könige*) when three boys,

often from the local church, dress as the three Kings and call on people in the community leaving their mark and a date as a house blessing for the coming year on the door lintel: e.g. 'C+M+B 1992'.

The next major festival comes with the shrovetide celebrations **Karneval**, *Fasching* and **Fastnacht**. The customs vary according to the region with *Karneval* being confined to the Rhineland, *Fasching* to Bavaria and *Fastnacht* to the allemanic region of Swabia and Baden and into Switzerland. Catholic regions tend overall to have many more festivals and customs than Protestant regions because of the traditional outlawing of symbolism in the Protestant church. The tradition of misrule and the reign of fools begins on the Wednesday night preceding Ash Wednesday (*Aschermittwoch*) and continues until midnight on Shrove Tuesday. The Lenten period (*Fastenzeit*) is traditionally a period of abstention. There are, however, still some celebrations with ritual, even pagan, roots which are designed to beat out the winter (*den Winter austreiben*). Large bonfires are lit across the regions on beacon hills and the fools of *Fasnacht* return to jump over the fire on *Funkensonntag*, a couple of weeks into the season of Lent.

Easter begins with the Palm Sunday processions and with houses displaying brightly decorated poles outside that have been blessed in church. Budding branches are brought in and decorated with painted wooden eggs to create an *Osterbaum* (Easter Tree) and Easter Sunday hand-painted and decorated eggs, chocolate rabbits and Easter eggs are dropped in the gardens by the Easter Rabbit (*Osterhase*) for children to find. The celebration of the coming of spring and of new life, with its roots in rural life, continues on May Day. Traditionally young people from the community go out into the woods and search for a large pine tree which is then erected on the town square or village green, displaying the coats of arms and symbols of the local **Vereine**, of the guilds and the traditional trades as well as of the place itself. The tree is decorated with ribbons and garlands and acts as a symbol of the appropriation of nature into the local community as well as clear celebration of fertility and youth.

The festivals and customs of the summer months are more diverse and disparate than the celebrations which are more obviously connected to the Christian calendar and its ritual heritage. There is a plethora of town and village festivals (e.g. *Stadtfeste*, *Dorffeste* and *Dorfhockete*) held in the open air or in large beer tents, with stalls and amusements and traditional food and drink. Beer benches are set up in the streets an on the market squares and local people come together to affirm and strengthen their allegiance to the local town. Many towns hold large processions and have created their own customs, celebrating their heritage in elaborate floats and with costumes and piped bands. In Ravensburg there is an annual children's theatre and pupils from the local secondary schools hold shooting competitions and parade through the beer gardens and the streets with drums and whistles. These festivals are similar in their exuberance to the *Karneval* and *Fastnacht* celebrations. The open-air character of these festivals has made them particularly popular and the number of towns or villages hosting an annual festival is ever increasing. The culmination of the summer festivals comes with the Beer and Wine festivals of late summer when the grape harvest has been gathered. The Munich **Oktoberfest** is perhaps the best-known example of such a festival but others are held in the wine regions in the south and along the Rhine.

The rural celebrations of the harvest are still marked in Germany. Again, in the Catholic south some churches commission a harvest carpet (*Ernteteppich*) depicting scenes from rural life and from the Bible and made entirely of the harvest fruits, laid out in front of the altar in the sanctuary of the church. Two saints' days punctuate the harvest season: Michaelmas and Martinmas. Martinmas sees *Martinimärkte* (St Martin's markets) and processions in the streets at night of children carrying lanterns.

Not all festivals and customs are celebrated seasonally or by everyone. Some customs and festivals act as markers of certain rites of passage beginning with *Kommunion* (first communion in the Catholic church) and *Konfirmation* or *Firmung* (confirmation). Even in non-practising families confirmation is seen as an important stage in a child's development to adulthood and it is an occasion for family gathering and for symbolic gifts. In the GDR this religious custom was replaced by the secular ***Jugendweihe***. The *Abifeste*

(***Abitur*** celebrations) and the *Abischerze* have a similar function, marking, as they do, the end of formal schooling. The *Abiturienten* (pupils taking their *Abitur*) arrange their own leaving ceremony and ball and also plan an intricate practical joke to play on the whole school in their final week. This may involve the capture and auctioning of all the staff, swapping entire school classes with the next school in the town, or, in 1995, many pupils attempted to wrap their school in the same way as Christo wrapped the Reichstag that same year. **Weddings** also have many customs associated with them.

Not all those resident in Germany celebrate the dominant customs and festivals, rooted as so many are in Christianity. The Muslim communities of Turkish and Bosnian minorities for instance celebrate at different times and in different ways, although their festival seasons may often coincide with the major festivals in Germany (see also **Islam in Germany**).

Further reading

Russ, J.M. (1982) *German Festivals and Customs*, London: Oswald Wolff (comprehensive account with illustrations).

ALISON PHIPPS

Feuchtwanger, Lion

b. 7 July 1884, Munich; d. 21 December 1958, Los Angeles

Writer (real name Jacob Arje)

After studying at Munich and Berlin universities, Feuchtwanger worked as a dramatic critic for *Schaubühne* in Berlin. His novel *Jew Suss* (*Jud Süß*, 1925) enjoyed international success. Being a Jew, he was proscribed in 1933. He lived in Southern France where he organized an intellectual resistance movement against the Nazis. When Vichy France interned him, he fled to Spain and Portugal, and lived from 1943 in Pacific Palisades, California. Among his numerous, mainly historical novels and plays, his *Josephus* trilogy (1932–45) most obviously relates Jewish history to the persecution and exile experienced by the Jews of his own time.

CHRISTIANE SCHÖNFELD

Feuilleton

This French word, denoting a supplement to a newspaper or magazine, comes from *'feuille'*: sheet of paper. In German newspapers, such as *Die* **Zeit**, **Frankfurter Allgemeine Zeitung** and the Swiss **Neue Zürcher Zeitung**, the feature articles of the *Feuilleton* are devoted to material such as news items, reviews, criticism and commentaries from the literary, musical and visual art world. It usually occupies a separate or at least clearly defined section within the newspaper and can also contain articles dealing with popular science, excerpts from literary works, poetry and sometimes even a serialized novel.

The German *Feuilleton* has its roots in the 'learned articles' in the moral weeklies which were popular during the Enlightenment, dealing mainly with moral instruction, interspersed with cultural news and occasionally literary criticism. The cultural importance of the *Feuilleton* has continued to grow, branching away from the short personal commentaries on moral instruction to more literary and culturally discursive criticism. Presently the *Feuilleton* is not only an all-encompassing medium for cultural and scientific discoveries, but has also become one of the most important areas for discourse, encouraging public thinking and socio-critical education. The *Feuilleton* gives voice to short-lived yet effective communications about complex issues of cultural life. It has ultimately become a significant cultural-political factor as an agent for new ideas and trends in the arts and lifestyle because of the work of important writers. Some well-known writers who have contributed to the development of the *Feuilleton* with their essayist writings are Kurt Tucholsky, Egon E. Kisch, Hans **Mayer**, Marcel **Reich-Ranicki**, Walter **Jens**, and Fritz Raddatz.

In the aftermath of the political division of the two Germanies, newspapers in the GDR were especially hard-pressed to find writers for their *Feuilletons*, as many had not returned from their exiles. The 1960s saw the emergence of a serious re-evaluation of the *Feuilleton*. Although the articles may still have dealt with superficial subjects and may have only been commentaries and reviews, they were expected to serve the interests of socialism as defined by the **SED**.

The *Feuilleton* of the unified Germany has continued to develop into an important forum for literary and cultural discussions. The authors of the feature articles for the *Feuilletons* usually write about their professions, i.e. dramatists write about the theatre, musicians and composers write about the concert and recording scene, etc. Books containing selections from various *Feuilletons* were published in the 1960s, further emphasizing the contribution made by these writers to Germany's cultural and intellectual life.

Up until the reworked *Feuilleton* in post-war Germany, a writer of a feature article was not regarded very highly, largely because of the facile writing style. The superficial usage of clever turns of phrase, brilliantly formulated yet ill-conceived solutions and illogical associations, whilst entertaining for the passive reader, did not stimulate intellectually. It was only once the morally instructive articles were displaced by discursive commentaries inviting the reader to think and reflect about the subject matter at hand that the *Feuilleton* gained a respected place in Germany's literary and cultural scene.

BETTINA BROCKERHOFF-MACDONALD

Feyerabend, Paul

b. 13 January 1924, Vienna; d. 11 February 1994, Genolier

Philosopher

Principally concerned with the relation between theory and experience, Paul Karl Feyerabend argued for a relativism in which all-encompassing theories can be 'incommensurable' with one another – not assessable by any single set of standards. He criticized the idea that science can be characterized in terms of its use of a method, and drew attention to social and political factors influencing the development of science. Seeking to dethrone science from its special place in western culture, he hoped to open the way for a light-hearted cultural pluralism in which different paths of inquiry are assigned equal social resources. Feyerabend liked to think of himself as an entertainer, rather than a professional philosopher.

See also: philosophy; Popper, Karl Raimund

JOHN PRESTON

Fichte, Hubert

b. 21 March 1935, Perleberg (Branden-burg); d. 8 March 1986, Hamburg

Writer and literary critic

Being partly Jewish in Nazi Germany, Fichte experienced the duality of being both an insider and outsider in German culture. This experience of bordering different cultures led him to travel and conduct research on the Marquis de Sade, the 'Leathermen' movement and voodoo. Noted for his concept of 'poetic anthropology/ethnology', Fichte focused on ethnography and language as artistic invocations of reality rather than mimetic representations. A gay critic, Fichte suggested that queer preference provoked this radically different 'aesthetic experience'.

KITTY MILLET

film, experimental

In the late 1950s, influenced by developments in music (serialism) and the visual arts, the Austrian structural filmmakers Peter Kubelka and Kurt Kren explored 'film as film', the materiality of celluloid, light and projection. They exerted a major influence on Birgit and Wilhelm Hein's *Raw Film* (*Rohfilm*, 1968), on Werner Nekes' *Kelek* (1968) and Dore O.'s *Alaska* (1968). These were the pre-eminent West German experimental filmmakers in the 1960s, who explored structure, rhythm and gaze. During the 1970s Klaus Wyborny, Heinz **Emigholz**, Valie **Export** and others enriched structural filmmaking by introducing fictional narratives and spoken text.

See also: New German Cinema

MARTIN BRADY

film: Austria

After WWII the Austrian film industry, which had been under Nazi influence throughout the period from 1938 to 1945, was taken over by the four Allied powers and used for their own ends. The Soviet authorities exercised total control over the parts they had seized. The western powers, on the other hand, especially the Americans and the British, soon handed over much of their powers to Austrian filmmakers and producers, while at the same time setting up their own film distribution activities in order not to lose control of the market. Austrian investment in the film industry focused around the activities of Creditanstalt-Bankverein, the biggest bank in the country, which led to the foundation of a distribution company and a film production company. During the 1960s and 1970s film production in Austria virtually came to an end. Most of the production sites either went into liquidation or were sold to estate agents or to the **ORF**, the Austrian radio and television company. In spite of various attempts, plans for a comprehensive revival of film production facilities in Vienna remain to be realized.

Most people who had dominated the Austrian film industry before and during WWII continued to influence the era after 1945 without major and long-lasting difficulties in spite of their past. The new films very much exploited the old Viennese clichés that represented an unrealistic dream world as opposed to the grim realities of the immediate post-war period, in many cases employing operetta-style music to create a light mood. The hardships of everyday life and the immediate past were hardly presented at all, as many of the film scripts were based on historical events and personalities of the Hapsburg era with the Austrian scenery as a pleasant backdrop, thus creating an Austrian variety of the *Heimatfilm*. These were mostly romantic love stories with stereotypical characters, evoking an atmosphere widely associated with *Gemütlichkeit*, and also serving as a vehicle for the presentation of tourist attractions, depicting idyllic regions like the Salzkammergut and the Wachau, or presenting the Vienna Boys' Choir, as in *Singende Engel* (Singing Angels), directed by Gustav Ucicky (1898–1961) in 1947, *Im Weißen Rössel* (White Horse Inn) (1952) by Willi Forst (1903–80) or *Der Förster vom Silberwald* (The Forester of the Silver Wood) (1954) by Alfons Stummer. The actors were mainly drawn from the major Austrian theatres. Paula Wessely (1908–) and Paul Hörbiger (1894–1981), as well as Hans Moser (1880–1964), who epitomized the grumpy Viennese stereotype, were the established stars despite their successes during the Nazi era.

The director Franz Antel (1914–), whose work covers various genres from the *Heimatfilm* to light comedies and soft porn, left his mark with the classic comedy *Hallo Dienstmann* (Hey Porter) (1952), and with his ambitious project *Stubborn Mule* (*Der Bockerer*) (1981), a film about a Viennese butcher who resisted the Nazis. With his three *Sissi* films (1955–7) about Elisabeth of Austria, the wife of Emperor Francis Joseph I, the well-established director and producer Ernst Marischka (1893–1963) created a cinematic myth and helped to launch the international career of Romy **Schneider** (1938–82) and Karlheinz Böhm (1928–).

Only few films dealt with the war and its aftermath. Examples are *Der weite Weg* (The Long Way Home) (1946) by Eduard Hoesch or *Der letzte Akt* (*The Last Act*) (1955), by the German director Georg Wilhelm Pabst (1885–1967), about the end of the Third Reich with Albin Skoda (1909–61) as Adolf Hitler and Oskar Werner (1922–84), who later made an international career.

Owing to the small Austrian market and the lack of funding, filmmakers were often forced to work for German producers and distributors. By the end of the 1960s commercial Austrian film making had come to a virtual standstill.

It took several years until a new generation of film directors emerged who were not under the spell of the traditions of the 1950s and 1960s. Modern Austrian films very often take up literary subjects, like *Das falsche Gewicht* (The Wrong Weight) (1978), an adaptation of a Joseph Roth text by Bernhard **Wicki** (1919–), Maximilian Schell's *Tales from the Vienna Woods* (*Geschichten aus dem Wienerwald*) (1979), based on a play by Ödön von Horváth, or Wolfgang Glück's *Der Schüler Gerber* (The Pupil Gerber) (1980), based on a novel by Friedrich Torberg. Axel Corti (1933–93) especially adapted a number of literary works for film and television, e.g. Gernot Wolfgruber's novel *Herrenjahre* (Master Years) (1983), and Joseph Roth's *Radetzkymarsch* (Radetzky March) (1993). Xaver Schwarzenberger (1946–) turned Gerhard **Roth**'s novel *Der stille Ozean* (The Pacific Ocean) (1983) into a feature film. Paulus Manker (1958–) made the play *Weiningers Nacht* (Weininger's Night) (1989) by Joshua Sobol into a film.

A highly critical strand of television and feature films deals with various aspects of Austrian history, mainly the Nazi era and the time after 1945. The six-part television series *Die Alpensaga* (The Alpine Saga) (1976–80), by Dieter Berner (1944–) with its screenplay by Wilhelm Pevny and Peter **Turrini**, introduced this new approach to Austrian history, which opposes the idyllic concepts of rural life that were one of the core elements of the earlier *Heimatfilm* movement and which shows a realistic view of the past.

Axel Corti's *Welcome to Vienna*, 1986, deals with the historical events immediately before and after the end of WWII. Wolfram Paulus' *Heidenlöcher* (Heathen Caves) (1986) is an accurate study of a local farming community in a remote Salzburg valley during the war with all its idiosyncrasies and its tendencies to co-operate with rather than to resist Nazi rule. Karin Brandauer (1945–92), one of the leading female directors, deals with similar themes in the film *Sidonie* (1990, based on a book by Erich Hackl) and in two parts of a four-part television series on **South Tyrol**, *Verkaufte Heimat* (The Bartered Homeland) (1988, 1989).

Film comedies, both funny and satirical, constitute another element of modern Austrian cinema. *Exit – nur keine Panik* (Exit – Don't panic) (1980) by Franz Novotny (1949–), and *Müllers Büro* (Müller's Office) (1986), a take-off on classical gangster movies by Niki List (1956–), exemplify Austrian humour. Peter Patzak (1945–), who later gained wide acclaim with his film *Kassbach* (1979), struck a similar note with the parodistic and often surreal television series about detective Kottan (starting in 1976).

Often hardly noticed by the public are a number of experimental filmmakers, among them Peter

Weibel (1945–) and Valie **Export** (1940–) as well as Ferry Radax (1932–), Kurt Krenn (1929–) and Peter Kubelka (1934–), who have played an important role in the development of Austrian cinema.

Whereas the international impact of modern Austrian cinema is limited, actors like Romy Schneider, Helmut Berger (1944–), Klaus Maria **Brandauer** (1943–) and Arnold **Schwarzeneg-ger** (1947–) became well-known in the world of film. The directors Billy **Wilder** (born 1906 in Galicia), Fred **Zinnemann** (1907–), and the director and producer Otto Preminger (1906–86), who emigrated to America in the 1920s and 1930s, made their way in the US and created films of lasting importance, like *Sunset Boulevard* (Wilder, 1961) or *High Noon* (Zinneman, 1952).

Further reading

Büttner, E. and Dewald, C. (1997) *Anschluß an morgen: Eine Geschichte des österreichischen Films von 1945 bis zur Gegenwart*, Salzburg and Vienna: Residenz-Verlag.

Steiner, G. (1995) *Filmbook Austria*, Vienna: Federal Chancellery, Federal Press Service.

GEORG HELLMAYR

film: FRG

Cinema in the FRG can be subdivided into five periods: the hesitant experiments – before the establishment of the two separate German states – of the post-war *Trümmerfilm* (cinema of ruins), the commercial success and artistic inertia of 1950s mass entertainment, the artistic aspirations of Young German Cinema (1962–9), the **New German Cinema** (through to the death of Rainer Werner **Fassbinder** in 1982), and contemporary cinema looking to regain the mass audience.

Wolfgang **Staudte**'s *The Murderers are Amongst Us* (*Die Mörder sind unter uns*, 1946) set the tone for the so-called *Trümmerfilm*. Scripted before the war was over, it addresses pressing moral conflicts amidst the ruins, as a doctor is confronted with his former commanding officer. Many titles of this time – e.g. Rudolf Jugert's *Film without a Title* (*Film ohne Titel*,

1947) and Harald Braun's *Between Yesterday and Tomorrow* (*Zwischen gestern und morgen*, 1947) – show how filmmakers thematized their search for new directions. Many had been working during the Third Reich and were forced to adjust to a situation in which every film was scrutinized by the Allies for its ideological content. Helmut **Käutner**'s *In Those Days* (*In jenen Tagen*, 1947), Erich Engel's *The Blum Affair* (*Die Affäre Blum*, 1948) and Staudte's *Rotation* (1949) were early attempts to see National Socialism in a historical context.

The 1950s, the decade of the **Economic Miracle**, were dominated by escapism and cinematic nostalgia. *Heimatfilme* (rustic regional romances) flourished in the wake of Hans Deppe's hugely successful *Grün ist die Heide* (Green is the Heath 1951), a melodrama with a reactionary and melancholy subtext on lost German lands, and the sentimental *Sissi* films with Romy **Schneider**, set in imperial Austria, are still popular today. These boom years at the box office (128 films were released in 1955 and in 1956 there were sixteen cinema visits per head) also marked an artistic nadir, although a few filmmakers did attempt to be more challenging. Georg Tressler's *The Hooligans* (*Die Halbstarken* 1956), introduced a realist tone, Rolf Thiele's *The Girl Rosemarie* (*Das Mädchen Rosemarie* 1958) spotlighted political corruption in the wake of the scandals surrounding the high-society prostitute Rosemarie Nitribitt, and Bern-hard Wicki's powerful anti-war film *The Bridge* (*Die Brücke* 1959) reminded audiences of the traumas of the war. A remarkable film which focuses directly on the psychological anxieties of the 1950s is Ottomar Domnick's *Jonas* (1957), scripted by Hans Magnus **Enzensberger**.

At the Berlin Film Festival of 1961 no film merited the Federal Film Prize. Testifying to the lack of artistic integrity in German cinema, this *impasse* created a platform for young writer-directors who allied themselves with Italian Neo-Realism and the French New Wave. These became the authors of the Oberhausen Manifesto, seen as announcing the new wave in Germany (see also **New German Cinema**).

It took time for any significant effects on feature filmmaking to be felt, and the most popular 1960s films were Edgar Wallace thrillers starring Klaus **Kinski**, and Karl May Westerns, beginning with

Harald Reinl's *Winnetou 1* (1963). Cleverly marketed soft-core porn films, generally of Bavarian origin, also challenged the supremacy of American cinema at the box-office.

Internationally, the 1970s in the FRG are associated with the intellectual, art-house successes of **New German Cinema**, challenging and often formally experimental features which appealed principally to the generation of the **student movement**. The films of Alexander **Kluge**, Jean-Marie **Straub**, Danièle **Huillet**, Volker **Schlöndorff**, Rainer Werner **Fassbinder**, Wim **Wenders** and Hans Jürgen **Syberberg** lacked mass appeal, although filmmakers were well supported by television, metropolitan repertory cinemas (the *Kommunale Kinos*) and distribution through **Goethe-Institut**s worldwide. From the mid-1970s the proportion of women filmmakers steadily increased, until by 1990 it was the highest of any film-producing country. Including the work of Claudia von **Alemann**, Jutta **Brückner**, Doris **Dörrie**, Ulrike **Ottinger**, Helke **Sander**, Helma **Sanders-Brahms**, Monika **Treut** and Margarethe von **Trotta**, women's film at first developed thematically and stylistically in parallel with the women's movement. Dörrie's box-office success with her comedy *Men* (*Männer*, 1985) marked a move away from feminism towards mainstream entertainment. Gay cinema, represented in particular by Rosa von **Praunheim** and Lothar Lambert, has remained a consistently prominent feature of German filmmaking since 1970.

Subsidy debates dominated the industry from the early 1980s. Those seeking to preserve funding defended cinema as art, pointing to New German Cinema as the paradigm, while those advocating the free market as a realistic context for the production of popular cinema looked to the 1950s. Although comedy emerged as a dominant characteristic after 1989, used as a political tool by filmmakers such as Christoph **Schlingensief**, and for light entertainment by Sönke **Wortmann**, Katja von Garnier, Detlev Buck, Sherry Hormann and others, the meeting of two distinct film traditions failed to provide fresh impulses. **Documentary film** in the FRG certainly benefited both from the momentous political events of autumn 1989 and from the stronger documentary tradition in the GDR (see **Böttcher, Jürgen**).

Andreas Voigt also surfaced as an important documentary filmmaker with *Last Year Titanic* (*Letztes Jahr Titanic*, 1990) following developments in Leipzig from the **Wende** to unification. Schlingensief's *The German Chainsaw Massacre* (*Das deutsche Kettensägenmassaker* 1992), a low-budget trash horror movie parodying consumerism through the story of a manic West German family hunting down East Germans at the border and turning them into sausages, provided an extreme example of the 'unification comedy', a peculiarly German genre for the 1990s.

See also: film festivals; film journals; film, experimental; film: GDR

Further reading

Bock, H-M. (1984ff) *Cine-Graph: Lexikon zum deutschsprachigen Film*, Munich: edition text + kritik (loose-leaf encyclopedia, entries provide biography, critical overview, bibliography and filmography).

Jacobsen, W. *et al.* (eds) (1993) *Geschichte des deutschen Films*, Stuttgart and Weimar: Metzler (covers 1895 to 1992 decade by decade, with chapters on documentary, experimental, and GDR cinema; also contains extensive bibliographies).

Knight, J. (1992) *Women and the New German Cinema*, London and New York: Verso (corrects previous histories of German film of the period by focusing on women's filmmaking).

Pflaum, H.G. and Prinzler, H.H. (1993) *Cinema in the Federal Republic of Germany*, Bonn: Inter Nationes (handbook with extensive filmographies and introductory essays on film in the FRG and GDR).

MARTIN BRADY AND HELEN HUGHES

film: GDR

GDR film production was determined by political rather than artistic considerations, its success judged by cultural rather than economic criteria. In line with Lenin's remark that it is the most important of the arts, film was expected to make substantial contributions towards the development of socialist society.

All films were planned, financed, produced, and distributed by **DEFA**, the country's state monopoly film company, which also regulated the import of foreign films. Feature film production was centred at the former Ufa studios in **Babelsberg**. Though directors did not have to submit to commercial pressures, they were caught between the expectations of their political masters and audience demands for attractive, convincing films.

Film content was influenced by changes in the political climate and accompanying debates about the function of art within socialist society. Depending on whether the country was going through a period of entrenchment or liberalism, film form and content wavered between doctrinaire **socialist realism** and critical realism.

Socialist realism regards film as a propaganda tool, operates with set patterns of plot and stereotype characters (positive heroes who achieve self-realization within a socialist collective), and rejects experiments with film form. Individuality, contradictions, or subtle hints at cracks in the socialist system are unacceptable. Critical realism identifies controversial issues, opens them up for critical debate, and allows formal experiments which enhance and deepen the understanding of that reality.

The most liberal period lasted from 1945 to 1949 when film occupied the centre of the Russian re-education programme. While the western Allies – particularly the US – attempted to prevent the re-emergence of a strong, competitive film industry in Germany the Russians sanctioned the founding of DEFA as early as November 1946 and prepared the ground for the creation of a large film company which could easily be controlled by the state. DEFA's early production policies reflected a humanist rather than a doctrinaire socialist perception of the world. The first generation of DEFA directors, which included Gerhard Lamprecht, Slatan Dudow and Erich Engel, established the long tradition of decidedly anti-fascist films. Ranging from Wolfgang **Staudte**'s *The Murderers Are Amongst Us* (*Die Mörder sind unter uns*, 1946) and *Marriage in the Shadows* (*Ehe im Schatten*, Kurt **Maetzig**, 1947) to the masterpieces of Konrad **Wolf**, they are DEFA's most important contribution to German Cinema.

Soviet concern over cracks in the socialist block (1948) and the emergence of two Germanies (1949) brought an end to liberal film policies. In November 1947 DEFA became a joint-stock company, and its shares were taken over by a subsidiary of the Socialist Unity Party **SED** and the Soviets. The *Künstlerischer Rat* (Artistic Advisory Board), appointed by the SED, took over production control. In 1952, the 'First Film Conference' demanded strict adherence to socialist realism and the abandonment of 'progressive-humanist' issues. In 1953, DEFA became a state company, and the following year production control went to the newly created Ministry of Culture.

A *Neuer Kurs* (New Course) introduced in the wake of Stalin's death (1953) brought a degree of liberalism and gave individual filmmakers greater autonomy and responsibility. It lasted until 1958 when the 'Second Film Conference' rescinded the 'New Course' and reinstated the objectives of 1952, since *Gegenwartsfilme* (films set in the present) placed too much emphasis on negative aspects of life in the GDR. Criticism focused particularly on the so-called 'Berlin Films' such as *Berlin – Corner of Schönhauser* (*Berlin – Ecke Schönhauser*, 1958) by Gerhard Klein and his script writer Wolfgang **Kohlhaase**. Shot on location they vividly captured the atmosphere and addressed the problems of rebellious young people in East Berlin.

The **Berlin Wall** (1961) generated a feeling of protection from negative western influences. Organized in small, relatively independent production units a new generation of directors, trained at film schools in Babelsberg, Prague and Moscow, began to look critically at life in the GDR. Their liberal optimism came to an abrupt halt in December 1965. In a speech to the Eleventh Congress of the Central Committee of the SED Erich **Honecker** chose two recently completed films – Kurt Maetzig's *I Am the Rabbit* (*Das Kaninchen bin ich*, about a corrupt public prosecutor) and Frank Vogel's *Don't Think I am Crying* (*Denk bloß nicht ich heule*, focusing on the generation conflict) – to launch a full-scale attack on the corrupting influences of the media. As a result, films by Frank **Beyer**, Jürgen **Böttcher**, Egon **Günther**, Gerhard Klein, Günter Stahnke, and Hermann Zschoche were stopped before completion and/or shelved, and their directors' careers interrupted or destroyed. Known as *Verbotsfilme* (forbidden films) or *Regalfilme* (shelved films) most of them did not reach the cinemas until 1989.

Ironically the period of entrenchment which followed seemed to come to an end with Honecker's election as Party Secretary in 1971. In an atmosphere of rapprochement between East and West Germany he boldly pronounced that there should be no taboos for artists who were firmly rooted in socialism. Though his statement did not lead to a genuine revision of his previous position, a number of films emerged which focused on the rights and problems of the individual. Frequently featuring female protagonists, the most popular and widely debated were Heiner **Carow**'s *The Legend of Paul and Paula* (*Die Legende von Paul und Paula*, 1972, scripted by Ulrich **Plenzdorf**) and *Solo Sunny* (1979) by Konrad Wolf and Wolfgang Kohlhaase.

When a new generation of filmmakers, amongst them Helmut Dziuba, Roland Gräf, Evelyn Schmidt, Rainer Simon, Erwin Stranka and Lothar Warneke, attempted to make critical films during the 1970s and 1980s, more often than not their work was hampered and blocked by ideological hardliners. As a consequence, some directors turned to filming literature. Creative freedom did not come until unification, by which time filmmakers were faced with different restrictions – those imposed by commercial considerations.

DEFA's entertainment films – frequently laced with ideological messages – included comedies, musicals, adventure films, children's films and, above all, *Indianerfilme* (films about Red Indians), the company's answer to the western – its most popular and successful film genre. Though most of them demonstrate a high professional standard, their technical excellence cannot compensate for their lack of formal and visual experimentation. More likely to survive the test of time are DEFA's **documentary films**, particularly those which observed and/or managed to question everyday GDR reality, such as Jürgen Böttcher's work or Winfried Junge's long-term project *Lebensläufe* (Personal Developments – the continuing record, begun in 1962, of the development of people from a provincial town who had entered school that year). Important from an ideological and historical point of view are also Andrew and Annelie **Thorndike**'s compilation films, and the investi-

gative, but manipulative documentaries of Walter Heynowsky and Gerhard Scheumann.

See also: cultural policy: GDR; DEFA; Eleventh Plenum

Further reading

Heimann, T. (1994) *DEFA, Künstler und SED-Kulturpolitik*, Berlin: VISTAS (analysis of the relationship between GDR cultural policies and film production from 1945 to 1959).

Pflaum, H.G. and Prinzler, H.H. (1993) *Cinema in the Federal Republic of Germany*, Bonn: Inter Nationes (revised, updated, and enlarged English translation of the standard reference work; includes a survey of GDR cinema and comprehensive bibliography).

Schenk, R. (ed.) (1994) *Das zweite Leben der Filmstadt Babelsberg. DEFA-Spielfilme 1946–92*, Berlin: Henschel (comprehensive survey of DEFA, includes filmography and content of every feature film produced).

HORST CLAUS

film: Switzerland

German-Swiss film production did not develop until the 1930s, and well beyond 1945 films tended to present an idealized picture of Switzerland. In 1963, the government began to provide limited funding for filmmaking, and from the early 1960s many noted documentary films examining contemporary society were made. Critical attitudes established in these works were an integral part of the feature films of the 1970s which portrayed the Swiss present and past in an often uncomfortable light. In the 1980s and 1990s, a second generation of directors came forward, and there was a more international character to the themes developed. In 1991 a German-Swiss film was awarded the Hollywood Oscar for Best Foreign Film, but in general German-Swiss films have not the international renown achieved by the work of leading French-Swiss directors. There are three major annual film festivals in Switzerland.

There was no significant German-Swiss production until the 1930s. Films, like all Swiss cultural life at that time, reflected the political climate of the endangered country. Thus, *Füsilier Wipf* (Rifleman Wipf) (1938) extolled values of sturdy independence and was seen by a third of the Swiss population. Later, *The Last Chance* (*Die letzte Chance*, 1945) portrayed Switzerland as a refuge for those fleeing from fascism and was much praised abroad. Ironically, both films were directed by Leopold Lindtberg, an Austrian Jew working in Switzerland in conditions of considerable difficulty. After 1945, German-Swiss films, with few exceptions, presented a picture of Switzerland increasingly divorced from contemporary reality.

By the mid-1960s, the less idealized views of Swiss history and society, which were establishing themselves generally, influenced films. The importance of the film as a cultural asset received recognition with the start in 1963 of financial support from the Confederation. This permitted a new departure for the German-Swiss film by promoting documentary films which examined aspects of contemporary Swiss life. The first notable film was Alexander Seiler's *Siamo italiani* (We are Italians) (1964), which, employing new technical methods which offered a more direct reflection of reality, examined the problems of foreign workers in Switzerland and introduced several films on groups on the periphery of society. A second broad theme of these films was the inadequacy of the democratic processes for the expression of opinion and change, for example, Jürg Hassler's *Krawall* (Riot) (1970) on the impact of the 1968 movement in Zürich, *Gösgen* (1978) on demonstrations against Swiss nuclear reactors, and *Züri brännt* (Zürich's Burning) (1981) on the youth protests of 1980 in Zürich. A third theme was the recent Swiss past, taken up by, amongst others, one of the most noted figures in the German-Swiss film, Richard Dindo. His *Schweizer im spanischen Bürgerkrieg* (Swiss in the Spanish Civil War) (1973) and *Die Erschiessung des Landesverräters Ernst S* (The Execution of the Traitor Ernst S) (1976) explored official Swiss attitudes to fascism. Dindo continued his examination of vindictive state power in the fates of four youths, *Dani, Michi, Renato und Max* (1987).

The provisions regarding financial support from the Confederation were altered in 1969 to include feature films. The 1970s have been called the best years of the 'New Swiss Film', and the committed

search for truth which is such a strong element in the documentary films was now often present in German-Swiss feature films. For example, Peter von Gunten's *Die Auslieferung* (The Extradition) (1974), the precisely researched historical reconstruction of the deportation of a Russian anarchist, permitted conclusions to be drawn about contemporary attitudes. The best-known of the iconoclastic films was Markus Imhoof's *The Boat is Full* (*Das Boot ist voll*) (1981), in which, in contrast to *Die letzte Chance*, the deportation of a group of German refugees back to certain death in Germany was harrowingly depicted. (The use of both standard German and Swiss dialect in this film underlines the problem of language for the German-Swiss filmmaker.) Even the comedy by Rolf Lyssy, *The Swissmakers* (*Die Schweizermacher*, 1978), the most successful German-Swiss film of all time, which followed the tribulations of a group of foreigners applying for Swiss citizenship, ironically showed one applicant finally rejecting the treasured status.

The 1980s and 1990s saw more works by women directors and also a move towards Third World themes in the documentary film. Two outstanding feature films in these years which drew on the strengths of the German-Swiss film developed in the two previous decades were *Alpine Fire* (*Höhenfeuer*, 1985), an examination of the restrictive and ultimately self-destructive Swiss myth of mountain life, and *Journey of Hope* (*Reise der Hoffnung*, 1990) by Xaver Koller, a depiction of the difficulties of Kurdish asylum-seekers in Switerland which, in 1991, won the Hollywood Oscar for the Best Foreign Film.

The Confederation, through the Film Section of the *Bundesamt für Kultur* (Federal Office of Culture), provides production support, makes awards to highly-regarded films, helps film promotion and the submission of films at international festivals. In 1995, 11 million Swiss francs were available, approximately two thirds for production, and one-third for the promotion and maintenance of the *Cinémathèque*, the film archive in Lausanne. Through *Pro Helvetia* (the Arts Council of Switzerland) seasons of Swiss films abroad are promoted. The Migros food and services co-operative, as well as other private bodies, also provide financial support for films.

Since 1947, there has been an annual international film festival at Locarno, since 1966 an
annual workshop for Swiss films at Solothurn, and
since 1969 an international festival of documentary
films at Nyon.

Further reading

Dumont, H. (1987) *Geschichte des Schweizer Films.
Spielfilme 1896–1965*, Lausanne: Schweizer Film-
archiv (a marvellously readable compendium of
all productions of the period).

Gersch, W. (1984) *Schweizer Kinofahrten. Begegnungen
mit dem neuen Schweizer Film*, Berlin: Henschel (a
review of Swiss films from the early 1960s from
the point of view of a GDR citizen).

Giger, B. *et al.* (1978) *Film in der Schweiz*, Munich:
Carl Hanser (essays by Swiss filmmakers and
critics).

Schlappner, M. and Schaub, M. (1987) *Vergangenheit
und Gegenwart des Schweizer Films (1896–1967)*,
Zürich: Schweizerisches Filmzentrum (essays by
the two authors on themes in Swiss films).

MALCOLM PENDER

film festivals

Film and video festivals provide opportunities to
film/video makers including publicity, critical and
artistic examination, exposure to programmers,
curators, distributors and buyers as well as
exchange between filmmakers. In an age of
increased economic competition and intensified
marketing, festivals have become more important
than ever. For the cineaste, festivals are often the
only venue to see many independent films that
would otherwise not find an audience in the
competitive film market.

Germany has several important festivals. Given
the unique developments and history of German
film production before, during and after the Third
Reich, festivals in Germany developed as intense
forums for discussion and agitation in order to
implement changes and to promote young filmmakers. The oldest festival, the Berlinale (Berlin
Film Festival), was founded in 1951 and remains
the largest and most respected international festival

after Cannes and Venice. The golden *Bär* (bear) is a
coveted prize. The Mannheim Internationale Film
Woche (International Film Week) became an
annual event in 1961, after a successful start in
1952. The *Filmtage* in Oberhausen (Oberhausen
festival) remains the festival with the most rigorous
artistic and political forum for discussion since its
inception in 1954. It was here, in February 1962
that the Oberhausen Manifesto, proclaiming the
death of the traditional German film, and
commonly perceived as the starting-point for the
New German Cinema, was formulated. The
smallest film festival in Germany originated in Hof
in 1967 and has become the place where new
German filmmakers are discovered.

When discussions were held in 1979 to found
the Internationale Münchner Filmwochen, controversial political appointments stalled the creation of the festival until 1983. The consequence
was that German filmmakers organized their own
festival in Hamburg in 1979 where sixty filmmakers signed the famous Hamburg Declaration
expressing hope for a renewed vigorous tradition of
German film production.

Women have not been absent from the festival
scene, indeed the Feminale, Germany's main
women's film festival, has grown from a small
national affair in 1984 into an international forum
held annually in Cologne. The Feminale has built
up a reputation for presenting unique films,
especially in the experimental sector. It also stresses
its role as a forum for information, exchange, and
debate.

In the former GDR, the Nationale Kinderfilm-
festival (National Children's Film Festival) takes
place in Gera and alternates every two years with
the Nationales Spielfilmfestival (National Feature
Film Festival) in Chemnitz. Schwerin is host to the
FilmKunstFest. Festivals held in other cities include
the experimental film festival in Osnabrück; the
International Animated Film Festival in Stuttgart;
the Experimental Short Film Festival in Bonn; the
International Children's Festival in Essen; the
Children's Film Festival in Frankfurt am Main; the
Göttingen Film Festival; the Interfilm Festival
Berlin (an international short film festival run by
the *Jungforum* section of the Berlin Festival); and the
Nordische Filmtage in Lübeck.

Political changes continue to affect the way in

which festivals are run. In 1996 the Koordination der Europäischen Filmfestivals (Co-ordination of European Film Festivals) was founded in order to promote European film and establish co-operation between festivals. The fact that the EU has increased its subsidies is an indication that festivals remain an important presence in marketing European films.

UTE LISCHKE-McNAB

film journals

Soon after the rapid development of technology and film in 1895, the print media began to promote film as a new art form. The cinema was, according to most critics, capable of both entertainment and enlightenment. By the late 1920s, the status of film and film criticism as a major force in German was firmly established.

Among the earliest film journals to appear were the *Internationale Film- und Kinematographen-Zeitung* (1906), *Der Kinematograph* (1907), *Organ für die gesamte Projektionskunst* and *Lichtbild-Bühne* (1908). *Film-Kurier*, published daily from 1919 to 1944 in Berlin, included perspectives on film, varieté, art, fashion, sport and the stock market. Lotte Eisner, the renowned German film historian and critic, was on the editorial board. *Film-Revue* published its first issue in 1947 with Marlene Dietrich on the cover. Oriented towards popular tastes, it was selling 400,000 copies by the mid-1950s.

After 1945 the Catholic and Protestant churches became prominent players in film criticism in their attempt to reclaim the social and cultural power denied them under Hitler and National Socialism. The churches led a campaign to ward off the secularization and commercialization of foreign and indigenous cultural practices. After the Catholic church began to publish *Filmdienst der Jugend* (Film Service for Youth) in 1947, which became *Film-Dienst* in 1949, one of the longest running film journals in Germany, the Protestant church founded the *Evangelischer Filmbeobachter* (Evangelical Film Observer) in 1948. Between 1948 and 1983 the Protestant church also published *epd Kirche und Film*. In 1984 the *Filmbeobachter* and *epd Kirche und*

Film merged into *epd Film* which became both a readable and critical journal.

By the mid-1980s, the general body of film journals consisted of those providing film criticism, information and comment; those which offered a network around independent productions; and those which established a forum for debating critical theory. Some journals have developed around theoretical positions and took authorship theory as their key framework in the 1950s and 1960s. In the 1970s, the discussions around notions of ideology and representation provided a way of constructing a political critique of film as representation in terms of its textual strategies and production of meaning. In recent years, some journals, notably *Cinema* (first published 1976), *Film* (1963) and *Filmkritik* (which became *Film und Fernsehen* in 1970), have incorporated debates on reading, address and reception, and the audience, as well as policy debates on matters such as censorship (see also **censorship: FRG**; **censorship: GDR**).

In 1974 Helke **Sander** set up the first German feminist film journal *Frauen und Film*. It was, and remains, the only European feminist film journal, providing a forum for exploring contemporary women's filmmaking and recovering the history of women's contribution to cinema throughout the twentieth century. An interesting overview of film and television in the former GDR is provided by *Film und Fernsehen* which first appeared in East Berlin in 1973. Published monthly by the *Verband der Film- und Fernsehschaffenden der DDR*, it contains essays, interviews, critical reviews and festival reports. The dedication of its current editor, Erika Richter, has ensured the journal's survival after the **Wende**.

Currently, journals reflect the broadened focus of film theory and criticism and, partly under the influence of feminism, have become more eclectic.

UTE LISCHKE-McNAB

Fink, Heinrich

b. 31 March 1935, Korntal (Bessarabia)

Theologian and academic

After studying Protestant theology, Fink became a lecturer at the Humboldt University in East Berlin, and in September 1979 was appointed Professor of Practical Theology. From 1980 to 1990 he was director of the Theology Section. Early in 1990 Fink was appointed rector of the Humboldt University and continued in this position until 1992 when details of his alleged involvement with the **Stasi** were revealed. It was alleged that he had worked as an informer from 1969 to 1989 under the codename 'Heiner'.

PETER BARKER

Fischer-Dieskau, Dietrich

b. 28 May 1925, Berlin

Baritone

One of the outstanding voices of the post-war years, Fischer-Dieskau made his debut in Freiburg in Brahms' *German Requiem* in 1947, and broadcasting the work with which his name became synonymous in later years, Schubert's *Winterreise*. Although active in the fields of oratorio and opera, his greatest fame resides with his *Lied* performances, especially Schubert, Schumann and Wolf, some of them on record with the English pianist Gerald Moore. Britten wrote the baritone part of the *War Requiem* with him in mind, and wrote for him the *Songs and Proverbs of William Blake*.

From 1970 he increasingly devoted his energy to conducting, primarily the choral works of J.S. Bach and the Mozart operas.

DEREK McCULLOCH

Fischer, Fritz

b. 5 March 1908, Ludwigstadt

Historian

Fritz Fischer, Professor of History in Hamburg from 1948 until becoming emeritus in 1973, became the subject of massive controversy on the publication of *Griff nach der Weltmacht* in 1961. This, and two subsequent books, *Weltmacht oder Niedergang* (1965) and *Krieg der Illusionen* (1969), exploded a comfortable conservative consensus by clarifying Germany's war aims before WWI, revealing the willingness of German politicians and military leaders to unleash war, and locating this in the context of domestic social tensions. The 'Fischer controversy' marked a key turning point in West German **historiography**, showing continuities between Imperial Germany and Hitler.

MARY FULBROOK

Fischer, Joschka

b. 12 April 1948, Langenburg

Politician

A founding member of the **Greens** and the most prominent representative of their 'Realo'-wing, Fischer was voted into the **Bundestag** in 1983. From 1985 to 1987 he was the first Green minister at *Land*-level (the red–green coalition in Hesse). He has upset and amused the public with his casual dress and unorthodox behaviour in parliament. The driving force behind the party's programmatic modernization in the 1990s, Fischer sought to enhance the Greens' economic competence. Since 1994 the leader of the Greens' parliamentary group, he was appointed Foreign Minister in Gerhard **Shröder**'s government in 1998. He is the author of widely read political studies (e.g. *Der Umbau der Industriegesellschaft*, 1989 and *Risiko Deutschland*, 1994).

INGOLFUR BLÜHDORN

Fischer Verlag

S. Fischer is the 'first name' in serious modern literature in Germany. Its authors included Hugo von Hofmannsthal, Arthur Schnitzler, Peter Altenberg, and Thomas **Mann**. The firm is also noted for its publication of world-class foreign authors (Bernard Shaw and Tolstoy) in translation. The founder,

Samuel Fischer, took his firm with him into exile in 1936, first to Vienna, then Stockholm, and finally New York. S. Fischer began publishing in Germany again in 1950 and has remained one of the most significant houses for contemporary literature. The firm issues a series of prestigious but inexpensive paperbacks under Fischer Taschenbuch Verlag.

JOHN B. RUTLEDGE

fitness movement

The modern fitness movement has its origins in infantry training exercises of the late seventeenth and eighteenth centuries. Friedrich Ludwig Jahn (1778–1852), convinced of the importance of personal fitness and hygiene for national health, initiated the *Turnbewegung* in Germany, resulting in the proliferation of gymnastics clubs. Germany's largest sport organization, the *Arbeiter-Turn-u. Sportbund*, founded in 1893, was abolished in 1933 by the Nazis and replaced by the *Deutscher Reichsbund für Leibesübung*. The post-war competition for pre-eminence in the Olympic Games and the increased visibility of women in sports heightened awareness of physical fitness and encouraged municipalities since the late 1960s to embrace the national *Trimm-dich* ('get fit') campaign by investing in fitness parks and jogging trails. Germany's interest in keeping the body fit in a machine age is further fuelled by the commercialization of sports through professionalized sponsors, the sports media and product advertising, and is accompanied by new university curricula in sport medicine, sport psychology and the sociology of sport.

See also: Olympic Games; sport: FRG

JENNIFER HAM

flags

The German national and merchant flag adopted in 1949 (Article 22 of the Basic Law) is a horizontal tricolour with three equal bands of black, red and gold, used previously in the Weimar Republic. The colours were originally used by early nineteenth-century independence supporters, and their connection with the colours in the arms of the Holy Roman Empire is coincidental. The official government and naval version has a gold shield in the centre with a black spread-eagle. The national flag used by the GDR placed the state emblem in gold in the centre of this tricolour (dividers superimposed upon an upright hammer, surrounded by a wreath of corn, decorated at bottom with a black–red–gold ribbon). Individual states have their own flags, of which the white and blue of Bavaria (either divided horizontally, or lozengy) is the most familiar.

The German flag has alternated in recent history between black–red–gold and black–white––red. The Hohenzollern Empire used a black––white–red horizontal tricolour as the national flag, but its war flag was white with a black cross, the upright slightly towards the hoist, outlined with a thin black line, and with a central white disk with a black edge on which was the imperial eagle. The tricolour, with the Iron Cross superimposed, filled the top part nearest the hoist. Hitler's Third Reich rejected the black–red–gold of Weimar, restoring the black–white–red tricolour. Nazism used flags extensively as emotional rallying-points, especially the red party flag, with a black swastika on a white central disc, declared a national flag by the Reichstag in 1935. The Nazi ensign was similar to the pre-1918 war flag, though red rather than white, with a swastika on the white centre disc, and just the Iron Cross in the canton. Since it is now illegal to display the swastika, **Neo-Nazism** has sometimes used the rather similar old imperial flag.

Austria's national flag is a horizontal tricolour of red–white–red, readopted in 1945, and supposedly commemorating a twelfth-century hero whose surcoat was completely stained with blood in battle except where his sword-belt kept the central portion white. The government flag has on the central stripe the emblem of the republic, a red–white–red shield superimposed on a black eagle in broken chains, with a civic crown and holding a hammer and sickle (representing industry and agriculture). The square Swiss flag is red with a white cross (with equal arms not touching the edge). It is of some antiquity and became, with the colours counterchanged, the symbol of the International Red Cross. **Liechtenstein**'s flag is halved horizontally, royal blue and red, with a crown on the blue near the hoist; that of **Luxembourg** is a red–white–blue horizontal tricolour, much like that of The Netherlands, but with a lighter blue. The ruling houses of both countries have their own flags.

Further reading

Crampton, W.G. (1984) *The New Observer's Book of Flags*, London: Warne.

Hattenhauer, H. (1984), *Deutsche Nationalsymbole* Munich: Olzog.

BRIAN MURDOCH

flea markets

Germans have a liking for shopping at outdoor markets. Beginning in the early 1980s, *Flohmärkte* or *Trödelmärkte* began to proliferate as outdoor shopping venues, given the economic downturn and a renewed sense of environmental awareness that encouraged recycling. The influx of **Gastarbeiter** and the later opening of the East brought many foreigners who traded and bartered goods. These locales quickly became flea markets, as, for example, the section near the Reichstag and the Brandenburg Gate in Berlin. Throughout the year, many cities in Germany hold special flea markets and it has become trendy for people of all ages to attend.

See also: recycling

UTE LISCHKE-McNAB

Fleischmann, Adolf Richard

b. 18 March 1892, Esslingen am Neckar; d. 28 January 1968, Stuttgart

Painter

Educated at the Stuttgart Academy, Fleischmann emigrated to France in 1938 where he became a member of the groups L'Equippe and Réalités Nouvelles. During the war he joined the Résistance and was interned several times. He temporarily lived in New York after the war before moving back to Stuttgart. Influenced by late impressionism, then expressionism and cubism, he explored the

possibilities of free abstraction in the 1930s. His late work from *c*.1950 went down in art history as a unique combination of constructivist elements and subtle colour nuances employing geometrical forms, divided in vertical and horizontal complexes.

Further reading

Wedewer, R. (1977) *Adolf Fleischmann*, Stuttgart: Gerd Hatje (standard monograph on Fleischmann).

INES SCHLENKER

Fleischmann, Peter

b. 26 July 1937, Zweibrücken

Filmmaker

Fleischmann's first feature film, *Hunting Scenes From Lower Bavaria* (*Jagdszenen aus Niederbayern*, 1968), has remained his most celebrated work. Based on a realist play by the Bavarian Martin Sperr, who also plays the lead role, this shocking portrait of the victimization and murder of a homosexual in a rural community inspired a wave of so-called critical or anti-*Heimat* films. The exposing of hypocrisy and injustice remained a feature of his subsequent work, much of it for television, including his 'anti-pornography' feature *Dorothea's Revenge* (*Dorotheas Rache*, 1973).

See also: New German Cinema

MARTIN BRADY

Fleißer, Marieluise

b. 23 November 1901, Ingolstadt; d. 2 February 1974, Ingolstadt

Writer

Most of Fleißer's major works were first published or performed in the Weimar period. But isolated from her literary contacts in Berlin after 1929 by an abruptly terminated relationship with Bertolt **Brecht**, effectively banned from writing by the Nazis, ostracized in Ingolstadt after 1933 and trapped in an oppressive marriage, she only began to reassert herself as a writer in the 1960s, exorcizing the trauma of Brecht in *Avantgarde* (1963) and revising her earlier work. Praised by the authors of the *Neues **Volksstück*** at the end of the 1960s and re-evaluated by feminist scholarship in the 1980s, she has become recognized as a distinctive twentieth-century voice.

Her early stories, such as *Ein Pfund Orangen* (A Pound of Oranges) (1929), typically portray the pseudo-emancipation of young women who have left traditional family role-structures for the supposed freedom of the urban *bohème*, but then discover, and collude in, their continued exploitation. *Purgatory in Ingolstadt* (*Fegefeuer in Ingolstadt*) (1923, premiered 1926, revised 1970–1) dramatizes pubertal anxieties and persecution in the religion-steeped claustrophobia of small-town Bavaria. *Pioneers in Ingolstadt* (*Pioniere in Ingolstadt*) (1926; premiered 1928, revised 1968, film version by Rainer Werner **Fassbinder** 1971), sets male-female relationships, Fleißer's central theme, in the specific structures of civil and military power and dependency, as the soldiers' sexual voraciousness encounters the illusions and subsequent disillusionment of the town's servant girls. The scandal over the 1929 Berlin production, engineered by Brecht and fanned by the right-wing press, permanently scarred Fleißer's relationship with her home town. In *Der Tiefseefisch* (The Deep Sea Fish) (1930), the fragmentary structure reflects the heroine's psychological bewilderment, storm-tossed between two men, polar opposites as writers but united in their assumed right to dispose over her career. Though Fleißer is often labelled a *Volksstück* writer, only *Der starke Stamm* (The Tough Breed) (1944–5; premiered 1950, revised 1972), a sarcastic comedy of greed, lust and ambition, really fits the category.

Fleißer's only published novel, *Mehlreisende Frieda Geier* (Frieda Geier, Traveller in Flour) (1931; revised as *Eine Zierde für den Verein*, 1972) weaves three themes into a fascinating literary document of the Weimar *Kleinbürgertum* (petit-bourgeoisie) and its mentality on the eve of fascism. The first is business: the anxieties of shopkeepers and craftsmen towards mechanization and capital-concentration. The second is sport: the male body, mass spectacle, and the ***Verein*** as fascistoid collective. The third theme is love: discrepant male and female expecta-tions, gender stereotypes, the revenge of a close community on a woman who challenges them. In Frieda, with her male haircut and clothes, and her determined sexual and material independence, Fleißer creates a figure who resists the normative pressures to which the author herself was later forced to succumb by politics, upbringing and material need. Such ironies of Fleißer's life should not, though, obscure her acute satirical insights and the intense, distinctive voice of her texts, which draws on Bavarian syntax and idiom but emphatically transcends regionalism.

Further reading

McGowan, M. (1987) *Marieluise Fleißer*, Munich: C.H. Beck.

MORAY McGOWAN

Floh de Cologne

The name of this Cologne-based rock band, founded in 1966, translates as 'Cologne Flea' and alludes to the famous Eau de Cologne (*4711*). They started as a political **cabaret**, but following the example of various American groups they increasingly linked their texts with **rock music**. Within the context of the **student movement** the group developed into one of the most radical German *Politrockgruppen*, sympathizing with the **DKP** and its Marxist–communist policies. Due to their radical left-wing stance, they were largely ignored by the media. After the decline of the student and **APO** protests, the group continued to attract a fringe following until its dissolution in 1984.

ANNETTE BLÜHDORN

Focus

This colourful, controversial magazine was set up by the publishers **Burda** in 1993. *Focus* has emerged as a viable alternative to **Augstein**'s Der ***Spiegel***, and is generally seen as supportive of a more conservative political line than its Hamburg competitor. Self-appointed 'the modern news magazine' and committed to, in its own words, 'facts, facts, facts', *Focus* has proved an unexpected success in Germany's crowded magazine market, with circulation of almost 800,000 weekly and an extended readership of over five million. Via Focus-TV and *Focus-online*, it has also made a great investment in its television and Internet presence.

ROBIN B. HODESS

folk music

In a German-speaking context, the untranslated English term 'folk music' is used as a generic label for forms of popular music featuring elements of Breton, Irish or Scottish traditional music. Beyond this, the term is also used for traditional music from east European countries, for the American folk or **protest song** as well as Latin-American music, particularly from Chile and Peru. As musical imports, all of these currents enjoy significant popularity in the German-speaking countries. In contrast with this folk music, the German term *Volksmusik* describes authentically German musical traditions which originated in past centuries from the lower strata of society. *Volksmusik* has always been played and sung by lay persons and has relied exclusively on oral tradition. In its characteristic simplicity it is opposed to *Bildungsmusik* and *Kunstmusik* (artistic music; see **music**) which was cultivated mainly in the educated and leisured upper classes. *Volksmusik* includes both vocal music (*Volkslied*), occasionally making use of regional dialects, and instrumental music which is often associated with traditional dances (*Volkstanz*). In the German-speaking countries, traditional instruments of *Volksmusik* are accordion, mouth-organ, the brass, dulcimer, zither and horn, such as alpenhorn or natural horn. As *Volksmusik* reflects social and regional cultures and identities, it varies greatly in style between different regions, particularly between the north and the south.

In Germany the writer and philosopher J.G. Herder (1744–1803), who coined the term *Volkslied* in 1773, was the first to develop an academic interest in *Volksmusik*. German romanticism idealized and cultivated *Volksmusik* as the expression of the true regional or national character. In the nineteenth century research into *Volksmusik* was firmly established as a field of academic enquiry. The gradual decline of this traditional musical culture has been much lamented and closely monitored; it has often been interpreted as an indicator of cultural decay. In contemporary culture, which is strongly shaped by the mass media and by technologies of sound recording and transmission, authentic *Volksmusik* and its oral tradition have largely become a phenomenon of the past. To some extent *Volksmusik* survives in the form of children's songs or in the context of regional customs and traditions. There is also some overlap between *Volksmusik* and certain Christian feasts (e.g. Christmas). Nevertheless, its innovative potential has virtually disappeared. Under the conditions of mass tourism and in the commercial interests of the **music** industry, *volkstümliche Musik* ('fakelore' rather than folklore) has become the modernized variety of *Volksmusik*. *Volkstümliche Musik* develops and commercially exploits elements of traditional *Volksmusik*. Since the late 1980s German *volkstümliche Musik* has enjoyed considerable popularity and has even established its own competition (*Grand Prix der Volksmusik*). However, in most cases it merely reproduces stereotypes without taking any genuine interest in original folklore. It can be regarded as a variant of the German ***Schlager***. Today the *Deutsches Volksliedarchiv* in Freiburg (established 1914) maintains the largest collection of traditional folk tunes and verses.

Further reading

Braun, H. (1985) *Einführung in die musikalische Volkskunde*, Darmstadt: Wissenschaftliche Buchgesellschaft (introduction to *Volksmusik*, its historical development and contemporary significance).

ANNETTE BLÜHDORN

food

Their drink is a liquor made from barley or other grains, which is fermented to produce a certain resemblance to wine. Their food is plain – wild fruit, fresh game, and curdled milk. They satisfy their hunger without any elaborate cuisine or appetizers. But they do not show the same self-control in slaking their thirst. If you indulge their intemperance by plying them with as much drink as they desire, they will be as easily conquered by this besetting weakness as by force of arms.

(Tacitus: *Germania*)

The prejudice persists that German cuisine is not one of the qualities of German culture, in fact that German fare not only does not reflect the depth of German intellectual life and history, but that it is the black sheep of German culture. The modern traveller thus often visits Germany despite its alimentary habits. However, food not only plays a crucial role in the German lifestyle, but can be exquisite and is certainly more varied than in Tacitus' description. Even so, the Roman historian writing about the customs of the barbarian German tribes does not denigrate German food in his *Germania*. He describes it as simple rather than bad.

Germans are a wise and moderate people when they do not drink, in Tacitus' opinion. Moderation as a form of self-control seems to have haunted the German alimentary discourse as diffused in cookbooks, nutritional handbooks and even literature, at least since the end of the nineteenth century. These texts are all very much preoccupied with the moral implications of a gastronomic pleasure which has historically been linked to the excesses of the aristocracy as the sociologists Georg Simmel and Norbert **Elias** pointed out in their seminal studies on table manners. The pleasure of eating – and the joy of commensality – have both become the undeclared object of the gastronomic interest that has gradually risen to occupy many spheres of culture in the past twenty-five years, from specialized publications to theoretical, historical, sociological and anthropological studies devoted to food and its symbolisms.

The interest in the culture of food consumption has strongly emerged in the years following the post-war starvation of 1946–8 and the *Freßwelle* ('guzzling wave') that followed in 1950 after the lifting of rationing restrictions. Food became an issue to 'study' especially in the period after the political revolts of the 1960s and 1970s. In particular, political movements such as the **Greens**

have indirectly brought to the surface of the cultural discourse the political relevance of the alimentary system, as strictly related to issues such as pleasure and desire on the one hand, and consumption on the other. A critique of consumption along with the attempt to reconcile the issue of the pleasure of eating with a conscious political criticism of bourgeois habits and the capitalist market economy has been part of the German political subconscious since the late 1970s. In this respect, Germany has undoubtly had a pivotal role in the raising of alimentary consciousness and in effecting the nutritional changes – which in Germany took the shape of a true alimentary revolution – that have occurred in the industrialized countries in the past twenty-five years. In the late 1980s and 1990s the gastronomic discourse as well as food-habits in Germany show less the ideological duty to eat according to a 'political consciousness' than an eclectic attitude towards food, one that is well represented by the conspicuous presence of health-food stores (*Reformhäuser*) and restaurants specializing in traditional and regional cuisine, as well as in the New German Cuisine, born under the influence of the French *nouvelle cuisine* in the early 1980s.

The revolution of the German diet, which according to some contemporary gastrosophes was due entirely to the cooks' endorsement of *nouvelle cuisine* and to others was brought about by the new healthy trends of the 1970s and 1980s, is mentioned in every culinary text published in the past twenty years. It is striking that no matter their position, all of these texts ascribe the radical change in German eating and cooking habits and their acquired love for 'light' and 'elegant' food to a reformation supposedly coming from above or outside: the French influence or the creative German chefs. In reading these texts, it appears as if by the hands of the great chefs a whole alimentary culture was changed. Gastronomy reveals itself here as still very much embedded in the old romantic ideal of cooking as a creative art and of the chef as a genius who affects and enlightens the people's vulgar taste. No one mentions in these culinary and critical texts the modifications of social strata and lifestyles brought about by the introduction of new technologies, by immigration or by medicine. On the other hand those who hold that a German cuisine will always be detectable and identifiable as such in spite of the French influences or the innovations introduced by new dietary precepts ignore the fact that such a traditional German cuisine does not exist in its 'singularity'. Just as there is not just one language but a multiplicity of dialects and customs, which bear the different histories of the various *Länder*, German cuisine and food customs vary from region to region.

The variety of the French as well as the eastern European flavours present in German cuisine testifies to the central position of Germany in Europe. German traditional dishes then not only bear traces of all the cuisines from the bordering countries, past and present, but also trace culinary – and hence cultural – borders within Germany. It is common knowledge, for instance, that northern and southern Germany are divided by the so called border of the white sausage (*Weißwurst-äquator*) and that if some dishes may be found all over the country their names are never the same. The many regionalisms of Germany can be simplified into a strategic geographical division of the country into five gastronomic regions: the north (including the city-states of Bremen, Hamburg and Berlin, and the North-Sea and Baltic-Sea coastal areas with Lübeck, Hanover and Brandenburg), the west (North Rhine-Westphalia, the lower Rhine: Münster, Dortmund, Düsseldorf and Cologne), the centre (middle Rhine and Rhineland-Palatinate, Hessen), the south (Baden-Württemberg with the Black Forest, Swabia, and Bavaria: Freiburg, Stuttgart, Würzburg, Nürnberg and Munich) and the east (from Thuringia to Saxony: Erfurt, Weimar, Halle, Leipzig and Dresden).

Thus, whereas *nouvelle cuisine* brought about a kind of homogenizing aesthetic principle of elegance and lightness, and an orientalizing eclecticism which paradoxically functioned to create a uniform style of cooking, the concomitant surfacing of the regional cuisines underscored the diverse identities of the German people. The rejuvenation of the country kitchen and regionalism paralleling the diffusion of *Bioläden* (organic food stores) contrasts with the increasing internationalist trend. Regional recipes and foods could then be viewed as the national culinary wave aimed at re-familiarizing the German consumer used to

foreign cuisine with the great diversity present on German territory.

What is German food then and in what ways does the concept of a national cuisine relate to that of a German identity today? Travel guides tend to place German cuisine within the international panorama and always attempt to classify food in regional or national terms. The same is true about cookbooks, especially those aimed at a foreign audience curious to master foreign cooking just like a language. The unification of Germany even led former Chancellor Helmut Kohl and his wife Hannelore to publish their own 'German' version of a culinary journey through the contemporary unified German nation. The point in the Kohls' cookbook is the indispensable presence of a harmonic cohabitation of identity and difference in the formation of a new German identity for a new unified nation.

The book, entitled *A Culinary Voyage through Germany* and published in 1996, was immediately translated into English as well as other foreign languages and it presents itself as a true travel guide, as the title suggests. A nostalgic and romantic gaze is offered by the memories of the Chancellor which complement the more technical and statistical information about cooking, markets, products and dietary changes given by Hannelore's conversations with master chef Alfons Schubeck. Food becomes yet another way to present Germany as a nation fond of its multifaceted traditions as well as its economic centrality and modernity which has only perfected the ancient pleasure of eating, as one may infer from the text. Germany re-presents itself to the nation as well as to the foreigner in this 'official' cookbook of the 1990s as an appetizing country, as rich in *savoir-vivre* as its historical and present competitor, France.

'*Kneipenkultur*' – the culture of pubs in German cities – remains an alternative to both expensive eating and a fortress against Americanization as defined by the parameters of the leftist ideology since the 1960s which revolted against the Coca-Cola generation and the mass consumption that started in the 1950s. Notwithstanding the yuppies' health trends of the late 1980s, or the political correctness of the activists of the 1970s, the 1950s have left a durable trace behind. This decade's fear of social instability, new crises, and thus hunger, is still evident in the statistics regarding the consumption of meat in Germany in the 1980s, a period in which health food, vegetarianism, and new diets had already entered the public domain. In the mid-1980s Germany was the only country where the consumption of meat did not decrease. Indeed, the Germans' consumption of traditional foods which in periods of crisis are too expensive, such as meat, and conspicuous goods, such as sugar and pastries (which require butter, chocolate, etc.), dominates the market. Not only do the German bakeries produce twelve hundred varieties of cakes and pastries and three hundred types of bread, but statistics show that each German consumes about 180 lb of bread and rolls each year. Today Germany is the European leader in bread consumption. According to a 1991 survey, Germans yearly consume 80 kg per capita, ahead of Italy (75 kg) and France (56 kg).

These statistics reconfirm the fact that the German traditional diet has not been abandoned at all and Germans still eat their traditional foods, from bread (originally introduced with white wheat by the Romans) to fifteen hundred different varieties of *Wurst*. Despite the success of the doner kebab (a meat pita sandwich), sausage remains one of the favourite items of German cuisine. Each person eats about 60 lb each year and 80 percent of all German households serve cold cuts of meat and sausage for supper.

The variety of the German people, mirrored by the myriad dishes that come to the German table, is reflected in the renewed interest in regional specialties, an interest which manifests itself also in the staggering number of restaurants and cookbooks specializing in *heimische Spezialitäten* (local cuisine). At the same time, in contrast with the more nationalist gastronomic agendas, an ethnic culinary diversity has become prominent after many years of immigration in Germany, and especially after the influence exercised by immigration on German tourism as it skyrocketed in the affluent 1980s. From the stigmatization of the immigrant as other, through the appropriation of immigrant food by the alternative political groups expressing their political solidarity with minorities, to their recodification as the healthiest, 'yuppy' cuisines, Italian as well as Asian food (Chinese, Indian and more recently Japanese, Thai and Indonesian) are now established components of the German diet. Tourism has played its part in this: following on the increase of tourism in the 1960s, more and more ethnic restaurants opened in Berlin and in a few years they represented half of the city's eating places.

Further reading

Counihan, C. and Van Esterik, P. (eds) (1997) *Food and Culture. A Reader*, New York: Routledge (collection of old and new essays about the symbolic meanings of food; invaluable reference).

Kohl, H. (1996) *A Culinary Voyage through Germany. Commentary by Chancellor Helmut Kohl*, Munich: Verlag Zabert Sandmann and New York, London and Paris: Abbeville Press (this cookbook is discussd in the above entry).

Olszewska Heberle, M. (1996) *German Cooking*, New York: Berkeley Publishing Group (see the introduction of this cookbook for a general description of German food).

Protzner, W. (ed.) (1987) *Vom Hungerwinter zum kulinarischen Schlaraffenland*, Stuttgart: Steiner-Verlag (series of articles about cooking, eating and starvation in contemporary Germany until the 1970s).

Rath, C.D. (1984) *Reste der Tafelrunde*, Frankfurt am Main: Rowohlt (excellent text about past and present eating habits in Germany and elsewhere; excellent bibliography).

Wierlacher, A. (1985) 'Opulente Fremde und fremde Opulenz', *Jahrbuch Deutsch als Fremdsprache* 11: 179–90 (symbolisms of eating and food in contemporary German literature).

—— (1987) *Vom Essen in der deutschen Literatur*, W. Kohlhammer Verlag (food in German literature; good bibliography).

—— (1994) *Kulturthema Essen*, Hamburg: Akademie Verlag (excellent collection of essays on food and eating by the most prominent scholars of cultural studies in Germany; excellent bibliography).

CECILIA NOVERO

forest

The German forest has become synonymous with Germans and Germany. Since the time the Roman historian Tacitus described the Germans as dwellers of the woods clad in skins of wild beasts or even tree bark, and possessing a natural nobility, German forests have become legendary. The mythology of the forest was visualized through the paintings of Caspar David Friedrich (for instance *Chasseur in the Forest*) and immortalized by the brothers Grimm in *Altdeutsche Wälder* (Old German Forests) and their collection of fables and fairy tales known as *Kinder- und Hausmärchen* in the early nineteenth century. Both painters and storytellers have evoked the image of a forest with monstrously deformed oaks, gnarled and twisted firs and beeches. The forest became the refuge from the cares of city and town, a spiritual habitat.

Yet it is also a sinister wood, Hansel and Gretel finding themselves at the witch's house and the Robber Bride finding herself among cannibals in her fiancé's woods. The objective of the Grimm brothers in their philological undertaking was to restore the lost unity of German culture by recovering whatever remained of the original oral traditions. Their stories, as allegories, were chiefly about the theme of restoration. Forests continue to play a prominent role in German art, culture, literature and film where patriotism and religion, antiquity as well as the present and the future merge.

Approximately one third of Germany's land mass is still covered by forest, including well-known areas such as the Black Forest and, in the eastern part of Germany, Thuringia. The *Land* of Rheinland-Pfalz has the highest proportion of forested land. Between thirty and forty million cubic metres of timber is felled annually.

Forests also remain important as recreation areas for the inhabitants of an industrial and densely populated country who regularly use the trails of the forests for fitness and recreation. The German government enacts strict forest preservation and forestry promotion laws, especially reforestation and forest management. Since the early 1980s there has been increasing forest depletion, **Waldsterben**, despite laws aimed at air pollution and acid rain caused by industry, the burning of domestic fuel, and also commercial agricultural practices. The poster for the film *Deutschland im Herbst* (Germany in Autumn, 1978), which subversively idealizes the beauty of the German forest, epitomizes the social, political and environmental decay of twentieth-century Germany (see also **Autumn, German**).

Forests have also been closely connected to the concept of **Heimat**, a phenomenon that is represented by the countless *Heimatfilme* which reached their production peak in the 1950s. In part, this is also a manifestation of longing for the memory of the forest and the land and a return to what was perceived to be primaeval wilderness. In truth, nowadays, it is about a past and a spirit of place that may be more Germanic myth than reality. Often confronted with political strife, or the loss of identity in their lives, Germans have searched elsewhere for peace in the forest.

See also: environmentalism; hunting

Further reading

Schama, S. (1996) *Landscape and Memory*, London: Random House (contains a chapter on the German forest referred to as *Der Holzweg*, meaning the 'track through the wood', but also 'the wrong track').

UTE LISCHKE-McNAB

FPÖ

The Freiheitliche Partei Österreichs (Austrian Freedom Party) was founded in 1955 as a party of the nationalist and liberal camps after its forerunner the Verband der Unabhängigen (Association of Independents), established in 1949, disintegrated. Between 1983 and 1987 the FPÖ participated in a coalition government with the Social Democrats (**SPÖ**).

Jörg **Haider**'s leadership (since 1986) has driven the party towards a populist, right-wing, strongly nationalist position and broadened its power base to more than 20 percent (1994, 1995) in spite of a split with a group of liberal members of parliament who formed the **Liberales Forum** in 1993.

GEORG HELLMAYR

Franke, Manfred

b. 23 April 1930, Haan (Rhineland)

Writer

Recognized for his innovative use of collage to document historical events, Manfred Franke is often compared to Alexander **Kluge**. His most notable work, *Mordverläufe* (Processes of Murder) (1973), documents the experience of a small town during *Kristallnacht* through the use of clippings and news articles. A broadcasting executive, he has published radio plays, essays, literary studies and autobiographical accounts.

KITTY MILLET

Frankfurt Book Fair

The Frankfurt Book Fair, which is held each October in Frankfurt am Main, is the largest international book trade fair in terms of the number of titles displayed and of the number of countries and publishers participating. Since 1993 it has also been known as the largest and most important meeting for the producers and sellers of multimedia. It is also a very important cultural event, with its 'focal themes' offering a forum for discussions of cultural questions and controversial topics, and integration of the literatures of lesser-known regions into the literary world.

The Frankfurt Book Fair is the world's oldest. The tradition of book fairs in Germany stretches back to the time of Gutenberg, whose new technology coincided with the beginning of book publishing and selling. For a long time Frankfurt am Main was the leading publishing centre. In the eighteenth century it was surpassed by Leipzig, which held the position until WWII. It is therefore not surprising that the first book fairs took place in Frankfurt am Main and Leipzig as early as in the fifteenth century. After the interruption caused by WWII, the Frankfurt Book Fair was re-established

in 1949 by the Professional Organization of Publishers and Sellers of the Book Trade Association in Frankfurt.

In the exhibition halls of the fair, the visitor finds printed and electronic books exhibited by publishers and multimedia producers from countries from around the world. Visitors to the Frankfurt Book Fair are usually writers, publishers, booksellers, librarians, agents, journalists, information brokers or readers.

Apart from the commercial side, the fair is also the book trade's 'window on the world' and a major cultural event. In the mid-1970s, the book fair began to concentrate more on its content and focal themes were introduced. Since 1988 there has been a different focal theme country each year. An extensive programme of events such as poetry readings, film evenings at local and regional museums and galleries, concert series, art exhibitions, theatre performances and other events showcasing the specific culture and arts of the focal country is organized by the featured country or region itself. These events usually last beyond the duration of the fair and even go beyond the city boundaries as the focal country or region presents itself in various communities throughout Germany.

The Frankfurt Book Fair also issues its own important publications such as the annual *Frankfurt Book Fair Catalogue* and the 'Who's Who at the Fair' list, which provides all exhibitors' addresses and publishing executives of exhibiting companies.

The fair culminates in the awarding of the Peace Prize of the German Book Trade Association. Previous winners include Max **Frisch**, Yehudi Menuhin, Teddy Kollek, Hans Jonas and Václav Havel.

BETTINA BROCKERHOFF-MACDONALD

Frankfurt School

Founded in 1923 as the Institute for Social Research at Frankfurt University by the Marxist philosopher Felix J. Weil, the School became a leading proponent of modernism in philosophy and social sciences, and the home of **Critical Theory**. Its most prominent director was **Horkheimer**, who together with **Adorno**, steered it away from

Marxist dogma with a return to the philosophy of Hegel and Schopenhauer. Threatened by National Socialism, the Institute moved to New York as the International Institute of Social Research, returning to Frankfurt am Main in 1950 where it produced the influential journal *Frankfurter Beiträge zur Soziologie*. Associates of the School were **Benjamin**, Herbert **Marcuse** and **Habermas**.

HANS J. HAHN

Frankfurter Allgemeine Zeitung

This newspaper, often known by its abbreviation *FAZ*, is widely regarded as the leading national (*überregional*) daily in Germany. The *FAZ*, whose conservative editorial position supports free market economics, has tended to report favourably on the Christian Democrats coalition, industry, and the Bundesbank. It has a weekday circulation around 400,000. In addition to its influential coverage of economics, the newspaper offers extensive attention to foreign affairs, largely through its network of foreign correspondents. The FAZ *Feuilleton*, or cultural section, is also very highly regarded. Established in 1949, the paper's majority owner is the non-profit FAZIT Foundation.

See also: newspapers

ROBIN B. HODESS

Frankfurter Rundschau

The *Frankfurter Rundschau* numbers among the four serious, responsible, supra-regional **newspapers** in Germany. Founded 12 August 1945, it was one of the very first presses to receive a licence from the American authorities. The *Frankfurter Rundschau* is an independent, progressive newspaper with a liberal orientation; it addresses issues of social tolerance and opposes discriminatory practices. Published six times a week, with a daily circulation in the mid-nineties of 185,000 (580,000 readers), it sets a high standard and is an influential model of critical journalism.

JOHN B. RUTLEDGE

Frauenliteratur

In Germany, the word *Frauenliteratur* can mean two different types of texts: hugely popular and cheap 'women's books' in the Mills & Boon fashion, and women's writing, which aspires to articulating the female experience in literary form. The latter acquired the name *Frauenliteratur* only in the 1970s in the wake of second-wave **feminism and the women's movement** evolving at that time. Since the 1980s the volume of women's writing has increased exponentially, and certain authors and works have been adopted into the literary canon while others have been absorbed into what is still thought of as mainstream literature. Most bookshops still have a shelf labelled '*Frauenliteratur*', and reputable publishing houses run series devoted to women and women's writing, for instance **Fischer** with *Die Frau in der Gesellschaft* (Woman in Society). Although *Frauenliteratur* might thus be perceived as a ghetto, certain tenets of feminist thought have become more accepted in German society in general while publishers have realized that women constitute the majority of the reading public and are supporting more women authors than ever. Therefore the dividing line between 'literary' women's writing and books written by women mainly for women solely for entertainment is becoming blurred.

Traditional women's books have always concentrated on romance featuring a heroine who embodies the traditional female values such as patience, self-sacrifice, modesty and chastity. They tend to end, after a series of misunderstandings, entanglements and near-disaster, in marriage affirming societal norms – even in a fairytale ending. Probably the most famous author of such books was Hedwig Courths-Mahler who enjoyed enormous popular success for several decades, in the FRG at least until the late 1950s (developments in the GDR were very different). From then on, partly as a result of greater educational investment during the '*Economic Miracle*' years, there was a period of decline for these bodice-rippers, at least in book form. Teachers would denounce them as trashy and young girls would be made to feel embarassed when caught reading them. There is still, however, a thriving business in *Heftchenromane* (cheap eighty-page booklets with thin paper covers which are stapled together in the middle). Medical romances, rural romances, 'working girl' romances and others are published weekly; particularly popular are romances set in aristocratic circles. *Heftchenromane* provide a pure form of escapist reading; research has shown that their women readers are fully aware of this despite the continuing fears of educationalists and social scientists that they might provide unsuitable role models and affirm outmoded societal norms.

In the FRG, the new women's movement which started in 1968 engendered amongst other discussions a reappraisal of woman's place in literature, both as author and as subject. Unsurprisingly, the conclusion was that women's voices had been silenced in this area as well as others in a patriarchal society. A different kind of literature was called for which would reflect women's experiences, aspirations and hopes in every sphere of society. Many of the early works were either documentary or autobiographical in character; they reflected the need to make women's voices heard. The most influential of these texts was Verena **Stefan**'s autobiographical book *Shedding* (*Häutungen*, 1975). Stefan concentrates on the themes of sexuality, stunted and unsatisfied in a male-dominated society, and language, which is equally male-dominated and does not allow her to talk about her body or her sexuality in other than male (and mainly derogatory) terms. The book had a stunning impact and provoked fierce discussions. Its themes have been taken up time and again by later writers. The search for a new identity defined by women themselves, a female subjectivity, became a central concern from the late 1970s. Writers such as Karin **Struck** and Christa **Reinig** developed this issue including reflections on class identity together with female identity. Women writers, although constantly battling against ghettoization and marginalization by the male literary establishment, gained in confidence and produced texts of every genre. The search for their own voice often led to innovative forms and styles. Women writers have enriched German literature immeasurably, yet in universities *Frauenliteratur* is still mostly taught and read by women and ignored by men.

In the GDR, where no women's movement existed and feminism was a dirty word, literature had a different function. Initially regarded as an educational tool by the political leadership, it later became the main forum of discussion in a country whose state-controlled media did not allow public debate. Burdened with the strictures of **socialist realism** and state censorship (see also **censorship: FRG**; **censorship: GDR**), women writers nevertheless managed to explore the boundaries of female existence and produced some of the most highly regarded works of GDR literature. As in the FRG, the diverging interests of women (individually and collectively) and the patriarchal state began to find literary expression from the late 1960s and were even more vigorously pursued after 'the women question' was officially declared solved in 1976. Although always relevant to the GDR context, many books by women explored more global concerns from a female perspective. Authors like Christa **Wolf**, Irmtraud **Morgner** and Helga **Königsdorf** to name but a few were read by both sexes, avoiding to some extent the ghettoization of their western counterparts and making the female voice heard more loudly.

See also: prose fiction: FRG; prose fiction: GDR

Further reading

Brinker-Gabler, G. (ed.) (1988) *Deutsche Literatur von Frauen*, Munich: Beck (collection of essays on women's writing in German from its beginnings to the 1980s with index and bibliography in two volumes; very thorough and invaluable for any student of German literature).

Watanabe-O'Kelly, H. (ed.) (1997) *The Cambridge History of German Literature*, Cambridge: Cambridge University Press (has chapters on 'The Literature of the German Democratic Republic' and 'German Writing in the West' (1945–90) which place women writers in the wider context of German literature; includes a comprehensive bibliography).

Weedon, C. (ed.) (1997) *Postwar Women's Writing in German: Feminist Critical Approaches*, Providence, RI and Oxford: Berghahn Books (contains essays on theory, overviews of women's writing in Germany, Austria and Switzerland as well as essays on individual authors; includes index and very useful bibliography).

GABRIELA STEINKE

Freemasonry

The world's largest and most widely established fraternal order evolved, according to tradition, from the guilds of stonemasons and cathedral builders of the Middle Ages. The first Grand Lodge began in England in 1717, and all other lodges derive their charters from it. German lodges date from the late 1730s, the oldest being the Hamburg Absalom zu den drei Nesseln. Currently, five German grand lodges exist, united under the Vereinigte Großlogen von Deutschland – Bruderschaft der Freimaurer (VGL) (United Grand Lodges of Germany – Brotherhood of Freemasons). The VGL mainly performs international representation functions for the five grand lodges: the Großloge der Alten Frein und Angenommen Maurer von Deutschland (GL AFuAMvD) (German Grand Lodge of Ancient Free and Accepted Masons); the Große Landesloge der Freimaurer von Deutschland (GLL FvD) (Grand Lodge of German Freemasons), also called Freimaurerorden; the Große National-Mutterloge 'Zu den Drei Weltkugeln' (GNML 3WK) or Grand National Motherlodge of the Three Globes; the American Canadian Grand Lodge Ancient Free and Accepted Masons (ACGL); and the Grand Lodge of British Freemasons in Germany (GL BFG). The GL AFuAMvD represents the largest, consisting of ten district lodges, 264 lodges, and accounting for between 60 and 70 percent of German Freemasons.

Before the Nazi ban on Freemasonry, German Masons numbered approximately 76,000. Beginning in 1945, German lodges began reforming, and in 1958 the different grand lodges united under the VGL. Dialogue between German Freemasons and the Vatican began in 1972 to reverse the Church's twelve declarations against Freemasons, issued between 1738 and 1918, and excommunications. The Pope announced the reversal in 1981, and welcomed German Freemasons back into the church.

Further reading

Kephart, C.I. (1964) *Concise History of Freemasonry*, Fort Worth, TX: Henry L. Geddie.
Robinson, J.J. (1989) *Born in Blood: The Lost Secrets of Freemasonry*, New York: M. Evans.

RONDALL R. RICE

Freie Volksbühne

The term names both the West Berlin association of the Volksbühne membership organization, founded by Social Democrats in 1890 to provide reasonably priced, socially-critical theatre to the working class, and the West Berlin theatre owned and managed by the organization until the early 1990s. The complex history of the Volksbühne movement and its Berlin theatres parallels the political tensions and shifts of the past century; the movement split over internal political tensions in 1892, was reunited in 1920, dissolved in 1933, re-established after the war and split again in 1947, with separate organizations and theatres in the East and West sectors. The post-war Freie Volksbühne (theatre) was established in West Berlin and moved into its own purpose-built theatre in 1963. Frequent changes in artistic directorship, tension between aesthetic aspirations and the traditionalist taste of its subscription-based audience, and the lack of a standing ensemble of players made for an erratic production record. It achieved international – and controversial – acclaim in the mid-1960s with the world premieres of 'documentary' dramas by **Hochhuth**, **Kipphardt**, and **Weiss**, directed by Erwin **Piscator**. The *Freie Volksbühne* (theatre) was closed after German unification.

KAREN RUOFF KRAMER

Freitag

Beginning life in 1946 under the title *Sonntag* as the cultural weekly of the **Kulturbund**, this newspaper served a useful function during the GDR's ideologically less constrained periods (e.g. the 'thaw' of the middle 1950s, the years after Erich **Honecker**'s accession to power) as a focus for debate on cultural life. Its editor of 1955–6, Gustav Just, was a prominent victim of the show-trials of 1957 alongside Wolfgang **Harich** and Walter **Janka**. Retitled *Freitag* for symbolical reasons during the *Wende* (*frei* meaning 'free' as well as being the first syllable of the German word for 'Friday'), the journal now devotes as much attention to the socio-political issues which impinge on cultural developments as to culture itself.

DENNIS TATE

Fremdwörter

Fremdwörter ('foreign words') is the term commonly used to designate lexical imports into German which for many speakers may still betray their foreign origin. If an import holds its ground, its spelling and even its original meaning may change, e.g. *der Keks*, now 'cookie/biscuit', from the English 'cakes'. While objectors have argued that large-scale importation of foreign words into German is unnecessary, detrimental to understanding and even the language's 'health' (*Fremdwörter* as *Fremdkörper* – 'foreign bodies'), more relaxed observers claim that the process is natural, inevitable, and that the long-term effect on the language – usefully extending its communicative range – can only be invigorating. Most foreign words brought into German nowadays come from English. The influence of Russian on the German used in the GDR was always relatively slight.

See also: dictionaries; language

Further reading

Drosdowski, G. *et al.* (1994) *Duden. Das Große Fremdwörterbuch*, Mannheim, Leipzig, Zürich and Vienna: Dudenverlag (wide coverage, with a pithy 'Introduction to the History and Function' of *Fremdwörter*).
Russ, C.V.J. (1994) *The German Language Today*, London: Routledge (pages 248–70 cover the development of German vocabulary).

GLYN HATHERALL

Fried, Erich

b. 6 May 1921, Vienna; d. 22 November 1988, Baden-Baden

Poet and translator

Erich Fried was a leading voice in the politicization of West German culture in the 1960s, and became one of the best known contemporary poets in the German language. A prolific writer, he attracted a wide readership through direct and often controversial treatment of sensitive political themes, and through his message of compassion, humanity and hope for the future. Fried shared with other members of the **Gruppe 47** a strong moral commitment deriving from the experience of fascism. As a prominent participant in demonstrations against the Vietnam War and in the **student movement** in the 1960s, opposition to **Berufsverbot** in the 1970s, and in the **peace movement** in the early 1980s, he came, alongside Heinrich **Böll**, to personify the 'conscience of the nation', though his socialist convictions were no longer widely shared. His short, aphoristic texts were familiar from posters and protest banners to many who did not normally read poetry.

Fried's lifelong concern was to combat injustice and inhumanity in his writing. The quality of his verse is undoubtedly uneven, and on occasion he was not above abusing poetry as a vehicle for political enlightenment. However, his best writing is both intellectually satisfying and deeply moving, combining simplicity of form and language with subtlety and complexity of allusion. In rhymeless texts often lacking regular rhythm, but making effective use of rhetorical structures and word play, he follows the arguments of his opponents through to absurd conclusions, exposing dangerous assumptions and attitudes. His political message is, however, balanced by personal self-discovery and reminders of the need in life for love and individual happiness.

Towards the end of his life his earlier poetry was republished, and since his death attention has focused on the young Fried as a Jewish émigré living in London. He participated in German and Austrian political and cultural organizations during the war, and became known for his German broadcasts on the BBC World Service between

1952 and 1968. Fried was also a gifted translator of English literature. The overnight success of his version of Dylan Thomas' radio play *Under Milkwood* (*Unter dem Milchwald*) in 1954 marked a turning point in his career, and his translations of the major Shakespeare plays are regularly used in Germany today.

See also: poetry: FRG; protest movements: FRG

Further reading

Goodbody, A. (1993) 'Erich Fried – German, Jew, British and Socialist: The Composite Identity of an Austrian Émigré', in R. Schmidt and M. McGowan (eds), *From High Priests to Desecrators: Contemporary Austrian Writers*, Sheffield: Sheffield Academic Press, pp. 83–103 (a biographical account, discussing influences and themes in Fried's work).

Kaukoreit, V. (1991) *Frühe Stationen des Lyrikers Erich Fried: Vom Exil bis zum Protest gegen den Krieg in Vietnam: Werk und Biographie 1938–66*, Darmstadt: Verlag Jürgen Häusser (the authoritative account of Fried's life and work up to the mid-1960s, with important insights into émigré life in London; contains comprehensive bibliographies).

Lawrie, S. (1996) *Erich Fried: A Writer without a Country*, New York: Peter Lang (focuses, like Kaukoreit's book, on Fried's life and work up to the 1960s).

AXEL GOODBODY

Friedrich, Götz

b. 4 August 1930, Naumburg; d. 12 December 2000, Berlin

Producer and theatre administrator

General intendant of the Deutsche Oper, Berlin from 1981, Friedrich trained as assistant to the influential opera director Walter Felsenstein. He also worked as Chief Producer at the Hamburg Opera (1973–81) and as Director of Productions at Covent Garden (1971–81), where he has mounted two productions of Wagner's *Ring* cycle. The intellectual complexity of his stagings, which might loosely be termed post-Brechtian within Felsen-

stein's vivid tradition, has often led to their controversial reception; this was especially the case at the **Bayreuth Festival**, where he staged *Tannhäuser, Lohengrin* and *Parsifal*.

BEATRICE HARPER

Fries, Fritz Rudolf

b. 19 May 1935, Bilbao

Writer

Born in Spain, Fries came to Germany in 1942 and is best known for his début novel *Der Weg nach Oobliadooh* (The Way to Oobliadooh) (1966). Although he was resident in the GDR, the novel was initially published in the FRG only. Fries' work contains elements of fantasy and modern narrative techniques such as interior monologue are applied. Other titles include *Das Luft-Schiff* (The Sky Ship) (1974), *Alexanders neue Welten* (Alexander's New Worlds) (1982), and *Die Väter im Kino* (The Fathers in the Cinema) (1990).

See also: cultural policy: GDR

HELEN L. JONES

Frisch, Max

b. 15 May 1911, Zürich; d. 4 April 1991, Zürich

Novelist and dramatist

His father's death in 1936 forced Frisch to abandon his study of German literature at Zürich University and train as an architect at the city's *Eidgenössische Technische Hochschule*, where he graduated in 1940. Despite service in the Swiss army during WWII, Frisch launched his own architectural practice in 1942 which he ran alongside his literary activities until 1954 when the collapse of his first marriage and the critical success of his third novel, *I'm not Stiller* (*Stiller*), led to his decision to write full-time. Frisch's life was marked by extensive travel. He lived for lengthy periods in New York, Berlin and Rome before returning to Switzerland in 1965. His relationship with Switzerland and the Swiss was always a difficult one, and although he became an encouraging father-figure to many younger Swiss writers, he remained until his death a controversial figure in his home country.

Frisch had published journalism and some fiction before the war, but his first major work was the *Sketchbook 1946–1949* (*Tagebuch 1946–1949*, published 1950), which brought him into contact with the tyro publisher, Peter **Suhrkamp**, who became a lifelong friend. The book's unique combination of socio-political commentary, philosophical reflection and short narratives (many of which contain the germs of later novels and plays) is characteristic of much of Frisch's work. The mosaic structure was repeated in the later diary, *Sketchbook 1966–1971* (*Tagebuch 1966–1971*, published 1972), but the fragmentary technique also determined the form of his three principal novels, *I'm not Stiller*, *Homo Faber* (1957, turned into a commercially successful film by Volker **Schlöndorff** under the title *Voyager*) and *A Wilderness of Mirrors* (*Mein Name sei Gantenbein*, 1964). Frisch's predominant theme is the problem of identity. His protagonists either attempt to deny the past in order to create a new identity (Anatol Stiller) or cling to an old one in order to avoid any examination of the self (Walter Faber). In *Gantenbein*, Frisch's most experimental work, the crisis provoked by a failed marriage leads to dizzying attempts by the anonymous narrator to invent credible stories to embody his experience. Frisch's deconstruction of male arrogance and inadequacy anticipates many of the preoccupations of a later generation of feminist writers. With his *Tagebücher*, this loose 'trilogy' represents Frisch's most lasting contribution to the twentieth-century European novel.

Paradoxically, Frisch's breakthrough came not in the novel, but in the theatre. In particular, the black comedy, *The Fire Raisers* (*Biedermann und die Brandstifter*, 1957), and the parable play, *Andorra* (1961), established his international reputation. Influenced technically by Thornton Wilder and Bertolt **Brecht**, these plays attack the private and public face of bourgeois hypocrisy. Where *Andorra* examines the deadly nature of prejudice, *The Fire Raisers* explores the implications of moral cowardice. Other plays concentrate on overtly political themes or, like the narrative fiction, on the problematic

nature of personal relationships, especially in the context of marriage.

Frisch's late work is characterized by an uncomfortably honest dissection of the problem of ageing and the fear of death. The candidly autobiographical *Montauk* (1975) is an elegiac account of a weekend with a young woman where the older man's experience and nagging memories vitiate his capacity for spontaneous enjoyment. His last play, *Triptych. Three Scenic Panels* (*Triptychon, Drei szenische Bilder*, 1978), though not a success on the stage, is an equally melancholy meditation on human transience and the impossibility of sustaining creative relationships. The short story *Man in the Holocene* (*Der Mensch erscheint im Holozän*, 1979) reduces these themes radically to the compass of an old man's disintegrating memory. The tragicomedy of an isolated individual's final desperate attempt to construct an intelligible world from fragments of knowledge stands as a telling metaphor for human alienation in a natural world utterly indifferent to the fate of humanity.

With growing fame, Frisch maintained a high profile in social and political matters, whether in terms of Switzerland or world affairs. Innumerable speeches and essays reveal a combative spirit which, despite deep moral scepticism, clung to the battered ideals of the Enlightenment. Whether accompanying the German Chancellor, Helmut **Schmidt**, on a diplomatic mission to China or attempting to dismantle the Swiss national myth in *Wilhelm Tell für die Schule* (William Tell for School Use, 1971), Frisch was committed to establishing the dialectic role of literature in the body politic. Fittingly, his last work – after a long period of silence – was an unexpected contribution to a bitter debate on the future of the Swiss army, one of the most fundamental institutions of the Confederation, which was unleashed by a referendum proposing its abolition. *Schweiz ohne Armee? Ein Palaver* (Switzerland Without an Army? A Palaver, 1989) takes the form of a dialogue between an old man, who had helped to guard the Swiss frontiers against Nazism, and his grandson, plagued with doubt about the morality of army service. Though this last foray into contemporary politics did not endear Frisch to the Swiss bourgeoisie any more than his novels and plays had done, his uncompromising voice and intellectual honesty will be missed as Switzerland urgently seeks to redefine her role in a rapidly changing Europe.

See also: culture: Switzerland

Major works

Frisch, M. (1976/86) *Gesammelte Werke in zeitlicher Folge*, ed. H. Mayer, 7 vols, Frankfurt am Main: Suhrkamp (standard edition).
—— (1989) *Schweiz ohne Armee? Ein Palaver*, Zürich: Limmat. (Frisch's contribution to the debate on the proposed abolition of the Swiss army).
—— (1990) *Schweiz als Heimat? Versuche über 50 Jahre*, ed. W. Obschlager, Frankfurt am Main: Suhrkamp (collection of all Frisch's work dealing with his difficult relationship with Switzerland).

Further reading

Butler, M. (1976) *The Novels of Max Frisch*, London: Oswald Wolff (close readings of *Jürg Reinhart, Die Schwierigen, Stiller, Homo Faber* and *Mein name sei Gantenbein*).
—— (1985) *The Plays of Max Frisch*, London: Macmillan (succinct discussions of the nine major plays).
Koepke, W. (1991) *Understanding Max Frisch*, Columbia, SC: University of Carolina Press (an accessible introduction to Frisch's main preoccupations).
Pender, M. (1979) *Max Frisch – His Work and its Swiss Background*, Stuttgart: Verlag Hans-Dieter Heinz (a good general study).
Petersen, J.H. (1978) *Max Frisch*, Stuttgart: Metzler (broad introductory survey with history of reception, assessment of research and bibliography).

MICHAEL BUTLER

Frischmuth, Barbara

b. 5 July 1941, Altaussee (Austria)

Writer

A member of the **Grazer Gruppe**, most of Frischmuth's novels deal with women searching for their identity and self-realization in modern society.

Her early works (see *Die Klosterschule*, 1968; *Amoralische Kinderklapper*, 1969) are characterized by an experimental approach to language, whereas her later writings use a traditional and fantastic style (see *Das Verschwinden des Schattens in der Sonne*, 1973; *Die Mystifikationen der Sophie Silber*, 1976).

ERNST GRABOVSZKI

Fritsch, Katharina

b. 14 February 1956, Essen

Sculptor

After being educated as a painter at the *Staatliche Kunstakademie* in Düsseldorf, Fritsch turned to sculpture. Her visual language is based on man-made prototypes of a wide range of objects, both banal and ritual, which are reproduced in series arranged in a specific symbolic order, or distributed as multiple art objects. The object's colour, and – frequently – symmetry together with the contrast of its formal qualities carry meaning in works that often appear monumental and hermetically sealed.

See also: sculpture

KERSTIN MEY

Fritz, Marianne

b. 1948, Weiz (Austria)

Writer

Fritz' novels (e.g. *Die Schwerkraft der Verhältnisse*, 1978; *Das Kind der Gewalt und die Sterne der Romani*, 1980) stand out from contemporary Austrian literature because of their complexity of language and content. They deal with mechanisms of supression in human relations and in society. Her twelve-volume novel *Dessen Sprache du nicht verstehst* (1986), the 'story' of the family Null, breaks all rules of conventional narration.

ERNST GRABOVSZKI

Fromm, Erich

b. 23 March 1900, Frankfurt am Main; d. 18 March 1980, Muralto (Switzerland)

Social scientist and psychoanalyst

A philosopher by training, Fromm co-founded in 1930 the South German Institute for Psycho-analysis in Frankfurt am Main. His linking of psychoanalysis and Marxism earned him a profes-sorship at the Institute for Social Research known as the **Frankfurt School**. When the Institute moved to New York, Fromm emigrated to the United States where he practised and taught analysis. In the late 1930s, his colleagues at the Institute rejected his revisions of Freud. Fromm combined his social and psychoanalytic interests with political work in the American Socialist Party and the international peace movement.

KALLIOPI NIKOLOPOULOU

Fuchs, Jürgen

b. 19 December 1950, Reichenbach (Saxony); d. 9 May 1999, Berlin

Writer and psychologist

Fuchs began to publish poetry and prose in the early 1970s. Due to his critical views, his works were censored and he could not complete his studies in Social Psychology. Imprisoned in No-vember 1976 for nine months, as described in *Gedächtnisprotokolle* (Notes from Memory) (1977), he was eventually expelled to West Berlin. Active in citizens' initiatives to dissolve the **Stasi** in 1990 (see also **citizens' initiatives: FRG; citizens' initiatives: GDR**), the West German government commissioned him to investigate the East German state security service. He now works as a writer and a psychologist in Berlin.

See also: censorship: GDR; dissent and opposition: GDR; poetry: GDR

MARGRIT FRÖLICH

Fühmann, Franz

b. 15 January 1922, Rochlitz/Rokytnice, (Czechoslovakia); d. 8 July 1984, (East) Berlin

Writer

The turbulence of Fühmann's literary career reflects the extraordinary historical experience of his generation. Brought up amongst the Sudeten German minority in the newly created state of Czechoslovakia, he became a teenage convert to National Socialism and had some of the poems he wrote as a soldier on the eastern front published in Goebbels' propaganda journal *Das Reich*. Four years in Soviet PoW camps turned him into a Stalinist and facilitated his rise to dubious cultural prominence in the GDR of the early 1950s. There then began a process of disillusionment, during which the real potential of a gifted author became evident in works – such as the autobiographical *Das Judenauto* (The Jews' Car) (1962) – which were still flawed by ideological distortions. Only after coming close to death through alcoholism, in the aftermath of the Soviet bloc's crushing of the 'Prague Spring' reforms of 1968, did Fühmann undergo the third, and decisive, 'conversion' which made him into a fearless critic of the stagnation of state socialism, both in his creative writing and his public role as a GDR intellectual. The despair he felt as East–West relations degenerated into the nuclear confrontation of the early 1980s probably contributed to his premature death.

Fühmann's undisputed literary breakthrough in both German states came with another autobio-graphical work, *Twenty-Two Days or Half a Lifetime* (*Zweiundzwanzig Tage oder Die Hälfte des Lebens*, 1973), which illustrated the inner conflicts of a generation which had 'come to socialism via Auschwitz'. He then adopted a stimulating diversity of narrative perspectives – mythical, biblical and futuristic as well as that of the contemporary observer of everyday life – in order to show why his socialist utopia had failed to develop. His essayistic work of the 1970s highlighted the impact of modernist authors such as Hoffmann, Barlach, Kafka and Joyce on his creative evolution, and paved the way for his last major work, *Der Sturz des Engels* (The Fallen Angel) (1982), which combines a frank account of key episodes in his life in the GDR with an empathetic reinterpretation of the work of his most important modernist forebear, Georg Trakl. By now he had redefined his identity in terms of the Central European cultural pluralism into which he had been born, and which his work as a translator and advocate of Czech and Hungarian literature had made increasingly attractive as he became alienated from the GDR. An ambitious attempt to encapsulate his experience within the framework of a huge metafictional work, *Im Berg* (In the Mine) had to be abandoned in 1983.

See also: prose fiction: GDR

Major works

Fühmann, F. (1992), *Twenty-Two Days or Half a Lifetime*, trans. L. Vennewitz, London: Faber (his most accessible work in English).
—— (1993), *Werkausgabe*, 8 vols, Rostock: Hinstorff (collection of the major works).

Further reading

Richter, H. (1992), *Franz Fühmann: Ein deutsches Dichterleben*, Berlin: Aufbau (full biography and extensive textual analysis).
Tate, D. (1995), *Franz Fühmann: Innovation and Authenticity*, Amsterdam: Rodopi (reassessment of his importance as a prose writer).

DENNIS TATE

Furtwängler, Wilhelm

b. 25 January 1886, Berlin; d. 30 November 1954, Baden-Baden

Conductor

Regarded as the leading German conductor of his time. Furtwängler's early ambitions as a composer were detoured by his appointment as the successor to Nikisch at both the Leipzig Gewandhaus and Berlin Philharmonic in the 1920s. Unlike many influential colleagues, Furtwängler remained in Germany during the Nazi regime, only fitfully distancing himself from politics; he resigned all official posts in 1934. His last years were both controversial and disappointed, his renewed international reputation marred by growing deafness. The mesmeric intensity of Furwängler's conducting was unique. It compelled players and audiences alike to discount the legendary awkwardness of his gestures. Recordings give some impression of the power of his work, especially in Beethoven, Wagner and Bruckner.

BEATRICE HARPER

Fussenegger, Gertrud

b. 8 May 1912, Pilsen (Bohemia)

Writer (also G. Dietz and G. Dorn)

Living through WWI had a strong influence on Fussenegger's early years. In 1921 she moved to Telfs (Tyrol) with her family. Starting in 1930, she studied history, art history, German and philosophy in Innsbruck and Munich, earning her doctorate in 1934. She later lived in Hall (Tyrol) and now lives in Leonding. Influenced by her family's Bohemian history, she employs an austere style and writes mainly novels, short stories and historical works, but has also written poetry, essays, ***Hörspiele*** (radio plays), and a libretto for an opera by Helmut Eder.

MARTINA S. ANDERSON

G

Gadamer, Hans-Georg

b. 11 February 1900, Marburg

Philosopher

Gadamer's autobiography *Philosophical Apprentice-ships* (*Philosophische Lehrjahre*, 1977) chronicles the impact of Paul Natorp's neo-Kantian philosophy, Martin **Heidegger**'s destruction of the western metaphysical tradition and Rudolf **Bultmann**'s existentialist theology on his philosophical educa-tion. His early philological and poetical approach to philosophy later developed into his idea of philosophical hermeneutics as expressed in his major work *Truth and Method* (*Wahrheit und Methode*, 1960). In the tradition of Humboldt's language of philosophy, Gadamer analyses the intersubjectivity of language and understanding and emphasizes the reciprocal relations between methodological ap-proach and knowledge, suggesting that hermeneu-tic reflection reveals the unexamined presuppositions handed down by tradition which inform the dualism between the natural and the human sciences.

THOMAS NOLDEN

Gaiser, Gerd

b. 15 September 1908, Oberriexingen; d. 9 June 1976, Reutlingen

Writer

Gaiser's œuvre is characterized by a conservative, humanistic attitude, and a concern with man's mythical conception of himself. His largely for-gotten publications of the 1940s show National Socialist influences. The post-war writings for which he is best known are concerned with the reorientation of people after the war, and a romantic critique of the materialism in the period of the **Economic Miracle**, for instance in *The Last Dance of the Season* (*Schlußball*, 1958; published in the US as *The Final Ball*).

JUDITH LEEB

Ganz, Bruno

b. 22 March 1941, Zürich

Actor

A member of Peter **Stein**'s legendary ensemble at the Berlin Schaubühne theatre, Ganz is known for sensitive and complex portrayals in classical plays (e.g. Shakespeare and Kleist) and in contemporary drama (Thomas **Bernhard**, Peter **Handke** and Botho **Strauß**). He has given remarkable, subtly understated performances in films including Wim **Wenders**' *The American Friend* (*Der amerikanische Freund*, 1977), Reinhard **Hauff**'s *Messer im Kopf* (*Knife in the Head*, 1978), Werner **Herzog**'s *Nosferatu* (1978), as well as *Wings of Desire* (*Der Himmel über Berlin*, 1987) and *Far Away, So Close* (*In weiter Ferne, so nah*, 1993) by Wenders. He is recognized as the most distinguished German-speaking actor of his generation, receiving the Iffland Ring award in 1996.

CHRISTIAN ROGOWSKI

garden gnomes

Gnomes, or *Gartenzwerge*, are a standard item of kitsch in German gardens and **Schrebergärten**, derived from stone dwarfs found in baroque gardens. In 1883 Philipp Griebel began the current tradition by crafting gnomes out of terracotta. They have become colourful, red-capped creatures made of ceramic or plastic and are a popular export item. Expensive in Germany, they caused a 'garden gnome controversy' in 1994 when Poland began to produce half a million inexpensive gnomes that invaded Germany and made local producers unhappy. This resulted in the creation of the Association for the Protection of Garden Gnomes and a Eurognome-94 symposium to protect German gnomes.

UTE LISCHKE-McNAB

Gastarbeiter

Gastarbeiter, literally 'guest-worker', is the term which was used in West Germany from the early 1960s onwards to describe those foreign workers who were recruited by West German companies on fixed-term contracts to fill the gaps in the labour force. The term was unknown in East Germany until the 1980s when a small number of workers came to the GDR to work, usually on five-year contracts, from socialist countries.

At the end of 1995 the number of foreigners living in Germany reached seven million. By far the largest proportion of these are foreign workers who originally came to West Germany on short-term contracts, and their dependants. The rapid growth of the West German economy from the early part of the 1950s meant that a constantly expanding workforce was needed. The return of more than 4 million prisoners of war, the influx of 4.7 million refugees and expellees of working age from former German territories in the late 1940s and early 1950s, and the 1.8 million migrants from East Germany up to the building of the Berlin Wall in 1961, ensured a constant supply of new workers for the expanding economy. But by 1960 unemployment had fallen below 1 percent and the influx of new workers had dried up. Therefore new sources of labour were required. From 1960 to the stop on recruitment in 1973 the number of foreign workers grew from 280,000 to 2.6 million.

The first treaty to supply foreign workers was with Italy in 1955, which was followed by further treaties with Spain and Greece (1960), Turkey (1961), Morocco (1963), Portugal (1964), Tunisia (1965) and Yugoslavia (1968). In the earlier years the largest numbers came from Italy, Spain and Greece, but from the end of the 1960s the numbers coming from Yugoslavia, and above all Turkey, increased rapidly; by 1980 a third of all foreigners in West Germany were Turks. The proportion of foreigners in the population rose from 1.2 percent in 1960 to over 7 percent in 1980; as a proportion of the working population they reached almost 10 percent in 1980, but fell back to just under 8 percent by the end of the 1980s. West Germany had therefore experienced a marked increase in its foreign population over a relatively short period of time without regarding itself as a country of immigration. Policy was directed at the workplace, since the foreign workers came to Germany on the principle of rotation; of the 16 million foreigners who settled in West Germany between 1960 and 1990, over 12 million returned home. This still leaves a sizeable figure who stayed, and as *Gastarbeiter* stayed for longer periods of time they brought their families to Germany, which led to the phenomenum of foreign children being born in Germany in increasing numbers. In November 1973, after the economic problems caused by the oil crisis, including rising unemployment, a stop was put on the signing of further contracts. The numbers of *Gastarbeiter* dropped below 2 million, but the increase in dependants, especially after the rules were relaxed in 1977, and the reluctance of those who were already there to leave Germany, has meant a steady growth in the numbers of foreigners overall; this increase was augmented in the 1980s and 1990s by the sharp rise in refugees and asylum-seekers (see **asylum, political**).

With the realization by the **SPD**-led coalition in the late 1970s that West Germany had acquired a sizeable foreign population, the first moves towards addressing some of the resulting social questions were made. In 1978 the first Federal Commissioner for foreigners was appointed, and the first official discussions on how best to promote integration on a long-term basis appeared in a memorandum in

1979. The new approach was however short-lived; even before the change to a Christian Democrat-led government in 1982, policy reverted to an emphasis on the encouragement of repatriation. The growing success of right-wing parties in the late 1980s, in the face of the steep rise in asylum-seekers, forced the government to introduce proposals for a new *Ausländergesetz* (Law on Foreign-ers). In this new law, which came into force on 1 January 1991, and replaced the original law of 1965, the rules governing the status of foreigners are laid down. Foreigners are not covered by Article 11 of the Basic Law guaranteeing freedom of movement. The *Ausländergesetz* governs the circumstances under which foreigners are allowed into Germany and their status in Germany. Most crucial for *Gastarbeiter* was the fact that they were now given the right under normal circumstances to German citizenship after fifteen years residence. Also children between sixteen and twenty-three were given the automatic right to German citizen-ship if they had attended a German school for six years. But the new law did not allow the right to dual citizenship which has meant that the number taking advantage of the new citizenship rules has remained low. Also it did not grant voting rights to foreigners in local elections.

Nevertheless, it is clear that progress has been made in Germany in the 1990s concerning the acceptance of *Gastarbeiter* into German society. Despite the outbreaks of hostility towards foreign-ers, leading in some cases to brutal attacks on asylum-seekers (such as in Hoyerswerda in 1991 and Rostock in 1992, which were partly fuelled by the insecurities of East Germans in the post-unification period), much progress has been made towards the integration of *Gastarbeiter* into German society, who represent the most stable communities of foreigners in Germany. There are now second and third generations who know no other home-land, despite the fact that they might still have a Turkish or other passport. In the 1994 general election two MPs of Turkish background were elected to the Bundestag. In certain cities, such as Berlin, Frankfurt am Main or Stuttgart, large communities of *Gastarbeiter* families have made their mark on the cultural landscape. A number of writers and artists from *Gastarbeiter* backgrounds have started to have their work recognized in

Germany (see **migrant literature**). The process is irreversible and has fundamentally changed the nature of German life.

Further reading

Bade, K.J. (ed.) (1993) *Deutsche im Ausland. Fremde in Deutschland*, Munich: Beck (a recent book on migrations affecting Germany and Germans).

Hentges, G. and Kühnl, R. (1993) 'Foreign Work-ers in Germany', *Debatte*, 1, 2: 54–70 (a recent article from a historical perspective).

PETER BARKER

Gauck, Joachim

b. 24 January 1940, Rostock

Joachim Gauck co-founded *Neues Forum* (NF), and became Special Federal Government Commis-sioner with responsibility for the files of the GDR Security Service (*Stasi*).

Gauck studied theology, and worked as a pastor in Rostock, supporting the church peace, environ-mental and human rights groups in Mecklenburg. He served on the NF Council and was a member of the *Volkskammer* for the Bündnis 90/Grüne alliance, chairing the parliamentary committee dealing with the dissolution of the *Stasi*. In 1991 he shared the Theodor-Heuss medal with five citizens' movements members including Jens **Reich** and Ulrike **Poppe** on behalf of the people of the GDR (see also **citizens' movements: GDR**).

BEATRICE HARPER

gay and lesbian culture in Germany

The enormous significance of Germany for con-temporary gay and lesbian culture begins with the establishment in 1897 of the first homosexual organization, the Wissenschaftlich-humanitäre Ko-mitee or WhK (Scientific Humanitarian Commit-tee), whose foundation can be taken to mark the emergence of the modern homosexual emancipa-tion movement. In 1898 Dr Magnus Hirschfeld, the Committee's central organizer, began its public work by introducing a petition to the German parliament for the removal from the Penal Code of §175, which criminalized any 'unnatural sex act committed between persons of the male sex'. The founding political activity of the WhK set off a rich and difficult struggle that laid the groundwork for contemporary lesbian and gay culture. While the WhK concentrated on political reform and scientific enlightenment to achieve social tolerance, other groups quickly formed that advocated homosexual emancipation as a means to broad cultural transformation. And although women like Toni Schwabe participated in the WhK their numbers remained small since §175 did not criminalize lesbianism and Hirschfeld's activities mainly interested men. That lesbian participation in political and social activity took place mainly in the organized women's movement which explains in part the absence of a distinct lesbian culture until after WWI. Such a distinction of gay and lesbian interests as well as reform versus integration-oriented directions continues until today.

An active and vibrant public sphere emerged during the Weimar Republic. Hirschfeld opened his Institut für Sexualwissenschaft (Institute for Sexual Science) in 1919. Early liberalization of censorship led to an explosion of gay, lesbian and transvestite publications. Publisher Friedrich Radszuweit founded the Bund für Menschenrechte (League for Human Rights) that by 1929 counted 48,000 members. The first gay film, *Different from the Others (Anders als die andern)* premièred in 1919 and the now classic lesbian film *Mädchen in Uniform* (Girls in Uniform) opened in 1931. Major urban centres saw the flourishing of bars, balls and cabarets oriented towards both lesbians and gays.

The Nazi takeover in 1933 put an end to tolerance, closing down the limited openings of Weimar. In 1935 a sharpened version of §175 entered the penal code and criminalized all 'sex offences' between males. Yet, although the point was highly debated, it still did not criminalize lesbianism – which does not mean that lesbians were free from persecution. The Nazi persecution of homosexuals differs significantly from the extermination of the Jews. If the Jews were the outside threat to the race, homosexuals were the became inner enemy of the racial state.

However, unlike being Jewish, being homosexual was not enough in itself to get one sent to a concentration camp. Nazi science tended to view homosexuality as acquired behaviour, forgivable if men and women 'returned' to their 'proper' roles as soldiers and mothers. Repeat offenders against §175 proved that their homosexuality was inborn and were subjected to castration and concentration camp sentences. It is estimated that between five and fifteen thousand of the approximately fifty thousand convicted men were sent to the camps and marked by the pink triangle. Because lesbians were assigned the black triangle for the larger category 'asocial', their number cannot be determined. How many more men and women were investigated by the *Gestapo*, entered into protective marriages, or committed suicide is unknown.

With the collapse of the Third Reich bars reopened almost immediately in the major cities. In Berlin Lotte Hahm and Kati Reinhart opened the lesbian bar *Max und Moritz* and organized lesbian balls in the old style into the 1960s. However the collapse did not bring liberation for gays and lesbians. Political organization was limited. The decimation wrought by the persecution of the last twelve years was compounded by the fact that the Federal Republic retained the Nazi version of §175 until 1969. During the next fifteen years conviction rates paralleled those of the Nazi period. The GDR did return §175 to the Weimar era's wording, but in both Germanys a conservative repressive heterosexual cultural agenda dominated until the rebellions of the 1960s. In Frankfurt am Main and Hamburg, a few 'homophile' organizations did emerge and, in the tradition of the WhK, they sought to present scientific arguments and encourage legal reform. They became significant sources of support for men convicted under §175. As women, lesbians experienced a particular form of oppression in the FRG under the conservative cultural agenda of the **Adenauer** period. The women, who had survived on their own and dug out the ruins of the war as *Trümmerfrauen*, were forced back into disesteemed jobs and traditional roles: secretary, housewife, mother. The GDR, on the other hand, required all its citizens to work and advocated in principle equality for women, providing lesbians with an important form of economic independence.

In the FRG reform of the penal code resulted mainly from an increase in electoral strength of the **SPD** in the 1960s. In 1969 §175 took on the form and purpose of 'protection' of minors, establishing twenty-one as the age of consent between males. This was significantly higher than the age of heterosexual consent. Four years later it would be reformed again, but a difference of 18 versus 14 remained. A number of groups emerged in this period of political liberalization. However a new form of activism only began in 1971 following the controversy around the television broadcast of Rosa von **Praunheim**'s film *Not the Homosexual is Perverse, But the Situation in which He Finds Himself* (*Nicht der Homosexuelle ist pervers, sondern die Situation, in der er lebt*). By 1972 'Homosexual Action Groups', gay activist groups modelled on radical US examples, had formed throughout the major cities. Perhaps the most active, the Homosexuelle Aktionsgruppe Westberlin (HAW) organized a series of spring gatherings that led to a nationwide exchange of ideas. The concept of 'coming out', with its attendant principles of cultural transformation through personal and social consciousness-raising, became the centre of political practice.

In its initial phase there was a women's group within the HAW, but it quickly broke off to follow a different political path. The lesbian movement took its inspiration from US radical separatists. The rejection of the traditional feminine roles of the Adenauer era and the assertion of a woman's right to self-determination were understood as not only matters of sexual behaviour. Lesbians saw themselves at the forefront of the feminist revolt against the male-dominated power structures. In this perspective gay men were often seen as a part of patriarchy, pursuing goals that opposed those of lesbians. Lesbians thus formed separate social and political organizations. The Itzehoe protests in 1973 against the trial of Marion Ihns and Judy Anderson, lesbians who had killed Ihns' abusive husband, strengthened the distinct lesbian leadership. One year later two major organizations emerged, the Lesbisches Aktions-Zentrum and Gruppe L 74 (Group Lesbos 74), the latter oriented more towards older professional women. The principle of coming out was central to these organizations as well.

In both gay and lesbian movements, the mid-1970s led to similar blossomings of cultural expression. Militancy provided many individuals with a sense of pride of lesbian and gay identity. The public sphere was transformed by bookstores, like the lesbian *Lilith* and the gay *Prinz Eisenherz* and through newspapers, like the gay *Siegessäule* and the lesbian *Unsere kleine Zeitung*. Publishers like *Frauenoffensiv*, *Orlanda*, *Amazonen* and *Rosa Winkel* supplied this public sphere with materials and information freed from the censorship of the established publishers. Authors like Christa **Reinig** and Hubert **Fichte** provided significant contributions to the genre of out lesbian and gay literature. The success of such endeavours in turn led the major publishers to establish lesbian and gay series to tap into this market. Women's Studies initiatives brought discussions of women's sexuality into the university setting as an object of study and research. The establishment of *Spinnboden e.V. Lesbenarchiv* and the *Schwules Museum* (Gay Museum) provided important sites for the documenting and archiving of lesbian and gay history. In addition to von Praunheim, filmmakers like Alexandra von Grote, Ulrike **Ottinger**, Monika **Treut**, Rainer Werner **Fassbinder**, and Frank Ripploh provided significant contributions to lesbian and gay cinema. Annual events like Christopher Street Day or the Pfingsttreffen der Lesben (Spring Gathering of the Lesbians) begun in the 1970s continue today, providing a sense of visibility and identification for both communities.

Starting in the early 1980s, the **AIDS** crisis transformed the Gay Rights Movement, robbing it of many of its leaders. The hysteria of the tabloids and talk shows and calls by conservative politicians for registration and internment of people with HIV made clear the need for education and community-organized support services. Gay men responded with heroic creativity and resiliency, and the general public responded caringly. Beginning with the 1983 AIDS issue of Der **Spiegel**, the media presented images and insight into the lives of gay men that ultimately promoted social acceptance. 1983 also saw the establishment of the first organization to confront the demands of the crisis, the Deutsche AIDS Hilfe (German AIDS Support). In addition to providing support to persons with AIDS, the AIDS support networks drew on the creative support of graphic artists and filmmakers like Wieland Speck to develop innovative and successful Safer Sex campaigns. Adding to the already existing infrastructure of support networks and group centres for lesbians and gays, the eventual state support and professionalization of AIDS care providers ultimately integrated and institutionalized the interests of gay men.

In the GDR organization proceeded slowly. The tireless work of Rudlof Klimmer, doctor and party member, had resulted in the removal of §175 in 1968, but no mass organization had ensued. Homosexuality was decriminalized, but homosexual political organization was treated as a threat to the state. The Homosexuelleninitiativ Berlin (Berlin Homosexual Initiative), founded in 1973, formed an underground scene until 1978. They met weekly in the space provided at the Gründerzeit Museum run by Charlotte von Mahlsdorf, the most famous transvestite of the GDR. As of 1982 the Protestant church acted as protective umbrella organization for, eventually, twenty-two regional groups, often with separate gay and lesbian subgroupings. In 1986 the state finally allowed the formation of official groups, the *Sonntags-Clubs* (Sunday Clubs), named after the day of their weekly meetings.) These groups espoused the goal of emancipation and integration into socialist society. Open discussion of lesbian and gay issues accelerated in the final years. Indeed the first gay film in the GDR, Heiner **Carow**'s *Coming Out*, was premièred under state sponsorship on 9 November 1989 – the same night that the Berlin Wall fell.

Lesbian and gay organization has accelerated, moving from self-help to professional status. Today centres and clubs receive official support from state and local administrations. In 1989 the Berlin Senate established the Fachbereich für gleichge-schlechtliche Lebensweisen (Department for Same-Sex Lifestyles) as an advisory organization to the city government. The longtime lesbian historian and activist Ilse Kokula was appointed as one of the first organizers. In 1994 §175 was struck completely from the books. Lesbian couples pursue alternative insemination and groups have formed advocating gay marriage as the next step in social integration. However, legal protections and official acceptance aside, lesbians and gays continue to be the targets of discrimination and violence. The rise of xenophobia and **neo-Nazi** organizations have resulted in an increase in the attacks on lesbians and gays, confronting many with the limits of integration and tolerance. Renewed militancy and calls for cultural transformation indicate that lesbians and gays are still struggling with the question of how – paraphrasing the film title – 'to change the situation in which they live'.

See also: feminism and the women's movement; Schroeter, Werner

Further reading

Baumgardt, M. *et al.* (1997) *Goodbye to Berlin? 100 Jahre Schwulenbewegung. Eine Ausstellung des Schwulen Museums und der Akademie der Künste 17. Mai bis 17. August 1997*, Berlin: Rosa Winkel.

Campe, J. (1988) *Andere Lieben: Homosexualität in der deutschen Literatur: Ein Lesebuch*, Frankfurt am Main: Suhrkamp.

Grau, G. (ed.) (1995) *Hidden Holocaust: Gay and Lesbian Persecution in Germany 1933–45*, New York: Casell.

Lemke, J. (ed.) (1991) *Gay Voices from East Germany*, Bloomington, IN: Indiana University Press.

Marti, M. (1992) *Hinterlegte Botschaften: Die Darstellung lesbischer Frauen in der deutschsprachigen Literatur seit 1945*, Stuttgart: Metzler.

Sillge, U. (1991) *Un-Sichtbare Frauen: Lesben und ihre Emanzipation in der DDR*, Berlin: LinksDruck.

Steakley, J. (1975) *The Homosexual Rights Movement in Germany*, New York: Arno.

RANDALL HALLE

Gehlen, Arnold

b. 29 January 1904, Leipzig; d. 30 January 1976, Hamburg

Philosopher and sociologist

Gehlen developed an 'elementary anthropology' that, influenced by Max Scheler's philosophical anthropology, conceives of humans as 'deficient beings', whose existence as a species is threatened by their natural inability to deal with life's hazards. Humans seek relief through self-disciplined modes of 'action' embodied in cultural forms and institutions such as language, law and morality. Gehlen joined the Nazi Party relatively early, in 1933. He remained an influential figure in **sociology** after 1945, though frequently under attack from the left, especially **Frankfurt School** members including **Adorno** and **Habermas**.

BRETT R. WHEELER

Geissendörfer, Hans W.

b. 6 April 1941, Augsburg

Filmmaker

An autodidact whose first feature film, *The Case of Lena Christ* (*Der Fall Lena Christ*, 1968), a portrait of the Bavarian writer, was produced for television, Geissendörfer continued to work in television in a range of genres, including psycho-dramas and a western-style adaptation of Schiller's *Don Carlos* (*Carlos*, 1971).

Geissendörfer has subsequently concentrated on producing polished literary adaptations, turning to authors as varied as Anzengruber, Ibsen, Patricia Highsmith, with *The Glass Cell* (*Die gläserne Zelle*, 1977), Thomas **Mann**, with *The Magic Mountain* (*Der Zauberberg*, 1981) and Friedrich **Dürrenmatt**, with *Justiz* (Justice) (1993).

See also: New German Cinema

MARTIN BRADY

George, Götz

b. 23 July 1938, Berlin

Actor

Götz George acted in several popular German films during the 1950s and 1960s, including two Wolfgang **Staudte** films, but was shunned by **New German Cinema** directors in the 1970s, when he worked mainly in television and theatre. During the 1980s and 1990s he became Germany's best-known domestic actor, especially for his role as Horst Schimanski in the television crime series *Tatort*, and lead roles in Dominik **Graf**'s *Die Katze* (The Cat) (1987), Helmut Dietl's *Schtonk!* (1991),

and Romuald Karmakar's *The Death-Maker* (*Der Totmacher*, 1995).

JONATHAN LEGG

German language: Austria

In Austria, German is the main state **language**, though the southeast corner includes minorities of native population, living in scattered pockets, who speak Slovene, Hungarian and Croat. The German language spoken throughout most of Austria consists of variants of the Bavarian dialect; the peculiarities of the national written standard are partly accounted for by dialect features and partly by the circumstances of the old Austrian Empire. Austria is very conscious of the pluricentric nature of the German language, and is reluctant to concede the final word on the linguistic norms of German to north German authorities.

With complete lack of regard for political boundaries, the Bavarian dialect group of German (generally known as *Bairisch*) sweeps from Bavaria in Germany across Austria in such a way that its central band includes both big cities, Munich and Vienna; similarly, the South (alpine) Bavarian subdivision embraces the Bavarian highlands as well as the Tyrol and Carinthia in Austria. The main exception on Austrian territory is the small western province of Vorarlberg, where Alemannic dialect is spoken, linking this region linguistically to German Switzerland.

Unlike the diglossic situation of the German language in Switzerland (see also **German language: Switzerland**), whereby the speakers switch deliberately from one form of the language to the other, the language forms used by most Austrians merge gradually into one another; the users slide up and down the sociolinguistic scale according to the circumstances.

Even educated speakers of German in Austria usually have a distinct accent, since the phonological norms of the Austrian national standard differ in many respects from the north German ones. Lexical 'Austriacisms' afford much more palpable distinctions. Many of the words of Germanic dialect origin are shared with Bavaria, though Austrians tend to have less compunction about committing them to paper, even in print. Many of the words of foreign origin, however, are more specific in their occurrence to Austria, as their use goes back to geographical and historical links between the former domains of the Austrian Hapsburgs – hence the numerous words of Italian and some of Slavonic and Hungarian origin.

A small number of morphological and syntactical deviations in the standard language, including linking devices in word formation and changes in plural forms and genders of nouns, as well as differing use of verb tenses and of prepositions, are significant because of their grammatical implications.

Austria has its own compact, one-volume official German dictionary, the *Österreichisches Wörterbuch*, which is a general dictionary of German incorporating a number of Austriacisms. However, some Austrians prefer to take the German **Duden** dictionaries as their ultimate authority; editions of these works since WWII have included many Austriacisms.

See also: German language: Switzerland

Further reading

Bundesministerium für Unterricht (1951–) *Österreichisches Wörterbuch*, Vienna: Österreichischer Bundesverlag (general dictionary of German, published in a number of successive editions for use in schools and offices in Austria).

Ebner, J. (1980) *Wie sagt man in Österreich? Wörterbuch der österreichischen Besonderheiten*, 2nd edn, Mannheim: Dudenverlag (a dictionary of Austriacisms, especially those occurring in print – in spite of the title!).

GRAHAM MARTIN

German language: Switzerland

From the linguistic point of view Switzerland is one of the most complex parts of German-speaking Europe. This small country on the southern periphery of the German-speaking area is split into regions where four different languages are spoken: French in the west, Italian in certain geographical protuberances in the south, Romansh in scattered pockets in the southeastern canton of the Grisons (its speakers being bilingual with German), and German in the rest of the country. German speakers are by far the predominant majority, comprising over 70 percent of the native population. While true bilingualism is relatively rare, the German used in Switzerland is affected by diglossia: forms of *Schweizerdeutsch* (Swiss German), spoken by all sectors of the population, are variants of the *Alemannisch* (Alemannic) **dialect**, while the written **language** is a version of standard German, which most German Swiss claim to have some difficulty in producing. Use of the dialect has spread from the 1970s on, and many obervers express alarm at its ever-increasing extent.

Although the term *Schweizerdeutsch* is frequently used to refer to the German spoken in Switzerland, there is no uniform variant, and the term is therefore a rather elastic concept covering a large number of individual dialects. Thus, although to the ears of many Germans from the north or even the centre of Germany, Swiss German may sound like a different language, it cannot be regarded as such because of the lack of norms governing it. There are certainly a number of common denominators amongst its features, some of which link it to allied forms of Alemannic dialect spoken in southwest Germany and western Austria, but the German Swiss have never been able to agree on normative forms of pronunciation, spelling, vocabulary or grammar.

There is a large degree of dissension amongst scholars as to the divisions of Alemannic in general and Swiss German in particular; the language of the Basel area is invariably assigned to *Niederalemannisch* (Low Alemannic), while the majority of the rest of German-speaking Switzerland is commonly labelled *Hochalemannisch* (High Alemannic). Important dialectal groupings occur around the large cities of Zürich and Bern. According to many authorities, each of the twenty-odd German-speaking cantons has its own typical dialect variant, and the further divisions are practically infinite.

The dialect was previously confined in Switzerland – as in other parts of the German-speaking area – to spoken usage, though it has always been used by all social strata amongst the German Swiss; such spoken usage was reproduced in print in literary contexts such as plays and poems. For most writing, such as newspapers, novels, reports and even personal letters, the standard language was traditionally used; speech on formal occasions such as lectures and addresses, as well as most broadcasting, followed the norms of the standard language, which the Swiss tend to refer to as *Schriftsprache* (written language). During WWII there was a tendency in Switzerland to move away from the language of the Nazis in Germany, and the dialect was increasingly used in domains where it had previously been avoided. After reverting to the previous state of affairs for a couple of decades after the war, dialect usage – as an indirect result of the sociological upheaval in western Europe at the end of the 1960s – again began to spread in Switzerland, and in subsequent decades it increasingly invaded domains which had previously been the preserve of the standard language. Thus the German-language electronic media (i.e. television and radio) in Switzerland are now dominated by dialect, more and more teaching in schools is carried out in dialect, and many people regularly write informal letters in dialect. Many German Swiss now show reluctance to switch to standard German when talking to German speakers from Germany or Austria, or to speakers of other languages, whether from their own country or abroad. In spite of endless protests from various quarters in Switzerland, there has been no sign by the late 1990s of an abatement in the spread of dialect usage, which is commonly referred to as the *Mundartwelle* (dialect wave). The potential problems most frequently cited are as follows:

(1) German-speaking Switzerland is in danger of isolating itself culturally from the rest of the German-speaking lands;
(2) the German Swiss are also in danger of creating a major cultural rift between themselves and the speakers of the country's other three languages, especially since the latter have only very limited opportunities of learning Swiss German.

The Swiss national version of the standard German language contains a number of peculiarities known as 'Helveticisms'. Apart from a number of differences in pronunciation, including speech rhythm, the major distinctions occur in the realm of vocabulary. Some words are clearly of Germanic origin, and their derivation from the Alemannic dialect can most readily be seen, while others are simply old-fashioned in general German usage. Words of foreign (in particular French) origin are especially popular in Swiss usage. Particularly intriguing are forms where the deviation has grammatical implications, e.g. differences in word formation, plural forms and genders of nouns, and the use of verb tenses.

There is no German-language dictionary published and generally accepted in Switzerland for use there. The German Swiss take **Duden** publications from Germany (which include a number of Helveticisms) as the norm for linguistic usage.

See also: German language: Austria

Further reading

Baur, A. (1983) *Was ist eigentlich Schweizerdeutsch?*, Winterthur: Gemsberg Verlag (covers all aspects of Swiss German, with particular reference to politics and sociolinguistics).

Lötscher, A. (1983) *Schweizerdeutsch. Geschichte, Dialekte, Gebrauch*, Frauenfeld: Verlag Huber (complements Baur's book, concentrating more on an analysis of linguistic features).

Meyer, K. (1989) *Wie sagt man in der Schweiz? Wörterbuch der schweizerischen Besonderheiten*, Mannheim: Dudenverlag (a dictionary of Helveticisms, especially those occurring in print – despite the title!).

Müller-Marzohl, A. (1994) 'Die Mundartwelle in der Schweiz', *Sprachspiegel* 6: 179–81 (a very concise presentation of Swiss diglossia and the phenomena and problems of the 'dialect wave').

Rash, F. (1998) *The German Language in Switzerland*, Bern: Peter Lang (a comprehensive survey of all aspects of the German language situation in Switzerland).

GRAHAM MARTIN

German Question

Sometimes referred to as the 'German Problem' in English, though invariably as *Die deutsche Frage* in German, the term 'German Question' has been used to characterize a range of issues relating to

German identity. In practice it is possible to reduce these to three interacting subsidiary questions: a 'who?' question (*who* are 'the Germans'?); a 'where?' question (*where* is '**Germany**'?); and a 'how?' question (*how* should Germany most appropriately organize its political life, at both the domestic and international levels?). The idea of a German Question thus has a much longer history, and far wider ramifications, than is implied by the restriction of the term to the problem of the division of Germany that became commonplace in the postwar years. The German Question in its broader senses did not just begin with the East–West split in the late 1940s, and nor was it 'solved' by German **unification** in 1990.

Germany's dubious distinction of belonging to the category of countries whose histories tend to be perceived as a 'question' or 'problem' has in modern times derived most obviously from the fact of the Third Reich, and the inevitable questions about the place of those twelve years in the country's preceding and subsequent history: why did it happen, could it happen again, and how could a repetition be prevented? The issue of the Third Reich is, however, embedded in an older set of problems relating to unavoidable basic givens of geography and demography: Germany, however defined, lies in the centre of Europe, it shares borders with no fewer than nine other countries, and its population is far and away the largest in Europe outside Russia. These simple facts of life, combined in the twentieth century with a powerful economy, have meant that whatever happens in Germany inevitably impinges on the rest of Europe, and indeed the whole world.

Early uncertainty about who the Germans actually were is already suggested by the range of names they have been given in other languages. Whereas, for instance, 'English', '*anglais*', and '*englisch*', or 'French', '*français*', and '*französisch*' clearly derive from the same roots and indicate some common agreement about who the people in question are, no such consensus is apparent in the case of 'German', 'allemand', and 'deutsch'. In fact, the French '*allemand*', together with its cognates in other Romance languages, refers originally to one specific Germanic tribe, the Alemanni, whilst the Finnish language has chosen another tribe, the Saxons, for its term for 'German'

– '*saksaa*'. In contrast with this over-specificity there is etymological vagueness in the terms used in English – the roots of the word 'German' are thought to lie in a Celtic word simply meaning 'neighbour' – while in the Slav languages the Germans are 'strangers' (the Russian '*nemeckij*', for instance). And as for the word '*deutsch*', its etymology implies nothing more than 'the people' (and its English cognate 'Dutch' has, to add still further to the confusion, subsequently settled on a different nation from the Germans to whom it once applied).

The 'who?' and 'where?' aspects of the German Question first came to the fore in the Napoleonic era. Where previously for a thousand years the varying incarnations of the loose and amorphous construct of the 'Holy Roman Empire of the German Nation' had meant little in terms of political or cultural identity, the Wars of Liberation (from French hegemony) brought the first stirrings of popular national sentiment, and the establishment, in 1815, of the 39-state *Deutscher Bund* (known in English as the 'Germanic Confederation'). The 1848 revolutions, which affected all of German-speaking Europe, highlighted questions about the degree of centralization appropriate to the German polity, but also about the geographical boundaries of 'Germany', and in particular the place of Austria with its substantial non-German-speaking populations. The Austro-Prussian War of 1866, and the subsequent establishment in 1871 of the Prussian-led German Empire, confirmed the exclusion of Austria from modern incarnations of the German state that has obtained – apart from the last seven years of the Third Reich – through to the present day.

The significance of the 'how?' element in the German Question is evident in the fact that twentieth-century Germans have experienced in turn all the major political systems that the century has had to offer: authoritarian monarchy (in the Wilhelmine Empire), parliamentary democracy (in the Weimar years and in the Federal Republic), fascism (in the Third Reich), and communism (in the GDR); they have also experienced various attempted coups, and – from 1945 to 1949 – occupation by foreign powers.

The Nazi years represented the most extreme set of answers to all three 'German Questions': an uncompromisingly racial definition of what it meant to be 'German', an aggressively expansionary redrawing of 'Germany', and one of the most virulent domestic political orders ever witnessed. The subsequent fate of the country – occupation and division – can be seen in terms of yet another attempt, this time on the part of the victorious allies, to come to grips with the German Question, now in the light of the disastrous answers imposed by the Nazis.

Both the Federal Republic and the GDR represented themselves as the natural heirs to the positive traditions of German history, and as the incarnations of an appropriate political system for the future of the German people. The post-war German Question thus became narrowed, for most Germans, to the choice between capitalism and communism and the stark division of Germany into two states epitomizing those two systems. For the outside world the determination of the wider place of 'the two Germanys' (the commonly used anomalous English plural was indicative of linguistic difficulties in conceptualizing the new situation) took on special urgency in the light both of the recent Nazi past and the present antagonisms of the Cold War. This was especially the case with the Federal Republic, the most populous and economically the most powerful state in Europe: the early governments under Konrad **Adenauer** affirmed that this was now a westward-looking country that had turned its back on the old ambiguous status of the 'land in the middle', while the emerging military and economic alliances of western Europe were designed as much as anything as anchors to keep the new Germany under control.

At the official level, the notion of the German Question in the sense of a division to be overcome was espoused by both German states in the early years, but only West Germany upheld this insistence through to the end. By the 1960s the GDR was already proclaiming that 'socialism' (in its own Marxist–Leninist sense of the term) must be the basis for any unification, and in the 1970s it abandoned the notion that there was one German nation, albeit divided into two separate states, for the claim that the stage had now been reached where there were quite simply two separate nations – a socialist one and a capitalist one – on former German soil.

Talk of an 'open German Question' thus became taboo in the East, but in the West too discussion was fraught with complications, and became much more constrained and muted after the *Ostpolitik* of the early 1970s. The 'where?' question was particularly problematic from the outset, as after the war the Allies excised substantial portions of German territory in the East, incorporating them into Poland (and, in the case of the former German city of Königsberg and its hinterland, into the Soviet Union under the Russian name 'Kaliningrad'), as a result of which 'Germany' is now significantly smaller than in any of its previous twentieth-century incarnations. The GDR (in keeping with the Soviet view) recognized the Oder-Neisse Line as the Polish western border from the outset, but in West Germany, particularly in the 1950s and 1960s, the idea was kept alive – not least because of pressure from the three million or so expellees – that Germany was divided not just into two, but into three (i.e. the FRG, the GDR and the 'eastern territories'). Recognition of the status quo was finally conceded by the **Brandt** government 'on behalf of the Federal Republic' in a 1970 treaty with Poland, but a definitive resolution of the matter, like everything else relating to the German division, was left for the 'Peace Treaty with Germany' that had never been signed and that, given that there *was* no 'Germany' to sign it with, seemed increasingly unlikely to materialize. In the event, these outstanding issues were to be dealt with in a quite unforeseen manner in the agreements that paved the way for unification in 1990.

Explicit engagement with the division of Germany in the cultural realm has been extraordinarily meagre (Christa **Wolf**'s novel *Divided Heaven* (*Der geteilte Himmel*, 1962) and various works by Uwe **Johnson** were notable exceptions). The Nazi past, and its implications for the present, have on the other hand been a staple and distinctive theme in much of the literature, theatre and cinema of post-1945 Germany (see also *Vergangenheitsbewältigung*). This was especially – though by no means exclusively – the case in West Germany, the GDR having conveniently absolved itself of responsibility for the legacy of the Third Reich by presenting itself as the state of the victims, and through its Marxist portrayal of fascism as an aggressively malignant variant of the capitalism that it had itself abolished.

Whilst writers have focused their attention on the reverberations of the Third Reich in the post-war present, historians have sought to trace the earlier paths that led up to 1933. Here the question that has excited most debate is that of German singularity – was there something special about Germany that made it uniquely susceptible to the calamity of Nazism? The assertion of a German 'special path' (*Sonderweg*) had had *positive* implications for German nationalists of the nineteenth and early twentieth centuries, reaching its degraded apogee in the Nazis' own messianic rhetoric of a German mission to save the 'Aryan race'. Post-Third-Reich historians focused on what were now perceived as distinctive *flaws* in the German past (notably the 'failed revolution' of 1848 and the 'feudalization of the bourgeoisie' in the Second Empire), but their premises in turn were increasingly relativized in the 1980s by arguments over whether Germany's history was any more or any less 'peculiar' than that of other countries – arguments that came to focus on the 'uniqueness' or otherwise of the **Holocaust** in the very public 'historians' quarrel' (***Historikerstreit***) of 1986.

The memory of the Third Reich has meant that perceptions of German history, past and present, can never elude the uncomfortable rhetoric of 'questions' and 'problems'. Unification, and the series of international agreements that accompanied it, may have resolved for the foreseeable future the 'where?' question and, in domestic politics, the 'how?' question (though the '***Ossi/ Wessi***' division is evidence of a still-unresolved 'who?' question), but other issues, such as Germany's exclusivist nationality law and its implications for the country's seven million foreign residents (***Ausländer***), or the role of the German armed forces on the global stage, or quite simply Germany's place, economically and politically, at the centre of post-Cold-War Europe, are still heavily tinged with perceptions of a German Question.

See also: flags; German studies; Hallstein Doctrine; historiography; history teaching; *Mitteleuropa*; national anthems; *Volk*

Further reading

Breuilly, J. (ed.) (1992) *The State of Germany: The National Idea in the Making, Unmaking and Remaking of a Modern Nation-State*, London and New York: Longman (twelve essays on aspects of the German Question from the Holy Roman Empire through to the 1990s).

Fritsch-Bournazel, R. (1992) *Europe and German Unification*, Oxford and Providence, RI: Berg (assesses the German Question from a post-unification perspective).

James, H. (1990) *A German Identity 1770–1990*, London: Weidenfeld & Nicolson (examines cultural, political, and – in particular – economic aspects of the German Question).

JOHN SANDFORD

German Studies

In response to demands for greater interdisciplinarity, in relation to a diversified spectrum of career opportunities and in defence of the attractiveness of the subject, German Studies has evolved out of the more traditional concerns with German language and literature. This development, inaugurated in the 1960s at some well-established British universities and polytechnics, has meant that the rough symmetry that existed between German ***Germanistik*** and the equivalent subject in English-speaking countries has been altered significantly. Before the development of German Studies had taken hold the curricular and research field of *Auslandsgermanistik* (*Germanistik* in non-German-speaking countries) closely corresponded to *Germanistik* in German-speaking lands, except that major provision for language teaching had to be made. 'German Language and Literature' was one of the modern philologies which flourished during the undisputed ascendancy of European nation states, while German Studies is a transdisciplinary terrain in which the study of German language and literary criticism have become optional elements within a wider programme of learning about modern Germany in a humanities or social-science context. In the Anglo-American educational systems, foreign modern languages (with the possible exception of Spanish) are not a growth area, with English having advanced to unchallenged supremacy as a *lingua franca* of globalized finance, trade and traffic. Nevertheless, a variety of motivations for studying German persist – from an educational interest in German culture, history and science to the necessity to communicate in what is still one of the most widely spoken languages in Europe. While as a single honours subject it has undoubtedly declined, the study of German has typically become part of a combination with other subjects in a changing framework of disciplinary orientations and boundary shifts in the organization of knowledge in the humanities and sciences.

These changes have by no means been universally welcomed within the academic community. In the first instance they have eroded the foundation of the subject in philology and literary analysis without as yet being able to offer a clear disciplinary canon of learning. Indeed German Studies now typically represents a multidisciplinary assemblage of programmes, which include aspects of social, political, economic, intellectual and cultural history, as well as studies in linguistics and practical language. Cultural history or cultural studies themselves embrace a diverse cluster of subjects such as literature, media of mass communication and women's studies.

This enormous range of disciplines and subjects is reflected in a major reorientation of appointments policies, particularly in the larger departments of German, where representatives of literary criticism now find themselves side by side with historians, political scientists and specialists in cultural studies, with all the attendant difficulties of establishing fruitful cross-disciplinary linkages. The felt necessity for organizing such fundamental changes within the subject area originate outside Germany. Hence for all their critical, even revolutionary, aspirations the earlier debates about *Germanistik* in Germany and elsewhere regarding the place and scope of literary history, methods of literary criticism, the orientations of modern linguistics and the critique of language have only had a limited influence on the development of

German Studies. This is because, in the first instance, the German discussions about *Germanistik* were motivated by the desire to uncouple the subject from its nationalist and National Socialist aberrations. A critique was required of German desires in the first half of the twentieth century to establish *Germanistik* as an all-embracing knowledge with the central mission of providing Germany with a national ethic founded in an assumed unique essence of Germanness. This was allegedly to be detected in the history of German poetic literature as well as in legends and fairy tales, folk culture and customs, German art and law. In *Germanistik – eine deutsche Wissenschaft* (*Germanistik* – a German Science) (1967) Eberhart Lämmert and others argued that the subject had to be cleansed of the mishmash of an ill-defined ideology of German exceptionalism and re-established as an unpretentious discipline subdivided into linguistics, literary history and literary aesthetics. Extra-poetic problems of language and literature were also to be addressed, but these received only a mention at this early stage in the debate. This critique of the mystifications of the poetic and of poets uniquely rooted in the spirit of the German people, combined with a critical examination of the fatal contributions of *Germanistik* to the *völkisch* elements of Nazi ideology, were still the leading preoccupations of Karl Otto Konrady's book *Literatur und Germanistik als Herausforderung* (Literature and *Germanistik* as a Challenge) (1974). Meanwhile an exploration of the international discourse on methodology was beginning to make its impact on the subject. The essays collected in *Ansichten einer künftigen Germanistik* (Approaches to a Future *Germanistik*) (1969) and *Neue Ansichten einer künftigen Germanistik* (New Approaches to a Future *Germanistik*) (1973) furnished information and insights into new critical practices such as structuralism, sociology of literature, modern linguistics, literary hermeneutics, reader-response theory, mass-media studies and communications theory. Helmut Kreuzer in his *Veränderungen des Literaturbegriffs* (Changed Notions of Literature) (1975) drew attention to the possibilities of encompassing *Trivialliteratur*, television and the British-inspired discussion on the chasm between scientific and literary culture. These debates were rehearsed further, and methodologically extended, in *New Ways in Germanistik*, which addressed the question, 'Why study literature?' and in particular 'Why study German literature?' in an age when national identity seemed eroded by tendencies towards cosmopolitan and multinational culture. However, despite raising new questions and touching on new areas of study the essays assembled in the above books, as indicated in their titles, remained cautiously confined to more or less traditional demarcations of the subject. Less surprisingly, it is the same disciplinary restraint which defines the parameters of the electronic databank for *Germanistik* (GERDA) that is being developed at the Free University of Berlin.

Although by the mid-1980s the study of German in Britain was increasingly modernized in response to the needs of commerce and industry, it was in the United States where the debates about German Studies as a multidisciplinary field were most explicit. An interdisciplinary organization, the German Studies Association, with its own journal and annual conferences, had been active since the late 1970s, first in the western United States and later coast to coast. In January 1989 the New York Office of the German Academic Exchange Service (**DAAD**) sponsored a conference in Scottsdale, Arizona, on *German Studies in the USA: A Critique of 'Germanistik'?* Three years later the DAAD organized another conference at the same venue on 'Post-Wall German Studies'. In 1994 a DAAD-sponsored 'Symposium on The Future of Germanistik in the USA' followed. The spring-1989 issue of *The German Quarterly*, published by the American Association of Teachers of German, had tackled '*Germanistik* as German Studies: Interdisciplinary Theories and Methods'. The same journal returned to the debate with a special issue on 'Culture Studies' in the autumn of 1996. The thrust of the argument was to explore possibilities of interdisciplinarity, not so much as a theory, but as a teaching and research praxis.

In Germany, too, traditional *Germanistik* began to be seen as too narrowly parochial and much wider perspectives demanded to be embraced under the umbrella of '*interkulturelle Germanistik*'. An academic society of that name was founded in 1984. It understands its academic procedures to be grounded in cultural anthropology and guided by the perception of the otherness of ethnicities, their

internal and external interaction, dissonance, assimilation and antagonism. Within the constitution of an intercultural hermeneutics an acute awareness of class- and group-specific cultural idioms, and practices of intercultural mediation, are promoted as the focus of study. With the thesis of German exceptionalism, Germany's catastrophically aberrant path into modernity, losing credibility amongst international historians, intercultural German studies seeks to interpret aspects of Germany within a European or intercontinental setting (see also **German Question**; **historiography**). In contradistinction to attempts earlier in the twentieth century at establishing a unified and normative *Deutschwissenschaft*, the idea of a homogeneous, isomorphic national culture is abandoned in favour of a conception of culture as one variant amongst others, composed of different building blocks depending on region, historical location and the degree of educational sophistication in a given social segment.

The constructivist pluralism of such arguments, while not necessarily yielding to randomness in the composition of meanings and life worlds, may yet prove unsatisfactory for explaining the rootedness of cultures in generic and unique traditions. However, the intercultural approach is predicated on the reinstatement of a broad concept of culture as a constitutive environment for all social activity. In recognizing the normative relativity of the indigenous model, German culture and language are set within a plurality and alterity of other cultures both within Germany and outside. Varieties of the foreign therefore become part and parcel of interpreting the specificity of the home-culture. *Germanistik* is being developed as an applied science of cultural studies. The approach to literature is fundamentally guided by the acknowledgement of its embeddedness in intertextual, transregional and transnational traditions; the contemporary German language is didactically presented as a variant of articulation for a multiculturally composed audience of learners in order to stress the interdependence of cultural formations. The teaching–learning situation is explicitly understood as a method of intercultural bridge-building and seeks to promote competence in intercultural understanding.

Such critical practices were neither as innovative

as was at first claimed, nor were they initially extended to fields other than German language and literature. However, the conferences on intercultural German studies soon responded to a broadening of its research areas and now encompasses *Sprachdidaktik* (language teaching methodology), *Linguistik* (linguistics), *Literaturforschung* (literary studies), *kulturvergleichende Landeskunde* (comparative area studies), *Fremdheitslehre und interkulturelle Kommunikation* (alterity studies and intercultural communication), *Medienforschung und Mediendidaktik* (media research and training) and *Übersetzungsforschung* (translation studies). Many of these were meanwhile also being considered within a reformed curriculum of German *Germanistik*. Given interculturalism's basic methodological premises it was logical to demand their application far beyond the confines of literary production, dissemination and reception. Not surprisingly, comparative intercultural studies can fruitfully address problems not only concerned with the inspiration of the literary imagination by a variety of national and transnational sources, but also with those of, say, comparative management cultures within and across the corporative identities of multinational companies. Clearly, the cultural determination of human behaviour affects collective operations within institutions, organizations, regions and nations.

Within this interpretative approach any given culture cannot escape being seen as a ghetto of socialization patterns which demand to be broken up and transgressed so as to achieve the creation of an intercultural subject aware of its limitations and open to the plurality of social and cultural models. Divergence and digression from, and contradiction and critical distance to inner-cultural anchorages as local or regional enfetterments is therefore presumed to become both a research programme and a behavioural norm. Hence intercultural hermeneutics as an interpretative paradigm poses challenges to the power structures which permeate culture. While undoubtedly the intention is to overcome cultural insularity and advance habituations of tolerance, there is a danger of dismissing the confinements of culture as an arbitrary enmeshment by prejudice, instead of recognizing cultural peculiarity as a specific attempt at evolving contexts of meaning. In order to guard against randomness and relativity, *Interkulturelle Germanistik* disavows monocultural hegemony and optimistically searches for intracultural standards in order to find a terrain where actors from different cultures can meet in fruitful exchange and mutual understanding.

German Studies today is therefore a portmanteau, accommodating both a multidisciplinary curriculum and an intercultural discipline, but also still enfolding the study of German language and literature as important or even core subjects.

Further reading

Conrady, K.O. (1974) *Literatur und Germanistik als Herausforderung*, Frankfurt am Main: Suhrkamp.

DAAD, New York (ed.) (1989) *German Studies in the USA: A Critique of 'Germanistik'?*, Arizona State University, Consortium for Atlantic Studies.

Denham, S., Kacandes, I. and Petropoulos, J. (eds) (1997) *A User's Guide to German Cultural Studies*, Ann Arbor, MI: University of Michigan Press (wide-ranging collection of essays and practical information by American Germanists).

Hermand, J. (1994) *Geschichte der Germanistik*, Reinbek bei Hamburg: Rowohlt (standard concise history).

Kolbe, J. (ed.) (1969) *Ansichten einer künftigen Germanistik*, Frankfurt am Main, Berlin and Vienna: Ullstein.

Kreuzer, H. (ed.) (1973) *Neue Ansichten einer künftigen Germanistik*, Munich: Hanser.

—— (1975) *Veränderungen des Literaturbegriffs. Fünf Beiträge zu aktuellen Problemen der Literaturwissenschaft*, Göttingen: Vandenhoeck and Ruprecht.

Lämmert, E. *et al.* (1967) *Germanistik – eine deutsche Wissenschaft*, Frankfurt am Main: Suhrkamp.

Lutzeier, P.R. (ed.) (1998) *German Studies: Old and New Challenges*, Bern: Peter Lang (a collection of papers written by British and Irish Germanists).

McCarthy, J.A. and Schneider, K. (eds) (1996) *The Future of Germanistik in the USA*, Nashville, TN: Vanderbilt University Press.

Sheppard, R. (ed.) (1990) *New Ways in Germanistik*, New York, Oxford and Munich: Berg.

Suhr, H. (ed.) (1992) *Post-Wall German Studies: A Challenge for North American Colleges and Universities in the 1990s*, New York: DAAD.

Wierlacher, A. *et al.* (eds) (1995) *Jahrbuch Deutsch als Fremdsprache. Intercultural German Studies*, vol. 21, Munich: iudicium verlag (special number on intercultural German Studies).

WILFRIED VAN DER WILL

Germanistik

The academic discipline which, in English-speaking universities, is traditionally known as 'German'. *Germanistik*, which has its origins in early-nineteenth-century attempts to construct a national cultural identity, was a major object of critique by the **student movement** of the late 1960s, not least for its complicity in the ideology of the Third Reich. Broadly Marxist-inspired reformulations of the discipline were widespread in the 1970s, but for all the subsequent widening of methodological approaches, it retains its traditional focus on German language and literature. *Germanistik* has long been the biggest humanities subject at most German universities, studied typically by those intending to teach German in secondary schools. (For a fuller discussion and further reading, see **German studies**).

JOHN SANDFORD

'Germany'

The notable fact that the *Bundesrepublik Deutschland* (Federal Republic of Germany) (1949) is the first German state to use the term '*Deutschland*' in its title indicates that the customary linguistic equation 'Germany' = '*Deutschland*' is imprecise and potentially misleading. Official titles for areas covered by the English term 'Germany' over the centuries have included *Heiliges Römisches Reich Deutscher Nation* (Holy Roman Empire of the German Nation), *Deutscher Bund* (Germanic Confederation), *Deutsches Reich* (German Empire), *Deutsche Republik* (German Republic) and *Drittes Reich* (Third Reich – literally 'Third Empire') – leaving the term '*Deutschland*' available to carry linguistic, cultural or, less happily, ethnic and pseudo-ethnic connotations. Certainly, the modern German state that eventually emerged in 1871 did not fully correspond to the prevalent notion of a nation-state: the unification that took place was deemed a *kleindeutsche Lösung* ('small-German solution'), excluding as it did Austria in particular: the new Empire's first head of state, King Wilhelm of Prussia, was crowned '*Deutscher Kaiser*' rather than '*Kaiser von Deutschland*'.

Today's '*Deutschland*' is synonymous with *Bundesrepublik Deutschland*, the country arrived at through the amalgamation of the FRG and the GDR under the title of the former in 1990. From the founding of West and East Germany in 1949 until their unification, however, the term '*Deutschland*' was denotatively and connotatively extremely complex. Initially, both the GDR and the FRG had ambitions to represent 'Germany'. In the former, the ruling party, the **SED**, christened their key newspaper **Neues Deutschland** and the (later abandoned) text of the East German **'national' anthem** referred to a *Deutschland, einig Vaterland* ('Germany, single fatherland'). '*Deutschland*', however, was dropped from the East German constitution in 1968, the acronym *DDR* having been cultivated to become the normal term of reference for the East German state amongst its citizens, and in 1974 the international vehicle identification mark 'D' – hitherto common to both states – was replaced on East German vehicles by 'DDR'. In titles of institutions etc. use of the adjective *Deutsch* . . . receded in favour of the noun phrase *der* (of the) *DDR*. The concept of representing a greater whole was also to the fore in the West German choice of anthem – the third verse of the *Deutschlandlied* – and in the country's official title, which was not '*Bundesrepublik Deutschlands*' (i.e. 'of' Germany, perhaps implying 'part of') but '*Bundesrepublik Deutschland*'. And there was less hesitation here about using '*Deutsch* . . .' in institutional titles, although *Bundes* . . . ('federal') was also common (less so: *Bundesdeutsch* . . .). For many years the West German government discouraged the use of 'BRD', this increasingly popular acronym being perceived (erroneously) to have been 'planted' by East Germans to equalize the international standing of the two states. Stigma was long attached to the use of 'DDR' in West Germany, some perceiving that such use marked the speaker as a GDR sympathizer: **Springer** newspapers used the (after all, convenient) abbreviation in inverted commas until 1989. During the early Cold War period, the range of 'synonyms' in popular use in West Germany for referring to East Germany was wide, and each in its own way revealing; everyday, negatively loaded referents for West Germany did not emerge in East Germany, in spite of the unrelenting application of negative descriptors ('imperialist', 'revanchist', etc.) in the GDR media.

See also: German Question

Further reading

Fuchshuber-Weiß, E. (1994) 'Namenkunde und Geschichtsunterricht: Deutschland zwischen 1800 und 1990. Ein Land wechselt Verfassungen und Namen', *Germanistische Linguistik: Reader zur Namenkunde IV,* 121–3: 259–75.

Glück, H. and Sauer, W.W. (1990) *Gegenwartsdeutsch,* Stuttgart: Metzler (particularly pages 7–22).

Latsch, J. (1994) *Die Bezeichnungen für Deutschland, seine Teile und die Deutschen. Eine lexikalische Analyse deutschlandpolitischer Leitartikel in bundesdeutschen Tageszeitungen 1950–91,* Frankurt am Main: Peter Lang.

GLYN HATHERALL

Geschonneck, Erwin

b. 27 December 1906, Bartenstein (Bartoszyce, Poland)

Actor

Raised in a working class enviroment in Berlin, Geschonneck joined the Communist Party in 1929. After surviving several Nazi concentration camps he joined Ida Ehre's Hamburg Kammerspiele (1945) and the **Berliner Ensemble** (1949). A star by the time he left the Ensemble in 1955, he continued to work mainly in film and television. His self-confident portrayal of proletarian characters and his insistence on the importance of the collective for the creative process made him a model socialist–realist actor. A committed communist throughout his life he joined the **PDS** after unification.

HORST CLAUS

Gielen, Michael

b. 20 July 1927, Dresden

Conductor

During his often controversial tenure at the Frankfurt opera (1977–87) Gielen ceaselessly renewed the repertory by engaging the most innovative producers, such as Ruth **Berghaus** and Willi Dekker. The exploratory, spectacular style of the Gielen era became a benchmark by which other theatrically aware opera companies have been judged. He also successfully collaborated with many leading composers, giving, for example, the premiere of B.A. **Zimmermann**'s hugely complex opera *Die Soldaten* at the Cologne Opera in 1965. Gielen now directs the Südwestrundfunk Orchestra Baden-Baden, maintaining Hans **Rosbaud**'s pioneering tradition.

BEATRICE HARPER

Gille, Sighard

b. 25 February 1941, Eilenburg (Saxony)

Painter and graphic artist

Gille studied painting in the master class of Bernhard **Heisig**. His portraits, figurative arrangements and landscapes have been influenced by the visual language of Otto Dix, Max Beckmann and Oskar Kokoschka. With imagery ranging from television viewers to the provocatice diptychon of *Gerüstarbeiter – Brigadefeier* (Scaffolding Worker – Team Celebrating) they are critical reflections on social reality. Gille sensuously celebrates in his paintings individual and collective desires and hopes with expressive gestures of colour and form.

See also: painting

KERSTIN MEY

Gisel, Ernst

b. 8 June 1922, Adliswil (near Zürich)

Architect

Apprentice draughtsman at Vogelsanger and

mason in Zürich 1938–40, Gisel went on to study interior design at Kunstgewerbeschule (Craft School) and ETH (Technical University) Zürich (1940–2). He worked for Alfred Roth (1942–4) before establishing his own practice in Zürich in 1945. He was Visiting Professor at the ETH Zürich 1968–9, and Guest Professor at the TU (Technical University) Karlsruhe 1969–71.

Gisel's large and varied œuvre prove him to be one of Switzerland's most versatile and adaptable architects. His designs are always functional, often displaying unusual compositions, originality of detail and a tremendous mastery of materials.

MARTIN KUDLEK

GmbH

Limited liability companies (the German term in full is *Gesellschaft mit beschränkter Haftung*) were first given their legal basis in Germany in 1892, and this institutional form spread throughout the world. Liability is limited to the assets of the business, which by law must have a minimum paid-up capital of DM 50,000. The managing director is chosen by the shareholders' meeting, but often directors are main shareholders. The limited company is Germany's favoured legal form for companies, and there are more than 250,000 GmbH. Supervisory boards may be created, and companies having more than 2,000 employees must have equality between shareholders' and employees' representatives.

CHRISTOPHER H. FLOCKTON

gmp

The architectural partnership gmp (von Gerkan, Marg und Partner) was established by Meinhard von Gerkan and Volkwin Marg in 1965 with offices in Hamburg, Berlin, Aachen, Leipzig and Brunswick.

Von Gerkan, Marg und Partner became known with their prize-winning design for Tegel Airport in Berlin (1965–74). Sound construction and a great ability to organize space distinguishes their build-

ings. Their œuvre is large and varied, reaching from modernizations and domestic buildings to large industrial schemes. The exhibition halls in Leipzig (1992–6) and the Lehrter railway station project in Berlin (1993-) represent two of their most prestigious works.

MARTIN KUDLEK

Goes, Albrecht

b. 22 March 1908, Langenbeutingen (Württemberg)

Writer

The contribution of Albrecht Goes to German literary life rests in his belief in the power of human compassion and creativity over evil. He served as a curate in Baden-Württemberg until 1953, and as a preacher in Stuttgart until 1973. His most famous work, *Unruhige Nacht* (Restless Night) (1949), is based on war-time experiences in the Ukraine. It recounts the night in which the padre prepares a deserter to meet the firing squad at dawn. Goes is renowned for his essays, especially on Mozart and Mörike, and a poetic output which spans over sixty years.

Further reading

Wirth, G. and Pleßke H.-M. (1989) *Albrecht Goes: Der Dichter und sein Werk*, Berlin: Union Verlag (critical appreciation of his life and works).

CHRISTOPHER YOUNG

Goethe-Institut

The 'Goethe Institute for the Cultivation of the German Language Abroad and the Promotion of International Cultural Co-operation Inc.' is a worldwide institution, with more than 150 branches in over seventy countries. Founded in 1951 as an independent, non-profit-making organization, with its head office in Munich, since 1976 it has become more closely associated with the Foreign Ministry, its task defined as the execution of comprehensive foreign culture policies, especially through the transmission of information about the FRG. In this, it is associated with the *Vereinigung internationaler Zusammenarbeit* (VIZ) (Association for International Co-operation), together with other institutions such as **Inter Nationes**, the **DAAD**, and the **Humboldt Foundation**. Most of its funding comes from the Foreign Ministry and its fortunes are related to the foreign culture policies of different administrations. Under Willy Brandt, 'culture' flourished as the third column of foreign policy but, in times of economic retrenchment, reduced funding has led to the closure of Goethe Institute branches.

In their host countries, branches liaise in particular with universities and schools, providing essential information and material for teachers of German. Libraries provide information about all aspects of German life, and specialized language courses lead to internationally recognized qualifications. In addition to language teaching, the promotion of culture and the arts has gained in importance with a broad definition of culture as everyday life, including German **science**, technology and socio-political debate.

In 1989 the Foreign Ministry made funds available to western European branches designed to stem a perceived decline in the popularity of German and to revive interest in Germany, and this initiative has had a considerable effect. It was part of a European integration programme designed to support European languages other than English. Adult education, too, has gained new prominence with particular emphasis on 'Business German'. In co-operation with the *Deutsche Industrie- und Handelstag* (DIHT) (German Industrial and Trade Association), special examinations for Business German have been introduced. There are sixteen institutes within Germany, primarily charged with teaching German as a foreign language and with the training of staff. With the end of the Cold War the home branches have gained in prominence as language centres for East European immigrants. At the same time new opportunities arose abroad, leading to a redistribution of funds and expansion into central and eastern Europe, especially Russia, Poland, Hungary and the Czech Republic, where there are some eleven million German speakers. In Hungary and elsewhere in eastern Europe, former teachers

of Russian are being retrained to teach German, reflecting a change in economic and cultural orientation. The Goethe Institute is chaired by Hilmar Hoffmann, former *Kulturdezernent* (Head of Cultural Affairs) of Frankfurt am Main, who was elected to the post of president in 1993.

The Herder-Institute in the former GDR played a similar role, though more restricted to language teaching; it continues as part of Leipzig University.

Further reading

Sturm, D. (1989) 'Goethe Institutes promote the German language abroad', *Bildung und Wissenschaft* 9, 10: 31ff.

HANS J. HAHN

Goldmann Verlag

Founded in Leipzig in 1922 by Wilhelm Goldmann (1897–1974), the firm was re-established in Munich in 1950. By the mid-1970s Goldmann had grown to be one of the largest German producers of popular, inexpensive mystery, science fiction and world literature paperbacks. The firm features series of non-fiction in law, education, psychology and economics. It also publishes editions of classical writers in 'thin-paper' editions. The **Bertelsmann** group acquired Goldmann in 1977 and until 1986 production at Goldmann was limited to paperback. Since then, however, Goldmann has reappeared in the hard-cover market in *belles lettres* and non-fiction.

JOHN B. RUTLEDGE

Gollwitzer, Helmut

b. 29 November 1908, Pappenheim; d. 17 October 1993, (West) Berlin

Theologian

Heavily influenced by Karl **Barth**'s theology and socialist political praxis, Gollwitzer similarly combined his theological insights with political concerns. He was involved in the resistance to the Nazi regime and, in the post-war years, in the fight against German rearmament and the repression of minorities, such as the student rebels of 1968. This theological–political nexus, which drew him to the left of the political spectrum, led him to support Gustav Heinemann's Gesamtdeutsche Volkspartei, and to oppose NATO and the Vietnam War.

MARK LINDSAY

Gombrich, Ernst

b. Vienna, 30 March 1909

Art historian

Gombrich studied in Vienna under Julius von Schlosser and Emanuel Loewy. He was recommended by Ernst Kris in 1936 to assist Gertrud Bing in the archives of the Kunstwissenschaft Bibliothek Warburg which moved from Hamburg to London in 1934. Gombrich served as Director of the Warburg Institute and as Professor of the Classical Tradition at the University of London between 1959 and 1976. His contribution to the art historical discipline is immense, his most famous publications being *The Story of Art* (1950), translated into thirteen languages, and *Art and Illusion* (1960), which engaged with the relationship between science and the humanities.

SHULAMITH BEHR

Gomringer, Eugen

b. 20 January 1925, Cachuela Esperanza (Bolivia)

Writer and art critic

The founder of *konkrete poesie* (concrete poetry) in Germany, Gomringer's 1953 *konstellationen* presented individual words with no apparent context in different spatial arrangements, thus enhancing the words' rhythmic and visual significance. This new linguistic artform inspired experimental writers such as Helmut **Heißenbüttel**, Max **Bense** and Franz Mon. Members of the **Wiener Gruppe**) published their first texts in *Spirale*, co-founded by Gomringer. Though his literary output remained small, the Swiss writer continued to

synthesize theoretical aspects of language, art and music in his teaching. He was an endowed Professor of Aesthetic Theory at the University of Düsseldorf; his chair later went to Oswald **Wiener**.

ANKE FINGER

Graevenitz, Gerhard von

b. 19 September 1934, Schilde (Brandenburg); d. 20 August 1983, Traubachtel in Hapkern (Interlaken, Switzerland)

Artist

Graevenitz was a leading exponent of kinetic art who established a German wing of the international 'Nouvelle Tendance' movement in 1962. This aimed to challenge artistic tradition, demystify the creative process, and promote greater viewer participation. Graevenitz's first works were white reliefs which altered optically when the viewer moved. His main body of work features objects whose controlled yet unpredictable movement explores kinetic and light effects. Graevenitz was particularly influential in The Netherlands, where he lived from 1970.

ALEX COOKE

Graf, Dominik

b. 6 September 1952, Munich

Filmmaker

Graf is an important figure in German cinema, as he was one of the first of a new generation of directors to turn their back on **New German Cinema** in favour of making popular genre films in the early 1980s. Graf has worked in a number of genres, receiving most attention for his action thrillers such as *Die Katze* (The Cat) (1987), which starred Götz **George**, and *Die Sieger* (The Winners) (1994), and for his contributions to the television series *Tatort* and *Der Fahnder*.

JONATHAN LEGG

Graf, Steffi

b. 14 June 1969, Brühl

Tennis player

Athleticism, a powerful forehand and serve allied to a fierce competiveness have made Steffi Graf into Germany's outstanding women's tennis player and one of the most successful women tennis players of all time. By late 1996, she had won twenty-one Grand Slam titles, including the Wimbledon singles title on seven occasions, and her career prize money totalled over £12.5 million. Her career has been troubled by frequent injury and family problems, including the jailing in August 1995 of her father on a charge of tax evasion on a part of her tennis income.

MIKE DENNIS

Grass, Günter

b. 16 October 1927, Danzig (now Gdańsk, Poland)

Writer

Grass achieved immediate fame when he was awarded the prize of the **Gruppe 47** in 1958 for his unfinished novel *The Tin Drum* (*Die Blechtrommel*), the publication of which a year later confirmed his prodigious talent. Since then he has remained a seminal figure in German literature with a world-wide reputation. He is also an accomplished graphic artist – he studied graphic art and sculpture in Düsseldorf from 1953 to 1956 – who invariably provides striking illustrations for the covers of his literary works. Since the 1960s he has subscribed to the ideal of the politically committed intellectual, something which has made him a significant and frequently controversial figure in German public life.

The Tin Drum was the first part of a trilogy which chronicles life in what between 1919 and 1939 was the Free City of Danzig (today's Gdańsk) under the control of the League of Nations and then under German control until 1945. It shows how, separated from their fellow-countrymen, many of its German citizens, in particular the lower middle-class, succumbed to National Socialism. The world

described is what Grass, the son of a grocer, experienced himself as a boy. As a member of a German-Polish family he was also aware of the tensions in the city between the two nationalities. However, the impact of Grass' early works was due not merely to their socio-political themes. They reveal an author of unparalleled literary imagination and a stylist capable of powerful and original imagery. Moreover, the treatment of the themes of sex and religion was such as to provoke accusations of blasphemy and pornography in the Germany of Konrad **Adenauer**.

It was with such a reputation among certain sections of society that Grass began to involve himself in politics. From the 1965 election onwards he was a vociferous, if initially not always welcomed, supporter of the **SPD**. His political commitment was based on the belief that writers should abandon ivory towers and play an active role as citizens. Like his fictional works, his views were based on personal experience. As a youth he had fallen prey to Nazi ideology and seen how it had led to mass destruction, including the loss of his home town and the expulsion of its German population. He saw in the pragmatic ideals of social democracy and in the figure of Willy **Brandt** models for a democratic society that avoided all extremes of right and left. These views were encapsulated in the 1972 work *From the Diary of a Snail* (*Aus dem Tagebuch einer Schnecke*), where the metaphor of the snail stands as the symbol of slow yet steady social progress.

From the mid-1960s political themes became more directly prevalent in Grass' literary works, which, in the eyes of some critics, now lacked the freshness of his earlier ones. Certainly his poetry and dramatic works which in the 1950s had owed much to the literature of the absurd turned to political themes. The 1966 drama *The Plebeians Rehearse the Uprising* (*Die Plebejer proben den Aufstand*) deals with the reaction of a theatre director in East Berlin – although not named, **Brecht** is clearly meant – to the 1953 workers uprising. Brecht's public lack of support is seen as part of a negative tradition, described in the words of the play's subtitle, as 'A German Tragedy'. This play, along with his reaction to the Berlin Wall, made Grass extremely unpopular in official GDR circles. Equally his anti-radical stance led to Rudi

Dutschke characterizing him as the students' main enemy.

The 1977 novel *The Flounder* (*Der Butt*) brought a return to the style of the early works. Skilfully woven around the Grimms' story of the fisherman and his wife, it has as its theme the role of women and food (Grass is a keen cook) in history from primitive society to the present. The general tone of the novel is, however, less optimistic; indeed in the 1980s, in the light of looming environmental crisis and the perceived increased threat of nuclear war, he took back the metaphor of the snail saying that it was moving too fast for the good of humanity. Most recently he has been a highly sceptical observer of the process of German unification.

Although he had always sought to maintain German cultural unity, Grass warned against German unification in a series of speeches after the events of 1989. He feared that unification would bring a return to German arrogance and the desire to dominate. The 1991 novel *The Call of the Toad* (*Unkenrufe*) envisages a growing negative German influence in the Polish territories that, like his native city, were once German. It was, however, the 1995 novel *Ein weites Feld* (Too Far a Field) that attracted massive critical attention because of its presentation of the unification process as a western takeover of the GDR and its warnings against potential German expansionism. By making the main protagonist Theo Wuttke an expert on the nineteenth-century novelist Theodor Fontane, Grass suggests parallels between post-1871 and post-1990 Germany. Not only did this political dimension meet with widespread disapproval, in aesthetic terms the novel was also exaggeratedly dismissed as 'unreadable'. Despite such condemnations, it immediately achieved bestseller status. Both reactions only underline Grass' unique role within contemporary German literary and political life.

See also: intellectuals; prose fiction: FRG

Major works

Grass G. (1965) *The Tin Drum*, Harmondsworth: Penguin.

—— (1966) *Cat and Mouse*, Harmondsworth: Penguin.

—— (1969) *Dog Years*, Harmondsworth: Penguin.

—— (1989) *The Flounder*, London: Picador.

—— (1994) *Werke*, Studienausgabe, 12 vols, Göttingen: Steidl.

—— (1995) *Ein weites Feld*, Göttingen: Steidl.

Further reading

Hollington M. (1980) *Günter Grass. The Writer in a Pluralist Society*, London: Marion Boyars (a good survey of Grass's prose, poetic and dramatic work as well as a consideration of his political role).

Keele A.F. (1988) *Understanding Günter Grass*, Columbia, SC: University of South Carolina Press (concentrates on prose works).

Neuhaus V. (1993) *Günter Grass*, Stuttgart: Metzler (good introduction to Grass with very useful bibliographical material).

STUART PARKES

Grazer Gruppe

This loose network of Austrian authors in the Styrian capital of Graz gathered around the journal *manuskripte* and its editor, Alfred Kolleritsch, during the 1960s. Its members included writers as well known as Peter **Handke**, and their work was marked by an aesthetic revolt against what was perceived to be the hegemony of conservative taste in Austria. Sometimes displaying a specifically postmodernist stance, with a cultivation of playfulness and fantasy, the writings of the Grazer Gruppe lacked the linguistic radicalism of the Vienna Group (Oswald **Wiener**) or the neo-Marxist politics of the **student movement**.

See also: Wiener Gruppe

RUSSELL A. BERMAN

Greens

Officially the German Green Party (Die Grünen) was founded in January 1980 in Karlsruhe. Based on the **FRG protest movements** which emerged in the 1970s the Greens centred their main activities around the issues of environmental protection and disarmament. The demands of the women's movement played another pivotal role in the party's history. In the 1980s the Greens entered several *Land* parliaments, obtained seats in the Bundestag and in the European Parliament, and built for the first time a red–green government coalition in 1985 with the **SPD** in Hessen. On the basis of their success the German Greens also played a major role in the European Green Movement. In the first post-unification parliamentary elections in the winter of 1990, however, the Greens failed to regain seats in the Bundestag, whereas the united East German citizens' movement obtained eight parliamentary seats. In 1993 the Greens and part of the citizens' movements of the GDR (**Bündnis 90**) merged into one party, Bündnis 90/Die Grünen. As an all-German party they returned to the Bundestag after the 1994 elections and after the 1998 federal elections became the junior partners in the first-ever 'red–green' coalition government at national level.

The period of foundation

The official foundation of the Green Party had been preceded by various local and regional events. The first 'Green List' of local election candidates had already evolved in 1977 as an amalgamation of different local citizens' initiatives (see also **citizens' initiatives: FRG**; **GDR**); the *Grüne Liste Umweltschutz* (GLU) (Green List for Environmental Protection) in Lower Saxony, for example, experienced a number of electoral successes at the local level in 1977 and obtained 3.9 percent of the votes in the 1978 *Landtag* elections. For the European Parliament elections in 1979 different local and regional Green Lists and organizations founded the Sonstige Politische Vereinigung DIE GRÜNEN (SPV). This association immediately received 3.2 percent (893,683) of the votes. With this positive response the groundwork was laid for the final foundation of a fully fledged federal Green Party in 1980.

One of the main controversies in the initial phase of the Greens concerned the relationship between *Ökosozialisten* (ecological socialists) and *Wertkonservativen* (value conservatives). The value conservatives feared that cadres from communist organizations might take over the Greens for their own purposes. In the end many value conservatives left the party. Later on the relationship between grassroots movements and the party itself evolved into one of the main controversies in the party. Many supporters of the green movement feared that party structures and participation in elections would lead to a disregard of grassroots work. Therefore many party members emphasized that non-parliamentary work should be – borrowing an image from soccer – the 'support leg' (*Standbein*) and the parliamentary work the 'striking leg' (*Spielbein*) of the party. This conflict, however, continued to exist and was one of the main issues between '*Fundis*' ('fundamentalist' party members) and '*Realos*' ('realist' party members) during the 1980s.

Organizational structure

The Green Party has about 50,000 members. They are organized in *Landesverbände* (*Land* Associations), *Kreisverbände* (Regional Associations), *Stadtteilgruppen* (Ward Associations) and *Bundesarbeitsgemeinschaften* (BAG) (specialist working groups at the national level). The *Bundesdelegiertenkonferenz* (BDK) (Conference of Delegates) is the highest tier of the party. It decides the political guidelines, the programme and coalition issues at the national level. In addition to this it elects the *Bundesvorstand* (Federal Executive) with two chairpeople as its head. The Executive is responsible for the political administration of the party. According to the decentralized principles of the Party Statute the *Land* Associations decide their political profile and coalition issues independently. This leads in practice to a great variety of political profiles in the different *Länder*. The *Länderrat* (Council of *Land* Delegates) represents and co-ordinates the interest of the *Land* Associations. Representatives of the *Bundesvorstand*, the *Bundestag* representatives and the *Bundesarbeitsgemeinschaften* participate in the *Länderrat*. All party offices and the lists for parliamentary elections are based on a strict quota (one woman, one man, and so on). The rotation system (a two-year limit on the holding of all offices), however, which was one of the main organizational principles, and a serious bone of contention in the beginning of the Green Party, has since been abandoned.

Political programme

The party's four principles sum up its political programme as ecological, grassroots democratic, social and non-violent. Initially the party concentrated on environmental and peace issues such as air and water pollution, acid rain, the death of the forest (**Waldsterben**), and the end of the arms race. For this reason the Greens were attacked by the established parties as a single-issue party with no interest in the economy and social welfare. In the course of the 1980s, however, experts in the party and its parliamentary groups developed a programme which covered all important societal issues in the FRG. The design of an ecological reform programme (*ökologisches Umbauprogramm*) underlined in this context the competence of the party not only in ecology but also in the economy. One of the programme deficits of the Greens was their failure to confront the issue of German unification: in general their attitude was hostile to what was perceived as the re-establishment of a German superstate, though some groups within the party had long seen the overcoming of the division of Germany as a key element in the 'healing' of Cold War Europe. The Greens' deliberate downplaying of this issue was one of the reasons why the party failed to react appropriately to the events of 1989–90 in the run-up to the first all-German elections.

Parliamentary groups

By the end of 1998 the Green Party was represented in the Bundestag (47 members), the European Parliament (12 members), the *Land* Parliaments of Baden-Württemberg, Bavaria, Berlin, Bremen, Hamburg, Hessen, Lower Saxony, North Rhine-Westphalia, Rhineland-Palatinate, Saarland, Saxony-Anhalt, and in the councils of hundreds of cities and smaller communities. Besides these they are in four red–green *Land* governments: Hessen, North Rhine-Westphalia Schleswig-Holstein and Hamburg). Contrary to the declared intention that parliamentary work should only be the 'striking leg' of party policy, in fact it dominates most public activities and utilizes the majority of the party's personnel resources.

Leadership

Although officially the Greens are anti-leadership-orientated, certain green politicians can be credited with forming the initial image of the party and became its unofficial public representatives. One of the most famous figures was Petra **Kelly**, who was a founding member of the party. She died in 1992 in tragic circumstances. Other well known politicians of the Green Party are Daniel **Cohn-Bendit**, Joschka **Fischer** and Antje Vollmer. Otto Schily, for years one of the most prominent figures of the Greens in the Bundestag, left the party in 1989 and joined the SPD. Jutta Ditfurth, a member of the 'fundamentalist' wing, left the party in 1991.

See also: environmentalism; parties: FRG; Schröder, Gerhard

Further reading

Frankland, E.G. and Schoonmaker, D. (1992) *Between Protest and Power: The Green Party in Germany*, Boulder, CO and Oxford: Westview Press (best general introduction in English).

Kolinsky, E. (ed.) *The Greens in West Germany: Organisation and Policy Making*, Oxford and Providence, RI: Berg (contains chapters on the Greens' position in the party system, and on policies and party organization).

Raschke, J. (1993) *Die Grünen: Was sie wurden, was sie sind*, Cologne: Bund-Verlag (lengthy and comprehensive analysis of the history and development of the Green Party and its different *Land* associations).

LOTHAR PROBST

Gregor-Dellin, Martin

b. 3 June 1926, Naumburg

Writer and editor

After work as an editor in publishing in Halle, Gregor-Dellin left the GDR in 1958. He was the West German **PEN** President from 1982 to 1988. He wrote an extensive biography of Richard Wagner and edited and annotated Cosima Wagner's diaries (see *Richard Wagner: Sein Leben, sein Werk,* *sein Jahrhundert*, 1980; and *Cosima Wagner: Tagebücher*, 1977); he has also edited the works of Bruno Frank and Klaus Mann. He wrote several novels and **radio** plays as well as essays on Franz Kafka and on writers and religion. He lives in Munich.

JAMES KELLER

GRIPS-Theater

GRIPS-Theater is Germany's foremost theatre company for children and young people. It is an offspring of the Reichskabarett, a political cabaret which functioned as mouthpiece of the 1968 **student movement** in West Berlin. Spicing its work with infectious music and witty lyrics, GRIPS – the word refers to a person's ability to think independently – addresses topical issues and aims to raise social awareness amongst people of all ages. The company's biggest successes include *Eine linke Geschichte* (A Tale of the Left) and *Line 1* (**Linie 1**), both written for older audiences by its manager and principal author Volker Ludwig.

See also: drama: FRG; theatres

HORST CLAUS

Gropius, Walter

b. 18 May 1883, Berlin; d. 5 July 1969, Boston

Architect

Gropius studied at the TH (Technical University) Berlin and Munich, and worked for Peter Behrens from 1907 to 1910, setting up private practice in 1910. He founded *Das staatliche Bauhaus* in Weimar in 1919, of which he was director until 1928. He built the new Bauhaus building when it moved to Dessau in 1925. In private practice from 1928 to 1933, he was a founder member and first president of CIAM (Congrès Internationaux d'Architecture Moderne) in 1928. He emigrated to Britain in 1934 where he was in partnership with Maxwell Fry from 1934 to 1936. Moving to the United States in 1937, he founded the firm The Architects' Collaborative. He was a Professor at Harvard

University Graduate School of Design from 1937 to 1952.

Gropius and **Mies van der Rohe** are usually seen as the most important German representatives of classical modernism. After the war German architecture saw a major revival of the Bauhaus, especially in style. Of the few buildings Gropius built in post-war Germany the block of flats in the Hansaviertel, for Berlin's Interbau exhibition of 1957, is the most famous.

See also: architecture

MARTIN KUDLEK

Grotewohl, Otto

b. 11 March 1894, Brunswick; d. 21 September 1964, (East) Berlin

GDR functionary

A leading member of the **SPD** in the 1920s, Grotewohl became chair of its Central Committee in Berlin in June 1945. He was instrumental in leading the SPD in the Soviet zone into a fusion with **KPD** in April 1946 to form the **SED**, despite having expressed his fear of communist coercion to a British representative in Berlin. In October 1949 he became the first Prime Minister of the GDR and in September 1960 a deputy chair of the Staatsrat (State Council).

See also: parties and mass organizations: GDR

PETER BARKER

Grün, Max von der

b. 25 May 1926, Bayreuth

Writer

Literature of the workplace has never made much impact in Germany, but with the establishment of the **Gruppe 61**, co-founded by Fritz Hüser and von der Grün, and coinciding with the publication of the latter's first works in the early 1960s, a significant new literary direction in Germany was ushered in. Von der Grün's aim was to draw the attention of the middle-class literary establishment to working-class culture. He used his own experiences as a miner to create a mixture of autobiography and fiction, which lends veracity to his works and gives them a documentary flavour.

Von der Grün was born into a religious, working-class family. After a commercial apprenticeship, he served in WWII, was a PoW in the US, and then became a miner for thirteen years in the Ruhr. In 1964 he was able to become a full-time writer and has published novels, short stories, essays and radio plays, and seen the filming of some of his works. He has also been translated into numerous languages.

His first novel evoked little response, but *Irrlicht und Feuer* (Will-'o'-the-Wisp and Fire) caused an immediate sensation and resulted in his being taken to court. He was accused of defaming his mining company, was acquitted, but none the less dismissed. The repercussions were widespread and the affair was seen as an example of industry, with its financial resources, trying to stifle the legitimate concerns of the ordinary worker. The situation paralleled the growing political and social unrest of 1960s Germany.

Von der Grün writes not only about the industrial Ruhr, but is a social critic with a sharp eye. His works reveal concern both with the individual in a materialistic society and with the worker's situation of total dependence in a mechanized, industrial world becoming increasingly automated, with resultant unemployment. Von der Grün questions this basic situation and explores the wider ramifications this has on family relationships and social issues.

Von der Grün has never been frightened of touching on sensitive matters, which has earned him attacks by friends and enemies. His reputation as an uncomfortable writer was reinforced in *Stellenweise Glatteis* (Icy Patches), which is based on authentic material. In it he examines the interrelationship of politics and economic self-interest and especially the highly questionable roles played by the unions, who were embarrassed by his book.

His importance lies not only in having provided graphic insights into working conditions, but also in his incorruptible eye as a social critic of modern Germany. He writes uncompromisingly in a simple and direct language about people he knows. He is concerned about the emotional impoverishment of the individual who is forced to conform in order to survive and whose dignity is threatened. Von der Grün clearly demonstrates an unflinching moral commitment.

Further reading

Reinhardt, S. (ed.) (1990) *Max von der Grün*, Frankfurt am Main: Luchterhand (a useful collection of short essays and biographical details).

Schonauer, F. (1978) *Max von der Grün*, Munich: Beck (a good introduction to the man and his works).

PETER PROCHNIK

Gründgens, Gustav

b. 21 December 1899, Hamburg; d. 7 October 1963, Manila

Actor and **Intendant**

An important and controversial figure in German theatre, Gründgens was director of the Berlin State Theatre under the Nazis from 1934 to 1945 and continued his career in post-war West Germany. As an actor he is remembered for his portrayal of Mephisto in Goethe's *Faust*. *Mephisto* was also the title Klaus **Mann** gave to his 1936 portrayal of an opportunistic actor. Banned in West Germany from 1966 to 1980 this novel was the basis for an Oscar-winning film directed by István Szabó.

Further reading

Goertz, H. (1982) *Gustav Gründgens*, Reinbek bei Hamburg: Rowohlt (volume in the 'ro-ro-ro' monograph series with textual and photographic material).

STUART PARKES

Grüner Punkt

This circular emblem on the packaging of goods produced for the German market signifies that a licence fee has been paid to the Duales System

Deutschland GmbH (DSD) which is thereby committed to collecting and disposing of the packaging waste outside the public system of waste disposal. DSD was established in reaction to a 1991 government decree which sought to reduce the use of product packaging and promote **recycling**. The emblem's implicit suggestion of environmental compatibility obscures the fact that satisfactory recycling facilities and markets for recycling products are not readily available. Hence its use has been heavily criticized by environmentalists.

INGOLFUR BLÜHDORN

Grützke, Johannes

b. 30 September 1937, Berlin

Artist

An artist whose work encompasses music, poetry, sculpture and set design, Grützke is best known for socially critical figural paintings. During his art school training in Berlin he rejected the prevailing influence of American and French abstract art by adopting a style of uncompromising realism. His dramatically composed, confrontational works dissect social convention and human psychology yet are not intentionally didactic. His influences range from renaissance and mannerist art through to the realism of Max Beckmann. In 1991 he completed a controversial 33 metre mural for the Paulskirche in Frankfurt am Main.

ALEX COOKE

Gruftis

Also known as Gothics or Goths, *Gruftis* (from 'Gruft', meaning 'tomb' or 'crypt') first appeared in German clubs in the early 1980s as a subgroup of the **punks**. Their unisex look – teased black hair, white make-up with black eyeliner and dark lipstick, and baggy black clothes – was inspired by British New Wave music icon Robert Smith, lead singer of The Cure. German *Grufti* bands include X-mal Deutschland, Deine Lakaien and Project Pitchfork. Members of this subculture often appropriate occult and mystic images. The word

has a second, unrelated meaning as a derogatory or self-ironic reference to people over the age of forty.

SABINE SCHMIDT

Gruner & Jahr

G&J, one of the largest European publishing conglomerates, publish more than seventy-two magazines and ten newspapers. Partly owned by **Bertelsmann**, G&J has mass media ventures in nine countries. They publish Germany's influential news magazines *Stern*, and *Capital*. G&J are also active in the United Kingdom (with *Best*, *Focus*, *Prisma* and *Here!*) and the United States. They are active in the women's magazine market in Germany (with *Brigitte* and *Frau im Spiegel*), the United Kingdom, the United States (with *McCall's* and *Family Circle*), France and Spain. Their newspapers include the *Berliner Kurier*, the *Berliner Zeitung* and the *Hamburger Morgenpost*.

JOHN B. RUTLEDGE

Gruppe 47

This group of writers had a major influence on the development of West German literature in the post-war period. It provided a focus for literary life at a critical time in a country lacking a cultural capital. At the time it was seen by its detractors as a symbol of left-wing dominance of cultural life, whereas recent critics have accused it of ignoring such vital topics as the Holocaust.

Despite its undoubted influence, it is difficult to pin down the essence of the group. It originated following the prohibition of the journal *Der Ruf* by the American authorities. One of the co-editors, Hans Werner **Richter**, invited a number of authors to meet together in September 1947 to read and discuss their texts. Following a further meeting two months later the group met biannually, and from the mid-1950s normally annually. Writers read their texts from what was known as the 'electric chair' and were then subject to spontaneous criticism. Over the years Walter **Höllerer**, Walter **Jens**, Joachim Kaiser, Hans

Mayer and Marcel **Reich-Ranicki** established themselves as the major critics.

One problem when discussing the Gruppe 47 is the lack of a clear membership. Richter, whose experience under Nazism led him to dislike all forms of organization, merely invited certain people to attend. There were many regulars but others were only present on one or two occasions. It is equally difficult to talk of a single group style of literature. If early meetings were dominated by texts associated with *Kahlschlag*, these were soon superseded by modernist writing influenced by Kafka. More consistent was the political line taken by writers associated with the group. Most authors were anti-fascist, non-ideological left-wingers. They protested against government actions during the **Spiegel Affair** and against the Vietnam War.

The influence of the Gruppe 47 had undoubtedly something to do with Richter's talent for publicity and his close links with leading publishers. The literary careers of Martin **Walser** and Günter **Grass** were launched by their being awarded the Gruppe 47 prize in 1955 and 1958 respectively. By the 1960s meetings were a media event, not least the excursion to Princeton University in 1966, which was justified by the hostility shown there to the Vietnam War. A year later at the meeting at the Pulvermühle in Franconia, group members were subjected to student demonstrations which accused them of a lack of social relevance. This was the last regular meeting of the group, with plans to meet in Czechoslovakia being thwarted by the Soviet-led invasion of 1968. The social and cultural upheavals associated with the student movement had led to a change of atmosphere that was less congenial to the established forms of the group. The necessary degree of consensus had disappeared.

Further reading

Arnold, H.L. (ed.) (1987), *Die Gruppe 47*, Munich: edition text + kritik (comprehensive survey of the group dealing with literary and political questions).

Mandel, S. (1973) *The Reflected Intellect*, Carbondale and Edwardsville, IL: South Illinois University Press (general survey of the group's activity and its literature together with list of authors and meetings).

STUART PARKES

Gruppe 61

Established in 1961 under the joint guidance of Fritz Hüser, Director of the Dortmund Library, and the novelist Max von der **Grün**, the literary movement Gruppe 61 was short-lived, but quickly became synonymous with 'workers' literature'. The group marked a new direction, but remained viewed with suspicion by Germany's cultural establishment. Works were written lacking formal, aesthetic elements, and reportages by the controversial Günter **Wallraff** became important features. Eventually the initial, emancipatory aim of workers' literature, which had been to break the social limitations imposed on the worker, was expanded to embrace literature about the workplace itself with an unambiguous socio-political message. Ideological differences, however, led to the group's early demise.

Further reading

Kühne, P. (1972) *Arbeiterklasse und Literatur*, Frankfurt am Main: Fischer (an indispensable survey).

PETER PROCHNIK

Gsovsky, Tatjana

b. 18 March 1901, Moscow; d. 29 September 1993, Berlin

Choreographer

Gsovsky spent much of her active life in **ballet** in Berlin, where she directed at the Städtische Oper and the Deutsche Oper for many years until 1966, continuing on retirement to direct the ballet school of the Deutsche Oper, of which she was created an honorary member in 1971. Her major creations include *Les Noces* (Stravinsky), *Labyrinth der Liebe* (Varèse) and **Blacher**'s *Tristan*, all in Berlin between 1961 and 1965.

DEREK McCULLOCH

Gstrein, Norbert

b. 3 June 1961, Mils (Austria)

Writer

Gstrein studied mathematics in Innsbruck, Stanford and Erlangen. His prose-writings (*Einer*, 1988; *Anderntags*, 1989; *Das Register*, 1992; *O₂*, 1993; *Der Kommerzialrat*, 1995), characterized by stylistic competence and formal skill, deal with loners deformed by their environment. By using a modified manner of the *Heimatroman* Gstrein depicts characters unable to find their identity in their native places.

ERNST GRABOVSZKI

Günther, Egon

b. 30 March 1927, Schneeberg (Saxony)

Filmmaker and writer

Of working-class background, Günther studied philosophy, German and education at Leipzig University, subsequently working as teacher, publishers' reader, writer and **Dramaturg** before turning to directing. On the surface the majority of his films are adaptations of literary works, but their main function is to address topical issues which, for political reasons, could not be examined in the context of a contemporary setting. Frustrated by the impossibility of dealing with the defects of socialist society Günther moved to West Germany at the end of the 1970s.

See also: Eleventh Plenum; film: GDR

HORST CLAUS

Gysi, Gregor

b. 16 January 1948, Berlin

Lawyer and politician

Son of GDR minister Klaus Gysi, Gregor trained as a lawyer and conducted a practice from 1971 which specialized in defending prominent dissidents, such as Robert **Havemann**, Rudolf **Bahro** and Bärbel **Bohley**. In the autumn of 1989 he led the renewal process of the **SED** and its transformation into the **PDS** (Party of Democratic Socialism). He was the leader of the PDS group in the Bundestag from December 1990 to October 2000 and was national party leader from January 1991 to January 1993. Since 1992 there have been allegations of involvement with the **Stasi**, which he has strenuously denied.

PETER BARKER

H

Haacke, Hans

b. 12 August 1936, Cologne

Sculptor and conceptual artist

Haacke's effective aesthetic interventions based on the incorporation of factual documentation into the realm of art have contributed to the establishment of an art that articulates moral and political responsibility. Files, photographs, advertisments and banal objects are used for provocative references to and comments on industrial civilization and those in power. Critical assessment of Germany's past and present figures prominently in his work. Although he has lived in New York for many years he is internationally regarded as highly representative of contemporary German art.

See also: documenta; sculpture

KERSTIN MEY

Haas, Ernst

b. 2 March 1921, Vienna; d. 12 September 1986, New York

Photographer

An innovator in early colour photography, Haas was a member of the progressive post-war photojournalist group 'Magnum' in Paris and New York, and enjoyed a successful career working for magazines such as *Life* and *Paris Match*. He moved to New York in the early 1950s, and pioneered the expressive qualities of colour photography, using innovative abstract compositions and camera motion techniques. He saw photography as visual poetry and constantly sought to interpret reality in new ways. His subjects ranged from everyday scenes to exotic landscapes and nature studies.

ALEX COOKE

Habermas, Jürgen

b. 18 June 1929, Düsseldorf

Philosopher and sociologist

Habermas is the main second-generation representative of the **Critical Theory** of the **Frankfurt School**. He is also the most eminent and controversial figure in contemporary German **philosophy**, having contributed to most of its main debates. Habermas was Theodor W. **Adorno**'s assistant from 1955 to 1959, then taught at Heidelberg and Frankfurt am Main, before becoming co-director of the Max Planck Institute in Starnberg in 1971. In 1983 he returned to Frankfurt am Main, where he has been Professor Emeritus since 1994.

Critical theory seeks to explain the development of modern capitalist society and to indicate how it might be freed from domination and exploitation. Habermas transformed this project by providing it with, first, a non-positivist methodology for the social sciences inspired by hermeneutics, and, second, new normative foundations in the form of moral standards for the assessment of ideologies and social formations. Adorno had condemned the

Enlightenment tradition, because for him reason was inevitably reduced to 'instrumental reason', the efficient marshalling of means in the services of ends which are left unjustified. By contrast, Habermas defends the ideals of the enlightenment – 'the project of modernity' – by developing a rich conception of rationality that includes a non-instrumental, ethical dimension. He explains rationality no longer by reference to the solitary reflections of a Cartesian ego, but by reference to a process of intersubjective communication aimed at understanding and consensus.

Habermas' early work was devoted to a critique of positivism (including Karl **Popper**'s critical rationalism) inspired by Kant and Marx. *Knowledge and Human Interests* (*Erkenntnis und Interesse*, 1968) argues that all knowledge depends on 'quasi-transcendental' human interests rooted in our natural history. The natural sciences presuppose the 'technical' interest in the prediction and control of nature, the social sciences the 'practical' interest in understanding other human beings, and the 'critical sciences' (psychoanalysis and critical social theory) the 'emancipatory' interest in freedom to which the other two interests are subservient.

After 1970, under the influence of analytic philosophy, Habermas took a linguistic turn from this anthropological epistemology to a *Theory of Communicative Action* (*Theorie des kommunikativen Handelns*, 1981) which makes explicit the various capacities needed for human interaction. According to Habermas, this approach provides a basis for critical theory, since the universal preconditions of linguistic communication include normative commitments with ethical implications. When we communicate, we make validity claims (to truth, moral rightness and sincerity). In assessing such claims we 'counterfactually anticipate' an 'ideal speech situation' in which all participants seek a rational consensus, in other words, an agreement not on the basis of coercion or deceit, but only through free and equal debate.

The theory of communicative action involves a consensus theory of truth and moral rightness: a statement is true or a norm justified if it would be accepted by all in an ideal speech situation. It also provides a non-positivistic methodology of the social sciences. They cannot adopt the 'objectivizing' attitude of causal explanation, but must seek to understand human practices from the perspective of their participants, by focusing on the explanations they themselves would give for their actions. But Habermas insists against relativists like Ludwig **Wittgenstein** and Hans-Georg **Gadamer** that they can nevertheless criticize these practices on theoretical and ethical grounds. In order to contribute to a discourse with their opponents, relativists have to abide by those standards of argumentation which they claim to be unjustified and optional.

The theory of communicative action also underpins an evolutionary theory of social development influenced by Lawrence Kohlberg and Niklas **Luhmann**. The process of modernization is characterized by the conflict between the aspirations to rational agreement implicit in human interaction (the 'life-world') and the economic and organizational pressures generated by complex social systems.

In recent years, Habermas has concentrated on using this apparatus to develop a defence of enlightenment ideals against the irrational tendencies which unite conservatives and postmodernists. This reflects his abiding role as an effective critic of German politics and culture, which ranges from his involvement with the **student movement** in the 1960s through his defence of public liberties to his attack on the trivialization of the Holocaust in the so-called historians' dispute (***Historikerstreit***).

Further reading

Bernstein, R. (ed.) (1985) *Habermas and Modernity*, Cambridge, MA: MIT Press (illuminating introduction, critical essays and Habermas' response).

Geuss, R. (1981) *The Idea of Critical Theory*, Cambridge: Cambridge Univeristy Press (a probing critical study).

McCarthy, T. (1978) *The Critical Theory of Jürgen Habermas*, Cambridge: Polity Press (rightly regarded as the standard account of the early and middle period).

Thompson, J.B., and Held, D. (eds) (1982) *Habermas, Critical Debates*, London: Macmillan Press (Habermas responds to various commentators).

White, S. (1988) *The Recent Work of Jürgen Habermas*, Cambridge: Cambridge University Press (useful on the foundations of ethics and the most recent work).

HANS-JOHANN GLOCK

Hacks, Peter

b. 21 March 1928, Breslau (now Wrocław, Poland)

Writer

Hacks wrote historical dramas in the GDR exemplifying the tenets of contemporary Marxist–Leninism, and developed a style of historical comedy with similarities to **Brecht** and **Dürrenmatt**, for instance *Der Müller von Sanssouci* (The Miller of Sanssouci) (1957). Plays like *Die Sorgen und die Macht* (Power and its Problems) (1959–62) examined critically the difficulties of establishing a socialist society in the GDR. Hacks also engaged with the dramatic tradition, particularly Shakespeare, in a number of adaptations. Later he subsided into a bland affirmation of the achievements of the GDR.

See also: drama: GDR; socialist realism

Further reading

Trilse, C. (1980) *Das Werk des Peter Hacks*, East Berlin: Volk & Wissen (critical study of work).

ARRIGO SUBIOTTO

Härtling, Peter

b. 13 November 1933, Chemnitz

Writer and critic

A prolific novelist, author of children's books and autobiographical fiction, Härtling focuses in many of his works on the theme of the social outcast.

Härtling's father died in a Russian PoW camp in Austria in 1945 and his mother committed suicide in the following year. He finished his schooling in Nürtingen (Württemberg), trained as a journalist and worked his way up to become editor of the local paper. From 1956 to 1962 he was literary editor of the *Deutsche Zeitung* and from 1968–73 chief editor of the Fischer publishing house.

During the 1950s Härtling published several volumes of poetry. His poetry's playful style is belied by expressions of unease at aspects of West German society. In the early 1960s he embarked on the first of a number of works of semi-fiction, a combination of biography and fiction in which he explores the lives of artists and their troubled relationship with society. The romantic poet Lenau in *Niembsch oder Der Stillstand* (Niembsch or the Standstill) (1964) was followed by *Hölderlin* (1976), *Die Dreifache Maria* (The Three Marias) (1982), *Waiblingers Augen* (Waiblinger's Eyes) (1987), *Schubert* (1992), and the collection of texts *Der Wanderer* (The Wanderer) (1988). Härtling discussed the problem of literary creation and that of recreating the past in his 1984 *Frankfurter Vorlesungen* (Frankfurt Lectures), and *Der Spanische Soldat oder Finden und Erfinden* (The Spanish Soldier or Finding and Inventing). The 1969 novel *Das Familienfest* (The Family Party) is the kaleidoscopic history of a Nürtingen family from 1857–1967; in *Janek* (1969) Härtling seeks to recover the memories of his youth only to discover that the memories are themselves shaped by the person remembering them. In *Zwettl. Nachprüfung einer Erinnerung* (Zwettl. Checking a Memory) (1973) the theme is the impossibility of reconstructing anything from the past.

Parent–child relationships, and also the treatment by society of emotionally deprived children, possibly reflecting Härtling's own childhood experiences, are the subjects of a number of works. In *Hubert oder die Rückkehr nach Casablanca* (Hubert or the Return to Casablanca) (1978) a son finds escape from his tyrannical Nazi father in the world of the cinema. Härtling examines his own past in much greater detail in *Nachgetragene Liebe* (Belated Love) (1980) and in *Herzwand* (The Wall of the Heart) (1990) in which he examines his own adolescence and his relationship to his own children. His first children's novel, the bestseller *Das war der Hirbel* (That was Hirbel) (1973) portrays a deprived child's longing for warmth and protection. It was followed by *Ben loves Anna* (*Ben liebt Anna*, 1979), *Crutches* (*Krücke*, 1988), and many more.

Other themes in Härtling's work are environmental issues, as in *Das Windrad* (The Windwheel)

(1983), and women's emancipation, as in the novel *Woman* (*Eine Frau*, 1974).

Further reading

Huish, I. (1991) 'The Adult Writer in a Child's World: Some Reflections on Peter Härtling and the *Kinderroman*' in A. Williams, S. Parkes and R. Smith (eds) *German Literature at a Time of Change 1989–1990*, Bern: Peter Lang.

MARGARET VALLANCE

Haesler, Otto

b. 13 June 1880, Munich; d. 2 April 1962, Wilhelmshorst (near Potsdam)

Architect

Haesler worked as a mason for L. Bernoully in Frankfurt am Main and H. Billing in Karlsruhe, establishing his own building office in Celle in 1906. He joined the *Ring* group in 1926.

Haesler's most important work is that of the late 1920s which demonstrates his interest in industrialization. His varied œuvre includes domestic designs, schools, hospitals and large *Siedlungen* (housing estates), such as *Dammerstocksiedlung Karlsruhe* (1927–9), planned with Gropius.

After WWII he mainly concentrated on the reconstruction of the East German town of Rathenow.

MARTIN KUDLEK

Häusser, Robert

b. 8 November 1924, Stuttgart

Photographer

Highly-regarded internationally, Häusser began to work primarily with black and white photography in the early 1940s. His pictures contain sharply-defined motifs which are often shot in static, symmetrical frontality. His subjects – desolate landscapes, uncanny still-lifes and isolated figures – provoke existential questions on the transience and alienation of life, and are all pervaded by a sense of melancholy. Häusser claims to seek the truth in his pictures by transforming the prosaic into the revelational. He rejects the idea of 'objective' photography and through exclusively representational work succeeds in expressing his own fundamental feelings and ideas.

ALEX COOKE

Hagen, Nina

b. 11 March 1955, (East) Berlin

Rock singer

Nina Hagen, the step-daughter of Wolf **Biermann**, began her musical career in 1973 with an East German rock band called Automobil. She emigrated to West Germany in 1976 to become the undisputed queen of German punk rock. Classically trained, the young Hagen had her first hit in 1978 with 'TV-Glotzer' (roughly: 'couch potato'), a warped multilingual reworking of the Tubes' 'White Punks on Dope'. Whereas her original work was sung in a mixture of German and English, her later albums, such as *NunSexMonkRock* (1982) and *Fearless* (1983) (featuring the club-hit 'Sarah', a homage to Sarah Leander) privilege the latter over the former.

MATTHEW T. GRANT

Hager, Kurt

b. 24 July 1912, Bietigheim, near Karlsruhe; d. 18 September 1998, Berlin

GDR politician

A veteran of the communist resistance to Hitler, Hager returned to the Soviet zone of Occupation from exile in England in 1946. After establishing himself as Professor of History in Berlin he was elected to the **SED**'s Central Committee, then became, for the entire period from 1963 to 1989, the Politbüro member responsible for ideological and cultural matters. He is notorious for his dismissal in 1987 of Gorbachev's reform policy of *glasnost'* as merely 'the neighbour changing his wallpaper'. Hager was expelled from the SED's successor party, the **PDS**, in 1990. He was inconclusively tried after unification for crimes allegedly committed during the 1930s.

DENNIS TATE

Hahn, Ulla

b. 30 April 1946, Brachthausen (Sauer-land)

Writer

Hahn studied literature, history, and sociology in Cologne, worked for two years as a journalist, then studied in Hamburg, earning her doctorate (with a dissertation on 1960s German protest literature) in 1975. In 1979, after teaching at the universities of Hamburg, Bremen and Oldenburg, she became a culture editor at Radio Bremen. She has worked since 1987 as a freelance writer in Hamburg. Hahn became a popular and commercially successful poet in 1981 with *Herz über Kopf* (Heart over Head), which addressed, as does much of her work, contemporary issues concerning love and personal relationships.

MARTINA S. ANDERSON

Haider, Jörg

b. 26 January 1950, Goisern (Salzkam-mergut)

Politician and party leader

Haider studied law and made an early career in the *Freiheitliche Partei Österreichs* (**FPÖ**). A member of the Austrian Parliament (from 1979–83, 1986–8 and 1992–), he gained the leadership of the party in 1986 and introduced a marked shift to the right. He became Prime Minister (*Landeshauptmann*) of the *Land* of Carinthia in 1988, but was ousted in 1991 because of remarks about the employment policies of the Nazis.

As a populist politician he is synonymous with the success of his party which he gave a youthful image as well as strong right-wing inclinations.

GEORG HELLMAYR

Haller, Fritz

b. 23 October 1924, Solothurn

Architect

Beginning his career as a draughtsman, Haller has been in private practice since 1949, and Professor at the TU (Technical University) Karlsruhe since 1977.

Haller became known with his steel construction systems which he often exposes (e.g. *Ausbildungszentrum der Schweizerischen Bundesbahn*, the Swiss Railways training centre in Murten, 1980–2). His architectural style is largely of functionalist nature, seeking solutions in the conventional rather than offering superficial, attention-grabbing originality.

MARTIN KUDLEK

Hallstein Doctrine

The Hallstein Doctrine was a guiding principle in West German foreign policy from 1955 to 1969 according to which diplomatic relations were refused to countries that recognized the GDR, on the basis that the FRG was the sole legitimate representative of the whole German people. The communist states of eastern Europe (except the Soviet Union as a 'special case') were affected, as were a number of third-world countries. The doctrine was named after Walter Hallstein, Secretary of State in the Foreign Office.

See also: Ostpolitik

JOHN SANDFORD

Handke, Peter

b. 6 December 1942, Altenmarkt (Griffen, Austria)

Writer

Handke was born to a working-class mother, who married his stepfather shortly after Handke was born. He spent the war years alternately in Griffen and in Germany, attended primary schools in Griffen and a Catholic boys' secondary school near Klagenfurt, completing the Abitur in 1961. While studying law at Graz University, he became active in the literary and cultural groups Forum Stadtpark and the **Grazer Gruppe**. After his first novel, *The Hornets* (*Die Hornissen*) was published in 1966, he abandoned his studies and devoted himself to writing. In an outburst attacking the literary establishment at the 1966 meeting of the **Gruppe 47** he made himself known as a provocative personality and an important spokesman for a new generation of post-war writers not preoccupied with the past. He established himself in the late 1960s and early 1970s as a playwright, novelist, poet, scriptwriter and essayist, whose work, marked by a persistent interest in language and the difficulties inherent in the human condition, has been influential in reforming the modernist literary tradition in Europe. Handke has consistently rejected the political engagement of German realist writers, addressing theory and politics in interviews and non-fiction works. He published a highly controversial travelogue about Serbia in 1995. He has received numerous awards, including Germany's highest literary honour, the Georg Büchner Prize, in 1973 and Austria's highest honour, the Grosser Österreichischer Staatspreis, in 1987.

Handke attended the 1966 meeting of the **Gruppe 47** in Princeton as an unknown writer. He caused a stir when he addressed the highly regarded authors gathered there with a harsh dismissal of their '*Beschreibungsimpotenz*' (descriptive impotence) and an argument against confusing words with the things they represent. After his first and most successful *Sprechstück* (language play), *Offending the Audience* (*Publikumsbeschimpfung*), debuted in Frankfurt am Main just a few months later, Handke's reputation as an important writer overshadowed his personality, though never fully. His early dramatic works challenged the theatrical conventions of plot, performer, and audience, and highlighted the contradictory powers of language to express individuality and to limit and distort that expression. In prose, he expressed the disjunction between subjective experience and the external world in dispassionate and extremely detailed language, often with no narrative purpose. He has been associated with Austrian linguistic philosophy, especially **Wittgenstein** and the **Wiener Gruppe**.

Handke, who considers himself a German writer and an Austrian, lived alternately in West Berlin, Paris, Frankfurt am Main and Salzburg between 1968 and 1979, and has since lived in Salzburg and Paris. He married the actress Libgart Schwarz in 1965, and their daughter, Amina, was born in 1969. Handke's most successful novel, *The Goalie's Anxiety at the Penalty Kick* (*Die Angst des Tormanns beim Elfmeter*), appeared as both a book and a film, directed by his friend Wim **Wenders** in 1971. That same year, his mother committed suicide; in 1972 Handke's memoir of her life, *A Sorrow Beyond Dreams* (*Wunschloses ˙Unglück*), appeared. In 1972 Handke and Libgart separated, and he published *Short Letter, Long Farewell* (*Der kurze Brief zum langen Abschied*), the first of several novels in which the characters struggle with a heightened awareness of their situations that results from or leads to the disruption of relationships.

After the publication of an unusual journal, *The Weight of the World* (*Das Gewicht der Welt*) in 1977, Handke's style underwent some changes as he turned to the themes of history and myth and experimented with traditional literary forms, such as the fairytale and the epic poem. The autobiographical account *Child Story* (*Kindergeschichte*), which explores a father's relationship to his child, is written in the style of Thucydides. Having earlier regarded his 1970 play *Der Ritt über den Bodensee* (*The Ride Across Lake Constance*) as the culmination of his dramatic work, Handke published his first work for the theatre in ten years in 1981, the dramatic poem *Walk About the Villages* (*Über die Dörfer*). Handke also incorporated the upheaval of the early 1990s in his work, treating Slovenia's new independence as a metaphor for isolation and homelessness in *Abschied des Träumers vom Neunten Land* (Departure of the Dreamer from the Ninth Land) in 1991. In 1995 Handke again made news when he published an attack on the media and a defence of Serbia in a travelogue *A Journey to the Rivers: Justice for Serbia* (*Eine winterliche Reise zu den Flüssen Donau, Save, Morawa und Drina, oder, Gerechtigkeit für Serbien*). A selection of responses by critics and other writers was published in 1996. His hometown of Griffen opened a museum for him in August 1997.

Major works

Handke, P. (1969) *Kaspar and Other Plays*, trans. M. Roloff, New York: Farrar, Straus & Giroux (includes *Offending the Audience*).

—— (1974) *The Innerworld of the Outerworld of the Innerworld*, trans. with a postscript by M. Roloff, New York: Seabury Press (selections in German and English from *Die Innenwelt der Außenwelt der Innenwelt*).

—— (1976) *The Ride Across Lake Constance and Other Plays*, trans. M. Roloff and K. Weber, New York: Farrar, Straus & Giroux.

—— (1977) *Three by Peter Handke*, New York: Avon Books (contains the novels *The Goalie's Anxiety at the Penalty Kick*, *Short Letter, Long Farewell*, and *A Sorrow Beyond Dreams*).

—— (1977) *A Moment of True Feeling*, trans. R. Manheim, New York: Farrar, Straus & Giroux.

—— (1984) *The Weight of the World*, trans. R. Manheim, New York: Farrar, Straus & Giroux.

—— (1985) *Slow Homecoming*, trans. R. Manheim, New York: Farrar, Straus & Giroux (contains *The Long Way Around*, *The Lesson of Mont-Sainte-Victoire* and *Child Story*).

—— (1992) *Theaterstücke in einem Band*, Frankfurt am Main: Suhrkamp Verlag (contains virtually all of his important plays and *Sprechstücke*).

—— (1996) *Walk About the Villages: A Dramatic Poem*, trans. with an afterword by M. Roloff, Riverside, CA: Ariadne Press.

—— (1997) *A Journey to the Rivers: Justice for Serbia*, trans. S. Abbott, New York: Viking.

Further reading

Firda, R.A. (1993) *Peter Handke*, New York: Twayne Publishers (general survey of Handke's life and works).

Hern, N. (1971) *Peter Handke: the Theatre and Antitheatre*, London: Woolf (analysis of his early plays).

Müller, A. (1993) *André Müller im Gespräch mit Peter Handke*, Weitra: Bibliothek der Provinz (four interviews from 1971, 1972, 1978 and 1988).

Schlueter, J. (1981) *The Plays and Novels of Peter Handke*, Pittsburgh, PA: University of Pittsburgh Press (analysis of his works).

Zülch, T. (ed.) (1996) *Die Angst des Dichters vor der Wirklichkeit: 16 Antworten auf Peter Handkes Winterreise nach Serbien*, Göttingen: Steidl (responses by journalists and writers to his *Journey to the Rivers*.)

MARIANNA McKIM

Hanka, Erika

b. 18 June 1905, Vincovci (Croatia); d. 15 May 1958, Vienna

Austrian ballerina and choreographer

After training in Austria and Germany Hanka joined the Folkwang Ballet company and was a principal with the Düsseldorf Opera from 1936–9 before taking up engagements in Cologne, Essen and Hamburg. In 1945 she was guest choreographer in Vienna, making her mark with her production of **Egk**'s *Joan von Zarissa*. She was appointed chief choreographer and ultimately ballet director of the opera in Vienna. Here she produced over fifty ballets, including **Egk**'s notorious *Abraxas*, as well as works by Richard **Strauß**, von **Einem**, and **Blacher** and Bartók's *Magical Mandarin*.

DEREK McCULLOCH

Harich, Wolfgang

b. 9 December 1923, Königsberg; d. 15 March 1995, Berlin

GDR dissident and philosopher

A brilliant academic with strongly held opinions, Harich helped found cultural institutions in the GDR in the early 1950s, but was imprisoned for eight years in 1957 for taking the leading part in an unsuccessful coup along the lines of Imre Nagy's reform socialist government in Hungary. He was subsequently partially rehabilitated, and published on literature, philosophy and ecology. Shortly before his death he published an account of political events in the 1950s under the title *Keine Schwierigkeiten mit der Wahrheit*.

See also: dissent and opposition: GDR

AXEL GOODBODY

Harnoncourt, Nikolaus

b. 6 December 1929, Berlin

Austrian conductor and early music
   specialist

In founding the Vienna Concentus Musicus in
1953, a chamber orchestra dedicated to performing pre-classical music on the original instruments
of that epoch, Harnoncourt became one of the
major protagonists of a performing revolution that
has changed the way audiences hear music of the
late renaissance and baroque eras. His interpretive
approach, fusing contemporary semiology, baroque
rhetoric and musicological research, has met with
resistance in Anglo-Saxon musical circles, but has
nevertheless marked the interpretive stance of a
generation of early music players. His later
attempts at grafting this perspective onto modern
orchestras have, paradoxically, met with more
universal praise. Outstanding among Harnoncourt's recordings is the first complete cycle of
J.S. Bach's *Cantatas*, undertaken with the Dutch
harpsichordist, Gustav Leonhardt.

BEATRICE HARPER

Hauff, Reinhard

b. 23 May 1939, Marburg

Filmmaker

Initially a director of light entertainment programmes for television. Following the critical
Heimatfilm Mathias Kneisl (1971), Hauff directed a
sequence of hard-hitting realist films during the
1970s and 1980s confronting contemporary issues
in West Germany, including state control in *Knife in
the Head* (*Messer im Kopf*, 1978), **terrorism** in
Stammheim (1985, based on the protocols of the trial
of the **Baader–Meinhof** terrorists), and the
Berlin Wall and division of Germany in *The Man
on the Wall* (*Der Mann auf der Mauer*, 1985), scripted
by Peter **Schneider**.

See also: film: FRG; New German Cinema

HELEN HUGHES

Hauptstadtfrage

In 1949 Bonn became the government seat of the
FRG, and East Berlin was declared capital
(*Hauptstadt*) of the GDR. Bonn was seen as a
temporary solution until Berlin could again be
capital of a unified Germany. This pledge was
confirmed in the Unification Treaty of 1990.
However, Bonn supporters tried to sabotage the
move: to them Bonn symbolized a stable liberal
democracy, while Berlin conjured up images of
Nazi Germany. In 1994 compromise legislation
was passed: most government bodies will move to
Berlin from the year 2000, the **Bundestag** will
meet in the renovated Reichstag, but the staff of
some ministries will remain in Bonn.

MONIKA PRÜTZEL-THOMAS

Haushofer, Marlen

b. 11 April 1920, Frauenstein (Upper
   Austria); d. 21 March 1970, Vienna

Writer

Having died before the women's movement
became a force in Europe, Haushofer was rediscovered when her novels were republished in the
1980s due to the significance of *Frauenliteratur*.
Focusing on the individual struggles of her female
protagonists to define themselves in a male-
dominated society, as in *The Wall* (*Die Wand*,
1963), her critical perspective marked a turning-
point in Austrian literature, paving the way for
feminist texts.

Further reading

Schmidjell, C. (1991) *Die Überlebenden*, Linz:
   Landesverlag (unpublished texts and critical
   essays).

PETRA M. BAGLEY

Hausmann, Manfred

b. 10 September 1898, Kassel; d. 6
   August 1986, Bremen

Writer and translator

Hausmann studied philology, art history and
philosophy and received his Ph.D. in Munich. He
was the editor for various newspaper *Feuilleton*s
and first gained fame with his early works of
youthful adventures, which had strong autobiographical features, detailing family life in a poet's
home. He achieved the greatest recognition with
his novels of the experiences of a late eighteenth-
century romantic era vagabond in the twentieth
century, detailing Hausmann's pessimistic, almost
nihilistic, view of the world. His poems are
influenced by the coastal landscape of the North
Sea, while his dramas are mainly secular and
Christian mystery plays.

BETTINA BROCKERHOFF-MACDONALD

Havemann, Robert

b. 11 March 1910, Munich; d. 9 April
   1982, (East) Berlin

GDR dissident and physicist

Havemann, who survived being condemned to
death as a member of the communist resistance by
the Nazis, and courageously stood up for the party
during the **June Uprising** in 1953, was dismissed
from all political and professional posts after
publicly criticizing Stalinist policies in 1964. He
was one of the GDR's most prominent dissidents
for over twenty years.

See also: Biermann, Wolf; dissent and
opposition: GDR; peace movement: GDR

Further reading

Woods, R. (1986) *Opposition in the GDR Under
   Honecker, 1971–85: An Introduction and Documentation*, Basingstoke and London: Macmillan (contains documents on the repressive measures

taken against Havemann in 1979 and extracts
from his writing).

AXEL GOODBODY

Heidegger, Martin

b. 26 September 1889, Meßkirch (Swabia); d. 26 May 1976, Freiburg

Philosopher

One of the most important German philosophers
of the twentieth century, Heidegger was instrumental in the development of **existentialism** as a
philosophical system. As pupil and successor of
Edmund **Husserl** in Freiburg, Heidegger's **philosophy** gained instant recognition in the 1920s
with the publication of *Being and Time* and became
at times virtually synonymous with German
philosophy in the 1950s, even though it was heavily
contested throughout by writers associated with the
Frankfurt School, and here especially by Theodor W. **Adorno**.

The central element of Heidegger's writings is a
critique of western metaphysical thinking, with its
emphasis on what he called 'presence' and
'availability' which led to a neglect of Being
(*Seinsvergessenheit*) in positivist, scientist and other
objectifying strands of thought. In his work
published before WWII this analysis led to the
formulation of new starting positions within
philosophy, of which the infamous 'being-to-
wards-death' is but one among many. After the
war, the thrust of his œuvre was increasingly
motivated by a critique of modern technique. The
resulting particular brand of cultural pessimism
shares much in motivation with the work of the
writer Ernst **Jünger**, although Heidegger's refusal
to succumb to a Nietzschean superman ethos
conceivably places his post-war publications within
reach of the roots of **alternative culture**.

Interest in Heidegger's work, though, is not
restricted to his philosophy; his involvement with
National Socialism and the lack of any apparent
Vergangenheitsbewältigung, or process of coming to terms with it, after 1945 was the root cause
of an affair similar in argumentative structure to
that of the **Historikerstreit** (Ott, 1993). Heideg-

ger's membership in the NSDAP and especially the acceptance speech of the *Rektor* position of Freiburg University delivered in 1933 – in which he employed the language of blood and soil to construct an alternative vision for German universities – was and continues to be interpreted by many commentators to discredit Heideggerian philosophy. Heidegger's own refusal publically to comment on the decisions he took during the 1930s, even after his right to teach at German universities was briefly suspended in the wake of the **denazification** process, disappointed many colleagues and commentators.

Among his pupils, Hans-Georg **Gadamer** and Herbert **Marcuse** deserve special mention, while Heidegger's intellectual and erotic relationship with Hannah **Arendt** (Safranski 1994: 166–72) has been the source of much speculation. After his death, Heidegger's philosophy became influential in the formulation of French post-structuralist philosophies.

Further reading

Lacoue-Labarthe, P. (1990) *Heidegger, Art and Politics*, trans. C. Turner, Oxford: Blackwell.

Ott, H. (1993) *Martin Heidegger: A Political Life*, trans. A. Blunden, HarperCollins: London.

Safranski, R. (1994) *Ein Meister aus Deutschland. Heidegger und seine Zeit*, Munich: Carl Hanser.

ULF STROHMAYER

Heimat

Heimat emerged in the late nineteenth century as a politically ambiguous term reflecting tensions between local loyalties and German national identity. Notoriously difficult to translate, it is perhaps best rendered by the word 'roots', which sidesteps the difficulty in English of expressing the meanings 'home' and 'homeland' while evoking some of the wider psychological connotations of the word. During the Third Reich, the discourse of *Heimat* also conveyed opposition to the modernizing process and the reactionary cult of roots. Following WWII it has been appropriated by the

German right, critiqued by the left, and reclaimed by the Greens and the new left.

Heimat designates political and psychological identity. Politically, it has served to forge identity in a Germany which has no neat coincidence between geography, the nation state and the community of German speakers. The idea of the rural *Heimat* bridges nation, region and immediate locality. In the shape of *Heimatfilme* (kitsch, nostalgic films which celebrated a German rural idyll), it was an important distraction from 1950s industrial reconstruction. However, in 1960s and 1970s film and literature it was subjected to a sharp critique and represented as an oppressive, rural fortress. Filmmakers and playwrights exposed the construction of *Heimat* as a set of repressive moral values (see **Kroetz, Franz Xaver**; **Fassbinder, Rainer Werner**; **New German Cinema**). The left-wing political writer Walter **Jens** also attacked *Heimat* as the material inheritance of the property-owning classes.

Heimat is frequently identified with utopia and nostalgia, which are located at the intersection of political and psychological meanings. Both are subject to the political ambiguity characteristic of the term. 1950s right-wing *Heimat* utopia is counterbalanced by the left utopian writings of Ernst **Bloch**. Nostalgia for the *Heimat* can be found on the left and right: in the Marxist critic Walter **Benjamin**, though his *Heimat* is urban, but also in the later right-wing discourse of the 'lost lands' of the east (see **refugees**). Psychologically, *Heimat* as loss signifies not only lost childhood, but the ruptured unity with the mother. Indeed, *Heimat* is especially closely identified with maternity. The identification of *Heimat* with motherhood emerges via the metaphor of the fertile mother earth.

The key concept of *Heimat* as community is dependent on language as a criterion for inclusion or exclusion. **Dialect** embodies the political ambiguity of *Heimat*. It is both a force for exclusion, and a positive feature of small communities that should be cherished. New left and green thinking in the 1980s attempted to recuperate *Heimat* from the conservative and nationalist right to construct a usable identity, based on community and environment. These attitudes are reflected in films such as Edgar **Reitz**'s 1984 saga *Heimat*. Unification has reaffirmed the importance of *Heimat* in questions of national and regional identity without resolving the essential ambiguity of the term.

See also: *Heimatliteratur*

Further reading

Hermand, J. and Steakley, J. (eds.) (1994) *Heimat, Nation, Fatherland: The German Sense of Belonging*, New York and Bern: Lang..

RACHEL PALFREYMAN

Heimatliteratur

Heimat literature alludes, often critically, to a century-old tradition linking character and a (usually provincial) place of origin as the (lost) basis of identity. Themes include the critique of a reactionary idyll (in the work of Franz Xaver **Kroetz** and Martin Sperr); blood-and-soil ideology and the lost lands in the east (in Horst **Bienek** and Siegfried **Lenz**); and the GDR as failed *Heimat* (in Uwe **Johnson**). Partially recuperated in green politics, *Heimat* is the antipode to multicultural hybridity or the postmodern nomadic subject (see **multiculturalism**; **postmodernism**).

Further reading

Pott, H.-G. (ed.) (1986) *Literatur und Provinz. Das Konzept Heimat in der neueren deutschen Literatur*, Paderborn: Ferdinand Schöningh.

ELIZABETH BOA

Hein, Christoph

b. 8 April 1944, Heinzendorf (Silesia, now Jasienica, Poland)

Writer

Hein's upbringing in the GDR's early years left him with no illusions regarding the nature of state socialism, but he remained there to become one of the outstanding authors of his generation. In 1958 he was obliged to become a boarder at a West Berlin grammar-school after being denied access, as the son of a Protestant pastor living in Saxony, to the local *Erweiterte Oberschule*, the only pathway to higher education within the GDR. Three years later, the building of the Berlin Wall closed this educational loophole, but he returned home to complete his Abitur at evening classes. Only after earning a living for some years in temporary jobs was he accepted as a student of philosophy in Leipzig in 1967. Between 1971 and 1979 he nurtured his long-standing ambition to become a dramatist, working (alongside Heiner **Müller**) as an assistant to Benno Besson at the **Deutsches Theater** and the Volksbühne in East Berlin, before opting for a career as a freelance author.

His breakthrough in the GDR came in 1980 with the performance of *Cromwell*, which uses the example of an English revolutionary leader corrupted by power as a parable to illuminate the failure of eastern European socialism to live up to its promises. It was as a prose writer, however, that Hein gained recognition in the West. *The Distant Lover* (*Der fremde Freund*, 1982) depicts the alienated existence of a forty-year-old career-woman, searching for a fulfilling relationship and a sense of purpose behind a façade of cynicism. Although the social context is that of the contemporary GDR, the story struck a chord with its West German readership, not least because of Hein's narrative skill in getting under the skin of his protagonist. *Horns Ende* (Horn's Death) (1985) adopted a multi-perspective approach in looking back at the 1950s and suggesting that the GDR was still failing to tackle its grim dual legacy of fascism and Stalinism, as illustrated by the fate of a nonconformist academic. A third novel, *Der Tangospieler* (The Tango Player) (1989) confronted the previously taboo subject of the Warsaw Pact's invasion of Czechoslovakia in 1968 and its dispiriting impact on Hein's generation of intellectuals. As the publication of all of these works was preceded by prolonged struggles with the cultural establishment, it was no surprise that Hein was at the forefront of the attack on censorship at the 1987 **Writers' Congress** (see also **censorship: FRG**; **censorship: GDR**).

The status achieved by Hein in this public role has been evident since the *Wende* through his extensive involvement, especially as editor of **Freitag**, in debates on the new moral responsibilities of ex-GDR intellectuals. The success of his latest novel, *Das Napoleon-Spiel* (The Napoleon Game) (1993), the portrayal of another alienated representative of his generation, has confirmed his continuing significance as a creative writer.

See also: drama: GDR; prose fiction: GDR

Further reading

Hein, C. (1990) *The Distant Lover*, London: Picador (translation of his first novel).
McKnight, P. (1994) *Understanding Christoph Hein*, Columbia, SC: University of South Carolina Press (full-length study of Hein's work).

DENNIS TATE

Heinrich, Jutta

b. 4 April 1940, Berlin

Writer

A radical feminist and active in the new women's movement, Heinrich accuses the hierarchy of the family structure and patriarchal power relations of responsibility for women's powerlessness and male aggression (see *Das Geschlecht der Gedanken* (The Gender of Thoughts) (1977).

In her play *Männerdämmerung* (Twilight of Men) (1990) she satirizes the chaos and destruction of the masculine order, with the male protagonist giving birth to a child which is his self.

See also: feminism and the women's movement

PETRA M. BAGLEY

Heisig, Bernhard

b. 31 March 1925, Breslau (now Wrocław, Poland)

Painter and graphic artist

Heisig has decisively shaped the profile of the GDR's representative painting abroad through renewing the genre of history painting. Past and present are interwoven in his images, and war and fascism as existential experiences figure prominently in his figurative work, as do the new media.

He was commisioned for a number of important portraits such as the one of ex-Chancellor Helmut Schmidt. For many years (1961–4; 1976–87) he headed the school of Graphics and Bookmaking in Leipzig.

See also: documenta; painting

KERSTIN MEY

Heißenbüttel, Helmut

b. 21 June 1921, Rüstringen (near Wilhelmshaven); d. 19 September 1996, Glückstadt

Writer

Heißenbüttel studied German literature and art history during WWII after returning from the Russian front. He worked at a Hamburg publishing house before he joined the *Süddeutscher Rundfunk* (SDR) in 1957 and replaced Alfred **Andersch** as the Director of the 'Radio Essay' in 1959, a position he held until his retirement in June 1981.

Together with Max **Bense**, Eugen **Gomringer**, Franz Mon, the authors of the Vienna Group (see **Wiener Gruppe**) and others, Heißenbüttel personified the link to a tradition in German literature that originated with the often politically-oriented linguistic experiments of the futurists, dada and surrealism, but also the work of Gertrude Stein and Ezra Pound. In the 1950s, this tradition, destroyed by the Nazis, was slowly re-established and thereafter located itself in direct opposition to the literary projects of the **Gruppe 47**. Though comparatively conventional in his writings until the late 1950s, Heißenbüttel considered himself part of this other literature: his 1955 visits to both a meeting of the Gruppe 47 and Max Bense and Eugen Gomringer at the *Hochschule für Gestaltung* in Ulm marked the beginning of his work with concrete poetry and experimentation in language.

His *Textbücher 1–6*, for example, begun in 1960, display an increasing desire for abstraction in language to detect new poetic possibilities for everyday contexts. The creative energy in these simultaneously highly theoretical and often hilarious vignettes results from his focus on language as a source for musical exploration as well as play that enables the author to dismantle the expectations of the reader. Parallel to this clever exploitation of literary and linguistic possibilities existed a socio-political concern with regard to Germany's past and present throughout his texts that lends itself to acquiring a unique perspective on the cultural conscience of the FRG.

Apart from writing numerous novels and volumes of short prose, Heißenbüttel was a prolific composer of the **Hörspiel** and collaborated with Karlheinz **Stockhausen** on musical productions. More important, however, are his essays on the theory of poetics and the history of literature (see his *Über Literatur*, 1966) that accompanied his literary output. These recoveries, among others, triggered German interests in authors such as Gertrude Stein. His essays, too, present a continued and almost utopian belief in the infinite existence of poetic realities to be discovered in language.

Further reading

Burns, R. (1975) *Commitment, language and reality*, Coventry: University of Warwick Occasional Papers in German Studies.

Heißenbüttel, H. (1981) *Helmut Heißenbüttel*, Munich: edition text + kritik (includes his earlier texts).

Rumold, R. (1975) *Sprachliches Experiment und literarische Tradition*, Bern: Herbert Lang.

ANKE FINGER

Heller, Eva

Writer

Heller's *With the Next Man Everything will be Different* (Beim nächsten Mann wind alles anders) (1987) popularized the genre of the satirical women's novel. By 1996, the story of a film student's struggles with love and career had seen thirty-three printings. The author's formula of poking fun at conventional gender relations also proved successful in *Der Mann, der's wert ist* (The Man Who's Worth It) (1993), *Erst die Rache, dann das Vergnügen* (Revenge before Pleasure) (1997), and in a number of cartoons. Heller holds a Ph.D. in sociology and

lives in Frankfurt-am-Main. She is the author of two children's books and several psycho-sociological studies. (The date and place of her birth are not publicly available.)

Major work

Heller, E. (1992) *With the Next Man Everything Will Be Different*, trans. K. Winston, New York: Random House (translation of *Beim nächsten Mann wird alles anders*).

SABINE SCHMIDT

Henselmann, Hermann

b. 3 February 1905, Roßla (Harz); d. 19 January 1995, (East) Berlin

Architect

Soon after the war Henselmann abandoned functionalism in favour of a more traditional style which he attempted to fuse with modernism. The first phase of the Stalinallee (1952–9) shows modern, Schinkelesque and Stalinistic elements.

In various positions, for instance as East Berlin's chief architect (1953–9) or director of the Institute for Town Planning and Architecture of the German Building Academy (1966–72), he had a decisive influence on the development of town planning and architecture in the GDR. He was mainly responsible for East Germany's *Plattenbauten* (industrially prefabricated blocks) and for replacing historical building stock with these.

MARTIN KUDLEK

Henze, Hans Werner

b. 1 July 1926, Gütersloh (Westphalia)

Composer

One of the most performed composers of his generation, much of Henze's prolific output falls into fundamentally traditional categories, such as symphony, opera or ballet. In each case, he has brought new, colourful and radical perspectives to bear, though rarely breaking the mould of the expected genre. The blend of sensual opulence and theatrical acuity displayed by such works as *König Hirsch* (1962) or *The Bassarids* (1965) easily explains the popularity of Henze's operas in the contemporary German repertory.

BEATRICE HARPER

Herburger, Günter

b. 6 April 1932, Isny im Allgäu

Writer and long distance runner

Herburger studied philosophy and Sanskrit in Munich and Paris at the Sorbonne. He read for the **Gruppe 47** in 1964. The themes of his fiction range from the boredom of everyday life to psychedelic symbolism. He also wrote about his marathons (see his *Lauf und Wahn* (Running and Madness) 1988). He worked in television for Süddeutscher Rundfunk from 1960 to 1964. He wrote **radio** plays, poems (*Das brennende Haus*, The Burning House, 1990), and several children's books. He was awarded the Bremen Literary Prize in 1973.

JAMES KELLER

Hermlin, Stephan

b. 13 April 1915, Chemnitz; d. 6 April 1997, Berlin

Writer (real name Rudolf Leder)

One of the most highly regarded poets and essayists in the GDR, Hermlin was born into a Jewish entrepreneurial family and grew up in Berlin. In 1913 he joined the Young Communists. After leaving school he worked in the printers' trade, was engaged in the anti-Nazi resistance movement and fought in the Spanish Civil War. From 1936 he was in exile, in Egypt, Palestine and Britain; in France and Switzerland he was interned in various camps. He participated in the Free Germany (*Freies Deutschland*) movement and worked on the periodical *Über die Grenzen* (Across the Frontiers).

In 1945 he returned to Germany, first to Frankfurt am Main where he worked for the radio.

In 1947 he moved to East Berlin where he played an active part in re-establishing cultural life in the Soviet occupation zone. He worked as a freelance writer, became a member of the German Academy of Arts, (*Deutsche Akademie der Künste*, DAK), and a member of the executive committee of the **PEN** centre. He received many prizes, including the Heinrich Heine prize in 1948 and the National Prize of the GDR in 1950 and in 1954.

Hermlin's literary output was not huge, but the quality of his essays and lyric poetry was always of a high standard. His first volume of poetry, *Zwölf Balladen von den großen Städten* (Twelve Ballads from the Big Cities), published in 1945, revealed a creative linguistic power and the influence of expressionist poets such as Georg Heym and the early works of **Becher**, as well as that of baroque poetry and that of Swinburne and Apollinaire. This was followed by *Die Straßen der Furcht* (Streets of Fear) (1947) and *Zweiundzwanzig Balladen* (Twenty-two Ballads) (1947) which like much of his work reflect the theme that was of great significance for him, the anti-fascist resistance, as in the story *Der Leutnant Yorck von Wartenberg* (1945) (inspired by the novella by Ambrose Bierce) and *Die Zeit der Gemeinsamkeit* (The Time of Community), about the Warsaw ghetto, both of which were republished in a volume of short stories *(Erzählungen)* in 1966.

Hermlin remained consistent in his belief in a better, communist future. During the Stalinist era he wrote panegyrics to the Soviet leader which were published in the collection *Der Flug der Taube* (The Flight of the Dove) (1952), and he remained a friend of **Honecker**. He also stands out as a man of integrity who was not afraid to speak out on behalf of other writers, such as Wolf **Biermann**, when he believed they were being unjustly attacked. As a critic and through works such as the radio play about Hölderlin, *Scardanelli* (1970), he helped to create a more liberal attitude to writers regarded as modernist.

In the twenty-seven prose texts of *Abendlicht* (Evening Light) (1979) he looks back at his own life in the context of the struggle against fascism. Hermlin also won widespread recognition for his sensitive translations of American, French, Latin American and Hungarian poetry.

MARGARET VALLANCE

Herrnstadt, Rudolf

b. 18 March 1903, Gleiwitz, Silesia (now Gliwice, Poland); d. 28 August 1966, Halle

Journalist and GDR functionary

A journalist in the 1920s in Berlin, Herrnstadt went into exile after 1933 and became editor in 1943 of the newspaper *Freies Deutschland* (Free Germany) for German PoWs in the Soviet Union. He returned to Berlin in May 1945, was editor of the *Berliner Zeitung* from 1945 to 1949 and of ***Neues Deutschland*** from 1949 to 1953. He became a member of the **Central Committee** of the SED in 1950 and a candidate member of the **Politbüro**, but was removed in July 1953 after being accused of involvement in a conspiracy against the party leadership.

See also: dissent and opposition: GDR

PETER BARKER

Herzog & de Meuron

This architectural partnership was established in Basel in 1978 by Jacques Herzog and Pierre de Meuron. After studying under Aldo Rossi and assistant teaching at the ETH (Technical University) Zürich, Herzog & de Meuron gained recognition with their first small projects. Their work often presents a successful synthesis between unusually formal and disciplined designs and spatial complexity and convincing architectural interpretations. Their work is also known for its high-quality detailing. The Fotostudio Frei in Weil (1982), the Goetz Collection in Munich (1992) and the locomotive depot Auf dem Wolf in Basel (1992–6) belong to their best-known buildings.

MARTIN KUDLEK AND BERTHOLD PESCH

Herzog, Thomas

b. 5 August 1941, Munich

Architect

Having studied in Munich and Rome, Herzog established his own practice in 1971. He has taught at the TH (Technical University) Munich since 1992.

Herzog is best known in connection with the development of solar technique in domestic architecture and with ecological building. Furthermore he came to fame with prefabricated designs (often to be partially self-erected), pneumatic constructions and timber construction. The Richter housing estate (1981–2) in Munich, the Linz Conference Centre (1991) and the Production Plant for Wilkhahn in Bad Münder-Eimbeckhausen (1993) are amongst his most acclaimed buildings.

MARTIN KUDLEK

Herzog, Werner

b. 5 September 1942, Munich

Filmmaker and writer

A leading director of the **New German Cinema** whose spectacular, impassioned feature films, controversial documentaries, and fiery character have earned him an international reputation as the pre-eminent romantic and visionary storyteller of post-war German cinema. An author and filmmaker decidedly suspicious of language and rational discourse, his films are characterized by breathtaking landscape imagery, the atmospheric use of music (cult band Popol Vuh and others), and narratives built around the generally futile attempts of heroic outsiders to achieve superhuman feats – be it to challenge the sun to a duel in *Signs of Life* (*Lebenszeichen*, 1967), find the lost gold of Eldorado in *Aguirre, Wrath of God* (*Aguirre, der Zorn Gottes*, 1972), transport a ship over a mountain in *Fitzcarraldo* (1982) or scale unclimbable peaks in the documentary *The Dark Glow of the Mountains* (*Gasherbrum – Der leuchtende Berg*, 1984) and the feature film *Scream of Stone* (*Schrei aus Stein*, 1991). The legendary demands made by Herzog on his cast and crew – most famously his alter-ego, the volatile Klaus **Kinski** – whilst shooting his epics in far-flung corners of the globe (the Amazon, Sahel and Sahara deserts, Australian outback and Patagonia) have necessitated equally heroic feats and prompted accusations of exploitation of both people and places.

Following a series of shorts with off-beat themes including body-building and malevolent chickens – creatures Herzog believes to be born evil – he shot his debut feature, *Signs of Life*, on the Greek island of Kos. It is an adaptation, set during WWII, of a novella by the German romantic writer Achim von Arnim. Prefiguring the obsessions of his later work, it is peopled by bizarre loners and outcasts, and is shot through with absurd and grotesque humour. Plagued by the heat – beautifully and oppressively captured by cameraman Thomas Mauch – and forced to conform, the protagonist Stroszek escapes into madness before being overpowered by his fellow soldiers. *Even Dwarfs Started Small (Auch Zwerge haben klein angefangen*, 1969) amplifies the theme of outcasts *in extremis* into a grotesquely compelling carnival of human folly, staged as a sequence of set-pieces worthy of Hieronymus Bosch. With a cast made up entirely of dwarfs, his macabre tale of a failed rebellion in a penal colony aroused hostility from the left, who read into it a savage parody of the student uprisings, ignoring the director's obvious empathy with his engaging protagonists. Dividing his time between feature filmmaking and documentaries, Herzog had followed his first feature with an experimental essay film charting his travels across Africa, *Fata Morgana* (1969), a mesmerizing combination of experimental documentary and mythologizing commentary. Before directing *Aguirre*, which was to bring him international acclaim, he directed his most celebrated documentary, *Land of Silence and Darkness (Land des Schweigens und der Dunkelheit*, 1971), a moving account of the life and work of the Bavarian deaf-mute Fini Straubinger, who campaigned tirelessly for the education and integration into normal society of fellow sufferers.

Aguirre, the first of five films with Kinski – *Fitzcarraldo* and *Cobra Verde* (1987) are very much in the same mould – took Herzog to Peru, and the fictitious story of the fanatical conquistador was produced with an international audience in mind. Grander in scale and less experimental than his previous work, it makes up for a certain lack of subtlety and characterization with ravishing cinematography and raw energy, culminating in an unforgettable image of Kinski floating down the Amazon on a raft colonized by screeching monkeys.

Alternating between the two poles of his romantic vision, Herzog turned for his next feature from the outsider to the outcast, from a childlike tyrant to an *enfant terrible*, and from the Amazon to the medieval Swabian town of Dinkelsbühl. *The Enigma of Kaspar Hauser (Jeder für sich und Gott gegen alle*, 1974) is the story of the legendary foundling discovered in Nürnberg in 1828, transformed by Herzog into a coruscating attack on the persecution of the individual by church and state. In its distrust of language, education and science, and incorporation of a 'villainous father' figure, Herzog's historical drama has an obvious contemporary slant. The tragic, inarticulate protagonist played by the remarkable actor Bruno S. – himself a victim of abuse and educationally subnormal – bears an unmistakable similarity to the deaf mutes in *Land of Silence and Darkness* and is the obverse of the characters embodied by Kinski. Lyrical, elegiac and stunningly shot by Jörg Schmidt-Reitwein (with dream sequences by experimental filmmaker Klaus Wyborny) the film was awarded three prizes at the Cannes Film Festival.

Herzog had dedicated *Kaspar Hauser* to the legendary film historian Lotte Eisner, thereby expressing his solidarity with pre-war German cinema. In 1978 he reinforced this proclamation and affirmed his position as a legitimate heir to German romanticism by directing a remake of F.W. Murnau's *Nosferatu* and a faithful, albeit rather stagey, adaptation of Büchner's fragmentary play *Woyzeck*, both with Kinski in the leading role.

For many commentators the 1980s and 1990s have seen Herzog treading water. However, whilst his feature films have indeed veered towards self-parody, most uncomfortably in Kinski's swollen performance as the adventurer *Cobra Verde*, Herzog has developed his considerable talents as a documentarist, with striking films on the war in El Salvador, South Saharan nomads, the Central African 'Emperor' Bokassa and, most controversially, an apocalyptic essay about the ecological catastrophe bequeathed by the Gulf War (*Lessons in Darkness*, 1992).

See also: Achternbusch, Herbert; film: FRG;
New German Cinema

Further reading

Corrigan, T. (ed.) (1986) *The Films of Werner Herzog:
Between Mirage & History*, New York and London:
Methuen (an excellent collection of essays on
themes and individual films, with a complete
filmography up to 1984 and a selected bibliography).

Herzog, W. (1980) *Of Walking in Ice*, New York:
Tanam Press (Herzog's poetic diary of his
barefoot pilgrimage from Munich to France in
1974 to visit the ailing film historian Lotte
Eisner).

—— (1980) *Screenplays*, New York: Tanam Press
(includes *Land of Silence and Darkness*, *Aguirre, Wrath
of God* and *The Enigma of Kaspar Hauser*).

MARTIN BRADY

Hesse, Hermann

b. 2 July 1877, Calw; d. 9 August 1962,
Montagnola (Switzerland)

Writer

Hesse's works have generally made their biggest
impact on the young, who felt a kinship with him as
they too sought to give meaning to their lives.
During the 1960s and 1970s his intense emotional
and mystical works generated a huge following
among the hippie generation for whom he became
a cult figure. Indeed, he has rightly been called the
spokesman of romantic idealists and wanderers.

From a pietistic background, Hesse rejected
Christianity early in life in favour of mysticism. His
personal crises and adolescent experiences form
the basis of many of his novels, which often read
like a spiritual odyssey. In reality, however, his
personal problems are universalized and become
the starting point for questioning and exploring the
critical tensions between traditional values and
modern life, and particularly the political changes
of the first half of this century.

Hesse first entered the book trade, but devoted
himself to writing after his first novel *Peter Camenzind*

was published in 1904. A visit to India lasting
several months was an escape from Europe and he
immersed himself in Indian mysticism.

The outbreak of WWI was a cataclysmic event
for Hesse and coincided with his wife being
committed to a mental institution and his own
nervous breakdown, which resulted in his having
Jungian psychoanalytic treatment. Psychoanalytic
concepts are important for a better understanding
of Hesse's later works for they made him aware of
the role of the subconscious in artistic creation. In
1924 he acquired Swiss citizenship and retired to
Montagnola where he remained for the rest of his
life. In 1946 he was awarded the Nobel Prize for
Literature.

Hesse's whole life was a confrontation with the
self, his work being a gradual unfolding and
awakening. In 1919 he caused a sensation with
Demian, a work that involves considerable spiritual
upheaval and which gave him a large, young
following. Not exactly autobiographical, it is about
a voyage of self-discovery. From now on he
exhorted the young to turn inward, to seek the
god within themselves. The shattering experience
of awakening leads to the 'Way Within' which
incorporates both responsibility and freedom of the
self. It is this opposition of chaos and unity and the
tension between these polarities that is the impulse
behind his work.

Subsequent novels grapple with the contradictory elements of life. Man is torn between two
poles, between religious and aesthetic impulses as
in *Narcissus and Goldmund* (*Narziß und Goldmund*,
1930) in which the reader witnesses the conflict
between a scholarly monk (moral asceticism) and
the wanderer greedy for life. Hesse sets his novels
in a utopian sphere rather than in reality. His last
novel *The Glass Bead Game* (*Das Glasperlenspiel*) (1943)
is a reflective and didactic allegory that seeks a
solution to being an outsider.

Further reading

Boulby, M. (1967) *Hermann Hesse*, Ithaca, NY:
Cornell University Press (a useful and comprehensive study).

Ziolkowski, Th. (1965) *The Novels of Hermann Hesse*,

Princeton, NJ: Princeton University Press (a seminal, critical study of theme and structure).

PETER PROCHNIK

Heym, Stefan

b. 10 April 1913, Chemnitz

Writer and journalist (real name Helmut Flieg)

Stefan Heym's life and writings reflect many of the major issues affecting Germany in the twentieth century. Born into an affluent Jewish family, he was caught up in controversy even before the Nazis' rise to power forced him to flee abroad. After a period in Prague he reached the US – and relative safety – in 1935. As well as journalistic work he wrote the popular anti-Nazi novel *Hostages* (1942).

He returned to Europe with the Allied invading forces and served after the end of the war with the US Radio in Frankfurt am Main, before being transferred back to the US at the end of 1945 and dismissed from the army because of alleged 'pro-Communist sympathies'. His subsequent works present an ever more critical analysis of capitalism, and in 1951 he moved to the GDR, where he began a life of popular but independent-minded journalism and increasingly critical fiction writing. A significant early project was *Der Tag X* (Day X), on the East German **June Uprising** of 1953, a work eventually shelved because of predictable political responses. It appeared in 1977 as *Five Days in June* (*5 Tage im Juni*). In general his works of the 1950s were those of the engaged socialist opposing the reality of the existing socialist system. For much of the 1960s he adapted historical and semi-historical material to analyse his particular interest in the wider theme of revolution, relating this to the events of 1848 in *The Lenz Papers* (*Die Papiere des Andreas Lenz*, 1963) and to the ambivalent figure of Lassalle in *Uncertain Friend* (*Lassalle*, 1969). By 1965 Heym's criticism of the GDR's refusal to come to terms with its own Stalinist past led to an almost total ban on his publication within the GDR. This official displeasure was reinforced in 1976 when he led protests at the expatriation of Wolf **Biermann** (see also **Biermann Affair**).

His works from the early 1970s drew much of their material from literary sources – Defoe in *The Queen against Defoe* (*Die Schmähschrift*..., 1970), and the Bible in *The King-David-Report* (*Der König David Bericht*, 1972), and demonstrate the relationship of the intellectual to a powerful leader, with evident echoes of Stalinism, while later *Collin* (1979) analyses the relationship of the contemporary intellectual to power. In another mythical/Biblical work *Ahasver* (1981) he contributed indirectly and ironically to the issue of the peace movement. He was active in the late 1980s in the protest movements that led to the end of the GDR.

After unification his alliance with the **PDS** (he briefly represented them in the *Bundestag*) caused renewed controversy, as did a number of highly critical short works on aspects of unification such as *Auf Sand gebaut* (Built on Sand) (1990) and *filz* (graft) (1992).

Further reading

Hutchinson, P. (1992) *Stefan Heym: The Perpetual Dissident*, Cambridge: Cambridge University Press (a study skilfully embracing biography and works).

Wolfschütz, H. and Töteberg, M. (1978) 'Stefan Heym' in H.L. Arnold (ed.) *Kritisches Lexikon zur deutschsprachigen Gegenwartsliteratur*, Munich: edition text + kritik (concentrates critically on aesthetic matters and evaluation; full, periodically updated bibliography).

JOHN WIECZOREK

Hilbig, Wolfgang

b. 31 August 1941, Meuselwitz (Thuringia)

Writer

Wolfgang Hilbig has rapidly established himself as one of the most notable poets and writers of prose to emerge from the former GDR. Born in Meuselwitz (Leipzig), he initially worked in manual trades and entered a writing career when he joined a *Zirkel schreibender Arbeiter* (a writing workers' group) which formed part of the Bitterfeld programme in the 1960s (see also **cultural policy: GDR**). Hilbig did not, however, produce a literature which toed the line of state doctrine and depicted the humanizing effect of the new socialist system on the means of production; on the contrary, his work is a graphic representation of individual alienation in a polluted, stagnated society.

His first publication, a volume of poetry entitled *abwesenheit* (absence) (1979), appeared in the FRG, although, with the support of Franz **Fühmann**, a selection of poetry and prose also appeared in the GDR in 1983 entitled *stimme, stimme* (voice, voice). As a result of his publication in the West Hilbig was charged and convicted of 'breaching currency regulations' (*Devisenvergehen*). He remained in the GDR until 1985, when he moved to the West on an open visa.

The term *Abwesenheit* has been applied generally to facets of Hilbig's work; his self-conscious exploration of what language makes absent and the reduction of the worker to a functional part of the state machinery are features of the poem of the same title. Both his poetry and his prose show how language does not serve reality, but serves the 'simulation' of reality instead, and this becomes particularly apparent in his novel *'Ich'* ('I') (1993). Here the main protagonist is an informer working for the **Stasi** who is observing 'Reader', a writer in the **Prenzlauer Berg** scene. The central character's assimilation of reality in his writing parallels the creation of a fiction of reality by the State Security Police. Another element of the novel that is typical of Hilbig's work as a whole is the exploration of the self, and the fragmentation of identity (it is significant that the 'ich' of the title is given in speech marks for it implies the question: who is 'I'?). The main character is commonly located in a landscape which has its real counterpart in the opencast mining sites outside Leipzig but which becomes the interior landscape of the self. In *Alte Abdeckerei* (Old Knacker's Yard) (1991), for example, a boy, or a young man, roams an industrial wasteland; the desolation and the stench of waste hold a fascination for the narrator who sees himself as a lone figure. Consequently he feels drawn towards the men who work in 'Germania II' (the site of the skinner's yard) who are shunned by the people of the town. In this sense he is not unlike Hilbig himself.

Further reading

Arnold, H.L. (ed.) (1994) *Wolfgang Hilbig*, Munich: edition text + kritik (consists of a collection of articles and a useful bibliography).

Wittstock, U. (ed.) (1994) *Wolfgang Hilbig – Materialien zu Leben und Werk*, Frankfurt am Main: Fischer (a general reference work containing articles on the author).

HELEN L. JONES

Hildebrandt, Dieter

b. 23 May 1927, Bunzlau (Silesia; now Bolesławiec, Poland)

Writer, actor and cabaret artist

After studying theatre in Munich, Hildebrandt founded a **cabaret**, the *Münchner Lach- und Schießgesellschaft*, with Sammy Dreschel in 1956, and became one of Germany's best-known political satirists. An advocate of the moral and democratic functions of cabaret, he has frequently fallen foul of the censor, especially in his television broadcasts for **ZDF** (1973–9) and SFB (from 1980). His writings include memoirs, sketchbooks, and a satire on the football world. But it is Hildebrandt's skill as a performer that gives his texts their humour and political bite.

JONATHAN LONG

Hildesheimer, Wolfgang

b. 9 December 1916, Hamburg; d. 21 August 1991, Poschiavo (Switzerland)

Writer and graphic artist

Hildesheimer trained as an artist, but is best known as a writer. His works include radio and stage plays, short stories, novels, biographical texts and numerous essays.

The son of a Jewish industrial chemist, Hildesheimer spent his youth in Germany and England. In 1933, his family emigrated to Jerusalem, where he studied art and interior design, continuing his studies at London's Central School of Arts and Crafts from 1937–9. He spent the war years as an

English teacher in Tel Aviv and an information officer for the British government in Jerusalem, before working as an interpreter at the Nürnberg Trials between 1946 and 1948.

His literary début was a 1952 collection of stories entitled *Lieblose Legenden* (Loveless Legends). These are elegant satires whose humour and lightness of touch contrasted strongly with much post-war fiction and enlivened early meetings of the **Gruppe 47**. He was also an important radio playwright and was awarded the *Hörspielpreis der Kriegsblinden* in 1955. Throughout the 1950s and 1960s he wrote numerous stage plays in the absurdist idiom, but these have dated, and it is as a prose writer that Hildesheimer is likely to be remembered.

Tynset (1965) brought Hildesheimer great critical acclaim: it won both the Büchner Prize and the *Bremer Literaturpreis* in 1966. *Tynset*'s sister text *Masante* (1973) exploits the same monological, associative form, but was to be Hildesheimer's last fictional narrative; in 1975 he proclaimed 'The End of Fiction', arguing that fictional models were inadequate to the task of 'expressing our situation' at a time when the forces that shape the individual life have become unknowable and the world threatens to destroy itself in nuclear apocalypse or environmental catastrophe. His next book, *Mozart* (1977), was a controversial biographical essay which set out to explode the myths surrounding the composer. It provoked an energetic musicological debate, and Hildesheimer's 'psychological' interpretations of Mozart's operas have exerted considerable influence on subsequent productions. His text *Marbot* (1981) is subtitled *Eine Biographie*, but applies the discourse of biography to a fictional subject, problematizing the fiction–reality distinction, and raising crucial questions about historical representation and the knowability of the past. After *Marbot*, Hildesheimer published no major work of literature. He devoted himself to the visual arts, and became a prominent spokesman on environmental issues.

As a writer, Hildesheimer resists categorization. Although a member of the Gruppe 47 and avowedly left-wing, he never advocated a politically engaged literature; nor do his works reflect a specifically Jewish consciousness. His literary concerns remained predominantly existential. But as a formal innovator Hildeheimer is consistently interesting, and as a master of German prose style he has few rivals in the literature of post-war Germany.

Further reading

Jehle, V. (1989) *Wolfgang Hildesheimer Materialien*, Frankfurt am Main: Suhrkamp (anthology of reviews and articles, plus bibliography of primary and secondary sources.)

Stanley, P.H. (1993) *Wolfgang Hildesheimer and his Critics*, Drawer: Camden House (annotated bibliography of primary and secondary sources).

JONATHAN LONG

Hillgruber, Andreas

b. 18 January, Angerburg (East Prussia; now Węgozgewo, Poland) 1925

Historian

Following appointments as a school director, a university lecturer in Marburg (1965–8), and then in Freiburg (1968–72), Hillgruber was appointed Professor of Modern History at the University of Cologne. His research focused primarily on twentieth-century military history, WWII, and international relations; he has also published source editions, and several survey works, including *Deutsche Geschichte 1945–82* and *Der Zweite Weltkrieg*. He sprang to prominence with the publication of *Zweierlei Untergang* (1986), a slim volume containing two controversial essays dealing with the 'destruction of the German Reich' and the 'end of European Jewry', key conservative texts of the **Historikerstreit**.

MARY FULBROOK

Hilmer & Sattler

This architectural partnership was established in Munich in 1974 by Heinz Hilmer and Christoph Sattler. Their approach to architecture and town planning seeks for solutions in the conventional, reacting against those evolving from ideology (e.g.

Le Corbusier's). In their domestic designs central halls are preferred to corridors and the use of traditional building materials and forms prevails. Their *Gemäldegalerie* (competition in 1986, begun 1992) in Berlin has to be understood as a conservative reaction to the buildings surrounding it (e.g. **Scharoun**'s *Staatsbibiliothek*). Their Potsdamer Platz town planning scheme (1991) relates to the traditional block-system of the late nineteenth century. Hilmer & Sattler strive for discreet adaptation rather than attention-grabbing gestures.

MARTIN KUDLEK

Hilsenrath, Edgar

b. 2 April 1926, Leipzig

Writer

Hilsenrath's novels are amongst the most important examples of post-war Jewish writing. With stark realism, *Nacht* (Night) (1978) gives an authentic portrayal of the bleak, brutalizing struggle for survival in the Romanian ghetto to which the young Hilsenrath himself had been deported. It is a world devoid of pity, solidarity, resistance or hope. In contrast, *Der Nazi und Der Friseur* (The Nazi and the Barber) (1977) is a grotesque satire both on the banality of fascism and on the theme of guilt and expiation as an SS-man and mass-murderer takes on the identity of one of his Jewish victims, becoming a respectable, middle-class Israeli citizen with a barber's shop in Tel Aviv.

DAVID ROCK

Hindemith, Paul

b. 16 November 1895, Hanau; d. 28 December 1963, Frankfurt am Main

Composer and performer

Hindemith started to play the violin at the age of nine, and at the age of thirteen his talents were recognized by the leading violinist Adolf Rebner who accepted him as a pupil and had him awarded a free place at the conservatory in Frankfurt am Main, where he remained a student until 1917.

Hindemith's facility with instruments was legendary, not only as a violinist and viola player (soloist in Walton's *Viola Concerto* at the BBC Promenade Concerts in 1929), but also as pianist and clarinettist. In 1915 he became leader of the orchestra at the Frankfurt Opera, earning money in addition in café orchestras and the like. In 1917 he was called up, but as a member of the regimental band remained behind the front line. His commanding officer then requested him to form a string quartet to play in private concerts, thus keeping him and his talents from the brunt of battle.

In the 1920s he achieved a more marked profile as a composer, his one-act operas *Mörder, Hoffnung der Frauen* and *Nusch-Nuschi* (based on a Burmese puppet play) creating scandals for their provocative attitude to sex. His string quartets, however, won him esteem as a serious composer, though his equally successful *Kammermusik Nr 1* brought to light a frivolous, quasi-dadaistic element to his music. He was also untiring in the promotion of outstanding music by other composers, including Schoenberg and Webern.

With no known interest in teaching he was made Professor of Composition at the conservatory in Berlin in 1927, and developed the interest in teaching that led to his treatise *Unterweisung im Tonsatz* (Instruction in Composition) and the composing of works for performance by amateurs.

His ideas and outspokenness did not befriend him to the Nazis, nor did his habitual performances with Jewish artists and composers. His music was boycotted, a move that was openly attacked by **Furtwängler** who had premiered his symphony *Mathis der Maler* in 1934. Hindemith was temporarily suspended from the conservatory, but shortly after reinstatement he left Germany for Switzerland and then the US. He remained there until 1953, being particularly associated with Yale, though his success as a teacher in the more liberal American climate was more restricted than had been the case in Germany. In 1953 he settled in Switzerland, teaching in Zürich until 1955, and devoting more time to conducting. He died unexpectedly of what was later confirmed in Frankfurt am Main as acute pancreatitis.

His output was prolific in all genres, and his wide-ranging interest in music led him not only to champion contemporary music but also to publish editions of works by the baroque composers Monteverdi, Vivaldi, Biber and Ariosti (like Hindemith a virtuoso of the *viola d'amore*), as well as cadenzas for Mozart concertos. Although his subsequent influence on composers has been limited, his effect on the development of music in Germany between the wars can hardly be overstated.

DEREK McCULLOCH

Hinstorff Verlag

The Rostock-based publishing house Hinstorff emerged from the obscurity of its traditional focus on Mecklenburg's regional culture to become the GDR's most radical literary publisher of the 1970s. Under the directorship of Konrad Reich, supported by his chief-editor Kurt Batt, Hinstorff won over the influential Franz **Fühmann**, who in turn helped to attract to its ranks the brightest talents of the younger generation, including Ulrich **Plenzdorf**, Jurek **Becker** and Klaus **Schlesinger**. Although forced back into line ideologically under new management after the **Biermann Affair**, Hinstorff retained something of its reputation for innovation.

See also: publishing: GDR

DENNIS TATE

Historikerstreit

The *Historikerstreit* (Historians' Dispute) blew up in West Germany in the year preceding the 1987 general election. The main issues revolved around the uniqueness or comparability of the Holocaust, and the implications of historical interpretations for national identity.

It was in part unleashed by a controversial piece by Ernst **Nolte** in the *Frankfurter Allgemeine Zeitung* (6 June 1986), 'The Past Which Will Not Pass Away'. Nolte suggested that the Holocaust was unique only in the technical means of murder used, gassing, but that in all other respects – mass deportations, death camps, the murder of entire social groups – it was comparable to atrocities such as the crimes of Stalin and Pol Pot; it was,

moreover, a defensive reaction to a prior 'Asiatic deed', the Gulag Archipelago.

Nolte's views were neither entirely new, nor isolated. Other conservative historians, such as Klaus Hildebrand, Andreas **Hillgruber** and Michael **Stürmer**, demanded a 'normalization' of the past and a relativization of Nazi crimes. Stürmer, an academic adviser to Chancellor Helmut **Kohl**, published a piece in the *FAZ* on 25 April 1986, 'History in a Land Without History', which sought to reappropriate history for the construction of a new national identity. Hillgruber, in the first of two essays in *Zweierlei Untergang*, presented an evocative description of the destruction of Prussia, self-consciously claiming empathy with the German soldiers and civilians struggling on the eastern front, and arguing against the notion of 1945 as 'liberation'. His brief, dry, almost appendix-like essay on the Holocaust failed to link the continued deaths in 1944–5 with the prolongation of war, and, after placing primary blame on Hitler, sublimated broader German responsibility into a more general anthropological question.

These apologetic tendencies were noted and vigorously attacked, first by the philosopher Jürgen **Habermas** in an article in *Die Zeit* (11 July 1986), 'A Kind of Settlement of Damages', and subsequently by left-liberal historians such as Martin **Broszat**, Jürgen **Kocka**, Wolfgang and Hans **Mommsen**, Hans-Ulrich Wehler and others. Once the controversy was unleashed, there was a stream of vitriolic articles in the highbrow press. Even when the dust appeared to have settled, an after-spate of ill-tempered books and polemics continued to fly.

Most observers agreed that the debate had produced more sound and fury than light. Little new empirical material was adduced; indeed, the lack of any empirical support of hypotheses couched as rhetorical questions was a notable feature of Nolte's articles. It did, however, register both the extent to which conservatives were prepared to break long-standing taboos, and also the degree of pluralism such that demands for a uniform national identity were effectively and energetically resisted.

See also: German Question; historiography; *Vergangenheitsbewältigung*

Further reading

Augstein, R. *et al.* (1987) 'Historikerstreit', Munich: Piper Verlag; trans. J. Knowlton and T. Cates, *Forever in the Shadow of Hitler?*, New Jersey: Humanities Press, 1993 (source texts).

Evans, R.J. (1989) *In Hitler's Shadow*, London: I.B. Tauris (provides commentary on the *Historikerstreit*).

Hillgruber, A. (1986) *Zweierlei Untergang. Die Zerschlagung des deutschen Reiches und das Ende des europäischen Judentums*, Stuttgart: Siedler (essay collection by the conservative historian, referred to in the entry).

Maier, C. (1988) *The Unmasterable Past*, Cambridge, MA: Harvard University Press (provides commentary).

Wehler, H.-U. (1988) *Entsorgung der deutschen Vergangenheit?*, Munich: C.H. Beck (provides commentary).

MARY FULBROOK

historiography

Historiography in the two Germanies was intimately related to the different political conditions obtaining in East and West. In the classic western view, a diversity of empirically open approaches in West Germany was contrasted with a view of GDR history as a legitimatory science (*Legitimationswissenschaft*) for the communist regime. In the official GDR view, western bourgeois historians merely camouflaged the underlying causes of historical change, and sustained a continuing false consciousness among the working masses. Nevertheless, while there were striking differences during the 1950s and 1960s, there were then moves towards a form of convergence in both topic and approach in the 1970s and 1980s.

Contrasts in the Cold War years

In the very early post-war years, there was still a diversity of historians and historical approaches in the Soviet occupation zone. But, as in other spheres, things began to be tightened up in 1948: non-Marxists were subjected to increasing pressure, and many were excluded or left for the West. Alexander Abusch's rather pessimistic view of German history was condemned by the SED in 1951, and a more optimistic approach was officially ordained. Clusters of historians who were potentially 'hostile to the state' were closely observed by the **Stasi**, and many subsequently left for the West. At the 1958 Trier Historians' Congress, East German historians broke away from the *Verband der Historiker Deutschlands*, and the new GDR *Deutsche Historiker-Gesellschaft* was founded in its place. By the late 1950s, the East German historical profession was becoming more streamlined, more politically conformist or constrained.

The Marxist stage theory of history entailed the struggle of 'progressive' and 'reactionary' forces in every age. Nazism was but one variant of the generic stage of 'fascism', based in imperialist monopoly capitalism. Thus there was nothing intrinsically and always bad about *German* history specifically: it was *capitalism* which was to blame for Hitler. Since the working class, the ultimate winner of history, was currently in power in the GDR – or at least, the vanguard party was ruling on its behalf in a transitional period – it was perfectly possible to write a more positive version of German history in terms of the history of class struggles. This more positive view was expressed in the 1950s by a concentration on revolutionary upheavals and the struggle for freedom. The German people – workers and peasants – were innocent; the ills of German history did not arise from the peculiarities of any specific German *Sonderweg* ('special path'), but from the oppressing imperialist capitalist classes (both agrarian and industrial).

The West German historical profession of the 1950s showed remarkable lines of continuity with the historical profession in Hitler's Germany, with very little change in personnel as a result of denazification. The continuities in methodological approaches and presuppositions were also notable, apart from a small minority of proponents of social and structural approaches to history (such as Theodor Schieder, Werner Conze and Karl Dietrich Bracher).

In an interesting, contradictory symmetry with East German views at the time, most West German historians tended to present Nazism not as intrinsic to the long sweep of German history, but rather as a broader European phenomenon – making use of the concept of totalitarianism to deliver a few sideswipes against communism at the same time. This incidentally also permitted them to ignore communist resistance to Hitler, such as the Red Orchestra, because it was allegedly in the service of an equally totalitarian cause. Gerhard Ritter, for example, saw the origins of totalitarianism in the French Revolution, and the association with mass politics had certain implicitly anti-democratic overtones. With distinguished exceptions, such as Karl Dietrich Bracher's magisterial survey of the rise and character of the Nazi dictatorship, there was a tendency to inflate the role of Hitler as a madman, a criminal surrounded by a small gang of evil henchmen, who had taken over an innocent country, the *Land der Dichter und Denker* ('land of poets and thinkers') and led it down evil paths. This view both served to condemn Nazism and Hitler as evil, while at the same time consolidating the notion that Nazism did not in any essential way either arise out of long-term trends in German history, or have any intrinsic relationship with the German people. Moreover, by emphasizing strategic and tactical mistakes made by a megalomaniac and increasingly unhinged Hitler, this interpretation also served to salvage a degree of honour for the Army and other élite groups. There was at the same time a marked unwillingness to deal with the **Holocaust** proper.

In order to show that there were 'acceptable' traditions leading into West Germany (an almost direct parallel to the GDR emphasis on communist resistance, progressive traditions, and their culmination in the GDR) the idea of an 'other Germany' was developed. The heroes of West German accounts at this time were the men involved in the largely conservative, nationalist resistance of the July Plot of 1944. It was not until much later that a new generation of left-liberal historians pointed out just how little many of those involved in the July Plot actually sympathized with or understood democratic ideas.

Convergence in the era of *détente*?

With the sea-changes in domestic political culture and relations between the two Germanies which began in the mid- and late 1960s, these historiographical patterns began to change in both states. In the West, there was an explosion of sociological and structural approaches, more history from below as well as history from above, more openness to a variety of forms of resistance to Nazism, providing a lively diversity of counterpoints to continued conservative tones which were revitalized in the course of the 1980s. In the East, GDR historians produced more 'top-down' history (rather than focusing on momentous battles and revolutionary turning-points), more emphasis on even the 'bad' aspects of popular opinion, and on other forms of resistance to Hitler than only communist opposition.

In the course of the 1960s in the GDR, the historical profession became more politically homogeneous, provincial and conformist; and historical research was subjected to five-year planning and stringent political control. The focus on revolutionary moments and class struggles was broadened with the ambitious enterprise embarked upon by Jürgen **Kuczynski** and his colleagues on the history of the German working class. The eight-volume *Geschichte der deutschen Arbeiterbewegung* was published in 1966; it was followed two years later by the first two general histories of Germany. Kuczynski brought refreshingly open perspectives to Marxist history.

In the 1970s, the conclusion of **Ostpolitik** was accompanied by a shift in historiographical approaches in the GDR. A theoretical debate on the distinction between heritage (*Erbe*) and tradition provided the precondition for opening the whole of German history as a legitimate field of inquiry, while recognizing that only certain elements of the historical legacy were deemed to be positive. There was a renewed interest in the role of 'great men' in history, with the publication of the massive, two-volume biography of Bismarck by Ernst **Engelberg**, and the accessible biography of Frederick the Great by Ingrid Mittenzwei. In 1983, the centenary of the death of Karl Marx, commemorations of this great founding father of communism were almost overshadowed by the extraordinary rehabilitation of Martin Luther as a national hero, on the occasion of the quincentenary of his birth. The reformation was now suddenly designated as the idealist precondition for Germany's 'early bourgeois revolution', the German Peasants' War, and Luther took a place alongside the old hero of the Peasants' War, Thomas Münzer, as a key forebear of the GDR. The renewed interest in Prussia as a field of historical investigation paralleled new approaches to the legacy of Prussia in West Germany in the early 1980s. There thus appeared to be striking similarities, not only in choice of topic, but also in approach: the causal role of ideas and great men had not previously been a notable feature of the materialist theory of history as interpreted in the GDR.

Even in the old and standard field of the history of the working classes and the labour movement, there were new theoretical approaches. Jürgen Kuczynski, for example, criticized earlier Marxist history for being one-sided and simplistic, and argued for a broader history from below. The account of Nazism presented by Kurt Pätzold and Manfred Weissbecker reinserted the role of the (admittedly misguided) German people in allowing Nazi anti-semitic policies to be carried out. No longer was there a simplistic distinction between the monopoly capitalist 'fascists' and the innocent people. Although a lot of GDR history was still strongly distorted by political purposes, some East German historians were able to adopt the 'sandwich principle' for the presentation of their research: a rich empirical filling was topped and tailed by a little dry bread of Marxist–Leninist theory. This meant at least a somewhat greater diversity in the offerings of East German historians, although censorship and political direction still prevailed.

In West Germany from the 1960s a variety of alternative voices began to challenge the predominant orthodoxy. The publication of Fritz **Fischer**'s re-examination of the origins of WWI in 1961 exploded a variety of taboos, while the **student movement** and the resurrection of neo-Marxist theories in the later 1960s challenged the prevailing climate of amnesia with respect to Nazi Germany. New perspectives on the Third Reich developed in the 1970s. Research such as the 'Bavaria project', based in the Munich Institut für Zeitgeschichte

under Martin **Broszat**, revealed the complexity of patterns of popular opinion and political dissent in the Nazi state. Interpretations by scholars such as Hans **Mommsen** and others delineated the complexity of structures of power in what increasingly appeared to be a 'polycratic' regime. Debates over the origins of genocide became increasingly sophisticated, as wider paradigms of interpretation – 'functionalist' or 'structuralist' – were deployed to reinterpret the Holocaust. The new interest in social and societal history was given a massive boost by the energetic and vigorous contributions of scholars associated with what became known as the Bielefeld School, most notably Hans-Ulrich Wehler and Jürgen **Kocka**. In the 1970s and 1980s there were diverse challenges to these approaches by practitioners of 'history from below': the history of everyday life, as well as the rise of new approaches such as feminist history. Similarly, the emphasis on a German *Sonderweg*, or special (and distorted) path to modernity, which firmly anchored the Third Reich in earlier disjunctures in German history, came under attack, with both theoretical and substantive research tending to undermine the premises on which it had been based.

By the 1980s there was a rich diversity of strands in West German historiography, giving rise to often very heated controversies. One such, which shed more heat than light, was the ***Historikerstreit*** of 1986–7. Demands from a number of conservative historians, most prominently from Ernst **Nolte**, Andreas **Hillgruber**, Klaus Hildebrand and Michael **Stürmer**, for a 'normalization' of the past and a relativization of Germany's crimes were met with heated counter-arguments by left-liberal historians and social theorists such as Jürgen **Habermas**, Hans-Ulrich Wehler and others. It was clear that history could not so easily be subverted to the construction of a conservative national identity in the Federal Republic.

Historiography after unification

The absorption of the former GDR into an enlarged Federal Republic led to a radical restructuring of the East German historical landscape, with many East German historians losing their jobs. Some observers discerned at least the seeds of a 'renationalization' of German history in the 1990s, although there were vigorous counter-currents and lively controversies.

Further reading

Fischer, A. and Heydemann, G. (eds) (1988) *Geschichtswissenschaft in der DDR*, Berlin: Duncker & Humblot.

Iggers, G. (ed.) (1991) *Marxist Historiography in Transformation*, Oxford: Berg.

Jarausch, K. (1991) *Zwischen Parteilichkeit und Professionalität. Bilanz der Geschichtswissenschaft in der DDR*, Berlin: Akademie Verlag.

Maier, C. (1988) *The Unmasterable Past*, Cambridge, MA: Harvard University Press.

Schulin, E. and Müller-Luckner, E. (eds) (1989) *Deutsche Geschichtswissenschaft nach dem zweiten Weltkrieg (1945–65)*, Munich: Oldenbourg.

Wehler, H.-U. (1988) *Entsorgung der deutschen Vergangenheit?*, Munich: C.H. Beck.

MARY FULBROOK

history teaching

History teaching has differed to some extent according to region in the Federal Republic. The main contrast was, however, between the GDR and the FRG.

In the GDR the teaching of history was integrally related to political education. History was seen as a means of legitimating the present, and of transforming historical consciousness in order to produce a 'socialist personality'. A uniform education system of 'polytechnic' schools presented a centrally controlled curriculum, and only politically reliable individuals could be entrusted with the teaching of history.

Historical development was presented in the GDR as a series of stages of progress, according to the Marxist–Leninist schema. Transitions from one stage to the next took place by means of revolutionary class struggles, culminating eventually in socialism: the GDR had thus reached a higher stage of development than the FRG. There was a clear moral message: villains and heroes were clearly depicted, and students were invited to

identify with the revolutionary heroes. In recent and contemporary history, the heroes were the working class and its vanguard communist party. School history lessons were complemented by visits to museums, exhibitions and sites of remembrance, which similarly highlighted a particular moral and political message.

History teaching in the FRG is directed towards the rather different goals of a democratic, pluralist society. Moreover, education is organized at the regional (*Land*) rather than the federal level: some areas have retained the traditional tripartite system (with some modifications and developments), while others have developed comprehensive systems. There was initially far less turnover of personnel in the West than the East, and in the 1950s and 1960s history was often taught by individuals who had been teachers, or had received their own education and training, under the Third Reich. The taboos and sensitivities were often simply evaded by ending the teaching of history at an earlier date. It was only in the 1970s and 1980s that a new generation was able to address the rise and character of the Nazi dictatorship more directly.

As in the East, so in the West history teaching is complemented by visits to museums, exhibitions, concentration camps and the like. In the 1980s there was a veritable boom in such public presentations of the artefacts of history. As far as the Nazi period is concerned, however, some studies have suggested that many West German schoolchildren react with a combination of horror and boredom, rather than acquiring more differentiated knowledge and understanding. Nevertheless, they at least had the chance of exposure to a wide range of evidence and debates, whereas children in the GDR, the self-proclaimed 'anti-fascist state', did not have the opportunity to explore alternative interpretations.

Further reading

Hearndon, A. (1974) *Education in the two Germanies*, Oxford: Basil Blackwell.

Meier, H. and Schmidt, W. (eds) (1970) *Geschichte, Geschichtsbewußtsein und sozialistische Gesellschaft. Beiträge zur Rolle der Geschichtswissenschaft, des Geschichtsunterrichts und der Geschichtspropaganda bei der Entwicklung des sozialistischen Bewußtseins*, East Berlin: Dietz Verlag.

Riesenberger, D. (1973) *Geschichte und Geschichtsunterricht in der DDR*, Göttingen: Vandenhoeck & Ruprecht.

MARY FULBROOK

Hochhuth, Rolf

b. 1 April 1931, Eschwege

Writer

Although Hochhuth has written a number of prose works, his reputation rests almost entirely on his plays and the controversial theses he expounds in them and in the historico-political research that usually accompanies them. Based on the model of Schiller's historical dramas, the plays often appear to be extremely anachronistic in aesthetic terms despite their closeness to the kind of documentary drama that was widespread in the 1960s. Speeches, often delivered in verse, are frequently reminiscent of lectures, while scenes are generally preceded by extensive stage directions and comment on their political significance. Successful productions, which have been numerous, invariably require considerable editing of the voluminous original.

What Hochhuth also shares with Schiller is the belief that the theatre is a moral institution. His concerns have extended from the attitude of the Roman Catholic church to the Nazi extermination of the Jews in his first work of 1963, *The Representative* (*Der Stellvertreter*), to the behaviour of West Germans in the former GDR after unification in the 1992 *Wessis in Weimar* (Westerners in Weimar). Almost invariably a major public storm has been created by the views advanced, helped by Hochhuth's own skill in publicizing his work. Attention was drawn to *Wessis in Weimar* by a controversy over whether he was justifying the terrorist murder of the head of the Treuhand privatization agency Detlev Karsten Rohwedder, whilst Chancellor Kohl is reported to have apologized to the Pope for Hochhuth's criticism of the church for failing to speak out against the Holocaust. The claim made in his second play *Soldiers* (*Soldaten*) of 1967 that Churchill connived in the death of the Polish wartime leader General Sikorski led to successful legal action against Hochhuth in England.

The controversies aroused by Hochhuth are a clear proof that writers can have social and political influence. His criticisms of government policy in 1965 provoked the notorious 'pincher' insult from the then chancellor, Ludwig Erhard, who dismissed intellectuals as no more than little yapping dogs. Hochhuth's revelations about the judicial career of the prime minister of Baden-Württemberg Hans Filbinger during the Nazi era led to the latter's resignation in 1978. Nevertheless, it is impossible to classify Hochhuth as a left-wing intellectual. He has supported the **F.D.P.**, whilst his belief in the significance of individual action is at odds with much modern political thinking. In many respects, he remains isolated among his fellow writers. His decision to purchase the **Berliner Ensemble** in 1995 proved universally unpopular.

Despite his many detractors, Hochhuth remains a major figure in German literature. The significance of the questions he raises is undeniable. Moreover, reactions to his views are a measure of society's tolerance and liberality.

Further reading

Arnold, H.L. (ed.) (1978) *Rolf Hochhuth*, Munich: edition text + kritik.

Hinck, W. (ed.) (1981) *Rolf Hochhuth – Eingriff in die Zeitgeschichte*, Reinbek bei Hamburg: Rowohlt (the title underlines the significance of the political dimension of Hochhuth's work).

STUART PARKES

Hochschule für Gestaltung

The Hochschule für Gestaltung (HfG) (the Academy of Design) in Ulm, founded in 1952 by the Geschwister Scholl Foundation, was planned as an experimental institution where students received a specialized training on a universal basis and were taught civil responsibility and technical skills. Originally conceived as a new Bauhaus aiming at improvement of quality, form and usefulness of everyday objects, the HfG, opened on 2 October

1955, later attempted to create a new link between design, science and technology. The *Ulmer Modell*, a special method of training, became the model for institutions in several countries. Yet, inner conflicts and defaming press campaigns added to the precarious financial situation. When federal funding stopped in 1967, the HfG had to close a year later.

See also: art colleges

Further reading

Lindinger, H. (ed.) *Ulm Design: The Morality of Objects* Cambridge, MA: MIT Press (comprehensive catalogue about the HfG).

INES SCHLENKER

Hochwälder, Fritz

b. 28 May 1911, Vienna; d. 20 October 1986, Zürich

Dramatist

Hochwälder fled the Nazis in 1938. Settling in Zürich, he turned to writing as a profession. During the 1940s and 1950s his plays, based on historical subjects but illuminating contemporary problems, enjoyed unprecedented international success, especially *Das heilige Experiment* (1943), translated as *The Strong are Lonely* (1956). Moral dilemmas and guilt as a universal human attribute are the main motifs. After 1955, Hochwälder abandoned historical plays and sought inspiration in the Viennese *Volkstheater* (popular folk theatre) refusing to the last any influence of modern theatrical theory.

Further reading

Daviau, D.G. (1988) 'Fritz Hochwälder', in D.G. Daviau (ed.), *Major Figures of Modern Austrian Literature*, Riverside: Ariadne Press (authoritative introduction to Hochwälder's life and works).

GABRIELA STEINKE

Höllerer, Walter

b. 19 December 1922, Sulzbach-Rosenberg (Bavaria)

Poet and publisher

Höllerer is a prolific writer and editor. He was a member of **Gruppe 47** and co-edited the influential literary journal *Akzente* from 1954–9. Since 1961 he has been the editor of *Sprache im technischen Zeitalter*, at that time the most influential German journal acknowledging the ever speedier entwining of literature, language and technology. Höllerer is also a very productive artist in his own right, producing poetry, films, novels, a play and essays.

HOLGER BRIEL

Höpcke, Klaus

b. 27 November 1933, Cuxhaven

GDR politician

Höpcke came to prominence as cultural editor of **Neues Deutschland** (1964–73) before being promoted to Deputy Minister of Culture (1973–89). Because of his responsibility for publishing he was referred to colloquially as the 'Minister of Books', but he was also the head of the GDR's literary censorship authority (see also **censorship: GDR**). He played a part in supporting the radicalization of culture in the **Honecker** era, but on a piecemeal basis which meant he was inevitably also involved in acts of repression which are now extensively documented. Since 1990 he has been a **PDS** member of the Thuringian *Land* parliament.

DENNIS TATE

Hörspiel: FRG

The German radio play (*Hörspiel*) came into being on 24 October 1924 with the transmission of Hans Flesch's *Zauberei auf dem Sender* (Magic at the Radio Station), a piece about a magician, anxious to demonstrate his powers, causing mayhem in a broadcasting studio while at the same time illustrating the ease with which a purely acoustic medium can transcend the confines of realism. During the following years, a number of the leading Berlin writers of the Weimar Republic either experimented with the *Hörspiel* form or broadcast radio adaptations of their works. (Brecht's *Lindbergh* and Döblin's *Berlin Alexanderplatz*, both 1929, are milestones in the second category.) As part of National Socialism's *Gleichschaltung* policy, radio plays were assigned either the task of political propaganda (e.g. Richard Euringer's *Deutsche Passion*) or fostering a mood of escapism.

After 1945 – for a variety of economic, cultural and aesthetic reasons – *Hörspiele* assumed a significant role in the cultural output of the individual zones of occupation and in the early FRG. Günter **Eich**'s *Geh nicht nach El Kuwehd!* (Don't go to El Kuwehd!) (1950), *Der Tiger Jussuf* (Yussuf the Tiger) (1952) and *Die Mädchen aus Viterbo* (The Girls from Viterbo) (1953), mark the beginning of an intense period of radio play production in the 1950s. Eich's *Träume* (Dreams) (1950), with its combination of surreal and lyrical elements, effectively captured the largely a-political, angst-ridden mood of the time. However, this should not lead to an underestimation of the sheer variety of works (satires, didactic parables, psychological monologues, conversation pieces and poetic legends) produced during the 1950s by such diverse authors as Ingeborg **Bachmann**, Heinrich **Böll**, Friedrich **Dürrenmatt**, Max **Frisch**, Wolfgang **Hildesheimer**, Martin **Walser** and Wolfgang **Weyrauch**.

All such pre-stereophonic forms are characterized by a conception of the *Hörspiel* as spoken word evoking a second (fantastic or plausible) reality in the listener's mind. With stereophonic radio's ability to spatialize language between the speakers or headphones the *Hörspiel* of the 1960s became primarily an exploration of language's materiality. As Klaus Schöning's pioneering 1969 anthology *Neues Hörspiel: Texte Partituren* demonstrates, the writers of the new-wave radio play (e.g. Peter **Handke** and Wolf **Wondratschek**) were also intent on widening their repertoire by including a variety of non-linguistic sounds and orchestrating simultaneous collages according to principles derived from electronic music. Subsequent experiments with authentic (*O-Ton*) collage-material have

failed to attract writers of the same stature as the '*Neues Hörspiel*' tendency which had for well over a decade engaged the radical talents of such major concrete poets as Ferdinand Kriwet, Ernst **Jandl**, Friederike **Mayröcker**, Franz Mon and Gerhard Rühm.

Further reading

Döhl, R. (1988) *Das Neue Hörspiel*, Darmstadt: Wissenschaftliche Buchgesellschaft.
Keckeis, H. (1973) *Das deutsche Hörspiel*, 1923–73, Frankfurt am Main: Athenäum.
Schöning, K. (ed.) (1992ff) *Geschichte und Typologie des Hörspiels*, 7 vols, Darmstadt: Wissenschaftliche Buchgesellschaft.
Schwitzke, H. (1963) *Das Hörspiel: Dramaturgie und Geschichte*, Cologne: Kiepenheuer & Witsch.
—— (1969) *Reclams Hörspielführer*, Stuttgart: Reclam.

JOHN J. WHITE

Hörspiel: GDR

In his 1973 survey *Das deutsche Hörspiel* Hermann Keckeis writes of a tension in the development of German radio drama that began during the Weimar Republic with the opposing theories of Richard Kolb and Hermann Pongs. Kolb insisted on the inner effect of the disembodied word, its aesthetic value, and its removal from mundane reality, a view that attracted lyric poets to the genre, especially in the subsequent Federal Republic of Germany. For Pongs – supported by Bertold Brecht, Walter Benjamin, Friedrich Wolf, Alfred Döblin and others in the *Arbeiterradiobewegung* (Workers' Radio Movement) – radio should be a collective experience, a medium to inform and educate the masses about contemporary social problems, albeit without ignoring the need for quiet contemplation. Such works – *Gegenwartsdramatik* (contemporary drama) – sought to achieve a balance between society and the individual and characterized much of the radio drama of the GDR, particularly in its later years.

In the 1950s, while *Hörspiel* authors in the FRG experimented with sound and form (*Das neue Hörspiel*), GDR authors and theorists struggled for free expression and tried to agree on a concept of realism that would also allow for the subjective emotion and contemplation advocated by Pongs. No attempt was made at experimentation with sound, although some formal innovations were made (monologue, dream sequences), as more well-known authors were attracted to the medium (e.g. Inge and Heiner **Müller**, Günter **Kunert** and Stephan **Hermlin**). The period from the mid-1960s was typified by works dealing with contemporary social problems concealed in a historical setting. Stefan Hermlin's *Scardanelli* (1970) was ostensibly a biography of Hölderlin, but dealt with the struggle between power and the human spirit; Günter Kunert's *Mit der Zeit ein Feuer* (In Time, A Fire) (1971), *Ehrenhandel* (Affair of Honour) (1972), and *Ein anderer K.* (A Different K.) (1976) had Dürer, Heine and Kleist as their main protagonists but contemporary issues as their essence.

O-Ton (collages of authentic recordings) was adopted in 1977, more than a decade after its use began in the FRG. The injection of such contemporary realism changed both the form and the content of GDR radio drama, and the *realistisches Gegenwartshörspiel* (realistic contemporary radio drama) became again, and remained, its hallmark. The *Hörspiel* in the GDR suffered less from censorship than any other genre, but much was written that could not be aired (e.g. Joachim **Walther**'s *Infarkt*, a play about a GDR citizen destroyed by his society, was written in 1975 but not broadcast until 1990).

In the final decade of the GDR, radio drama went through immense changes. New authors were attracted by its relative freedom from censorship – particulary true of the *Kinderhörspiel* (children's radio drama) – and a clear note of revolt emanated from them. In 1982 Günther Rückert's *Dame vor Spiegel* (Woman at a Mirror) was allowed to portray a totally pessimistic view of GDR society and its destructive effect on an individual. The 'Nalepa-Sound' (named for the street in which the *Rundfunk der DDR* had its main studios) was famous throughout the industry in Europe where it won many prizes. The sound combined realistic themes, professional authors and actors, and a great deal of original music. Its demise is regretted by most in the industry, East and West.

See also: *Hörspiel*: FRG

Further reading

Keckeis, H. (1973) *Das deutsche Hörspiel 1923–1973*, Frankfurt am Main: Athenäum.

Underwood, P. (1993) *Authority and Rebellion: The GDR Kinderhörspiel*, dissertation, Knoxville, TN: University of Tennessee.

Würffel, S.B. (1978) *Das deutsche Hörspiel*, Stuttgart: Metzler.

PENNY J. UNDERWOOD

Hoflehner, Rudolf

b. 8 August 1916, Linz

Painter and sculptor

In the 1950s, Hoflehner was a leading exponent of Austrian abstract sculpture along with Fritz **Wotruba**. Using welding machinery, he fashioned blocks of iron into forms suggestive of the human figure, and these became increasingly aggressive in appearance. In 1967 Hoflehner took the unconventional step of abandoning sculpture in favour of painting. Here he developed the theme of human struggle and suffering, depicting contorted, fleshy forms reminiscent of Francis Bacon. In the late 1970s his work focused on representational human figures, which continued to convey a sense of violence and suffering.

ALEX COOKE

Hofmann, Gert

b. 29 January 1931, Limbach (Saxony); d. 1 July 1993, Erding

Writer

A prolific writer of radio plays from the 1960s onwards, Hofmann moved from the GDR to West Germany in 1951. Much of his work, some of it autobiographical and including novels and short stories, deals with the Nazi past and its manifestations in the present, the role of art and the artist, and questions social values. Works include *Balzac's*

Horse (*Balzacs Pferd*, 1978) and *Die Überflutung* (The Flood) (1979) (both radio plays), *The Spectacle at the Tower* (*Auf dem Turm*, 1982), *Our Conquest* (*Unsere Eroberung*, 1984) and *Parable of the Blind* (*Der Blindensturz*, 1985).

Further reading

Butler, M. (1994) 'Ein hoffnungsloser Moralist: Some observations on the Narrative World of Gert Hofmann', *German Life and Letters* 47, 3: 375–84.

MARGARET VALLANCE

Hollein, Hans

b. 30 March 1934, Vienna

Architect

Hollein studied engineering and architecture at the Academy of Fine Arts in Vienna, and gained an M.Arch. from Illinois Institute of Technology and Berkeley. He worked in the USA, Sweden and Germany before establishing a private practice in Vienna in 1964. He has been Visiting Professor at numerous American universities, Professor at Düsseldorf Academy of Fine Arts since 1967, and has also taught at Vienna Academy since 1976.

Hollein's architecture is characterized by an idiosyncratic fusion of art, design and architecture, often using expensive materials and expressive and suggestive detailing. The Milan Pavilion (1968) gave him an international reputation which was secured by his Viennese shop-conversions and the Mönchengladbach Museum (1972–82).

MARTIN KUDLEK

Holocaust

The term is derived from *holocaustus*, the translation into Greek of the Hebrew *olah*, 'a burnt offering dedicated *exclusively* to God'. Over time, *holocaust* came to denote total destruction, especially by fire. Since the 1960s, *Holocaust* acquired the meaning which is the subject of this article: the planned exclusion of Jews from civic society and their physical destruction through organized mass killings. In Germany, Nazi terms such as 'final solution' ('*Endlösung*') or 'Extermination of the Jews' ('*Judenvernichtung*') are still widely used. The word 'Holocaust' itself gained widespread currency after the showing on German television of the American series of that name in 1979. The death toll of the Holocaust has been estimated at six million, one million of them babies and young children. In 1933, European Jewry numbered 8.6 million; by 1945 three out of four had perished. Along with the Holocaust, the Nazi regime carried out other mass murders. Victims included a quarter of a million Gypsies, three million Soviet PoWs, tens of thousands of Soviet commissars, and over ten million Czechs, Poles, Serbs, Russians and others, some of them partisans, most of them, however non-combatants or slave labourers. As archives open in eastern Europe, an upward revision of the numbers, including victims of the Holocaust, is likely. In particular the number of civilians murdered in the Soviet Union has been previously underestimated.

After the installation of Adolf Hitler as Chancellor on 30 January 1933, the preparatory phase of the Holocaust began. Jews in Germany faced persecution and the destruction of the economic and social foundations of their lives. The elections on 5 March 1933 were already accompanied by numerous anti-Semitic incidents including the destruction of the synagogues in Dresden and Göttingen. On 1 April 1933 the Nazis called on Germans to boycott Jewish shops while SA hordes smashed business premises and violently assaulted many Jews. Six days later, the 'Law for the Restoration of the Civil Service' dismissed so called non-Aryans – defined as everyone with at least one Jewish grandparent – from public service including all levels of state administration and teaching. An employment ban for doctors, lawyers, actors and writers followed. On 25 April, the number of Jews allowed to attend schools and universities was severely restricted. On 10 May, there was public burning of 'un-German' books. On 15 September 1935, the infamous Nürnberg Laws deprived Jews of their German citizenship, banned intermarriage and excluded them from employment, education and social participation. Exclusion even extended to attending a theatre, cinema or swimming pool.

After the *Anschluß*, Nazi anti-Jewish measures also applied in Austria. On 28 October 1938, 20,000 Jews whose status as naturalized Germans had been declared void by the Nazis were driven into the no-man's land between Germany and Poland. In protest, a 17-year-old boy, whose parents were among those deported, shot a member of the German embassy in Paris on 7 November 1938. The Nazis used the incident to move from exclusion to physical attacks and murder: on 9 and 10 November 1938, SA and SS formations burnt and destroyed virtually all synagogues in Germany, vandalized shops and homes, murdered scores in the streets and imprisoned several thousand Jews in concentration camps. By September 1939, 300,000 Jews had fled Germany; of the 210,000 who remained, 170,000 were murdered in the Holocaust.

During WWII, persecution became the Holocaust, exclusion equalled murder. The euthanasia programme foreshadowed the death camps. Between spring 1939 and August 1941, over one hundred thousand mentally and physically handicapped patients were selected by a 'medical commission' and murdered through gassing in specially constructed mobile vans or gas chambers. Following protests from the German public (but not from the medical profession) euthanasia was ostensibly suspended although killings did continue.

After the Nazi invasion of Poland in September 1939, Jews suffered extensive pogroms, lost all economic and social rights, were expelled from their homes, 'concentrated' in overcrowded ghettos in large cities, or used as slave labour. Hunger and disease caused many deaths. As early as 21 September 1939 a letter by the SS General and Chief of Police, Heydrich, announced that the measures of 'resettlement' were in preparation for an 'ultimate objective'. That this objective was genocide became evident in the course of WWII, in particular after the invasion of the Soviet Union in June 1941. Following on the heels of the German Army were four SS units, the *Einsatzgruppen*, subdivided into mobile murder squads. Reinforced by more than twenty-six police battalions, consisting of Lithuanians, Latvians, Estonians, Ukrainians, Germans, Austrians and others, they had, by November 1942, murdered over one million Jews as well as tens of thousands of Gypsies and communist officials.

More 'efficient' methods of mass murder were sought than shootings over execution pits. In December 1941, experiments to use mobile vans for gassing and to dispose of the bodies in crematoria ovens resulted in the first death camp, Chelmo near Łódź, and a mass transfer of Polish Jews for gassing from nearby ghettos. On 20 January 1942 Heydrich, assisted by Eichmann, presided over the Wannsee Conference, attended by state and SS officials involved in the deportation of Jews from occupied lands. The resulting administrative co-ordination, particularly with the Ministry of Foreign Affairs, marked a further stage in the process of genocide. New death camps were established in 1942: **Auschwitz**, Belzec, Majdanek, Sobibor and Treblinka. The six million Jews who perished in the Holocaust came from Poland, the Soviet Union, Lithuania, Latvia and Estonia; from Czechoslovakia, Hungary, Romania, Bulgaria, Greece and Yugoslavia; and from Austria, Germany, Italy, France, Belgium, Denmark and Norway.

As the populations in the ghettos, weakened by starvation and illness, were sent to their deaths, Jewish resistance began to be organized. In 1943 there were a series of uprisings, the most famous in the Warsaw Ghetto (in April and May), in the Bialystock ghetto (August), and in the Sobibor and Treblinka death camps. Other acts of revolt occurred in several smaller ghettos, including an organized break-out from the Kovno ghetto.

The Holocaust was spearheaded by the SS but could not have been carried out without Hitler's knowledge and approval and the active co-operation of the army, the police, major and minor state, regional and local officials, construction firms, industrial giants like IG Farben (who supplied the death camps with the poisonous gas, Zyklon B), architects to design and engineering firms to build the gas chambers and crematoria, medical practitioners, railway managers, guards, train drivers and so on. Rumours of mass shootings and death camps abounded and there were many eye-witness accounts of the deportations and atrocities. Most Germans remained indifferent to the Holocaust (or claimed to obey orders) and only a handful took the side of the victims.

See also: *Historikerstreit*; *Vergangenheitsbewältigung*

Further reading

Cesarani, D. (ed.) (1994), *The Final Solution: Origins and Implementation*, London: Routledge (this collective volume brings together experts on the Holocaust and the history of Nazi Germany; based on new archive materials from eastern Europe, chapters cover the development and scope of the Holocaust, the role of SS and German army as well as responses to the Holocaust in Germany, occupied Europe, the US and Britain).

Gilbert, M. (1986), *The Holocaust: The Jewish Tragedy*, London: Collins (based on a vast collection of personal evidence, eye-witness accounts, diary entries, retrospectives, interviews, and also on Nazi documents and decrees, Gilbert's book presents a history of the Holocaust from its preparatory phase in the 1930s to the shattered lives of its few survivors).

Krausnick, H. *et al.* (1968) *Anatomy of the SS State*, London: Collins (originally published in German, this seminal study puts special emphasis on the role of the SS, the German army and state admininstration and aims to clarify the decision-making process that resulted in the Holocaust, and identify the perpetrators of genocide both in the bureaucracy and in the murder squads and death camps).

Lanzmann, D. (1985) *Shoah. An Oral History of the Holocaust*, New York: Pantheon (this book consists of the text of Lanzmann's film which recreates the horrors of the Nazi death camps through the accounts of survivors and also shows how many ordinary people knew about or contributed to the Holocaust).

EVA KOLINSKY

Holthusen, Hans Egon

b. 15 April 1913, Rendsburg (Schleswig-Holstein)

Poet and critic

Holthusen established his reputation after 1945 as a poet of a defeated Germany. Unlike many poets, he was prepared to tackle uncomfortable themes such as war and guilt when much of the population preferred to think only of the future. This poetic vein ran dry by the early 1950s, giving way to an influential series of books devoted to literary criticism and the moral value of literature. By the 1960s the conservative Holthusen was in conflict with the left in German literature, pariculary Günter **Grass** and H.M. **Enzensberger**.

ANTHONY BUSHELL

Holzbauer, Wilhelm

b. 3 September 1930, Salzburg

Architect

Holzbauer studied at the Vienna Academy of Fine Arts, and was a founding member of *Arbeitsgruppe 4*. Since 1977 he has been a professor at the Vienna Academy of Applied Arts.

Holzbauer's large projects convince by the compact and clear organization of complex functional sequences without creating cramped spaces. His smaller designs also demonstrate spatial virtuosity and a great desire for material quality. Some of his more important buildings are the housing project *Wohnen Morgen* in Vienna (1973–9), Salzburg University Science Faculty (1978–86), and the Biological Centre in Frankfurt Main (1988–93).

MARTIN KUDLEK

Honecker, Erich

b. 25 August 1912, Neunkirchen (the Saar); d. 29 May 1994, Santiago (Chile)

GDR functionary

The son of a miner who was a member of the Communist Party in the Saar, Honecker himself became a full member of the **KPD** in 1929. He was sent for party training to Moscow in 1930–1 and returned to the Saar to become a full-time official in the communist youth movement (KJVD). In December 1935 he was arrested in Germany as a communist activist and sentenced in 1937 to ten years in prison. He served his sentence in Brandenburg prison, and just before the end of the war, in March 1945, he escaped from prison and lived underground until the capitulation.

When the KPD leadership returned to Germany in April and May 1945, Honecker was put in charge of youth affairs and supervised the setting up of the Free German Youth (**FDJ**) in March 1946. In 1950 he became a candidate member of the **Politbüro**, and a full member in 1958. During this period his rise up the hierarchy of the **SED** owed much to his strong support for Walter **Ulbricht**, the First Secretary of the SED. As Secretary for Security from 1958 Honecker was responsible for the planning and execution of the building of the **Berlin Wall** in 1961, in collaboration with the Soviets. During the 1960s Honecker came to be seen as the natural successor to Ulbricht, and when Ulbricht was forced to resign in 1971 under Soviet pressure, Honecker was the obvious successor.

Initially, there were hopes of a more flexible leadership in the GDR, especially in the cultural sphere, and the change in government in the FRG in 1969 had also led to the prospect of a more relaxed relationship between the two German states. Honecker's speech in 1972 which spoke of 'no taboos' in the cultural field, and the signing of the Basic Treaty in December 1972, according the GDR a degree of recognition by the FRG, increased these hopes. During the ensuing years, the GDR did achieve much greater international recognition, but hopes of a more liberal cultural policy were dashed by the '**Biermann Affair**' in 1976.

In 1980 Honecker made a state visit to Austria, the first to a western country, which was a sign of the GDR's greater acceptance by the international community. After much diplomatic bargaining he was finally allowed to visit West Germany in 1987. But at home there were signs of growing unrest, first because of the failure of the economy, and second as a reaction against the repressive activities of the security services. After Gorbachev's rise to power in the Soviet Union, Honecker showed his increasing ideological rigidity by his total rejection of any move in the direction of the reforms being introduced in the Soviet Union. Honecker's serious illness in 1989 increased his isolation from reality, which forced a group of Politbüro members, probably with Soviet support, to engineer his removal from the top position in the SED in October 1989.

After his removal from power he was protected by the Soviet army which flew him to Moscow secretly, together with his second wife, Margot, in March 1991. When the Soviet Union started to collapse later that year, he sought asylum in the Chilean embassy in Moscow. His daughter had married a Chilean exile during the Pinochet years. After great pressure from Bonn on the Chilean government, Honecker was forced to leave the embassy in July 1992, and he was returned to Germany. He was charged with manslaughter in relation to the shootings on the borders of the GDR. His health was, however, deteriorating, and the trial was suspended shortly after its opening in November 1992. Honecker was allowed to fly with his wife to Chile early in 1993, but he survived for only another year before succumbing to cancer.

Further reading

Borkowski, D. (1987) *Erich Honecker*, Munich: Bertelsmann (biography of Honecker).

Michel, K. and Spengler, T. (eds) (1993) *In Sachen Erich Honecker*, Berlin: Rowohlt, (collection of essays on Honecker's political life).

Przybylski, P. (1991) *Tatort Politbüro. Die Akte Honecker*, Berlin: Rowohlt (commentary on Honecker's political life with extracts from files on Honecker).

PETER BARKER

Honecker, Margot

b. 17 April 1927, Halle

GDR functionary (neé Feist)

A functionary in the **FDJ** in the late 1940s and 1950s, she married Erich **Honecker** in 1953. In 1963 she became Minister of Education in the GDR and a member of the **Central Committee** of the SED. After the suspension of the trial against her husband in January 1993 because of ill-health, she accompanied him to live in Chile, where she remained after his death in May 1994.

PETER BARKER

Honneth, Axel

b. 18 July 1949, Essen

Philosopher

Honneth's works mark an important innovation in the tradition of the Critical Theories of the **Frankfurt School**. Central to his thought is the argument, put forward especially in *Kritik der Macht* (*Critique of Power*) (1986), that **Critical Theory** simplifies structures of social domination by neglecting the ethical dimension to human behaviour. Honneth seeks to ground his own socio-critical ethics in the conflictual dialectics of interpersonal recognition, which is strongly indebted to Hegel's early reflections on law and right. He attempts to refigure critical theories of law, value and power by asserting moral consensus, or recognition, as the ground of social formation and solidarity. This is seen especially in *Kampf um Anerkennung* (*Struggle for Recognition*) (1992).

CHRIS THORNHILL

Horkheimer, Max

b. 14 February 1895, Stuttgart; d. 7 July 1971, Nürnberg

Philosopher and sociologist

Director of the **Frankfurt School** from 1931, widely considered founder of **Critical Theory** with a series of articles in the *Zeitschrift für Sozialforschung* (see especially 'Traditionelle und kritische Theorie', 1937). Horkheimer's later works move away from Marxism and towards a re-evaluation of Schopenhauer and the Jewish tradition.

Further reading

Gumnior, H. and Ringguth, R. (1973) *Max Horkheimer*, Reinbek bei Hamburg: Rowohlt (concise overview of life and work).

Schmidt, A. and Altwicker, N. (eds) (1986) *Horkheimer heute: Werk und Wirkung*, Frankfurt am Main: Fischer (also contains detailed bibliographies of primary and secondary literature).

GÜNTER MINNERUP

Horn, Rebecca

b. 24 March 1944, Michelstadt (Hessen)

Performance artist, video artist, sculptor and filmmaker

Rebecca Horn is a multimedia artist with an international reputation who executed her first body-art performances in 1968. Subsequent performances frequently involved choreographed rituals and body 'extensions' (wings and feelers) to explore identity and sexuality. As well as video recordings of performances she has produced numerous films – including the feature-length experimental films *La Ferdinanda* (1981) and *Buster's Bedroom* (1990). Since the early 1980s she has concentrated on large-scale installations, often involving musical instruments and kinetic elements, which combine natural and mechanistic materials to powerful and poetic effect.

MARTIN BRADY

Hotter, Hans

b. 19 January 1909, Offenbach am Main

Bass baritone

Hotter trained as an organist and choirmaster, but later studied singing and was renowned as the leading Wotan (in Wagner's *Ring* cycle) of the postwar years. He created roles in two of Richard Strauß's later operas, *Friedenstag* and *Capriccio*, in Munich, and was a mainstay of the **Bayreuth Festival** from his debut in 1952. From 1961–4 he produced as well as sang in the *Ring* cycle at Covent Garden. He appears in the first commercially recorded *Ring* cycle (Decca), singing with enormous authority, his huge, warm voice inflected with great verbal imagination.

BEATRICE HARPER

HPP

The architectural partnership of Hentrich, Petsching und Partner (HPP), established in Düsseldorf in 1953, has a large, sometimes uninspired œuvre dominated by office and administration buildings of Miesian nature. The Thyssen Skyscraper in Düsseldorf (1957–60) is the best-known, representing a prototype of German *Wirtschaftswunder* (**Economic Miracle**) architecture.

MARTIN KUDLEK AND BERTHOLD PESCH

Hrdlicka, Alfred

b. 27 February 1927, Vienna

Sculptor and graphic artist

After studying painting and sculpture under Fritz **Wotruba**, Hrdlicka only became well known during the 1960s. Today he is one of the most popular, though controversial Austrian sculptors. In his figurative sculptures, drawings and prints he reflects on history and events of the day. Exploration of the causes of fascism plays an important part in his work, which is generally centred around violence and sexuality. He has also expressed his political commitment in a number of provocative public monuments and polemical texts.

See also: sculpture

KERSTIN MEY

Huchel, Peter

b. 3 April 1903, Lichterfelde (near Berlin); d. 30 April 1981, Staufen (Breisgau)

Writer

Huchel's life was characterized by stark contrasts. On the one hand, he was thrust into the middle of highly political conflicts as editor in chief of the GDR literary journal *Sinn und Form* from 1949 until his involuntary resignation in 1962, and on the other hand, he was forced to live in isolation and under state observation in Wilhelmshorst near Potsdam from 1963 until his move to West Germany in 1971. As the editor of *Sinn und Form*

he refused to comply with official demands that the journal become a cultural mouthpiece for the mission of **socialist realism** in the GDR. Rather, Huchel insisted on creating an international literary journal which was geared towards intellectuals in both Germanys. Although he faced opposition from within the political apparatus from early on, he had strong supporters, like Bertolt **Brecht** and Johannes R. **Becher**. Huchel was not a member of any one ideological group. His humanist intellectualism found itself at odds with the official cultural programme of the GDR, formulated, for instance, in 1959 in the ***Bitterfelder Weg*** manifesto, which outlined a literature production by and for workers towards the common goal of socialism. He moved to West Germany in 1971, and settled in Freiburg.

Huchel wrote mainly poetry. In the 1920s and 1930s he earned his livelihood by writing approximately thirty-five radio plays, only half of which still exist. Huchel's poetry is strongly characterized by the use of nature imagery, undoubtedly a result of his childhood experiences on his grandfather's farm in Alt-Langerwisch outside Berlin. The language of nature is often interpreted as a code for political criticism, as exemplified in some of his most famous poems such as 'Hubertusweg' and 'Der Garten des Theophrast'. Nature represents a realm of exact observation without pointing to a metaphysical significance. Huchel's style has evolved from writing mostly in rhyme in his early poetry to predominantly free verse in his later work. Much of his poetry is as aesthetically powerful as it is difficult to analyse. The hermetic quality of the images in his later work is often compared to that in Paul **Celan**'s poetry. Huchel poems have brought him numerous literary prizes.

See also: poetry: GDR

Further reading

Parker, S. (1988) 'Visions, Revisions and Divisions: The Critical Legacy of Peter Huchel' in *German Life and Letters* 41, 2 (engages Vieregg (1988) in a spirited exchange over the proper critical evaluation of Huchel's work and biography).

Vieregg, A. (1986) *Peter Huchel*, Frankfurt am Main: Suhrkamp Taschenbuch Materialien (contains a selection of critical essays, interpretations of individual poems, accounts of personal encounters and a bibliography; Vieregg is the editor of Huchel's collected works in two volumes).

—— (1988) 'The Truth about Peter Huchel?' in *German Life and Letters* 41, 2 (Huchel's political views during and immediately after WWII are of particular interest).

REINHILD STEINGRÖVER McRAE

Huillet, Danièle

b. 1 May 1936, Paris

Filmmaker

Huillet is a modernist and politically radical collaborator with Jean-Marie **Straub**. Appalled by the 1950s Paris university atmosphere, she prepared to enter film school (IDHEC), then joined Straub in the FRG to begin their Bach film. She had early credits as an assistant director but was subsequently recognized as a more equal partner whose role emphasizes production, sound, rehearsal of actors and editing. She is also an actress and French translator of German and Italian texts for several productions.

Further reading

Heberle, H. and Stern, M.F. (1982) 'Das Feuer im Innern des Berges', *Frauen und Film* 32: 4–12 (among countless Straub and Huillet interviews, the only one with Huillet alone).

BARTON BYG

Humboldt Foundation

Named after Alexander von Humboldt (1769–1859), the natural scientist and explorer, the *Humboldt-Stiftung* was established in Berlin in 1860 and, following war-time disruption, re-emerged in 1925 and 1953. Its brief is to provide financial assistance to foreign academics for research in Germany and also to sponsor German academics researching abroad. In 1992 over 2,000 senior academics from eighty-four countries re-ceived assistance, in a proportion of 65 percent to scientists, 25 percent to arts scholars and 11 percent to engineers. Special awards include American scholarships for young German scientists, awards for foreign arts scholars, and for Franco-German co-operation.

HANS J. HAHN

humour

Mark Twain once said the German sense of humour is no laughing matter. However, in spite of the traditional view of German humour as, at best, wooden, and, at worst, sadistic (the word *Schadenfreude* is, after all, notoriously untranslatable) there is plenty of evidence for a German sense of humour. The late twentieth century has seen a renaissance in the fashion for comedy clubs and cabaret as well as the continuation of humour traditions such as slapstick, carnival and practical jokes, and, in the 1990s, a wave of highly successful comic films.

In spite of the differences in humour between Britain and Germany, British humour is very popular in Germany and is perceived as black, deadpan or dry and thoroughly exotic. Several popular British comedy shows and comedians are particularly celebrated in Germany, notably *Monty Python*, *Fawlty Towers* and Rowan Atkinson's *Mr Bean*. Similarly derivative comedy programmes such as a German-style *Candid Camera*, or *Herzblatt*, the German equivalent of *Blind Date* demonstrate similarities in humour and the extent to which some comedy is indeed translatable.

One of the rituals of the German New Year celebrations is the television screening of ***Dinner for One***, starring Freddy Frinton as a drunken butler serving dinner to an eccentric English Lady, Miss Sophie. This short film was made in Hamburg in 1963 and is shown in English without subtitles because it relies on the visual impact of slapstick for its humour.

Slapstick dominates the humour of the ***Volkstheater***, the popular theatre, in Germany. Comic plays relying for their humour on mistaken identity, or rags to riches scenarios, are populated by comic buffoonery and highly visual slapstick scenes enjoy much success. Comic plays performed in popular theatres such as the Rebstöckle, in Stuttgart, or the **Ohnesorg-Theater** in Hamburg are often recorded and televised. *Karneval* also represents a further aspect of German slapstick humour with the rule of the fool, cross-dressing and elaborate costumes providing an escape into humour before the serious business of Lent.

In contrast to the slapstick humour of the popular German theatre and of *Karneval* is the tradition of **cabaret**. Cabaret has provided a forum for satirical, political comment over the past century and cabaret clubs such as the Distel in the former GDR provided a focus both for satirical comment on the communist regime before unification and then for further comic reflection on political progress following the *Wende*.

German jokes reflect both the political and the slapstick nature of German humour as well as highlighting attitudes within Germany to the various regions. The East Frisians bear the brunt of much humour and they are portrayed in jokes as backward and slow rural people. However, the Austrians, Swabians and Bavarians suffer a similar fate, for example:

How does an Austrian know that Lake Constance has dried up? By the dust thrown up by his oars when rowing.

Political jokes and jokes marking unification abound, often mocking the Trabant:

How do you increase the value of a Trabi up to DM 100? Fill up the tank.

ALISON PHIPPS

Hundertwasser, Friedensreich

b. 15 December 1928, Vienna; d. February 2000, on board the Queen Elizabeth II in the South Pacific

Architect and artist (real name Friedrich Stowasser)

Influenced by the *Jugendstil*, Hundertwasser employs a kaleidoscopic, decorative style of painting. This is echoed in architectural ideas which are characterized by a feeling of organic growth and express his desire to harmonize man and nature.

Since the 1950s he has travelled the world championing ecological causes; in 1981 he received the Austrian Prize for Nature Protection. In 1983 work began on the *Hundertwasser-Haus* in Vienna, a small housing project demonstrating his attempt to 'rehumanize' modern architecture. Since 1974 he has lived mostly in New Zealand.

ALEX COOKE

hunting

Hunting is one of the oldest activities of humankind. Although initially providing the means for survival, hunting today is a sport as well as a profession. The codification of hunting as a sport coincided with the emergence of modern sport in the nineteenth century. The first hunting law was passed in Germany in 1848 and was linked closely to land ownership. Hunting has traditionally remained an activity of the upper classes, although historically lower-class participants were identified as such by the varieties of game they could hunt. Hunting remains an exclusive activity, though today this is a result of legal requirements rather than class affiliation.

Hunting in Germany is regulated by a plethora of related laws such as the National Hunting Act, the Hunting Season Act and provincial hunting and seasons laws of the respective *Länder*, as well as laws on wildlife, weapons, food hygiene and the environment. In addition, the German Hunting Association is responsible for the administration of hunting throughout Germany. Prospective hunters must undergo a stringent examination process before a hunting licence can be issued.

In recent years, hunting has been condemned in the popular press as a cruel, inhumane blood sport. However, hunting associations maintain that hunting's poor image is a result of a few irresponsible hunters and a campaign of misinformation. Hunters play a vital role in the maintenance of forests. As a result of urbanization and expanded living spaces, forests diminish at an alarming rate and animals left to reproduce further endanger the forest, as it is unable to sustain constant growth of fauna. Hunters play an important role in the maintenance and control of animal populations that ensures the healthy survival of forests.

More than simply a profession or sport, hunting plays a significant role in the cultural memory of Germans. Germans have traditionally cultivated a bond to outdoor life and have romanticized forests to a large extent, and hunters have played an important part in the traditional understanding of German life. The relationship between forests, hunting and traditional village life in Germany has been eulogized in numerous plays, stories, poems and songs throughout German history, and hunting jargon (*Jägersprache*), with its hundreds of specialist terms, has long been a distinctive element in the vocabulary of the German language.

See also: sport: FRG; sport: GDR

TARA MAGDALINSKI

Husserl, Edmund

b. 8 April 1859, Proßnitz (now Prostějov, Czech Republic); d. 27 April 1938, Freiburg

Philosopher

As founder of phenomenology, Husserl exercised a deep influence on divergent philosophical figures in Germany (e.g. Martin **Heidegger** and Theodor W. **Adorno**) and France (e.g. Jean-Paul Sartre, Maurice Merleau-Ponty and Jacques Derrida). Reacting to the scientific relativism of historicism and psychology at the turn of the century, he sought to restore a foundational role for transcendental consciousness in the constitution of experience, which in later writings was reformulated as an intersubjective life-world, mobilized as a cultural universal against the particularist chauvinism of fascism.

See also: existentialism; philosophy

BRETT R. WHEELER

I

IBA

The general theme of the Internationale Bauausstellung Berlin (International Building Exhibition, or IBA) (1984–7) was '*Wohnen in der Innenstadt*' (the inner city as a residential area). In 1979 the Bauausstellung Berlin GmbH was created by the Berlin House of Deputies, to organize the exhibition as a vehicle for urban development and improvement throughout West Berlin, taking account of the historical city fabric and avoiding massive acts of demolition such as had been commonplace in the 1960s and 1970s.

In opposition to functionalist ideas that saw the *tabula rasa* as the starting point for all planning and building, the new direction embraced the *genius loci* as a vital planning factor. J.P. **Kleihues**, who co-directed the planning organization, Aldo Rossi, Gottfried **Böhm** and Rob **Krier** were the main exponents of such an approach.

Hardt-Waltherr Hämer was in charge of the 'critical reconstruction' and 'careful renovation' of schemes dealing with existing urban fabric which was complemented with new construction under Kleihues' direction. The renovation schemes focused on Luisenstadt and Kreuzberg's SO 36 district (often re-implementing the nineteenth-century town structure as laid down in Kleihues' overall planning scheme), while new building projects were built in Tegel, Prager Platz, the southern Tiergarten area, and Friedrichstadt. Designs were selected through competitions, often engaging runners-up for parts of the overall scheme. Many of the world's most acclaimed architects and planners made up the two hundred or so firms working for the IBA.

Moore-Ruble-Yudell won the planning competition for the harbour basin in Tegel with housing and separated social facilities that closely follow the site's natural outlines while managing to lock a strong sense of community into the scheme. The buildings are of different size and character, ranging from historicizing architecture (e.g. MRY's curving housing blocks and villas by Tigerman and Stern) to very abstract terraced house and villa designs by BJSS (see **Schultes, Axel**) and Poly-Steinbach-Weber. Other important architects working on this site are Gumbach, Hejduk, and Portoghesi. **Peichl** built a phosphorous elimination plant and more housing in other parts of Tegel.

The master plan for the Prager Platz was made by Gottfried Böhm. The buildings by Böhm, Krier and Aymonino echo the historical piazza-shape while presenting different architectural solutions.

Hans **Hollein**'s *Kulturforum* in the southern Tiergarten area binds together the already existing buildings (the *Nationalgalerie*, *Philharmonie* and *Nationalbibliothek*, etc.) with Stirling's *Wissenschaftszentrum* and Rob Krier's Rauchstraße. His plan depends on multi-party villas and shared communal spaces. He designed three villas, others were built by Grassi, Hermann and Valentin, Hollein, Nielebock, Rossi and Tonon. More IBA schemes are to be found to the south, most importantly **Ungers**' U-shaped housing block on Lützowplatz and Greotti's gateway building on Lützowstraße.

In South Friedrichstadt the IBA developed a badly war-damaged area, employing very diverse schemes by such architects as Eisenman, Hejudk,

Herzberger, **Kollhoff**, Koolhaas, Krier, Martorell-Bohigas-Mackay, Rossi and **Ungers**.

The IBA Berlin is not only important because it produced some of the most outstanding designs of the 1980s on an international level and offered many good solutions for West Berlin's housing problem and modernization, but also because it offers a model for other city developments, including the unified Berlin itself.

See also: architecture; Berlin building boom; reconstruction

Further reading

Bauausstellung Berlin GmbH (1987) *Internationale Bauausstellung Berlin 1987: Projektübersicht*, Berlin: Felgentreff und Goebel.

MARTIN KUDLEK

industrial relations

The West German industrial relations system has retained most of its key characteristics since the early post-war period: neo-corporatist in its organization, there is a high degree of centralization in its collective bargaining and wide application across plants and regions of its wage agreements. With unification, this system was applied unchanged to East Germany, and the western unions assumed bargaining rights there in late 1990.

This trade union structure took its form in 1945 largely under the auspices of the Allies, and particularly Great Britain. Their concern was to create industrial trade unions and so overcome the confessional and ideological differences which had so fragmented the union movement during the Weimar Republic. By 1949, therefore, when the DGB (*Deutscher Gewerkschaftsbund*) trade union federation first issued its programme, there were sixteen, later to become seventeen, trade unions, largely organized by the main industrial branch.

There are exceptions to this industrial basis, however. The DAG (*Deutsche Angestellten Gewerkschaft*) white-collar union rejected this industrial organization in 1947 and demanded the right to recruit members in administrative functions throughout the economy: it is not affiliated to the DGB and now has a membership of half a million, or perhaps 5 percent of all trade union members. The small Christian trade union federation *Christlicher Gewerkschaftsbund Deutschlands* has 300,000 members and, lastly, the DBB (*Deutscher Beamtenbund*) civil service federation has 800,000 members and plays an important role, since its civil servants are not allowed to strike. Its separate position also reflects the special status of union membership. The 'density', is of the order of 34 percent in the DGB branches and 70 percent in the public service.

The centralized nature of the system is displayed by the high level at which wage bargaining takes place, the broad coverage and validity of the collective agreement, and the particular legal restrictions imposed. The Collective Bargaining Agreement Act of 1949, revised in 1969, draws on many aspects of the Weimar Republic legislation, and imposes a 'peace obligation' before strike action may be called. Recourse to arbitration is commonly taken, and indeed is viewed as part of negotiation procedures. There are several agreements, from the 'framework collective agreement' and the 'framework collective wage agreement', which set the rights, conditions, and job classifications, to the more important annual collective wage agreement. Employers may choose to pay rates and premiums above the tariff for their branch and region. The wide application arises from the fact that, if an employers' federation signs an agreement with the union federation, all employers who are members of their federation must pay the tariff wage to all their employees in that sector. Such agreements have spread more widely by application to the service sector, which has low levels of unionization. Pilot agreements for the rest of the economy tend to be those of the metalworkers in Baden-Württemberg. The high degree of union organization can be matched by employers' discipline, such as the resort to 'lock-outs' by the engineering employers. To call a strike, a union must attain a 75 percent share of members' votes cast. At plant level, the works' councils play ever more important roles, particularly in approval of flexible working patterns and reductions in hours.

Further reading

Koch, K. (1989) *West German Industrial Relations*, chapter 4 in K. Koch (ed.) *West Germany Today*, London: Routledge (good overview of industrial relations structures and objectives of the social partners).

CHRISTOPHER H. FLOCKTON

Innerhofer, Franz

b. 5 May 1944, Krimml (near Salzburg)

Writer

Innerhofer's first three autobiographical novels describe the boy Holl's progression from material and emotional deprivation as an unloved illegitimate child on an isolated farm, in *Beautiful Days* (*Schöne Tage*) (1974), through his apprenticeship as a blacksmith and factory worker, in *In Shadow* (*Schattseite*) (1975), to growing political consciousness as a university student, in *Die großen Wörter* (Grand Words) (1977). The narrative technique of *Schöne Tage*, particularly, evokes a near-speechless, brutalized world behind the idyll of rural Austria. Subsequent works like *Der Emporkömmling* (The Upstart) (1982) have not matched this remarkable trilogy.

MORAY MCGOWAN

intellectuals

Intellectuals in the German-speaking countries have imposed upon public consciousness to a far greater extent than in Great Britain and the United States (or, following Sartre's death, in France). They have spoken out on rearmament (1950s), NATO membership (1950s), the Vietnam conflict (1960s), federal elections, as well as on the legacy of **Auschwitz**, the **Holocaust**, and the need for *Vergangenheitsbewältigung*. They have also addressed **environmentalism** (1980s), *Gastarbeiter*, **abortion law**, **literature**, the **German Question**, and, more recently, German **unification**.

The intellectual class is defined more broadly in the German-speaking states than in Anglo-Saxon countries. Consequently, intellectuals include authors (e.g. Heinrich **Böll**, Max **Frisch**, Christa **Wolf**, Stefan **Heym**, Peter **Handke**, Martin **Walser**, Hans Magnus **Enzensberger**, and, most famously, Günter **Grass**), songwriters (Wolf **Biermann**), historians (the liberal Martin **Broszat**, or the conservatives Michael **Stürmer** and Ernst **Nolte**), sociologists (Ralf **Dahrendorf**), psychologists (Alexander **Mitscherlich**), political philosophers (Jürgen **Habermas**), literary critics (Emil **Staiger** and Marcel **Reich-Ranicki**), or even the editor of the *Der Spiegel* (Rudolf **Augstein**).

German intellectuals are characterized by their high public profile, their propensity to speak out on issues unrelated to their professional lives, and by their willingness to become politically engaged. Their favoured medium is the 'arts' (*Feuilleton*) section of newspapers such as *Die Welt* and the *Frankfurter Allgemeine Zeitung*. The FRG, Austria and Switzerland each have a highly developed public sphere in which citizens might observe – and occasionally contribute to – intellectual debate in newspapers, public meetings, and through citizens' initiatives. Another medium is the television talk show, a forum which is satirized in Martin Walser's novel, *Das Einhorn* (1966) as self-indulgent games-playing. In the GDR, intellectuals created an alternative public space in literature. Operating on a more metaphorical level, the arts offered non-conformist perspectives even within state censorship. Intellectual dissent ranged from Christa **Wolf**'s socialist-humanist critiques to the radicalism of the **Prenzlauer Berg**. Stefan **Heym** and Christa Wolf, moreover, campaigned in 1989 and 1990 for the GDR as an alternative to both communism and capitalism. The resurgence of intellectual voices during the *Wende*, however, often obscures the longer history of grassroots dissent and opposition (see also **dissent and opposition: GDR**).

In the fledgling FRG, writers in particular quickly established themselves as the 'conscience of the nation'. The *Gruppe 47*, initiated by Hans Werner **Richter** and Alfred **Andersch**, poignantly, if impotently, contrasted the crass materialism of the 1950s **Economic Miracle** with its own moral agenda. The **Spiegel Affair** of 1962 inaugurated a more directly 'political' mood. Authors forced the resignation of the Defence

Minister Franz Josef Strauß following his attempts to restrict press freedom. From the mid-1960s, however, intellectual consensus disintegrated, despite joint agitation against the Emergency Laws and the Vietnam conflict. Thus, Günter Grass's electioneering on behalf of the **SPD** in the 1965 and 1969 elections angered many who destested the party's collusion with the **CDU** in the Grand Coalition of 1966–9. Conversely, Grass condemned Martin Walser, Peter **Weiss** and Erich **Fried**, for whom international injustice was more pressing than domestic reform. Grass also dismissed Hans Magnus Enzensberger and Peter Weiss for their romantic attachment to socialism in Cuba and North Vietnam, and for their association with the apparent extremism of the **student movement** and the Extra-Parliamentary Opposition (**APO**).

In the 1970s, disillusionment in the West following the failure of '1968' frequently led to introspection (the **'New Subjectivity'**). Alternatively, in the FRG, intellectuals campaigned against the **Berufsverbot**, and against the state's paranoid response to **terrorism**. In this period, then, the historical gulf between *Geist und Macht* (intellect and power) was palpable. Heinrich Böll protested against state interference in citizens' private lives in his book *Die verlorene Ehre der Katharina **Blum***, and, in an article, against the witchhunt against Ulrike **Meinhof**. In the GDR too, state control worried intellectuals. In the East the **Biermann Affair** of 1976 provoked widespread protest, as a result of which Stephan **Hermlin** and Christa Wolf were censured. Christa Wolf, Jurek **Becker**, Günter de **Bruyn**, Sarah **Kirsch**, Ulrich **Plenzdorf** and Volker **Braun** were also expelled from the **Writers' Union of the GDR**.

The main issues of the 1980s, in both East and West, were the **peace movement**, nuclear weapons and the environment. In the FRG, Heinrich Böll was active on all of these fronts until his death in 1985. Grass was also active, although he distanced himself from the SPD, and spent much time in India. Simultaneously, the rise of the Green Party (*Die Grünen*) and of citizens' initiatives rendered intellectuals' intervention superfluous. In the East, too, environmentalism, sexual freedom and political reform were furthered more by citizens' movements operating within the churches

than by established intellectuals (see also **citizens' movements: GDR**).

In the FRG, a separate strand of intellectual activity in the 1980s focused upon **historiography**. The 1983 federal elections, which brought the CDU to power, encouraged conservative re-evaluations of the Nazi period. The 1986 ***Historikerstreit*** centred upon charges levelled by Jürgen Habermas against the conservative historians Andreas Hillgruber, Ernst Nolte and Michael Stürmer. Habermas perceived in attempts to 'relativize' the FRG's Nazi past a conservative agenda to re-establish a dangerous form of partriotism. Links were made to the commemoration of SS graves at **Bitburg** in the presence of President Reagan, and to Chancellor **Kohl**'s decision to build historical museums in Bonn and Berlin.

Conservative reappraisals have continued into the 1990s. Emboldened by the CDU-engineered unification, right-wing commentators have declared the bankruptcy of liberal-left intellectuals. An argument about the East German writer Christa Wolf has escalated into a dismissal of post-war literature in *both* East *and* West. For commentators such as Ulrich Greiner and Frank Schirrmacher, intellectual engagement has been a moral pose struck for aesthetic purposes. The ferocity of such criticisms has forced a re-evaluation of intellectual engagement in the FRG, as well as in Austria and Switzerland. It has also cast doubt upon the sincerity of intellectual dissent in the former GDR, and upon the credibility of those in the West who promoted GDR writers as progressive voices. The result of such reassessments is uncertainty as to the intellectuals' role. All three German-speaking states await a new intellectual generation and a new intellectual style.

Further reading

Bullivant, B. (1994) *The Future of German Literature*, Oxford: Berg (literary intellectuals in East and West; survey of intellectual and literary disputes since unification).

Burns, R. (ed.) (1995) *German Cultural Studies. An Introduction*, Oxford: Oxford University Press (chapters on GDR culture, including the Biermann Affair, on intellectual protest in the FRG and on intellectual debate and political culture since unification).

Burns, R. and van der Will, W. (1988) *Protest and Democracy in West Germany. Extra-Parliamentary Opposition and the Democratic Agenda*, London: Macmillan (intellectuals' involvement in political protest in the FRG).

Goodbody, A. and Tate, D. (eds) (1992) *Geist und Macht: Writers and the State in the GDR*, Amsterdam: Rodopi.

Parkes, S. (1986) *Writers and Politics in West Germany*, London: Croom Helm.

STUART TABERNER

Intendant

This term is roughly equivalent to artistic director of a theatre. In German theatres it is not uncommon for a leading actor to hold such a position.

See also: *Dramaturg*

SEÁN ALLAN

Inter Nationes

Founded in 1952 as an independent, non-profit making institution, with the aim of promoting German cultural policies abroad, Inter Nationes was set up by the Adenauer government with its Head Office in Bonn, to emphasize the new role of Germany in post-war Europe and as a counter to GDR propaganda. Together with other institutions such as the **Goethe-Institut**, the **DAAD** and the **Humboldt Foundation**, it is part of the *Vereinigung internationaler Zusammenarbeit* (VIZ) (Association for International Co-operation). VIZ is funded by a number of federal institutions: the Foreign Ministry, the Press and Information Office, Ministry of Economic Co-operation, and Ministry of Economic Affairs. Inter Nationes circulates its information to foreign politicians, academics and journalists who further disseminate news and comments on the Federal Republic. This aspect of its work inevitably means that it, together with the other institutions in VIZ, can be subjected to governmental pressure, affecting its objective handling of information and its capacity for self-criticism.

A more specific function of Inter Nationes is its information service to schools, universities and other cultural and educational establishments, covering the intellectual, cultural and moral life of contemporary Germany. This service concentrates particularly on the provision of audiovisual and print media, either producing its own information or subsidizing and purchasing material produced on the open market. Audiovisual resources include documentary films, feature films and television drama, while its printed material specializes in educational, socio-political and broadly cultural matters. Occasionally it also contributes funds for the translation of new German literature and of specialist scientific and technical publications. Its regular periodicals include the monthly cultural magazine *Prisma* and a bimonthly newsletter *Kulturchronik*, circulated in five languages. This material is made available on a non-commercial basis, either as a donation or through its lending service.

Inter Nationes also organizes educational visits to Germany and arranges contacts for foreign visitors. With the end of the Cold War, Inter Nationes, as an element of Germany's foreign culture policy, sought to expand into central and eastern Europe, assisting with the establishment of Goethe Institute libraries and other cultural enterprises. Recently, in compliance with the federal government's European policy, Inter Nationes has begun to introduce a German contribution to European cultural activities. It has also played a major role in updating the German image since unification. The current director of *Inter Nationes* and chair of VIZ is Dr Dieter W. Benecke, who also chairs the Adenauer Foundation, and who has been seen as a controversial figure with a somewhat narrowly pro-German interpretation of national culture and its image abroad.

Further reading

Weissmann, A. (1989), 'Inter Nationes', *Bildung und Wissenschaft* 9, 10: 30.

HANS J. HAHN

Irving, David

b. 24 March 1938, Hutton (near Brentwood, Essex)

Revisionist historian

David Irving, the attention-seeking author of more than thirty books, most on Nazi Germany, created public and scholarly controversy in 1976, when he argued that Adolf Hitler may not have ordered the destruction of European Jewry. His reputation suffered but remained intact until 1988, when he proclaimed that no Jews ever died by gassing in the Nazi camps (a claim not made in his books, many of which are first-rate). His subsequent banning from Germany and several other countries has only strengthened his support in 'far-right' and neo-Nazi groups. Despite his ban, Irving still manages to 'slip' into Germany, where his books sell well and lectures attract crowds.

JOEL S.A. HAYWARD

Iser, Wolfgang

b. 22 July 1926, Marienberg (Saxony)

Literary theorist

Together with Hans Robert **Jauß**, Iser is one of the foremost proponents of **Reception Theory**, an approach to literary studies which flourished from the late 1960s to the early 1980s at the University of Constance, where he was Professor of English and Comparative Literature. In his work, Iser puts forward a phenomenological account of reading based on the notion of an 'implied reader'.

Further reading

Holub, R.C. (1984) *Reception Theory: A Critical Introduction*, London and New York: Methuen (contains a bibliography of Iser's major contributions to Reception Theory up to 1982).

SEÁN ALLAN

Islam in Germany

After the members of the Protestant and Catholic churches, Muslims make up the third largest religious group in Germany. Numbering some 2.7 million in total, the majority (approximately 94 percent) are Sunnites, whilst the remaining 6 percent are Shiites or belong to other Islamic minority groups. Even if these differences are ignored, Muslims still cannot be regarded as a homogeneous group since it is important to distinguish between, on the one hand, those who are committed believers and live in accordance with the 'Sharia', and on the other, those who adopt a more relaxed attitude to their faith and lead a more secular existence. Moreover, practising Muslims in Germany have their origins in some forty-eight different nations (mainly African and Asian) many of which have extremely varied cultural traditions. The vast majority of Muslims – some 2.05 million (76 percent) – are Turks, followed by Tunisians and Lebanese. The majority originally came to Germany as **Gastarbeiter** or in search of political asylum (see also **asylum, political**).

Practising Muslims often have difficulties in observing their religious duties and rituals within German society. For in spite of their considerable presence in the workforce, little heed is paid to the particular demands made upon them by their faith. An additional problem is the very limited number of mosques, a problem that is exacerbated not only by lack of funds but also by opposition on the part of the indigenous German population to the building of such religious centres. Further problems are caused by the often extreme contradictions between German social structures and the traditions of Islamic culture, which in most cases is extremely patriarchal. These contradictions often lead to conflicts above all for second-generation Muslims whose traditional values have been influenced simultaneously by those of the west. For such Muslims the significance of their Islamic faith is waning and young second-generation Muslims often do not really feel at home in either culture.

Similarly, ensuring a religious upbringing in accordance with Islamic traditions also leads to difficulties. Since most schools in Germany are co-educational, the situation of Muslim girls often leads to conflicts between schools and families especially in respect of activities such as school trips, sports events, etc. in which both sexes participate. Moreover, many parents opt to send their children to special Koran schools to ensure that they are brought up in the traditions of Islam, thereby placing them under an additional burden on the one hand, and accentuating cultural differences on the other.

There are a wide variety of organizations serving the Muslim population and there are a number of well-established, representative bodies, for instance the *Arbeitskreis Islamischer Gemeinden* (Islamic Communites' Working Group) and the *Islamrat für die BRD* (FRG Islamic Council). Needless to say, first-hand experience of Muslims plays an important role in shaping the way Germans view Islam today. The expansion of tourism (especially into such areas as Turkey, Tunisia and Morocco) has enabled many Germans to experience Islamic culture in its original context and to engage productively with the culture, a development which is to be welcomed since Islam is now firmly established in Germany and – in view of the high birth-rates within the Muslim minority – the Muslim population is set to increase in the future.

See also: *Ausländer*, minorities, non-German

Further reading

Kolinsky, E. (ed.) (1996) *Turkish Culture in German Society Today*, Oxford and Providence, RI: Berghahn (includes a chapter on Islam in Germany).

Stiftung Lesen (1996) *Leseempfehlung Islam*, Bonn: Bundeszentrale für politische Bildung (contains a 100-page list of titles relating to all aspects of Islam.)

BIRGIT RÖDER

J

Jahnn, Hans Henny

b. 17 December 1894, Stellingen (near Hamburg); d. 29 November 1959, Hamburg

Writer

A committed pacifist, Jahnn took refuge from WWI in Norway. His writing, especially his plays, is written in an expressionist style and is character-ized by elements of paganism, sexual excess and extreme brutality. His work was banned by the Nazi regime and he eventually emigrated to Denmark, returning to Hamburg in 1945. He is best known for his plays *Pastor Ephraim Magnus* (1919) and *Medea* (1926), as well as his first novel *Perrudja* (1929) and the trilogy *Fluß ohne Ufer* (River Without Banks) (1949–61).

SEÁN ALLAN

Jandl, Ernst

b. 1 August 1925, Vienna; d. 9 June 2000, Vienna

Writer

After conscription in 1943 and release from a PoW camp three years later, Ernst Jandl studied German and English at Vienna University, qualifying as a grammar school teacher in 1949. In 1950 he completed a Ph.D. on Arthur Schnitzler and spent 1952 to 1953 as an exchange teacher in England where he came into contact with Erich **Fried**. He began to write in conventional forms in the early 1950s, but rapidly moved towards experimental poetry in concert with Gerhard Rühm and H.C. **Artmann**. In 1954 he met Friederike **Mayröcker** who became his partner and close collaborator in numerous avant-garde projects. After intermittent periods of leave, Jandl gave up school-teaching in 1977 on the grounds of ill-health. Without sharing the extreme position of such scourges of the Austrian establishment as Thomas **Bernhard**, he is noted for his social and political commitment. For example, he was one of the co-founders of the *Grazer Autorenversammlung* in 1973 aimed at helping younger writers in Austria. Although his work encompasses radio plays and texts for the theatre, it is Jandl's brilliant performances of his own sound poetry which have established his internatonal reputation as the foremost exponent of experi-mental literature in the German language.

Jandl's work has affinities both with the expressionist poetry of August Stramm and the iconoclasm of the dadaists Hugo Ball, Raoul Hausmann and Kurt Schwitters. His own auda-cious experiments with language and form are rooted in what he has called '*gründliche Simplizität*' ('basic simplicity'), that is, a concentration on the basic building blocks of communication in order to combat the cacophony of official jargon, political discourse and mind-numbing cliché which assails the individual in modern society. Thus common to all his work is the belief in the emancipatory function of literature. Normative grammar and aesthetic hierarchies are radically blurred in order to jolt language, and thus perception, out of stereotyped modes of expression. Jandl himself places his poetry in four categories: poems which evolve from exploring the patterns of everyday speech; '*Sprechgedichte*' ('speaking poems') where the semantic charge of words is exploded by distortion, punning and startling disjunctions of syntax; pure sound poetry in which meaning is located only in the phonetics of articulation itself; and visual (concrete) poetry where the arrangement of words on the page forms an integral part of the aesthetic structure.

Although Jandl has been the focus of scandalized reaction, above all in the conservative artistic circles of post-war Austria, the hallmark of his work is paradoxically its accessibility. For however experimental, Jandl's poetry rarely loses contact with empirical reality. This is best seen in a '*Sprechgedicht*' like '*schtzngrmm*', which conveys the futility of war by the elision of every vowel on the principle, as Jandl puts it, that 'war does not sing!'. Constructed on the single word, '*Schützengraben*' (trench), the poem reproduces the brutal sounds of battle in a vocal crescendo, culminating in the bleak syllable, 't-tt' ('*tot*' meaning 'dead'). Similarly, from apparently nonsensical words ('lepn/nepl') his 'ode auf N' builds up to a fierce denunciation of the cult of heroism, as the extended syllable 'naaaaaaaaaaaa' ('*Narr*' meaning 'fool') unleashes the name 'Napoleon' in a donkey-like bray. On the other hand, the gentler side of Jandl's talent finds expression in such visual poems as '*erschaffung der eva*' ('creation of eve') in which the creation story is graphically suggested by a radical reduction of means. Shaped as a tree, the words 'god', 'rib', 'eve' and 'adam' are configured with an aesthetic economy which not only pleases the eye, but releases multi-layered meanings, not least with the echo of an earlier German baroque tradition. Such creations reveal Jandl's capacity to provide provocatively witty structures within which listeners or viewers can freely move to discover their own creativity.

Jandl's later work has turned to more autobiographical themes in which the darker side of his personality comes to the fore. The same gift for surprise is evident, but the pain of transience and fear of death predominate. Yet even here bitterness is controlled by a characteristic self-irony in which black humour counters despair. If, as Ludwig **Wittgenstein** argued, the limits of our language define the limits of our world, Jandl's formidable energies remain properly focused on the need to extend such artificial and oppressive barriers to human potential.

See also: Grazer Gruppe; literature: Austrian; Wiener Gruppe

Further reading

Arnold, H.L. (ed.) (1996) *Ernst Jandl*, Munich: *edition text + kritik* (four poems by Jandl, collection of essays and bibliography).

Riha, K. (1991) 'Ernst Jandl', in H.L. Arnold (ed.), *Kritisches Lexikon zur deutschsprachigen Gegenwartsliteratur* (general survey with bibliography, regularly updated).

Schmidt-Dengler, W. (ed.) (1982) *Ernst Jandl. Materialienbuch*, Darmstadt and Neuwied: Luchterhand (articles on poetry, theatre and political commitment).

Siblewski, K. (ed.) (1990) *Ernst Jandl. Texte, Daten, Bilder*, Frankfurt am Main: Luchterhand (biographical data and essays on all aspects of Jandl's work).

MICHAEL BUTLER

Janka, Walter

b. 29 April 1914, Chemnitz; d. 17 March 1994, Potsdam

Janka was an anti-fascist activist who spent part of his exile (1941–7) in Mexico, where he gained the reputation as a publisher which led to his appointment in 1952 as head of the **Aufbau Verlag**. His reformist Marxist views turned him into a 'counter-revolutionary' victim of the GDR show-trials of 1957, abandoned to his fate by old friends like Johannes R. **Becher** and Anna **Seghers**. He re-emerged from obscurity in October 1989, when his memoir *Schwierigkeiten mit der Wahrheit* (Difficulties with the Truth) appeared. He was formally rehabilitated by the **PDS** in 1990.

DENNIS TATE

Janowitz, Gundula

b. 8 February 1939, Berlin

Soprano

After studying singing in Graz, Janowitz was engaged by Karajan for the Vienna Opera in 1960, with her first major parts as Pamina in *The Magic Flute* and Dido in Purcell's *Dido and Aeneas* in 1961. A year earlier she had also performed for Wieland Wagner as a Flower Maiden in Bayreuth. Throughout the 1960s and 1970s she consolidated her reputation as a lyric soprano in all the major opera houses and concert halls of Europe, with a Covent Garden debut in 1976.

DEREK McCULLOCH

Jaspers, Karl

b. 23 February 1883, Oldenburg; d. 26 February 1969, Basel

Psychologist and philosopher

Jaspers was a representative of **existentialism** as it was developed from the 1930s onwards. One-time friend and later adversary of Martin **Heidegger**, Jaspers was prohibited from teaching in Nazi Germany from 1937 until 1945 since he refused to renounce his Jewish wife. In the post-war period, he opposed restorative tendencies in the FRG – in the absence of any **denazification** worthy of that name – and became actively involved in the fight against nuclear arms and NATO. He redefined the role of the intellectual in the first two decades of the FRG as a public activist. Jaspers received the German book trade's Peace Prize in 1958.

See also: intellectuals; philosophy; protest movements

ULF STROHMAYER

Jauß, Hans Robert

b. 12 December 1921, Göppingen

Literary theorist

Together with Wolfgang **Iser**, Jauß is one of the foremost proponents of **Reception Theory**, an approach to literary studies which flourished from the late 1960s to the early 1980s at the University of Constance, where he was Professor of Romance Languages. In his work, Jauß argues for a new form of literary historiography derived from Marxism and formalist aesthetics.

Further reading

Holub, R.C. (1984) *Reception Theory: A Critical Introduction*, London and New York: Methuen (contains a bibliography of Jauß's major contributions to Reception Theory up to 1982).

SEÁN ALLAN

jazz

Germany has established itself as the centre of Europe's jazz scene with Berlin and Frankfurt am Main distinguishing themselves as jazz metropolises that serve as important stages for both international and German musicians. Although the immediate post-war period was characterized by a proliferation of American jazz, which can be attributed to the radio broadcasts of the American Forces Network (AFN), German jazz musicians began to find their own distinct style and creative edge in a relatively short time following the formation of the German Jazz Federation (Deutsche Jazz Föderation) in 1950. The federation helped to promote German jazz musicians by organizing workshops and obtaining gigs and record contracts for its members. The federation was also responsible for the establishment of the first German jazz festival one year later. This festival, held annually in Berlin, continues to be one of the most popular musical events in Europe. The most well known German jazz musicians include Wolfgang Daner, Manfred Schoof and Albert Mangelsdorff.

Although there was a general distrust of western

music in the former GDR, jazz was supported in solidarity with African Americans, who were often depicted as 'the oppressed race of capitalism'. The **FDJ** (Free German Youth) formed numerous jazz clubs that were among the popular forms of entertainment. Jazz records produced in the GDR were in high demand and smuggled over into the FRG to a wide audience.

The development of jazz in Germany runs parallel to the country's political history. In the early twentieth century, jazz was a popular musical import from America, identified with ragtime and dance music. During the rise of National Socialism, jazz was declared illegal and became part of the racist, anti-Semitic Nazi propaganda machine that declared jazz to be a blend of decadent 'negro rhythms and Jewish feeling'. During 1940–5, there was a jazz revival in the form of swing music promoted by rebellious students tired with the cultural policies of Nazi Germany. These students were harshly punished, and jazz music became marked by these events as an anti-authoritarian, defiant, musical form of expression.

The social significance of jazz was explored by one of Germany's most important intellectuals, Theodor **Adorno**, who formulated a highly controversial and profound critique of jazz and its regressive character.

It is possible to get a professional degree in jazz at various musical colleges in Germany, including the Darmstadt Jazz Institute, which houses Europe's largest jazz archives and publishes the jazz magazine *Coda*.

Further reading

Adorno, T. (1936) 'Über Jazz' in *Zeitschrift für Sozialforschung* 5: 235–59 (technical essay that discusses the social impact of jazz in psychoanalytic and Marxist terms).

Lange, H.H. (1966) *Jazz in Deutschland*, Berlin: Colloquium (standard history of jazz in Germany, including biographies of the most influential German jazz musicians).

LISA YUN LEE

Jelinek, Elfriede

b. 20 October 1946, Mürzzuschlag (Styria)

Writer

Austrian Marxist–feminist writer and dramatist known for her acerbic wit and biting exposés of patterns of oppression in daily life.

Jelinek's early experimental pop novel *wir sind lockvögel baby!* (we are decoys baby!) (1970) was followed by the novel *Women as Lovers* (*Die Liebhaberinnen*, 1975), which was much acclaimed by the women's movement for its Marxist–feminist critique of the institution of marriage. *The Piano Teacher* (*Die Klavierspielerin*) (1983), her most personal book, deals with female sexuality and rewrites the myth of the artist. *Lust* (1989), a work of anti-pornography, further exposes the unequal power relations between men and women. *Wonderful, Wonderful Times* (*Die Ausgesperrten*, 1980) uncovers the continuation of fascist tendencies in 1950s Austria, while *Oh Wildnis, oh Schutz vor ihr* (Oh Wilderness, Protect Us From It) (1985) tackles the politics behind green issues. Of her plays, *Was geschah, nachdem Nora ihren Mann verlassen hatte oder Stützen der Gesellschaft* (What Happened after Nora left her Husband or Pillars of Society) (1982) examines the theme of women and work; *Burgtheater* (1984) created a furore for its unwelcome probing of Austria's Nazi past; *Wolken. Heim* (Clouds. Home) (1990) examines the cultural background to German fascism; and *Totenauberg* (an invented place name) (1991) explores the links between nature, fascism, and German philosophy. *Stecken, Stab und Stangel*, like most of her plays, was premièred in Germany, at the Deutsches Schauspielhaus in Hamburg on 12 April 1996. Jelinek has published translations from French, Spanish and English, including works by Thomas Pynchon, and is also the author of a number of radio plays and screenplays, including that for the film of Ingeborg **Bachmann**'s novel *Malina*. Always keen to explore new media, she has now begun to publish texts on the internet.

Strongly influenced in her early work by the **Wiener Gruppe**, the **Frankfurt School**, and the works of Bertolt **Brecht** and Roland Barthes, Jelinek has always, as a Marxist writer, been concerned to demonstrate the uncomfortable truths hiding behind the surface appearances of everyday life. Most frequently targeted objects of her attack are the media, **Heimatliteratur**, the family as a locus of oppression, German imperialism and the comfortable myths of Austrian identity. Her principal aesthetic tools are grotesque exaggeration, irony, montage and language play. Her characters are deliberately unrealistic, being fragmented, postmodern cyphers for the messages she wishes to convey. In 1998 she was awarded the prestigious Büchner Prize.

Further reading

Bartsch, K. and Höfler, G. (eds) (1991) *Dossier 2: Elfriede Jelinek* Graz: Droschl (essays and bibliography).

Fiddler, A. (1994) *Rewriting Reality*, Oxford: Berg (the only major study of Jelinek in English; includes bibliography).

Janz, M. (1995) *Elfriede Jelinek*, Stuttgart: Metzler (full-length study stressing that Jelinek has always been first and foremost a Marxist; includes bibliography).

Johns, J.B. and Arens, K. (eds) (1994) *Elfriede Jelinek: Framed by Language*, Riverside, CA: Ariadne Press (essays and bibliography).

BRIGID HAINES

Jens, Walter

b. 8 March 1923, Hamburg

Writer and intellectual

Walter Jens is both a well-known author and a prominent literary critic and public intellectual. A founding member of **Gruppe 47**, Jens' critical social engagement was present from his first novel, *Nein – Die Welt der Angeklagten* (No – The World of the Accused) (1950), an anti-utopian account of a depersonalizing absolute state. Jens became professor of rhetoric and classical philology in 1956 and Ordinarius in 1965 at the University of Tübingen. Despite his academic background, however, beginning in 1962 Jens achieved prominence as television critic for *Die Zeit* under the

pseudonym Momos. Together with his wife Inge (married 1951) he was awarded the Theodor-Heuss prize for their written work as well as their political engagement. Jens has been Honorary President of **PEN** since 1982 and Honorary President of the Berlin Akademie der Künste since 1989.

Jens himself divided his work into three stages. In his early prose writings, he explored the significance of ancient Greek myths as well as the New Testament in re-thinking contemporary questions of truth and freedom. In the second stage of his writings, he focused more on literary criticism. In his influential collection of critical essays *Statt einer Literaturgeschichte* (Instead of a History of Literature) (1957) he argued for a greater connection of the poetic text with biography and authorial intention, positing that the concept of art should include science and philosophy as well. In the fictive exchange of letters between an author and a literary critic (both figures representing Jens himself) entitled *Herr Meister. Dialog über einen Roman* (Herr Meister. A Dialogue About a Novel) (1963), Jens examined the possibility and impossibility of literary production in the face of a melancholy brought about by the tension between tradition and the present. This dialectical self-conversation, simultaneously self-critique and self-justification, represented Jens' farewell to the novel form.

Without abandoning his fascination with mythology and religion, in the later stage of his life Jens has focused more on his role as engaged public intellectual, positioning himself both as radical democrat and an unorthodox socialist. He has proven himself to be a master rhetorician, adept at both public lectures and religious sermons, sometimes blurring the boundaries between the two. In *Von Deutscher Rede* (On German Speech) (1969) he argued for a connection between rhetoric and morality, while his *Republikanische Reden* (Republican Speeches) (1976) placed the literary at the centre of the constellation of literature, rhetoric and politics.

Jens has also been actively involved in mass media, particularly television, both as a critic and as a writer of television plays.

Further reading

Hinck, W. (1993) *Walter Jens, un homme de lettres, zum 70. Geburtstag*, Munich: Kindler (monograph includes an extensive bibliography of Jens' work).

Jens, W. and Jens, I. (1994) *Vergangenheit-gegenwärtig: biographische Skizzen* Stuttgart: Radius (joint auto-biographical account of Walter and Inge Jens).

MICHAEL RICHARDSON

Jochum, Eugen

b. 1 November 1902, Babenhausen; d. 2 March 1987, Munich

Conductor

A vivid and emotionally involved interpreter of the central German repertory, Jochum avoided Nazi interference during his wartime tenure as General Music Director of the Hamburg State Opera. In 1949 he formed the Bavarian Radio Symphony Orchestra, which he raised to the first rank. In the 1960s and 1970s he held important posts in Amsterdam and London while appearing as a guest internationally. The generosity of his music-making is preserved in cycles of the symphonies of Beethoven, Brahms and Bruckner, each recorded twice.

BEATRICE HARPER

Johansen, Hanna

b. 17 June 1939, Bremen

Writer (also wrote as Hanna Muschg)

Johansen has lived since 1972 in Zürich. Her stories and novels represent an ongoing reflection on the *condition féminine* (Samuel Moser), which she probes with childlike openness and Socratic persistence. In her most recent works, *Kurnovelle* (Spa Novella) (1994) and *Die Universalgeschichte der Monogamie* (Universal History of Monogamy) (1997) she inquires – at times painfully, at times with delicate humour – into the disjunctions in relationships between men and women. Writing initially as Hanna Muschg, Johansen has also written internationally successful stories for children that explore basic philosophical issues in dialogues involving both animals and humans.

JEFFREY GARRETT

Johnson, Uwe

b. 20 July 1934, Cammin (now Kamin Pomorski, Poland); d. 22 February 1983, Sheerness (England)

Writer

Born in Pomerania, now part of Poland, Johnson grew up first in Anklamm and then in Güstrow in the province of Mecklenburg in the GDR. After studying German in Rostock and Leipzig, he moved to West Berlin in 1959, just before the appearance of his first novel *Speculations About Jacob* (*Mutmaßungen über Jakob*). Johnson lived in West Berlin until 1974, apart from two years in New York, where he began to write the four-volume *Anniversaries* (*Jahrestage*). The last ten years of his life were spent in growing isolation in Sheerness on the Isle of Sheppey, where *Anniversaries* was finally completed in 1983. Johnson's work is profoundly marked by his experience of Nazism, the division of Germany and the **Holocaust**, and is remarkable for its historical detail, complex narrative structures, and highly individual language. First labelled 'the writer of the two Germanys', he is now widely seen as one of the most important figures in German literature since the war.

After having been sent by his parents for six months (1944–5) to a Nazi élite school near Posen, Johnson became in his youth a convinced socialist and supporter of the GDR. However, as a student in Rostock he clashed with the local leadership of the Free German Youth (**FDJ**) over its treatment of the Protestant youth organization in May 1953. Excluded from the university, he was reinstated in the aftermath of the **June Uprising** in 1953 but transferred to the University of Leipzig in 1954, where he studied under Hans **Mayer**.

The Rostock incident formed the basis for his first novel *Ingrid Babendererde*, whose subject matter and disregard for the canons of **socialist realism** made it unacceptable to GDR publishers. Though the **Suhrkamp Verlag** also refused to publish it (it appeared only in 1985, after his death), it began Johnson's close relationship with Peter Suhrkamp and his successor Siegfried Unseld. It also established the pattern for his future writing, focusing on the interplay between historical and political events and individual consciousness from a Marxist, materialist point of view increasingly influenced by the thought of such figures as Walter **Benjamin**.

On completing his studies in 1956 Johnson was largely unemployed while writing *Speculations About Jacob*, the story of the love between Jakob Abs, a railway worker in the East, and Gesine Cresspahl, now in the West, at the time of the Hungarian uprising and the Suez crisis in 1956. Published in the West in 1959, it immediately established his reputation as one of Germany's leading young writers; its uncompromisingly modernist structure, a montage of narrative, dialogue and interior monologue, reflected Johnson's admiration for William Faulkner and his conception of the novel as a 'quest for truth' ('*Wahrheitsfindung*').

Johnson's reputation as the 'writer of the two Germanys', though unwelcome to him, was apparently confirmed by his next two major works. *The Third Book About Achim* (*Das dritte Buch über Achim*) in 1961 explored the differences in attitudes and assumptions which prevent a western journalist, Karsch, from writing a biography of a celebrated GDR sportsman, the cyclist Achim; *Two Views* (*Zwei Ansichten*) of 1965 depicted the effects of the **Berlin Wall** on two individuals, one from the East and one from the West.

Johnson left the GDR in 1959, just before *Speculations About Jacob* appeared, and settled in West Berlin; however, he did so reluctantly, remaining socialist in outlook and critical of the FGR. In 1961 his position between the two Cold War camps involved him in a fierce public controversy with the writer Hermann **Kesten** and the CDU politician Heinrich von Brentano. Johnson took part in meetings of **Gruppe 47** but, though close to leading writers such as Günter **Grass**, Martin **Walser**, Max **Frisch** and Ingeborg **Bachmann**, he remained sceptical throughout the turbulent 1960s about the writer's ability to influence public events directly.

In the four-volume novel *Anniversaries*, conceived during Johnson's two-year stay in New York

(1966–8), Johnson widened the historical scope of his work, tracing the family history of Gesine Cresspahl, the central figure of his closely-knit fictional world, from the early 1930s to the early years of the GDR. This story is told by Gesine to her daughter Marie, in a so-called 'pact' with the narrator, in daily, dated instalments over the 366 days from 21 August 1967 to 20 August 1968 and is interspersed with an account of their lives in New York and with daily extracts from the *New York Times*, reporting such events as the Vietnam war, the death of Robert Kennedy, and the Prague Spring. Overshadowed by the disasters of German history this century, the work reflects its central character's, and Johnson's, quest for a more just society. Gesine is given new hope by the Prague Spring, to which she would like to contribute; its crushing on the last day of Johnson's year – a coincidence which could not have been anticipated when the work was planned – is not reported in the text.

In addition to its painstakingly researched historical detail, *Anniversaries*, like all Johnson's work, creates a powerful sense of place, evoking both the beloved, lost landscape of Mecklenburg and the modernity of New York; as a novel of the modern city, it has been compared to Dos Passos' *Manhattan Transfer* and **Döblin**'s *Berlin Alexanderplatz*.

The first three parts of *Anniversaries* appeared in quick succession between 1970 and 1973, but work on the fourth volume was severely impeded by writer's block experienced as a result of the breakdown of Johnson's marriage, which occurred after his move to Sheerness in 1974. This link between Johnson's private life and the progress of the novel indicates the strong autobiographical elements present in *Anniversaries*, as in all his writing. Johnson provides his own account of his work in his Frankfurt lectures of 1979, published in *Begleitumstände* (Accompanying Circumstances) of 1980.

Since his sudden death in 1984 Johnson's reputation has continued to grow, especially since 1989 in his native East Germany, where he was hitherto unpublished and rejected. He is seen increasingly as perhaps the most important writer to emerge from the GDR, providing the most historically complete and detailed picture of that society in its first decades. Johnson's papers are now housed in the Uwe Johnson Archive at the University of Frankfurt.

See also: modernism; prose fiction: FRG; prose fiction: GDR

Major works

Johnson, U. (1959) *Mutmaßungen über Jakob*, Frankfurt am Main: Suhrkamp; trans. U. Molinaro, *Speculations about Jacob*, London: Jonathan Cape, 1963.

—— (1961) *Das dritte Buch über Achim*, Frankfurt am Main: Suhrkamp; trans. U. Molinaro, *The Third Book about Achim*, London: Jonathan Cape, 1968.

—— (1965) *Zwei Ansichten*, Frankfurt am Main: Suhrkamp; trans. R. Winston and C. Winston, *Two Views*, London: Jonathan Cape, 1967.

—— (1970, 1971, 1973, 1985) *Jahrestage* 4 vols, Frankfurt am Main: Suhrkamp; 2 vol. abbreviated trans. L. Vennewitz and W. Arndt, *Anniversaries. From the Life of Gesine Cresspahl*, New York, Harcourt Brace Jovanovich, 1975 and 1987.

—— (1975) 'Berliner Stadtbahn (Veraltet)', in *Berliner Sachen*, Frankfurt am Main: Suhrkamp (an important essay on Johnson's ideas on narrative).

—— (1980) *Begleitumstände. Frankfurter Vorlesungen*, Frankfurt am Main: Suhrkamp.

—— (1985) *Ingrid Babendererde. Reifeprüfung 1953*, Frankfurt am Main: Suhrkamp.

—— (1988) *'Ich überlege mir eine Geschichte...' Uwe Johnson im Gespräch*, ed. E. Fahlke, Frankfurt am Main: Suhrkamp.

Further reading

Bond, D.G. (1993) *German History and German Identity: Uwe Johnson's 'Jahrestage'*, Amsterdam and Atlanta, GA: Rodopi.

Riordan, C. (1989) *The Ethics of Narration. Uwe Johnson's Novels from 'Ingrid Babendererde to 'Jahrestage'*, London: Modern Humanities Research Association.

GRAHAM JACKMAN

Jonke, Gert

b. 8 February 1946, Klagenfurt

Writer

Gert Friedrich Jonke was one of a group of writers emerging in the late 1960s who were to challenge an Austrian literary establishment content with the cosy narrating of historical themes or the uncritical evocation of a timeless bucolic world. Jonke's attack, in contrast to some of his contemporaries, did not initially take his work primarily into the field of direct social criticism. He has preferred to draw on a repertoire of linguistic, mathematical and surrealist structures to rupture traditional narration whilst simultaneously aiming to expose the fragmenting and disintegrating nature of contemporary society.

ANTHONY BUSHELL

journalism

The profession of journalism has been defined in terms of the journalist's social status as a writer, editor and/or reporter for the press. However, journalism also refers to the process of creating and structuring texts and programmes for print media (**newspapers** and **magazines**), audiovisual media (**radio, television**, film and documentaries), online electronic services and **advertising**. Journalism is characterized by a dynamic tension between its mission to inform and influence the public sphere and, conversely, to reflect and articulate public opinion and interests.

Article 5 of the Federal Republic's Basic Law protects journalists from external intervention and guarantees freedom of expression. The profession's self-regulation through the German Press Council (Deutscher Presserat) and a critical readership are considered additional guarantors of a free press. In the GDR, journalists – who were admitted to the profession only on completion of a four-year course at the 'Sektion Journalistik' at the University of Leipzig – were expected to assist in the development of a 'socialist consciousness' among the populace in accordance with the Marxist–Leninist precepts of the **SED**.

Journalists in the FRG participated in, and became targets of, the economic and political conflicts of the 1960s and 1970s. The imprisonment of the *Spiegel* editor Rudolf **Augstein** in 1962 and the critique of capitalist media embodied in the **APO** and **student movements** signified the politicization of journalism. Media mergers in the print sector intensified conflicts between owners' commercial interests and journalists' pursuit of editorial independence. Journalists raised issues of unionization, co-determination (*Mitbestimmung*), and (unsuccessfully) challenged the sole right of the owners to determine editorial content (*Tendenzschutz*).

A combination of unions (*IG Medien, Deutsche Journalisten Union* and *Rundfunk-Fernseh-Film-Union*) and professional associations (*Deutscher Journalisten Verband*) represent journalists in trade negotiations. Although unions have advocated educational norms for the study of journalism which – unlike other professions – has no uniform curricular guidelines, the profession and employers have only agreed upon a more or less obligatory traineeship (twelve to eighteen months) following the **Abitur** or degree programme.

Area specialization and media diversification have enlarged the scope of journalism. Politics, business, culture, sports and local news are augmented by reports on travel, automobiles, fashion, food and dining, or health. Journalism also increasingly functions as a service profession by packaging 'infotainment'.

As pressures for market share and ratings have grown, investigative journalism (epitomized by Günter **Wallraff**) has lost ground to the pursuit of sensational stories (e.g. the forged Hitler diaries in *Stern*). The expansion of commercial **broadcasting** in the late 1980s accelerated trends towards *Bildjournalismus* (visual mediation of content in print and broadcast media) and so-called *Gefälligkeitsjournalismus*, which 'accommodates' the positions of various interest groups in content. Critics point to the blurring of boundaries between advertising and editorial content, the trend towards visual mediation of content, and the 'levelling' or superficial treatment of issues as further evidence of the disintegration of a journalism which can contribute and respond to public discourse and is now increasingly shaped by the market dynamics of entertainment.

See also: mass media: FRG; mass media: GDR

Further reading

Humphreys, P.J. (1994) *Media and Media Policy in Germany: The Press and Broadcasting since 1945*, 2nd edn, Oxford and Providence, RI: Berg (deals with mass media in general, but also addresses issues relating to journalism).

Professional issues are treated in the journal *Journalist*.

BURKARD HORNUNG AND MARK W. RECTANUS

Judaism

Post-Shoah Judaism in Germany is a controversial and contentious project. Where before the **Holocaust** there had been some half a million German Jews, the basis of the 'new Jewish communities' after the war was provided by approximately 15,000 eastern European displaced persons, 8,000 German Jews and 3,000 returnees. The historical divisions within Judaism of orthodoxy, conservative, and reformed no longer existed; the refugee populations at the time were primarily secular. Since the subsequent resettlement of Jews in Germany would entail mainly immigrants, Judaism and Jewish identity had to be re-imagined.

The first wave of post-Shoah immigration to West Germany began in 1952 with the Luxembourg Agreement, which stipulated that former German citizens in exile were entitled to reparations and repossession of land. (The GDR, on the principle that communists had also been victimized by the Nazis, never accepted responsibility for reparations; the Jewish community there remained proportionately much smaller than that in the FRG.) In the 1960s and 1970s, Sephardic Jews from Arab countries and Israelis began to immigrate as well, followed in the 1980s and 1990s by Jews from Russia. Hitherto, the lack of Jewish educational programmes and schools in Germany had made these immigrant communities primarily dependent on Israel and the US for rabbinical guidance and religious instruction.

Jews in Germany are organized officially through the auspices of the Central Council (Zentralrat der Juden in Deutschland), whose chairperson (currently Paul Spiegel) is supposed to be the spokesperson for the entire Jewish community. Although some estimate that community at about 80,000, only 40,000 are actual 'dues-paying members' of *Gemeinden* – the eighty-odd institutional congregations recognized by the government. A marked characteristic of the Jews in Germany is the heterogeneous composition of the *Gemeinden*. Alternatives to professed registration in the *Gemeinde* include the neo-orthodox Adass Jisroel, the Lubavitcher Hasidim, the Centrum Judaicum in Berlin, and the Jewish Culture Club (Jüdischer Kulturverein). Although some Jews choose membership both in alternative groups *and* the *Gemeinde*, more often they affiliate with either the one or the other. The conflict over membership in the *Gemeinde* or affiliation with alternatives reflects the characteristic fears of Jews in Germany regarding the past Shoah and the re-emergence of neo-Nazi persecution (see also **skinheads**), and Jewish communities are confronted on a daily basis with the dilemma of 'invisibility' versus 'visibility' within German society as a whole.

The size of the Jewish community in Germany has increased dramatically in the 1990s as a result of the steep rise in the immigration of Jews from the former Soviet Union – in particular Russia and Ukraine. The majority of these immigrants – for the most part young, educated and secular in outlook – have settled in the big cities, especially Berlin (which has the largest Jewish *Gemeinde* in the country), but also Frankfurt am Main, Munich, Cologne, Düsseldorf, and Hamburg. Although German Jews have tended to retain their positions of power in the governing councils of the larger communities, there has been a distinct 'Russification' of Jewish life in Germany which has been especially marked in many of the smallest *Gemeinden*, where the original German Jews have found themselves minoritized by the new immigrants from the East.

The immigration of Russian Jews is governed by an agreement of 1991 between the federal and *Land* governments and the Central Council, which guarantees the new arrivals access to generous welfare benefits and integration programmes. Officially Germany's ongoing project of ***Vergangenheitsbewältigung*** means that Jewish affairs are very much part of the public consciousness of the country, receiving prominent coverage in the media, while the small Jewish community itself enjoys generous support from the public purse and a guaranteed role in public events and state bodies.

See also: churches and religion

Further reading

Bodemann, M. (1996) *Gedächtnistheater: die jüdische Gemeinschaft und ihre deutsche Erfindung*, Hamburg: Rotbuch.

Brenner, M. (1997) *After the Holocaust: Rebuilding Jewish Lives in Postwar Germany*, Princeton, NJ: Princeton University Press.

Burgauer, E. (1993) *Zwischen Erinnerung und Verdrängung: Juden in Deutschland nach 1945*, Reinbeck: Rowohlt.

Cohn, M. (1994) *The Jews in Germany, 1945–93: The Building of a Minority*, Westport, VA: Praeger.

Gilman, S. (1995) *Jews in Today's German Culture*, Bloomington, IN: Indiana University Press.

Rabinsbach, A. and Zipes, J. (1985) *Germans and Jews After the War*, Bloomington, IN: Indiana University Press.

Stern, S. (ed.) (1995) *Speaking Out – Jewish Voices from United Germany*, Berlin: Edition Q.

KITTY MILLET

Jüngel, Eberhard

b. 5 December 1934, Magdeburg

Protestant theologian

Shaped by his conflicts with the dictatorial ideology of the GDR, the notion of freedom became central to Jüngel's theologizing. Opposed to anthropological interpretations of faith, he maintains that the event of faith corresponds to the event of truth, which is the event of God's coming to the world. Reflecting the influence of **Barth**, **Bultmann**, Fuchs and Ebeling, faith and truth remain central categories in his theology. Holding that theology is free, Jüngel therefore opposes theological concepts that are based on socio-political analysis and works on a theological response to atheism.

MAGDA MUELLER

Jünger, Ernst

b. 29 March 1895, Heidelberg; d. 17 February 1998, Riedlingen

Writer

Ernst Jünger's remarkable and controversial writing career stretched over some seventy-five years. His perspective was all-embracing, and the diverse and disparate range of his intellectual interests earned him both praise and denigration. He focused on the decay of bourgeois society, the depersonalization of modern man, death, war, revolution, technology, drugs, the mythological and the psychological. Added to these are his unusual and fascinating travel journals, and an abiding interest in entomology and nature, to which he attaches metaphysical meaning.

Already in 1913 his wanderlust had manifested itself when he ran away and joined the Foreign Legion. At the outbreak of WWI Jünger enlisted in the German army, was wounded and became a highly decorated officer for his fearless combat patrols as part of an élite corps of assault troops. After the war he studied philosophy and zoology and then became a full-time writer. During WWII he served in France and Russia, recalling his experiences in his journals. After the cessation of hostilities he continued his extensive travels.

Jünger's favourite literary forms are the diary and essay. In 1920 he published his military experiences in an astonishing book *The Storm of Steel* (*In Stahlgewittern*) in which war, contact with the elemental, became the most decisive experience through which man, through supreme exertion, could attain self-realization. Further accounts of apocalyptic warfare followed. Writing in cold, impersonal, emotionless language, Jünger aestheticizes war and endows it with mystical meaning. This detachment is typical of Jünger, who sees warfare as a positive means of laying the foundations of a new society.

Following a brief flirtation with nationalist politics, which led to his hostility towards capitalist democracy and his being labelled right-wing, Jünger returned to the idea of a new society in *Der Arbeiter* (The Worker). This figure, moulded by fire and blood on the battlefield, would create a new state of militant totalitarian functionalism. At great risk to himself in 1939 Jünger published *On the Marble Cliffs* (*Auf den Marmorklippen*), an allegory set in a mythical landscape about the rise of tyranny that had Hitler in its sights, although Hitler decided nothing should be done to the author.

Jünger also tried writing novels, without success except for *Die Zwille* (The Catapult) in 1973, which is an interesting novel of social and psychological self-development. Experiments with hallucinogens and various mind-altering substances go back many years and are detailed in *Annäherungen* (Approaches), which reinforces his reputation as an adventurer. Jünger was always prepared to take both physical and intellectual risks in his efforts to escape the monotony of bourgeois life.

Jünger's wide interests, endless curiosity and individual standpoints make it difficult to compartmentalize him, but over his long life he ranged over enormous intellectual areas which may account for the contradictions in his position. Essentially, however, he remained an élitist and loner following his own way.

Further reading

Arnold, H.L. (ed.) (1990) *edition text + kritik 105/106*, Munich: edition text + kritik (general essays by diverse hands).

Meyer, M. (1990) *Ernst Jünger*, Munich: Hanser (a comprehensive survey of themes).

PETER PROCHNIK

Jürgens, Curd

b. 13 December 1912, Munich; d. 18 June 1982, Vienna

Actor

Known not only for his strong-man roles, but the infamous scandals in the German popular press, Jürgens made his film debut in 1935 and acted in over fifty films before he finally made his mark as General Harras in *Des Teufels General* (*The Devil's General*, based on Carl **Zuckmayer**'s work, directed by Helmut **Käutner** 1954). Thereafter he made eighty more films, not counting television roles. He also directed four films. He was typically cast as a macho character.

UTE LISCHKE-McNAB

Jugendweihe

The *Jugendweihe* is a secular form of confirmation in Germany which has been in existence since the nineteenth century, but the practice became particulary associated with the GDR after its institutionalization there in 1954. A central committee for the *Jugendweihe* was set up in November 1954, and the first ceremonies were performed in the spring of 1955 when just under 18 percent all fourteen-year-olds took part. The official ceremony took place at the end of the eighth year of the Polytechnical High School at the age of fourteen at which pupils were received into the ranks of adults. It included a vow to socialism and a statement of support for the GDR.

The ceremony was preceded by a period of preparation in which pupils had to attend ten special classes and take part in particular outings, for example to a former concentration camp. At the ceremony participants received a book, *Vom Sinn unseres Lebens* (Concerning the Meaning of Our Life) which aimed to provide pupils with the basis for becoming good 'socialist citizens'. The *Jugendweihe* developed very quickly into an important social occasion, and the official ceremony was often followed by a party at which participants were also given presents by their relatives.

Participation in the *Jugendweihe* was officially voluntary, but in practice there was pressure both at school and in society in general to participate. By 1960 the number of participants had risen to 87.8 percent, and in the 1980s this figure rose to over 98 percent. In theory, the *Jugendweihe* could be combined with a religious confirmation, but when it was introduced the churches at first refused to allow pupils who had participated in the state ceremony to be admitted to confirmation. When it

became almost universal practice in the 1960s, however, the Protestant church changed its policy and allowed pupils who had taken the state oaths to proceed to confirmation, sometimes after a year's grace. The number of people proceeding to religious confirmation continued to decline, however, and in the late 1980s represented only about 10 percent of fourteen-year-olds. The Catholic church continued to campaign against the state ceremony to the end of the GDR.

When the GDR disappeared as a state in 1990, it was expected that the *Jugendweihe* would also disappear. Although there was initially a steep drop in the numbers, they started to increase again in the early 1990s, partly because the ceremony represented a part of East German identity. The content of the ceremony after unification has lost its socialist character and reverted to one in which a young person is received in a general way into adult life.

PETER BARKER

June Uprising

The uprising in the GDR which took place on 16 and 17 June 1953 started as a protest by industrial workers against new work norms which had been announced at the end of May. The strikes quickly turned into a political protest against the policies of the **SED**, which in the summer of 1952 had announced a programme of measures designed to transform the GDR into a socialist state on the Soviet model. The SED lost control of the situation and on 17 June the Soviet Union used tanks to quell the revolt. The official figure for casualties was 21 dead and 187 injured, but the real figure was much higher.

See also: dissent and opposition: GDR

PETER BARKER

Jungk, Robert

b. 11 May 1913, Berlin; d. 14 July 1994, Salzburg

Scientific journalist and futurologist (real name Robert Baum)

Being of Jewish origin Jungk left Germany in 1934 and worked as a foreign correspondent in Prague, Zürich and London. From the 1950s he was actively involved in the protests against Germany's rearmament. In 1968 he took on a professorship in West Berlin. His writings focus on the ethical implications of modern science and technology, particularly nuclear technology. His books on Hiroshima (*Strahlen aus der Asche*, 1959) and on the anti-democratic character of nuclear technology (*Der Atomstaat*) (The New Tyranny: How Nuclear Power Enslaves Us, 1977) became core texts of the anti-nuclear and **peace movements** during the 1970s and 1980s.

INGOLFUR BLÜHDORN

K

Kabel, Heidi

b. 27 August 1914, Hamburg

Actress

Star actress of the **Ohnsorg-Theater** (OT) from 1932, Kabel became nationally popular through her roles in televised OT *Volksstücke*, for instance *Mudder Mews* (Mother Mews) and *Wenn der Hahn kräht* (When the Cock Crows); through extensive OT tours; and through television series like *Kleinstadtbahnhof* (Small-town Station) or *Rummelplatzgeschichten* (Fairground Tales). The typical Kabel role combines strong will, traditional values, folk wisdom, sharp tongue, matronly eroticism, occasional skittishness and peasant craftiness in outwitting more 'sophisticated' characters.

MORAY McGOWAN

Käsemann, Ernst

b. 12 July 1906, Bochum-Dahlhausen; d. 16 February 1998, Tübingen

Protestant Theologian

After his imprisonment for opposing Nazism, Käsemann became the Professor for New Testament at the universities of Mainz (1946), Göttingen (1951) and Tübingen (1959). A critical student of **Bultmann**'s theology, he initiated the latest stage of the problematic question about the historical Jesus (1954), asserted that Christian faith has to focus on the crucified and not the resurrected God (1967), and that justification of the godless was the core of all Christian proclamation. His theology of the suffering God led to the development of a profound alternative that draws political consequences from his biblical exegeses for social justice and a restructuring of the church. His provocative scholarship has elicited extreme responses.

MAGDA MUELLER

Kästner, Erich

b. 23 February 1899, Dresden; d. 29 July 1974, Munich

Writer

Kästner is known chiefly for the social satire *Fabian* (1931), written during the Weimar Republic, and for his popular children's books, especially *Emil and the Detectives* (*Emil und die Detektive*) (1928), filmed in 1930, and *Das doppelte Lottchen* (The Two Lotties) (1949), filmed in 1951. He bore witness to the crimes committed in the Third Reich in *Die Schule der Diktatoren* (The School of Dictators) (1956) and in his diary *Notabene 45* (N.B. 45) (1961). After the war he founded two cabaret companies in Munich, and edited a magazine for young people, *Der Pinguin* (The Penguin), until 1949. During the first half of the 1960s he edited humorous anthologies. His last published work was a children's book, *Der kleine Mann und die kleine Miss* (The Little Man and the Little Miss) (1967). He also translated T.S. Eliot's *Old Possum's Book of Practical Cats* (1952).

MARGARET VALLANCE

Käutner, Helmut

b. 25 March 1908, Düsseldorf; d. 20 April
1980, Castellina (Italy)

Filmmaker and actor

Building on experience in cabaret, Käutner
became a leading director of comedies and
melodramas during the final years of the Third
Reich, despite efforts by Goebbels to suppress his
work for its perceived escapism. *In Those Days* (*In
jenen Tagen*, 1947), an attempt to confront the Nazi
past, and the prize-winning anti-war film *The Last
Bridge* (*Die letzte Brücke*, 1954) were followed by
numerous literary adaptations (including three
films based on texts by Carl **Zuckmayer**) and,
increasingly, work in the theatre, opera and
television.

See also: film: FRG

MARTIN BRADY

Kagel, Mauricio

b. 24 December 1931, Buenos Aires

Composer

Many labels have been applied to Kagel: expressionist, dadaist, surrealist, but he is first and
foremost an iconoclast, whose innovative musical
and theatrical compositions struck at the very heart
of the cultural pretensions of West German society.
Based in Cologne since 1957, he has eagerly
appropriated mass media (especially an inventive
series of television films) to expound his singular
perspective, never more finely honed than when
mocking the worship of icons, such as Beethoven in
Ludwig van or Johann Sebastian in the *Sankt Bach
Passion*. All of this does not detract from musical
invention of a high order, placing Kagel in the first
rank of European composers.

BEATRICE HARPER

Kahlschlag

This term, normally used to refer to the clearing of
forests, was employed by Wolfgang **Weyrauch** in

1949 to refer to authors' efforts to forge a new path
for literature in the post-war turmoil. More
generally it is used of attempts by certain writers,
associated with the beginnings of the **Gruppe 47**,
to rid their writing of the language and rhetoric of
Nazism. The best-known example of *Kahlschlaglite-
ratur* is Günter **Eich**'s poem 'Inventur', which
largely consists of an enumeration of possessions.
Critics have pointed out that the process was in
reality less radical than the proclamations of intent.

STUART PARKES

Kamnitzer, Heinz

b. 10 May 1917, Berlin

Writer, journalist and historian

Kamnitzer was from 1970 to 1989 President of the
GDR **PEN** club. Forced to emigrate under the
Nazis, he returned to Germany in 1946. From
1950 to 1954 he was Professor of History at the
Humboldt University Berlin, and from 1953 to
1955 he jointly edited the *Zeitschrift für Geschichtswissenschaft* with Alfred Meusel and Leo Stern.
From 1955 he became a freelance writer and
journalist with a particular interest in the relations
between literature and society (Arnold Zweig).

MARY FULBROOK

Kant, Hermann

b. 14 June 1926, Hamburg

Writer and (ex-)cultural functionary

In the GDR of the 1960s, Hermann Kant's rise to
prominence was widely publicized as an exemplary
success-story. The son of a working-class family,
who had originally trained as an electrician, he had
emerged from a PoW camp in Poland to become,
in 1952, one of the first graduates of the *Arbeiter-
und Bauernfakultäten* (Workers' and Peasants' Faculties) which had been established at the GDR's
universities in order to democratize access to
higher education. This had paved the way to the
study of German literature at the Humboldt
University in Berlin and then to an impressive

literary debut as an independently-minded, but ultimately loyal author with a welcome sense of humour.

Kant's first novel, *Die Aula* (The Assembly Hall) (1965), was a partly autobiographical account of his generation's experience, focused on his years at the ABF in Greifswald and published just after these faculties had been disbanded with their transitional educational task evidently completed. *Die Aula* not only enjoyed immense popularity in the GDR as a prime example of a literature liberating itself from the propagandist simplifications of the 1950s; it was also taken seriously in the West and later became a set-text on school and university courses. His next novel, *Das Impressum* (Editorial Details) (1972) was eagerly awaited, not least because its publication had been delayed for three years for unspecified political reasons, but it proved disappointingly complacent about the contemporary GDR, as seen through the eyes of its protagonist, a newspaper editor about to become a government minister. Kant finally managed to fulfil the literary potential evident in *Die Aula* in an absorbing, sober account of his experience as a PoW, *Der Aufenthalt* (Temporary Abode) (1977). He then appeared to be frittering away his talent in volumes of shorter prose, which were often entertaining but only at the price of avoiding engagement with significant contemporary issues.

This loss of creative direction coincided with Kant's elevation to the presidency of the GDR **Writers' Union** (1978–90), the most demanding of his new roles in a career development which turned him into a compliant 'multi-functionary' (Corino 1995) and left him little time for serious writing. Any ambitions he might have had to mediate effectively between his fellow-authors and the SED's cultural establishment were thwarted by his failure to maintain the trust of either side in the increasingly fraught atmosphere which followed the **Biermann Affair**. Despite his protestations that he had done his utmost during his years of office to promote the work of his colleagues in the face of enormous political pressures, the recent evidence of his prolonged involvement with the **Stasi** has dealt a final blow to his already battered credibility.

See also: prose fiction: GDR

Further reading

Corino, K. (ed.) (1995), *Die Akte Kant*, Reinbek bei Hamburg: Rowohlt (a hard-hitting exposure of Kant's involvement with the Stasi, going back to the 1950s).

Kant, H. (1991), *Abspann: Erinnerung an meine Gegenwart*, Berlin: Aufbau (an attempted self-defence, especially regarding his role in the Writers' Union).

DENNIS TATE

Karajan, Herbert von

b. 5 April 1908, Salzburg; d. 16 July 1989, Anif (Salzberg)

Conductor

Wilhelm **Furtwängler**'s successor as Chief Conductor of the Berlin Philharmonic (1955–88), as well as Music Director of the Vienna Staatsoper (1957–64) and Artistic Director of the **Salzburg Festival** (1956–88), Karajan was one of the most successful and influential of conductors. A consummate technician, he had little time for contemporary music, but gained huge renown for the polish and insight of his performances of the classics, particularly of Beethoven, Bruckner, Richard **Strauß** and Wagner. An eager explorer of new technologies and their commercial potential, he left over 500 recordings in various visual and audio media.

BEATRICE HARPER

Karat

The GDR rock band Karat was founded in 1975. Like the **Puhdys** and **Silly** they were officially approved by the GDR authorities, despite being famous for couching in metaphors whatever may appear ideologically offensive. With its indefinite promise of hope for a golden future beyond all the miseries of everyday life, their 1979 song *Über sieben Brücken mußt du geh'n* (Seven Bridges You Have to Cross) became a kind of alternative anthem in the East. Karat was the first GDR group to receive a

West German 'golden disc' (1983) after selling over 500,000 copies of this song in the FRG.

ANNETTE BLÜHDORN

Karneval

Karneval, like **Fastnacht**, is a shrovetide festival, but confined to the Rhineland regions and in particular to the city of Cologne. Both *Fastnacht* and *Karneval* are culturally Catholic ritual celebrations and involve an inversion of normal power structures for a strictly delimited period of time. For the period of *Karneval* a Carnival king is crowned who inverts the normal power structures and ushers in the rule of fools for the *Karneval* period. The other two focuses for the *Karneval* rule of fools are the virgin, usually a man in drag, and the peasant. These men are elected on the eleventh day of the eleventh month at 11.11 am when the *Narrenzeit* ('Fooltide') begins and culminates, after much preparation by the *Narrenzunft* (the 'Fools' guilds') and by the *Narrenrat* (the 'Fools' council'), in the shrovetide celebrations. Election to these offices brings much publicity but also a financial burden. The city of Cologne is estimated to spend in excess of a million Deutschmarks on *Karneval*.

Karneval is marked by huge processions which snake through the medieval city centres and are watched by up to a million people on the streets. Tonnes of toffees are thrown to the crowds from the floats. The main procession is on *Rosenmontag* (the Monday before shrove Tuesday) but the Thursday, known as *Weiberfastnacht*, is the women's *Karneval*. Women are excluded from the power structures of *Karneval* but they may exact revenge on the Thursday by cutting off men's ties. The obvious Freudian element to these gestures requires little analysis. Bright, gaudy costumes, often supplied by costumiers at considerable expense, face paints, special *Narrenhüte* (Fools' hats) masks etc, are worn to some degree by the majority. The processions run over several days and floats from the *Karneval* guilds as well as from local schools and other **Verein**e (local institutions) are able to represent aspects of the city's history as well, on occasion, as political issues such as environmentalism. The imagination and creative energy which is paraded through the streets during *Karneval* is astounding, as is the popularity and the loyalty of natives to the festivities. The historical floats usually stop short of celebrating modern German history, though some satirize contemporary politicians. Military uniforms and pipe bands abound, often with women dressed as soldiers disobeying orders and demonstrating a cult of nostalgia for a medieval past.

Accompanying the processions and the costumes are the fancy-dress balls and the dancing in huge beer tents and on the streets at night. There are recitals of local poetry and also familiar dialect songs, which are songs only sung during the *Karneval* season in the streets often as a spontaneous chorus.

Karneval ends with the return of normal rule to the mayor and with the Rhineland suffering from an immense communal hang-over on Ash Wednesday.

ALISON PHIPPS

Karsunke, Yaak

b. 4 June 1934, Berlin

Writer

Co-founder of the left-wing periodical *Kürbiskern* (Pumpkin Seed) in 1965 and editor until 1969, Karsunke was active in the Extra-Parliamentary Opposition (**APO**). Trained as an actor, he appeared in two of **Fassbinder**'s first films. He wrote several volumes of experimental poetry, e.g. *Kilroy & andere* (Kilroy & Others) (1967); plays, the most successful of which, *Die Bauernoper* (The Peasants' Opera), was first performed in 1973; and ballet libretti. The influence of **Brecht** is shown in his questioning of prevailing political ideologies and the combination of entertainment and political dialectic. He is the translator of Arnold Wesker.

MARGARET VALLANCE

Kasack, Hermann

b. 24 July 1896, Potsdam; d. 10 January 1966, Stuttgart

Writer

Although he had published poetry and plays between the world wars, Kasack's reputation rests on his prose works written after 1945, which accurately convey the bleak pessimism of early post-war Germany. *The City Beyond the River* (*Die Stadt hinter dem Strom*, 1949) is a dream-like, allegorical vision of a devastated region peopled by 'dead souls' and controlled by oppressive authorities. Subsequent works are satirical parables about self-serving state mechanisms and the depersonalization of the individual with echoes of Karl **Jaspers**' philosophy.

Further reading

Mainland, W.F. (1966) 'Hermann Kasack' in B. Keith-Smith (ed.) (1966) *Essays on Contemporary German Literature*, London: Wolff (a useful introduction).

PETER PROCHNIK

Kaschnitz, Marie Luise

b. 31 January 1901, Karlsruhe; d. 10 October 1974, Rome

Writer

Kaschnitz emerged as one of the few poets writing after Germany's defeat in 1945 who were able to write convincing poetry, in a technical and moral sense, about the experience of war. This early poetry was marked by a mastery of formal structure which gave way to loser forms in her later works as a more subjective voice developed. Her years in Italy had made her alive to classical forms and the potency of mythology. She was also a distinguished writer of short stories.

ANTHONY BUSHELL

Kelly, Petra

b. 29 November 1947, Günzburg (near Ulm) d. 1 October 1992, Bonn

Politician

Petra Kelly was a founder member of the German Green Party (**Greens**) and, at least internationally, its most famous representative. Throughout the 1980s, she was also a most charismatic and internationally recognized figurehead of the German **peace movement**. She struggled for global disarmament and solidarity and the uncompromising protection of human rights. As one of the first spokespersons of the Greens she helped to build up the popularity of green ideals, yet towards the end of the 1980s her influence within the party declined. Following a period marked by personal problems and political frustration in the early 1990s, Petra Kelly died under tragic circumstances, which, although officially categorized as a murder carried out by her partner Gert Bastian, come close to a joint suicide.

Youth and education

Petra Kelly owes her surname to her stepfather J.E. Kelly, an American lieutenant-colonel of Irish origin. She was first educated in a Catholic convent school in Günzburg and then attended High School in the US (1959–66). From 1966 to 1970 she studied World Politics and International Relations in Washington. During her university years she became politically active and built up contacts with Democrats like Robert Kennedy and Hubert Humphrey. Following her first degree she obtained an MA at the University of Amsterdam (1970–1). In 1971 she started to work for the European Communities in Brussels. When she left Brussels in 1982 she was member of the executive of the EC's Economic and Social Committee.

The Green Politician

As a great admirer of Willy **Brandt**'s reform policies Petra Kelly joined the **SPD** when Brandt became Federal Chancellor. In 1972 she also became a member of the 'Federal Association of Environmentalist Citizens' Initiatives' (*Bundesver-*

band *Bürgerinitiativen Umweltschutz*, BBU) (see also **citizens' initiatives: FRG**). Infuriated about the government's support for **nuclear power** and generally disappointed by the lack of significant political changes during the 1970s, she left the SPD in 1979 and devoted her political energy to the social movements. She became a member of the executive committee of the BBU and, in the run-up to the 1979 European Elections, she helped to found the Green Party. As their leading candidate she secured the party 3.2 percent of the German vote. In the following years she ran as the Greens' top candidate in various *Land* and regional elections using what she called the 'anti-party party' to bring social movement concerns to the attention of decision-makers in Bonn. From 1980 to 1982 she was one of three spokespersons of the party's Federal Executive Committee, and after the federal elections of 1983 she was one of the first Green members of the *Bundestag*. In accordance with the party's policy of rotating its MPs, she should have left this post in 1985. Her refusal to do so triggered off controversial debates about the usefulness of rotation. In the following years she never identified with specific ideological groupings within the party. She rejected political compromises and tactical alliances. Although committed to the Greens, her first loyalty was not to the party but to her own radical pacifism.

Her personal utopia

The most formative experience in Petra Kelly's life was the illness and early death of her half-sister Grace Patricia who was diagnosed as having cancer at the age of seven and died three years later. Her sister's suffering as well as her own impaired health (renal disease) made the fear of cancer one of the most powerful motivating forces in her tireless political struggle. Despite her commitment to human rights campaigns, women's issues and minority groups all over the world, her strongest concern was the life-destroying capacity of nuclear technology. For Kelly, the development of nuclear energy since the 1970s and the nuclear arms race of the 1980s had inaugurated the age of global apocalypse, and all social and political debate now had to be focused on questions of life and survival. It was her deepest belief that the

destruction of mankind is the most heinous crime imaginable. Any action leading in this direction had to be radically condemned. Against the inhumane and uncontrollable politics of destruction she struggled for social solidarity, responsibility and empathy. Following the examples of Rosa Luxemburg, Mahatma Gandhi and Martin Luther King she never campaigned in a spirit of hatred or bitterness but always sought to understand her political enemies as human beings. For her commitment and achievements she was awarded the Alternative Nobel Prize in Stockholm (1982).

Gert Bastian

Her relationship with general Gert Bastian started in 1980. Bastian had been a soldier for twenty-four years before resigning from the Bundeswehr in protest against NATO nuclear weapons. He drafted the Krefeld Appeal against the stationing of American Pershing and cruise missiles on German territory which was signed by some five million people. He became an active member of the peace movement and the Greens, and then Petra Kelly's most committed supporter. Although he was considerably older than Petra Kelly, they had an intimate relationship which lasted until their tragic death. Gert Bastian shot Petra Kelly while she was asleep and then killed himself. There was no indication of any dissent between them, nor of any plans for a joint suicide. Petra Kelly had become increasingly frustrated, exhausted and frail since the Green Party had failed to gain Bundestag representation in the 1990 elections. For support she relied exclusively on Bastian, who was then almost 70 and arguably overburdened with this responsibility. It had been Petra Kelly's wish never to outlive her partner, yet her strict principles of non-violence and her reverence for human life make it difficult to assume her tacit consent to the deed.

Further reading

Kelly, P. (1984) *Fighting for Hope*, London: Chatto & Windus (detailed deliberations on her principles and political views).

Raschke, J. (1993) *Die Grünen. Wie sie wurden, was sie sind*, Cologne: bund (academic analysis of the historical development of the Green Party; includes Petra Kelly's political contribution).

Schwarzer, A. (1994) *Eine tödliche Liebe. Petra Kelly und Gert Bastian*, Munich: Heyne (analysis of the relationship between Kelly and Bastian).

INGOLFUR BLÜHDORN

Kempe, Rudolf

b. 14 June 1910, Niederpoyritz (Saxony); d. 12 May 1976, Zürich

Conductor

Principal oboeist of the Leipzig Gewandhaus for seven years, Kempe emerged as a conductor of international distinction after WWII, holding operatic posts in Dresden (1949–52) and Munich (1952–4), and frequently appearing at Covent Garden. His lyrical, lucid approach shed unexpected light on the operas of Wagner and Richard **Strauß**, which he recorded with great success. He held important symphonic posts with the Royal Philharmonic (1963–75), the Zürich Tonhalle (1965–72) and the Munich Philharmonic (1967–76).

BEATRICE HARPER

Kempff, Diana

b. 11 June 1945, Thurnau (Oberfranken)

Writer

Kempff's début was with a largely overlooked volume of poetry *Vor allen das Unnützliche* (Above All, the Superfluous) (1975) that drew on, among other things, the Japanese haiku tradition. She received acclaim for her autobiographical novel, *Fettfleck* (Grease Spot) (1979), a monologue that tells the story of a troubled, overweight girl struggling with the pressures of society and the unhappy marriage of her parents. She writes poetry, novels and **Hörspiele** (radio plays).

MARTINA S. ANDERSON

Kempowski, Walter

b. 29 April 1929, Rostock

Writer

Kempowski was born into an affluent shipbuilding family. After a youth marked by WWII he was arrested in 1948 for 'economic espionage', sentenced to twenty-five years imprisonment but released in 1956. He moved to the West where he eventually worked as a village school-teacher – an important phase of his life – until 1979. In 1980 he founded an archive for German biographies.

After his first longer published work, *Im Block: Ein Haftbericht* (In the Prison Block: A Report from Jail) (1969), which detailed the events of his own imprisonment, Kempowski concentrated on the series of novels that earned him the reputation of the 'chronicler of the German middle classes'. The first of these, *Tadellöser & Wolff* (1971, television film 1975 by Eberhard **Fechner**), chronicled events in his family from the years leading up to WWII to 1945 and established the pattern for subsequent works: deliberately avoiding reflection and moral judgements, Kempowski, from the point of view of a youth from ten to sixteen years old, creates a heavy weave of contemporary reality out of the interplay of individually remembered local events, quotations, family rituals and sayings, the material of everyday life. The quantity of information presented (Kempowski's archive of slips of paper, his *Zettelkasten*) did not encourage nostalgia (although many of his older readers responded at least initially with this – and many younger readers looked on these works as collections of source material on 'how their parents lived'). Instead, by presenting the family without idyll and emphasizing its limitations in the face of the social reality surrounding it, Kempowski creates a unique amalgam of autobiography, local (Rostock) history and contemporary history in the form of a family chronicle. Other novels followed, drawing the family saga from the turn of the century up to events of the 1960s: *Uns geht's ja noch gold* (We're Still Doing Fine) (1972); *Ein Kapitel für sich* (A Chapter in Itself) (1975); *Aus großer Zeit* (From the Good Old Days) (1978); and *Schöne Aussicht* (Good Prospects) (1981), and so on.

Kempowski also wrote a number of radio plays and other, semi-documentary works, based on questioning his fellow Germans about their memories, for instance *Haben Sie Hitler gesehen?* (Did You See Hitler?) (1973), as well as works relating to his life as a teacher, such as *Unser Herr Böckelmann* (Our Mr Böckelmann). In a new departure Kempowski published his four-volume work, *Das Echolot: Ein kollektives Tagebuch Januar und Februar 1943* (The Echo-Sounder: A Collective Diary for January and February 1943) (1993) in which, abandoning any fictional framework, he presents a patchwork of extracts from letters and diaries from a wide range of people, as well as registers of births and deaths, instructions to journalists from press conferences, and so on.

Further reading

Dierks, M. (1978) 'Walter Kempowski', in H.L. Arnold (ed.) *Kritisches Lexikon zur deutschsprachigen Gegenwartsliteratur*, Munich: edition text + kritik, 1978 (periodically updated, full bibliography of works and secondary literature).

Riley, C. (1997) *Walter Kempowski's Deutsche Chronik: a Study in Ironic Narration*, Frankfurt am Main and New York: P. Lang (full-length study of the narrative of Kempowski's early works, with bibliography).

JOHN WIECZOREK

Kertész, István

b. 28 August 1929, Budapest; d. 16 April 1973, Tel Aviv

Conductor

Kertész's early teachers in Budapest included Kodaly at the Liszt Ferenc Academy, while Klemperer, then at the Budapest Opera, influenced him as a conductor. In 1955 Kertész himself was conducting there. Following the uprising in 1956, he moved to Germany and became naturalized. His first post was at Augsburg, then later Cologne. From 1960 he enjoyed considerable popularity as a conductor, not only of opera. His Covent Garden début was in 1960, followed by a three-year

contract with the London Symphony Orchestra with whom he went on a world tour. A conservative conductor, he nevertheless mastered an exceptionally wide repertoire and showed great affinity with the music of Britten, Bartók and Stravinsky, as well as Dvořák and Mozart.

DEREK McCULLOCH

Kesten, Hermann

b. 28 January 1900, Nürnberg; d. 3 May 1996, Riehen (Basel)

Writer

Kesten's early success with stories and novels that brought the gaze of an urbane moralist to bear on questions of individual freedom and responsibility, for instance *Josef sucht die Freiheit* (Joseph in Search of Freedom) (1927) was followed by exile in The Netherlands and France (1933–40) and the US (1940–9). Anti-Nazi and anti-communist, Kesten is best known in the FRG as a literary polemicist and an essayist specializing in portraits of his fellow-writers, as in *Meine Freunde die Poeten* (My Friends the Poets) (1953). Kesten devoted himself as critic, translator, anthologist and editor to furthering and disseminating the liberal-humane tradition in German and European literature. He was President of FRG **PEN** from 1972 to 1976.

GRAHAM BARTRAM

Keun, Irmgard

b. 6 February, 1905, Berlin; d. 5 May, 1982, Cologne

Writer

Keun is best known for her pre-WWII novels set in the last days of the Weimar Republic, the first years of Nazi rule, and the time of her exile. Acute observation of everyday detail provides important insights into the period. Her books were banned by the Nazis; Keun fled Germany in 1936 returning illegally in 1940. Disenchantment with post-war Germany, changes in literary fashion and chronic alcoholism prevented her from emulating her pre-war successes. She lived in obscurity until her rediscovery in the late 1970s in the wake of renewed interest in women's writing.

See also: *Frauenliteratur*

GABRIELA STEINKE

Keusch, Erwin

b. 22 July 1946, Zürich

Filmmaker

Keusch moved to Germany from Switzerland in 1968. An autodidact, he directed short experimental films and documentaries from 1968 and fiction films for television from 1973. His breakthrough came with *The Baker's Bread* (*Das Brot des Bäckers*) in 1976, a witty and perceptive, semi-autobiographical milieu study set in a provincial bakery. During the late 1970s he directed documentaries about football, Werner **Herzog**, and a Hamburg sex club. His subsequent feature films, including *The Flyer* (*Der Flieger*, 1987), the story of a world-record-breaking hang-glider flight in Bolivia, are documentary in style.

See also: New German Cinema

MARTIN BRADY

Khittl, Ferdinand

b. 1924, Franzensbad (Františkovy Lázně, Czechoslovakia); d. 27 February 1976, Bad Reichenhall

Filmmaker

Khittl moved to Germany in the early 1950s after serving in the merchant navy. A distinguished industrial and documentary filmmaker, and co-signatory of the Oberhausen Manifesto, he directed his only feature film in 1961, the experimental 'docu-fiction' essay *The Parallel Street* (*Die Parallelstraße*). Received enthusiastically at film festivals abroad, this unjustifiably neglected *tour de force* is a challenging philosophical odyssey, a parable of life, death and the transitory nature of human en-

deavour combining documentary sequences filmed across the globe with a bizarre Kafkaesque trial.

See also: New German Cinema

MARTIN BRADY

Kiefer, Anselm

b. 8 March 1945, Donaueschingen

Artist

A pupil of Horst Antes and Joseph **Beuys**, Kiefer first came to prominence in 1969 with *Occupations* (*Besetzungen*), a series of photographs of the painter himself giving the Nazi salute in different locations across Europe. Consistently controversial, his large-scale paintings (incorporating materials such as straw, glass, charred wood and plants), sculptures, and vast lead books tackle taboo themes from German history, for example in the painting *Germany's Spiritual Heroes* (*Deutschlands Geisteshelden*) (1973); philosophy, mythology, and culture, including a striking series of paintings based on Paul **Celan**'s poem *Death Fugue* (*Todesfuge*).

See also: painting

MARTIN BRADY

Kinski, Klaus

b. 18 October 1926, Zoppot (East Prussia, now Sopot, Poland); d. 22 November 1991, Labunita (California)

Actor

Kinski was a specialist in the depiction of extreme emotions through exaggerated gestures and overwrought delivery, in innumerable stage appearances, recitations and film roles. His performances in the Edgar Wallace films of the 1960s contributed considerably to their commercial success, similarly his role in Sergio Leone's spaghetti western *For a Few Dollars More* (1965). In the films of Werner **Herzog** his style reaches its apotheosis in five tumultuous title roles beginning with the insane Spanish conquistador in *Aguirre, Wrath of God* (*Aguirre, der Zorn Gottes*, 1972).

See also: film: FRG

HELEN HUGHES

Kinski, Nastassja

b. 24 January 1961, Berlin

Actress

Daughter of actor Klaus **Kinski**, Nastassja Kinski has enjoyed a remarkable, if uneven, career in Hollywood and European art cinema, in films by Roman Polanski, Francis Ford Coppola, Paul Schrader and Lina Wertmüller. Her debut at age fourteen in Wim **Wenders**' *Falsche Bewegung* (Wrong Move) (1975) established her image as alluring enigmatic waif, later reinforced by Richard Avedon's famous pin-up poster showing her nude with a snake. She occasionally challenges that mould, for instance with her complex performance as an estranged wife in *Paris, Texas* (1984) and as the angel Raphaela in *Far Away, So Close* (*In weiter Ferne, so nah*, 1993), both by Wenders.

CHRISTIAN ROGOWSKI

kiosks

Kiosks have been in existence in Germany since the last century. At first only to be found in larger cities, now they can be found practically everywhere. Due to the stringent opening hours of German shops, kiosks provide the population not only with newspapers, books and magazines, but also with snacks and alcoholic and non-alcoholic beverages, oftentimes being focal neighbourhood meeting places.

HOLGER BRIEL

Kipphardt, Heinar

b. 8 March 1922, Heidersdorf (Silesia); d. 18 November 1982, Munich

Writer and *Dramaturg*

The worldwide attention attracted by Kipphardt's 1964 documentary drama on the political respon-sibility of the scientist, *In the Matter of J. Robert Oppenheimer* (*In der Sache J. Robert Oppenheimer*), has obscured the formal and thematic range of his work, marked by critical rationalism, political commitment and restless energy.

Trained as a psychiatrist, he practised in East Berlin before becoming chief **Dramaturg** at the **Deutsches Theater** from 1950. He produced short stories and a number of satirical comedies, notably *A Shakespeare Urgently Wanted* (*Shakespeare dringend gesucht*) (1953), which mocks the stagnation of state-controlled culture. Frustration at this culture drove Kipphardt to West Germany in 1959. Appointed chief *Dramaturg* at the Munich Kammerspiele in 1969, he was sacked in 1971 in a controversy over Wolf **Biermann**'s *Der Dra-Dra*.

The General's Dog (*Der Hund des Generals*) (1962), uses Brechtian techniques (songs, projections, flashbacks and newsreels) in a critique of post-war West Germany's uncritical reinstatement of war criminals (see also **Vergangenheitsbewälti-gung**). *In der Sache J. Robert Oppenheimer* is more directly documentary, being based on the actual hearing in 1954 at which the atom scientist Oppenheimer answered charges of communist sympathies. The single set and interrogatory structure heighten the sense of an authentic tribunal. Yet documentary literature is in fact always tendentious, and this necessitates aesthetic intervention. Kipphardt not only condensed the 3,000-page transcript of the hearing, but reapportioned it for dramatic effect. Moreover, his Oppenheimer undergoes a conversion to the idea of the scientist's moral responsibility. *Sedanfeier* (Sedan Anniversary Celebration) (1970), by letting documents from the Franco-German War of 1870 speak for themselves, like a gym teacher's praise of physical fitness as the path to a heroic death, transforms them aesthetically into a grotesque parody of militarism. In the 1970s Kipphardt explored the artistic psyche in a mosaic of texts and genres: the television play *Leben des schizophrenen Dichters Alexander März* (Life of the Schizophrenic Poet Alexander März) (1975), the novel *März* (1976), *März-Gedichte* (März Poems) (1977) and the stage play *März, ein Künstlerleben* (März. An Artist's Life, 1980). His *Traumprotokolle* (Dream Protocols) (1981) are a radically frank record of 160 dreams from the period 1978 to 1981.

Joel Brand (1965), dramatizing Adolf Eichmann's attempt to trade one million Jews for ten thousand lorries, links thematically to *Bruder Eichmann* (Brother Eichmann), also begun in the 1960s but premièred only in 1983. *Bruder Eichmann* returns to the document-based investigation of historical reality; but as the title (echoing Thomas Mann's essay 'Bruder Hitler') suggests, the focus is not comfortable moral indictment of an incomprehensible monster, but the 'banality of evil' (Hannah Arendt), the psychological dynamic which makes an essentially ordinary man capable of administering genocide.

Further reading

Karbach, W. (1989) *Mit Vernunft zu rasen: Heinar Kipphardt*, Oberwesel: Verlag Loreley-Galerie.

MORAY McGOWAN

Kirch, Leo

b. 21 October 1926, Würzburg

Media entrepreneur

Leo Kirch owns one of Germany's most extensive media empires. The son of a winemaker in Franconia (Bavaria), Kirch got his start in the media industry by developing a niche in the area of film licensing. Today, Kirch not only possesses Europe's largest collection of film rights, but runs multiple television networks and is part-owner of Germany's largest newspaper publisher, Axel Springer Verlag. Kirch was known for his close relationship with the former chancellor Helmut Kohl and for his reluctance – unlike Axel **Springer** – to promote himself as a public figure.

Since the mid-1950s, Kirch has developed a truly international media concern, with holdings in Germany, Switzerland, Austria, France, Spain and beyond. The Kirch Group is also a multimedia business. It consists of film and television production companies, commercial television networks, synchronization and video production businesses, film leasing and theatres, merchandizing, and music, as well as print media organizations. Kirch is perhaps best known for his involvement in the launch of private television in Germany in the mid-1980s. His television interests include SAT.1 and the pay-television Premiere channel. In addition, Kirch placed part-ownership of the Pro 7 channel in the hands of his son, Thomas, thereby extending the family's influence in the media industry. Today SAT.1 and Pro 7 are the second and third largest private channels in the Federal Republic. The combined net income of Kirch's television ventures is more than DM 2 billion per annum.

Kirch spent several years seeking greater control of the press giant, Axel Springer Verlag (with its influential *Die Welt* and *Bild* newspapers) – a struggle he won in the mid-1990s. Kirch's long-term acquisition of substantial parts of Germany's media industry, as well as media businesses in both western and eastern Europe, have long made him suspect in the eyes of those opposed to such a concentration of media power. Kirch's mixture of media and politics (SAT.1 has often been referred to as an unashamed champion of Helmut Kohl), however 'behind-the-scenes', has brought comparisons with the Italian media mogul turned politician, Silvio Berlusconi. Since the mid-1990s, however, Kirch's media empire has acquired increasing debt (largely as a result of heavy investment in the launch of the first German digital television service) and has come under growing financial pressure, forcing Kirch to place shares in Pro 7 on public offer.

See also: broadcasting

Further reading

Radtke, M. (1994) *Ausser Kontrolle: Die Medienmacht des Leo Kirch*, Bern: Hans Erpf.

ROBIN B. HODESS

Kirche im Sozialismus

Kirche im Sozialismus (a church within socialism) was the term used from 1971 to 1989 by the Protestant churches in the GDR to describe their role in the socialist society of the GDR.

The GDR was the only country in central and eastern Europe in which a Soviet-backed government confronted a nominally majority Protestant church. The Evangelical Church in Germany (EKD), founded after WWII, had at first as members the Protestant *Landeskirchen* in both East and West Germany (see also **churches and religion**). However, attempts to hold the EKD together failed, following the refusal in the late 1950s of the GDR authorities to deal with the EKD, and the building of the **Berlin Wall** in 1961, which made meetings of church representatives from east and west increasingly difficult. On 10 June 1969, the eight Protestant *Landeskirchen* on the territory of the GDR dissolved their membership in the EKD and formed the Federation of Evangelical Churches in the German Democratic Republic (BEK).

In 1971, a meeting of the BEK's synod in Eisenach described the role of the Protestant churches in the GDR as being to be 'neither a church alongside, nor against, but within socialism' (*Nicht Kirche neben, nicht gegen, sondern im Sozialismus*). In the years that followed, the term 'church within socialism' was used as a shorthand to describe a political course of the BEK avoiding the extremes of total assimilation or total resistance to the SED. Influential in this period were Bishop Albrecht **Schönherr** (the first chairman, 1969 to 1981, of the BEK) and Manfred **Stolpe** (director of the BEK secretariat and then deputy chairman of the BEK).

Kirche im Sozialismus can also be seen as the most characteristic aspect of the church policy of the SED under Erich **Honecker** (1971 to 1989). The GDR government officially recognized the BEK in 1971, after which meetings at various levels were held, culminating in a meeting, on 6 March 1978, between leaders of the BEK and Honecker. Following this meeting, the Protestant churches were able to build churches on new housing estates, gained access to GDR radio and television, and took an increasing role in international ecumenical affairs. The 1983 *Lutherjahr*, in which both state and church marked the 500th anniversary of the birth of Martin Luther, was a significant event in strengthening the self-confidence of the churches.

The description *Kirche im Sozialismus* was never completely accepted by all clergy or church leaders. In 1976, the self-immolation of pastor Oskar Brüsewitz in protest against SED policies on the churches was a startling and sombre token of this dissent.

Following protests by the churches against the introduction in 1978 of military training (*Wehrerziehung*) in state schools, and the promotion in response of programmes of education for peace by churches, the Protestant churches began to provide an umbrella for an alternative youth-based subculture, particularly after the introduction of the annual *Friedensdekade* ('ten days for peace'), under the slogan 'Swords into Ploughshares'. Increasingly, peace groups meeting under the umbrella of Protestant churches were followed by ecology groups, civil liberty groups and even gay and lesbian groups. This started a debate within the church about its boundaries, and conflicts between the groups and church leaders grew in the 1980s. The state authorities attempted at the end of 1987 and the beginning of 1988 to take advantage of these tensions by mounting a series of arrests of activists.

By the mid-1980s the description *Kirche im Sozialismus* increasingly lost relevance as the SED leadership insisted on an increasingly dogmatic definition of socialism. On 5 March 1989 the then BEK chairman (Bishop Werner Leich of Thuringia) called publicly for the use of the term *Kirche im Sozialismus* to be dropped. A meeting of the BEK synod in September 1989, at which it had been intended to abandon the term, concentrated instead on a series of demands for the political reform of the GDR. Further reflection on the term became irrelevant in the course of the *Wende* and German unification.

Since the *Wende* there has been an increasingly critical debate about the role of the Protestant churches in the GDR, fuelled in part by the revelation of meetings between high level church representatives (in particular, Manfred Stolpe) and the Stasi.

See also: peace movement: GDR

Further reading

Besier, G. (1983) *Der SED-Staat und die Kirche: Der Weg in die Anpassung*, Munich: C Bertelsmann Verlag.

—— (1994) *Der SED-Staat und die Kirche, 1969–1990:*

Die Vision vom 'Dritten Weg', Frankfurt am Main: Propyläen.

—— (1995) *Der SED-Staat und die Kirchen 1983–1991: Höhenflug und Absturz*, Frankfurt am Main: Propyläen (a magisterial, but also controversial, trilogy about the Protestant churches in the GDR, drawing on archival material of the churches, the state archives and the archives of the Stasi; includes comprehensive bibliography).

Schröder, R. (1995) 'Kirche im Sozialismus', in *Materialien der Enquete-Kommission 'Aufarbeitung von Gechichte und Folgen der SED Diktatur in Deutschland'*, hrsg. vom Deutschen Bundestag, vol. 6, 2: pp. 1164–1429, Nomos Verlag: Baden-Baden (includes comprehensive documentary appendix and bibliography).

STEPHEN BROWN

Kirsch, Sarah

b. 16 April 1935, Limlingerode (Harz)

Poet

The daughter of a telephone engineer, Sarah Kirsch studied biology at the University of Halle. From 1963 to 1965 she was enrolled at the Johannes R. Becher Institute for Literature in Leipzig. In 1968 she moved to East Berlin, but in 1977 crossed to West Berlin – one of the many artists and writers who left the GDR in the wake of the **Biermann Affair**. Since 1983 Kirsch has lived in the small village of Tielenhamme in Schleswig-Holstein.

Two themes dominate Kirsch's poetic world: the transience of love and the fragility of nature in the modern world. Her early work must be read against the background of cultural policy in the GDR (see also **cultural policy: GDR**). Demands that literature should serve the development of a socialist society inevitably conflicted with Kirsch's need to express intensely private concerns. 'Das Ding Seele dies bourgeoise Stück' ('the thing called soul this bourgeois fragment'), as she once put it half-ironically, cannot be wished away by ideology. Thus her love poetry, predominantly the expression of pain and anger at personal betrayal, points also

to wider defects in human relationships under pressure from inimical social forces.

Since her departure from the GDR and Berlin, Kirsch's poetry and short prose compositions have continued to explore the fractured nature of human relationships and man's destructive exploitation of his environment. Paradoxically, these universal themes are encapsulated in sharp observations of minute detail – domestic incident, flowers, plants and birds – which reveal the eye of a trained scientist. Employing the traditional ingredients of romantic nature poetry – in Kirsch's case the marshes and flat, empty skies of her Schleswig-Holstein home where only man-made dikes protect the inhabitants from apocalypse – the poet transmutes bitter experience into the discipline of objective form. Personal happiness is seen as the fleeting echo of a long lost idyll. Kirsch's inclination towards debilitating pessimism is tempered, however, by her wry sense of humour and a melancholy courage in the face of constant disappointment. Though there is a danger, especially in her more recent work, that idiosyncratic syntax can turn into formulaic mannerisms, Kirsch's best work possesses a unique tone and an admirable control over material which in lesser hands could easily dissolve into sentimentality.

See also: poetry: GDR

MICHAEL BUTLER

Kirst, Hans Hellmut

b. 5 December 1914, Osterode (East Prussia); d. 23 February 1989, Bremen

Writer and film critic

Kirst voluntarily entered the German army in 1933, fighting on various fronts during WWII. He began publishing novels in 1950 and achieved bestseller success with the Gunner Asch novels (known as the '08/15' trilogy in German). In all he produced over forty novels with a total worldwide circulation of over fifteen million. Some novels were filmed. Much of his work is concerned with army life, WWII and the remilitarization of West Germany. He also produced a number of detective novels and worked as a film critic in television and with various Munich newspapers.

Further reading

Kirst, H.H. (1985) *Das Schaf im Wolfspelz. Ein deutsches Leben*, Herford: Seewald (Kirst's autobiography).

MAGGIE SARGEANT

Kirsten, Wulf

b. 21 June 1934, Klipphausen (near Dresden)

Poet

Kirsten set out in the early 1960s to raise a poetic monument to the landscape and people of rural Saxony, in a fresh, 'unpoetic' idiom. Though he initially embraced modernization, his gaze soon came to rest on political and social stagnation and the ecological crisis in the GDR, against which he reacted with a mixture of anger and resignation.

Further reading

Goodbody, A. (1990) 'The Romantic Landscape in Recent GDR Poetry: Wulf Kirsten and Volker Braun', in H. Gaskill *et al.* (eds), *Neue Ansichten: The Reception of Romanticism in the Literature of the GDR*, Amsterdam and Atlanta, GA: Rodopi, pp. 191–211 (focuses on Kirsten's affinity with the romantics).

AXEL GOODBODY

kitsch

Kitsch is an aesthetic category virtually synonymous with bad taste. Although there is no consensus about the etymology of kitsch, some scholars have suggested that it derives from a word meaning 'to grease' or 'to scrawl'. The archetypal image conjured by kitsch is that of the **garden gnomes**. Kitsch is associated with pictorial, literary or musical works which are emotionally charged and highly sentimental.

Although cheap mass-produced religious icons, schmaltzy music, plastic flowers and overly dramatic romantic paintings are considered typical kitsch in Germany, kitsch has no inherent structural properties. Rather, it is a culture- and context-dependent concept. Kitsch is a distinctly modern phenomenon that is contingent upon certain preconditions, including urbanization, the emergence of a middle class, mass production and technological progress. The designation of kitsch cannot be divorced from its socioeconomic relevance because kitsch is defined in opposition to high-art and considered to be a product of mass culture.

In post-war Germany, art was not immune to the prevailing forces of production, and kitsch flourished in the environment of commodification and rabid consumption created by the so-called **Economic Miracle**. In unified Germany, the cheap mass-produced products issued by the government during the GDR, such as colourful hen-shaped plastic egg holders, have taken on the status of kitsch.

In academic discussions of kitsch many thinkers, including Saul Friedlander and Susan Sontag, have made kitsch a central focus in debates concerning aesthetics and politics and the mobilization of the masses during Nazi Germany.

Further reading

Calinescu, M. (1987) *Five Faces of Modernity: Modernism, Avant-Garde, Decadence, Kitsch, Postmodernism*, Durham: Duke University Press (standard discussion of the important aspects of kitsch, although not specific to Germany).

Friedlander, S. (1984) *Reflections of Nazism: An Essay on Kitsch and Death*, New York: Harper & Row (an important meditation on the central role of kitsch and its importance to the cultural practices of the National Socialists).

LISA YUN LEE

Kiwus, Karin

b. 9 November 1942, Berlin

Poet

Karin Kiwus became famous with her very first collection of poetry, *Von beiden Seiten der Gegenwart* (From Both Sides of the Present) (1976). Here she carefully draws a sensitive and private picture of the 1970s. Gone is the programmatic poetry of the 1960s; Kiwus is one of the main proponents of the **New Subjectivity** (*Neue Subjektivität*) poetry movement which draws upon personal rather than collective or political sentiments. Her second collection, *Angenommen später* (Assumed Later) (1979) continues this undertaking.

HOLGER BRIEL

Kleiber, Carlos

b. 3 July 1930, Berlin

Conductor

Carlos Kleiber, the son of Eric Kleiber (music director of the Berlin Staatsoper between the world wars, first conductor of Berg's *Wozzeck* in 1925), is the most highly regarded of living German conductors. Since his early 'apprentice' jobs at the Deutsche Oper am Rhein, Zürich and Stuttgart, he has shunned permanent posts and concentrated on a small number of works, brilliantly and often explosively performed with the finest European orchestras, interspersed with a series of no less legendary cancellations.

BEATRICE HARPER

Kleihues, Josef Paul

b. 11 June 1933, Rheine

Architect

Having studied at the TU (Technical University) Stuttgart and Berlin (1955–9) and the École Nationale Supérieure des Beaux-Arts, Paris (1959–60), Kleihues worked for Poelzig in Berlin (1960–2). He has been an architect and town planner in private practice in Berlin since 1962, and Professor of Design and Architectural Theory at Dortmund University since 1973. He co-organized the 1987 **IBA**.

In his architectural work Kleihues combines human and playful elements with a strict 'Schinkelesque' purism. His reputation as an inspired town planner was confirmed with the redevelop-

ment of Friedrichstadt for which he managed to engage the apex of internationally renowned architects.

MARTIN KUDLEK

Kleine Zeitung

This Austrian daily newspaper, based in Graz, Styria, was founded in 1904. It was turned into a Nazi publication after the *Anschluß*, the annexation of Austria by Nazi Germany in 1938. Three years after its closure in 1945 the paper was re-established by the Catholic Press Association of Styria. With a print run of 280,000 (1997–8) it is the leading daily paper of southern and south-eastern Austria, competing for the market leadership in this area with the Viennese tabloid **Neue Kronen Zeitung**. It is a respected, independent, conservative paper without party political preferences.

GEORG HELLMAYR

Klemperer, Otto

b. 14 May, 1885, Breslau (now Wrocław, Poland); d. 6 July 1973, Zürich

Conductor

Klemperer was both an iconoclast and a traditionalist, and his musical and theatrical direction of Berlin's Kroll Oper, from 1927 to 1931, exemplified the adventurousness – the 'new sobriety' ('*neue Sachlichkeit*') – of the Weimar Republic. Of Jewish birth, Klemperer emigrated in 1933 and conducted the Los Angeles Philharmonic until 1939. Despite fluctuating health, he resumed his European career after 1945, notably with the Philharmonia in London from 1955, where his series of recordings are an impressive testimony to the immensity, and ruthlessness of his musical imagination.

BEATRICE HARPER

Klier, Freya

b. 4 February 1950, Dresden

Writer, theatre director and co-founder of the *Solidarische Kirche*

After her early release from prison for attempting to flee the country, Klier studied acting and directing, becoming Director of the Schwedt Theatre in 1982. She was active in the early stages of the autonomous peace movement in 1980, distributing an unofficial women's questionnaire from 1983 to 1984. While suffering *Berufsverbot* from 1985, she had unofficial performances in churches of politically critical programmes. In 1986 she started work on a book, *Jugend und Erziehungswesen der DDR* (Young People and the GDR Education System). After administering an unofficial questionnaire among young people, she was arrested in 1988, her manuscripts were seized, (later released to West Berlin), and she was forced to leave the GDR.

BEATRICE HARPER

Kluge, Alexander

b. 14 February 1932, Halberstadt

Filmmaker, writer and television producer

Kluge is a key figure in post-war German cinema – often referred to as 'the father of the **New German Cinema**' – and co-signatory of the landmark Oberhausen Manifesto. An auteurist, Brechtian filmmaker, he himself has repeatedly claimed Heinrich von Kleist as his mentor. As well as owing a debt to Jean-Luc Godard and the French New Wave, his literary, intellectually challenging cinema is firmly rooted in his own work as a writer. His films are, typically, essayistic assemblages of fictional, documentary and archive material with constantly shifting frames of reference. Kluge frequently overlays this material with his own ironic voice-over commentary and intersperses it with Brechtian intertitles, organizing the result into a series of associatively connected episodes. According to Kluge a film 'is composed in the head of the spectator'. His stylistic and thematic pluralism, what he has termed a 'rich totality of many determinations and relations', has led commentators to view him as a postmodernist, a label which he himself rejects. A staunch advocate of the collaborative film as a forum of democracy, and of the cinema as a modern equivalent of a classical amphitheatre for informed political debate, he initiated a trilogy of collective films, beginning in 1978 with *Germany in Autumn* (*Deutschland im Herbst*), a critical response to the one-sided media response to the **Baader–Meinhof** group, in which he worked alongside Rainer Werner **Fassbinder**, Volker **Schlöndorff**, Edgar **Reitz** and others. The democratic function of collective artistic production lies, according to Kluge, in the creation of so-called 'counter-public spaces' (*Gegen-Öffentlichkeit*), a notion which he has investigated theoretically in his expansive philosophical tracts co-authored by Oskar Negt, including *History and Obstinacy* (*Geschichte und Eigensinn*) (1981) and in practice by turning from cinema to television as a forum for his creative work in the late 1980s, working as an independent maverick producer for private satellite channels including RTL and SAT 1.

Having studied law, history and church music in the 1950s, Kluge began to practice as a lawyer in 1958, and for a time worked as legal advisor to Theodor W. **Adorno**. *Brutality in Stone* (*Brutalität in Stein*), a short documentary co-directed with Peter Schamoni in 1960, is a remarkably assured precursor of his mature style, tackling the theme of Nazi ideology by focusing on its architecture in a disjointed montage of texts, documents, archive footage, commentary and music, juxtaposed with tracking shots of the surviving ruins.

His programmatically-titled first feature, *Yesterday Girl* (*Abschied von Gestern*, literally 'good-bye to yesterday', 1967), starring his sister Alexandra in the lead role, helped put Kluge and New German Cinema on the map. Based on a story from his collection *Case Histories* (*Lebensläufe*, 1962), it tells the tragic story of a Jewish refugee from the GDR seeking a new life in the West but constantly frustrated by the materialism of the FRG and her own past. Although more linear than much of his later work it is typical of his style in its freewheeling narrative and ironic humour. It was followed a year later by the more experimental and intellectually demanding *Artistes at the Top of the Big Top:*

Disorientated (*Die Artisten in der Zirkuskuppel: Ratlos*). A brilliantly inventive montage of reflections on ideology, cinema and the pitfalls of utopian thinking, it has become one of the most celebrated films of the period and features a powerful central performance from Hannelore Hoger as the sardonically tenacious Leni Peikert who inherits a circus and determines to make it into an enlightened 'reformed circus', an unattainable dream which becomes a thinly-veiled allegory of the New German Cinema itself.

In his subsequent work Kluge has remained consistent in his stylistic approach, and – with the exception of *Strongman Ferdinand* (*Der starke Ferdinand*, 1975), an untypically straightforward and accessible satire on state security and surveillance – has tended to construct his films around fiercely independent female protagonists. In *Occasional Work of a Female Slave* (*Gelegenheitsarbeit einer Sklavin*, 1973) Alexandra Kluge plays a Frankfurt am Main housewife who runs an illegal abortion clinic to support her large family. When the clinic is forced to close she turns to an idiosyncratic brand of political action – selling sausages wrapped in political flyers. For her part, Hannelore Hoger reappeared in 1979 as an eccentric history teacher in *The Patriot* (*Die Patriotin*), a dense montage of reflections on German history, the aftermath of the 1977 'German Autumn', and the legacy of romanticism.

In 1983 Kluge united his two principal female leads in an expansive essay on the allure of opera, *The Power of Emotion* (*Die Macht der Gefühle*). This ambitious collage marks the emergence of Kluge's later style, in which the individual episodes become increasingly hermetic and unconnected and linear narrative is rejected entirely. For some commentators this marks the beginning of a gradual decline in potency, as Kluge rejects larger forms in favour of the anecdote and the aperçu, and retreats behind increasingly specious estrangement devices. His most recent films, including *Odds and Ends* (*Vermischte Nachrichten*, 1987), certainly lack the emotional impact and wit of his earlier work, and resemble piecemeal collections of sketches and jottings. As such they form a bridge to his recent television work, which has drawn heavily on his cinema films. His vast output of magazine programmes on topical cultural issues, including the *Ten to Eleven* series, bring together clips, recycled footage, music and interviews. The hard-hitting *Das goldene Vlies und die Catchpenny-Drucke in Blei* (The Golden Fleece and the Catchpenny Prints in Lead) (1992), a meditation on violence and its representation in myth and the arts, was produced as a response to the Gulf War and earned him an Adolf Grimme prize.

See also: New German Cinema; television

Further reading

Kluge, A. (ed.) (1983) *Bestandsaufnahme: Utopie Film*, Frankfurt am Main: Zweitausendeins (a weighty and well-illustrated stock-taking of twenty years of New German Cinema).

Liebmann, S. (ed.) (1988) *Alexander Kluge*, October 46 (special issue on Kluge with translations of selected writings, critical essays and a revealing interview).

MARTIN BRADY

Klump, Brigitte

b. 23 January 1935, Groß-Linichen (Pomerania)

Writer

After finishing her **Abitur**, Klump worked as an editor in East Berlin, where she, along with other non-party members, was sent to Karl Marx University in Leipzig for indoctrination. Helene **Weigel** got her a directing internship with the **Berliner Ensemble**. Klump escaped from the GDR in 1957 and studied journalism at the Freie Universität in West Berlin. *Das rote Kloster* (The Red Cloister) (1978) describes the brainwashing methods that she experienced in Leipzig and depicts her encounters with Wieland Herzfelde, Wolf **Biermann**, and Reiner **Kunze**.

MARTINA S. ANDERSON

Knef, Hildegard

b. 28 December 1925, Ulm

Actress, singer and writer

Knef appeared in Wolfgang **Staudte**'s *Die Mörder sind unter uns* (The Murderers Are Among Us) (1946) and scandalized German audiences with a brief nude scene in Willi Forst's *Die Sünderin* (The Sinner) (1950). She performed internationally in films by Henry Hathaway, Carol Reed and Claude Chabrol, and starred on Broadway in Cole Porter's *Silk Stockings* (1954–6). After 1963 Knef established herself as 'the greatest singer in the world without a voice' (Ella Fitzgerald), later also earning literary recognition for her song lyrics, her autobiography, *The Gift Horse* (*Der geschenkte Gaul*, 1970), and a book on her battle with cancer.

CHRISTIAN ROGOWSKI

Kneipe

Usually translated as 'pub' or 'bar', the *Kneipe* is a specifically urban institution, in contrast to the rural *Gasthaus*. A meeting-place with its own rites, traditions and patterns of communication, the *Kneipe* is part of **popular culture**.

Further reading

Dröge, F. and Krämer-Badoni, T. (1985) *Die Kneipe. Zur Soziologie einer Kulturform*, Frankfurt am Main: Suhrkamp (a sociological study of the *Kneipe* as a cultural form, includes bibliography).

JANET STEWART

Kocka, Jürgen

b. 19 April 1941, Haindorf (now Blogocice, Czech Republic)

Historian

A prominent left-liberal West German social historian, Kocka taught at Bielefeld from 1973–88, then moved to a Chair at the Free University Berlin, with stints in the US. Kocka's prolific publications combine explicit theoretical concerns with detailed empirical research, including books on class structure in WWI, employees in Germany and the US, the German bourgeoisie, working classes and underclasses since 1800, and social history and historiography. Kocka's many editorial roles include joint editorship of *Geschichte und Gesellschaft* since 1974. Kocka has also played a key role in the German historical profession and in the development of GDR history.

MARY FULBROOK

König, Barbara

b. 9 October 1925, Reichenberg (Liberec, Bohemia)

Writer

Of German-Hungarian-Czech ancestry, König fled to Bavaria after WWII and worked as a journalist. She edited for the *Deutsche Nachrichtenagentur* (DENA) in Bau Nauheim, then for the *Neue Zeitung* in Frankfurt am Main (for seven years). She joined **Gruppe 47** in 1950. In 1950 she also spent a year studying journalism and creative writing in the US. Until 1953, she edited the magazine *kontakt*. König writes novels, essays and radio and television scripts, focusing on the problem of identity, as in the novel *Die Personenperson* (The People Person) (1965).

MARTINA S. ANDERSON

Königsdorf, Helga

b. 13 July 1938, Gera

Writer and mathematician

At the time her first collection of stories, *Meine ungehörigen Träume* (My Impertinent Dreams), appeared in 1978, Helga Königsdorf had an established reputation as a research professor at the GDR Academy of Sciences in Berlin. Her wry feminist critiques of gender relations, and 'insider' parodies of the shortcomings of academic institutions in this volume, and two anthologies published in the decade that followed, were the basis of her considerable popularity. A longer narrative, *Re-*

spektloser Umgang (Disrespectful Companionship) (1986) probed much deeper into the question of scientific responsibility and ethics by means of hallucinatory dialogues between the narrator, a contemporary woman scientist, and Lise Meitner, who – in denial of her own gender identity and the destructive potential of the research – worked with Otto Hahn on nuclear experiments before fleeing Nazi Germany. As the narrator comes to recognize correspondences between herself and Meitner, she accepts Meitner's 'charge' to embrace alternate ways of knowing and to use her knowledge for humane ends. Like many of Königsdorf's protagonists, the narrator bears autobiographical traces, including the death of her Jewish grandmother under the Nazis.

Königsdorf's intense political involvement in the months before and after German unification is documented in three volumes of commentary and interviews published in 1990, reflecting her need to acknowledge the belated sense of complicity as well as the loss of human dignity that many experienced at this time.

Ungelegener Befund (An Inconvenient Discovery) (1990), written before unification, returns to some of the themes of *Respektloser Umgang*. In the process of trying to organize a memorial for his late father, the protagonist – himself an academic – discovers letters that point to the father's advocacy of Nazi racial biology. Despite East Germany's self-proclaimed anti-fascist legacy the son also discovers that his own contemporaries prefer to overlook this 'inconvenient discovery', a disturbing commentary on the continuing presence of the past that may underlie the protagonist's concealment of his own homosexuality.

Since unification some topics of Königsdorf's earlier texts have reappeared in her fiction. *Gleich neben Afrika* (Right near Africa) (1992), for example, is narrated by a writer who must come to terms with her past investment in the GDR system while simultaneously confronting the impact of the new market economy on her present life. *Im Schatten des Regenbogens* (In the Shadow of the Rainbow) (1993) returns to the milieu of the 'Institute for Numerographics' (*Zahlographie*), where staff now must confront their loss of position, privilege and even housing as a result of post-unification restructuring and reevaluation. Seemingly unaffected by such problems is the 'successful', but dysfunctional family of *Die Entsorgung der Großmutter* (Disposing of Grandmother) (1997), where the children communicate only by computer and describe the parents as 'Moneymonks... people who measure the value of everything only in money'. The parents neatly resolve the burden of responsibility for the grandmother by abandoning her on a bench in a faraway town, leaving her to spend her days in the company of stray cats. While the theme of postunification trauma is absent from the surface of this novel, it can be read as a critical allegory of values in unified Germany.

Major works

Königsdorf, H. (1978) *Meine ungehörigen Träume*, Berlin: Aufbau.
—— (1982) *Der Lauf der Dinge*, Berlin: Aufbau.
—— (1986) *Respektloser Umgang*, Berlin: Aufbau
—— (1988) *Lichtverhältnisse*, Berlin: Aufbau.
—— (1990) *Ungelegener Befund*, Berlin: Aufbau.
—— (1990) *Adieu DDR: Protokolle eines Abschieds*, Hamburg: Rowohlt.
—— (1990) *Aus dem Dilemma eine Chance machen: Reden und Aufsätze*, Hamburg: Luchterhand.
—— (1990) *1989 oder Ein Moment Schönheit: Eine Collage aus Briefen, Gedichten, Texten*, Berlin: Aufbau.
—— (1992) *Gleich neben Afrika*, Berlin: Rowohlt.
—— (1993) *Im Schatten des Regenbogens*, Berlin: Aufbau.
—— (1994) *Über die unverzügliche Rettung der Welt: Essays*, Berlin: Aufbau.
—— (1995) *Unterwegs nach Deutschland: Über die Schwierigkeit, ein Volk zu sein: Protokolle eines Aufbruchs*, Hamburg: Rowohlt.
—— (1997) *Die Entsorgung der Großmutter*, Berlin: Aufbau.

Further reading

Conacher, J.E. (1994) 'Pressing for Change: The Case of Helga Königsdorf', in E. Boa and J. Wharton (eds), *Women and the Wende: Social Effects and Cultural Reflections of the German Unification Process*, German Monitor 31, Amsterdam: Rodopi.
Gerber, M. (1991) 'Impertinence, Productive Fear

and Hope: The Writings of Helga Königsdorf',
in M. Kane (ed.), *Socialism and the Literary
Imagination*, Oxford: Berg.

Haines, B. (1992) ' "Botschaft aus einem seltsamen
Land": Helga Königsdorf and Her Critics', in A.
Goodbody and D. Tate (eds), *Geist und Macht:
Writers and the State in the GDR*, German Monitor
29, Amsterdam: Rodopi.

PATRICIA HERMINGHOUSE

Koeppen, Wolfgang

b. 23 June 1906, Greifswald; d. 15 March
1996, Munich

Writer (also wrote as Jakob Littner)

As a chronicler of post-war German history,
Koeppen gained international recognition with
his trilogy *Pigeons on the Grass* (*Tauben im Gras*, 1951),
Treibhaus (Hothouse) (1953), and *Death in Rome* (*Der
Tod in Rom*) (1954), as well as with his autobiographically inspired text *Jugend* (Youth, 1976). He
was awarded the Büchner Prize in 1962.

He grew up in East Prussia and studied at the
universities of Hamburg, Greifswald, Berlin and
Würzburg. He worked as a *Dramaturg*, an actor, and
a journalist (mainly for left-wing journals such as
Rote Fahne and *Vorwärts*). In 1933, his only
permanent employment ended with the closure of
the *Berliner Börsen-Courier*. His first novel *Eine
unglückliche Liebe* (An Unhappy Love) was published
in 1934 when he moved to The Netherlands. He
returned to Berlin in 1938, and soon went into
hiding south of Munich to avoid conscription. Both
this first novel and his second one, *Die Mauer
schwankt* (The Wall is Swaying) (1935), republished
in revised form under the title *Die Pflicht* (The Duty)
(1939), address themes which are characteristic of
Koeppen's works: the problem of identity and the
conflict between reason and emotion, between
order and disorder, between artist and bourgeois.

After WWII he wrote *Jakob Littners Aufzeichnungen
aus einem Erdloch* (Jakob Littner's Notes From a Hole
in the Ground) (1948) under the pseudonym Jakob
Littner (republished in 1992 under his real name),
the story of a Jewish stamp dealer who survived the
Holocaust. *Pigeons on the Grass* (*Tauben im Gras*, 1951)

was the first of three satirical novels criticising post-
war German society and politics. Glimpses of one
day in the lives of about thirty people of different
class, gender, nationality and race in Munich in
1948 construct – by way of inner monologue,
montage and almost cinematic simultaneity – a
picture of an occupied Germany which is both
pessimistic and hopeful. In 1953, the novel *Das
Treibhaus* (see also the 1987 film by Peter Goedel)
analyses the political developments of the young
FRG. Keetenheuve, a social-democratic member of
the German parliament, who has returned from
exile believing in the possibility of change and a
new beginning, fights in vain for a new peaceful
and democratic Germany and against the old
nationalistic and militaristic forces which are
already promoting rearmament. Deeply disappointed, Keetenheuve commits suicide. The last
novel of the trilogy *Tod in Rom* (Death in Rome)
(1954) is the first decidedly critical analysis of
Germany's fascist past, the failing of denazification,
and the danger of a return of fascism.

The analytic clarity with which Koeppen
critically outlines the conservative post-war developments of the FRG was both highly praised and
severely denounced by literary critics. His trilogy
was formally and thematically too courageous for
the literary landscape of the early Adenauer era,
which hampered its potential success. Further
publications such as his three books on travel,
Nach Rußland und anderswohin (To Russia and Elsewhere) (1958), *Amerika-Fahrt* (American Journey)
(1959) and *Reisen nach Frankreich* (Travels in France)
(1961), were often interpreted as a retreat into a
less political mode of writing.

Further reading

Burgess, G. (1987) 'Wolfgang Koeppen', in K.
Bullivant (ed.) *The Modern German Novel*, Leamington Spa: Berg.

Greiner, U. (1976) *Über Wolfgang Koeppen*, Frankfurt
am Main: Suhrkamp.

CHRISTIANE SCHÖNFELD

Kohl, Helmut

b. 3 April 1930, Ludwigshafen

Politician; German Federal Chancellor
1982–98

A member of the **CDU** since 1947, Kohl began his
political career in his home *Land* of Rheinland-
Pfalz. As chancellor he was initially widely
dismissed as an amiable but bumbling figure, but
he went on to display his qualities as an astute,
canny and determined politician when he seized
the opportunity of the collapse of communism to
push through the rapid **unification** of the two
German states. His enthusiastic espousal of an
ever-closer **European Union** was less popular
with the German electorate. By 1996 he had
overtaken **Adenauer**'s record as the country's
longest-serving chancellor, but was replaced by
Gerhard **Schröder** in 1998.

See also: food

JOHN SANDFORD

Kohlhaase, Wolfgang

b. 13 March 1931, Berlin

Writer

The son of a machine fitter, Kohlhaase was the
GDR's most renowned and prolific author of film
scripts. He had his first articles published while still
at school; he worked as trainee writer for youth
journals and as assistant *Dramaturg* for **DEFA**
before turning freelance in 1952. In collaboration
with director Gerhard Klein he created the so-
called 'Berlin Films', a popular genre about young
East Berliners inspired by Italian neorealism. He
later entered into another successful partnership
with Konrad **Wolf** with whom he co-directed *Solo
Sunny* (1979).

See also: film: GDR

HORST CLAUS

Kolbe, Uwe

b. 17 October 1957, (East) Berlin

Writer

Kolbe met Franz **Fühmann** in 1976, who was
instrumental in publishing Kolbe's poetry in *Sinn
und Form*. To further his career, be attended the
Johannes R. Becher Institute (1980–1). His first
book, *Hineingeboren* (Born Into It), became a
metaphor for the younger generation of writers in
the GDR. Because of the poem 'Kern meines
Romans' (Key to My Novel) in which Kolbe
arranged a series of nouns and verbs to create an
acrostic of anti-government sentiments, he was
forbidden to publish (1982–5). He also served as
editor of *Mikado*, a private literary magazine with
Lothar Trolle and Bernd Wagner.

CAROL ANNE COSTABILE-HEMING

Kollhoff, Hans

b. 18 September 1946, Lobenstein
(Thuringia)

Architect

Kollhoff studied in Karlsruhe; he has taught at the
ETH (Technical University) Zürich since 1990,
and has been in private practice in Berlin since
1978.

Kollhoff's designs react against the growing
discrepancy between appearance and construction
in architecture by focusing on the development of
the idea of the tectonic. Solid, well-crafted details
and the frequent use of stereotyped clinker façades
distinguish his buildings. His skyscraper cluster
proposal for the Alexanderplatz competition in
Berlin won Kollhoff the first prize in 1991.

MARTIN KUDLEK AND BERTHOLD PESCH

Konsalik, Heinz G.

b. 28 May 1921, Cologne

Writer (real name Heinz Günther)

Wounded whilst in active service during WWII,

Konsalik worked as a dramatist and journalist from 1946 to 1950. Since 1953 he has written prolifically (over 130 novels translated into thirty-four languages with an international circulation of over sixty-nine million). His work, usually dismissed as '*Trivialliteratur*', is generally set against a backdrop of WWII, of which it often presents a romantic picture.

MAGGIE SARGEANT

Kortner, Fritz

b. 12 May 1892, Vienna; d. 22 July 1970, Berlin

Actor and director

A leading actor on stage and screen during the Weimar Republic, Kortner is renowned for his dramatic range and expressive virtuosity; his most famous stage roles included Shylock and Richard III. His brooding presence as Dr Schön in F.W. Murnau's *Pandora's Box* (*Die Büchse der Pandora*, 1929) established his international reputation. Returning from Hollywood after the war, he regained his status as a leading director and actor for cinema, theatre, and television. In the 1960s his achievements as an actor and director were documented on film by Hans Jürgen **Syberberg**.

HELEN HUGHES

KPD

Founded at the beginning of 1919, the Kommunistische Partei Deutschlands (KPD) survived the Nazi period underground and in exile. In the Soviet zone it enjoyed the special support of the occupying power and, after its merger in 1946 with the **SPD**, it assumed the dominant role in the **SED**. In the West the Cold War and the **Economic Miracle** combined to deprive the KPD of the substantial working-class support it had enjoyed in the Weimar years. It won only sixteen seats on the basis of a 5.7 percent share of the vote in the 1949 Bundestag elections, which sank to 2.2 percent (and hence no seats) in 1953. In 1956 the party was banned as unconstitutional, but re-emerged in the guise of the

DKP in 1969. Small Marxist splinter groups also adopted the name 'KPD' in the 1960s and 1970s and in the GDR after the **Wende**.

JOHN SANDFORD

Krabbe, Katrin

b. 22 November 1969, Neubrandenburg

Athlete

A member of the Neubrandenburg sports club, Krabbe became one of the GDR's leading sprinters in the late 1980s. Although she became world champion in the women's 100 m and 200 m in 1991, her career suffered a severe setback when the International Amateur Athletic Federation imposed a four-year ban, subsequently reduced to two years, for taking clenbuterol.

MIKE DENNIS

Kraftwerk

The brain-child of Florian Schneider and Ralf Hutter, Kraftwerk is arguably the most important and influential band to emerge from Germany in the post-war period. Purveyors of electronic music, the group grew out of the contact between classical avant-gardism and pop culture in the late 1960s. Featuring repetitive rhythmic figures and spare, laconic lyrics, the group produced internationally successful dance music whose influence could be heard from the discotheques of the 1970s to the techno-raves and **Love Parade**s of the 1990s. Their first hit single, 'Autobahn' (1974), offered a synthetic reproduction of a car trip through the Ruhr valley.

MATTHEW T. GRANT

Krauß, Angela

b. 2 May 1950, Chemnitz

Writer

Known for her perceptive short stories about life and work in the GDR, *Das Vergnügen* (Pleasure)

(1984), *Glashaus* (1988), and the radio play *Meine Oma stirbt nie* (My Granny Will Never Die) (1988), Krauß became known in the 1990s for a new form of realism in which she heightens moments of ordinary life through experimental use of language. Her prose work includes *Der Dienst* (The Service) (1990), and *Die Überfliegerin* (The High-Flier) (1995), a collection of texts *Schöne Aussichten* (Beautiful Views) (1990), and the film scenario *Im Sommer schwimme ich im See* (In the Summer I Swim in the Lake) (1992).

MARGARET VALLANCE

Krautrock

Krautrock was an experimental **rock music** scene flourishing in the early and mid-1970s mainly in Berlin, Düsseldorf, Hamburg, Munich and Cologne. Dubbed 'Krautrock' by its fans in the British music press (who nowadays reassure one another that the German musicians involved took no offence!), its origins in the 1960s **student movement** gave it a political hue expressed in the communal social organization of some of the bands, and sometimes in their music. Krautrock was influenced by psychedelia, the electrocuted New York vision of the Velvet Underground, and the more austere manifestos of Karlheinz **Stockhausen** and minimalism. Partly by manifesting a sense of humour, the music avoided the pomposity and superstar affectations plaguing British and American 'progressive' rock. With hindsight, it was also a more important contribution to the recognizably artistic edge of **popular culture**, a contribution whose influence has resurfaced repeatedly, most notably in the **punk** explosion of the mid- to late 1970s and the hip-hop culture of the 1980s. In the latter, **Kraftwerk** take their place alongside James Brown as progenitors of contemporary dance and club culture.

A run-down of the best-known bands follows.

Amon Düül II, an offshoot from the communal band Amon Düül, produced wild, driving, primitive rock influenced by the longer psychedelic trips of the Pink Floyd.

Can, whose membership included classically-trained musicians, initially pursued an experimental approach, developing new modes of expression. They were strongly influenced by the Velvet Underground, partly in their use of vocals as effects, rather than information channels. But the bizarre vocals and song-structures mean that some of their early albums are probably more fêted than played. Even when toning down the radicalism for chart singles, they failed completely to tarnish their early avant-garde reputation.

The anarchic and fractured approach of Faust incorporated elements of many musical styles, sometimes presented in a cut-up format. Uncomfortable listening alternated with sublimely beautiful song elements presented within unfamiliar structures.

The first couple of **Kraftwerk** albums, produced before they became the purest (albeit ironical) expression of modernist technological romanticism, exhibit a flailing but challenging experimentalism.

Neu! clearly prefigured punk in their concise, repetitive but highly-charged short pieces.

Popol Vuh, consistently interesting, went through several phases which explored the possibilities of 'world music' years before the concept was coined. They are at their best, perhaps, on the 1972 acoustic album *Hosianna Mantra*, but are better-known for providing the soundtracks to more than one Werner **Herzog** film (most notably the lush Amazonian dreamscape of *Aguirre, Wrath of God*).

The early albums of Tangerine Dream, who quickly developed into a synthesizer-only band, achieve a superb balance of experimentalism and hearer-friendliness. (Enjoy the portentous song titles too!) Unfortunately, their move to the Virgin Record label and the subsequent success of 'Phaedra' (1973) betokened a shift into unthreatening Jean-Michel Jarre territory.

Some of the bands (e.g. Kraftwerk and Popol Vuh) never really went away; others (Can and Tangerine Dream) faded or split; and recently reactivated versions of others (Faust, Amon Düül II and Neu!) are still around. It is ironic that although Krautrock has few identifiable roots in the traditions of black music, it should have provided many of the technologically-driven beats behind Grandmaster Flash, Afrika Bambaata and others which reinvigorated dance music in the early 1980s.

Further reading

Cope, J. (1995). *Krautrocksampler*, London: Head Heritage (superb enthusiast's introduction which revealed Kosmische Musik to new generations of fans).

Freeman, S. and Freeman, J. (1996). *The Crack in the Cosmic Egg*, Leicester: Audion Publications (definitive discography, history, and geography of the scene).

JOHN PRESTON

Krawczyk, Stephan

b. 31 December 1955, Weida (Thuringia)

Singer

Krawczyk comes from a working-class family and joined the **SED** in 1976. He studied concert guitar and made his only record in the GDR in 1982. He became part of the alternative cultural scene in **Prenzlauer Berg** and left the SED in 1985. He was forbidden to perform publicly, but continued to give performances in churches and private rooms. In January 1988 he was arrested for displaying an unofficial slogan at the official Rosa Luxemburg demonstration in East Berlin and was forced to leave the GDR for West Germany under the threat of imprisonment.

PETER BARKER

Krechel, Ursula

b. 4 December 1947, Trier

Writer

Since the 1970s, when she began her writing career with the theatre piece *Erika* (1974), a collection of reports about the feminist movement titled *Selbsterfahrung und Fremdbestimmung* (Experience of Self and Definition of the Other, 1975), and the poetry volume *Nach Mainz* (Toward Mainz, 1977), Krechel has explored the interconnectedness of social issues, quotidian detail and literature. A focus on women's issues motivates her initial publications, such as the dramatic scenes comprising *Erika*, in which the main character struggles against conventions regarding marriage and professional roles that constrain her efforts to become independent. While the quotidian details and unaffected tone of *Verwundbar wie in den besten Zeiten* (Vulnerable in the Best of Times, 1979) situated her early poetic style within 'New Subjectivity', Krechel's essay 'Life in Quotation Marks' ('*Das Leben in Anführungszeichen*', 1979) registered the author's observation that a fundamental shift had occurred in the way literature expresses connections between experience and knowledge. Her subsequent publications display a continuing, increasingly nuanced preoccupation with questions of authenticity, women's writing and the relation between contemporary texts and literary tradition as adumbrated in this early essay.

Krechel studied German literature, theatre and art history in Cologne, and worked for two years as a *Dramaturg* before becoming a freelance writer and eventually settling in Frankfurt am Main. Her search for the tangible subject matter and transparent language, which she interpolates into poems alongside literary allusions, cinematic images and references to contemporary politics, surfaced already in *Nach Mainz*, where one poem mused that 'On many days a poem lies in the street'. Her subsequent work has displayed technical adeptness with innovative lyrical forms (including narrative poetry, verse sequences, montage and heteroglossia) and a preference for texts composed of loosely connected segments.

A prolific poet, who has been awarded the Elisabeth Langgässer Literature Prize and has published the collections *Rohschnitt* (Raw Cut) (1983), *Vom Feuer lernen* (Learning from the Fire) (1985), *Kakaoblau* (Cocao Blue) (1989), *Technik des Erwachens* (Technique of Awakening) (1992), *Landläufiges Wunder* (Customary Miracle) (1995) and *Ungezürnt* (Not Angered) (1997), she is one of the few among her generation of authors to show a breadth of poetic voice that accommodates both the long poem forms and precise, lyrical observations. *Rohschnitt*, a cycle of sixty poems, explicitly makes use of cinematic montage to narrate the self-defining journey of three women. Krechel similarly employs episodically structured, prose narrative in *Zweite Natur* (Second Nature, 1981) and *Die Freunde des Wetterleuchtens* (The Friends of the Sheet-Lightning, 1990), which centre around domestic scenes.

An article bringing to light the forgotten work of Irmgard Keun (in 1979) and two collections, *Lesarten* (Ways of Reading) (1991), comprised of close readings of poems, and *Mit dem Körper des Vaters spielen* (Playing with the Body of the Father) (1992), which contains interpretive essays, give evidence of Krechel's sustained efforts to redefine the poetic canon, come to terms with recent literary theory, and articulate feminine forms of writing throughout her career.

Major works

Krechel, U. (1974) 'Erika: Ein Stück', *Theater heute* 8: 37–46.

—— (1975/1983) *Selbsterfahrung und Fremdbestimmung: Bericht aus der Neuen Frauenbewegung*, Darmstadt and Neuwied: Luchterhand.

—— (1977) *Nach Mainz: Gedichte*, Darmstadt and Neuwied: Luchterhand.

—— (1979) *Verwundbar wie in den besten Zeiten*, Darmstadt and Neuwied: Luchterhand.

—— (1981) *Zweite Natur: Szenen eines Romans*. Darmstadt and Neuwied: Luchterhand.

—— (1982) *Lesarten*, Darmstadt and Neuwied: Luchterhand.

—— (1983) *Rohschnitt*, Darmstadt and Neuwied: Luchterhand.

—— (1985) *Vom Feuer lernen*, Darmstadt and Neuwied: Luchterhand.

—— (1989) *Kakaoblau*, Salzburg and Vienna: Residenz Verlag.

—— (1990) *Die Freunde des Wetterleuchtens*, Frankfurt am Main: Luchterhand.

—— (1992) *Mit dem Körper des Vaters spielen: Essays*, Frankfurt am Main: Suhrkamp.

—— (1992) *Technik des Erwachens*, Frankfurt am Main: Suhrkamp.

—— (1995) *Landläufiges Wunder*, Frankfurt am Main: Suhrkamp.

—— (1997) *Ungezürnt: Gedichte, Lichter, Lesezeichen*, Frankfurt am Main: Suhrkamp.

Further reading

Mielke, R. (1986) 'Ursula Krechel', in H.L. Arnold (ed.), *Kritisches Lexikon der deutschsprachigen Gegen-wartsliteratur*, Munich: edition text + kritik, pp. 1–14.

CHARLOTTE MELIN

Kreisky, Bruno

b. 22 January 1911, Vienna; d. 29 July 1990, Vienna

Diplomat and politician; Austrian Chancellor from 1970 to 1983

An active socialist who emigrated to Sweden from 1938 to 1946, Kreisky was a member of the Austrian team of negotiators who achieved the liberation of Austria from Allied occupation in 1955. He was Foreign Minister from 1959 to 1966, and formed a socialist minority government in 1970, winning three subsequent elections (1971, 1975 and 1979) with clear majorities. He resigned after the 1983 elections.

He advocated equality in society and in the welfare system, and was a supporter of the rights of the Palestinians in the Middle East conflict.

GEORG HELLMAYR

Křenek, Ernst

b. 23 August 1900, Vienna; d. 23 December 1991, Palm Springs (California)

Composer

Křenek began his studies at the age of sixteen, moving to Berlin where he joined Scherchen and Busoni. His first major compositions date from the early 1920s and include his first string quartet and first symphony. His early influences appear to have been Bartók and the neo-classicism of Stravinsky, whom he met in Paris. His first opera experience in Germany was at the opera houses in Kassel and Wiesbaden (1925–7). His first major triumph was the opera *Jonny spielt auf*, in which he coupled the mellifluence of Puccini to the 'seasoning of jazz'. The libretto by Křenek himself has been translated into eighteen languages. During the 1930s he was branded a *Kulturbolschewist* and in 1938 he emigrated to the US, leading an active life both as teacher and composer. From 1950 he made annual return visits to Europe, writing operas for stage and television for the next twenty years, though *Sardakai* written in two parts in 1967 and 1969 indicated some disillusionment with the very medium in which he so excelled. The sheer breadth of his eclecticism makes him peculiarly difficult to categorize.

DEREK MCCULLOCH

Krenz, Egon

b. 19 March 1937, Kolberg (Kołobrzeg, Poland)

GDR functionary

After a series of posts in youth organizations in the GDR in the 1960s, Krenz became a full member of the **Central Committee** of the **SED** in 1973 and of the ***Politbüro*** in 1983. He was regarded as Erich **Honecker**'s chosen successor as General Secretary of the SED. After Honecker's resignation on 18 October 1989, Krenz was appointed as General Secretary and as chairman of the *Staatsrat* (State Council). As head of the Politbüro, he authorized the decision to open the **Berlin Wall**, but his political position became untenable. He resigned from the *Staatsrat* on 7 December and was excluded from membership of the reformed SED-**PDS**. In 1997 he was imprisoned for 6½ years for his responsibility for deaths at the German–German frontier.

PETER BARKER

Krier, Rob

b. 10 June 1938; Grevenmacher (Luxembourg)

Architect

Krier studied at the TU (Technical University) Munich from 1959 to 1964. He worked for **Ungers** from 1965 to 1966 and **Otto** from 1967 to 1970. He has been an architect and town planner in private practice in Vienna since 1976, and Professor at the TU Vienna since 1975.

Krier is best known for the development of planning typologies which relate to archetypal patterns and historical models. These were first put into practice with his suggestions for the re-planning of Stuttgart's city centre (1974) and later laid down in his book *Stadtraum in Theorie und Praxis* (The Urban Space in Theory and Practice) (1975). His most famous planning and building work was realized for the Internationale Bauausstellung Berlin (**IBA**) (Ritterstraße 1977–80, and Rauchstraße 1980–5).

MARTIN KUDLEK

Krips, Josef

b. 8 April 1902, Vienna; d. 13 October 1974, Geneva

Conductor

After a traditional pre-war apprenticeship in smaller opera houses, Krips became a major figure in the reconstruction of post-war Viennese musical life. A born Mozart specialist, he created and conducted an ensemble of singers which guaranteed the quality of the Vienna Staatsoper's performances at a precarious time. In 1946 he conducted *Don Giovanni* for the reopening of the **Salzburg Festival**. He later held a number of appointments with American and British orchestras and recorded much of his preferred Mozartian repertory.

BEATRICE HARPER

Kristl, Vlado

b. 24 January 1923, Zagreb

Filmmaker, painter, poet, video artist and dramatist

Kristl was a partisan during the German occupation of Yugoslavia and a leading 'informal' painter and animator in Zagreb during the 1950s. Exiled to Germany in 1963, he became the most celebrated experimental filmmaker of the 1960s, producing anarchic, chaotic and politically subversive features such as *The Dam* (*Der Damm*, 1964), and animated and live action shorts, such as

Madeleine Madeleine (1963). He made formally more experimental films after 1967 under the influence of New American Cinema, and developed 'Video Theatre' performances in the 1970s, and post-modernist painting and rebellious poetry in the 1980s.

See also: film, experimental

MARTIN BRADY

Kroetz, Franz Xaver

b. 25 February 1946, Munich

Writer, actor and theatre director

Kroetz is one of the most successful authors of the *Neues* **Volksstück**, with more than forty plays in countless productions worldwide by the mid-1990s. Most are domestic dramas. In the early ones the figures direct the aggressions their social deprivation has generated – but which their impoverished language cannot articulate – towards themselves, their families or their unborn children. Thus suicides, domestic murders, and attempted or successful abortions are central motifs: *Request Concert* (*Wunschkonzert*) (1971); *Game Crossing* (*Wildwechsel*) (1971); *Michi's Blood* (*Michis Blut*) (1971). Shocking stage images, such as the knitting-needle abortion in *Homework* (*Heimarbeit*) (1971) or the masturbation and defloration scenes in *Farmyard* (*Stallerhof*) (1972), ensured these plays a scandalous notoriety fuelled by Kroetz' often intemperate pronouncements. However, they are not merely sensationalized slice-of-life dramas; the rhythmic pattern of the scenes, and the dialogue, though based on a Bavarian lower-class sociolect, are highly crafted.

Kroetz' commitment to the **DKP** from 1972–80 led him to a brief flirtation with Agit-Prop (e.g. *Münchner Kindl*, 1972), and, in Oberösterreich (*Upper Austria*, 1972), *Das Nest* (1974), *Mensch Meier* (1977) and *Der stramme Max* (Big Max, 1978), to portray more typical members of the German working class and moments of awakening political consciousness. He also sought a mass audience for these plays via television. In contrast to the early plays, the characters' improved socio-economic situation and articulacy mean that when faced by crisis (typically, unemployment or pregnancy as threats to consumer prosperity), they are able to realize the other-determined nature of their lives. This enlightenment is as much moral as political (e.g. *Das Nest*) and conservative attitudes often underlie the plays' social criticism. None the less they were among the most performed of the mid-1970s.

In the 1980s, Kroetz continued to address key social issues such as technology and identity in *Nicht Fisch, nicht Fleisch* (Neither Fish Nor Fowl, 1980), unemployment in *Furcht und Hoffnung in der BRD* (Fear and Hope in the FRG, 1983), and the crisis of peasant identity in the face of agricultural modernization in *Dead Soil* (*Bauern sterben*, 1984). But he also sought to escape, in his own words, the '*Wohnküchen-Gasherd-Realismus*' ('living-room/gas-cooker realism') of his family plays, in part through a return to the radicality of the forms and motifs of his early work. His novel trilogy *Der Mondschein-knecht* (The Moonshine Lad, 1981), portraying the progression of a crippled peasant boy to skilled typesetter and trade union activist, exemplified the synthesis of the subjective and the political Kroetz now sought. Increasingly, Kroetz also stresses his self-perception as a Christian writer. *Der Dichter als Schwein* (The Poet as Swine, 1988), *Bauerntheater* (*Peasant Farce*, 1991), and his travel notes, for instance *Brasilien – Peru – Aufzeichnungen* (1991), address, often mockingly, a writer's crises of political impotence and aesthetic stagnation. His response to unification was the sarcastic cabaret *Ich bin das Volk* (I Am the People, 1994). Throughout his career Kroetz has also directed and acted, both for stage and television.

Further reading

Mattson, M. (1996) *Franz Xaver Kroetz. The Construction of a Political Aesthetic*, Oxford: Berg.

MORAY McGOWAN

Krolow, Karl

b. 11 March 1915, Hanover

Poet, translator and critic

One of the most gifted and enduring lyrical voices of the FRG since the country's foundation, Krolow's technical mastery of form and his assimilation of other European influences, especially French and Spanish, rescued German (FRG) poetry from much of its isolation and clumsiness in the immediate post-war period. Initially indebted to Wilhelm **Lehmann** and Oskar Loerke, Krolow's poetry developed beyond that of the German nature poets to engage with contemporary issues. Krolow has been a major force in promoting and interpreting the work of other poets.

See also: poetry: FRG

ANTHONY BUSHELL

Kronauer, Brigitte

b. 29 December 1940, Hamburg

Writer

Kronauer was born in Essen and studied pedagogy at universities in Cologne and Aachen. She worked as a schoolteacher until she became a full-time writer in 1971. She now lives with her husband and their friend the painter Dieter Asmus in the Hamburg suburb of Nienstedten.

After ten years of writing stories Kronauer won instant fame with her first novel, *Frau Mühlenbeck im Gehäus* (Mrs Mühlenbeck in Her House) (1980) in which an energetic, outgoing widow and the nameless narrator, a withdrawn, fragile, highstrung teacher, reflect two radically different experiences of a woman's existence. Her minute and sensuous descriptions of everyday situations, people, animals and nature do not reproduce reality or reflect an imagined world. Exposed to the focus and clarity of Kronauer's blinding vision, the scenes freeze, inert objects move and familiar gestures reveal a new meaning. Her prose is artificial and highly constructed – to a point where the mind behind it seems more calculating than poetic. A narrating 'I' and individual protagonists or groups of characters are juxtaposed, the one observing, reflecting and writing, while the other aggressively embraces life. The narrators are strangely objective and so impersonal that no reader would take them as autobiographical.

The confusing and elusive experience of reality is also the general subject of Kronauer's intricately structured subsequent novels. Rita Münster's love changes her view of herself and the world (*Rita Münster*, 1983), while her complement, the scholar Matthias Roth in *Berittener Bogenschütze* (Bowman on Horseback) (1986), studies passion in Joseph Conrad to transcend his banal life. The author's most innovative novel, *Die Frau in den Kissen* (The Woman in the Pillows, 1990), draws upon the heritage of the *nouveau roman*, much as do her early stories. A panorama of life in its multifaceted fragmentation, it is populated with fleeting characters and mediated through an obsessive eye and mind. In her most recent, more conventionally narrated novel *Das Taschentuch* (The Handkerchief, 1994) the narrator's naïve attempts to remember the nondescript pharmacist Willy Wings and his conventional family life is a satirical commentary on how post-war Germany reinvents its history. *Die Einöde und ihr Prophet. Über Menschen und Bilder* (The Wasteland and its Prophet. About Men and Paintings) (1996), a collection of stories and essays about painting, is the author's latest attempt to mirror life in its myriad reflections.

Kronauer's work also includes a substantial body of stories – *Die gemusterte Nacht* (The Patterned Night) (1981) and *Schnurrer. Geschichten* (Schnurrer. Stories) (1992) – as well as critical essays and prose studies – *Die Revolution der Nachahmung* (The Revolution Of Imitation) (1975); *Aufsätze zur Literatur* (Essays on Literature) (1987); and *Die Lerche in der Luft und im Nest. Zu Literatur und Kunst* (The Lark Airborne and in its Nest. On Literature and Art) (1995).

JUTTA ITTNER

Krug, Manfred

b. 8 February 1937, Duisburg

Actor and singer

A steelworker by profession, Krug lived in West Germany until the age of twelve when his father moved to the GDR. In 1957, after two seasons as trainee actor with the **Berliner Ensemble**, he turned freelance film and television actor, singer and jazz musician. Though professionally and financially successful he left the GDR in the wake of the **Biermann Affair** and became a star in West German television series. He is best known as Robert Liebling, a lawyer from the Berlin district of Kreuzberg in *Darling Kreuzberg* (*Liebling Kreuzberg*), created for him by his friend Jurek **Becker**.

HORST CLAUS

Kubin, Alfred

b. 10 April 1877, Leitmeritz an der Elbe (Bohemia; now Litoměřice, Czech Republic); d. 20 August 1959, Zwickledt (Austria)

Draughtsman, graphic artist and writer

Kubin studied art in Munich in 1898 and encountered the etching tradition of Max Klinger. By 1900, he developed his own technique of pen and ink drawings in black and white that suited his symbolist, dream-like imagery. These served as illustrative material in various books and literary journals and as independent works of art exhibited in numerous venues. Kubin was also a talented writer and his mystical, visionary novel *Die andere Seite* was published in 1909. Holdings of his œuvre can be found in the Kubin-Archiv in Hamburg, the Städtische Galerie im Lenbachhaus in Munich, and the Oberösterreichisches Landesmuseum.

SHULAMITH BEHR

Kuczynski, Jürgen

b. 17 September 1904, Elberfeld; d. 6 August 1997, Berlin

Economic historian

Kuczynski began his distinguished academic career in the GDR after returning from wartime exile in England. He established the Institute for Economic History (part of the Academy of Sciences (see also **academies**)) and continued his prolific research output after retirement, notably with the six-volume *Geschichte des Alltags des deutschen Volkes* (History of the Everyday Life of the German People) (1980–5). Despite his reputation as an internal critic of the SED he acknowledged, in his post-unification autobiography *Ein linientreuer Dissident* (A Loyal Party Dissident) (1992) the failure of his generation of intellectuals to promote significant reform.

DENNIS TATE

Kühn, Dieter

b. 1 February 1935, Cologne

Writer

Kühn has written stage and radio plays, novels and texts belonging to the hybrid genre of 'imaginative historiography'. The first of these, *N* (1970), is a biography of Napoleon. Its self-conscious mingling of fact, fiction and conjecture established a form of historical novel which, with variations, informs much of Kühn's subsequent work. He has received several literary prizes, including the *Hörspielpreis der Kriegsblinden* (1974) and the Hermann Hesse Prize (1977). He was *Stadtschreiber* (town scribe) of Bergen-Enkheim from 1980–1.

Further reading

Klüppelholz, W. and Scheuer, H. (eds) (1992) *Dieter Kühn*, Frankfurt am Main: Suhrkamp.

JONATHAN LONG

Küng, Hans

b. 19 March 1928, Sursee (Switzerland)

Theologian and writer

Küng studied theology at the Gregorian University in Rome, was ordained in 1954, gained a doctorate in Paris in 1957, and undertook pastoral work in Switzerland. Since 1963 he has been Professor (now emeritus) and Director of the Institute of Ecumenical Research, Tübingen. He was made official theological adviser by Pope John XXIII in 1962. He has received many prizes and honours, having written numerous influential books on theological (especially ecumenical) topics designed for a wide audience of Christians of different denominations and non-Christians. He is also interested in the environment and global responsibility.

Further reading

Küng, H. (1994) *Große christliche Denker*, Munich and Zürich: Piper (demonstrates his popular and ecumenical approach to Christianity particularly well).

BRIAN MURDOCH

Kulka, Peter

b. 20 July 1937, Dresden

Architect

Having taken an apprenticeship as a mason, Kulka studied engineering (1954–8) and architecture at the Hochschule für Bildende und Angewandte Kunst Berlin-Weißensee (1958–64). He worked with **Henselmann** in 1964 and **Scharoun** from 1965 to 1968 in Berlin. He has been in private practice since 1969; he has been partners with Herzog, Köpke, Siepmann and Töpper in Bielefeld. Since 1979 he has had his own office in Cologne, and an office in Dresden since 1991. He was a professor at the RWTH (Technical University) Aachen from 1986 to 1992.

Modern building materials and innovative construction techniques distinguish most of Kulka's buildings. One of his most interesting designs is the

Sports Stadium Chemnitz 2002 (begun 1994, in collaboration with Ulrich Königs) with its invisible roof-construction.

MARTIN KUDLEK

Kulturbund

The *Kulturbund zur demokratischen Erneuerung Deutschlands* (Cultural Alliance for German Democratic Renewal) was created in the Soviet zone in 1945 as an organization dedicated to restoring cultural unity on a broad anti-fascist basis. It was given its own publishing house, the **Aufbau Verlag**, and the author Johannes R. **Becher** became its first president. After initial success in attracting the support of liberals throughout Germany, it came overtly under the control of the SED and was banned in the western zones. The *Kulturbund der DDR*, as it renamed itself in 1974, was classified as a 'mass organization', and as such held twenty-two seats in the **Volkskammer**, with a further 2,760 delegates sitting on local authorities in the GDR (see also **parties and mass organizations: GDR**). Its original function as a forum for authors became redundant with the establishment of a separate GDR **Writers' Union**.

DENNIS TATE

Kunert, Günter

b. 6 March 1929, Berlin

Writer

Since 1979, when Kunert left the GDR, after two years of harassment by the authorities following his signature of the Biermann petition (see also **Biermann Affair**), his name has been familiar to the West German public from his books, interviews and articles in the press, and he is one of the most widely discussed writers in the German language today. The hallmark of his poems, essays, and other literary work is uncompromising pessimism. This may be explained on a biographical level by the trauma of childhood discrimination as the son of a half-Jewish mother in the Third Reich, and subsequent humiliating public censure and **Stasi** surveillance in the GDR. Like his West German contemporary Hans Magnus **Enzensberger**, Kunert attacked the tyranny of 'instrumental' reason in the 1960s, vehemently rejecting the contemporary euphoria for progress and technology, and took a lead in expressing ecological concerns.

Kunert's literary career began in the early 1950s with didactic verse influenced by **Brecht**, which played a part in the creation of a GDR national consciousness based on anti-fascism and belief in a better future under socialism. However, this was soon replaced by sombre '*Warngedichte*', poems drawing attention to political and social problems, seeking to stimulate unease and provoke an active response in readers. His insistence on remembering the crimes against humanity committed in the Third Reich and his suggestion that life in the GDR was characterized by social alienation of the individual led to public censure and private intimidation. He responded first with bitter allusions between the lines of his poems, then with open confrontation in a literary debate in 1966, when he cited **Auschwitz** and Hiroshima as examples of the true achievements of progress and technology. His essays and poems in the late 1960s and 1970s reveal growing disillusionment with socialism, and he came to adopt a cyclical view of history, arguing that art should be free from any political or social obligation. Since the 1980s Kunert's poetry has been characterized by stark apocalyptic images reflecting a feeling of existential exile, from which artistic creativity alone can provide respite.

See also: poetry: FRG; poetry: GDR

Further reading

Arnold, H.L. (ed.) (1991) *Günter Kunert*, Munich: edition text + kritik 109 (contains informative essays exploring aspects of Kunert's writing, and a select bibliography of secondary literature).

Dunne, K. (1995) *Der Sündenfall: a parabolic key to the image of human existence in the work of Günter Kunert 1960–1990*, Frankfurt am Main: Peter Lang (a useful introduction to Kunert focusing on religious imagery and the existential dimension in his prose and poetry).

Kasper, E. (1995) *Zwischen Utopie und Apokalypse. Das lyrische Werk Günter Kunerts von 1950 bis 1987*, Tübingen: Niemeyer (a comprehensive study of Kunert's poetry, interpreting key poems and giving much background information).

Riedel, N. (1987) *Internationale Günter Kunert-Bibliographie*, vol. 1, *Das poetische und essayistische Werk in Editionen, Einzeldrucken und Übersetzungen*, Hildesheim: Olms (standard bibliography of Kunert's works).

AXEL GOODBODY

Kunstausstellung der DDR

The Kunstausstellung der DDR was the central and representative exhibition of fine arts, and later applied arts too, held every five years in Dresden since the Große Deutsche Kunstausstellung of 1946. Organized by the State and the Artists' Association of the GDR, the overview – until 1971 under the title 'Deutsche Kunstausstellung' – mirrored the ideological function of the visual arts. Therefore, it was mainly works that could be accommodated within the expanding framework of **socialist realism** that were selected by the respective juries. Figurative art in traditional media continued to dominate all ten exhibitions.

See also: cultural policy: GDR; design; painting; sculpture

KERSTIN MEY

Kunze, Reiner

b. 16 August 1933, Oelsnitz (Erzgebirge)

Writer

Kunze's place in official GDR literary history is almost non-existent. After studying philosophy and journalism in Leipzig from 1951 to 1955, Kunze began working as a teaching assistant in journalism at the Karl-Marx University in Leipzig. Although his first poems were published in 1959, he did not attain the status of free writer until 1962. Repeated trips to Czechoslovakia influenced his writings. As a show of solidarity with Czechoslovakian reformers during the Prague Spring, Kunze resigned from the **SED** in 1968, provoking the GDR to prohibit his publications. In 1969 the West German Rowohlt publishing house printed *Sensible Wege* (Sensitive Ways). This publication in the West prompted open attacks against Kunze at the 6th Writers' Congress.

A momentary thaw in the GDR's restrictive policy occurred in 1973 when Reclam published 30,000 copies of *Brief mit blauem Siegel* (Letter with Blue Seal), which contained numerous texts that had only previously appeared in the West. Shortly thereafter (spring 1974), Kunze gave an officially sanctioned public reading of his poetry during the **Leipzig Book Fair**. Prior to 1974, Kunze's only contacts with the reading public were clandestine gatherings in churches, which did not have to obtain permission for religious gatherings. In order to maintain an air of legality, a pastor would say a brief prayer before the reading and offer a blessing at its conclusion.

Kunze is most famous for *Die wunderbaren Jahre* (The Wonderful Years), which S. Fischer published in 1976. This collection of short prose pieces describes momentary aspects of life for 'typical' GDR youth. Combining miniatures, anecdotes, quotations and discussions, Kunze created an ironic portrayal of the contradictions inherent in the GDR's totalitarian system. As a result of the publication of this text (for which Kunze had indeed received the requisite permission from the GDR's licensing bureau), he was expelled from the Writers' Union. This was overturned in 1989. Until 1977 he resided in Greiz in the province of Thuringia; after receiving permission to move to West Germany with his family, they set up residence in Obernzell-Erla in the vicinity of Passau.

The western media praised the publication of *Die wunderbaren Jahre* in 1976, but they denounced Kunze and the film a few years later. Although he was awarded the Bavarian film prize in 1979 for his adaptation, the media questioned Kunze's motivation, denouncing him for his membership of the SED. As a citizen of the West, Kunze, in the eyes of the media, had forfeited his right to criticize the GDR.

Since his move to the West, Kunze has continued to write. He has been instrumental in breaking the silence surrounding the involvement of the **Stasi** in the repression of writers. His own file comprises twelve volumes totalling 3,491 pages and encompasses the time period from 16 September 1968 until 19 December 1977, the day of his departure for the West. In 1990, Kunze published excerpts from his file in the documentary book *Deckname 'Lyrik'* (Codename 'Poetry'), a compilation that made Stasi documentation accessible to the general public.

See also: cultural policy: GDR; dissent and opposition: GDR

Major works

Kunze, R. (1959) *Vögel über dem Tau. Gedichte*, Halle: Mitteldeutscher Verlag.

—— (1962) *Aber die Nachtigall jubelt. Heitere Texte*, Halle: Mitteldeutscher Verlag.

—— (1969) *Sensible Wege*, Reinbek bei Hamburg: Rowohlt.

—— (1970) *Der Löwe Leopold. Fast Märchen, fast Geschichten. Kinderbuch*, Frankfurt am Main: S. Fischer.

—— (1973) *Brief mit blauem Siegel*, Leipzig: Reclam.

—— (1973) *Zimmerlautstärke*, Frankfurt am Main: S. Fischer.

—— (1976) *Die wunderbaren Jahre*, Frankfurt am Main: S. Fischer (this was made into a film in 1979).

—— (1986) *eines jeden einziges leben. gedichte*, Frankfurt am Main: S. Fischer.

—— (1989) *Das weiße Gedicht. Essays*, Frankfurt am Main: S. Fischer.

—— (1990) *Deckname 'Lyrik.' Eine Dokumentation*, Frankfurt am Main: S. Fischer.

—— (1993) *Am Sonnenhang, Tagebuch eines Jahres*, Frankfurt am Main: S. Fischer.

Further reading

Feldkamp, H. (ed.) (1987) *Reiner Kunze: Materialien zu Leben und Werk*, Frankfurt am Main: Fischer (interviews and critical articles about Kunze's literary works).

Graves, P. (ed.) (1985) *Three Contemporary German Poets: Wolf Biermann, Sarah Kirsch, Reiner Kunze*, Leicester: Leicester University Press (collection of poems with an introduction).

Wallmann, J.P. (1977) *Reiner Kunze: Materialien und*

Dokumente, Frankfurt am Main: Fischer (interviews and critical articles).

Wolff, R. (ed.) (1983) *Reiner Kunze: Werk und Wirkung*, Bonn: Bouvier (historical information and analyses of Kunze's early works).

CAROL ANNE COSTABILE-HEMING

Kurier

This Viennese daily paper was founded in 1945 by the American military authorities, and directed against Soviet attempts to influence Austrian politics. It was sold to Austrian owners in 1954. It is the flagship of a publishing house that also produces various magazines (e.g. *profil* and *trend*). In 1988, 45 percent of the shares were sold to the German WAZ (Westdeutsche Allgemeine Zeitung) Group. Since 1988 it has been distributed by **Mediaprint**, a joint enterprise of *Neue Kronen Zeitung* and *Kurier*. This conservative tabloid with strong affiliations with the **ÖVP** (Austrian People's Party) is the third largest daily paper in Austria (selling 307,000 copies in 1997

GEORG HELLMAYR

Kursbuch

A West German journal founded in 1965 by Hans Magnus **Enzensberger**, *Kursbuch* ('timetable') still appears quarterly within united Germany. The journal's focus is contemporary, theoretical and radical. *Kursbuch* has been identified with the FRG's left-liberal intellectual tradition, although it publishes across political divides. Issues initially accented the arts, with much original material. Edition 15 (1968), however, declared the 'Death of Literature', reflecting contemporary politicization. *Kursbuch* has subsequently emphasized politics, and, latterly, 'lifestyle'. The journal has featured **environmentalism** (33, 1973); feminism (35, 1974; 47, 1977) (see also **feminism and the women's movement**); citizens' initiatives (50, 1977) (see also **citizens' initiatives: FRG**; **citizens' initiatives: GDR**); youth (54, 1978; 113, 1993); **minorities** (62, 1980) and **unification** (101, 1990).

STUART TABERNER

L

Laederach, Jürg

b. 20 December 1945, Basel

Writer

Laederach began his career with short prose in 1974, partly influenced by the tradition of linguistic experiments that originated in the 1950s and 1960s in opposition to the bourgeois literature of the **Gruppe 47**. His often absurd, yet humorous texts focus on his protagonists' inane existence in everyday language and culture and simultaneously proclaim and undermine their idiosyncratic identities. Loosely affiliated with the **Grazer Gruppe**, the Swiss author concentrates on unearthing the linguistic possibilities of his grotesque scenarios and thus prevents the reader's identification with the characters via layers of irony in, for example, *Flügelmeyers Wahn* (Flügelmeyer's Madness), 1986.

ANKE FINGER

Lampe, Jutta

b. 13 December 1937, Flensburg

Actress

Lampe worked for much of her early career under Peter **Stein** at the Schaubühne Berlin, where she appeared in celebrated productions of Brecht's *Die Mutter*, Gorki's *Summer Guests* and Kleist's *Prinz Friedrich von Homburg*. She has also enjoyed a successful film career, appearing in filmed versions of the above plays and Margarethe von **Trotta**'s *Sisters or the Balance of Happiness* (*Schwestern oder die Balance des Glücks*) in 1979, and *The German Sisters* (*Die bleierne Zeit*) in 1981.

SEÁN ALLAN

Land

A *Land* is an administrative regional unit within the German federal structure, with its own parliament (*Landtag*) and government, and with, in particular, exclusive legislative competence in cultural matters. Before unification West Germany was divided into ten *Länder* and West Berlin; with unification the special status of Berlin was relinquished and five new East German *Länder* joined the FRG, thus creating sixteen *Länder*: Baden-Württemberg, Bayern, Berlin, Brandenburg, Bremen, Hamburg, Hessen, Mecklenburg-Vorpommern, Niedersachsen, Nordrhein-Westfalen, Rheinland-Pfalz, Saarland, Sachsen, Sachsen-Anhalt, Schleswig-Holstein and Thüringen. Criticism of the ineffectual size of the smaller *Länder* (the city states Berlin, Bremen and Hamburg) has mounted.

See also: Bundesrat; federalism

MONIKA PRÜTZEL-THOMAS

Lander, Jeannette

b. 8 September 1931, New York

Writer and critic

Born to Polish-Jewish émigré parents, Lander grew up in a Yiddish-speaking household in an African-

American neighbourhood of Atlanta, Georgia. Married to the German writer Joachim Seyppel from 1950 to 1982, she studied English and German literature in the US before moving in 1960 to West Berlin, where she completed a dissertation on W.B. Yeats. In 1984 to 1985, she spent a year in Sri Lanka. These experiences, including her complex relationship to language (Yiddish, Black English and German), are reflected in her novels of the years 1971, 1972 and 1993. In addition to fiction, she has written radio plays, television scripts, a Jewish cookbook and a book on Ezra Pound.

Major works

Lander, J. (1971) *Ein Sommer in der Woche der Itke K.*, Frankfurt am Main: Insel.
—— (1972) *Auf dem Boden der Fremde*, Frankfurt am Main: Insel.
—— (1976) *Die Töchter*, Frankfurt am Main: Insel.
—— (1980) *Ich, allein*, Munich: AutorenEdition.
—— (1993) *Jahrhundert der Herren*, Berlin: Aufbau.
—— (1996) *Eine unterbrochene Reise*, Berlin: Aufbau.
—— (1998) *Robert*, Berlin: Aufbau.

Further reading

Adelson, L. (1993) 'Jeannette Lander's *Ein Sommer in der Woche der Itke K.* Jews and Other Others: On Representations and Enactments', in *Making Bodies, Making History*, Lincoln, NB: University of Nebraska Press.

PATRICIA HERMINGHOUSE

Lang, Helmut

b. 10 March 1956, Vienna

Fashion designer

Lang is one of the leaders of European minimalist fashion design. After a succession of low-paid jobs in Vienna, Lang set up his own made-to-measure fashion studio in 1979. Within five years his was a full powered ready-to-wear label with equal emphasis on men's and women's wear. With a licensed sunglasses collection and a diffusion jean-

swear line he is following the route taken by Calvin Klein. Named International Designer of the Year at the Council of Fashion Designers of America awards in 1996, Lang has capitalized on the success he encountered following his first collection in a Viennese exhibit at the Centre Pompidou in Paris in 1986. He straddles the world of academia and business as he is also professor of the masterclass of fashion at the University of Applied Arts in Vienna.

ADRIAN MURDOCH

Langer, Bernhard

b. 27 August 1957, Anhausen

Golfer

Twice winner of the American Masters, in 1985 and 1993, and a member of the European Ryder Cup team on eight occasions, Langer is undoubtedly the greatest German golfer ever and has made an important contribution to the development of the game in Germany. His overcoming of a putting affliction known as the 'yips' is testimony to his tenacity as a player and to a strong determination rooted in a deep religious faith.

MIKE DENNIS

language

German is the majority language and the official language of the state in Germany, Austria, Liechtenstein and the German-speaking part of Switzerland, henceforward referred to as the 'German-speaking countries', and it is the language of the largest single linguistic group in Switzerland as a whole. It is also spoken by substantial minorities in many other states in Europe, and in the Americas, Australia and Namibia, and it retains a role as a language of international communication in central Europe. It has the second largest number of native-speakers of any language in Europe, after Russian. Total numbers of speakers of languages are hard to determine, but, as a first language, German probably ranks seventh in the world, ahead of French, with ninety to a hundred million speakers. For its speakers it is very often a crucial element in their sense of their ethnic or national identity.

German belongs to the Germanic sub-group of the Indo-European language family. This means that it is closely related to the other Germanic languages, i.e. the Scandinavian languages, English, Frisian, Dutch, Yiddish and *Lëtzebuergesch* (Luxembourgish), the entire sub-group having probably been a single language or a group of closely related dialects about two thousand years ago. It is less closely related to the other Indo-European languages, this whole family probably having been a single language or group of similar dialects some time before 3,000 BC. Most, but not all, of the languages of Europe, of Iran and of the Indian subcontinent belong to the Indo-European family; several of them, such as English and Spanish, have also been spread in recent centuries to many other parts of the world.

Language relationships of this kind manifest themselves in similarities in basic vocabulary and grammatical structures. The similarities between German and other Germanic languages are obvious; many similarities between German and non-Germanic Indo-European languages are only clear to specialists.

Language families have played a prominent part in modern German thought, much of our knowledge of them deriving from nineteenth-century German scholarship. They have frequently been linked to race: speakers of Indo-European languages, known as *Indogermanisch* (Indo-Germanic) in German, were long thought to represent an Aryan race, elevated to a master-race by the National Socialists. Actually the link between language and race is generally so tenuous as to be virtually non-existent, given the frequent acquisition, throughout history, of the language of a powerful group by less powerful groups and individuals.

The term 'Germanic' implies that the other Germanic languages derive from German; this is not the case, German being simply one of several Germanic languages.

The relationship between German and English can be clearly seen in very large numbers of closely parallel common words like *Haus*/house, *Mann*/man, *Sonne*/sun, *Arm*/arm etc. Similar grammatical phenomena include the formation of different

tenses of many common verbs with vowel change, where, for example English 'sing, sang, sung' correspond to German '*singen, sang, gesungen*'. Some similarities are not actually due to relationship, but to both English-speakers and German-speakers having taken new words from prestigious European languages, particularly French and Latin.

Despite many similarities, there are substantial grammatical differences between English and German, German retaining some significant characteristics, such as grammatical gender and a case system, originally common to all Indo-European languages, which have been lost in English.

Language plays a major role in modern German politics as perhaps the most obvious defining characteristic of the nation. Language plays a similar part in many nations in Europe and elsewhere, but in many others a historic territory or a shared majority religion are equally important. In contrast, the extent of German territory was debatable until 1990, and the Protestant–Catholic religious cleavage is still politically significant. This focus upon the language entails many problems, given the diversity and spread of German.

German is extremely diverse compared to most other languages, with different dialects often being scarcely mutually intelligible (see also **dialect**). These dialects are nevertheless considered to be varieties of a single language largely because they do share some clear similarities, and also because there has developed alongside them, since the late fifteenth century, a relatively uniform standard language used in most written communications and in modern times also used increasingly in speech, particularly by the educated. The standard language is well understood by the overwhelming majority of German-speakers, although it has distinct national varieties in Germany, Austria and Switzerland, and differs appreciably within Germany particularly between north and south (some east–west differences also developed during the division of Germany). One variety, *Lëtzebuergesch*, used to be regarded as a German dialect, but now has the status of a separate language; it is scarcely comprehensible to German-speakers unless they know a dialect from the area close to **Luxembourg**, and it now has its own distinct standard form, although standard German (often in a Luxembourg form with a few local characistics) is still the most widespread written language in the Grand Duchy, and French is also used, actually enjoying a higher public profile than German.

German is, or was until recently, spread across more states than any other language in Europe, with substantial minorities in most central and eastern European countries and the former USSR; in the west there are significant German-speaking minorities in eastern Belgium, Alsace-Lorraine in France, and **South Tyrol**/Alto Adige in Italy as well as a smaller group in Jutland in Denmark.

The close link between language and nationalism has had important political consequences. Under National Socialism it led to a belief that areas in Europe where German was spoken, particularly if they bordered on the German-speaking countries, should be united with Germany; this was a major pretext for the invasions of Poland and Czechoslovakia. In the post-war period it led to demands by the FRG that the Soviet Union and other eastern European countries allow 'the Germans' to return to their homeland. When the Iron Curtain disappeared and such people were free to move to Germany there was anxiety at this substantial and rapid influx of *Aussiedler* (the term used for ethnic Germans from Eastern Europe 're-settling' in Germany), but also dismay that many of them, particularly from the former Soviet Union, did not actually speak German; many of them saw their Germanness in less clearly linguistic terms, or had simply preserved a memory that their families had once been German-speaking.

In the other German-speaking countries the link between the language and German nationalism can be something of an embarrassment. In Austria it has led to the cultivation of the various Austrian regional dialects, and a rather vigorous promotion of the somewhat distinct Austrian standard German, a process not without contradictions and complexities (see Ammon 1995). In Switzerland the national variety of standard German has been in sharp decline since WWII, having been marginalized in speech, even the speech of the intelligentsia, and in broadcasting, by resurgent Swiss-German dialects (*Schwyzertütsch*). It is, however, still the dominant written form (see Ammon 1995). The German language is also important in

Austrian nationalism, in distinguishing Austrians from other groups in the former Hapsburg Empire.

Not only are there numerous German-speaking minorities in other countries, but German used to be the major language of wider communication in central and eastern Europe. Despite the determined efforts of the Soviet Union in the post-war period, it was not ousted from this role by Russian, and there are informal reports of, for example, Hungarian and Polish officers communicating in German during Warsaw Pact manœuvres. There is evidence that, since the end of the Cold War, this international use of German has increased again quite strongly, despite the immense attraction of English.

Each of the German-speaking countries contains minority language groups, which, given the language–nationalism link, have suffered various degrees of discrimination. Many of these groups are indigenous, the languages in question often having been present in the territory as long as or longer than German. There are other Germanic languages in Germany: Danish and North Frisian in Schleswig-Holstein. Further languages belong to other sub-groups of the Indo-European family; the Slavonic sub-group is represented by Sorbian in eastern Germany and by Croatian and Slovene in Austria, and the Romance sub-group (modern descendants of Latin) by Romansh or Rhaeto-Romance which is spoken in parts of Switzerland where German is the majority language. The non-Indo-European Hungarian is spoken in a small area of Austria. Given the multilingual nature of the Swiss state, Romansh-speakers have been subject in modern times to little deliberate discrimination, while, at the other extreme, speakers of the Slavonic languages have not found it easy to maintain separate linguistic identities, Sorbian, for instance, having been the object of severe discrimination under National Socialism. Jews in Germany have probably not constituted a linguistic minority for at least two hundred years, having abandoned the minority language Yiddish for varieties of German (often with a few peculiarly Jewish characteristics). However, since Yiddish is closely related to German, the transition point between German-influenced Yiddish and Yiddish-influenced German is not easy to determine. Yiddish was used by several millions in central and eastern Europe before the war, but now survives chiefly in Russia, Israel and the United States, and to some extent in Britain. The contemporary German state is relatively tolerant and supportive of indigenous linguistic minorities.

All of the German-speaking countries are home to substantial numbers of speakers of non-indigenous minority languages, who, often despite lengthy residence, usually have no citizenship rights, and whose residence is theoretically temporary (see also **Gastarbeiter**). Official interest in their languages often extends little beyond making sure that they can understand essential communications, and research has focused almost entirely on the varieties of German used by first generation immigrants. Most of the languages in question are other Indo-European languages, chiefly Romance (Italian, Spanish and Portuguese), Slavonic (Croatian and Serbian), and Greek; however, the largest single group speaks the non-Indo-European Turkish.

Like other languages which play a clear role in national identity, German has often experienced the phenomenon of purism. Purism attempts to purge the language of words of foreign origin. Purism is usually advocated by scholars and politicians, and only at certain periods in history; most users of most, but not all, languages will happily 'borrow' words from other languages with which they come into contact, particularly for new artefacts or alien flora and fauna, but also for familiar objects and concepts if the other language and its speakers enjoy power and prestige; it is probably true to say that most users of a language are either unaware of purism, or regard it as irrelevant. German hence has numerous words from neighbouring languages, particularly French, but also Italian, with smaller numbers from Slavonic languages and Hungarian; currently the main source of borrowings is English. It also uses very large numbers of words of Latin and Classical Greek origin, as do most European languages. Purists have made sporadic, almost entirely unsuccessful attempts to purge the language of such words. Interestingly the National Socialists did not advocate purism, and it has had little political significance since WWII, apart from attempts in the GDR to minimize the use of English loans. Where purism has succeeded,

however, is in creating an impression that thousands of words of the language, including many everyday words, and many words which have no clear alternatives, are actually 'foreign words' (**Fremdwörter**), which ideally should not be used, and which are in some sense more difficult than words of native origin. Most such 'foreign words' are thoroughly integrated into the language, and some are even German coinages, not occurring in the apparent source language, such as *Showmaster* ('presenter of television show'), only apparently from English. Even though purism is now politically dead, it is still active in education and publishing where the most influential series of dictionaries, Duden, still includes a separate *Fremdwörterbuch* (dictionary of 'foreign words' used in German).

See also: German language: Austria; German language: Switzerland; minorities, German; minorities, non-German

Further reading

Ammon, U. (1995) *Die deutsche Sprache in Deutschland, Österreich und der Schweiz*, Berlin: de Gruyter.

Clyne, M.G. (1995) *The German Language in a Changing Europe*, Cambridge: Cambridge University Press.

Russ, C.V.J. (1994) *The German Language Today*, London: Routledge.

Wells, C.J. (1985) *German. A Linguistic History to 1945*, Oxford: Clarendon.

STEPHEN BARBOUR

Lattmann, Dieter

b. 15 February 1926, Potsdam

Writer and cultural functionary

Lattmann aptly described himself as a 'politico-literary multi-purpose figure'. He was the first chairman of the **Verband deutscher Schriftsteller** and an SPD member of parliament from 1972 to 1980. The problems of this experience – SPD stalwart Herbert Wehner suggested parliament was no place for poets – are documented in *Die Einsamkeit des Politikers* (The Loneliness of the

Politician) (1977) and *Die lieblose Republik* (The Cold Republic) (1981). His interest in the **German Question** is reflected in the 1985 novel *Die Brüder* (The Brothers), which portrays a family split, like Lattmann's own, by the division of Germany.

STUART PARKES

Lauda, Niki

b. 22 February 1949, Vienna

Racing driver and businessman (full name Andreas-Nikolaus Lauda)

Lauda won the Formula One World Championship in 1975 and 1977 for Ferrari, as well as in 1984 for McLaren. After a nearly fatal accident in 1976 he became an enigmatic character in motor racing. He founded a private passenger airline with which he broke the virtual state monopoly of Austrian Airlines. As one of the most popular sportsmen in Austria he is also regarded as a symbol of the free entrepreneurial spirit.

GEORG HELLMAYR

Lavant, Christine

b. 4 July 1915, Groß-Edling, Lavantal (Carinthia); d. 7 June 1973, Wolfsberg (Carinthia)

Writer

As in the case of her compatriot and contemporary Christine **Busta**, Lavant's childhood of extreme hardship and her religious faith profoundly coloured her verse. Unlike Busta, however, Lavant displayed a more individual approach to language once her initial indebtedness to Rilke had been overcome. She established her literary reputation relatively late with her collections *Die Bettelschale* (The Begging Bowl) of 1956 and *Der Pfauenschrei* (The Cry of the Peacock) of 1962. The baroque-like qualities of her poetry have been attributed to her Austrian background.

ANTHONY BUSHELL

legal system: FRG

Since the middle ages, the German legal system has been shaped by the adoption of principles of Roman law which largely replaced the less systematic Germanic customary law, and later by the codification of the nineteenth century, which drew on the French law codes compiled under Napoleon I. After the disruptions of the Hitler era, guarantees for inalienable human rights were written into a new constitution (see also **constitution: FRG**), the Basic Law, and the **Federal Constitutional Court** ensures that the principles of the Basic Law are observed at all times.

In contrast to an English system based on common law statutes and precedents, the distinctive feature of the German legal system is systematic written codification, complete with general and specific principles that can be applied to new situations. The task for German judges is to apply the rules of the law codes, not to create law. In theory case-law is not a formal source of law. However, in practice, decisions of higher courts are taken as guidelines by the judges. A prime example for this is the binding decisions of the **Federal Constitutional Court**.

German law divides into civil law (*Zivilrecht*) and public law (*Öffentliches Recht*). Public law covers the legal relationships between the state and its citizens, and defines the extent of activities for state institutions. It includes constitutional law (*Staatsrecht*), criminal law (*Strafrecht*), criminal procedural law (*Strafprozeßrecht*) and administrative law (*Verwaltungsrecht*). Civil law regulates legal affairs between private individuals and is largely based on the **BGB**, the civil code. In modern times it has been extended to include commercial law (*Handelsrecht*), company law (*Gesellschaftsrecht*) and the bulk of labour law (*Arbeitsrecht*). A newer development is hybrid codes, like environmental laws, which combine elements of both civil and public law.

The extensive codification of German law has led to a situation where battles that were lost in politics are often pursued a second time round through the courts. This strategy has frequently proved successful. Examples are the contesting by members of the **CDU/CSU** of the various reforms of abortion legislation (see also **abortion law**), which was then partly reversed through their action in the Constitutional Court; and court action brought by environmental groups against the approval of construction plans for several nuclear power stations.

German judges are all legally qualified and in tenured state employment, which gives them independence. German courts are divided vertically into ordinary courts which deal with civil and criminal cases, and specialized administrative courts. This latter category comprises labour courts (*Arbeitsgerichte*), often playing the role of an industrial tribunal; social courts (*Sozialgerichte*) that deal with social security matters; financial courts (*Finanzgerichte*) in charge of fiscal concerns; and administrative courts (*Verwaltungsgerichte*), before which the decisions of state authorities can be challenged. The German court structure has also three to four horizontal layers of courts and appeal courts, on local, regional and finally federal level, with the Federal Constitutional Court as the highest appeal court.

See also: civil rights

Further reading

Foster, N. (1996) *German Legal System and Laws*, London: Blackstone Press.

MONIKA PRÜTZEL-THOMAS

Lehmann, Wilhelm

b. 4 May 1882, Puerto Cabello (Venezuela); d. 17 November 1968, Eckernförde

Writer

Lehmann revitalized nature poetry in the late 1920s through his precise botanical and ornithological observation. His poetic method, finding images in natural phenomena, historical and mythological figures for the experience of a mystic communion with nature, permitting escape from contemporary political reality, influenced a generation of younger poets.

Further reading

Schäfer, H.-D. (1969) *Wilhelm Lehmann: Studien zu seinem Leben und Werk*, Bonn: Bouvier (remains the standard account of his life and work).
Scrase, D. (1984) *Wilhelm Lehmann: A Critical Biography. Volume I: The Years of Trial (1880–1918)*, Columbia, SC: Camden House (a detailed account of Lehmann's early life).

AXEL GOODBODY

Leipzig Book Fair

Although most aspects of publishing in the ex-GDR were centred on Berlin, Leipzig retained something of the international status it had enjoyed in the book-trade since the eighteenth century. Not only was the state-run distribution network based there; its traditional Spring Fair became the major event in the GDR's publishing calendar. Although it paled into insignificance compared with its traditional rival, the **Frankfurt Book Fair**, it provided an invaluable opportunity during the détente years for GDR publishers and their authors to communicate with their western counterparts.

See also: publishing: GDR

DENNIS TATE

Leiser, Erwin

b. 16 May 1923, Berlin; d. 23 August 1996, Zürich

Documentary filmmaker

Leiser emigrated to Sweden after the pogrom against Jews ('*Reichskristallnacht*') of November 1938, and became a journalist and a translator of German literary works into Swedish. A documentary filmmaker since 1959, he relocated to Zürich in 1961. The director of many portraits of artists, a documentary about poverty in the world, and two films about Hiroshima, he is best known for his numerous critical documentaries that explore the Nazi past and the Holocaust.

See also: documentary film

MARGRIT FRÖLICH

Lemper, Ute

b. 4 July 1963, Münster

Singer, actress and dancer

The cosmopolitan and multilingual Ute Lemper is often compared to Marlene **Dietrich**. She began her singing career at fifteen and studied acting at the Max-Reinhardt-Seminar. She has appeared in productions of *Cats*, *Cabaret* and *The Blue Angel*, and in several films, including *Prospero's Books* and *Prêt-à-porter*. As a singer, her repertoire ranges from Kurt Weill's political songs and Edith Piaf's *chansons* to compositions by Michael Nyman.

Recordings

Lemper, U. (1989) *Ute Lemper Sings Kurt Weill*.
—— (1991) *Crimes of the Heart*, Sony Music (pop).
—— (1992) *Songbook* (Michael Nyman compositions), Decca/Argo.
—— (1993) *Illusions*, Fontaine.
—— (1993) *Ute Lemper Sings Kurt Weill, vol. 2*.
—— (1995) *City of Strangers*, Decca.
—— (1995) *Espace Indecent*, Polydor France
—— (1997) *Berlin Cabaret Songs*, Decca.

SABINE SCHMIDT

Lenz, Hermann

b. 26 February 1913, Stuttgart

Writer

Until Peter **Handke**'s advocacy in 1973, Lenz was little respected for his lack of political engagement, but is now recognized as an outstanding proponent of '*neue Innerlichkeit*' (Büchner Prize 1978, Würth Prize 1997). Lenz is best known for two series of autobiographical novels upholding the cultivation of the inner sphere as the path to survival in a barbaric century. The trilogy of *Der innere Bezirk* (The Inner Precinct) (1961–80) chronicles the years 1935–50. *Verlassene Zimmer* (Departed Rooms)

(1966) began a cycle of to date nine novels, of which *Freunde* (Friends) (1997) is the latest, recounting the life of Lenz's alter ego, writer Eugen Rapp.

JEFFREY GARRETT

Lenz, Siegfried

b. 18 March 1926, Lyck (East Prussia)

Writer and cultural critic

Although Lenz is a writer with a long, prolific career that began in 1951 with the novel *There Were Hawks in the Sky* (*Es waren Habichte in der Luft*) and the short story collection *So zärtlich war Suleyken* (How Sweet was Suleyken), he is perhaps best known for his 1968 novel *The German Lesson* (*Die Deutschstunde*), a text that investigates the recent past and reveals in the microcosm of a small German-Danish town the social and mental attitudes that gave rise to the atrocities of the Nazi era. The novel was adapted as a film and translated into nineteen languages, which catapulted Lenz into the status of internationally recognized proponent of post-war German literature with the likes of Heinrich **Böll** and Günter **Grass**. Like Böll and Grass, Lenz was also a member of the **Gruppe 47**.

Lenz's technique of evoking local history to depict and lay bare larger social dynamics finds an interesting parallel in **Grass**'s writing, who like Lenz grew up in what today is Poland. Both in many of his short stories and in novels like *Local History Museum* (*Heimatmuseum*, 1978), Lenz nods to the distinctive qualities of his home region but in opposition to the mythologizing qualities implied by the word **Heimat**, a project Lenz himself once formulated as 'homeland without homesickness' ('*Heimat ohne Sehnsucht*'). Making use of this stance, Chancellor Willy **Brandt** in fact invited both Grass and Lenz to attend ceremonies officially recognizing the permanence of Poland's western border (see also **Ostpolitik**). Nevertheless, some critics have attempted to align those texts that deal with his home region with the sentimental and politically suspect genre of **Heimatliteratur**, with the implication that Lenz's writing should not be taken seriously.

A split of critical consensus marks the reception of Lenz's œuvre. Detractors find that Lenz's writing lacks an innovative, hallmark literary style and that his serious works are too solemn and his comical texts too flimsy. Lenz's texts have been valued, in turn, for the questions they raise about the Nazi past, their non-trivial treatment of conflicts of responsibility and duty and studies of individuals as they act in limiting circumstances. These issues have been related to Lenz's own experiences in WWII and moral awakening which led him to desert the German army towards the end of the war. Additionally, Lenz defines his characters relative to others in the texts; their appearance in pairs and other constellations is an important feature of his narratives.

Beyond short stories and novels, Lenz has produced an impressive array of radio and stage plays (see also *Hörspiel*), essays and interviews. Lenz has also received a large number of literary prizes.

In the 1960s Lenz campaigned for the **SPD**. Interestingly, Lenz never joined the party. He took his action rather out of the conviction that it represented his views more closely than any other and that the issues the country faced were critical ones that required action. Most recently, Lenz was a vocal critic of German **unification**.

Further reading

Murdoch, B. and Read, M. (1978) *Siegfried Lenz*, London: Oswald Wolff (discussion of Lenz's life and his major works by genre).

Reber, T. *Siegfried Lenz*, Berlin: Colloquium (discussion of Lenz by theme).

Wagener, H. (1976) *Siegfried Lenz*, Munich: C.H. Beck (essays on Lenz's major works and his position in post-war German literature and a bibliography).

Wolff, R. (1985) *Siegfried Lenz. Werk und Wirkung*, Bonn: Bouvier (collection of articles on Lenz's writing and an interview with Lenz).

PETER M. McISAAC

Lettau, Reinhard

b. 10 September 1929, Erfurt; d. 17 June 1996, Karlsruhe

Writer and academic

Both a writer and political activist, Reinhard Lettau was noted for his radio plays, dramatic pieces and literary works, and from 1967 to 1991 held the post of Professor of German Literature at the University of California at San Diego. Never satisfied with cultural critique from behind the safety of a desk, Lettau found himself taken into custody more than once for his political activism. As one of the major figures emerging from the West German **student movement** of the 1960s, Lettau remained committed to leftist politics throughout his career.

KITTY MILLET

Leutenegger, Gertrud

b. 7 December 1948, Schwyz (Switzerland)

Writer

In Leutenegger's works, which embrace prose, poetry and drama, an aethetics of the **New Subjectivity** – mingling of reality and dream; apocalyptic and utopian motifs; echoes of poetic realism and the Alpine village tale – subserves a global vision of environmental and psychic transformations accompanying modernization. Urban decay in Zürich or Berlin and declining Swiss or Italian village life (in *Vorabend*, 1975 and *Meduse*, 1988), Swiss zenophobia and patriarchies old and new (in *Nineve*, 1977 and *Gouverneur*, 1981), despoliation of the Alpine **Heimat** by agribusiness (*Kontinent*, 1985) are juxtaposed with modernization in gerontocratic China (*Kontinent*) or radiation sickness, urban alienation and rural poverty in Japan (*Acheron*, 1994).

ELIZABETH BOA

Liberales Forum

The Austrian political party Liberales Forum was founded in February 1993 as a classical liberal party by five members of the **FPÖ** (among them spokeswoman *Heide Schmidt*) who left the FPÖ because of its strong right-wing tendencies. Since then this parliamentary group has tried to establish itself in regional elections with limited success. In national elections the party was able to gain the support of the liberally minded middle-class electorate, especially in Vienna, thus outpacing the **Greens** in the 1995 December elections.

Its party platform is based on human-rights issues, the importance and independence of the individual, and a free market economy.

GEORG HELLMAYR

libraries

Using the well-resourced libraries of Germany, Austria and Switzerland, some of which have been in existence for over a thousand years, can be a daunting task. There is strong regional provision, and a bewildering array of library types. Fortunately, published material, a selection of which is listed at the end of this entry, provides addresses and telephone numbers, summarizes the range of holdings in the larger libraries, and the scope of specialized collections, and lists the documentation required of users. Library organization in the German-speaking states is remarkably similar in structure.

Ecclesiastical foundations constitute the oldest stratum. The library at the Swiss monastery of St Gall (Stiftsbibliothek St Gallen), founded in 719, now contains some 150,000 volumes, 2,000 manuscripts and 1,635 incunabula. Some were re-established after a period of disuse, such as the library of the Benedictine monastery at Niederaltaich, first founded in the eighth century and again in 1918. Another Benedictine foundation, the Benediktiner-Erzabtei St Peter in Salzburg, also founded in the eighth century, now houses a special music collection with 3,000 scores, including Mozart and Haydn, as well as 120,000 books, 1,300 manuscripts and 1,000 incunabula. Other ecclesiastical libraries are relatively new: for instance, the Bischöfliche Zentralbibliothek Regensburg was established in 1972 and now has 250,000 volumes.

From the fourteenth century onwards, however, territorial rulers, the new universities and the municipalities gradually replaced the church as major patrons. Their collections form the basis of the regional research libraries we know today. Examples of the first category are the Herzog August Bibliothek in Wolfenbüttel, founded in 1572, and the Fürstlich Fürstenbergische Hofbibliothek in Donaueschingen, founded in 1723. Wolfenbüttel has 720,000 volumes, including a special collection of imprints from the sixteenth to eighteenth centuries, and almost 12,000 manuscripts. Donaueschingen is smaller, but also has an important collection of incunabula.

University libraries generally have a central repository and libraries in individual departments. The University of Cologne, for example, has 2.2 million volumes centrally and probably as many again distributed around the 123 individual research institutes. In Bremen (founded 1660, 2.2 million volumes), Frankfurt am Main (founded 1484, 4 million volumes) and Göttingen (founded in 1734, 3.5 million volumes, probably the first academic library in the modern sense with policies for acquisition and reader access), the university libraries also function as regional state libraries. In Austria, the landscape is dominated by Vienna (founded 1365, 5 million volumes), which is also supplemented by 63 institute libraries. In Switzerland, the university library in Bern (1.7 million volumes) is actually larger than the National Library (Schweizerische Landesbibliothek, 1.2 million volumes) and the University of Basel (founded after 1460) also has a large collection (2.7 million volumes). In Zürich, the canton, university and city libraries are combined in the Zentralbibliothek Zürich (established 1914, 2.4 million volumes).

Town libraries are generally smaller, but may still contain interesting collections. The Bibliotheca Bipontina (in Zweibrücken), for example, inherited the books of the Dukes of Zweibrücken. As one might expect, town libraries often specialize in matters of local interest. In the Stadtbibliothek Braunschweig, founded in 1861, we find material on the city of Brunswick, the surrounding area, and local personalities such as the mathematician and astronomer Karl Friedrich Gauß (1777–1855), and the novelists Friedrich Gerstäcker (1816–1972), Ricarda Huch (1864–1947) and Wilhelm Raabe (1831–1910). Similarly, the Stadtarchiv und Wissenschaftliche Stadtbibliothek Soest documents the history of Soest, Westphalia, and the Hanseatic League.

The German constitution decrees that the *Länder* are responsible for most academic libraries (*Universitäts-Bibliotheken*, *Staats-Bibliotheken* and *Landes-Bibliotheken*), federal involvement being limited to government institutions, national archives and the like (e.g. the Bundesarchiv and Deutsche Bibliothek). Germany's regional character has meant that there has never been one single copyright library in Germany. Before the war, the Deutsche (originally Preußische) Staatsbibliothek (founded in 1661) together with the Deutsche Bücherei in Leipzig (established 1912) collected German imprints. After the war, the Staatsbibliothek **Stiftung Preußischer Kulturbesitz** took over the role of the Deutsche Staatsbibliothek in West Berlin, while the Deutsche Bibliothek in Frankfurt am Main mirrored the role of the Deutsche Bücherei. After unification, the German authorities were faced with about 7 million volumes in the Deutsche Staatsbibliothek, 5 million volumes in the Deutsche Bücherei, 4.1 million in West Berlin and 2.27 million in Frankfurt am Main. The result of the ensuing reorganization is a National Library in Frankfurt am Main, opened in May 1997, with 7 million books and electronic titles. The new library therefore now takes the place of the Bayerische Staatsbibliothek in Munich as the largest library in the German-speaking world, but the latter can be seen as a supplementary copyright library. It has 6 million volumes, 36,000 current periodicals, 18,553 incunabula and almost 3 million music scores.

In Germany, government documents are available in federal libraries (e.g. the library of the Deutscher Bundestag, founded 1949, 1 million volumes), seats of regional government (e.g. Senatsbibliothek Berlin, founded 1949, 418,000 volumes), and the courts (the library of the Kammergericht Berlin was established in the eighteenth century and has almost 200,000 volumes). Similarly, Switzerland has a number of government libraries attached to the Federal Parliament (Bundeshaus) and the ministries, as well as other public offices. This situation is largely mirrored in Austria.

In addition, libraries are operated by private companies such as Henkel (founded 1910, 100,000 volumes). These mainly contain technical reports and other reference works for corporate needs, but some, such as the Ciba-Geigy library in Basel (founded 1884), provide a public loans service as well. Other specialized libraries are devoted to single authors. One example is the Thomas-Mann-Archiv in Zürich, established in 1956.

Further reading

Bartz, B., Opitz, H. and Richter, E. (eds) (1991) *World Guide to Libraries*, 10th edn, Munich: Saur.

—— (1993) *Handbuch der Bibliotheken Bundesrepublik Deutschland, Österreich, Schweiz*, Munich: Saur.

Gebhart, W. (1977) *Spezialbestände in deutschen Bibliotheken. Bundesrepublik Deutschland einschließlich Berlin (West)*, Berlin: de Gruyter.

Welsch, E. K, Danyel, J. and Kitton, T. (1994). *Archives and Libraries in a New Germany*, New York: Council for European Studies.

JONATHAN WEST

Liebeneiner, Wolfgang

b. 6 October 1905, Liebau (Lower Silesia; now Lubawka, Poland); d. 28 November 1987, Vienna

Actor and filmmaker

A gifted craftsman, Liebeneiner's career represents revealing continuities and ruptures in German cinema. Head of the **Babelsberg** film academy under the Nazis, he made 'apolitical' entertainment movies and the notorious pro-euthanasia propaganda film *Ich klage an!* (*I Accuse!*) in 1941. After the war, he directed Wolfgang **Borchert**'s play *The Man Outside* (*Draußen vor der Tür*, 1947) and its film version *Liebe '47* (1949), before returning to his trade mark comedies and family melodramas, including *Die Trapp-Familie* (1956) and *Die Trapp-Familie in Amerika* (1958). Later worked primarily for television, with popular mini-series like *Tom Sawyers* *und Huckleberry Finns Abenteuer* (*The Adventures of Tom Sawyer and Huckleberry Finn*, 1968).

CHRISTIAN ROGOWSKI

Liechtenstein

The Principality of Liechtenstein (*Fürstentum Liechtenstein*) is by far the smallest independent German-speaking state today and one of the smallest sovereign states in the world. It covers an area of 160 square kilometres and its population (early 1990s) is just over 30,000. It is situated in alpine parts, being squashed between the east of Switzerland and the west of Austria. It is divided into eleven *Gemeinden* (communes); Vaduz is the capital.

In its origins, the country was an obscure part of the old Holy Roman Empire, becoming a principality within the Empire in 1719 after the territory had been purchased by the Austrian noble family of Liechtenstein. Since 1866 – the end of the German Confederation – Liechtenstein has been free of all political ties, as it avoided being incorporated into Bismarck's German Empire in 1871. In the latter part of the nineteenth century the country had a customs union with Austria, and since 1924 it has had one with Switzerland, whose currency it uses.

The monarchy is the main distinctive feature of the country's political system, differentiating it most clearly from its republican neighbours to the west and east. The latest constitution (of 1921) confirms the constitutional monarchy, but leaves considerable powers with the Prince (*Fürst*) as head of state. In theory the powers of the people were put on a par with those of the Prince, though in practice the then Prince and his next two successors simply did not exercise their full powers. When Prince Hans-Adam II ascended the throne on the death of his father in 1989, however, he insisted on assuming the full powers of the sovereign as laid down in the state constitution, with particular reference to the country's foreign affairs. His attitude caused a considerable controversy, both within the country and abroad.

The people are represented by an elected Diet (*Landtag*), with twenty-five members in one chamber. A government of five members is appointed by the Prince on the nomination of the Diet. The Diet and Government are largely made up of representatives of two major political parties: the Vaterländische Union (Fatherland Union) and the Fortschrittliche Bürgerpartei (Progressive Citizens' Party). Since the elections of 1993, one minor oppositional grouping, the Freie Liste (Free List), has also been represented in the Diet. Each of the two major political parties has a daily newspaper as its organ of publication.

The country's legal system, while fully independent of those of its neighbouring states, nevertheless has strong ties with both of them. Liechtenstein law is an amalgam of Austrian, Swiss, and indigenous statutes. Moreover, the judicial system conventionally includes a small number of Swiss and Austrian judges appointed to the benches of all the major courts.

The education system consists of general schools at all the usual levels, from *Kindergärten* up to the one state-run *Gymnasium*. There are also specialized establishments in the country like the School of Music, the School of Art, the College of Engineering (*Fachhochschule*), and a special school for the handicapped. For other specialized forms of education and training there are arrangements in place with a number of institutions, for instance teacher-training establishments and various vocational colleges, in neighbouring parts (especially in Switzerland). There is no institution of full university status in Liechtenstein.

The state religion is Roman Catholic, but there are also a couple of small Protestant churches. From time immemorial the territory of the present Principality belonged to the Swiss diocese of Chur; in 1997, however – in a move that was highly controversial both inside and outside the state – the Vatican created an Archdiocese of Vaduz, with a native Liechtensteiner as archbishop.

As to the economy, Liechtenstein can be considered a prosperous country. Its manufacturing industry covers a considerable range of products, some of them highly technological in nature. The country has three established general-purpose banks. Because of the favourable taxation laws, coupled with banking secrecy, a large number of 'letter-box' firms are registered in Liechtenstein but do not actually operate there; there are continual efforts on the part of the authorities to tighten up the regulations governing these firms so as to minimize dangers of money laundering and financial scandals.

The country belongs fairly and squarely to the German-speaking area of Europe. Article 6 of the state constitution runs: 'The German language is the national and official language.' The spoken language is the Alemannic dialect of German, which links Liechtenstein particularly to its western neighbour, German-speaking Switzerland (see **German language: Switzerland**), as well as its eastern neighbour, the Austrian province of Vorarlberg. The written language used in Liechtenstein contains many Helveticisms, but also a few remaining Austriacisms.

From a cultural point of view, the Principality is internationally renowned for the Prince's art collection, a small portion of which is accessible to the general public in changing exhibitions in a gallery in Vaduz. A national museum in Vaduz contains various displays illustrating the country's history from prehistoric to modern times. Given its very restricted population, the country has produced a considerable number of graphic artists and a fair number of practising musicians. On the whole, writers have been a relatively rare phenomenon in the population.

Since the 1970s, Liechtenstein has begun to acquire an increasing presence on the world scene. In 1990 the country was admitted to membership of the United Nations, in 1991 to EFTA, and in 1995 to the European Economic Area. Previously it had been content to let Switzerland represent it in most international organizations, but Liechtenstein's moves to join the UNO and the EEA were particularly significant in that Swiss voters had decided *not* to associate themselves with these organizations.

In general terms Liechtenstein enjoys excellent relations with its two neighbour-states. To an outside observer, Austria appears to adopt a benign and largely generous attitude to its tiny neighbour, while the hard-nosed Swiss, with whom Liechtenstein has a considerable number of practical links, tend to expect full financial participation in order to cement neighbourly relations.

Further reading

Meier, R.A. (1993) *Liechtenstein*, World Bibliographical Series, Oxford: Clio Press (an annotated bibliography on various aspects of the country).

Schulamt des Fürstentums Liechtenstein (1993) *Fürst und Volk. Eine liechtensteinische Staatskunde*, Vaduz: Amtlicher Lehrmittelverlag (a full account of the country's development and present-day political institutions; richly illustrated).

GRAHAM MARTIN

Liedermacher

The term *Lied* (song) in a late twentieth century German context connotes less the *Kunstlied* (art song) of Schubert or the eighteenth and nineteenth-century *Volkslied* (folk song) than the songs of contemporary singer-songwriters (*Liedermacher*). Since the early 1960s, German-language *Liedermacher* (male and female) have been an active and visible segment of the popular music scene in the two German states (until unification in 1990), Austria and German-speaking Switzerland.

Some leading *Liedermacher* are Franz Josef **Degenhardt**, Wolf **Biermann**, Konstantin **Wecker**, Reinhard Mey, Georg Danzer and Hannes Wader with dozens more in the succeeding tiers, including variations such as *Rock-Liedermacher* Udo **Lindenberg** and an array of *Liedermacher* groups or bands (e.g. **BAP**, bots, Schmetterlinge, and Biermösl Blosn). Some popular *Liedermacher-innen* have been Kristin Horn, Ina Deter and the feminist group Schneewittchen. The term *Liedermacher* was allegedly coined by Biermann in the early 1970s, replacing such less catchy labels as *Songpoet* and *Politbarde*. In music stores, *Liedermacher* are frequently found today under the label *Deutsche Interpreten*.

Distinctive is the *Liedermacher*'s multiple function as lyricist, composer and accompanist (initially and still commonly on acoustic guitar), and singer of his or her own songs. The label emphasizes the songsmith's craft, in the sense of Brecht's neologism '*Stückeschreiber*' (literally 'writer of plays'), rather than the artistic inspiration of the *Dichter* (author/poet). *Liedermacher* songs are often socially critical texts seeking to heighten public consciousness about societal ills such as prejudice, intolerance, the unreconstructed Nazi past, class injustice and the corrosive effects of post-war affluence. *Liedermacher* are almost invariably linked to various positions in the German left from moderate **SPD** to radical **DKP**.

Influences on *Liedermacher* come largely from abroad, with the Anglo-American folk boom of the 1960s (e.g. Bob Dylan, Joan Baez, Phil Ochs and Tom Paxton) and the post-war French *chanson* (e.g. Georges Brassens) dominant forces. The Chanson Folklore International festivals at Burg Waldeck in the Hunsrück were epochal events from 1964 to 1969 for the identity of German *Liedermacher*, and a surprising number of singer-songwriters who appeared at the festivals are still active. In addition to the outspokenly political *Liedermacher* are those whose songs are more subjective and personal, such as Rainhard Fendrich, Ludwig Hirsch, Herbert Grönemeyer, Georg Danzer and Christof Stählin. The more popular *Liedermacher* tour regularly throughout German-speaking Europe.

A small number of right-wing singer-songwriter groups (e.g. Endsieg, Störkraft, Volkszorn, and Böhse Onkelz) surfaced briefly in the post-unification sobering-up of the early 1990s but faded soon thereafter; their topical songs were militantly xenophobic and gave voice to a distinct frustration particularly among disaffected, unemployed youth (**skinheads**) in the cities and the new German states of the East. Many music stores refused to carry their CDs. Several solidarity concerts by liberal and left-wing counter-groups were also held in the early 1990s, for instance 'Arsch huh, Zang ussenander' (Stand Up and Show Your Teeth) in Cologne on 9 November 1992), in response to violence against asylum-seekers and other foreigners, particularly from Turkey.

See also: protest songs

Further reading

Lassahn, B. (1982) *Dorn im Ohr: Das lustige Liedermacher-Buch*, Zürich: Diogenes (useful cross-sectional anthology of *Liedermacher* songs from Biermann to Wecker).

Nyffeler, M. (1978–1983) *Liedermacher in der Bundesrepublik Deutschland*, Bonn: Inter Nationes (six audio cassettes with songs and transcribed texts, appeared annually, invaluable resource for study of *Liedermacher*).

Rothschild, T. (1980) *Liedermacher: 23 Porträts*, Reinbek bei Hamburg: Rowohlt (biographies and sample songs of *Liedermacher*, some idiosyncratic choices).

RICHARD J. RUNDELL

Lilienthal, Peter

b. 27 November 1929, Berlin

Filmmaker

Lilienthal emigrated to Uruguay with his parents in 1939, returning to Berlin in 1954. He worked in television from 1960. His experiences as a Jewish exile are central to his films, in which outsiders, rebels and uprootedness feature prominently. Most of his films are literary adaptations, including *Malatesta* (1970), his debut feature, and *Head Teacher Hofer* (*Hauptlehrer Hofer*, 1974), the story of a revolutionary teacher at the turn of the century. His most celebrated film, *David* (1979), is a powerful story of a Jewish boy in the Third Reich.

See also: film: FRG

HELEN HUGHES

Lind, Jakov

b. 10 February 1927, Vienna

Writer and dramatist

Lind led a cosmopolitan existence after fleeing from the Nazis in 1938, settling in Palestine for five years; he worked as a sailor, detective, film agent and actor. Lind reflects the horrors of his past in his work. Grotesque visions are conjured up, often expressed in surrealist language, as in *Eine Seele aus Holz* (A Soul of Wood) (1962) and his novel *Eine bessere Welt* (A Better World) (1966). Resident in London since 1954, he began writing in English in the 1970s, translating his novels into German.

MARGARET VALLANCE

Lindenberg, Udo

b. 17 May 1946, Gronau (Westphalia)

Rock musician

The self-proclaimed godfather of German rock, Udo Lindenberg and his Panikorchester first appeared in the early 1970s singing a savvy, hip and uncouth form of rock music. With his trademark fedora and bad-boy persona, Lindenberg sang such hits as 'Alles klar auf der Andrea Doria' (Everything's in Order on the Andrea Doria) and 'Reeperbahn', a homage to the Beatles' time in Hamburg. Lindenberg was one of the first to write rock lyrics in colloquial German, almost single-handedly granting legitimacy (and commercial success) to this genre. His career has spanned more than two decades and his live performances have become legendary for their spectacular excess.

MATTHEW T. GRANT

Linie 1

This hit musical revue by Volker Ludwig (book, lyrics) and Birger Heymann (music) is about a pregnant girl from West Germany travelling through Berlin in search of her rock-star lover (its first night was at the **GRIPS-Theater**, Berlin, on 30 April 1986). The title refers to underground line no. 1 which, prior to unification, connected West Berlin's Zoo Railway Station (the city's principal point of arrival) with Kreuzberg (the centre of its alternative scene). Reinhard **Hauff**'s cinematic interpretation of this vivid portrait of Berlin life through the eyes of a teenager, featuring most of the members of the original cast, was the opening film of the 1988 Berlin Film Festival.

HORST CLAUS

literary criticism: FRG

Literary criticism in the FRG changed completely during the decades following 1945, and became less élitist, as the number of students and university lecturers increased rapidly in the late 1960s. The situation, in general, benefited from the growing variety of literary approaches and from the widespread attention to international theories. Literary criticism thus has become a highly specialized field within the literary culture of the FRG. In the late 1990s, these approaches are differentiated between the various functions of literary analysis and evaluation. Not only critics within the mass media, but also more and more scholars nowadays wonder whether such specialist notions are of any relevance to German cultural and social life. The reason these doubts arise has much to do with the developments in politics and culture since 1945.

When Germany had been liberated from Nazi barbarism and the western Allies began their democratic re-education programmes, the majority of those Germans dealing with culture sought consolation in their cultural past, the era of Goethe especially. Those with a literary education as well as scholars looked for human values within the so-called masterpieces of literature. It was an ideal of humanity rather than history they were interested in when they responded to and paraphrased supposedly autonomous works of art from the late eighteenth century. People thought that literature could help them with the problems of life, and besides deriving comfort from existentialist thought (e.g. that of **Heidegger**) there were several who hushed up their own direct involvement in fascist ideology. (For details see Hermand 1994: 114–23.)

Throughout the 1950s German intellectuals, favouring an idealistic concept of literature, avoided social issues. In 1955 Emil **Staiger**, who, with Benno von Wiese and Wolfgang Kayser, was for many years one of the leading critics, published his influential book, *Die Kunst der Interpretation* (The Art of Interpreting). He stressed the reader's emotional response as crucial to understanding literary texts. It was a similarly restricted idea of hermeneutics that **Gadamer** developed in his most important work, *Truth and Method* (*Wahrheit und Methode*, 1960). At the end of the decade, Gadamer's approach led to a vigorous debate with the sociologist and critical Marxist **Habermas**, when the intellectual atmosphere had changed completely. Formalism, the second major trend in post-war German literary criticism, had been established as early as the late 1940s. Although Kayser's introductory work, *Das sprachliche Kunst-*

werk (The Literary Work of Art) (1948), had concentrated on stylistic issues and on the forms of literature and therefore avoided much of the ontology of the Staiger school, he and his successors also kept to a strictly intrinsic literary approach. Nevertheless, the German formalists in the second half of the 1950s managed to catch up with international theoretical debates by occupying themselves with the older Russian formalists (e.g. Shklovskii and Tynianov), the Prague school (e.g. Mukařovsky, Jakobson and Wellek), and chiefly with the American New Criticism of the 1940s (e.g. Ransom, Brooks, Warren and Jakobson). This methodological broadening was accompanied by an extension of the range of literary subjects; bourgeois modernist works became the formalists' favourite object of study (e.g. those of Baudelaire, Heym, Rilke, Trakl, Benn and Kafka).

Thus a strengthening of liberal tendencies heralded radical changes, which took place when the political climate changed after the mid-1960s. Literary criticism in the FRG began to concern itself with political and social problems; the **Frankfurt School**, which had returned to Germany in 1949, for some years played a leading role in the process of emancipation. **Horkheimer**'s and **Adorno**'s analyses of fascist structures and of modern bourgeois society came eventually to serve as a basis for the critical discussion of German history. **Critical Theory**, further developed by Habermas' communication theory and by Herbert **Marcuse**'s psychoanalytic study *Eros and Civilization* (*Triebstruktur und Gesellschaft*, 1955), established a Marxist perspective in the cultural debates of the FRG that had been inconceivable in the decades before (see Türcke and Bolte 1994: 69–97). Besides those who proclaimed the **'Death of Literature'**, critics committed themselves to neglected traditions within German literature (e.g. Lessing, Jacobin literature, 'Vormärz', naturalism, socialist literature in the Weimar Republic, etc.). Popular fiction and mass media became the subject of scholarly interest, which meant the beginning of **Reception Theory** (in **Jauß**, Weinrich and **Iser**). Several social histories of German literature were planned in the early 1970s; however, they lost their materialist orientation as, in the second half of the decade, sociology itself moved away from Marxist positions.

New Subjectivity then became the paradigm of the later 1970s as the reform movement ran out of steam. Social relevance was no longer the key term for literary criticism; it was replaced by more individual concepts of authenticity and identity. Romantic, *fin de siècle* and female writers in general came into vogue. New, internationally based approaches were added to those of the late 1960s. French post-structuralism (e.g. in Lacan, Barthes, Foucault, Derrida and Kristeva) and American deconstruction (de Man) have been discussed in a broad debate on **postmodernism** since the 1980s. Scepticism about totality and the process of enlightenment, notions of otherness and non-identity, and concepts of intertextuality were absorbed in an abstract, often merely in a technical way by critics who were socially disillusioned.

Nevertheless, a crucial result of the theoretical debates is that no single major discourse dominates literary criticism in the 1990s. Meanwhile feminist and gender studies, as well as the ideas of the American new historicism and of a European history of civilization, have arrived on the scene. Objections are raised to this methodological profusion. In reality, the development can be a process of democratic pluralism as long as there is agreement on the criteria used to evaluate the different approaches. What is necessary is a discussion about their functions and relevance within a highly specialized late capitalist society.

Further reading

Fohrmann, J. and Müller, H. (eds) (1988), *Diskurstheorien und Literaturwissenschaft*, Frankfurt am Main: Suhrkamp.

Hermand, J. (1994), *Geschichte der Germanistik*, Reinbek bei Hamburg: Rowohlt.

Hoy, D.C. and McCarthy, Th. (1994), *Critical Theory*, Oxford, UK and Cambridge, MA: Blackwell.

Kimmich, D., Renner, R.G. and Stiegler, B. (eds) (1996), *Texte zur Literaturtheorie der Gegenwart*, Stuttgart: Philipp Reclam jun.

Türcke, C. and Bolte, G. (1994), *Einführung in die kritische Theorie*, Darmstadt: Wissenschaftliche Buchgesellschaft.

GERT VONHOFF

literary criticism: GDR

In the immediate post-war years there was a consensus between politicians and writers in the Soviet zone of Germany that literature had a crucial part to play in the ideological reorientation of the population. Literary criticism was assigned a dual role: it was to draw the attention of the public to works of literature which contributed to the development of the nation, and to keep a watchful eye out for potentially damaging writing. The liberal policy initially pursued was, however, succeeded in the early 1950s by campaigns against 'formalism' and the prescription of **socialist realism** as defined by Georg **Lukács**. Walter **Ulbricht**'s successful containment of the political challenges of 1953 and 1956 led to a progressive tightening of state control over literature. The liberal Leipzig professor Hans **Mayer** was relieved of his post and left for the West. Criticism was now in practice concerned with clarifying the writer's, and sometimes indeed the critic's own ideological position, rather than with the assessment of literary quality. In a grotesque overestimation of the influence of literature on workers, subject matter, approach and even individual themes were prescribed by cultural functionaries.

From the early 1960s onwards, a new generation of writers asserted the right to subjectivity and began to deal with social problems more frankly. This was reflected in a series of heated public debates on individual publications and the role of literature in society, in which the balance gradually shifted away from ideological and aesthetic prescription. At the same time the study of literature in the GDR began to emerge from sterile subordination to the Marxist–Leninist interpretation of history. Traditionally preoccupied with the material conditions of literary production and embracing a broad conception of culture, it now produced innovative work in literary sociology. In the early 1970s a new 'communicative-functional' theory emphasizing the dialogue between writer and reader was expounded by the academics Dieter **Schlenstedt** and Manfred Naumann, which integrated elements of contemporary **Reception Theory**.

In the uncertain political climate of the late 1970s and 1980s, the views of the ideologically safe critics Annemarie Löffler, Mathilde Dau and Werner Neubert were used in a subtle game of intimidation, and censorship continued right up to 1989. However, Hans and Eva Kaufmann, Sylvia and Dieter Schlenstedt, Ursula Heukenkamp, Bernd Leistner and others sought to mediate between writers and the state by offering system-affirming interpretations and playing down controversial aspects of their work.

See also: censorship: GDR; cultural policy: GDR; publishing: GDR

Further reading

Grant, C. (1995) *Literary Commmunication from Consensus to Rupture. Practice and Theory in Honecker's GDR*, Amsterdam and Atlanta, GA: Rodopi (a detailed study of developments in literary theory and literature as a form of social communication).

Lehmann, J. (1991) 'Vom "gesunden Volksempfinden" zur Utopie: Literaturkritik der DDR im Spannungsfeld von Zensur und Literatur', in H.L. Arnold (ed.), *Literatur in der DDR. Rückblicke*, Munich: edition text + kritik (a short critical account of literary criticism between 1949 and 1989).

Münz-Koenen, I. (1991) 'Die Literaturwissenschaft der DDR in einem institutionalisierten Diskurssystem', *Jahrbuch für Internationale Germanistik* 23, 2: 34–48 (discusses legitimation of the state and opposition in literary studies in the GDR).

AXEL GOODBODY

literature: Austria

As a consequence of the common language and also of the more powerful German publishing industry modern Austrian literature has been closely linked with German literature since WWI in spite of the fact that most Austrians regard their body of literature as a separate entity on the basis of its cultural background and the multi-ethnicity of its origin. According to Claudio Magris' theory of the Hapsburg myth, the bureaucratic traditions, the Emperor as a symbolic supranational link between the various peoples, and the hedonistic way of life that characterized the Austro-Hungarian Empire provided a prevalent influence on twentieth-century Austrian literature and can be seen in the works of many Austrian authors who spent their formative years in the Hapsburg Empire (among them Fritz von Herzmanovsky-Orlando, Hermann **Broch**, George **Saiko**, and Heimito von **Doderer**).

In response to the Nazi takeover of Austrian territory and its rich cultural heritage, one of the characteristics in the aftermath of WWII was the recurring theme of Austrian identity, which was often taken up as a reaction to the horrors of the Third Reich and in order to distance the country from the German influence on Austrian literature of the previous years. However, many authors of Austrian origin or from the area of the former Hapsburg Empire found a new lease of life in Germany and were favourably received there. Nevertheless, the historical background, the traditions, and the identity of these authors remained Austrian, and it was this ambiguous relationship that had a considerable effect on the cultural rivalry and affinity between the two nations.

The legacy of WWII and the effects of the German occupation of Austria from 1938 to 1945 revived an independent Austrian tradition that deliberately established links with the distant past and often neglected the times of the autocratic regime in Austria (1933–8) and the people's involvement in the activities of the Third Reich (1938–45).

The literary scene was torn between those who had left or had been forced to leave the country and those who had not only stayed but had even supported the regime in many cases. Altogether the response of writers to their experience between 1933 and 1945 was varied and often changed as the disastrous events of the Third Reich unfolded.

Many supporters of the former Nazi regime tried to publish after 1945, but remained unsuccessful. However, a number of authors like Paula Grogger (1892–1984) and Karl Heinrich Waggerl (1897–1973), who had welcomed the advent of the Nazis more or less openly in 1938, were able to re-establish their artistic reputation.

After 1945 many authors who had fled Nazi rule did not return to Austria, like Hermann Broch (1886–1951), whose literary works in the tradition of James Joyce were gradually published and had considerable influence on Austrian literature.

The novel *Auto da Fé* (German title *Die Blendung*), written by the émigré Elias **Canetti** (1905–94) from 1930 to 1931, became known to a wider public only when it was republished in the 1960s. Canetti's philosophical work *Crowds and Power* (*Masse und Macht*, 1960) is a sharp analysis of mass phenomena and their relationship with the power structure of society. He was awarded the Nobel Prize for Literature in 1981. The novels of George Saiko (1892–1962), written in the 1930s, were printed after the war and showed similarities with Musil's and Broch's texts. The novels by the artist and author Albert Paris Gütersloh (1887–1973) as well as some of Fritz von Herzmanovsky-Orlando's (1877–1954) grotesque texts evoked symbols and images of Austria's past. Gertrud **Fussenegger** (1912–) represented the realistic tradition of the pre-war period, both in drama and fiction. Before turning to fictional texts Christine **Lavant** (1915–73), who was partly influenced by Rainer Maria Rilke, became well-known for her poetry which focused on life in the country. Fritz **Hochwälder**'s (1911–86) dramas with their traditionally composed structure made him the most successful Austrian playwright of the 1950s and 1960s.

Literary journals like traditionally-minded *Der Turm* (The Tower) (Vienna 1945–8), published by the Österreichische Kulturvereinigung (Austrian Cultural Association), *Plan* (Vienna 1945–8), founded by Otto Basil, which became a springboard for the young generation of writers, and *Das Silberboot* (The Silver Boat) (Salzburg 1946–52) provided publishing facilities for the authors of the day, including émigrés like Erich **Fried** and Elias Canetti. The young emerging writers drew on their own personal experiences of the war, but – unlike in Germany – did not feel responsible for the horrors of the past. Authors such as Franz Kafka (1883–1924), Robert Musil (1880–1942) and Karl Kraus (1874–1936) exerted considerable stylistic influence. Many of these publications ceased to exist in the wake of the currency reform of 1947, but anthologies like *Stimmen der Gegenwart* (Voices of the Present), published between 1951 and 1956 by Hans Weigel (1908–91), still introduced the young generation of authors to the reading public, even though their immediate impact was comparatively minor as the young writers were – at least until 1952 – virtually ignored by the press and the publishing houses. As a consequence a number of authors, among them Ilse **Aichinger** (1921–) and Ingeborg **Bachmann** (1926–73), left for Germany in order to find new audiences and publishers there.

Whereas Hans Weigel was the dominant father figure of the young generation of the late 1940s and early 1950s, it was Heimito von Doderer (1896–1966) who was the artistic focal point with his innovative novels *The Strudlhof Steps* (*Die Strudlhofstiege*, 1951) and *The Demons* (*Die Dämonen*, 1956). Naturalist in his narrative approach, Doderer composed his texts carefully and provided them with plots driven by the individual fate of characters rather than by their intentions. They helped to establish a new tradition independent of distant forerunners and had considerable influence on authors like Herbert Eisenreich (1925–86).

Among the young generation Paul **Celan** (1920–70), the son of German-speaking parents in Romania, wrote elaborate poetry under the impression of the horrors of the Third Reich, as in 'Death Fugue' ('Todesfuge', 1951).

Ilse **Aichinger** (1921–) came to the fore in these years, especially with her remarkable novel *Die größere Hoffnung* (The Greater Hope, published in English as *Herod's Children*) (1948), in which she presents the story of a young Jewish girl in Nazi-occupied Vienna. Her style was far from realistic and thus provided a new insight into the sufferings of the Jewish community.

Ingeborg Bachmann impressed with her early volumes of enigmatic poetry *Die gestundete Zeit* (Borrowed Time) (1953) and *Anrufung des Großen Bären* (Invocation of the Great Bear) (1956) and her radio plays such as *The Good God of Manhattan* (*Der gute Gott von Manhattan*) (1958). Ilse Aichinger and Ingeborg Bachmann are only two of a number of female authors like Christine **Busta** (1915–87), Marlen **Haushofer** (1920–70), and Herta Kräftner (1928–51) who came to the fore in the 1940s and 1950s and who wrote both narrative texts and poetry.

Under the influence of the Art Club, an avant-garde meeting point of artists of all kinds, the Vienna Group (**Wiener Gruppe**) emerged, but

was for a long time unnoticed by the general public. These young writers, such as Hans Carl **Artmann** (1921–), Gerhard Rühm (1930–), Oswald **Wiener** (1935–), Konrad Bayer (1932–64) and Friedrich Achleitner (1930–), devoted their attention to language experiments as well as to the use of the Viennese dialect. Artmann's *Med ana schwoazzn dintn* (In Black Ink) (1958), a collection of poems in dialect, epitomized the vernacular of Vienna. The surreal tendencies of the Vienna Group were partly shared by Ernst **Jandl** (1925–) and Friederike **Mayröcker** (1924–), who achieved considerable critical acclaim for the visual and acoustic effects they created in their concrete poetry and also in their innovative radio plays.

As the social situation of authors in the 1950s gradually improved, the artistic rift between the more traditional wing and the literary avant-garde, with their liking for surrealism, deepened.

The actor and author Helmut **Qualtinger** (1928–87) and his partner Karl Merz (1906–79) established themselves as the leading political satirists with a series of highly critical revues, in which they exposed the attitudes of the decades of the **Economic Miracle**, most importantly in the all too realistic monologue *Herr Karl* (1961), in which the Nazi spirit lingering behind the façade of the petty bourgeois becomes apparent.

In the early 1960s Graz became another focal point of Austrian literature with the emergence of the **Grazer Gruppe**, a free association of young and in many ways innovative authors that centred around the Forum Stadtpark (founded in 1959 by Emil Breisach) and its literary journal *manuskripte* under the editorship of the author Alfred Kolleritsch (1931–). In 1966 a new literary era was ushered in, when Peter **Handke** (1942–), the most prominent member of the Graz Group, turned against literary realism and the **Gruppe 47**, an informal group of mainly German writers. His concern with language and its various uses dominates most of his plays, like *Kaspar* (1967), and narrative texts alike and made him one of the leading figures of contemporary Austrian literature. His translations of Austrian Slovene authors, especially Florian Lipus (1937–), helped to promote this strand of literature. In his novels Gerhard **Roth** (1942–), also a member of the Graz Group, deals with the perception of reality and the attempts by his protagonists to find their own identity. Often provocative, Wolfgang Bauer (1941–) and Peter **Turrini** (1944–) attempted to revive the tradition of the *Volksstück* and aimed to show the limits of human expression through language and – in the case of Turrini – to deliver a strong political message.

Franz **Innerhofer** (1944–) depicts the hardships of life under the authoritarian structures of rural life in his autobiographical account *Schöne Tage* (Beautiful Days) (1974). Reinhard P. Gruber (1947–), and Gert Friedrich **Jonke** (1946–) tried to oppose the cliché-ridden country novel. The prose of Alois Brandstetter (1938–) revolves around typically Austrian settings and exposes the use of language in an ironic way.

Thomas **Bernhard** (1931–89), a solitary figure in the literary scene, became the leading protagonist of Austrian literature in the 1980s. His novels, for instance *Frost* (1963) and *Holzfällen* (Woodcutters) (1984), as well as his extremely critical plays such as *Heldenplatz* (Heroes' Square) (1989), often under the spell of isolation, illness and death, are driven by aggression against and contempt for the society from which he wanted to distance himself. The artistically remarkable texts of Elfriede **Jelinek** (1946–) are equally critical of society, but are also carried by a passionate feminism.

The 1980s saw the continuation of many of the trends that dominated Austrian literature in the 1970s, with a strong tendency towards autobiographical accounts, the criticism of modern Austria, and a return to mythical stories.

In his plays, which are often set in his local Tyrolean environment, Felix Mitterer (1948–) dramatizes the predicaments of outsiders in the harsh world of the Austrian countryside. In a stylistically very interesting way the stories of Norbert **Gstrein** (1961–) take up the problems of human communication and the loss of identity among the rural population. Evelyn **Schlag** (1952–) discusses the self-realization of her protagonists (often artists) in circles where human relationships prove to be difficult. Her texts are especially remarkable for their description of nature. With his novel about the Austro-Hungarian Arctic expedition of 1872 to 1874, titled *Der Schrecken des Eises und der Finsternis* (The Horrors of Ice and Darkness) (1984), Christoph **Ransmayr**

(1954–) revealed his stylistic craftsmanship, and his novel *Die Letzte Welt* (The Last World) (1988) is one example of a series of texts which turned to mythical themes, another example of which is the 'Demeter Trilogy' (1986–90) of Barbara **Frischmuth** (1941–). The strongest attack yet against modern society in the 1990s was made by Werner **Schwab** (1958–94) in provocative plays which are almost limitless in their aggression.

Through the years the themes of Austrian literature, which were still partly influenced by the past, the Hapsburg Empire in particular, and by the immediate experience of the war, have been replaced by a concentration on private problems within the boundaries of families or on personal relationships. Many authors devoted their attention to the problems of self-expression through language, the limitations of language, and language experiments. In addition, many modern works of literature revolve around Austria as a focus of identity and around the way in which Austrians deal with each other and with their immediate historical past.

See also: culture: Austria

Further reading

Daviau, D.G. (ed.) (1988) *Major Figures of Modern Austrian Literature*, Riverside, CA: Ariadne Press.

Markolin, C. (1995) *Modern Austrian Writing: A Study Guide for Austrian Literature, 1945–1990*, New York: Lang.

Schmidt, R. and McGowan, M. (eds) (1993) *From High Priests to Desecrators: Contemporary Austrian Writers*, Sheffield: Sheffield Academic Press.

GEORG HELLMAYR

literature: Switzerland

The literature of German-speaking Switzerland was, in 1945, the only literature being written in German in a country which had been neutral during WWII. Swiss society, the political and social structures of which had survived intact, expected writers to continue to affirm these structures as they had done during the hostilities. Yet, in the second half of the 1940s, some writers, notably

Max **Frisch** (1911–91) and Friedrich **Dürren-matt** (1921–90), ran counter to this expectation by asking why the country had been spared. From the late 1950s onwards, German-Swiss writers increasingly questioned the values of a conservative society proud of its special historical and political traditions. Literary works gradually left restricted concerns behind and presented universal issues in a Swiss setting, as the work of the greatest German-Swiss literary figure, Gottfried Keller (1819–90), had done. Contemporary issues such as the impediments in society to the development of the individual and the relentless encroachment of economic pressures on the individual's freedom, the despoliation of the environment, and social attitudes to sickness and death featured in the writing of the 1970s and 1980s. Writers presented through the model of Switzerland – so envied by others as an idyll of prosperity – the negative consequences of the consumerism and technological advance which affected the rest of the developed world. After the deaths of the internationally acclaimed Dürrenmatt and Frisch at the beginning of the 1990s, established and new writers assured continuity in the literary achievement which has made the contribution from German-speaking Switzerland to literature in German so consistently important since the 1950s.

The context of the literature written in German-speaking Switzerland is determined by two factors, political history and language. First, the German-Swiss are citizens of a state which has political structures and traditions quite distinct from those of Germany, but they are culturally part of German-speaking Europe, in which Germany plays the leading role. Second, the language of everyday spoken communication is German-Swiss **dialect** which, although a form of German, has considerable differences from the standard German in which the German-Swiss conduct much formal and most written communication. Thus the writer Hugo Loetscher (1927–) has claimed of his German-Swiss fellow-countrymen that they are bilingual within the one language. The greater part of the literature from this area of Switzerland is written in standard German, so that a novel containing a conversation between two German-Swiss in Zürich, for example, will not reflect how they would actually speak. It is argued that this imparts to the German-Swiss reader a strong awareness of the artificiality of literary conventions.

The literatures of French, German and Italian Switzerland relate much more to three major European literatures than to each other, but the Swiss political dimension has often caused the themes of German-Swiss literature to be different from those of German literature. On the one hand, the successful reception after 1945 of Dürrenmatt and Frisch was related to Switzerland's neutrality: during WWII, the main Zürich theatre, the Schauspielhaus, where their first plays were performed, had been the only important German-speaking stage not under Nazi domination, and Frisch in particular was able to address themes arising from the recent hostilities in a way quite impossible for a German writer in the immediate post-war period. On the other hand, the dominating theme of post-war German literature, *Vergangenheitsbewältigung* (coming to terms with the past), does not figure in German-Swiss writing of the same period. Frisch's seminal novel *I'm not Stiller* (*Stiller*, 1954) presents Switzerland as a place of stagnation fearful of the future, and Dürrenmatt's play *The Visit* (*Der Besuch der alten Dame*, 1956), is a morality tale about Swiss materialism. Both these works provide for younger writers models of dissent from established views, and mark the beginning of a gradual radicalization of literature in German-speaking Switzerland which was initially very much at odds with the expectations of a conservative public. Frisch's two plays *The Fireraisers* (*Biedermann und die Brandstifter*, 1958) and *Andorra* (1961), which depict blinkered self-satisfaction and moral irresponsibility, were successful throughout the world.

The special nature of Switzerland, for long a literary theme, ceased to offer a focus of interest after *I'm not Stiller*. Writers became interested in their immediate locality as the setting for the specific limitations to the life of the individual. Additionally, an awareness of the importance of the place of work as an often negative influence emerged in literary texts by a new generation of writers who started publishing at the beginning of the 1960s: Hugo Loetscher, Otto F. Walter (1928–94), Jörg **Steiner** (1930–) Adolf **Muschg** (1934–) and Peter **Bichsel** (1935–). Bichsel's *And Really Frau Blum Would Very Much Like to Meet the Milkman* (*Eigentlich möchte Frau Blum den Milchmann* *kennenlernen*) (1964), the best-known text of this period, is a volume of short pieces of prose, small snapshots which present a fragmented reality, and its enormous success well beyond Switzerland revived an interest in a widely used German-Swiss short form and in its earlier practitioners, notably Robert Walser (1878–1956).

A second important volume published in the 1960s, albeit with a resonance restricted to German-speaking Switzerland, was the collection of poems in dialect by Kurt Marti (1921–), *rosa loui* (Rosenloui Glacier) (1967). Literature in dialect had been the vehicle for traditional, highly conservative views of a largely rural Switzerland. In *rosa loui* a range of contemporary concerns were presented in language, which had a great impact because everyone speaks a version of it, and the book became one of the most notable and impressive contributions to a dialect revival from the mid-1960s onwards, which involved both poets and *chansonniers*.

The manifestations in Switzerland of the 1968 **student movement** were very much more restricted than those which convulsed France and West Germany. None the less, the political failure of the movement and the ability of existing power structures to withstand change influenced German-Swiss literature of the 1970s. Much writing challenged the view which cherished Switzerland as an area of unchanging stability, seeing instead the country as a repressive capitalist society intolerant of modes of perception other than its own. Accordingly, the tone of much post-1968 writing is sombre, but its focus, in contrast to more subjective trends in West Germany, remains broadly on the social framework in which the individual lives. Writers who started publishing at this time include Urs Widmer (1938–), Gerhard Meier (1917–) and Christoph Geiser (1949–).

There had been attempts by writers in the 1960s to define the role played by Switzerland in WWII and in particular her relationship to Nazi Germany, for example in the 1964 novel *Die Hinterlassenschaft* (The Legacy) by W.M. Diggelmann (1927–59). The themes of the 1970s also assess the Swiss body politic in the sober post-1968 atmosphere. As *I'm Not Stiller* had viewed Switzerland from prison, Muschg's 1974 novel *Albissers Grund* (Albisser's Reason) views the country from a hospital, and E.Y. Meyer's great 1977 novel *Die Rückfahrt* (The Journey Back) presents the example of Switzerland as a warning of the dangers of western consumerist technology which has arrogantly sundered its links with the knowledge of the past. The theme of death and dying within this society, so envied by others for its unrivalled prosperity, occurs frequently during the 1970s, in novels, plays and autobiographical accounts, the best-known of the latter being Fritz Zorn's *Mars* (1977). Sensationally, this best-seller claimed that there was a causal link between the terminal cancer of its author and the life-denying attitudes of his upper-class Swiss upbringing.

It was not until 1971 that Swiss women were granted the vote at federal level, and the theme of restricted space has been identified in women's writing at the end of the 1970s and the begining of the 1980s, whilst other books by women deal with the social stigma attaching to physical disablement. A large number of women writers came to the fore at this time, for example Erica **Pedretti** (1930–), Maja Beutler (1937–) and Margrit Schriber (1939–). *Vorabend* (The Evening Before) (1975), the depiction by Gertrud **Leutenegger** (1948–) of a Swiss political woman, appeared in the same year as the great feminist cult book in West Germany, *Sheddings* (*Häutungen*) by Verena **Stefan** (born 1947 in Switzerland). By the mid-1980s, with the arrival of Helen Meier (1929–) and Ilma Rakusa (1946–), amongst others, women's writing was making a major contribution to German-Swiss literature.

By the beginning of the 1980s, the works of many writers were reflecting a concern with the protection of the individual against the incursion of the forces of modern society and so, increasingly, the themes of German-Swiss literature were coming to represent, within the framework of traditional German-Swiss literary motifs, wider global issues. For example, the motif of the Swiss house, traditionally the symbol of physical protection and spiritual values, became, in a number of works since about 1970, the vehicle for the expression of the preoccupations of a world beset by industrial retrenchment, ecological impoverishment and existential unease, for instance in Frisch's *Man in the Holocene* (*Der Mensch erscheint im Holozän*, 1979), and O.F. Walter's *Zeit des Fasans* (Time of the

Pheasant) (1988). The manner in which traditional German-Swiss literary forms were being used by writers to show change was a feature of writing in the 1970s and 1980s, at a time when literary themes were becoming much less influenced by national ethos. For example, the highly successful 1983 novel *Cow* (*Blösch*) by Beat Sterchi (1949–), which took the form of the *Bauernroman* (novel of farming life), does not praise the values of country life, but instead tells the story of a Spanish foreign worker quitting Switzerland, the place of mechanized farming and prosperity, because of the existential cost to the individual.

Towards the end of the period, Martin R. Dean's novel *Der Mann ohne Licht* (The Man without Light) (1988) is representative of a move forwards in that it portrays an unproblematic break with outmoded forms, passing in review the attitudes of the older and the contemporary generation and imparting a sense of emancipation and an awareness of intellectual and emotional choice about future courses of action. It was a suitable start to the 1990s since, in one sense, an era had come to a close with the deaths of Dürrenmatt and Frisch, in 1990 and 1991 respectively. Continuity was assured, however, by those who had become the older generation by then, notably by Adolf Muschg with his epic novel on the Parsifal theme, *Der rote Ritter* (The Red Knight) (1993), and by Peter Bichsel with his collection of short pieces *Zur Stadt Paris* (At the City of Paris) (1993). Additionally, a new generation was having success with first works: Nicole Müller (1962–) with a description of a broken relationship between two women *Denn das ist das Schreckliche an der Liebe* (For That Is What Is Terrible About Love) (1992), and Peter Weber (1968–) with his successful *Der Wettermacher* (The Weather Maker) (1993), a novel set in his native East Switzerland. This continuity was recognized by the wider German-speaking world: Max Frisch won the premier German literary award, the *Büchner* Prize, in 1958, and Adolf Muschg won it in 1994.

See also: cultural policy and institutions: Switzerland; culture: Switzerland

Further reading

Böhler, M. (1989) 'Swiss Literary Culture since 1945: Productive Antagonisms and Conflicting Identities', *German Quarterly* 62: 293–307 (the best essay in English on the complex situation of the German-Swiss writer).

Burkhard, M. (1981) 'Gauging Existential Space: The Emergence of Women Writers in Switzerland', *World Literature Today* 55: 607–12 (a key essay).

Butler, M. and Pender, M. (eds) (1991) *Rejection and Emancipation: Writing in German-Speaking Switzerland 1945–1991*, Oxford: Berg (two introductory essays on political and literary trends, followed by essays on ten writers).

Flood, J. (ed.) (1985) *Modern Swiss Literature – Unity and Diversity*, London: Wolff (nine essays on aspects of all the literatures of Switzerland).

Pezold, K. (ed.) (1991) *Geschichte der deutschsprachigen Schweizer Literatur im 20. Jahrhundert*, Berlin: Volk und Wissen (the standard work of reference for all authors and trends of the period).

Waidson, H.M. (1984) *Anthology of Modern Swiss Literature*, London: Wolff (a translated selection from the literatures of Switzerland).

MALCOLM PENDER

Literaturstreit

The '*deutsch–deutscher Literaturstreit*' (German–German literary conflict) broke out during the summer of 1990 as the Federal Republic and the ex-GDR moved rapidly towards unification. It was sparked off by the appearance of Christa **Wolf**'s text *What Remains* (*Was bleibt*), originally written in 1979 as an account of the author's reactions to finding herself under surveillance by the **Stasi** in the aftermath of the **Biermann Affair**, but only released for publication in a revised version after the opening of the Berlin Wall in 1989, when the GDR's critical intellectuals saw an opportunity for a 'renewal of socialism' within the frontiers of their own state. By the time it was published, in June 1990, their hopes had been swept aside and replaced by profound uncertainty regarding their role in a unified Germany.

Some West German critics – notably Ulrich Greiner in *Die Zeit* and Frank Schirrmacher in the *Frankfurter Allgemeine Zeitung* – read Wolf's text as a belated attempt to curry favour by presenting herself as a victim of the SED regime, and responded by arguing that, despite her international literary reputation, she was just as much a privileged 'state poet' as authors who had consistently supported the party line. While leading West German intellectuals like Walter **Jens** and Günter **Grass** sprang to Wolf's defence, insisting on a differentiated assessment both of the integrity and of the creative achievements of GDR authors, it became clear that some of her critics regarded this battle only as the first in a concerted campaign against all forms of '*Gesinnungsästhetik*' (politically tainted aesthetics), directed at mainstream works of West German literature as well. When established authors like Hans-Magnus **Enzensberger**, Martin **Walser** and Botho **Strauß** appeared to support this right-wing realignment of German cultural life, fears were aroused that the spirit of the 1970s *Tendenzwende* was being enshrined as the orthodoxy of the new Germany.

This sense of a concerted campaign at odds with the pluralistic credentials of the Federal Republic has returned at regular intervals through the 1990s, in relation to the general issue of the involvement of GDR intellectuals with the Stasi, the practicalities of amalgamating various parallel East–West literary institutions, and the integrity of other ex-GDR authors such as Stefan **Heym** (when he was running for election to the Bundestag in 1994) and Stephan **Hermlin** (the subject of a sweepingly critical monograph by Karl Corino in 1996). It provides a reminder of how far the process of cultural unification still has to run.

Further reading

Deiritz, K. and Krauss, H. (eds) (1991) *Der deutsch-deutsche Literaturstreit*, Hamburg: Luchterhand (full documentation of the original debate).

Durrani, O., Good, C. and Hilliard, K. (eds) (1995) *The New Germany: Literature and Society Since Unification*, Sheffield: Sheffield Academic Press.

Goodbody, A. and Tate, D. (eds) (1992) *Geist und Macht: Writers and the State in the GDR*, German Monitor 29, Amsterdam: Rodopi.

Hahn, H.-J. (ed.) (1995) *Germany in the 1990s*, German Monitor 34, Amsterdam: Rodopi (all three volumes deal extensively with post-'Wende' intellectual conflicts).

Wolf, C. (1993) *What Remains and Other Stories*, London: Virago.

DENNIS TATE

Loest, Erich

b. 24 February 1926, Mittweida (Saxony)

Novelist

Loest is a realist whose work is often close to his own experience. Although imprisoned in 1957 and subject to Stasi surveillance, described in *Die Stasi war mein Eckermann* (The Stasi Was My Eckermann) (1991), Loest managed, after a series of detective stories, to publish his critical portrayal of GDR society *Es geht seinen Gang oder Mühen in unserer Ebene* (Things Go Along or Difficulties on our Plain) in 1978 in limited editions. He moved to the West in 1981, but continuing concern with eastern themes is visible in his works published since unification. Loest became vice-chairman of the **Verband deutscher Schriftsteller** in 1984, and is currently chairman.

STUART PARKES

Löwith, Karl

b. 9 January 1897, Munich; d. 25 May 1973, Heidelberg

Philosopher

Löwith's early works, especially *The Individual as Fellow Man* (*Das Individuum in der Rolle des Mitmenschen*, 1928), constitute a critique of Heideggerian ontology, to which they oppose a relational theory of communication – an antecedent of modern dialogism. Löwith is famous for his work on historicism, especially *Meaning in History* (initially in English, 1949), which he denounces as secular eschatology. Renowned also are his theory of secularization, and his works on the legacy of Hegel, in which he explains Marx, Nietzsche and

Kierkegaard within the context of Hegel reception. His thought shows an affinity with Jacob Burckhardt, whose stoical, anti-progessivist sense of historical being mirrors his own.

CHRIS THORNHILL

Lorenc, Kito

b. 4 March 1938, Schleife (Saxony)

Poet and Dramatist

Under the influence of Johannes **Bobrowski**, Lorenc developed into the most influential Sorbian poet of his generation. He has published poetry in both German and Sorbian, the most representative of which was collected in *Wortland. Gedichte aus zwanzig Jahren* (Word Land. Poems from Twenty Years) (1984). He is also known as a translator of poetry, especially from Slav languages. His anthology of Sorbian literature in a bilingual edition, *Sorbisches Lesebuch* (Sorbian Reader) (1981), provides the most comprehensive survey of Sorbian literature available.

See also: minorities, non-German

PETER BARKER

Lorenz, Konrad

b. 7 November 1903, Vienna; d. 27 February 1989, Vienna

Zoologist, ethologist and philosopher

Lorenz shared the Nobel Prize for Medicine in 1973 for his work in ethology, but his attempts to apply biological theory to a wide range of social and cultural questions are intensely controversial. In *On Aggression* (*Das sogennante Böse*), which appeared in English translation in 1966, he argued, largely on the basis of analogies with animals, that much of human aggressive behaviour is instinctive. His final book, The *Waning of Humaneness* (*Die acht Todsünden der zivilisierten Welt*), published in 1983, presented a sombre picture of humanity threatened by cultural and genetic decline.

Further reading

Deichmann, U. (1996). *Biologists under Hitler,* trans. T. Dunlap, Cambridge, MA: Harvard University Press (contains important archival research into Lorenz's membership and activity in the Nazi party and how this affected his theories).

BORIA SAX

Loriot

b. 12 November 1923, Brandenburg

Cartoonist, writer, actor and director (real name Bernhard Victor ('Vicco') Christoph-Karl von Bülow)

After studying painting and graphics at the Academy of Arts in Hamburg in the late 1940s, Loriot (who adopted as his pseudonym the French word for the 'oriole' in his family's coat of arms) worked as a cartoonist and freelance artist with **Stern** and **Quick** magazines. In 1967 he joined **ZDF** television as an author and moderator of the satirical series *Cartoon* and *Loriots Telekabinett*. His humour derives especially from the earnestness with which his characters encounter the pitfalls of the everyday. A highly successful writer, he is known in German-speaking countries for his sophisticated play with language and situations from real life, as well as his invention of the characters Wum and Wendelin (1977). Since 1985 he has also gained fame as a theatre and film director, actor and opera producer. Elected to the Bavarian Academy of Fine Arts in 1993, he has received many awards for his work.

MAGDA MUELLER

Love Parade

The Love Parade is the largest gathering of the German Techno movement held annually in Berlin. Officially, the event has the status of a political demonstration; the seriousness of its political ambitions, however, may be questioned. The first Love Parade (1989) was attended by a few hundred young people dancing 'for peace, fun, and pancakes' (*Für Friede, Freude, Eierkuchen*) through the centre of Berlin behind lorries playing Techno music. The event has since evolved into a mass gathering of over a million dancers thus presenting considerable problems for the Berlin authorities. Nevertheless, the Love Parade is widely supported as a major attraction and economic factor.

ANNETTE BLÜHDORN

LPG

LPGs (in full Landwirtschaftliche Produktionsgenossenschaften) were agricultural co-operatives created after the Second Party Conference in July 1952 which decreed the 'planned building of socialism' in the GDR. By 1960 about 85 percent of land was farmed by co-operatives. Initially only the arable land was farmed collectively, but from 1959 there was strong pressure to bring all the land and equipment into collective ownership. Although opposed by the larger farmers, and now much criticized for their inefficient and un-ecological farming methods, the LPGs brought about an unprecedented improvement in material living conditions for much of the rural population. In theory rights of possession remained intact, which caused problems when many LPGs were dissolved after unification.

PETER BARKER

Luchterhand Verlag

Founded in 1924 by Hermann Luchterhand, the firm was one of the first to publish legal and offical sets in loose-leaf form. The firm begin publishing literature in 1955 and has become one of Germany's most influential publishers of *belles lettres*. Peter **Bichsel**, Günter **Grass**, Peter **Härtling**, Anna **Seghers**, Gabriele **Wohmann** and Christa **Wolf** number among its authors. When the Dutch publishing group Kluwer acquired the house in 1987, former Luchterhand authors protested strongly. The literary section was then sold to Arche Verlag (Zürich). Literary publishing has continued under the name 'Luchterhand

Literaturverlag', which issues *belles lettres* and literary criticism.

JOHN B. RUTLEDGE

Luckhardt, Hans and Wassili

Hans: b. 16 June 1890, Berlin; d. 12 October 1954, Bad Wiessee

Wassili: b. 22 July 1889, Berlin; d. 2 December 1972, West Berlin

Architects

Both brothers were important representatives of expressionist architecture and members of the Novembergruppe and the Gläserne Kette. In 1921 they set up a practice in Berlin which Alfons Anker was to join in 1924. During the Nazi regime their building activity deteriorated, only to pick up again in 1951 with the Berlin Pavilion for the Constructa in Hanover. The Landesversorgungsamt Bayern in Munich (1954–7, sadly pulled down in 1989) was the last major project they planned together.

After Hans' death, Wassili built the Cottbuser Tor apartment building in Berlin (1956), a widely copied scheme with the balconies set into the façade to form loggias. Later important works include university buildings in Berlin.

MARTIN KUDLEK

Lübbe, Hermann

b. 31 December 1926, Aurich (Ostfriesland)

Philosopher

Together with Odo Marquard and other former pupils of Joachim Ritter, Hermann Lübbe belongs to the Ritter School of German philosophy, which, among other things, stresses the finitude of man, warns against the dreams of philosophical and political do-gooders, and embraces modern capitalist society. His main themes are the dynamics of social change; the way history and historiography contribute to individual and social identity; the inadequacy of **Critical Theory** with its oscillation between the equally misguided extremes of cultural pessimism and utopianism; the importance of religion; and the undesirability of a European superstate.

HENK de BERG

Luhmann, Niklas

b. 8 December 1927, Lüneburg; d. 6 November 1998, Orlinghausen

Sociologist

Niklas Luhmann was one of the most influential social theorists of recent decades. Central to Luhmann's thinking is his sociological systems theory, which views the various functional areas of society (law, politics, economics, science, art, etc.) as self-referential or 'autopoietic' systems, i.e. as processes with their own internal dynamics that cannot be causally influenced. Among his numerous publications the books *Social Systems* (*Soziale Systeme*, 1984) and *Ecological Communication* (*Ökologische Kommunikation*, 1986) gained particular prominence.

Further reading

de Berg, H. (1995) 'Select Annotated Bibliography to Luhmann's Systems Theory and Its Applications in Literary Studies', *Poetics Today* 16 (4): 737–41.

HENK de BERG

Lukács, Georg

b. 13 April 1885, Budapest; d. 4 June 1971, Budapest

Cultural theorist

During his years of exile from the Third Reich, which he spent in the Soviet Union in close contact with the leadership of the **KPD**, Lukács consolidated the position he had begun to establish in the Berlin of the early 1930s as German communism's dominant cultural theorist. Although scornful of the dogmatic narrowness with which the principles of **socialist realism** had been expounded at the

Soviet Writers' Congress of 1934, Lukács was only marginally less authoritarian in his theoretical writings of the 1933–45 period. He insisted that contemporary German writers should build on the cultural heritage of the 'progressive' bourgeois literature of the eighteenth and nineteenth centuries, as exemplified by the classical *Entwicklungsroman* and the fictional realism of Balzac or Tolstoy. When practising German writers-in-exile such as Bertolt **Brecht** or Anna **Seghers** argued the case for different literary traditions or for adapting the techniques of modernism, their views were brusquely rejected. Even though Lukács chose to return home to Hungary, his programmatic essays – such as *Fortschritt und Reaktion in der deutschen Literatur* (Progress and Reaction in German Literature) (1945) – were being widely promoted in East Germany within months of the end of the war as the key to the development of a new anti-fascist culture, and the clarity of his line of argument was to prove inspirational to many young readers, at least in the short term.

The years between 1945 and the abortive Hungarian uprising of 1956 are full of contradictions as far as Lukács' impact on GDR culture is concerned. In Hungary his political views on democratizing society proved unacceptably 'revisionist' as the Cold War intensified, and his cultural theories were discredited. In the GDR, however, his books continued to dominate literary debate and establishment figures like Johannes R. **Becher**, the author who became the state's first Minister of Culture, still saw him as a key figure in the GDR's pursuit of a distinctive cultural identity. Only after 1956, when Lukács narrowly avoided execution for his role in the uprising, did the GDR agree to toe the Soviet line and ban his work, although its continuing influence on official cultural policy remained obvious. This ban meant, however, that Lukács' more differentiated later volumes *The Meaning of Contemporary Realism* (*Wider den mißverstandenen Realismus*, 1963) and *Solzhenitsyn* (1970) did not reach a GDR readership.

After his death a cautious debate was permitted on the true extent of his importance to GDR literature, but by then the issue was largely historical, since a plurality of literary approaches to his elusive goal of realism was now being tolerated. His reputation suffered a further blow with the publication of *Die Säuberung* (The Purge) (ed. Reinhard Müller, 1991), which exposes the involvement of the exile KPD leadership, including Lukács, in the Stalinist purges of 1936–7.

See also: prose fiction: GDR

Further reading

Löwy, M. (1979), *Georg Lukács: From Romanticism to Bolshevism*, London: New Left Books (good account of his ideological development).

DENNIS TATE

Luxembourg

While standard German remains constitutionally one of the official languages of the Grand Duchy of Luxembourg, much of its prestige has been surrendered to the two other official languages, French and *Lëtzebuergesch*, the use of standard German now being restricted largely to the written form, where it can be found in newspapers and a large number of fictional and non-fictional texts.

Lëtzebuergesch, the national language, is genetically a West Moselle Franconian dialect of German. Its isolation from the mainstream of German culture for many centuries has produced a language sufficiently remote from standard German as to be unintelligible to speakers of that language, while standard German itself becomes known to Luxembourgers only through its use in school. Colloquial varieties of German do not exist in Luxembourg, their place being taken by *Lëtzebuergesch*, which has its own sub-varieties, the main variety (*koine*) being that of the Alzette river valley.

The presence of three languages in Luxembourg has inevitably led to a trilingual literary tradition. While Luxembourg literature written in French began with Félix Thyes (1830–55), the first poet of international rank was Marcel Noppeney (1877–1966). Other French-language authors include Paul Palgen (1883–1966), Nicolas Ries (1876–1941), Willy Gilson (1891–1974), Nicolas Konert (1891–1977), 'Edmond' Dune (Hermann Dune, 1914–89) and Albert Borschette (1920–).

French has since the nineteenth century been the intellectual, administrative and political language of the country, replacing German as the medium of instruction in senior schools (hence the use of German in newspapers to reach a wider audience than might come from such schools alone). Because of the high numbers of foreign nationals in Luxembourg (at the 1991 census the resident population of 384,634 comprised 70.5 percent Luxembourgers, 10.2 percent Portuguese, 4.96 percent Italians, 3.43 percent French, 2.67 percent Belgians, 2.31 percent Germans, 0.87 percent Dutch, 0.83 percent British, 0.65 percent Spaniards and 3.58 percent others), French is often used as the first language of spoken contact. French habits have also penetrated the Grand Duchy in other ways. The cuisine, for example, is largely French, and was brought back by generations of young Luxembourg women who entered service in households in Lorraine in order to improve their French.

At the spoken level, standard German has little currency outside schools, where it is used as a vehicle language introduced in lower classes in order to teach basic literacy. Its use in church services, which was formerly widespread, is now receding.

Luxembourg literature written in standard German began with Nikolaus Welter (1871–1951) and Batty Weber (1860–1940). Other authors include Jean-Pierre Erpelding (1884–1974), Hermann Berg (Wilhelm Weis, 1885–1970), Nikolaus Hein (1889–1969), Paul Henkes (1898–1985), Albert Hoefler (1899–1950), Jean-Pierre Decker (1901–72), Joseph Funck (1901–78), Nicolas Heinen (1906–88), Gregor Stein (Pierre Grégoire, 1907–91), Christophe Klausener (Willy Schmit, 1917–82), Henri Blaise (1924–), Anise Koltz (1928–) and Roger Manderscheid (1933–).

Among Luxembourg German-language authors published in Germany perhaps the best-known is Alex Weicker (1894–1986), whose novel *Fetzen* (Tatters) (1921) brought Luxembourg to the forefront of the German literary scene.

In the field of fine art, Joseph Kutter (1894–1941), the Grand Duchy's most acclaimed artist, studied in Munich and came strongly under the influence of German expressionism. Kutter's masterpiece 'Man with Injured Finger' (1930) now hangs in the Musée National d'Art Modern, Paris.

The rise of *Lëtzebuergesch* as the premier national language can be traced back to the country's independence (1839), and particularly to the threat of German annexation during the Franco-Prussian War (1870–1). The German occupation of Luxembourg during WWI reinforced the feeling of national union, while the German occupation and attempted Nazification of Luxembourg between May 1940 and September 1944, together with the subsequent destruction of the northern section of the country in the Battle of the Bulge (December 1944 to March 1945), made *Lëtzebuergesch* the symbol of resistance and the chief pillar of national identity.

At the end of WWII, *Lëtzebuergesch*, which as late as 1938 had been ruled out as a parliamentary language, became the *de facto* spoken language of the Chamber of Deputies and all administration. However, the use of *Lëtzebuergesch* in written form, which had been restricted to plays and recitational works produced by those able to devise and use spelling systems for the language, proved to be problematic. None the less, one daily newspaper, *D'Union* (The Union), which had begun as a resistance monthly in 1944, was published entirely in *Lëtzebuergesch*. Soon this proved too complicated for typesetters and translators, and caused the newspaper to resort increasingly, and then completely (in 1948), to German.

Little headway was therefore made in promoting written forms of *Lëtzebuergesch*, although the tradition of plays, poems and short stories begun by Michel Lentz (1820–93), Dicks (Edmond de la Fontaine, 1832–91), Michel Rodange (1827–76) and Caspar Mathias Spoo (1837–1914) was continued and expanded by Joseph Keup (1891–1981), Jacques Kintzele (1874–1965), and 'Tit' Schroeder (Theodor Schroeder, 1911–86). In speech, however, *Lëtzebuergesch* became increasingly dominant, reinforced by regular radio broadcasting (1959) and television programmes (1968), as well as theatrical performances, and recordings of popular songs. In the meantime, easy access to spoken standard German from German television transmitters, and a subsequent flood of loanwords into *Lëtzebuergesch*, came in the early 1970s to be seen by language activists as a corrosive influence, which might in the end cause *Lëtzebuergesch* to be overwhelmed and assume the status of a German dialect instead of a national language. Consequently in 1971 a language support group, Actioun Lëtzebuergesch (Operation Lëtzebuergesch), was set up, and in addition to publishing its own journal, *Eis Sprooch* (Our Language) (1971–93), also had active members who produced dictionaries from German (1974), French (1980 and 1988), Portuguese (1980), and English (1982) into *Lëtzebuergesch*, with a short *Lëtzebuergesch*-to-French dictionary appearing in 1989. In 1975 AL was also instrumental in causing the orthography of the *Luxemburger Wörterbuch* to be adopted by the Luxembourg Government as official.

Pressure from Actioun Lëtzebuergesch, the former Resistance groups, and those who had been forced into military service for the Nazis (*Enrôlés de force*), arose in 1980 to ensure that *Lëtzebuergesch* gained constitutional recognition as the national language. This came in 1984, when the constitution was revised to allow the official use of *Lëtzebuergesch* 'as far as possible' in spoken and written form by civil servants. This has since led to an upsurge in the use of *Lëtzebuergesch* for newspaper announcements, advertisements, street furniture, supermarket items, headings of articles written in German, etc, and has generally made Luxembourgers more conscious of the rising status of their own language. The number of radio stations broadcasting *Lëtzebuergesch* has also increased significantly since 1991, when new legislation was introduced. The domains of use for *Lëtzebuergesch* are therefore expanding within the Grand Duchy, and there is strong evidence to suggest that this will continue to be the case.

Further reading

Newcomer, J. (1984) *The Grand Duchy of Luxembourg. The Evolution of Nationhood 963 A.D. to 1983*, New York and London: Lanham.

Newton, G. (ed.) (1996) *Luxembourg and Lëtzebuergesch: Languages and Communication at the Crossroads of Europe*, Oxford: Oxford University Press.

Tockert, J., Bruch, R., Palgen, H., Comes, I., Hess, J., Ludovicy, E. and Meyers, J. (eds) (1950–77) *Luxemburger Wörterbuch*, 5 vols, Luxembourg: Grand-Ducal Institute; reprinted as *Lëtzebuerger Dixionär*, 2 vols, Luxembourg: Kraus, 1995.

GERALD NEWTON

M

Maaz, Hans-Joachim

b. 17 February 1943, Niedereinsiedel
(now Dolní Poustevna, Czech Republic)

Psychiatrist and psychotherapist

Since 1980 Maaz has been head physician at a Protestant clinic for psychotherapy and psychosomatic medicine in Halle. Fighting for psychoanalytic and body-oriented forms of therapy, he touched upon the taboos of the East German state. He is widely known for his best-selling book *Behind the Wall: the Inner Life of Communist Germany* (*Der Gefühlsstau: Ein Psychogramm der DDR*) of 1990, in which he examines a specific East German sociopsychological disposition and traces its remnants in the unified Germany.

MARGRIT FRÖLICH

Mack, Heinz

b. 8 March 1931, Lollar (Hessen)

Environmental artist

Along with Otto **Piene**, Mack was a founder member of the **Zero Group**. Initially an abstract painter, he abandoned painting in the 1950s in favour of a more studied exploration of the effects of movement and light. 'Light Reliefs' and 'Light Sculptures' led in the 1960s to experiments with vibrating light towers in desert landscapes. He produces theatre-sets, sculptures, and air, light and water constructions. He has had countless public art commissions in Germany, such as the 1992 'Piazetta' square for the Neue Deutsche Museen.

ALEX COOKE

'Made in Germany'

On 23 August 1987, the commercial designation of origin 'Made in Germany' was 100 years old. Extensive FRG media coverage of the centenary, including explicit references in West German **advertising**, revealed the importance of the national trade mark as a source of German self-esteem in a decade punctuated otherwise by a number of sombre fortieth anniversaries relating to the Third Reich and WWII. The centenary of 'Made in Germany' symbolized the resilience of German industry and the continuity of its achievement, which in 1986 culminated in the FRG becoming the world's leading exporter.

'Made in Germany' was brought into being in 1887 by the then world export champion Great Britain as a protectionist measure aimed at preventing unscrupulous German companies from plagiarizing or adapting British trade marks and hallmarks as a means of overcoming Germany's reputation for producing 'cheap and nasty' products. But forcing German firms to identify the provenance of German-made products which might otherwise be mistaken for British ones only served to enhance the image of things 'Made in Germany'. The year 1887 marks the point at which Germany began to increase its share of world exports and Britain's share began its inexorable decline.

After 1949, the **Economic Miracle** which took place in the FRG led West Germans to regard themselves as the true heirs and custodians of the 'Made in Germany' tradition, though many FRG products bore the label 'Made in West Germany' to distinguish them from goods originating in the GDR. This practice continued not only after the GDR abandoned the 'Made in Germany' mark in the late 1970s in favour of 'Made in GDR', but also to a significant extent in the period immediately following German **unification**. This time, the companies concerned were worried that products from the new *Länder* would dilute the good image of 'Made in Germany'. 'Made in Germany' was seen by others as the key to unifying all German workers under one standard of quality, and it was adopted as a publicity gimmick by the **Treuhand**. Some commentators argue that the 'Made in Germany' concept is no longer relevant in the era of globalization, its place having been taken by brand-related selling-points such as 'Made by **Mercedes**'. But 'Made in Germany' remains a powerful and extensively deployed marketing instrument.

See also: Trabant; *Vergangenheitsbewältigung*; Volkswagen

Further reading

Head, D. (1992) *'Made in Germany': The Corporate Identity of a Nation*, London, Sydney, Auckland: Hodder & Stoughton (examines the origins of the label and its importance both to German firms and to German national identity).

—— (1995) '"Made in Germany" in the 1990s', *German Monitor* 34: 171–8 (discusses the progress of 'Made in Germany' in the context of German unification and the Single European Market).

James, H. (1989) *A German Identity*, London: Weidenfeld & Nicolson (discusses modern Germany's preoccupation with economic success and identifies the importance of industrial products for Germany's national culture).

DAVID HEAD

Maetzig, Kurt

b. 25 January 1911, Berlin

Filmmaker

The son of the owner of a film laboratory, Maetzig grew up in a film-making environment, studied in Paris and Munich (gaining a Ph.D. in 1935), and joined the illegal Communist Party in 1944. As a founder-member of **DEFA** he initiated the weekly GDR newsreel *Der Augenzeuge* (*The Eyewitness*) in 1946 before turning to directing feature films. He was amongst those who set up the GDR's Film School in Babelsberg (1954). An influential, politically committed filmmaker, Maetzig sees the strength and responsibility of film in its ability to uncover social relationships and reveal the distribution of power.

See also: Eleventh Plenum; film: GDR

HORST CLAUS

magazines

Since the eighteenth century magazines have been in existence in Germany and their distribution has steadily increased. Generally, they can be divided into four distinct groups: (1) entertainment, general information and leisure magazines, (2) special interest magazines, (3) vocation-specific magazines, and (4) advertisement magazines. Of these, the first group has the greatest social impact, with a combined circulation of *c*.120 million per issue. Most of them are weeklies or monthlies.

The most important political weeklies are *Der Spiegel*, **Stern** and **Focus**. *Spiegel* is the oldest, having been founded in 1947 by Rudolf **Augstein**. It can reasonably claim to have influenced political events in the FRG as no other magazine has. At the time of its inception, it was based on the American *Time* magazine, but *Spiegel* adopted a much more leftist/Social Democrat stance.

The next group is general leisure magazines, with **Quick**, *Neue Revue*, *Das Goldene Blatt*, *Neue Post* and **Bunte** leading the way. Their subject matter includes jet-set gossip, reports on international royalty, human interest stories and advice columns.

In the case of *Quick* and *Neue Revue*, nudity is added in order to boost their circulation.

Yet another group is that of women's magazines. Of those, the most prominent are *Brigitte, Tina, Bella* and various German editions of international women's magazines such as *Elle*. A growing market is that of men's magazines. While German versions of *Playboy* and *Penthouse* have existed for decades, as have sports magazines (*Kicker*) and motoring magazines (*Auto Zeitung*), other, newer magazines such as the German version of *Men's Health* and men's lifestyle magazines were launched only recently.

Political, women's and lifestyle magazines have been available for a long time. The creation of another group, though, had to do with the advent of television. Germany's oldest television programme weekly, *Hör Zu*, was also the first major magazine to appear in Germany after the war. It came out in 1946, although, with no television available yet, more as a lifestyle and radio magazine. Other television guides have followed, such as *TV Hören und Sehen* and, more recently, *TV Movie* and *TV Spielfilm*, and together they have some of the biggest circulations in the market.

The 1980s was the decade of the youth or yuppie lifestyle magazine. Up until then, the youth market had been catered for by *Bravo*, but it became increasingly old-fashioned. Following the revolutionary lay-out style Neville Brody had introduced in the UK in *The Face*, two Austro-German magazines, *Wiener* and *Tempo*, cornered the market with witty reporting, irreverent attitudes and controversial stories and photographs. Both did much to rejuvenate the up till then somewhat staid German-language market. However, they did not last; with more competition from other magazines and the death of yuppiedom at the end of the 1980s, they lost much of their readership and subsequently ceased publication.

Another event which has re-shaped the German magazine market was German unification. Suddenly a whole new unknown market segment of 16 million people had appeared. And while German publishing houses were quick to buy old GDR publishing ventures, many of them did not survive capitalism. Starting in 1992–3, a backlash against western publications made the situation even more complex. With almost 1,000 titles available, changes in the structure of the market, and also in the magazines themselves, are occurring with increasing rapidity.

See also: Burda; Gruner & Jahr; mass media: FRG; *Super-Illu*

Further reading

Faulstich, W. (ed.) (1994) *Grundwissen Medien*, Munich: Fink (basic facts and bibliographies on the German media).

Humphreys, P. (1994) *Media and Media Policy in Germany. The Press and Broadcasting since 1945*, 2nd edn, Oxford: Berg (the most exhaustive overview of German media in English).

Meyn, H. (1996) *Massenmedien in der Bundesrepublik Deutschland*, Berlin: Volker Spiess (an overview of recent developments in German mass media).

HOLGER BRIEL

Maizière, Lothar de

b. 2 March 1940, Nordhausen

Lawyer and politician; GDR Prime Minister, March–October 1990

Originally a musician in the GDR, de Maizière changed to law for health reasons and from 1976 was a lawyer in Berlin. In November 1989 he became leader of the CDU in the GDR, and from November 1989 to March 1990 deputy chairman of the Council of Ministers (*Ministerrat*). With the electoral success of the conservative Alliance for Germany in the first free elections to the People's Chamber in March 1990, he succeeded Hans **Modrow** as Prime Minister. In October 1990 he became a deputy leader of the all-German CDU, but had to relinquish this post in September 1991 after allegations that he had acted as an informer for the **Stasi**.

PETER BARKER

Mann, Klaus

b. 18 November 1906, Munich; d. 22
    May 1949, Cannes

Writer

The son of Thomas **Mann**, Klaus Heinrich Mann
started out as a *Dramaturg* in Berlin and
subsequently established a theatre ensemble there
together with Gustaf **Gründgens**, Pamela Wedekind, and his sister Erika Mann. In 1933 he left
Germany and went eventually to Paris during
which time he collaborated with Aldous Huxley,
André Gide and his uncle, Heinrich Mann, on *Die
Sammlung*, an anti-fascist periodical. In 1936 he
emigrated to the US, returning to Europe in 1945
to fight in the North African campaign as a soldier
in the US army. He is best known for his 1936
novel about Gustaf Gründgens' compromise with
the Nazis, *Mephisto* (*Mephisto. Roman einer Karriere*),
which was made into an Oscar-winning film
(starring Klaus Maria **Brandauer**) by István
Szabó in 1981. Mann committed suicide in 1949.

SEÁN ALLAN

Mann, Thomas

b. 6 June 1875, Lübeck; d. 12 August
    1955, Kilchberg (Zürich)

Writer

Thomas Mann, one of the most outstanding
writers of the twentieth century and recipient of
the Nobel Prize in 1929, was the son of a
prosperous businessman and Senator, Johann
Mann, of Lübeck. Mann's mother, Julia da Silva-
Bruhns, was of South American descent. After the
death of their father in 1891, the family moved to
Munich. Mann's first novel *Buddenbrooks: The Decline
of a Family* (*Buddenbrooks*), of 1901, enjoyed international success. In 1905, Mann married Katja
Pringsheim, the daughter of a professor of mathematics at Munich university, with whom he had six
children (see also **Mann**, Klaus). Both in essays
and lectures he had warned of the rise of
barbarism, and when Hitler came to power in
1933, Mann – who was in Switzerland at the time
– was advised by his children not to return to
Germany. He emigrated to the US via France and
Switzerland, where he lectured at Princeton
University from 1938 until he settled in Pacific
Palisades, California, in 1941. In 1952, he returned
to Switzerland, where he died three years later.

His numerous works include *Death in Venice* (*Der
Tod in Venedig*, 1912), *The Magic Mountain* (*Der
Zauberberg*, 1924), *Joseph and his Brothers* (*Joseph und
seine Brüder*, 1933–1943, 4 vols), *Lotte in Weimar* (*Lotte
in Weimar*, 1939), *Germany and the Germans* (*Deutschland und die Deutschen*, 1945) and *Doctor Faustus* (*Doktor
Faustus*, 1947). Influenced by the great realists of
the nineteenth century, such as Tolstoy, Dos-
toievsky, Flaubert and Fontane, realism in Mann's
own work only serves to construct a transparent
surface. The reader breaks through the surface by
way of an underlying structure of leitmotif, which
creates ironic narratives both real and symbolic.
The ambivalence of decline and decay (often of an
artistic mind) is a motif which runs through almost
all of Mann's work, especially in *Buddenbrooks*, *Death
in Venice*, and *The Magic Mountain*. The most
vitalistic of Mann's protagonists is Joseph, the
picaresque hero of his great biblical exile novel
Joseph and his Brothers, who raises the question of
humanitarianism and searches for the essence of
the human being. Nothing remains of this sphere
of classical humanitarianism in Mann's last major
work *Doctor Faustus*. In this story of 'the life of the
German composer Adrian Leverkühn as told by a
friend', Leverkühn symbolizes the degeneration of
Germany in Mann's lifetime. Mann passes judgement on his native country, which made a contract
with the devil in 1933. However, the Nazi era only
indirectly enters the story of Leverkühn, as it is only
during the Third Reich that his friend Serenus
Zeitblom writes the story down. This frame or
foreground nevertheless allows the reader to
recognize in Leverkühn Mann's interpretation of
the ambivalent curse on the essence of German
nature.

Further reading

Fetzer, J.F. (1996) *Changing Perceptions of Thomas
    Mann's Doctor Faustus: Criticism 1947–1992*, Co-
    lumbia, SC: Camden House.

Travers, M. (1992) *Thomas Mann*, London: Macmillan.

CHRISTIANE SCHÖNFELD

Marcuse, Herbert

b. 19 July 1898, Berlin; d. 29 July 1979, Starnberg

Social Philosopher

As a student of philosophy in Berlin and Freiburg, Marcuse was strongly influenced by the existentialism of his teachers **Husserl** and **Heidegger**, but had also been close to the socialist labour movement since joining the USPD in WWI and becoming a member of the Workers' and Soldiers' Councils during the 1918 revolution. He joined the Frankfurt Institute for Social Research (**Frankfurt School**) in 1933, the year of its emigration to the US, but unlike **Adorno** and **Horkheimer** did not return to Germany after the war. He continued to work at the US State Department until 1954 when he took up a professorship at Brandeis University. Marcuse rose to prominence in both the US and Germany in the 1960s when his writings exerted a major influence on the **student movement** of 1966–9 which, in contrast to the indifference and hostility displayed towards political activism by Horkheimer and Adorno, he embraced with enthusiasm.

Marcuse's thought was attractive to the 'New Left' of the 1960s because its integration of elements of **Marxism** and Freudian psychoanalysis seemed to offer a theoretical explanation for the failures of the 'Old Left' and the new revolutionary vanguard role of marginal groups like students. In *Soviet Marxism* (1958), *Eros and Civilization* (1955) and *One-Dimensional Man* (1964), Marcuse argued that classical Marxism, in neglecting the importance of the repression of sexual libido ('eros'), had been an insufficiently radical negation of modern society and indeed, in its contemporary forms of Stalinism and social democracy, had become part of the repressive apparatus itself. The consumerist abundance created by modern technology had led to the complete integration of the industrial working class

and the loss of revolutionary class consciousness in a 'totally administered society'. It was left to 'the substratum of the outcasts and outsiders, the exploited and persecuted, of other races and other colours, the unemployed and the unemployable... outside the democratic process' (*One-Dimensional Man*) to lead the fight for liberation. Human emancipation, for Marcuse, was more than the socialization of the means of production and a planned economy: it required the release of the individual from libidinal repression and the eroticization of all social relations and human activity.

Further reading

Katz, B. (1982) *Herbert Marcuse and the Art of Liberation*, London: New Left Books (intellectual biography).

Kellner, D. (1984) *Herbert Marcuse and the Crisis of Marxism*, London: Macmillan (includes detailed bibliography).

GÜNTER MINNERUP

Marcuse, Ludwig

b. 8 February 1894, Berlin; d. 2 August 1971, Munich

Philosopher, literary critic and journalist

Also known under the pseudonym Heinz Raabe, Marcuse participated in the Berlin psychoanalytic circle. In 1933 he emigrated to France and in 1938 to the United States, where he was professor of philosophy, culture, and history at Los Angeles until his return to West Germany in 1962. His books include studies on literature, philosophy, and music, but he is best known for his provocative work on obscenity.

KALLIOPI NIKOLOPOULOU

Maron, Monika

b. 3 June 1941, Berlin

Writer and journalist

Strongly influenced by surrealism, Maron became known for her scathingly satirical commentaries on GDR society.

Born during the bombardment of Berlin in WWII, Maron reflects in her novels the experiences of childhood spent in the aftermath of the destruction; death and the problematic nature of human relationships feature frequently in her work. Step-daughter of Karl Maron, GDR Minister of the Interior from 1955–63, she grew up in the privileged world of the political élite which she later rejected. After studying drama and art in Berlin, she became a reporter on the staff of the weekly *Wochenpost*. From 1976 she worked as a freelance writer, moving to Hamburg in 1988. After German unification she returned to live in Berlin.

Too critical to be published in the GDR, her first novel *Flight of Ashes* (*Flugasche*, 1981), portraying a young female journalist's struggle for personal and professional integrity, illustrates the dilemma faced by East German journalists. It was one of the first works to deal with the subject of industrial pollution. The confrontation between Josefa, the young journalist, and the high functionary who requires her to compromise in the interests of political expediency represents the generation conflict which features in much of her work. Her following plays and novels, *Das Mißverständnis* (The Misunderstanding) of 1982 and *The Defector* (*Die Überläuferin*) of 1986 satirize aspects of life in the GDR through the use of surreal fantasies. In all of her work there comes a point in the narrative where the protagonist withdraws from her surroundings to inhabit another world from which she surveys her life, a kind of surreal inner emigration. Her most attractive characters are rebels and anarchists.

In the early 1980s when a growing body of critical literature was tolerated, the GDR cultural authorities were about to allow the publication of *Flight of Ashes* when Maron engaged in a public correspondence with the West German writer Joseph von Westfalen in the pages of *Der Spiegel*.

This was published under the title *Trotzdem herzliche Grüße* (Best Wishes, Anyway) in 1988.

Maron challenges the Stalinist past of her parents' generation in *Silent Close No. 6* (*Stille Zeile Sechs*) of 1991, in which her protagonist confronts the aged functionary Professor Beerenbaum with the fate of German communists who were arrested by Stalin's secret police. She defiantly rejects the alibi of the struggle against fascism used by her elders who fought for socialism but colluded in its self-destruction. In *Animal triste* (1996) her protagonist ponders the treacherous nature of human love from the vantage-point of extreme old age.

Further reading

Kane, M. (1990) 'Culpabilities of the Imagination: The Novels of Monika Maron', in A. Williams, S. Parkes and R. Smith (eds), *Literature on the Threshold: the German Novel of the 1980s*, Oxford: Berg.

Schmidt, R. (1994) 'From Surrealism to Realism: Manika Maron's *Die Überläuferin* and *Stille Zeile Sechs*', *German Monitor* 31: 247–55.

MARGARET VALLANCE

Marxism

The fate of Marxism as an intellectual current in Germany cannot be separated from the fate of the political movements rooted in Marxism. Until 1933, the mass support for Marxist politics (in the social-democratic or communist variant) exerted a strong gravitational pull on the literary, artistic and philosophical intelligentsia, and much of the rich cultural production of the Weimar Republic was influenced by Marxism. The Third Reich violently disrupted this tradition, suppressing Marxism in all its manifestations, forcing its leading representatives into an exile from which many would never return, and even physically eradicating them.

After 1945, the re-emergence of Marxism in the political and cultural life of Germany was conditioned, and some would say deformed, by the Cold War and the division of the nation into two states. In East Germany, Marxism (more precisely, Soviet-style Marxism–Leninism as espoused by the **SED**) became the official ideology of the state, while in the West the intellectual and political climate was dominated by a militant anti-Marxism for at least two decades: the **KPD** (*Kommunistische Partei Deutschlands*), which had already lost most of its pre-war support, was banned in 1956 and not allowed to reconstitute itself as the **DKP** (*Deutsche Kommunistische Partei*) until 1969.

Militant anti-communism not only affected communists, however, but also exerted pressure on the Social Democrats and the trade unions to purge themselves of Marxism and Marxists – one **CDU** election poster of the time was captioned 'All roads of Marxism lead to Moscow'. When the **SPD** formally renounced Marxism as its official programmatic platform with the adoption of the Godesberg Programme in 1959, it was probably as much in response to this pressure as in response to the **Economic Miracle** and a desire to 'modernize' the party. In the **trade unions**, the Marxist intellectuals Viktor Agartz and Theo Pirker were dismissed from the DGB's official Economic Research Institute (WWI) in 1955 and membership of the Communist Party declared incompatible with membership of a DGB union.

As an intellectual current outside the organizations of the labour movement, the influence of Marxism during the Cold War era was almost entirely confined to a small number of university departments such as the politics and sociology seminars led by Wolfgang Abendroth and Werner Hofman in Marburg and the Institute of Social Research in Frankfurt (the **Frankfurt School** – Theodor **Adorno**, Alfred Schmidt, later Jürgen **Habermas** and Oskar Negt). It was also at the universities that the **SDS** (*Sozialistischer Deutscher Studentenbund*), formerly the SPD's student organization but expelled from the party in 1961, survived as an independent group with the support of left-wing professors and maintained a thread of continuity for radical Marxist thought in student politics.

The SDS played a crucial part in the **student movement** and extra-parliamentary opposition of 1967–8 not just in terms of activist leadership, but also by injecting into the movement its characteristically intense preoccupation with theory. For a few years after 1967, just about every variant of

Marxism ever invented was excavated to find a following among an eager audience of rebellious students. Theoretical debate filled the columns of widely-read journals such as *Konkret* and ***Kursbuch*** as well as the catalogues of commercial publishing houses. A new generation of young Marxist intellectuals proceeded to fill some of the vacancies in the rapidly expanding German universities, especially in the humanities and the social sciences. The radical momentum created by the student movement carried with it much of the critical intelligentsia in the arts, especially literature, theatre and film where a number of prominent authors, producers and directors (**Enzensberger**, **Walser**, **Wallraff**, **Weiss** and **Fassbinder**) associated themselves with Marxism or Marxist-influenced cultural and political movements.

In the continued absence of any real working-class radicalism, however, this renaissance of Marxism proved a short-lived intellectual fashion: attempts at forming student-based 'revolutionary parties' inevitably foundered, the ***Berufsverbot*** limited the employment prospects for avowed Marxists in public service, and although radical activism continued, this was now gradually reoriented towards ecological, 'green', rather than class issues.

In the GDR, where 'Marxism–Leninism' was the official ideology, all significant academic and cultural production had to be couched in Marxist terms, of course. Yet even oppositional, dissenting or non-conformist individuals and currents tended to adopt Marxist positions, often counterposing their 'true' Marxism against the doctrines of the state: prominent 'dissidents' such as Ernst **Bloch** (who left the GDR in 1961), Robert **Havemann**, Wolfgang **Harich**, Wolf **Biermann**, Stefan **Heym** and Rudolf **Bahro** were all, in their different ways, concerned with formulating an explicitly Marxist critique of the East German regime. Many other intellectuals and writers who never broke with the regime in public, from Bertolt **Brecht** to Heiner **Müller**, from the historian Jürgen **Kuczynski** to the film director Konrad **Wolf**, frequently transgressed the 'party line' to make genuinely original contributions to the rich tradition of German Marxist culture.

Such achievements have found little recognition after unification, when even a writer like Christa **Wolf** found herself under attack for collaboration with the SED and **Stasi**. In Germany today, the political, cultural and intellectual influence of Marxism is once again marginal, and even the **PDS**, the successor party to the **SED**, lists Marx and Engels as only one of the contributory influences on its programme.

See also: APO; dissent and opposition: GDR

Further reading

Anderson, P. (1976) *Considerations on Western Marxism*, London: New Left Books (discusses evolution of western, including German, Marxism from the 1930s to 1970s).

Graf, W.D. (1976) *The German Left Since 1945*, Cambridge and New York: The Oleander Press (focuses on impact of Cold War anti-communism).

Markovits, A. and Gorski, P. (1993) *The German Left: Red, Green and Beyond*, New York: Oxford University Press (comprehensive survey up to, and including, unification).

GÜNTER MINNERUP

mass media: FRG

The **Federal Constitutional Court** has, in successive verdicts, repeatedly affirmed the crucial role of media freedom (guaranteed in Article 5 of the constitution (see also **constitution**)) in the functioning of the democratic system. In accordance with the federal principle, responsibility for the media lies with *Länder*. Individual media are covered in detail under the headings listed below.

See also: advertising; ARD; broadcasting; censorship; journalism; magazines; newspapers; publishing: FRG; radio: cultural role (FRG); television; ZDF; (and names of individual publications)

JOHN SANDFORD

mass media: GDR

The mass media in the GDR were – in accordance with a dictum of Lenin's – allocated the threefold task of '**propaganda**, agitation, and organization'. Their function was to disseminate the **SED** viewpoint and to create a 'socialist consciousness' among the population; western notions of 'pluralism' and of the 'watchdog' role of the media were thus rejected.

State control over the press was exercised by the government press office, and over **broadcasting** by government committees for radio and television, whilst overall Party control lay with the **Politbüro** and the Central Committee's Department for Agitation and Propaganda. The selection and presentation of news was prescribed centrally by these bodies in accordance with principles of Marxist–Leninist 'partisanship' (*Parteilichkeit*), and further control was ensured by the fact that the media were serviced by only one news agency, the state-run **ADN**. Conformity among journalists was ensured through careful selection of politically reliable candidates for the job and obligatory training at the *Sektion Journalistik* at the University of Leipzig.

Publication of newspapers and magazines was dependent on the acquisition of a government licence: in practice, licences were restricted largely to the parties and mass organizations, and the overall structure of the press – with circulations determined by government-controlled allocation of paper – scarcely changed from the beginning of the GDR right through to 1990. All parties and mass organizations published central dailies in Berlin, of which the SED's **Neues Deutschland** and the **FDJ**'s *Junge Welt*, with circulations of over a million each, were by far the biggest. The regional press was dominated by the SED *Bezirkspresse* – 14 dailies, subdivided into 218 local editions, for each of the *Bezirke* outside Berlin (see also **Bezirk (GDR)**). Periodicals were subject to comparable forms of control, and ranged from academic and theoretical Party organs to large-circulation popular magazines such as the general-interest *NBI—Neue Berliner Illustrierte* (circulation 730,000), the women's weekly *Für Dich* (930,000), and – with the largest sales of all – the television and radio listings magazine *FF-Dabei* (1,400,000).

Broadcasting was highly centralized, with two countrywide television channels, and three main radio services. However, whereas western press products were unobtainable in the GDR, television and radio programmes from West Germany and West Berlin could be picked up over much of the country, and for most East Germans watching western television was a normal daily activity. The response by GDR television was minimal: its dourly dogmatic news programmes were hardly watched, and only in the area of entertainment were attempts made to incorporate some of the production values that were luring viewers to the western channels. Total ideological control over citizens' minds thus proved impossible, and the cumulative effect of the 'nightly reunification of the Germans around the television set' was an important factor in the eventual collapse of the GDR.

See also: publishing: GDR; Schnitzler, Karl-Eduard von

Further reading

Holzweissig, G. (1989) *Massenmedien in der DDR*, West Berlin: Verlag Gebr. Holzapfel (standard concise survey of GDR media).

JOHN SANDFORD

Masur, Kurt

b. 18 July 1927, Brieg (Silesia)

Conductor

A leading figure in East German musical life. Masur's conducting, with its probity and discipline, exemplifies the finest traditional values. His appointments included the chief conductorships of the Dresden Philharmonic Orchestra (1955) and the Komische Oper, Berlin (1960) before he became music director of the Leipzig Gewandhaus in 1970. In the upheavals of 1989 Masur took personal responsibility for making the orchestra's concert hall available to the public. It became a key forum and thus a safety valve in turbulent times. This demonstration of exemplary public conduct earned Masur even greater international approba-

tion. Ever faithful to Leipzig, he has since also been appointed music director of the New York Philharmonic (1991).

BEATRICE HARPER

Mattes, Eva

b. 14 December 1954, Tegernsee

Actress

Mattes's portrayal of Beppi in **Kroetz**'s *Stallerhof* (Hamburg 1972) established her remarkable presence and emotional range, developed in her lead roles in Shakespeare (Desdemona, Katharina, Portia, Rosalind), especially directed by Peter Zadek, in Schiller's *Maid of Orleans* and *Maria Stuart*, Lorca's *Yerma*, Büchner's *Woyzeck* (Maria) and Kleist's *Penthesilea*, but also in numerous contemporary plays, and television and film work, such as Helma **Sanders-Brahms**'s *Deutschland bleiche Mutter* and Mattes's own *Ein Mann namens EVA*, exploring gender and sexuality through the complex identity of R.W. **Fassbinder**.

Further reading

Bernd Sucher, C. (1988) *Theaterzauberer. Schauspieler. 40 Porträts*, Munich: Hanser.

MORAY McGOWAN

Mattheuer, Wolfgang

b. 7 April 1927, Reichenbach (Vogtland)

Painter, graphic artist and sculptor

Influenced by nineteenth-century realism and the imagery of Max Beckmann and Pablo Picasso, Mattheuer developed a clear and objective figurative language. Reverting to classical mythology provided a means to articulate his critical position regarding the social situation in the GDR and the German past. In his paintings and prints he established a figurative-metaphorical style that founded his international reputation as one of the main representatives of **socialist realism** 'made in GDR'. Since the 1970s he has also worked as a sculptor in the figurative tradition.

See also: documenta; painting

KERSTIN MEY

Maurer, Georg

b. 11 March 1907, Reghin (Romania); d. 4 August 1971, Potsdam

Writer

Maurer worked as a writer in the GDR upon his return from Russian captivity after WWII. He taught at the Johannes R. **Becher** Literary Institute in Leipzig from 1955 until his death. In teaching younger GDR writers such as **Braun**, Mickel, and **Kirsch**, he greatly influenced the development of the GDR lyric. Maurer's poetry and essayist writings explored the fundamental concepts of love and work in opposition to bourgeois **modernism**. Influenced by **Bloch**'s philosophy, Maurer hoped to achieve a better communication between humankind and nature in his writings.

See also: poetry: GDR

BETTINA BROCKERHOFF-MACDONALD

Max-Planck-Gesellschaft

This most prestigious non-university association for the promotion of research, founded in 1948, replaced the Kaiser-Wilhelm-Gesellschaft. It administers approximately seventy Max-Planck-Institutes which focus on basic research in the natural sciences, medicine, law, history and social sciences. Its headquarters are in Munich, with a president elected for six years by the senate, the latter consisting of representatives from **science**, finance, and the federal and regional governments. Funded equally by federal government and the *Länder*, it receives an annual budget in the region of fifteen million marks, 60 percent of the national research budget.

HANS J. HAHN

May, Ernst

b. 27 July 1886, Frankfurt am Main; d. 12 September 1970, Hamburg

Architect

May studied at University College, London (1907–8), at the Technical University (TH) Darmstadt (1908–10) and the TU Munich (1912–13). He worked for Raymond Unwin in London from 1910 to 1912. Amongst numerous occupations, he was architect and town planner in Russia (1930–3) and Kenya (1937–54), and head of the Planning Office of Neue Heimat in Hamburg (1954–60). He was in private practice in Hamburg from 1960 to 1970, and taught at the TH Darmstadt.

May is one of the most influential German town planners of the twentieth century and was decisively involved in the reconstruction of German cities after WWII. In this period he demonstrated his town planning skills in Hamburg, Bremen, Bremerhaven and Wiesbaden.

MARTIN KUDLEK AND BERTHOLD PESCH

May, Gisela

b. 31 May 1924, Wetzlar

Actress and singer

Having studied drama in Leipzig from 1940–2, she took engagements in Dresden, Danzig and Görlitz. After 1945 she was a *chanson* singer in Halle, and with the **Berliner Ensemble** since 1961. Her work shows the influence of **Weigel**, Piaf and Lenya. As an actress, she is best known for her *Hello, Dolly!* (Metropoltheater Berlin) of 1970, *Mrs Warren's Profession* (*Frau Warrens Gewerbe*) of 1973, and *Mother Courage and Her Children* (*Mutter Courage und ihre Kinder*) of 1978, which defined her as a character actress specializing in sardonic but cagey women. She has toured theatres in Europe, Australia and the US. As an interpreter of songs with texts by Brecht, Tucholsky, Kästner and Brel, she has made about twenty-five recordings. She has appeared in films since 1956, television since 1958.

RICHARD J. RUNDELL

Mayer, Hans

b. 19 March 1907, Cologne

Literary critic

A lucid analyst of German literature in its socio-historical context, Mayer was appointed professor at Leipzig University in 1948. Among the many students he influenced were aspiring authors like Christa **Wolf** and Uwe **Johnson**. He clashed with the GDR establishment because of his insistence on modernist awareness as the basis of a credible socialist culture, and was forced to leave in 1963. Since retirement he has produced a two-volume autobiography, *Ein Deutscher auf Widerruf* (German Subject to Review), published 1982–4, and a perceptive analysis of the GDR's early years, *Der Turm von Babel* (The Tower of Babel) in 1991.

DENNIS TATE

Mayröcker, Friederike

b. 20 December 1924, Vienna

Writer

Published for the first time in 1946, Friederike Mayröcker is perhaps Austria's most prolific post-war female writer and poet. Life-long companion of concrete poet Ernst **Jandl**, Mayröcker's early *lange Gedichte* (long poems) and prose texts – including 1956's *Larifari* and 1966's *Tod durch Musen* (Death by Muses) – were clearly influenced by her peripheral association with the language experimentations of the **Wiener Gruppe** (see also **Artmann, Hans Carl**; **Wiener, Oswald**).

After her transfer to the major publishing house, Rowohlt, in 1968, and her early retirement from teaching in 1969, Mayröcker began to evolve her idiosyncratic prose style with which she persisted for the next two decades (see for instance *Das Licht in der Landschaft* (1975) and *Lection* (1994)). This style is characterized by an abundance of neologisms and compounds, borrowings from other languages (especially English), lack of punctuation and capital letters, fusion of real fact and surreal fantasy, and a process of *Exzerpieren* (excerpting) and *Decollage* with phrases taken from literature, dreams and the printed matter of daily life. Critics have consis-

tently referred to the musicality and rhythmicality of Mayröcker's prose which offsets its verbal difficulty. Mayröcker has published more than twenty volumes of prose since the early 1970s, and seven novels, including *Die Abschiede* (The Farewells) of 1980, *Das Herzzerreißende der Dinge* (The Heartrending Nature of Things) of 1985, *Mein Herz mein Zimmer mein Name* (My Heart My Room My Name) of 1988, and *Stilleben* (Still Life) of 1991. Only one of Mayröcker's prose works, *Reise durch die Nacht* (1982), has been translated into English: *Night Train*, translated by Beth Bjorklund, appeared in 1992.

Mayröcker's poetry publications within this period have been regular but less profuse (see her *Ausgewählte Gedichte 1944–1978* (Selected Poems), published 1979, and *Gute Nacht, guten Morgen* (Good Night, Good Morning), 1982). She has authored several books for children, often consisting of her own illustrations, as in (1981) *Ich, der Rabe und der Mond* (I, the Raven and the Moon (1981)). She has also written several experimental – 'stereophonic' – radio plays. For the radio play *Fünf Mann Menschen* (Five Man Men) which she co-wrote with Ernst Jandl, Mayröcker was awarded the *Hörspielpreis der Kriegsblinden* (the radio award of those blinded in the war) in 1968.

Friederike Mayröcker has been awarded numerous literary awards and honours in Austria and Germany, including the *Ehrenzeichen für Wissenschaft und Kunst der Republik Österreich* (the Austrian republic's honorary award for arts and sciences) in 1987, and the prestigious 'Friedrich Hölderlin Prize' in 1993. However, her work remains largely unknown on a popular level in the German-speaking countries. A Friederike Mayröcker Archive was set up by Marcel Beyer at the Wiener Stadt- und Landesbibliothek (the Vienna city and district library) in 1993. Friederike Mayröcker lives today in Vienna.

Further reading

Beyer, M. (1992) *Friederike Mayröcker: eine Bibliographie*, Frankfurt am Main and Berlin: Peter Lang (the standard bibliography of Mayröcker's work to date).

Lindemann, G. (ed.) (1979) *Friederike Mayröcker. Ein Lesebuch, Gedichte, Prosa, Hörspiele, mit Zeichnungen der Autorin*, Frankfurt am Main: Suhrkamp (an anthology of three decades of Mayröcker's work).

ANGHARAD PRICE

Mechtel, Angelika

b. 26 August 1943, Dresden

Writer (also A. Eilers)

Mechtel grew up in the Rhineland, Munich and Würzburg, and has worked as a factory worker, maid and shop assistant. She joined **Gruppe 61** in 1965. A writer of short stories, novels, poetry, essays, documentary reportage, children's books and radio and television scripts, she is known for her often surreal depictions of the brutality and violence lying below the surface of everyday life. She is active in political causes and writers' unions, and these interests are reflected in her work. She is especially concerned with the situation of women and children. Her husband is the writer and journalist Wolfhart Eilers.

MARTINA S. ANDERSON

Meckel, Christoph

b. 12 June 1935, Berlin

Writer and graphic artist

Son of the poet and writer Eberhard Meckel, he briefly studied graphic design in Freiburg and Munich. Since 1956 he has worked as an independent graphic artist and writer. Meckel's work is extensive, multilayered as well as artistic: he has published over thirty books (lyrics, short stories, and novels) as well as graphic arts, children's books and illustrations to Voltaire, Brecht, and others. Influenced by his interest in visual arts and journeys to Africa and Europe, Meckel's poetic language is full of sensuality and magic.

Further reading

Loquai, F. (ed.) (1993) *Christoph Meckel*, Eggingen: Edition Isele.

AMINIA BRUEGGEMANN

Mediaprint

Austrian media conglomerate Mediaprint was founded in 1988 as a joint subsidiary of ***Neue Kronen Zeitung*** and ***Kurier***, and is thus largely owned by the WAZ (*Westdeutsche Allgemeine Zeitung*) Group. The dominating press distributor in Austria, Mediaprint is in a commanding position with a market share of 47 percent of all Austrian daily papers.

Mediaprint and its subsidiaries have led to an increasing awareness of press concentration and the need for market control by law.

GEORG HELLMAYR

Mehring, Walter

b. 19 April 1896, Berlin; d. 3 October 1981, Zürich

Writer and cabaret author

Together with Kurt Tucholsky, Mehring was the most important representative of 1920s Berlin **cabaret**. Influenced by expressionism and Dada, his critical, often satirical texts used montage techniques drawing on sources such as political speeches, news headlines and literary quotes. He introduced elements of the ***Schlager*** and jazz rhythms into the *chanson*. His distinctive ballad style was imitated and further developed by Bertolt **Brecht**. Being of Jewish descent, Mehring had to leave Germany in 1933. He never fully succeeded in re-establishing his career thereafter.

ANNETTE BLÜHDORN

Meinhof, Ulrike Marie

b. 7 October 1934, Oldenburg; d. 9 May 1996, Stuttgart-Stammheim

Left-wing journalist, then terrorist

As a journalist for the satirical left-wing magazine *Konkret*, Meinhof often expressed sympathy in her articles for the aims and strategies of the **student movement** and **terrorism**. She authored the television play *Bambule*. After helping to free **Baader** in 1970 Meinhof went underground and provided the intellectual justification for the violent strategy of the Baader–Meinhof group, and participated in bank robberies and bomb attacks. Arrested in June 1972, she committed suicide by hanging herself in prison after falling out with **Ensslin** and Baader.

Further reading

Krebs, M. (1988) *Ulrike Meinhof*, Reinbek bei Hamburg: Rowohlt.

MONIKA PRÜTZEL-THOMAS

memorials

Memorials perform a psychological and a symbolic function and represent physical, socially negotiated sites through which a local or a national identity may be celebrated and consecrated for future generations. Memorials in German culture mark or celebrate significant events in national and in local histories or they venerate the deeds of famous people perceived, by their time, or by later generations, to have made a culturally significant contribution. Memorials in Germany may thus be said to be iconographic representations personifying culturally significant deeds and their perception in time and in space. It is possible to discuss memorials either as officially sanctioned, by those in power, or as buildings or other sites deemed to be of historical or cultural significance. The so called *Naturdenkmäler* (natural monuments) are an example of this particular category and may include listed buildings or trees which have received a preservation order.

Perhaps the most famous and most nationally symbolic of contemporary German memorials, both within and outside of the German context, are those which act as a physical memorial to the tragic course of German history throughout the twentieth century. Many of these memorials are housed in Berlin but other examples may be found across the country. It was the policy of post-war governments to erect or preserve monuments to Germany's shame linked to the desire to keep the memory of the National Socialist period and its consequences alive so as to prevent a repeat of history. The phrase 'lest we forget' is thus not so much associated with the commemoration of the nation's dead as with the remembrance of the worst excesses of Germany's more recent past. Such memorials, which include former concentration camps such as Dachau, are termed *Mahnmal* or *Gedenkstätte*, carrying senses of memorial, warning and remembrance. Other striking examples of this most distinctive aspect of the culture of memory in Germany, at a national level, include the site in Berlin used by the Nazis for the execution of members of the resistance and the house of Dietrich **Bonhoeffer**. The *Gedächtniskirche* (Memorial Church) in the centre of former West Berlin is the shell of the cathedral bombed by the Allied Forces during WWII, which was left to act as a poignant reminder of the destruction and devastation of war, as was the *Frauenkirche* in Dresden.

Since unification in 1990 a debate concerning the role of memorials in the former East Germany has developed as the old icons and ideological heroes fell from favour under the new democracy. The visible dismantling of monuments to Lenin or the re-naming of streets formally named after Red Army heroes or working-class artists together with the change of Karl-Marx-Stadt back to its previous name of Chemnitz are all tangible examples of the cultural change. The **Berlin Wall**, for many years the symbol of the Cold War and a poignant symbol of the separation of Germany into two politically incompatible states, has now become a memorial, with sections under preservation orders, to this period in modern German history.

Whereas many of the nationally significant memorials in Germany offer no cause for celebration, the plethora of local monuments across Germany demonstrates both the fragmented nature of German identities and the relative safety of localized veneration. Local memorials enable an assertion of local identity over and above the relatively young and fragile national identity and the difficulty of expressing national pride. By celebrating and consecrating the lives and deeds of either local citizens or significant local events certain ideals may be personified and the creativity or political acumen of the local may be asserted in opposition to the national. It is often the case that the cult which forms around the honour of a person or of an event is out of proportion to its relative significance. In this way local poets and artists may be venerated without their work gaining national acclaim, or similarly events such as village or *Verein* anniversaries may become excessively marked by memorials.

Local or civic monuments are invariably erected in public space, space which is also symbolically sensitive. Attempts to erect 'modern art' monuments in such space regularly meet with opposition, unlike culturally acceptable monuments such as statues, fountains and plinths. The cultural policy of the German government seeks to encourage unusual or reactive artistic approaches in the creation of new public monuments (see also **cultural policy: FRG**). However, although local monuments and memorials display a greater sense of pride than many of the national memorials, pains are taken to remember the Nazi past at a local level too.

ALISON PHIPPS

Mensching, Steffen

b. 27 December 1958, (East) Berlin

Poet and clown

Over the 1980s Mensching kept his distance both from the GDR's self-declared avant-garde, the **Prenzlauer Berg** poets, and the state-sponsored literary scene to which he – as a graduate of the *Becher-Institut* in Leipzig – could also have had easy access. He made his independent breakthrough with the 1983 volume *Erinnerung an eine Milch-glasscheibe* (Memory of a Frosted Glass Pane), but also enjoyed widespread popularity in his double act with Hans-Eckardt **Wenzel** as satirically

minded clowns. His first post-unification collection of poems is *Berliner Elegien* (Berlin Elegies) of 1995.

DENNIS TATE

Mercedes-Benz

The largest division within Germany's biggest company, Stuttgart-based Daimler-Benz, and the marque of the division's motor vehicles, which are known simply as Mercedes. Dubbed the '**Volks-wagen** of the affluent', Mercedes cars are also favoured by German taxi-drivers. The three-pointed Mercedes star, chosen by Gottlieb Daimler (whose cars were named after the daughter, Mercedes, of an early backer) to signify powered transport on land, sea and in the air, has come to symbolize German industrial power. Tamils seeking **political asylum** in the 1980s referred to the FRG as 'Mercedes-land'.

See also: 'Made in Germany'; motor car

DAVID HEAD

Merkur

Merkur, Deutsche Zeitschrift für europäisches Denken (German Journal for European Thought), is often regarded as the outstanding German literary journal of the post-war era and has outlived most of its contemporaries. It first appeared in February 1947 under French licence, and the intention of the editor Hans Paeschke was that it should encourage moral and intellectual responsibility, reflecting the pre-occupation of early post-war German journalism. Modelled on Wieland's *Teutscher Merkur*, and drawing on Enlightenment thought, it has particularly conveyed a sense of European belonging. Contributors have included Denis de Rougemont, Hans Egon **Holthusen**, Theodor **Adorno**, Jürgen **Habermas** and Hans Magnus **Enzensberger**.

CLARE FLANAGAN

Mey, Reinhard

b. 21 December 1942, Berlin

Singer-songwriter

Mey trained as industrial manager, then started a degree in business management. He began his musical career in the mid-1960s, with his first album being released in 1966. His performances at the festival Chanson Folklore International (see also **music**) were successful, and since the 1970s he has been fully established as author and singer of sensitive-lyrical, humorous and satirical songs. Having released over 30 albums, Mey is one of the best known singer-songwriters in Germany; however, he has often been criticized for lacking political commitment. Occasionally, his songs are regarded as *Schlager*. In 1994 he was awarded the *Deutscher Kleinkunstpreis* for '*Chanson*'.

ANNETTE BLÜHDORN

Mielke, Erich

b. 28 December 1907, Berlin; d. 21 May 2000, Berlin

GDR functionary

A communist party activist in the 1920s and 1930s, Mielke fled into exile after involvement in the murder of two policemen in Berlin in 1931. From 1936 to 1939 he fought in the Spanish Civil War. He returned to Germany in 1945, and, together with Wilhelm **Zaisser**, established a secret police force in the Soviet zone. From 1950 he was Secretary, from 1957, Minister for State Security. In May 1976 he became a full member of the **Politbüro**. Mielke was responsible for the development of the **Stasi** into an extensive network spying on GDR citizens. In October 1993 he was convicted of the 1931 murders, but released owing to bad health.

PETER BARKER

Mies van der Rohe, Ludwig

b. 27 March 1886, Aachen; d. 17 August 1969, Chicago

Architect

Mies began his career by working for his father's stonemason business. Moving to Berlin in 1905, he worked for Bruno Paul from 1905 to 1907, set up a private practice in 1908. He was Director of the Werkbund exhibition *Weißenhofsiedlung* in Stuttgart (1927), Director of the Bauhaus (1930–3) and President of CIAM (Congrès Internationaux d'Architecture Moderne). After emigrating to the US in 1938, he set up a private practice in Chicago, and became the Director of Architecture at IIT (Illinois Institute of Technology – formerly Armour Institute).

Mies and **Gropius** are usually seen as the most important German representatives of classical modernism. Although Mies's work was an inspiration for many of Germany's post-war architects, he himself built very little outside America during that time. His National Gallery in Berlin, 1962–8, represents his last 'masterwork'.

See also: architecture

MARTIN KUDLEK

migrant literature

The emergence of migrant writing in the FRG can be closely linked to the beginning of organized labour migration in the late 1950s. However, the first literary texts written by immigrants only appear in the 1970s. Isolation, hard physical labour and bad living conditions were reasons for a delayed production of texts. These unfavourable basic conditions also meant that the first generation of labour immigrants was always under represented in migrant literature. The first texts were published in mother-tongue immigrant newspapers, replacing the pre-literary forms of expression which had dominated so far. The simple narratives and poems concentrated on the immediate accounts of the experience of immigrant workers. Often they showed much suffering under poor living conditions, language problems, discrimination by the

Germans, and homesickness. In this respect writing had primarily a therapeutic purpose.

The 1980s were characterized by the emergence of infrastructures which fostered the widening and the establishment of migrant literature on the German book market. Writing competitions, supported by the Institute for German as a Foreign Language at the University of Munich, resulted in the publishing of anthologies by a leading paperback company and the setting up of the Adalbert-von-Chamisso-Award in 1985. The Institute's activities helped make migrant literature available to a wider German public. Many of its programmatic writings, however, revealed an ethnocentric view of migrant culture, rating the literary articulation of immigrants as an exotic addition to a self-contained homogeneous German literature. In addition to these initiatives by the dominant majority, groupings emerged from among the authors themselves.

In the light of the recruitment freeze of 1974 and the following period of settlement, many authors turned against the retrospectiveness of their compatriots which often emerged in their literature and instead pleaded for a stronger literary examination of migrant reality in West Germany. This change of attitude led to the foundation of the Polynationale Literatur- und Kunstverein (PoLiKunst) and the publishing collective Südwind (both in 1980).

The leading members of these groups insisted upon the terms *Gastarbeiterliteratur* (literature of labour immigration) and *Literatur der Betroffenheit* (literature of involvement) to characterize their literary activities. These terms pointed to the main topic of this literature and referred to its political aims. PoLiKunst and Südwind intended to create solidarity among the various migrant groups. They also wanted to inform the West German public about the reality of ethnic minorities in their society in order to enforce political change. The multinational approach of these groupings resulted in the authors using German as their language of communication and literature. During the 1980s several anthologies by the groups were distributed by alternative publishing houses, thereby increasing the German readerships' awareness of migrant writing. Unfortunately, these anthologies also contributed to the reception of this literature as a homogeneous creation which should be valued mainly as a reflection of '*Gastarbeiter*'- reality. Apart from the multinational groups PoLiKunst and Südwind, bilingual initiatives like the Greek-German publishing house Romiosini were set up by immigrants who intended to free the literatures and languages of their home countries from their '*Gastarbeiter*' image by publishing bilingual editions and translations of 'classics' such as Seferis.

From the start there were authors like Aras **Ören**, who did not join any groups and continued to write in their mother tongue, in order to stay in close contact with their culture of origin, even in the foreign land. Others returned to their home countries and contribute to the extensive *Deutschlandliteratur* which describes the effects of migration from the perspective of the people in the catchment areas.

Today migrant literature in the German Federal Republic presents itself as a very diverse phenomenon, which is coined by the different national, cultural and social backgrounds of the authors and can be characterized by its richness of literary forms. The awarding of renowned prizes to immigrants can be seen as a sign of the increasing recognition this literature receives by the German-speaking public. Its reception is still not free from prejudice, however.

See also: Biondi, Franco; Gastarbeiter; Özakin, Aysel; Özdamar, Emine Sevgi; Pazarkaya, Yüksel; Schami, Rafik

Further reading

Chiellino, C. (1995) *Am Ufer der Fremde. Literatur und Arbeitsmigration 1870–1991*, Stuttgart and Weimar: J.B. Metzler Verlag.

Fischer, S. and McGowan, M. (1995) 'From Pappkoffer to Pluralism. Migrant Writing in the German Federal Republic', in R. King *et al.* (eds), *Writing Across Two Worlds. Literature and Migration*, London: Routledge, 39–56.

Reeg, U. (1988) *Schreiben in der Fremde. Literatur nationaler Minderheiten in der Bundesrepublik Deutschland*, Essen: Klartext-Verlag.

Teraoka, A. (1987) 'Gastarbeiterliteratur. The Other Speaks Back', *Cultural Critique* 7: 77–101.

Weigel, S. (1992) ' Literatur der Fremde – Literatur

in der Fremde', in K. Briegleb and S. Weigel (eds), *Hansers Sozialgeschichte der deutschen Literatur Band 12: Gegenwartsliteratur seit 1968*, Munich: dtv, pp. 182–229.

SABINE FISCHER

minorities, German

There are German-speaking minorities scattered throughout the world. In at least twenty-seven countries in the world there are still significant German-speaking communities in which German is the mother tongue. These communities are the result of German colonization in eastern and central Europe in the Middle Ages, of changes in the borders of the German and Austrian states after 1919 and 1945, and of emigration in the nineteenth and twentieth centuries for economic or political reasons, mostly to North and South America, and Australia.

The German communities in central and eastern Europe go back in some cases to the twelfth century. By the middle of the fourteenth century, German settlements had extended far beyond the Elbe into Poland, Hungary, Bohemia and along the Baltic to Estonia, Latvia and into Russia. The so-called Saxons of Transylvania are the oldest Germanic group in eastern Europe, having moved into what at that time was Hungarian territory in the twelfth century. These Saxons did not come from what is known today as Saxony, but the western part of the Rhineland, Westphalia, Hessen and Bavaria. By the thirteenth century there were over 300,000 Germans, who acquired political and religious autonomy which lasted until the incorporation of Transylvania into the Hungarian part of the Dual Monarchy in 1876. The second significant migration of Germans into the western part of present-day Romania, the Banat, came in the eighteenth century. The so-called Swabians of the Banat came initially also from the western Rhineland, but were joined by German-speakers from other parts of Germany and Austria. By 1918 there were over 300,000 in the Banat. Unlike other German groups outside the new German borders of 1945, the Romanian Germans were not expelled, but were not given any status as a

minority until 1956. During the Nazi period there were over 700,000, but more than 100,000 died in the war and a number fled. The first census in 1948 put their number at 345,000, but this figure has gone down steadily as it became easier to emigrate to West Germany as *Aussiedler*, foreign nationals who can demonstrate that they are of German stock in accordance with Article 116 (1) of the Basic Law, and as a result are automatically granted German nationality. The increasingly nationalistic policies of the Romanian government in the 1970s and 1980s accelerated the emigration, so that by 1990 there were only 200,000 left, and the disappearance of this German minority is a definite possibility.

There are also significant German-speaking minorities in Hungary and the northern and western states of the former Yugoslavia, the so-called 'Danube-Swabians', which are the result of similar migrations, in particular in the eighteenth century, from the German states and Austria. These minorities have declined steadily since 1945 as a result of assimilation and emigration, and the numbers who maintain German as their first language are relatively small.

The other major German group in eastern Europe are the Germans of Russia, of which the two largest groups are the Volga and the Black Sea Germans. At the first Russian census in 1897 there were nearly 1.8 million people who gave German as their first language. Both groups came to Russia in the eighteenth and nineteenth centuries as part of a settlement policy started by Catherine the Great. During the nineteenth and into the twentieth century they maintained their ethnic identity; the settlement area of the Volga Germans around Saratov was even declared an Autonomous Soviet Republic in 1924. But the invasion of the Soviet Union by the German army in 1941 led to the deportation of many German groups into Siberia and Central Asia. Despite this the census of 1979 showed a population of German nationality of nearly 2 million, the fourteenth largest ethnic group in the Soviet Union, although only 1.1 million declared their first language to be German. More than 100,000 Soviet Germans emigrated to West Germany as *Aussiedler* in the 1980s, and the numbers continued to rise in the 1990s, nearly 150,000 in 1990 alone, despite more restrictive conditions being imposed by Germany in 1991. Many of these *Aussiedler* have great problems of assimilation on arrival in Germany; their lack of German and their cultural background mean that they are often treated as foreigners by Germans. Despite this continued emigration, the number of Germans in the countries of the former Soviet Union is still substantial; the last census of 1989 produced a figure of over 2 million.

The most significant German-speaking minority which resulted from border changes is in **South Tyrol**, which has been part of Italy since the collapse of the Austro-Hungarian Empire and the implementation of the St Germain Treaty in 1919. The fascist period in Italy brought increasing pressure to assimilate, and the pact between Hitler and Mussolini in June 1939 provided for the transfer of the German-speakers of South Tyrol to the German Reich. By the end of 1943 about 75,000 of the 267,000 German-speakers had migrated to the Reich. Despite strong opposition from its population, South Tyrol was handed back to Italy after a decision by the Allied Foreign Ministers in April 1946. An agreement was signed in September 1946 between Austria and Italy which guaranteed certain rights to the minority, which were then incorporated in the Peace Treaty of February 1947. But only in the area of education with the provision of bilingual schools was the agreement implemented. In other areas, such as employment rights, it was not put into practice. This failure on the part of the Italian government to implement the agreement increased support for the Südtiroler Volkspartei (South Tyrol People's Party) and resulted in a growing number of attacks on government property in the 1960s. This pressure led to the signing of a new agreement in November 1969, the so-called 'Packet', and the Autonomy Statute of 1972 which guaranteed the rights of all three linguistic groups in South Tyrol: the German-speakers, the Ladins and the Italians. The main advance since 1972 has been in the area of employment where 5,000 posts in the civil service are reserved for German-speakers. The German-speaking minority has been growing in numbers, and unlike other minorities has shown no inclination to assimilate. At the last census in 1981 there were about 280,000 German-speakers registered in South Tyrol.

The other German-speaking minority which was created by the defeat of Germany and Austria in 1918 is that in Denmark. In a referendum in February 1920 three-quarters of the population in North Schleswig voted to become part of Denmark. This left a German-speaking minority of about 25,000. After 1945 the area reverted to Denmark amidst strong hostility to the German-speakers, many of whom had served in the German army during the occupation of Denmark. The Germans were, however, allowed to form their own party, the *Bund Deutscher Nordschleswiger* (The League of German North Schleswigers); in 1953 it gained one seat in the Danish parliament which it lost in 1964 having failed to win 2 percent of the vote. The Bonn–Copenhagen declarations of March 1955 resulted in the free development of the minorities on both sides of the border (see also **minorities, non-German**) especially in the area of bilingual education. There are no exact figures on the number of German speakers, but estimates put the figure at around 20,000.

The German-speaking minorities of Silesia in Poland and the Sudetenland in the Czech Republic are perhaps the most politically sensitive because of the way in which the German populations of these regions were expelled in 1945–6. Only about 60,000 German speakers remain in the Czech Republic, but in 1983 Poland had about 1.1 million people of German origin who have the right to German citizenship according to the criteria established by the Federal Republic, most of whom were in Silesia. This group, a large number of whom spoke little or no German, were not recognized as a separate ethnic group by the Polish government, but as Poles who had been 'Germanized'. After the political changes in Poland in the 1980s greater recognition was given to the German minority, but a large number decided to leave and go to West Germany as *Aussiedler* towards the end of the 1980s: 250,000 in 1989 and 134,000 in 1990. But the numbers fell in 1991 to 40,000 after the stricter rules introduced in January 1991.

The shifting of frontiers on Germany's western borders has also produced substantial German-speaking minorities. In the cantons of Eupen and Malmédy in Belgium there are over 60,000 German speakers as a result of border changes after WWI and the inclusion of German-speaking areas in the original Belgian state of 1830. However, the most controversial area has been that of Alsace-Lorraine, which since the Franco-Prussian War (1870–1) has passed back and forwards between Germany and France four times. On each occasion the new political authority has instituted a policy of discrimination in favour of its own language and culture. Since 1945 Alsace-Lorraine has been part of France and seems likely to remain in France.

The language situation in Alsace-Lorraine is complicated: the official language is French, and since 1945 the French government has encouraged the settlement of French speakers from other parts of France, and does not recognize German as an official language. The German that is spoken by over one million people is in the form of a number of dialects, and is strongest in rural areas of Alsace. Alsatians and Lorrainers of German origin do not regard themselves as Germans, and only a small minority have a command of High German, whereas the majority of German dialect speakers have a full command of French. Assimilation pressures were strong, especially in the immediate post-war period as a reaction against the German occupation. There has as a result been little pressure on the part of the German-speakers themselves for greater cultural autonomy, and although German dialects are still strong amongst the rural population, the identity of the younger generation is becoming more and more French.

Further reading

Bade, K.J. (ed.) (1993) *Deutsche im Ausland. Fremde in Deutschland*, Munich: Beck (a recent book on migrations affecting Germany and Germans).

Born, J. and Dickgiesser, S. (1989) *Deutschsprachige Minderheiten*, Mannheim: Institut für deutsche Sprache (useful for recent statistics).

Stephens, M. (1976) *Linguistic Minorities in Western Europe*, Llandysul, Wales: Gomer Press (the most comprehensive volume in English).

PETER BARKER

minorities, non-German

There are two major groupings of non-German minorities in the German-speaking countries: ethnic groups which have lived in predominantly German-speaking states for centuries (indigenous groups) and are nationals of the respective states, and other ethnic groups which have come to Germany recently under particular circumstances (see also **asylum, political**; *Gastarbeiter*; **refugees**). The indigenous groups are small in number and have over the centuries been subject to strong assimilatory pressures. In Germany there are three significant groups: the Danes and the Frisians in Schleswig-Holstein and the Sorbs in eastern Saxony. In Austria there are a number of small Slav and Hungarian groups, of which the most significant are the Slovenes of Carinthia and Styria, and the Croats and Hungarians of the Burgenland. In the German-speaking part of Switzerland the Rhaeto-Romans form a minority in the eastern Grisons canton. Finally, there are the Sinti and Roma who, despite persecution during the Nazi period, are present in significant numbers in Germany and Austria.

The Danish minority in Schleswig

The presence of a Danish minority in South Schleswig within the present German borders stems from the referendum held in 1920 after the Treaty of Versailles, as a result of which the border was redrawn, leaving approximately 20,000 Germans in Denmark and a larger number of Danes in Germany. After 1945 this border was re-established despite some pressure from Denmark to move the border southwards. In 1955 the Bonn-Copenhagen Declarations laid down the principles concerning the linguistic and cultural rights of the Danish minority. They laid the basis for the establishment of Danish schools and publications, and the suspension of the 5 percent hurdle for the political party representing the interests of the Danish and Friesian minorities, the *Südschleswigscher Wählerverband* (SSW), which guaranteed it representation in the state parliament. Between 1949 and 1953 this party had one seat in the Bundestag through gaining 5.4 percent of the vote in Schleswig-Holstein. From 1955 it was represented in the

Schleswig-Holstein state parliament, with one or two seats; in the 1996 election the SSW gained 2.5 percent and two seats in the Schleswig-Holstein parliament. There is no article in the Basic Law guaranteeing the rights of ethnic minorities, despite intense pressure for the inclusion of a minorities clause in 1993–4, but clauses were included in the constitution of Schleswig-Holstein of 13 December 1949 granting the freedom to identify with a national minority and establishing the right of parents to send their children to a Danish school.

The North and East Friesians

The other significant ethnic minority in north Germany, the Frisians, has a history of settlement in western Europe which goes back to the early Middle Ages. The Frisian language belongs to the North Sea coastal branch of the West-Germanic language group, and shows considerable similarity to English. The largest group of Frisian speakers, West Frisians, is situated in The Netherlands, but two further groups, the North Frisians who settled on the East coast of the North Sea in the ninth century, and the East Frisians who established a colony in the Saterland near Oldenburg in the thirteenth century, live in Germany. In these two areas the Frisian language has been gradually pushed back by Low German; in the Saterland East Frisian speakers are now confined to three villages and number no more than one thousand. In Schleswig, on the coastal strip from Husum to the Danish border, and on the North Sea islands of Helgoland, Amrum, Föhr and Sylt there are about 10,000 North Frisian speakers and some bilingual schools. Since 1945 some interest has been shown in support for the Frisian language in Germany, but the number of speakers is now so small and the assimilatory pressures so strong that its future as a living language is in doubt.

The Sorbs of Lusatia

Similar problems are being experienced by the Slav minority in eastern Saxony and Brandenburg, the Sorbs or Wends. They are the only survivors of the western Slav tribes which settled in the area between the Oder and the Elbe in the fifth and sixth centuries. From the tenth century these Slav tribes became subject to colonization by the Germans. The present-day Sorbs are the descendants of the two largest Sorbian tribes, the *Milceni* (Upper Sorbs), and the *Luzici* (Lower Sorbs), and their respective dialects have developed into two separate written languages, Upper and Lower Sorbian. In 1900 there were about 150,000 speakers, about two-thirds of whom were monolingual, but the number now is down to under 50,000, and all are bilingual.

After 1945 the Sorbs were all contained within the Soviet zone, and under the influence of the Soviet nationalities policy, which gave a limited degree of cultural autonomy to linguistic minorities, the Sorbs started to gain in the 1950s some of the cultural institutions they needed to recover from the repressive policy of the Nazi period when the Sorbian language was banned from all official use and Sorbian cultural institutions and publications were closed down. In return for this limited degree of cultural autonomy Sorbian institutions, in particular the main cultural organization the **Domowina** (Homeland), were forced in the 1950s to submit to the political pressures of the ruling communist party, the **SED**. For the Sorbs this meant putting the development of a socialist society above their own national interests. They had remained a rural community of small farmers, but in the 1950s they were required to submit to the pressures of collectivization into **LPG**s. Also, the fact that Lusatia, the traditional homeland of the Sorbs, contained rich deposits of lignite, brought about the destruction of many Sorbian villages through open-cast mining, and resulted in the construction of large power stations, thereby bringing in large numbers of Germans into the area, which further diluted the Sorbian communities. These communities had in any case been affected by the influx of **refugees** from Silesia and the Sudetenland after 1945. As a result, there has been a steady decrease in the number of Sorbian speakers, despite the establishment of a network of Sorbian schools in some of which Sorbian is the language of instruction.

The Sorbian community has also been affected by the disruptions of the post-unification period. Sorbian institutions, especially the *Domowina*, were criticized for their complicity with communism; most of the institutions, such as the Domowina publishing house, have survived the political changes with the help of state subsidies through the Stiftung für das sorbische Volk (Foundation for the Sorbian People), established in 1991. However, because of high unemployment, as well as the new opportunities to travel, many young Sorbs are leaving Lusatia, and the numbers of children studying their own language is declining. The states of Brandenburg and Saxony have included clauses in their constitutions guaranteeing the rights of the Sorbs as an ethnic minority, the radio stations have increased the number of Sorbian broadcasts, and Brandenburg television (ORB) has given the Lower Sorbs a monthly television programme, but unification has brought about an intensification of assimilatory pressures, and the Sorbian-speaking population is expected to further decline.

Ethnic minorities in Austria

The indigenous ethnic minorities in modern-day Austria are essentially a result of the break-up of the multi-ethnic Hapsburg Empire after 1919 and the resulting re-drawing of borders. There is an essential difference between the largest minority groups, the Slovenes, Croats and the Hungarians, which was determined by their geographical position within the Austro-Hungarian Empire. The Croats and Hungarians of the Burgenland, Austria's eastern-most province, were situated in the Hungarian-ruled part of the Empire, in which there was no separation of Church and State, and in which minority languages such as Croatian continued as the language of church and school. In Carinthia (Kärnten), where the Slovene minority is centred, Church and State were separated in 1869; as a result anti-clerical policies intensified assimilatory pressures, and pro-Slovenian groups became closely associated with clerical politics. The differences between the two areas were intensified by the experiences of the Nazi period; in the Burgenland there was little opposition to the Nazis, and many Croats joined the NSDAP, while the Hungarians' 'mother country' was in any case an ally of Germany. In Carinthia the Slovenes provided the main opposition within Austria to Nazi domination, and 3,500 Slovenes joined Tito's

partisans in the guerilla war against the German army.

After 1945 these historical differences affected the way in which relations between minority groups and the German-speakers developed, with a sharpening of antagonism in Carinthia, and a lack of conflict in the Burgenland. This became clear after the conclusion of the State Treaty of 1955; Article 7 gave official recognition to the Slovene and Croatian minorities, and incorporated the right to bilingual education and the use of the minority languages in official contexts. The ability of Austria's central government to impose such general principles on the state government of Carinthia was directly challenged by the re-establishment of the Carinthian Home Guard (KHD) in 1956 which campaigned against the bilingual school system introduced in 1945. In 1959 it forced the watering-down of the bilingual school law and the weakening of the position of Slovene as an official language. The most violent confrontation came when an attempt was made to put in place the final provision of the State Treaty, namely the erection of bilingual place-names. In 1972 bilingual signs were put up in 205 places, but these were almost immediately torn down by German-nationalist groups. Slovenian was therefore subject to a serious campaign of harassment which means that it has progressively declined as an everyday language. Whereas in 1951 over 42,000 people declared themselves Slovene-speaking, by 1991 this number had declined to just over 20,000. The number of Croats in the Burgenland has also declined, from around 30,000 in 1951 to just under 20,000 in 1991, but there has been little of the hostility experienced in Carinthia. Bilingual primary education was reintroduced in 1945, but its extension to the secondary sector did not come until the late 1980s; in 1992 the first bilingual grammar school was established.

The setbacks of 1972 forced the central government to rethink its minorities policies. In 1976 it introduced a new law which was, however, rejected by all the minority groups themselves, with the exception of the Hungarians in the Burgenland, who were for the first time given official status. The Slovenes and the Croats regarded the new law as a reduction of their rights established in the State Treaty of 1955 and refused to send delegates to the advisory councils set up by the law. The 1980s saw both groups attempting to re-establish the principles of 1955 through the law with some success; in 1987 Croatian was recognized as an official language in six out of seven regions of the Burgenland, and a Slovenian bilingual school was finally opened in Klagenfurt, the capital of Carinthia, against the wishes of the state leader, **Haider**. Both groups also gained access to the media with radio and television programmes in the late 1980s. But the initial hopes of further liberalization after the political changes of 1989–90 in Central Europe have been shattered by a number of bomb attacks from 1994–5; for example on the bilingual school in Klagenfurt.

The Rhaeto-Romans of Switzerland

Rhaeto-Romansh is the smallest of the four national languages of Switzerland (see also **cultural policy and institutions: Switzerland**). Its speakers are the descendants of the inhabitants of the valleys of the Grisons, who were forced after the invasion of the Roman legions in 15 BC to speak a kind of Vulgar Latin. They have links with the Ladins of **South Tyrol** and the Friulans further east in that the languages of all three areas derive from Latin. By the fifteenth century the area of settlement had become economically dominated by the Germans; the major town of the area, Chur, was by that time a German town. But Romansh remained the dominant culture of the villages and valleys of the eastern and northern Grisons, and literary languages started to develop from the seventeenth century. Until 1938 Romansh was not recognized as a national language, but after Mussolini's attempts to claim the Grisons, it was made a national language in amendments to the constitution. It did not however become an official language, except locally in the Grisons. The situation in the schools varies from area to area, but in the Romansh-speaking areas now, the first three classes of the primary school are normally conducted in Romansh, but with German also taught. There are no secondary Romansh schools. Particularly with the advent of tourism as the major economic force in the region, the numbers of mother-tongue Romansh speakers has been declining; less than 1 percent of the Swiss population describe themselves as Romansh speakers, numbering less than 50,000 people.

The Sinti and Roma

The Sinti and Roma, popularly referred to indiscriminately as 'gypsies' in English, are the descendants of groups which left southern Asia in the eighth to tenth centuries and moved into Europe via Iran, Egypt and the Balkans. It is not always possible to make an exact distinction between Sinti and Roma; the Sinti moved out of the Balkans into central and western Europe at the end of the fourteenth century, probably to escape from areas coming under Ottoman control, while the larger numbers of Roma groups stayed in the Balkans. Since the nineteenth century, but especially in the twentieth century, many Roma groups have as a result of political pressures also moved into Central Europe.

Before WWII, Germany had a large, predominantly Sinti population, but under the 1935 Nürnberg Laws, they were deported into concentration camps and mostly murdered. Exact figures are disputed, but estimates of between 200,000 and 600,000 are cited. For those who survived it was difficult to become reintegrated into Germany, since they had been declared 'stateless' by the Nazis and often had difficulty in proving their earlier German nationality. From the 1960s new waves, primarily of Roma, came into West Germany as *Gastarbeiter*, mostly from Yugoslavia. Some of these have acquired German nationality under the more relaxed rules of the late 1980s and 1990s. Since the political changes in central and eastern Europe a large number have come into Germany, seeking asylum from renewed economic and hostile pressures, particularly from Romania. This increased presence of a minority which many Germans still regard as tending towards unsocial, if not criminal, behaviour has intensified public intolerance towards the Sinti and Roma. There are around 50,000 Sinti and 30,000 Roma living in Germany, and similar numbers in Austria, but these figures exclude those who came in as *Gastarbeiter*, since they are classified under their country of origin.

Further reading

Baumgartner, G. (1995) *6 X Österreich. Geschichte und aktuelle Situation der Volksgruppen*, Klagenfurt: DRAVA Verlag (a recent summary of the situation of minorities in Austria).

Schmalz-Jacobsen, C. and Hansen, G. (eds) (1995) *Ethnische Minderheiten in der Bundesrepublik Deutschland*, Munich: Beck (a recent collection of essays on a wide range of minorities in Germany).

Stephens, M. (1976) *Linguistic Minorities in Western Europe*, Llandysul, Wales: Gomer Press (the most comprehensive work in English).

PETER BARKER

Mira, Brigitte

b. 20 April 1915, Hamburg

Actress and singer

A trained operetta singer, Mira had a motley career in theatre, cabaret, musical films and television before her discovery as a serious actress by the **New German Cinema**. She achieved international recognition in R.W. **Fassbinder**'s 1973 film *Ali – Fear Eats the Soul* (*Angst essen Seele auf*) as Emmy, the lonely charwoman in love with a Moroccan immigrant. She now primarily works for television, in popular series such as 1978's *Drei Damen vom Grill* (*Three Ladies from the Hot-Dog Stand*), usually portraying resolute elderly Berliners.

CHRISTIAN ROGOWSKI

Mitscherlich, Alexander

b. 20 September 1908, Munich; d. 26 June 1982, Frankfurt-am-Maim

Physician and psychoanalyst

A leading social critic until his death in 1982, Mitscherlich was involved in rebuilding the psychotherapeutical profession after WWII. He was a founding member of key institutions designed to overcome both the destruction wrought by the Nazi antipathy for Freudian psychology and some practitioners' collaboration with Nazism. He was one of several founders of the German Society for Psychotherapy and Depth Psychology and the German Psychoanalytic Union in 1949. In founding the first major post-war psychoanalytic journal, *Psyche: Zeitschrift für Psychoanalyse und ihre Anwendungen* (Psyche: Journal of Psychoanalysis and its Applications) in 1947, Mitscherlich sought to promote a socially critical 'psychoanalytic humanism' that differed significantly from the German bourgeois establishment.

Mitscherlich attended the Nürnberg Doctors' Trial of 1946 as a representative of the German medical association. Together with fellow physician Fred Mielke, he documented the proceedings in a report titled *Wissenschaft ohne Menschlichkeit* (Science without Humanity), which exposed some of the most gruesome of medical experiments conducted on concentration camp inmates during the Third Reich. However, the association never distributed the bulk of the ten thousand copies and the report was ignored by mainstream medical journals. It was not released for general publication until 1960, under the title *Medizin ohne Menschlichkeit* (Medicine without Humanity). Constantly aware of the legacy of the Third Reich, he remained a tireless advocate of a more humane and livable West German society until his death. His two best-known works remain *Society Without the Father* (*Auf dem Weg zur vaterlosen Gesellschaft*) of 1963, in which he elaborates the paradox of increasing subordination to convention and bureaucracy in a world of growing 'subjective autonomy', and *The Inability to Mourn* (*Die Unfähigkeit zu trauern*) of 1967, a seminal psychological analysis of Germans' inability to face up to their guilt in the Third Reich, co-authored with his wife, Margarete **Mitscherlich** (-Nielsen). *Die Unwirtlichkeit unserer Städte* (The Inhospitableness of Our Cities, 1965) criticized the contemporary city planning for contributing to a dysfunctional society.

As the main founder and head of the Sigmund Freud Institute in Frankfurt am Main, Mitscherlich was instrumental in shaping the West German psychiatric profession. He authored, co-authored, or edited many of the profession's standard textbooks in the 1960s and 1970s. However, the most important works in psychiatry deal with themes that reflect his progressive political views and a preoccupation with collective psychology (e.g. *Freedom and Lack of Freedom in Illness*; *The Idea of*

Peace and Human Aggression; *Tolerance: Investigation of a Concept*).

See also: psychology; *Vergangenheitsbewältigung*

MICHAEL R. HAYSE

Mitscherlich (-Nielsen), Margarete

b. 17 July 1917 Graasten (Denmark)

Psychoanalyst, social critic and writer

Together with her husband, Alexander **Mitscherlich**, with whom she co-founded the Sigmund Freud Institute in Frankfurt am Main, Margarete Mitscherlich played a key role in reviving Freudian psychoanalysis in Germany after WWII. *The Inability to Mourn* (*Die Unfähigkeit zu trauern*), published in 1967, was co-written with her husband, and remains her most widely discussed book. Beginning in the 1970s, Mitscherlich's research and writing focused increasingly on women's and gender psychology (e.g. *The Peaceable Sex: On Aggression in Women and Men* (1987)).

See also: psychology; *Vergangenheitsbewältigung*

MICHAEL R. HAYSE

Mitteldeutscher Verlag

This publishing house was established in the East German industrial town of Halle with a brief to promote the work of young authors. It rose to prominence in the 1960s in the context of the ***Bitterfelder Weg*** as the main publisher of the literature inspired by that much-heralded 'cultural revolution', notably Erik Neutsch's 1964 novel *Spur der Steine* (Trail of Stones). Although it retained the loyalty of some authors of this generation (Günter de **Bruyn**, Volker **Braun**) after they achieved wider recognition in the 1970s, its reputation waned following clashes with authors such as Erich **Loest** over issues of censorship (see also **censorship: FRG**; **censorship: GDR**). It finally ceased publishing in 1995.

See also: publishing: GDR

DENNIS TATE

Mitteleuropa

The geopolitical notion of *Mitteleuropa* (Central Europe) begins some two hundred years ago with the birth of modern German nationalism at the time of the Napoleonic Wars. Geographically it encompassed the central European plain, stretching from the Rhine to the Vistula, and often further beyond, and from the Baltic to the Adriatic. Its dubious reputation reached its peak with the appearance of Friedrich Naumann's best-seller *Mitteleuropa* (1915), advocating the fusion of East-Central Europe all the way to the Black Sea under German hegemony and with Austria-Hungary as a junior partner. After imperial Germany's defeat in 1918 the geopolitical ambitions of German élites were revived by the racial obsession of combining spatial conquest (*Lebensraum*) with a neo-Darwinist human engineering, which involved the physical removal and destruction of entire ethnic groups like the Jews, Gypsies and Slavs. With Germany divided between four powers in 1945 there was every indication that the ghost of *Mitteleuropa* had been buried for good.

Since the mid-1980s, however, *Mitteleuropa* has undergone a surprising metamorphosis in the context of German, as well as non-German, Central Europe. Instead of geopolitical determinants, this time the cultural dimension seemed to have gained the upper hand. Several factors in the mid-1980s helped the reappearance of *Mitteleuropa* as the new untried attractive force which was supposed to cut across the blocs and to help in removing the Iron Curtain. Its popularity among the intellectuals had to do with the vagueness of its contents. Inspired by an eccentric Italian literary group of the 1970s led by Claudio Magris (*Movimento Mitteleuropeo*), Austrian intellectuals were allured by the nostalgia of the Hapsburg monarchy returning at least in fantasy. Images of a bygone cultural landscape from Czernowitz to Trieste – conveniently leaving the German past and Russian present out – began to fill the agenda of articles and scholarly conferences. The East European participants (e.g. Milan Kundera and György Konrád) reflected on the post-Yalta world of former *Mitteleuropa* being betrayed by the West and unalterably occupied by an alien people from the East. The object of the exercise, nevertheless, was a vague fusion with 'the West', and ignorance, at first, of Germany and 'the **German Question**'. Those two questions suddenly appear as the central argument in the Prague Appeal of mid-1985, in which dissident intellectuals demanded German unification as the precondition for an all-European unity.

The West German reaction to *Mitteleuropa* was confused at the beginning. Individuals like Karl Schlögel tried to impose their own idealistic vision of a pre-Bismarckian *Mitteleuropa* resuscitated. The political left, however, exploited the new idea as a device for disengaging the two nuclear super-powers in the centre of Europe. For some, at the time of the 1980s 'Euro-missile' controversy, it meant in the first place weakening the US dominance over western Europe and then dismantling NATO to create a nuclear-free zone in the centre of the continent.

German unification in 1990 seems to have temporarily disrupted this process of rediscovering and redefining the cultural roots of Central Europe. Since then the search for a new identity has been pursued by each nation of Central Europe individually – without much reference to the common *Mitteleuropa* heritage. An interesting but short-lived experiment, launched in 1990 by the Italian foreign minister De Michelis, was a scheme bringing together countries of the Danube basin along with Italy and Poland, but avoiding Germany, clearly designed to keep the latter from trying to dominate Central Europe. The last remnant of a non-German scheme in Central Europe, still formerly surviving since 1991, is the Visegrad group of three East European countries, Czechoslovakia, Hungary and Poland (four after 1993 when Czechoslovakia was divided). Renamed CEFTA (Central European Free Trade Agreement), the scheme is politically impotent and cannot substitute for the original vision of *Mitteleuropa*.

Further reading

Ash, T.G., Judt, T., Gellner, E. Milosz, C. and Rupnik, J. (1990) in the special issue of *Daedalus*, Winter 1990, devoted to Central Europe.

Busek, E. and Brix, E. (1986) *Projekt Mitteleuropa*, Vienna: Überveuter.

Glotz, P. (1985) *Manifest für eine neue europäische Linke*, Berlin: Siedler.

Hanak, P. (1986) 'Gab es eine mitteleuropäische Identität in der Geschichte?', in *Europäische Rundschau* 2: 3–16.

Jaworski, R. (1987) 'Die aktuelle Mitteleuropadiskussion in historischer Perspektive', *Historische Zeitschrift* 247.

Konrád, G. (1985) *Antipolitics: An Essay*, trans. R.E. Allen, San Diego, CA: Harcourt, Brace, Jovanovich.

Kundera M. (1984) 'The Tragedy of Central Europe', *The New York Review of Books*, 26 April.

Meyer, H.C. (1955) *Mitteleuropa in German Thought and Action 1815–1945*.

Papcke S. and Weidenfeld W. (eds) (1988) *Traumland Mitteleuropa? Beiträge zu einer aktuellen Kontroverse*, Darmstadt: Wissenschaftliche Buchgesellschaft.

Riemeck, R. (1983) *Mitteleuropa. Bilanz eines Jahrhunderts*, Frankfurt-am-Maim: Fischer.

MILAN L. HAUNER

modernism

Since Roman antiquity, the term 'modern' has referred to the present time, set in contrast to a past, in order to distinguish the two moments and to suggest an evaluative distinction: 'modern' marks either a superiority over older culture or a deplorable decline from it. This distinction can be traced through the usage during the Middle Ages and Renaissance, until it is posed decisively in the aesthetic and philosophical debates of the seventeenth and eighteenth centuries as part of the Enlightenment in England, France and Germany. While classicism ascribed a normative status to Greco-Roman culture, closely related ideas of human perfectibility and historical progress challenged these same norms and led to the exploration of an alternative and specifically modern aesthetics. Especially in the wake of the establishment of an aesthetics of autonomy and romantic notions of progressive art, each work became subject to its own criteria, rather than to expectations or rules inherited from classical authors. Consequently any serious work of art would have to be modern, by responding to the exigencies of its own times. Indicating contemporaneity or currency, the term pervades nineteenth-century critical debates and is adopted in German, often polemically, by advocates of naturalism and later literary movements around the turn-of-the-century, particularly in the form of '*die Moderne*'.

Modernism, strictly speaking, refers to the innovative literature of the early twentieth century, especially English-language authors such as T.S. Eliot, James Joyce and Ezra Pound. It is sometimes used more broadly to refer to wider experimentation in literature in that period, but particularly writing that is self-reflective and highly formal, as opposed to literature with emphatic communicative, political or cultural-political aspirations, which is frequently described as 'avant-garde'. With reference to German material, 'modernism' may therefore refer either narrowly to authors comparable to the Anglo-American modernists, e.g. Thomas **Mann**, Musil and **Benn**, or to the broader range of innovative writing especially through the Weimar Republic, from Hofmannsthal and George through the expressionists to **Brecht** and **Fleißer**. The premier orthodox Marxist critic Georg **Lukács**, opposed modernism as an expression of imperialism and decline. Nazi cultural policy attacked modernism as 'cultural bolshevism', although some recent critics have begun to explore aspects of a fascist modernism. Even after 1945, modernism faced considerable opposition. In the GDR, innovative art and literature were sometimes denounced with the pejorative term '*modernistisch*', whereby objections were couched within the terms of Marxist aesthetics: modernism was viewed as excessively formalistic or subjective, ignoring the objective processes of historical progress. In the FRG of the Adenauer era, modernism made some headway against conventional or conservative taste, but it was frequently viewed with suspicion, an indication of a loss of cultural balance. In both East and West Germany, the resistance to modernism implicitly relied on an assumption about the normative status of nineteenth-century aesthetic conventions.

Modernism gained credibility in post-war Germany due to a combination of factors: the influence of the international art world and the cultural tastes brought by the western occupying powers; the gradual recovery of the indigenous German modernist heritage which had been suppressed during the Nazi era; the centrality of aesthetic innovation in the philosophy of the **Frankfurt School**, especially the influential work of Theodor **Adorno**. His advocacy of modern music, particularly the twelve-tone music of Arnold Schönberg, contributed to a high standard of intellectual expectations for the arts in general: the rigorously constructed, hermetic work of art, as opposed to the commercial products of the 'culture industry', was cast as the only viable alternative to alienation. The formal coherence of the work was viewed as the aesthetic corollary to a history of rationalization, as well as a protest against the suffering caused by that history. For Adorno, the work of art always conveys a criticism towards the present moment, and it is therefore 'modern'. In contrast, Peter Bürger places a weight on the distinction between 'modernism' and 'avant-garde'. Modernism represents the consistent result of the autonomy aesthetics articulated around 1800 by Goethe, Schiller and the romantics, who initiated a process of formalization that culminated in the symbolism of the late nineteenth century. Modernism attempted to maintain the separation of 'life' and 'art', while the more political avant-garde attempted to overcome it. Jürgen **Habermas** presents a third variant of modernism theory by treating the autonomization of art as a component of a history of modernity which, in terms derived from the work of Max Weber, is characterized by the emergence of separate value spheres. The autonomization of art in modernism allows for the development of refined sensibility, on the one hand, while, on the other, it preserves a realm of freedom against avant-garde efforts to collapse art and politics, which can only mean making art subservient to the state. The premier social philosopher of the FRG, Habermas is concerned furthermore with the challenge of 'postmodernity', particularly as it has emerged in the philosophy of post-structuralist thinkers. His account of modernity relies on the Enlightenment legacy of an expectation of human progress, and precisely this historical trajectory is denounced by the advocates of the post-modern condition, such as Jean-François Lyotard. While aesthetic modernism typically linked the difficulty of hermetic form to an emancipatory agenda, post-modern art is often self-consciously recognizable, drawing on familiar quotations from popular culture or other sources, and often quite distant from or sceptical towards aspirations towards self-criticism.

Further reading

Berman, R.A. (1986) *The Rise of the Modern German Novel: Crisis and Charisma*, Cambridge, MA: Harvard University Press (an account of the emergence of modernist literature in Germany in its relations to German social theory).

Bürger, P. (1984) *Theory of the Avant-Garde*, Minneapolis, MN: University of Minnesota Press (a discussion of the institution of art, its relation to classical-romantic aesthetics, and the rise of the historical avant-garde of the early twentieth century).

Habermas, J. (1987) *The Philosophical Discourse of Modernity*, Cambridge, MA: MIT Press (a set of lectures discussing the problems of modernity in European philosophy from Hegel to Luhmann).

Hewitt, A. (1983) *Fascist Modernism: Aesthetics, Politics, and the Avant-Garde*, Stanford, CA: Stanford University Press (a comparativist exploration of the theoretical resonance between aspects of the historical avant-garde and the modernist aspirations of fascism).

Lyotard, J.-F. (1984) *The Postmodern Condition: A Report on Knowledge*, Minneapolis, MN: University of Minneapolis Press (the principal account of postmodernism as an alternative to the philosophy, rhetoric and aesthetics of modernism).

RUSSELL A. BERMAN

Modrow, Hans

b. 27 January 1928, Jasenitz (near Ueckermünde)

GDR functionary and politician

A prisoner of war in the Soviet Union, Modrow returned to Germany in 1949 and joined the **SED**. In 1973 he became leader of the SED in Dresden, but did not become a member of ***Politbüro*** until 8 November 1989. On 13 November he was appointed Prime Minister and attempted to build coalition governments to save the GDR. He was, however, forced to bring forward elections to the ***Volkskammer*** (People's Chamber) from May to March 1990 and to accept the idea of unification. He became a deputy leader of the **PDS** in December 1989, and was elected to the Bundestag in 1990.

PETER BARKER

Moltmann, Jürgen

b. 8 April 1926, Hamburg

Protestant theologian

Moltmann first came to prominence in 1964 with the publication of *Theology of Hope* (*Theologie der Hoffnung*), which was strongly influenced by *Das Prinzip Hoffnung* by the Jewish Marxist Ernst **Bloch** with its eschatological philosophy and biblical motifs. Moltmann's theology has had an explicit political dimension, arguing that the God of the Bible is not 'apolitical' but a partisan in the struggle against the forces of injustice. Moltmann's later work has been increasingly influenced by feminist theology as well as concentrating on creation and the environment.

Further reading:

Bauckham, R. (1997) *The Theology of Jürgen Moltmann*, Edinburgh: T. and T. Clark (includes bibliography).

STEPHEN BROWN

Moltmann-Wendel, Elisabeth

b. 25 July 1926, Herne

Theologian and writer

Since the early 1970s, Moltmann-Wendel has been one of the pioneers of feminist theology in Germany, initially helping the insights of North American feminist theology to become better known in the German language area. Her writings have concentrated on finding role models for women in the biblical narratives and a psycho-social interpretation of Christianity.

Further reading:

Scherzberg, L. (1991) *Sünde und Gnade in der feministischen Theologie*, Matthias-Grünewald-Verlag, Mainz (devotes a chapter to Moltmann-Wendel alongside other feminist theologians).

Woltmann-Wendel, E. (1997) *Autobiography* (*Wer die Erde nicht berührt, kann den Himmel nicht erreichen ... Autobiographie*), trans. J. Bowden, London: SCM Press (includes bibliography).

STEPHEN BROWN

Mommsen, Hans

b. 5 November 1930, Marburg an der Lahn

Historian

Following periods in Tübingen and the *Institut für Zeitgeschichte* in Munich (1960–1) and Heidelberg (1963–8), Hans Mommsen became Professor of Modern History at Bochum (retired 1996). Along with his twin brother Wolfgang, Hans continued the family tradition of historical scholarship. He made his reputation with his second book, *Beamtentum im III. Reich* (1996), a study of the civil service in the Nazi years. A series of pathbreaking essays in the 1970s and 1980s contributed to the development of a more complex view of structures of power in the Third Reich, known as the 'structuralist' or 'functionalist' (as opposed to the 'intentionalist') interpretation of Nazi Germany.

MARY FULBROOK

Moníková, Libuše

b. 30 August 1945, Prague; d. 12 January 1998, Berlin

Writer

A Czech novelist and academic who wrote in German, Moníková's 1981 novel *Eine Schädigung* (Damage), about a brutal rape symbolizing the rape of Czechoslovakia in 1968, signalled what was to be her most enduring theme: her problematic Czech identity. *Pavane für eine verstorbene Infantin* (Pavane for a Deceased Infanta) of 1983 develops this theme using the metaphor of a voluntary disability chosen by the female narrator. *Die Fassade. M.N.O.P.Q.* (The Façade. M.N.O.P.Q.) of 1987 explores Czech history and culture on an epic scale. *Treibeis* (Drift-Ice) of 1992 and *Verklärte Nacht* (Transfigured Night) of 1996 deal with exile and with a return home to Prague in the changed climate after the 'Velvet Revolution' respectively. Moníková also published a book of plays in 1990, *Unter Menschenfressern* (Among Cannibals), and two volumes of essays, *Schloß, Aleph, Wunschtorte* (Castle, Aleph, Dream Tart) of 1990, and *Prager Fenster* (Prague Windows) of 1994.

BRIGID HAINES

Monk, Egon

b. 18 May 1927, Berlin

Theatre and television director

Monk collaborated with **Brecht** and Erich Engel in the early years of the **Berliner Ensemble** (1949–53), on several productions like *Mother Courage* (*Mutter Courage*) and *The Tutor* (*Der Hofmeister*). He was solely responsible for *The Beaver Coat and The Red Cock* (*Biberpelz und roter Hahn*), *Urfaust* and *The Rifles of Señora Carrar* (*Die Gewehre der Frau Carrar*). Monk joined the Norddeutscher Rundfunk, Hamburg, in 1955, and made an impact as head of television drama from 1960–8. Subsequently he was active as a freelance television director.

ARRIGO SUBIOTTO

Morgner, Irmtraud

b. 22 August 1933, Chemnitz; d. 6 May 1990, (East) Berlin

Writer

Born into a family with a tradition of railway employment, Irmtraud Morgner trained as a Germanist at the University of Leipzig and worked briefly as an editorial assistant before publishing her first story, *Das Signal steht auf Fahrt* (The Signal Is On Go), in 1958. Although like much of her subsequent work, it treated problems of gender relations and equality, she subsequently disavowed it, along with her first novel, *Ein Haus am Rand der Stadt* (A House on the Outskirts of Town) (1962), as too subservient to the tenets of **socialist realism**. Her next novel, *Rumba auf einen Herbst* (Autumn Rumba) of 1965, marked such a break with the conventions of that doctrine that it could not pass censorship, although she did include excerpts from it in the intermezzos of her most famous novel, *Leben und Abenteuer der Trobadora Beatriz nach Zeugnissen ihrer Spielfrau Laura* (The Life and Adventures of the Troubadour Beatriz as Told by Her Minstrel Laura.

The radically new style and approach that led to the non-publication of *Rumba* in the wake of the **Eleventh Plenum** was apparent in her 1969 *Hochzeit in Konstantinopel* (Wedding in Constantinople), a Scheherazade-like cycle of stories related by a woman on a pre-nuptial honeymoon with an ambitious physicist, whom she finally leaves. Her next works, *Gauklerlegende. Eine Spielfraungeschichte* (Legend of the Trickster: A Lady Minstrel's Tale) of 1971 and *Die wundersamen Reisen Gustav des Weltfahrers* (The Strange Journeys of Gustav the World Traveller) of 1972, contain elements that anticipate the *Trobadora* novel. In this immense work of fantasy, the foremost twelfth-century woman troubadour, Beatriz de Dia, returns to life during the Paris May revolution of 1968 and, through her subsequent friendship with the tram driver Laura Salman in the GDR, encounters the reality of life in this so-called 'promised land for women'. Linking up with underground matriarchal forces in a quasi-Faustian pact, Beatriz participates in Morgner's attempt to effect the 'entrance of women into history' by creating a legendary 'history', much of it in a humorous vein. Underlying Morgner's attempt to create a new 'functional genre', with its free use of montage and transgression of traditional forms, is her utopian desire to create the 'novel of the future', corresponding to the more fragmented 'life rhythms' of creative women.

In the 1983 sequel to this novel, *Amanda: Ein Hexenroman* (Amanda: A Witch Novel), the Faustian theme becomes more prominent, the pessimism more insistent. Beatriz returns as a siren who, unable to be heard in her warning against nuclear devastation, resorts to writing a book, while Laura now has two sides: that of the typical GDR woman and of the underworld witch Amanda.

Morgner's death in the year of German unification precluded completion of this 'Salman Trilogy' (*Das heilige Testament*). Regretting that her writing had at least indirectly helped to sustain the GDR political system and rejecting the appellation 'feminist', she remained convinced, however, that women had more to gain in socialism than capitalism.

Major works

Morgner, I. (1959) *Das Signal steht auf Fahrt*, Berlin: Aufbau.
—— (1962) *Ein Haus am Rand der Stadt*, Berlin: Aufbau.
—— (1968) *Hochzeit in Konstantinopel*, Berlin: Aufbau.
—— (1971) *Gauklerlegende. Eine Spielfraungeschichte*, Berlin: Eulenspiegel.
—— (1972) *Die wundersamen Reisen Gustav des Weltfahrers: Lügenhafter Roman mit Kommentaren*, Berlin: Aufbau.
—— (1974) *Leben und Abenteuer der Trobadora Beatriz nach Zeugnissen ihrer Spielfrau Laura. Roman in dreizehn Büchern und sieben Intermezzos*, Berlin: Aufbau.
—— (1983) *Amanda. Ein Hexenroman*, Berlin: Aufbau.
—— (1991) *Der Schöne und das Tier*, Frankfurt: Luchterhand.
—— (1992) *Rumba auf einen Herbst*, Hamburg: Luchterhand (did not pass censorship in 1965).
—— (1998) *Das heilige Testament: Ein Roman in Fragmenten*, ed. R. Bussmann, Hamburg: Luchterhand.

Further reading

Lewis, A. (1995) *Subverting Patriarchy: Feminism and Fantasy in the Works of Irmtraud Morgner*, Oxford: Berg.

Pietsch, H. (1990) 'Goethe as a Model for Feminist Writing? The Adaptation of a Classical Author in Irmtraud Morgner's *Amanda*', in G. Bauer Pickar and S. Cramer (eds), *The Age of Goethe Today: Critical Reexamination and Literary Reflection*, Munich: Fink.

Von der Emde, S. (1995) 'Irmtraud Morgner's Postmodern Feminism: A Question of Politics', in J. Clausen and S. Friedrichsmeyer (eds), *Women in German Yearbook 10*, Lincoln, NE: University of Nebraska Press.

PATRICIA HERMINGHOUSE

motor car

The motor car has been of pivotal economic and social importance in Germany since the war. Prior to **unification**, the car epitomized differences between the two German states. In the FRG, it was 'the **Economic Miracle** outside the front door', for it had contributed significantly to economic recovery and was seen not only as one of the main rewards of industrial success, but also as a national status symbol. The GDR's anachronistic cars, made by backward production methods and without regard to consumer requirements, came to embody 'the command economy on wheels'.

Germany, the birthplace of the motor car, is the third largest producer of cars in the world after Japan and the United States of America. In 1996, 110 years after Carl Benz was granted a German patent for what is today recognized as the world's first automobile, German manufacturers accounted for a total of just under 7 million cars, 4.54 million of which were produced in Germany itself. As a result of the strong deutschmark and high production costs in the FRG, an increasing number of German cars are no longer **'Made in Germany'**. The major manufacturers of cars in Germany (ranked in order of German-based production in 1995–6) are **Volkswagen**, Opel (owned by General Motors since 1929), **Mercedes-Benz** (part of the Daimler-Benz Group),

BMW (Bayerische Motoren Werke), Ford, and Audi (part of the Volkswagen Group). German unification brought about the demise of GDR car marques and the construction of Volkswagen and Opel car-production facilities near the sites of the main GDR car plants. Car production in the former GDR has since doubled. Three major foreign car producers are now German owned: SEAT (Spain) and Skoda (Czech Republic) by the Volkswagen Group, and Rover (UK) by BMW.

In 1996, the number of cars registered in Germany exceeded 40 million for the first time. Over 80 percent of all German households now have at least one car, and the German car market is distinguished by the consistent dominance of major German car marques. German car manufacturers have pioneered ways of making cars recyclable and reducing air pollution caused by them, but the rise in traffic density has undermined efforts to reduce fuel consumption and emissions, making the car an environmental issue in the FRG. Nevertheless, Germany is still very much a car society and remains the only EU member state in which there is no speed limit on motorways.

See also: *Autobahn*; recycling; Trabant; *Waldsterben*

Further reading

Sachs, W. (1990) *Die Liebe zum Automobil*, Reinbek bei Hamburg: Rowohlt (a lively history of Germany's enthusiasm for and incipient disillusionment with the motor car).

Wolf, W. (1996) *Car Mania. A Critical History of Transport*, London and Chicago, IL: Pluto Press (a wide-ranging critique of the motor car containing many observations on the car's position in German society).

Wood, J. (ed.) (1985) *Great Marques of Germany*, London: Octopus Books (tells the story of Germany's most famous car companies).

DAVID HEAD

Mühl, Otto

b. 16 June 1925, Grodnau (Austria)

Artist and filmmaker

Initially active as an 'informal' painter and sculptor, he became a prominent member of the Viennese Actionist movement during the 1960s, staging erotic performances based on psycho-analytical theories of abreaction. A number of taboo-breaking, orgiastic *Materialaktionen* (Material Actions), including *Mama and Papa* (*Mama und Papa*) of 1964, were recorded by the filmmaker Kurt Kren. In the mid-1970s he founded the controversial AA-Kommune (Analytical Action Commune) in Friedrichshof to promote alternative modes of communal living. Sentenced in the late 1980s to seven years imprisonment for rape and child abuse.

See also: Nitsch, Hermann

MARTIN BRADY

Müller, Heiner

b. 9 January 1929, Eppendorf (near Chemnitz); d. 30 December 1995, Berlin

Dramatist and theatre director

By the late 1980s, Müller was viewed in the FRG and by the international theatre avant-garde, and even, grudgingly, in the GDR – of whose history he was both a product and a bitter critic – as the major German dramatist since **Brecht**. 'I believe in conflict; apart from that, in nothing', he once declared, and the negative energies of unresolved conflict characterize his work. He deploys a bewildering range of Brechtian, Artaudian and postmodernist techniques (see **postmodernism**), and a vast knowledge of European literature since the Greeks, in blood-drenched collages of the catastrophes of European enlightenment humanism in general, and German history in particular.

Broadly, there were three phases to Müller's work, complicated by the delaying effects of censorship and his practice of rewriting and recycling material. First, so-called *Produktionsstücke*

(production pieces) of the 1950s and early 1960s, like *Der Lohndrücker* (The Wage-Shark), co-authored in 1957 with his wife Inge Müller, or *Der Bau* (The Building Site (1965)). These plays focus on the conflicts of the early GDR's transition from capitalism. Thematically related to **socialist realism**, and overtly endorsing its goal of socialist consciousness, the plays in fact resist proletarian heroics in favour of a more credible view of the contradictions of creating a new Germany with the old Germans. Variously interpreted as critically constructive or downright condemnatory of the GDR and its prospects, in either event these plays brought Müller into conflict with the authorities, for instance in his exclusion from the Schriftstellerverband (**Writers' Union**) in 1961.

In his second phase, in the 1960s and early 1970s, Müller turned to adaptations and reworkings of classical themes (*Herakles 5* in 1966 and *Prometheus* in 1968), of Brecht, Shakespeare (*Macbeth* in 1972) and Soviet writers like Gladkow (*Cement/ Zement* (1974)). However, this strategy of indirect critique did not, for example, prevent *Macbeth* from being accused of pessimism and escapism. *Philoktet* (1966) uses the myth of Philoctetes, marooned on an island by Odysseus during the Trojan War, to address the contradiction between humanistic ideals and the realities of a rule which represses these ideals in the present with the declared goal of realizing them in the future. The play indicts not only Stalinism but more widely the repression of freedom by means of manipulative reason, which is not unique to socialist states.

It is to challenge this instrumentalization of reason, but also to express a vision of history as endless slaughter, that Müller, in his third phase from the mid-1970s until his death, radically intensified his representations of conflict. In keeping with the postmodern dissolution of unitary conceptions like historical progress or the integral individual subject, the unities of time, place, plot and character are exploded. But so too are the rational causalities sought by Brechtian theatre: for example, Müller's view of fascism takes much more account of the irrational and subconscious. In *The Battle* (*Die Schlacht*) of 1975 (first version 1951), *Germania* (*Germania Tod in Berlin*) of 1977, *The Road of Tanks* (*Wolokolamsker Chaussee*) of 1985–9, or the posthumously premiered *Germania 3* (1996), extreme images of murder, betrayal, brutal sexuality or cannibalism link the GDR with the disasters of German history. Parallel scenes stress fateful links: between Hitler and Stalin, the communist worker and his fascist brother, twin systems of oppression and moments of individual and class betrayal. In *Gundling's Life Frederick of Prussia Lessing's Sleep Dream Scream (Leben Gundlings Friedrich von Preußen Lessings Schlaf Traum Schrei)*, the title's syntactic fragmentation presents history as blocks of rubble not coherent construction, and Prussia is a cabinet of horrors, mocking the GDR's claim to be heir to the progressive traditions of the Prussian Enlightenment.

Müller argued repeatedly in interviews that not only capitalism, or socialism, but the whole historical tradition of European patriarchy was played out. In *Despoiled Shore Medeamaterial Landscape with Argonauts (Verkommenes Ufer Medeamaterial Landschaft mit Argonauten)* Jason is killed by his own ship, the rapacious colonist destroyed by his own technology of colonization. The potential for historical change lies, if anywhere, in those excluded from this tradition, be it women, or the Third World. Both in form and content, *Hamletmachine (Die Hamletmaschine*, 1987) dismantles the Enlightenment individual by paralleling (*Hamlet – Machine*) the artistic subject/artist Hamlet as moulder of his material and the machine as symbol of dominance over nature. Moreover, a 'Hamlet Machine', cloning Hamlets industrially, dethrones the autonomous individual. Meanwhile, in the 'ruins of Europe' Ophelia's monologue of resistance to her socially defined gender role generates revolutionary energy. Similarly, in *The Mission (Der Auftrag*, 1987), the true revolutionary is not the privileged intellectual Debuisson – whose participation in the discourse of power has compromised him, like Hamlet (the western male intellectual) – but the black slave Sasportas, for whom oppression and exclusion are direct physical reality.

Müller's texts can be intensely, if often funereally, poetic in their own right. But they are largely monologic, since the horrors of history have invalidated the drama of interacting self-determining subjects, whether bourgeois or proletarian. Thus non-verbal images too are central to Müller's work: he admired the performance art of Robert Wilson (with whom he co-operated on several projects) and the dance theatre of Pina **Bausch**. Müller's work as director, and – in his last years – co-manager of the post-GDR *Berliner Ensemble*, was troubled and erratic. His 1990 *Hamlet*, rehearsed throughout the turmoil of 1989, was an eight-hour necrology for the GDR as a decayed and doomed state. His interviews, for instance *Gesammelte Irrtümer* (Collected Errors) of 1986, bristle with dialectic aphorisms: 'I am an optimist: I believe in the Fourth World War'. His 1992 autobiography *Krieg ohne Schlacht* (War Without Battles) does not wholly defuse accusations of collaboration with the **Stasi**, but remains a fascinating, black-comic document.

Further reading

Fiebach, J. (1990) *Inseln der Unordnung. Fünf Versuche zu Heiner Müllers Theatertexten*, Berlin: Henschel.

Fischer, G. (ed.) (1995) *Heiner Müller: ConTEXTS and HISTORY*, Tübingen: Stauffenburg.

Müller, H. (1995) *Theatremachine*, translated and introduced by M. von Henning, London: Faber.

Schmidt, I. and Vaßen, F. (eds) *Bibliographie Heiner Müller*, Bielefeld: Aisthesis (primary and secondary works to 1992).

Teraoka, Arlene (1985) *The Silence of Entropy and Universal Discourse. The Postmodernist Poetics of Heiner Müller*, New York, Bern and Frankfurt am Main: Lang.

MORAY McGOWAN

Müller, Herta

b.17 August 1953, Nitzkydorf (Banat, Romania)

Writer

Born in the German minority of the Banat, Müller is a prolific novelist and essayist whose works portray the narrow bigotry of German-Romanian village life, the human destruction of the Romanian dictatorship, and the rootlessness of the political exile. As a student she joined the *Aktionsgruppe Banat*, a group of Romanian-German writers seeking freedom of expression under the Ceausescu dictatorship. After completing her studies she worked as a translator in a machine factory until she was fired for refusing to co-operate with the secret police. During this time she wrote the short stories that make up the collection *Niederungen* (Lowlands), but she had difficulty satisfying the censors, and it was not published until 1982, and then only in radically modified form. In this work Müller depicted the zealously fascist mentality of the German minority, its hypocrisies and its ruthless oppression of non-conformists.

Müller was working as a teacher when her uncensored manuscript of *Niederungen* was smuggled to the West and published by the *Rotbuch Verlag* to instant critical acclaim. After 1985 she was forbidden to publish in Romania. She emigrated in 1987 and settled in Berlin.

Her novel *The Land of Green Plums* (*Herztier*, 1994) is a particularly rich portrayal of life in the Romanian dictatorship, in that Müller links the repressive childhood of her narrator with the brutal oppression of the state. It is in many respects a *roman à clef* about her friends in the *Aktionsgruppe Banat*. In it, as in all her works, the oppressiveness of theme is alleviated by the stark beauty of her prose and the unexpected flashes of humour behind some of her imagery.

Many of Müller's works reflect aspects of her own history – the efforts to get an exit visa, the problems of resettlement in the West, the feelings of alienation that plague the political exile. She has also produced collages which blend pictorial images with dense word imagery, such as the collection *Der Wächter nimmt seinen Kamm* (The Watchman Takes His Comb) of 1992.

Müller has been an outspoken critic of those East German writers who collaborated with the **Stasi**, and withdrew from PEN as a protest against its decision to merge with its former GDR branch. She has won a dozen literary prizes, including the Kleist Prize and the European literary prize 'Aristeion'.

See also: minorities, German

Further reading

Bauer, K. (1996) 'Zur Objektwerdung der Frau in Herta Müllers *Der Mensch ist ein großer Fasan auf der Welt*', in *Seminar* 32, 2: 143–54 (a feminist interpretation of Müller's 1986 novel *The Passport*).

Eke, N.O. (ed.) (1991) *Die erfundene Wahrnehmung. Annäherung an Herta Müller*, Paderborn: Igel Verlag (interpretive essays of both individual works and the main motifs in Müller's fiction; good bibliography).

Krauss, H. (1993) 'Fremde Blicke. Zur Prosa von Herta Müller und Richard Wagner', in W. Delabar and W. Jung (eds), *Neue Generation – neues Erzählen*, Opladen: Westdeutscher Verlag, pp. 69–76 (this essay compares Müller's works with those of her husband and compatriot Richard Wagner).

BEVERLEY DRIVER EDDY

Mueller-Stahl, Armin

b. 17 December 1930, Tilsit

Actor

An accomplished violinist, composer and singer of *chansons*, painter and book author, Mueller-Stahl obtained a diploma as music teacher before turning to acting. Besides his appearances on the stage he worked in film (especially with Frank **Beyer**), television, radio and dubbing. After signing a letter of protest in the context of the '**Biermann Affair**' he was forced to leave the GDR. He made his West German debut in **Fassbinder**'s *Lola*, and embarked on a career which led to Hollywood and work with directors such as Costa-Gavras, Barry Levinson and Jim Jarmusch.

HORST CLAUS

multiculturalism

Since neither German state in the post-war period developed official immigration policies, the concept of a multicultural society received no official status. West Germany allowed immigration for foreign workers on fixed-length contracts from the mid-1950s onwards, and as a result had acquired a sustantial foreign population by the mid-1970s (see also **Gastarbeiter**). In response, the **Brandt** and **Schmidt** governments, and a number of cities with substantial foreign populations, such as Frankfurt and West Berlin, introduced programmes designed to promote integration and the idea of multiculturalism.

PETER BARKER

Muschg, Adolf

b. 13 May 1934, Zollikon (Switzerland)

Writer and academic

By believing aesthetic experience to compensate for the vagaries of 'reality', Muschg espouses a 'politics' in his fiction which stresses the individual's responsibility for self-fulfilment. Thus aesthetic experience leads the individual to imagine the fulfilment of need through literature. In *Literatur als Therapie?*, Muschg modifies this position by excluding the writer from literature's therapeutic function: literature is therapeutic for the artist's audience but never for the artist. Much of his work is concerned with questions of guilt, resignation and the responsibility of the intellectual. Muschg has held the post of Professor of Literature in Zürich since 1970.

KITTY MILLET

museums

Germany's museums have a wide range of functions: to display ethnographic and anthropological collections, art treasures, representations of local, ethnic and national history, science and technology, to name the most prominent. German museums number over 3,000 and are administered at the federal, state, and municipal levels. Private museums also make up a significant segment of Germany's museums.

As in other European countries, notably France, Britain and Italy, the oldest collections were amassed to prominently display royal, aristocratic, and ecclesiastical wealth and privilege. Only after the French Revolution were these collections made accessible to all with the goal of public erudition and participation in a common culture, a policy that was further institutionalized as ever-increasing numbers of museums were built in the course of the nineteenth century. The expectation that public and private museums be accessible to the general public regardless of class or educational background remains staunchly entrenched in Germany, and museums typically offer significant discounts to students and senior citizens. Germany's museums receive over 100,000 million visitors per year and special exhibitions (see also **art exhibitions**) often generate intense interest.

Germany differs from other European countries in that its museum offerings are spread out over many different cities. While Berlin boasts an impressive range of museums, the concentration relative to the rest of country is not analogous to Paris or London. Cities such as Munich, Frankfurt am Main, Düsseldorf, Hamburg, Cologne, Dresden, Kassel and Bonn have world-class institutions, often found in clusters such as the 'museum mile' in Bonn. This decentralization of culture results partially from the fact that prior to unification in 1871 Germany consisted of many smaller principalities who founded local institutions. Germany continues to construct museums locally, making its museums more accessible to people living outside the capital. Germany likewise has no binding national museum policy, although co-operation in restoration, security and research is fostered through the **Stiftung Preußischer Kulturbesitz** and the *Deutscher Museumsbund* (German Federation of Museums), an agency to which all museums belong.

A feature peculiar to **Berlin** is the existence of two versions of many institutions. These museums were split due to the cold war, with east and west claiming to be the continuation of pre-war museums. Although these museums have been rejoined after German unification, many continue to be housed in separate buildings. Most recently intense debate has centred on the founding of a national Jewish museum in Berlin to commemorate the **Holocaust**. This museum would augment the exhibitions and **memorials** to the victims of Nazi atrocities.

Further reading

Calov, G. (1969) *Museen und Sammler des 19. Jahrhunderts in Deutschland*, Berlin: De Gruyter (treatment of collection in the formative period of museum development).

Grasskamp, W. (1981) *Museumsgründer und Museums-stürmer. Zur Sozialgeschichte des Kunstmuseums*, Munich: Beck (a good overview of the political contingencies surrounding museums over the last two centuries).

PETER M. McISAAC

music

Since the beginning of the twentieth century it has become common practice in the German-speaking countries to differentiate between *E-Musik* (*Ernste Musik*, serious music), *U-Musik* (*Unterhaltungsmusik*, light music), and *Volksmusik* (**folk music**). Although it is not restricted to the classical epoch, *E-Musik* is often referred to as *klassische Musik* (classical music). It comprises symphonies, sacred music, opera, chamber music, etc. and is generally considered as a form of artistic expression. Traditionally, it has been accessible mainly to the upper-middle class and educated strata of society and has been regarded as more aesthetically sophisticated than *U-Musik*. In contemporary German-speaking society it is still considered as culturally and educationally valuable (*Bildungsmusik*) and therefore massively subsidized by public bodies. *U-Musik*, i.e. operetta, musical, different kinds of popular music (see also **Jazz**; **rock music**; Schlager, serves the prime purpose of entertainment. Its aesthetic value is undermined by its orientation towards the taste of the majority, its dependence on quickly changing fashions, and the commercial principles shaping its production as well as its reception. The evolution of *U-Musik* is closely connected to the emergence of urban mass culture and modern technologies of sound transmission and reproduction. *Volksmusik*, including folk songs, folk tunes, dances, etc. is closely linked to regional customs and traditions. Accordion, mouth-organ, dulcimer (*Hackbrett*) or zither evoke feelings of German *Gemütlichkeit* (conviviality) and *Heimat*. Increasing mobility, tourism and the mass media have significantly changed its original character, but despite its commercial transformation it still contributes to the stabilization and reproduction of specific regional identities, particularly in rural and tour-istically attractive areas. The boundaries between these three categories of music have always been fluid, and the implicit value judgements problematic. Nevertheless they are still characteristic of contemporary German culture. Particularly after the Nazi experience of the Third Reich, *Volksmusik* and certain kinds of traditional *U-Musik* smacked of *Heimat* and *Deutschtümelei* (sentimental Germanomania), whilst the newly emerging Anglo-American popular music was, for a long time, widely resented as banal and purely commercial. This explains the German bias towards *E-Musik*, which is significantly stronger than in Britain, for example.

E-Musik since 1945

After the Nazi era, which had celebrated for example the work of Wagner, but discredited more experimental forms of music as degenerate, a radically new start was felt to be necessary. An important point of departure was the work of Paul **Hindemith** (1895–1963), who in the 1920s and 1930s had supported the pioneers of 'New Music', and emigrated to the US in 1940. There were also composers such as Boris **Blacher**, Karl Amadeus Hartmann, Wolfgang Fortner and Carl **Orff**, who had remained silent during the Nazi period or withheld their works. The most radical breach with tradition was symbolized by the work of Karlheinz **Stockhausen** (born 1928) who, on the basis of Arnold **Schönberg**'s (1874–1951) concept of twelve-tone music, developed the genre of serial music. For Stockhausen and the musical avant-garde, the regular international **Darmstadt Festival** became an important inspiration and forum for the exchange of ideas. Slightly more conventional than these New Music composers was a second strand of musical renewal with representatives like Hans Werner **Henze** or Giselher Klebe, who sought to breathe new life into traditional music by combining it with elements of new experimental music.

Whilst leading composers were trying to find radically new, authentic forms of musical expression, public musical culture in the 1950s began to re-establish itself on the basis of traditional *E-Musik*. The avant-garde composers sought to capture in their music the fundamentally uprooting and destructive experience of modernity – with the **Holocaust** as its most perverse expression. But in line with the dominant post-war approach of suppressing the Nazi past and avoiding confrontation with it, the public preferred to stick with musical traditions, which were cultivated particularly by the large **opera** houses. Newly built **concert halls** and newly founded or re-established **orchestras** followed a similar approach, leading to the tripling of concert subscriptions between 1953 and the end of the decade. A well-known representative of this musical restoration was Herbert von **Karajan** (1908–89), leader of the Berlin Philharmonic Orchestra (since 1955) and the Vienna State Opera (since 1956), as well as director of the annual **Salzburg Festival** (since 1956). Amongst the major music festivals which were founded or re-established in the early 1950s was the **Bayreuth Festival**, which continues to attract a conservative and wealthy audience.

The intellectually demanding avant-garde music which systematically militated against established musical patterns and expectations remained a minority interest. It gained some recognition amongst the politically and aesthetically open-minded generation of the 1960s, but already in the early 1970s serial music was superseded by the more aesthetically pleasing work of the first post-war generation of composers like Wolfgang **Rihm** (born 1952), who initiated a revival of more traditional methods of composition. Their work is known as *Neotonale Musik* (neo-tonal music) or *Neoromantische Musik* (neo-romantic music). Contemporary music throughout the German-speaking countries is characterized by the simultaneity of experimental, avant-garde approaches and revived musical traditions. Aesthetic pluralism and the postmodernist 'anything goes' lead to individualization and prevent the emergence of large or even dominant aesthetic or compositional schools.

In the GDR the development of musical culture was strongly determined by the administrative structures of the state. As early as 1951 the official 'Association of Composers and Musicologists of the GDR' was founded as a sub-division of the *Kulturbund*. In accordance with the instructions of the Ministry of Culture, the association gave guidance concerning the officially desired musical development (see also **cultural policy: GDR**). It remained deeply sceptical *vis-à-vis* musical experiments in the West. Most GDR composers therefore distanced themselves from avant-garde music.

U-Musik since 1945

Building on the **cabaret** and operetta tradition of the 1920s and 1930s (Marlene **Dietrich**, Zarah Leander and Hans Albers) the German *Schlager* became the dominant form of light music in the immediate post-war period. By the mid-1950s, the *Schlager*-market had successfully been re-established. Its escapist imagery of a world without political or social tensions was a welcome counterweight to the strains of post-war reconstruction. Love, passion and the yearning for faraway places (*Fernweh*) or homely cosiness (*Heimweh*) were the main subjects for Peter **Alexander**, Freddy Quinn, Caterina Valente and others. From the 1960s the increasingly banal German *Schlager* came under pressure from American rock'n'roll and British beat. Heino and the blond child star Heintje continued to serve the unpolitical older clientele, whilst the younger generation turned towards the new trends from overseas. During the 1980s, however, the *Schlager* was influenced by the German New Wave (*Neue Deutsche Welle*), and has experienced a kind of revival since then.

Two important German currents which emerged from the politicized climate of the 1960s were first the singer-songwriter movement (see **Liedermacher**) and second, the attempt to establish a genuinely German rock music. For the singer-songwriter movement the annual festival Chanson Folklore International at the Burg Waldeck was an important stimulus and opportunity for co-operation. A prime example of the strong political commitment of many singer-songwriters is Franz Josef **Degenhard**. Their **protest songs** espoused the leftist ideas of the **student movement**. Contemporary representatives of this current have turned towards more entertainment-oriented or poetical forms of expression (e.g. Reinhard **Mey** and Konstantin **Wecker**). The most important motor of the second strand was Udo **Lindenberg**. Since the early 1970s he has successfully established the tradition of *Deutschrock*, which was imitated and further developed by a wide range of younger musicians (see also **Kraut-rock**).

In the GDR the field of *U-Musik* was strictly controlled by the state authorities. After 1953 only officially approved, professional musicians were allowed to perform publicly. Pressures for political correctness and loyalty to the system severely restricted their freedom of expression. In 1958 a quota system was introduced requiring 60 percent of dance and light music played in public to be produced in the GDR or other communist countries. Nevertheless, the influence of Anglo-American rock music could not be suppressed, and the government therefore sought to control youth culture by trying to establish an independent East German rock music (with German-language lyrics) as a conformist alternative. With certain bands like **Karat** and the **Puhdys** the emerging GDR rock gained some popularity in the West, but by and large it remained an isolated phenomenon.

To date the lion's share of *U-Musik* on the German market has consisted of Anglo-American imports, but German popular music is gradually gaining ground. During the early 1990s, the percentage of German-language songs listed in the German charts has risen steadily. In its most recent varieties, however, German *U-Musik* has largely abandoned lyrics. Techno music is widely considered as a genuinely German product. With the Berlin **Love Parade** (founded in 1989) as its main annual event now attracting almost one million young people, it has developed into the most outstanding innovation of musical youth culture in the 1990s. Unlike in Britain and the US, operetta and musical never gained great importance in the German-speaking countries. Only in the 1980s did new purpose-built venues for major Broadway musicals begin to attract a significant number of people.

Musical culture

In the German-speaking countries musical culture is to a significant extent shaped by the activities of musical lay-persons. About one-third of the German public play a musical instrument; active involvement in choirs and orchestras and private music circles is widespread. The two main churches provide a framework for much of this lay culture. Major parish churches traditionally have their own professional choirmaster (*Kantor*), who, beyond his function as the official church organist, conducts the church choir and occasionally even an affiliated orchestra. Membership in church choirs is free of charge. Even in small cities, they regularly perform the major choral works of sacred music composed for the different occasions throughout the ecclesiastic year. Most of the well-known contemporary choirs such as the Dresden Kreuz-Chor, the Leipzig Thomaner-Chor or the Regensburg Domspatzen have their origin in this church choir tradition. In a more secular context, a wide range of brass bands, folk groups and other instrumental groups, often affiliated to public institutions or social clubs, provide further opportunities for musical activity. Traditionally such groups play an important role in the community life of rural areas.

Musical education of the wider public is taken care of by a range of state-funded and private institutions. Music schools are available in all medium-sized and large cities. They supplement the general musical education provided as part of the school curriculum, and make instrumental classes accessible to large sections of society. In Germany, the Association of Music Schools (*Verband deutscher Musikschulen*) supports the national young musicians' festival Jugend musiziert, an annual competition which involves about 10,000 children and teenagers. Public and private conservatoires and colleges of music (*Musikhochschulen*) provide training for young musicians up to professional level. Some of the most renowned colleges of music are in Hamburg, Hanover, Aachen, Munich and Vienna. In the whole sector of musical education the emphasis is still strongly on serious music. Only in the 1980s has the Hamburg College of Music introduced a degree in Popular Music.

The German music market is the third largest in the world after the US and Japan. The lion's share of the total turnover is taken by *U-Musik* with *E-Musik* making up for approximately 12 percent (see also **music industry**).

Further reading

Dahlhaus, C. and Danuser, H. (eds) *Neues Handbuch*

der Musikwissenschaft (13 vols), vol. 7 (1984) *Die Musik des 20.Jahrhunderts*, Laaber: Laaber Verlag (development of serious music in a political, sociological and philosophical context).

Dahlhaus, C. and Eggebrecht H.H. (eds) (1995) *Brockhaus-Riemann Musiklexikon*, Mainz: Piper-Schott (most authoritative work of reference in the field of music and musicology).

Eckhardt, A., Jakoby, R. and Rohlfs, E. (eds) (1995) *Musikalmanach 1996/97 – Daten und Fakten zum Musikleben in Deutschland*, Kassel: Bärenreiter and Bosse (regularly updated statistical details about musical culture in Germany).

Griffiths, P. (1994) *Modern Music: A Concise History*, revised edition, London: Thames and Hudson (traces the new directions of music from the beginning of the century to the 1970s, focusing on the European countries).

Mühe, H. (1996) *Unterhaltungsmusik*, Hamburg: Kovac (historical development of light music).

ANNETTE BLÜHDORN

music festivals

A music festival consists of performances by world-renowned artists of important works of music and can last over weeks, even months. As Germany is and was the birthplace of so many well-known composers, such as J.S. Bach, L. van Beethoven, G.F. Händel, P. **Hindemith**, A. **Schönberg**, K. **Stockhausen**, and performers, such as the violinist Anne-Sophie Mutter and the conductor Herbert von **Karajan**, it is not surprising that there are roughly more than a hundred local and regional music festivals in Germany. The oldest music festival, held every ten years, is the Oberammergau **Passion Play** in Upper Bavaria, and the most well-known is perhaps the Richard Wagner Festival in Bayreuth, which has been an annual event since 1876 (see also **Bayreuth Festival**).

Not only does each major city have a major music festival, but many small towns and regions throughout Germany honour either a composer or just a musical genre itself with a festival. They are usually held annually, biannually or at various yearly intervals during the spring and summer months, not only to garner the widest audience, but also because many of these performances are open-air. Bonn, for example, stages its International Beethoven Festival every three years. The great classical works are still very popular in many parts of Germany and there are a great number of traditional festivals devoted to the works of individual composers of classical music, such as the George Frideric Handel music festivals in the cities of Halle and Göttingen, and festivals devoted to Richard Strauß in Munich and Garmisch-Partenkirchen. Berlin honours Johann Sebastian Bach with its Bach Festival in July. The Austrian-born composer Wolfgang Amadeus Mozart is not only honoured in his native country by the world-famous **Salzburg Festival**, but also in Germany by Mozart's Heritage in Dresden in May, and the Würzburg Mozart Festival in June. The musical festival held at **Donaueschingen** between 1921 and 1929 (and renewed there in 1950) was an important force in furthering avant-garde music in that period.

There are, however, festivals which are also devoted to either a particular musical genre, such as classical music, opera, ballet, or jazz, or ones that mix these genres. Munich has its Opera Festival in July, Frankfurt am Main holds its Frankfurt Festival in September. Stuttgart not only hosts the European Music festival during August and September, but also stages a Jazz Festival in April, while Berlin has its Jazz Festival in November. The Munich Ballet Days take place in March while the Hamburg Ballet Festival with the Hamburg State Opera Company takes centre stage in May. The romantic Castle Festival is held every year in August in Heidelberg and northern Germany is well-represented by the Schleswig-Holstein Music Festival. This extremely popular festival – a big musical event in a provincial setting – was founded by the pianist and conductor Justus Frantz in 1986 and brings internationally famous musicians to this northernmost German state. Every summer the Rhinegau Music Festival brings together first-class soloists and ensembles devoted to both old and new music.

BETTINA BROCKERHOFF-MACDONALD

music industry

In the wider sense of the term, the music industry (*Musikwirtschaft*) refers to all aspects of the production and sale of music-related goods. Apart from music retail shops, this includes the work of concert agencies, the manufacture and sale of musical instruments as well as the huge market in hi-fi equipment. In a more restricted sense the term describes the production and commercial exploitation of music itself, i.e. performance, reproduction and distribution of music. The production – the interaction between composer, interpreter and recording technician – is the creative heart of the music industry. In economic terms, the recording industry and the music publishers are its most important parts. The base of the music market is formed by the music consumers, including the buyers of records, concert-goers and the home-audience for publicly broadcast music.

In all German-speaking countries musical works are secured by a copyright act (*Urheberrechtgesetz*) that protects the material and non-material interests of composers (and authors). The rights of commercial exploitation include broadcasting and performing rights as well as rights of reproduction in audio and audiovisual media. Most composers do not exercise their property rights personally but enter into contractual agreements with publishers or **broadcasting** companies. National societies (*Verwertungsgesellschaften*) centrally administer and control the commercial exploitation of property rights. In Germany, the most important organization of this kind is the *GEMA* (*Gesellschaft für Musikalische Aufführungs- und Mechanische Vervielfältigungsrechte*). The Austrian organization is called *AKM* (*Gesellschaft der Autoren, Komponisten und Musikverleger*). In Switzerland the equivalent society is the *SUISA* (*Société Suisse pour les droits des auteurs d'œuvres musicales*).

Music publishers originally dealt with the production and sales of printed music and musical literature. In Germany, well-established publishers following this tradition are Bärenreiter in Kassel, Breitkopf and Härtel in Wiesbaden and Schott in Mainz. Well-known Austrian publishers are Doblinger and Universal-Edition, both located in Vienna. In the context of the modern music industry, however, music publishers increasingly focus on the exploitation of musical rights and work in close co-operation with record companies. About one third of German music publishers deal with serious music, and two-thirds with light music. Due to the internationalization of the pop-market, most formerly independent German publishers have become subsidiaries of British and American media concerns like EMI Publishing and Warner Chappell.

Among the eight countries which dominate the world turnover of record sales, Germany is third after the US and Japan. In the early 1990s about 230 million records were sold. Compared to the early 1970s this represented a dramatic increase of about 250 percent. This was due to the rapid development of the youth market in rock and pop music during the 1970s which went hand-in-hand with the increasing availability of electronic luxury goods like hi-fi systems. After some decline in sales in the early 1980s, the introduction of the compact disc (CD) in 1983 once again boosted the German record market. Since about 1990 CD-sales have outstripped sales of other formats (vinyl, cassettes). Parallel with this development, the age-profile of consumers shifted significantly. Whilst in the early 1980s teenagers made about 35 percent of record purchases, they only accounted for 20 percent a decade later. At the same time, the numbers of consumers aged between twenty and forty rose from about 37 to almost 50 percent. This is due first to the higher costs of CDs in relation to previous formats; second, the rock-generations of the 1960s and 1970s continued to be interested in music as they moved into adulthood. The age-group over fifty (about 35 percent of the German population) accounts for only 14 percent of the total turnover of the music market. All in all, the whole sector strongly relies on about 10 percent of the total German population.

The recording industry distinguishes between pop and classical music in the same way that broadcasting differentiates between light and serious music (see also **music**). At the beginning of the 1990s German language pop's share of the domestic market levelled off at about 30 percent, with international pop music making up about half of the total turnover. The market share of classical music was around 12 percent. Altogether the recording market had a volume of DM 3.67 billion in 1990 (DM 2.25 billion in 1980). Most of this (in 1990, 81 percent) is in the hands of five companies which are all subsidiaries of international media concerns: BMG Ariola (**Bertelsmann**), EMI Electrola (Thorn-EMI), PolyGram (Philips), Sony Music Entertainment (Sony; until 1990 CBS, Columbia Records) and Warner Music Germany (WEA International). Despite this dominance of the media giants, some small independent labels continued to be successful, especially during the early 1980s when they promoted an authentic German New Wave (*Neue Deutsche Welle*).

For the music industry, radio and television play a significant role. On the one hand their music programmes are an essential means of advertising CDs and concerts; on the other hand, they are a serious form of competition, particularly with regard to the possibilities of private copying. In German public service television broadcasting, the proportion of music programmes is only 5 percent; in commercial television it varies according to the thematic emphasis of each channel. The public service radio corporations devote about 60 percent of their programme time to music, one-third to serious music and two-thirds to light music. Commercial channels put stronger emphasis on musical entertainment. In both public service and commercial music programmes, international pop figures prominently. The availability of new digital technologies is likely to initiate dramatic changes in the economic and legal framework of the German music industry.

Further reading

Brodbeck, K.-H. (1991) *Musikwirtschaft*, Munich: Ifo-Institut für Wirtschaftsforschung (on economic aspects of the German music industry).

Moser, R. and Scheuermann, A. (eds) (1992) *Handbuch der Musikwirtschaft*, Starnberg and Munich: Josef Keller Verlag (particularly informative on the legal side of the German music industry).

Shemel, S. and Krasilovsky M.W. (1988) *This Business of Music*, 5th edn, New York: Billboard Publications (general introduction).

ANNETTE BLÜHDORN

myth

Ever since the eighteenth century myth has been a major source of inspiration for German-speaking authors. The tendency in Weimar classicism to idealize Greek heroes and heroines (e.g. Goethe's Iphigenia and Hölderlin's Hyperion) gradually gave way to the more profound recognition that myths illuminate the whole spectrum of human experience, and that their morally shocking dimensions also need to be confronted, as Kleist did in his *Penthesilea*. The subsequent rediscovery of Germanic myth proved more problematic once Goethe's portrayal of Faust, as the incarnation of human striving for self-fulfilment, had been eclipsed by epic themes like the Nibelung saga (popularized in Wagner's operas), which were open to abuse for chauvinistic purposes, most ominously during the Third Reich.

In post-1945 divided Germany two contrasting responses to this complex legacy were evident. In the Federal Republic the widespread desire for a fresh start ('**Kahlschlag**') led to the relative neglect of mythic subject-matter, whereas GDR cultural policy sought to rehabilitate the 'positive heroes' of myth (rarely, however, its heroines) as integral parts of the new state's literary heritage (see also **cultural policy: GDR**). This encouraged simplistic portrayals of figures like Prometheus (the personification of creativity), Odysseus (the returning exile), Hercules (the productive worker) and Faust (the committed intellectual) as forerunners of socialism. Works portraying the same figures in a more ambivalent light, from Hanns **Eisler**'s *Johann Faustus* (1952) to Franz **Fühmann**'s *Prometheus* (1974), represented frontal challenges to this strategy and were often subject to censorship (see also **censorship: FRG**; **censorship: GDR**).

From the 1970s authors in both German states found unexpected common ground as they recognized the potential of myth to highlight contemporary gender issues. Christa **Wolf**'s *Kassandra* (1983) achieved international success in linking a psychologically persuasive portrayal of the much-maligned Trojan princess with an historical analysis of the disastrous long-term effect of the marginalization of women's perceptions, culminating in the nuclear weapons confrontation of the Reagan–Brezhnev era. But it was only one work among many presenting traditionally discredited mythic women in a more sympathetic light. Medusa was transformed from a caricature of ugliness and vindictiveness into a model of resistance to patriarchal destructiveness in Stefan **Schütz**'s ambitious eponymous novel of 1986 and was identified by Sigrid Weigel (in the title of her influential monograph) as epitomizing women's traumatic historical experience. Medea's reputation as the deranged murderess of her own children underwent equally radical change in Heiner **Müller**'s *Medea-Material* of 1982, Elfriede **Jelinek**'s *Krankheit oder Moderne Frauen* (Illness or Modern Women) of 1987 and Wolf's *Medea* (*Medea. Stimmen*) of 1996. This latest cycle in the appropriation of myth may now, however, be close to exhausting its creative potential, as the more obtrusive element of political partisanship in Wolf's post-unification treatment of the Medea story suggests.

Further reading

Bernhardt, R. (1983) *Odysseus' Tod – Prometheus' Leben: Antike Mythen in der Literatur der DDR*, Halle: Mitteldeutscher Verlag (a differentiated account which fails, however, to question GDR literature's preoccupation with heroes).

Weigel, S. (1989) *Die Stimme der Medusa: Schreibweisen in der Gegenwartsliteratur von Frauen*, Reinbek bei Hamburg: Rowohlt (highlights the shift of creative focus to mythic women).

DENNIS TATE

N

Nadolny, Sten

b. 29 July 1942, Zehdenick (Havel)

Writer

Nadolny's best-selling *Die Entdeckung der Langsamkeit* (*The Discovery of Slowness*) (1983), uses Franklin's 1840s polar expedition to invoke the virtues of slowness and duration in opposition to the contemporary world of information and sensation overload; themes anticipated in *Netzkarte* (*Railpass*) (1981), a teacher's would-be therapeutic odyssey through West Germany, and developed in *Selim oder die Gabe der Rede* (*Selim or the Gift of Speaking*) (1990). Here two contrasting perspectives and narrative traditions (the German Alexander and the Turk Selim) interweave in a panoramic novel of the Federal Republic.

MORAY McGOWAN

names, personal

Surnames

Since surnames are relatively stable and unaffected by fashion, normally being inherited rather than chosen, they have always attracted the attention of, for instance, historians and etymologists. As far as the general public in post-war Germany is concerned, it is the shifting legal position of such names that has been of most interest. As gender discrimination has attracted increasing attention, post-war surname legislation has introduced a significant measure of marital and parental choice.

Since 1994 both marriage partners may retain their pre-marital surname, or alternatively be registered in either partners' name. A partner using the other partners' surname may also prefix or suffix his or her own surname to create a double surname. All children of a marriage must bear the same surname: if the parents cannot agree on this, the decision is delegated to a guardianship court (*Vormundschaftsgericht*). This last ruling responds to a 1991 Federal Constitutional Court declaration that the requirement that the father's surname be given to a child if he and the mother are unable to agree on which of the parents' surnames it should receive was unconstitutional.

Forenames

By comparison with the UK and US, German law on forenames ('given' or 'first' names) is restrictive. The child's sex is required to be recognizable in the forenames given: if one of the forenames is ambiguous, the other must be clearly male or female as appropriate. Forenames have to be recognizable as 'real' names – single letters, Sr., Jr. etc. certainly won't do – and must not prejudice the child's interests, as perceived by the registrar, or those of a third party: names must not be nonsensical or offensive. In the GDR it was also required, in the case of more than one forename being given, that the forename by which the person was to be commonly called should be underlined on registration.

Forenames are inherently unstable, being subject, despite the levelling effect of social pressures, to a significant degree of parental choice. Through international contacts and the pull of rapidly changing fashions, the stock of names on which parents can choose to draw is also becoming ever wider. In such a context, some conflict with the gate-keepers is inevitable: what in Germany to one registrar is a known name, clearly marked for sex, to another may be an unmarked and fanciful invention. Both rejections and acceptances for girls have been documented in West Germany *vis-à-vis*, for instance, the names *Carol*, *Andy* and *Ana*. An appeal in 1982 against a registrar's decision not to allow *Nicola Robin* for a boy on the grounds that *Nicola* was not clearly a male name was upheld on the basis that (a) *Nicola* could indeed be a male name (of Italian origin), and – ironically in view of practice in the English-speaking world – (b) the second forename chosen, *Robin*, was exclusively marked as male. Generally acknowledged male/ female names such as *Heike*, *Kai*, *Helge* are rarely allowed through without another forename which is appropriately sex-specific. Since Germany has no centralized equivalent of the UK 'General Register Office', students of German naming fashions have to obtain data from individual local register offices, a time-consuming procedure which has resulted in there being as yet no wholly reliable statistics on parents' naming preferences in Germany. Borna, near Leipzig, served as the thermometer of East German naming fashions, its statistics being recorded by Johannes Schultheis in the now defunct journal *Sprachpflege*. A similar service, with data collected over a wider area, was provided for West Germany by Walter Seibicke and published annually in *Der Sprachdienst*, the journal of the *Gesellschaft für deutsche Sprache*, which now serves the whole of Germany, continues to advise register offices on naming issues and also operates an answering service for parents with name queries.

Naming trends in the post-war period have shown a move away from names of a more obviously 'German' character (e.g. *Günt(h)er*, *Gustav*, *Helmut*, *Werner*, *Gisela*, *Gerda*, etc.) towards imports from Scandinavia (e.g. *Birgit*, *Ingrid*, *T(h)orsten* and *Sven*), France (e.g. *André*, *Michèle*, *Marcel*, *Nadine* and *Nicole*) and the English-speaking world (e.g. *Mike*, *Kevin*, *Patrick*, *Dennis*, *Vanessa*, *Jennifer* and *Jessica*), but also increasing recourse to the international Hebrew-Greek-Latin name stock (e.g. *Andreas*, *Marc/kus*, *Matthias*, *Florian* and *Sebastian*). Such recourse can also, of course, create throw-backs to naming practices of the past (*Maria* and *Paul*, for example, have re-emerged), but a renewed taste for eighteenth- and nineteenth-century names closely associated with monarchy (e.g. *Ernst*, *Wilhelm*, *Ludwig*, *Viktoria* and *Augusta*) has yet to be detected. The following (real-life) family tree is quite representative of German naming trends over two centuries: born circa 1770 Franz Joseph and Therese > 1800 Johann Martin and Maria Ursula > 1830 Franz Xaver and Ursula > 1870 Bernhard and Caroline Katharine Sophie > 1900 Albert and Eleonore Marie Elisabeth > 1930 Hermann and Edith > 1960 Ulrich and Bettina > 1990 Alexandra-Katharina, Dominik and Nicolas Philipp. The names Christian, Michael, Stef/phanie and Christine/a were particularly prominent in the 1980s but are now receding. On the basis of available statistics, the ten names most frequently chosen in Germany in 1995 for girls include, in both the new and the old federal states, Maria, Laura, Julia, Anna/e, Sophia/e, Sarah and Lisa, and for boys Alexander, Maximilian, Luc/kas and Tobias. Differences between north and south, or between Catholic and Protestant areas, may well be greater than those between East and West. The spread of different names used for girls is invariably larger than that used for boys.

Further reading

Debus, F. (1985) 'Zur Namengebungs-Norm in der DDR', *Germanistische Linguistik: Sprachliche Normen und Normierungsfolgen in der DDR* 82–3; 141–68.

—— (1987) 'Personennamengebung der Gegenwart im historischen Vergleich', *Zeitschrift für Literaturwissenschaft und Linguistik: Namen* 67: 52–73.

Naumann, H. (ed.) (1994): *Das große Buch der Familiennamen. Alter, Herkunft, Bedeutung*, Niedernhausen: Falken.

Seibicke, W. (1991) *Vornamen*, Frankfurt am Main: Verlag für Standesamtswesen (both this and the surname book below contain much useful material about names in addition to annotated lists).

Seibicke, W. and Jacob, L. (1996). 'Die beliebtesten Vornamen des Jahres 1995', *Der Sprachdienst 2*, 96: 41–7.

GLYN HATHERALL

national anthems

Traditionally, Germans have not been happy with their national anthem. Sung to the melody of the second movement (*'poco adagio cantabile'*) of Joseph Haydn's *Kaiserquartett* (1797), the *Lied der Deutschen* (Song of the Germans) (1841) by August Heinrich Hoffmann von Fallersleben was tainted by much abuse and some misunderstanding. With its infamous first lines, *'Deutschland, Deutschland über alles / Über alles in der Welt'* (Germany, Germany, above all, / above everything in the world), which were anticipated by Heinrich Joseph Collin's *Österreich über alles* (Austria Above All) (1809), the song seemed to indicate nothing but unbridled national chauvinism. Falsely translated into English as 'Germany, Germany first of nations, / Over all in this wide world,' the lines were often read as an imperialist call to arms for the Teutonic conquest of the entire world. In a similar spirit the French translation *'Si, pour se défendre et attaquer, / Elle s'unit fraternellement'* (for *'Wenn es stets zu Schutz und Trutze / Brüderlich zusammenhält'*) gives the idiomatic phrase of communal protection an aggressive twist which could only confirm what had been read into the ambiguous statement. But the author was just the opposite of a nationalist aggressor. Best known for his popular children's songs, Hoffmann von Fallersleben was a dissident writer at odds with the Prussian authorities, a liberal who was forced to resign his professorship at the university of Breslau and expelled from Prussia because his collection of poems, cleverly entitled *Unpolitische Lieder* (Apolitical songs) (1841), were deemed too political. In fact, he was in a kind of shortlived exile when he wrote the *Lied der Deutschen* on 26 August 1841, on the then-British island of Helgoland which was to be exchanged for Zanzibar to become German territory in 1890.

Popularized in collections of patriotic and student stongs, Hoffmann von Fallersleben's song quickly pushed aside Ernst Moritz Arndt's *Was ist des Deutschen Vaterland?* (What is the German's Fatherland?) (1813) as the most popular song to address the question of German national identity in the face of foreign intervention (Napoleon) and domestic repression (Metternich). While after 1871 the official hymn of the newly created Imperial Reich, *Heil dir im Siegerkranz* (Hail to You in the Crown of Victory) hailed the emperor's military strength, the German people increasingly adopted the *Lied der Deutschen*. Rooted in the liberal democratic tradition of 1848 which is most clearly expressed in the third strophe (*'Einigkeit und Recht und Freiheit'* – unity and right and freedom), the song took on the role of an unofficial hymn countering the dynastic exhortation – in quite the same way Hoffmann had pitted his text against the dynastic anthem of the Holy Roman Empire, *Gott erhalte Franz den Kaiser* (God Save Franz the Emperor), which Haydn used in his *Kaiserquartett*.

It was in this republican spirit that on 11 August 1922 a social democrat, the first president of the Weimar Republic, Friedrich Ebert, declared the popular song the official national anthem. But just as some fanatical soldiers in the battle of Langemarck on 11 November 1914 had plunged to their death, singing *'Deutschland, Deutschland über alles'* along with Max Schneckenburger's anti-French *Wacht am Rhein* (Watch on the Rhine) (1841), the Nazis coupled the first strophe with an anthem of their own, the *Horst-Wessel-Lied* (*'Die Fahne hoch'* – Raise the flag) by one of the first 'martyrs' of their movement. Thus, after the end of the Third Reich, the national anthem was shelved and on most occasions replaced with the last movement of Beethoven's ninth symphony, the *Ode to Joy* (*An die Freude*) based on a text by Schiller (*'Freude, schöner Götterfunken'* – Joy, beautiful divine spark). On one historic occasion, however, when the first FRG Chancellor, Konrad **Adenauer**, was officially saluted on a state visit to Washington D.C., the military band, for lack of a German anthem, resorted to playing a silly ***Schlager*** of the 1940s, *Heidewitzka, Herr Kapitän*, which enraged the chancellor so much that he insisted in a correspondence with the first FRG President, Theodor Heuss, on restoring the German anthem. Heuss only reluctantly agreed to have the *Deutschlandlied* (with only the third strophe to be sung on official occasions) reinstated – but not by official decree, instead by mere publication of his letter to Adenauer (dated 6 May 1952) in the Federal Law Gazette.

While singing the dreaded first strophe of the *Deutschlandlied* has definitely been unwanted in the FRG, the GDR counterpiece of 1949, Johannes R. **Becher**'s *Auferstanden aus Ruinen* (Risen From the Ruins), also written to fit Haydn's melody but set to music by Hanns **Eisler** (with allusions to a popular tune of the 1930s, Hans Albers' *Good-bye Johnny*), could no longer be sung after 1971 when the reference to German unity, 'Deutschland, einig Vaterland' (Germany, united fatherland), no longer corresponded to the revised constitution which rejected the notion of a German nation larger than the socialist state.

After the fall of the **Berlin Wall** there was a public debate in the early summer of 1990 which national anthem would be best for the soon-to-be-unified Germany; '*Einigkeit und Recht und Freiheit*' clearly won over Bertolt **Brecht**'s *Kinderhymne* (Children's hymn) of 1950 ('*Anmut sparet nicht noch Mühe*' – Save neither grace nor labour) and Becher's hymn of 1949. While the second strophe of the *Deutschlandlied*, though no longer sung as part of the national anthem, is devoted to '*deutsche Frauen*' (German women), the third strophe, with its exclusive reference to 'brotherly' unity, has irked some feminists, but not as much as the Austrian anthem, *Heimat bist du großer Söhne* (Home You Are of Great Sons), which, though written by a woman (Paula von Préradovic), praises only the sons and not the daughters of the fatherland. With 'freedom' now guaranteed, the call for 'unity' which is generic to most national anthems is increasingly questioned as it does not reflect the growing cultural diversity of a struggling nation in which the initial euphoria of 1989–90 has clearly faded.

See also: German Question

Further reading

Kuhn, E. (1991) *Einigkeit und Recht und Freiheit. Die nationalen Symbole der Deutschen*, Frankfurt am Main and Berlin: Ullstein Verlag.

Seeba, H.C. (1986) ' "Einigkeit und Recht und Freiheit": The German Quest for National Identity in the 19th Century', in P. Boerner (ed.), *Concepts of National Identity. An Interdisciplinary Dialogue. Interdisziplinäre Betrachtungen zur Frage der nationalen Identität*, Baden-Baden: Nomos Verlagsgesellschaft.

HINRICH C. SEEBA

nature

This unspecific term most commonly denotes the totality of what exists independent of humanity, organizes and reproduces itself according to its own laws, and provides the basis of human life and civilization. In strongly urbanized societies the term often refers in a more restricted way to the (still cultivated) countryside surrounding the cities. In German culture, the forests are traditionally seen as the incarnation of nature. Hence, their decline since the 1970s has been a focal point of the environmental movement (see also **Waldsterben**; **pollution**; **environmentalism**). Germany is known for its high environmental standards and public awareness, reflected in strong environmental organizations and an outstandingly successful Green Party (see **Greens**). Germany has ten national parks covering a total of 7,002 km^2. Amongst others, these include the Black Forest, the *Bayerischer Wald* and the Lüneburg Heath. In addition there are some 4,888 nature reserves covering 6,200 km^2. Several other categories of protected areas further contribute to the conservation of nature in Germany.

In German culture, the appreciation of nature originates around the beginning of the nineteenth century. During the romantic era, which sought to counterbalance the one-sidedness of philosophical rationalism and the rapidly developing natural sciences, the portrayal of idealized nature was a central theme in popular and fine art. The term *Naturdenkmal* (monument of nature) was coined in 1799 (by A. v. Humboldt). The first ensemble of a human building and its surrounding natural environment to be put under official protection were the ruins of *Burg Drachenfels* (1828). With the progress of industrialization and the emergence of social problems in the rapidly expanding cities, the concept of nature became a focus for unfulfilled human desires, the longing for **Heimat**. Larger conservationist movements, ramblers' associations and life-reform groups, arguably the precursors of today's environmentalism, emerged towards the end of the nineteenth century.

In the contemporary debate (since the 1970s) a mixture of old and new interpretations of nature can be discerned: it appears as the object of the natural sciences, the creation of God, a finite resource, an ecological equilibrium, the lost paradise, a social utopia, etc. These multiple concepts of nature are reflected in the plurality of strategies for its protection. Concern for nature is normally directly related to concern for the future of humanity. In most contexts the idea of naturalness represents a normative principle for human behaviour. Nature and naturalness imply moral infallibility and they are relied upon to keep the destructive potential of human civilization under control. The stability of nature is the desired antidote to the acceleration of civilizatory change.

See also: environmental literature; *Heimatliteratur*; protest movements

Further reading

Dominick, R.H. (1992) *The Environmental Movement in Germany*, Bloomington and Indianapolis, IA: Indiana University Press (a history of environmentalism since the nineteenth century).

Landeshauptstadt Stuttgart, Kulturamt (ed.) (1994) *Zum Naturbegriff der Gegenwart. Kongressdokumentation*, Stuttgart: Friedrich Frommann Verlag (on the meanings of 'nature' in the contemporary debate).

Sieferle, R.P. (1984) *Fortschrittsfeinde? Opposition gegen Technik und Industrie von der Romantik bis zur Gegenwart*, Munich: Beck (on the genealogy of the ideas of nature and its conservation).

INGOLFUR BLÜHDORN

Naturtheater

Naturtheater is a form of popular outdoor theatre, performed in small towns and villages in southern Germany. The plays are performed by the indigenous population after being written, or transposed into dialect by local dramatists. The scale of active participation, and the size of the audiences, have made *Naturtheater* a major cultural phenomenon in Germany during the twentieth century. A wide range of plays are performed in *Naturtheater* ranging from popular comedies to classics such as Schiller's *William Tell*. The Reutlingen Naturtheater has a long tradition of performing popular German comedies since its establishment in 1928. In Hayingen the work of the resident dramatist, actor and director, Martin Schleker, enjoys particular success, drawing audiences from a radius of 100 kilometres.

ALISON PHIPPS

Nay, Ernst Wilhelm

b. 11 June 1902, Berlin; d. 8 April 1968, Cologne

Painter and graphic artist

Nay's early, figurative œuvre assimilated influences from cubism and expressionism. The Third Reich accordingly denounced him as a 'degenerate' artist. Until 1949 his paintings' style and subject matter struck a balance between figuration and abstraction, whereafter the latter prevailed. Nay's characteristic brushstrokes and spatial composition grounded his expressive abstraction in contingency, marking a contrast to the impersonal and absolutist abstraction favoured by painters like **Baumeister**. Between 1955 and 1965, with an increasingly decorative and strongly colourful style, Nay was esteemed as the leading German representative of European abstraction.

DANIEL KOEP

Neckermann

Founded in 1963 as a subdivision of the renowned Neckermann mail-order company NUR, Neckermann und Reisen GmbH + Co. KG (Neckermann and Travel) rapidly developed into the main German provider of package holidays for worldwide organized tourism in the 1970s, introducing cheap air travel to the masses, with its own hotels, tourist clubs, cruise ships and tourist sport facilities.

The sobriquet '*Neckermänner*' ('Neckermen') became synonymous with the criticism of mass tourism. Neckermann also contributed to the rationalization of the organization of mass tourism, for instance introducing computerized booking. The founder, Josef Neckermann, was an Olympic champion in dressage horsemanship.

See also: vacations and tourism

JUDITH LEEB

neo-expressionism

Neo-expressionism is regarded more as a slogan of convenience than as a term applicable to a specific movement. It refers to the re-emergence of a painterly figural tradition in the 1980s that distanced itself from the tendency towards abstraction and *Art Informel* of the post-war period. Its range, however, encompasses different generations of artists and numerous artistic practices, from the *Pandämonium* manifestoes of Georg **Baselitz** and Eugene Schönebeck of the early 1960s, to the *Heftige Malerei* (Angry Painting) exhibition held at Haus am Waldsee in Berlin in 1980, featuring the works of Rainer Fetting, Bernd Zimmer, Helmut Middendorf and Salomé.

The renewal of an expressionist idiom has been interpreted as a search for self-identity; German expressionism came in for particular censure in the 1937 'Degenerate Art' exhibition. Viewed as an act of defiance, the restoration of this legacy reinscribed artistic 'authenticity' as central to the creative process. Hence, Anselm **Kiefer**'s mixed media negotiations of German landscape, myth and history, as well as Baselitz's 'primitivist' inverted paintings, have been seen to comply with this paradigm. Of the same generation, Karl-Horst Hödicke's city scenes were of great inspiration to his students at the Hochschule für Bildende Künste in Berlin. The expressionist technique and colour intensity of his paintings were achieved by using *Kunstharz* (or synthetic resin) – a mixture of inexpensive household pigments on a base of oil and acrylic.

The exploitation of this medium and gestural painterliness reached a climax in the cityscapes of his students Fetting, Middendorf and Zimmer, in which the artifice of the **Berlin Wall** or apartment blocks sweep away traces of organic life. Critically considered in the context of Die Neuen Wilden (The New Fauves), the artists chose subjects that reflected their engagement with the art and club scenes of Berlin, Salomé focusing on the homosexual subculture of the city's night life. As in the case of Hödicke's circle, who founded an artists' co-operative in Berlin in 1964, the Galerie Großgörschen 35, Die Neuen Wilden set up their Galerie am Moritzplatz in the decaying area of Kreuzberg in 1977. However, the growing importance of the art market gradually supplanted avant-garde notions of communal artistic interaction.

Hence, the origination of the term neo-expressionism cannot be separated from the context of dealership and critical reception at the time. Of particular importance to its promotion was the Galerie Michael Werner, which moved from Berlin to Cologne in 1968. The gallery of Paul Maenz in Cologne also staged pivotal exhibitions, such as Mülheimer Freiheit in 1981. The increasing capitalization of the art market led various commentators to question the motivations of the artists, Benjamin Buchloh being particularly vociferous about the revisionism of new figuration. Donald Kuspit, the American art critic, was equally instrumental in bringing such debates to the attention of an international audience.

Further reading

Buchloh, B.H.D. (1981) 'Figures of Authority, Ciphers of Regression: Notes on the Return of Representation in European Painting', *October* 16: 39–68.

Krens, T., Govan, M. and Thompson, J. (1989) *Refigured Painting: The German Image 1960–88*, New York: Solomon R. Guggenheim Museum.

Kuspit, D. (1993) *The New Subjectivism: Art in the 1980s*, New York: Da Capo (includes pivotal articles of the early 1980s from *Art in America* and *Artforum*).

SHULAMITH BEHR

neo-nazism

The term 'neo-nazism' refers to political parties, organizations or groups in post-war Germany which espouse all or part of National Socialist ideology, glorify Hitler as a political leader, and show their allegiance to Nazism through a use of Nazi-style language, symbols and actions. In 1993, the annual report by the Office for the Protection of the Constitution, which monitors political extremism in Germany, listed 77 groups with a total of 42,400 members, among them three political parties with 32,000 members between them, excluding the **Republikaner** (23,000 members) whose place on the far right of the political spectrum is not deemed to conflict with the constitutional commitment against National Socialism. Thirty-one groups were classified as neo-nazi. While right-extremism and neo-nazism hardly differ with regard to their ideologies, neo-nazi groups adopt more provocative languages and actions, including the use of violence.

As a right-extremist opposition against the democratic system and German political developments since 1945, neo-nazism is based on four key themes. First, German nationalism which purports a superiority of Germans and rejects the territorial settlement after 1945. Even German unification failed to meet the demands for a 'greater' Germany in the borders of 1937 or even of 1941/2). Second, anti-communism entails the summary rejection of all communist or left-wing groups and activities as alleged dangers to the German people and its interests. Until the collapse of the eastern bloc, anti-communism linked neo-nazi with German mainstream politics. Third, racism and xenophobia emulate the Nazi policies of persecution and the use of violence against foreigners. Since the early 1970s, hostility from the extreme right and neo-nazi acts of violence have been directed against **Gastarbeiter**, and since the late 1980s also against asylum seekers. Fourth, anti-Semitism of the extreme right justifies the Nazi persecution of the Jews, vilifies **Vergangenheitsbewältigung** and admissions of German guilt, and purports that the **Holocaust** never happened. In neo-nazism, anti-Semitism is enacted as desecration of Jewish cemeteries, concentration camp memorials and synagogues and as acts of physical violence against individuals who are taken to be Jews.

Neo-nazism in post-war Germany developed in four phases. The first phase began with the creation of right-extremist political parties by former members of the Nazi party and officer corps in 1948–9 and ended with the banning by the Federal Constitutional Court of the Socialist Reichs Party (SRP) in 1952 after it gained 11 percent of the vote in *Land* elections in Lower Saxony. During the second phase (1952–72), various right-extremist successor parties attempted to mobilize the right-extremist potential which had been estimated at up to 15 percent in the FRG. Between 1966 and 1968, the National Democratic Party (NPD) entered seven *Land* parliaments, failed at the 5 percent hurdle in the Bundestag elections in 1969 and had lost all parliamentary representation by 1972. In addition, the *Deutsche National Zeitung* (circulation over 100,000), affiliated mass organizations like the Deutsche Volksunion and a plethora of groups from paramilitary gangs (Wehrsportgruppe Hoffmann) to clones of the Hitler Youth (Wiking Jugend) disseminated Nazi-style ideologies, often with funding from nazi organizations in the United States and elsewhere in Europe. The third phase of neo-nazism commenced in 1972 when young right-extremists of the Aktion Widerstand turned against the NPD and other proponents of the 'old right' ostensibly to fight against the government's **Ostpolitik** but also to infuse a more aggressive approach in a political camp whose older activists only harked back to the Nazi years and whose leaders were too fearful of risking a party ban to challenge the constitutional consensus.

The 1970s saw the rise of the extra-parliamentary radicalism of the far right which has since been termed neo-nazi. The ideological assumptions and targets were the same as before: nationalism, anti-communism, foreigners, anti-Semitism with the dual focus of attacking Jews and denying the Holocaust. This new radical approach changed the face of neo-nazism in Germany. It attracted young people (in the past, Nazi orientations predominated among older generations). Nazi successor parties, as the Nazi party itself, had attracted above average support from the well-educated middle classes, self-employed and farmers. The neo-nazi groups of the

1970s and later attracted the less well-educated, blue collar and unskilled workers, apprentices and pupils in non-advanced types of schools (*Hauptschulen*). The generation change in neo-nazism went hand in hand with an increase in offences with a right-extremist motivation, in particular offensive daubings or acts of aggression against foreigners and Jews. The fourth phase began in the mid-1980s when a neo-nazi youth culture of **skinheads** and street gangs emerged in the West alongside established right-extremist organizations and in the East in open defiance of socialist anti-fascism. After unification, the two youth cultures combined to produce a new-style of neo-nazism: criminal offences with right-extremist motives rose from about 300 to well over 2,000 per annum, one in four of those commited in the new *Länder*, 80 percent by young people under the age of twenty. Neo-nazi attacks resulted in six deaths in 1992 and in seven deaths in 1993 as well as twenty attempted murders. Since unification Turks, asylum seekers and Jews have been in the forefront of neo-nazis attacks but the disabled, the homeless and anyone who appears non-German also become ready targets.

Official figures suggest that organized right-extremism doubled from 21,000 in 1993 to 42,000 in 1993, excluding the Republican party which does not count as right-extremist at the federal level. Neo-nazi organizations had 1,100 members in 1983 and 1,500 (a 30 percent increase) in 1993. In addition, official reports listed 5,600 unaffiliated neo-nazi skinheads, other estimates arrive at considerably higher numbers. From a radical dimension within the organized extreme right, neo-nazism in Germany has become a facet of contemporary youth culture, backed by anti-Semitic and xenophobic computer games, jokes, cartoon characters and a discourse which has absorbed Nazi aims and language but is considered 'normal' outside extremist organizations as much as inside them. In an attempt to quell the rise of neo-nazism among young people several neo-nazi groups and skinhead bands have been banned since 1990 and German courts have begun to pass stiffer sentences against right-extremist offenders. However, the nationalism, racism and anti-Semitism which had been the hallmark of neo-nazism inspired a protest culture among young Germans who regard themselves as losers in an increasingly mobile and affluent society. Their ideological orientations no longer depend on membership in a right-extremist organization – in the new *Länder*, organized right-extremism is virtually non-existent – nor does their use of violence depend on clearance from a neo-nazi leader.

Further reading

Bergmann, W. and Erb, R. (eds) (1994) *Neonazismus und rechte Subkultur*, Berlin: Metropol Verlag (the book consists of specialist chapters on anti-Semitism and xenophobia among young Germans, on attitudes to violence and case studies of neo-nazi groups, their language, activities and membership, in particular in the new *Länder*).

Bundesminister des Inneren (ed.) *Verfassungsschutzbericht* Bonn, annually since 1961 (although these reports tend to imply that neo-nazism and right-extremism are no more relevant in Germany than in any other western democracy and numbers on membership developments and offences may be higher than stated there, the reports constitute a good source to trace the long-term development of neo-nazism in Germany).

Willems, H. (1993) *Fremdenfeindliche Gewalt. Einstellungen, Täter, Konflikteskalation*, Opladen: Leske & Budrich (the book contains the findings of a detailed empirical survey on the acceptance of violence among young people generally and specifically the use of violence against foreigners; the survey includes a wealth of data on the social and economic background of activists and offenders, on the regional distribution of xenophobic violence, and its place among Germany's young people).

EVA KOLINSKY

Neue Deutsche Literatur

Established in 1953 as the monthly journal of the GDR **Writers' Union**, *Neue Deutsche Literatur* remained in the shadow of its more independently-minded rival **Sinn und Form**, despite its undoubted importance both as a forum for pan-German literary dialogue (until the building of the Berlin Wall) and as the launching-pad for young GDR authors. It has emerged from the *Wende* (now as a bi-monthly publication) strengthened by the presence of authors like Christa **Wolf** and Christoph **Hein** on its editorial board and by its renewed commitment to contemporary German literature as a whole.

DENNIS TATE

Neue Kronen Zeitung

The *Neue Kronen Zeitung* is the largest Austrian daily paper (printrun: 1,120,000). In 1959 Hans **Dichand** and Kurt Falk revived the old title *Die Kronen Zeitung* (originally founded 1900) with financial support from trade unions. After a long lawsuit Dichand and Falk became joint owners. In 1987 Dichand bought out Falk and sold 50 percent of his shares to the German WAZ (Westdeutsche Allgemeine Zeitung) Group.

A populist tabloid which commands more than 40 percent of the national readership, the *Neue Kronen Zeitung* has exerted a decisive influence on Austrian politics (e.g. the introduction of abortion laws, the anti-nuclear movement and ecological conflicts). Commercially it is trying to expand into other markets (e.g. cable television, local radio and mobile phone systems).

GEORG HELLMAYR

Neue Zürcher Zeitung

Founded in 1780, the *Neue Zürcher Zeitung* is the best-known serious German-language daily newspaper in Switzerland. It has a very high, internationally recognized standard of news reporting and feature articles, and editorially adopts politically conservative views. Since 1951, the *Neue Zürcher Zeitung* has published an accompanying monthly magazine in English, the 'Swiss Review of World Affairs', and since 1991, a monthly supplement to the main paper, 'NZZ-Folio', each issue of which carries features and articles devoted to one topic of current interest. Some 90 percent of sales come from readers' subscriptions (circulation in 1995 was approximately 154,000 daily).

MALCOLM PENDER

Neues Deutschland

Neues Deutschland ('ND'), a daily newspaper founded in 1946, was the central organ of the **SED** from 1950 until 18 December 1989. With more than 1 million copies, the Berlin-based daily was the most important newspaper in the GDR. After the political changes in East Germany, it became the party-owned newspaper of the **PDS** with sales of some 70,000 copies per day in 1996.

As the central organ of the SED, *Neues Deutschland* was, like the state-owned press agency **ADN**, the most important instrument of the East German **Politbüro** and its party **propaganda**. Controlled by the Department of Agitation and Propaganda, its press coverage affirmed the ideological line of SED party politics, and in prioritizing agitation over information, often concealed vital facts from its readers. As a result of its increasingly stifling and doctrinal journalism, over the years most critical East German readers lost their interest in the paper.

After the political changes in the fall of 1989 and the subsequent demise of the GDR, *Neues Deutschland* underwent a substantial transformation, both structurally and politically. The previously leading ideologues were replaced and a critical confrontation with its own past eventually took place. Yet due to the paper's previous affirmation of party politics and its high percentage of mandatory subscriptions by enterprises, mass organizations and leading party members, already by June of 1990 its sales figures had dropped by 70 percent. Like all East German newspapers, *Neues Deutschland* had to downsize its staff – from 530 people during the existence of the GDR to only one hundred in 1994. With the exception of *Neues Deutschland*, all East German newspapers were bought by large publishing conglomerates from the West. Since it is owned and financed by the PDS, *Neues Deutschland* is the only East German newspaper that remained economically independent from these large enterprises, yet therefore less competitive.

Under these revised conditions, *Neues Deutschland* has redefined its purpose as being a critical left-wing voice of pluralist views. Carrying the subtitle *'Sozialistische Tageszeitung'* (socialist daily newspaper), it often provides oppositional perspectives to German government politics, especially with regard to matters that are disadvantageous to the new *Länder* (the former GDR). The close connection with the PDS and left-wing politics is reflected also in the papers' readership. The paper has regained the interest of many East German intellectuals and is also read by the economically less well-off in the East. It is less successful in attracting a younger readership (most of its readers are over fifty) as well as those who believe that the paper may not have effectively abandoned its communist past. While *Neues Deutschland* remains marginal with readers in the West, it is the leading national newspaper in the eastern part of Germany.

See also: journalism; mass media: GDR; newspapers

Further reading

Holzweißig, G. (1989) *Massenmedien in der DDR*, Berlin: Holzapfel (standard survey of GDR media).

MARGRIT FRÖLICH

Neues Forum

The largest citizens' movement in the GDR (see also **citizens' movements: GDR**), Neues Forum was established in winter 1989. After the release of a founding declaration demanding democracy, free elections and a free press, more than a hundred thousand GDR citizens joined the movement. Grassroots democracy, decentralized structures and citizens' self-representation instead of representation through parties were the essential principles. After the first free elections to the GDR parliament in March 1990 Neues Forum split into different factions. This was the beginning of a continuing decline. The largest group was integrated in **Bündnis 90**; only a small group of activists stayed in the Neues Forum.

See also: citizens' initiatives: GDR; *Wende*

LOTHAR PROBST

Neuss, Wolfgang

b. 3 December 1923, Breslau (now Wroctaw, Poland); d. 5 May 1989, Berlin

Cabaret artist

Sent to the eastern front in 1941 and wounded several times, Neuss became West Germany's leading satirical **cabaret** artist in the 1960s. He received prizes for his work on radio and television and for his 1964 record *Das jüngste Gericht* (The Last Judgement). The record of his joint performance with Wolf **Biermann** in *Wolf Biermann (Ost) zu Gast bei Wolfgang Neuss (West)* (1965) captures the iconoclastic wit of the two artists. A drop-out in the 1970s, he made a limited comeback in the 1980s.

MARGARET VALLANCE

New German Cinema

Although there is general agreement that the death of Rainer Werner **Fassbinder** in 1982 marked the end of West Germany's new wave of art-house cinema, a variety of dates have been proposed for its inception. 1962 was the year in which a group of twenty-six young filmmakers, spurred on by the French *nouvelle vague* and Italian neo-realism, signed the defiant Oberhausen Manifesto renouncing 'conventional German cinema' and 'the influence of commercial partners'. The year 1965 saw the debut feature of Jean-Marie **Straub** and Danièle **Huillet** and the founding of the Kuratorium junger deutscher Film to subsidize films by new directors. In 1966 Volker **Schlöndorff**'s first literary adaptation, *Young Törless (Der junge Törless)*, was well received at Cannes, and Alexander **Kluge**'s programmatically titled *Abschied von gestern* (*Yesterday Girl*, literally 'good-bye to yesterday') won eight prizes including a Silver Lion in Venice. 1967 saw the feature film debut of Edgar **Reitz**. A persistent lack of funding, the absence of suitable production and distribution infrastructures, and the disenchantment of audiences and critics alike with German cinema meant that the 'new cinema' proclaimed in the manifesto was slow to make its mark. This period of frustrations and setbacks has often been termed 'Young German Cinema', with the New German Cinema proper heralded in 1969–70 by the first features of Rainer Werner **Fassbinder**, Werner **Schroeter**, Rosa von **Praunheim** and Wim **Wenders**, members of a younger generation who were able to benefit from the funding organizations and statutes instituted by the 'Oberhausener'. This confusion over dates and terminology stems in part from the fact that, unlike its French and Italian prototypes, the New German Cinema was decidedly heterogeneous, with a diverse, often antagonistic group of *Autorenfilmer* (auteurist writer-directors) following their own political and aesthetic programmes. Indeed it is really only the rejection of commercial mass entertainment cinema and a conspicuous 'literariness' which unite Kluge's Brechtian montages, Schlöndorff's polished literary adaptations, Werner **Herzog**'s neo-romanticism, Wenders's road movies, Fassbinder's politicized melodramas and Hans-Jürgen **Syberberg**'s spectacular historical pageants.

Summing up the spirit of the early years, director Rudolf **Thome** has written: 'We wanted a cinema that looked like the films of Hawks and Godard. A cinema that was fun. A cinema that was simple and radical'. The heavy reliance on foreign models explains why this period is dominated by American-style gangster movies and *nouvelle vague* references. A peculiarly German feature of the New German Cinema, on the other hand, is its predilection for literary adaptation, both of contemporary authors as in Schlöndorff and Margarethe von **Trotta**'s *The Lost Honour of Katharina Blum* and Schlöndorff's *The Tin Drum*, and classical texts as in Fassbinder's *Fontane Effi Briest*, Helma **Sanders-Brahms**'s *Das Erdbeben in Chile* (The Earthquake in Chile) and Herzog's *Woyzeck*. Indeed a number of directors, including Schlöndorff, Straub, Huillet, Peter **Lilienthal** and Hans W. **Geissendörfer**, concentrated almost exclusively on literary adaptation.

The experiences of what has become known as the 'fatherless generation' help to explain not only the filmmakers' fascination with America, but also their preoccupation with the past and

memory (in particular the Third Reich), and the superabundance of narratives revolving around outsider figures. The New German Cinema is rightly celebrated as political cinema, but this assertion has to be qualified. Certainly Fassbinder, Kluge, Straub, Huillet, von Trotta, Schlöndorff and Reinhard **Hauff** were what film historian Thomas Elsaesser terms 'contentist' filmmakers, addressing such topical themes as *Gastarbeiter*, the press and **terrorism**. The culmination of terrorist activity in the '**German Autumn**' of 1977 indeed spawned a mini-wave of its own, comprising the collective film *Germany in Autumn* (*Deutschland in Herbst*, 1977–8), Hauff's *Knife in the Head* (*Messer im Kopf*, 1978) and *Stammheim* (1986), Fassbinder's *The Third Generation* (*Die dritte Generation*, 1979), and von Trotta's *The German Sisters* (*Die bleierne Zeit*, 1981). Certain themes, however, remained virtually taboo, most conspicuous amongst them the Holocaust and German division. Moreover, few films on National Socialism pre-date the mid-1970s. In stark contrast to their contentist colleagues, Herzog, Schroeter and Wenders belong to Elsaesser's catagory of 'sensibilist' filmmakers, focusing on states of mind and favouring images (especially landscapes) and music over words.

The renaissance of German art-house cinema in the 1970s – the decade during which Fassbinder, Herzog, Schlöndorff, Wenders and Syberberg gained international audiences and critical acclaim – made little impression on the home market, and the achievement of the New German Cinema is, ultimately, that of a prestige export product. Summing up the impact of his generation at home, Hauff concluded that 'on the arts pages we are strong, in the film industry we are marginal figures'. In 1978, the *annus mirabilis* of the New German Cinema, the share of the home market captured by German films sank to 8 percent. Without what Herzog has termed the 'artificial respiration' of government subsidy and prizes – and without television co-production – he and his colleagues would have been unable to work. As long as the government felt it was benefiting from the positive image of German cinema abroad it was willing to maintain the life-support machine, but in the new political climate of the early 1980s Minister of the Interior Friedrich Zimmermann decided that the time had come to stop funding oppositional voices. The filmmakers' equivocal stance on terrorism and the controversy in Bavaria surrounding Herbert **Achternbusch**'s 'blasphemous' film *Das Gespenst* (The Ghost) (1982), were used to justify the change in policy.

This crisis was underlined by the death of Fassbinder in 1982, by which time Wenders, Schlöndorff and Herzog were all working abroad. This marks the end of the second great flowering of German film, although the main protagonists have continued to work as *Autorenfilmer* in an increasingly hostile climate.

See also: documentary film; film festivals; film, experimental; film: FRG

Further reading

Corrigan, T. (1994) *New German Cinema: The Displaced Image*, Bloomington, IA: Indiana University Press (an updated edition of a classic study which examines representative films).

Elsaesser, T. (1989) *The New German Cinema: A History*, Houndmills, London: BFI Macmillan (a standard work, organized chronologically and by theme; contains extensive filmographies).

Sandford, J. (1980) *The New German Cinema*, London: Oswald Wolff (a detailed and lively analysis of seven major directors).

MARTIN BRADY AND HELEN HUGHES

New Subjectivity

New Subjectivity (also known as New Sensibility and New Inwardness) describes the dominant literary trend in West Germany in the 1970s, a decade characterized by a pronounced interest in subjective forms of writing and a thematic concern with personal experience and the nature of individual identity. The trend is generally assumed to have begun around 1973 and to reflect changes in the broader socio-political climate. There had been a period of intense political activity in the late 1960s which climaxed in the **student movement**, a context within which literary concerns had been neglected in favour of commitment to the political collective. But by the early 1970s, the disintegration of the student movement, the advent

of **terrorism**, and the state's repressive response to it had given rise to a collective mood of disappointment and resignation which provided the impulse for a return to literature as a medium in which to explore the personal concerns of the individual.

Poets such as Jürgen Theobaldy and Nicolas **Born** focused on everyday private experience and plays by Botho **Strauß** and Thomas **Bernhard** explored individual identity crises. Two novels by former political activists published in 1973, Karin **Struck**'s *Klassenliebe* (Class Love) and Peter **Schneider**'s *Lenz*, gave expression to a widespread concern that individual needs had been neglected during the protest period, while autobiography and the autobiographical novel provided forms within which a number of writers focused on the individual's disoriented search for a sense of self in an apparently meaningless world, a theme common to the fiction of Strauß, Born and Peter **Handke**.

New Subjectivity in fact provides an umbrella term for an extremely diverse range of subjective writing which encompasses a number of discrete trends, including the so-called *Vater-* and *Mutterromane* (which focus on the life of the writer's parent), *Verständigungstexte* (texts concerned to communicate a sense of shared experience to a specific target group), and the new wave of women's writing which emerged during the decade. It has proved a useful label for all those works of the 1970s and early 1980s which focused on individual experience, largely at the expense of, but also on occasions as a medium for, political statements.

Further reading

Bullivant, K. (1987) 'Realism and "New Subjectivity"', in *Realism Today, Aspects of the Contemporary West German Novel*, Leamington Spa: Berg (detailed readings of a number of representative texts).

DeMeritt, L.C. (1987) *New Subjectivity and Prose Forms of Alienation. Peter Handke and Botho Strauß*, New York: Lang (surveys the trend before focusing on two writers)

McCormick, R.W. (1991) *Politics of the Self. Feminism and the Postmodern in West German Literature and Film*, Princeton, NJ: Princeton University Press (an in-depth study of the New Subjective trend in two media).

McGowan, M. (1989) 'Neue Subjektivität', in K. Bullivant (ed.) *After the 'Death of Literature': West German Writing of the 1970s*, Oxford: Berg (an informative analysis of aspects of the trend).

JOANNE LEAL

newspapers

The daily newspaper market in Germany is characterized by a predominance of regional and local titles, relatively low individual circulations, and a lack of 'national' papers in the British sense. Long-term trends have been marked by growing concentration of ownership and a diminution in the number of independent editorial units. The general tone of the daily press tends, with one major exception, to be serious and sober, and newspaper-buying habits are marked by high degrees of readership loyalty, encouraged by the practice of subscription as the preferred method of purchase. Explicit party-political attachments are not a feature of the German press.

For most Germans, *the* daily paper is the one published locally. These publications have circulations that range from (typically) just a few thousand to (exceptionally) a hundred thousand or more, and are normally morning, rather than evening, papers. They usually cover not just local matters, but the whole range of international, national and regional news as well. Such papers may well also appear in other local editions in other towns and districts in the region – often as a result of take-overs, mergers and other co-operation agreements between previously independent local papers.

The distinction between 'local' and 'regional' papers is not always clear, as what may be perceived as an example of the former may in fact be a sub-edition of the latter, but in general the titles of the regional papers are well-known – though they are not always readily available – outside their home area, and they have circulations that by German standards are decidedly large (i.e. well over 100,000). This is especially the case in East Germany, where the former SED district papers, bought up by western concerns after privatization, have a virtual monopoly of the regional market, and sales figures well in excess of those of their western counterparts (see also **mass media: GDR**). Politically, the local and regional press in both East and West tends to be middle-of-the-road.

The German papers best-known abroad fall into the category of the 'supra-regional dailies' (*überregionale Tageszeitungen*). These are papers that are readily available nationally (and internationally), but which none the less have their roots – and their highest sales – in a particular region. Four papers are traditionally accorded this status: the **Süddeutsche Zeitung**, published in Munich, the **Frankfurter Allgemeine Zeitung** (*FAZ*) and **Frankfurter Rundschau**, both published in Frankfurt am Main, and Die **Welt**, published in Berlin. All four are 'serious' papers, differing in their politics, their degree of regional attachment, and their readership appeal: the *Süddeutsche* and the *Frankfurter Rundschau* are both left-of-centre politically, and the *FAZ* and *Die Welt* right-of-centre; while the *Süddeutsche* and the *Frankfurter Rundschau* have distinct strongholds in Bavaria and the Frankfurt am Main area respectively, the other two are less regionally rooted. In terms of readership appeal the *FAZ* is undoubtedly the most earnest and 'heavyweight' in its style and coverage, followed by the *Frankfurter Rundschau* and the *Süddeutsche*, with *Die Welt* aiming itself more at the middle market.

Apart from the specialist cases of the financial daily *Handelsblatt* and the 'alternative' *tageszeitung*, the only paper with a truly 'national' distribution is the **Bild** (though it too appears in a number of distinct regional editions). *Bild*, founded in 1952 by Axel **Springer**, is the exception that proves the rules of German newspaper publishing: not only its countrywide reach and its huge circulation (over four million, the biggest on the continent), but its brash and sensationalist style (this latter emulated by only a handful of strictly local big-city papers) are quite atypical of the rest of the German press. Reaching around a third of the population every day, *Bild* has always been a force to be reckoned with in the shaping of public opinion, though the strident right-wing populism and dubious journalistic practices that brought it notoriety in earlier decades have abated since Springer's death in 1985.

The Sunday paper habit is little developed in Germany, the only two significant examples of the genre being Sunday editions of *Bild* and *Die Welt*. Serious weekly newspapers, on the other hand, play an important role in providing the national forum for political and cultural debate that cannot so readily be offered by the decentralized daily press. Pre-eminent among the weeklies is the liberal *Die Zeit*, which sells close on half a million copies; smaller in circulation (and in size) are the Catholic *Rheinischer Merkur*, the Protestant *Sonntagsblatt*, and *Wochenpost*, a former GDR title with a specifically East German focus. *Die Woche*, launched in 1993, has attempted to woo a readership looking for something more colourful, catchy, and less daunting than the earnest pages of *Die Zeit*.

Statistics indicate a slow but steady decline in the number of daily titles in Federal Republic since the 1950s, a process that resumed in the 1990s after the sudden increase brought by the addition of East Germany. By the late 1990s there were some 380 daily papers, selling between them a total of 30 million copies. These outwardly healthy figures mask the fact that only about a third of these papers are independent units, and that the number of districts where only one local paper is published has increased to the point where for around half the population there is – given the German preference precisely for these local papers – in effect only one relevant daily paper on offer.

Newspapers in Austria

The Austrian press structure reflects both the disproportionate role of Vienna in the country's cultural life, for which there is no equivalent in Germany, and at the same time the countervailing strength of regional allegiances. Seventeen daily papers appear in Austria, and nearly three-quarters of sales are accounted for by those based in Vienna. By far the biggest share of the market is held by the **Neue Kronen Zeitung**, which is read by around 40 percent of the country's adult population, followed at some distance by **Kurier** and **täglich Alles**, which have a readership share of around 12 percent each. All three of these of these papers are at the 'popular' end of the spectrum, and are Vienna-based (although the *Neue Kronen Zeitung* also prints in Graz, Klagenfurt, Linz and Salzburg). The country's second-biggest city, Graz, is the home of the middle-market **Kleine Zeitung**, which also has a share of overall readership of around 12 percent. Other parts of the country have their own regional papers, but only one – the **Salzburger Nachrichten** – forms part of the trio of Austria's most respected 'quality' dailies, the other two being the Vienna-based *Der* **Standard** and *Die* **Presse**. Each of these papers has an overall readership share from around 4 percent to 5 percent. All of the papers mentioned here describe themselves as politically independent.

(For related entries on the Austrian press see also **Arbeiterzeitung**; **Bacher, Gerd**; **Dichand, Hans**; **Mediaprint**; **profil**; **Wiener Zeitung**).

Newspapers in German-speaking Switzerland

The structure of the Swiss press is highly decentralized, not just a result of the multilingual cultural geography of the country (see also **German language: Switzerland**), but even more as a reflection of the highly localized organization of Swiss public life, for even within the individual language regions papers typically have a small geographical range. The number of daily titles is high (over 100 in the mid-1990s; the following statistics refer to this period), and there are another 150 or so papers that appear on a less frequent basis, but individual circulation figures tend to be low (nearly half the dailies sell less than 10,000 copies, and only eight exceed 50,000). Swiss newspapers are typically earnest in tone, and decidedly conservative in their layout, and often in their political stance too.

Undoubtedly the best-known and most prestigious Swiss daily – both at home and abroad – is the **Neue Zürcher Zeitung**, a journal of record of redoubtable thoroughly; half of the *NZZ*'s daily sales of around 150,000 are in the Zürich area, where its main competitor is the more liberal *Tages-Anzeiger*, which sells around 280,000 copies. The two other main serious papers in the German-speaking cities are the *Berner Zeitung* (128,000) and the *Basler Zeitung* (115,000). The biggest-selling paper in Switzerland as a whole, however, is **Blick** (355,000 copies daily), which fits none of the normal patterns of Swiss journalism: it is a newcomer (launched in 1959), is sold predominantly through retail outlets rather than by subscription, is brash and sensationalist in makeup and tone, and has an even distribution throughout its language area.

Further reading

Humphreys, P.J. (1994) *Media and Media Policy in Germany: The Press and Broadcasting since 1945*, 2nd edn, Oxford and Providence, RI: Berg (detailed account of media organization and policy issues through to the post-unification period; two chapters are devoted to the press).

Meyn, H. (1996) *Massenmedien in der Bundesrepublik Deutschland*, Berlin: Colloquium Verlag (introduction to structure of the media and problems of press – and broadcasting – freedom; regularly updated.)

Sandford, J. (1976) *The Mass Media of the German-Speaking Countries*, London and Ames: Oswald Wolff and Iowa State UP (covers the history of the German press up to the mid-1970s, with chapters also on Austria and Switzerland).

JOHN SANDFORD

Niemöller, Martin

b. 14 January 1892, Lippstadt; d. 6 March 1984, Wiesbaden

Protestant church leader

Niemöller, a WWI submarine commander ordained in 1924, initially welcomed National Socialism, but – soon disillusioned – became a prominent member of the Confessing Church, opposed to National Socialist influence in the Protestant churches. Niemöller was held in concentration camps from 1937 to 1945, and after played a major role in the Evangelical Church in Germany as head of its Foreign Relations Department (1945–56) and President of the Evangelical Church in Hessen-Nassau (1947–64); and in the World Council of Churches as an executive member (1948–61), and WCC president (1961–8). He was an outspoken opponent of the

FRG's western integration and rearmament, nuclear weapons and the US involvement in Vietnam.

Further reading

Bentley, J. (1984) *Martin Niemöller*, Oxford: Oxford University Press (includes select bibliography).

STEPHEN BROWN

Nitsch, Hermann

b. 29 August 1938, Vienna

Performance artist and painter

First active as a painter in the style of abstract expressionism, Nitsch founded his Orgien-Mysterien Theater (Orgies Mysteries Theatre) in 1961 and became a leading member of the Viennese Actionists. His large-scale performances or *Gesamtkunstwerke*, often lasting many days, involve audience participation, animal slaughter, quasi-religious sacrificial rituals and live music. Intended to function cathartically, the performances owe an acknowledged debt to ancient Greek drama, Wagnerian opera and psychoanalytical theory. Relics from the performances – including despoiled vestments and vast blood paintings – are frequently exhibited in conventional gallery spaces.

See also: Mühl, Otto

MARTIN BRADY

Nöstlinger, Christine

b. 13 October 1936, Vienna

Writer

One of the most popular and prolific authors for children in the German language, Nöstlinger is acclaimed for both her humour and her insights into children's lives and problems. She has been credited with breaking the mould of traditional children's literature, particularly in her depiction of unusually strong and independent girl characters and her criticism of the Austrian school system and the family. She has also published poems in

Viennese dialect and written for the Austrian press, radio and television. She is the recipient of numerous national and international prizes for children's books.

GABRIELA STEINKE

Nolte, Ernst

b. 11 January 1923, Witten (Ruhr)

Historian

Trained as a philosopher, Nolte moved into history and became Professor of Modern History at the Free University of Berlin in 1973, following a stint at Marburg from 1965. His comparative studies of European fascism (1963 and 1966) received widespread critical acclaim; but his massive volume on Germany and the Cold War (1974) already signalled a controversial attempt to relativize Nazi crimes, while his book on Marxism and industrialization (1983) introduced the view that fascism was a reaction to Marxism. These views became central elements in the *Historikerstreit*, which was unleashed by the publication of the text of a speech by Nolte.

MARY FULBROOK

Nossack, Hans Erich

b. 10 January 1901, Hamburg; d. 2 November 1977, Hamburg

Writer

Now translated into many languages, Nossack's work gained recognition after 1945. His percipient novels and essays are basically accounts or reports, primarily concerned with the question of personal identity, and containing scathing criticism of postwar German society. His works tend to be existentialist, challenging accepted norms and probing unknown and uncertain spheres. *The Impossible Proof* (*Unmögliche Beweisaufnahme*, 1956) confronts the central problem of trying to live by two different realities, and examines the relationship between what is real and unreal. His works, written in the first person, are not autobiographi-

cal, but inner explorations investigating the possibilities of human existence.

Further reading

Kraus, J. (1981) *Hans Erich Nossack*, Munich: Beck (provides a useful overview).

PETER PROCHNIK

Novak, Helga Maria

b. 8 September 1935, Berlin

Writer

Influenced by Bertolt **Brecht**, Novak's poetry and ballads are critical of state power and bureaucratic injustice, and coincide with the revoking of her GDR citizenship. Nazism, the formation of the GDR and the Cold War provide the structure for her autobiographical writings, *Die Eisheiligen* (The Ice Saints) (1979) and *Vogel federlos* (Featherless Bird) (1982). She rejects her brutal adoptive mother, swapping the discipline at home for the regime of a Communist boarding-school. Recalling one of the main tenets of the women's movement, she presents private issues as having political relevance.

See also: feminism and the women's movement; *Frauenliteratur*

PETRA M. BAGLEY

nuclear power

During the 1970s and 1980s, the use of nuclear energy was one of the most controversial issues in Germany, a catalyst for the formation of strong protest movements which contributed significantly to the shaping of contemporary **political culture**. The first nuclear power plant (Obrigheim) began operating in 1968. Today a total of twenty power stations provide about 34 percent of Germany's electricity. An expansion of the capacities is not projected. Used fuels are sent to La Hague (France) and Sellafield (UK) for reprocessing.

Germany's nuclear programme was devised by the government of Chancellor Helmut **Schmidt** in response to the 1973–4 OPEC oil embargo. Its aim was to make the national economy less dependent on fuel imports and thereby secure and continue what had been achieved through the **Economic Miracle**. The idea of basing further economic development on nuclear energy conflicted, however, with the then emerging demand for qualitative instead of quantitative growth. The public was worried about evidence of nuclear installations contaminating the environment and increasing the risk of cancer through their 'normal' radiation as well as their radioactive waste. The question of the safe and long-term storage of these wastes remained unanswered. There were fears that a 'nuclear state' (*Atomstaat*) would develop in which democratic rights of information and participation would be restricted, in order to make the dangerous technology less vulnerable to acts of sabotage or terrorism. Furthermore, the political climate of the Cold War gave rise to anxieties that nuclear power plants would become targets of military attacks, thus turning any conventional war into a nuclear war.

Large-scale protests began in Wyhl in the southwest of the country, where citizens' initiatives from Germany, France and Switzerland jointly demonstrated against a projected power plant (1975) (see also **citizens' initiatives: FRG**). Similar action followed in Brokdorf, Gorleben, Grohnde and other places, often involving tens of thousands of people and regularly culminating in serious clashes with the police. Towards the end of the 1970s the anti-nuclear movement merged into the new **peace movement**. Its political networks provided the basis for the formation of the **Greens**. Throughout the 1980s the projected reprocessing plant in Wackersdorf was a focal point of protests as it could have produced plutonium suitable for nuclear weapons. The 1986 disaster at Chernobyl intensified dissent even further. Even more than before, nuclear technology became the symbol of the unmanageability of today's 'risk society'.

The 1989 decision to give up the Wackersdorf project reflected a re-orientation of official strategy in Germany. Whilst nuclear power had formerly been celebrated as a cheap and unlimited source of energy, experts now consider the technology as uncompetitive unless heavily subsidized by the state. Decentralized gas-fired power stations are regarded as more profitable. In 1998 the new **Schröder** government promised that in the long term all German nuclear power plants would be closed down.

See also: environmentalism

Further reading

Burns, R. and Will, W.v.d. (1988) *Protest and Democracy in West Germany*, London and Basingstoke: Macmillan (anti-nuclear movement in the context of political protest in general).

Jungk, R. (1979) *The New Tyranny: How Nuclear Power Enslaves Us*, New York: Fred Jourdan Books and Grosset & Dunlap (a political criticism of nuclear technology).

INGOLFUR BLÜHDORN

NVA

The Nationale Volksarmee (NVA) (National People's Army) served a dual function in the GDR, functioning both as East Germany's military contingent to the Warsaw Pact Treaty Organization and as an important domestic pillar of support to the **SED** regime. Officially founded on 18 January 1956 in response to the establishment of the **Bundeswehr**, the NVA inherited equipment, personnel and a well-developed system of bases from East Germany's existing 'barracked people's police'. Soviet advisors played a crucial role in organizing and training the NVA, which adopted Soviet military training procedures, doctrine and equipment. Service in the NVA was voluntary until 1962 (i.e. until the option of evading conscription by escaping to the West was finally removed by the construction of the **Berlin Wall**), after which a draft system compelled young East German males to complete eighteen months of military service. Pacifists could not opt out of military service, but were allowed to join unarmed construction units – albeit in the face of official disapproval and consequent hindrance to their later career prospects.

The NVA consisted of land and air defence forces, a navy and border troops. Training and exercises focused on conflict between NATO and the Warsaw Pact, in which NVA forces would occupy West Berlin and join other Pact forces in offensive operations designed to fight on the enemy's territory. By 1989, the NVA numbered over 170,000 active duty personnel. Foreign observers consistently ranked its units among the Warsaw Pact's best trained and equipped forces.

The SED kept tight control over the NVA through a 'political administration' which paralleled the military chain of command. Over 99 percent of officers belonged to the party, as did most career-enlisted personnel. SED and **FDJ** organizations existed at every level of the military. Party assemblies, political training sessions and a political schools disseminated SED dogma throughout the NVA. Service personnel were encouraged to develop hatred for the capitalist and 'imperialist' west while strengthening their devotion towards the party, the socialist community of nations and the USSR. The NVA's political administration waged a decades-long struggle against the tendency on the part of military specialists and technocrats to emphasize 'professional' matters at the expense of political training, successfully upholding the primacy of socialist politics within East Germany's military organization.

NVA units participated in the Soviet suppression of Czechoslovakia in 1968, yet remained in the barracks during East Germany's velvet revolution of 1989. Following German unification, most NVA equipment was destroyed or sold, and all but a few bases were closed. The Bundeswehr accepted some 25,000 junior officers and career-enlisted personnel into its ranks on a trial basis.

Further reading

Numerous German books and articles have appeared since 1989 which incorporate material from GDR archives, but the only English-language monograph on the subject remains T. Forster's 1980 publication.

Backerra, M. (ed.) (1992) *NVA. Ein Rückblick für die Zukunft. Zeitzeugen berichten über ein Stück deutscher Militärgeschichte*, Cologne: Markus.

Bald, D. (ed.) (1992) *Die Nationale Volksarmee. Beiträge zu Selbstverständnis und Geschichte des deutschen Militärs von 1945–1990*, Baden-Baden: Nomos.

Forster, T. (1980) *The East German Army: The Second Power in the Warsaw Pact*, London: Allen & Unwin.

Naumann, K. (1993) *NVA: Anspruch und Wirklichkeit nach ausgewählten Dokumenten*, Berlin: E.S. Mittler.

DOUGLAS PEIFER

occupation

After military defeat in May 1945, Germany was subjected to four-power occupation. Occupation policies differed from zone to zone, with great impact on politics, economy and society.

In 1944, the European Advisory Commission planned for a temporary occupation by the US, Britain and the USSR. At the Yalta conference (February 1945), a French zone was agreed. At the Potsdam conference (July to August 1945), it was decided that Germany as a whole should be administered by an Allied Control Council, but each power had the right of veto and zonal military commanders were responsible to their own governments (see also **Potsdam Agreement**).

The US, whose zone in southern Germany had no access to the sea, was given an enclave around Bremen. Berlin came under four-power control. The Soviets *de facto* altered Germany's eastern boundaries, compensating Poland for territory lost to the USSR by giving Poland part of East Prussia (the USSR taking the other part) and German territory east of the Oder and Neisse rivers, annexations not agreed by the western powers. Germany had to absorb millions of refugees from these lost territories.

Differences soon emerged between the zones. In the Soviet zone, the Communist party (**KPD**) was first to be licensed, followed by a refounded **SPD**, a new conservative Christian CDU, and a liberal party, the LDPD. In April 1946 the KPD and SPD merged to become the **SED**. Two puppet parties, the NDPD and DBD, were set up, and from 1948 politics was increasingly controlled by the SED,

backed by the Soviet military administration (SMAD). Radical denazification, land reform in September 1945, and reforms of industry and finance in 1946, dramatically altered economy and society in the Soviet zone.

In the West, a variety of democratic political parties were founded, including the **CDU**, the SPD, and several liberal parties later forming the **F.D.P.**. A degree of local and regional self-government was reintroduced. Despite limited attempts at decartelization and decentralization, there was no real restructuring of the capitalist economy.

Disagreements over reparations soon led to a breakdown of relations between the western powers and the USSR, while France proved obstinate in relation to the coal-rich Saar, the industrial Ruhr areas, and the left bank of the Rhine. In 1946, the British and Americans decided that the German economy should be rebuilt rather than living standards depressed. At the beginning of 1947, the British and American zones merged into the Bizone. With the announcement of the Truman doctrine concerning the containment of communism in 1947, and the introduction of Marshall Aid in 1948, emerging Cold War rifts became greater. In March 1948 the Soviets marched out of the Allied Control Council; in June 1948 they imposed a blockade on Berlin following currency reform in the western zones. In April 1949, following lengthy discussions on the foundation of a West German state, the French merged with the Bizone. By October 1949, the two opposing states, the Federal Republic and the German Democratic Republic had been founded.

Further reading

Fulbrook, M. (1991) *The Divided Nation: Germany 1918–1990*, chap. 6, London: Fontana.

Naimark, N. (1995) *The Russians in Germany*, Cambridge, MA: Harvard University Press.

MARY FULBROOK

Oder–Neisse line

The Oder and Neisse rivers became the new border between a shrunken post-war Germany and a Poland which had been shifted eastwards by the USSR. The redrawn boundary was viewed as provisional by the western Allies, pending a peace conference. Nor was there agreement over which branch of the Neisse river should constitute the border, and the USSR simply appropriated the fertile area east of the western branch for Poland. It was only in the course of 1990 that West German Chancellor Helmut **Kohl** belatedly agreed the Oder–Neisse line as Germany's eastern border.

See also: occupation

MARY FULBROOK

Oelze, Richard

b. 29 June 1900, Magdeburg; d. 27 May 1980, Posteholz (near Hameln)

Painter

Along with Max Ernst and Hans Bellmer, Oelze is one of the leading figures in German surrealist painting; unlike them he worked primarily within Germany itself, having studied at the Bauhaus schools during the 1920s. A reclusive character, he exhibited in the two major surrealist exhibitions in London in 1936 and Paris in 1938, but only began to receive proper critical recognition in the 1960s. His pre-war work features fantastic, monochromatic scenes of organic landscapes and figures. After the war, amorphous, anthropomorphic visions dominate, which evoke both mystery and unease.

ALEX COOKE

Ören, Aras

b. 1 November 1939, Bebek-Istanbul

Writer and radio journalist

In Ören's work, written in Turkish, but translated and directed equally at a German readership, and set very largely in Berlin (where he has lived since 1969, and worked for the Turkish programme of the Sender Freies Berlin since 1974), the social experience of labour and other migrants, and the psychological consequences, are central themes. But Ören locates them within European working-class experience as a whole, and his work, one of the first major œuvres by a migrant writer in contemporary Germany to gain wide critical recognition, is not **Gastarbeiter** literature. His work links at times to *Arbeiterliteratur*, for instance the story *Bitte nix Polizei* (Please, No Police) (1981), where an illegal immigrant's fear of officialdom is embedded in a mosaic of working-class experience. Especially in the longer poems *Was will Niyazi in der Naunynstraße?* (What does Niyazi Want in the Naunynstraße?) (1973), *Der kurze Traum aus Kagithane* (The Brief Dream from Kagithane) (1974) and *Die Fremde ist auch ein Haus. Berlin-Poem* (The Alien Place, Too, is a House) (1980), the Berlin district of Kreuzberg, once a German proletarian quarter, and now also the largest Turkish settlement outside Turkey, is represented as a place which manifests what Ören terms the 'bloody wound' of European history as a continuum of class and ethnic exploitation. The language mixes everyday details, class-struggle rhetoric and consciously literary syntax. Later volumes invoke more explicitly German and Turkish poetic traditions (the latter previously rejected by Ören as decayed and dishonest) without abandoning critical awareness of migrant experience's material causes, for instance in *Deutschland – ein türkisches Märchen* (Germany – a Turkish Fairytale) (1978), echoing Heinrich Heine, and possibly Wolf **Biermann**, and *Mitten in der Odyssee* (In the Midst of the Odyssee) (1980). The existential restlessness which migration unleashes is explored in *Gefühllosigkeiten. Reisen von Berlin nach Berlin* (Unfeelingnesses. Journeys from Berlin to Berlin) (1986) or *Dazwischen* (In Between) (1987). The central theme of Turkish-German experience as a complex, individually variegated amalgam remains, but now the poems are generally shorter, more epigrammatic and more metaphoric. The novel *Die verspätete Abrechnung* (The Delayed Reckoning) (1988) explores the semi-autobiographical narrator's tangled cultural roots in a way not possible in the poetry. *Berlin Savignyplatz* (1995) recycles figures and motives from *Bitte nix Polizei* in a novel of self-reflexive narratological rumination. *Wie die Spree in den Bosporus fließt* (As the Spree flows into the Bosporus) (1991), Ören's exchange of letter poems with the Berlin German writer Peter **Schneider** (Ören in Berlin, Schneider in Istanbul), presents the cities less as polar opposites than places of complex interchange in European metropolitan culture.

See also: migrant literature; minorities, non-German

Further reading

Chiellino, C. (1995) *Am Ufer der Fremde. Literatur und Arbeitsmigration*, Stuttgart: Metzler, pp. 307–39.

Gott, G.M. (1994) *Migration, Ethnicization and Germany's New Ethnic Minority Literature*, Ann Arbor, MI: UMI, pp. 162–201.

MORAY McGOWAN

ÖVP

The Österreichische Volkspartei (Austrian People's Party) is a conservative Christian Democratic Party. Founded in April 1945, it was Austria's biggest party and led all governments until 1970, mostly in coalition with the Social Democratic Party (**SPÖ**). From 1966 until 1970, the ÖVP held one-party government under Josef Klaus. Their opposition period lasted from 1970 to 1987. Since then the ÖVP has been the junior partner in the grand coalition with the SPÖ with a share of the votes of about 30 percent.

The ÖVP consists of several sub-organizations to represent all sectors of society, both regional and social.

GEORG HELLMAYR

Özakin, Aysel

b. 7 September 1942, Urfa (Turkey)

Writer

Aysel Özakin was already an award-winning writer before she sought asylum in West Germany in 1981 as a result of the Turkish military coup. In Turkey she was known particularly for her sophisticated representation of processes of female identity formation. Her protagonists, exclusively intellectual Turkish women, develop their own images of self in conflict with fixed categorizations of 'class' and 'gender', as in *Die Preisvergabe* (The Presentation of the Award) (1979). In Germany she broadened her main theme whilst emphasizing the important influence of ethnocentric stereotyping on the development of a bi-cultural female identity.

Özakin, who defines herself as a cosmopolitan writer, saw her literary work in Germany limited because of her nationality and the fact that she was an immigrant. Literary critics expected her to write texts about the problems of Turkish labour immigrants and labelled her 'the Turkish woman without a head-scarf', thus associating her with an underpriviledged social class to which she did not belong. The social distance between the writer and the immigrant worker population becomes particularly clear in the 1982 volume of narratives *Soll ich hier alt werden?* (Am I to Grow Old Here?). Özakin's disappointment about her own degradation and the restriction of her creativity as a writer in Germany led to her turning away from German as a language of literature and resulted in her eventual emigration to Great Britain (circa 1990).

See also: migrant literature

Further reading

Wierschke, A. (1996) *Schreiben als Selbstbehauptung. Kulturkonflikt und Identität in den Werken von Aysel Özakin, Alev Tekinay und Emine Sevgi Özdamar: mit Interviews*, Frankfurt am Main: Verlag für Interkulturelle Kommunikation.

SABINE FISCHER

Özdamar, Emine Sevgi

b. 10 August 1946, Malatya (Turkey)

Theatre producer, actress and writer

Özdamar's great love for the theatre is evident in all her work. It especially expresses itself in the diverse alienation techniques with which she attacks western clichés about the orient. In her 1986 play *Karagöz in Alamania* (Blackeye in Germany) for example, which combines elements of the epic and the absurd theatre with those of the traditional Turkish shadow play, she exaggerates common **Gastarbeiter** stereotypes and breaks them down in an ironic fashion. Her 1992 novel *Das Leben ist eine Karawanserei* (Life is a Caravanserai) confronts these prejudices with a differentiated image of Turkish culture. This novel, which portrays the childhood and youth of a woman in the Turkey of the 1960s, presents Turkish identity as a shimmering kaleidoscope, moulded by continual changes of location and numerous encounters with people of different social and cultural origin. Finally, in her 1990 narrative *Mutterzunge* (Mother Tongue) Özdamar develops a provocative model for the development of a multicultural female identity. Under the influence of German culture a female Turkish immigrant experiences the loss of her mother-tongue and consequent emotional alienation from her homeland. Whilst learning Arabic, the language of her grandfather, she rebuilds her cultural roots. A dream-like scene, in which the Arabic language seizes possession of the protagonist's body, suggests the submission of a modern Turkish woman to a long-gone male-dominated and oppressive culture. Here Özdamar deliberately plays with anti-Islamic stereotypes. The dream puts these clichés on stage. It reveals their fictional character, distorts and undermines them.

See also: migrant literature

Further reading

Wierschke, A. (1996) *Schreiben als Selbstbehauptung. Kulturkonflikt und Identität in den Werken von Aysel Özakin, Alev Tekinay und Emine Sevgi Özdamar: mit*

Interviews, Frankfurt am Main: Verlag für Interkulturelle Kommunikation.

SABINE FISCHER

Ohnsorg-Theater

The Ohnsorg-Theater was founded in Hamburg in 1902 by Richard Ohnsorg (and later named after him), to provide popular entertainment in the *Niederdeutsch* (or *Plattdeutsch*) dialect. The Ohnsorg-Theater's blend of **Volksstück** comedy – slick plotting, stock characters and traditional values, in plays like *Tratsch op de Trepp* (Scandal on the Stairs) – attracts critical and academic scorn but remains immensely successful; television broadcasts (over eighty plays since 1954) made it, and its star Heidi **Kabel**, household names. An overlap with *Blut und Boden* values allowed the Ohnsorg-Theater to flourish under Nazism; attempts (e.g. by Walter Ruppel, director 1986–94) to shake off this taint by introducing *Niederdeutsch* versions of **Brecht** or even R.W. **Fassbinder** proved short-lived.

MORAY McGOWAN

Oktoberfest

The Oktoberfest, despite its name, does not take place in October but at the end of the summer in September. The festival dates back to 1810 and lasts for sixteen days. It has become one of the hallmarks of the city of Munich, attracting visitors from all over the world. It is essentially a beer festival with sites such as the famous *Hofbräu Haus* serving *Maße* (litre glasses) of beer to thousands of customers, who, it is estimated, consume approximately 4.5 million litres of beer. The festival also plays host to a large fairground with side stalls, traditional delicacies from Bavaria, such as *Bretzen* (large pretzels) and *Weißwurst* (white sausage).

ALISON PHIPPS

Olympic Games

The 1916 Berlin Olympics were cancelled because of WWI. The successful 1936 Berlin Olympics were considered a showpiece for the Nazi government. Germany was banned from the 1948 London Olympics. The GDR and FRG were forced to compete as one team until 1964. Separate GDR and FRG teams participated under one flag and anthem in 1968 (Mexico), whereas separate teams competed in the 1972 Munich Olympics, which were marred by the massacre of eleven Israeli athletes and officials, spawning the immortal phrase 'the Games must go on'. The Olympics were a source of increasing nationalism and national expression for both German states during the 1970s and 1980s. After the *Wende*, sports federations and the National Olympic Committees unified and the united team has competed successfully since the 1992 Barcelona Olympics.

See also: sport: FRG; sport: GDR

Further reading

Guttmann, A. (1992) *The Olympics. A History of the Modern Games*, Urbana, IL: University of Illinois Press (includes section on Germany).

TARA MAGDALINSKI

opera

Germany's rich and diverse operatic tradition was to re-emerge after WWII and by the end of the 1960s had reached, and in many ways surpassed, its earlier achievement, variety and vibrancy. The deep tradition of an operatic culture in German society allowed a speedy restoration of the musical infrastructure and by the 1990s Germany had over seventy music theatres, supported through a generous system of subsidies, allowing a flourishing operatic scene. The founding of the GDR and the FRG, marked, in musical terms, an end of an operatic heritage and also a new beginning. The annual international New Music course held in Darmstadt from 1946 played a crucial role for young German composers in identifying new musical directions. The year 1949 saw the deaths of Richard Strauß and Hans Pfitzner, who exemplified a late and post-romantic operatic tradition. Austria's great operatic past had been closely linked to Germany but after 1945 evolved a

different, conservative, style. The **Salzburg Festival** and the restored Vienna Opera House established for Austria an international reputation, based primarily on the traditional opera repertoire. The creation of two German republics continued the divide of those composers who had remained in Germany during the National Socialist period and those who had gone into exile. The cultural roots of the two republics were to be subject to a fierce competition emanating from the juxtaposition of a pluralist democracy and an authoritarian state.

In the first period of the GDR opera was inhibited through the tight control of culture by the **SED**. Some works, such as those of Hanns **Eisler** (1898–1962) and Paul **Dessau** (1894–1979) reflected a commitment to the ideology of socialist realism. Dessau and Bertolt **Brecht** collaborated on the opera *Die Verurteilung des Lukullus*, a work concerned with the misery war can bring. The emphasis by the SED on works with a socialist dimension led to the importation into the repertoire of works by composers such as Alan Bush (1900–95); the 'workers' operas' *Wat Tyler* and *Die Männer von Blackmoor* being given numerous performances. The political leadership and the cultural isolation of the GDR meant that composers only achieved a degree of internationalization from the late 1970s onwards as the Cold War moved towards détente. The political strictures gave rise to a critical appoach to operatic productions, particularly by the opera producers Harry Kupfer and Götz **Friedrich**. Satire also became an acceptable vehicle for opera to test the boundaries of SED tolerance. Reiner Bredemeyer's (1929) first opera, *Candide*, with a libretto by Gerhard Müller and performed in Halle/Saale in 1986, belongs to this category. The first two operas from Georg Katzer (1935), *Das Land Bum-Bum* (1978) and *Gastmahl oder Über die Liebe* (1988) employs the device of satire. Paul-Heinz Dittrich (1930), on the other hand, wrote a number of scenic chamber works, experimental in combining literature, music, space, light and visual images. His abstract works, such as *Die Verwandlung*, from Kafka, and *Spiel* (1987), from Beckett, puzzled the authorities. As the GDR neared its end the composer Siegfried Matthus (1934) used the bicentenary of the French Revolution to recall the egalitarian rights of the people in his opera *Graf Mirabeau* (1989). The opera was produced with Karlsruhe and Essen and also appeared on East and West German television; it was to adumbrate the new unified Germany. Katzer's third opera, *Antigone oder Die Stadt*, was premièred (Berlin, 1991) in the new Germany.

In the FRG the availability of opera was an essential component of official cultural policy. Medium and smaller German cities either restored or built new theatres which were able to present the classical operatic repertoire. The federalist structure of the FRG had a beneficial impact on creating a diverse operatic scene. Music festivals add to a flourishing music and opera landscape. Major festivals are hosted by Dresden, Eisenach, Weimar, Eutin, Bonn, Munich, Würzburg, Göttingen, and Bayreuth (see also **Bayreuth Festival**). Some of these venues provided a new generation of composers with the opportunity to have their work performed. However, it was Berlin, Hamburg and Cologne which allowed for new opera to be premièred from the 1960s to the 1980s. **Henze**'s early operas *König Hirsch* (1956) and *Der junge Lord* (1965) were presented in Berlin as was his later *Musikdrama, Das verratende Meer* (1990). Hamburg's contribution was to première Henze's important work *Der Prinz von Homburg* (1960) and the influential instrumentally focused theatre production of *Staatstheater* (1971) by Mauricio **Kagel** (1931), which marked a break with the linear evolution from composers such as Berg and Schönberg. Opera Stabile, a chamber opera group founded in Hamburg in 1973, provided opportunities for new and experimental opera. However, it was Bernd Alois **Zimmermann** (1918–70) who had the most emphatic impact on the contemporary German opera scene with his work, premièred at Köln, *Die Soldaten* (1965). The vast orchestral forces made it a very German opera, the complex stage directions required new technology, but the subject matter, taken from a play by the eighteenth-century writer Lenz, went to the heart of the German public's preoccupation with the horrors of war. The *Nationaltheater* in Munich provided a conservative programme for its audiences until in 1978 it produced Aribert **Reimann**'s (1936) adaptation of Shakespeare's *King Lear, Lear*, a work of great technical intricacies and enormous musical control. Reimann's opera *Das Schloß* (1992), after Kafka, firmly underlined the significance of

Literaturoper for the German opera scene. The Munich Biennale, founded in 1988, has provided an important platform for the younger generation of German composers to experiment. These include Wolfgang **Rihm** (1952) and Udo Zimmermann (1943). Karlheinz **Stockhausen** (1928) has a distinct place within the constellation of contemporary German opera composers. It is not only the wealth of creative ideas, from electronic music to improvisation, from the American influence of John Cage to the construction of a universal music, that gives Stockhausen his prominence. It is also his visionary construct, of Wagnerian proportions, which will enable him to complete his monumental theatre cycle *Licht* by the year 2003. Despite these new and exciting young composers the repertoire of the German opera house remains firmly rooted in the late eighteenth and nineteenth centuries.

Further reading

Belkins, G. and Liedtke, U. (ed.) (1990) *Musik für die Oper. Mit Komponisten im Gespräch*, Berlin: Henschel.

Brockhaus, F.A. (1982) *Der Musik Brockhaus*, Mainz: F.A. Brockhaus and B. Schott Söhne.

Hermann, S. and Hermann, N. (1992) *Deutsche Oper im 20. Jahrhundert. DDR 1949–1989*, Bern and Berlin: Peter Lange.

Thrun, M. (ed.) (1995) *Neue Musik seit den achtziger Jahren. Ein Band zum deutschen Musikleben, Band 2*, Regensburg: Con Brio Dokument Band 5, Con Brio Verlagsgesellschaft.

Tschulik, N. (1987) *Musiktheater in Deutschland: die Oper im 20*, Jahrhundert: Vienna.

KARL KOCH

orchestras

Germany in particular has a rich variety of orchestras, reflecting the energy and diversity of its musical life. The *International Who's Who in Music* lists 169 orchestras (as against 10 for Austria, 19 for Switzerland and 45 for France). Indeed, most towns of any size fund their own orchestras, often attached to **theatres** and **opera** houses. Many of the great German orchestras were founded in the nineteenth century, but the growth of broadcasting has provided fresh impetus for new foundations.

The leading German orchestra is probably the Berlin Philharmonic, founded in 1882. The Philharmonic Hall, destroyed in the war, was replaced by a new building in 1963. Famous conductors include Wilhelm **Furtwängler**, and more recently the towering figure of Herbert von **Karajan**, who died in 1989. It is now conducted by Claudio Abbado. Indeed, German orchestras attract a large number of foreign conductors and soloists, and German musicians find work abroad. Thus the pianist Daniel Barenboim is General Music Director of the Staatskapelle Berlin; James Conlon of the Gürzenich-Orchester in Cologne; the American Dennis Russell Davies, now Music Director of the Stuttgart Chamber Orchestra, handed on his baton at the Beethovenhalle in Bonn to the Frenchman Marc Soustrot. On the other hand, Kurt **Masur** has directed the New York Philharmonic, and Christoph von Dohnányi was the Chief Conductor of the Cleveland Orchestra. Berlin is well provided with orchestras, largely as a result of unification. For example, the *Berliner Sinfonie-Orchester* and the *Deutsches Symphonie-Orchester Berlin* in the east of the city is matched by the Berlin Symphony Orchestra in the west. Also worthy of note is the *Orchester der Deutschen Oper Berlin*, founded 1912, which also numbered Wilhelm Furtwängler among its former conductors.

Germany's strong regional structure is reflected in its cultural activities and in its music. Even smaller towns may have orchestras of international renown, such as the Bamberg Philharmonic, directed by Horst Stein, but the major orchestras are in major centres. The *Sächsische Staatskapelle Dresden*, which also plays for the opera, and whose former conductors include Karl **Böhm**, has its origins in the sixteenth century. The *Dresdner Philharmonie* (director Michel Plasson) was founded in 1871. The *Philharmonisches Staatsorchester Hamburg* gave its first concerts in 1829, but rose to new heights under the directorship of Karl Muck (1859–1940). The *Philharmonisches Kammerorchester Hamburg* gave a celebrated performance of Bach's piano concertos with Helmut **Schmidt** as one of the soloists. The North German Radio Symphony Orchestra (NDR-Symphonieorchester) was formed from the Hamburg Radio Orchestra in 1951.

Munich has a number of notable orchestras, including the Bayerisches Staatsorchester, the Bach Collegium München, the Münchner Symphoniker and two orchestras (the Rundfunkorchester and the Symphonieorchester) of Bavarian Radio, but the Munich Philharmonic is probably the best known. It was formed in 1924 on the basis of the orchestra of Franz Kaim, a wealthy patron of German music, who also built the concert hall. Since 1928 it has been the official orchestra of the city and is now directed by Sergiu Celibidache. Stuttgart is also a major musical centre, with several major orchestras including the Stuttgart Philharmonic, the Staatsorchester Stuttgart and the Radio-Sinfonieorchester Stuttgart. Of particular note is the Stuttgart Chamber Orchestra, founded by Karl Münchinger in 1945. The Orchester der Württembergischen Staatstheater Stuttgart was founded at the beginning of the sixteenth century to provide music at court, as was the Orchester des Nationaltheaters Mannheim (founded 1720). The Gewandhausorchester (literally 'cloth-hall orchestra') has played since 1981 in the new *Gewandhaus* in Leipzig, two hundred years after its first concert in the banqueting hall of the original *Gewandhaus*. The orchestra grew out of the Leipzig Collegium musicum, formerly directed by Georg Philip Telemann and after 1729 by Johann Sebastian Bach, the Grosse Concert founded by Leipzig businessmen in 1743, and the Musikübende Gesellschaft founded by J.A. Hiller in 1775. It has been directed since 1980 by Professor Kurt Masur, and numbers Wilhelm Furtwängler and Felix Mendelssohn-Bartholdy among its former conductors.

The *Collegia musica* were loose associations of music lovers, which became an important moving force in German musical culture, as they gradually allowed audiences and therefore fostered a tradition of public performances. Many smaller groups have taken on the name *Collegium musicum* in an attempt to recreate an atmosphere of inclusive playing and performance, many often using original instruments. Universities provide fruitful ground for this activity. Examples of similar groups are the Concentus musicus (Vienna), associated with Nikolaus **Harnoncourt**, the Leonhardt-Consort under the direction of Gustav Leonhardt, and the Musica antiqua Köln with Reinhard Goebel.

In Austria, the Vienna Philharmonic has the longest tradition – it was founded in 1842 and regular concerts began in 1860 – and the most illustrious list of former conductors, including Hans Richter (from 1875–98), Gustav Mahler (from 1898–1901), Wilhelm Furtwängler (from 1927–8; 1938–54), and Claudio Abbado (1971). Herbert von Karajan, took the orchestra to New York in 1989 after an association of thirty years. The orchestra is self-governing, plays for the Vienna State Opera and regularly performs at the **Salzburg Festival** (which also boasts the Mozarteum Orchester). The Vienna Symphony Orchestra was founded in 1900 as the Wiener Konzertverein Orchester and merged with the Verein Wiener Tonkünstler in 1921. It is administered by the Gesellschaft der Musikfreunde, Wiener Konzerthausgesellschaft, the Bregenz Festival and Austrian Radio. In 1934 it became Vienna's main broadcasting orchestra.

In Switzerland, Zürich has a long musical tradition. The *Tonhalle-Orchester Zürich* was founded in 1868. The Collegium Musicum Zürich has maintained its reputation under the leadership of Paul Sacher for over half a century.

See also: concert halls

Further reading

Duckles, V.H. (1974) *Music Reference and Research Materials. An Annotated Bibliography*, 3rd edn, London and New York: Macmillan.

Grove's Dictionary of Music and Musicians (1961) 5th edn, 10 vols, London: Macmillan (look under German towns and cities).

Marco, G.A. (1984) *Information on Music: A Handbook of Reference Sources in European Languages. Vol. III: Europe*, Littleton, CO: Libraries Unlimited.

Music in Germany '94, Bonn: Inter Nationes (this is an annual publication).

JONATHAN WEST

ORF

The Österreichischer Rundfunk Fernsehen (ORF) (Austrian Broadcasting Corporation) was founded in 1967 after the 1966 Broadcasting Act (following a widely supported petition to parliament) laid the foundation for a modern radio and television company. Its forerunner organizations, however, go back to 1924 when the first Austrian Broadcasting Corporation was established. Regular television broadcasts started in 1957.

The 1974 Broadcasting Act ensured the legal independence of the company and required fairness, objectivity and independence of reporting from the ORF. In 1984 the principle of the freedom of the arts was added to its charter.

Since its beginnings the ORF has enjoyed a monopoly position in Austria. With the advent of cable and satellite television in the 1980s new competition (mainly from Germany) emerged and led to a considerable change in programming. The 1993 Regional Radio Act laid the legal basis for the operation of private radio stations under special licensing regulations.

Four programmes on FM radio and two television channels as well as medium and short wave programmes are broadcast by the ORF. One FM radio channel (Österreich 1) is devoted to classical music, the arts and serious talk radio, whereas Österreich 3 (Ö3) is orientated towards international youth culture featuring mainly English and American pop music. Österreich 2 operates from nine regional radio stations that serve the nine *Bundesländer* with a mix of Austrian and German folk music and regional programmes.

Blue Danube Radio, the fourth radio channel, which mainly broadcasts in English with parts of the programmes in French and German, was introduced in 1979 to cater for the international community of Vienna. Since 1992 it has been broadcast throughout the country.

In 1984 the Austrian Broadcasting Corporation started to produce a satellite programme under the title 3sat in co-operation with the German stations **ZDF** and (since 1993) **ARD** as well as the Swiss **SRG**.

The ORF is run by a director-general who is elected by a board of trustees who are nominated by various social groups and who represent a cross-section of the listeners and viewers. Even though the ORF is legally independent the positions of director-general and of the programme controllers are carefully selected according to the political balance of power.

Most of the television programmes are imports from Germany or international film distributors. However, the ORF has proved to be a devoted supporter of local film artists, dramatists and freelance television and radio journalists. Owing to the broadcasting regulations the ORF has to dedicate a certain amount of its resources to cultural activities which among other things makes it a forum for traditional as well as avant-garde artists. Broadcasts from various theatres and opera houses, traditional music and live sports programmes, especially in winter, are important features of Austrian radio and television.

Financially the ORF relies on licensing fees as well as on advertising which is, however, limited by law. In addition to its programming expenses the ORF also has to finance its own terrestrial transmitter network.

See also: broadcasting

Further reading

Ergert, V. and Andics, H. *et al.* (1974) *50 Jahre Rundfunk in Österreich*, Salzburg: Residenz-Verlag.
Fritz, D. (1987) *Die Organisation des ORF*, Innsbruck: Universitätsverlag.
Österreichischer Rundfunk: Almanach, Vienna (published annually).

GEORG HELLMAYR

Orff, Carl

b. 10 July 1895, Munich; d. 29 March 1982, Munich

Composer

Few composers can have made their name so completely and universally on the strength of one work as has been the case with Orff and his *Carmina Burana*, first performed in Frankfurt am Main in 1937. The work epitomizes Orff's search for a medium in which music is only part of the overall spectacle, ideally comprising music, drama and dance. Other works in similar vein exploit translations into German from Greek tragedy and Shakespeare (e.g. *Ein Sommernachtstraum*). Orff's musical idiom is direct, primitive and triadic. His other main contribution was in the field of education, where he believed that all children, with appropriate resources, can be drawn into the music-making process. The plethora of quality instruments now owned by most primary schools bears testimony to his influence. But the much advertised Orff–Kodaly method is a compromise hotch-potch that would have been sanctioned by neither composer, whose aims and approach had little in common.

DEREK MCCULLOCH

Ortheil, Hanns-Josef

b. 5 November 1951, Cologne

Writer

Ortheil's novels anatomize social situations and historical contexts, usually of the post-war period, through their protagonists (e.g. *Fermer*, 1979 and *Hecke*, 1983). His first critical success, *Schwerenöter* (Philanderer) (1987), contrasts the development of two brothers in a changing society from the currency reform of 1948 to the **student movement** and the rise of the **Greens**. In *Agenten* (Agents) (1989) he incisively yet non-moralistically describes the mentality and way of life of German yuppies, of both the professional and cultural ilk, whose behaviour is fashioned by a complicated and closely observed negotiation of styles and tastes.

JUDITH LEEB

Ossi/Wessi

These slang terms have come into use since unification to denote citizens of the former GDR and old Federal Republic, respectively. They are usually used in a negative sense and stemmed from the increased feeling of alienation between the citizens of the two former German states after unification. *Wessis* were seen by the easterners as arrogant know-alls who were ruthless in their exploitation of the post-unification situation, while *Ossis*, seen from a western perspective, lacked the sophistication, and self-reliant independence and flexibility of West Germans.

See also: unification

PETER BARKER

Ossowski, Leonie

b. 15 August 1925, Ober-Röhrsdorf (Osowa Sién, Poland)

Writer (née von Brandenstein; also known as Jolanthe Kurtz-Solowjew and Jo von Tiedemann)

Leonie Ossowski writes novels, short stories, children's books and scripts for documentary film and television. In 1945 she fled to Thuringia and then Swabia. She has worked as a factory worker, retail clerk and photolaboratory assistant. She earned her initial success with two **DEFA**-commissioned film scripts: *Zwei Mütter* (Two Mothers) (1957) and *Stern ohne Himmel* (Star without Sky) (1958). *Die große Flatter* (The Big Flutter) (1977), a story of orphans in West Berlin, earned success both as a book and as a film.

MARTINA S. ANDERSON

Ostpolitik

Ostpolitik is a term used primarily to refer to the steps taken by the **Brandt** government in the early 1970s to improve and 'normalize' relations between West Germany and the communist countries of eastern Europe. As a result of Brandt's initiatives non-aggression treaties were entered into with the Soviet Union and Poland in 1970, whilst in parallel negotiations the four wartime Allies reached an agreement in 1972 clarifying the status of West Berlin. A succession of agreements between the GDR and the Federal Republic culminated in the Basic Treaty signed in 1972 (effective from 21 June 1973), in which the two German states, after two decades of minimal communication, agreed to develop 'normal good-neighbourly relations on the basis of equality' – though stopping short, at West Germany's insistence, of full diplomatic recognition. The *Ostpolitik*, for which Brandt was awarded the Nobel Peace Prize, was a cornerstone of the overall East–West détente of the 1970s. In the cultural sphere it bore belated fruit in the form of the 1986 Cultural Agreement, in which the two German states undertook to co-operate in such spheres as art, education, science, sport and youth exchanges.

See also: *Abgrenzung*; German Question; Hallstein Doctrine

JOHN SANDFORD

Ottinger, Ulrike

b. 6 June 1942, Konstanz

Filmmaker

Ottinger began as a photographer and a painter. A self-taught director and camerawoman, her visually striking fiction and documentary films explore outsiders and unusual communities. She uses fiction to investigate social artifice in her feminist pirate film *Madame X* (1977), and presents a brash portrait of Berlin sub-culture in *Ticket of No Return* (*Bildnis einer Trinkerin*, 1979). Camp, operatically stylized, and frequently parodistic, her fiction films have provoked lively debate amongst feminist critics. Ottinger's anthropological fascination with the exotic led to documentaries on China, and a splendid eight-hour study of Mongolian nomads (*Taiga*, 1992).

See also: film: FRG

HELEN HUGHES

Otto, Frei

b. 31 May 1925, Siegmar (Chemnitz)

Architect

Otto studied at the TU (Technical University) Berlin from 1948 to 1952, established his private practice in 1952 and ran his architecture studio from 1958 to 1968 in Berlin, and in Warmborn since 1968. He founded the Development Centre for Lightweight Construction, Berlin, in 1957. Otto has held the posts of Professor and Director of the Institute for Lightweight Structures, Stuttgart University from 1964 to 1991, and Visiting Professor at numerous universities and institutes.

As an exceptionally innovative constructor and visionary, Otto's influence is felt throughout the world. He is also responsible for some of the most interesting and unusual buildings in Germany, for instance the roof-construction of the Olympic stadium in Munich (1968–72), with **Behnisch**.

MARTIN KUDLEK AND BERTHOLD PESCH

P

painting

As a result of the division of Germany into two states with different socio-economic structures, ideological aims and cultural values, art after the war developed in different directions. After a short period of revived pre-war traditions during the late 1940s and early 1950s, painting in West Germany became strongly dominated by a confluence of the western European and American abstract movement, ranging from the late 1940s American Informel and French Tachisme to minimalism and concept art of the 1970s. Spontaneous expressivity, which prevailed in abstract painting of the 1950s, was followed by a phase of self-reflexive geometric works. In the course of the 1960s the West German art scene grew increasingly pluralistic, gradually embracing new media such as performance, happenings and video, pop art, photo-realism and hard-edge painting, as well as conceptual positions and purist aesthetics. The multiplicity of experiments and individual styles coincided with a gradual dissolution of the hegemony of international styles. During the early 1980s figurative expressive and critical realist concepts gained international recognition as the new 'German art'. The late 1980s and early 1990s were marked by increasingly hedonistic approaches to painting, with frequent references to both its history and internal structure. Painting in the GDR was based on state commission and was in general politically and rhetorically motivated. It was required to depict and communicate the features and aims of the new society. Particularly during the 1950s and early 1960s the Soviet concept of

socialist realism functioned as an aesthetic guideline. Portraits of exemplary workers, collective work in industry and agriculture, industrial land-scapes and history painting concerned with class warfare pointed to the construction of a new society. As a result of a more liberal cultural policy in the early 1970s the scope for experiments with different modes of expression and pictorial means gradually increased. In the 1980s painting began to turn towards the internal aspects of the medium without completely losing sight of social reality. A younger generation of artists in particular explored the formal capacity of the picture as a sign for the vigorous articulation of the self rather than as an illustration of aesthetic doctrine. Painting after German unification is characterized by increasingly hedonistic approaches to artistic tradition in the context of new media and popular culture. With the exception of Berlin, where the two systems have clashed, the unification process has hardly left any traces in the practice of artists in the former West. Art in the former GDR has been affected by a radical change in its underlying conditions.

The East–West division in painting began in the immediate post-war period with the return of an older generation of artists from exile or 'inner emigration'. Many artists with abstract orientations settled in the West, whilst those who had come out of the Assoziation Revolutionärer Bildender Künstler (Association of Revolutionary Artists) or who worked in the tradition of social realism went to East Germany. However, after 1945, successful attempts were made to reunite artists belonging to different directions in exhibitions like the *Deutsche*

Kunstausstellung in Dresden in 1946. Only to a certain degree did German pre-war movements such as expressionism, surrealism, bauhaus and critical realism provide a common thread for post-war developments in West and East Germany.

Painting in the FRG

By the 1950s painting in the FRG was dominated by abstraction. Older artists such as Willi **Baumeister** and Ernst Wilhelm Nay continued their abstract expressive concepts, whilst French Tachisme gained currency in West Germany, mediated by Hans Hartung's calligraphic subjective ciphers and Wols's graffiti-like images. Emil **Schumacher** and other members of the ZEN group, founded in Munich in 1949, oriented themselves towards the strongly gestic character of Asian calligraphy and the meditative philosophy of Zen Buddhism. Not only was abstraction embraced by many younger artists like K.O. Götz and K.H.R. Sonderborg as a new orientation and an opportunity to catch up with the modernist movement which had been completely excised by the Third Reich, but it was in line with a cultural policy under **Adenauer** that aimed for a rapid westernization of the FRG (see also **cultural policy: FRG**). Artists with strong affinities towards surrealism such as Richard Oelze remained on the periphery of the art scene. Realist and verist concepts as exemplified by Werner Heldt shared a similar fate. And so did the mythical-expressive figurations of H.A.P. Grieshaber and Horst Antes. Reactions against the hegemony of the subjective lyrical gestures of Tachisme and American Art Informel came from different directions. In 1955, Konrad Klapheck began to depict banal objects, such as a Continental typewriter, in a laconic austere manner. An interest in colour, light and movement was shared by Heinz **Mack**, Otto **Piene** and Günther **Ücker** – the nucleus of the **Zero Group**. Based on an optimistic feeling for life and an enormous confidence in their own creativity they established a style of 'concrete abstraction' in a multitude of forms: installations, projects, exhibitions and publications. The anarchic SPUR ('track' or 'trace') group of artists emerged in 1958. In opposition to bourgeois contentions, their members cultivated a brutalist

and interventionist aesthetics that erupted in spontaneous events, political actions and colourful sensual works. Other artists such as Gerhard Graubner and Raimund Gierke produced highly self-reflexive, geometrical spaces in colour and monochrome. During the late 1950s and 1960s painting came under the influence of a diversity of artistic innovations ranging from Anglo-American pop art to minimalism and concept art. During that time Joseph **Beuys** became prominent as an artist and teacher. To the present day, his subversive strategies aimed at rupturing and expanding the boundaries of art, his mythical and political concerns, social and intellectual activities as well as his multidimensional aesthetic concept have provided enormous stimuli for other artists. Early works by Gerhard **Richter**, Sigmar **Polke** and Wolf **Vostell** made critical and sarcastic references to German everyday reality and pictorial conventions. Richter's concept of 'capitalist realism' alluded to the doctrines of **socialist realism** east of the border. These approaches were taken further in the actions of Happening and Fluxus artists in the wake of the **student movement**. The belief in social and cultural change of the late 1960s soon evaporated, and by the beginning of the 1970s artists had withdrawn into 'individual mythologies', as apparent in the work of Anna Oppermann and Jochen Gerz. Only a few German artists incorporated conceptual strategies in their work, amongst them Hanne **Darboven**, and Hans **Haacke**, who both moved eventually to New York. These latter explored in detail their potential for critical political commentaries. Due to the federal structure of West Germany, painting developed in several centres at different times. Whilst painting in the Rhineland and Berlin played a crucial part during the early years, Düsseldorf was the leading centre in the 1960s. By the end of the 1970s the focus had shifted towards Berlin and Cologne, when expressive figurative concepts, which had already begun to emerge in the early 1960s, finally received international recognition as the new 'German Art'. A sense of immediacy and vibrancy that marked this so-called **neo-expressionism** stems particularly from the formative energy of eruptive creativity. Anselm **Kiefer**, Georg **Baselitz**, Markus Lüpertz, Jörg Immendorff and A.R. **Penck** amongst others reasserted a pictorial dialogue between narrative content – referring to history, social reality and mythology – and form and meaning as a condition for critical intervention. The self in the context of ambiguous subjective experience of metropolitan life was thematized in the painting of a younger generation of artists such as Helmut Middendorff, Salome, Rainer Fetting, Albert Oehlen, Ina Barfuss, Georg Dokoupil and Walter Dahn. During the 1980s a number of artists moved away from their initially figurative concepts towards an exploration of the material conditions of painting, for instance Richter; or towards the construction of virtual realities married to renewed concerns for simplicity, formal rigidity and intensity, as in the cases of Polke and Christa Näher. Heterogeneous elements and discourses are fused in the complex multimedial works of Rosemarie **Trockel**, Georg Herold, Günther Förg and others who came to the fore mainly after the second half of the 1980s.

Painting in the GDR

Art of the immediate post-war period dealt with the horror of the recent past, addressing collective and individual suffering, pain and grief in generalized terms that oscillated between condemnation and solemnity, as in the work of Hans Grundig, Wilhelm Lachnit and Karl Hofer. Only a few artists were concerned with cautiously optimistic visions of a new beginning. With the foundation of the GDR art faced new requirements. The representation of the new social forces – the workers and farmers – remained the central subject for painting, firmly based on the concept of **socialist realism**. Murals, often executed by specially commissioned groups of artists, and large-scale paintings in particular served to propagate the new ideology to a wide audience. By the early 1970s artistic approaches took on a more individual and critical quality, with reflections on social reality becoming broader and more complex. Despite the fact that cultural politics in the GDR strongly emphasized a '*sozialistische Nationalkunst*' (socialist national art), painting was shaped by regional differences. Whilst in Berlin an urban realism coupled with inwardness and a subdued use of colour prevailed, as in the pictures of Harald Metzkes and Nuria **Quevedo**, Dresden's baroque

tradition can be traced in tendencies towards a vibrant palette and the dynamic pictorial structures of painters like Curt Querner and Theodor Rosenhauer. An emphasis on constructive elements characterized the Halle 'school' exemplified by the work of Willi **Sitte**. Metaphorical and allegorical encodings influenced by Max Beckmann and Max Klinger provided a fertile soil for artists in Leipzig. Since the participation of Werner **Tübke**, Bernhard **Heisig** and Wolfgang **Mattheuer** in the **documenta** 7 in Kassel 1977, these highly complex and cerebral images typical of the Leipzig school became virtually synonymous with art 'made in GDR'. Extensive references to history and mythology were employed and read as critical commentaries on the present political situation. The bias of cultural policy towards representation and ideological commitment resulted in numerous painters leaving the East and settling in the FRG. Other artists, like Georg Altenbourg and Carlfriedrich Claus, eventually found a niche for their abstract personal notations and formal experiments. From the late 1970s onwards an increasing number of artists, most of whom were born in the GDR, searched for innovative means of expression to symbolize 'instable' subjectivity and new experiential horizons, amongst them Hartwig Ebersbach, Walter Libuda, Jürgen Wenzel, Angela Hampel, the '*Autoperforationsartisten*' and Strawalde. Their works, performances and public actions mocked the political and ceremonial, and articulated environmental problems and social deformations, gender conflicts and violence in society with self-confident vehemence. Unification led to a broadening of horizons and aesthetic concepts as well as shock and new constraints amongst artists in East Germany. Their reorientation shows itself in changes of medium, in format, material and formal principles, and in an overall tendency towards less overtly political subjects.

Further reading

Damus, M. (1991) *Malerei der DDR. Funktionen der bildenden Kunst im Realen Sozialismus*, Reinbek bei Hamburg: Rowohlt (comprehensive survey of painting in the GDR).

—— (1995) *Kunst in der BRD 1945–1990*, Reinbek

bei Hamburg: Rowohlt (comprehensive overview of art in the FRG).

Feist, G. and Gillen, E. (eds) (1988) *Stationen eines Weges. Daten und Zitate zur Kunst und Kulturpolitik der DDR 1945–1988*, West Berlin: Museumspädagogischer Dienst (comprehensive survey of main developments of art in the socio-cultural context of the GDR).

Joachimides, C., Rosenthal, N. and Schmied, W. (eds) (1986) *German Art in the 20th Century. Painting and Sculpture 1905–1985*, Munich: Prestel (overview of painting and sculpture in Germany and the FRG).

Krens, T., Govan, M. and Thompson, J. (eds) (1989) *Refigured Painting. The German Image 1960–88*, Munich: Prestel (overview of neo-expressionist painting in the FRG).

Staerk, B. (1994) *Contemporary Painting in Germany*, Sydney: G+B International (introduction to the development of figurative painting mainly in the FRG).

Thomas, K. (1985) *Zweimal deutsche Kunst nach 1945: 40 Jahre Nähe und Ferne*, Cologne: DuMont (concise overview of early developments of painting in the FRG and GDR).

KERSTIN MEY

Palermo, Blinky

b. 2 June 1943, Leipzig; d. 17 February 1977, Kurumba (Maldives)

Artist

Palermo was a pupil of Joseph **Beuys** in Düsseldorf, where he studied from 1962 to 1967. He collaborated with Gerhard **Richter**, Sigmar **Polke** and Imi Knoebel. Working at the border between painting, sculpture and installation, he developed an architectonic variant of constructivism and colour-field painting using simple geometrical shapes and predominently primary colours. He devised a series of large-scale gallery installations involving minimal interventions, usually in the form of spare, geometric wall-painting. Palermo was also active as a graphic artist, producing sketches in the style of Beuys, and as a printmaker.

See also: painting

MARTIN BRADY

Palitzsch, Peter

b. 11 September 1918, Deutmannsdorf (Chmielno, Silesia)

Theatre director, manager and artistic director

Palitzsch collaborated with Bertolt **Brecht** at the **Berliner Ensemble**. He refused to return to the GDR after the construction of the **Berlin Wall**. He held the posts of Artistic Director at the Württembergisches Staatstheater until 1972 and Director of the City Theatre Frankfurt until 1980. In 1992 he was Co-director of the Berliner Ensemble. He has directed various plays all over Germany and abroad as a freelancer. He débuted as an opera director with Aribert **Reimann**'s *Gespenstersonate* (1984) and film director with *Sand* (1971). His entire work is determined by his sceptical view of modern society mixed with optimism from a Marxist point of view. Theatre for Palitzsch becomes a tool of historical orientation and a great game of fantasy at the same time.

See also: drama: GDR

Further reading

Mennicken, R. (1993) *Peter Palitzsch. Regie im Theater*, Frankfurt am Main.

MATHIAS BAUHUF

Pannenberg, Wolfhart

b. 2 October 1928, Stettin (now Szczecin, Poland)

Theologian

Pannenberg exemplifies the generation of German theologians immediately preceding and continuing after WWII, who begin to seriously revise the major tenets of Christian doctrine. Influenced heavily by Karl **Barth** and Karl **Jaspers**, he is best known for his theory of 'revelation as history', initially articulated in his 1965 publication, *Offenbarung als Geschichte*. Pannenberg rejects traditional and evangelical Christianity's belief that the Bible constitutes 'the word of God': revelation is not in the word but in the history of the church's experience with the word.

See also: Moltmann, Jürgen; religion

KITTY MILLET

Papenfuß-Gorek, Bert

b. 11 January 1956, Stavenhagen (Mecklenburg)

Poet

The most accomplished and linguistically inventive of the **Prenzlauer Berg** poets of the ex-GDR, Papenfuß-Gorek established his iconoclastic reputation in the late 1970s through his readings in pubs to punk rock accompaniments. He achieved wider literary recognition when a collection of his poems, *dreizehntanz* (thirteendance), was published by the **Aufbau Verlag** in 1988. In post-unification Germany he has maintained an increasingly independent momentum as a 'regenerator of the language' in volumes such as *tiské* (illustrated by A.R. **Penck**, 1990) and *nunft* (with its accompanying CD, 1992).

Further reading

Kane, M. (1995) 'The Poetry of Bert Papenfuß-Gorek' in P. Brady and I. Wallace (eds) *Prenzlauer Berg: Bohemia in East Berlin?*, Amsterdam: Rodopi, pp. 67–86.

DENNIS TATE

Paradigmawechsel

The term 'paradigm shift' denotes fundamental changes occuring in the theoretical assumptions underlying any field of intellectual enquiry. The Copernican revolution in science, which led to the abandonment of the idea of the earth as the centre of the universe, is a classic case of *Paradigmawechsel*. Changes of paradigm necessitate both the reinter-

pretation of existing knowledge and the radical reformulation of research objectives. A new paradigm creates a fundamentally new world(-view). The concept is most commonly used in philosophical contexts (e.g. in J. **Habermas** and N. **Luhmann**), where it refers to the transition from traditional subject-centred theories to contemporary communicative (inter-subjective) theories.

INGOLFUR BLÜHDORN

parties (social)

Family gatherings for birthdays, anniversaries, weddings, christenings and Christmas are very important in German-speaking countries. They tend to be more formal than other occasions such as the big parties on New Year's Eve or during the *Karneval* season. Informal dinner parties among friends are also common, as are barbecues, neighbourhood potlucks and block parties, or office parties. Many festivities are organized by clubs devoted to sports, shooting or gardening (see also **Schrebergarten**). German get-togethers can last three to ten hours, and alcohol (mostly beer, wine and *Sekt* – sparkling wine) is usually involved. The concept of *Gemütlichkeit* (a cozy feeling of well-being and togetherness) traditionally governs the party atmosphere.

SABINE SCHMIDT

parties: FRG

Political parties represent social groups and their interests in parliament and government and each can be characterized by its social basis, organization and claim to political power. In German political history, parties were excluded from government before 1918 and deemed expendable even during the Weimar democracy. These legacies of non-recognition were evident in party splintering and anti-system radicalization. After 1945, parties and the political system in which they operated were recast with two broad purposes in mind. The first was to prevent a resurgence of the Nazi Party or a similarly anti-democratic political force. To this end, the NSDAP and its affiliated organizations were banned by the Allies in 1945 while the Basic Law stipulated in 1949 that all political parties had to subscribe to the democratic consensus as a precondition of their legality. The second purpose concerned stability. In order to prevent splintering, the Allies licensed a limited number of parties across the political spectrum: the **KPD**, **SPD**, **F.D.P.** (or its regional predecessors), **CDU** (**CSU** in Bavaria) and the Catholic Centre Party; while the FRG introduced the 5 percent electoral hurdle. This made it more difficult for smaller parties to enter parliaments and obstruct governing majorities.

Although over 130 political parties have competed in elections in the FRG since 1945 and the First Bundestag in 1949 included 12 different political parties, the party system in the FRG has been characterized by a process of *concentration*. By the mid-1950s, CDU/CSU, F.D.P. and SPD dominated the Bundestag; by the 1970s, they also dominated regional parliaments. In 1949, the two strongest parties, CDU/CSU and SPD, between them had won 60.2 percent of the vote; by 1957, the concentration on the two big parties had risen to 82 percent; it peaked with 91.2 percent in 1976. The smaller F.D.P. has tended to remain below 10 percent yet has been represented in the Bundestag since 1949 without interruption and served longer in government coalitions than either CDU/CSU or SPD. In the 1990s, it lost representation in several *Land* parliaments and hovered precariously close to the 5 percent hurdle of parliamentary elimination.

One of the key features of post-war German party development was the success of the *Volkspartei*. Traditionally, political parties had aimed at representing the interests or ideological preferences of a specific social group. In 1945 most parties continued to focus on class or ideology while CDU and CSU deliberately broadened their base from a Catholic to a Christian platform in order to attract conservative voters from all social or religious backgrounds. As the governing party during the economic recovery of post-war Germany which improved the living standards of all social groups, the CDU/CSU succeeded in incorporating the electorate right of centre and contributed significantly to the formation of a democratic **political culture**. From 31 percent in 1949 the CDU/CSU soared to 50.2 percent, its

'electoral miracle' in 1957. With the exception of 1972 and 1998, it has been the strongest political party in the Bundestag. This CDU/CSU dominance has given the German party system a right-of-centre slant.

The first post-war decade saw SPD votes stagnate around 30 percent. While CDU and CSU incorporated new voters and social groups, the SPD only mobilized its traditional clientele. The transformation of the SPD from a 'class party' to a *Volkspartei* came into effect with the Godesberg Programme in 1959 which relinquished Marxist aims, endorsed the capitalist order and accepted Germany's integration into the western power bloc. By the late 1950s, the ban on the right-extremist SRP in 1952 and the Communist Party in 1956 had produced a party system of the centre: all parties with Bundestag representation shared a consensus on the political system, the social order and on key policies. After the transformation of the SPD all 'established' parties could be considered potential coalition partners in a polity where all governments have been coalitions. By 1966, the CDU/CSU dominance had been reduced sufficiently for the SPD to join a Grand Coalition; from 1969 to 1982, the SPD governed in coalition with the FDP; in 1982, a CDU/CSU and F.D.P. coalition regained control. In electoral terms, the 1950s were a decade of CDU/CSU dominance, the 1960s saw the emergence of the SPD as a potential CDU/CSU rival and as an advocate of social equality and a voice of the younger generation; in the 1970s, the two *Volksparteien* seemed set to eliminate smaller parties while opposition found an increasingly extra-parliamentary voice. The rise of the **Greens** halted the convergence of the two *Volksparteien* at the centre and generated two party blocs and potential coalition partners: CDU/CSU and F.D.P. to the right; SPD and Greens to the left of centre.

The Greens were the first party to pass the 5 percent hurdle and enter the Bundestag (in 1983) since the short-lived refugee protest party BHE in 1953. Their support emanated from **citizens' movements** and they claimed to voice issues which had been ignored by 'established' parties. Green environmentalism encompassed conservationist and ecological concerns but also propagated 'new politics', an agenda of social and political participation which reflected the preferences of educated new middle class voters of the younger generations. In the course of social and economic modernization, the *Volksparteien* found their support weakening: CDU and CSU could no longer rely as firmly on religious orientations or on women's votes as in the founding years of the FRG while the SPD had to target the educated new middle class as blue-collar employment declined and its working-class milieu all but disappeared. Young Germans of the post-war generations have their own expectations of how parties should relate to citizens, how policies should be transparent and how party organizations should involve their members. In the 1970s, these expectations translated into interest in politics, increased electoral turnout (over 90 percent) and a doubling of party membership (from 2 to 4 percent of the electorate). In the 1980s and 1990s, *Parteienverdrossenheit* – a disaffection with political parties – spread especially among the under twenty-fives. While the Greens pioneered 'basic democracy' in their party organization and set out to challenge traditional hierarchies, the other parties have yet to recast their culture and break the 'iron law of hierarchy' (Michels, 1957). The introduction of women's quotas in the Greens (1985) and the SPD (1988) responded to participatory demands but also constitutes an attempt to ensure that in their composition party organizations and parliaments reflect the society they represent and provide access for all citizens to political decision-making.

Further reading

Michels, R. (1957) *Zur Soziologie des Parteiwesens in der modernen Demokratie*, Stuttgart: Klett.

Smith, G. *et al.* (eds) (1992) *Developments in German Politics*, Basingstoke: Macmillan (a textbook with chapters written by subject specialists on key aspects of German political development including the party system and case studies of the main political parties).

Stoess, R. (ed.) (1990) *Parteienhandbuch*, 2 vols, Opladen: Westdeutscher Verlag (the handbook includes well researched articles on the origins, organization, programme and electoral performance of all political parties in the FRG since 1945 and is an invaluable source of information;

the first volume also includes a book-length introduction to the emergence of the party system).

EVA KOLINSKY

parties and mass organizations: GDR

The **SED** was the single most influential and powerful body in the GDR. Its leadership role was enshrined in the GDR constitution, a role which was recognized unreservedly by the mass organizations and the other four 'allied' political parties – the Christlich-Demokratische Union (CDU), Liberal-Demokratische Partei Deutschlands (LDPD), Demokratische Bauernpartei Deutschlands (DBD) and Nationaldemokratische Partei Deutschlands (NDPD). The CDU and the LDPD, both licensed by the Soviet authorities in 1945, resisted the hegemonic tendencies of the SED until finally succumbing at the beginning of the 1950s. The NDPD and the DBD, on the other hand, were pliant instruments from the time of their foundation in 1948 and were deployed by the SED and the Soviet Military Administration to attract former soldiers and farmers and to erode the middle-class constituency of the Christian and Liberal Democrats. The 'allied' parties performed an important transmission function in that they transmitted the decisions and policies of the SED with a view to securing compliance with official policy among members not under the direct organizational control of the SED. The outward appearance of a multi-party system was a useful propaganda device both at home and abroad and the CDU and LDPD performed a modest role as a bridgehead to similarly named parties in West Germany. Although the 'allied' parties were represented in the **Volkskammer** and the local and regional assemblies, they were denied permission to establish their own political organizations in the armed forces, the enterprises and the universities.

Among the most important of a wide range of mass organizations were the Freie Deutsche Jugend (**FDJ**), Freier Deutscher Gewerkschaftsbund (**FDGB**), Demokratischer Frauenbund

Deutschlands (**DFD**), Kulturbund der DDR (KB) and the Vereinigung der gegenseitigen Bauernhilfe (VdgB). The latter body, the Farmers' Mutual Aid Association, provided equipment and other facilities for those engaged in agriculture. The mass organizations enjoyed a large membership, that of the FDGB and the FDJ numbering 9.6 and 2.3 million respectively in the late 1980s. Like the other mass organizations, such as the Ernst Thälmann Pioneers and the German Gymnastics and Sports Association, their organizational structure was based on the Leninist principle of democratic centralism, and SED members formed the nucleus of their executives. Such bodies, while acting as 'transmission belts' of the SED, also sought to cater for the specific interests of their members. These two functions were not easily reconciled and caused much dissatisfaction among members.

See also: political culture: GDR

Further reading

Gotschlich, H. (ed.) (1994) *'Links und links und Schritt gehalten . . .' Die FDJ: Konzepte – Abläufe – Grenzen*, Berlin: Metropol Verlag.

Weber, J. (ed.) (1994) *Der SED-Staat: Neues über eine vergangene Diktatur*, Munich: Olzog Verlag.

Zimmermann, H. (ed.) (1985) *DDR Handbuch*, 3rd edn, Cologne: Verlag Wissenschaft & Politik.

MIKE DENNIS

Passion Plays

The medieval and early modern traditions of theatrical portrayals of the sufferings of Jesus during Christian Holy Week were revived in several areas of German-speaking Europe after 1945, but only the Oberammergau Passion Play has proven to have had substantial durability and impact.

Rooted in liturgical drama, processions and mystery plays, versions of the Passion Play were widely performed in the German states, Austria and Switzerland until the eighteenth century, after which they became rare. Only the Oberammergau Passion Play, first performed in 1634 and normally repeated at ten-year intervals, has maintained continuity. Several other towns have sought to revive the play, with mixed success, including Altomünster, Amberg, Freiburg im Breisgau, Kemnath, Lohr am Main, Neumarkt in der Oberpfalz, Nördlingen, Sömmersdorf and St Margarethen in the Federal Republic, Heiligenstadt in the former German Democratic Republic, and Erl, Mettmach, and Thiersee in Austria. The Luzern Passion Play in Switzerland was not revived.

Oberammergau's play was first given to carry out a vow made in 1633 that, if the village were saved from the plague, it would perform the Passion Play each decade, forever. The text was rewritten in the nineteenth century by two priests, Othmar Weis and Joseph Daisenberger, as a melodrama based loosely on the Gospels, interspersed with tableaux from the Old Testament. The music was written by the village schoolmaster, Rochus Dedler, in the style of Handel. In 1950 and 1960 the play was performed virtually unchanged from the earlier versions.

Critics objected that this traditional Oberammergau play showed a stereotype of a 'Jewish plot' as the cause of Jesus's suffering and death. They charged that such anti-Semitism was unworthy and offensive, especially after the **Holocaust**. Traditionalists in the village responded that they were only being true to the Bible, and that they had no anti-Semitic intent. Controversies surrounded the productions of 1970, 1980 and 1984 (an extra, 350th anniversary, season). Reformers within the village won control of the play in the late 1980s and began serious reforms for the 1990 season. The same group is preparing further reforms for the season of 2000.

The culture of Oberammergau, a southern Bavarian village of 5,000 people, is dominated by the play. Crafting and selling religious wood carvings is a major industry. Following carefully guarded traditions, only villagers can perform in the play, so families cultivate dramatic and musical skills and vie for the best parts each time the play is performed. The vast majority of the town is Roman Catholic, though since 1945 some Protestants and Eastern Orthodox families have settled there. There is no Jewish population.

The Oberammergau Passion Play lasts all day long, with approximately one hundred performances each season playing to a total of 500,000 visitors. About half of those who attend are foreigners who purchase elaborate tour packages with the Passion Play as a centrepiece. Thus the play has a major economic impact, not only on the village, but on the entire region.

Further reading

Friedman, S. (1984) *The Oberammergau Passion Play: A Lance Against Civilization*, Carbondale, IL: Southern Illinois University Press (a highly critical account of anti-Semitism in the Oberammergau Passion Play).

Henker, M. (ed.) (1990) *Hört, sehet, weint und liebt: Passionsspiele im alpenländischen Raum*, Munich: Haus der Bayerischen Geschichte (illustrated scholarly catalogue for an exhibition on Passion Plays).

GORDON R. MORK

Pausewang, Gudrun

b. 3 March 1928, Wichstadtl (Bohemia; now Mladkov, Czech Republic)

Writer and schoolteacher

A very popular and prolific writer for both adults and children, Pausewang initially drew on her experiences as a schoolteacher in South America. Since the 1980s she has turned increasingly towards environmental, anti-war and Third World topics. *Last Children* (*Die letzten Kinder von Schewenborn*, 1983) and *Fall-Out* (*Die Wolke*, 1987), which describe life after a nuclear attack and after an accidental nuclear fallout respectively, excited prolonged controversy concerning the suitability of the topic for young readers. Several autobiographical books about her youth and displacement trace the development of her political consciousness.

GABRIELA STEINKE

Pazarkaya, Yüksel

b. 24 February 1940, Izmir (Turkey)

Writer

Pazarkaya, who writes in Turkish and German and publishes in both countries, is seen as one of the pioneers of Turkish *Deutschlandliteratur*. His volume of poems *Irrwege* (Wrong Tracks, published 1968 Istanbul) is one of the first literary explorations of the problems of foreign workers. The author went to Germany as a student in 1957 and witnessed the Turkish labour migration that started on a large scale in the late 1960s. Confrontation with the extreme discrimination experienced by Turkish people motivated him to analyse his own image of Germany. The brutal social reality was incompatible with the ideal of a Germany of poets and thinkers which Payarkaya had acquired during his education in Turkey. This discrepancy between reality and imagination is clearly expressed in Pazarkaya's most famous poem 'Deutsche Sprache' (German Language) (1989). Pazarkaya is even better known through his diverse cultural activities than through his literary work. He played a leading role in the publication of the Turkish-German magazine *Anadil* (Mother Tongue) (1980–3) and influenced the programme of the Ararat publishing house (founded in 1977). Pazarkaya translated the texts of famous Turkish authors such as Nazim Hikmet and wrote essays about Turkish literature, culture and migration. His activities are intended to inform the German readership about Turkey, thus liberating Turkish culture from its minority status.

See also: *Gastarbeiter*; migrant literature

Further reading

Chiellino, C. (1988) 'Gespräch mit Yüksel Pazarkaya', *Die Reise hält an. Ausländische Künstler in der Bundesrepublik*, Munich: Beck, pp. 100–10.

Riemann, W. (1983) *Das Deutschlandbild in der modernen türkischen Literatur*, Wiesbaden: Harrassowitz.

SABINE FISCHER

PDS

The Partei des Demokratischen Sozialismus (PDS) (Party of Democratic Socialism) is the successor to the **SED** (Socialist Unity Party) which was the dominant political party in the GDR from its foundation in 1949 to the collapse of Communist power in November 1989. At the emergency SED party conference in December 1989, convened after the deletion on 1 December of Article 1 of the GDR constitution (see also **constitutions: GDR**) concerning the leading role of the SED, it was decided not to dissolve the SED, but to rename it SED-PDS. On 4 February 1990 the party executive committee decided to drop SED altogether from the name of the party, shortly before the party's first conference at the end of February. The decision not to dissolve was made primarily because of the loss of capital and buildings which would have resulted from a dissolution. But a further crucial factor was that the SED could not follow the path of the Polish and Hungarian Communist Parties, namely to dissolve itself and then reform in the centre ground of social democracy; that position had been occupied by the refounded SDP/SPD in the GDR since the autumn of 1989.

The leaders of the PDS came originally from the reform wing of the SED; the two leading figures initially were the prime minister of the GDR from November 1989 to March 1990, Hans **Modrow**, and Gregor **Gysi** who became its first chairman. In the first free elections to the **Volkskammer** (People's Chamber) on 18 March 1990 the PDS received 16.4 percent of the vote, with its highest poll, 30.2 percent, in East Berlin. In subsequent elections in 1990 this share of the vote fell, reaching its lowest point in the federal elections of 2 December, 11.1 percent on the territory of the GDR. This percentage entitled them to only 17 seats in the Bundestag. Despite the fact that the party had seats in all the five new *Land* parliaments in the East (average percentage vote 11.6 percent), the SED-PDS had in the space of a year gone from being the party of power in the GDR to a minor opposition party. It had also lost the vast majority of its members; in November 1989 the SED still had 2.1 million members, but by June 1990 the PDS figure had fallen to 350,000. Also, whereas only 17 percent of the membership was over sixty years old in 1989, by the middle of 1990 51 percent were in this age bracket.

The scene was therefore set for the rapid disappearance of the PDS. But, partly because of the negative consequences of unification for many East Germans in the post-unification period, and partly because of the public relations skills of its leader, Gregor Gysi, the PDS recovered from this lowpoint. Despite the handicap of still being regarded as the successor to the SED, and despite having a hard-line communist wing, the 'Communist Platform', it managed to develop its image as the party which was best able to represent eastern interests in what was seen by a number of people in the East as a takeover by the West. The PDS was able to fulfil this role primarily because, despite its loss of members, it still had the largest, and most active and experienced, membership in the eastern *Länder*, and its ability to mobilize support at election times became particularly apparent during the elections of 1994. In all the *Land* elections in the East it increased its proportion of the vote substantially. The most significant result was that in Sachsen-Anhalt in June 1994, after which a minority SPD/Green government assumed office, and was able to govern with PDS co-operation. For the first time the PDS was not totally isolated from all the other political parties. In the October 1994 federal election it increased its vote in the East to just under 20 percent, but failed to make any breakthrough in the West, polling only 0.9 percent. As a result it fell below the 5 percent hurdle in the whole of Germany, but was able to re-enter the Bundestag with 30 seats as a result of achieving four directly elected seats in East Berlin. PDS electoral fortunes were further enhanced by its success in the elections to the city parliament in Berlin in October 1995, when it consolidated its position as the strongest party in eastern Berlin, achieving over 40 percent of the vote in some districts. In September 1998 it increased its seats in the Bundestag to 36.

See also: elections: FRG; elections: GDR; parties: FRG

Further reading

Barker, P. (ed.) (1998) *The Party of Democratic Socialism in Germany: Modern Post-Communism or Nostalgic Populism?*, Amsterdam and Atlanta, GA: Rodopi.

Gerner, M. (1994) *Partei ohne Zukunft? Von der SED zur PDS*, Munich: Tilsner (a comprehensive study).

PETER BARKER

peace movement: FRG

The peace movement is one arm of the new **protest movements** which emerged in the 1980s. Local peace groups and national network organizations, supported in part by the **SPD**, the **trade unions**, the **Greens** and church groups, mobilized hundred of thousands of citizens against the arms race, the stationing of cruise and Pershing II missiles, the Star-Wars programme of Ronald Reagan, and the strategy of deterrence. The Krefelder Appell (Krefeld Declaration), a collection of signatures against NATO's decision to deploy new missiles in Europe, was signed by more than 9 million West Germans. In June 1982 one of the largest protest meetings in the history of the FRG with more than 500,000 participants was held by the peace movement in Bonn. The spectrum of activities also included acts of civil disobedience such as blockades of military facilities and missile bases.

Origin and history of the FRG peace movement

The development of a new peace movement in the 1980s is to be seen in the context of earlier disarmament movements. A broad opposition to the rearmament of the FRG had already evolved at the beginning of the 1950s. In the late 1950s protest focused on the issue of whether or not the **Bundeswehr** should receive atomic weapons. Under the slogan '*Kampf dem Atomtod*' (Fight Nuclear Death) thousands of people demonstrated against the armament policy of the **Adenauer** government. The SPD, the DGB (the parent organization of all trade unions in the FRG) and church groups supported this protest movement. In the 1960s peace activists started the Easter March Campaign, a pacifist movement against the inter-

national arms race and nuclear tests. The student protest against the Vietnam War at the end of the 1960s gained more public attention but this protest was part of the wider **student movement** rather than of a more comprehensive peace movement. In the second half of the 1970s, after a period of détente, international conflicts and the arms race between the superpowers led to new tensions. The Reagan administration issued in 1980 a new armament programme and intensified propaganda against the Soviet Union. Many Germans feared that their country would provide the battleground for a nuclear war between the superpowers. Against this background they refused to accept the strategy of deterrence and criticized particularly the stationing of Pershing II missiles in their country. This was the starting point for the development of a large new peace movement. Parallel to this development a peace movement also arose in the GDR. Under the roof of the Protestant church independent peace groups started to criticize not only the NATO deployment decision but also the armament policy of the Soviet Union and of the GDR government. In some cases these groups initiated protest campaigns together with peace activists from the FRG (see also **peace movement: GDR**).

In the wake of the lost battle against the deployment decision the mass protest of the peace movement wound down and took on a more institutionalized structure in the second half of the 1980s. The peace movement retained, however, the ability to mobilize thousands of citizens in a short time. When the Gulf War started some hundreds of thousands of Germans protested in public meetings.

The composition of the peace movement

The peace movement is politically and ideologically an association of very heterogeneous currents. One can differentiate between (a) supporters from the old and new left (e.g. the **DKP**, left-wing Social Democrats, undogmatic left, radical left, trade-union members); (b) pacifist and Christian peace groups (e.g. the German Peace Society – United War Resisters, the 'Living without Armaments Initiative', Reconciliation Action/Service for Peace, Pax Christi); (c) green and alternative peace groups (e.g. the Federal Association of Independent Peace Groups, Grassroots Revolution – Federation of Non-Violent Action Groups); (d) more conservative oriented peace groups (e.g. members of the **CDU** and established organizations); and (e) militant grassroots groups. In addition to this, initiatives from certain occupational sectors (teachers, lawyers, physicians and scientists), and peace study experts completed the diversity of the movement. Even soldiers from the **Bundeswehr**, organized in the Darmstädter Appell (Darmstadt Declaration), participated in the peace movement.

In keeping with its perception of itself as a decentralized and grass-roots movement, the peace movement regarded the local peace groups as its true backbone. For the purpose of co-ordination and communication, network organizations such as the Koordinierungsausschuß der Friedensbewegung (Co-ordination Committee of the Peace Movement) were founded.

Political concepts of the peace movement

In keeping with the ideological heterogeneity of the peace movement different concepts of peace were held. The minimum consensus was the rejection of the stationing of cruise and Pershing II missiles. More positively formulated concepts argued for a new security policy. They called for disengagement, disarmament, nuclear-free zones in central Europe, and a nuclear test ban. Some groups focused their activities on the issue of arms exports, while pacifist-oriented groups favoured the concept of social defence. Because of the absence of a formal peace treaty between the wartime Allies and Germany, some concepts were dominated by the idea of a peace settlement for the whole of Germany. Controversies between different currents of the peace movement centred around the question of whether or not the Soviet Union was a 'natural' ally of the movement. Most of the grassroots groups insisted that the peace movement was independent of the power blocs and owed no loyalty to any of the superpowers. Political and ideological differences in the wake of the end of the Cold War and particularly during the Bosnian War led to the organizational dissolution of the peace movement in the 1990s.

Further reading

Burns, R. and van der Will, W. (1988) *Protest and Democracy in West Germany*, London: Macmillan (contains chapters on the peace movement in the 1950s and 60s, and on the 'new peace movement' of the 1980s).

Johnstone, D. (1984) *The Politics of Euromissiles*, London: Verso (discusses the issues that gave rise to the 1980s peace movement).

Leif, T. (1990) *Die strategische Ohn-Macht der Friedensbewegung: Kommunikations- und Entscheidungsstrukturen in den achtziger Jahren*, Opladen: Westdeutscher Verlag (examines structures of the West German peace movement in the 1980s).

Wasmuht, U.C. (1987) *Friedensbewegungen der 80er Jahre: Zur Analyse ihrer strukturellen und aktuellen Entstehungsbedingungen in der Bundesrepublik Deutschland und den Vereinigten Staaten von Amerika nach 1945*, Gießen: Focus Verlag (comprehensive analysis of the evolution and development of the peace movement in the FRG and in the US).

LOTHAR PROBST

peace movement: GDR

The peace movement that emerged in the GDR in the 1980s had to function within a system that condemned it as superfluous, obstructive, and illegal, because – so it was claimed – socialism alone was the surest guarantor of world peace. Independent peace activists remained a small but growing minority, operating largely in scattered local initiatives under the umbrella of the Protestant churches. In the course of the decade their agenda was extended increasingly explicitly to civil-rights issues, and their groupings provided the nuclei of the citizens' movements of the **Wende** (see also **citizens' movements: GDR**).

The GDR peace movement first came to wider attention in the early 1980s (largely through the West German media, as the GDR media resolutely ignored it) in the context of the worldwide peace protests of the time. Its roots lay in the campaign to improve the provisions for conscientious objectors that had begun in the early 1960s, and in opposition to the pre-military training that was introduced into school syllabuses in 1978.

Although the threat of nuclear war now became a major concern, it saw this – in contrast to the 'official' peace movement of the GDR government and many western peace movements – as just one issue among many. Thus it defined 'peace' and its preconditions very broadly, and attended to wider social, environmental, third-world and gender issues.

Inevitably civil rights matters had to be addressed, as these concerned the very possibility of independent debate and protest, but the peace movement never expressly challenged the socialist system, and shied away from describing itself as an 'opposition'. This was in many ways a reflection of its symbiosis with the Protestant **Kirche im Sozialismus**: the peace movement needed the church as this was the only 'space' (both literal and metaphorical) for independent thought and action in the GDR, while the church took the predominantly youthful members of the peace movement under its wing partly out of a sense of Christian obligation, but also because many pastors and congregations shared their views and concerns.

Official harassment, persecution and discrimination were the common experience of many in the movement, with the state being particularly unwilling to tolerate activity that spilled beyond the churches. (Even wearing the 'Swords into Ploughshares' emblem in public was criminalized.) Thus Pastor Rainer Eppelmann was arrested for disseminating the 'Berlin Appeal' ('Make Peace Without Weapons') that he and Robert **Havemann** had written in 1982, and further arrests ensued in 1988 when independent campaigners joined the annual official rally commemorating the communist martyrs Rosa Luxemburg and Karl Liebknecht.

Several campaigners, such as Bärbel **Bohley**, Gerd and Ulrike **Poppe**, and Rainer Eppelmann, came to prominence at the time of the *Wende* as organizers of the citizens' movements and as participants in the **round tables**. For a brief moment the principles of the peace movement took centre stage, and were instrumental in ensuring the non-violent nature of the revolution; but in 1990 they were quickly overtaken by the rush to unification.

See also: dissent and opposition: GDR; uranium mining

Further reading

Neubert, E. (1997) *Geschichte der Opposition in der DDR 1949–1989*, Berlin: Chr. Links Verlag (includes detailed coverage of the peace movement and its progeny).

Rüddenklau, W. (1992) *Störenfried: DDR-Opposition 1986–1989*, Berlin: BasisDruck (richly documented coverage of events in the last three years of communist rule).

Sandford, J. (1983) *The Sword and the Ploughshare: Autonomous Peace Initiatives in East Germany*, London: Merlin (covers the period up to early 1983; includes selected documents in English translation).

JOHN SANDFORD

Pedretti, Erica

b. 25 February 1930, Sternberg (now Šternberk, Czech Republic)

Writer and sculptress

Pedretti's artistic œuvres, situated in the indeterminate margins of autobiography and fiction and freely combining elements of both, represent a lifelong exploration of language and identity formation in a multilingual world. Forced to flee her childhood home in 1945, she later settled in Switzerland as an adopted homeland. Her prose and sculptures challenge the conventional interpretations of an autobiographical project, and characterize communication as spoken language juxtaposed with visual images to represent the world and multicultural societies. She has been recognized with numerous literary and art prizes, including the Ingeborg Bachmann Prize in 1984. Her prose works include *Heiliger Sebastian* (Saint Sebastian) (1973), *Valerie, oder das unerzogene Auge* (Valerie, or the Uneducated Eye) (1986), *Engste Heimat* (Most Narrow Homeland) (1995), numerous short stories and radio plays.

See also: literature: Switzerland

ANNE BLUME

Peichl, Gustav

b. 18 March 1928, Vienna

Architect

Having studied at the Vienna Academy of Fine Arts under Clemens Holzmeister from 1949 to 1953, Peichl established a private practice in Vienna in 1953. He has held the post of Professor at the Vienna Academy of Fine Arts since 1973.

Peichl gained international recognition with the first of five studios for the Austrian broadcasting service **ORF** (1968–81). From the mid-1970s he has combined his expressive, often symbolic machine aesthetic with an interest in ecological building, of which the *EFA-Erdfunkstelle* (ground receiving station) in Aflenz (1976–80) is a good example. His *Bundeskunsthalle* in Bonn (1989–92) moves towards a calmer monumentality held in stone with ironic (postmodern) touches to it.

MARTIN KUDLEK

PEN

The numerous tensions in the German branches of the International Association of Poets, Playwrights, Editors, Essayists, and Novelists have reflected political developments. After the Cold War precipitated a split in the original all-German association, unification did not bring the eastern and western PEN clubs together, with former GDR émigrés particularly reluctant to accept many of their former colleagues. Only in 1998 was it agreed that the two should merge, with formal unification planned for the autumn of that year. As president of the International PEN in the 1970s Heinrich **Böll** was subject to exaggerated criticism for not doing enough for dissident Soviet writers.

STUART PARKES

Penck, A.R.

b. 5 October 1939, Dresden

Painter, sculptor, graphic artist and musician (real name Ralf Winckler; also known as Mike Hammer)

Ralf Winckler, alias A.R. Penck, alias Mike Hammer, started as a self-educated artist in the GDR.

In 1980, he moved to the FRG, and settled in London in 1983. He became internationally known as part of the German new expressionists movement. He operates with standardized visual signs often on a monumental scale. The images have an affinity to cave paintings, the art of children or graffiti. Visual and verbal language are interwoven. He has also established himself as a Free Jazz musician.

See also: Baselitz, Georg; painting; sculpture

KERSTIN MEY

Petersen, Wolfgang

b. 14 March 1941, Emden

Filmmaker

Petersen directed several television films in the 1970s, but the huge international success of his war film *The Boat* (*Das Boot*, 1981) and the English-language fantasy film *The Neverending Story* (*Die unendliche Geschichte*, 1984, based on the book by Michael **Ende**) drew him to Hollywood. After his first two American features flopped, Clint Eastwood rescued his career by demanding his services for *In The Line of Fire* (1993). With this film, Petersen became a high profile Hollywood A-List director, and he consolidated his reputation as an accomplished maker of action thrillers with *Outbreak* (1995).

JONATHAN LEGG

Peymann, Claus

b. 7 June 1937, Bremen

Theatre director and artistic director

Peymann started out at the student drama studio in Hamburg. In 1966 at the Frankfurt Theater am Turm (TAT) he staged work by Peter **Handke** and Gerlind **Reinshagen**. At the Munich Kammer-spiele and the Hamburg Schauspielhaus he directed Heiner **Müller** and Thomas **Bernhard**. The latter was to become his favourite dramatist. In 1970 he co-founded the Berlin Schaubühne. He was Managing Director at the Württembergisches Staatstheater in Stuttgart, but in 1977 refused the extension of his contract. From 1979 he was Co-Director at the Schauspielhaus Bochum, and since 1986 Director of the **Burgtheater** in Vienna. Peymann's work is a synthesis of enlightenment and utopia in which the latter is revealed by the exaggeration of wrong and hypocritical attitudes.

Further reading

Sucher, C.B. (1990) *Theaterzauberer. 10 Regisseure des deutschen Gegenwartstheaters*, Munich and Zürich.

MATTHIAS BAUHUF

philosophy

The background of post-war Germanophone philosophy

Ever since the times of Kant and Goethe, Germans have been fond of regarding themselves as '*ein Volk der Dichter und Denker*' ('a people of poets and thinkers'). In the nineteenth century, German academic philosophy provided an institutional and intellectual model for western philosophy. Moreover, most of the great innovators outside academic philosophy (Schopenhauer, Marx, Nietzsche, Frege, Freud and Wittgenstein) wrote in German. As a result, twentieth-century philosophy is largely the invention of German speakers. This holds not just of continental philosophy – Hegelianism, Marxism, existentialism, phenomenology, hermeneutics and psychoanalysis – but also

of analytic philosophy, which was shaped decisively by Frege, Wittgenstein and the logical positivists of the Vienna Circle. From Kant to the end of the twentieth century, one concern has united these otherwise diverse traditions, namely the question whether philosophy can preserve a separate role in view of the progress of the empirical sciences. Unlike their Anglophone and Francophone colleagues, Germanophone philosophers have tended to resist the attempt to reduce philosophy either to the natural sciences or to a branch of *belles lettres* unrestrained by academic standards of truth or rationality.

The rise of Nazism had relatively little impact on the content of mainstream academic philosophy. Its main philosophical consequence was that certain movements were driven abroad – Marxism, psychoanalysis, logical positivism – while individuals like Karl **Jaspers** and Edmund **Husserl** were silenced. As a result of emigration, post-war German philosophy was for some years rather provincial. Its subsequent development was partly determined by who did and who did not return. That process was also characterized by three features – continuity, revival and reappropriation – which have dominated, respectively, the three main trends: phenomenology and hermeneutics, dialectical philosophy, and analytic philosophy.

Phenomenology and hermeneutics

Continuity is most pronounced in the phenomenological tradition and its off-shoots in **existentialism** and hermeneutics. Husserl's phenomenology is less a doctrine than a *method*. It aims to establish philosophy as a non-empirical yet rigorous science by avoiding speculative system-building in favour of descriptions of what is present to us in consciousness. The fundamental feature of consciousness is intentionality, its being about or directed at things; phenomenology 'brackets' or disregards the physical world in order to concentrate on the intentional structures through which we are related to it. Because of its methodological character, phenomenology could be applied to all areas of philosophy, in ways that often diverged from Husserl's own ideas. As a result, it has been a live tradition in the Federal Republic of Germany (e.g. in Elizabeth Ströker), partly inspired by the publication of Husserl's *Nachlaß* (posthumous writings) from 1954 onwards.

Nevertheless, phenomenology had a far greater impact through its influence on the existential phenomenology of Husserl's pupil Martin **Heidegger**. In *Being and Time* (*Sein und Zeit*, 1927) Heidegger's central concern was the 'question of being', namely of what makes various entities the kinds of things they are. The distinguishing feature of *Dasein*, i.e. of human existence, is that humans are concerned with their own 'Being' (*Sein*), notably with the practical choices they face. Heidegger rejected Husserl's bracketing, because our existence is too practically engaged with the world for such an abstraction. But he agreed that we should bracket the scientific world-picture in order to reveal the everyday practical significance things have for us.

After the war, Heidegger moved from this existential ontology to a direct mediation of Being itself, which is no longer regarded as something humans do, but as something that happens to them (see his rebuff to Sartre in 'On Humanism', 1947). However, this existential mysticism was too oracular and idiosyncratic to exert a lasting influence on German academic philosophy. It is no surprise, therefore, that the main development of Heidegger's thought (its 'urbanization' according to Habermas), Ernst-Georg **Gadamer**'s *Truth and Method* (*Wahrheit und Methode*, 1960), harks back to the early Heidegger. For Gadamer, phenomenology, and thereby philosophy in general, is hermeneutics, i.e. the investigation of the method of interpretation, because the fundamental structures and limits of human existence are determined by interpretation, of Being in Heidegger, and of sense (*Sinn*) in Gadamer. That interpretation is essentially mediated by language. It is also universal: there are no brute facts or raw data, only the attempt of interpreters to merge their 'horizon', their historically shaped prejudices and conceptual commitments, with that of the interpreted individual, text or tradition. As a result, philosophy turns into a dialogue with texts and with the history of their effects. Thus Gadamer transforms philosophical hermeneutics, the study of philosophical interpretation, into hermeneutic philosophy, a kind of philosophizing that evolves essentially around the idea of interpretation.

Dialectical philosophy: neo-Marxism and the Hegel renaissance

Dialectical philosophy in the FRG was shaped by three factors, all of which highlighted the philosophical, and in particular the Hegelian, aspects of **Marxism** against the economistic determinism of Marxist orthodoxy. The first was Georg **Lukács**' *History and Class-Consciousness* (*Geschichte und Klassenbewußtsein*, 1923), which resisted the determinist model of economic base and ideological superstructure by insisting that the proletariat needs to develop a reflective consciousness if a successful revolution is to come about. Lukács's Hegelian brand of Marxism was further fuelled by the discovery of Marx's early Paris manuscripts in the 1920s. The third factor was the founding of the Institute of Social Research in 1923. After emigrating to New York in 1933, the Institute returned to Frankfut am Main in 1950 under the directorship of Max **Horkheimer** and Theodor W. **Adorno**.

The **Critical Theory** of this so-called **Frankfurt School** attempts to explain the development of modern capitalist society in a way which would at the same time indicate how it might be freed from relations of domination and exploitation. Critical theory rejected the Marxist verdict that pure theory, i.e. philosophy, has simply been superseded by revolutionary practice. Before the war, it was an interdisciplinary project which tried to combine neo-Marxist sociology, dialectic philosophy and Freudian psychoanalysis. After the war, philosophy came to dominate. In *The Dialectic of Enlightenment* (1947) Horkheimer and Adorno moved from a renunciation of capitalism to a renunciation of the Enlightenment tradition as a whole, on the grounds that rationality inevitably reduces to 'instrumental reason', the efficient marshalling of means in the service of controlling and manipulating nature and society.

Critical theory had an enormous impact on the **student movement** of the 1960s, strengthened by the often parallel influence of Ernst **Bloch** and Herbert **Marcuse**. However, the death of Adorno in 1969, the collapse of the student movement, the dogmatic hardening of Marxist positions, and the rise of **terrorism** (sometimes blamed on critical theory) diminished its political influence and fuelled a neo-conservative philosophical journalism (e.g. Herman **Lübbe**). As a major force, critical theory survived mainly through the work of Jürgen **Habermas**. Habermas transformed critical theory yet again. Instead of condemning reason as such, he tried to develop a conception of reason with a non-instrumental, ethical dimension.

In *Knowledge and Human Interest* (*Erkenntnis und Interesse*, 1968) Habermas contrasts the technical dimension of human knowledge stressed by orthodox Marxists and the early Frankfurt School alike, with a 'practical' dimension, namely that of interpersonal communication. At the same time he rejects the universal claims of Gadamer's hermeneutics in the name of a neo-Marxist critique of ideology, by insisting that both the technical and the practical dimensions of knowledge are subservient to an 'emancipatory' interest in human freedom and flourishing. From 1970 onwards, Habermas took a linguistic or 'communicative' turn, which was inspired by Niklas **Luhmann**'s system-theory on the one hand, analytic philosophy of language on the other, and culminated in *Theory of Communicative Action* (*Theorie des kommunikativen Handelns*, 1981). In recent years, he has applied this theory to a defence of Enlightenment ideals against both traditionalism and postmodernism.

Although inspired by it, dialectical thought in the FRG has not been confined to Marxism in even the widest sense. There has also been a renaissance of Hegelianism. Notable attempts have been made to revive Hegelian-cum-Aristotelian ideas in moral and political philosophy, and to reconstruct Hegel's theoretical philosophy, especially his logic, out of its Kantian roots (e.g. in Rüdiger Bubner and Dieter Henrich). For obvious political reasons, academic philosophy in the GDR was confined to Marxism. In comparison to dialectical thought in the FRG (or even in other communist countries), that Marxism was not just orthodox but dogmatic. Philosophical questions and positions were treated almost exclusively according to the ideological exigencies of the **SED** (with the exception of some purely formal work, which could get by with paying lip-service to 'the classics of Marxism' in the Preface). Original thinkers like **Bloch** and his pupil Wolfgang **Harich** were either silenced or exiled.

The reappropriation of analytic philosophy

Many pioneers of analytic philosophy were driven out of *Mitteleuropa* by the Nazis. As a result, analytic philosophy had to be rediscovered after the war. This process, in particular the assimilation of Ludwig **Wittgenstein** and Karl **Popper**, played an important role in making Germanophone philosophy more modern and international. It took several forms. Some philosophers without prior allegiances embraced analytic philosophy wholeheartedly, and became mainstream analytical philosophers. This holds true especially of the Munich School of Wolfgang Stegmüller, and of related developments in Austria, which were facilitated by historical and personal links with the pre-war Vienna Circle. Stegmüller and his pupils (e.g. Eike von Savigny) deserve the main credit for reintroducing analytic philosophy, thereby enabling a growing number of German analytic philosophers to participate in the international debate.

Other German philosophers approached analytic philosophy from their own indigenous perspective (many of them taught for some time at Heidelberg, Gadamer's university). One important example of this approach is the work of Habermas and Karl-Otto Apel, which, among other things, involves a critical hermeneutics. They have used Wittgensteinian and pragmatist ideas to defend the hermeneutic distinction between the causal explanations provided by the natural sciences and the understanding of human action and speech sought by the social sciences against positivist objections. At the same time, they have attacked the relativistic tendencies in Wittgenstein and Gadamer by insisting that certain moral principles have universal validity because they are tacitly presupposed in any intersubjective communication. Habermas uses this idea to provide critical theory with an objective moral standard by which to judge ideologies and social formations, and Apel for a renewal of transcendental philosophy, in which Kant's preconditions of experience are replaced by preconditions of intersubjective communication.

Other attempts to combine analytic and continental philosophy have been less influential, but also less eclectic. For example, Ernst Tugendhat and Wolfgang Künne have pursued questions derived from phenomenology and hermeneutics (e.g. concerning the nature of philosophy and the objects of thought) by using analytical tools in ways that advance both the continental questions and the analytic methods.

The philosophy of science constitutes a substantial and lively part of German analytic philosophy, due mainly to the ongoing debates between three main movements. The first is Stegmüller's Munich School, which represents the post-positivist mainstream, but has also made novel contributions to the structuralist account of scientific theories. The second is Popper's critical rationalism. It came to prominence as a result of the 'positivism debate' (*Positivismusstreit*) in the 1960s between Popper and his German lieutenant Hans Albert on the one hand, and Adorno and Habermas on the other. As a result, critical rationalism came to be seen as the great alternative to the Frankfurt School. Originally, critical rationalism was a philosophy of science based on the idea that all knowledge is fallible. But in Germany critical rationalism became best known as a political philosophy of liberal outlook, which avoids both conservativism and Marxism by favouring piecemeal social change. The **SPD**, **F.D.P.** and **CDU** have all scrambled to lay claim to Popper's political legacy.

The third and most indigenous movement of German philosophy of science is the constructivism of the Erlangen School founded by Paul Lorenzen. Constructivism tries to explain and justify concepts taken for granted by other positions through methodic steps that start from simple linguistic activities. The programme started with the foundations of logic and mathematics, but was later extended to the natural sciences ('proto-physics') and to ethics.

General trends

In quantitative terms, German philosophy remains dominated by historical and exegetical work ('The Concept of History from Augustine to Dilthey'). The standard of scholarship is high, but the writing is often turgid. Although it has traditionally been characterized by the competition of different schools, it has recently evolved (partly for reasons of funding) around collaborative and interdisciplin-ary projects, like the monumental *Historisches Wörterbuch der Philosophie* (Historical Dictionary of Philosophy) edited by Joachim Ritter, the 'rehabilitation of practical philosophy', the theory of action, and an abiding concern with philosophical anthropology, which goes back to the work of Arnold **Gehlen** and Helmuth **Plessner**. German philosophy remains closely linked to broader political and social concerns, e.g. in Tugendhat's defence of the peace movement or Habermas' contribution to the historians' dispute (***Historikerstreit***). However, this link has not always been fruitful. Thus a curious alliance of the religious right and the dogmatic left has managed to suppress any debate of bioethical issues because of their alleged connection with fascism. Contemporary philosophy in Germany and Austria is more diverse than philosophy in the Anglophone world; but it has yet to recapture the originality and eminence it possessed before the rise of Nazism.

Further reading

Bubner, R. (1981) *Modern German Philosophy*, Cambridge: Cambridge University Press (the standard work on post-war philosophy in the FRG; highly instructive).

Glock, H.J. (1997) 'Insignificant Others: The Mutual Prejudices of Anglophone and Germanophone Philosophers', in C. Brown and T. Seidel (eds), *Cultural Negotiations*, Tübingen: Günther Narr Verlag.

Pyle, A. (ed.) (1994) Special Issue of *Cogito* 8, 3 (a very useful collection of recent survey articles).

Roberts, J. (1988) *German Philosophy: An Introduction*, Cambridge: Polity.

Schnädelbach, H. (1984) *Philosophy in Germany 1831–1933*, Cambridge: Cambridge University Press (a brilliant account of the roots of post-war German philosophy).

Stegmüller, W. (1969) *Main Currents in Contemporary German, British, and American Philosophy*, Dordrecht: Reidel (transmitted ideas of emigrants to post-war German philosophers).

Sutton, C. (1974) *The German Tradition in Philosophy*, London: Weidenfeld & Nicolson (argues for the existence of a distinctively German tradition).

HANS-JOHANN GLOCK

Pieck, Wilhelm

b. 3 January 1876, Guben; d. 7 September 1960, (East) Berlin

GDR functionary

A leading member of the **KPD** in the 1920s and 1930s, he spent the Nazi period in emigration, mostly in the Soviet Union. He returned to Germany with the Red Army on 1 July 1945 and was chair of the KPD until April 1946, then, after its fusion with the **SPD**, co-chairman with **Grotewohl** of the **SED** until April 1954. He was the first, and only, President of the GDR from its foundation in October 1949 until his death.

PETER BARKER

Piene, Otto

b. 18 April 1924, Laasphe (Westphalia)

Environmental artist

Founder of the **Zero Group** with Heinz **Mack**. Piene's earliest 'fire' and 'smoke' pictures were an exploration of light effects which he developed further in kinetic light sculptures and 'light ballets'. In the late 1960s Piene began 'sky art' projects, involving large open-air constructions which expressed a utopian search for harmony between man, nature and the cosmos. An example was his 700-metre 'Olympic Rainbow' at the 1972 Munich Olympics. In 1974 Piene became Director of the Centre for Advanced Visual Studies in Cambridge, Massachusetts, where he was made Professor Emeritus in 1992.

ALEX COOKE

Pietraß, Richard

b. 11 June 1946, Lichtenstein (Saxony)

Writer and editor

A member of the first generation of writers to grow up entirely in the GDR, Pietraß worked initially in industry, and then, after studying clinical psychology, began working in publishing. His first volumes

of lyric poetry appeared in the 1970s, establishing him as an acute observer, rather than an overt critic, of life in his country. His imaginative handling of language is reflected in his numerous translations, which include the poems of Seamus Heaney. Since the **Wende** he has been a member of the editorial board of the journal **Neue Deutsche Literatur**.

JOHN SANDFORD

Piontek, Heinz

b. 15 November 1925, Kreuzburg (Silesia; now Kluczbork, Poland)

Writer

Piontek first gained recognition with nature poems, which were partly rhyming, full of rustic pictures and melodic lyricism. His poetry has increasingly become more precise, laconic, sharply reflective and pointed, while retaining a rational-poetic style. He has also written short stories and novels and published essays and highly regarded anthologies. In addition, he has translated John Keats and has written several **Hörspiele** (radio plays). Thematically he is concerned with communication, with achieving the 'what is humanly possible in poetry'. In 1960 he received a grant for the **Villa Massimo** and he was awarded the Büchner Prize in 1976.

BETTINA BROCKERHOFF-MACDONALD

Piscator, Erwin

b. 17 December 1893, Ulm; d. 30 March 1966, Starnberg

Theatre director and producer

The most renowned director of Weimar Berlin, Piscator established Das Proletarische Theater in 1920. He was known for technological innovation (multiple stage levels, simultaneous rendering of scenes, integration of projections and film strips) and political engagement. Dismissed from the Volksbühne in 1927 for pro-communist agitation, he established the famous Piscator Bühne. Exiled in the USSR, Paris and the US, he returned to the

FRG in 1951. He directed highly acclaimed productions of 'documentary' dramas (of **Hochhuth**, **Kipphardt** and **Weiss**) at the **Freie Volksbühne** from 1963 to 1965.

Further reading

Piscator, E. (1963) *Das Politische Theater*, Reinbek bei Hamburg: Rowohlt (Piscator's major texts).

KAREN RUOFF KRAMER

Plenzdorf, Ulrich

b. 26 October 1934, Berlin

Writer

Plenzdorf's name will always be indissolubly linked with the GDR's literary 'thaw' of the early 1970s, because he had the good fortune to have a text on the central socio-political issue of the generation gap, written in a refreshingly unorthodox colloquial register, available for publication, as Erich **Honecker** announced the start of a new era of literature 'without taboos'. The cautious publication of *Die neuen Leiden des jungen W.* (The New Sorrows of Young W.) in the journal **Sinn und Form** in the spring of 1972 was followed by its spectacular public success in a dramatized version all across the GDR. This in turn provoked a vigorous debate about the need for a revitalization of GDR culture along the lines indicated by Plenzdorf's text.

The irony of this overnight triumph was that *Die neuen Leiden* was the reworking of a rejected film-script by a **DEFA** author who had few literary pretentions. Plenzdorf's primary interest lay in the cinema, yet his work for DEFA was strewn with difficulties. His first major script, *Karla* (directed by Herrmann Zschoche, 1965), recounting the frustrations experienced by a young teacher, fell victim to the blanket ban on new films imposed at the SED's **Eleventh Plenum**. Only in the wake of *Die neuen Leiden* was he permitted to reach the GDR's viewing public with his *Legende von Paul und Paula* (directed by Heiner Carow, 1973), the story of a love transcending the state's new class divide, which enjoyed the same huge success as his play.

The fame which this dual breakthrough brought Plenzdorf made him a marked man as soon as Honecker's liberalization receded. The film version of *Die neuen Leiden* (directed by Eberhard Itzenplitz, 1976) had to be made in the FRG, while the sequel to *Paul und Paula*, the *Legende vom Glück ohne Ende* (Legend of Neverending Happiness) (1979) finally appeared in book form after being blocked by DEFA. Although it never quite generated the same public enthusiasm as his works of the early 1970s had done, Plenzdorf's nostalgic portrayal of an organic socialist community in working-class Berlin stood in stark contrast to Honecker's brave new world of featureless housing estates and insincere conformism. He extended this line of attack in the adaptations of the prose work of other GDR authors for stage and/or screen which then became his main creative outlet, such as *Glück im Hinterhaus* (Happiness in a Rear Tenement) (1980) and the ecologically orientated *Insel der Schwäne* (Island of Swans) (1983), both directed by Zschoche.

After unification Plenzdorf relished the new opportunities afforded by his first direct access to television drama, taking over the popular **ARD** detective series *Liebling Kreuzberg* (Darling Kreuzberg) from Jurek **Becker** in 1992 and locating its episodes amidst the social tensions of contemporary Berlin.

See also: drama: GDR; prose fiction: GDR

Further reading

Plenzdorf, U. (1990), *Filme*, Frankfurt am Main: Suhrkamp (collection of his screenplays).

Thomaneck, J. (1988), *Die neuen Leiden des jungen W*, Glasgow: University of Glasgow (part of the series 'Introductory Guides to German Literature').

DENNIS TATE

Plessen, Elisabeth

b. 15 March 1944, Sierhagen (Schleswig-Holstein)

Writer

Brought up on the estate of her aristocratic family, Plessen's first novel *Mitteilung an den Adel* (Message to the Nobility, 1976) achieved notoriety for its revelations about the German nobility and began the trend of autobiographical writings about the deceased father, known as *Väterliteratur*. Rejecting her father's values, she seeks to create her own identity, whilst coming to terms with the loss of a powerful, authoritarian parent. Plessen co-edited with Michael Mann the memoirs of Thomas **Mann**'s wife Katja.

See also: *Frauenliteratur*; New Subjectivity

PETRA M. BAGLEY

Plessner, Helmuth

b. 4 September 1892, Wiesbaden; d. 12 June 1985, Göttingen

Philosopher and sociologist

Together with Max Scheler (1884–1928) Plessner was the founding father of philosophical anthropology, an empirically oriented philosophical current which sought to establish anthropology as the *prima philosophia*, a position the Aristotelian tradition had accredited to metaphysics. In 1926 Plessner became professor in Cologne. He emigrated to The Netherlands in 1933, where he then held a Professorship at Groningen University. His Groningen lectures became the basis for his highly controversial book on German culture and identity *Die verspätete Nation* (*The Beloved Nation*) (1959). From 1951 Plessner was Professor of Sociology in Göttingen.

INGOLFUR BLÜHDORN

Plievier, Theodor

b. 12 February 1892, Berlin; d. 12 March 1955, Avegno (Switzerland)

Writer

Pliever authored one of the best German novels about the WWII, *Stalingrad* (1948). Based on the eye-witness accounts of PoWs which Plievier acquired during his involuntary exile in the Soviet Union (1934–45), it accurately depicts the horrors of modern warfare and its effect on soldier and citizen. The novel became a bestseller in the UK and the US. In Germany it fuelled the debate about the responsibility of the German people for the war. It was followed by *Moskau* (1952) and *Berlin* (1954).

JOHN B. RUTLEDGE

Pluhar, Erika

b. 28 February 1939, Vienna

Actress and singer

Pluhar studied acting at the Max-Reinhardt-Seminar, and has been engaged at the **Burgtheater**, Vienna, since 1959. She specializes in vulnerable, romantic roles and songs with Austrian flavour. She has appeared in several films including *Liebe ist kein Argument* (Love is No Argument) (1984) and *Die Brüder* (The Brothers) (1976) and on television, in *Gemeinsam: Erika Pluhar und Fado* (In Common: E.P. and Fado) (1980). Since 1972 she has been active as a *chanson* singer, has made several recordings: *Pluhar singt Biermann* (Pluhar sings Biermann), *Narben* (Scars), and *Über Leben* (About Life). A book of her own song texts and poems, *Über Leben: Lieder und ihre Geschichten* (About Life: Songs and Their Stories) was published in 1982.

RICHARD J. RUNDELL

poetry: FRG

Whilst committed communist poets could serve the newly created German Democratic Republic and Austrian poets had a restored homeland after 1945 in which to write, the position of West German poets immediately following WWII was less clear. The maturer poets in the late 1940s and early 1950s had come of literary age during the Weimar period or, in many instances, in the days of the Empire. Before the Allied occupation in 1945 they had lived through twelve years of National Socialism, an ideology to which a few of the country's greatest poets such as Gottfried **Benn** had initially succumbed. This ideology had reduced poetry to exaltation and bombast and provided an impoverished diet on which the younger poetic talents emerging in 1945 had been educated. Significantly, exile had been primarily the lot of German prose writers whereas poets had remained within Germany during the Hitler period. Thus the inauspicious legacy for poetry in the newly created Federal Republic of Germany had been its poets' isolation from the world outside and the impoverishment of the German language.

It is therefore not surprising that many of the early volumes of poetry appearing in the provisional West German state displayed considerable technical and thematic uncertainty. Older poets clung to established forms, younger poets floundered or produced imitations of Rilke. Rudolf Hagelstange, Hans Egon **Holthusen** and Marie Luise **Kaschnitz** were amongst the more able poets capable of treating the theme of Germany's recent collapse, both in material and moral terms, yet none broke away immediately from essentially traditional poetic forms.

A strong vein of nature poetry, some of it metaphysical in its intent, flourished in the late 1940s and 1950s, particularly in the work of Wilhelm **Lehmann**, Elisabeth Langgässer, Oda Schaefer and Günter **Eich**. This was not a new venture but a continuation of a school of poetry that had existed before the war.

A key figure in the rejuvenation of modern German poetry was Karl **Krolow**, who was able to assimilate foreign influences, to demonstrate that the German language was still capable of great finesse, at a time many voices claimed that the language was creatively dead in the wake of Nazism, and to develop his own work beyond the thematic cul-de-sac to which nature lyric threatened to reduce German poetry.

Within a decade of the Federal Republic's foundation the '**Economic Miracle**' and Chancellor Adenauer's clear alignment of West Germany's politics with those of the western Allies had given the country its firm contours. This provided a social context in which, and against which, poets could respond. Hans Magnus **Enzensberger**'s *verteidigung der wölfe* (the defence of the wolves) of 1957 helped re-establish the tradition of the political poem, a form viewed with distaste by many German poets following the experience of National Socialism's politicization of all art. Enzensberger attacked the habits of the bourgeoisie, thus continuing a favourite theme of two of the most naturally talented German poets: Heinrich Heine and Bertolt **Brecht**. Resident in East Germany after the war, Brecht was virtually ostracized in the West despite his outstanding natural poetic gifts.

The political lyric was to be but one line of development in modern (West) German poetry; a second line was to be found in experimentation with language. Dadaism and surrealism had already been taken up by German poets around the time of WWI. Now in a prospering West Germany a group of poets began to experiment with the basic elements of language: sound and the visual appearance of the printed word as text. Much of this work, sometimes playful and sometimes anarchic in intent and offered under the banner of 'concrete poetry', challenged the very notion of poetry, and it was undoubtedly meant to discomfort or amuse the reader by turns. The best known proponents of this form of poetry were Helmut **Heißenbüttel**, Eugen **Gomringer** and the Austrian Ernst **Jandl**.

The political poetry of the 1960s, heightened by the hostile response of many West German writers and poets to American involvement in Vietnam, gave way in the 1970s to more private concerns. Neither overtly political poetry nor abstract montages could sustain indefinitely what market there was for poetry. With material needs satisfied and with the arrival of a younger generation of poets free from any involvement with Nazi Germany, the value of individual experience began to be cultivated in a movement loosely styled 'new subjectivity', one that was not necessarily apolitical. Two of its leading exponents, Rolf Dieter **Brink-**

mann and Nicolas **Born**, died young. Ironically it was East Germany that was to provide the momentum for much of West German poetry in the 1970s and 1980s as a stream of major poetic talent fled from East Germany, a state which had shown hostility to the very idea of the cultivation of the individual sphere and an intimate voice in poetry. Amongst the most striking gains for contemporary West German poetry was the arrival of Sarah **Kirsch**, Günter **Kunert** and Reiner **Kunze** from the German Democratic Republic.

More recent poetry has shown remarkably broad and often eclectic tastes: exotic travel, feminism and the problems of ecology (but a persistently and noticeably absent theme has been the concern of West German poets for the fate of their fellow Germans in the German Democratic Republic). Despite their diversities, many younger poets raised entirely within the Federal Republic, such as Ulla **Hahn**, Peter Maiwald and Hans-Ulrich Treichel, have not sought to depart radically from traditional verse structures, including rhyme.

Further reading

Breuer, D. (1988) *Deutsche Lyrik nach 1945*, Frankfurt am Main: Suhrkamp (collection of essays dealing with individual movements and poets in contemporary German poetry).

Knörrich, O. (1978) *Die deutsche Lyrik seit 1945*, Stuttgart: Alfred Körner Verlag (standard history of German poetry in the first quarter of a century following the end of WWII).

ANTHONY BUSHELL

poetry: GDR

The high regard in which GDR poetry was held in the West in the 1970s and 1980s suffered a sharp reversal on the unification of the country, when East German literature was dismissed by leading West German critics as practically worthless. Not only were the political views of GDR writers, who had previously enjoyed a 'political bonus' in the West as dissidents in a socialist state, now discredited: their writing was also seen as lacking genuine aesthetic quality. A more detached judge-ment suggests that GDR poetry included imaginative writing of lasting value, speaking of individuals and their needs, alongside aesthetically weaker verse, some of which may be remembered as a vehicle for open or allegorically cloaked political criticism.

In the absence of open public debate on social and political issues in the GDR media, poetry functioned, despite its limited readership, as a counter-discourse to official language. Poets took a prominent part in the flowering of GDR literature in the liberal phase in the early 1960s, and again in demanding intellectual freedom and voicing public concern with political, social, and ecological developments after Erich **Honecker** came to power in 1971. The expatriation of the dissident poet and songwriter Wolf **Biermann** (see also **Biermann Affair**) in 1976 marked a crucial turning-point in GDR culture. However, Bier-mann's stance of open opposition was the exception rather than the rule, most contemporaries seeking rather a *modus vivendi* with the state, which offered a living from commissions and generous print runs of their work by western standards.

The first phase of GDR poetry in the 1950s was characterized by eager participation in the propagation of a GDR socialist national consciousness and the transmission of political slogans in conventional verse forms, though there were notable exceptions (e.g. Bertolt **Brecht**, Peter **Huchel** and Johannes **Bobrowski**). Volker **Braun** was at the centre of a group of new talents who emerged in the early 1960s, asserting the right to subjectivity in an often hostile atmosphere, and exploring techniques of poetic modernism such as intertextuality. A third generation of poets who came on the scene in the final decade of the GDR's history, the **Prenzlauer Berg** writers, were characterized by inventive language manipulation and indifference towards socialist ideals. Of their number, the Dresden-born poet Durs Grünbein has gone on to gain spectacular critical acclaim in the 1990s.

See also: *Literaturstreit*

Further reading

Berendse, G.-J. (1990) *Die 'sächsische Dichterschule'*.

Lyrik in der DDR der sechziger und siebziger Jahre, Frankfurt am Main: Peter Lang (traces the breakthrough to intellectual and aesthetic modernism in the 1960s and 1970s).

Emmerich, W. (1996) *Kleine Literaturgeschichte der DDR*, Leipzig: Gustav Kiepenheuer Verlag (the post-unification edition of this comprehensive standard work gives a thoughtful reassessment of GDR poetry alongside prose and drama).

Geist, P. (1994) 'Die Schatten werfen ihre Ereignisse voraus: Nachsichtendes zur Lyrik aus der DDR', in J.H. Reid (ed.), *Reassessing the GDR. Papers from a Nottingham Conference*, Amsterdam and Atlanta, GA: Rodopi (a stimulating review of the achievements of GDR poetry).

Lermen, B. and Loewen, M. (1987) *Lyrik aus der DDR. Exemplarische Analysen*, Paderborn: Schöningh (presents ten poets with biographical information, and interpretations of a handful of poems by each).

AXEL GOODBODY

Politbüro

The Politbüro of the **Central Committee** (ZK) of the **SED** was in practice the highest decision-making body within the SED, and therefore in the GDR. Formally it was elected by the ZK, and a member of the Politbüro was required to report to each meeting of the ZK on its activities. The General (up to 1976 First) Secretary of the ZK always chaired the Politbüro, and each member was responsible for a particular, specialist area. From 1981 there were twenty-one full members and these were the most influential figures in the SED.

PETER BARKER

political correctness

Political correctness in language represents an attempt to achieve social and political aims by manipulating linguistic usage. It has usually been used to further political aims which could be broadly categorized as liberal. Its most common manifestation is the promulgation of vocabulary to replace terms which are seen as discriminatory against minorities or disadvantaged groups.

It is perhaps best known to a wider public through conservatives' attempts to discredit it. These attempts have often been successful, since avoiding common but discriminatory vocabulary frequently involves the substitution of longer, circumlocutory expressions, which can easily be ridiculed as pretentious.

Political correctness is broadly parallel in German and English, with attempts to combat through changing usage phenomena such as racism, sexism and discrimination against disabled people. The public is probably more aware of attempts to use language to change political reality in German than in English, since for forty years opposing attempts to achieve this were made in the Federal Republic and the GDR (see Good, 1989).

An area of contrast between German and English is found in the avoidance of sexist language. In English this involves largely the replacement of vocabulary, but in German the problems are more intractable because of the system of grammatical gender; at least on a small scale, the vocabulary of a language can be changed fairly rapidly, and by deliberate manipulation, but changes to the grammatical system usually happen slowly and independently of conscious intervention. The problems in German can be illustrated by many nouns denoting occupations, such as *Lehrer* ('teacher'). This is a masculine noun, which is used to refer to males, but was always also used when the gender of the person was unknown or irrelevant. Its plural form, also *Lehrer*, was used to refer to men, or to mixed groups. The use of *Lehrer* and other similar occupational terms has been attacked by feminists for its implication that the 'normal' person employed in the profession in question is a man. There is a feminine equivalent, *Lehrerin*, but this can be seen as a grammatically derived form implying a secondary or subordinate status for female teachers; and it is never used for mixed groups. (Feminine forms like *Lehrerin* were in sharp decline in the GDR, both men and women increasingly being referred to as *Lehrer*). There has even been an unsuccessful suggestion that the grammatical system could be altered, to combat discrimination, allowing the gender of nouns simply to change depending on the referent: hence

Lehrer could be masculine when referring to a man, feminine when referring to a woman, and neuter if the person's gender was unknown or irrelevant (see Pusch, 1984). 'Politically correct' writers and speakers have adopted the less drastic option of using *Lehrerin oder Lehrer* ('female or male teacher') in the singular where gender is unknown or irrelevant, and *Lehrerinnen und Lehrer* in the plural for mixed groups. This can unfortunately be ridiculed for its unwieldiness, although in writing shorthand forms such as *LehrerIn* (singular) and *LehrerInnen* (plural) have gained considerable currency.

See also: language

Further reading

Clyne, M.G. (1995) *The German Language in a Changing Europe*, Cambridge: Cambridge University Press.
Good, C. (1989) *Zeitungssprache im geteilten Deutschland*, Munich: Oldenbourg.
Pusch, L.F. (1984) *Das Deutsche als Männersprache*, Frankfurt-am-Main: Suhrkamp.

STEPHEN BARBOUR

political culture: FRG

'Political culture' links two apparently disparate realms: politics and culture. As a concept of analysis it was introduced by Almond and Verba in *The Civic Culture* (1963) and aims at describing how the institutional structures of a political system relate to patterns of political support and participation, a task as complex as 'nailing a pudding to a wall'. By the mid-1980s, *'politische Kultur'* had entered the German language as a metaphor for good political credentials, decent style and an adherence to democratic values.

In Germany, political culture research has concentrated specifically on the traces of authoritarian and Nazi traditions in post-war democracy. Almond and Verba showed that the political culture was not yet democratic in the 1950s: Germans were proud of their own national character and the economic performance of the country, while parliamentary government or party pluralism did not elicit much support. Studies commissioned by the Americans for their zone of occupation had revealed earlier that the majority of Germans were preoccupied with their own economic hardship and took no interest in the political reconstruction around them. When the Basic Law was agreed in 1949, most took no notice and two-thirds declared not to know whether their democratic constitution was a good thing or not.

Since then, the political culture has been transformed as Germans began to accept democracy, its processes and principles. In a replica study of the *Civic Culture* David Conradt showed in 1980 that Germans had developed 'affective support' for their democratic institutions and no longer made their support conditional on economic strength or on policy outcomes.

Post-war German political culture emerged over time in seven phases. During the first phase (1945–9) Germans complied with the installation of democracy without taking an active part in it. Turnout at elections was high because it was perceived as a citizen's duty towards the state, not as an opportunity to influence the composition of parliament and through it the course of politics. In 1950, one in three Germans would still have preferred a one-party government, about 40 percent would have preferred a government without parliament while over 90 percent were convinced that they had been better off before 1945 than afterwards. The second phase of German political culture (1949–63) is identical with the Adenauer era. In their political behaviour, Germans were 'democrats by the book' (Eldinger 1968), well-informed about the organizational structure of their political system, able to name their political leaders or recall key issues of the day. Turning out to vote still meant performing a duty rather than exercising a right. Party preferences were determined by social class, denomination and ideology. The party-system remained divided into hostile 'camps' with the CDU/CSU on one side and the SPD on the other. Economic stability was the key concern of the electorate and democracy essentially a *Schönwetterdemokratie*, a fair weather system, which would elicit support as long as economic growth was assured, and might falter at the first signs of crisis.

During the third phase of political culture

(1963–69) the two main political parties began to resemble one another in their policies and even formed a coalition between 1966 and 1969. Political orientations had also changed. The post-war generations who now reached voting age had grown up in a democracy and began to choose between political parties rather than remain affiliated to a given camp. While the 1950s had been dominated by CDU and CSU, the 1960s seemed to be dominated by CDU/CSU and SPD together without room for opposition. In protest against an alleged cartel of the *Volksparteien*, the right-extremist NPD entered seven *Land* parliaments while the **student movement** began to campaign at extra-parliamentary level for an improvement of the democratic quality of Germany's institutions and political processes. Democracy itself was judged as lacking in democracy.

The fourth phase of political culture (1969–74) is best characterized by **Brandt**'s dictum '*mehr Demokratie wagen*', the first SPD-led government's pledge to extend democratic participation. Electoral turnout, party support, party membership, interest in democracy and in taking an active part all reached an all-time high which was to last until the late 1970s. At the same time, Germany saw the rise of **neo-nazism** and of left-wing terrorism and a policy of exclusion against 'radicals' as potential destroyers of the democratic political system itself (see also **Berufsverbot**) From the outset, post-war democracy had derived a 'negative identity' from the division of Germany and its contrastive proximity to communism. Fear of communism within its own ranks (more so than fear of persistent nazi orientations) proved a powerful means to curtail opposition and enforce consensus. After **Ostpolitik** and détente anti-communism lost its edge among the post-war generations who found their expectations of more democracy unmet by the political realities of the day.

The fifth phase of German political culture (1974–82) saw the retreat of the SPD from democratic innovation to a focus on economic stability; it also saw the emergence of post-materialism as a social and political force among the educated, the young and the new middle class. In the past, material hardship had tended to dominate lives and constrain policy agendas. As material conditions improved, more and more individuals aspired to enhance the quality of their lives (not merely ensure material survival) and articulated policy preferences more freely. In Germany, these 'new politics' generated citizens' initiatives (see also **citizens' initiatives: FRG**), anti-nuclear, peace and environmental movements and the **Greens**. New politics also inspired a new debate about 'democracy from below' and the link between institutional structures and citizens. From an 'old politics' perspective, democracy is based on support by the citizens for a given political system. From a 'new politics' perspective, a political culture is democratic if the institutions reflect the views of the citizens and respond to them.

This assertiveness and diversity has characterized German political culture in its sixth phase (1982–90). Increasingly, voters judge the competence of a political party by its success or failure to address specific issues. At the eve of unification, the link between institutions and citizens had become more flexible but also more volatile, with party support and approval of the democratic quality of established processes likely to be withheld altogether. Non-voting, non-acceptance of party organizations and disdain for the practicalities (not the principle) of parliamentary democracy have gained ground notably among young Germans. Since unification, German political culture entered a seventh phase with a newly divided detachment from democracy: in the west, many find the democratic quality of life lacking and wish for a better democracy while many East Germans have yet to develop affective support for the democracy which came with unification and wish for a different system or no democracy at all.

Further reading

Almond, G. and Verba, S. (1963) *The Civic Culture*, Boston, MA: Little Brown.

Conradt, D. (1980) 'Changing German Political Culture', in G. Almond and S. Verba (eds), *The Civic Culture Revisited*, Boston, MA: Little Brown.

Edinger, L. (1968) *Germany*, Boston, MA: Little Brown.

Kaase, M. (1983) 'Sinn oder Unsinn des Konzepts 'Politische Kultur' für die vergleichende Politikforschung, oder auch: der Versuch, einen Pudding an die Wand zu nageln', in M. Kaase and

H.-D. Klingemann (eds), *Wahlen und politisches System. Analysen aus Anlaß der Bundestagswahl 1980*, Opladen: Westdeutscher Verlag.

Kolinsky, E. (1991) 'Socio-Economic Change and Political Culture in West Germany', in J. Gaffney and E. Kolinsky, *Political Culture in France and Germany*, London: Routledge.

EVA KOLINSKY

political culture: GDR

The term political culture entered the mainstream of comparative communist studies in the early 1970s. Lucien W. Pye, one of the pioneers of the concept, defined it as 'the set of attitudes, beliefs and sentiments which give order and meaning to a political process and which provide the underlying assumptions and rules that govern behavior in the political systems' (Pye, in Sills, 1968: 218). While some analysts have restricted the concept to subjective orientations, others have opted for a broader category encompassing not only what people think but also patterns of action. This latter approach was often employed in the study of communist systems as the lack of accessible survey data prompted some scholars to use forms of political behaviour to infer the attitudinal content of political culture.

As there was no unified political culture in the GDR and other communist states, and in order to capture its diversity, other categories were devised, such as 'official', 'élite', 'dominant' and 'sub-' political cultures. The GDR's 'official' culture, propagated by a myriad of state and party organizations over which the **SED** exercised tight control, constituted an ambitious experiment in political socialization aimed at the elimination or undermining of many pre-existing and traditional structures. The 'official' culture was based on a wide range of sources: the 'revolutionary' traditions of German communism, Marxist–Leninist notions of socialist democracy, the role of the SED as the leading force in society, the primacy of collective and societal beliefs over private and individual ones, the state direction of the economy and the elimination of exploitation based on social class and gender. Furthermore, the claim of the GDR to be an anti-fascist and socialist state was intrinsic to the SED élite's conception of the GDR's moral superiority over its West German capitalist rival.

The components of the 'official' culture were neither static nor free of ambiguity. This is exemplified by the SED's German policy. Whereas until 1970 to 1971 the SED leadership was officially committed to the restoration of a united German state and nation (although much of this was lip service, especially after 1961), the Honecker regime pursued the thesis of two separate German nations as part of its *Abgrenzung* policy. The FRG and the GDR were, so GDR ideologues claimed, developing as separate nations on the basis of their respective capitalist and socialist orders. This class theory of the nation was significantly modified in the mid-1970s to early 1980s when elements of 'traditional' German culture were incorporated into official doctrine. For instance, various aspects of Prussian history and of the work of such ambiguous figures as Frederick the Great, Luther and Bismarck were interpreted in a positive rather than, as hitherto, a primarily negative light.

Another feature of the 1970s was the emergence of an 'alternative' political sub-culture embedded in the small ecological, women's, gay, human rights and, above all, peace groups. Under the protective umbrella of the Protestant church, the latter itself a survival from the 'traditional' political culture, the groups sought to define alternative positions to the SED on issues of women's identity, environmental protection, military security and direct democracy. The groups finally emerged from their niches towards the end of the 1980s and played an active role in the demolition of SED rule in 1989. They were, however, unsuccessful in their aspiration to reconstruct the GDR on the basis of a reformed socialism.

The 'dominant' political culture, a term sometimes applied to 'mass' political cognitions, feelings and beliefs, was difficult to delineate not only because it was so heterogeneous but also because of the lack of substantial field research free of blatant ideological bias. Congruence between 'official' and 'mass' culture could not be inferred from overt forms of political behaviour such as voting and political rallies as much of this was ritualistic and, in a monocratic system, the pressure to conform intense. On the other hand, the emigration, between 1949 and 1961, of over two and a half million people from the GDR and a high rate in the later 1980s may be regarded as a reliable indicator of an appreciable deficit in the political legitimacy of the SED regime. Before the **Wende** in 1989 investigations into the political culture of the GDR had to rely heavily on interviews of émigrés, memoirs, literature, social scientific publications and so forth. Although since 1989 the voluminous declassified archival material and access to the East German élites and populace have made it possible to provide a more differentiated representation of the political culture of the GDR, it still remains an extremely difficult task to delineate attitudinal structures across different generations, time periods, confessions and political groupings. However, what does appear to be clear is that GDR political culture was deeply impregnated by an authoritarianism which had its roots in the traditional *Obrigkeitsstaat* of the Second Reich and the Third Reich as well as in the Leninist–Stalinist structures imposed on the GDR by the Soviet authorities, and that certain officially propagated values such as gender equality and public ownership enjoyed considerable popular support. It is also apparent, for example from the investigations undertaken since the 1970s by the Leipzig Institut für Jugendforschung, that young people's commitment to many of the basic values of the SED declined sharply in the final decade of SED rule.

Whilst the SED failed to produce an assembly line of socialist personality clones, forty years of intensive political socialization and the impact of different structures to those prevailing in the old FRG have nevertheless produced a pattern of political orientations and beliefs which, combined with the socio-economic and psychological problems associated with the unification process, have contributed to a mental divide between many east and west Germans which cannot be removed as quickly as the physical barrier of the Berlin Wall.

See also: citizens' movements: GDR; *Ossi/Wessi*

Further reading

Förster, P. and Roski, G. (1990) *DDR zwischen Wende und Wahl. Meinungsforscher analysieren den Umbruch*, Berlin: LinksDruck Verlag.

Minkenberg, M. (1993) 'The Wall after the Wall. On the Continuing Division of Germany and the Remaking of Political Culture', *Comparative Politics* 26, 1: 53–69.

Niemann, H. (1993) *Meinungsforschung in der DDR. Die geheimen Berichte des Instituts für Meinungsforschung an das Politbüro der SED*, Cologne: Bund-Verlag.

Sills, D. (ed.) (1968) *International Encyclopedia of the Social Sciences*, New York: Macmillan.

MIKE DENNIS

Polke, Sigmar

b. 13 February 1941, Oels, Poland

Painter

Polke's diverse work refuses tight categorizations. During the 1960s he took banal family snapshots or seemingly trivial mass-media images as a point of departure for his paintings. Through exposing the banal as banal, and by rupturing and undermining media rhetoric, he established a critical distance to and political consciousness of immediate social reality. Humour and irony functioned as means of subversion. Later he turned away from representational art. Experimenting with chemical reactions on the canvas he sought to undermine the claim to authentic artistic creation.

See also: documenta; painting

KERSTIN MEY

pollution

Anthropogenic emissions into the natural environment endangering plant and animal life as well as human health. Public concerns first surfaced towards the end of the nineteenth century with the formation of protest movements and conservationist organizations. Since the 1970s environmental pollution has been generally recognized as an important social and political issue. In the FRG increasingly serious pollution arising from growing affluence triggered off large-scale protests leading to the formation of the **Greens**. The country has since taken efforts to implement strict standards of pollution control and environmental protection.

See also: environmentalism; *Grüner Punkt*; *Heimat*; nature; recycling; *Waldsterben*

INGOLFUR BLÜHDORN

Poppe, Gerd

b. 25 March 1941, Rostock

Physicist and co-founder of the citizens' movement, *Initiative für Frieden und Menschenrechte* (IFM)

Involved in the GDR **peace movement** since 1968, Poppe became a conscientious objector in 1975. Between 1980 and 1989 he was forbidden to travel abroad, but maintained contact with east European oppositional movements. He co-founded the IFM in 1986, and contributed to several illegal samizdat publications, for instance *grenzfall*. Elected speaker of the IFM (1989) he represented it at the central **Round Table** and was later chairman of the *Volkskammer* parliamentary group, *Bündnis 90/Die Grünen*. A member of the Bundestag from 1990, he did not stand for re-election in 1998.

BEATRICE HARPER

Poppe, Ulrike

b. 26 January 1953, Rostock

Political activist

Poppe co-founded the first independent *Kindergarten* in East Berlin in 1980. She was a founding member of *Frauen für den Frieden* in 1982, and was held in custody in 1983 under suspicion of treason. She participated in peace and human rights groups, including the *Initiative für Frieden und Menschenrechte* and *Frieden konkret*, and the discussion group 'Absage an Praxis und Prinzip der **Abgrenzung**'. A founding member of *Demokratie Jetzt* in 1989,

Poppe represented it at the central **Round Table**. Poppe works as an educational administrator at the Evangelical Academy, Berlin-Brandenburg.

BEATRICE HARPER

Popper, Karl Raimund

b. 28 July 1902, Vienna; d. 17 September 1994, Croydon

Philosopher

An independently-minded philosopher of science, Popper saw the central problem of **philosophy** as that of 'the growth of knowledge'. He developed the 'critical rationalist' approach to scientific, social, psychological and political phenomena, according to which knowledge grows by the critical testing and elimination of proliferated theories.

The thriving intellectual environment of Vienna in the second decade of the century kindled Popper's interest in the problem of demarcating science from non-scientific activities. Although his early work was influenced by the Logical Positivists of the Vienna Circle, he vigorously resisted many of their central tenets, and acquired a reputation for being their 'official opposition'. His first published book, *The Logic of Scientific Discovery* (*Logik der Forschung, 1934*) (1934), advanced the 'falsification-ist' view that scientific theories are falsifiable: phenomena which would refute the theory, were they observed, can be specified in advance. Einstein's theory of relativity is a good example of a testable scientific theory, Popper argued, but Freudian psychoanalysis is unfalsifiable, and there-fore unscientific. In later works he explained the basis of this approach: science comprises a tradition of *critical* discussion, a tradition in which bold testable conjectures are put forward and then critically evaluated by reference to (among other things) experience. It can be viewed entirely in terms of creative guesses and (logically impeccable) deductive inferences, and scientific progress is revealed as a succession of theories which, although false, nevertheless approach ever nearer to the truth. Metaphysics, to which positivists are allergic, Popper construed as acceptable proto-scientific speculation.

Popper spent the years during WWII working on his social and political philosophy, presented in 1945 as *The Open Society and Its Enemies* and *The Poverty of Historicism*. Plato, Hegel and Marx were criticized for the totalitarian implications of their utopias, and for their 'historicist' view that the task of social scientists is to make prophecies. Marx's theory of society was shown to be falsifiable, but also falsified. (Marx's disciples, such as the advocates of **Critical Theory**, were later berated for turning their mentor's view into an unfalsifiable creed). Paralleling Friedrich Hayek's critique of collectivist social planning, Popper proposed that because social phenomena are inherently unpredictable, social scientists should help politicians engage in 'piecemeal social engineering', rather than holistic revolutionary transformations. Explanation in the social sciences, he suggested, should be in terms of how the agents view 'the logic of the situation'.

In response to the incipient relativism of 1960s philosophy of science, Popper construed Alfred Tarski's semantic theory of truth as a rehabilitation of the 'objectivist' correspondence theory. He also introduced his own commonsense metaphysics, comprising a pluralistic ontology of three 'worlds': physical phenomena, mental phenomena, and logico-linguistic phenomena. Because inhabitants of these different realms interact, none is causally closed, so determinism and materialism are myths.

Popper consistently pursued an objectivist approach to knowledge, in contrast to the 'subjectivist' approach of commonsense and traditional philosophy according to which knowledge has 'sources'. He later drew parallels between his own falsificationist theory of science and Darwin's theory of evolution by natural selection. Despite a thinning-out of the critical rationalist school, his work continues to be influential among certain German and Anglo-American philosophers.

Further reading

Miller, D. (ed.) (1985) *Popper Selections*, Princeton, NJ: Princeton University Press (excellent anthology of selections from Popper's work).

O'Hear, A. (1980) *Karl Popper*, London: Routledge & Kegan Paul (lively and detailed critical study of many aspects of Popper's philosophy).

Popper, K.R. (1945) *The Open Society and its Enemies*, 2 vols, London: Routledge & Kegan Paul (part of Popper's 'war effort' – his critique of the totalitarian social theories of Plato, Hegel and Marx).

—— (1959) *The Logic of Scientific Discovery*, London: Hutchinson (powerful presentation of the falsificationist view of science, only published in English long after the German original – *Logik der Forschung*, Vienna: Springer, 1934).

Schilpp, P.A. (ed.) (1974) *The Philosophy of Karl Popper*, LaSalle, IL: Open Court (includes Popper's autobiography, together with critical essays on his work, and Popper's replies).

JOHN PRESTON

popular culture

The development of popular culture in West Germany was marked by commercialization, escapism, and the embracing of American popular culture. The mass media of television, cinema and pop music form the main components of popular culture in Germany, together with 'event'-based leisure-time activities (sports, organized parties, etc.). The term *Erlebnisgesellschaft* (society of experiences) describes the recent emphasis German society places on these 'events'.

A classist social system that equalled education with culture reinforced a perceived gap between élite 'high' and mainstream 'low' culture. This gap still has not completely closed, but it has narrowed: since 1986, the number of Germans who regularly attend concerts, opera, and theatre performances has risen by 150 percent, while attendance at art exhibitions has quadrupled. Robert Wilson's sophisticated *Black Rider/Alice in Wonderland/Time Rockers* trilogy at the Hamburg Thalia Theater became a crossover success with traditional theatre audiences and young rock music fans. An open-air performance by opera singers Luciano Pavarotti, Placido Domingo and José Carreras in Munich attracted 67,000 spectators in 1996.

The cultural rebuilding of post-war Germany faced huge obstacles due to the rupture caused by the twelve-year National Socialist regime. After 1933, thousands of artists from all fields were forced into exile or killed. With the end of WWII, most of the cultural production of the Third Reich fell into deserved oblivion. Following denazification and re-education by the Allies, a number of artists continued their careers – some of them despite their association with Nazi Germany, others coming out of 'inner emigration'. Returning emigrants, such as author Thomas **Mann** and actor Peter Lorre, often were ignored or disdained for having gone into exile. Many Germans seemed reluctant to deal with the immediate past. A true regeneration was not achieved; when prominent supporters of the National Socialist regime gained important positions in the FRG after its founding in 1949, most of the public reacted apathetically. Economic and political stabilization did not lead to many creative innovations; consumers looked for distraction and entertainment.

Contributing to the escapist tendencies of popular culture in the 1950s and 1960s was the *Wirtschaftswunder* (**Economic Miracle**), which brought a general increase in the standard of living. A widespread nostalgia for a remote, idyllic past found its expression in commercial paintings, music, popular literature and film. *Heimatfilme* and *Volksmusik* served to reaffirm the (imagined) ties to the homeland and to a mythical way of life that emphasized honour, simplicity, beauty of the land, family life and romantic love. In the 1950s, however, many Germans were able to afford **vacations** in the Mediterranean for the first time. Italy and later Spain became attractive, romanticized destinations. Popular music reflected the desire for an idyllic, individualistic everyday life as well as the fascination with the newly accessible foreign cultures in German-language *Schlager* songs. **Food** and **fashion** were also influenced. Since the 1980s, Germans have increasingly chosen vacations outside of Europe, and they continue to have the highest leisure travel frequency in the world.

The development of forms of popular culture in East Germany depended on governmental rules as to content, design, and opportunities to appear in public. The gap between high and popular culture also existed in the GDR. Government initiatives such as the encouragement of workers in the late 1950s to participate in the production of literature and visual art were ideologically motivated. Youth

cultures could not grow and flourish the way they did in West Germany. Western influences were sometimes accepted, as in the 1964 Youth Law which allowed certain new music and dance styles, or during a period of cultural liberalization in the early 1970s. But in many ways, East Germany remained more culturally conservative because the citizens' access to innovative outside influences remained limited.

In 1946, publisher Ernst Rowohlt helped to democratize reading by making both international and German literature affordable: his *Rowohlt Rotations Romane* books were printed in large quantities on cheap paper and sold at a very low price. By the end of 1953, he had sold eight million copies of one hundred different titles. However, *Groschenromane*, cheap romance novels for women and adventure novels for men, became even more successful, especially the series about the FBI agent Jerry Cotton (since 1955) and the Perry Rhodan **science fiction** series (since 1961).

Decreases in working hours (by 1974, a forty-hour week was common) as well as increases in annual vacation days gave West Germans more free time. The standard of living rose steadily, and many families could afford to buy time-saving household appliances as well as entertainment appliances such as **television** and stereo sets. Watching television became by far the most popular leisure activity. Similar to developments in other countries, the development of popular culture in post-war Germany has been greatly influenced by television. Programming began in West Germany in 1954 and in East Germany in 1956. By the late 1970s, practically all West German households owned at least one television set. The FRG used transmitters strong enough to broadcast western programmes to most of the GDR. Many East Germans therefore were well-informed about aspects of daily life in West Germany, and they liked the same shows as their neighbours to the West.

Not surprisingly, many of the best-known representatives of German popular culture are television personalities. Stars like Rudi **Carrell**, Hans-Joachim Kulenkampff, Hans Rosenthal and Wim Thoelke drew large audiences (up to 80 percent of households with televisions) for the monthly ninety-minute live variety shows, many of them broadcast concurrently in Germany, Austria and Switzerland. Frank Elstner designed and initially hosted one of the most successful game shows on German television: debuting in 1981, *Wetten daß...?* continues to attract up to twenty million viewers and is now presented by the actor, entertainer and talk-show host Thomas Gottschalk. In the 1970s, Dieter Thomas Heck and Ilja Richter hosted popular playback music shows; Heck's featured the German *Schlager* charts, while Richter presented international stars.

A long tradition of high-quality crime thriller series exists with programmes like *Tatort* (in which actors Götz **George** and Manfred **Krug** made names for themselves), *Der Kommissar, Der Alte* and *Derrick*. *Polizeiruf 110* is an East German programme now in nationwide syndication. The popularity of dialect theatre indicates the continuing importance of the concept of **Heimat**; productions by the Bavarian *Komödienstadl* and the Hamburg-based **Ohnsorg-Theater** have regular slots on television. While dramatic series have long been common, sitcoms are still rare. Today's numerous **soap operas** had precursors in family drama series such as *Unsere Nachbarn heute abend* (1954–60) or *Familie Hesselbach* in the 1960s. The longest-running one, *Lindenstraße*, about a Munich neighbourhood, debuted in 1985. In the late 1980s, the new private television stations began to produce soaps, among them the popular *Gute Zeiten, schlechte Zeiten* (Good Times and Bad), which was initially derided for using an amateur cast.

As a consequence of unification, most of the programmes and performers from the former GDR were absorbed by West German television. In his weekly show *Der schwarze Kanal*, Karl Eduard von **Schnitzler** criticized West German television programmes for twenty-nine years. The programme, an ironic cult favourite for viewers in the FRG, was cancelled in 1989. The live television youth programme *1199* started just before the 1989 revolution. Controversial for its open political criticism and its western design, it set record viewer ratings, but was reduced to a harmless entertainment show in 1990. A similar fate befell radio DT64, a programme from the 1960s which occupied a niche for alternative programming but was cancelled in 1992. Two East German television stations still broadcast GDR movies and series; some popular shows such as *Ein Kessel Buntes* preserve a few sources of identity. On television as in other areas of culture, West German culture proved dominant while much of East German culture disappeared or is limited to the five new states.

Since the 1950s, West German critics and artists have complained that German culture is endangered by outside influences. Consumers have supposedly surrendered to Hollywood movies, American and British popular music, and American television shows. The presence of US popular culture in German everyday life is indeed impossible to overlook, but it tends to be incorporated into German culture rather than imitated. In film, American influence is due to the Allied decentralization policy after the end of WWII which hampered the restoration of a national film culture and facilitated imports of American movies to the western zones. Sport continues to play a major role. Some twenty-six million Germans were organized in member associations of the German Sports Federation in 1996. In the 1990s, young Germans discovered American basketball, football, and skateboarding not only as leisure activities but as influences on their fashion, music and even their speech. German adaptations of British and American musicals play in permanent venues (e.g. *Cats* in Hamburg, *Starlight Express* in Bochum and *Sunset Boulevard* in Wiesbaden). An initial period of imitation gave way to original productions, and the musical business now grosses about DM 400 million per year.

In West German popular music, Ted Herold and Peter Kraus were groomed to give German interpretations of American rock'n'roll and introduce an alternative to *Schlager*. The Berlin band Ton Steine Scherben initiated political rock music in the late 1960s and 1970s. It was followed by experimental and electronic rock music with bands like Can, Faust, Neu, Tangerine Dream, **Kraftwerk**, and later Einstürzende Neubauten. The British punk movement influenced young musicians in the late 1970s. Many wrote German lyrics (Abwärts, Die **Toten Hosen**, Nina **Hagen**): some infused pop with punk elements, a style that became known as *Neue Deutsche Welle* (represented by Nena, Ideal, Extrabreit and others) but quickly peaked and eventually became quite similar to *Schlager*.

The music cable channel Viva aided the rise in popularity of German music. Started in 1993 (Viva II debuted in 1996), Viva plays 40 percent local product, with an emphasis on dance and pop. German-language hip-hop is represented by bands like Die Fantastischen Vier. German techno was introduced in clubs in the late 1980s and has changed from a major subculture into mainstream. DJs like West Bam or Marusha, and Viva VJs like Heike Makatsch and Stefan Raab have replaced musicians as pop stars. The annual **Love Parade** started as an underground weekend rave in Berlin in the late 1980s and now attracts several hundred thousand visitors each July. *Schlager* is on the wane (the market share in 1995 was only 6.1 percent), but domestic dance pop and rock, as well as *Volksmusik*, have increased their shares. A number of rock musicians, singing in English and German, enjoy durable careers. Bands like **BAP** and the Scorpions, and singers like Udo **Lindenberg**, Marius Müller-Westernhagen, Herbert Gröne-meyer and Heinz Rudolf Kunze are household names.

East German bands often reflected the development of western rock music. Some, like **Karat**, **Silly** and **Puhdys**, were fairly popular in the West before unification; singer-songwriters (*Liederma-cher*) such as Bettina Wegner and Stefan Kraw-czyk have been unable to maintain their audiences. Among East German entertainers, the classically trained pop band Die Prinzen has enjoyed the biggest post-unification success.

In 1978, German film held 8 percent of the West German market; the share rose slightly, but significantly to 11 percent in 1996. Hit movies like *The Most Desired Man* (*Der bewegte Mann*, 1994) by Sönke **Wortmann** (based on a best-selling gay comic by Ralf König), *Keiner Liebt mich* (Nobody Loves Me) (1994) by Doris **Dörrie**, *Jailbirds* (*Männerpension*, 1996) by Detlev **Buck**, and the animated *Werner – Das muß kesseln* (Werner – It's Got to be Really Cool) (1996) attract mass audiences. The most successful German movies in the 1990s are a result of a new interest in comedy, sparked by imported American television sitcoms. The activities of comedians like Heinz Erhardt and Wolfgang Neuss in the 1950s and 1960s, or later **Loriot** and

Otto **Waalkes** ranged from political satire and ironic understatement to language humour. Since 1979, the satirical magazine *Titanic* has published new and established writers and cartoonists, including Robert Gernhardt, Bernd Eilert, F.K. Waechter, Chlodwig Poth, Hilke Raddatz and Max Goldt. Recent German comedy is frequently criticized for a perceived lack of sophistication but at the same time praised for an uninhibited nature not seen before, with performers like Helge Schneider and Wigald Boning walking the fine line between silliness and comic absurdity.

See also: Bitterfelder Weg; comics; film festivals; rock music; sport: FRG; sport: GDR; television; television drama

Further reading

Burns, R. (ed.) (1995) *German Cultural Studies*, Oxford and New York: Oxford University Press (comprehensive survey of modern German culture with separate analyses of East and West Germany).

Hermand, J. (1986) *Kultur im Wiederaufbau. Die Bundesrepublik Deutschland, 1945–1965*, Munich: Nymphenburger (part 1 of the history of post-war culture).

—— (1988) *Die Kultur der Bundesrepublik Deutschland, 1965–1985*, Munich: Nymphenburger (contains numerous invaluable facts and committed analyses).

SABINE SCHMIDT

pornography

Pornography, the visual representation of sexually explicit material, is a regulated form of free speech in Germany. This means that although there are forms of pornography legally available for mass consumption, there are certain types of pornography that are illegal and punishable by high fines and imprisonment. Included within this group are child pornography and hard-core sexual violence, which along with neo-nazi material are outlawed in Germany.

Germany has some of Europe's most stringent youth morals protection laws in the audiovisual media, and any stores carrying pornography and indexed for excessive violence are off limits to minors. With the proliferation of electronic media such as the World Wide Web, the regulation of pornography has proven to be increasingly difficult. Germany has been at the forefront of creating laws to punish those who are considered to be aiding the distribution of illegal forms of pornography over the Internet. These laws have generated many public debates since they are regarded by some as baseless, unenforceable forms of censorship (see also **computers**; **censorship: FRG**).

Even as there are relatively strict laws governing the type of pornography that should be made available, Germany is known for its liberal attitude concerning the depiction of nudity in various forms of mass media. Popular magazine covers often depict nude women or men in images that other countries, such as the United States, might consider inappropriate and pornographic. Likewise, German television channels regularly schedule softcore pornography that is shown during late-night viewing hours.

LISA YUN LEE

postmodernism

Postmodernism is a term used to describe a variety of pluralistic architectural, artistic, literary, musical and philosophical endeavours since the late 1960s. A central feature of postmodernism is its attention to multiple styles, perspectives and traditions. Postmodern architecture, art, literature, and philosophy utilize eclecticism, collage, parody and pastiche. Postmodernism sometimes is equated with deconstruction and poststructuralism.

The influence of postmodernism is most evident in contemporary German **architecture**. Postmodern architecture emphasizes a combination of styles and traditions. The works of Frank Gehry, the Vitra Design Museum in Weil am Rhein, Bernard Tschumi, Zentrum für Kunst und Medientechnologie in Karlsruhe, and **Coop Himmelblau**, design for the Ronacher Theatre in Vienna, demonstrate a blending of architectural styles and a reconceptualizing of traditional notions of architectural space. Other examples of postmodern architecture can be found in Berlin, Düsseldorf, Frankfurt am Main and Hamburg.

In addition to its impact on architecture, postmodernism's combination of styles, perspectives and traditions has influenced the visual arts in German culture. Postmodern **painting** and **sculpture**, with their tendency towards contrast and opposition, have played an important role in shaping today's German art scene.

In the performing arts, avant-garde theatre emphasizes the opposition between high and mass culture. Avant-garde theatre, like the visual arts, blends texts of popular culture from film and television with works from traditional modern drama. Musical postmodernism in contemporary German culture ranges from the multicultural and multi-ethnic sound of popular music to the activist and iconoclastic message of hard core punk.

In German literary culture, postmodern fiction represents a genre that redefines narrative structure, time and identity. Postmodern fiction often departs from traditional notions of linearity. The German novelist Christoph **Ransmayr** is noted for his imaginative use of time. Other contemporary German writers, such as Botho **Strauß** and Patrick **Süskind**, also depart from traditional notions of time and character development. Issues of gender, race and sexual identity are included as themes in postmodern fiction. These literary themes are often carried over into film by directors such as Monika **Treut** who explores social issues. The multiple styles of postmodern fiction and postmodern film emphasize flashbacks, out-of-sequence events and explorations of the human situation through various themes of identity and social conflicts.

Postmodernism plays an influential role in German culture studies. A number of German social theorists and philosophers have had an impact on the development of postmodernism. Ludwig **Wittgenstein**'s theory of language is regarded as a prelude to postmodernism. Theodor **Adorno**, a central figure in the **Frankfurt School**, anticipated the non-foundational philosophy of French postmodernism with his understanding of negative dialectics. Contemporary postmodern continental philosophy rests upon the German philosophical tradition since Immanuel

Kant. Postmodernism, philosophy and culture studies come together in a wide variety of academic disciplines and social sites. The meaning of postmodernism in Germany is continually shaped by cultural life.

See also: Critical Theory; cultural studies; multiculturalism

Further reading

Huyssen, A. (1995) *Twilight Memories: Marking Time in a Culture of Amnesia*, London: Routledge.

VICTOR E. TAYLOR

Potsdam Agreement

Following the Potsdam Conference (17 July to 2 August 1945) the three great powers issued a joint communiqué. France was not present. The USSR (Stalin), the US (Roosevelt then Truman) and Britain (Churchill then Attlee) agreed that Germany should never again pose a threat to world peace, and should be demilitarized, denazified, democratized and decentralized. A shrunken Germany should provisionally be jointly administered by the occupying powers. Reparations should be taken in kind from each zone, with equipment from the more industrialized western zones being exchanged for foodstuffs and raw materials from the Soviet zone.

See also: occupation; Oder-Neisse line

MARY FULBROOK

Praunheim, Rosa von

b. 25 November 1942, Riga (Latvia)

Filmmaker

Praunheim worked as assistant to Gregory Markopoulos and collaborated with Werner **Schroeter** before making raucous genre parodies and the feature *Not the Homosexual is Perverse, But the Situation in Which He Finds Himself* (*Nicht der Homosexuelle ist pervers sondern die Situation, in der er lebt*, 1971). A controversial and hotly-debated film, it flaunts

negative gay stereotypes in order to subvert them. Often deliberately amateurish, camp and colourfully transgressive, his subsequent feature films and documentaries (including the hard-hitting 'AIDS-Trilogy', 1989–90) are political and highly entertaining.

See also: gay and lesbian culture in Germany; New German Cinema

HELEN HUGHES

Prenzlauer Berg

Prenzlauer Berg, at the time arguably the most rundown inner-city area of East Berlin, gave its name to a new kind of literature that developed in the GDR in the 1980s. That the writers in question gathered in this district reflected their apparently total alienation, both in political and aesthetic terms, from official literary life.

Whereas many of the generation of GDR writers who were born before the creation of that state and whose childhood had partly been spent under Nazism, for example Volker **Braun** and Christa **Wolf**, maintained hopes of a reformed but still socialist GDR, the younger Prenzlauer Berg authors, whose whole life had been spent in the GDR, no longer harboured any such aspirations. Moreover, they eschewed the largely realist aesthetic of their elders to write in a fiercely modernistic style which was influenced by their reception of French literary theory. Other forebears include the 'concrete poetry' of Helmut **Heißenbüttel** and Ernst **Jandl**. Preferred forms were poetry and short prose texts which frequently ignore grammatical conventions such as capitalization of nouns.

Publication possibilities for such works were naturally almost non-existent within the official cultural policy of the GDR. Accordingly, there developed a number of self-produced small-circulation magazines, of which the best-known is *adrianefabrik*, which managed to print up to a hundred copies. At the same time Prenzlauer Berg was increasingly hailed in the FRG as a new kind of GDR literature in which politics no longer dominated or stifled artistic creativity.

At no time was it fully accurate to speak of a

homogeneous Prenzlauer Berg literature. Since unification, however, the conditions that created the phenomenon have changed totally. Moreover, perceptions have been affected by the discovery that two of its leading protagonists, Sascha **Anderson** and Rainer **Schedlinski**, had supplied information on fellow-writers to the **Stasi**, which was keen to keep tabs on any kind of unofficial activity. In 1991 Wolf **Biermann** denounced Anderson as 'Sascha Arschloch' ('Arsehole') and dismissed his kind of a-political writing as aesthetic game-playing that the Stasi could easily tolerate. It has even been claimed that the whole phenomenon of Prenzlauer Berg was a Stasi creation. Although such attacks exaggerate Stasi influence and ignore that many associated writers were persecuted, it remains fair to say that the reputation of Prenzlauer Berg, as a synonym for GDR literary dissidence, has been tarnished.

See also: cultural policy: GDR

Further reading

Arnold, H.L. (ed.) (1990) *Die andere Sprache. Neue DDR-Literatur der 80er Jahre*, Munich: edition text + kritik (contains many texts associated with Prenzlauer Berg as well as explanatory essays).

Böthig, P. and Michael K. (eds) (1993) *MachtSpiele. Literatur und Staatssicherheit im Fokus Prenzlauer Berg*, Leipzig: Reclam (collection of essays on the Stasi and literature, many of which deal with Prenzlauer Berg).

Leeder, K.J. (1991) '"Poesie ist eine Gegensprache": Young GDR Poets in Search of a Political Identity', in A. Williams, S. Parkes and R. Smith (eds), *German Literature at a Time of Change 1989–1990*, Bern: Peter Lang (contains sensitive interpretations of works by many poets associated with Prenzlauer Berg).

STUART PARKES

Presse, Die

Die Presse is a highly respected Viennese daily paper, originally founded as a liberal paper in 1848 to reflect the new-found freedom of the press. Between 1938 and 1945 it was published under Nazi control. Relaunched in 1945 by Fritz Molden, it has been published weekly since January 1946 and daily since October 1948. In 1991 it was taken over by the publisher of the **Kleine Zeitung**, Styria Verlag, from the long-time owner Bundeswirtschaftskammer, the Federal Economic Chamber.

Die Presse (with a daily print run of around 125,000 copies in 1998) is one of Austria's leading liberal newspapers catering for the educated independently minded establishment.

GEORG HELLMAYR

Prey, Hermann

b. 11 July 1929, Berlin

Singer

After singing as a boy with the Berlin Mozart Choir, Prey moved on to the Hochschule für Musik to study singing. His first success came with winning a competition organized by the Hessischer Rundfunk in 1951. Thereafter came major contracts with the opera houses in Wiesbaden (1952), Hamburg (1953), Vienna (1957) and Bavaria (1959), Prey also appearing in Salzburg in that year. In the 1960s came significant debut performances in New York and Bayreuth, with his debut in Covent Garden in 1973. Although slightly overshadowed by **Fischer-Dieskau**, Prey's reputation in Mozart operas was formidable, recording the title role of *Figaro* for Karl Böhm (though more often seen on stage as the Count).

DEREK McCULLOCH

profil

The weekly Austrian news magazine *profil*, published in Vienna, was founded in 1970 by Oscar Bronner, and sold to the **Kurier** Group in 1973. It specializes in serious investigative journalism. Several political scandals were uncovered by its staff, leading to shake-ups in Austrian politics and the church. Its style is entertaining and critical, at times leaning to the left, even though it is published by the conservative *Kurier* Group. With a print run of about 90,000 a week (1998) it is regarded as the most popular and the most serious news magazine in Austria.

GEORG HELLMAYR

propaganda

As an instrument of government, propaganda has played a prominent role in twentieth-century Germany, both the Third Reich and the GDR having created complex propaganda machines that sought to shape the minds of their own citizens as well as foreign opinion. In the open society of the FRG the preconditions for propaganda have been lacking: inasmuch as a West German propaganda effort *has* existed, it was a feature above all of the early Cold War years, and typically directed at the GDR.

The word 'propaganda' is notoriously difficult to define, not least because of its widespread use as a loose term of abuse. All concerted attempts at influencing opinion, such as political campaigns, advertisements or the manifold activities of 'public relations' firms, have aspects of propaganda about them, but those engaging in such activities do not normally use the term of themselves because of its negative connotations. Propaganda in the narrower sense of state manipulation of opinion requires a closed society in which the propagandist's message is the only one available. Even then, its effectiveness is only partial: evidence suggests that it has much more success in reinforcing existing opinions than in creating new ones.

In the GDR, the term 'propaganda' was used negatively of any perceived western attempts at 'confusing' opinion, but it was also used positively of officially sanctioned activities in the GDR itself aimed at instilling and strengthening Marxist-Leninist attitudes among the population. As in all communist countries, the notion of 'propaganda' went hand-in-hand with that of 'agitation'. The former, in accordance with a distinction deriving from Lenin, was seen as aiming itself primarily at the converted, seeking to refine and develop the convictions they already held, while 'agitation' focused more on concrete issues and sought to inspire the masses to action.

In practice, the distinction meant little, and *Agitation und Propaganda* was an omnipresent feature of life in the GDR, not least in cultural policy and the **mass media** (see also **cultural policy: GDR**). Overall responsibility for the formulation of propaganda lay with the SED's **Politbüro**, while the Central Committee had specifically designated departments for agitation and propaganda. A complex system of political education courses of varying lengths and sophistication kept party members abreast not only with the basics of Marxist-Leninism but also with received views on a whole panoply of current issues.

Despite its sealed borders, the GDR was not the hermetically closed system that propaganda requires if it is to flourish. The ready availability of West German radio and television over much of the country gave the population access to alternative sources of information and opinion, thereby constantly providing foils to the determined orthodoxy that characterized their own country's propaganda efforts.

JOHN SANDFORD

prose fiction: FRG

It is often said that the post-war West German novel began in 1959, the year of the appearance of Heinrich **Böll**'s *Billiards at Half-Past Nine* (*Billard um halb zehn*), Günter **Grass**'s *The Tin Drum* (*Die Blechtrommel*) and Uwe **Johnson**'s *Speculations About Jakob* (*Mutmaßungen über Jakob*). All three of these novels are marked by modernist narrative techniques; Böll and Grass share the concern, largely missing up to that point, to place the Nazi past within a greater historical context, while Johnson, recently arrived from the GDR, had written the first important novel on the division of Germany. The year 1960 also saw the emergence of Martin **Walser** as a major novelist with a series of social satires focused on the anti-hero Anselm Kristlein; the title of the first of these, *Halbzeit* (Half Time), was regarded as programmatic. With these works, it was felt, the German novel had shaken off a certain provinciality and was rejoining the European mainstream as well as an older German tradition of novel-writing. Grass, for example, was parodying the German *Entwicklungsroman*.

This is, of course, unfair to the literary production of the preceding decade and a half. It is true that the astonishingly numerous post-war examples of utopian or dystopian fiction, such as *City Beyond the River* (*Die Stadt hinter dem Strom*, 1949) by Hermann **Kasack** and *We are Utopia* (*Wir sind Utopia*, 1943) by Stefan **Andres** are now largely forgotten. The insecurity prompted by the experience of bombing raids, refugees, displaced persons and vast troop movements made **existentialism** popular and this was reflected in a tendency, not least in the war novels of the time such as Böll's *And Where Were You, Adam?* (*Wo warst du, Adam?*, 1951), Gerd **Gaiser**'s *The Last Squadron* (*Die sterbende Jagd*) and Hans Werner **Richter**'s *They Fell from God's Hand* (*Sie fielen aus Gottes Hand*, 1974), to focus on the tragic helplessness of the individual rather than to investigate causes and social structures. A similar existentialist standpoint is to be found in Alfred **Andersch**'s resistance novel *Flight to Afar* (*Sansibar oder der letzte Grund*, 1957). The cultural policies of the National Socialists had excluded most of the experimental techniques of the European and American avant-garde, illustrated in the novels of James Joyce, which now were enthusiastically embraced by writers such as Arno **Schmidt**, but can be found, for example, in Wolfgang **Koeppen**'s *Tauben im Gras* (Pigeons in the Grass) (1951). Kafka, too, was a crucial influence in these years in the fiction of Hans Erich **Nossack** and others. Partly under the influence of Ernest Hemingway, the short story, a genre relatively new to German fiction, found powerful exponents in Wolfgang **Borchert**, Böll and Wolfdietrich **Schnurre**. Koeppen and Böll are today, however, seen as having made the most important contributions of these years to the salvaging of respectability from the ruins left by the Third Reich, both through their sophisticated employment of narrative techniques and through their critique of a society which was suppressing all memory of the past.

Nevertheless, *The Tin Drum* (1959) was the first post-war German novel to make an international impact, and it was followed by further successes by Grass and by Böll; the latter went on to become the FRG's only recipient of the Nobel Prize for literature with his novel *Group Portrait With Lady* (*Gruppenbild mit Dame*) (1972). The 1960s, in fiction as in politics, were the final years of the hegemony of the **CDU**, culminating in the **student movement** and **APO**; they were a decade of debate and controversy. Texts, rather than novels or stories, were propagated by writers such as Franz Mon and Helmut **Heißenbüttel**, who were sceptical about the continued viability of fiction in the technological age, as was Wolfgang **Hildesheimer**, whose novels constantly play with the relation between fiction and reality. By contrast, an important new departure for the West German literary scene was the founding of the **Gruppe 61** as a forum for the publication of literature which centred on working-class life; its foremost member, Max von der **Grün**, was to write a number of novels which were close enough to the reality of the shop floor to lead to court cases. A more concrete depiction of social reality is likewise to be found in the literary beginnings of Alexander **Kluge** and Dieter **Wellershoff**, both of whom were developing conceptions of literary realism distinct from their predecessors. This was related to a more overt political stance among writers, culminating in the declaration in the influential journal *Kursbuch* in 1968 that fiction 'was dead' (see also **'Death of Literature'**) and that writers should devote themselves to documentation of the kind exemplified in the writings of Günter **Wallraff**. Hans Magnus **Enzensberger**'s *Der kurze Sommer der Anarchie* (The Short Summer of Anarchy) (1972) on a Spanish Civil War leader, and Manfred **Franke**'s *Mordverläufe* (The Course of Murder) (1973), tracing the events of the pogrom of 9 November 1938 in a small German town, are among the more interesting products of this programme.

A counter-movement, however, **New Subjectivity**, in which social reality was mediated through the individual, soon set in. Biographical novels, often on literary figures of the past, became fashionable, and were frequently linked to a preoccupation with the phenomenon of madness (e.g. Peter **Härtling**'s *Hölderlin* of 1976 and Heinar **Kipphardt**'s *Dorothea Merz* of 1976). Partly under the influence of the ecology movement, the concept of *Heimat*, long discredited by its association with National Socialism, was rehabilitated, scrutinized and celebrated in novels such as Siegfried **Lenz**'s *Local History Museum* (*Heimatmuseum*, 1978) and Martin Walser's *The Inner Man* (*Seelenarbeit*, 1979).

An important impetus here was the emergence of a women's literature, much of which was semi-autobiographical or confessional in nature. Most notable among these novels were Karin **Struck**'s *Klassenliebe* (Class Love) (1973), a complex, if rambling meditation on becoming both a writer and a mother, and Verena **Stefan**'s *Shedding* (*Häutungen*, 1975), a frank description of the narrator's discovery of her own sexuality. Christa **Reinig**'s *Entmannung* (Emasculation) (1976), by contrast, employs irony, parable and montage in its witty deconstruction of male–female relationships and the myths (ranging from Clytemnestra to Faust) which support them. Brigitte **Kronauer**, Anne **Duden** and the Romanian-German Herta **Müller** are among the many contemporary women writers of fiction who have developed a distinctive tone.

German fiction has traditionally been used as a forum for the discussion of issues of the day. Thus the upheavals of the later 1960s and after became the subject matter for numerous novels of the time. Peter **Schneider**'s *Lenz* (1973) is the prototypical text of New Subjectivity, as its focalizer-protagonist, the student Lenz, becomes disillusioned with the arid discussions of his Marxist friends in Berlin and learns that the individual with his private needs and neuroses can still have a part to play in societal change. Uwe **Timm**'s *Heißer Sommer* (Hot Summer) (1974) is a more extended account of the phases of the student movement, but likewise departs from pure documentation in the direction of individual focalization. The aftermath of the protest movement – **Berufsverbot** and urban **terrorism** – inspired novels by Schneider, Peter **Chotjewitz**, Böll and F.C. **Delius** among others. All of these have in common the accusation that the repressive measures taken by the state are the exact counterpart to the terrorism of the Red Army Faction. In the 1980s, the fear of a Third World War and nuclear annihilation gave rise to a number of novels, such as Grass' *The She-Rat* (*Die Rättin*, 1986), which anticipated the apocalypse. Most recently, unification and its concomitant problems have been the topic of novels by Walser, Delius and Grass.

The presentation of the Third Reich took on fresh dimensions from the late 1960s onwards. The earlier concentration on the existential helplessness of the individual gave way to a broader picture, in which documentation and subjectivity underwent a fruitful symbiosis. In *The German Lesson* (*Deutschstunde*, 1968) Siegfried Lenz employs the child's perspective of Grass's *The Tin Drum* without the grotesque, demonic features of that novel; he also introduces a link to the present day, which is a further important characteristic of this literature, which does not merely show what happened but suggests how this relates to today's readership. Thus Böll's *Group Portrait With Lady* (*Gruppenbild mit Dame*, 1971) is the account of a present-day investigation into resistance and complicity in Nazi Germany; the current social status of the various characters is a comment on contemporary society. Rolf **Hochhuth**'s *A German Love Story* (*Eine Liebe in Deutschland*, 1978) documents the harrowing fate of an affair between a Polish PoW and the farmer's wife for whom he works. The first, and probably best, volume of Walter **Kempowski**'s six-volume family chronicle, *Tadellöser und Wolff* (1971), is a montage of fragments of everyday life in the Third Reich; here, by contrast to Hochhuth's novel, the horror is understated, present in the odd phrase which reminds the reader of the real nature of Nazi society. One fashionable trend consisted of the so-called 'father novels'; reflecting the recognition of the generation of the student movement that their elders had a past yet to be uncovered. Such texts as Bernward **Vesper**'s *Die Reise* (The Journey) (1977) and Ruth **Rehmann**'s *Der Mann auf der Kanzel* (The Man in the Pulpit) (1979) find the narrators in search of the past of their respective fathers.

The Nazi past plays a central role in what are arguably the two most important German novels since *The Tin Drum*, Uwe Johnson's *Anniversaries* (*Jahrestage*, 1983) and Peter **Weiss**'s *Die Ästhetik des Widerstands* (The Aesthetics of Resistance) (1975–81). Both are extremely long (four volumes the former, three the latter). *Anniversaries* takes as its starting point the year 1968, with its political demonstrations against the Vietnam War at the one end and the suppression of democratic socialism in Czechoslovakia at the other. These events are set within a historical montage, partly documentary, including excerpts from the *New York Times*, partly fictitious (the biography of the chief protagonist). Weiss focuses on resistance to fascism, initially in Spain, later in the closing years of Nazi rule in Germany itself. His novel is partly a socialist *Entwicklungsroman*, partly a historical novel, partly a series of interpretations of works of art from a socialist point of view, one of the senses of the novel's title.

At the opposite end of the political spectrum is the novel of the New Right, whose chief proponent is Botho **Strauß**. Novels such as *Devotion* (*Die Widmung*, 1976) and *Der junge Mann* (The Young Man) link an anti-enlightenment critique of late twentieth-century civilization with postmodernist narrative structures, fragmentation, the absence of a reconstructible story-line, and multiple focalization. Strauß, more obviously in his plays for the theatre, is preoccupied with **myth**, and the reinterpretation of myths or creation of new ones has been a prominent feature of the recent German novel, as in Michael **Ende**'s cult children's novel *The Neverending Story* (*Die unendliche Geschichte*, 1979) or Helmut Krausser's *Melodien* (Melodies).

Possibly the most interesting and potentially fruitful development in the recent German novel has been the emergence of a literature from the substantial Turkish minority, in which not only the experiences of this group are articulated but forms and images from the 'other' culture intermingle with the German. Interestingly, too, many of the authors are women, the best-known of whom is Emine **Özdamar**, whose *Das Leben ist eine Karawanserei* (Life is a Caravanserai) (1992) was a resounding success (see also **migrant literature**).

Further reading

Bance, A. (1980), *The German Novel 1945–1960*, Stuttgart: Heinz (chapters on the post-war novel in relation to the historical context and individual interpretations of novels by Böll, Andersch and Gaiser).

Bullivant, K. (ed.) (1987) *The Modern German Novel*, Leamington, Hamburg and New York: Berg (essays on individual authors including Andersch, Böll, Grass, Johnson, Koeppen, Lenz, Schneider, Strauß and Walser).

—— (1994) *The Future of German Literature*, Oxford: Berg (informative account mainly of the development of the German novel since the war in the light of unification).

Ryan, J. (1983), *The Uncompleted Past. Postwar German Novels and the Third Reich*, Detroit, MI: Wayne State University Press (chapters on *The Tin Drum, Flight to Afar, Billiards at Half-Past Nine, Cat and Mouse, The German Lesson* and on documentary texts).

Weedon, C. (ed.) (1997) *Post-War Women's Writing in German. Feminist Critical Approaches*, Providence, RI and Oxford: Berghahn (general historical surveys and essays on Duden, Rehmann and Özdamar).

J.H. REID

prose fiction: GDR

Any post-*Wende* reassessment of the development of prose fiction in the GDR needs to recognize that there was always a basic conflict between the objectives of an ideologically determined cultural policy (articulated in the dogmatic terms of **socialist realism**) and the determination of some, if not all, of the authors committed to the state to write in a creatively authentic way about their experiences (see also **cultural policy: GDR**). Even though the emphasis placed by the **SED**'s cultural theorists on the production of conventional novels as the most effective means of reaching a wide audience was misguided – their ignorance of the greater potential of new mass media like television is difficult to grasp from today's perspective – it ensured that this underlying conflict was regularly ignited by works of fiction (and autobiography) which failed to conform to their ideological expectations. The full extent of the struggle waged by independently-minded prose writers against party orthodoxy has only become clear since the collapse of state socialism, and a history of GDR fiction which takes this properly into account still has to be written. When it is, it will show that even the more 'timeless' prose works produced by authors living in the GDR – Christa **Wolf**'s *The Quest for Christa T.* (*Nachdenken über Christa T.*, 1969) is generally regarded as being the first of them – are still recognizably 'East German' in the sense that they were originally intended for a GDR readership, aiming to extend the frontiers of socialist realism rather than to reject it out of hand. Conversely, a new literary history will have to acknowledge the significant role still being played by ex-GDR prose writers in the culture of unified Germany and carefully weigh up the elements of continuity and change in their creative evolution since 1989 which have made this possible.

The Ulbricht era (1945–71)

The years of the Cold War, which reached its grim climax with the building of the **Berlin Wall** in August 1961, offered little scope for an effective challenge to the dogma of socialist realism, yet the outlines of an alternative fictional aesthetic are clearly detectible throughout the early post-war period. One of the first (and most popular) novels to be published in the Soviet occupation zone was Anna **Seghers**'s *The Seventh Cross* (*Das siebte Kreuz*, 1942), which makes significant use of the allegedly 'decadent' modernist technique of montage in creating an atmosphere of suspense as its protagonist makes his escape from Nazi persecution. Other western exiles, such as Stephan **Hermlin**, showed a similar disregard for socialist realism in the stories he wrote describing his wartime experience in occupied France, published in 1949 as part of his collection *Die Zeit der Gemeinsamkeit* (The Time of Solidarity), which powerfully convey heightened states of anguish and alienation.

Even after the hardline imposition of the policy which decreed that the only valid fictional task for the 1950s was the production of '*Aufbauromane*' (construction novels) celebrating the pioneering economic achievements of the new GDR, there were windows of opportunity. The mid-1950s cultural 'Thaw' gave a new generation of prose-writers, notably Franz **Fühmann**, a chance to switch their attentions to a subject they really knew something about, the experience of war, with the narrative emphasis shifting towards the psychological investigation of their susceptibility to Nazi propaganda, in a liberating way which eventually also obliged them to reject the propagandist role they had taken on in their adopted homeland. Yet the novel which could have encouraged a real qualitative improvement in early GDR prose writing, Uwe **Johnson**'s *Speculations About Jacob* (*Mutmaßungen über Jakob*, 1959), was dismissed out of

hand, and its author forced into exile, because of its unacceptably critical focus on the repressive nature of GDR society in the 1950s. Johnson's multi-perspective narrative structure, depicting the efforts of the group of individuals closest to the young protagonist, amidst the intellectual uncertainties created by the Cold War, to reconstruct the circumstances which have led to his mysterious death, established a yardstick by which the authenticity of fiction subsequently published in the GDR could be judged, but it took at least two decades before his literary contemporaries who had remained in the GDR could admit that this was the case.

Surprisingly, perhaps, it was the crisis which culminated in the building of the Berlin Wall which paved the way for a modest 'cultural revolution' in the 1960s, since the SED's strategy for regaining a degree of popular legitimacy, following the trauma of August 1961, involved an acceptance that its officially fostered industrial literature had lost all credibility. Although the obvious beneficiaries were authors of a new wave of open-ended industrial novels, exemplified by Christa Wolf's *Divided Heaven* (*Der geteilte Himmel*, 1963), aiming to generate a genuine dialogue with their disaffected readership about the mistakes made in the 1950s, the longer-term effect of this period of liberalization was the scope it provided for the publication of more adventurous novels such as Johannes **Bobrowski**'s *Levin's Mill* (*Levins Mühle*, 1964). Bobrowski's revival of the traditions of oral storytelling proved inspirational in pointing a way beyond the mere surface realism of conventional GDR novels. His humorous narrator has no inhibitions about blending historical facts and fantasy in his account of nineteenth-century life in a divided German-Polish-Jewish community (a story which may still contain a political message, but of a more subtle kind than those pedantically underlined by the omniscient narrators of socialist realist fiction). Although the impact of works like *Levin's Mill* was not visible for several years, following the return to cultural repression at the infamous **Eleventh Plenum** of December 1965 (Wolf's *Christa T.* was one of the few innovative proseworks of the later 1960s to find a way through the censorship process), the floodgates were released following Erich **Honecker**'s promotion to SED leader in

1971 and his promise that there would henceforth be 'no taboos' for authors 'firmly rooted in socialism'.

The Honecker era (1971–89)

The retarding effects of two decades of unenlightened cultural policy were evident in the nature of some of the prose works which enjoyed public success in the aftermath of Honecker's liberalization. Ulrich **Plenzdorf**'s *Die neuen Leiden des jungen W.* (The New Sorrows of Young W.) (1972) was essentially a GDR variant on an American original, J.D. Salinger's *Catcher in the Rye* (1951), similarly focused on a teenager telling the story of his rebellion against authority in the jargon of his peer-group, yet it met the profound need of the détente years to renew links with western culture and its anti-authoritarian values. The politically more controversial novels of older authors like Stefan **Heym** and Erich **Loest** also depended heavily on familiar strategies, in their case the narrative techniques and the simplified characterization of popular fiction. The real creative progress achieved in the 1970s occurred elsewhere, and three important strands can be identified. First there is the liberation of creative fantasy (following the lead given by Bobrowski) in the work of female authors, especially Irmtraud **Morgner** in her montage-novel *Trobadora Beatriz* (Beatrice the Troubadour) (1974), which subjects the experience of women in the contemporary GDR, allegedly a 'promised land' of equal opportunities, to the often satirical scrutiny of a medieval poet who has just awoken from a Sleeping Beauty-like repose. Second, the need for an alternative literary heritage to the Weimar classicism enshrined in SED cultural policy is demonstrated in a succession of biographical novels, such as Gerhard Wolf's *Der arme Hölderlin* (Poor Hölderlin) (1972), which not only emphasize the arrogant way aspiring authors of the classical era were treated by Goethe and Schiller, but also draw attention to the vitality of the techniques of prose-writing evolved by previously underrated nineteenth-century figures such as Kleist, Hoffmann and Büchner. Third, there is a wave of largely autobiographical works by authors who grew up during the Third Reich, such as Fühmann's *Twenty-Two Days or Half a Lifetime*

(*Zweiundzwanzig Tage oder Die Hälfte des Lebens*, 1973), acknowledging that, despite all the rhetoric about the GDR as an anti-fascist state, there had been no clean break with National Socialism after 1945. Only now was it becoming clear to them that the task of ***Vergangenheitsbewältigung*** (coming to terms with their past) would not be complete until they dealt with the continuing legacy of the Third Reich, all too visible in the methods used by the Warsaw Pact states to crush the democratic reform movement in Czechoslovakia in 1968.

The factor which all of these innovative GDR prosewriters of the early Honecker era had in common was their renewed faith in the longer-term potential of eastern European socialism to develop into something approaching a Marxist utopia. These hopes were, however, soon to be dashed again, in the years after the **Biermann Affair** (1976), when they were persecuted for their refusal to submit to the authority of the SED leadership. They soon came to recognize that state socialism was degenerating into political and economic paralysis. This growing pessimism is reflected through the 1980s in prose works, notably Christa Wolf's feminist reworking of the myth of the Trojan war, *Cassandra* (*Kassandra*, 1983), which take a dispirited view of a world apparently heading towards nuclear and ecological disaster. The bleakness of the contemporary GDR itself is exposed in novels such as Günter de **Bruyn**'s *Neue Herrlichkeit* (New Glory) (1984) and Christoph **Hein**'s *Horns Ende* (Horn's Death) (1985). With hindsight it seems no coincidence that this virtual abandonment of political hope is articulated in prose which has now achieved the modernist sophistication which makes it stimulating to a wider international readership. The reasons why such major authors continued to live and publish in the GDR right up to 1989 are, however, only just beginning to be explored in autobiographical works like de Bruyn's *Vierzig Jahre* (Forty Years) (1996).

GDR prose-writers in unified Germany

Following the collapse of the GDR its established prose-writers found themselves under immediate pressure, especially from West German cultural media, to produce large-scale works which might contribute to a comprehensive *Vergangenheitsbewälti-gung* of the kind neither German state had achieved after the demise of the Third Reich. The unrealistic nature of these expectations is reflected by the fact that de Bruyn's autobiography, published seven years later, has been heralded as the first such work to come anywhere close to meeting them. The cultural life of unified Germany has been dominated by heated public debates about the integrity (or lack of it) of GDR authors, notably the controversy ignited by the publication of Wolf's *What Remains* (*Was bleibt*, 1990) and her insistence that there are positive elements within the legacy of the GDR, even though she too was spied on by the Stasi. The authors themselves had consequently neither the opportunity nor the clarity of perspective during this turbulent transition to produce new fiction taking stock of their achievements and failures as committed intellectuals. Important novels subsequently published, such as Hein's *Das Napoleon-Spiel* (The Napoleon Game) (1993) and Wolf's *Medea* (1996), represent tentative moves forward, with their deliberately restricted narrative focus and their adherence to fairly familiar thematic ground. The eagerly awaited 'great novel' about life in the GDR may still be some way off.

Further reading

Emmerich, W. (1996) *Kleine Literaturgeschichte der DDR*, Leipzig: Kiepenheuer (includes a detailed account of each phase in the development of GDR fiction).

Faber, E. (ed.) (1995 onwards) *Die DDR-Bibliothek*, Leipzig: Faber & Faber (collection of edited reprints, mainly of works of fiction, aiming to provide a historical record of GDR literature).

Fox, T. (1993) *Border Crossings: An Introduction to East German Prose*, Ann Arbor, MI: University of Michigan Press (survey focused mainly on works available in translation).

Goodbody, A., Tate, D. and Wallace, I. (1995) 'The Failed Socialist Experiment: Culture in the GDR', in R. Burns (ed.), *German Cultural Studies: An Introduction*, Oxford: Oxford University Press (provides an overview of prosewriting in its wider cultural context).

Reid, J.H. (1990) *Writing without Taboos: The New*

East German Literature, Oxford: Berg (deals mainly with proseworks of the Honecker era).

Wehdeking, V. (1995) *Die deutsche Einheit und die Schriftsteller*, Stuttgart: Kohlhammer (includes analyses of post-unification work of ex-GDR prosewriters).

DENNIS TATE

prostitution

Prostitution, the selling of sexual services for money, is legal in Germany. According to recent statistics, German men spend an estimated DM 12.5 billion ($8.4 billion) per year buying sex. As in other countries, there is an official or unofficial red-light district in every major city. Sex-clubs, peep shows and Eros Centres serve as organized bordellos. Prostitution's legal status is muddy, however, as a contract between a prostitute and a client would be considered immoral and would not stand up in court.

There are currently two major political collectives that promote the rights of prostitutes: HYDRA in Berlin, and HWG (Huren wehren sich gemeinsam – Prostitutes Resist Together) in Frankfurt am Main. Supported by radical feminist groups and social parties such as the **Greens**, they argue for the recognition of prostitution as a legitimate profession. Currently, prostitutes must pay taxes on monies they have earned, but they are not granted official state benefits, such as health insurance, unemployment benefits, or social security.

In Germany, all prostitutes must carry a health card and attend clinics every two weeks. In the current **AIDS** generation, there is an increased concern for public health, and HIV-positive prostitutes have become the focal point of a controversial suggestion to make the names of those who are HIV-positive a matter of public record, as in the former GDR.

The overwhelming majority of prostitutes in Germany's major cities are poor, immigrant women. There has been heightened attention and concern for the illegal promotion of forced prostitution, which has increased since the fall of the Iron Curtain. Many unsuspecting women are lured into Germany from eastern Europe and forced into slavery as prostitutes. As they are virtually illegal immigrants, they are immediately shipped out of the country, making it almost impossible to prosecute those who are responsible.

LISA YUN LEE

proT

proT, an experimental theatre company, was founded in Munich in 1969 by charismatic author, director, actor and filmmaker Alexeij Sagerer, writer and director of all of its productions. Initially drawing on performance art and the muscular humour of Bavarian folk theatre, for instance in *G'schaeg'n is G'schaeg'n* (What's Done is Done) (1969) Sagerer soon introduced live music and experimental film into his *'unmittelbares Theater'* (direct theatre), to most striking effect in the raucous, poetic and visually spectacular *Tieger von Äschnapur* (Tieger of Eschnapur) trilogy (1977–84). From 1980 proT became increasingly formalist – embracing video and installation – but without sacrificing its anarchic humour.

MARTIN BRADY

protest movements: FRG

Usually the term 'protest movements' characterizes citizens' initiatives (see also **citizens' initiatives: FRG**), action groups, alternative projects, environmental and **peace movement**s, the women's movement and Third-World solidarity groups which emerged in the FRG in the course of the 1970s. Some theories and descriptions start from the assumption that these protest movements already had their forerunners and developed in waves: from the more traditional protest against the rearmament of the FRG in the 1950s to the **student movement** in the 1960s, and then to the ecological and pacifist movements in the 1970s and 1980s (see also **Greens**). The principal characteristics of the protest movements are decentralized structures, direct democracy, anti-leadership-orientation, no fixed ideology, diverse and often changing issues, anti-power orientation, and various forms of protest activities. Co-ordination and communication between the different movements and groups are managed by network organizations. These network organizations mobilized hundreds of thousands of demonstrators in Bonn and other places during the protest against the stationing of cruise and Pershing II missiles in the FRG in 1981–3. The protest movements challenged with their activities the traditional party system and had a democratizing impact on the **political culture** of the FRG. Even the established parties were forced to integrate some of the protest issues into their political programme, and the **Greens** evolved in 1979 out of these movements.

Political scientists point out that the protest movements represent a new type of political formation and call them 'new social movements' in contrast with older ones like the labour movement. The new social movements do not centre their activities around issues of wealth distribution and political power but around issues dealing with the quality of life. In this respect they are post-materialistic and value-oriented. This orientation corresponds with the social-structural composition of the protest movements: various investigations have shown that their participants are mainly rooted in segments of the new middle class.

See also: dissent and opposition: GDR

Further reading

Brand, K.-W. (1982) *Neue soziale Bewegungen. Entstehung, Funktion und Perspektive neuer Protestpotentiale*, Opladen: Westdeutscher Verlag (fundamental analysis and description of the new protest movements).

Burns, R. and van der Will, W. (1988) *Protest and Democracy in West Germany*, London: Macmillan (the standard survey in English).

Roth, R. and Rucht, D. (ed.) (1987) *Neue soziale Bewegungen in der Bundesrepublik Deutschland*, Frankfurt am Main and New York: Campus Verlag (essays on the development of several protest movements).

LOTHAR PROBST

protest songs

In part parallel to, in part influenced by, the topical song movements in the US and Britain in the early 1960s, but with roots in political *chansons* of the 1920s, protest songs in Germany were the staple of German-language **Liedermacher** well into the late 1970s and, in isolated instances, into the 1990s. Two masters of the genre are Franz Josef **Degenhardt** and Wolf **Biermann**, although most serious singer-songwriters have written and sung protest songs.

German protest songs are the province of the political left. They embody the conviction that songs can make a political difference, although they are usually performed before like-minded audiences. Whether or not songs change people's minds, they may well serve to heighten consciousness of sociopolitical issues, often with economic or class-conscious underpinnings. Such songs articulate opposition against an attitude, behaviour or condition which needs changing.

One book of 'critical' songs groups them thematically: against destruction of the environment, against bourgeois morality (*Spießertum*) and self-delusion, against authoritarian child-rearing, against power and domination in the wrong hands, against war and rearmament, etc. While US protest songs focused on civil rights and opposition to the Vietnam war, German protest songs of the 1960s and 1970s protested the Grand CDU-SPD Coalition under Kurt Georg Kiesinger, the presence of unrepentant Nazis in West German government, restrictive laws (*Berufsverbot*), labour-union causes, disputes over such matters as worker involvement in corporate decision-making (*Mitbestimmung*), and, after 1980, unemployment.

Biermann's songs, written until 1976 in the GDR, attacked the staid, repressive practices of the SED bureaucracy, guilty of entrenched power and not genuine communists at all. Degenhardt's songs, siding after 1972 with a **DKP** point of view, were no less powerfully wrought, and dealt frequently with international solidarity. Both Biermann and Degenhardt, although no longer supportive of one another, continued to record CDs and appear on concert tours well into the mid-1990s. Their student audience of 1968 remained faithful to them even after the **Wende** of 1989 to 1990.

Coming to grips with German unity gave some Liedermacher new energy with protests against the alleged brutality of West Germany's capitalist annexation and colonization of East Germany.

Protest songs by less well-known but no less proficient and musically gifted *Liedermacher* and rock singers such as Walter Mossmann, Dieter Süverkrüp, Hannes Wader, Konstantin **Wecker**, Lerryn, Kristin Horn, Udo **Lindenberg**, Ina Deter, Klaus Hoffmann, Angi Domdey (for the group Schneewittchen), Herbert Grönemeyer, Hans Scheibner, Hanns Dieter Hüsch and Christof Stählin attacked the complacent attitudes which characterized affluent, post-war West German society's self-centred indifference.

A single umbrella under which German protest songs can be gathered is the theme of intolerance – of political dissidents, of those who think and act differently from the majority, of outsiders, of foreigners and of oppressed minorities. One can assert that German *Liedermacher* protest songs are thus a reaction to the perversion of popular music during the Nazi era and an attempt to integrate international influences into a German political art form.

Further reading

Klusen, E. and Heimann, W. (1978) *Kritische Lieder der 70er Jahre*, Reinbek bei Hamburg: Rowohlt (anthology of protest songs).
Stern, A. (1976) *Lieder aus dem Schlaraffenland: Politische Lieder der 50er-70er Jahre*, Oberhausen: Asso (639-page anthology of protest songs).

RICHARD J. RUNDELL

psychology

Many schools of modern psychology were begun by Germanophones in the nineteenth century, including psychoanalysis and experimental psychology. The interwar years (1919–32) provided a rich, if unstable environment for research, which was destroyed by Nazism. Since 1945 German psychology has become more eclectic, taking from previously dominant schools that which seems most useful.

Each of the major psychological approaches (behaviourist, psychoanalytic, Gestalt and humanistic) found supporters in central Europe between the wars. Most influential was Max Wertheimer's Gestalt psychology. Gestalt psychologists such as Kurt Koffka and Wolfgang Köhler studied the ways in which perceptions are formed and how the processes are determined by context, configuration and meaning.

Separately, Sigmund Freud in Vienna founded psychoanalysis which spread quickly to Zürich and from there to Berlin and Munich. Psychoanalysis thrived in German-speaking Europe as did theories put forward by the competing depth-psychologists Alfred Adler and Carl Gustav Jung. The rise of Nazism forced many analysts to emigrate, and psychoanalysis spent the war in exile. Freud's death in 1939 ended the early stages of psychoanalytic theoretical development and left theoreticians such as Erich **Fromm** and Erik Erikson free to creatively diverge from Freud's formulations.

During the war military psychologists were widely employed and industrial psychology received a boost from wartime productivity needs. In 1941 German universities began issuing psychological diplomas signalling an increased professionalization. As a discipline which requires freedom of thought however, psychology suffered badly under the Nazis.

Lost lives, scattered communities and destroyed facilities were the main obstacles to renewed psychological research in Germany after 1945. Gestalt psychology continued to dominate much of psychological discussions in central Europe through the mid-1960s. The advent of the computer gave birth to information-processing conceptions in perception and cognition theory. Subfields such as these were largely products of Anglo-American work, generally disliked by older psychologists, and consequently reflect West Germany's post-war political and cultural adaptation to Cold War circumstances. Since 1970 Gestalt psychology's influence has waned in favour of cognitive and humanistic explanations. Contemporary German psychologists concern themselves particularly with psychoanalysis, social adjustment theory, and analysis of motivation. Applied psychology most successfully integrated itself into the everyday fabric of German society and culture: educational, industrial, child welfare and vocational training are areas in which psychologists have been increasingly employed.

Further reading

Ash, M.G. (1995) *Gestalt Psychology in German Culture, 1890–1967*, Cambridge: Cambridge University Press.

Duhrssen, A. (1994) *Ein Jahrhundert psychoanalytische Bewegung in Deutschland: die Psychotherapie unter dem Einfluß Freuds*, Göttingen: Vandenhoeck & Ruprecht.

Krampen, G. and Wissenhutter, J. (1993) 'Bibliometrische Befunde zur Entwicklung der Teildisziplinen der Psychologie', *Psychology Rundschau* 44, 1: 25–34.

van Rappard, H.V. (1979) *Psychologische as Self-Knowledge: The Development of the Concept of the Mind in German Rationalistic Psychology and its Relevance today*, trans. L. Faili, Assen: Van Gorcum.

Semin, G.R. and Krahe, B. (eds) (1987) *Issues in Contemporary German Social Psychology: History, Theories and Application*, London and Beverly Hills, CA: Sage Publications (published in English for the first time these essays are a fine guide to the German intellectual tradition).

DAVID D. LEE

public opinion

Public opinion has been an active area of social scientific study and analysis in the FRG since the 1950s, when it was watched particularly closely as a barometer of the establishment of democratic attitudes in post-Nazi Germany. Private firms as well as leading universities have kept apace with the sophisticated tools of public opinion research that are today called on in the fields of marketing and political communication, the latter above all during elections. However, the study of public opinion in Germany also has a more theoretical branch, where it has followed the traditions of systems theory and Critical Theory, linking it more closely to sociology than to the practical work of survey research.

The first studies of public opinion in Germany

were conducted as early as 1945 by the US Office of Military Government for Germany, assessing attitudes towards topics from radio listening to food shortages. This tradition of American interest in German public views continued under the US Information Agency, which examined German (and other European publics') attitudes towards a variety of political developments on the continent. Following in this tradition, German institutes for the study of public opinion soon emerged, and public opinion became a staple of most academic courses in journalism and mass communication. On the applied side of public opinion study, leading survey research firms in the FRG include Infratest, Emnid, Institut für Demoskopie Allensbach, Forsa and Gesellschaft für Konsumforschung (GfK).

Germany's best known public opinion researcher is Elisabeth Noelle-Neumann, who, together with her husband, set up the Institut für Demoskopie Allensbach in 1947. Noelle-Neumann's conservative political leanings have made her the trusted advisor of Chancellors Adenauer and Kohl in matters of public opinion. She has also made her mark on the academy, developing a theory of public opinion based on the dominance of certain opinions and known as the 'spiral of silence'. According to Noelle-Neumann, members of the public tend to express (and act on) opinions only when they believe such opinions are widely held. Otherwise, they are fearful of being isolated in minority positions and are reluctant to indicate their real attitudes, a phenomenon which leads to their spiralling 'silence'. Above all, Noelle-Neumann has employed this theory to explain why, in her view, (conservative) voters have had their opinions neglected by the (liberal) German media, with considerable consequences in both opinion polls and the voting booth. Although often contested, the 'spiral of silence' has made Noelle-Neumann one of the only German communications researchers who is known internationally.

Working in the critical theoretical tradition (and until his retirement, based at Frankfurt University, the intellectual 'home' of his **Frankfurt School** teachers), Jürgen **Habermas** has also made a significant contribution to academic literature on public opinion. In his 1962 book, *Structural Transformation of the Public Sphere*, Habermas has traced the growth of a bourgeois public sphere from eighteenth-century European coffee-houses through its decline in the mass media climate of twentieth-century late capitalism. Throughout this and other work, Habermas has emphasized the intrinsic role of a reasoning public in modern society's political sphere. Another important contributor to the study of public opinion in Germany has been Niklas **Luhmann**. Luhmann, whose work is based on systems theory, has focused on the function rather than the influence of public opinion. In so doing, he has emphasized the system structures that bring certain topics to attention and has detached the study of public opinion from its otherwise normative, political status.

Further reading

Merritt, A. and Merritt, R. (eds) (1970) *Public Opinion in Occupied Germany*, Urbana, IL: University of Illinois.

Noelle-Neumann, E. (1992) *The Spiral of Silence: Public Opinion – Our Social Skin*, 2nd edn, Chicago, IL: University of Chicago Press.

ROBIN B. HODESS

publishing: FRG

The German book publishing industry is frequently associated with Gutenberg's invention of movable type in the fifteenth century. Today, over 2,000 publishers and 4,000 booksellers in the Börsenverein des Deutschen Buchhandels (the publishers' and booksellers' trade association) produce, distribute and sell approximately 50,000 new titles and 20,000 new editions annually. Fiction (designated as *belles-lettres* or *Belletristik*) represents the largest proportion of new titles and accounts for half of the paperback book production in Germany. A highly-efficient distribution system, or so-called intermediate book trade (*Zwischenbuchhandel*), serviced by publishers and wholesalers allows customers to receive most books within twenty-four hours of placing an order. While the largest wholesalers, Koch, Neff & Oetinger (KNOE), Lingenbrink (Libri) and **Bertelsmann**, stock about 150,000 titles, over 500,000 titles are actually available from publishers and distributors. Book chains (Hugendubel and Montanus Aktuell) as well as department stores (Karstadt, Kaufhof and Hertie) have garnered higher percentages of retail sales through mass-market merchandising in their large, urban stores. Confronted with increasing competition from the chains and shrinking profit margins, small and medium-sized booksellers have tailored their marketing and customer service to special audiences ('niche markets') by focusing on subject categories (e.g. antiquarian, arts, ecology, contemporary fiction, film, hobbies, religion, scientific and technical, travel and women's writing).

Although the continuous emergence of new publishers and booksellers suggests a diverse and dynamic publishing environment, economic concentration has increased in the German book market and throughout much of the European Union (EU). In Germany, roughly 9 percent of publishers account for over 80 percent of sales, and about 10 percent of booksellers earn 63 percent of all bookstore sales. Mergers and acquisitions have contributed to greater concentration as firms such as Bertelsmann and Georg von Holtzbrinck evolved from print-based publishers into multinational media conglomerates which co-ordinate numerous, highly-specialized publishing subsidiaries. The segmentation of publishing and bookselling into diverse 'niche markets' within publishing groups reflects both the shifts in reader interests and the economic impact of licensing rights for paperbacks and audiovisual media, particularly as books are thematically integrated into other forms of media production, such as book and film/television 'tie-ins' of best sellers. The success of foreign (predominantly English-language) bestsellers translated into German also signifies the internationalization of the German book market and the integration of publishing into a global communications industry, within which book publishing is merely one sector.

While market specialization is a response to more complex patterns of media use and consumption (in print and audiovisual formats), programmatic divisions within the publishing industry also reflect historical differences in the production, distribution and use of a wide range of books subsumed under the general rubric 'book publishing'. Major divisions and several notable publishers within these areas include: fiction and non-fiction (S. **Fischer**, Carl Hanser, Hoffmann und Campe, **Luchterhand** Literaturverlag, Kiepenheuer & Witsch, R. Piper, **Rowohlt**, **Suhrkamp**/Insel); scientific, technical, and medical (Gustav Fischer, Carl Hanser, Springer, Thieme and Urban & Schwarzenberg); professional and academic (C.H. Beck, Campus, Kohlhammer, Luchterhand, J.B. Metzler and Max Niemeyer); encyclopedias, textbooks, and general reference (**Brockhaus**, Cornelsen, Kindler, Klett, Langenscheidt and **Reclam Verlag**); children and young adults (Beltz & Gelberg, Oetinger, Ravensburger and Thienemann); art and photography (Hirmer and Prestel); religion (Echter, Herder and Kösel); and travel guides (Baedeker, DuMont and Polyglott).

Although most of these divisions are dominated by firms in the FRG, a number of highly-visible publishers in Austria and Switzerland represent a significant cultural presence within German-language publishing. Diogenes (Switzerland) and Residenz (Austria), for example, are internationally recognized as premier literary publishers. The market presence of West German publishers is even more conspicuous in the new *Länder*, where the state-owned publishing firms were dissolved or acquired (e.g. **Aufbau**) after unification. Others, such as Insel or Reclam Verlag Leipzig, were 'reunited' with their counterparts in the West (as branch operations) after forty years of separation. Although small presses have been modestly successful in the East, growth in publishing and bookselling has been sporadic at best and will only improve gradually with economic stabilization.

Beginning in the 1960s, economic pressures to achieve greater market share within publishing sectors, to acquire new and more profitable operations and develop 'synergy' with existing publishing programs (coupled with the realization that small, independent publishing was economically precarious) led to acquisitions of independent publishers by medium-sized and large firms. Suhrkamp, for example, expanded from a medium-sized publisher of fiction into a larger publishing group with its own fiction and professional publishing subsidiaries (Deutscher Klassiker Verlag, Insel, Nomos and Suhrkamp/Insel Taschenbuch).

Langenscheidt exemplifies a family-operated firm which grew into an international publishing group (with over twenty-four subsidiaries) by expanding its core programmes in dictionaries, reference works and encyclopedias through the acquisition of the Bibliographisches Institut & F.A. Brockhaus (publishers of **Duden** reference works) and investments in travel guides (APA Insight Guides, Baedeker and Polyglott). Holtzbrinck consolidated its position as a multimedia publisher through acquisitions in literary publishing (Droemer Knaur, S. Fischer and Rowohlt), textbook and academic publishing (Diesterweg, Metzler and Schroedel), as well as investments in general and professional publishing. Bertelsmann, considered the world's largest book publisher, exemplifies the expansion of multinational publishing through extensive domestic and foreign acquisitions in **book clubs** and music clubs, magazine publishing and multimedia. Despite significant differences, these publishers reflect the trend towards internationalization and concentration as publishers attempt to retain and expand their market share through growth strategies.

Publishers have become adept at producing books in a variety of formats and licensed editions (e.g. book-club editions, high-quality paperback boxed sets and limited-printing collectors' editions (see also **book clubs**)). The paperback provided much of the economic impetus for the expansion of German publishing during the 1960s and 1970s. Although paperbound books had been published in Europe since the sixteenth century, mass-production and distribution was a result of modern technological advances in printing and binding. After WWII, Ernst Rowohlt and his son H.M. Ledig-Rowohlt responded to the severe material shortages in Germany by utilizing newspaper presses to produce an inexpensive series of paperbacks called the *Rowohlt-Rotations-Romane* (more commonly known as the *ro-ro-ros*). Although some publishers (Fischer, Goldmann, Herder, List and Ullstein) soon followed Rowohlt with their own paperback series, many booksellers and publishers (e.g. Peter Suhrkamp) rejected the paperback as an inferior and inappropriate medium for disseminating literature. Others preferred to sell their rights to new publishers specializing in paperbacks, such as Deutscher Taschenbuch Verlag (**dtv**) which was

established in 1961 by a group of hardcover publishers to reprint their own titles. The initial reluctance to publish paperbacks dwindled as their economic success and popularity surged. In 1963, Peter Suhrkamp's successor, Siegfried Unseld, introduced a literary series in paperback (*Edition Suhrkamp*) which became an icon of literary culture in the FRG and marked the new acceptance of the paperback among leading literary publishers. Suhrkamp, S. Fischer, Carl Hanser, Kiepenheuer & Witsch, Luchterhand and Rowohlt recognized the market for paperback series which addressed literary, social and political issues of interest to the growing numbers of university students, intellectuals and young professionals. Publishers employed higher-grade paper stock and sophisticated book-cover designs (such as Willy Fleckhaus's rainbow of colours for the *Edition Suhrkamp*) in order to create cosmopolitan, urbane or avant-garde images for their series. By the 1970s, the sophisticated, 'upscale' image of literary series, which included original fiction and non-fiction by contemporary authors, had engendered recognition among influential literary critics and definitively secured the paperback's acceptance as a legitimate and a profitable publishing format.

These social, technological and economic forces simultaneously fostered the growth of numerous new, small and alternative presses with literary programmes and sociopolitical agendas (e.g. Frauenoffensive, Rotbuch, Verlag der Autoren and **Wagenbach**). A significant number of the alternative presses have become an institutionalized sector within German publishing by attracting and maintaining a core of dedicated readers concerned with cultural and social issues, for instance ecology, feminism, the Third World and more recently, multiculturalism. However, these issues have also been integrated into the extensive programmes of larger publishers, requiring small presses to reformulate their publishing programmes, form co-operative ventures, and develop more extensive contacts with specialized booksellers. The Mainz Minipress Fair is a small-press alternative to the international **Frankfurt Book Fair**. Many small presses specialize in limited-edition books for collectors. Yet, larger publishers have also entered this market, for example with a series of 'bibliophile paperbacks' produced by Harenberg.

Economic support for small booksellers and publishers has been fostered through the system of retail price maintenance or net pricing (*feste Ladenpreise*) which allows publishers to establish a base or net price for a new title, below which it may not be sold (with the exception of book-club or specially-licensed editions). Thus, customers will find the same price for a new publication in all retail outlets, ensuring that independent booksellers will not be undersold through 'price-cutting wars' with book chains. However, net pricing has been undermined by publishers who have granted extraordinary discounts of over 50 percent to chains and by discounting out-of-print books (*Modernes Antiquariat*). After the demise of net pricing in the UK (the Net Book Agreement) in 1997, many publishers and booksellers questioned the future of retail price maintenance in Germany. (The EU has banned it for trade across national borders.) Independent booksellers are concerned that its elimination in Germany will accelerate the growth of large retail chains and hinder the growth of small, independent booksellers and publishers.

The function of book publishing as part of an international communications industry is most visible at the annual **Frankfurt Book Fair** – the world's largest trade fair for buying and selling book rights. Publishers, booksellers, librarians, agents, authors, translators and the media gather to examine over 100,000 new titles from more than 2,400 publishers and 95 countries. The Frankfurt Book Fair exemplifies the importance of mediators (agents, translators and reviewers) in the publishing industry. Although literary agents (representing German authors) are less common in Germany than in the UK and the US, they play a pivotal role in brokering translation rights to German publishers. Approximately one book in seven is a translation into German and almost 75 percent of these are from English. In the fiction category (*Belletristik*), 45 percent of all new titles are translations (78 percent of which are from English). Yet, relatively few new fiction titles in German are licensed for publication in the UK or US (averaging about 25 licenses per annum), underscoring the socio-cultural and economic dominance of the English language within international

media markets. As translations have become a significant segment within German publishing, translators have attempted to negotiate more equitable compensation for their work, in part through the Association of German Authors (**Verband deutscher Schriftsteller**).

The Frankfurt Book Fair accentuated the convergence of print and electronic publishing when it announced 'Frankfurt Goes Electronic' as a thematic emphasis during the early 1990s. The Fair also presented book rights online over the World Wide Web. While German publishers have utilized computerized printing and publishing technologies in book production, distribution and marketing for several decades, new ventures in publishing books in electronic media (CD-ROM) or online represent a small, but growing segment of publishing. Increasingly, publishers conceptualize the dissemination of texts in both print and electronic media. Thus, they are expanding the notion of publishing as a process of selecting, acquiring, refining (editing), mediating, disseminating, marketing and licensing intellectual property – regardless of its material form.

See also: publishing: GDR

Further reading

Weidhaas, P. (1995) 'Germany', in P. Altbach and P. Hoshino (eds), *International Book Publishing: An Encyclopedia*, New York: Garland (a good overview of German publishing within the context of the international publishing industry).

Wittmann, R. (1991) *Geschichte des deutschen Buchhandels: Ein Überblick*, Munich: C.H. Beck (an excellent historical survey of German publishing).

Statistical data on German publishing and bookselling may be found in the annual editions of *Buch und Buchhandel in Zahlen*, Frankfurt am Main: Buchhändler-Vereinigung. Current trends in German publishing and bookselling are reported in the trade journals *Börsenblatt für den Deutschen Buchhandel* and *Buchreport*.

MARK W. RECTANUS

publishing: GDR

Publishing in the GDR was structured and developed according to the principles of state socialism, with the 'Central Administration for Publishing and the Book Trade' within the Ministry of Culture at the pinnacle of a carefully controlled hierarchy. The stated aim was entirely laudable: to create what Johannes R. **Becher** called a '*Literaturgesellschaft*', a society of readers in which literature would play a significant role in influencing the course of the new state's development. Prices were kept low as a means of encouraging everyone to purchase and collect books of their own and thus put an end to a bourgeois privilege of previous eras. Sales figures were very impressive by western standards: the average edition of a new publication ran to 25,000 copies and the number of books purchased annually worked out at an average of eight or nine per member of the population. About a third of the books published were works of creative literature (*Belletristik*) and sixteen publishers out of a total of seventy-eight were primarily concerned with the production of literary works. There was an emphasis on maintaining traditional standards of quality which allowed publishing houses to employ far more staff than their western counterparts, and the difference in proofreading and editorial precision was often striking when GDR and FRG editions of the same text were compared. The whole publication process was, however, much slower in the GDR, with the combination of the state's limited printing capacity and paper supply, the extensive vetting of any politically sensitive material as well as this commitment to quality meaning that there was often well over a year between the author's delivery of a text to the publisher and its eventual appearance.

Publishing houses were established after 1945 according to a preconceived division of labour. New firms were created in order to give each of the GDR's political parties and mass organizations its own outlet, such as the **Dietz Verlag** for the **SED**, the Buchverlag Der Morgen for the Liberal-Democratic Party, the **Aufbau Verlag** for the **Kulturbund** and the Verlag Neues Leben for the Freie Deutsche Jugend (**FDJ**). Publishers of creative literature had to maintain distinctive profiles, with Aufbau concentrating on major authors of the exile years, the **Mitteldeutscher Verlag** fostering new talent, the Kinderbuchverlag enjoying a near monopoly on children's literature, and so on. Famous names from the history of the German book-trade, associated with its traditional centre in Leipzig, such as **Reclam**, Brockhaus, Kiepenheuer and Insel, were preserved under state ownership after their owners had moved to the FRG and re-established themselves there, creating a confusing East–West duplication of names which were now completely unconnected. Distribution was also centralized in Leipzig, with the annual **Leipzig Book Fair** as the focus for new publications.

Although this system had obvious organizational advantages, its in-built rigidity caused political tensions as soon as individual publishers sought to expand their base or modify their image. The new flexibility promised after Erich **Honecker** came to power led some publishers to challenge the status quo. The **Hinstorff Verlag** in Rostock, whose original brief had been to develop a regional profile as the GDR's publisher of Low German and Scandinavian literature, began to attract the rising generation of critically-minded authors who had lost patience with the conservatism of firms like Aufbau, and rapidly gained a reputation both inside and outside the GDR as its most innovative and politically provocative publisher. After the **Biermann Affair** the SED attempted to restore order by dismissing Hinstorff's director, Konrad Reich, and replacing him with a party loyalist, but recognized that it could not entirely turn the clock back in what was now a prestigious and commercially successful firm. Even more revealing was the SED's response to the initiative of a group of authors in 1974–5 to break the state's monopoly on publishing by organizing, editing and producing their own anthology of *Berliner Geschichten* (Berlin Stories). The full extent of the campaign of intimidation conducted against the initiators of the anthology, Ulrich **Plenzdorf**, Klaus **Schlesinger** and Martin Stade, and the other authors willing to contribute to it, by cultural bureaucrats and the Stasi, has only become clear since the collapse of the GDR, but this was a fundamental challenge to state-controlled publishing which had to be suppressed at all costs.

Since unification the publishing network in the ex-GDR has been changed, if not as radically as other institutions of state socialism. The wholesale privatization process organized by the **Treuhand** has transformed management structures and allowed the Leipzig-based firms to be reunited with their western namesakes, but most of the publishing houses created after 1945 have managed to survive in a slimmed-down form. Aufbau, easily the biggest of the GDR's literary publishers, overcame the turbulence of the *Wende* with the help of funds from the SED's successor, the **PDS**, before being bought by the Frankfurt businessman Bernd Lunkewitz. While losing the limited rights it had originally held to publish GDR editions of authors 'owned' by FRG firms and losing some of its prestigious GDR authors (notably Christa **Wolf**) to western rivals, Aufbau has retained a sufficiently attractive range of authors to remain solvent, even if (like other ex-GDR publishers) it has had problems in extending its distribution network into western Germany. The most encouraging aspect of 1990s publishing in the new *Länder* has been the emergence of new locally-based firms, such as Galrev (*Verlag* spelt backwards), collectively owned by some of the **Prenzlauer Berg** poets, or Faber & Faber, owned by the ex-director of Aufbau, Elmar Faber, whose idea of creating a '*DDR-Bibliothek*' of historically important and/or creatively innovative works of the period up to 1989 has attracted considerable interest.

See also: censorship: GDR

Further reading

Emmerich, W. (1996) *Kleine Literaturgeschichte der DDR*, Leipzig: Kiepenheuer (includes a clear account both of the original structure of GDR publishing and post-unification changes).

Plenzdorf, U. *et al.* (eds) (1995) *Operativer Schwerpunkt Selbstverlag*, Frankfurt am Main: Suhrkamp (contains both the planned anthology of '*Berliner*

Geschichten' and a documentation of the way its publication was blocked).

DENNIS TATE

Puhdys

GDR rock-band, founded in Berlin in 1969. One of the few groups which were officially tolerated by the state on the basis of its strict 'qualitative' assessment criteria, the Puhdys were allowed to perform publicly in the GDR and abroad, but state control severely restricted their scope for political expression. Their records were also available in West Germany, where the band attained some popularity. The Puhdys played cover versions of Anglo-American songs as well as their own compositions with German lyrics. By the early 1990s, the band had sold about fifteen million albums.

See also: Karat; Silly

ANNETTE BLÜHDORN

punks

The mostly urban punk subculture developed in the late 1970s and was inspired by the British punk movement. Punks became a politically and culturally active protest group that emphasized general opposition to authority and traditional social values rather than presenting alternative ideas. This attitude was also expressed through creative hair styles, use of everyday objects as jewellery, and deliberately careless dress. West German punks were squatters, published fanzines and started bands such as ZK, Die **Toten Hosen**, Die Ärzte, Slime and Abwärts. In Berlin and Hanover, punks continue to organize annual demonstrations which ritually end in run-ins with the police.

SABINE SCHMIDT

puppet theatre

In Germany, puppet theatre spans both high and popular culture, an intersection in which adults and children attend together the often symbolically-charged puppet plays. This phenomenon reflects a changed tradition in German-speaking countries after 1945. Originally for adults, puppet theatre had been an important tool in the imagining of German identity. In fact, Goethe and Lessing felt that German aesthetic experience and identity were revealed in this genre. Post-1945 puppet theatre relies primarily on Rhineland rod puppets, marionettes and stick figures.

KITTY MILLET

Q

Qualtinger, Helmut

b. 8 October 1928, Vienna; d. 29
   September 1986, Vienna

Dramatist and actor

Qualtinger started his career in 1946 as a satirist,
writer and playwright. During the 1950s Qualtinger was a member of several satirical revues. His
best known work is *Der Herr Karl* (1961, co-written
with Carl Merz), a one-act play on an opportunistic
petty bourgeois. Qualtinger has played numerous
roles on television and in films.

ERNST GRABOVSZKI

Quevedo, Nuria

b. 18 March 1938, Barcelona

Graphic artist and painter

In 1952 Quevedo emigrated with her parents to
the GDR. After being educated as a graphic artist
she started as an illustrator of literature, Spanish
prose in particular. Since 1971 she has worked as a
figurative painter. Here, too, a tendency towards
the expressive interpretation of the subject prevails.

Her mature work shows a rigorous realism which
refers to the tradition of Goya and Velázquez. In
drawings such as the series on Cassandra she
vehemently discusses existential questions of mankind.

See also: painting

KERSTIN MEY

Quick

Hovering in name between the English 'quick' and
the German *erquicken* (to revive, to refresh), this
weekly periodical thrives on sensational news
stories and the regular feature of scantily-clad
women on its front cover. It had its heyday in the
1970s and early 1980s, with a circulation figure of
around one million. However, due to the diversification of the German print media in the 1990s, it
has lost some of its ground to newer and even more
daring publications. Nevertheless, it remains a
popular periodical in the realm of the **Regenbogenpresse**.

See also: magazines; mass media: FRG

HOLGER BRIEL

R

Rad, Gerhard von

b. 21 October 1901, Nürnberg; d. 31
   October 1971, Heidelberg

Protestant theologian

Rad taught theology at various German universities, latterly Heidelberg, specializing in Old
Testament studies, notably questions of form. His
two-volume *Theologie des Alten Testaments* appeared in
numerous editions, the last in 1965 to 1966. He
contributed Genesis volumes to the translation and
commentary project *Das Alte Testament Deutsch*. Most
of his works are translated into English. With
Walther Eichrodt, Otto Eissfeldt and others he is
one of the most influential Old Testament scholars
of the century.

Further reading

Laurin, R.B. (1970) *Contemporary Old Testament
   Theologians*, London: Marshall, Morgan & Scott.
Spriggs, D.G. (1974) *Two Old Testament Theologies*,
   London: SCM.

BRIAN MURDOCH

radio: cultural role

The regional structure of **broadcasting** in the
FRG and the dominance (exclusively, until the
early 1980s) of the public service principle has
meant that radio has from the outset played an
important role in the promotion and dissemination
of high culture – not least in the field of **music** and
the distinctive German genre of the *Hörspiel* (radio
play) (see also **Hörspiel: FRG**). By the 1960s all
the regional corporations were broadcasting at
least three radio services, usually on FM, and
including in each case a 'serious' channel providing
classical music, radio plays, literary criticism,
discussions and talks. As most listeners are within
range of more than one corporation's offerings, the
availability of such programming is unusually high
in Germany. In the post-war decades a major role
in the spread of Anglo-American pop culture was
played by the radio services of the British and,
especially, American forces in Germany, which had
a large following particularly among young people,
in their turn influencing the programming policies
of the German stations themselves.

In Austria and Switzerland too, the provision by
the public-service corporations of a radio channel
devoted to 'serious' programming has been a
significant element in cultural life. In the GDR
such programming was found in particular on the
FM service Radio DDR II (see also **Hörspiel:
GDR**), but tight state control and the expressly
propagandistic mission of the broadcasting services
(see also **propaganda**) led many listeners to tune
in by preference to western programmes.

The advent of commercial radio in the FRG in
the 1980s has led to a great increase in the number
of stations – mostly local and nearly all dominated
by popular fare aimed at a mass audience. The
development of digital radio will multiply even
more steeply the number and variety of services
available, and accelerate further the process of
audience fissiparation and the creation of ever
more radio sub-cultures that have been one of the

most distinctive developments in the medium over the past two decades.

JOHN SANDFORD

Rahner, Karl

b. 5 March 1904, Freiburg im Breisgau; d. 30 May 1984, Innsbruck

Catholic theologian

Ordained a priest in 1932, Rahner taught in Jesuit colleges and became Professor of Dogmatic Theology at Innsbruck in 1949. From 1964 to 1967 he held a chair in Munich (1964–7), and from 1967 to 1971 in Münster. He served at the Second Vatican Council (1962–5) as *peritus* (an expert, or official theologian). He was appointed by Pope Paul VI (1969) to assess trends in theology since the Council; he frequently urged the Pope to evaluate channels of power within the church. Considered a transcendental Thomist, Rahner's theological anthropology was influenced by the philosophy of Martin **Heidegger**.

MAGDA MUELLER

railways

Since 1 January 1994 the national railway system in Germany has been operated by the state-owned Deutsche Bahn AG. This company, the largest German transportation enterprise, replaced the western German Deutsche Bundesbahn and the eastern German Deutsche Reichsbahn. It was created as part of a structural reform under which operations were split into four main sectors responsible for the passenger business, freight, maintenance and infrastructure. The German government began privatization of each sector in 1997. Germany also has municipally owned underground and surface (*S-Bahn*) railways.

Further reading

Offizieller Jubiläumsband der Deutschen Bundesbahn: 150

Jahre Deutsche Eisenbahnen (1985) Munich: Eisenbahn-Lehrbuch Verlagsgesellschaft.

RICHARD A. HAWKINS

Rainer, Roland

b. 1 May 1910, Klagenfurt

Architect

Rainer studied at the TH (Technical University) Vienna 1928–33. He has been in private practice in Vienna since 1947. His posts have included Chief Town Planning Officer of Vienna (1958–63), Professor of Housing and Town and Country Planning at the TH Hanover (1953–4) and Professor of Building and Design at the TH Graz.

Rainer's architectural interest ranges from town planning to the smallest domestic buildings, embracing these matters on an essentially humane basis. His low-rise, high-density Gartenstadt Puchenau near Linz (1963–7), built around private atrium spaces, illustrates these ideas. His first important municipal building is his Town Hall in Vienna (1953–8). His entire œuvre relies on simple materials and clear construction, resulting in straightforward yet intricate spaces.

MARTIN KUDLEK

Raiser, Konrad

b. 25 January 1938, Magdeburg

Protestant theologian

Since 1993, Raiser has been General Secretary of the World Council of Churches. *Ecumenism in Transition* (*Ökumene in Übergang*) (1991) expounds Raiser's belief that ecumenism needs a paradigm shift (see also **Paradigmawechsel**) away from the unity of the church to encompass humankind and the whole of creation. Raiser was one of four East and West German theologians who initiated the *Berliner Eklärung* in February 1990, criticizing the *Loccumer Eklärung* of January 1990, in which East and West German Protestant church leaders called for speedy re-unification of German Protestantism.

See also: churches and religion

Further reading

Raiser, K. (1991) *Ecumenism in Transition (Ökumene in Übergang)*, trans. T. Coates, Geneva: WCC Publications.

STEPHEN BROWN

Ranke-Heinemann, Uta

b. 2 October 1927, Essen

Theologian

Daughter of the former president of the FRG, Gustav W. Heinemann, she converted to Catholicism and was the first female professor of Catholic theology in the world. Having criticized the church's position on mixed (Protestant and Catholic) marriages (1979), sexuality, and the doctrine of immaculate conception (1987), Ranke-Heinemann lost her Catholic professorship (New Testament and History of the Old Church) and became Professor of Religion (free of the influence of the church) at the University of Essen. She is internationally known for her engagement against napalm and nuclear weapons and for peace as well as her ongoing critique of misogynous tendencies in the Catholic church.

MAGDA MUELLER

Ransmayr, Christoph

b. 20 March 1954, Wels (Austria)

Novelist

Ransmayr has been acclaimed for his 1988 novel *The Last World (Die letzte Welt)*, widely viewed as a postmodern masterpiece. The narrator leaves Rome to seek the banished poet Ovid but encounters strange figures in a timeless world that is increasingly subject to decay. Less praised was *Morbis Kitahara* (1995), which portrays a defeated country which, unlike post-war Germany, is being returned to a pre-industrial state.

Further reading

Murath, K. (1996) 'The Function of Allegory in

Christoph Ransmayer's Novel *Die letzte Welt'*, in A. Williams, S. Parkes, J. Preece (eds), *Contemporary German Writers, Their Aesthetics and Their Language*, Bern: Peter Lang.

STUART PARKES

Rasp, Renate

b. 3 January 1935, Berlin

Writer (also Rasp-Budzinski)

Rasp studied art and acting in Berlin and Munich, and worked in the television industry before becoming a writer. Her first story *Der Spaziergang nach St Heinrich* (The Walk to St Heinrich) (1967) appeared in an anthology edited by Dieter **Wellershoff**. She was celebrated as the discovery of 1967 after publishing *A Family Failure (Ein ungeratener Sohn)*, a bestseller translated into English by Eva Figes. Her works explore familial and personal relationships, gender roles, and questions of identity. She was a member of **Gruppe 47**. Since 1973, has divided her time between Munich and Newquay in Cornwall.

MARTINA S. ANDERSON

Rathenow, Lutz

b. 22 September 1952, Jena

Writer and political activist

Rathenow made his reputation almost exclusively on the basis of manuscripts smuggled out of the GDR and published abroad. His first book, a collection of short stories entitled *Mit dem Schlimmsten wurde schon gerechnet* (Prepared for the Worst) (1980), led to his temporary arrest, which provoked wide international protests. He refused to emigrate and went on to publish many additional books including *Contacts* (1987), the only collection of his writings available in English translation. In 1996 he received the Adenauer Prize for his prose collection entitled *Sisyphos*.

BORIA SAX

Reception Theory

Reception Theory is an approach to the study of literary (and other) texts which focuses not on the relationship between author and text but on that between text and reader. The term is usually used to refer to the pioneering work carried out by Hans Robert **Jauß** and Wolfgang **Iser** from the mid-1960s to the mid-1980s at the University of Constance.

In his early work, Jauß took the German academic establishment to task for its neglect of history in literary studies. He proposed a new approach to the study of literature that would combine the Russian Formalists' emphasis on the crucial role played by the recipient in arriving at judgements of aesthetic quality with the Marxist view of literature as part of a larger process of historical developments. Central to his theory is the notion of a 'horizon of expectation' (*Erwartungshorizont*), in other words the set of literary, social and cultural expectations which each reader brings to a text. The task of literary scholars is to reconstruct the 'horizon of expectation' for works from past eras. The more the reader's own horizon of expectation is called into question by his or her encounter with that of the work itself, the greater the aesthetic merit of the work in question. In this way, literature ceases to be simply a reflection of history generally and assumes a 'socially formative function', shaping the consciousness of the reader and thereby fulfilling its emancipatory potential. Some years later, however, Jauß revised his theory, pointing out that although suitable for dealing with certain types of avant-garde literature, it was less adequate as a hermeneutic device when applied to 'affirmative' modes of writing such as medieval literature and that it understated the relationship between aesthetic pleasure and the cognitive and communicative efficacy of art.

In his work Wolfgang Iser offers a phenomenological account of the act of reading. Central to his theory is the notion of an 'implied reader' (*implizierter Leser*) who is said to embody all the predispositions necessary for a literary work to exercise its effect. During the reading process, the reader is confronted with a framework of 'indeterminacies' which must be resolved. But whereas in the case of everyday speech such indetermina-cies can be resolved with reference to a given set of conventions, in the case of fiction readers have to discover the conventions underlying the text for themselves, a process which for Iser is 'tantamount to bringing out the meaning'. The nature of the reader's response will depend to a large extent on the particular experiences which make up each individual's 'prevailing' thought-system. None the less, anxious to avoid the notion that the possibilities of interpretation are limitless, Iser suggests that there is 'something' which acts as a constraint on interpretation, although what this is is never really spelled out.

Both Jauß's and Iser's theories of reception have provoked considerable debate. In the early 1970s, Jauß was taken to task by GDR scholars – notably Claus Träger and Manfred Naumann – who criticized his historiographical approach on the grounds of its inherently 'bourgeois bias'. Iser's theory – and in particular the vexed question of the indeterminacy of meaning – led to a vigorous exchange of views with the American critic Stanley Fish.

Further reading

Holub, R.C. (1984) *Reception Theory: A Critical Introduction*, London and New York: Methuen (clear overview of the major theorists together with a critique of their work).

SEÁN ALLAN

Reclam Verlag

In 1867 the Leipzig publishing firm of Reclam, directed by Hans Heinrich Reclam, initiated the *Universal-Bibliothek* – a series of slight, inexpensive paperback editions of classical texts. A godsend to generations of students, even before WWII the number produced was 280 million with some 7,600 different texts available. Following the post-war division of Germany and the passing into state ownership of the Leipzig house, the company's proprietors emigrated to the West and set up afresh in Stuttgart. Each 'house of Reclam' continued the tradition of the *Universal-Bibliothek* in their respective parts of Germany, with the Leipzig company performing a particularly important function in GDR cultural life by producing volumes of contemporary foreign literature (especially poetry) in high-quality translations. Since unification the firms have come under single management, but the Leipzig series has retained its separate identity. Reclam also produces a series of guides to art, opera, novels and drama.

See also: publishing: FRG; publishing: GDR

JOHN B. RUTLEDGE AND DENNIS TATE

reconstruction

Plans for the reconstruction of German cities destroyed in the war had already been made under the Nazi regime. In most cases elements of these plans found their way into Germany's rebuilt urban and rural fabrics. As in most other fields the notion of a '**Stunde Null**' (zero hour) remains a myth.

The first phase of reconstruction was dominated by the clearance of 400 million cubic metres of rubble (see also **Trümmerfrauen**) and the provision of emergency accommodation for the bombed-out population and refugees. The largely destroyed economy, the paralysation of initiative until the 1948 monetary reform, and allied restrictions, delayed reconstruction. The discussion between traditional and progressive planners remained theoretical until *circa* 1949. These years were dominated by the mere drawing up of plans, in many cases utopian visions. By the mid-1950s these had been rendered outdated by the ever growing demands of the economic boom and were only realized partially.

The destruction of towns was generally seen as a chance to undo former shortcomings. Inadequate planning laws and restriction of planners' powers were later seen as the main reasons for not realizing this chance. Although these powers were given in the East, they were soon made subordinate to GDR party politics, resulting in monotonous and 'inhumane' townscapes after the total industrialization of building.

In the West, the lack of federal regulations led to the fragmentation of planning. This explains why most West German towns could choose different models of reconstruction. Although a consensus based on the retention of a town's elementary ground plan seems to have existed among most planners, due to the more or less intact underground infrastructure, their ideas varied greatly and again often conflicted with political and economic interests. Reconstruction has to be seen as a mediation process between these three, often multi-poled forces, resulting in different reconstruction schemes for most towns.

Nevertheless three basic reconstruction models can be differentiated: *Wiederaufbau* (the recreation of historical building stock), *Neubau* (the construction of completely new buildings), and *Aufbau* (new building that relates to the historical building stock in style, material and form).

Strict *Wiederaufbau* only really happened connected to singular 'monument-islands'. On a larger scale Freudenstadt in Baden-Württemberg comes closest to this model.

The bulk of German reconstruction falls under the remaining two categories, and even these types are hardly ever found in pure form throughout a whole town. Kassel, Hanover and Kiel represent different *Neubau* models of relative purity. *Neubau* often did not exclude *Wiederaufbau* as first experiments in Brunswick (Burgplatz and Altstadtmarkt) demonstrate. The extent of war-destruction was often responsible for meagre 'monument-islands' in *Neubau* towns (e.g. Deichstraße in Hamburg). In other cases (e.g. St Martin in Cologne, Römerberg in Hamburg and Schnoorviertel in Bremen) modern reconstructions helped complete larger monument island areas.

Munich and Karlsruhe represent successful *Aufbau* cities, although again much of the two other categories played into their reconstruction. Small towns were most likely to apply this model too: Rastatt is a good example. Virtually all villages were rebuilt accordingly. One can safely say that no large town's reconstruction relied solely on one model and it has to be emphasized that each town's reconstruction represents a unique planning approach.

See also: town planning

Further reading

Diefendorf, G. (1994) *In the Wake of War*, Oxford: Oxford University Press.

MARTIN KUDLEK

recycling

The term most commonly refers to the re-use of scrap materials, reprocessing of domestic waste, purification of sewage water, etc. For the environmentally aware public the term has strongly positive connotations; environmentalists are more sceptical. Germany achieves a recycling quota of about 66 percent for paper and cardboard, 55 percent for glass, 95 percent for ferrous metals, 48 percent for sheet metal, 14 percent for aluminium and 25 percent for plastics. It is often regarded as the recycling nation *par excellence*.

The recycling of scrap metal, textiles and paper has a particularly long tradition. Scrap dealers used to make a living from collecting re-usable materials in residential areas. For charities the collection of old newspapers etc. was a welcome source of extra income. Up to the 1970s these activities were not motivated by environmental considerations. The same applies to the former GDR, which operated an efficient system of collecting secondary raw materials, but only in order to combat its chronic shortage of resources.

With the advent of mass consumerism and the wide recognition of environmental problems, recycling increasingly became a necessity, often requiring substantial financial input. A shortage of suitable dumping sites for domestic refuse as well as the need to save energy and material resources stimulated a change of behaviour patterns. During the 1980s city councils established a network of publicly accessible collection points for glass, paper, metal and other materials covering the whole of the country. In the early 1990s separate dustbins for paper and for biodegradable kitchen and garden wastes (compost) were distributed to households.

Following the government's 1991 *Verpackungsverordnung* (packaging decree), which sought to alleviate the so-called *Müllnotstand* (refuse emergency) by stipulating recycling quotas for most packaging materials, a controversial debate developed about the ecological usefulness of recycling and its dubious function as a way of condoning the ecological sins committed by an ecologically unsustainable consumer society. Environmentalists drafted an alternative, if unsuccessful, waste management bill prioritizing, as a matter of principle, the avoidance of waste over its recycling. Industry established the *Duales System Deutschland GmbH* (DSD), which set up a commercial scheme for collecting, sorting and recycling packaging materials, financing its activities through licence fees charged for the ***Grüner Punkt***. However, the practice of commercializing the disposal of waste remained highly controversial. DSD practice demonstrated that satisfactory recycling facilities and technologies are often not available and that markets for recycling products cannot easily be established. In several cases the refuse was illegally disposed of in Third World countries. Even where materials are successfully reclaimed, recycling in practice always means 'downcycling', the manufacturing of lower-grade products.

See also: environmentalism

Further reading

Altner, G. *et al.* (eds) (1992; 1995) *Jahrbuch Ökologie 1992*; *Jahrbuch Ökologie 1995*, Munich: Beck (on the debate about official waste policies and possible alternatives).

Gandy, M. (1994) *Recycling and the Politics of Urban Waste*, London: Earthscan (comparative study of large cities including Hamburg).

Rohlfs, H.H. and Schäfer, U. (eds) (issued annually) *Jahrbuch der Bundesrepublik Deutschland*, Munich: Beck/dtv (for statistical data).

INGOLFUR BLÜHDORN

re-education

Re-education was the Allies' positive policy complementing attempts at denazification in post-war Germany: the Germans, subjected to twelve years of Nazi propaganda and indoctrination, should be re-educated to learn the virtues of democracy as understood by the Allies. This, of course, meant very different things in the East and the West.

In both East and West, great emphasis was laid on the media, and in particular the licensed press, as a medium for re-education. In the western zones, the growth of a democratic press run by the Germans under close Allied supervision was perhaps one of the more successful aspects of re-education policies, and laid the foundations for the subsequent newspaper and journal landscape of West Germany. The same was true of the licensed radio stations, although these rapidly came under the political control of the new democratic parties. The showing in cinemas of films such as *Todesmühlen*, designed to rub into Germans the horrors of the Nazi concentration camps and make them realize the errors of their ways and the sins of their former leaders, seems to have been less effective as a means of transforming West German political culture. In the Soviet zone, the manifest political distortions in the press provoked a generally cynical reaction among the populace, and failed to produce the desired re-education in any genuine sense.

Schools were initially closed and former teachers subjected to stringent political controls on both sides. In the Soviet zone, over three-quarters of schoolteachers lost their jobs (with marked regional variations). Politically reliable and often very young 'new teachers' were rapidly trained in short courses and brought in to fill the vacancies. Nazi schoolbooks were jettisoned and the school system overhauled with the abolition of confessional schools in the Law for the Democratization of German Schools in 1946.

School reform in the western zones was much more patchy and incomplete. Although Nazi schoolbooks were replaced by old textbooks from the Weimar period, many teachers survived denazification in the West. The traditional tripartite schooling system was retained, as were confessional schools, and American proposals for reform were effectively resisted by the Germans. Universities were affected by potential reforms even less than schools, with both the system and the staff in higher education remaining largely untouched.

Reorientation seminars, organized visits to Britain and the US, the setting up of American and British cultural centres in Germany, and the organization of political education courses, all made contributions over time to re-education in West Germany. But most studies suggest that transformation in West German political culture came less as the effect of such policies on particular individuals, than as a by-product of the passage of time. Younger generations, socialized in new circumstances, developed different attitudes and orientations from those of their parents' and grandparents' generations. Similarly communist propaganda and indoctrination in the East was often too blatant to be swallowed wholesale: changing patterns of political culture were the result of changing generational experiences and expectations rather than a consequence of re-education.

MARY FULBROOK

refugees

Germany has experienced two major waves of refugees since 1945: the first in the period immediately after 1945 comprising displaced persons in Germany, and Germans and other groups in Europe who were fleeing from the Soviet Army; and the second in the 1980s which resulted from West Germany's liberal position on political asylum (see also **asylum, political**).

There were two major groups of refugees in Germany in the immediate post-war period. The first group of about 11 million people comprised foreigners who had been brought to Germany during the Nazi period, many as forced labour. They were classified by the Allies as displaced persons and collected into camps before being offered the opportunity to return to their countries of origin. By the end of September 1945 over 5 million people had been returned to their countries of origin. The only groups which were forced to return were Soviet displaced persons, who were repatriated forcibly to the Soviet Union in accordance with the agreement made between the western Allies and Stalin at Yalta in February 1945. Some of these were murdered on their return. A large number of displaced persons did not want to return to their original countries, and in 1947 a resettlement programme, mostly to North America and Australia, was started by the United Nations Refugee Relief Agency which lasted until 1951. Only about 150,000 displaced persons remained in Germany.

The advance of the Red Army into East Prussia in the summer of 1944 and into Poland in the autumn caused the flight of the German population. By the summer of 1945 it was clear that Germany was going to lose East Prussia, the parts of Pomerania and Silesia to the east of the **Oder-Neisse line**, and that the Sudetenland was going to be returned to Czechoslovakia. This expulsion of the German population had been discussed by the Allies at the conferences of Teheran (1943) and Yalta (1945), and had then been confirmed at Potsdam in August 1945. At least 2 million Germans lost their lives in the process; the first census in October 1946 registered about 9.6 million expellees in the four zones. By the next census in West Germany in September 1950 the number had risen by a further 2 million. The expellees were distributed through the four zones on a quota basis, but the largest number went to the agrarian states. In 1950 they represented 21.1 percent of the population in Bavaria, 27.2 percent in Lower Saxony, 33.0 percent in Schleswig-Holstein and 42.5 percent in Mecklenburg. In the autumn of 1949 a federal Ministry for Expellees was established and its task was to further the process of integration. Its success can be measured by the fact that although the political grouping set up to represent their interests, the Block der Heimatvertriebenen und Entrechteten (BHE) was a political force in the early 1950s, by the early 1970s it had almost disappeared from the scene. The Ministry for Expellees was disbanded in 1969.

PETER BARKER

Regenbogenpresse

Regenbogenpresse (literally 'rainbow press') is the generic term given to the lower end of the German weekly magazine market. The name originates from their colourful reporting practices and prolific usage of photography. While much of the reporting is international in scope, human interest stories from within Germany also feature, mostly focusing on the lives of the rich and famous, scandals and diverse social indiscretions and personal infidelities. It was also known in the 1960s as the *Sorayapresse* because of its obsession with the wife of the then Shah of Persia.

See also: magazines; mass media: FRG

HOLGER BRIEL

Rehmann, Ruth

b. 1 June 1922, Siegburg

Writer

Rehmann began writing in the 1950s and has addressed such themes as individual isolation in *Illusionen* (Illusions) (1959), the question of guilt under National Socialism in *The Man in the Pulpit. Questions for a Father* (*Der Mann auf der Kanzel. Fragen an einen Vater*, 1979), and the Writers Congress of 1947 in *Unterwegs in fremden Träumen. Begegnungen mit dem anderen Deutschland* (Travelling in Foreign Dreams. Encounters With the Other Germany) (1993). As well as novels she has also produced a collection of short stories entitled *Paare* (Couples) (1978).

HELEN L. JONES

Reich, Jens

b. 26 March 1939, Göttingen

Molecular biologist and political activist

After studying medicine Reich became Professor of Biomathematics in East Berlin in 1980. Refusing to break off contact with West German citizens, he lost the post as Head of Department at the Central Institute for Molecular Biology in 1984. In 1988 he wrote a series of articles in *Lettre Internationale* under the pseudonym Thomas Asperger. After 1985 Reich joined various oppositional groups, co-founding the **Neues Forum** (NF) in 1989 and representing it in the Bündnis 90/Die Grünen parliamentary group in the *Volkskammer*. In

1994 he stood as an independent candidate for the federal presidency.

His publications include *Energy Metabolism Cell* (1981), *Rückkehr nach Europa* (Return to Europe) (1991) and *Abkehr von den Lebenslügen* (Leaving Life-Lies Behind) (1992).

BEATRICE HARPER

Reichart, Elisabeth

b. 19 November 1953, Steyregg (Austria)

Writer

Reichart studied history and German at the University of Salzburg and received a doctoral degree in 1983 after successfully defending a dissertation on the anti-fascist resistance movement in the lake district of Austria (Salzkammergut). She began her writing career in 1979, publishing in anthologies and journals as well as writing for radio. Austrian history, particularly as it relates to the Third Reich, provided the backdrop for her first two novels. Later novels are guided by the pursuit of the female perspective, as they pointedly reveal the inadequacies of language particularly as it relates to women in contemporary society.

CAROL ANNE COSTABILE-HEMING

Reichlin/Reinhart

The Reichlin/Reinhart architectural partnership was set up in 1970 by Bruno Reichlin and Fabio Reinhart. From 1972 to 1974 both were assistants to Aldo Rossi at the ETH (Technical University) Zürich.

Reichlin and Reinhart's architectural approach represents a synthesis between vernacular tradition and modern rationalist architecture. They became known with their villa designs that depend on Palladian motives, most of which are found in the Ticino (e.g. Sartori Haus, Riveo, Vallemaggia, 1976–7). The Motel Castello near Bellinzona (1988–91) is an example of their recent work.

MARTIN KUDLEK

Reich-Ranicki, Marcel

b. 2 June 1920, Włocławek (Poland)

Literary critic

Reich-Ranicki survived the Warsaw ghetto to become the – increasingly controversial – doyen of West German literary critics, invariably expressing his aesthetic and political preferences in a trenchant manner. Reich-Ranicki was one of the regular critics at meetings of the **Gruppe 47** between 1958 and 1967 and literary editor of the ***Frankfurter Allgemeine Zeitung*** from 1973 to 1988. He remains prominent through his appearances on the television programme *Das literarische Quartett*. Recent controversies include the storm in 1994 over alleged post-war espionage for Poland and reaction to his vehement rejection of **Grass**'s 1995 novel *Ein weites Feld* (A Wide Field).

STUART PARKES

Reimann, Aribert

b. 4 March 1936, Berlin

Composer and pianist

From 1955 to 1959 Reimann studied piano, harmony and counterpoint (under Pepping) and composition (under **Blacher**) at the Hochschule für Musik in West Berlin, also spending some of the final year in Vienna. Various operas and orchestral works have been published (mostly with Schott) but he also made his name as an accompanist to **Fischer-Dieskau**. Of his operas *Lear* (1978) is perhaps the best known.

DEREK McCULLOCH

Reimann, Brigitte

b. 21 July 1933, Burg (near Magdeburg); d. 20 February 1973, (East) Berlin

Writer

Among the most talented of the GDR's rising authors of the 1950s, Reimann came to prominence for the wrong reasons, through the success of her conformist story *Ankunft im Alltag* (Arrival in Everyday Life) (1961), promoted as an exemplary product of the **Bitterfelder Weg**. Her autobiographical novel *Franziska Linkerhand*, published in 1974 after her death from cancer has, in contrast, enjoyed enduring popularity in both parts of Germany as an authentic portrayal of a young architect's struggle to fulfil her potential in a male-dominated society.

See also: prose fiction: GDR

DENNIS TATE

Reinig, Christa

b. 6 August 1926, Berlin

Writer

Christa Reinig was born and brought up in a working-class district of East Berlin. After 1945 she became an office helper, a factory worker and then studied art history and Christian archaeology at the Humboldt University before moving permanently to the FRG in 1964, where she has been the recipient of many literary awards. A supporter of **feminism and the women's movement**, her move in that direction occurred around 1974. The catalyst was her great indignation at the trial of two lesbians accused of hiring someone to kill the husband of one of them. Reinig has since focused in her work on the deplorable treatment of women by society and become involved with more radical feminism, even though belonging to an older generation.

Reinig has written novels, stories, radio plays and is an excellent poet. Her early verse, written in the GDR, was considered politically suspect for its pessimism and feelings of estrangement. Her characters are outcasts and marginalized, and the inhuman situation they found themselves in ran counter to socialist ideology, hence the authorities banned her from further publication.

In her unusual autobiographical novel written in 1974, *Die himmlische und die irdische Geometrie* (Heavenly and Earthly Geometry), she objectifies herself by using dialogues between the philosopher Immanuel Kant and de Sade, Satan and J.S. Bach. The work is not linear, but consists of episodic associations. Reinig's sparkling powers of satire, irony, wit and black humour are clearly demonstrated in the complex structure of *Entmannung* (Emasculation) (1976) in which she expresses her concern about the physical and psychological violence perpetrated by men against women. The novel must be understood as a metaphor about what being a woman really means, as she cleverly reverses male and female roles.

None of Reinig's texts convey comforting messages or reassurances, although occasionally she voices hopes for an alternative future without violence. Her vision is uncompromising since she makes her readers ask themselves uncomfortable questions as she confronts them with the unexpected and unfamiliar. Reinig is a provocative writer who has sometimes been ridiculed and condemned as being unrealistic in her aims. Her concern is for a radical transformation of existing conditions. Women must create their own futures and not rely on traditional female characteristics to achieve their aims. To Reinig all is perfectly clear, and she does not attempt a theoretical recasting of the current situation.

A life-long interest in astrology has led her to explore the structures of mythic patterns in her narratives, in which she establishes a connection between contemporary life and **myth**. In *Die Frau im Brunnen* (The Woman in the Fountain) the tensions between two women, one devoted to mathematics and the other to the world of plants and animals, are used to explore the experience of fear and pain before the approach of death.

Further reading

Brügmann, M. (1986) *Amazonen der Literatur*, Amsterdam: Rodopi (includes a study of *Entmannung*).

Puknus, H. (ed.) (1980) *Neue Literatur der Frauen*, Munich: Beck (contains a short but perceptive essay on Reinig).

PETER PROCHNIK

Reinshagen, Gerlind

b. 4 May 1926, Königsberg

Writer

Reinshagen's work engages critically yet poetically with a society blind to its own deformations. The 1976 play *Sonntagskinder* (Sunday's Children), a child's-eye view of everyday life in Nazi Germany, reveals the disastrous results of opportunism and political naïvety. Workplace settings, for instance in the novel *Rovinato* (1981) and the play *Ironheart – Eisenherz* (1982), contrast with texts interweaving memory, fantasy and reality, in plays like *Die Clownin* (The Clown) (1986) and *Medea bleibt* (Medea stays) (1995), and the Berlin novel *Die flüchtige Braut* (The Runaway Bride) (1984).

Further reading

Kiencke-Wagner, J. (1989) *Das Werk von Gerlind Reinshagen*, Frankfurt am Main, Munich, Bern, New York and Paris: Lang.

MORAY McGOWAN

Reisekader

Kader (cadres) in the **SED** in the GDR were, in accordance with Marxist–Leninist principles, the leading individuals, functionaries and specialists in all areas of GDR life. *Reisekader* (travelling cadres) were the representatives of the SED and other institutions in the GDR who were allowed to travel abroad, particularly to non-socialist countries, to represent their institutions. In the GDR, where the right to foreign travel, except to a small number of socialist countries, was a privilege, only those representatives who were regarded as politically reliable, although not necessarily members of the SED, were accorded the status of *Reisekader*.

PETER BARKER

Reiser, Rio

b. 9 January 1950, (West) Berlin; d. 20 August 1996, Fresenhagen

Singer, lyricist and actor (real name Ralph Möbius)

In the late 1960s, Reiser founded the band Ton Steine Scherben: it became known for its agitprop lyrics and for jump-starting German-language rock music. Reiser's slogans '*Keine Macht für niemand*' ('no power to no one') and '*Macht kaputt was euch kaputt macht*' ('destroy what destroys you') entered everyday speech. In 1985, Reiser began a solo career in mainstream pop. He wrote songs for musicals and other pop singers and acted occasionally. He remained politically active for gay rights and as a member of the **PDS**.

Recordings

Reiser, R. (1971) *Warum geht es mir so dreckig?*
—— (1972) *Keine Macht für niemand.*
—— (1986) *Rio I*, Columbia
—— (1995) *Himmel und Hölle*, Columbia

SABINE SCHMIDT

Reitz, Edgar

b. 1 November 1932, Morbach (Hunsrück)

Filmmaker

A co-signatory of the Oberhausen Manifesto, his early work comprised experimental shorts such as *Speed* (*Geschwindigkeit*, 1962). His first feature, *Meal Times* (*Mahlzeiten*, 1967), a portrait of an independent young woman, established the meticulous realist style which has characterized his subsequent work. The eleven-hour cinema and television series *Heimat* (1984), a novelistic chronicle of life in a Hunsrück village between 1919 and 1982, was an enormous success worldwide, and was followed by *Heimat – The Second Generation* (*Die zweite Heimat*, 1993), a semi-autobiographical study of students in Munich during the 1960s.

See also: *Heimat*; New German Cinema

MARTIN BRADY

Republikaner

In 1995, because of xenophobic tendencies and contacts with neo-nazis, the Republikaner were declared a right-wing extremist party with anti-constitutional aims by the Bundesamt für Verfassungchutz (the German equivalent to MI5). Founded in 1983 in Bavaria, they enjoyed a short spell of relative popularity between 1989 and 1992, capitalizing on the **asylum** debate. Under the charismatic leadership of Franz Schönhuber (replaced in 1994), they gained seats in the European Parliament and the *Land* parliaments of Berlin and Baden-Württemberg with 7.1, 7.5, and 10.9 percent of the vote respectively. After achieving only 1.9 percent in the federal election of 1994, they have experienced diminishing political significance.

Further reading

Jaschke, H.G. (1994) *Die Republikaner. Profile einer Rechtsaußen-Partei*, Bonn: J.H.W. Dietz.

MONIKA PRÜTZEL-THOMAS

Reschke, Karin

b. 17 September 1940, Krakow (Poland)

Writer and actress

Reschke became an actress after breaking off her study of German literature in Munich. She also worked as a radio intern and contributor to several magazines and newspapers. She published her first prose in 1980, the autobiographically-inflected *Memoiren eines Kindes* (A Child's Memoirs), and has worked as a freelance writer since 1984. Her works address the personal development of women and the obstacles with which society confronts them. Her biggest success was *Findebuch der Henriette Vogel* (1982), a fictional diary of Henriette Vogel, who committed suicide with Heinrich von Kleist.

MARTINA S. ANDERSON

Richter, Gerhard

b. 9 February 1932, Dresden

Painter

Richter studied in Dresden and, from 1961, in Düsseldorf. One of the most successful and eclectic painters of the FRG, he co-founded 'capitalist realism' (1963), initially painting banal images (often lifted from newspapers) in a pop-influenced, photorealist style. Consistently cool and analytical, his subsequent output has seen abrupt stylistic and thematic shifts, and included *48 Portraits* (1971–2) based on encyclopedia photographs, colour charts (from 1966), cityscapes (from 1968), grey monochromes, cloud and *memento mori* paintings, superrealist and soft-focus portraits and landscapes, and vast, brilliantly coloured, gestural abstractions.

See also: painting

MARTIN BRADY

Richter, Hans Werner

b. 12 November 1908, Usedom; d. 23 March 1993, Munich

Writer and journalist

One of the personalities most closely associated with post-1945 cultural recovery in western Germany, Richter is remembered primarily for his efforts to revive the practices of political and literary criticism. His most celebrated contribution to this was the founding of the **Gruppe 47**. Originally a book dealer by trade, Richter had an erratic period of adjustment to the Third Reich. His involvement with the Communist Party, his subsequent ejection from it, his brief spell in exile and his attempts at resistance are early testimony to his active but non-conformist politics. He served with the German army from 1940 until 1943, when he was taken prisoner by American troops in Italy. In camp in the US, he became involved in the psychological warfare programme, eventually contributing to a journal for German PoWs, *Der Ruf* (The Call). On his return in 1946, the publication was relaunched as an American-licensed contribution to **re-education** in Germany. Together with fellow editor Alfred **Andersch**, he presided over the journal's hostile approach to **denazification** policies and, possibly as a result of this, both lost their licence to edit in 1947. Richter, whose objection to the theory of collective guilt had already caused friction with the PoW publication, was seen as the more political of the two editors, and his efforts to introduce another journal, *Der Skorpion* (The Scorpion), were quashed by the licensing authorities. His criticism of fellow Germans exposed him to further attack, and dismissal of his middle-ground politics of the time as naïve and idealistic still prevails. Within Gruppe 47, Richter became a significant promoter of post-war literary development and 'father' of West German literary criticism. His passionate commitment to free exchange of critical ideas and the positive response to this among other writers ensured the survival of the group as a regular forum, and Richter as its convener, until the late 1960s.

Richter's own literary output has to some extent been overshadowed by these political and often controversial distinctions, but it underlines the nature of his concerns. His 1949 novel *Die Geschlagenen* (The Vanquished) draws on his own experience, relating the capture of a German soldier in Italy and his subsequent internment in the US. Significantly, the novel reflects both Richter's distinction between the ordinary soldier and political authority and his concern with anti-war literature. Similarly, the 1951 novel *Sie fielen aus Gottes Hand* (They Fell From the Hand of God) uses the background of war and camp life in a cautionary way. His early works, then, are clearly influenced by wartime experiences, and while later texts depart from this, all are set in twentieth-century Germany.

Richter continued to flout political conformism, for instance in his well-publicized meetings with East German writers and simultaneous condemnation of the repressive regime. Preoccupied always with the role of the writer in society, he figured in the West German media until his death.

Further reading

Embacher, E. (1985) *Hans Werner Richter: Zum literarischen Werk und zum politisch-publizistischen Wirken eines engagierten deutschen Schriftstellers*, Frankfurt am Main, Bern and New York: Lang.

Neunzig, H.A. (ed.) (1979) *Hans Werner Richter und die Gruppe 47*, Munich: Nymphenburger.

Nickel, A. (1994) *Hans Werner Richter – Ziehvater der Gruppe 47*, Stuttgart: Heinz.

CLARE FLANAGAN

Richter, Karl

b. 15 October 1926, Plauen; d. 15 February 1981, Munich

Conductor, organist and harpsichordist

A product of the Leipzig tradition of Bach interpretation, Richter settled in Munich in 1951, where he founded the Munich Bach Orchestra and Chorus. His rigorous performance criteria and unfussy interpretations set the standard in the playing and singing of Bach's music, especially his Passions and Cantatas, for most of the late 1950s and 1960s, only to be superseded by the exploratory innovations of the period instrument movement, as exemplified by **Harnoncourt**.

BEATRICE HARPER

Riefenstahl, Leni

b. 22 August 1902, Berlin

Filmmaker, photographer, writer and actress (real name Berta Helene Amalie Riefenstahl)

With *Triumph of the Will* (*Triumph des Willens*, 1935) and *Olympiad* (*Olympia*, 1938) Riefenstahl established her reputation as a documentary filmmaker. Her feature films received less attention. After WWII, she concentrated on photography, spending time in Africa and publishing books about the Nubian people. In her seventies, she took up scuba diving and worked in underwater photography. Often criticized for being non-apologetic about her past, Riefenstahl still enjoys international critical acclaim as a director and photographer.

Further reading

Riefenstahl, L. (1991) *Leni Riefenstahl: A Memoir*, New York: St Martin's Press (autobiography).

The Wonderful, Horrible Life of Leni Riefenstahl (British documentary film, 1993).

Salkeld, A. (1996) *A Portrait of Leni Riefenstahl*, London: Jonathan Cape (biography).

SABINE SCHMIDT

Riemann, Katja

b. 1 November 1964, Bremen

Film and television actress

After beginning her career in theatre and television, Riemann proved herself to be a prolific actress in a series of romantic comedies in the early 1990s, the dominant film genre of the period in German mainstream cinema. She starred in many of the most commercially successful films of this time, such as Katja von Garnier's *Making Up!* (*Abgeschminkt!*, 1992), Sönke **Wortmann**'s *The Most Desired Man* (*Der bewegte Mann*, 1994) and Rainer Kaufmann's *Talk of the Town* (*Stadtgespräch*, 1995).

JONATHAN LEGG

Rihm, Wolfgang

b. 13 March 1952, Karlsruhe

Composer

A product of the Darmstadt Summer Courses, Rihm soon established himself as one of the most brilliant composers of his generation. His challenging chamber opera *Jakob Lenz* (1978) has become the most performed of contemporary music-theatre works in Germany, and later operas, such as *Hamlet-Maschine* (1986), based on a play by Heiner **Müller**, have confirmed the intensity of his response to text. His chamber music reveals a Schumannesque obsessiveness and romanticism within a completely modern language.

BEATRICE HARPER

Rilling, Helmuth

b. 29 May 1933, Stuttgart

Conductor and church musician

Rilling's early studies were at the Musikhochschule in Stuttgart with Nepomuk David and Hans Grischkat. He came to prominence with his chamber choir, the Gächinger Kantorei, consisting mainly of fellow students, named after the village in the Schwäbische Alb where the twenty singers met to rehearse. Many of these formed the backbone of the Figuralchor of the Gedächtniskirche in Stuttgart, where he became organist in 1957. Other appointments – many of them at one time running concurrently – included the Kirchenmusikschule in Spandau (West Berlin) and the Musikhochschule in Frankfurt am Main. In 1965 he founded the Bach-Collegium in Stuttgart as an instrumental ensemble for performances and recordings with his Stuttgart choirs. An outstanding choral conductor, he has a penchant for a suave, legato style of performance which has placed his many Bach recordings in the 'romantic' camp, apparently untouched by the 'authentic' movement in the performance of eighteenth-century music.

DEREK McCULLOCH

Rinser, Luise

b. 30 April 1911, Pitzling (Bavaria)

Writer

Banned from writing in 1940 and imprisoned by the Nazis in 1944, Rinser was married to the composer Carl **Orff** from 1954 to 1959. Her first publication after the war was a *Gefängnistagebuch* (Prison Diary) (1946), followed by *Jan Lobel from Warsaw* (*Jan Lobel aus Warschau*, 1947), the story of an escaped Jewish prisoner. Her later novels depict, often from a woman's perspective, the struggle for personal freedom and responsibility and reflect her own brand of religious humanism in their criticism of post-war materialism. Her work raises moral issues involving love and marriage, religious faith, guilt and redemption.

MARGARET VALLANCE

rock music

Rock music in Germany developed under the shadow of Anglo-American rock. The groups which emerged in the mid- to late 1960s, such as Can, Amon Düül, Tangerine Dream and Guru Guru, to name but a few, modelled themselves on Pink Floyd and the Grateful Dead, tended to sing songs in English, and played a hallucinatory brand of drone rock. While commercial success was fleeting (and even as late as 1989 domestic product only accounted for about one third of total music sales in Germany), many of these groups exercised a lasting influence on the underground and alternative rock scene at home and abroad.

The 1970s brought with them two major breakthroughs for German Rock Music. On the one hand, there was Udo **Lindenberg** and his Panikorchester singing ironic rock songs in German, which paved the way for German language pop music separate from the hyper-kitsch **Schlager** tradition. On the other hand was **Kraftwerk** – an electronic band which combined the spacey synth-rock of Tangerine Dream with the avant-garde sensibility of the German classical tradition, especially the work of Karlheinz **Stockhausen**. Kraftwerk is by far the most important German Rock band of all time, having spawned followers and imitators in the realm of disco, new wave, punk, hip-hop, rap, techno and ambient music.

In the 1980s a number of groups continued in the pioneering footsteps of Udo Lindenberg producing rock in German both in and out of the mainstream. First and foremost among these bands is the 'kölschrock' band **BAP**. Nena, Marius Müller Westernhagen and Herbert Grönemeyer also belong in this tradition. On the alternative side of things, the *Neue Deutsche Welle* (new German wave) brought forth groups singing in German but with a more (or less) anti-commercial sensibility. Important groups and singers from this period are Nina **Hagen**, Fehlfarben, Ideal, Trio and Die **Toten Hosen**.

Initially criticized as a symptom of western decadence, rock music in East Germany was cautiously allowed to evolve under the watchful eye of the **FDJ** during the 1970s. Though some groups were able to achieve an amount of local notoriety, among them the **Puhdys** and Pankow,

East German rockers either had to emigrate, as in the case of Nina **Hagen**, or wait for the fall of the Berlin Wall to get their due. The Leipzig-based group, Die Prinzen, have been the most successful in this regard.

The end of the Cold War and the collapse of the Berlin Wall ushered in a new era for German rock music with a proliferation of musical styles. Germany has its share of techno bands (KMFDM being one of the best known), alternative rock bands (Tocotronic, first and foremost), and hip-hop bands (die fantastischen Vier), not to mention more notorious right-wing bands like the Böhsen Onkelz. Now, as before, international success depends on a band's willingness or interest to sing in English, but the German scene has enough history to actually support bands who sing to Germans in German about life in Germany.

See also: Krautrock

MATTHEW T. GRANT

Rosbaud, Hans

b. 22 July 1895, Graz; d. 29 December 1962, Lugano

Conductor

As Chief Conductor of the Südwestfunk Baden-Baden Orchestra (1948–62), Rosbaud premièred many scores by the leading members of the European post-war generation – for example, Pierre Boulez's *Le Marteau sans Maître* – which renewed German creative musical thinking in the post-war period. In 1954 he led the world première of Schönberg's unfinished opera *Moses und Aron*. His unostentatious conducting style and passionate objectivity has been a great influence, and his creative example is often cited by such eminent practitioners as Boulez and Christoph von Dohnanyi.

BEATRICE HARPER

Roth, Friederike

b. 6 April 1948, Sindelfingen

Writer

Roth earned her doctorate in linguistics and philosophy in Stuttgart (with a dissertation on the aesthetics of Georg Simmel) in 1975. From 1976 to 1979 she taught anthropology and sociology at the Fachhochschule Esslingen. Since 1979 she has worked as a dramatic producer for the SDR (South German Radio). She writes poetry, prose, *Hörspiele* (radio plays) and drama. She is known for her use of language, which some critics identify as 'feminine'. Her works explore philosophical questions and tensions between elevated and colloquial language. Major themes include feminist concerns, sexual relationships, death and other aspects of contemporary life.

MARTINA S. ANDERSON

Roth, Gerhard

b. 24 June 1942, Graz

Writer

Shaped by his experiences as a medical student and computer worker, Roth's protagonists inhabit the margins between normality and madness. Their futile attempts to order the exhausting stream of impressions and information without becoming perceptually deadened are often described in a clinical, scientific tone, as in *The Autobiography of Albert Einstein* (*die autobiographie des albert einstein*, 1971). Roth's seven-part cycle about life in the Austrian provinces includes his masterpiece *Landläufiger Tod* (Ordinary Death) (1984) about the mute Franz Lindner reinventing the world as a microcosm of natural and human village history.

JUDITH LEEB

Round Table

The Round Table was the model of grass-roots democracy established at every level of GDR society following the collapse of the SED regime, as a forum for working out the political institutions of a revitalized state. The central Runder Tisch, which met every week in Berlin between 7 December 1989 and 12 March 1990, included representatives from **Modrow**'s provisional government, other political parties, citizens' movements and the churches (see also **citizens' movements: GDR**). It drafted more than a hundred bills, including a social charter and a democratic constitution, but its work was largely ignored by the **Volkskammer** elected on 18 March, which paved the way for rapid unification.

DENNIS TATE

Rowohlt-Verlag

A quality publisher and a major participant in post-war German literature, the Rowohlt-Verlag was founded by Ernst Rowohlt in 1908. Reconstituted in 1945 and led by Heinrich Maria Ledig-Rowohlt, it moved to its own building in Reinbek near Hamburg in 1960. Rowohlt has published works of important German writers (e.g. Fallada, **Rühmkorf**, Toller and Tucholsky) and provided Germany with translations of major figures of modern world literature (e.g. Pinter, Durrell, Camus and Balzac). Various paperback series, such as the '*ro-ro-ro monographien*', provide an important source of practical information. The firm is now part of the Holtzbrinck publishing group.

JOHN B. RUTLEDGE

Rühmann, Heinz

b. 7 March 1902, Essen; d. 3 October 1994, Berg (Starnberger See)

Film actor and director

Rühmann directed a number of films, including *Briefträger Müller* (Postman Müller) (1953), but is better known as a comic actor who appeared in over a hundred films in a career spanning some sixty-seven years. Rühmann first shot to fame in *Die Drei von der Tankstelle* (Three from the Petrol Station) (1930). His on-screen persona was typically that of the down-trodden 'little man' struggling against adversity, a role he fulfilled most notably in *The Good Soldier Schweyk* (*Der brave Soldat Schwejk*) (1960). His best-known films include *Quax der Bruchpilot* (Quax, the Crash-Happy Pilot) (1941) and *Die Feuerzangenbowle* (The Punchbowl) (1944).

SEÁN ALLAN

Rühmkorf, Peter

b. 25 October 1929, Dortmund

Writer

Rühmkorf is the maverick virtuoso among the writers of his generation. His early poetry already shows improvisatory brilliance in relation to the canon. Through parody and techniques of variation Rühmkorf updates Eichendorff, Heine, Holz and **Benn**. Since *Irdisches Vergnügen in g* (Earthly Delight in g[ravity]) (1959) rhyming forms have been accompanied by free verse with a conversational tone. *Kunststücke* (Tricks) (1962) includes an essay theorizing parody and contradiction as techniques through which a poem's relation to the past give it critical force.

Poetry has a political dimension according to Rühmkorf both because it acts as a lie-detector in relation to contemporary slang, clichés or catch-phrases, and because it can provide a model of social coherence. Genuinely popular verse, from the walls of public lavatories or in the scurrilous rhymes of schoolchildren, is revealed as a subversive force in the anthology *Über das Volksvermögen* (On the Power of the People/On the National Wealth) (1967). But poetry also involves a commitment to personal experience and sensuality. The two spheres are strictly separated in Rühmkorf's poetics, which he calls a theory of 'schizography' – writing split between the personal and the political.

The personal takes many forms. Three self-portraits provide landmarks in his work: the first in 1958, the next in 1978 in *Haltbar bis Ende 1999* (Use by end 1999); the third 'Selbst III/88' (Self III/88) is a prescient meditation on growing older in a German landscape which seeks new kinds of integration through the sensual and the sexual. (The tumultuous year 1968, he has said, was too preoccupied with street politics to encourage self-portraiture.) Rühmkorf's diaries from 1989 to 1991, *TABU I*, published in 1995 represent his fullest attempt to register personal alienation from the politics of **unification**. In many poems, however, personal pleasure is celebrated in sex, alcohol and what Rühmkorf calls 'experimenting with the world via every available orifice'.

The political dimension of Rühmkorf's work mounts a broad polemic against the (West) German establishment, both political and artistic. His critical career began in the student paper *Zwischen den Kriegen* (Between the Wars) edited with his friend Werner Riegel, and continued with contributions to the Hamburg *Studentenkurier* (Student Courier), later *konkret*. The pseudonymous column *Leslie Meiers Lyrikschlachthof* (Leslie Meier's Lyric Slaughterhouse) attacked the quietism, modishness and technical incompetence of contemporary poetry. Reviving the **Gruppe 47** boycott of the 1960s, Rühmkorf was active in the **PEN** and **Verband deutscher Schriftsteller** campaign against the **Springer** press in the early 1980s.

Three plays as well as the 'enlightened' fairytales of *Der Hüter des Misthaufens* (The Keeper of the Dunghill) (1983) extend his political critique to other forms. Rühmkorf's achievement is to hold together polemic and personal celebration in writing which increasingly registers the vicissitudes and *ressentiments* of a self-confessed pessimist.

Further reading

Durzak, M. and Steinicke, H. (eds) (1989) *Und sie bewegt sich doch*, Reinbek bei Hamburg: Rowohlt (important collection of critical essays).

Rühmkorf, P. (1992) *Komm raus!*, ed. K. Wagenbach, Berlin: Wagenbach (a broad selection of poems, critical essays and polemics).

ANTHONY PHELAN

Runge, Erika

b. 22 January 1939, Halle

Television producer and writer

A specialist in 'transcript literature', Runge produced *Bottroper Protokolle* (Bottrop Transcripts)

(1968) and *Frauen. Versuche zur Emanzipation* (Wo-men. Attempts at Emancipation) (1969), the latter containing texts in which women talk to the interviewer about their lives in response to questions about how successful West German law has been in implementing sexual equality. In *Eine Reise nach Rostock, DDR* (A Journey to Rostock, GDR) (1971) men and women living in the district of Rostock talk about various aspects of their lives. In *Berliner Liebesgeschichten* (Berlin Love Stories) (1987) the topic is love.

MARGARET VALLANCE

S

Sachs, Nelly

b. 10 December 1891, Berlin; d. 12 May 1970, Stockholm

Writer

With Paul **Celan**, Sachs is the most important representative of German **Holocaust** literature. She emigrated to Stockholm in 1940, where she wrote mainly poetry about the persecution of the Jewish people – the suffering of both victims and survivors – as in *In den Wohnungen des Todes* (In the Houses of Death) (1947). For a selection of her poetry in English translation see *O the Chimneys* (1967). Despite an identification with the victims, the author writes in a conciliatory tone which tries to discover an eschatological glimpse of hope even in the horrors of the Holocaust. In 1966, she was awarded the Nobel Prize for literature.

See also: *Vergangenheitsbewältigung*

CHRISTIANE SCHÖNFELD

Saiko, George Emmanuel

b. 5 February 1892, Seestadtl (Bohemia; now Ervěnice, Czech Republic); d. 23 December 1962, Rekawinkel (Lower Austria)

Writer

Despite his modest œuvre, principally two novels, *Auf dem Floß* (On the Raft) (1948) and *Der Mann im Schilf* (The Man in the Reeds) (1955), and two collections of short stories, Saiko remains a major figure in contemporary Austrian writing. His works are associated with the magic realism school, in which the chaotic and irrational are given form and therefore a measure of rationality. The writer is seen to be equipped no less than the psychiatrist to articulate consciously those forces that would otherwise remain hidden.

ANTHONY BUSHELL

Salzburg Festival

Inaugurated in 1920 with Hofmannsthal's *Jedermann* produced by Max Reinhardt, the Salzburg Festival had become an important international event by the next decade. When Toscanini withdrew from the **Bayreuth Festival** because of its Nazi associations and subsequent ban on Jewish artists in 1933, it was to Salzburg that he came. Though the post-war festival has seen such important premieres as the operas *Die Liebe der Danae* by Richard **Strauß** (1952) and *The Bassarids* by **Henze** (1966), the focus of attention has been on expensively cast and conservatively staged operas, especially, and understandably, by Mozart. Conductors Wilhelm **Furtwängler** and Herbert von **Karajan** were the dominant figures. After Karajan's death (1989) attempts have been made to alter this balance, to the dismay of Salzburg's ostentatiously gourmet public.

BEATRICE HARPER

Salzburger Nachrichten

This Austrian daily paper, published in Salzburg, was founded by the American military authorities in 1945 to cater for western Austria. Handed over to Austrian owners in autumn 1945, it has become one of the most respected independent broadsheets in Austria. It is traditional in its set-up, but famous for the quality of its style. Originally a regional publication, it has also introduced a national edition to compete with the main dailies published in Vienna. With its daily print run of around 100,000 copies (1998) it is on a par with the quality papers *Die **Presse*** and *Der **Standard***.

GEORG HELLMAYR

Sander, Helke

b. 31 January 1937, Berlin

Filmmaker

One of the first women filmmakers in the FRG to train at a film college (the Berlin dffb), she prepared the ground for the success of women's film in the 1980s, co-organizing the Women's Film Seminar in Berlin in 1973, and founding the journal *Frauen und Film* (Women and Film) in 1974. Her semi-autobiographical feminist features, including *The All-Round Reduced Personality* (*Die allseitig reduzierte Persönlichkeit – REDUPERS*, 1977) and *The Subjective Factor* (*Der subjektive Faktor*, 1981), focus on women's struggle for expression and equality.

See also: film: FRG; feminism and the women's movement

HELEN HUGHES

Sander, Jill

b. 27 November 1943, Wesselburen (Holstein)

Fashion designer

Sander's designs are often called 'minimalist', but the Hamburg-based designer prefers the word 'pure'. Her styles have catered exclusively to an internationally upscale clientele since her first 'Jill

Sander' store outside Germany was set up on Paris's Avenue Montaigne in 1993 – emphasizing beauty and elegance over originality, and with price tags to match. What sets Sander apart from many designers is, first, that she is publicly traded, and second, an extreme measure of obsession with managing her image. The stores that carry her have a strict line to toe when it comes to display and merchandizing, including paying for the in-store shops. In the mid-1990s she dramatically reduced her US retailers because some of the stores were not doing it exactly the way she wanted it done.

ADRIAN MURDOCH

Sanderling, Kurt

b. 19 September 1912, Arys (East Prussia)

Conductor

At the age of twenty-one Sanderling worked for the Städtische Oper in Berlin as a répétiteur, but was soon forced by the political situation to leave Germany. He moved to Moscow, where he was engaged almost immediately by the Moscow Radio Symphony Orchestra, first as guest, then as resident conductor. In 1941 he took over the Leningrad Philharmonic Orchestra. After almost twenty years he finally returned to Germany, first conducting the (East) Berlin Symphony Orchestra before becoming chief conductor of the Dresdner Staatskapelle. Thereafter he was in much demand throughout Europe, conducting in London the Gewandhausorchester in 1970 and returning to conduct the New Philharmonic Orchestra from 1972. His interpretation of the romantic and early twentieth-century repertoire won him particular acclaim.

DEREK McCULLOCH

Sanders-Brahms, Helma

b. 20 November 1940, Emden

Filmmaker

Sanders-Brahms is a director of emotionally charged fiction films about women, which owe a stylistic debt to Rainer Werner **Fassbinder**. She first reached a wide audience with the television drama *Shirin's Wedding* (*Shirins Hochzeit*, 1976) focusing on the fate of a Turkish woman in Germany. Her most celebrated film, *Germany, Pale Mother* (*Deutschland, bleiche Mutter*, 1979–80), is a compelling and semi-autobiographical piece of feminist mourning, retelling the history of Germany during and after WWII from a woman's perspective. She subsequently directed European co-productions (*Laputa*, 1986), and is active as a polemicist.

See also: New German Cinema; film: FRG

HELEN HUGHES

satire

This mode of representation finds narrative expression in literature, drama, film, television and cabaret, as well as in journalism and in the fine arts (graphic arts, paintings and sketches). Sarcasm, ridicule, irony, the grotesque, etc. serve as means of indirect criticism of and attack on individuals, moral or political opinions, events, social conditions and ideologies.

Satire always stands in a close critical relationship to a given socio-political context. As a connotative mode, it depends upon the common socialization and cultural background of both artist and audience, as it invites the latter's complicity in recognizing and responding to subtextual meaning, cloaked in such formal distortion as comical exaggeration and dramatic excess. Through the assessment of cultural products that have utilized the satirical mode in various eras and political and national regimes, it is possible to draw concrete conclusions about the status of the public sphere and possibilities for social criticism in the respective time and place, and gather information about contemporary values, mores, social constraints and conflicts.

Within narrative forms of representation satire is often employed concurrent with other modalities such as humour or melodrama. Examples of literary satire in the FRG after 1945 include Günter **Grass**'s *The Tin Drum* (*Die Blechtrommel*, 1959), Martin **Walser**'s *Ehen in Philippsburg* (Mar-

riages in Philippsburg) (1957) and Heinrich **Böll**'s *The Clown* (*Ansichten eines Clowns*, 1963). Satirical novels from the GDR include Fritz Rudolf **Fries**'s *Der Weg nach Obliadooh* (The Way to Obliadooh) (1966), Volker **Braun**'s *Hinze-Kunze-Roman* (The Hinze-Kunze-Novel) (1985) and Thomas **Brussig**'s *Helden wie wir* (Heroes Like Us) (1995) – a satirical account of life in the GDR that appeared following German unification. Exemplary of satire in the dramatic genre is Max **Frisch**'s *The Fire Raisers* (*Biedermann und die Brandstifter*) (Switzerland 1958; originally produced in 1953 as a radio play), and in television the author and satirist Dieter **Hildebrandt** with his television series *Notizen aus der Provinz* (Notes from the Countryside) (FRG: **ZDF**, 1973–9), and *Scheibenwischer* (Windscreen Wiper) (FRG: **ARD**, beginning in 1980).

Political **cabaret** is the most prevalent medium for satire. Well-known contributions to post-war cabaret include *Die Hinterbliebenen* (The Bereaved) (Bad Reichenhall, 1945–9), and *Frischer Wind* (Fresh Air) (1946–9); later prominent samples from West German political cabaret are *Die Stachelschweine* (The Porcupines) (West Berlin, 1949–present), *Münchner Lach- und Schießgesellschaft* (Munich Society for Laughter and Shooting) (1956–present), *Rationaltheater* (Munich) (1965–94) and ***Floh de Cologne*** (Flea de Cologne) (1966–83). The most important cabarets produced in the GDR and still running today are *Die Distel* (The Thistle) (East Berlin, founded in 1953) (see also **Distel, Die**), *academixer* (Leipzig) (founded in 1966), *Die Pfeffermühle* (The Peppermill) (Leipzig, founded in 1954) and *Herkuleskeule* (Hercules' Mace) (Dresden, founded in 1954).

Important satirical magazines in the FRG are *Simplicissimus* (1954–67, a successor of the first *Simplicissimus* which was founded in 1896 and discontinued in 1944), *Pardon* (1962–82) and *Titanic* (beginning in 1979). In the GDR, *Frischer Wind* (Fresh Air) (founded 1946) was succeeded in 1954 by *Eulenspiegel*.

Further reading

Gaier, U. (1967) *Satire: Studien zu Neidhart, Wittenwiler, Brant und zur satirischen Schreibart*, Tübingen: Niemeyer (still provides the most prevalent working definition of satirical writing in close correspondence with its socio-political context).

Jacobs, D. (1996) *Untersuchungen zum DDR-Berufskabarett der Ära Honecker*, Frankfurt am Main: Lang (the political function of East German cabaret and prevalent topics addressed in the 1970s and 1980s as illustrated through the study of four political cabarets in the GDR).

SYLVIA KLÖTZER

Sawallisch, Wolfgang

b. 26 August 1923, Munich

Conductor and pianist

Sawallisch held the posts of Musical Director and later General Director of the Bavarian State Opera (1971–93), and was active as an opera and symphonic conductor internationally. Like **Böhm**, he is an outstanding exponent of Wagner and Richard **Strauß**, in which respect he is regarded as an upholder of traditional values. His running of the Bavarian State Opera was seen as exemplary in this regard. Since 1993 he has been Musical Director of the Philadelphia Orchestra.

BEATRICE HARPER

Schädlich, Hans Joachim

b. 8 October 1935, Reichenbach (Saxony)

Writer

Unable to publish in the GDR, Schädlich moved to the West following the **Biermann Affair**, where his 1977 work *Versuchte Nähe* (Attempted Proximity) was widely praised. Since unification he has been extremely critical of former GDR colleagues and remains best known as a former dissident, with less attention being paid to the challenging aesthetic and linguistic dimensions of his work.

Further reading

Bond, D.G. (1996) ' "Die Suche nach dem Was und dem Wie": Hans Joachim Schädlich', in A. Williams, S. Parkes and J. Preece (eds), *Con-*

temporary German Writers, Their Aesthetics and Their Language, Bern: Peter Lang.

STUART PARKES

Schall, Ekkehard

b. 29 May 1930, Magdeburg

Actor

Schall studied acting in Magdeburg, worked in 1948 in Frankfurt an der Oder, and joined the **Berliner Ensemble** in 1952. He is best known for high-profile, sly, 'dialectical' roles in Brecht plays (e.g. Arturo Ui, Puntila, Azdak, Galileo and Coriolanus). He has had film roles as Eilif in *Mutter Courage und ihre Kinder* (Mother Courage and Her Children), and in *Der arme Hassan* (Poor Hassan), *Berlin – Ecke Schönhauser* (Berlin, Corner of Schönhauser Boulevard), *Wolf unter Wölfen* (Wolf Among Wolves), *Die Bestie* (The Beast), and in *Wagner*. From 1977 to 1991 he was Acting Artistic Director at the Berliner Ensemble. He received an OBIE for 'An Evening with Ekkehard Schall' (New York, 1985). He is married to Brecht's daughter Barbara (1930–).

RICHARD J. RUNDELL

Schami, Rafik

b. 23 June 1946, Damascus (Syria)

Writer

Rafik Schami was already active as a writer before his emigration to Germany in 1971. In Syria he wrote short prose, songs and plays. He was the publisher and co-author of a wall news-sheet in the old quarter of Damascus until it was banned in 1969. He went to Germany to study and work. Since 1982 he has been a professional writer. As the son of Aramaic Christians, Schami had to face the consequences of a minority existence at a very early age. These experiences continued in West Germany, although in a modified way, and form the main theme of his writing.

Schami falls back upon his preferred genre of 'alternative' tales to present the problems of ethnic minorities in German society. His writing style takes up the eastern traditions of verbal narrative, yet produces a clear reference to German reality and follows an informative and critical path, appealing to the German majority to see engagement with foreigners as a valuable way of gaining knowledge and to recognize the right of minorities to their 'otherness'. With regard to the minority the stories attempt to emancipate, by clarifying the dangers of assimilation and representing solidarity and willingness to learn as successful strategies for the changing of power relationships. As a leading figure in PoLiKunst and the publishing group Südwind Schami attaches a significant role to literature in the fight for minority rights. The revolutionary force of literature is represented metaphorically in his tale *Südwind*, in which the dividing wall between a rich land-owner and a poor farming family is brought down by being dug under.

From 1985 Schami turns explicitly to children's literature, because he believes that the children's imagination and their sense of justice can be a powerful means of correcting society. He also pays close attention to the representation of his own childhood memories, to make up the information deficit of the German readership with regard to the social, cultural and political situation in Syria, as in *Eine Hand voller Sterne* (A Hand Full of Stars) (1987).

The art of story-telling is a another theme which can be followed through all of Schami's work. It is depicted as an effective non-violent means in the fight against the powerful and against the advance of purely consumption-oriented ways of communication, for instance in *Erzähler der Nacht* (Narrators of the Night) (1989). The author intends to demonstrate the subversive power of verbal narrative by telling his tales openly in direct contact with his German-speaking public.

The socially critical presentation of German society, a fairytale style of writing, and an oriental performance style have contributed to the enormous success of Schami's texts on the German book market and by doing so have raised the recognition level of migrant writing. On the other hand they have unintentionally promoted the acceptance of texts by Arab writers as an exotic enrichment of German national literature.

See also: migrant literature

Further reading

Reeg, U. (1988) *Schreiben in der Fremde. Literatur nationaler Minderheiten in der Bundesrepublik Deutschland*, Essen: Klartext-Verlag.
Tantow, L. (1988) 'Rafik Schami', in H.L. Arnold (ed.) *Kritisches Lexikon zur deutschsprachigen Gegenwartsliteratur Band 7*, Munich: edition text + kritik.

SABINE FISCHER

Scharoun, Hans

b. 20 September 1893, Bremen; d. 25 November 1972, (West) Berlin

Architect

Scharoun studied at the TH (Technical University) Charlottenburg, Berlin (1912 to 1915), and was in private practice in Insterberg (1919–25) and Berlin (1932–72), before holding the positions of City Planning Officer of Berlin (1945–7), Professor of Town Planning at the TU Berlin (1946–58) and President of the Berlin *Akademie der Künste* (1955–68). He was a founder of the *Planungskollektiv Berlin* in 1946.

In his thirties, Scharoun belonged to Germany's avant-garde and he soon became one of the most celebrated architects after the war. His style evolves around an organic expressionism of which the Berlin Philharmonie (1956–63) and the Berlin Staatsbibliothek (1964–78) are fine examples.

MARTIN KUDLEK

Schattner, Karljosef

b. 24 August 1924, Gommern (Magdeburg)

Architect

Schattner, who studied under **Döllgast** in Munich, has taught in Darmstadt, Munich and Zürich since 1985. From 1957 onwards he has been head of the *Diözesanbauamt* (diocese building control office) in Eichstätt where most of his buildings stand. Although their formal language is unmistakably modern (he is mentally close to Carlo Scarpa), these designs are placed into the baroque town's historical context with the greatest sensibility. Schattner's best-known projects are the Institute for Psychology and Journalism (1985–8) and the additions and alterations to the Schloß Hirschberg (1987–92).

MARTIN KUDLEK AND BERTHOLD PESCH

Schedlinski, Rainer

b. 11 November 1956, Magdeburg

Writer

Following a series of temporary jobs in industry, Schedlinski settled in East Berlin in 1984. An active member of the **Prenzlauer Berg** alternative culture, Schedlinski published books on art. His literary and essayistic endeavours focused on the inability of the written word to capture the essence of objects as visual media could. From 1986 to 1989 he was the editor of the unofficial literary magazine *ariadnefabrik* (ariadne factory). In 1974 he was contacted by the **Stasi** and worked as an unofficial informant until 1989. Schedlinski later confessed and apologized publicly for his actions.

CAROL ANNE COSTABILE-HEMING

Scherchen, Hermann

b. 21 June 1891, Berlin; d. 12 June 1966, Florence

Conductor

A true original, Scherchen assisted **Schönberg** while still a teenager and ferociously pioneered new music up to his death. After 1954 he returned to West Germany from Swiss exile to teach at the **Darmstadt Festival**, but his political and aesthetic radicalism ensured he never again obtained a permanent post in his native country. Equally adventurous in the classics, his passionate and philological approach to Bach anticipated the current baroque revolution by three decades. An acute portrait of him appears in **Canetti**'s memoirs, *Das Augenspiel*. In 1919 he founded the influential journal *Melos*. His *Lehrbuch des Dirigenten* (Conductor's Textbook) (1929) remains a classic.

BEATRICE HARPER

Schilling, Niklaus

b. 23 April 1944, Basel

Filmmaker and cameraman

Niklaus Schilling made his first 8mm film in 1961 with his brother, the painter Alfons Schilling. He moved to Germany in 1965. *Night Shades* (*Nachtschatten*, 1971), his debut feature, is a darkly expressionist *Heimatfilm*. He has appropriated and subverted classic genres to reflect on themes as diverse as the German romantic spirit, in the melodrama *Rheingold* (1977), the East–West division, in the thriller *The Willi Busch Report* (*Der Willi-Busch Report*, 1979), and filmmaking itself. Renowned for his technical skill as a cinematographer, he has experimented with Steadicam and video.

See also: New German Cinema

MARTIN BRADY

Schilling, Tom

b. 23 January 1928, Halle

Dancer and choreographer

After training with the ballet school in Dessau, Schilling's first engagements came at the opera houses in Dresden (1945) and Leipzig (1946–52), and then the Nationaltheater in Weimar (1953–6). As director of ballet and chief choreographer he moved back to Dresden in 1956, and from 1965 was artistic director and chief choreographer at the Komische Oper in (East) Berlin. His major productions include **Egk**'s *Abraxas*, Gershwin's *An American in Paris* and Prokofiev's *Romeo and Juliet*.

DEREK McCULLOCH

Schirdewan, Karl

b. 14 May 1907, Stettin (now Szczecin,
Poland); d. 15 January 1998, Potsdam

GDR functionary

A communist party activist in the 1920s and 1930s,
Schirdewan was imprisoned during the Nazi
period. After 1945 he worked in the **SED** party
apparatus in Berlin and Saxony. In 1952 he worked
closely together with Walter **Ulbricht** and became
a full member of the **Politbüro** in July 1953. In
February 1958 he was removed from all his
functions, and severely reprimanded, after being
accused, together with the head of State Security
Ernst Wollweber, of attempting to form an
oppositional faction within the party leadership.
He was rehabilitated by a commission of the SED-
PDS in January 1990.

See also: dissent and opposition: GDR

PETER BARKER

Schlag, Evelyn

b. 22 December 1952, Waidhofen an der
Ybbs (Austria)

Writer

Equally renowned for her poetry and prose fiction,
Schlag's themes embrace isolation and longing,
and her heroines, often students or artists in search
of renewal and fulfilment, evolve by experiencing
changes of setting, new sexual encounters, and life-
threatening illnesses, as in *Die Kränkung* (The Injury)
(1987). Eroticism and the rural landscape dominate
much of her work.

See also: literature: Austria

Further reading

Riemer, W. (1993) 'Evelyn Schlag's *Die Kränkung*:
Resurrecting Katherine Mansfield', *Modern Austrian Literature* 26, 2: 107–25 (about the heroine's
alter ego).

BEVERLEY DRIVER EDDY

Schlager

'*Schlager*' is the German word for 'hit'. In contrast
to **rock music** in Germany, which developed in
the mid-1960s and was dominated by groups
emulating successful anglophone rock groups, the
Schlager, which has its roots in the popular melodies
and operettas of the late nineteenth century, is a
domestic musical commodity produced for domestic consumption. *Schlager* are pop songs sung in
German reflecting the traditional themes of pop
music: love, melancholy, nostalgia and fantasy.
Schlager are further subdivided into '*Schnulzen*', or
particularly sentimental love songs, and '*Evergreen*',
or *Schlager* which have stood the test of time. Aside
from these generic or formal markers, however, a
Schlager is defined in the final instance by
commercial success (generally, sales in excess of
20,000 units).

The *Schlager* has had an ambivalent relation to
folk music, and in the 1950s it was feared that
the radio-driven dissemination of *Schlager* would
bury the rich tradition of folk music in Germany.
However, with the rise in popularity of beat and
rock music, the dividing line between *Schlager* and
folk became blurred. The two merged becoming a
conservative bastion of popular **music** in the
German language. It was in the figure of Heino
(Heinz-Georg Kramm), who at the outset of his
career in 1965 was referred to as the '*gesunder
Gegenpol zu der modischen Beathysterie*' (healthy antidote to fashionable beat hysteria), that the two
realms achieved their perfect union. Heino's
trademark blonde hair and dark glasses made
him both a caricature and pseudo-mod icon of
Schlager culture as he sang songs like 'Babysitter
Boogie-Woogie' or 'Caramba, Caracho, ein Whis-
key'. At the same time, his work also revealed the
intense nationalism of *Schlager* culture with his
renditions of 'Kein schöner Land in dieser Zeit'
(No More Beautiful Land in This Time) or 'Hohe
Tannen' (Tall Firs).

Of course, *Schlager* culture was not always so
ideologically loaded. More often than not, Schlager
were simply schmaltzy pop tunes, such as the child
star Heintje's 'Mama', or bucolic idylls like Jürgen
Drews' 'Ein Bett im Kornfeld', or even mellow soft
rock ballads like Howard Carpendale's 'Deine
Spuren im Sand'. Moreover, *Schlager* were often

knock-offs of Anglo-American hits, a good example being Juliane Werding's 'Am Tag, als Conny Kramer starb' (On the Day That Conny Kramer Died), which was a thinly veiled reworking of the Band's 'The Night They Drove Old Dixie Down'.

The increasing commercial viability of the German language rock music pioneered by Udo **Lindenberg** and others marked the decline of *Schlager* kitsch in the 1980s. This reversal of fortunes has relegated the traditional *Schlager* to the realm of fantasy and nostalgia it so often evoked.

Further reading

Fischer, H. (1965) *Volkslied, Schlager, Evergreen*, Tübingen: Tübinger Vereinigung für Volkskunde (sociological study of *Schlager* in everyday life).

Kayser, D. (1975) *Schlager, das Lied als Ware*, Stuttgart: Metzler (cultural materialist analysis of the *Schlager* form).

Mezger, W. (1975) *Schlager: Versuch einer Gesamtdarstellung*, Tübingen: Tübinger Vereinigung für Volkskunde (analysis with extensive list of references).

MATTHEW T. GRANT

Schlenstedt, Dieter

b. 30 August 1932, Blankenburg (Harz)

Literary critic

Schlenstedt is the most influential GDR-based commentator on its own literature, a status deriving both from his openness to 'western' literary theories (such as reception aesthetics) and from his close personal links with many leading authors. He held a research professorship in literary history in the GDR Academy of Sciences from 1976 until its post-unification dissolution, and was President of the eastern German branch of the international writers' organization **PEN** from 1991 to 1997. He is best known for his volume *Die neue DDR-Literatur und ihre Leser* (The New GDR Literature and its Readers) (1979).

DENNIS TATE

Schlesinger, Klaus

b. 9 January 1937, Berlin

Writer

Part of the generation of creatively innovative GDR authors who established their careers in the wake of **Honecker**'s promise of 'no taboos', Schlesinger was then expelled in 1979 from the **Writers' Union** for protesting against the emergence of new forms of repression. He emigrated to West Berlin in 1980 but retained close links with GDR cultural life. He published one of the first post-*Wende* autobiographical accounts of this process of disillusionment, *Fliegender Wechsel* (Rapid Changeover) (1990) and a highly praised novel about growing up in divided Berlin, *Die Sache mit Randow* (The Randow Affair), 1996.

See also: prose fiction: GDR

DENNIS TATE

Schlingensief, Christoph

b. 24 October 1960, Oberhausen

Filmmaker

Schlingensief began filmmaking at the age of eight, making over twenty films before the controversial, anarchic feature *100 Years of Adolf Hitler* (*100 Jahre Adolf Hitler*) (1989), a riotous recreation of Hitler's last hours featuring Udo Kier and Margit Carstensen, earned him a reputation as *agent provocateur*. Two bloodthirsty, slapstick pastiches of unification and its aftermath – *The German Chainsaw Massacre* (*Das deutsche Kettensägenmassaker*) (1990), and *Terror 2000* (1992) – refined his trademark splatter-movie style and owe a conspicuous debt to the hysterical frenzy of the post-**Baader-Meinhof** films of Rainer Werner **Fassbinder**.

See also: film: FRG

MARTIN BRADY

Schlöndorff, Volker

b. 31 March 1939, Wiesbaden

Filmmaker and producer

When he took over the management of the **Babelsberg** film studios in Potsdam in 1992 Schlöndorff saw the possibility of fulfilling his abiding dream of a commercially thriving, popular German cinema. His appointment to this prestigious post was a consequence of his career as an internationally successful director in the FRG during the 1970s, producing a string of successful literary adaptations which culminated in the Oscar-winning *Tin Drum* (*Die Blechtrommel*, 1979), coupled with his experience in Hollywood during the 1980s.

Although one of the major filmmakers of the **New German Cinema**, Schlöndorff is not strictly an *Autorenfilmer* (auteurist writer-director), preferring to use scriptwriters or base his films on literary works. After gaining experience in France, and working as assistant to Alain Resnais, he based his debut *Young Törless* (*Der junge Törless*, 1966) on the novella by Robert Musil depicting the harshness of life in a military academy. Its quintessentially German setting allowed him, in his own words, 'to establish certain links with German film traditions – Stroheim and Lang'.

In his second feature, the Kleist adaptation *Michael Kohlhaas* (*Michael Kohlhaas – Der Rebell*, 1969), some commentators saw parallels between the protagonist's rebellion against social injustice and the increasingly violent struggles of the **student movement** in the FRG. *The Sudden Fortune of the Poor People of Kombach* (*Der plötzliche Reichtum der armen Leute von Kombach*, 1970), one of a number of critical *Heimat* films of the early 1970s, is based not on a literary text but on chronicles from the year 1822.

The Lost Honour of Katharina **Blum** (***Die verlorene Ehre der Katharina Blum***, 1975), co-directed with his wife Margarethe von **Trotta**, has become, like Heinrich **Böll**'s story on which it is based, a landmark in the history of **terrorism** in the FRG and the involvement of **Bild**. Together with an episode in the collective film *Germany in Autumn* (*Deutschland im Herbst*, 1978), also scripted by Böll, it constituted a major contribution to the debate on how the media should respond to politically motivated violence. In sharp contrast, *Coup de Grâce* (*Der Fangschuß*, 1977) is a stark adaptation of a novel by Marguerite Yourcenar. Strikingly shot in black and white, it features a vigorous performance from silent film star Valeska Gert.

Schlöndorff was well-established as a director of polished literary adaptations by the time he took on Günter **Grass**'s complex and innovative novel *The Tin Drum*, translating the manic, child-like voice of the narrator, Oskar Matzerath, into a highly sensual, visually baroque sequence of spectacular set pieces.

During the 1980s Schlöndorff, like many German filmmakers, turned to international co-productions, adapting the works of non-German authors such as Marcel Proust, Arthur Miller and Margaret Atwood, and dividing his time between Germany and America. In 1990 he turned to the Swiss author Max **Frisch** for his film *Voyager* (*Homo Faber*, 1991) and in 1996 directed a second big-budget feature on the Third Reich, *Der Unhold* (The Fiend).

See also: film: FRG; New German Cinema

HELEN HUGHES

Schmeling, Max

b. 28 September 1905, Klein-Luckow (Pomerania)

Boxer

A successful, yet controversial boxer of the 1920s and 1930s, Schmeling became Germany's first European champion in 1927 (Light Heavyweight), German Heavyweight Champion in 1928, and World Heavyweight Champion from 1930 to 1932. His international victories stirred the nation's pride. He was presented as a perfect Aryan by Hitler, although Schmeling was not a Nazi. His bout against African-American Joe Louis (1936) was touted as a demonstration of Aryan superiority over 'racially inferior Negroes'. Disowned by the Nazi regime after losing to Louis in 1938, Schmeling returned to boxing in 1947 and retired in 1948. He remains a contemporary German sporting hero and a symbol of athletic ability and fair play.

See also: sport: FRG; sport: GDR

Further reading

Forster, M. (1987) *Max Schmeling: Sieger im Ring, Sieger im Leben*, Munich (biography of Schmeling).

Schmeling, M. (1977) *Erinnerungen*, Frankfurt am Main: Ullstein (Schmeling's memoirs).

TARA MAGDALINSKI

Schmidt, Arno

b. 18 January 1914, Hamburg; d. 3 June
1979, Bargfeld (near Celle)

Writer

Arno Schmidt's literary output, spanning the period from 1949 (*Leviathan*) to the posthumously published *Julia oder die Gemälde* (Juliet or the Paintings) of 1979, comprises nine novels, six collections of stories, a psychoanalytical study of Karl May (*Sitara*), a biography of Fouqué, four volumes of radio essays on largely underrated eighteenth- and nineteenth-century writers, numerous translations from the English (including Faulkner, Fenimore Cooper and Poe) and a significant body of literary theory. While having quickly been recognized as one of the more inventive and hermetic prose-writers in post-war German literature, Schmidt achieved fresh notoriety with *Zettel's Traum* (Bottom's Dream) (1970), an A3-format, typewritten, multi-columned experimental novel composed in a mixture of idiosyncratic German and quirkish portmanteau wordplays bearing witness to an obsession with *Finnegans Wake*. Schmidt's subsequent novels – *Die Schule der Atheisten* (The Atheists' School) (1972), *Abend mit Goldrand* (Evening edged in Gold) (1975) and *Julia oder die Gemälde* – were all published as typescripts in the same massive format and displayed a similar combination of Joycean neologism and preoccupation with sexual innuendo via etymological games.

The majority of Schmidt's early fiction represented an impressive attempt to work systematically through four notional '*Versuchsreihen*' (test series) of prose experiments, each focusing on a particular mental paradigm: recollection, for instance in *Die Umsiedler* (The Displaced) (1953); what he called '*Musivisches Dasein*', the selective registering of experience, most successfully explored in *Das steinerne Herz* (Heart of Stone) (1956); the '*längeres Gedankenspiel*' (extended freeplay of thought), the mind's compulsive tendency to construct alternative thoughts to the reality it is registering, the best example of which is *Kaff auch Mare Crisium* (Dead-end Village also Mare Crisium) (1960); and dream. Schmidt's guiding assumption was that all of these psychological activities had become a challenge to writers to invent a new medium to express them. Yet for all their novel orthography and typography his 'solutions' were intended as refinements of literature's realistic repertoire. The underlying theory is to be found in Schmidt's *Berechnungen I-III* (Calculations I-III) (1959, 1980), while his later preoccupation with Joyce and Freud is documented in *Der Triton mit dem Sonnenschirm* (Triton with Parasol) (1969). Although first and foremost important as stylistic experiments, Schmidt's fictions convey a powerful sense of cultural pessimism and disquiet at the excesses of the Cold War; the later novels are increasingly characterized by solipsism, esotericism and self-referentiality. Schmidt's *magnum opus*, *Zettel's Traum*, is predicated on the assumption that from middle age onwards the mind develops a receptivity to the alleged libidinous substratum of language, a modified Freudian thesis that became a pretext for the sexual decodings and spoof etymologies which are an extreme version of the earlier '*längeres Gedankenspiel*' mode.

Further reading

Drews, J. (ed.) (1982) *Gebirgslandschaft mit Arno Schmidt: Grazer Symposion 1980*, Munich: edition text + kritik.

Minden, M.R. (1982) *Arno Schmidt: A Critical Study of his Prose*, Cambridge: Cambridge University Press.

Schardt, M. and Vollmer, H. (eds) (1990) *Arno Schmidt: Leben: – Werk – Wirkung*, Reinbek bei Hamburg: Rowohlt.

Weninger, R. (1995) *Framing a Novelist*, Columbia, SC: Camden House.

JOHN J. WHITE

Schmidt, Helmut

b. 23 December 1918, Hamburg

Politician; German Federal Chancellor 1974–82

Schmidt became Chancellor on the resignation of Willy **Brandt**, under whom he had served as Minister of Defence and Minister of Finance. Changing political and economic circumstances meant that the vision of the Brandt interlude had to be abandoned for crisis-management, and Schmidt – with his image of an urbane 'fixer' – steered the German economy with relative success through the global turmoil of the 1970s. His government also had to confront the **terrorism** of the traumatic 'German **Autumn**' of 1977, and rifts in the **SPD** over **peace movement** concern at NATO rearmament at the beginning of the 1980s. His downfall was occasioned when his **F.D.P.** coalition partners deserted him over economic policy.

JOHN SANDFORD

Schmidt, Siegfried Johannes

b. 28 October 1940, Jülich

Philosopher and literary theorist

After seminal work in linguistics and pragmatics in the early 1970s, Siegfried J. Schmidt turned to literary studies and became one of the founders of *empirische Literaturwissenschaft* (empirical theory of literature). In the 1980s he played a key role in German social thought as one of the exponents of radical constructivism – a theory of knowledge as a social construction. In his most recent work Schmidt incorporates some of the key insights of Niklas **Luhmann**'s systems theory while preserving the central tenets of radical constructivism.

HENK de BERG

Schneider, Peter

b. 21 April 1940, Lübeck

Writer

One of Germany's best-known political essayists, Schneider achieved fame with his novel *The Wall Jumper* (*Der Mauerspringer*) in 1982, which depicts the effect of the Berlin Wall on people's lives.

Whilst a student in Berlin in the 1960s Schneider published literary criticism and essays in newspapers and periodicals such as *Die* **Zeit**, *Neue Rundschau* and *Neue Deutsche Hefte* and in 1965 wrote speeches for the **SPD** election campaign. From 1967 to 1971 he was active in the **student movement** in Berlin and Italy, combining political activism with literary production. An essay entitled 'Phantasy in Late Capitalism and the Cultural Revolution' published in Hans Magnus **Enzensberger**'s periodical *Kursbuch* in 1969 represented the views of left-wing **intellectuals** involved in the student movement. Schneider, like Wolf **Biermann**, donated the money from a literary prize to the **APO**. His opposition to the Vietnam War earned Schneider a reputation as a dangerous radical, and when he attempted to enter the teaching profession he found his way barred by a **Berufsverbot**.

By this time, however, Schneider had become an established writer. His story *Lenz* (1973) 'remains the iconic text of the student movement' (Riordan) but his growing doubts about the radical movement are reflected in plays such as *Geschäftszeichen 1Aa5* (Reference 1Aa5) (a collage of historical and contemporary political scenes performed in 1975) and *...schon bist du ein Verfassungsfeind* (...you are already an enemy of the Constitution) (1975), as well as in his collection of political texts *Ansprachen* (Addresses) (1970). The stories in *Die Wette* (The Bet) (1978) reflect the changing political perspective of the New Left and also men's position in relation to the women's emancipation movement. His only fictional approach to the question of violence and politics is in the screenplay to Reinhard **Hauff**'s film *Messer im Kopf* (A Knife in the Head) (1978). He also collaborated with Hauff on the film version of *Der Mauerspringer*, entitled *Der Mann auf der Mauer* (The Man on the Wall) (1982).

The deep impression made by a reading tour through South America in 1980 and a journey through China in 1985 is reflected in essays and the play *Totoluque* on the downfall of the Aztecs (1985). Schneider's correspondence with the convicted terrorist Peter-Jürgen Boock, *Ratte tot* (Rat dead) was also published in 1985. His controversial combination of fact and fiction in the story *Vati* (Daddy) based on the revelation that Rolf Mengele, who had probably been to school with Schneider, had gone to Brazil to visit his father, the war criminal, Josef Mengele, was published in 1987.

In a collection of anecdotes published after the collapse of the Berlin Wall, *The German Comedy. Scenes of Life After the Wall (Extreme Mittellage: Eine Reise durch das deutsche Nationalgefühl)* (1990), Schneider portrays the insecurities and paradoxes of the German identity crisis in the absence of the Wall.

In 1992 Schneider's first novel *Couplings (Paarungen)* was published, set in pre-unification West Germany, combining humour with story-telling and essayistic analysis. *Vom Ende der Gewißheit* (The End of Certainty) (1994) contains further essays.

Further reading

Riordan, C. (ed.) (1993) *Vati*, Manchester: Manchester University Press (German text with introduction and notes in English).
—— (1995) *Peter Schneider*, Cardiff: University of Wales Press (a collection of essays on different aspects of Schneider's life and work, including an interview).

MARGARET VALLANCE

Schneider, Rolf

b. 17 April 1932, Chemnitz

Writer

Schneider's varied literary output includes plays for theatre and radio, parodies, travel books, short stories and novels. His early work deals particularly with Germany's recent past, but in the 1970s he focused increasingly on life in the GDR. The 1979 novel *November* (November) was inspired by the expatriation of Wolf **Biermann** and by the letter

of protest issued by leading GDR intellectuals, including Schneider. In 1979 his membership of the **Writers' Union** was withdrawn. In the 1990s he has produced perceptive essays on the GDR and on socio-political developments in Germany.

IAN WALLACE

Schneider, Romy

b. 23 September 1938, Vienna; d. 29 May 1982, Paris

Actress

Schneider was idolized in Germany for her role as the beautiful Empress Elisabeth of Austria in the *Sissi* films (1955–7), a trilogy of sumptuous, tearful biopics whose popularity came to epitomize 1950s escapism in Germany. Managing eventually to escape being typecast in similarly sugary roles, she demonstrated her considerable acting ability through acclaimed performances in Luchino Visconti's stage production of *'Tis Pity She's a Whore* in Paris (1963–5) and in such varied films as Orson Welles' *The Trial* (1962), Luchino Visconti's *Ludwig* (1972), and Claude Sautet's *Mado* (1976).

See also: film: FRG

HELEN HUGHES

Schnitzler, Karl-Eduard von

b. 28 April 1918, Berlin

Television presenter and political commentator

Schnitzler presented the East German television programme *Der schwarze Kanal* (The Black Channel), which sought to address the problem of GDR citizens watching and being influenced by western television, portraying it as being engaged in anti-socialist political manipulation. Despite his intellectual abilities, von Schnitzler's style of reporting and his political intolerance meant that he was not accepted by the GDR citizens, and a part of the demonstrations in 1989 demanded that he resign, which was realized when he presented the programme on 30 October 1989 for the last time.

See also: mass media: GDR

JONATHAN McHAFFIE

Schnurre, Wolfdietrich

b. 22 August 1920, Frankfurt am Main; d.
9 June 1989, Kiel

Writer

Permanently scarred by his experiences of Nazi
Germany, Schnurre became one of the leading
advocates and practitioners of an ethically and
politically committed literature in the immediate
post-1945 years. His reputation rests on his short
stories, but he also wrote poetry, radio and
television plays, novels and a wide range of essays
on contemporary social, political, and cultural
issues. Founder member of the **Gruppe 47**.

See also: *Hörspiel: FRG*; *Kahlschlag*; *Stunde Null*;
Vergangenheitsbewältigung

Further reading

Blencke, K. (1993) *Wolfdietrich Schnurre: Der Nachlaß*,
Paderborn: Igel.

RODERICK H. WATT

Schönberg, Arnold

b. 13 September 1874, Vienna; d. 13 July
1951, Hollywood

Composer

Having revolutionized modern music by abandoning tonality in 1907 and pioneering twelve-tone
(serial) composition in the early 1920s, he spent his
final years in Hollywood, having left Berlin in
1933. His radical post-war compositions, combining twelve-tone constructivism and expressionist
emotional intensity, include the *String Trio* Op. 45
and *A Survivor from Warsaw* Op. 46 for speaker,
chorus and orchestra, a passionate lament for the
victims of the Holocaust. Championed by Theodor
W. **Adorno**, his music exerted an enormous

influence on post-war composers including Karlheinz **Stockhausen** and Hans Werner **Henze**.

MARTIN BRADY

Schönherr, Albrecht Freiedrich

b. 11 September 1911, Katscher (Upper
Silesia; now Kietriz, Poland)

Protestant church leader

Schönherr, a student of **Bonhoeffer**, was a prime
mover in the formation of the Federation of
Evangelical Churches in the GDR, founded in
1969 by the eight member churches in the GDR of
the Evangelical Church in Germany, and its first
chairman (1969–81). In 1973 he became Bishop of
the eastern region of the Evangelical Church in
Berlin-Brandenburg, having been, since 1967, its
episcopal representative (*Bischofsamtsverwalter*). The
high point of his term of office was the meeting of
6 March 1978 between federation representatives
and Erich **Honecker**, which brought some
improvements for the situation of the church in
the GDR (see also ***Kirche im Sozialismus***).

Further reading

Schönherr, A. (1979) *Horizont und Mitte: Aufsätze,
Vorträge, Reden, 1953–1977*, East Berlin: Evangelische Verlagsanstalt (a collection of Schönherr's
most important speeches and papers).
—— (1992) *Gratwanderung*, 2nd edn, Leipzig:
Evangelische Verlagsanstalt (a post-*Wende* review
of the history of the GDR churches).

STEPHEN BROWN

Schorlemmer, Friedrich

b. 16 May 1944, Wittenberge (Altmark)

East German pastor and civil rights
activist

After studying theology Schorlemmer became a
pastor in Halle. In 1978 he became a lecturer at
the Protestant seminary in Wittenberg and became
involved with oppositional groups. In 1988 he

presented his 'Twenty Wittenberg Theses' to the Protestant Church conference which criticized conditions in the GDR. He was a co-founder of the citizens' group, *Demokratischer Aufbruch* (Democratic Awakening) in September 1989, but after this group joined forces with the CDU in January 1990, Schorlemmer moved to the SPD, and was from May 1990 the SPD leader on the Wittenberg town council. He is now a lecturer at the Protestant Academy in Wittenberg.

See also: citizens' movements: GDR

PETER BARKER

Schottroff, Luise

b. 11 April 1934, Berlin

Protestant theologian

Schottroff, since 1986 Professor for New Testament at Kassel, was initially prominent because of her 'materialist interpretation of the New Testament' which attempted to counter traditional biblical interpretation through social historical methodology. Increasingly influenced by the peace and women's movements, she now describes herself as a 'feminist liberation theologian', concentrating on the social history of early Christianity and feminist interpretation of the New Testament.

Further reading

Gössmann, E. *et al.* (1991) *Wörterbuch der feministischen Theologie*, Göttingen: Gütersloher Verlagshaus Gerd Mohn (Schottroff is a co-editor of this book which includes a select bibliography of her major works).

Schottroff L. (1995) *Lydia's Impatient Sisters: A Feminist Social History of Early Christianity*, trans. B. Rumscheidt and M. Rumscheidt, London: SCM Press.

STEPHEN BROWN

Schrebergarten

Also termed *Kleingarten* (small garden) or *Laube* (leafy retreat), this term derives from the Leipzig orthopaedist Daniel Gottlob Moritz Schreber (1808–61) who advocated gardening and gymnastics to restore the health of the urban population. Colonies of *Schrebergärten* stand on the outskirts of most German towns, offering flat-dwellers relaxation, quiet, fresh air and produce, and ranging from allotments with a simple hut to landscaped lawns (with gnomes, ponds and fountains) round an elaborate weekend-cottage. These idyllic retreats are often organized in, and regulated by, *Kleingartenvereine* (small garden associations), and sometimes surrounded by barbed wire and locked gates. In the GDR, state attempts to regulate *Kleingarten* production of, for instance, honey, strawberries or rabbit meat, conflicted with the pursuit, typical of the GDR as a *Nischengesellschaft* (niche society), of private space away from ideological blandishments.

MORAY McGOWAN

Schreier, Peter

b. 29 July 1935, Meissen

Tenor

Schreier joined the Kreuzchor in Dresden in 1945, moving on to the Musikhochschule there in 1956 and entering the school of opera attached to the Dresden Opera in 1959. Although his repertoire is broad, it is as the evangelist in the Bach Passions and in the lyrical roles in Mozart operas that he is most recognized. Since the 1980s he has been increasingly active as a conductor, notably of Bach cantatas.

DEREK McCULLOCH

Schröder, Gerhard

b. 7 April 1944, Mossenberg/Lippe

Politician; German Federal Chancellor 1998–

A member of the **SPD** since 1963, Schröder became Minister-President of his home state of Lower Saxony in 1990. As the party's chosen chancellor candidate in the 1998 federal election, he traded on his popular image of a new breed of centre-left politician in the mould of Britain's Tony Blair. The outcome, in which the SPD vote exceeded that of the **CDU/CSU** for only the second time in a national election, brought to an end sixteen years of government under Helmut **Kohl**, and was widely perceived as marking a generational change in the political history of the Federal Republic. As previously in Lower Saxony, Schröder formed a coalition with the **Greens**, bringing them into government for the first time at national level. Major reforms promised by the new 'red–green' government included an overhaul of the citizenship laws that would grant German nationality to nearly half the country's *Ausländer* population, and, over the longer term, the phasing out of **nuclear power**. Its policies on economic reform were more cautious.

JOHN SANDFORD

Schroeder, Margot

b. 29 April 1937, Barmbek (Hamburg)

Writer

A former bookseller, Schroeder began to publish in 1972 with the **Hörspiel** (radio play) *Ehebefragung* (Marriage Interrogation). She also writes novels, poetry, children's books and essays. Her work focuses on the family life of workers and the lower middle class, written from a socially critical, feminist point of view, contrasting realistic description and dialogue with poetic elements. Schroeder became known with *Ich stehe meine Frau* (I Stand My Ground) (1975), which portrays the successful organization of a tenants' initiative by a working-class housewife. Her early novels were widely read by the women's movement.

MARTINA S. ANDERSON

Schroeter, Werner

b. 7 April 1945, Georgenthal (Thuringia)

Filmmaker, theatre and opera director

Schroeter is the most distinctive, visionary and provocative director on the outer limits of the **New German Cinema**, whose influence on other filmmakers (including Rosa von **Praunheim**, Hans Jürgen **Syberberg** and Ulrike **Ottinger**) has been much greater than his success at the box office.

He passed the entrance examination to the Munich School for Television and Film but left after a few weeks. Between 1967 and 1969 he directed around sixteen striking experimental shorts which were screened at a number of festivals and acclaimed by Wim **Wenders** amongst others.

His ambitious debut feature, *Eika Katappa* (1969), fused international underground cinema – influences include Kenneth Anger, Gregory Markropoulos and Andy Warhol – gay, religious and mythological iconography, fervent melodrama, Verdi, popular music, and German romanticism into a heady and camp mixture of baroque tableaux, sumptuous lighting, and operatic gestures. It established an inimitable style which he was to refine over the next decade. The 1970s saw a gradual shift in his films from the experimental, rough-edged style of the caustic satire *The Bomber Pilot* (*Der Bomberpilot*, 1970) and the ecstatic brilliance of the film considered by many, including Schroeter himself, to be his masterpiece, *The Death of Maria Malibran* (*Der Tod der Maria Malibran*, 1971), towards a more cosmopolitan, polished aesthetic incorporating narrative and neo-realist elements, most notably in the psychological drama *Regno die Napoli* (1978) and the expansive *Gastarbeiter* melodrama *Palermo or Wolfsburg* (*Palermo oder Wolfsburg*, 1980).

From as early as 1970 Schroeter received generous funding from television, principally **ZDF**, and was able to produce eight feature-length films in as many years, drawing on a relatively stable group of actresses experienced at translating his complex, emotionally-charged scenarios into eloquent, often painfully moving gestures and actions. Pre-eminent amongst them were Magdalena Montezuma, Christine Kaufmann and Ellen Umlauf. Following Montezuma's death shortly after shooting *The Rose King* (*Der Rosenkönig*, 1984–6), a febrile and visually sumptuous celebration of the romantic quest for pure (gay) love, Schroeter directed only one feature film, *Malina* (1990), a glossy, big-budget adaptation of the novel by Ingeborg **Bachmann**, starring Isabelle Huppert (clumsily dubbed into German) and Mathieu Carrière. Co-scripted by the Austrian writer Elfriede **Jelinek**, this European co-production was not able to afford Schroeter the international breakthrough his œuvre deserves.

As well as producing a number of striking, politically engaged documentaries during the 1980s, including his passionate assault on the Marcos regime in the Philippines, *The Laughing Star* (*Der Lachende Stern*, 1983), Schroeter has been active as a theatre and opera director since 1972, when he staged Lessing's *Emilia Galotti* at the Deutsches Schauspielhaus in Hamburg. As controversial as his films, to which they often owe a considerable debt in their ambitious stylization and 'high-camp' theatricality, his numerous stage commissions have kept him at the centre of cultural life in Germany.

See also: New German Cinema

Further reading

Jansen, P.W. and Schütte, W. (1980) *Werner Schroeter*, Munich and Vienna: Hanser (a detailed survey with an extensive interview, annotated filmography, and bibliography).

MARTIN BRADY

Schubert, Helga

b. 7 January 1940, Berlin

Writer

Schubert's background as a psychotherapist explains the coolly ironic observation of human weakness that characterizes her work. Two volumes of short stories, portraying life in the GDR, conveying details of scene and situation that border on the satirical, with particular emphasis on the lives of women, were published in both East and West Germany in the 1970s and 1980s. In 1990 *Judasfrauen* (Judas Women), a collection of short stories based on documentary material, analyses cases of women informers in the Third Reich. She has also written radio plays and film scripts, for instance *Die Beunruhigung* (Unease) (1982).

MARGARET VALLANCE

Schürmann, Joachim

b. 24 September 1926, Viersen

Architect

Schürmann studied at the TH (Technical University) Darmstadt from 1946 to 1949, and established a private practice with his wife Margot in Cologne in 1956, with an office in Salzburg since 1991. He held the post of Professor at the TH Darmstadt from 1966 to 1969.

Schürmann's varied œuvre reaches from restoration to town planning work. His architectural approach leads on from classical modernism although functionalism never overtakes the human dimensions of his work. Schürmann understands how to adapt his designs to their environment sensitively, but without subordination. Some of his more important designs are St Stephan in Cologne (1958–61) and his buildings for the post office in Cologne (1980–90).

MARTIN KUDLEK

Schütz, Helga

b. 2 October 1937, Falkenhain (Zlotoryje, Poland)

Writer

For many years a scriptwriter for **DEFA**, Schütz turned to literature in the 1970s with the stories *Vorgeschichte oder Schöne Gegend Probstein* (Prehistory or Beautiful District of Probstein) (1971), *Das Erdbeben bei Sangerhausen* (The Earthquake near Sangerhausen) (1972) and *Festbeleuchtung* (Party Lights) (1976) featuring autobiographical elements such as the forced abandonment of villages in Silesia towards the end of WWII. Novels written in the 1980s, though firmly rooted in the GDR, still feature the search for a lost family background, such as *In Annas Namen* (In Anna's name) (1989) and its post-**Wende** sequel *Vom Glanz der Elbe* (Of the Shining Elbe) (1995).

MARGARET VALLANCE

Schütz, Stefan

b. 19 April 1944, Memel

Writer

After a career as an actor Schütz started writing plays, strongly encouraged by Heiner **Müller**. The plays, expressionistic and critical (e.g. *Odysseus' Heimkehr*, 1972; *Kohlhaas*, 1975), were hardly performed in the GDR. In 1980 he moved to the FRG. His first novel (*Medusa*, 1986), hailed and criticized with equal vigour, was one of the most artistically innovative GDR analyses of the decade. Later works portray, in a unique fictional tone, human deformation in consumer societies (e.g. *Katt*, 1988; *Schnitters Mall*, 1994).

Further reading

Jucker, R. (ed.) (1997) *Stefan Schütz*, Munich: edition text + kritik (essays on Schütz's life and work; includes bibliography).

ROLF JUCKER

Schultes, Axel

b. 17 November 1943, Dresden

Architect

Schultes studied at the TU (Technical University) Berlin from 1962 to 1969, setting up private practice in partnership with Bangert, Jansen and Scholz as BJSS in 1972. He left BJSS to form Axel Schultes Architekten in 1991.

Schultes's architecture is characterized by a massiveness of elemental form which is combined with sharply cut openings and often contrasted with more playful elements such as confusing vistas and unusual spatial qualities (e.g. the Kunstmuseum, Bonn, 1985–92). His greatest success as a town planner is the first prize in the Berlin Spreebogen competition (1991) in which 835 planners from 44 countries took part (see also **Berlin building boom**).

MARTIN KUDLEK

Schumacher, Emil

b. 29 August 1912, Hagen (Westphalia);
d. 4 October 1999, Ibiza

Painter

Schumacher is a leading exponent of German abstract painting. In the 1950s he was heavily influenced by French abstraction, but soon asserted a distinctive style by introducing three-dimensional elements into his paintings. He reached the acknowledged highpoint of his career in the 1960s with intensely-coloured, viscous works delineated by scratches and marks which suggested a 'dialogue' between artist and material. He later introduced asphalt, lead, stone and wood into his painting and also produced ceramic work. Although never representational, his works often evoke a romantic sense of the powers of nature.

ALEX COOKE

Schumacher, Michael

b. 3 January 1969, Hürth-Hermühlheim (near Cologne)

Racing driver

Schumacher began his racing career at the age of five and found early success after winning the national Junior Karting Championships at fifteen. He began racing cars in 1988, first entered the Formula One in 1991 and became the youngest driver to win back-to-back World Championships in 1995. Schumacher is a national icon and one of the leading sports stars in Europe. The media's portrayal of the rivalry between Schumacher and England's Damon Hill parallels other sporting rivalries between these two nations, particularly in soccer.

See also: Lauda, Nicki; sport: FRG

TARA MAGDALINSKI

Schutting, Julian

b. 25 October 1937, Amstetten (Lower Austria)

Writer (formerly Jutta Schutting)

Schutting first started publishing prose and poetry in the early 1970s. Not known outside the German-speaking world, Schutting owes allegiance to the European avant-garde and to the Viennese avant-garde of the 1950s. Equally keen to perpetuate the traditions of a specifically Austrian history, culture and literature, Schutting has sought to revitalize 'high' literature, though his work is of uneven quality. The best introduction to the best of Schutting is available in one volume, Reclam's *Findhunde. Prosa*, edited by Gisela Steinlehner, first published in 1988. Following a sex change, revealed for the first time in *Wienerin* (6 September 1989), Jutta Schutting has published as Julian Schutting.

HARRIET MURPHY

Schwab, Werner

b. 4 February 1958, Graz; d. 1 January 1994, Graz

Dramatist

Schwab rapidly rose to prominence following the production of *Volksvernichtung oder Meine Leber ist sinnlos: Eine Radikalkomödie* (Genocide or My Liver is Senseless: A Radical Comedy) at the Munich *Kammerspiele* in 1991, one of a cycle of post-modern farces entitled *Fäkaliendramen* (Faecal Plays). That same year he was named as 'new dramatist of the year' by the magazine *Theater heute*. His provocative plays are characterized by their blasphemy and obscenity, their broken and contradictory structure and their neologistic idiom.

SEÁN ALLAN

Schwaiger, Brigitte

b. 6 April 1949, Freistadt (Austria)

Writer

With the bestselling first novel *How Does the Salt Get into the Sea* (*Wie kommt das Salz ins Meer*, 1977), her ironically bitter account of a suffocating marriage, Schwaiger began the intimate exploration of autobiographical experience also characteristic of her later work, including the account of her childhood, *Mein Spanisches Dorf* (My Spanish Village) (1978), and the portrait of her father, *Lange Abwesenheit* (Prolonged Absence) (1980).

Further reading

Wolfschütz, H. (1978 ff) 'Brigitte Schwaiger', in H.L. Arnold (ed.), *Kritisches Lexikon zur deutschsprachigen Gegenwartsliteratur*, Munich: edition text + kritik (a critical survey of Schwaiger's work with bibliography).

JOANNE LEAL

Schwarz, Rudolf

b. 15 May 1897, Strasbourg; d. 3 April 1961, Cologne

Architect

Schwarz studied at the TH (Technical University) Berlin (1915–19), and the State Academy of Arts under Poelzig (1919–23). He was in private practice in Frankfurt am Main and Cologne (1953–61), and held positions as Chief City Planner (*Generalplaner*) of Cologne (1946–52) and Professor of Town Planning at the Kunstakademie Düsseldorf (1953–61).

Schwarz is best known for his churches. He developed his designs out of the relationship between built form and liturgy and the wish for symbolical expression. Schwarz also has to be remembered for planning Cologne's reconstruction after WWII. Two important post-war buildings are St Anna in Düren (1951–6) and the Wallraf-Richards Museum in Cologne (1955–7).

MARTIN KUDLEK

Schwarzenegger, Arnold

b. 30 July 1947, Graz

Actor and body builder

An award-winning body builder (Mr Universe; Mr Olympia), Schwarzenegger left Austria to study in the US. He used his Austrian heritage to promote his image as an alien *Übermensch* with automaton-like delivery of minimal lines and became the world's leading box office attraction (*Terminator* 1984, grossed over $100 million). His career was carefully orchestrated as he built up his financial empire through astute collateral marketing. He married Maria Shriver (Kennedy) in 1985, was appointed Chairman of the President's Council on Physical Fitness and Sport in 1990, and invested in the Planet Hollywood restaurant chain where he promotes his mother's Austrian *Apfelstrudel* (apple strudel).

UTE LISCHKE-McNAB

Schwarzer, Alice

b. 3 December 1942, Wuppertal

Journalist and writer

A leading figure of the West German women's movement, in 1971 Schwarzer led the campaign for a woman's right to a 'dignified abortion', and in 1975 gained further notoriety with the publication of *Der 'Kleine Unterschied' und seine Großen Folgen* (The 'Little Difference' and its Enormous Consequences), in which she identified sexuality as the source of women's oppression. An admirer of De Beauvoir, she has published other works on the position of women in society, and since 1977 has edited the feminist magazine **Emma**.

See also: feminism and the women's movement

JOANNA McKAY

Schwarzkopf, Elisabeth

b. 9 December 1915, Jarotschin (Posen; now Jarocin, Poland)

Soprano

One of the outstanding women singers of the post-war generation, after her Berlin debut in 1942 Schwarzkopf was invited by Karl **Böhm** to the Vienna Opera. She made her debut in Covent Garden in 1952. A year later she married Walter Legge, the artistic director of EMI records, for whom she made numerous recordings. As is often the case, fashions change, so that many of these recordings sound precious today and the voice and enunciation uneven, though her recording of Richard **Strauß**'s *Four Last Songs* remains remarkable by any standards.

DEREK McCULLOCH

Schweiger, Til

b. 19 December 1963, Freiburg

Film and television actor

After appearing in the popular television soap opera *Lindenstraße* and the crime series *Die Kommissarin* and *Polizeiruf 110*, Schweiger starred in several hit feature films in the early 1990s. These included Wolfgang Büld's car comedy *Manta, Manta* (1992), Sönke **Wortmann**'s *The Most Desired Man* (*Der bewegte Mann*, 1994) and Detlev **Buck**'s *Jailbirds* (*Männerpension*, 1995). Schweiger became one of the best-known leading men of early 1990s German popular cinema, with his brash macho image bringing him pin-up status.

JONATHAN LEGG

Schygulla, Hanna

b. 25 December 1943, Katowice (Poland)

Actress

Sometimes compared with Marlene **Dietrich** and Kristina Söderbaum, Hanna Schygulla emerged from Munich subculture in the 1960s, where she was a founder-member of the *antiteater* group. Her career is closely associated with Rainer Werner **Fassbinder**, and she starred in many of his films, becoming a household name in Germany for her title role in *Fontane Effi Briest* (1974) and internationally celebrated for her dramatically nuanced performance in *The Marriage of Maria Braun* (*Die Ehe der Maria Braun*, 1978). She has also starred in films by Wim **Wenders**, Margarethe von **Trotta**, Volker **Schlöndorff** and Jean-Luc Godard.

HELEN HUGHES

science

Up to the 1930s Germany's scientific reputation was very high, a situation which changed dramatically under the Nazis, when many eminent scientists emigrated. Nevertheless, recent international comparisons demonstrate that Germany has re-established a powerful position in scientific research. Expenditure on research and technology, as a percentage of her GDP, indicates that Germany ranks only after the US and Japan. Two-thirds of funding comes from industry, followed by the federal and *Länder* governments. An analysis of different disciplines indicates that Germany scores well above average on research in energy, chemistry and life sciences, with information and communication sciences, physics, biotechnology and medicine as average, and engineering science now below average. The greatest growth areas, both in Germany and worldwide, are in biotechnology, applied microbiology, communication and computer sciences, together with medicine and materials research with Germany's contribution particularly strong in environmental sciences. As elsewhere, German science is increasingly developing at an international level. The **Humboldt Foundation** and the **DAAD** are the most prominent bodies responsible for publicly funded exchange projects employing German and foreign scientists. German co-operation in science and technology involves agreements with over thirty countries; the JET and ITER programmes in nuclear fusion and COST (international co-operation outside the EU) in applied research are prime examples. Every four years the federal government publishes a comprehensive report, detailing the aims and focus of research developments and financial support.

Public funding for research in 1991 amounted to DM 25.07 million, half going to the natural sciences, 7.6 percent to medicine and 17 percent to arts and social sciences. This is co-ordinated by the Bundesministerium für Forschung und Wissenschaft (Federal Ministry for Science and Research) under whose authority the Wissenschaftsrat (Science Council) was founded in 1957 as an administrative body responsible to the federal and *Länder* governments. It is charged with developing a comprehensive strategy for the promotion of scholarship and for a structural programme of research within and outside universities. Still the main arena for research, especially basic research, **universities** are the only institutions which cover all scientific disciplines. Closely linked with them are the seven **academies** of science, whose remit is the promotion of long-term projects. The largest and most prestigious centres for scientific research are the institutes administered by the Max-Planck-Gesellschaft where research of the highest international standard is carried out. Applied research is directed and executed by the Frauenhofer Society with its fifty institutes undertaking commissioned projects for industry. Several private donors such as the Volkswagen and Fritz Thyssen Foundations provide significant funds for individual research projects. In total, nearly half a million people work in German science and research.

Further reading

Federal Ministry for Research and Technology (1996) *Report of the Federal Government on Research*, Bonn: Bundesministerium für Forschung und Technik (an official report with much statistical data).

Schneider, C. and Maier-Leibnitz, H. (1991) 'The Status of Academic Research in the Federal German Republic: A Report on Two Surveys and the Testimony of Individual Scientists', *Minerva* 29, 1: 27–60 (discusses scientific research and development at German universities).

HANS J. HAHN

science fiction

The term 'science fiction' (SF), in use in English since before 1930, entered popular German vocabulary untranslated around 1960. Precursors of German science fiction can be found in the works of the romantics, whose preoccupation with magnetism, mesmerism, magical optics and automata was frequently reflected in their literary productions (e.g. E.T.A. Hoffmann's *Der Sandmann*, a source of Offenbach's *Tales of Hoffmann* of 1881).

The *Romantik*-inspired demonization of technology, continuing as a motif in German naturalism (G. Hauptmann) and horribly confirmed by the industrialized carnage of WWI, inspired a host of early German writers and filmmakers who emphasized the sinister, anti-humanistic forces of technological change, for instance Alfred Döblin with *Berge, Meere und Giganten* (Mountains, Oceans, and Giants) (1924) and Fritz Lang with *Metropolis* (1927).

A popular, progress-affirming and more utopian strain in German fantastic writing – the true antecedent of modern German SF – dates from Jules Verne (1828–1905) and Paul Scheerbart (1863–1915). Bernhard Kellermann (1875–1951) recounts in *Der Tunnel* the building of a passage under the Atlantic, and Hans Dominik (1872–1945) wrote numerous popular novels celebrating German technological bravura. Curt Siodmak (1902–) wrote novels in the 1930s that introduced many modern SF staples, including teleportation in *Bis ans Ende der Welt* (To the End of the World) (1933) and lasers in *Rache im Äther* (Revenge in Space) (1932).

The devastation of WWII and the division of Germany caused a rupture in both the philosophical-dystopian and technophile-utopian manifestations of the genre: post-war German fantastic writing developed in the shadow of foreign influences rather than within the heretofore robust indigenous tradition. By far the livelier cultivation of science fiction was in the socialist East, where class warfare was projected into outer space, as in Eberhardt del'Antonio's *Titanus* (1959), or aliens intervened in the class struggle on earth, as in Alexander Kröger's *Sieben fielen vom Himmel* (Seven Fell from the Skies) (1969). Influenced by the more reflective and philosophical form of science fiction developed by Stanislaw Lem and other eastern

European writers, later East German writers dealt with basic moral questions, as in Rainer Fuhrmann's *Die Untersuchung* (The Investigation) (1984), lifting the genre occasionally above triviality.

If the science fiction writing of the eastern half of Germany was dominated by the political and cultural agenda of the occupying Soviets, West Germany willingly succumbed to a flood of popular SF literature from the US and Britain. Seizing the commercial opportunity, the Moewig publishing company introduced the enormously popular 'Perry Rhodan' series in 1961, printed in up to 300,000 copies by the 1970s. Perry Rhodan fan clubs counted tens of thousands of members. Perry Rhodan authors were usually Germans writing under Anglo-sounding pseudonyms, for instance 'Clark Darlton' (Walter Ernsting). Other publishers of popular SF series in Germany today, such as the Heyne Verlag in Munich, publish mainly translations.

Science fiction in Germany today remains in the mould of the modern Anglo-American tradition, and as such is mainly 'the belletristic vehicle of a technocratic ideology' (Manfred Nagl), with Roland Emmerich's 'Hollywood' movie *Independence Day* (1997) the most successful imitation of the type to date.

JEFFREY GARRETT

Scientology

The Scientology sect was founded by the American science-fiction writer L(afayette) Ron(ald) Hubbard (1911–86), following the publication of his book *Dianetics* (1950). Claiming some 8 million followers all over the world (30,000 in Germany), Hubbard's organization has sought recognition as *The Church of Scientology* for tax reasons in the US and elsewhere. Scientology is based on a system of Hubbard's mysterious truths and revelations, as well as a hierarchy of illumination. Public concern about the sect has been especially forceful in Germany, where the federal and *Land* governments have placed it under observation for its 'totalitarian' and 'anti-democratic' principles, and where films starring Hollywood Scientologists such as Tom Cruise and John Travolta have been picketed and boycotted. The Scientology organization in its turn has compared the 'victimization' of its German members to that of the Jews in the 1930s, and the US State Department has expressed concern at 'human-rights abuses' in Germany.

FREDERIC M. KOPP

sculpture

Despite divergent developments in sculpture in the two German states, the anti-classical figurative style of the pre-war period provided a common thread and prevailed between 1945 and 1949. During the 1950s sculpture in the FRG quickly came under the influence of a supranational confluence of western European and American abstract art. Representational sculpture was pushed into the background where it remained until **neo-expressionism** revived the figure. In the GDR figurative conceptions based on the doctrine of **socialist realism** established themselves in the 1950s and formed the core of sculptural experience throughout the state's history. The unification process has left sculptors in the former FRG generally untouched, whilst in the former GDR the conditions on which the production, function and understanding of art were based have suddenly ceased to exist. The dominance of the art-market has had a disruptive impact, particularly on the practice of those artists exploring figurative possibilities.

Sculpture in the FRG

After the war sculpture, with its need for material and facilities, was affected by an absence of private patrons and state commissions. As an extremely public medium it suffered from the lack of suitable spaces. In addition, the appropriation by the Nazi regime of those figurative concepts that were not part of the avant-garde, and its megalomaniac and melodramatic perversions resulted in a general under-representation of sculpture in the post-war re-emergence of German art. Measured and timeless images of man citing the tradition of the nude figure, inward calmness and spirituality marked the work of an older generation of artists such as Kolbe, Scheibe, Marcks, Mataré and –

from the early 1960s onwards – Seitz and Grzimek. Until the early 1950s abstract sculpture such as the metal objects by Uhlmann and Hartung played a marginal role. When abstract art gained dominant influence it came to the fore in the shape of associative organic objects or reduced sculptural core forms, followed by more open and complex sculptural structures under the influence of Art Informel. During the later 1960s and 1970s sculpture expanded beyond its generic boundaries embracing new modes of expression such as minimal and conceptual art. By the end of the 1970s many artists had turned away from the optimistic rationality of the previous years, from a predilection for abstract ideas, pure material and geometric forms. An urge to trace individual experience and sensuality led to an emphasis on personal style and manifested itself in the use of new media such as performance, happenings, fluxus and video. By the beginning of the 1980s **neo-expressionism** reinstated a figurative language on the basis of eruptive outbreaks of creative force that resulted in intense formal gestures. Above all it was Joseph **Beuys** who broadened the understanding of art by insisting on the creative potential of man and by demanding that thought is sculpture. Both his work, centred around the visualization and transcendence of functional and situational relationships, and his personality, provided vital stimuli for the middle and younger generation of artists ranging from **Baselitz** and Lüpertz to Ruthenbeck, **Horn**, Mucha, Schütte and **Trockel**. The latter have become internationally recognized since the late 1980s. Although liberal pluralism best describes their disparate works, they have in common a close relation between their objects and installations and the surrounding space, as well as a saturation with complex meaning.

Public sculpture in the FRG

Monuments of the post-war period referred to the terror of the Nazi regime, war, persecution and death in stylized personifications of suffering, pain and grief. Abstract-organic metaphors relating to the contemporary situation surfaced by the end of the 1950s. The *Kunst am Bau* programme (a percentage of the sum for the construction of a public building has to be spent on art) provided a tool for the commission of architecture-related sculpture. During the late 1960s and 1970s stereometric forms and rational module-like structures were employed to articulate a reconciliation between art and technology, an optimism rooted in the German **Economic Miracle**. Since the 1980s public sculpture has become increasingly pluralistic in style and depended on initiatives such as the *Skulptur Projekte* in Münster, in 1977, 1987 and 1997.

Sculpture in the GDR

A figurative style that followed the anti-classical and realist traditions of the 1920s established itself in the 1950s in alignment with the doctrine of **socialist realism**. From the beginning, the instructive potential of representational sculpture was appropriated by the state to construct and circulate new meanings within a wider political culture, hence the importance of public sculpture. Memorials for the victims of the Nazi dictatorship – the Buchenwald memorial by **Cremer** being an outstanding example – and statues of the new heroes, stylized workers and peasants marked by social and historical attributes, as well as exemplary portraits, fulfilled this function. The liberalization of the cultural climate at the beginning of the 1970s widened the scope for individual aesthetic positions, and allowed for the articulation of ambiguous subjective experience. However, experiments beyond the traditional framework of sculpture were either officially ignored or annexed to the applied arts, and treated accordingly by the critics. Non-figurative sculpture, performances, happenings, video and so on existed at the periphery until the late 1980s, confined to an insider audience, for their showing was restricted to the few private galleries, a number of smaller communal spaces, or the church. The relatively homogeneous appearance of mainstream sculpture in the GDR remained unchallenged.

See also: art; documenta

Further reading

Franzke, A. (1991) 'New German Sculpture. The Legacy of Beuys', in A. Papadakis, C. Farrow and N. Hodges (eds), *New Art. An International Survey*, London: Academy Editions (useful focus on the influence of Beuys on recent sculpture in the BRD).

Joachimides, C., Rosenthal, N. and Schmied, W. (eds) (1986) *German Art in the 20th Century. Painting and Sculpture 1905–1985*, Munich: Prestel (overview of art in Germany and the FRG).

Mensch-Figur-Raum. Werke deutscher Bildhauerkunst des 20. Jahrhunderts (1988) Berlin: Staatliche Museen zu Berlin (East), Nationalgalerie (introduction to the understanding of sculpture in the GDR and its traditions).

Skulptur Projekte in Münster 1987 (1987) Cologne: DuMont (influential project of sculpture in the public sphere).

SkulpturSpannungen. Skulptur heute (1986) Cologne, Berlin and Munich (contemporary sculpture in the FRG and beyond).

KERSTIN MEY

SDS

No single factor was more significant in shaping the political character of the West German **student movement** than the *Sozialistischer Deutscher Studentenbund* (SDS) (League of German Socialist Students). The radical transformation that the SDS itself underwent in the course of its twenty-year history is graphically illustrated in the development of its two most prominent leaders: while one of its earliest chairmen, Helmut **Schmidt**, became a leading Social Democrat and Federal Chancellor, one of its last and best known spokesmen, Rudi **Dutschke**, helped found the party which, as the real heir to the student movement, came to pose such an electoral threat to the **SPD**, namely *Die Grünen* (see also **Greens**).

Founded in Hamburg in September 1946 the SDS was initially motivated by anti-fascism and a morally defined anti-capitalism. Formally independent of the SPD, the SDS nevertheless identified with the policies of that party, and following the massive electoral defeat the latter sustained in 1953 it was actually the Berlin SDS which first proposed the wholesale modernization of Social Democracy that, some five years later, was to be expressed formally in the Godesberg Programme (1959). This consensus did not extend, however, to the remilitarization of Germany, which the SDS consistently opposed. In May 1960 a right-wing faction split off from the SDS to found a rival organization which won the backing of the SPD, and in the following year the rift was completed when the SPD leadership declared party membership incompatible with that of the SDS.

Far from dissolving into insignificance the now autonomous SDS vigorously set about developing its positions in theoretical debate, much of which was conducted in the journal *neue kritik* and in discussions with the New Left in Britain and America. While ultimately concerned to rouse the West German public from its state of depoliticization, the SDS initially focused its energies on university politics. Its memorandum on higher education of 1961, one of the inaugural documents of the student protest movement, argued for a wide-ranging reform of universities which would shake off 'the thousand-year dust' clinging to old institutions of power. This idea was popularized in one of the most famous campaign slogans of the student movement, *Unter den Talaren, der Muff von tausend Jahren* (Underneath the professorial gowns there lies the reactionary sediment of a thousand years), the typically ironic tone of which very much reflected the iconoclastic spirit brought to the SDS at the Free University of Berlin by a group of 'situationists'. Banded together in political communes, the most notorious being the *Kommune 1*, they specialized in spectacular 'happenings' and other forms of 'subversive action' designed to taunt and ridicule authority. Their techniques of provocation went as far as advocating arson in department stores in order to give the population 'an authentic Vietnam feeling' (advice taken literally by Andreas **Baader** and Gudrun **Ensslin** in April 1968). The Vietnam War had been a focus of SDS activity since the highly successful 'Vietnam semester' it organized at the Free University in autumn 1965, and in May 1966 the SDS sponsored a Vietnam congress at Frankfurt University where the 2,200 participants heard the main speaker, Herbert **Marcuse**, analyse the war as an egregious example of western imperialism.

On 2 June 1967 another act of violence, this time rather closer to home, served to ignite further the spirit of anti-authoritarianism. During a demonstration in West Berlin against a visit by the Shah of Iran the student Benno Ohnesorg was shot dead by a policeman, an act interpreted by the SDS as a political murder on behalf of a system lurching towards fascism. Similarly, the extremely comprehensive security measures adopted by the police at the ensuing mass demonstrations were seen as a dress rehearsal for the proclamation of a state of emergency and the suspension of democracy. Such interpretations could only gain any plausibility in a situation where many believed that, through the formation of the Grand Coalition and its assent to the Emergency Laws, parliament had abdicated its role as watchdog of government and guarantor of the constitution. The ensuing political vacuum was to be filled by an Extra-Parliamentary Opposition (**APO**). This term developed a double meaning in SDS circles: on the one hand, it referred to a specific campaign against the proposed Emergency Laws, on the other it signalled a broad social movement led by the students against established politics and culture. In the latter sphere the chief target was the **Springer** press which the SDS, clearly betraying the influence on it of **Frankfurt School** theory, saw as epitomizing the manipulative powers of the 'culture industry'. When on 11 April 1968 a *Bild* reader shot Rudi Dutschke, this triggered a further explosion of mass protest which both marked the climax of the efforts of the SDS to forge an alliance between students and workers and inaugurated unprecedented levels of violence and vandalism.

By the summer of 1968, when the Emergency Laws were finally passed by parliament, it was apparent to the SDS that the transition from particularized protest to wholesale opposition to the political system could not be achieved by its policy of openly confronting the state. A more gradual process, a 'long march through the institutions', was required which meant extending its political activity into the schools and factories. By the spring of 1970 a situation had been reached where the SDS decided on its own dissolution, having dispersed itself in various *Basisgruppen* (local action groups) out of which grew a number of Marxist–Leninist parties (*K-Gruppen*). Ironically, in view of the origins of the SDS, the main impact was, however, on the SPD, whose youth wing (Jusos), ideologically enlivened by the influx of some 100,000 new members, now embarked on a 'dual strategy' combining party-political involvement with grassroots extra-parliamentary mobilization.

Further reading

Albrecht, W. (1994) *Der Sozialistische Deutsche Studentenbund (SDS): Vom parteikonformen Studentenbund zum Repräsentanten der Neuen Linken*, Bonn: Dietz Verlag (monumental study concentrating on pre-1960s developments).

Fichter, T. and Lönnendonker, S. (1977) *Kleine Geschichte des SDS*, Berlin: Rotbuch (concise but incisive study of the SDS's organization and strategy debates).

ROB BURNS AND WILFRIED VAN DER WILL

SED

The Sozialistische Einheitspartei Deutschlands (SED) (The Socialist Unity Party of Germany) was the leading political party in the Soviet zone of Germany and the German Democratic Republic from its foundation in April 1946 to its reformation into the SED-**PDS** in December 1989. It was founded in April 1946 from an amalgamation of the **KPD** and the **SPD** which had been the first political parties to be re-established in the Soviet zone in June 1945. The KPD had originally resisted suggestions from the SPD of an immediate amalgamation, but the failure of communist parties to make significant electoral gains in Austria and Hungary in the autumn of 1945 convinced the Soviet Union and KPD leaders of the necessity of such a merger. In the only open vote in the SPD on the issue – in West Berlin in March 1946 – 82 percent voted against a merger, and the SPD, led by Otto **Grotewohl** in Berlin, was fearful of being forced into an unequal partnership with the KPD, but under strong pressure from the Soviet Union it had no choice but to agree.

At the first party conference on 21 and 22 April 1946 the principle of parity of representation of the two parties in the structure of the SED was established. Also the 'principles and aims' of the new party stressed the 'German road to socialism': the immediate imposition of the Soviet model was not envisaged. These aims had, however, been devised with the all-German context in mind, and with the intensification of the Cold War, and the growing division between the two parts of Germany, the SED started in the summer of 1948 to move towards a party on the Soviet model. The 'Party of the New Type' was formally declared at the party conference in January 1949, and the principle of parity, which had already been extensively undermined, was revoked. With this change the SED moved from being a mass Marxist party to one based on cadres with a strongly hierarchical structure. The principle of 'democratic centralism' which made party decisions binding on all its members and bodies and forbade the existence of factions within the party became the organizational principle of the SED. A **Politbüro** was elected which effectively became the most powerful body of the SED.

The SED was not the only political party in the Soviet zone, but since July 1945 the other parties had been bound together with the KPD/SED in an anti-fascist Unity Front with the leading role being played by the KPD/SED. With the foundation of the GDR in October 1949 the SED established its position as the dominant political body in the GDR. It occupied all leading positions in the government with one chairman, Wilhelm **Pieck**, as President, and the other, Otto Grotewohl, as Prime Minister. At its Third Party Conference in July 1950 the executive committee of the party was replaced by the **Central Committee**, with its most influential figure, Walter **Ulbricht**, as its General Secretary. A secretariat of the Central Committee was established at the same time, and it was this group which supervised and controlled the entire party apparatus. Although the other parties continued to exist, they did so in the 'National Front' alongside the mass organizations and under the complete domination of the SED which had control over who was selected as candidates for election on single lists.

In June 1953 the party received a severe shock to its authority in the **June Uprising**, but it managed to recover and to continue to restructure the institutional structures and the economy of the GDR along Marxist–Leninist lines. Despite various attempts to oust him, Ulbricht maintained his position as leader, and after 1958 ruled unchallenged until his removal in 1971. After the closing of the borders in 1961 the SED allowed some liberalization of the economy with the New Economic Policy and a relaxation in cultural policy, but the crushing of the reform programme in Czechoslovakia in 1968 brought to an end any possibility of change. Article 1 of the second constitution of the GDR in 1968 formalized the leading role of the SED, and this role remained unchallenged until the autumn of 1989.

After Erich **Honecker** took over as First Secretary in 1971 any hopes of profound changes in the party were not realized. The structures and practices of the SED were confirmed in the party programme and statute in 1976, which remained in force until 1989. The inability of the SED to change and adapt was highlighted after 1985, when the party rejected any move in the direction of Gorbachev's reform programme in the Soviet Union. This inability led directly to its downfall in November 1989 and the removal of its leading role from the constitution on 1 December 1989.

See also: constitutions: GDR; elections: GDR; parties and mass organizations: GDR; political culture: GDR

Further reading

Herbst, A., Stephan, G.R. and Winkler, J. (1997) *Die SED: Geschichte, Organisation, Politik: Ein Handbuck*, Berlin: Dietz.

PETER BARKER

Sedlmayr, Walter

b. 6 January 1926, Munich; d. 14 July 1990, Munich

Actor

Sedlmayr worked with **Achternbusch**, **Fassbinder** and **Schlöndorff** and also acted in obscure

Heimatfilme. His death created more headlines than his entire career as the police searched for his killers in the gay community as well as in Munich high society for many years. A typical character actor, he played the leading role in Hans Jürgen **Syberberg**'s 1972 *Ludwig's Cook (Theodor Hierneis oder: Wie man ehem. Hofkoch wird)*.

UTE LISCHKE-McNAB

Seeler, Uwe

b. 5 November 1936, Hamburg

Soccer player

During his playing career with SV Hamburg between 1954 and 1972, Seeler was one of Germany's most popular footballers. An acrobatic and industrious centre forward, he scored forty-three goals in his seventy-two appearances for West Germany, and captained his country in the World Cup in 1966 and 1970.

MIKE DENNIS

Seghers, Anna

b. 19 November 1900, Mainz; d. 1 June 1983, (East) Berlin

Writer (real name Netty Radvanyi, née Reiling)

Anna Seghers is widely regarded as one of the most important German women writers of the twentieth century, although her communism made her a controversial figure during the Cold War. Born the only child of well-to-do Jewish parents, she studied art history and Chinese in Heidelberg and Cologne before marrying in 1925 a Hungarian Marxist, the sociologist Laszlo Radvanyi. She joined the **KPD** in 1928 and the League of Proletarian Revolutionary Writers one year later. Forced into exile in 1933, she fled first to Paris and then to Marseilles. In 1941 she and her family finally reached Mexico City, where she was to spend the remainder of an unusually productive exile as a leading member of a lively émigré community of German communists. She returned to Germany in 1947 and settled in

East Berlin, where she committed herself to building a new, socialist Germany and enjoyed public prominence as President of the **Writers' Union of the GDR** (1952–78).

Seghers achieved early fame with the award of the prestigious Kleist Prize in 1928. Her subsequent work provided clear evidence of her political convictions but was seldom sufficiently orthodox to satisfy party dogmatists. Her major literary achievements, both published in English during WWII, are the novels *The Seventh Cross* (*Das siebte Kreuz*), which became a bestseller, received a Book of the Month award, and was turned into a successful Hollywood film, and *Transit Visa* (*Transit*), which draws on her experience of the frantic scramble among refugees for a safe passage out of Vichy France. Much of the work which she produced after returning from exile fell well short of her best, however. The enormous prestige she enjoyed in the GDR has been questioned in recent years, notably after Walter **Janka**'s attack on her integrity, but her reputation in unified Germany remains high. She is one of the few eminent people from the GDR who were made honorary citizens of Berlin before 1989 and still retain that status today, and the street in Berlin-Adlershof where she lived for many years has been renamed Anna-Seghers-Straße.

See also: cultural policy: GDR

Major works

Seghers, A. (1928) *Der Aufstand der Fischer von St. Barbara*, Berlin: Kiepenheuer; trans. M.L. Goldsmith, *The Revolt of the Fishermen*, London: Mathews & Marrot, 1929.

—— (1942) *Das siebte Kreuz*, Mexico: El libro libre; trans. J.A. Galston, *The Seventh Cross*, Boston, MA: Little, Brown & Co, 1942 (the successful 1944 Hollywood adaptation, *The Seventh Cross*, was directed by Fred Zinnemann and starred Spencer Tracy).

—— (1948) *Transit*, Konstanz: Weller; trans. J.A. Galston, *Transit*, Boston, MA: Little, Brown & Co, 1948.

Further reading

Argonautenschiff. Jahrbuch der Anna-Seghers-Gesellschaft Berlin und Mainz E.V. (1992) Berlin and Weimar: Aufbau (essays on the work as well as previously unpublished texts by Seghers herself).

Wallace, I. (ed.) (1998) *Anna Seghers in Perspective*, Amsterdam and Atlanta, GA: Rodopi (collection of essays on various aspects of Seghers's work).

Zehl Romero, C. (1993) *Anna Seghers*, Reinbek bei Hamburg: Rowohlt (survey of life and work, with numerous photographs).

IAN WALLACE

sex shops

In the wake of the liberalization of public attitudes in the 1960s, an industry providing 'sex education' films and sex aids began to appear in Germany. At first, this development was restricted to sex cinemas, but soon sex shops also opened.

Following further decriminalization, and pioneered by such countries as Sweden, Denmark and The Netherlands, these shops proliferated in the 1970s, for the first time offering hard-core **pornography** legally. While independent sex shops still exist, most of them are run by conglomerates such as Beate **Uhse** and Dr Müller. At first only located in red-light districts, they can now be found in small towns and villages all over Germany. Beate Uhse was also the first to introduce 'mobile sex shops' to the ex-GDR, where pornography was banned.

HOLGER BRIEL

Silly

The East German rock band Silly was founded in 1978. Silly's success was due to singer Tamara Danz (1952–96), the complex melodies and the sensitive portrayals of the East German malaise of the 1980s. Their second LP *Mont Klamott* (1983) was voted GDR Rock Record of the year. Other records include *Bataillon d'amour* (1986) and *February* (1989) (a farewell to the GDR).

See also: rock music

Further reading

Schumann, D. (director) (1987; sequel 1994) *flüstern und SCHREIEN*, DEFA (a documentary film about East German rock music).

MARGRIT FRÖLICH

Simmel, Johannes Mario

b. 7 April 1924, Vienna

Writer

Simmel is by far the best-selling post-war German-language author. Although frequently shunned by the German literary establishment, his novels have been well received in the English-speaking world and are increasingly being taken seriously in Germany. They are based on real events, and also seek to portray the context of the action authentically. Simmel uses straightforward language, but weaves complex plots. The novels champion individuals against the big battalions of government and business.

Simmel rejects the distinction made more sharply in Germany between writing as high art and writing as entertainment, seeing himself in the tradition of Fallada, Maugham and Hemingway. Action-packed plots, spiced with sex and crime, package his message for a larger readership in a way of which Brecht might have approved. *Niemand ist eine Insel* (Nobody Is an Island) (1975) confronts the problems of handicapped children, but the bait for the reader is the glamorous film industry. He often draws on his own professional experience. Simmel's early work as a script writer provides the backdrop for *Ich gestehe alles* (I Confess Everything) (1952), in which an American script writer with a year left to live rediscovers himself. Simmel's training as a journalist enables him to write about the intrigues of the publishing industry in *Der Stoff aus dem die Träume sind* (The Stuff that Dreams are Made Of) (1971) and provides a vehicle for other novels: *Gott schützt die Liebenden* (God Protects Lovers) (1957); *Die im Dunkeln sieht man nicht* (You Can't See the Ones in the Shadows) (1985); and *Doch mit den Clowns kamen die Tränen* (But the Clowns Brought the Tears With Them) (1987). Such powerful themes are found again: love in *Love is*

Just a Word (1969; *Liebe ist nur ein Wort*, 1963); the effects of Cold-War politics on post-war Germany in *Dear Fatherland* (1969; *Lieb Vaterland magst ruhig sein*, 1965; *Double Agent – Triple Cross* 1980); and biological warfare research in *The Ceasar Code* (1970, 1976; *Und Jimmy ging zum Regenbogen*, 1970). Many of Simmel's books deal with the legacy of WWII. *It Can't Always be Caviar* (1965; *Es muß nicht immer Kaviar sein*, 1960), tells of a reluctant secret agent, whose culinary skills enable him to escape from the enemy; *Mich wundert, daß ich so fröhlich bin* (I'm Surprised I'm So Cheerful) (1949), explores the self-discovery of seven people trapped in an air-raid shelter; *Cain '67* (1971; *Alle Menschen werden Brüder*, 1967), publicized the existence of Nazi organizations in post-war Germany when this was still a taboo subject. First-person narrative, wise counsellors (usually police inspectors), and references to evocative music all play their parts in Simmel's work.

Further reading

Schlicht, K. (1989) *Die Figur des Erzählers bei Johannes Mario Simmel. Ein Beitrag zur narrativen Gestaltung des modernen Unterhaltungsromans*, Marburger Studien zur Germanistik 12, Marburg: Hitzeroth (contains useful bibliography and interview with Simmel).

Simmel, J.M. (1992) 'Schriftsteller und Politik', *Neue deusche Literatur* 40: 153–63.

JONATHAN WEST

Sinkel, Bernhard

b. 19 January 1940, Frankfurt am Main

Filmmaker

Sinkel trained as a lawyer before turning to film (with Alf Brustellin). He worked as a scriptwriter and for television. His first feature, *Lina Braake* (1975), was hailed as a revival of German comedy, and was a huge success with critics and at the box office thanks to Sinkel's crisp dialogue and outstanding performances from ageing stars Lina Carstens and Fritz Rasp. The thriller *On Ice* (*Kaltgestellt*, 1981) explores the political climate in the FRG following the Baader–Meinhof crisis. After Brustellin's death in 1981, Sinkel worked mainly for television.

See also: New German Cinema

MARTIN BRADY

Sinn und Form

Launched in 1949 as the bi-monthly cultural journal of the GDR's Academy of the Arts, *Sinn und Form* achieved international recognition under the editorship of Peter **Huchel** (1949–62) both for its preservation of a sense of German cultural unity and for its emphasis on literary quality despite Cold War pressures. It regained something of its prestige in the **Honecker** era through its publication of the controversial work of authors such as Ulrich **Plenzdorf**, Volker **Braun** and Franz **Fühmann**. Since the **Wende** it has helped to promote a historical understanding of GDR culture by publishing previously suppressed documents.

DENNIS TATE

Sitte, Willi

b. 28 February 1921, Kratzau (Chrastava, Czechoslovakia)

Painter and graphic artist

Influenced by Léger and Picasso, Sitte sought to renew the principles of **socialist realism** through using achievements of modern art. His figurative paintings focus on the depiction of working people who are often represented as nude and dynamic bodies. Many of his paintings were commissioned by the state. From 1974 to 1988, he headed the Artists' Association of the GDR, where he tried to increase the social influence of artists, their social security and freedom to move, yet he remained reserved against the experiments of young artists.

See also: cultural policy: GDR; documenta; painting

KERSTIN MEY

skinheads

In West Germany the first groups of skinheads emerged in the late 1970s, but it was not until the beginning of the 1980s that the broadening of the movement's base was seen. As in Great Britain – where they had originated years earlier – skins were part of a youth sub-culture which was an expression of revolt against the older generation and their norms. They originally defined themselves as non-racist, rooted in working-class traditions and anti-political. The skinheads in Germany replaced the **punks**, who by now had become too fashionable for many whose self-definition was based on the sense of belonging to a sub-culture.

Although from their very beginnings skins proclaimed that they saw themselves as non-political, the vast majority of them could be said to hold right-wing ideas. As the left was for many associated with political opposition, bourgeois attitudes and boredom, the extreme political right provided much better opportunities to provoke the establishment (for example with Nazi symbols and slogans). It also provided the environment the skins were looking for: a display of machismo-masculinity, a sense of comradeship, and the acceptability of boozing and rioting – in their eyes tantamount to the quintessence and the very substance of their self-image.

The football stadiums were the main playground for the first generation of skinheads, and thus for many young people football spectatorship was the beginning of their involvement with the skinhead culture. However, when their aggressive behaviour barred them from the football grounds many changed their outfit and hairstyle and turned into today's football hooligans.

Due to the fact that the skinheads shared some values and attitudes with the political right, especially towards foreigners and the left wing, neo-nazi organizations sought to gain access to the scene. Initially they seemed to be successful in targeting various skinhead groups and involving them in some spectacular events as was the case when the Germans played the Turkish national football team in 1983. Yet soon afterwards skinheads started to keep their distance again for fear of getting involved in any organized political activities and they realized that they were used as thugs by the neo-Nazis.

During the next few years it was not so much the case that skinheads joined Nazi organizations but vice versa: larger numbers of young neo-Nazis joined Skinhead groups since this seemed to be the quickest way of earning a reputation of being cool, hard and unmistakably right-wing. These attitudes only remotely resembled the original values of the movement, and the original skinheads and those sympathizing with them started to feel alienated from their own origins. In the mid-1980s this split manifested itself in the foundation of the German section of 'SkinHeads Against Racial Prejudice' (SHARP) – an anti-racist skin organization founded in the US. Since then skinheads have been deeply divided, although the media still portray them as a homogeneous mainly right-wing phenomenon.

To a much lesser degree and encountering considerably more suppression, skinhead groups emerged in the GDR at about the same time as in West Germany – since this seemed to be a most effective way of annoying the state authorities. They copied the style and attitudes of their western counterparts without knowing much about the origins of the sub-culture. But only the collapse of the 'first anti-fascist state on German soil', as the GDR defined itself, brought about an inflation of skinheads and hooligans who now follow in the footsteps of their western counterparts.

Further reading

Farin, F. and Seidel-Pielen, E. (1995) *Skinheads*, Munich: Beck (gives an up-to-date account of the development of the Skinhead culture in Germany).

ASTRID HERHOFFER

Sloterdijk, Peter

b. 26 June 1947, Karlsruhe

Philosopher, writer and cultural critic

Known for his theories of the subject during the 1980s, and within the critical debates of 'New Subjectivity', Sloterdijk writes in the tradition of the **Frankfurt School** of **Critical Theory**. In his major work *Critique of Cynical Reason* (*Kritik der zynischen Vernunft*) (1983), he attempts to revitalize contemporary theories of the subject by returning to the history and philosophy of cynicism and by restoring the body in theoretical accounts of subjectivity. He has taught in Karlsruhe and Frankfurt am Main and is currently a freelance writer.

KALLIOPI NIKOLOPOULOU

soap operas

Soap operas are a relatively new genre in Germany's televisual history. One of the reasons for this is that until the mid-1980s German radio and television **broadcasting**, being public institutions, did not have private sponsorship. In the US, where soap operas originated, they were initially sponsored by detergent manufacturers, whose target audience were housewives, who, it was hoped, would buy their products.

While television programmes in Germany which would qualify as soap operas due to their serial contents did exist, such as *Familie Hesselbach* (The Hesselbach Family), they did not fulfil one important prerequisite: they were not aired on a daily basis. With the advent of private television this changed, and nowadays programmes such as *Verbotene Liebe* (Forbidden Love), *Gute Zeiten, Schlechte Zeiten* (Good Times, Bad Times), *Geliebte Schwestern* (Beloved Sisters) and *Marienhof* are broadcast on a daily basis on both private and public stations.

One aspect which distinguishes German series from their American counterparts is the time of their airing. Generally speaking, daytime television has not caught on in Germany; instead, what has caught the eye of the viewers are the *Vorabendsendungen* (pre-prime-time broadcasting) between 17.50 and 20.00 (see also **advertising**). It is during that time slot that German soap operas are shown.

Another American series, *Dallas*, had a strong impact on the acceptability of soap operas in Germany. Before being shown in Germany, it had already shifted audience make-up in the US itself.

While it went out only once a week, it was much more lavishly produced than the daily soaps, yet still retained their 'cliff-hanger' quality, i.e. the individual episodes were not conclusive in themselves, but at least one plot strand always awaited its resolution in the following week's episode. It went on to become a worldwide success. While in Germany there was still much ideological opposition to the televisual presentation of the American (business) dream, its huge audience rating spoke for itself, and in the wake of *Dallas* comparable German weeklies started to be broadcast. Many of these shows had a distinctive 'German' theme to them, the most prominent being *Schwarzwaldklinik* (Black Forest Hospital) which ran for several seasons and broke many audience records. Another, *Lindenstraße*, has been on the air for more than ten years and has become Germany's longest-running soap opera. Its decisive approach to German topics, focusing on minorities in Germany, everyday problems of everyday people, and tackling general prejudices, has begun to make it acceptable even to its former critics.

See also: television

HOLGER BRIEL

socialist realism

Despite the hostility of returning exiles such as Bertolt **Brecht**, the Soviet doctrine of socialist realism was imposed on all spheres of culture in the GDR in the early 1950s. Attempts had been made by Marxist critics of the calibre of Georg **Lukács** to evolve a more flexible theory for a German socialist culture, which would place much more emphasis on the humanistic heritage of Goethe and Schiller, but Cold War pressures encouraged the GDR's censorship authorities to insist on the adoption of the Stalinist criteria established at the Soviet Writers' Congress of 1934 (see also **censorship: GDR**). Their dogmatic interpretation of what constituted the 'objective reflection of reality', a 'partisan perspective', 'typical' conflicts and the 'positive hero(ine)' threatened to destroy the credibility of GDR culture as a whole in its formative years. Hans Marchwitza's 'construction novel' *Roheisen* (1955) exhibits all the worst features

of this endeavour to present propaganda as literature.

Although the idea of a distinctively East German road to socialist realism re-emerged in 1959 with enthusiastic SED backing in the context of the ***Bitterfelder Weg*** campaign, it appeared to have little substance. Only when the creative intellectuals who had been urged to gain first-hand experience of industrial life began to relate their findings to the grim reality of the post-1961 period, as symbolized by the Berlin Wall, did an authentic culture begin to emerge. Christa **Wolf**'s *Divided Heaven* (*Der geteilte Himmel*, 1963), which was also made into a successful **DEFA** film the following year (directed by Konrad **Wolf**), is the key work in this process of cultural emancipation from the straitjacket of socialist realist theory. The immense popularity of *Der geteilte Himmel* in both genres nevertheless suggested that the underlying socialist realist goal of making serious culture widely accessible might after all be attainable.

Such hopes were rapidly dashed, however, first by the renewal of ideological interference at the infamous **Eleventh Plenum** of 1965, then by the growing recognition amongst the authors and filmmakers themselves that the pursuit of 'subjective authenticity' (Christa Wolf) was incompatible with the narrow industrial focus of socialist realism. By the 1970s even an author like Stefan **Heym**, whose narrative style and treatment of character in his politically controversial novel *Five Days in June* (*Fünf Tage im Juni*, 1974) has much in common with socialist realism, was heralding the end of a literature which was 'neither socialist nor realistic'. It is equally significant that a leading literary critic like Dieter **Schlenstedt** was able in 1979 to publish a comprehensive study of GDR literature which made no reference to the state's official literary doctrine. In the 1980s it was a meaningless cliché found only in formal ideological discourse.

See also: prose fiction: GDR

Further reading

Chung, H. (ed.) (1996) *In the Party Spirit: Socialist Realism and Literary Practice in the Soviet Union, East*

Germany and China, Amsterdam: Rodopi (provides a range of comparative perspectives).

Scriven, M. and Tate, D. (eds) (1988) *European Socialist Realism*, Oxford: Berg (includes a chapter on the GDR).

DENNIS TATE

sociology

An analytical distinction can be made between German sociology and sociology in Germany: whereas German sociology assumes the existence of a particular theoretical and methodological tradition which mirrors the history and local culture of Germany, sociology in Germany describes the practical structure of the discipline in that country (the location of sociological research, national sociological journals, national professional bodies etc.). Both aspects are considered in turn below.

Since the war, German sociology has been characterized by controversy, over the question of continuity or change, and over the issue of the nature of sociology itself. In fact, continuity, through a re-orientation to the theoretical traditions of classical German sociology, and change, through interaction with American sociology, typify the development of German sociology. The debate on the nature of sociology has involved discussion both of the proper object of sociological research and of the methodology best suited to conducting such research, and has contributed to the existence of diverse schools of sociology. Sociology in Germany developed in a similar fashion to sociology in Austria and Switzerland. Due to its ideological orientation in the GDR, however, sociology developed differently there.

German sociology

The orthodox view of texts written on the history of German sociology since WWII has emphasized the influence of American sociology and argued that post-war German sociology developed in the context of the hegemony of US sociology, as illustrated by the new importance attached to empirical social research in Germany. Certainly, the reception of American sociology in general, and the structural functionalism of Merton and Parsons in particular, has had a major influence on the development of German sociology and has also played an important role in debates focused around the question, 'what is sociology?'.

The 'Americanization' of German sociology can, however, be questioned. Although American sociology has been influential in the development of post-war German sociology, particularly in empirical research, this influence has been neither one-sided nor merely uncritically accepted. The enforced exile of many German sociologists during the war led to interaction between German and American sociology. This can be illustrated by the case of the Institute for Social Research in Frankfurt am Main, which emigrated to the US and continued its work at the 'New School for Social Research' in New York (see also **Frankfurt School**). Furthermore, reception of American sociology has been critical and has involved the adaptation of American sociology to the German context as in the case of the social theory advanced by Jürgen **Habermas** or Niklas **Luhmann**. Habermas's reconstructive sociology synthesizes elements of Parsons's structural functionalism with the sociology of Max Weber, while Luhmann developed his systems theory from a critical reception of Parsons and Merton. The importance of Habermas's and Luhmann's theories to contemporary world sociology lends further credibility to the hypothesis that interculturality and interaction paint a truer picture of the development of German sociology than the notion of 'Americanization'.

Interaction with American sociology has been partnered by German contemporary sociology's re-orientation to the classical sociology (represented by Max Weber, Georg Simmel and others), and also its continuing concern with the 'dialectics of modernity' (Münch, 1993). Münch traces this concern with the contradictory nature of modern society through the work of contemporary German sociologists, from Theodor **Adorno** and Max **Horkheimer**, through Habermas and Luhmann and finally to Ulrich Beck's (1992) analysis of 'risk society'. Re-orientation to classical sociology and continuing concern with dialectical change have been identified, along with a blurred boundary between sociology and **philosophy**, and a strong resistance (for example, Habermas's critique of postmodernity) to the work of the French post-structuralists, as markers of a German sociology.

Yet even if a 'German' sociological tradition, characterized by continuity and change, can be identified, there is little consensus within German sociology on the nature of the discipline itself. Both the object of sociological analysis and the appropriate methodology are highly contested areas. Insight into the controversy which is typical of German sociology can be gained through consideration of the circumstances which produced the *Positivismusstreit* (the debate over positivism) in Germany sociology, or through exploration of the continuing debate between Habermas and Luhmann, representatives of **Critical Theory** and systems theory respectively.

German sociology in the 1950s and early 1960s, which provided the backdrop for the *Positivismusstreit*, was characterized by a three-way constellation of schools of thought, each competing for a hegemonic position in the field of sociology, situated in Cologne, Frankfurt am Main, and Dortmund and Münster, and led by René König, Adorno and Helmut Schelsky, respectively. König was concerned to divest sociology of its connections to cultural critique and to social philosophy, and to establish sociology based on positivism as a practical social scientific discipline, which could be defended as academically legitimate. In the early 1950s, Adorno echoed König's main themes, by positing empirical research as a corrective to the speculation of the humanities, and yet neo-Marxist critical theory, as propagated by the Frankfurt School, also represented the continuing relationship of social research to social philosophy within the German context. From 1957, however, Adorno returned to a position critical of positivism, of *Realsoziologie* (mere description of phenomena, lacking both interpretative and theoretical understanding) which he regarded as the 'thinning-out' of sociological thematics. And Schelsky, also a positivist, defined his work in comparison both to the Cologne and to the Frankfurt schools, subscribing neither to empirical social research influenced by American sociology nor to cultural sociology and social philosophy. Instead, he intended to develop a new programme based on

a transcendental 'theory of society', but it was, however, never realized. Nevertheless, much of Adorno's criticism of positivism may have been directed at Schelsky's work which Adorno saw as providing legitimation for the social status quo.

The debate between Habermas and Luhmann began in the 1970s and focuses on the nature of modern society. Luhmann developed a model of society as a system and argued that the assumption that complex modern societies can be understood and organized by individuals is untenable. Habermas argued against Luhmann's radical functionalism, stating that complete systems control is not possible. The concept of the autonomous 'system' in Habermas' later work on 'communicative action' does make concessions to Luhmann's position, and yet Habermas rejects Luhmann's radical functionalism and champions the notion of the 'lifeworld' (the collection of shared meaning and values of a society) which is conceived as having its own logic and thus not being reducible to the 'system'.

Continuation of controversy in the field of sociology in Germany has fuelled the debate on the future of sociology. In many countries, a sense of crisis in sociology has been articulated and, in the German context, disenchantment with sociology was expressed by Ralf **Dahrendorf** as early as the 1960s, and later reiterated by Schelsky in his 'anti-sociology'. A collection of articles published under the title *Jenseits der Utopie* (Beyond Utopia) in 1991 reflects on the positive and negative moments of 'disenchanted sociology'. This collection seeks to explore and understand sociology's sense of crisis as a consequence of contemporary sociologists' failure to understand sociology's double aim, which is to interpret social life and also to be self-reflexive. Strategies to develop a sociology which fully addresses this double aim should relativize the sense of crisis and allow the (re-)creation of a sociology which provides *Zeitdiagnose* (diagnosis of the times), by exploring the everyday phenomena through which culture and society are articulated. Its concerns must be simultaneously at the level of a theory of society, and at the level of analysis of a spatially and temporally located society, and indeed, *Zeitdiagnose*, the theory of society and analysis of a particular society, must be interlinked rather than allowed to develop separately.

One attempt to create such an integrated model of sociology, bridging the divide between empirical and theoretical work, and between quantitative and qualitative research methods, is represented by the conception of sociology as a *dritte Kultur* (a third way) between science and artistic production (Lepenies, 1985). In this attempt to overcome the sense of crisis in sociology, contemporary sociology in Germany acknowledges its relationship to, and, at the same time, its distinction from, *Kulturwissenschaft* (**cultural studies**), while retaining the search for synthesis related to models of dialectical change.

Sociology in Germany

The German Sociological Association was first founded in 1909. It was re-established in 1946 and publication of the *Kölner Zeitschrift für Soziologie* (Cologne Journal of Sociology) was resumed in 1948–9. New chairs in sociology were appointed in the immediate post-war period, although major expansion of sociology in the university sector did not take place until the 1960s.

Sociology in Austria

The *Wiener Gesellschaft für Soziologie* (Viennese Sociological Society) was founded in 1907, although the Austrian Sociological Association was not established until 1950, and the first university degree courses in sociology were not offered until 1966, following the creation of chairs in sociology in the early 1960s. As in West Germany, general expansion in the universities in the late 1960s and 1970s favoured sociology. The younger generation of fully-trained sociologists took over the Austrian Sociological Association in the mid-1970s and publication of the *Österreichische Zeitschrift für Soziologie* (Austrian Journal of Sociology) began in 1976. Theoretically, Austrian sociology was influenced by debates in both Germany and the US, but there was no formation of specific schools within Austria.

Sociology in Switzerland

The Swiss Sociological Association was founded in 1955, but the majority of its members were not professional sociologists until the 1970s. Professionalization and institutionalization of sociology in Switzerland took place in the 1970s and included publication of the *Schweizer Zeitschrift für Soziologie* (Swiss Journal of Sociology) in 1975 – a bilingual (French and German) journal. Despite the fact that the journal is published bilingually, language barriers have hindered collaboration between French-speaking and German-speaking sociologists in Switzerland. It is difficult in Switzerland, as in Austria, to distinguish clear schools of sociology.

Sociology in the GDR

In the GDR, the term 'sociology' was initially excluded by the Institut für Gesellschaftswissenschaften des Zentralkomitees der SED (The Central Committee of the SED's Institute for the Study of Society), who preferred to label their Marxist–Leninism as *Gesellschaftswissenschaft* (study of society). An obligatory introductory course in *Gesellschaftswissenschaft* formed the ideological basis for all academic studies. However, the late 1950s saw official recognition of the importance of empirical social research and in the 1960s, through professionalization and internationalization, the label 'sociology' was adopted, with a corresponding analytical separation of Marxist from bourgeois sociology. This could not resolve the tension between an ideologically-oriented *Gesellschaftswissenschaft* and the application of professional social research.

Further reading

Beck, U. (1992) *Risk Society. Towards a New Modernity*, London: Sage.

Fleck, C. and Novotny, H. (1993) 'A Marginal Discipline in the Making: Austrian Sociology in a European Context', in B. Nedelmann, and P. Sztompka (eds), *Sociology in Europe. In Search of Identity*, Berlin: Walter de Gruyter (critical analysis of history of Austrian sociology; includes bibliographical details).

Lepenies, W. (1985) *Die Drei Kulturen. Soziologie zwischen Literatur und Wissenschaft*, Munich and Vienna: Hanser.

Levy, R. (1989) 'Weshalb gibt es (k)eine Schweizer Soziologie?', *Schweizer Zeitschrift für Soziologie* 15,

3: 453–87 (analysis of Swiss sociology; comparison with Germany and Austria).

Lother, P. (1991) *Dogma oder Wissenschaft? Marxistisch–Leninistische Soziologie und staatssozialistisches System in der DDR*, Frankfurt am Main: IMSF (critical analysis of history of sociology in GDR).

Lüschen, G. (ed.) (1979) *Deutsche Soziologie seit 1945*, Opladen: Westdeutscher Verlag (collection of essays on history of German sociology since 1945; includes bibliographical details).

Müller-Doohm, S. (1991) *Jenseits der Utopie*, Frankfurt am Main: Suhrkamp (collection of essays on contemporary sociology; includes bibliographical details).

Münch, R. (1993) 'The Contribution of German Social Theory to European Sociology', in B. Nedelmann and P. Sztompka (eds), *Sociology in Europe. In Search of Identity*, Berlin: Walter de Gruyter (differentiation of post-1945 German sociology from American and 'European' sociology).

Schafers, B. (1995) *Soziologie in Deutschland*, Opladen: Leske & Budrich (history of sociology in Germany; theoretical controversies in German sociology; includes bibliographical details).

JANET STEWART

Sölle, Dorothee

b. 30 September 1929, Cologne

Protestant theologian

A prominent political theologian, Sölle's first book, *Christ the Representative* (*Stellvertretung*) (1965) received wide attention but its 'death of God theology', and her anti-Vietnam War activities, made her a controversial figure. In 1968, Sölle started the *Politisches Nachtgebet* ('political evening prayers') in Cologne, linking prayer and political commitment. She was guest professor at Union Theological Seminary, New York, from 1975 to 1987. Her radicalism and many themes in her earlier theology prefigured feminist theology, whose insights in turn influenced her later work. In the 1980s, she was a prominent figure in the peace movement.

Further reading

Bentley, J. (1982) 'Dorothee Sölle: Political Theology' in J. Bentley (ed.) *Between Marx and Christ*, London: Verso (a British overview of Sölle placing her in the context of Christianity and Marxism in the twentieth century).

Scherzberg, L. (1991) *Sünde und Gnade in der feministischen Theologie*, Mainz: Matthias-Grünewald-Verlag (devotes a chapter to Sölle including a bibliography).

STEPHEN BROWN

South Tyrol (Südtirol)

South Tyrol, located in the north of Italy, consists of the mostly German-speaking Bozen (Bolzano) District and the mostly Italian-speaking Trentino. After WWI South Tyrol, until then a part of the Austro-Hungarian Empire, came under Italian rule (1919). Under Mussolini attempts were made to increase the Italian element of the population in the Bozen District. After 1945 a treaty between Italy and Austria (the 'Gruber-De-Gasperi Agreement') granted administrative and cultural autonomy as well as equal rights to the German- and Ladin-speaking population in the newly founded, Italian dominated, province Trentino-Südtirol (Alto Adige). Delays to its implementation led to a terrorist campaign in the 1960s and to diplomatic tensions between Austria and Italy that were settled in an accord in 1969 (the *Südtirolpaket*).

See also: minorities, German

GEORG HELLMAYR

Sparschuh, Jens

b. 14 May 1955, Karl-Marx-Stadt (now Chemnitz)

Writer

The author of novels, radio plays, essays and stories for children, Sparschuh shot to prominence with the comic novel *Der Zimmerspringbrunnen* (The Indoor Fountain) (1995), in which Hinrich Lobek, an unemployed former citizen of the GDR, achieves unexpected success establishing a new eastern German market for indoor fountains produced in the west. The impact of unification on his life is treated with light-hearted irony, although there are disturbing indications that Lobek once worked for the **Stasi** or at least learned to behave like them.

IAN WALLACE

spas

The German health-care system covers most of the cost of a four-week stay in one of the 384 state-certified spas. Patients may go to a spa about once every three years, either as part of a therapy or as preventive medicine. The word *Bad* in a place name denotes the town's certification, usually based on the presence of healing springs, medical facilities and a spa culture that dates back to the nineteenth century. Spas often specialize in treatments of respiratory tract, circulation and skin problems. A patient's stay (*Kur*) is supervised by a doctor, the *Badearzt*, and also includes relaxation and cultural activities.

SABINE SCHMIDT

SPD

The Sozialdemokratische Partei Deutschlands (SPD) is – together with the **CDU** – one of the two big political parties in the Federal Republic. Its average share of the vote in the fourteen federal elections from 1949 to 1998 has stood at 37.5 percent, compared with the CDU/CSU's 44.1 percent. The SPD has been in government at the federal level (from 1966 to 1969 as part of the 'grand coalition' with the CDU, from 1969 to 1982 in coalition with the **F.D.P.** and from 1998 in coalition with the **Greens**). At the *Land* level it has its main strengths in the Protestant north and centre of the country, where it has over the years formed governments in various patterns of coalition, and sometimes on its own. In elections it tends to gain most support in urban areas, and among working-class and young voters; party membership on the other hand is more white-collar. The SPD has traditionally been the party with most support among the country's intellectual and cultural

establishment, and SPD municipal and *Land* governments have a record of sympathetic sponsorship of artistic activities.

The SPD is Germany's oldest political party: although it adopted its present name in 1891, it was founded in 1875 as the Sozialistische Arbeiterpartei (Socialist Workers' Party), which in its turn traced its beginnings to the foundation by Ferdinand Lassalle of the Allgemeiner Deutscher Arbeiterverein (General German Workers' Association) in 1863. Despite official persecution, the party established itself as the natural political home of much of the rapidly growing urban working class in the Second Empire (1871–1918), and had become the biggest single party in the *Reichstag* by the time of WWI. It maintained this position throughout the 1920s, but – although it set its stamp more than any other party on the polity of the Weimar Republic (1918–33) – it was constrained in government by the need to operate in unstable multi-party coalitions, by the turbulent social, political and economic conditions of the time, and by the bitter hostility of the Communists (**KPD**), with whom it had to compete for the working-class vote. The Nazis banned the party when they came to power, and its activists were forced into exile or underground, with many ending up in prisons and concentration camps.

After the war, the Social Democrats' feeling that their hour had finally come turned out to be a serious misjudgement of the mood of the German people, who gave more support in federal elections in the late 1940s and 1950s to the newly-founded CDU. (In the Soviet zone the post-war SPD was short-lived: it was merged in April 1946 with the KPD to form the **SED**.) The Social Democrats' Marxist rhetoric (which had always been at variance with the cautious reformism and determined anti-communism of their practice when in office), and their neutralist foreign-policy stance, did not go down well in these Cold-War years with a West German electorate tired of outdated sloganizing and entranced with the growing prosperity of the **Economic Miracle**. Accordingly, a 'new-look' SPD was fashioned in the Bad Godesberg Programme of 1959, declaring itself to be no longer just a party of the working class, but a 'catch-all' party (*Volkspartei*) – with new policies to match – like its main rival the CDU. The moderate centre-left policies adopted at Bad Godesberg have characterized the party's stance over the subsequent decades.

The economic downturn of the mid-1960s led in 1966 to the formation of a grand coalition government, the SPD's first taste of power at the federal level. The fact that the CDU Federal Chancellor, Kurt Georg Kiesinger, was a former Nazi alienated many on the left, but its new 'responsible' role in Bonn undoubtedly enhanced the SPD's image among the electorate, and in 1969, after securing the allegiance of the F.D.P., the party was able to form a government under Willy **Brandt**. This was the high point in the SPD's relationship with the country's intellectuals, with prominent writers such as Günter **Grass** campaigning vigorously on its behalf, and the 1972 federal election was the only one before 1998 in which the party's share of the vote, at 45.8 percent, surpassed (though still only marginally) that of the CDU/CSU. Brandt's brief period in office (terminated in 1974 when it emerged that he had unwittingly been harbouring an East German spy – Günter Guillaume – as one of his closest aides) was distinguished by its reformist zeal, not least in the shape of the **Ostpolitik**. The remaining eight years of SPD government (under Helmut **Schmidt**) were marked by less adventurous policies, given the need to manage the effects of the 1973 oil crisis. Schmidt's government was ousted in 1982 when disagreements over economic policy led to the collapse of the coalition with the F.D.P.

During the **Kohl** years the SPD suffered from a lack of clear political direction and distinctive leadership. The debate over NATO missile deployments in the early 1980s provoked tensions between the anti-militaristic instincts of many party members and the leadership's desire to preserve a pro-western consensus (see also **peace movement: FRG**). The emergence of the Greens led to the erosion of the voter base on the left and among young people, obliging the party to enter into 'red-green' coalitions in both local and *Land* assemblies. It was also wrong-footed by the **Wende**, its perceived lack of enthusiasm for rapid **unification** leading to an unexpectedly poor showing in its pre-war strongholds in Saxony and Thuringia in the East German election of March 1990 and in the

first all-German federal election of October that year. It was later to improve its position as the 'blossoming landscapes' promised by Kohl failed to materialize in the East, though it has to compete with the **PDS** for the left-wing vote there. In the 1998 federal elections the SPD achieved an unprecedented 5.7 percent lead over the CDU/CSU, and, under its new leader Gerhard **Schröder**, formed the first-ever 'red–green' coalition government at national level.

See also: parties: FRG; SDS

Further reading

Miller, S. and Potthoff, H. (1991) *Kleine Geschichte der SPD*, Bonn: Dietz (despite its modest title, a standard and substantial history of the party; nearly half the book consists of invaluable tables, diagrams and documentation; a shorter, earlier edition appeared in 1986 in English translation as *A History of German Social Democracy*, published in Leamington Spa and New York by Berg).

Padgett, S. (ed.) (1993) *Parties and Party Systems in the New Germany*, Aldershot and Brookfield, VT: Dartmouth Publishing (on the situation after unification; numerous references to the SPD, including a chapter on its place in the left as a whole).

Padgett, S. and Burkett, T. (1986) *Political Parties and Elections in West Germany*, London and New York: Hurst & St Martin's Press (includes a chapter on the SPD through to the mid-1980s).

Parness, D. (1991) *The SPD and the Challenge of Mass Politics*, Boulder, CO and Oxford: Westview Press (on the SPD's difficulties defining its role in the FRG).

JOHN SANDFORD

spelling reform

In July 1996 the countries where German is used as an official language agreed on a new system of orthography, to be introduced in schools from August 1998. The old system, which dates back to 1902, is permitted to co-exist with the new one until 2005. The *Rechtschreibreform* proposals, which have been variously dismissed as misguided, confusing and costly to implement, have led to much heated debate.

The spelling reform is the result of years of deliberation by scholars from Germany, Austria and Switzerland, culminating in a conference in Vienna in November 1994 attended also by delegations from Belgium, Denmark, Hungary, Italy (**South Tyrol**), **Liechtenstein**, **Luxembourg** and Romania. The proposals were approved by all participants, and in April 1995 the final version of the new system was submitted to the relevant authorities. To enable government officials, institutions, publishers and the public to acquaint themselves with the changes, the proposals were made available by the Tübingen-based Gunter Narr publishing house.

The new rules seek to simplify German spelling and punctuation through greater standardization, whilst preserving traditions in order to ensure that texts written in the old system will remain readable. Two of the most distinctive features of German orthography – the initial capitalization of nouns and the letter 'ß' – are retained: indeed, the reforms extend the use of capitalization, though the 'ß' will be used in fewer circumstances (and, as before, not at all in Switzerland which uses 'ss' in all situations). Inconsistencies in the spelling of certain words as compounds or separately are removed (in favour of the latter principle); previously obligatory uses of the comma will be made optional; and there is some simplification of word-division and the spelling of words borrowed from foreign languages. In all, the number of spelling rules in German has been reduced from 212 to 112.

The proposals very quickly provoked controversy in Germany, in particular because of the upheaval and expense involved in introducing changes that are ultimately so minor as to be sure to invite calls for yet another round of reforms in the future. The only beneficiaries, it has been claimed, are the producers of school textbooks and reference works. Protest declarations have been issued (signed by prominent writers such as Günter **Grass** and Siegfried **Lenz**), courts up and down the country have delivered numerous (often contradictory) verdicts on the reform, and individual *Länder* (who are responsible for the education system) have vacillated over its implementation, and even, in one case (Schleswig-Holstein), been obliged to reverse it after a legally-binding referendum. However, the eventual introduction of the new rules in schools and in official documents is beyond doubt.

See also: Duden

Further reading

Deutsche Rechtschreibung: Regeln und Wörterverzeichnis. Text der amtlichen Regelung (1996) Tübingen: Gunter Narr Verlag (the official statement on the spelling reform).

Heller, K. (1996) *Rechtschreibreform 2000: Die aktuelle Reform. Wörterliste der geänderten Schreibungen*, Stuttgart: Klett Schulbuchverlag (one of the many lexica of the new spellings).

BIRGIT RÖDER

Sperber, Manès

b. 12 December 1905, Zablotov (eastern Galicia); d. 5 February 1984, Paris

Writer and psychologist

Raised in a *shtetl* community and educated in Vienna, Sperber worked with Alfred Adler in the 1920s, taught psychology in Berlin in the late 1920s and early 1930s, and fled Nazi Germany for Paris in 1934. As a youth, he was active in the Zionist movement and in 1927 he joined the Communist Party, which he left again in 1937. Most famous for his novel trilogy, *Like Tears in the Ocean (Wie eine Träne im Ozean*, 1961), which reflects his disillusionment with communism, and his autobiographical trilogy, *All our Yesterdays (All das Vergangene…*, 1974–7), he was the recipient of the Goethe Prize, the Büchner Prize, and other awards.

NOAH ISENBERG

Spiegel Affair

In 1962, after Der **Spiegel** had published a report critical of West German military policy, Conrad Ahlers, its author, and the magazine's publisher, Rudolf **Augstein**, were arrested and the *Spiegel* offices occupied by the police. In the event, the threatened legal proceedings were not brought, but the ensuing public outcry led to the resignation of the Defence Minister, Franz Josef Strauß. The '*Spiegel* Affair', as it became known, was seen as a test of press freedom and the democratic credentials of the still-young FRG, as well as a symptom of dangerous arrogance on the part of the government as **Adenauer**'s long chancellorship approached its end.

JOHN SANDFORD

Spiegel, Der

A weekly news magazine, established in 1947 by Rudolf **Augstein**, *Der Spiegel* (the title means 'The Mirror') has a ruthlessly investigative approach to the news which combines minute attention to factual detail with a style that often verges on sensationalism. Left-liberal in its politics, it has functioned from the outset as a gadfly to the establishment. It is also known for its waywardly playful handling of the German language. It has a circulation of around one million. Its status as the sole German news magazine was challenged in 1993 with the launch of *Focus*.

See also: magazines; *Spiegel* Affair

JOHN SANDFORD

SPÖ

Founded in 1889 by Victor Adler, the Sozialdemokratische Partei Österreichs (SPÖ) (Austrian Social Democratic Party) developed from a traditional left-wing party of the working classes to a broadly based organization comprising all sectors of society. In 1934 it was abolished by the autocratic Dollfuß regime, but was reconstituted in 1945 as the 'Socialist Party of Austria' when Social Democrats and Revolutionary Socialists merged. It remained the second largest party until 1970 when Bruno **Kreisky** became Chancellor. Since then it has remained in power as the strongest party even though its share of the votes decreased from more than 50 to less than 40 percent in the mid-1990s. In 1991 it was renamed

as the 'Social Democratic Party of Austria' in order to emphasize the democratic element which is an integral part of the party platform.

Politically it proclaims its commitment to freedom, equality and social justice as well as international solidarity.

GEORG HELLMAYR

sport: FRG

From participation to spectating, sport has been an integral part of the cultural development of Germany. In addition, sport has been linked to Germany's political development, specifically to the emergence of a German nation. In order to understand the significance of sport in the FRG, it is essential to first give a brief overview of German sports history.

Turnen (gymnastics) was the first organized physical activity in Germany and was developed in order to strengthen Prussian youth in the face of military defeat. Friedrich Ludwig Jahn and advocates of his system of gymnastics were keen to develop a sense of nationhood in response to French occupation during the early nineteenth century. Gymnasts remained suspicious of sport, a distinctly English phenomenon, though sport became widespread during the twentieth century. The political links between sport and German nationalism were clearly present throughout the nineteenth and twentieth centuries, and governmental national sport during the twentieth century is well documented.

The organization of national sport suffered from severe fragmentation during the Weimar Republic. The decentralized organization of sport and the allegiance of sports clubs to conservative or socialist political parties as well as to religious groups during the Weimar era led to the highly centralized and structured organization of sport in Nazi Germany, and was a major influence in the formation of a uniform sports system in the FRG. Although attempts were made to depoliticize sport after WWII, sport remained a feature of the German political landscape.

Following WWII, the Allies tried to dismantle the sports system that had existed under the Nazi regime, and sporting events could not be held in occupied zones without the permission of the local military authority. The foundation of the redevelopment of sport in Germany was the Allied Control Directive 23 of 17 December 1945, which outlined the decentralization, demilitarization and denazification of sport in Germany, and promoted the organization of sport on the local level. Other directives were issued that forbade the participation of former Nazis and those involved in Nazi sporting clubs and sports administration in any organized sporting event. German sport recovered quickly from the ravages of war, which indicated the significance of sport to the German people. In some areas, football training resumed a week after the end of the war and organized clubs emerged only six weeks after Germany's capitulation. In June 1945, for example, 32 soccer teams participated in a round-robin competition for a prize from the Stuttgart mayor. By the end of 1945, leagues in the American zone had been re-established and a new season began.

With the emphasis on constructing a sports system from below, separate national sports organizations in the FRG and GDR only gradually emerged after the local, regional and state levels were established, and despite the directives, organizers were drawn largely from the former sports administrators of Nazi Germany. A convicted war criminal, Karl Ritter von Halt, became the Honorary President of the German Athletics Federation and once again became Germany's International Olympic Committee (IOC) representative. Some researchers have suggested that this was because the most experienced sports administrators found themselves involved with Nazi sport without having any particular political affiliations. Others have suggested that the dominant image of the Nazi regime as a monolithic society, in which citizens had little individual determination of their lives, actually functioned to assist the return of many of these officials. Ultimately, there was no complete **denazification** in German sport.

A legacy of the Allies' attempts to decentralize German sport is the dual organization of sport by region and by sport. Sport in the FRG was organized in a two-tiered system with national bodies for individual sports, as well as local and regional sports administrations organized by *Länder.*

Individual clubs are generally multi-sport and are organized locally and regionally. Individual sports within local clubs are governed by national federations, which are responsible for holding national championships and other inter-regional competitions and for selecting national teams. Both tiers are incorporated into the Deutscher Sportbund (DSB), which has been the national body for German sport since its inception in 1950. The DSB does not, however, exercise executive power, and member organizations retain financial and administrative autonomy. The sports system of the FRG was based on several main principles, including East–West rivalry, specifically competition with the GDR, and on principles of access to sport for all members of society. Whereas élite sport has typically been organized at the federal level by the DSB and the Bundesanstalt für Leistungssport, the organization, provision of facilities and funding of 'Sport for All' programmes remain within the jurisdiction of the various Ministries of Culture and Education in Germany's *Länder*, and rest on millions of volunteers.

The importance of sport in the education of Germany's youth remained at the forefront of concern in the FRG as educators were conscious of the abuse of school sport during the Third Reich. School sport was an area that received almost immediate attention, as the DSB first made official statements about the place of school sport in its overall programme in the early 1950s. Students should have access to a daily physical education lesson to balance their intellectual development. In addition, the DSB stressed the importance of health as a major component of physical education, a direct reaction to the state of the nation's health following WWII. Physical education, however, was not included as a separate chapter in official school curricula until 1973. Sport was recognized as an independent area of education that makes specific contributions to individual, social and cultural development. Some suggest that the increased interest in physically educating West Germany's youth had more to do with East Germany's sporting success than with a real concern for the health and well-being of young people. Certainly the increased interest in school sport coincided with preparations for the Munich Olympics, as host cities traditionally perform well. The DSB, however, claims that the primary emphasis is not on performance and élite sport, but rather on participation and education.

German sport has always been strongly linked to the emergence of nationhood. The *Turner* first used their system of gymnastics to develop a sense of collective identity in the face of military defeat and occupation. Nazi Germany also employed sport and other physical activities to generate a sense of the German nation, based on views of Aryan physical supremacy. This trend has not abated, and sport in the FRG was closely connected to the emergence of a national awareness or state consciousness amongst West Germans. The return of West Germany to international sporting competitions such as the World Cup or the Olympics saw a resurgence of national pride in the nation. The German soccer team's 1954 World Cup victory provides, however, possibly the best example of the power of sport in constructing national identity. Newspapers captured the importance of the victory in one slogan, '*Wir sind wieder wer*' ('we are someone again'). The victory coincided with the German *Wirtschaftswunder* (**Economic Miracle**), and these slogans marked the FRG's 'coming of age', and heralded a return to national and international respectability in the post-war era.

Despite the importance of soccer and the significance of international victories, it was the Olympic Games that increasingly became an avenue promoting national awareness. Success in international competition, in particular against the Soviet bloc and the GDR, were interpreted as a demonstration of the inherent superiority of the national political and economic system of the FRG. West Germany's most notable return to the international stage came in 1972, when the **Olympic Games** were hosted by Munich. The eyes of the world once again turned to Germany, and Germany took the opportunity to display a return to respectability, much as the 1936 Olympics were supposed to. West German sport's greatest and worst moment came in Munich in 1972 during the Games. Eleven Israeli athletes and officials were murdered after being taken hostage, to which IOC President, Avery Brundage, responded with the famous words 'the Games must go on'. The GDR successfully competed at the 1972 Olympics, which heralded the dawn of a new era of sporting rivalry.

International success returned two years later when the FRG won the 1974 Football World Cup, losing only one match to the GDR. This success did much to restore a sense of national pride in the FRG; however, the emergence of the GDR as a powerful sporting nation during the 1970s reinforced a growing rivalry between East and West and was a significant factor in the rise of East German nationalism. Sport in both the FRG and GDR became a showcase of national political and economic superiority, as well as a demonstration of international importance. As Germany was a focal point of the Cold War, encounters with the East on the sports field became metaphors for a greater struggle.

German unification promised the fusion of two strong sports programmes, and officials from the FRG anticipated that the gold medal performances of East German athletes would boost their own international performance. Indeed, the fusion of the DSB and the (East) Deutscher Turn- und Sportbund (DTSB) preceded the unification of the GDR and FRG. The dismantling of East German institutions and structures prompted some to speculate on the appropriateness of the term 'unification', and this was the case in sport too. According to the Unification Treaty, the FRG's sports administration model was to be extended to the five new states. In other words, unification of the sports systems, as with other institutions, meant the disappearance of the GDR's equivalent. The DTSB and DSB did not unify, but rather the DTSB was subsumed by the DSB, which is clearly evidenced by the almost complete dismissal of the DTSB's staff. Individual sports federations merged with their West German counterparts and countless sports and physical culture institutions were closed down, with the exception of the Research Institute on Sport and Physical Culture in Leipzig, the Research Institute on Equipment in Berlin and the Doping Test Laboratory in Kreischau. Essentially, the unification of the two sports systems was supposed to be representative of the higher aims and values attached to political and social unification.

Physical activity has traditionally been a structured part of West German life, and activities such as gardening, hunting and hiking in addition to organized individual and team sports, have remained popular. Despite the emergence of alternative forms of leisure, statistics suggest that around one third of all citizens of the FRG are affiliated with sports clubs, and that as many as 45 percent of all Germans regularly participate in physical activities. Participation rates in particular sports, such as golf and tennis, have risen dramatically following the international successes of German athletes such as Bernhard **Langer**, Steffi **Graf** and Boris **Becker**, yet the most popular national sport remains soccer with over 5.5 million members of the German Football Federation, and hundreds of thousands of spectators at professional games each week. Gymnastics and tennis are the next two most popular sports with 4.6 and 2.3 million club members respectively.

See also: hunting; sport: GDR

Further reading

Magdalinski, T. (1996) 'Historical Interpretation and the Continuity of Sports Administrators From Nazi to West Germany', *Sport History Review* 27, 1: 1–13 (analyses the structural continuity of the West German sports system from the Nazi sports system).

Palm, J. (1991) *Sport for All: Approaches from Utopia to Reality*, Schorndorf: Verlag Karl Hofmann (discusses the 'Sports for all' system in the FRG).

Ueberhorst, H. (ed.) (1981) *Geschichte der Leibesübungen. Teilband 2: Leibesübungen und Sport in Deutschland vom ersten Weltkrieg bis zur Gegenwart*, Berlin: Bartels & Wernitz (comprehensive volume on the development of sport in Germany; part of a larger collection documenting the world history of sport).

TARA MAGDALINSKI

sport: GDR

Sport was expected not only to contribute to the well-being of GDR citizens and the reproduction of labour but also to the development of key characteristics of the socialist personality such as discipline, honesty, a collective spirit and a will-ingness to defend the homeland. Furthermore, the successes in international competition and a high level of popular participation in sport were intended to demonstrate the superiority of the socialist system over capitalism and to help reduce the legitimacy deficit of the GDR.

Given its political significance, the development of sport was supervised by the highest SED bodies, including the **Politbüro**, and high-performance sport was monitored by Main Department XX/3 of the Ministry of State Security. As part of the highly-centralized sports system typical of communist states, the army, the Ministry of Education and the largest mass organizations such as the **FDGB** and the **FDJ** co-operated closely with the main central sports bodies, the State Secretariat for Physical Culture and Sport (created in 1970 after the dissolution of the State Committee for Physical Culture) and the German Gymnastics and Sports Association (Deutscher Turn- und Sportbund der DDR, DTSB). The State Secretariat drew up the annual and long-term sports plans and oversaw the development of sports science and research as well as the training of officials. The DTSB, founded in 1957, had a large membership (3,658,671 in 1988) and presided over an elaborate network of about 10,600 sports communities in factories, agricultural co-operatives, colleges, the army, police and the residential areas. The sports communities were normally subdivided into sections providing facilities for intensive training and general sports groups for members with less specialized interests. Another link in the chain, the Society for Sport and Technology (Gesellschaft für Sport und Technik, GST), was mainly responsible for the pre-military training of young people from the age of fourteen. In addition, most pupils and students at school, college and university were timetabled to spend at least two hours per week on curricular sport.

Mass sport often had a competitive edge. For example, the famous children's and youth *Spartakiaden* held each year at local level, and biannually at regional and central level, stimulated a high level of performance and participation. The Joint Sports Programme of the DTSB, FDGB and FDJ encouraged not only active forms of relaxation such as walking and swimming but also the competitive spirit of participants. The badge 'Ready to Work and Defend the Homeland' was the main element in the programme and was intended to underpin two of the SED's basic ideological goals. Over four million people were awarded one of the bronze, silver and gold medals in 1983. Despite these high participation rates, the SED failed to attain its stated goal of 'sport for everyone in every place, several times a week'. Employed women and shift workers exhibited low rates and many East Germans deliberately abstained from institutionalized sport as they regarded sport as a leisure activity to be pursued individually or among members of the family. The poor quality of many sports halls, playing fields and open-air swimming pools was another disincentive.

The SED leaders were more successful in attaining their targets in top-level sport. Élite sport was promoted from 1954 onwards – especially after the entry of a separate GDR team in the 1968 Mexico Olympics – and the GDR's so-called 'diplomats in tracksuits' were a major weapon in the SED's attempt to break the country's diplomatic isolation. In terms of medals, the GDR became one of the world's top sports nations. Its athletes gained 25 medals (9 gold) at the 1968 Olympics and 102 (37 gold) in Seoul in 1988. The secret of success lay in the clear delineation of strategic goals, a vast organizational network geared to these goals, and the widespread use of performance-enhancing drugs. A key figure in the promotion of élite sport was Manfred Ewald, the President of the DTSB from 1961 to 1988. Medal intensive sports such as track and field, swimming and gymnastics were identified as prime targets rather than the less promising tennis, badminton and hockey. Highly-gifted children were selected early in their school life for development at one of the twenty-five élite boarding sports schools and talented performers were concentrated in about thirty well-endowed sports clubs and the sports associations of the armed forces and the **Stasi**. The Deutsche Hochschule für Körperkultur und Sport in Leipzig, founded in 1950, became world famous for its systematic training of thousands of top coaches and instructors. Powerful incentives were on offer to the élite: foreign travel, payments in western currency, bonuses, good career opportunities and, as in the case of Katarina **Witt**, the enjoyment of a high profile in public life.

From the late 1960s, drugs, notably anabolic steroids, were used to an unparalleled degree as part of a comprehensive doping project organized by top SED and state organs. The scientific centre of the project was Leipzig's Forschungsinstitut für Körperkultur und Sport, which from its foundation in 1969, in conjunction with sports club officials and trainers and partner institutions such as the Academy of Sciences, was responsible for the systematic doping not only of thousands of leading athletes such as the sprinters Marlies Göhr and Marita Koch, the shot putters Udo Beyer and Ulf Timmermann and the long jumper Heike **Drechsler** but also many talented children.

Further reading

Berendonk, B. (1992) *Doping. Von der Forschung zum Betrug*, Reinbek bei Hamburg: Rowohlt.

Deutscher Bundestag (ed.) (1995) *Materialien der Enquete Kommission 'Aufarbeitung von Geschichte und Folgen der SED-Diktatur in Deutschland'*, volumes 3/1 and 3/2, Frankfurt am Main: Suhrkamp.

Holzweißig, G. (1981) *Diplomatie im Trainingsanzug*, Munich and Vienna: R. Oldenbourg.

Kleine Enzyklopädie Körperkultur und Sport (1979) Leipzig: Bibliographisches Institut.

MIKE DENNIS

Springer, Axel

b. 2 May 1912, Altona (Hamburg); d. 22 September 1985, (West) Berlin

Publicist and publisher

Axel Cäsar Springer created one the most extensive and influential publishing empires in post-war Germany. In the **Economic Miracle** years of the 1950s and 1960s, Springer pursued his dream of creating a politically influential publishing house, one committed to the freedoms and aspirations of the FRG. Indeed, in a divided Berlin, there was scarcely a physical artefact that stood so clearly as a symbol of West German principles and post-war successes as the Axel Springer headquarters in the Kochstraße, a high-rise located just metres from the Berlin Wall.

The middle-class son of a local publisher and printer from Hamburg's Altona district, the young Springer intended to go to Berlin as a journalist for Ullstein Publishers, a plan disrupted by the Nazi seizure of power. Springer avoided being drafted into military service, working in the family business and in a cinema during the war years. After 1945, Springer remained in Hamburg, where he got one of the first publishing licences (for a women's magazine) from the British authorities there. He quickly re-established the family publishing house and launched his first big venture, the *Hamburger Abendblatt* newspaper. In 1952, Springer founded ***Bild***, whose initial focus on photos (hence its title) was soon replaced with the popular tabloid format. *Bild* was an enormous success, catapulting Springer into the category of major publishers, and was followed soon after with the acquisition of the national newspapers *Die **Welt*** and *Welt am Sonntag*. By 1960, Springer had acquired a majority holding in Ullstein Publishers and planned to move the headquarters of his expansive print empire to Berlin, a commitment he kept despite the construction of the Berlin Wall. The magazines *Hör zu*, *Twen*, and *Eltern* became part of Springer's holdings over the course of the 1960s.

Axel Springer's achievements as a publisher and, particularly, his political engagement, made him a living legend, but a controversial one. From early on, the newspapers of the Axel Springer Verlag came to be associated with conservative values, offering unequivocal support for German unification, the reconciliation of Jews and Germans (and therein support for Israel), resistance to all forms of political totalitarianism, and the social market economy. In 1958, Springer even travelled to Moscow to meet with Khrushchev and to plead the case of German unity. While Springer was in tune with the political consensus of the Adenauer years, his position became much more tenuous in the fiery political climate of the late 1960s. Not only was Springer to become an outspoken critic of Brandt's ***Ostpolitik***, he was also subject to the wrath of students and others who felt that his newspapers, above all *Bild*, had provoked the situation that led to the shooting of the student protest leader Rudi **Dutschke**. In Berlin, Springer's high-rise headquarters became the site of extensive protest and, for some, were less a beacon of freedom and democracy than a symbol of entrenched power and of the continuities with Germany's fascist past. In fact, the Springer headquarters in Hamburg were targeted by Red Army Faction terrorists in 1973.

Married several times, Springer nevertheless had no obvious successor for his publishing empire. The most likely candidate among his children, his son Axel Junior, had worked as a photographer but took his own life in 1980. In order to secure the future of the Springer Verlag, Springer turned to the **Burda** family, who themselves ran one of Germany's leading publishing companies. The Springer Verlag had gone public in the 1970s, with Springer retaining 100 percent of the shares. In 1983, Burda received approximately a quarter of Springer shares, on the agreement that they would protect the integrity of the Springer Verlag after Springer's death.

Axel Springer died in autumn 1985. Earlier that year, Springer had collaborated with the **Kirch** Group in launching the private television channel, Sat1, which proved the beginning of Springer's diversification into the multimedia marketplace. Despite Springer's express wishes that Kirch himself not gain power within the Springer Verlag, Kirch waged a long battle after Springer's death to gain a greater share of this most political – and influential – print empire, a battle he won in the mid-1990s.

Axel Springer, who was most proud of the honours which recognized his service to Berlin and Jerusalem, left behind a contested empire. In the late 1990s, the Axel Springer Verlag continues to be a financial success, with its newspapers still upholding many of the conservative positions associated with Springer himself. Nevertheless, the Springer house is no longer the united empire its founder so carefully created.

See also: newspapers

Further reading

Lohmeyer, H. (1992) *Axel Springer: Ein deutsches Imperium*, Berlin: Bastei-Lübbe.

Müller, H.D. (1969) *Press Power: A Study of Axel Springer*, London: Macdonald.

Naeher, G. (1991) *Axel Springer: Mensch, Macht, Mythos*, Erlangen: Straube.

ROBIN B. HODESS

SRG

Most of Switzerland's radio and broadcasting services are provided by the independent Schweizerische Radio- und Fernsehgesellschaft (SRG) (Swiss Broadcasting Corporation). Because it has the responsibility of producing and broadcasting programmes for the whole country, its job is made more difficult than other channels such as **ARD** and **ZDF** in Germany, or **ORF** in Austria, in that it has to broadcast in all of the country's three main languages. To this end the umbrella organization SRG is divided into three main parts, each responsible for a different area: RDRS (Radio- und Fernsehgesellschaft der deutschen und der rätoromanischen Schweiz) for German and Romansh speakers, RTSR (Société de radiodiffusion et télévision de la Suisse romande) for French speakers, and CORSI (Società cooperativa per la radiotelevisione nella Svizzera italiana) for Italian ones. There is also an overseas service, similar to the BBC's World Service, called Swiss Radio International, which broadcasts in seven languages.

The proportion of programmes made for each language is carefully laid down. For television, German makes up almost 40 percent of the programmes, with French and Italian making up almost a third and a quarter respectively. It is a similar story for radio.

In 1993 a fourth television channel, S Plus, was introduced. It was a landmark in Swiss television because schedules were partly supplied by private programme makers. Many of the programmes are sports oriented. Two years later it was renamed Schweiz 4 (Switzerland Four).

Although Lausanne set up the third public radio service in Europe in 1922, SRG proper was founded in 1931 when the various independent regional radio stations in Switzerland joined together. The organization came into its own during WWII when it was broadcast all over Europe and perceived as a neutral voice. Regular television broadcasts did not start until 1958.

See also: broadcasting; German language: Switzerland

ADRIAN MURDOCH

Staeck, Klaus

b. 28 February 1938, Pulsnitz (near Dresden)

Graphic artist, publisher and lawyer

Since the late 1960s Staeck has been Germany's most outspoken political artist. His training was autodidactic. After early woodcuts (1964–7), he turned to photomontage in the tradition of John Heartfield. His images, frequently polemic, deliberately provocative and always critical, confront current political, social and ecological issues. In order to ensure their maximum circulation, Staeck has produced them as posters and postcards in large editions. His openly political role has made Staeck a controversial artist. He has successfully fought off many attempts of censorship against exhibitions and publications of his work.

DANIEL KOEP

Staiger, Emil

b. 8 February 1908, Kreuzlingen (Switzerland); d. 28 April 1987, Horgen (Switzerland)

Literary theoretician

From 1943 onwards Staiger was Professor of German Literature at the University of Zürich. He influenced post-war literary criticism with his 'immanent' approach to literature, attempting to understand literary works detached from their social and political background. This approach is expounded in *Grundbegriffe der Poetik* (Basic Concepts of Poetics, 1946) and *Die Kunst der Interpretation* (The Art of Interpretation) (1955).

ERNST GRABOVSZKI

Standard, Der

This Viennese daily paper was founded by Oscar Bronner in 1988 with the financial support of the German **Springer** Group. In 1995 Oscar Bronner bought back the shares of the German owners. Originally conceived as a paper to cover financial and economic topics, it developed into a full-size independent broadsheet. Since its introduction it has led to a wider and more profound coverage of hitherto neglected economic issues by other serious papers. Its daily print run of about 108,000 copies (1998) makes it one of the leading papers of the country.

GEORG HELLMAYR

Stasi

'Stasi' is the abbreviated form of 'Staatssicherheit' (State Security), by which the state security organization of the GDR has universally come to be known. It was founded in 1950, and during the lifetime of the GDR increased its power and influence in the East German state to become a large spying machine which penetrated every aspect of life in the GDR through its permanent staff and its extensive network of unofficial informers (*inoffizielle Mitarbeiter* – IM). It had twelve principal departments covering the different areas of activity in the GDR including an external spying section, HVA (Hauptverwaltung Aufklärung) which was responsible for all spying activities outside the GDR. When political change came to the GDR in the autumn of 1989, the Stasi was the most hated institution in the state structure for the majority of GDR citizens.

The Stasi had its roots in two organizations set up by the Soviet military administration: a police department set up in 1945, K5, responsible for countering opposition to denazification and democratization in the Soviet zone, and a secret police organization, the SSD (State Security Service), created by Erich **Mielke** with Soviet backing on his return to Berlin. On 8 February 1950, the formal existence of such an organization, which represented an amalgamation of K5 and the SSD, was announced in the Law on the Creation of a Ministry for State Security. Very little information about the purpose of this organization is contained in the Law; the only indication is that the new ministry was taking over what was previously a department in the Ministry of the Interior responsible for the protection of the economy. It is clear from its activities, however, that its main purpose was to counter what were regarded as internal and external threats to the GDR.

After two short periods in office by the first two ministers, Wilhelm Zaisser (1950–3) and Ernst Wollweber (1955–7), Mielke took over and remained in charge until the dissolution of the Stasi in 1989. The Ministry was in principle a state organization responsible to the **Volkskammer** and the Council of Ministers, but in practice it was the 'sword and shield' of the **SED**, set up to protect the power of the Communist Party in the administration of state power in the GDR, and reported directly to the leader of the SED. In the 1950s and 1960s the Stasi directed its activities mainly against individuals and organizations regarded as hostile to the GDR. Although this involved spying on GDR citizens, the main threat was seen as coming from outside, in particular from West Germany. In the 1950s the Stasi was involved in a number of spectacular kidnappings of individuals in West Germany, most of whom had held office in the GDR before fleeing to the West. Great emphasis was also put on placing spies in the political and administrative structures of West Germany. Their most significant success was the placing of a spy, Günter Guillaume, in the office of the then West German Chancellor, Willy **Brandt**. Guillaume was unmasked in 1974, but the affair was one of the main causes contributing to Brandt's resignation shortly afterwards.

During the 1970s the emphasis of Stasi activities changed after the normalization of relations with the FRG during the period of détente. The end of the 1970s saw a growth in oppositional activities in the GDR with the development of an independent **peace movement** and women's and ecological groups. The Protestant church, the only organization not under direct control of the state, was a particular target because of its role in providing a protective forum for some of these groups. It was during this period that the Stasi increased its use of informers to infiltrate groups which the SED regarded as hostile. Estimates of the number of IMs involved are as high as 500,000, and it was the extensive nature of the Stasi's snooping on individuals which has caused the most bitterness, in particular concerning the extensive nature of the data collected, with files on more than half the adult citizens of the GDR. This bitterness came to a head in the political turmoil of the autumn of 1989, and many of the demonstrations were directed specifically against the Stasi.

The abolition of the Stasi was announced by Hans **Modrow** in his maiden speech to parliament on 17 November 1989. It was to be replaced by an *Amt für Nationale Sicherheit* (Office for National Security), but suspicions within the population remained high that the Stasi was continuing under a new name, especially since the head of the new office, Wolfgang Schwanitz, was a former deputy to Mielke. Modrow was forced to abolish the new office before it established a real identity; its powers were transferred to other agencies, and the government, together with the **Round Table**, concentrated on the process of winding up the structures and personnel of the Stasi. This process was to prove to be contentious with accusations that Stasi officers were secretly destroying records. On 15 January 1990 a crowd of demonstrators, led by one of the citizens' groups, **Neues Forum**, invaded the Stasi headquarters in Berlin in the Normannenstraße, to try and prevent the further destruction of records. In April the new Minister of the Interior, Peter Diestel, confirmed that many Stasi records had been destroyed, and expressed the view that it would be better for all the records to be destroyed. But fierce opposition to this course was expressed, especially by citizens' groups in the GDR. The West German government supported this view, especially after June 1990 when it was discovered from the files that the GDR had given sanctuary to terrorists from West Germany. As a result, a law was passed on 20 December 1991 which gave both GDR citizens and foreigners the right to view their files. The revelations which ensued, especially concerning the unmasking of informers, and the role played in this by the Federal Commissioner responsible for the Stasi documents, Joachim **Gauck**, have been one of the most controversial aspects of the post-unification period.

See also: dissent and opposition: GDR; unification; *Wende*

Further reading

Fricke, K.W. (1991) *MfS Intern. Macht, Strukturen, Auflösung der DDR-Staatssicherheit*, Cologne: Verlag Wissenschaft und Politik (the standard work in German on the Stasi so far).

Gill, D. and Schröter, U. (1991) *Das Ministerium für Staatssicherheit. Anatomie des Mielke-Imperiums*, Berlin: Rowohlt (account by activists involved in the dissolution of the Stasi).

Wolfe, N.T. (1992) *Policing a Socialist Society. The German Democratic Republic*, Greenwood Press: Westport, CT (an American account of the police force and the Stasi).

PETER BARKER

Staudte, Wolfgang

b. 9 October 1906, Saarbrücken; d. 19 January 1984, Zigarski Vrh (Slovenia)

Filmmaker

Staudte directed his first films during the Third Reich. Until 1955, when he settled in the FRG, Staudte worked in both East and West Germany. *The Murderers are Amongst Us* (*Die Mörder sind unter uns*, 1946), the first post-war German feature film, vigorously confronted the legacy of National Socialism, a theme dominating his subsequent films for the cinema and, increasingly, television. These included children's films, thrillers and literary adaptations, most famously *The Underdog* (*Der Untertan*, 1951), based on Heinrich Mann's novel.

See also: film: FRG; film: GDR

MARTIN BRADY

Stefan, Verena

b. 3 October 1947, Bern

Writer

Stefan moved to Berlin in 1968 where she worked

with the women's group Brot und Rosen (Bread and Roses). She edited the *Women's Handbook* (*Frauenhandbuch Nr 1*). She is known principally for her outspoken, surrealist collection of autobiographical sketches, poems and dreams entitled *Shedding* (*Häutungen*, 1975), a seminal text for the women's emancipation movement. This work influenced publishers' attitudes to women's writing and helped to initiate the literary fashion of women writing for women with its rejection of the language of male sexuality. She published a volume of poetry *Mit Füßen und Flügeln* (With Feet and Wings) in 1980.

MARGARET VALLANCE

Steffann, Emil

b. 31 January 1899, Bethel (Bielefeld); d. 23 July 1968, Mehlem (Bonn)

Architect

Largely self-taught, Steffann worked as town and country planner in Lorraine from 1941 to 1944 with Rudolf **Schwarz**.

After the war, Steffann returned to Lübeck in 1946 where he worked on reconstruction and planning, choosing a respectful approach comparable to that of **Schwarz** and **Döllgast**, engaging in an interpretative reconstruction based on the formal language of modernism. A radical reduction of form and an immediacy of materials form the basis for his sensuous yet ascetic spaces as seen in his *Kartäuserkloster* Marienau (1962–4) and many other churches.

MARTIN KUDLEK

Steidle, Otto

b. 16 March 1943, Munich

Architect

Steidle has been in private practice in Munich since 1966, as Steidle und Partner since 1969, with a second office in Berlin from 1981. He gained his professorship at the Gesamthochschule Kassel in 1979, from 1981 at the TU (Technical University) Berlin.

Steidle's interest in prefabricated and ecological building is reflected in such experimental designs as the Genter Straße Building (1969–72), which is extendable within its prefabricated construction system (a project accomplished together with D. and R. **Thut**). Semi-open meeting spaces and an anti-monumental, elementary formal language (often verging on the improvised) are typical of his designs.

Important recent projects are the Gruner + Jahr publishing house, Hamburg (1990), and buildings for Ulm University (1993).

MARTIN KUDLEK

Stein, Peter

b. 1 October 1937, Berlin

Theatre director

Stein is Germany's most renowned living theatre director. He directed his first play in 1967; by 1970 brilliant productions in Munich, Bremen, and Zürich had established him as one of Europe's great directors. In 1970 he organized the legendary Schaubühne am Halleschen Ufer in West Berlin, initially a politically engaged theatre co-operative. Stein's work shows Brechtian influence and is marked by clarity, visual perspicuity, and proximity to the real. He left the Schaubühne in 1985; from 1991–7 he was Dramatic Director of the **Salzburg Festival**.

Further reading

Patterson, M. (1981) *Peter Stein. Germany's Leading Theatre Director*, New York: Cambridge.

KAREN RUOFF KRAMER

Steiner, Jörg

b. 26 October 1930, Biel (Switzerland)

Writer

Deeply influenced by his early teaching experience in a school for delinquent children, Steiner is credited with notable – and widely noted –

innovations in his early prose works such as *Strafarbeit* (Penal Labour) (1962) and *Schnee bis in die Niederungen* (Snow Down to Low-Lying Areas) (1973). He is equally well known for children's books created with graphic artist Jörg Müller, for instance *The Bear who Wanted to Be a Bear* (*Der Bär der ein Bär bleiben wollte*) (1976) and *Die neuen Stadtmusikanten in Aufstand der Tiere* (*The Animal's Rebellion*) (1990), translated into many world languages.

JEFFREY GARRETT

Steinert, Otto

b. 12 July 1915, Saarbrücken; d. 3 March 1978, Essen

Photographer

Originally trained as a doctor, Steinert became highly influential in post-war Germany, both practising and teaching photography. He organized three pioneering exhibitions entitled 'Subjective Photography' in 1952, 1954 and 1958. These aimed to promote individual creativity, innovation and high standards in black and white photography. Steinert's work is characterized by its formal experimentation, strict composition and strong tonal contrasts. From 1959 he was Professor of Photography at the Folkwang School in Essen, which was initially one of only two major photography schools in post-war West Germany.

ALEX COOKE

Stern

The magazine *Stern* has been one of Germany's two largest-circulating photo-journalism weeklies since its founding in 1948, and is the leading publication of the media empire of **Gruner & Jahr**. Its brash, often iconoclastic reporting style and sensationalist flair have attracted both readers and criticism. Its occasionally savvy reporting emphasizes images over text and a greater degree of humour than its more serious rival, *Der **Spiegel***. *Stern* suffered a crisis of public credibility following its 'discovery' and promotion of the so-called

'Hitler Diaries' in 1984, which were exposed as forgeries.

See also: magazines

MICHAEL R. HAYSE

Stich, Michael

b. 18 October 1968, Pinneberg

Tennis player

A powerful server with a delicate touch on the volley, Stich was one of Germany's leading tennis players. He won the Wimbledon men's singles title in 1991 and, in partnership with **Becker**, an Olympic men's doubles gold medal in 1992.

MIKE DENNIS

Stiftung Preußischer Kulturbesitz

This umbrella organization was founded in 1961 to foster co-operation among West Berlin museums that curate collections that were at one time Prussian holdings; it was extended after unification to include collections in East Berlin. Included are the Egyptian Museum, the Antiquities Collection, the Painting Gallery, the Copper Etching Cabinet, the Arts and Crafts Museum, the Coin Museum (in the Bode Museum), the Museum for East Asian Art, the Museum for Late Antiquities and Byzantine Art, the Museum for Anthropology, the Museum for Indian Art, the Museum for Islamic Art, the Museum of German Culture, the Museum of Pre- and Early History, the National Gallery, the Sculpture Collection and the Middle Eastern Museum.

See also: museums

PETER M. McISAAC

Stockhausen, Karlheinz

b. 22 August 1928, Burg Mödrath (near Cologne)

Composer

A pioneer in the theory and production of music who in the 1950s developed many of the electronic techniques now taken for granted, Stockhausen is one of the central figures in post-war European music. As student, and later teacher at the Darmstadt Summer Courses he evolved an imaginative response to the serialism of Schönberg and Webern; his work at this time is exemplified by the extraordinary *Gruppen* (1957) for three orchestras. Later developments brought the increased use of 'live electronics' into the concert hall; in 1970 he performed cycles of these pieces at the Osaka World Fair for six months. The natural grandeur of his sound world and scale of his thought have in the last fifteen years found an outlet in the projection and completion of a cycle of seven operas, collectively titled *Licht*.

BEATRICE HARPER

Stolpe, Manfred

b. 16 May 1935, Stettin (now Szczecin, Poland)

Lawyer and politician

After studying law in the GDR, Stolpe entered the service of the Protestant Church of Berlin-Brandenburg in 1959. From 1969 to 1982 he was head of the Secretariat of the Protestant Church Federation in the GDR, and from 1982 Consistorial President for Berlin-Brandenburg. In 1990 he became leader of the **SPD** in Brandenburg, and after state elections in October 1990 Minister-President of Brandenburg. In the state elections of September 1994 Stolpe was re-elected after the SPD gained an absolute majority. Since the opening of the **Stasi** archives in 1992 there have been allegations that Stolpe had too close a relationship with the Stasi in his liaison role with the GDR state.

PETER BARKER

Stoph, Willi

b. 9 July 1914, Berlin; d. 13 April 1999, Berlin

GDR politician

After war service Stoph held a number of functions in the **SED** in the late 1940s and 1950s concerned with the economy. In 1953 he became a member of the **Politbüro** and in September 1964 succeeded Otto **Grotewohl** as chair of the *Ministerrat* (Council of Ministers), which post he held, except between 1973 and 1976, until the resignation of the Ministerrat on 13 November 1989. He was accused of corruption and on 4 December was expelled from the SED. He was arrested in May 1991 and detained until August 1992, but released after his trial in November 1992 on charges relating to the shoot-to-kill policy on the East German border.

PETER BARKER

Straub, Jean-Marie

b. 8 January 1933, Metz

Filmmaker

With Danièle **Huillet**, his partner in both personal and professional life, Straub has been a reference point for cineastes since the early 1960s. Straub-Huillet films are marked by austere modernism and commitment to formal simplicity, with sparing use of edits and camera movements, and devotion to live sound. The screenplays excerpt but do not adapt 'texts' from other media – novels, operas, letters, etc.

Like others of the French New Wave, Straub began working with a student film club and writing criticism, then assisted on films by Astruc, Renoir, Rivette and Bresson. Bresson greatly influenced Straub and Huillet's restrained approach to visual composition, acting and sound, which also relates to 'Brechtian' aesthetics, 'political modernism' and the New Left of the 1960s (with similarities to Alexander **Kluge** and Jean-Luc Godard). Many interviews document Straub and Huillet's careful work methods and their refusal to be 'accessible'.

To avoid Straub's conscription for the Algerian War, he and Huillet moved to Munich in 1958 and since 1969 have resided in Rome. Their initial four German films secured their place in film history: two short films based on texts by Heinrich **Böll**, a radical and austere Bach film, and a short featuring Rainer Werner **Fassbinder** and other actors from the Action-Theater.

Straub and Huillet often choose texts for their resistance to adaptation, then stage them as 'oratorios' set in dramatic landscapes – Kafka's *Amerika* in Hamburg; Hölderlin, Brecht and Schönberg in Italy. Only in 1997 did they shoot a feature entirely in a studio – Schönberg's one-act opera *Von heute auf morgen* (From Today to Tomorrow), the first opera ever filmed entirely with live sound.

Such innovation using classical cinema technology is also characteristic. Four separate 'original' negatives exist of their Empedocles film; *Antigone* was shot from a single camera axis (at eye level and four metres above ground). Their 1989 film *Cézanne* juxtaposes Cézanne's works and the landscapes where they originated with his words about the layers of truth in the appearance of the world and refusing to conform to the expectations of others (especially wealthy patrons); this text is also a good introduction to the modernism of Straub and Huillet.

Further reading

Byg, B. (1995) *Landscapes of Resistance: The German Films of Danièle Huillet and Jean-Marie Straub*, Berkeley, CA: University of California Press (contains extensive bibliography, especially in English).

Jansen, P.W. and Schütte, W. (eds) (1976) *Herzog/ Kluge/Straub*, Munich: Hanser (includes interview with Straub and Huillet).

Roud, R. (1971; 1972) *Jean-Marie Straub*, London: Secker & Warburg and the British Film Institute; New York: Viking (the first book in English on Straub and Huillet; contains script of *Not Reconciled*).

Schütte, W. (ed.) (1984) *Klassenverhältnisse. Von Danièle Huillet und Jean-Marie Straub nach dem Amerika-Roman 'Der Verschollene' von Franz Kafka*, Frankfurt am Main: Fischer (includes screenplay, interview and essays on the Kafka-film).

Walsh, M. (1981), *The Brechtian Aspect of Radical Cinema*, K.M. Griffiths (ed.), London: British

Film Institute (essays on political and formal aspects, especially of Bach and Schönberg films).

BARTON BYG

Strauß, Botho
b. 2 December 1944, Naumburg
Writer

Strauß was, by 1980, the leading West German playwright alongside F.X. **Kroetz**. In the 1980s and 1990s, his prose and essays, always scornful of left-liberal social criticism, displayed increasing religiosity and cultural conservatism. His essay 'Anschwellender Bocksgesang' (Goatsong [Greek: tragedy] Growing Louder) in *Der Spiegel* (1993) controversially espoused right-wing ideas. His richly allusive, multidimensional texts make him one of the most-studied contemporary writers.

From the start, Strauß's plays challenged realist representation through self-conscious, indeed playful theatricality. After the bewildering surrealism and dream psychology of *Die Hypochonder* (The Hypochondriacs) (1972), *Bekannte Gesichter, gemischte Gefühle* (Familiar Faces, Mixed Feelings) (1975) uses ballroom dancing as a metaphor for empty relationships and failed communication. *Trilogie des Wiedersehens* (Trilogy of Reunion) (1977), a tapestry of the fluctuating relationships of seventeen visitors to an art exhibition, began a critical fashion of seeing Strauß as the seismographer of West Germany's cultural climate. Lotte, central figure of *Groß und klein* (Big and Little) (1978), finally unhinged by human indifference and the silence of God, signals the demise of the rationalistic, secular humanism of 1960s and 1970s culture in favour of **postmodernism** and a new religiosity. In *Kalldewey, Farce* (1981) gender conflict and the promise of the irrational in a supposedly mythless world lead to a black comedy of literal dismemberment. *Der Park* (The Park) (1983) shows an attempt to suffuse the modern world with the magic eroticism of *A Midsummer Night's Dream* foundering on contemporary apathy and viciousness. *Besucher* (Visitors) (1988) uses the theme of a play rehearsal to dissolve – as much of Strauß's work seeks to do – the boundaries between art and reality. *Die Zeit und* *das Zimmer* (Time and the Room) (1988) combines whimsical playfulness with Heideggerian ideas. *Schlußchor* (Closing Chorus) (1990), with its disruption by a voice calling '*Deutschland!*' and closing image of a woman dismembering a (Prussian) eagle, mocked the pathos of unification. In *Ithaka* (1996) he stages the final sections of Homer's *Odyssey*.

In the 1970s, Strauß's prose explored, more radically yet also with more irony than most writers of **New Subjectivity**, the self-dissolution that results from intense self-scrutiny, for instance in *Theorie der Drohung* (Theory of Menace) (1974), *Die Widmung* (Devotion) (1976) and *Tumult* (Rumor) (1980). The loose, associative form of the sketches and essays in *Paare, Passanten* (Couples, Passers-By) (1981) was exemplary for much 1980s writing, as was its abandonment of the critical dialectics of **Adorno**. The vast novel *The Young Man* (*Der junge Mann*, 1984), displays open-edged form, multiple levels, time planes and focalizations, intertextual borrowings, interpolated romantic novellas, irrational dream-logic, complex self-irony, allegories and set-pieces of social satire and cultural-philosophical dispute. *Niemand Anderes* (No-one Else) (1987) intensifies Strauß's rejection of 'sociocentric thought'. His later prose, like the *Fragmente der Undeutlichkeit* (Fragments of Obscurity) (1989), seeks a mystical non-understanding in which quasi-religious revelation is possible. Like Peter **Handke**, Strauß also revives the aloof stance of the *Dichter* (writer, poet) as privileged visionary.

Further reading

Adelson, L. (1984) *The Crisis of Subjectivity. Botho Strauß's Challenge to West German Prose of the 1970s*, Amsterdam: Rodopi.

MORAY MCGOWAN

Strauß, Richard

b. 11 June 1864, Munich; d. 8 September 1949, Garmisch-Partenkirchen

Composer

A monumental figure in the music of the late nineteenth and early twentieth centuries, Strauß was seen early on as the natural successor to Wagner and Brahms, and his tone-poems *Macbeth* (1886–91) and *Don Juan* (1889) quickly entered the international repertoire. From the twentieth century his attention moved to opera, with the composition of *Salome* (1905), *Elektra* (1908), *Ariadne auf Naxos* (1912–16) and *Der Rosenkavalier* (1910), the latter achieving immense popularity despite, or because of, its deliberately conservative style. The latter three operas were collaborations with Hofmannsthal. Despite frequent allegations to the contrary Strauß suffered under Hitler, especially for his unwillingness to cease collaborations with Jewish librettists (his daughter-in-law Alice and her children were Jewish), and his *Metamorphosen* for twenty-three solo strings was written in 1945 as an elegy for musical life in Germany. Strauß came to Britain in 1947 at the invitation of Thomas Beecham. He was officially 'denazified' in 1948, and died a year later, telling his daughter-in-law that dying was just as he had depicted it in his tone-poem *Tod und Verklärung* (1889).

DEREK McCULLOCH

street names

Early street names tended to be descriptive, indicating for instance status (*Hauptstraße*), location (*Am Kanal*), topography (*Sandweg*), directional orientation (*Charlottenburger Chaussee*) or some attribute of one or more of the street's inhabitants (*Schmied-*, *Judengasse*). But as towns expanded in the eighteenth and particularly the nineteenth centuries, too many new names were needed for street names to continue to be arrived at either 'naturally' or spontaneously: local residents might propose but people in power (monarchs or their representatives, town councils and later even political parties) decided what streets were officially to be called. Many of the new names chosen were overtly commemorative – initially of monarchs, hence for instance the *Karl-*, *Wilhelm-*, *Heinrich-* and *Friedrichstraßen* found in Germany today. As more and more names were needed, the stock of major national figures such as writers, musicians, generals, or national events such as battles fought and won, was also dipped into.

As political ideologies and systems have come and gone, street names have been left to proclaim the past, and controversy has ensued, particularly in Germany since 1989, but by no means only then. The names of National Socialism's most prominent 'heroes' (e.g. Adolf Hitler, Horst Wessel and Albert Schlageter), once seen on many street signs in both Germany and Austria, disappeared quickly after the war, either through local initiatives or by decree of the occupying power, but less obvious instances of Nazi street-naming practice are still apparent, for instance in the non-restoration of many of the Jewish names which were banned from Germany's street signs in 1938, or in the WWI fighter pilots commemorated with pomp and ceremony in street namings in Neutempelhof, Berlin in 1936.

By the early 1950s the GDR, which propagated 'anti-fascism' as one the mainsprings of its legitimacy, had systematically purged its streets not only of the fascist but also of Germany's 'imperialist-monarchist' past. But the GDR authorities, with more political control over such matters than pertained in West Berlin or the FRG, also vigorously marketed its own ideology through commemorative street names, the function of which, according to H. Kögler, was 'to give clear expression to the *Weltanschauung* of the ruling' (working) 'class in our state and by this means, also, to bring above all young people into contact with revolutionary and progressive cultural traditions' (translated from Fleischer *et al.*: 1987). Leaders of resistance to National Socialism commemorated in East German street signs were consequently communists (in West Germany, non-communists). German, GDR and foreign communist leaders (e.g. Karl Marx, Ernst Thälmann, Wilhelm **Pieck** and Ho Chi Minh) were also honoured, but above all close links with the Soviet Union were widely proclaimed. Not only did the names of, for instance, Russian writers (Gorki was a favourite) and politicians (particularly Lenin) appear in the streets, but the Russian street name pattern of '*Ulitsa* (street) + qualifying noun in the genitive case' (as in Straße der Aktivisten) became commonplace. Halle alone, prior to 1989, had seventeen names of this syntactic type, whereas in

West Germany the pattern is rare. Some of the 'genitive' names in the GDR were so long and/or so pervasive that they were popularly abbreviated (e.g. Straße der DSF for Deutsch-Sowjetischen Freundschaft), thereby, Kögler (as above) argued, regrettably losing the communicative force the namers intended. Since **unification**, most local authorities in the former GDR have sought to remove the strongest reminders of 'a failed regime' from their street signs: Dresden and Magdeburg have each experienced over sixty post-unification street-name changes. Karl-Marx-Platz in central Leipzig reverted to Augustusplatz, first named thus in 1839 after a King of Saxony, even before unification. (Karl-Marx-Stadt became Chemnitz again earlier still – by referendum.) In central Berlin, until 1990 controlled by the GDR, name changes have proved particularly controversial, particularly where older 'imperial' names have been restored. Berlin having regained its status as capital, the issue of (re-)naming 'representative' streets in the centre shifted from the jurisdiction of the local authority to the Senate, the governing body for the whole of Berlin, and national politicians and newspapers also expressed views which conflicted with those of many if not most local inhabitants. So great is the potential for controversy inherent in the commemorative naming of streets that Jens **Reich**, in *Die Zeit* (1 February 1991) under the title *Rebhuhnweg überlebt* (Partridge Way Survives), has argued the case for 'timeless' names only. Certainly, the more political the person or event whose name a street receives, the more likely that a change will be perceived to be necessary in due course. The following names have all in the course of time applied to a single street in Berlin: Kasernenstraße (to 1831); Königgrätzer Straße (1867–1915); Budapester Straße (1915–25); Friedrich-Ebert-Straße (1925–33); Hermann-Göring-Straße (1933–45); and Ebertstraße (officially from 31 July 1947). The Prussian victory over the Austrians at the battle of Königgrätz (Sadowa) occasioned the triumphalist change in 1867; the need to cultivate good relations with Austria-Hungary, now Germany's ally, led to the change in 1915. Friedrich Ebert, first president of the Weimar Republic, was commemorated immediately after his death in 1925 (today a period of five years is normally required to elapse after a person's death before their name can be used on a street sign) but in 1933 Ebert's name was removed in favour of (the still living) Hermann Göring. Finally(?) Ebert was re-instated, unofficially, in 1945. Commemorative names are least vulnerable when they belong to non-political figures (e.g. Beethoven and Goethe) or those whose once prominent position in society is forgotten over time, so that the name of the street becomes to most users a familiar and therefore cherished label with no other significance. One of the founding fathers of German stenography, Franz Xaver Gabelsberger (1789–1849), is an outstanding figure in this category: there is hardly a German-speaking town that does not have its *Gabelsbergerstraße*.

Further reading

Azaryahu, M. (1991) *Von Wilhelmplatz zu Thälmann-platz. Politische Symbole im öffentlichen Leben der DDR*, Gerlingen: Bleicher.

Berliner Geschichtswerkstatt (1988) *Sackgassen. Keine Wendemöglichkeit für Berliner Straßennamen*, Berlin: Nishen (a lively collection of articles on arguably objectionable names from the past).

Fleischer, W. *et al.* (1987) *Wortschatz der DDR*, Leipzig: VEB Bibliographisches Institut.

Koß, G. (1990). *Namenforschung. Eine Einführung in die Onomastik*, Tübingen: Niemeyer (pages 89–93 give a useful overview of the study of street names).

Meyer, H., and Mende, H.-J. (project leaders) (1993) *Wegweiser zu Berlins Straßennamen*, Berlin: Edition Luisenstadt (whereas most compendia of street names record only current names, this series meticulously documents, in exceptional level of detail, all names, both present and past).

GLYN HATHERALL

Strittmatter, Erwin

b. 14 August 1912, Spremberg; d. 31 January 1994, Dollgow (Brandenburg)

Writer and dramatist

One of the most successful writers of prose fiction in the GDR, Strittmatter grew up in a village in Lower Lusatia which had a mixed German and Sorbian population. This ethnic background is reflected in his works and is central to his last major work in three volumes, *Der Laden* (The Shop) (1983, 1987 and 1992). His father was a baker, and after the *Volksschule* (elementary school) Erwin took an apprenticeship as a baker, and then had a succession of jobs as agricultural labourer, waiter and chauffeur before being called up into the army. He deserted shortly before the end of the war and returned to Lusatia in 1945 to work again as a baker and labourer. He joined the **SED** in 1947, had several positions in local administration while working part-time as a journalist and started to write fiction. His first novel, *Ochsenkutscher* (Ox-cart Driver) (1951), is set in Lower Lusatia and portrays the changes in a small village in the Weimar Republic. This novel contains most of the major features of Strittmatter's prose works: the use of a childlike, naïve narrative perspective, usually linked to the development of one central character; the attempt to link the tradition of the village story to social and political change; and the use of humorous and erotic episodes to produce a down-to-earth style accessible to a wide readership.

Strittmatter's first play, *Katzengraben* (Cat Ditch) (1953), brought him into contact with Bertolt **Brecht** and was performed at the **Berliner Ensemble**. It portrays village life in the period 1947–9 after the land reform in the Soviet zone and presents the human and social conflicts resulting from the changes. A second play, *Die Holländerbraut* (The Dutchman's Bride) (1960), written in verse, developed the theme of the inseparability of human and political questions. But it is above all his prose works, *Tinko* (1954), also made into a film (1957), the three-part trilogy, *Der Wundertäter* (The Miracle Worker) (1957, 1973 and 1980), whose central character, Stanislaus Büdner, bears strong autobiographical traits, and the controversial novel, *Ole Bienkopp* (Old Bienkopp) (1963), which presented some of the contradictions of GDR socialism as experienced by ordinary people, for which Strittmatter is best known. His writing depended strongly on his talent for story-telling, and his collections of short stories, such as *Ein Dienstag im September* (One Tuesday in September) (1969) or *Die blaue Nachtigall oder der Anfang von etwas* (The Blue Nightingale or the

Beginning of Something) (1972), represent his most successful work.

Strittmatter identified closely with the GDR. He was First Secretary of the **Writers' Union** from 1959 to 1961, and one of its deputy chairmen from 1961 to 1978, but he tended to keep his distance from public political involvement. In 1958 he became a member of his local **LPG**, and in the 1970s and 1980s in particular he preferred to stay in the countryside and avoid Berlin. Evidence of the fact that in his writing he had stayed close to the concerns of ordinary people in eastern Germany was provided by the huge success of the third part of *Der Laden*, which became a bestseller in that part of Germany in 1992.

PETER BARKER

Struck, Karin

b. 14 May 1947, Schlagtow bei Greifs-wald

Writer

Regarded as an early feminist writer (see also **feminism and the women's movement**), Struck has written works that are typical of the 1970s trend towards **New Subjectivity** with its focus on confessional and autobiographical writing. Mirroring the mood of the time, *Klassenliebe* (Class Love) was an enormous best-seller in 1973. It describes the disintegration of her personality, her alienation from her class roots and her painful inability to reconcile her political commitment and personal, sensual experience. Struck's themes and manner of writing remain essentially the same: highly emotional, self-obsessive, and concerned with unstable relationships.

Further reading

Ader, S. and Schrimpf, H.J. (eds) (1984) *Karin Struck. Materialien*, Frankfurt am Main: Suhrkamp (a very useful source book).

PETER PROCHNIK

student movement

Although the beginnings of the student movement were to be found on the campus of Berkeley University in California and its most spectacular demonstrations were on the streets of Paris in 1968, it was nevertheless in Germany that it produced its most widespread and long-lasting results. Indeed, 1968 can be seen as a watershed in the history of the Federal Republic, marking the beginning of a period when the assumptions and values prevailing during the 1950s and 1960s were increasingly called into question and revised.

In the development of the West German student movement three distinct phases can be discerned. In the first, in which the movement was virtually synonymous with the **SDS** and most of its activities were focused on West Berlin, its energies were initially channelled into a campaign to reform the antiquated German university system. More generally, the spirit of anti-authoritarianism that informed the movement manifested itself not only in its capacity to (re-)invent new forms of political practice (such as happenings, sit-ins and teach-ins) but also in the private sphere as the students began to evolve new lifestyles epitomized by the communes and *Wohngemeinschaften* (house- or flat-sharing communities) that sprang up in most university towns. The second phase began on 2 June 1967 when a demonstration in West Berlin against a visit by the Shah of Iran culminated in the police shooting of the student Benno Ohnesorg. These events triggered an explosion of protest throughout the FRG, which was concentrated in the universities and driven by two issues: opposition to the proposed Emergency Laws and the campaign against the **Springer** press. It also enabled the **SDS** to become the driving force within the loose coalition of oppositional groupings which, since the mid-1960s, had come to be known as the **APO**. With the escalation of violence that followed the shooting of the SDS leader Rudi **Dutschke** on 11 April 1968 and the passage of the Emergency Laws through parliament two months later, the APO disintegrated and in the spring of 1970 the SDS dissolved itself.

The third phase of the student movement was characterized by its sectarianism: one response was the formation of dogmatic and highly centralized Marxist–Leninist parties, while an even tinier minority opted out of conventional politics altogether in order to wage a 'people's war' against the state by pursuing a strategy of urban **terrorism**. Considerable though the impact of the latter was on the political life of the FRG in the following decade, the real legacy of 1968 was the spirit of anti-authoritarianism which the student movement had kindled originally and which continued to reproduce itself at various sites of political and social protest throughout the 1970s and 1980s, notably as realized in the women's movement, the citizens' initiatives (see also **citizens' initiatives: FRG**), the **peace movement** and, ultimately, in the foundation of *Die Grünen* (see also **Greens**).

Further reading

Bauss, G. (1977) *Die Studentenbewegung der sechziger Jahre in der Bundesrepublik und Westberlin*, Cologne: Pahl Rugenstein Verlag (overview of events and debates in the 1960s).

Burns, R. and van der Will, W. (1988) *Protest and Democracy in West Germany*, Basingstoke: Macmillan Press (situates the student movement within the broader context of extra-parliamentary politics in the FRG).

Schneider, P. (1974) *Lenz*, Berlin: Rotbuch Verlag (seminal prose narrative partly based on Schneider's own experiences as a leading figure in the student movement).

ROB BURNS

students

The term *Student* applies only to those in higher education, both undergraduate and post-graduate, though the attainment of a first academic degree confers the right to use the title *Akademiker* (graduate). Until the 1970s students at German **universities** concentrated on academic pursuits, never enjoying the traditional extra-curricular social intercourse experienced in Britain and the US. Since then, about half of all students have taken up activities such as athletics or have joined cultural associations, with only 5 percent belonging to political groups.

Student profiles differ markedly between traditional universities and the specialized *Fachhochschulen* (FHS): students at the former tend to be younger on matriculation (21.6 years compared to 23.2 years at FHS but older on graduation (28.8 years as to 27.3 years at FHS). The lengthy study period engaged in by German students has engendered repeated debate. However, a large proportion of all students have previously acquired some vocational training or follow a part-time study-programme. In addition, about two-thirds have to supplement their income while studying and almost all students have vacation jobs. Since the 1960s the number of women at university has increased from 28 percent in 1960 to 42 percent in 1992, levelling off since the 1980s as a result of poorer employment prospects and decreasing state support. There has also been a noticeable change in the social composition of students, with an increase in working-class students from 5 percent in 1960 to 15 percent in 1980. A more traditional pattern has since developed, though *Fachhochschulen* still recruit more working-class students.

Social differences between students in the old and new *Länder*, obvious at the time of **unification**, have declined in significance. In 1992, students in the new eastern *Länder* were on average younger by three years, women were more strongly represented, especially in science and technology, and 20 percent of the age group went into higher education, compared to 36 percent in the old *Länder*. On the other hand, significantly more students in the new *Länder* came from academic backgrounds. While students' living expenses tended to be considerably cheaper, their lifestyle was far more modest. In the new *Länder* 88 percent of students received support from **BAföG**, compared to 28 percent in the West.

Students are obliged to join the *Deutsches Studentenwerk*, which promotes student welfare, in matters such as halls of residence and the refectory (*Mensa*). The *Allgemeiner Deutscher Studentenausschuß* (ASTA) (Students' Union) represents students in most *Länder*; its remit including academic, social and cultural issues. According to a 1991 survey, the typical German student is single, lives in a rented apartment, either alone, with a partner or in a group, owns a car and spends most on accommodation, followed by food and transport. Graduate unemployment has risen steadily since the mid-1970s and by 1993 had reached 4.7 percent. Following a worldwide tendency, German students today no longer form an exclusive élite and are more integrated into the general pattern of employment.

Further reading

Preisert, H. (1994) *Higher Education in Germany*, Bonn: Federal Ministry of Education and Science (a good survey on social trends and employment patterns).

HANS J. HAHN

Stürmer, Michael

b. 29 September 1938, Kassel

Historian

Following brief stints at Darmstadt and Kassel, Stürmer became Professor of History at Erlangen University in 1973. His early academic research focused on Bismarck and Imperial Germany, and on craft-work and court culture in the eighteenth century. Stürmer's academic activities were decidedly politicized in the 1980s, when he became a close adviser to the CDU Chancellor Helmut Kohl. A proponent of a new geopolitical determinism emphasising Germany's central European location, in his popular writing Stürmer harnessed history to the purpose of constructing a conservative national identity. He supported Ernst **Nolte** and Andreas **Hillgruber** in the *Historikerstreit*.

MARY FULBROOK

Stunde Null

May 1945 was often designated as *Stunde Null* or 'zero hour', the moment when the clock of German history was reset and Germans could make a new start, the historical slate wiped clean.

The myth was an important element in the rebuilding of personal and political life in both East and West Germany. The notion of a deep caesura allowed many Germans to block out the recent past, devoting their energies to the construction of new lives and identities in the 1950s.

For historians, 1945 remained for a long time a professional divide. 'History' ended in 1945; political science and sociology took over professional responsibility thereafter. However, historians gradually overcame their own 'zero hour' and debates developed over continuities and discontinuities, 'missed opportunities' or 'restoration' rather than radical reform, at least as far as West Germany was concerned.

The most radical turnover of personnel and transformation of structures occurred in the Soviet zone of occupation, which in 1949 became the GDR. The expropriation of large estates in September 1945, and the nationalization of sections of industry and finance in 1946, served to revolutionize East German society and xeconomy. Agrarian *Junkers* and industrial capitalists were ousted from positions of power, authority and control. In law, politics, administration and education there was a massive transfer of personnel. Only in vital areas such as medicine, or politically sensitive areas such as religion, was such radical transformation not effected.

But even in East Germany, there was no complete *Stunde Null*: the new state, had to work with the people it had, and former Nazis and fellow-travellers had to come to terms with the new regime. The establishment of new structures of power and changing cultures and mentalities took place only gradually and partially. And many of the political forms of the new regime – though not its aims or ideology – were reminiscent of the dictatorship it had displaced.

In the West, continuities were much more apparent. A modified form of capitalism ('social market', less state directed, somewhat decartelized) continued: although the Nazi political and military élites were ousted, continuities with conservative élites from the Weimar period were perhaps epitomized by the election of Konrad **Adenauer** as West Germany's first Chancellor; continuities in the civil service, judiciary, education and other professions were striking. Apart from the prosecution of a handful of war criminals, **denazification** was relatively piecemeal and ineffective.

In both West and East, more deep-rooted changes in society and political culture arguably took place in the 1960s than in 1945. But viewed in the longer sweep, total military defeat and occupation in 1945 broke the destructive cycle of domestic tension, militant nationalism and expansionist politics which had characterized Germany since the late nineteenth century. In that sense, perhaps, the notion of a *Stunde Null* is apposite; but even then, it has less to do with domestic breaks than with a changed international environment, and a divided nation in a world split by the Cold War between the new superpowers.

MARY FULBROOK

Süddeutsche Zeitung

This left-liberal newspaper is the largest national (*überregional*) daily in Germany, with a weekday circulation of approximately 400,000. The *Süddeutsche* was founded in 1945 as the first newspaper under the American authorities in Bavaria. Although read throughout the country, it has particular resonance in its home state of Bavaria, whose traditionally conservative politics provide an interesting backdrop for this Munich-based newspaper. With over forty foreign correspondents, the *Süddeutsche Zeitung* offers a wide spectrum of information as well as quality investigative journalism, making it one of the print media's leading opinion makers in the Federal Republic.

See also: newspapers

ROBIN B. HODESS

Süskind, Patrick

b. 26 March 1949, Ambach am Starnberger See (Bavaria)

Writer

Süskind achieved rare international success for a book written in German with his 1985 historical novel *Perfume* (*Das Parfüm*). Although regarded by some academic critics as trivial literature, this story of a murderer who uses his talents as a perfume maker to gain power over crowds is masterfully narrated. Other works were less successful, with the exception of the play *Der Kontrabaß* (The Double

Bass) (1984), a single-hander about a musician's frustrations.

Further reading

Parkes S. (1990) 'The Novels of Patrick Süskind: A Phenomenon of the 1980s', in A. Williams, S. Parkes and R. Smith (eds), *Literature on the Threshold*, Oxford: Berg.

STUART PARKES

Suhrkamp Verlag

Founded in 1950 by Peter Suhrkamp (1891–1950), former editor of the S. **Fischer** Verlag, the firm has become one of the most highly regarded publishers and a shaper of German intellectual life. Suhrkamp authors include **Brecht**, **Adorno**, **Hesse**, **Enzensberger**, and **Kasack**, as well as major British and American writers in translation. Upon the death of Suhrkamp, Siegfried Unseld took over directorship of the firm, introducing the series '*edition suhrkamp*' (devoted to theoretical issues) and the 'Red Series' (focusing on younger writers of the past ten years). Suhrkamp has helped to form the intellectual geography of Germany.

JOHN B. RUTLEDGE

Sukowa, Barbara

b. 2 February 1950, Bremen

Actress

Educated at the Max Reinhardt Acting School in Berlin, Sukowa is a striking and versatile stage actress who made her film debut at the peak of the **New German Cinema**. Her memorable performances include Rainer Werner **Fassbinder**'s *Berlin Alexanderplatz* (1980) and the title character of his melodrama *Lola* (1981). She shared a best actress Golden Phoenix award at the Venice Film Festival in 1981 with Jutta Lampe for her role in Margarethe von **Trotta**'s *Marianne and Juliane* (*Die bleierne Zeit*, 1981). She also played the title role in von Trotta's *Rosa Luxemburg* (1986) for which she was named best actress at Cannes.

UTE LISCHKE-McNAB

Super-Illu

This East Berlin weekly magazine, founded in 1991, is published by **Burda**, and aimed at **Ossi** readers. Its down-market contents include advice columns, tittle-tattle about television stars, and sexy stories. Though it has a large circulation of 570,000 copies per week, *Super-Illu*'s sales are confined almost exclusively to the East.

MICHAEL HÄNEL

Syberberg, Hans Jürgen

b. 8 December 1935, Nossendorf (Pomerania)

Filmmaker, theatre director and author

Syberberg is a visionary director whose explorations of the German psyche, outspoken diagnoses of contemporary social ills and aesthetic programme – a daring conflation of Brechtian estrangement and romantic inwardness, of expansive monologues and baroque imagery – have made him the most controversial filmmaker of the **New German Cinema**. Best known for his spectacular 'German Trilogy' – *Ludwig – Requiem for a Virgin King* (*Ludwig – Requiem für einen jungfräulichen König*, 1972), *Karl May* (1974), and the eight-hour *Hitler, a Film from Germany* (*Hitler, ein Film aus Deutschland*, 1977) – he has also directed challenging documentaries and literary adaptations, all in the unshakeable belief that Germany can only come to terms with its past and take on a spiritual role at the heart of Europe by celebrating and commemorating its rich cultural heritage. A robust idealist, he considers art the blueprint for a better world.

Educated in Rostock before moving to the FRG in 1953, he gained formative experience when asked by Bertolt **Brecht** in 1952 to film stage productions at the **Berliner Ensemble**. He worked in television before making his first feature-length documentaries from 1965, investigating unorthodox aspects of German cultural and social life (Fritz **Kortner**, Romy **Schneider**, the eccentric Counts Pocci, and the Bavarian sex-film industry). For his first feature films he turned to Tolstoy (*Scarabea*, 1968) and Kleist (*San Domingo*, 1970), transforming his source material into lively and unconventional polemics against social degeneration.

With *Ludwig*, a sumptuously theatrical portrait of the 'fairy-tale king', Syberberg pioneered the distinctive style which characterizes his work up to and including his adaptation of Wagner's *Parsifal* (1982). Operatic, flamboyant, and often, in the manner of Werner **Schroeter**, markedly camp, it is, according to Syberberg, a style fusing 'immobility, extended takes, epic clarity, estrangements, pathos and irony, placing dream and vision alongside lucidity and clear-headed analysis – a technique of association and framing which eschews arbitrariness in the choice of props, costumes, music, sounds, etc'.

Whilst *Karl May* examines the home-spun mythology of the popular nineteenth-century author in a more elegiac style – casting Helmut **Käutner** in the title role – the four-part *Hitler* is the apotheosis of Syberberg's trilogy, employing vast back projections and a panoply of props, costumes, musical and literary quotations to analyse and exorcise the 'Hitler in us'. It provoked heated debate and was supported by commentators as diverse as Michel Foucault, Susan Sontag and Heiner **Müller**.

After *Parsifal*, Syberberg engaged on a remarkable ten-year project of monologue films, with Edith **Clever** as the sole actress, all of which began life as stage productions. After the six-hour elegy *Night* (*Nacht*, 1984) they concentrated on Kleist (*Penthesilea*, 1988; *Die Marquise von O*, 1989). Ascetic, minimal and radiantly lyrical, these films unjustly received less attention than their director's strident literary polemics against social and cultural decay.

See also: New German Cinema

Further reading

Stewart, H. (ed.) (1992) *Syberberg: A Filmmaker from Germany*, London: British Film Institute (contains essays, a full filmography and selected bibliography).

MARTIN BRADY

T

Tabori, George

b. 25 May 1914, Budapest

Dramatist, theatre director and actor

A Jewish Hungarian, Tabori emigrated to England in 1936, then the US, where he worked as an intelligence officer, scriptwriter (for Hitchcock and Losey) and translator (of Brecht and Frisch). He returned to Europe circa 1970, directing in Bremen, Munich and Vienna; his ensemble approach used Strasbergian method acting, psychodrama and meditation techniques. Most of his family were exterminated, but plays such as *Cannibals* (1968), *Jubilee* (*Jubiläum* 1983) and *Mein Kampf* (1987), many translated and/or co-authored by Ursula Grützmacher-Tabori, address this 'event beyond tears' with taboo-breaking black humour.

Further reading

Gronius, J.W. and Kässens, W. (1989) *George Tabori*, Frankfurt am Main: Fischer.
Ohngemach, G. (1989) *George Tabori*, Frankfurt am Main.

MORAY McGOWAN

täglich Alles

The tabloid *täglich Alles*, published in Vienna, is the second largest newspaper in Austria (390,000 copies, 1998), founded in 1992 by Kurt Falk, the former partner of Hans **Dichand**, with the proceeds from the sale of his shares in the tabloid *Neue Kronen Zeitung*. This inexpensive colour paper covers a large variety of topics to please every possible reader, hence the title *täglich Alles* (Everything Everyday). Originally it was set up to compete with its key rival, the *Neue Kronen Zeitung*.

GEORG HELLMAYR

Taut, Max

b. 15 May 1884, Königsberg; d. 26 February 1967, (West) Berlin

Architect

Bruno's younger brother (see also **architecture**), Max Taut took an apprenticeship as a carpenter. He studied at the building trade school, Königsberg, from 1903 to 1905, and worked with Hermann Billing in Karlsruhe from 1906 to 1911, setting up private practice in 1906 in partnership with Franz Hoffmann (1918–50) and his brother Bruno (1923–31). He was barred from public work during the Nazi period (1933–45). He was Professor at the Akademie der bildenden Künste, Berlin from 1945 to 1954.

After the war Taut played a major part in the **reconstruction** discussions. His architectural work followed on from his 1920s designs, creating some important post-war buildings and housing estates, for instance the Methfesselstraße high-rise building in Berlin (1954–5), and the August Thyssen estate in Duisburg (1955–64).

MARTIN KUDLEK

taz

This abbreviation stands for the *Tageszeitung* (Daily Paper), a left-wing newspaper founded in Berlin in 1979. The *taz*, originally conceived of as a radical newspaper produced by an egalitarian editorial collective, was an outgrowth of the **student movement** and the ecological and citizens' movements of the late 1960s and 1970s (see also **citizens' movements: GDR**). In the mid-1990s, the *taz* had a daily circulation of just over 60,000, yet it is considered a national (*überregional*) newspaper, a profile it has gained in great part due to its issues-based, activist journalism. Still 'alternative', the *taz* has sought to retain its grassroots supporters by thematizing issues that would otherwise not attain prominent coverage in more mainstream papers. While the *taz* continues to have a young, well-educated readership, it has professionalized considerably over time. The newspaper has suffered from repeated financial crises, several of which have threatened its existence in recent years.

See also: newspapers

ROBIN B. HODESS

telephones

The broad distribution of private telephones from the 1960s onwards facilitated social mobility for West Germans (in the beginning of the 1960s, 14 percent of households had telephone facilities compared to 93 percent in 1988). In contrast, in the GDR there was a waiting list of up to twenty years for private telephones, and an antiquated and unreliable service, the modernization of which was one of the major infrastructural tasks undertaken following unification. The flotation of the state-owned Deutsche Bundespost telephone service as Deutsche Telekom AG in 1996 started a boom in private participation in the stock market. At the beginning of 1998 the state telephone monopoly was abolished.

JUDITH LEEB

television: cultural role

German broadcasting has undergone a sea change in the years since the arrival of cable and satellite technologies in the mid-1980s. Depending on one's perspective, the result is either an explosive multiplication of choices, as measured in both the availability of channels and new, more popular programming formats, or the gradual loss of politically critical, aesthetically innovative programmes in favour of a uniform appeal to the lowest common denominator. Of West German television's traditional strengths, the critical and aesthetically cutting-edge *Fernsehspiel* (**television drama**), the ethnographic mini-series, the personal, independent documentary, the feature on literary or cultural issues, and the hard-hitting political news magazines, only the latter have made it into the new transnational media landscape without being seriously compromised. The others, especially on the commercial channels, have been increasingly replaced by popular American programming fare or German imitations (especially game shows) as well as a flood of exhibitionist talk shows.

On the other hand, Germans clearly have more options than they did when two licence-fee-based public television networks, **ARD** and **ZDF**, enjoyed a monopoly status, amplified only by a chain of regional 'Third Programmes' – subsidiaries of the decentralized ARD network. Nowadays, more than thirty channels provide viewers with a wide variety of choices, including both commercial and non-commercial stations featuring the entire bandwidth of regular television programming, as well as channels specializing in sports, news, the arts, children's television, women's issues and pay-per-view.

News

Compared with American or British news broadcasts, German television news (*Tagesschau*, *heute* and *RTL aktuell*) is rather staid. Broadcasts tend towards the semi-official, providing viewers with a maximum of hard news in only fifteen to twenty minutes (half an hour for the late news, *Tagesthemen* and *heute-journal*). Far more aggressive are the many news magazines, produced by the public television stations, for instance *Panorama*, *Monitor*, *Report*,

Plusminus, *Weltspiegel* and *auslands-journal*. *Panorama*, named after its British model, has distinguished itself through hard-hitting, independent journalistic reportage, and during the ***Spiegel* Affair** of 1962, created an electronic public sphere that amplified the nationwide mass protests against the Adenauer administration's censorship of a critical print publication. However, the critical reportage of many ARD news magazines has led to repeated interference by conservative politicians, resulting in dismissals of critical journalists and even attempts at dissolving the ARD network altogether in favour of the politically more docile ZDF and commercial channels. In the 1990s several news magazines produced by major print publications have been produced (e.g. *stern-tv*, *Spiegel-TV*), while *Phoenix*, a new channel sponsored by the public television stations, provides coverage of major *Bundestag* debates.

Fictional programmes

The most original product of German television is the *Fernsehspiel* (television drama), a form that evolved from British and American roots into a distinctly German genre with its gritty realism and focus on contemporary social issues. While a number of *Fernsehspiele* have had an impact on West German culture, it is two mini-series that have caused the biggest stir. In 1979, the German broadcast of the American series *Holocaust* shocked the entire nation into a personal, emotional confrontation with the legacy of the mass murders of the Third Reich, while, in 1984, Edgar **Reitz**'s *Heimat* catalysed a nationwide search for a post-Holocaust identity, a 'usable past'.

The serial format evolved late on German television. Germany's first soap, *Lindenstraße* (Linden Street), did not start until 1985. Instead, long-running police series provided the formulaic predictability and familiarity with a returning cast of characters. The most successful of these have been *Der Kommissar* (The Inspector), *Tatort* (Scene of the Crime) and *Derrick*, and since 1990 also *Polizeiruf 110* (Police Emergency 110), formerly a production of GDR television. *Tatort* is probably the most noteworthy among these, since it has not only attracted some of the best writers and directors, but also reflects the regional structure

of the ARD network in that the individual episodes are produced by different regional subsidiaries of ARD and reflect local customs, dialects and geographic particularities.

West German television has also played a major, if ambiguous, role in the emergence of **New German Cinema** between 1962 and the mid-1980s. The *Film-Fernseh-Abkommen* (Film-Television Agreement) of 1974 provided the frequently 'difficult,' non-mainstream films of **Fassbinder**, **Herzog**, **Wenders**, and others with both a secure funding base and a guaranteed exhibition space. On the other hand, this may have contributed to the demise of New German Cinema by providing an all-too-comfortable niche, where filmmakers obsessed with artistic self-actualization would thrive in blissful ignorance of their audiences' interests and desires. There is no doubt, however, that Germany's lively **documentary film** culture would not exist without television sponsorship.

Arts and letters

West German public television has always considered coverage of literature and the arts part of its journalistic mission. In the 1960s, 1970s and 1980s there was rarely a significant theatrical event that would not find its way to German television screens. Archived by most German university video libraries (German copyright law permits the recording and archiving of public television materials for research purposes), these tapes now constitute an invaluable resource for anyone interested in the history of the German stage. Likewise, the never-ending need for original scripts has produced television adaptations (from both FRG and GDR television) of nearly every significant text in German literary history, of which many are also archived by German universities. In addition, there is German television's own critical discourse on literature and the arts, comprising interviews with authors and artists, magazines dedicated to cultural news (*Kulturweltspiegel*, *Titel*, *Thesen*, *Temperamente*, *aspekte*, and countless others, many of them in the regional 'Third Programmes'), literary game shows, debates (e.g. *Das literarische Quartett*, hosted by the famously combative Marcel **Reich-Ranicki**), readings and even an occasional original television play or series by a literary author (most notably Dieter **Wellershoff**, Gabriele **Wohmann** and Jurek **Becker** whose sophisticated comedy series *Liebling – Kreuzberg* is among the most popular shows on German television), although German writers, by and large, have steered clear of collaborations with broadcasting stations.

Television culture in the GDR

Although it is difficult to assess the actual role played by government-controlled television in the cultural and social life of the former GDR, biographical media research suggests that it was negligible compared to the role played by the reception of West German programmes in the GDR. Karl Eduard von **Schnitzler**'s *Schwarzer Kanal* ('Black Channel'), a propaganda attempt at discrediting West German broadcasts by adding a GDR commentary to them, was seen mostly as a source of amusement. GDR television news, *Die aktuelle Kamera* (Current Camera) was given no credit for accuracy, but was widely viewed for reading 'between the lines' of official government pronouncements. The show for which many GDR viewers tuned in regularly to their own broadcasting stations was *Polizeiruf 110*, a police series which many viewers credited for its gritty authenticity as well as its relatively realistic depiction of everyday life in the GDR. The only other area in which GDR television made a mark for itself is through its careful and lavish adaptations of major German literary works, some of which were purchased and broadcast by West German stations.

See also: broadcasting; Dinner for One; mass media: FRG; mass media: GDR

Further reading

Humphreys, P. (1990) *Media and Media Policy in Germany*, Oxford: Berg.

Kirschner, J. (1997) *Fischer Handbuch Theater, Film, Funk und Fernsehen*, Frankfurt am Main: Fischer (helpful bibliographical guide to secondary literature and archival sources).

Monatshefte (1990) 82, 3 (focusing on *Teaching German Media*, this provides a practical introduction to German Media Studies in English; includes notes on archival resources and substantial bibliographies).

Sandford, J. (1976) *The Mass Media of the German-Speaking Countries*, London: Oswald Wolff (outdated, but still an invaluable survey for anyone interested in German media history).

MICHAEL E. GEISLER

television drama

From early imitations of American models, television drama (*Fernsehspiel*) has evolved into the signature genre of Germany's public television stations **ARD** and **ZDF**. Focusing on contemporary social and political issues, the *Fernsehspiel* frequently employs a syncretist approach, fusing elements of documentary and fiction in a Brechtian attempt to transcend the traditional reception of fictional drama. Comprising a wide variety of aesthetic forms, the *Fernsehspiel* may be a 'live' drama, a sociological or psychological case study, a political dossier, an experimental avant-garde video, an adaptation of a literary work, a historical reconstruction or even a mini-series. The best screenwriters (and directors) have achieved a reputation rivalling that of literary authors: Dieter Meichsner, Wolfgang Menge, Egon Monk, Rolf Hädrich, Heinrich Breloer and Dieter Wedel. A number of literary authors (Dieter **Wellershoff**, Gabriele **Wohmann** and Heinar **Kipphardt**, among others) have written original screenplays for *Fernsehspiele*, often adapting them for stage works or novels later.

Most eclectic is ZDF's 'Little Television Workshop' ('Das kleine Fernsehspiel'). Since 1962, this late-night programming slot has provided funding and exhibition space for both German and international avant-garde filmmakers, among them Alexander **Kluge**, Rosa von **Praunheim**, Robert Wilson, and Meredith Monk. The so-called *Kamerafilm* model puts the individual filmmaker in complete control of his or her own production.

Over the years, *Fernsehspiele* have played a major role in catalysing public debate: In 1958, Meichsner's *Besuch aus der Zone* ('Visitor From the Soviet Zone') used the perspective of a visitor from communist East Germany to critique conditions in Adenauer's Economic Miracle, provoking debates all the way to the German parliament. In 1973, Menge's *Smog*, a fictional dramatization of authentic smog alert procedures, engendered a nationwide debate on environmental issues and succeeded in mainstreaming what had been a fringe concern up to that point.

The television plays produced by GDR television served mostly propaganda purposes, often in the form of East–West crime and spy capers, historical dramas glorifying the victory over fascism and the creation of a new socialist society, and, in the context of the **Bitterfelder Weg**, the integration of intellectuals into the production process. Exceptions are occasional texts addressing everyday problems in the GDR with the kind of gritty realism that has been a hallmark of **DEFA**. However, here, too, independent writers and directors (such as Klaus Poche, Frank **Beyer** and Egon **Günther**) risked immediate censorship, which prompted many of them to emigrate to the West. More important are GDR television's well-crafted (if aesthetically conservative) adaptations of German literature, some of which were also shown in the West.

Since the advent of cable and satellite, the *Fernsehspiel*, one of the costliest television genres, has suffered severe cutbacks. However, the spectacular success of Wedel's 1991 mini-series *Der große Bellheim* (The Great Bellheim), about the generational shift from the founders of the 'Economic Miracle' to business-school-educated executives, suggests that the genre has not run out of steam quite yet. Whatever its future prospects, for the years from 1952 to 1989 the *Fernsehspiel* remains one of the most significant bodies of texts for anyone interested in the history of West German mentality.

See also: broadcasting; mass media: FRG; mass media: GDR; television

Further reading

Collins, R. and Porter, V. (1981) *WDR and the Arbeiterfilm*, London: BFI (well-researched case study of experimental German television drama in the 1960s and 1970s; focus on 'workers' films').

Hickethier, K. (1980) *Das Fernsehspiel der Bundesrepublik Deutschland*, Stuttgart: Metzler (though outdated, still the best single volume on the history and aesthetics of German television drama).

MICHAEL E. GEISLER

Tendenzwende

Originally a journalistic term, *Tendenzwende* was used to describe the transformation of the intellectual and political climate between the resignation of Willy **Brandt** in 1974 and the return to power of the Christian Democrats under Helmut **Kohl** in 1982. The *Tendenzwende* thus coincides with the Chancellorship of Helmut **Schmidt**, whose rhetoric of cautious crisis management contrasted sharply with Brandt's flamboyant reformist ambitions, and unfolded against a backdrop of steadily rising unemployment, the confrontation with **terrorism**, and the renewed deterioration of East–West relations into the 'second Cold War'.

A combination of events and trends steadily eroded the foundations of the 'social-liberal' programme as originally defined by Willy Brandt: the worsening of the economic climate following the oil crisis restricted the budgetary space for costly social reforms, the increasingly repressive response to the terrorist threat (**Berufsverbot**, expansion and centralization of the police, legal restrictions on the rights of defence lawyers) all undermined the civil liberties credentials of the government, and the resumed arms race of the late 1970s frustrated the continuation and consolidation of Brandt's '*Neue* **Ostpolitik**'. The **SPD** found itself embroiled in increasingly bitter internal faction fights between left and right and losing electoral support first on its right (to an increasingly confident and strident CDU/CSU) and then on its left (to the **Greens**). In 1976, in his first campaign as leader of the opposition, Helmut Kohl fought under the polarizing slogan 'Freedom or Socialism' and achieved the second-best result (48.6 percent) for his party in the history of the Federal Republic. Four years later, it was probably only the adoption by the CDU/CSU of an even more right-wing candidate for the chancellorship, Franz Josef Strauß (who was mistrusted by more liberal Christian Democrat voters), that postponed once again a change of government which had seemed increasingly inevitable. The 'moral and spiritual turn' proclaimed by Kohl on becoming Schmidt's successor in 1982 (when the liberal **F.D.P.** abandoned Schmidt's government coalition) was, in fact, only the completion of the creeping *Tendenzwende* of the previous decade.

Among the critical intelligentsia, an increasing disillusionment with left-wing politics of both the reformist and revolutionary kind gave rise to various reorientations: a retreat from politics into a 'new inwardness' (*neue Innerlichkeit*); a postmodern rejection of all 'grand narratives' of progress in favour of a hedonistic, eclectic and consumerist culture; or a new commitment to the politics and lifestyles of the feminist, pacifist and ecologist 'new social movements'.

See also: New Subjectivity

Further reading

Burns, R. (ed.) (1995) *German Cultural Studies. An Introduction*, Oxford: Oxford University Press (see especially the essays by Bullivant and Rice, and Burns and van der Will).

Lübbe, H. *et al.* (1975) *Tendenzwende? Zur geistigen Situation der Bundesrepublik*, Stuttgart: Deutsche Verlagsanstalt (collection of contemporary essays).

GÜNTER MINNERUP

Tennstedt, Klaus

b. 6 June 1926, Merseburg; d. 11 January 1998, Kiel

Conductor

A product of the Leipzig Conservatory, Tennstedt emigrated to the West in 1971 having held operatic positions in Halle and Dresden. After a notable Boston Symphony Orchestra debut in 1974 he was in demand internationally, and became principal conductor of the London Philharmonic Orchestra in 1983. His volatile and romantic response to such composers as Mahler is in some contrast to the objectivity of the younger generation's, which accounted for Tennstedt's great popularity with audiences until illness began to curtail his activities in the late 1980s.

BEATRICE HARPER

terrorism

Terrorism is a form of extremism that tries to reach its political objective of putting a new political system in place through systematic acts of violence, mostly directed against the ruling élite, in order to mobilize the 'oppressed'. Both left-wing and right-wing extremists can resort to terrorism. However, in Germany, violent, right-wing attacks against foreigners or other minorities do not really fit this definition; they lack both vision and organization.

Left-wing terrorism in the FRG has its roots in the **student movement** of the 1960s with its utopian aim of a 'free' socialist society without war, hunger or oppression. In 1968, as a protest against the Vietnam War and the 'capitalist consumer society', an arson attack was committed on a department store in Frankfurt am Main. Subsequently, in 1970, the perpetrators, Gudrun **Ensslin** and Andreas **Baader**, together with the journalist Ulrike **Meinhof**, the lawyer Horst Mahler and others, formed the Baader–Meinhof group or Red Army Faction (RAF). Before their arrest in 1972, they committed bank robberies and bomb attacks, targeting US installations in Germany, and also the police and judiciary. Closely identifying with liberation movements in the Third World, they styled themselves 'urban guerrillas', for which they had received training in a Palestine camp. Their strategy was intended to provoke the state into losing its 'democratic camouflage' and show its 'true fascist face'. In the early days they received some sympathy and practical help from left and liberal intellectuals.

RAF terrorism peaked in 1977, with several murders of high-ranking members of the establishment, committed by a 'second generation' of terrorists. Among the victims were the Chief Federal Prosecutor Siegfried Buback, the Chief Executive of the *Dresdner Bank* Jürgen Ponto, and the President of the Employers' Federation Hanns-Martin Schleyer. A quieter phase followed the hysteria of the 'German **Autumn**' (*deutscher Herbst*) of 1977, which saw first an unsuccessful attempt at freeing imprisoned terrorists through hijacking a Lufthansa aeroplane to Mogadishu, then the suicide of Baader, Ensslin and Raspe in prison, and finally the murder of the kidnapped Schleyer.

In the 1980s, 'revolutionary cells' continued to murder representatives of the political and economic élites. Their last victim (on 1 April 1991) was D.K. Rohwedder, the President of the **Treuhand**. Many of the second generation terrorists had been harboured by the **Stasi**, the East German state police, and given new identities. They were arrested after the collapse of the Honecker regime. The only police encounter, in June 1993, with a 'third generation' of terrorists resulted in the death of a policeman and a terrorist in Bad Kleinen in Mecklenburg-Vorpommern.

The year 1992 had seen a turning point in RAF thinking: some of the imprisoned terrorists offered a cessation of the 'armed struggle'. This followed a policy of reconciliation from the government with the offer of parole for most of the long-term prisoners.

In April 1998 the RAF finally announced that it was disbanding, and conceded that its focus on the 'armed struggle' had been a mistake.

Further reading

Becker, J. (1977), *Hitler's Children. The Story of the Baader-Meinhof Gang*, London: Granada.
Butz, P. (1993), *RAF. Terrorismus in Deutschland*, Munich: Knaur.

MONIKA PRÜTZEL-THOMAS

Tetzner, Gerti

b. 29 November 1936, Wiegleben (Thuringia)

Writer

Tetzner's *Karen W* (1974) was one of several novels by women writers in the mid-1970s to handle the subject of a woman's struggle for personal and professional emancipation in the GDR. She is the author of several children's books, such as *Maxi* (1979), in which the protagonist struggles to find a new identity, whilst questioning problems in everyday life and the environment.

MARGARET VALLANCE

Thate, Hilmar

b. 17 April 1931, Dölau (near Halle)

Actor

Trained in the acting methods of Stanislavski and **Brecht**, Thate ranks amongst the most versatile character-actors in the German language. During his time with the **Berliner Ensemble** (1959–70) and the **Deutsches Theater** (1971–9) he achieved particular acclaim for his interpretation of roles in productions directed by Manfred **Wekwerth**. His Richard III (1972) has been called a milestone in German Theatre History. As a consequence of signing a protest note in connection with the **Biermann Affair** he left the GDR in 1980. Thate is married to the actress Angelica **Domröse**.

HORST CLAUS

theatres

Theatre plays a central role in German culture; Germany boasts the best-organized theatre system and, despite the massive budget cuts implemented since German unification, the greatest subsidies in the world. In 1996 to 1997 there were 809 registered publicly-run and independent theatres in Germany with a total seating capacity of 276,529. Because the arts are the domain of the *Länder*, the legal structure and subsidy policies vary from **Land** to *Land*; the most heavily subsidized theatres are the *Staatstheater* (national theatres), *Landestheater* (provincial theatres) and *Stadttheater* (city theatres), but many commercial and independent theatres also receive public subsidies. Subsidies to the 355 publicly run theatres alone totalled nearly DM 3.9 billion in 1996 to 1997. The artistic personnel of German theatres currently totals 27,313, of which 41 percent are women.

At the end of the war, German theatre had been isolated from the international arena for a dozen years; it was morally discredited, and many theatres lay in ruins. All German theatres had been closed by the Nazis in September 1944: by the end of the war, 98 theatres had been totally destroyed in Allied bombing, and a further 88 were lost in the redefinition of the German borders. Bertolt **Brecht** produced his epic on the Thirty Years' War, *Mother Courage (Mutter Courage)*, at the **Deutsches Theater** in 1949 on a bare stage, commenting that the set lay outside the theatre – the ruins of Berlin. A 'ticket' to the theatre in the early period was sometimes a piece of coal, which was used to heat the theatre.

The centrality of theatre in German cultural life is reflected by the devotion of scarce resources to its rebuilding even in the desperate post-war years. Companies were re-established and buildings rebuilt with surprising speed; in the season 1947 to 1948, artistic personnel in German theatres already numbered 23,523 – only 4,000 fewer than in 1996. Authorization for productions rested initially with Allied control commissions; although the policies of the western and Soviet authorities differed from the outset, and a marked East–West divide emerged in the German theatre scene, the biographies of many playwrights, directors and actors document substantial movement of dramatic artists between East and West in the initial post-war years (as late as 1961, some theatre professionals and performance artists travelled daily from their homes in West Berlin to work at theatres in the East until the **Berlin Wall** rendered the border impassable.) Despite the very different theatre cultures which developed in the FRG and the GDR, both perpetuated the traditions of massive state subsidy, repertory structure and civil servant status for technical and artistic personnel (in public- or state-run theatres). When Germany was unified in 1990, the most-respected theatres of the GDR were integrated into the FRG subsidy system.

Unification of the country had a strong impact on German theatre: eastern theatres were confronted with the aesthetic, financial and ideological challenges of adapting to a market economy, including loss of a large portion of their traditional audience and radical reductions in personnel. Western theatres have undergone notable budget cuts and have had to adapt to the concerns of a changing public sphere and new institutional competitors. The effects of unification have been most drastic in Berlin, where a number of prominent theatres (most importantly the **Freie Volksbühne**, Schiller Theater, Schloßpark-Theater and Renaissance Theater) were closed in their traditional form: because a large portion of the staff of these theatres were non-terminable civil servants, the Minister of Culture has in some cases leased the buildings and staff to private impresarios.

Despite reductions in subsidies, German theatres are still heavily supported by the public purse. There are currently 59 registered theatres in Berlin alone, which in the 1995 to 1996 season together received subsidies of DM 468,522,000 (approximately 87 percent to public institutions, 13 percent to independents); subsidies per seat, per performance were, at the Berliner Ensemble, DM 285, and at the Schaubühne am Lehniner Platz, DM 193. Baden-Württemberg has per capita the largest number of theatres and the highest subsidies (over DM 290 million in 1997); guest performances in rural areas by independent troupes are supported directly through the Ministry of Agriculture.

Theatre-going in Germany is a tradition enjoyed by a relatively broad spectrum of the populace. The long-standing tradition of the **Freie Volksbühne** (SPD-aligned subscription organization for the working class), ticket-subsidies to school classes, the large number of children's theatres and puppet-theatres, the practice of company outings to the theatre (a strong tradition in the GDR), widespread subscription schemes and the relatively low price of tickets have made theatre-going a feasible activity for people of many classes. Whereas it is undoubtedly true that the majority of theatre-goers tend to be middle-aged and educated, the very broad range of theatres – from avant-garde to boulevard and, increasingly, to musical theatre – appeals to audiences of very different composition. Particularly in Berlin (at least in quantitative terms the indisputable capital of German theatre), the diversity of German theatre audiences is striking: the tradition-dashing Volksbühne attracts the young, vocal and unruly;

the pristine Schaubühne am Lehninerplatz a highly educated audience of critical devotees; the Theater des Westens (a musical theatre) the older middle classes (including busloads of tourists from the old *Länder*); the **GRIPS-Theater** (a didactic youth theatre) teenagers, children, parents and teachers; the **Deutsches Theater** an educated audience with a strong eastern component; the Maxim-Gorki-Theater an age-diverse audience which expects both intellectual *niveau* and traditional entertainment. Countless off-theatres in Berlin attract young audiences with subculture-specific or multicultural productions (one of the best Berlin theatres is the Theater Kreatur – a largely Polish ensemble whose productions are marked by stunning visuals and a primordial physicality). The theatres of the ex-GDR encourage public interaction by arranging exchanges with directors and cast members in foyer-discussions or specially arranged meetings for students after performances. The role of the theatre critic in Germany also contributes to the vitality of theatre-going; every major local and supra-regional paper publishes reviews of the premières of the major theatres and occasional articles on trends and developments.

There is no consensus as to which German theatre is best; indeed, the laurel is passed, appropriately, between several theatres, depending upon the success of new premières and the taste of the reviewer. Virtually all of the top German theatres maintain impressively broad repertories. In Berlin, the two theatres which most openly compete for the top national ranking are the Schaubühne am Lehninerplatz and the Deutsches Theater; the Schaubühne, with one of the technologically most advanced buildings in the world (a Bauhaus structure by Mendelssohn, fully modernized in 1983), is known for absolute precision in acting, highly innovative staging, and impeccable taste, but is criticized for having become overly aestheticist and hermetic; the Deutsches Theater, which achieved international fame as Max Reinhardt's theatre in the 1920s and was the best GDR theatre when the city was reunited, is more traditionalist in style and repertory but is unique in its stylizations and the playful irony of many of its productions. At least two other Berlin theatres are also among the best in

the country, though neither of them currently enjoys, across the board, a reputation equal to that of the Schaubühne or the Deutsches Theater. The Volksbühne (particularly the productions of its maverick Artistic Director, Frank Castorf), is at present the most daring renegade among German theatres, noted for radical deconstruction of – some would say disregard for – the dramatic text. The **Berliner Ensemble**, which enjoyed international fame in the 1950s under the direction of Bertolt Brecht, has recently made headway – despite difficulties of adjustment after unification (due in part to disputes over the production rights of Brecht's plays, which are intimately linked with the tradition of this house, and the aesthetic stagnancy which marked many productions in the final decades of the GDR) – in regaining a reputation as one of Germany's top theatres. The 1995 production of Brecht's *Der aufhaltsame Aufstieg des Arturo Ui* brought very high acclaim; after unification the Berliner Ensemble was reorganized as a public corporation with five artistic directors (the most important of whom was Heiner **Müller**, who died in late 1995), and its repertory diversified; in 1999 Claus Peymann will become artistic director. Of Berlin's four most renowned theatres, three are in East Berlin.

To acknowledge Berlin as Germany's theatre capital is not to say that there are not theatres of equal rank elsewhere. Among the very top ensembles in the country are the Deutsches Schauspielhaus and the Thalia Theater in Hamburg, the Schauspiel and the Theater am Turm in Frankfurt am Main, the Düsseldorf Schauspielhaus, the Schauspiel in Cologne, the Nationaltheater in Mannheim, the Kammerspiele (with one of the largest repertories in Germany) and the Bayerisches Schauspielhaus in Munich, Schauspielhaus in Bochum (one of Germany's most innovative theatres which has been managed by some of the best directors in Germany), the Schauspiel Bonn, the Theater der Stadt in Heidelberg, the Landestheater in Tübingen (LTT), and the Stadttheater in Konstanz. The most notable theatres in the new *Länder* (outside Berlin) are the Staatsschauspiel Dresden, the Staatstheater Cottbus, the Hans-Otto-Theater in Potsdam, the Schauspiel in Leipzig, the Deutsches Nationaltheater in Weimar, the Freie Kammerspiele in Magdeburg, the Staatstheater in Schwerin, the Theater Vorpommern in Stralsund/Greifswald and the Volkstheater in Rostock, and the Kleisttheater in Frankfurt an der Oder.

As in most sectors of a country burdened by the staggering cost of unification, financial constraints are currently the central concern and most-discussed issue in German theatre life. Given the fact that roughly 83 percent of theatre budgets are covered by subsidy, shortfalls in subsidy are having a significant impact on the theatre scene. Theatre closures, reduction in the number of new productions, and great fluctuation in management have characterized recent years. A trend towards more commercially viable genres is detectable; the musical – a genre in which a single production often enjoys a run of many years and draws as much as 80 percent of its audience from outside the region – is growing in popularity. Specially erected houses have been built or are being planned for long-run musicals (*CATS*, *Phantom of the Opera*, *Starlight Express*, *Miss Saigon*, etc.) in Bochum, Essen, Stuttgart, Duisburg, Niederhausen and Bremen; a new 'musical hall' has been built at the Potsdamer Platz in Berlin, and many public theatres have now added musicals to their repertories.

This trend towards entertainment theatre is likely to exacerbate a syndrome which resulted from the largely classicist and 'big-name' repertory of most German theatres, and which has marred the otherwise exemplary state of German theatre for decades: the inability of young, experimental playwrights to get their plays produced.

See also: drama: FRG; drama: GDR

Further reading

Deutsches Bühnenjahrbuch (published annually) Hamburg: Verlag der Bühnenschriften-Vertriebsgesellschaft (report of the German theatre guild, published annually since 1889).

Hofmann, J. (1985) *Theaterbuch Berlin*, Berlin: Verlag Klaus Guhl (excellent handbook on Berlin theatres, theatre professionals, policies, structure of theatre scene).

Patterson, M. (1976) *German Theatre Today*, London: Pitman (an English-language overview of German theatre including statistics on major productions).

Steets, B. (1994) *Theateralmanach*, Pullach im Isartal: edition Schmidt (annual statistic overview of German theatre scene; includes data on all major theatres).

Theater Heute is the best critical journal of German theatre; it publishes reviews of all major premières, interviews with directors and actors, regular regional overviews of the scene, and texts of new plays.

KAREN RUOFF KRAMER

theology

In 1945 German theologians stood at a crossroad. The primary challenge they had to face was coming to terms with the atrocities committed against Jews by Christians in the name of Germany. The options were to deny ethical and moral responsibility for these crimes, to portray surviving members of the Confessing Church as heroes, to engage in a combination of the above, or to come to terms with the Nazi past. Not surprisingly, theologians escaped into an ambivalent mixture of these options. As early as October 1945, leading members of the Protestant church in Germany acknowledged Germany's guilt in general and the failures of Christians in Germany during the twelve years of the Nazi regime in particular. Nevertheless, it took until 1950 before the Synod of that same church publicly referred to the crimes against the Jews. Finally, from 1967 on, a painful but revealing dialogue between Jews and Christians emerged, which was fostered by committed individuals and facilitated by ecumenical meetings. However, not until the 1970s did theologians – in particular Eberhard Bethge (1909–) and Rolf Rendtorff (1925–) – reflect on the fundamental theological relevance of the Shoah (or Holocaust) for any rethinking of Christian theology in Germany. Today, the Jewish-Christian dialogue remains an ongoing process of mutual learning, wherein traditional notions, such as the absoluteness of Christianity, are evaluated and considered obsolete.

Furthermore, after 1945, the Old Testament and its relevance to the Christian church started to play a meaningful role. The Bible moved into the centre of discourse, and theology focused on biblical studies. Generations of theologians remained extremely influenced by Karl **Barth** (1886–1968) in his rejection of liberal theology, and by Rudolf **Bultmann** (1884–1976) in his reception of the philosophy of Martin **Heidegger** (1889–1976) in particular, and by Bultmann's appropriation of **existentialism** in general. While Bultmann's emphasis on 'form criticism' had dominated New Testament scholarship, it was nevertheless the Bultmannians Ernst **Käsemann** (1906–98) and Günther **Bornkamm** (1905–90) who insisted that the foundation of Christian faith is inseparable from Jesus. Their argument that Christians must confirm Jesus's life moved New Testament scholarship to an intensive effort to re-evaluate the 'historical Jesus.' Gerhard Ebeling (1912–) and Ernst Fuchs (1903–83) also focused on the historical Jesus as witness of faith. By continuing in Bultmann's tradition, both Ebeling and Fuchs emphasized hermeneutics as an essential reflection on language. While biblical scholarship had rediscovered the significance of eschatology and the Kingdom of God in Jesus's words and actions, the Protestant Jürgen **Moltmann** (1926–) and the Catholic Johannes Metz (1928–) alike grounded their systematic theologies in eschatology. This means that their theologies emphasized the dimension of the unexpected and the principally new and Moltmann- and Metz-developed theological ground for social reforms. By adopting the category *docta spes* (learned hope) of Ernst **Bloch** (1885–1977), Moltmann sketched out in accordance with Bloch's *Philosophy of Hope* (*Das Prinzip Hoffnung*, 1959) his *Theology of Hope* (*Theologie der Hoffnung*, 1964). The quality of Christian hope is defined as an expression of faith in the ultimate triumph of the crucified Christ, and the *cross* of Christ expresses that God is love. Moltmann understands God as a Trinitarian community of equals, a God who could experience the agony of enslaved people as told in the Exodus story and in the agony of the Son. Moltmann's goal of mediating Christianity and modernity has culminated in his political theology and in his social doctrine of the Trinity. For Moltmann, theology has to be involved in the struggle for emancipation through political power

at the national and international level. Wolfhard **Pannenberg** (1928–) shared the renewed interest in eschatology; he did not emphasize social change but accepted the challenge to hold up faith to contemporary philosophy.

The 1960s did not pass without posing essential questions about theology and its position in society. Not surprisingly, established values of contemporary society were called into question and a passion for social justice emerged in theology. The rediscovery of Paul Tillich's (1886–1965) *Vermittlung* (Mediation) of philosophy and theology, and his intellectual association with members of the **Frankfurt School** fuelled theologians' commitment to social change. Helmut **Gollwitzer** (1908–93) combined Karl Barth's Christian humanism with a Marxist critique of society and ideology. He favoured a political polarization of the church through careful attention to the message of the Bible. Gollwitzer became a hero of the German New Left, along with Dorothee **Sölle** (1929–) who subscribes to the so-called God-is-dead-Theology and combines moral political conscience with political action. Challenging those concepts dealing with Marxist ideology and promoting changes in society, Eberhard **Jüngel** (1934–) vehemently opposed theological concepts that understood faith as an anthropological category and as an expression of the human subject. Jüngel's anti-anthropological turn reasserted faith as divine truth.

Practical theology and *Seelsorge* (pastoral care) changed fundamentally under the appropriation of both Freudian and Jungian schools of thought in psychology and psychoanalysis. The recent surplus of trained theologians makes them especially employable in other jobs in the larger field of social work and supportive human services.

Certain similarities prevail in both the Protestant and Catholic church, and in their recent theological-historical developments. Nevertheless, significant differences exist due to the ecclesiological structure.

The Catholic theologian Karl **Rahner** (1904–84) propagated that mystery understood as a matter of religious faith lay at the heart of all human understanding. Later, he shifted from eternal truth to a search for truth centring his theology around evolutionary growth understood as nature moving towards grace and the word moving towards the Kingdom of God. In 1961, the Catholic church was de-hierarchized and redefined as the whole 'pilgrim of God.' This democratization changed the role of the laity and opened the church for ecumenical dialogue. Already in 1960, the Swiss-born Catholic theologian, Hans **Küng** (1928–), had fundamentally challenged the church by calling for a reform of mandatory celibacy, and in 1971 questioned papal infallibility. As a result of this dispute, his canonical mission to teach in the Catholic faculty in Tübingen was revoked in 1979. He continued to function as a Professor and Director of the Institute for Ecumenical Research. The Institute sponsored critical research and provided an intellectual home for feminist theologians as well. Küng remains fully committed to scientific theology, questions fundamental issues of Christology, continues to be involved with interfaith dialogue, and seeks to respond adequately to the postmodern condition with a critical ecumenical theology.

Modernism and **postmodernism** have raised serious questions for all religious denominations. Since the early 1980s, feminist theology has formulated problems of gender and centred around women. While Elisabeth **Moltmann-Wendel** (1926–) discusses the sociological position of women in church and society, numerous others assert essential differences between men and women.

After the unification of Germany in 1989, theologians who lived their faith and worked in the church in the GDR began to examine specific problems resulting from these societal conditions. Dealing with the socialist past, the involvement of the Protestant church with the SED state, and the question of its Christian responsibility and identity, continues to provoke ethical reflections on post-unified German theology.

See also: churches and religion; Kirche im Sozialismus

Further reading

Bethge, E. (1979) *Am gegebenen Ort*, Munich: Chr. Kaiser.

Rendtorff, R. and Henrix, H.H. (eds) (1988) *Die Kirchen und das Judentum*, Munich: Chr. Kaiser.

Rendtorff, R. and Stegemann, E. (eds) (1980) *Auschwitz: Krise der christlichen Theologie*, Munich: Chr. Kaiser.

Siegele-Wenschkewitz, L. (ed.) (1988) *Verdrängte Vergangenheit, die uns bedrängt: feministische Theologie in der Verantwortung für die Geschichte*, Munich: Chr. Kaiser.

MAGDA MUELLER

Thome, Rudolf

b. 14 November 1939, Wallau (Lahn)

Filmmaker

Thome worked initially as a film critic. His early films – influenced by Godard and Hawks – earned him the epithet 'feminist', and his memorable second feature, *Red Sun (Rote Sonne*, 1969), tells the macabre story of a women's commune resolved to murder every male lover within five days. The simplicity, directness and keen eye for milieu and psychology of his subsequent films, including the romance *Berlin Chamissoplatz* (1980) and 'forms of love' trilogy begun in 1987 with *The Microscope (Das Mikroskop)*, have elicited comparisons with Eric Rohmer.

See also: New German Cinema

MARTIN BRADY

Thorndike, Andrew and Annelie

Andrew: b. 30 August 1909, Frankfurt am Main; d. 14 December 1979, (East) Berlin

Annelie (née Kunigk): b. 17 April 1925, Klützow (now Kluczewo, Poland)

Documentary filmmakers

Andrew Thorndike (an employee of Ufa's Industrial Film Unit before WWII, whose ancestors came from Scotland via America) and his wife Annelie (a school teacher) made their first joint documentary in the GDR in 1952. After the return of confiscated German films by the Russians in 1954, they became known for increasingly sophisticated and complex compilation films. The

Thorndikes manipulated the visual material to promote their socialist convictions and underpin the socialist position in the propaganda war with the west in general, and the FRG in particular.

See also: documentary film; film: GDR

HORST CLAUS

Thut, Doris

b. 12 February 1945, Vienna

Architect

A pupil in E.A. Plischke's master class in Vienna, Thut also studied under Sep Ruf in 1967 in Munich, where she went into private practice in 1968. She has taught at the FH (Technical University) Munich since 1990.

In addition to theoretical work connected to the designing process and client participation, Doris Thut, together with her husband Rolf, is one of the pioneers of experimental domestic building (see also **Steidle**). The creation of poly-contextual environments and communal living are main themes in her work. Next to the Genter Straße building (1969–72), the Max-Planck-Straße housing project (1982–4) and a sports hall in Munich (1979–80) are her best-known designs.

MARTIN KUDLEK AND BERTHOLD PESCH

Timm, Uwe

b. 30 March 1940, Hamburg

Novelist

A realistic writer who has always stressed the political dimension of his work, Timm took part as a student in the events of 1967–8, which provide the backdrop to his 1974 novel *Heißer Sommer* (Hot Summer), the story of a Munich student's efforts to negotiate the world of sex and drugs as well as that of politics. He turned subsequently to historical and Third World themes, for instance in *The Snake Tree* (*Der Schlangenbaum*, 1986). The 1993 novella *Die Entdeckung der Currywurst* (The Discovery of Curry

Sausage), set in Hamburg in 1945, effectively combines humour and pathos.

STUART PARKES

Toten Hosen, Die

Die Toten Hosen (which means 'dead beats') are the most successful punk band to emerge from the German New Wave **punk** scene in the early 1980s. Taking their musical style from the Sex Pistols, 999 and other pioneering British punk groups, the Toten Hosen have parlayed their rebellious attitude and ironic social commentary into a surprising commercial success, selling more than 750,000 copies of their 1996 release 'Opium für das Volk'. Well-known for taking a stand against right-wing radicalism and racism, the Toten Hosen also made headlines when the **Schlager** singer Heino sued their singer, Campino, for appearing in public as '*der wahre Heino*' (the true Heino).

MATTHEW T. GRANT

town planning

Post-war town planning in Germany often depended on schemes presented during the Nazi era (e.g. in Munich and Düsseldorf), although many plans were drawn up reflecting the Weimar Republic's modern town planning ideals (e.g. **Scharoun**'s plans for Berlin). Reichenow's publications *Organische Stadtbaukunst* of 1948 and *Die autogerechte Stadt* of 1959, Schwagenscheidt's *Raumstadt* of 1949 and *Die gegliederte und aufgelockerte Stadt* of 1957 by Göderitz, Rainer and Hoffmann stand for the modern trends of the time. The Hansaviertel in West Berlin and the reconstruction of Mainz and Nürnberg were executed according to aspects of these.

With the *Städtetag* (town-planning convention) in 1960, criticism of the abandonment of the town's traditional spatial fabric caused by functionalist ideals set in, reaching a climax with Alexander **Mitscherlich**'s *Die Unwirtlichkeit unserer Städte* of 1965. The politics of disintegration and concentration were nevertheless retained, thus continuing the urban exodus and the simultaneous building up of the surrounding countryside. The new town structures and satellite towns required ever more efficient traffic systems as the motorcar became an increasingly dominant factor in town planning. Large shopping complexes emerged on the outskirts of towns, extracting commercial power and social life from the inner cities. The cry for a greater focus on town life in the early 1970s merely resulted in higher density in the newly built up areas. Despite increasing scientific input into town planning these areas have far more problems attached to them than the old inner-city building stock they were supposed to relieve. The 1970s also saw a reconsideration of traditional pre-war urban spaces which often took on nostalgic traits in the suppression of its shortcomings. The oil-crisis and the discussion over growth limits triggered off an environmental consciousness that also embraces the built environment (see also **environmentalism**; **IBA**). In addition the new understanding of urban culture manifested itself in the squats of the 1980s.

Another important planning task from the 1980s onwards is the environmental improvement of the *Großsiedlungen* (large-scale housing estates), scarcely twenty years old, in order to avoid the further decline of socially heterogeneous areas. Here, as in the Hansaviertel in Hamburg, the regaining of public space through architectural restructuring is characteristic. Another theme of recent town planning is the restructuring of disused industrial fabric (e.g. IBA Emscher Park in the Ruhr, 1987–97). Finding new usages for abandoned industrial and commercial areas in the Ruhr and many other towns has become an experimental area for contemporary town planning, ranging from the geometric space-additions in Potsdam-Kirchsteigfeld to ecological projects in Freiburg-Rieselfeld and car-free living in Bremen.

In the GDR the *16 Grundsätze des Städtebaus* (sixteen principles of town planning) of 1950, according to which Eisenhüttenstadt was planned, were soon abandoned in favour of the example of **Henselmann**'s Stalinallee. This model only asserted itself for a short while too, due to the party-political take-over of architecture and town planning. What followed was the total industrialization of building, resulting in the destruction of historical building stock and a mass of monotonous prefabricated *Großsiedlungen* that still dominate East German townscapes today.

See also: Berlin building boom; reconstruction

MARTIN KUDLEK AND BERTHOLD PESCH

Trabant

This small car manufactured from 1958 to 1990 by the VEB Sachsenring in Zwickau is the only mass production car in history with non-metal bodywork (Duroplast). Dubbed the '**Volkswagen** of the eastern bloc' and the 'command economy on wheels', the anachronistic 'Trabi' became a symbol for the GDR's economic mismanagement (delivery times of between twelve and fifteen years). It lived up to its name (suggesting a travelling companion) in 1989 during the motorized exodus of GDR citizens to the FRG. It was named 1989 Car of the Year in *Time Magazine*, and is the inspiration for countless Trabi jokes.

See also: 'Made in Germany'; motor car

DAVID HEAD

trade unions

After WWII the British occupation authorities helped refound and restructure trade unions in western Germany into a small number of industrial unions. These industrial unions formed a confederation in 1949, the Deutscher Gewerkschaftsbund (DGB). Based in Düsseldorf, the DGB has sixteen affiliates representing workers in both eastern and western Germany. The largest and strongest DGB affiliate is IG Metall, the metal workers' union. It had over 2.8 million members in 1996 and is one of the world's largest single unions. In 1997 *IG Metall* merged with another DGB affiliate, the GTB textile and clothing union, reducing the number of DGB affiliates to fifteen.

The DGB co-ordinates the activities of its affiliates, and represents them at national level. For most of the post-war period the DGB has been a partner in the 'social market economy' of the FRG alongside the employers and federal government.

German employees are also represented by three other national organizations. Founded in 1946, the Deutsche Angestellten-Gewerkschaft (DAG) (German Union of Salaried Employees) is the largest of these organizations, with about half a million members. It represents all white-collar workers in every industrial sector, so is not an industrial union. The DAG competes for members with DGB affiliates, principally in the public, financial and retail sectors.

The Deutscher Beamtenbund (DBB) (German Civil Servants' Federation), with about 800,000 members, is an organization for *Beamte* which was founded in 1950. The DBB regards itself as a professional association rather than a trade union. The DBB has to compete with the DGB for members, and about as many *Beamte* belong to the former as the latter.

The Christlicher Gewerkschaftsbund Deutschlands (CGB) (Christian Trade Union Federation) was founded by prominent Christian trade unionists who broke away from the DGB in 1955. It has about 300,000 members among its affiliated unions. However, the CGB failed to achieve a significant level of support, partly because there remains a strong minority presence of Christian Democrats in DGB unions.

Following the collapse of the GDR, some four million eastern German workers joined DGB trade unions during 1990 and 1991. The first half of the 1990s saw the emergence of an economic crisis, partly caused by the high cost of German economic and monetary unification, which resulted in a substantial increase in unemployment. Between 1991 and 1998 trade union membership in Germany fell by 3.3 million from 11.8 to 8.5 million. The membership of the DGB is becoming increasingly older as it has failed to attract younger workers as members. In January 1995 the DGB adopted a new corporate design as part of a campaign to reverse the decline in membership.

The main activity of the DGB is political lobbying. However, the DGB also supports some cultural activities. The most important of these is the Ruhrfestspiele Recklinghausen. This is an annual theatre festival co-financed by the German trade unions and the town of Recklinghausen. The DGB also promotes worker education. Since the introduction of the European Single Market

the DGB has sought to improve the cultural competencies (e.g. languages) of its members.

Further reading

DGB-Bundesvorstand (1996) *Symposium: Kultur wohin? Wege ins nächste Jahrtausend*, Düsseldorf: DGB Dokumentation.

Gehrke, R., Johannson, K. and Wagner, E. (eds) (1996) *Räume schaffen: Neue Ansätze kultureller Weiterbildung von Arbeitnehmerinnen und Arbeitnehmern*, Essen: Klartext/PRO.

Randlesome, C. (1994) *The Business Culture in Germany*, Oxford: Butterworth-Heinemann.

RICHARD A. HAWKINS

Treuhand

When the Treuhandanstalt (Trust Body) was set up on 1 March 1990 by the government of the GDR under Hans **Modrow** its stated task was 'the administration of state property in the interests of the general good'. Its purpose was to protect state-owned industry from collapse or privatization. After the victory of the conservative 'Alliance for Germany' two weeks later on 18 March, which signalled the imminent implementation of monetary and social union with West Germany, the aim of the Treuhand was changed to that of overseeing the privatization of the East German economy. A new Treuhand Law was introduced on 17 June 1990, two weeks before monetary union, which made it clear that the purpose of the Treuhand now was to restructure East German industry in such a way as to make it capable of competing in a free market economy. Paragraph 8(1) states that the main means of achieving this was privatization, but the same paragraph also makes it clear that those companies which could not be made competitive through restructuring would have to be closed, and their assets disposed of. The Treuhand was therefore caught from the outset between two policy directions; one of rapid privatization at any cost, and one which wanted to play a more positive industrial-political role which took into account the social costs of high unemployment and de-industrialization.

In the summer of 1990 the Treuhand became the largest state-owned holding company in the world. It took responsibility for more than 8,000 firms on 40,000 sites, including 100 Combines (*Kombinate*), with more than 6 million employees. It also took over more than 30,000 commercial units and over 8.5 million acres of agricultural and forestry land, about 40 percent of the territory of the GDR. In addition it assumed responsibility for all **Stasi** buildings and the assets of GDR parties and organizations, about 4,000 properties in all. On **unification** the Treuhand, which had a central office in Berlin and fifteen regional offices, took over responsibility for all state enterprises of the GDR and was charged in Articles 23 and 25 of the Unification Treaty with the reduction of the debts of these enterprises through the restructuring and privatization of the East German economy.

In the latter part of 1990 and the early part of 1991 the Treuhand presided over the collapse of East German industry. The resulting unrest in the new states as a result of rapidly increasing unemployment threatened to get out of control in the spring of 1991. In response the Treuhand started to build in contractual obligations into privatization contracts. New owners were now required to provide guarantees with regard to investment and employment levels, thereby reducing the danger of asset-stripping or closure to eliminate competition. The change in direction was too late for the first head of the Treuhand, Detlev Rohwedder, who was assassinated by terrorists in April 1991. His place was taken by Birgit Breuel who, until the dissolution of the Treuhand, presided over a policy which took industrial-political considerations more into account, especially in relation to such large industries as the chemical and ship-building industries. On 31 December 1994 the Treuhand was duly wound up having privatized over 14,000 enterprises, and responsibility for the administration of the Treuhand's responsibilities was taken over by the Bundesanstalt für vereinigungsbedingte Sonderaufgaben (Federal Office for Special Tasks Resulting from Unification).

See also: *Wende*

Further reading

Cuming, M. (1992) 'The Confused Role of the Treuhand', *German Monitor* 25: 25–40.

Flug, M. (1992) *Treuhand-Poker. Die Mechanismen des Ausverkaufs*, Berlin: Ch. Links Verlag.

PETER BARKER

Treut, Monika

b. 6 April 1954, Mönchengladbach

Filmmaker

Internationally successful filmmaker who came to prominence in the late 1980s with her irreverent, semi-documentary explorations of lesbian sexuality and sado-masochism. *The Virgin Machine* (*Die Jungfrauenmaschine*, 1988), the story of a young German woman coming-out in New York, the comedy *My Father is Coming* (1991), featuring Alfred Edel as a father forced to come to terms with his daughter's homosexuality, and the documentary *Female Misbehaviour* (1983–92) are humorously taboo-breaking, post-feminist investigations of sexual desire, with guest appearances from commentators as diverse as Camille Paglia and porn-star Annie Sprinkle.

See also: film: FRG

HELEN HUGHES

Trockel, Rosemarie

b. 13 November 1956, Schwerte

Sculptor and painter

Through various aesthetic strategies Trockel has established a female perspective within the international visual arts. Although her objects and images refer to the domestic sphere of housework and crafts, traditionally the realm of women, their messages are often deliberately ambivalent within a feminist context. Through the use of labels, symbols and emblems as patterns on knitwear, for instance, expectations are subverted. She seeks to disrupt and undermine familiar patterns of perception and thought with laconic irony and a complex play of allusions and associations.

See also: sculpture

KERSTIN MEY

Trotta, Margarethe von

b. 21 February 1942, Berlin

Filmmaker, screenwriter, and actress

Margarethe von Trotta has been one of the major and best known female directors to emerge from the **New German Cinema**, working first as an actress in the 1960s and early 1970s in films by Herbert Achternbusch, Reinhard Hauff, Rainer Werner Fassbinder and Volker **Schlöndorff** (whom she married in 1971), before she began writing screenplays and directing her own feature films to international critical acclaim. Von Trotta's cinematic œuvre has been consistently concerned with the intersections of female personal identity and political themes in German contemporary society and post-war history from a feminist perspective. Psychologically complex relationships between women as sisters or friends are prominent in many of her films, suggesting von Trotta's interest in the internal world and repressed doubles of her characters; they are, however, always placed in the specific realist context of the political and historical dimension of those relationships, as in *Marianne and Juliane* (*Die Bleierne Zeit*, 1981), about the **Ensslin** sisters and 1970s **terrorism** in West Germany, and *Rosa Luxemburg* (1986), a historical dramatization of the public and private life of the famous Polish socialist revolutionary.

After first collaborating with Schlöndorff as a co-director and co-writer on several films, such as *The Lost Honour of Katharina Blum* (1975), she directed her first solo film *The Second Awakening of Christa Klages* (1977). Her 1979 interior drama, *Sisters or the Balance of Happiness*, was followed by the internationally lauded *Marianne and Juliane* (1981), which received the Golden Lion at the Venice Festival. *Sheer Madness* (*Heller Wahn*, 1983) portrayed the intense but fraught friendship between two women as a mirror for the contemporary women's

movement and political and social changes in Europe.

During a six-year residence in Italy, von Trotta completed *The Three Sisters* (*Paura e amore*, 1988), loosely based on Chekhov's play; *The Return* (*Die Rückkehr*, 1990), about the intricacies of a love triangle, female friendship and jealousy; and *The Long Silence* (*Zeit des Zorns*, 1993), which examines the government corruption in contemporary Italy through the emerging political consciousness of the wife of an assassinated anti-Mafia judge. In 1994, von Trotta returned to Germany to direct *The Promise* (*Das Versprechen*), a story of two lovers separated for twenty-eight years by the **Berlin Wall**. Co-written with novelist Peter **Schneider**, *The Promise* marked the director's return to the fusion of fictional drama and recent German history, and represented the first feature film since **unification** to examine the traumatic period of the years of the Wall.

See also: feminism and the women's movement

Further reading

Elsner-Sommer, G. (1990), 'Margarethe von Trotta', in N. Thomas (ed.) *International Dictionary of Films and Filmmakers*, London: St James Press (contains filmography and selected bibliography up to 1990).

Linville, S. (1991) 'Retrieving History: Margarethe von Trotta's *Marianne and Juliane*', *PMLA* 106, 3: 446–58 (a detailed analysis of von Trotta's acclaimed film).

EVA RUESCHMANN

Trümmerfrauen

Literally 'rubble women', the concept of *Trümmerfrauen* has come to epitomise a particular moment of post-war life. With many men dead, imprisoned, or not yet returned home, much of the work of rebuilding from the ruins was undertaken by women. Lines of women formed to pass buckets, bricks and boulders from one to another, restoring some semblance of order in the ruins of bombed German cities. These lines symbolized the 'hour of the women', when women not only cared for their dependants (young, old and wounded) but also laboured in areas traditionally preserved as masculine domains.

MARY FULBROOK

Tübke, Werner

b. 30 July 1929, Schönebeck/Elbe

Painter and graphic artist

With his unconventional individual style and visual expressiveness Tübke makes a distinctive contribution to the development of twentieth-century figurative art. He ranges far and wide across the German painterly tradition from the renaissance to the baroque in his painstakingly executed works and concentrates on history painting as a means of critical reflection on the present. From 1976 to 1987 he was commissioned by the GDR state for a monumental panoramic painting for a Peasants' war memorial in Bad Frankenhausen. Recently he has established himself as an opera stage-designer.

See also: documenta; painting

KERSTIN MEY

Turrini, Peter

b. 26 September 1944, St Margarethen (near Klagenfurt)

Writer

Turrini is often reductively described as a **Volksstück** author; yet even *sauschlachten* (pig-killing) (1972), despite its bucolic setting, exaggerates and inverts *Volksstück* stereotypes to excoriate its sentimentalizing of the family. *Kindsmord* (Child Murder) (1973), *Josef und Maria*, a reworking of the nativity (1980), or his championing of minorities, reflect a strong sensitivity to outsider experience. His widely-viewed television series (with Wilhelm Pevny) *Die Alpensaga* (1974–6) on the socio-economic crisis of the Alpine peasantry underlined his left-wing commitment. The play *The Slackers* (*Die Minderleister*) (1988) passionately attacks capitalist forms of technological change.

MORAY McGOWAN

U

Uecker, Günther

b. 13 March 1930, Wendorf

Painter, sculptor, performance artist and filmmaker

Uecker has become almost exclusively associated with nails, which he employed as his preferred material from the late 1950s, arranging them in abstract, systematic configurations on board, furniture and other wooden surfaces before over-painting them white. The nails – often organized in tight wave-patterns – generate striking optical effects of light and shades as in *White Picture (Weißes Bild*, 1959). He joined the **Zero Group** in 1961, developing kinetic works. During the 1980s he produced large-scale installations, often addressing metaphysical themes, and began to use ash in the wake of the Chernobyl explosion.

MARTIN BRADY

Uhse, Beate

b. 25 October 1919, Cranz (East Prussia) (now Selenogradsk, Russia)

Chain sex store executive

Beate Uhse (née Köstlin) is the world's largest vendor of sex-related materials. With sex shops in every major Germany city and in other countries, her chain boasts annual sales of $80 million. The firm is known for attention to quality; the mail order business is extensive. In celebration of her fiftieth year of business, Uhse opened a museum of erotica in Berlin in 1996. A widely-recognized personality, Uhse served in the Luftwaffe, the first woman to fly a German fighter plane.

See also: sex shops

JOHN B. RUTLEDGE

Ulbricht, Walter

b. 30 June 1893, Leipzig; d. 1 August 1973, (East) Berlin

GDR functionary

A communist activist in the 1920s and 1930s, Ulbricht led the first group of communist function-aries to return to Germany from the Soviet Union in April 1945. He was the central figure in the establishment of the **KPD**, then the **SED**, as the leading political force in the Soviet zone with Soviet backing. From 1950 to 1953 he was General Secretary, and from July 1953 to May 1971 First Secretary, of the SED. Ulbricht was the crucial figure in the Sovietization of political and economic structures in the GDR in the 1950s, and the decision to build the **Berlin Wall** in August 1961.

PETER BARKER

Umsiedler

Umsiedler (resettlers) was a term that was used in the GDR to describe those Germans who had been forced to leave the areas that Germany lost at the end of WWII, such as Silesia and the Sudetenland, and resettle in Germany. For political reasons terms such as *Vertriebene(r)* (expellee) and *Flüchtling* (refugee), which were the normal terms in West Germany, were not used officially in the GDR, in order to avoid the impression that force had been used.

See also: refugees

PETER BARKER

Ungers, Oswald Mathias

b. 7 December 1926, Kaiseresch (Eifel)

Architect

Ungers studied at the TH (Technical University) Karlsruhe under **Eiermann** from 1947 to 1950, and has been in private practice in Cologne since 1950 and Berlin since 1964. He taught at the TU Berlin and Kunstakademie Düsseldorf.

Most of Unger's work up to the 1960s is dominated by domestic buildings. As commissions decreased in the 1970s he concentrated on competitions (e.g. Bremen University, 1977). Since the late 1970s he has realized many large building projects while fully developing his strict architectural language based upon the square, and becoming one of Germany's most important representatives of **postmodernism** (e.g. Architekturmuseum Frankfurt am Main, 1984). Winning the competition for the new Wallraf-Richards Museum in Cologne (1996) was especially important to him.

MARTIN KUDLEK

unification

In the first phase of the political *Wende* in the German Democratic Republic in the autumn of 1989 many sections of GDR society believed in the possibility of a reformed independent state. But by December 1989, revelations about corruption and abuse of power by the communist party (**SED**) and the realization of the true state of the economy meant that large numbers of GDR citizens now saw the only possible path as that of unification

with West Germany. This conviction was expressed in the election victory of the conservative Allianz für Deutschland (Alliance for Germany) on 18 March 1990, and unification was achieved on 3 October 1990 at a speed which nobody had previously envisaged.

Ever since the division of Germany into two states in October 1949, unification was present as a possibility; sometimes at the forefront of political activity, and at others, especially in the 1970s and 1980s, pushed into the background. For the forty-one years of separation the ultimate goal of West German policy was unification, while in the GDR official policy in the 1950s was that of unification on the basis of neutrality, a vision very different from that of the West. The building of the Berlin Wall in 1961 represented the symbolic abandonment of that policy by the GDR, although it was not until the amended constitution of 1974 that the GDR emphasized the idea of a separate socialist nation. Three years earlier, West Germany had signed the *Grundvertrag* (Basic Treaty) as the culmination of Willy **Brandt**'s *Ostpolitik* which accorded the GDR a limited recognition, but fell short of recognizing it as a foreign state. West Germany maintained its right to represent all Germans by according GDR citizens West German citizenship on application. During the 1970s and 1980s successive West German governments, whilst maintaining the pledge to bring about unification, in practice concentrated on improving relationships with the other German state.

When political change came to the GDR in the autumn of 1989, unification was not in the forefront of the debate. The emphasis was on reform of the GDR's political structures. The mood changed in November 1989. On 28 November, the West German Chancellor, Helmut **Kohl**, presented a ten-point plan to the Bundestag in response to the offer by the new GDR Prime Minister, Hans **Modrow**, on 17 November to establish close co-operation between the two states. In point five of his statement Kohl reiterated the commitment of his government to achieving unification, without indicating a timescale. Kohl's statement coincided with a change in the mood of the GDR population. For the first time calls for rapid unification with West Germany started to be heard at demonstrations throughout the GDR.

This change was a direct reaction to revelations of corruption and abuse of power by SED functionaries, in particular concerning the activities of the **Stasi**. The true state of the GDR economy was also becoming apparent, and it became clear that it could not be saved without the immediate help of its prosperous neighbour. Continuing emigration to West Germany after the opening of the borders on 9 November was a clear sign of desperation and spelt the end of the GDR as a separate state.

In December 1989 the GDR government under Modrow struggled to keep alive the idea of a reformable GDR. It was helped by the fact that a number of foreign leaders, most notably Mrs Thatcher from Great Britain and President Mitterrand of France, publicly expressed doubts about the idea of German unification. During a visit to the GDR from 20 to 22 December President Mitterrand expressed his fear that unification could upset the delicate political balance of Europe. But the two German states had already agreed on steps towards establishing a confederation in a meeting between Kohl and Modrow in Dresden on 19 December. By the end of 1989 only the successor party to the SED, the SED-**PDS**, and some sections of the **citizens' movements**, were insisting that the GDR should continue as a separate state. On 15 January 1990 over 150,000 people demonstrated in Leipzig in favour of unification. Three days later all the parties in the West German Bundestag, except the **Greens**, declared their support for unification. The Modrow government, in a desperate attempt to keep control of the political situation, agreed on 28 January to the bringing-forward of the **Volkskammer** elections from May to 18 March. On the same day eight representatives of opposition groups on the *Runder Tisch* (**Round Table**) agreed to take up positions as Ministers without Portfolio in the government. Modrow himself was now reconciled to the inevitability of unification. On 30 January he met the Soviet president, Mikhail Gorbachev, who expressed the view that the Soviet Union had in principle no objections to unification. Thus the last remaining obstacle to unification was removed, and on 1 February Modrow presented his declaration on the 'path to German unity' in East Berlin. Modrow's concept differed markedly from that of Kohl's, since he saw unification starting on the

basis of a German confederation which would assert its neutrality from previous military and political ties. On 13 February Modrow visited Bonn, and agreement was reached on the introduction of monetary and economic union, the first concrete step to unification. On the following day the foreign ministers of the two German states and those of the four occupying powers met in Ottawa and agreed on a '2 + 4' formula for a conference which would settle the external aspects of unification.

The initial framework for unification was thus established before the *Volkskammer* elections. The election campaign was dominated by two questions: first the basis on which monetary union would take place; and second by what route and at what speed unification would happen. The Social Democrats favoured the slower route via a confederation and Article 146 of the West German Basic Law which first required a referendum in the two German states on a new constitution. The conservative Alliance for Germany campaigned for unification via Article 23 by which individual *Länder*, which had yet to be reconstituted in the GDR, could apply to join the Federal Republic. This latter route represented a much faster path to unification since the Basic Law would be taken as the constitutional basis of the unified German state. The East German people gave the largest number of votes (48.15 percent) to the Alliance for Germany and only 21.84 percent to the SPD, thus confirming that the faster route was the preferred option for nearly half the population of the GDR. When the conservative Prime Minister Lothar de **Maizière** came to build his government he decided to include ministers from the SPD and the liberal alliance in order to bring together the broadest possible political spectrum to negotiate the terms for unification.

The immediate concern for the new GDR government was the negotiation of the conditions of monetary, economic and social union. The **Bundesbank** was already making it clear that to give parity to the East German mark would spell economic disaster. The leaking of their views at the end of March caused an outcry in the GDR which led to widespread demonstrations on 5 April. In the event the West German government decided to risk a conversion rate of 1:1 for wages, pensions, rents and savings up to certain amounts, while credits and debts were converted at a rate of 1:2. The aim was to stop the continuing emigration from East to West, and to prevent the total collapse of the East German economy. In order to encourage investment from West Germany the treaty laid down the introduction of a social market economy and the social security system of West Germany. The state treaty on monetary, economic and social union was signed by the Finance Ministers of both states on 18 May, passed by both parliaments on 22 June, and put into effect on 1 July. The transfer of the West German economic system to the GDR represented the first stage in the unification process. It was criticized in both parts of Germany for the speed with which it exposed the East German economy to immediate open competition, for which it was not prepared, thereby accelerating the collapse of the economy and increasing unemployment. But the introduction of the West German mark did lay the economic basis on which political union could take place.

Before that could happen, however, the future status of a unified Germany in relation to military and political blocks had to be clarified. The incorporation of the GDR into the European Union was fairly straightforward, since special trading arrangements between the GDR and the European Community already existed via its special trading arrangements with West Germany. At the Dublin conference on 28 April 1990 the European Council welcomed unification. On the question of NATO membership, the Soviet Union and many political groupings within the GDR favoured neutrality. West Germany and its western allies were strongly in favour of the new Germany being a full member of NATO. In discussions between Kohl and Gorbachev on 15 and 16 June, the Soviet Union granted the future Germany its full sovereignty and the right to decide its future alliances. At a further meeting a month later, Gorbachev accepted the idea of Germany belonging to NATO, which paved the way for the final agreement on 12 September on the '2 + 4' Treaty. In this treaty the final withdrawal of occupation troops from the whole of Germany, including Berlin, by the end of 1994 was agreed. The western Allies were allowed to keep NATO troops in the western parts, but only German troops would be allowed to be stationed on former GDR territory, and atomic weapons would be excluded. The treaty signalled the end of the Four-Power agreements on post-1945 Germany and gave it back its full sovereignty. It also declared that the borders of a united Germany were final, including the **Oder-Neisse** frontier with Poland.

Unification was originally due to take place in December 1990 to coincide with federal elections. But the mounting domestic crises in the GDR in the summer of 1990 caused the date to be brought forward to 3 October, the earliest possible date after the external questions of unification had been settled. The negotiations on the unification treaty were dominated by West German politicians, but major points of conflict occurred over the question of property restitution and the Abortion Law. In the first question the western view prevailed, and the principle of restitution before compensation was established in the 'Ruling on the Property Question' of 15 June which was incorporated into the Unification Treaty. The period 1945–9 was excluded, ostensibly at the request of the Soviet Union. The disputes concerning the restitution of property have dogged the post-unification period and in many instances have adversely affected investment decisions. On the abortion question no compromise could be found (see also **abortion law**), but a last-minute agreement postponed the decision until a future date whilst allowing the different laws in the two parts of Germany to continue until the end of 1992. This question was not finally settled until the summer of 1995. The Volkskammer passed a resolution on unification with the Federal Republic via Article 23 on 23 August with the necessary two-thirds majority. The Unification Treaty was then signed by the two states on 31 August and passed by both parliaments on 21 September. At midnight on 2 October the GDR ceased to exist and the new German state came into being.

See also: Treuhand; *Wende*

Further reading

Fritsch-Bournazel, R. (1992) *Europe and German Unification*, Oxford: Berg (commentary together with documents in English on the European dimension of unification).

Glaessner, G-J. (1992), *The Unification Process in Germany*, London: Pinter (an account by one of the major German commentators on unification).

Gransow, V. and Jarausch, K. (1994) *Uniting Germany. Documents and debates, 1943–1993*, Oxford: Berghahn (a comprehensive collection of documents in English).

Jarausch, K. (1994) *The Rush to German Unity*, Oxford: Oxford University Press (a recent American account).

Osmond, J. (ed.) (1992) *German Reunification: A Reference Guide*, Harlow: Longman (contains a series of chapters by different authors and statistics).

PETER BARKER

universities

The majority of German universities were established within the Holy Roman Empire during the fifteenth and sixteenth centuries under the aegis of local princes, with an administration and curriculum which reflected a united European culture. A decisive process of modernization began in the early nineteenth century with the reforms of Wilhelm von Humboldt (1767–1835), introducing a closer relationship between study and research, together with the concept of academic freedom. Universities subsequently enjoyed virtual autonomy in teaching and research, confining themselves almost exclusively to the pursuit of knowledge, in contrast to British and American universities where social and pedagogic aspects have more emphasis. Humboldt's reforms served to enhance the reputation of German universities throughout the nineteenth century, giving them a prime position in international scholarship and in German cultural and public life, where professors enjoyed an elevated social position. Student numbers and the general appreciation of scholarship tended to be higher in Germany than elsewhere, the student population rising from 15,000 in 1830 to 130,000 in the 1920s, with a drastic reduction during the Third Reich. The number of universities remained fairly constant until a small increase occurred in the 1920s, with a second period of expansion in the 1960s seeing new foundations such as Bochum, Regensburg, Düsseldorf, Konstanz and Bielefeld. German universities generally focus on basic and theoretical knowledge rather than vocational education, and the sacred unity of teaching and research promotes the learning process as the natural development of a student's intellectual and personal qualities.

The university is governed by a *Rektor*, elected from amongst the professors for a term of office of between two and four years, supported by a *Kanzler* (chancellor), responsible for administrative matters and for the budget. Universities, as institutions of the individual *Länder*, are regionally funded, and since 1964 also receive federal support (50 percent of larger investment and building programmes). The *Wissenschaftsrat* (Science Council), established in 1957, is responsible for co-operation between federal and *Land* governments and, together with the *Rektorenkonferenz* (Standing Conference of University Vice-Chancellors), for the co-ordination and formation of a common policy within the university sector.

A comprehensive reform of higher education was slow to start, hindered by those same reactionary forces within society and politics which affected the whole of the education system. The conservative nature of German universities, particularly their authoritarian, undemocratic structures, did not become a topic for public debate until the 1960s. In the wake of the **student movement** reforms were introduced, designed to make the university system more transparent and to give students and junior academics a constitutional role and equal representation with university professors. Further efforts were made to introduce more debate and participation in the teaching process and to break down the often rigid divisions between subjects and disciplines. Universities became more integrated into the public sphere, with a corresponding erosion of their élitist image, accelerated by easier access for the *Begabungsreserven* (educational reserves). A new experimental type of university, the *Gesamthochschule* (comprehensive university), amalgamated traditional universities with teacher training and engineering institutions. The new *Fachhochschulen* provided an alternative to universities in the more applied subject areas such as business studies and engineering. The five-fold expansion in student numbers since the early 1960s was initially accompanied by a corresponding growth in resources and public support. Universities were seen to strengthen the Federal Republic's industrial position and met a general demand for increased access to higher education.

The late 1970s and 1980s saw a change in public perception, as new priorities took precedence; law and order and socio-economic issues gained in importance over education. Rejecting the emancipatory fervour of the 1960s, society became more sceptical and began to question the alleged correlation between academic expansion and economic progress. **Postmodernism** rejected the belief in an 'unfinished project of modernity' (**Habermas**) and the integration of university and society lost favour. The university reform programme, in particular its more democratic aspects, was halted. The 1976 *Hochschulrahmengesetz* (Framework Act for Higher Education) saw an end to public debate on higher education and reversed several of the earlier reforms: the tripartite principle of the *Gruppenuniversität* (group university), with equal representation for professors, non-professorial staff and students on all university panels, was abandoned in favour of the previous professorial majority. The *akademischer Mittelbau* (non-professorial faculty) lost much of its status, and the *Land* authorities placed restrictions on the legal framework for university self-government. Since the 1980s a reduction in funding has seen the student–teacher ratio rise sharply from 9:1 (1971) to 18:1 (1991) and library resources and technical equipment no longer meet an acceptable standard.

As today's student population approaches two million, the traditional university concept is under stress from such numbers and from the demands of a modern high-tech society. The 1990s have seen a new crisis in higher education and the need for far-reaching university reforms has resurfaced. The study period is perceived as too long in comparison to international norms, while **students** are seen as overqualified for many posts. Failure rates have become unacceptably high, with drop-out rates approaching 40 percent in the early semesters. Insufficient emphasis is given to the pedagogical quality of university teaching and to an obligation to teach rather than accept research contracts or administrative roles in industry or the public sector. Slogans such as 'Mehr Ehre für die Lehre' (more honour to teaching) and 'Prüf den Prof' (test the professor) illustrate the students' demand for improved pedagogical skills, whilst some professors oppose such moves as *Verschulung der Universität* (universities becoming schools).

Further reading

de Rudder, H. (1994) 'The Quality Issue in German Higher Education', *European Journal of Education* 29, 2: 201–19 (discusses recent concerns about quality assurance in higher education and the prospect for a realistic basis for mass education).

Führ, C. (1995) 'The German University: Basically Healthy or Rotten?', in D. Phillips (ed.), *Education in Germany*, London and New York: Routledge (a survey of university reform and analysis of developments in the early 1990s).

Preisert, H. and Framhein, G. (1994) *Higher Education in Germany*, Bonn: Federal Ministry of Education and Science (comprehensive and critical overview).

HANS J. HAHN

uranium mining

Uranium mining was initiated in Thuringia and Saxony immediately after WWII. The Soviet-German 'Wismut AG' became one of the world's largest producers of uranium but showed little regard for the safety of miners and the surrounding environment. The situation – which involved environmental, human rights and military issues – began to concern the **peace movement** in the latter years of the GDR. Although closed down after unification, the mining sites still represent one of the most serious threats to the environment of the former GDR. Substantial investment has now been made to clear the damage and alleviate the situation of former miners now suffering from cancer.

Further reading

Hambeck, L. *et al.* (1996) 'Sanierung der Wismut-Halden', *Internationale Zeitschrift für Kernernergie (atw)* 41, 2: 103–7.

INGOLFUR BLÜHDORN

V

vacations and tourism

Germans are renowned for their wanderlust and travel more than most other nationalities. Tourism is the fourth largest sector of the German economy, providing around 7 percent of jobs, and 6 percent of the gross national product (including domestic services for travel abroad). Since the late 1960s more Germans holiday abroad than within Germany, increasing from 20 to 70 percent of tourists between the mid-1950s and the late 1990s. Spain, Austria and Italy are the traditional top three favourites with North America and other long-haul destinations growing rapidly in popularity since the 1980s. While mass tourism was seen as a means to flaunt West Germany's economic affluence, the limitations on travel abroad became a major focus of popular unrest aimed at the restricted life-style in the GDR.

For the majority of West Germans, average annual paid vacation increased from nine days in the 1950s to 30 days in the 1990s, partly thanks to the *Bundesurlaubsgesetz* (Federal Vacation Law) passed in 1963. This, together with the introduction of the 'long weekend' (i.e. including Saturday) in the late 1950s and the increased economic affluence of the working class in the 1960s, contributed to the emergence of mass tourism, often in the form of package holidays. Travel became the main activity during vacations by the late 1970s; while in the early 1950s only 20 percent spent their vacation travelling, by 1996 72 percent of Germans went on a journey of at least five days (or two weeks on average).

Tourism is organized by both dedicated non-governmental organizations and federal and state ministries. The main private organizations are Deutscher Fremdenverkehrsverband (German Organization for Foreign Visitors) and the Deutsche Zentrale für Tourismus e.V. (German National Tourist Office), an umbrella organization of travel offices, hotels, airlines, railway, bus companies, spas, and so on. While private organizations focus mainly on the marketing and rationalization of tourism, federal and state ministries attempt to stimulate local tourism, with programmes such as '*Familienferien in Deutschland*' ('Family holidays in Germany') or '*Unser Dorf muß schöner werden*' ('Our village must be more beautiful').

Discussions of German tourism have evolved with its changing character. Although only a few could afford travel in the late 1950s, tourism was much debated, especially mass tourism, against which rather snobbish middle-class criticisms were directed. In contrast, the writer Hans Magnus **Enzensberger** understood this new phenomenon as a search for a freedom that Germans were unable to find at work or in their daily lives. As mass tourism became widespread in the 1960s, the tourism debate shifted to the ecological problems it engendered, and also the power-relations between tourists and indigenous locals. The concept of *sanftes Reisen* (soft travel), developed in response by German and Swiss sociologists, involved greater consideration for local practices and opinions. A recent variant of soft travel is cultural tourism, involving shorter trips to museums, exhibitions, festivals and musical venues. Its popularity is indicative of a renewed interest in local (often German) traditions and culture. This includes

Erinnerungstourismus (memory tourism), which provides the experience of culture as a theme event, rather than as educational as was the caste in the nineteenth-century tradition of the *Bildungsreise* (educational journey), involving theme trips, such as 'the Luther year' or 'tracing knights and princes'.

Since the war, tourism has been seen as a testing ground for relations between West Germans and other nationals. In contrast, criticism of the restrictive GDR regime by ordinary East Germans shortly before 1989 focused increasingly on their confinement to vacation sites within the GDR or occasionally other eastern bloc countries. Tourism was organized by state organizations, in particular the workers' companies and the **FDGB** who had their own vacation facilities. Travel was highly subsidized, and therefore cheap. Comparatively more East Germans travelled each year (70 to 80 percent, versus 65 to 70 percent of West Germans in the 1980s). However, the stay was shorter (an average of thirteen versus seventeen days), and usually involved being sent to destinations according to what was available, which sometimes meant nondescript backwaters within the GDR. Only 10 to 20 percent organized their holiday individually. After 1989 the inhabitants of the former GDR quickly adopted West German travel patterns, increasingly preferring to organize their own trips to foreign destinations, often by car.

Tourism is a big money-maker in Austria, and in Switzerland, the birthplace of modern tourism. In Switzerland, for example, it makes up 6 percent of the gross national product. A little over half of visitors to Switzerland come from abroad, the bulk of whom are German, with a similar pattern in Austria. In both countries, various state institutions and interest groups work in close collaboration both to stimulate tourism, and protect the natural environment that it depends on.

See also: Neckermann

Further reading

Dreyer, A. (ed.) (1996) *Kulturtourismus*, Munich and Vienna: R. Oldenbourg (on the development of cultural tourism as a specifically German travel practice).

Enzensberger, H.M. (1996) 'A Theory of Tourism', *New German Critique* 68: 117–35 (originally published in German in 1958, this pioneer text of modern tourism offers a systematic theory of tourism, understanding it in terms of social criticism: mass tourism contains the paradox of attempting to fulfil the need for freedom while containing in its very form the restriction of freedom).

Needham, P. (1996) 'Leisure Industries: Travel Distribution in Germany', *Travel & Tourism Analyst* 5: 65–87 (an up-to-date overview of German tourism in English with a focus on private tourist institutions in English from the perspective of the travel industry).

Opaschowski, H. (1996) *Tourismus. Systematische Einführung – Analysen und Prognosen*, Opladen: Leske und Budrich (the standard, newly updated version of *Tourismusforschung* from 1989, with an overview of the motivation research, history and theory of German tourism. Does not cover the GDR).

Schildt, A. (1995) *Moderne Zeiten. Freizeit, Massenmedien und 'Zeitgeist' in der Bundesrepublik der 50er Jahre*, Hamburg: Christians (the most comprehensive sociological study on the emergence of tourism in the post-war period, its material conditions, and debates anticipating and surrounding tourism).

JUDITH LEEB

Valentin, Barbara

b. 15 December 1940, Vienna

Actress

A screen actress who has appeared in a wide range of films in Germany and the US. A celebrated star of commercial cinema embracing horror films such as *Ein Toter hing im Netz* (A Dead Man Hung in the Net, 1959) and soft-porn (including Leigh Jason's *Festival of Girls*, 1959), the actress once dubbed 'big breasted Barbara' featured in a number of films of the **New German Cinema** including Rainer Werner **Fassbinder**'s *Fear Eats the Soul* (1973), Herbert **Achternbusch**'s *Rita Ritter* (1983) and

Walter Bockmayer's raucous *Heimatfilm* parody *Die Geierwally* (1987).

See also: film: FRG

MARTIN BRADY

Valentin, Karl

b. 4 June 1882, Munich; d. 9 February 1948, Munich

Cabaret performer and film actor (real name Valentin Ludwig Fey)

Valentin was a brilliant cabaret artist and German comic film actor of the Weimar period. He wrote and performed scenes of caustic irony in strong Bavarian dialect characterized by absurd logic, human miscommunication and comic physicality, often in concert with his female partner, Liesl Karlstadt. He acted in over fifty films, usually based on his cabaret pieces, and collaborated with Bertolt **Brecht** on the film *Geheimnisse eines Friseursalons* (Secrets of a Barber Shop). Valentin was banned from the stage by the Nazis, whom he openly parodied, and died in penury.

KAREN RUOFF KRAMER

Van Ackeren, Robert

b. 22 December 1946, Berlin

Filmmaker and cameraman

Van Ackern trained as a cameraman and started filmmaking in 1964. He worked initially both as a director and cameraman (for Werner **Schroeter**, Rosa von **Praunheim** and others). Notable for their explicit violence, frank sexuality, and bold stylization, his own films often confront social and sexual taboos by compounding social realism with the clichés of melodrama, as in *Harlis* (1972) and *Purity of Heart* (*Die Reinheit des Herzens*, 1980). *The Woman in Flames* (*Die flambierte Frau*, 1983), his most popular film, is a raunchy romance set in the world of prostitution.

See also: New German Cinema

MARTIN BRADY

variety theatre

Variety theatres, also called *Varietés*, *Singspielhallen* or *Tingeltangel*, combined features of circus, cabaret and music hall, staging a panoply of numbers in review format such as gymnastics, trapeze, clowning, tableaux, pantomime, skits, singing, juggling, wrestling, modified striptease, film screenings and unusual human and animal feats. Begun in nineteenth-century bars and beer halls, variety theatres, such as the Metropoltheater and the Wintergarten in Berlin, and the Krystallpalast in Leipzig, skyrocketed in popularity in the 1890s, attracting international stars, such as Enrico Rastelli, Yvette Guilbert, Fritzi Massary, the Tiller Girls and the Ziegfield Follies, and composers, such as V. Hollaender and P. Lincke. Forced to close in the late 1950s because of the success of television and striptease bars, variety theatres burgeoned again in the late 1970s after the Wintergarten in Berlin reopened. The variety theatre tradition is carried on today by the Tigerpalast in Frankfurt am Main, the Schmidt Theater in Hamburg, the Scheinbar and Chameleon theatres in Berlin, Munich's Lustspielhaus, and the travelling *Verzehrtheaters*: Panem et circenses and Palais des Fous.

See also: circus; popular culture

Further reading

Jelavich, P. (1985) *Munich and Theatrical Modernism: Politics, Playwriting and Performance 1890–1914*, Cambridge: Harvard University Press (a thorough account of popular theatre of this era).

JENNIFER HAM

VEB

Volkseigene Betriebe (VEB) were socially-owned enterprises promoting reconstruction in the Soviet occupation zone and offering a traumatized population the chance of self-management at factory level. In 1946, 4,000 industrial firms were expropriated, and by 1950 there were 6,000 VEB, alongside 17,500 private firms. The latter halved in number over the 1960s and became VEB with full state ownership in 1972. Central planning of several thousand VEB required their grouping into branch and district associations (*Vereinigungen – VVB*) subject to industrial ministries. Under Honecker, the fusion of VEB into 126 centrally-led industrial combines and 95 district-managed combines reduced the nominally autonomous VEB to mere plants.

Further reading

Deutsches Institut für Wirtschaftsforschung Berlin (ed.) (1985) *Handbuch DDR-Wirtschaft*, Hamburg: Rowohlt (full survey of the East German economy).

CHRISTOPHER H. FLOCKTON

Verband deutscher Schriftsteller

The Verband deutscher Schriftsteller (VS) (Union of German writers) was founded in 1969 amid talk of the 'end of modesty' and 'the unity of the loners' to represent writers' interests. Early euphoria, felt at the first congress in Stuttgart in 1970 when Chancellor Brandt spoke of the vital social role of writers, has since evaporated. Some members resigned because of closer links to the trade unions; the VS is now part of the media workers' union IG Medien. There was a mass exodus including Günter **Grass** and Uwe **Johnson** in the 1980s when the executive was felt to be dominated by **DKP** supporters. The VS has been less rocked by German unity than **PEN** and certain **academies**.

STUART PARKES

Verbindungen

Verbindungen (student fraternities), originating in the seventeenth century as regional associations, have been a traditional feature of German **universities**. They gained prominence during the Napoleonic wars as beacons of national liberalism, forming the *Burschenschaft* federation in 1815. They later became increasingly nationalist and reactionary and to this day most *Verbindungen* exclude women. Dissolved during the Third Reich, *Verbindungen* regrouped after 1945, some continuing the practice of duelling, others involved with political, religious or social issues. *Alte Herren* (alumni) support their *Verbindung*, their 'old-boy-network' promoting the careers of former members, and having significant influence during periods of unemployment.

HANS J. HAHN

Verein

There is a German saying that when two Germans meet they establish a *Verein* (club). *Vereine* are of fundamental importance to both the definition of identity and the organization of social and cultural behaviour in contemporary German society. It is estimated that one in four Germans is a registered member of a *Verein* and that there are over 300,000 *Vereine* in the whole country. The institutionalization of the sports clubs, amateur dramatics societies, history groups and so on, is a process which has taken place during the twentieth century and has led to the establishment of complex structures and modes of organization. Institutionalization may be regarded as a process of empowerment of the grassroots giving access to a degree of political representation, eligibility for various funds and status. It also brings with it legal, financial, political and administrative responsibility. The creation of an institution enables controls, many of which are bureaucratic, to be exerted upon the practices of a group of people and on a culture, and may thus even hinder its development.

Vereine are sources of common activities and loyalty. Many Germans devote much of their leisure time to the work of the *Verein* and spend time staffing stalls to raise money, performing plays, holding musical evenings, hosting annual dinner-dances and celebrating various anniversaries, both of long-standing members who are often given token rewards for their loyalty, and of the *Verein* itself. Anniversaries give members of *Vereine* the opportunity for nostalgia and *Festschriften* (souvenir booklets) are produced to mark significant jubilees.

There is a clear relationship between the formation and consequent upholding of a tradition and the creation of a *Verein* or an institution to maintain it. Once a practice has been established, the *Verein* functions as a necessary, organizational support. In German law a *Verein*, once officially acknowledged, enjoys certain rights, privileges and responsibilities. There are five different official categories of *Verein* established in the *Bürgerliches Gesetzbuch* (Civil Law Code). The important distinction is essentially between the *wirtschaftlicher Verein* (pursuing economic activities) and the *Idealverein* (pursuing non-economic activities).

The legal status of the *Verein* is, for the majority of the members of *Vereine* and even for their leaders, of secondary importance. The civic status of the *Verein* is, however, one of the central defining features of both individual and collective identity in Germany. In Hornberg, for example, the CDU chair knew that Hornberg, with its population of 4,875, boasted a grand total of forty-six *Vereine* as of May 1993. In Fridingen, Josef Hagel, the ninety-year-old member of the *Kulturring* (cultural club) saw the existence of twenty-five *Vereine* in a village with a population of 3,000 as particularly positive. Once a *Verein* has been given legal status it has the right to add the abbreviation 'e.V.', meaning '*eingetragener Verein*', (registered *Verein*), thus further demonstrating the importance of the status of the institution in the public sphere.

ALISON PHIPPS

Vergangenheitsbewältigung

Although there was broad agreement on the need for 'coming to terms with the Nazi past' as both a moral imperative and a political necessity in post-war Germany, the form and content of such *Vergangenheitsbewältigung* has been the subject of bitter public controversies. Different views of the origins and the nature of the Nazi regime have implied different concepts of the requirements for a successful *Vergangenheitsbewältigung* ranging from the abolition of capitalism (the basis of the GDR's claim to have eradicated the roots of fascism) to acts of individual repentance.

In the immediate post-war years, the prevailing 'anti-fascist' consensus among German political parties was that big business had played a crucial part in Hitler's rise to power and that post-fascist reconstruction would therefore have to include strong anti-capitalist measures. The future of Germany, however, lay in the hands of the occupying powers and, with the beginning of the Cold War, the two emerging German states were increasingly shaped by the strategic interests of the United States and the Soviet Union. In the West, the conflation of fascism and communism under the common heading of 'totalitarianism' allowed former Nazis to atone for their crimes by participating in the struggle against communism, while a similar conflation of fascism with capitalism allowed the East Germans to disclaim any responsibility for the Nazi past. (The GDR, in contrast to the FRG with its claim to be the legal successor of the Third Reich, never paid compensation to the victims of Nazism.)

The **Adenauer** government restored the majority of those affected by Allied **denazification** to their careers and generally turned a blind eye to the past affiliation of civil servants and the academic and business élites. The 1950s and 1960s saw a continuing series of revelations concerning prominent figures in public life, often fed by East German documentations (*Braunbücher*) – the controversies surrounding Adenauer's advisor Globke, the Federal President Lübke, and the Chancellor of the Grand Coalition (1966–9) Kurt Georg Kiesinger being only the best-known examples.

For much of the 1950s, the (West) German legal authorities remained either unwilling or unable – because of continued Allied control of the files – to make much headway in the prosecution of Nazi crimes. The setting up of a central investigation agency in 1958 (Zentrale Stelle der Landesjustizverwaltungen zur Aufklärung von NS-Verbrechen) brought some change, culminating in the spectacular **Auschwitz** Trial of 1964. The legal *Vergangenheitsbewältigung* continued to be hampered, however, by the increasing difficulties of finding reliable evidence, bureaucratic delays and, critics have argued, the lack of enthusiasm on the part of the legal apparatus largely inherited from the Third Reich. During the 1960s, the Bundestag repeatedly debated, and eventually adopted, extensions to the thirty-year statute of limitation for the crimes of murder and genocide in order to enable continued investigation and prosecution.

Although it was a major theme in much of the literature of the post-war years, public discussion of the Nazi past remained muted until the 1960s, when the war generation was gradually replaced in positions of influence and the Cold War confrontation with communism began to abate. The student and youth rebellion and the rise to power of the Social Democrats created a new political climate for *Vergangenheitsbewältigung*. The Third Reich, largely excluded from history lessons in the 1950s, became a compulsory subject in the school curricula. A widely discussed book by the psychoanalysts Alexander and Margarete **Mitscherlich**, *Die Unfähigkeit zu trauern* (The Inability to Mourn) (1967), helped to refocus the attention of *Vergangenheitsbewältigung* on the mental mechanisms which had allowed ordinary Germans to 'forget' the Nazi past. A new generation of left-leaning academic historians began to investigate the roots of Nazism in previous German history (under the strong influence of the Anglo-Saxon theories of a German *Sonderweg*), clashing in the bitter ***Historikerstreit*** of 1985 to 1986 with more conservative colleagues seeking to overcome the obstacle presented by Hitler to a 'healthy' national identity.

Although the era of the Nazi trials and revelations about the past of prominent individuals is drawing to an end, public sensitivity to all aspects of *Vergangenheitsbewältigung* shows no sign of abating. Events such as the screening of the American television series *Holocaust* in 1979, the visit to the **Bitburg** military cemetery (which includes the graves of Waffen SS members) by Chancellor Kohl and President Reagan in 1985, the publication of Daniel Goldhagen's *Hitler's Willing Executioners* and the travelling exhibition about war crimes committed by regular *Wehrmacht* units continuously rekindle public interest. The long shadow cast by the Third Reich over almost every aspect of contemporary Germany is also visible in the fact that almost every important issue, from abortion law to European integration, tends to be viewed through the prism of avoiding a repetition of the Nazi past.

Since the collapse of the GDR and the unification of Germany in 1990, the term *Vergangenheitsbewältigung* has also been used in relation to the **SED** regime, especially in the context of legal proceedings against former GDR leaders and members of the GDR's security forces and revelations about individuals emanating from the ***Stasi*** (State Security) files.

See also: German Question; Judaism; prose fiction: FRG; prose fiction: GDR; re-education; *Volk*

Further reading

Dudek, P. (1992) 'Vergangenheitsbewältigung. Zur Problematik eines umstrittenen Begriffs', in *Aus Politik und Zeitgeschichte. Beilage zur Wochenzeitung Das Parlament*, B 1–2, pp. 44–53.

Faulenbach, B. (1987), 'NS-Interpretationen und Zeitklima. Zum Wandel in der Aufarbeitung der jüngsten Vergangenheit', in *Aus Politik und Zeitgeschichte. Beilage zur Wochenzeitung Das Parlament*, B 22, pp. 19–30.

Gauck, J. (1991), *Die Stasi-Akten. Das unheimliche Erbe der DDR*, Reinbek: Rowohlt (Gauck is director of the federal institute administering the East German state security archives.)

Hoffmann, C. (1992), *Stunden Null? Vergangenheitsbewältigung in Deutschland 1945 und 1989*, Bonn: Bouvier (concentrates on legal aspects; equates Third Reich and GDR as 'totalitarian').

Mitscherlich, A. and Mitscherlich, M. (1967) *Die Unfähigkeit zu trauern. Grundlagen kollektiven Verhaltens*, Munich: Piper (classic critique of German Vergangenheitsbewältigung by left-wing psychoanalysts).

Mohler, A. (1980) *Vergangenheitsbewältigung*, Krefeld: Sinus (conservative-nationalist critique of *Vergangenheitsbewältigung*).

GÜNTER MINNERUP

Verhoeven, Michael

b. 13 July 1938, Berlin

Filmmaker

Verhoeven's best-known films address questions of guilt and resistance in the Nazi era, and the inability of Germans to come to terms with their past. In *The White Rose* (*Die weiße Rose*, 1982), a group of Munich students risk their lives attempting to expose atrocities during the Third Reich, in *The Nasty Girl* (*Das schreckliche Mädchen*, 1989), a schoolgirl investigates the awkward past of her village during the Nazi era, and in *Mother's Courage* (*Mutters Courage*, 1995), a woman struggles to escape incarceration in a concentration camp.

JONATHAN LEGG

Vesper, Bernward

b. 1 August 1938, Frankfurt an der Oder;
   d. 15 May 1971 (suicide), Hamburg

Publicist and writer

Vesper's vast, autobiographical fragment *Die Reise* (The Journey) appeared posthumously in 1977. When his partner (in real life, Gudrun **Ensslin**) turns to terrorism, the narrator, trapped in a love–hate relationship to his father (Nazi poet Will Vesper), resorts to hallucinogenic drugs. Originally to be called *Der Trip* or *Der Haß* (Hatred), *Die Reise* is a monument to a generation caught between parents they rejected but yearned to love, a materially saturated society, a protest movement tearing itself apart, and part-understood and indiscriminate rebellion via drugs, sexual and social experiment.

MORAY McGOWAN

video

Since its emergence in the early 1950s, video in the FRG, as in other western countries, has been used in an infinite number of social, commercial, communicative, pedagogical, scientific and artistic contexts, and by television stations for live broadcasts, while it had comparatively little impact in the GDR.

In the 1960s, video art developed in West Germany as a genre of its own within the visual arts. Its beginnings are linked to the international Fluxus movement, the happenings, and the challenge of traditional forms of art. In the early stages, video artists provocatively rejected television for its manipulative power (pioneers being the Korean-born composer Nam June Paik in his 1963 exhibit in Wuppertal and Wolf **Vostell**). Between 1968 and 1970, *Westdeutscher Rundfunk* in Cologne broadcast art videos and Gerry Shum, the founder of the first 'video gallery', initiated art video productions by artists in 1969. In 1977, **documenta** 6 was dedicated to video. It opened with video performances by three artists (Joseph **Beuys**, Douglas Davis, Nam June Paik) that were broadcast worldwide via satellite. By the mid-1970s, video in the visual arts was regarded as a promising new medium for video art recordings, the presentation of video performances, video installations and video sculptures.

In addition to its impact in the visual arts, video also plays an important role in alternative media practices concerned with social and political issues. In the aftermath of the **student movement** and out of the ensuing critical debates about the bourgeois mass media, video became a medium for the creation of a counter-public sphere. Throughout cities in West Germany, Switzerland and Austria, independent media labs and centres, video workshops and alternative systems of video distribution emerged during the 1970s and early 1980s. In adapting media theories from the 1920s (e.g. those of Bertolt **Brecht**, Walter **Benjamin** and Sergej Tretjakov), the media groups used video as a means for intervening in social and political processes, allowing marginalized perspectives to reach a critical audience. The subject matters of their productions included anti-nuclear protests and environmental activities; the women's movement and the **peace movement**; neighbourhood projects and protests; and youth protests, squatters, alternative life styles and subcultures. Whereas the initial euphoria of the politically-engaged video movement has vanished, numerous critical documentary videos about a wide range of topical social and political as well as historical issues are being produced each year in the German-speaking countries. Subjects include minorities, human rights, women, gay lifestyles, AIDS, handicapped people, unemployment, homelessness, neo-nazism, the political changes in East Germany, the Holocaust, anti-fascism, national socialism, and so on.

Whereas video has established itself in the documentary genre of the German-speaking countries and is also used for experimental videos, or for videos blending fact and fiction (pioneers are Gerd Conradt and Michael Klier), its significance in the fiction genre remains marginal. The most prominent representative of this genre is Niklaus **Schilling**. He was the first one to use video for feature-length fiction films and for experiments with computer animation and image simulation.

See also: alternative culture; documentary film; feminism and the women's movement; film, experimental; film: FRG

Further reading

Arbeitsgemeinschaft der Filmjournalisten, Hamburger Filmbüro (eds.) (1987) *Neue Medien contra Filmkultur?* Berlin: Spiess.

Herzogenrath, W. (ed.) (1983) *Videokunst in Deutschland 1963 – 1982*, Stuttgart: Hatje.

MARGRIT FRÖLICH

Vienna (Wien)

The capital of Austria and one of the nine provinces (*Bundesländer*), Vienna was until 1918 the centre of the Hapsburg Empire. Covering an area of 414 square kilometres and with a population of some one and a half million, Vienna is situated in the east of the country on the banks of the river Danube at the crossing point of two major traffic routes, the Danube valley and the north–south route linking the Baltic Sea with the Mediterranean. The historic centre was built on the site of a Celtic settlement as well as a Roman camp of the first century AD.

Its diverse population is a result of Vienna's geographical position and the historical development of the Austro-Hungarian Empire, which attracted people from many central and eastern European countries. Owing to the size of the city in comparison with the rest of Austria Vienna dominates the country in many respects.

All major political and economic organizations and institutions as well as most major firms have their headquarters in Vienna. The residences of the Federal President and the government, the Parliament and the law courts are situated there. It is also the centre of the Austrian media, with many important newspapers and the headquarters of the main television and radio company (**ORF**).

St Stephen's Cathedral, the Imperial Palace (the Hofburg), the summer residence of the Emperor at Schönbrunn, the Ringstraße (a circular road with a series of public buildings built around the first district in historical styles) and Belvedere Palace are traditional tourist attractions. Vienna is also famous for its *Jugendstil* buildings like the Secession and the station buildings of the former city railways. Innovative blocks of council flats were built in the 1920s and 1930s and reflect the social democratic traditions of the city.

A modern underground system as well as the traditional trains, trams and buses provide convenient public transportation throughout the city.

Vienna is one of the three headquarters of the United Nations (since 1979), hosting major UN organizations (e.g. UNIDO and IAEA), which are housed in a large building complex of the 1970s. In addition other international organizations (e.g. OPEC) have their headquarters in Vienna.

Famous museums, such as the Museum of Fine Arts, the Albertina Collection of Graphic Arts, the Austrian Gallery in the Belvedere, the Museum of the Twentieth Century and a forthcoming Museum of Jugendstil underline the international importance of the city's art collections.

Strong emphasis is laid on the theatrical traditions of the city with a series of conventional theatres (e.g. the **Burgtheater**, the Akademietheater, the Theater in der Josefstadt and the Volkstheater) as well as a number of fringe theatres (e.g. the Serapions Theater and the Schauspielhaus). The operatic tradition is represented by the internationally renowned Vienna State Opera (the Wiener Staatsoper), which performs operas and ballets in their original language, whereas the Volksoper produces German versions of operas and musicals as well as ballets. Since the 1970s an increasing number of musicals have been produced in Vienna (at the Theater an der Wien and the Raimund Theater). Widely known concert halls (e.g. the Großer Musikvereinssaal and the Wiener Konzerthaus), excellent orchestras (e.g. the Vienna Philharmonic Orchestra), and the annual Vienna Festival round off the cultural ambitions of the city.

Further reading

Csendes, P. (1990) *Geschichte Wiens*, Vienna: Verlag für Geschichte und Politik.

Czeike, F. (1990) *Wien und Umgebung: Kunst, Kultur und Geschichte der Donaumetropole*, Cologne: DuMont.

Schorske, C. (1980) *Fin-de-siècle Vienna: Politics and Culture*, New York: Knopf (also published in 1981 by Cambridge University Press).

GEORG HELLMAYR

Villa Massimo

Villa Massimo was founded in Rome in 1913 and financed by the art-loving Jewish industrialist Eduard Arnhold as an institution abroad where professional German artists could live and work for a period in tranquillity. After 1945 it was funded by the German government, and in addition to artists and architects it now hosts writers, composers and photographers for subsidized stays of up to twelve months. Villa Massimo (Accademia Tedesca) is administered by the Deutsche Akademie whose juries select appropriate bursary holders. Exhibitions, concerts, readings and lectures are held there, often in close collaboration with the **Goethe-Institut**.

ARRIGO SUBIOTTO

Vilsmaier, Joseph

b. 24 January 1939, Munich

Filmmaker and cameraman

Already a successful cameraman, Vilsmaier directed a series of features backed by the Bavaria film company aimed at achieving a larger, more commercial market than the auteurist filmmakers of the 1970s and early 1980s. His films fit programmatically into genres such as the historical drama *Autumn Milk* (*Herbstmilch*, 1988) set in the Third Reich; the anti-war film *Stalingrad* (1991); the *Trümmerfilm Rama Dama* (1990), a nostalgic attempt to recapture the flavour and success of post-war popular cinema; and the literary adaptation *Brother of Sleep* (*Schlafes Bruder*, 1995).

See also: film: FRG

HELEN HUGHES

visual arts: Austria

Visual arts in the post-war period in Austria were marked by a lack of local traditions that could be followed easily. Even though important artists were still active like Herbert Boeckl (1894–1966), Alfred **Kubin** (1877–1959) and Oskar Kokoschka (1886–1980), their impact on the young generation of the day was minimal, as they had either left the country or had been suppressed by the authorities during the Nazi era.

Soon Wolfgang Hutter (1928–), Anton Lehmden (1929–), Arik Brauer (1929–), Rudolf Hausner (1914–95) and Ernst Fuchs (1930–) formed a new school of painting, the Viennese School of Fantastic Realism. Whereas their techniques were derived from the old traditional masters, their themes were of a new mythological and fantastic nature, which can be seen as a reaction to both the naturalist tendencies of Third Reich artists as well as a move away from expressionist trends of the 1920s and 1930s. They are heavily influenced by the teachings of Sigmund Freud, which were, however, only slowly being accepted by Austrian society.

The Galerie nächst St Stephan (Gallery near St Stephen's), founded by the open-minded priest Otto Mauer (1907–73), became the main centre of contemporary art in the 1950s and 1960s and the focal point of a group of progressive artists, among them Arnulf Rainer (1929–).

Influenced by Josef Dobrowsky (1889–1964), both Josef Mikl (1929–) and Wolfgang Hollegha (1929–) turned to abstract painting. Oswald Oberhuber (1931–), who was originally influenced by painters like Léger and Chagall, and Max Weiler (1910–) developed their highly independent styles.

The painter Friedensreich **Hundertwasser** (1928–) combines irregular shapes and strong colours with ecological themes and creates architecture based on his understanding of human nature.

In the 1960s the new movement 'Wiener Aktionismus' came to the fore and concentrated on happenings and performances that were intended to extend the perception of reality and led up to the artistic climax of the 1968 student movement. To this group belong Otto **Müehl** (1925–), Günter **Brus** (1938–), and Hermann **Nitsch** (1938–), who created a controversial form of performances that combined orgiastic and Christian elements in order to achieve cathartic effects on the part of the viewer (*Orgien Mysterien Theater*).

Maria Lassnig (1919–), who also made experimental films, gained international recognition with her two-dimensional style. In the 1980s an informal group of young artists – among them Hubert Schmalix (1952–) and Siegfried Anzinger (1952–) – devoted themselves to painting large pictures with highly expressive images akin to contemporary trends in other European countries and the US.

Fritz **Wotruba** (1907–75) became the leading figure of Austrian sculpture with works dominated by carefully composed blocks of bronze or stone. The design of St George's Church in Vienna is representative of his style. Alfred **Hrdlicka** (1928–), who also works as a painter, is well-known for his figurative expressionist sculptures which often carry his anti-fascist convictions. In contrast to Hrdlicka, Walter Pichler (1936–) creates abstract objects of utmost simplicity.

In spite of considerable talent, however, the international influence of Austrian art after WWII has remained limited.

Further reading

Kunst- u. Ausstellungshalle der Bundesrepublik Deutschland (ed.) (1996) *Kunst aus Österreich 1896–1996*, Bonn and Munich: Prestel.

GEORG HELLMAYR

visual arts: Switzerland

With a high density of excellent museums and galleries within their small country, the Swiss are better known as curators than artists. Building on a group of painters and sculptors who first acquired international recognition outside of national borders in the first half of the century, Swiss artists have struggled to establish a supportive scene interested in innovation and socio-critical dialogue. The driving forces for advancement have usually come first from outside Switzerland's borders, with native interest and patronage favouring art traditional in theme and form. Over time sponsorship of artists has interested a broader public, with more freedom to experiment with alternative forms, and daring, critical expression. In the early twentieth century, Switzerland was a magnet for creative minds from neighbouring countries torn by war, attracting the founders of Dada. During the same time many creative Swiss left the country to make their name abroad, including Paul Klee, Charles Le Corbusier, Meret Oppenheim and Sophie Taeuber-Arp. A group of artists born since the 1920s brought new waves of fantasy to art both in Switzerland and internationally. Jean Tinguely's self-destructing motorized sculptures were acclaimed for their societal relevance in an advanced industrial age. Concrete art had its start in Zürich under the influence of Max **Bill**. Alberto Giacometti established a style in his minimal stick figure forms, striking in their expressionism.

A new movement in Swiss art began in the 1970s, together with Paul Nizon's critical essay *Diskurs in der Enge* (Dialogue in the Narrow). Alienated by their homeland, artists turned to new forms of social and critical expression, often employing video and film in experimental forms of installation and performance. With government and bank sponsors hesitant to endorse artists who questioned or mocked national character, many left for abroad. Others, determined to found and support a tradition of artistic and critical expression at home searched for other means.

With the help of private sponsors they sought alternative spaces to produce and display their work. Old factories were turned into vital cultural centres, offering changing exhibitions and forums for discussion. Since the late 1980s, traditional art institutions, for the sake of survival and relevance, have shown a growing tendency to support contemporary art. Aside from the large metropolitan centres, smaller cities also inspire and support an active art scene with spaces dedicated to contemporary art. Artists gaining attention include Pipilotti Rist, the video team Peter Fischli and

David Weiss, Ben Vaultier, and Biefer Zgraggen. Contradicting the traditional resistance to change in Switzerland, development and recognition of Swiss visual arts has come from artists and sponsors taking risks, allowing criticism of their small land, and questioning the possibility of a future for it outside the European Community.

See also: art collections; cultural policy and institutions: Switzerland; culture: Switzerland; Hochschule für Gestaltung

Further reading

Fischer, R. and Russek, P. (1991) *Kunst in der Schweiz*, Cologne: Kiepenheuer & Witsch (essays by and about contemporary Swiss artists and curators, with addresses of museums, art foundations and galleries).

Lüthi, H. and Huesser H. (1983) *Kunst in der Schweiz 1880–1980*, Zürich: Orell Füssli (overview of art in Switzerland, with colourplates and illustrations).

The quarterly publication *Kunst & Architektur in der Schweiz* and bimonthly *Kunst-bulletin* are good sources of information.

ANNE BLUME

Volk

Like other words closely associated with nationalism and Nazi propaganda (*Ein Volk, ein Reich, ein Führer*), '*Volk*' was tinged with ambiguity and regarded with considerable suspicion after 1945 by anti-fascist intellectuals and writers: 'Nothing, no sense of nationhood, however idyllically coloured...can dispel **Auschwitz**' (Günter **Grass**, *Two States – One Nation*). There are, however, four distinct meanings and usages of '*Volk*'.

First, the colloquial one of 'the common people' as distinct from the privileged, educated or wealthy. Second, the democratic usage of '*Volk*' as a collective of citizens as in 'popular sovereignty' or 'the power of the people'. Third, the romantic-nationalist notion of the '*Volk*' as a community of fate, linked by a common history, culture, mentality and consciousness. Fourth, the racist concept of a common biological origin, the 'blood and soil' (*Blut*

und Boden) ideology uniquely identified with the adjective *völkisch* (which relates to '*Volk*' roughly as 'racist' relates to 'race') as used by the Nazis and their immediate predecessors.

The close affinities between the romantic-nationalist and National Socialist notions of '*Volk*' have informed a school of post-war historiography that sees the Third Reich as the culmination of irrational, anti-western tendencies in German nationalism, mirroring the Nazi self-image as the most radical German nationalists but also downplaying the crucial difference between nationalism and racism.

A significant and problematic relic of past cross-contaminations between nationalism and racism is the fact that German citizenship law derives from the *ius sanguinis* (blood law), a quasi-biological definition of nationality which gives the descendants of German emigrants (*Volksdeutsche*) automatic rights to German citizenship not enjoyed by the children of **Ausländer**. Reform has been promised by the new **Schröder** government.

During the Cold War, the term *deutsches Volk* became disputed territory between the FRG and the GDR in the battle for the high ground on the **German Question**. For the West, it was used to denote the continuing unity of East and West Germans as a *Kulturnation*, while the East, after initially applying the *Volksfront* (popular front) tactic against the 'imperialist splitters', eventually argued that the socio-economic and political differences between the two systems had given rise to two different nations, socialist and capitalist (two-nations theory). The demonstrations leading to the demise of the GDR in 1989 and 1990, with their decisive switch from the slogan '*Wir sind das Volk*' (which demanded democratic participation) to '*Wir sind ein Volk*' (which demanded unification) dramatically highlighted the continuing tension between the popular-democratic and the ethnic-nationalist dimensions of the term.

See also: *Vergangenheitsbewältigung*

Further reading

Emmerich, W. (1971) *Zur Kritik der Volkstumsideologie*, Frankfurt am Main: Suhrkamp (critique of the peculiarly German academic discipline of *Volks-kunde*).

Grass, G. (1990) *Two States – One Nation? The Case Against German Reunification*, London: Secker & Warburg (articulates the anti-fascist suspicions of the nationalist terminology and concepts contaminated by the Third Reich).

Kosing, A. (1976) *Nation in Geschichte und Gegenwart*, (East) Berlin: Dietz Verlag (authoritative, and sophisticated, statement of East German position under Honecker).

GÜNTER MINNERUP

Volkskammer

The Volkskammer (People's Chamber) was the Parliament of the GDR. Although in theory it was the supreme organ of state, power lay elsewhere, in the SED **Politbüro**. The outcome of elections was determined in advance in a unitary list of candidates drawn up by the National Front. Although the 500 members of the Volkskammer (463 before 1963) were spread across the five political parties and the main mass organizations, the **SED** had an inbuilt majority as many representatives of the Mass Organizations were also party members. Plenary sessions of the Volkskammer were infrequent, only lasting for one or two days. The Chamber remained a pliant body until the **Wende**, when it became the scene of lively debates.

See also: parties and mass organizations: GDR

MIKE DENNIS

Volksstück

Though with origins in eighteenth- and nineteenth-century **Volkstheater**, and still many points of contact to it, *Volksstück* now refers to one of two related, but essentially antagonistic, genres.

The first is the commercialized popular drama (usually comedy) exemplified by the Hamburg **Ohnsorg-Theater** or the Bavarian television *Komödienstadel*. In plays like *Hühner aus Nachbars Garten* (Chickens from Next Door), *Der Bauerndiplomat* (The Peasant Diplomat) or *Geld regiert die Welt* (Money Makes the World Go Round), stock figures trapped in the amber of a stylized (usually rural) idyll and within narrow regional, class and gender stereotypes – the lusty farmer, the shrewish widow, the cheerful cowman, the nimble-witted waiter, the patronizing but eventually hoodwinked (and in Bavarian *Volksstücke*, for example, preferably Prussian) city-slicker – act out stock situations: inheritance, cuckoldry, mistaken identity and the hindrances to young love. The stage language simulates dialect for comic effect. Subtlety is sacrificed to crude comedy and the happy ending. Where modernity encroaches on this world, then it is as a threat to be defeated by moral backbone, homespun wisdom, and native wit.

The second genre is the *Neues Volksstück* (*NV*), which emerged in the late 1960s with the work of Martin Sperr, R.W. **Fassbinder** and F.X. **Kroetz**, and which does not draw on these popular comedies, except sometimes to negate them explicitly, as in Peter **Turrini**'s *sauschlachten*. These plays were sometimes also labelled *Neuer Realismus* because they seemed to cut through existing stage conventions to say 'this is how the broad masses of the population really think, feel, talk and act'. However, they actually had literary models, namely Marieluise **Fleißer**'s and Ödön von Horváth's *Volksstücke* from the Weimar period and their portrayals of provincial mentality, power structures as reflected in male–female relationships, and false consciousness as revealed in inauthentic language. The *NV* sought to expose material, emotional and linguistic deprivation, latent or actual violence behind the façade of the **Economic Miracle** and the purportedly classless society. This critique of capitalism led many *NV* authors to invoke Bertolt **Brecht**; but the historical optimism implicit in the articulate, class-conscious proletarian Matti in Brecht's *Volksstück*, *Puntila and his Servant Matti* (1940–8) is almost wholly absent from the *NV*. Sperr (e.g. *Hunting Scenes from Lower Bavaria*, 1966) and Fassbinder (e.g. *Katzelmacher*, 1969) explore how groups define outsiders in order to persecute them, demonstrating the fascism inherent in the enshrinement of *Ruhe und Ordnung* (well-behaved order) as civic virtues. The work of Kroetz characteristically has a more domestic focus, seeking to portray social deformation as it manifests itself in intra-family violence, identity crisis and self-immolation.

With directors the *NV* was a brief fashion, exhausted by the latter 1970s. However, Kroetz and Turrini especially, and with them a second wave of writers, for instance Felix Mitterer, Thomas Strittmatter and Kirsten Specht, continued to explore the socio-economic and psychological crises of ordinary people under capitalism. Fitzgerald Kusz's highly successful critical comedies on political and environmental themes, originally in Franconian dialect but widely transferable, represent a noteworthy blend of the two types of *Volksstück*.

Further reading

Aust, H., Haida, P. and Hein, J. (1989) *Volksstück. Vom Hanswurstspiel zum sozialen Drama der Gegenwart*, Munich: C.H. Beck.

MORAY McGOWAN

Volkstheater

The history of *Volkstheater* and its reception are chequered. It is indeed possible to suggest that the meanings of the term in various cultural or historical contexts are so varied as to make it impossible to reach a unifying definition. The richness of heritage and diversity of aesthetic and political agendas which have seen the form as a potential vehicle make the Viennese *Volkstheater* of the nineteenth century, the professional *Volkstheater* venues in German cities of today, and the critical *Volkstheater* championed by academics, the broadsheet media, and critical dramatists, seem far removed from the popular belief in *Volkstheater* as a theatre from the people, for the people and by the people. *Volkstheater* is both a traditional bourgeois institution and a movement; it has both form and content; it is home to various genres such as the farce, the comedy and the melodrama, and it is perceived to have a genre of its own, a genre rooted in the local cultural context and dialect, celebrating roots and aesthetic traditions which belong to the people. While encompassing the impulse towards the traditional and expressing a sense of belonging it is also a form which demonstrates radical tendencies, politically and critically reflecting upon the life of everyday people and urging action. Dramatists of the *Volkstheater* include the ever-popular Nestroy and Raimund from the heydays of the Viennese *Volkstheater*, critical **Volksstück** dramatists such as **Kroetz**, and local dramatists writing their own plays for amateur production such as Martin Schleker and Paul Wanner. For some *Volkstheater* is spectacle, such as the *Karl-May-Festspiele* or the ever popular musicals which tour the German institutional *Volkstheater* stages in the regional capitals showing the latest international hit such as *Cats* or *Phantom of the Opera*.

It is perhaps most helpful to differentiate between the different forms of *Volkstheater* by dividing those deriving their being from patterns of late capitalist consumption, in other words professional popular theatre, and those which, although dependent on consumers, are concerned with expressing an identity of the people incorporating local perceptions of everyday life from both the past and the present day, in other words the folk theatre or community theatre. The spectacle, the published work of critical *Volkstheater* writers, and performance by professionals may thus be found in the institutionalized forms of the *Volkstheater*, those which see their heritage as stemming from early nineteenth-century Vienna, where travelling theatre found a permanent home and became urbanized. Theatre that is still clearly from the people, for the people and by the people, although no longer the rural folk form of the past, may then be seen as community *Volkstheater*, encompassing forms such as the ever popular children's theatres, the **GRIPS-Theater**, youth theatres, **Naturtheater**, open-air theatre, amateur theatre, etc.

Further reading

Brady, D. and McKormick, J. (1978) *People's Theatre*, London: Croom Helm (an excellent introduction to the theory and practice of popular theatre in Europe).

Hein, J. (1978) *Das Wiener Volkstheater: Raimund und Nestroy*, Darmstadt: Wissenschaftliche Buchgesellschaft (a discussion of the concept and the history of the *Volkstheater* focusing the Viennese tradition and the work of Nestroy and Raimund).

McGrath, J. (1989) *A Good Night Out. Popular Theatre: Audience, Class and Form*, London: Methuen (a practical discussion of the significance of popular theatre for political and community drama in the context of Britain; this is a useful point of comparison for *Volkstheater* as community theatre or political theatre in Germany).

Sondergeld, E. (ed.) (1992) *Handbuch Amateurtheater*, Heidenheim: BDAT (a comprehensive guide to amateur theatre in contemporary Germany, published to celebrate the centenary of the Amateur Theatre Association in Germany in 1992).

ALISON PHIPPS

Volkswagen

Based in Wolfsburg in Lower Saxony, Volkswagen AG was founded as a state-owned enterprise in 1938. For many years Volkswagen (the name means 'people's car') manufactured one of the world's best-selling cars, the 'Beetle'. The federal government privatized 60 percent of Volkswagen in 1965 and its remaining 20 percent share in 1988. The Lower Saxony government retains 20 percent. Volkswagen has become a major multinational carmaker with subsidiaries in, for example, Spain, the Czech Republic, Brazil, Mexico and China.

Further reading

Tolliday, S. (1995) 'From 'Beetle Monoculture' to the 'German Model': the Transformation of Volkswagen, 1967–1991', *Business and Economic History* 24, 2: 111–32.

RICHARD A. HAWKINS

Vostell, Wolf

b. 14 October 1932, Leverkusen

Multimedia artist

Under the influence of neo-Dada and American happenings, Vostell devised and practised 'décollage' from 1954, tearing down posters, erasing images and overpainting photomontages. He first incorporated a television into a painting in 1958 and began to use spare parts from cars in sculptural assemblages. A leading member of the German Fluxus movement, he concentrated on video during the 1970s. He has created numerous large-scale installations and performances – often including **video** – to address topical issues, including the student protests and Vietnam. He responded to the ***Wende*** with a striking series of paintings and prints.

MARTIN BRADY

Waalkes, Otto

b. 22 July 1948, Emden

Comedian, actor and comic book artist

The East Frisian joker, Germany's most popular entertainer, is simply known as Otto. In 1972, after two years of studies at the Hamburg Academy of Fine Arts, he began his career as a stand-up comedian. Following live appearances and the release of various recordings, he starred in his own television show in 1973. His work also includes over ten books, including *Otto: Das Buch* (Otto: The Book) (1980), and the two greatest commercial successes in the history of German cinema, *Otto: Der Film* (Otto: The Movie) (1985) and *Otto: Der Neue Film* (Otto: The New Movie) (1987).

FREDERIC M. KOPP

Wagenbach-Verlag

The publishing firm founded by Klaus Wagenbach (1930–) in Berlin in 1964 specializes in contemporary literature, cultural studies and politics. Wagenbach is the publisher of intellectuals such as Erich **Fried**, Wolf **Biermann**, Johannes **Bobrowski** and of significant foreign literature in translation. The firm publishes *Tintenfisch* and *Freibeuter*, important cultural journals, and is a major force in literary discussion. Editorial policy tends towards social engagement. In the 1960s and 1970s Wagenbach published texts by the extra-parliamentary opposition. In 1975 the series 'Rotbuch/Politik' split off from Wagenbach to become Rotbuch Verlag.

JOHN B. RUTLEDGE

Wagner, Richard

b. 10 April 1952, Lovrin (Banat, Romania)

Writer

Wagner was a member of the literary and political Banat Action Group in the 1970s until its destruction by the Securitate. His early concrete poetry displays the understatement, irony and laconic style which are distinguishing features of his later works. The diversity of forms employed since he came to Germany in 1987 is testimony to the range of experiences distilled into his works. His roots are always inherent in his prose writing: usually set in Berlin, the only German city where unification can be experienced directly, it draws its black humour and unique insights from Wagner's critical awareness of the often curious ways in which the past lives on in the present in this cosmopolitan meeting-point of east and west.

DAVID ROCK

Wagner, Wieland

b. 5 January 1917, Bayreuth; d. 17
October 1966, Munich

Producer and stage designer

It fell to Wieland and his brother Wolfgang
Wagner, the composer's grandchildren, to restore
the **Bayreuth Festival** after 1945. Renouncing
the figurist aesthetic of his parents, (with its
undeniable Nazi associations), Wieland forged a
simplified yet strongly symbolist approach to
Wagner's work, moving the operas out of realistic
settings into the realm of Jungian or mythical
archetypes. The fierce controversy which greeted
his early efforts was replaced by acceptance, and
Wieland's approach soon became the *lingua franca*
of Wagnerian staging. Many of his productions of
other composers' operas were for the Stuttgart
State Opera.

BEATRICE HARPER

Waldheim, Kurt

b. 21 December 1918, St Andrä-Wördern

Diplomat and politician; Austrian President from 1986 to 1992

Waldheim was Austria's representative at the UN
(1964–7, 1970), and Foreign Minister (1968–70).
After an unsuccessful campaign for the Austrian
presidency (1971) he became Secretary-General of
the UN (1971–81) where he tried to mediate
between conflicting factions, also giving support to
Third World countries and the PLO.

Elected Austrian President in 1986 after a
campaign in which he had to admit to his role in
the German Army during WWII, his reluctance to
face the truth was representative of the hitherto
prevalent way of dealing with Austria's past. Until
then Austria was only seen as a victim of Nazi
Germany without taking the involvement of a
considerable part of the population in Nazi
activities and the **Holocaust** into account. The
subsequent political discussion led to a new and far
more critical assessment of Austria's role during the
period of Nazi occupation.

Further reading

Mitten, R. (1992) *The Politics of Antisemitic Prejudice:
The Waldheim Phenomenon in Austria*, Boulder, CO
and Oxford: Westview Press.

GEORG HELLMAYR

Waldsterben

The 'death of the **forest**' as a consequence of
environmental pollution is not a problem peculiar
to Germany, but due to the significance of the
forests in German culture the phenomenon has
received more attention there than elsewhere.
About 29 percent of Germany's surface area is
wooded; official reports classify about 40 percent of
the trees as visibly and a further 24 percent as
seriously damaged.

The romantic love of forests, which has become
an integral part of the German sense of **Heimat**
and cultural identity, dates back to the early
nineteenth century when overuse by loggers and
farmers had almost completely destroyed the oak
and beech forests which originally covered the
whole of Germania. Since the romantic era, the
dark and mysterious forest as the source of
Germanic strength and inspiration has been
celebrated in countless poems, paintings and other
works of fine and popular art. Even today, most
Germans regard the forests, rather than the seaside
or the open countryside, as the incarnation of
nature and naturalness.

First incidences of trees dying in the immediate
vicinity of industrial facilities were described in the
mid-nineteenth century. Problems recurred regularly, but no systematic research was undertaken,
until in the 1970s widespread and increasingly
serious damage to coniferous as well as deciduous
trees alerted forestry experts and scientists. In 1981
the news magazine *Der **Spiegel*** brought the issue
to the awareness of the general public. Several
organizations for the protection of the forests were
founded, 'Robin Wood' being one of the most
original and committed ones.

In 1984 the federal government presented its
first official report (*Waldschadensbericht*) documenting
the state of the forests across the country. Since
then, annual reports have monitored the steadily

worsening situation. Generally forests in the southern *Länder* are more affected (around 70 percent
damaged) than those in the north of Germany
(around 50 percent damaged). Montane forests are
more threatened than those in lower regions. Due
to the low environmental standards in the former
GDR, the situation is particularly desolate in the
new *Länder* with up to 87 percent of trees damaged
in Mecklenburg-Vorpommern. Across the country,
oak trees (a German symbol of stability, quality and
tradition – hence the oak-leaf on some German
coins) and fir trees (popular because of the German
tradition of the Christmas tree) are particularly
affected (85 and 90 percent respectively). Until the
late 1980s sulphur-dioxide emitted from coal-fired
power stations was regarded as the main cause of
the damage (acid rain). Today, filters have more
than halved German SO_2 emissions, yet car
exhaust fumes and emissions from agro-industry
have proved equally damaging.

Further reading

Bode, W. and Hohnhorst, M.v. (1994) *Waldwende –
Vom Försterwald zum Nadelwald*, Munich: Beck (on
strategies for ecological change).

Dominick, R.H. (1992) *The Environmental Movement
in Germany*, Bloomington and Indianapolis, IN:
Indiana University Press (on the significance of
the issue within German culture and the
environmental movement).

See '*Waldzustandsbericht*', an annual publication of
the federal government, for recent figures and
research into the causes.

INGOLFUR BLÜHDORN

Wallraff, Günter

b. 1 October 1942, Burscheid (near
Cologne)

Writer

In the 1970s and 1980s Günter Wallraff developed
a reputation for candid, socially critical reportages
of contemporary German society. He first began
writing in the 1960s, and created a storm when he
infiltrated the **Bild** newspaper editorial offices and
unveiled malpractices in his book *Der Aufmacher. Der
Mann, der bei BILD Hans Esser war* (The Lead Story.
The Man who was Hans Esser at BILD) (1977).
Legal action was taken against him by the
Springer publishing house, and his methods of
investigation (unless serving the public interest)
were declared to be illegal by the **Federal
Constitutional Court**. The pattern of infiltration, revelation and legal repercussions was to
continue, however, when he disguised himself as a
Turk, acquired work through sub-contractors, and
exposed the unscrupulous working practices of
firms who exploit foreign workers by 'selling' their
labour force to larger companies such as Thyssen.
The results of his infiltration in this case, *Lowest of
the Low* (*Ganz unten*, 1985), appeared both as a book
and a documentary film and again he faced legal
action. This particular reportage became a best-
seller, yet its commercial success also generated
criticism and not just from those whom Wallraff
had exposed: Turkish associates, for example,
accused him of exploitation, and he was accused
of claiming authorship of sections which he had not
written himself.

There can be no doubt that Wallraff has made
an invaluable contribution to revealing abuses in
German society by documenting the exploitation
of those groups whose voices otherwise fail to reach
the public ear. His work is characterized not simply
by the reporting of observations from outside: he
enters situations in order to experience them at first
hand. Also, rather than restricting his reportages to
his individual observations, he creates a montage
using the accounts of others, letters, extracts from
reports and so on. The use of the first person invites
the reader to identify with the narrated experience,
and at the same time the evidence outside the
reporting first person demands the reader's critical
engagement. Wallraff belonged to **Gruppe 61** and
yet his focus on documentation rather than fiction,
and on politics rather than aesthetics represented a
minority in the group, and divisions led to the
breakaway Werkkreis Literatur der Arbeitswelt
(Working Group for Literature of the Working
World) in 1970, of which he was a formative
member.

Two years after *Ganz unten*, Wallraff documented
the regular surveillance and telephone tapping
carried out by the German authorities that led to

his temporary residence in The Netherlands in *Akteneinsicht* (Viewing the Files) (1987); he continues to maintain a residential base there and in Cologne.

Further reading

Linder, C. (ed.) (1986) *In Sachen Wallraff: Von den Industriereportagen bis Ganz unten, Berichte, Analysen, Meinungen und Dokumente*, Cologne: Kiepenheuer & Witsch (contains a useful collection of documents and articles).

Wallraff, G. (1986) *Lowest of the Low*, cameraman J. Gfrörer (the documentary *Ganz unten*, available with English subtitles).

—— (1990) *Der Aufmacher*, ed. and introduced by J. Sandford, Manchester: Manchester University Press (includes a 35-page introduction in English on Wallraff and the issues raised by his work).

—— (1994) *Enthüllungen*, Göttingen: Steidl (a collection of extracts of Wallraff's reportages 1968–87).

HELEN L. JONES

Walser, Martin

b. 24 March 1927, Wasserburg (Lake Constance)

Writer and dramatist

One of West Germany's most influential post-war writers, Walser observes with a critical and satirical eye the development of a prosperous middle-class society whose main criterion of success is based on social prestige and conformity at the expense of individual self-realization.

The son of a publican, Walser was called up for military service in 1944 and was later taken as a PoW. From 1946 to 1951 he studied languages, literature and history at the university of Tübingen, writing his thesis on Kafka. From 1949 to 1957 he worked for South German radio, first in entertainment, then in politics and current affairs. He also directed and began writing radio plays. In 1953 Walser joined the **Gruppe 47**. He visited the US, frequently as a guest professor.

Walser's first short stories are somewhat Kafkaesque in flavour as in the collection *Ein Flugzeug über dem Haus* (A Plane over the House) (1955), where he presents ordinary events in an unexpected, perhaps shocking, context. Three novels followed in which he examines West German society through the portrayal of middle-class protagonists in their struggle for upward social mobility or in their desperate attempts at staving off social decline. The first, *Marriage in Phillipsburg* (*Ehen in Philippsburg*, 1957), chronicles the process of adaptation and conformity, and the gradual loss of identity, in the figure of Hans Baumann who tries to become integrated into Phillipsburg society. For Walser the task of literature is to shed intellectual enlightenment by penetrating taboo areas of human consciousness. In the following novels, *Halbzeit* (Half time) (1960) and *The Unicorn* (*Das Einhorn*, 1966) Walser's protagonist Anselm Kristlein seeks to make his way in society and support his family but continually finds himself having to satisfy the expectations of others rather than realize his own hopes. Typically Walser's heroes withdraw from the external world in order to reflect upon their own predicament with the ultimate aim of regaining their capacity for action.

In the 1960s Walser brought new political themes to the somewhat conservative world of West German theatre. In *Rabbit Race and Detour* (*Eiche und Angora*, 1961–2) the comic figure of Alois and his belated attempts to adapt to new political conditions portray fascism not as a historical phenomenon but as a contemporary problem. *Der Schwarze Schwan* (The Black Swan) (1961–4) illustrates the apparently suicidal nature of protest against political conformity under Nazi rule. Another theme that occupied Walser in his early plays was the problematic nature of human relationships as in *Abstecher* (Detour) (1961) and *Die Zimmerschlacht* (Domestic Battle) (1962–3).

The dramatic satire *Überlebensgroß Herr Krott* (The Larger-than-life Mr Krott, first performed in 1962) sheds light on Walser's plays of this period. The wheelchair-bound capitalist who has already outlived himself, but cannot manage to die, terrorizes the already intimidated inhabitants of a surreal landscape. Walser is here using the public nature of theatre to pose questions about political power and its effect on human relationships. He also illustrates how conservative structures are able to prevent change, as in *Lügengeschichten* (Lying Stories) (1964).

The Vietnam War led Walser to a more radical political position. He criticized himself for having swallowed government placebos and expressed critical sympathy with the student left and the **DKP** (West German Communist Party). His own work became more sharply focused: from the reconstruction of middle-class individuality he began to pose a political alternative. He tried to help others publish work that had been hitherto unpublished, for instance Kessler's *Der Schock* (The Shock), a report from the world of the sub-proletariat. In his foreword to Erika **Runge**'s *Bottroper Protokolle* (Bottrop Transcripts) (1969) he expressed his support for working-class literature in its own right and joined the **Gruppe 61**. In *Fiction* (1970) there is a suggestion that the individual can only be saved in a socialist alternative and in *Die Gallistl'sche Krankheit* (Gallistl's Disease) (1972) the protagonist Gallistl tries to distance himself from the conditions causing his mysterious illness and through his communist friends finds the will to oppose.

In *Sauspiel* (Pig's Game) (1975) Walser takes the Peasants' Revolt as the background to reflect his experiences with conservative opponents, whereas the characters of Horn in the novel *Beyond all Love* (*Jenseits der Liebe*, 1976) and Hahn in the novella *A Runaway Horse* (*Ein fliehendes Pferd*, 1978) are merely trying to find strategies of survival. For Walser the prospects for self-realization seemed to be fading, as were hopes for a socialist alternative. The novel *The Inner Man* (*Seelenarbeit*, 1979) is a story of social degradation whose protagonist is linked with Horn and Hahn in the novel *The Swan Villa* (*Das Schwanenhaus*, 1980) and *Letter to Lord Liszt* (*Brief an Lord Liszt*, 1982) by his suffering and sense of social impotence. The satirical quality of Walser's earlier work has ceded to one of irony, showing the victims of the rat race in a highly competitive capitalist society.

From the mid-1980s Walser was deeply concerned with the **German Question**. He had moved from his earlier position of scepticism towards the idea of German unification (in 1978 he had argued for 'keeping the German wound open') to one of passionate pro-unity. The novel *Dorle und Wolf* (1987) features **Stasi** activity and

marital problems. The characters in the novel *Jagd* (Hunt) (1988) seem content to return to a 'safe' world after their brief attempt at breaking away from it. In his post-unification bestseller *Die Verteidigung der Kindheit* (The Defence of Childhood) (1991) Walser's protagonist attempts to preserve the memory of his childhood in a divided Germany.

Further reading

Parkes, K.S. (1986) *Writers and Politics in West Germany*, London and Sydney: Croom Helm (contains a chapter on Walser).

—— (1994) 'Looking Forward to the Past: Identity and Identification in Martin Walser's *Die Verteidigung der Kindheit*', in A. Williams and S. Parkes (eds), *The Individual, Identity and Innovation. Signals from Contemporary Literature and the new Germany*, Bern: Peter Lang.

Pilipp, F. (1994) (ed.) *New Critical perspectives on Martin Walser*, Columbia, SC: Camden House (a more recent collection of critical essays).

Sinka, M. (1982) 'The Flight Motif in Martin Walser's "Ein fliehendes Pferd" ', *Monatshefte* 74: 212–26.

Waine, A. (1987) 'Martin Walser', in K. Bullivant (ed.), *The Modern German Novel*, New York and Leamington Spa: Berg (general discussion of Walser's work).

MARGARET VALLANCE

Walter, Erich

b. 30 December 1927, Fürth

Dancer and choreographer

Walter received his early training at ballet schools in Nürnberg, his first major engagement being with the municipal theatre in Nürnberg (1947), followed by Göttingen and Wiesbaden. From 1953 to 1964 he was ballet master in Wuppertal. During this time he was also guest choreographer in Berlin, Hanover and Vienna. In 1964 he became director of ballet at the Deutsche Oper am Rhein in Düsseldorf.

DEREK McCULLOCH

Walther, Joachim

b. 6 October 1943, Chemnitz

Writer

Walther made his breakthrough in the GDR as the author of radio-plays, stories – including the best-selling *Ich bin nun mal kein Yogi* (I'm No Yogi) (1975) – and the ostensibly historical novel *Bewerbung bei Hofe* (Application for a Position at Court) (1982). Since unification he has built on his extensive editorial experience of the same period, devoting himself to exposing the extent of SED – and particularly **Stasi** – control of literary life, in the volumes *Protokoll eines Tribunals* (Protocol of a Tribunal) (1991) and *Sicherungsbereich Literatur* (Safeguarding the Literary Sphere) (1996).

See also: writers' union: GDR

DENNIS TATE

Wander, Maxie

b. 3 January 1933 Vienna; d. 20 November 1977 Kleinmachnow (near Berlin)

Writer

Maxie Wander, a high-school dropout, was born in Vienna, the daughter of a Viennese petrol station attendant in 1933. She worked at various jobs including as a housemaid, factory labourer and office worker. She married writer Fred Wander, a concentration camp survivor and Communist Party member, with whom she moved to the GDR in 1958.

Wander's major contribution to German culture and the only work to be published during her lifetime was her collection of seventeen interviews with GDR women (*Frauenprotokolle)*, entitled *Guten Morgen, du Schöne. Protokolle nach Tonband* (Good Morning, Beautiful. Transcripts from the Tape Recorder). The book, published in the GDR in 1977 and the FRG in 1978, was an instant bestseller in both countries.

Wander's book, while part of the confirming tradition of *Protokolliteratur* by women as exemplified in the 1973 book by Sarah **Kirsch**, *Die Pantherfrau*.

Fünf unfrisierte Erzählungen aus dem Kassettenrecorder (*The Panther Woman. Five Tales from the Cassette Recorder*), also differed from Kirsch's earlier work. The five women interviewed by Kirsch are almost completely lacking in a critical consciousness and identify mainly with men and men's roles. Wander's interviewees, in contrast, express discontent and (a limited) criticism of GDR societal conditions. The book's central theme is the emancipation of the individual from compulsory societal roles, a theme that was ground-breaking at the time. Concentrating especially on private roles and relationships, Wander and her interviewees fit into the tradition of the GDR type of 'feminism' where discontent was expressed in the private, rather than the public, realm. Wander's questions focus on daily life, work, love, sexuality, emancipation and oppression, and demonstrate how, in spite of the GDR's official claims of achieving equality, structures of oppression continued to exist in the reality of women's lives.

Wander also intended to publish volumes of interviews with men and children, but these projects were never completed due to her untimely death from cancer in 1977.

Further reading

Pickle, L.S. (1982) ' "Unreserved Subjectivity" as a Force for Social Change: Christa Wolf and Maxie Wander's *Guten Morgen, du Schöne*' in M. Gerber *et al.* (eds) *Studies in GDR Culture and Society 2*, Washington, DC: University Press of America, pp. 217–30 (Pickle analyses Wolf's introduction to Wander's book in the context of her other works, and compares the stories told by the women Wander interviewed to Wolf's female characters).

Wander, M. (1984) 'Waiting for a Miracle. Ruth B., Waitress, Unmarried, One Child' in E.H. Altbach *et al.* (eds) *German Feminism: Readings in Politics and Literature*, Albany, NY: SUNY Press, 170–7 (while Wander's *Guten Morgen* has not been translated in its entirety, this anthology and the following both contain one interview in translation).

—— (1993) 'Ute G., 24, Skilled Worker, Single, One Child' in N. Lukens and D. Rosenberg (eds and trans.) *Daughters of Eve: Women's Writing from* the German Democratic Republic, Lincoln, NB and London: University of Nebraska Press, pp. 39–48.

Wolf, C. (1984) 'In Touch', in E.H. Altbach *et al.* (eds) *German Feminism: Readings in Politics and Literature*, Albany, NY: SUNY Press, pp. 161–9 (Wolf's original introduction to Wander's volume is translated in this volume; in it, Wolf discusses the importance of Wander's work and also introduces the concept of *Berührung*, or 'touching').

BRENDA L. BETHMAN

Wecker, Konstantin

b. 1 June 1947, Munich

Singer-songwriter, film music composer and poet

The son of an opera singer, Wecker studied composition at the music conservatory in Munich, has written music for films such as *Die weiße Rose* (The White Rose) (1983) and acted in plays and films. Best known as a singer-songwriter (***Liedermacher***) with numerous LPs since 1972, his breakthrough song 'Willy' in Bavarian dialect (1977) attacked neo-Nazi tendencies in West Germany. He accompanies himself on piano, and has given numerous concerts. Wecker is more individualistic and subjective than is typical of the 1968 *Liedermacher* generation, with a dramatic performance style and stocky, rough-hewn appearance. He has published several volumes of poetry. His novel *Uferlos* (Shoreless) (1992) was an autobiographical treatment of his cocaine addiction. He was arrested for cocaine possession in 1996.

See also: protest songs

RICHARD J. RUNDELL

weddings

Weddings are examples of ritual celebrations marking transitional phases, or boundaries, as the identities of bachelor and spinster change to become man and wife. The celebrations permitted during the wedding are culturally negotiated, and, in the context of contemporary Germany, they display regional variations. The format of the wedding celebrations is both a matter of law, imposed nationally, and a matter of specific social, familial and cultural execution.

It is a requirement of law in Germany for a civic wedding ceremony to take place even if it is to be followed by a church service. The civic ceremony is conducted by the *Standesbeamter* (the registrar), following the posting of the intention to marry outside the local town hall several weeks before the actual ceremony. Before the ceremony takes place the genealogy of the couple must be verified and a family name stipulated. During the civic ceremony the choice of both family name and the changes to the surnames are made public. Two witnesses (*Trauzeugen*), often close friends or members of the family, are required to sign the legal documentation.

The tradition of hosting a party for friends prior to the wedding ceremony is known as the *Polterabend*. This is jointly hosted by the couple, and friends bring crockery and a variety of porcelain items which are then ritually smashed outside the couple's home, or in the yard. The superstition *Scherben bringen Glück* (pieces of porcelain bring luck), underlies the ritual.

On the day of the ceremony a variety of 'surprises' await the couple. In some regions of Germany a large *Hochzeitsbaum* (wedding tree) may be erected outside the couple's home festooned with ribbons and baby clothes. The couple travel to the church or the registry office together with their two witnesses and once the ceremony is over it is traditional for *Kaffee und Kuchen* (coffee and cakes) to be served to all guests. Some guests are invited solely to this part of the celebration. The cakes are usually provided by members of the family and close friends. The wedding breakfast is served in the evening, often following a regional menu, and during this time wedding gifts are presented to the couple. Most couples hire a dance band for the evening and they lead off the dancing with the bridal waltz, closely followed by their respective parents and the witnesses. Traditional ballroom dancing is the norm and young people are usually given the option of learning to dance as part of their schooling.

In some regions of Germany it is traditional for

the bride and her bouquet to be kidnapped during the course of the evening. She is usually taken to a local hostelry and it is the task of the witness to find her and her bouquet again whilst the bridegroom is left to dance with a broom. In the meantime the kidnappers and the bride treat themselves to champagne, paid for eventually by the witnesses, and make paper hats, known as *Narrenhüte* (Fool's hats) as a symbol of misrule.

ALISON PHIPPS

Wegner, Bettina

b. 4 November 1947, Berlin

Singer-songwriter

As a cult figure and the moral voice of the anti-bureaucratic youth movement of the 1970s GDR, Wegner produced songs that expressed dreams of a peaceable world, for instance *Sind so kleine Hände* (Such Tiny Hands) (1978). After years of persecution she moved to West Berlin in 1983.

MICHAEL HÄNEL

Weigel, Helene

b. 12 May 1900, Vienna; d. 6 May 1971, (East) Berlin

Actress

Weigel established her career as an actress during the Weimar Republic. She married Bertolt **Brecht** in 1929 and spent her post-1933 exile with him in Scandinavia and the US. She returned in 1948 to become Director and leading actress of the **Berliner Ensemble**. She reached an international audience through touring productions of Brecht's plays, especially as the protagonist of *Mother Courage* (*Mutter Courage*). After Brecht's death she continued his work of producing definitive performances of his plays but later attracted criticism for turning the Ensemble into a 'museum'.

DENNIS TATE

Weil, Grete

b. 18 July 1906, Munich

Writer

Weil was traumatically ejected from her high-bourgeois, assimilated background, and confronted with her Jewish identity, by the experience of exile, life in hiding in Amsterdam, and her husband's death in the Mauthausen concentration camp, which haunt her usually autobiographical narratives. *Meine Schwester Antigone* (Antigone, My Sister) (1980), her major novel, features a complex meditation on the Antigone figure: a symbol of principled rebellion and the duty to mourn, but also an alibi for the inaction of the narrator. Other major texts include the novella *The Last Trolley from Beethovenstraat* (*Tramhalte Beethovenstraat*) (1968), and the novel *The Bride Price* (*Der Brautpreis*) (1988).

MORAY McGOWAN

Weill, Kurt

b. 2 March 1900, Dessau; d. 3 April 1950, New York

Composer

Weill's earliest formal training was in the Hochschule für Musik in Berlin in 1918, but disappointed by the institution he returned home to assist in the 'court opera' of his home town, before moving to the newly-formed opera company in Lüdenscheid, Westphalia, subsequently returning to Berlin to study under Busoni, or rather his assistant Philipp Jarnach. Soon after he began his collaborations with the playwright Georg Kaiser, and their opera *Der Protagonist* (The Protagonist) in 1926 met with great success. Also at this time began his remarkable (though short) collaboration with **Brecht**, while continuing his joint ventures with Kaiser. *The Threepenny Opera* (*Die Dreigroschenoper*) in 1928 proved an international success, Weill's wife Lotte Lenya singing the role of Jenny. The political situation in the 1930s saw him the butt of public abuse, the aim of which was to ban his works from the German stage. Weill realized what was happening and a few weeks after the infamous fire at the Reichstag he left for

Paris, where he was persuaded to re-open his association with Brecht in *The Seven Deadly Sins* (*Die sieben Todsünden*), which was given a poor reception, though Weill considered it to be one of his best scores. He withdrew from Parisian musical life to the outlying village of Louveciennes, aided and abetted by Milhaud and Honegger. Shortly after he emigrated to the US, where his relationship with Broadway was likewise characterized by early failure, though he later began to understand better what the American public liked. This, in turn, failed to endear him to the European public.

The patchy nature and reception of his works, the loss of most of his early works and the neglect of many of his later ones, make an overall assessment of his importance peculiarly difficult. Until that happens, we must be grateful for the continuing success of *Die Dreigroschenoper*.

DEREK McCULLOCH

Weimann, Robert

b. 18 November 1928, Magdeburg

Cultural theorist

Weimann became the GDR's internationally best-known cultural theorist, his specialist interest in English drama leading him to an early awareness of the importance of the 'western' theories of new criticism and reception aesthetics for a developing Marxist understanding of cultural production. He was appointed to a research professorship in literary theory in the GDR's Academy of Sciences in 1969 and became Vice-President of the Academy of the Arts in 1978. He is particularly admired for his work on Shakespeare, for instance *Shakespeare und die Macht der Mimesis* (Shakespeare and the Power of Mimesis) (1988).

DENNIS TATE

Weimarer Beiträge

Weimarer Beiträge was the GDR's leading journal in the field of literary criticism and cultural theory, founded in 1955 under the aegis of the Centre for Research into German Classical Literature in

Weimar. Its regular features in the years up to 1989 included interviews with GDR authors and round-table discussions on new literary works. Informative but rarely controversial, it was exposed to healthy internal competition following the launch of the Berlin-based *Zeitschrift für Germanistik* in 1980. The journal was taken over by the Viennese publisher Passagen Verlag after unification and now has a broader interdisciplinary focus.

DENNIS TATE

Weisenborn, Günther

b. 10 July 1902, Velbert; d. 26 March 1969, (West) Berlin

Writer, dramatist and *Dramaturg*

Weisenborn was actively interested in both political and innovative theatre, and his work is characterized by anti-war themes, for instance in *U-Boot S4* (Submarine S4) (1928), and anti-fascist themes. He was arrested in 1942 for his connection with a plot against Hitler. Co-founder with Karl-Heinz Martin of the Hebbel Theater in Berlin in 1945, he wrote plays, including *Die Illegalen* (The Illegals) (1946), as well as historical accounts such as *Der lautlose Aufstand* (The Silent Rebellion) (1953) concerning German resistance to Nazism.

See also: drama: FRG; theatres

MICHAEL RICHARDSON

Weiss, Peter

b. 18 November 1916, Nowawes (Berlin); d. 10 May 1982, Stockholm

Writer

The son of a Jewish textile manufacturer, Weiss grew up in Berlin and Bremen, but emigrated with his parents in 1934 via Prague to England. He spent most of his life in permanent exile, settling in Sweden in 1939, where he was granted citizenship in 1949 and married the stage designer, Gunilla Palmstierna. Weiss remained a peripheral – though significant – figure in post-war German culture, expressing his hard-won moral, political and aesthetic views in several clamorous and often controversial plays.

In his early years Weiss painted, mainly in the surrealist manner, then tried his hand at making experimental documentary films. After 1960 writing became his main concern. His first prose works were characterized by a style of precise, unemotional description, indebted to Kafka and the French *nouveau roman*, through which he attempted to establish autobiographical clarity. *Leavetaking* (*Abschied von den Eltern*, 1961) and *Vanishing Point* (*Fluchtpunkt*, 1962) record this search for identity against the pressures of family and heritage.

Weiss shot to international prominence in 1964 with the vibrant play *Marat/Sade* (*Die Verfolgung und Ermordung Jean Paul Marats, dargestellt durch die Schauspielgruppe des Hospizes zu Charenton unter Anleitung des Herrn de Sade*), a collage of styles and themes influenced by **Brecht** and Antonin Artaud to create 'total theatre'. Reason and argument, violence and sexuality, madness and sanity conflict and merge in a fast-moving action in which Marat's defence of collectivism and revolution is opposed to de Sade's assertion of anarchic individualism. The three interacting time levels emphasize the historical significance of the collision between revolution and reaction, conscious reason and instinctive drives.

A year later Weiss touched a raw nerve in German society with *The Investigation* (*Die Ermittlung*, 1965), a chillingly stark dramatization of the lengthy Frankfurt am Main trial of **Auschwitz** war criminals. The impact of this play was all the more powerful for its documentary style cast in the form of an oratorio in eleven cantos, a structure echoing Dante's *Inferno*. Weiss persisted with idiosyncratic dramatic forms in politically agitatory works like *Song of the Lusitanian Bogey* (*Gesang vom lusitanischen Popanz*, 1967), an indictment of Portuguese colonial oppression in Angola, and *Vietnam Discourse* (*Vietnam-Diskurs*, 1968), as well as his rehabilitation of Stalin's rival in *Trotsky in Exile* (*Trotzki im Exil*, 1970).

Weiss spent the last decade of his life composing the massive 'novel', *Die Ästhetik des Widerstands* (The Aesthetics of Resistance) (in three volumes published in 1975, 1978 and 1981), in reality a three-volume autobiographical reflection masked as the life of a fictitious working-class narrator, born in 1917, who experiences the events of the Third Reich, the Spanish Civil War, prolonged exile in Czechoslovakia and Stockholm, and the communist diaspora. In effect Weiss meditates on the history of the European left, resistance and exile, rigid party loyalty and individual freedom of choice. This imaginative reconstruction is interwoven with elaborate analyses of great works of art – the Pergamon frieze, Géricault's painting *The Raft of the Medusa*, Picasso's *Guernica* and Kafka's *The Trial* – to justify a Marxist aesthetic as a necessary element in left-wing resistance, especially during hard times. *Die Notizbücher 1971–80* (The Notebooks 1971–80) (published 1981) accompanied the gestation of this impressive work and illuminate Weiss' methods and intentions.

Weiss was a committed Marxist, intellectually and emotionally, who nevertheless pursued his vision of a 'third way', rejecting both unreflective subservience to party dictates and right-wing betrayal of the principles of a just society. His uncompromising rectitude earned him vilification from both right and left, which reinforced his sense of exile – to the extent that he even felt himself a stranger in the German language.

Further reading

Hilton, I. (1970) *Peter Weiss: A Search for Affinities*, London: Wolff (introductory monograph with selection of work, in English).

ARRIGO SUBIOTTO

Weizsäcker, Carl-Friedrich von

b. 28 June 1912, Kiel

Philosopher and physicist

The son of a diplomat, von Weizsäcker became a physicist in the 1930s. During WWII he worked on the German atomic bomb project. After internment in England he returned to West Germany and started his career as a philosopher. From the 1950s, he has participated in public political debates, advocating nuclear disarmament, support of the Third World and ecological awareness. Although he turned to fundamental religious and ethical questions in the 1980s, his presence was still felt in everyday politics. He is the elder brother of the former Federal President Richard von Weizsäcker.

GABRIELE METZLER

Weizsäcker, Richard von

b. 15 April 1920, Stuttgart

Politician; German Federal President from 1984 to 1994

Regarded by many as the most distinguished of the Federal Republic's presidents, Weizsäcker was widely respected as a moral authority. His sensitive but firm insistence on the need for Germany to continue to acknowledge moral responsibility for the crimes of the Nazi past was most famously expressed in his speech to the Bundestag on 8 May 1985 on the fortieth anniversary of Germany's defeat. In 1993 he attacked the political establishment for its 'power-crazy' behaviour, which, he said, was causing a dangerous cynicism among ordinary people. A leading Protestant churchman and a member of the CDU, Weizsäcker was mayor of West Berlin from 1979 to 1984.

See also: *Bundesversammlung*

JOHN SANDFORD

Wekwerth, Manfred

b. 3 December 1929, Köthen

Theatre director

As one of **Brecht**'s star pupils Wekwerth became an assistant director at the **Berliner Ensemble** in 1951. Consolidating his reputation after Brecht's death, he rose to Director-in-Chief of the Ensemble between 1960 and 1969 before going freelance for eight years (including a period at the National Theatre in London). He returned to the Ensemble as its manager between 1977 and 1991. Wekwerth simultaneously extended his influence over GDR cultural life as a whole, becoming Vice-President of the Academy of the Arts (1974–82) and then, succeeding Konrad **Wolf**, its President (1982–90).

DENNIS TATE

Wellershoff, Dieter

b. 3 November 1925, Neuß (Rhineland)

Writer and literary theoretician

Wellershoff's output includes short stories, drama, lyric poetry and television plays, but he is best known for his experimental novels, for instance *Einladung an alle* (All Welcome) (1972), and radio plays. His essays and theoretical writings, such as *Literatur und Veränderung* (Literature and Change) (1969), and the collection *Der Roman und die Erfahrbarkeit der Welt* (The Novel and the Knowability of the World) (1988) reflect and inform his creative work, which is indebted in particular to the French *nouveau roman*. His concept of a liberating 'new realism' that penetrates beyond deceptive surface reality lay behind the founding of the Cologne School in the mid-1960s, which also included Nicolas **Born**, Rolf Dieter **Brinkmann**, and Günter **Herburger**.

JOHN SANDFORD

Welt, Die

First published on 2 April 1946 as a twice-weekly newspaper in the British zone, *Die Welt* is today considered the most right-wing of the main German national dailies. Owned by the Axel **Springer** concern it incurs losses of up to DM 40 million a year with a circulation of 216,000 copies. Its recent move from Bonn to the new capital Berlin seems not to have alleviated the problem, and the attempt by Thomas Löffelholz, editor since 1995, to adopt a more liberal stance has provoked direct political interference from Leo **Kirch**, who owns a 35 percent share in Springer.

See also: journalism; newspapers

ROLF JUCKER

Weltbühne, Die

Die Weltbühne, a weekly paper for politics, arts and business, began publication in 1918, having evolved out of the theatre journal, *Die Schaubühne*, founded by Siegfried Jacobsohn in 1905. After

Jacobsohn's death in 1926, the editorship was assumed by Carl von Ossietzky (1889–1938) with some early assistance from Kurt Tucholsky and was sustained until the journal was banned in 1933. When von Ossietzky was sentenced for treason at the 'Weltbühne-trial' of 1931, his former teacher, Hellmut von Gerlach, filled the position. Between 1933 and 1939 the exiled William S. Schlamm (1904–78) and Hermann Budzislawski (1901–78) continued to publish issues in Prague, Zürich and Paris under the revised name Die Neue Weltbühne until the journal was banned in Paris with the onset of WWII. Von Ossietzky's widow, Maud, assumed editorship of Die Weltbühne in co-operation with Hans Leonard in 1946 in East Berlin, and the journal was to become (albeit with a restricted print-run) one of the GDR's most independent-minded cultural publications. After Leonard's death in 1966, Hermann Budzislawski took over his position and in 1974 became sole editor, following Maud von Ossietzky's death. In 1992, Dr Helmut Reinhardt bought Die Weltbühne from the **Treuhand**. Because of a legal battle between the new editor and the heirs of previous editors, the final issue appeared in 1993.

SYLVIA KLÖTZER

Wende

The term, Wende, when used in a political context, means a change in political direction. It was used in West Germany in 1982 to describe the change from a Social Democrat-led government coalition to one led by the Christian Democrats because radical changes in government policy were expected. The term was then applied in 1989 to the transformation of the German Democratic Republic from a communist dictatorship to a state which started to introduce democratic structures. When political changes started to happen in the GDR in the autumn of 1989, there was uncertainty as to whether these changes should be described as a 'revolution' or as a Wende. Wende is the term which has become the most commonly used; the term revolution implies the deliberate use of violence, and one of the major features of the changes in the GDR was the lack of violence on the part of those

demonstrating for change, and the restraint, albeit reluctant, of the authorities in the face of those demonstrations.

The Wende started with the first major change in direction in the GDR, the forced resignation of the leader of the **SED** (Socialist Unity Party) and head of state, Erich **Honecker**, and finished with the election of a conservative government on 18 March 1990. Up until October 1989 the SED and the GDR government had resisted a number of pressures to change course: from GDR citizens emigrating illegally in the summer of 1989 via third countries or through the occupation of West German embassies in eastern Europe; from the protests of opposition groups, especially after the monitoring of the local elections in May 1989, leading to the foundation of citizens' groups, such as **Neues Forum** (New Forum), in September 1989; and from the demonstrations in favour of a reform of socialism in the GDR on 6–8 October at the time of Mikhail Gorbachev's visit to East Berlin for the fortieth anniversary of the founding of the GDR. During his visit the Soviet leader warned the SED leadership of the dangers of not introducing fundamental reforms, but was ignored by the inner core of the leadership, led by Honecker and **Mielke**, who from the accession to power of Gorbachev in 1985 had firmly resisted any temptation to follow the Soviet Union's path of reform. On the Monday after the official celebrations, 9 October, 70,000 people demonstrated in Leipzig for reform, when the famous slogan Wir sind das Volk (we are the people) was heard. It was on this day that fears were expressed of a bloody suppression of the protests. But in the event, partly as a result of the intervention of a group of leading figures in Leipzig, led by the musical director of the Leipzig Gewandhaus Kurt **Masur**, no force was used by the authorities. The crucial factor was the refusal of the Soviet authorities to intervene militarily on the side of the GDR government.

This demonstration proved to be a turning point. At a specially convened meeting of the **Central Committee** on 18 October, Honecker offered his resignation from all his functions 'on health grounds'. In fact, a group within the **Politbüro**, including his successor as General Secretary of the SED, Egon **Krenz**, had forced him to resign. Krenz made a speech on radio and television that evening in which he talked of the SED having introduced a *Wende*. He referred to the failure of the SED to respond to demands for change, and announced that the party was now ready to open a dialogue with other groups in society. One of his first actions was to sanction the preparation of a new law on the regulations governing the right of GDR citizens to travel abroad. In the following week however growing waves of demonstrations against the SED and Krenz developed. When he was put up for election as head of state in the **Volkskammer** on 24 October twenty-six deputies voted against him, with the same number of abstentions, and his stay in office was brief. On 4 November the largest demonstration for reforms that the GDR had ever seen, of over one million people, took place on the Alexanderplatz in the centre of East Berlin. Three days later, the government under Willi **Stoph** resigned, and the following day the entire Politbüro was forced to go. On 8 November the Ministry of the Interior recognized *Neues Forum* as a legal organization, a status which had been denied it on 21 September. On 9 November, in what was the most fateful decision for the future of the GDR, Günter Schabowski, Information Secretary to the Central Committee, announced at a press conference that the country's border's were to be opened 'with immediate effect until the passing of a new Travel Law'. The forces controlling the crossing points at the **Berlin Wall** had not been informed of this decision and were totally unprepared when large numbers of people started appearing at the frontier demanding to be allowed to go to West Berlin. Serious incidents were avoided by the yielding of the guards to the pressure of the crowds, and the frontier was opened. One of the leaders of Neues Forum, Bärbel **Bohley**, commented that same day that this decision spelt the end for a reformed GDR.

On 13 November a new government was installed under the reform-minded SED leader from Dresden, Hans **Modrow**, and on 17 November he was confirmed by the Volkskammer as the head of a new government. But this new government still contained a majority of SED ministers, seventeen out of twenty-eight, and the demonstrations continued throughout the GDR, with demands being made for the removal of the SED's claim to the leading role in government and for the introduction of a new electoral law. Under pressure from these demonstrations, Krenz, who was still head of state, announced on 23 November that the SED was prepared to consider removing Article 1 of the constitution which contained the clause relating to the SED's leading role. This measure was passed by the Volkskammer on 1 December.

Another major strand of protest was directed against the former SED leadership with allegations of corruption and abuse of power. A major focus for these protests was the **Stasi** which, although its abolition and replacement by an Office for National Security had been announced by Modrow on 17 November in his maiden speech, was still present as a visible force in society. The events of 7 and 8 October when a large number of people had been arrested and mistreated were still fresh in people's minds, and despite the announcement by Modrow, also on 17 November, of an investigation into allegations of misconduct, there was widespread suspicion that Stasi officers would be allowed to carry on quietly as before. This pressure led to the start of a police investigation on 30 November into charges of corruption and abuse of power against six former leading members of the SED, including Honecker. On 3 December the Politbüro and the Central Committee resigned and the Politbüro member responsible for the economy, Günter Mittag, and the trade union leader, Harry Tisch, were arrested on charges of misappropriation of state funds; two days later Honecker and Mielke were put under house arrest, and the following day Krenz handed in his resignation as head of state. On 7 December the **Round Table** (Runder Tisch), a forum formed to set in motion dialogue between the old parties and the opposition groups, met for the first time. In the space of a week the power of the SED in government had been fatally weakened. A week later the SED held a hastily convened special congress which resisted calls for the dissolution of the party but took the first step towards becoming a democratic party by changing its name to SED-**PDS**, the 'Party of Democratic Socialism'.

Alongside these fundamental political changes in the GDR, the debate about its future as a separate state had become a major topic. The West German

Chancellor, Helmut **Kohl**, had presented his ten-point programme to the Bundestag on 28 November in which he outlined a plan for 'overcoming the division of Germany and Europe', without giving any indication of a possible timescale. On the same day, a group of writers, artists and opposition representatives had presented an alternative plea, '*Für unser Land*' (for our country), for the maintenance of an independent GDR as a 'socialist alternative to the Federal Republic'. The following day Krenz and Modrow added their signatures to the document. But the tide of public opinion had turned away from the idea of a reformed GDR. On 4 December, on demonstrations throughout the GDR, the slogans '*Deutschland einig Vaterland*' (Germany one Fatherland – a quotation from the East German national anthem) and '*Wir sind ein Volk*' (we are one people) were heard for the first time. On 19 December Modrow and Kohl met for the first time and started negotiations about a confederation of the two states.

Any chance of the GDR remaining independent was undermined by revelations about the true state of the economy which was far worse than official statistics had suggested. The problem faced by the Modrow government was to prevent the GDR spinning out of control both politically and economically. The Round Table had already recommended on 7 December that elections should take place on 6 May the following year, but after the turn of the year criticism of what the opposition groups considered to be the continuing privileged position of the SED-PDS increased, as well as fears that the government was allowing the Stasi to continue to exist under the guise of the Office for National Security. On 15 January a demonstration organized by Neues Forum invaded the former headquarters of the Stasi in the Normannenstraße in Berlin to try and prevent further incriminating files being destroyed. On the same day Modrow offered the Round Table the task of supervising the dissolution of the secret service. By the end of January Modrow conceded that his government was no longer capable of controlling an orderly path to democracy. On 28 January he gave in to pressure from the Round Table to bring forward the elections to the Volkskammer to 18 March, and two days later he agreed in a meeting with Gorbachev in Moscow to

the unification of Germany, which he presented in a three-stage plan in Berlin on 1 February. Finally, on 5 February Modrow's proposal to the Volkskammer that the government should be broadened to include eight Ministers without Portfolio from opposition groups was accepted, and a 'Government of National Responsibility' was formed.

The rest of February was dominated by the political preparations for the election. On 5 February, the three conservative groups in the GDR, the **CDU**, DSU (German Social Union) and Demokratischer Aufbruch (Democratic Awakening) came together, under pressure from Kohl, to form the Allianz für Deutschland (Alliance for Germany); on 7 February the citizens' groups, Neues Forum, Democracy Now and the Initiative for Peace and Human Rights, formed the Bündnis 90 (Alliance 90); a week later the **Greens** and the Unabhängiger Frauenverband (the Independent Women's Association) agreed on an electoral alliance; and on 11 February the liberal parties, **F.D.P.**, LDPD and the Deutsche Forumspartei (German Forum Party), united in the Bund freier Demokraten (Federation of Free Democrats). The Social Democrat Party (SDP) had already changed its name on 13 January to **SPD** to signal their formal alliance with the West German Social Democrats. In the meantime, Gorbachev agreed on 11 February in a meeting with Kohl and Hans-Dietrich Genscher to German unification and Modrow accepted in a meeting with Kohl on 13 February the necessity for a swift monetary union with West Germany to stave off the possible economic collapse of the GDR and continuing emigration to West Germany. As a result, the speed at which unification should be accomplished, and the conditions under which it should be completed, became the focus of the election. The political grouping which promised the fastest route, the Alliance for Germany, won a surprisingly convincing victory, 48.15 percent of the vote, more than twice its closest rival, the SPD with 21.84 percent. The former communists, now the PDS, only managed to gain 16.33 percent, while Alliance 90, which had been in the forefront of the *Wende*, failed to make any impact with 2.19 percent. The advent of a conservative government, under the CDU leader, Lothar de **Maizière**, completed the political *Wende*, and paved the way for rapid unification within eight months.

See also: unification

Further reading

Abbey, W. (ed.) (1993) *Two into One: Germany 1989–1992. A Bibliography of the Wende*, London: University of London, Institute of Germanic Studies (includes a useful bibliography).

Bundeszentrale für politische Bildung (ed.) (1991) *Die Wende in der DDR*, Berlin: Müller Verlag (useful collection of documents and factual information).

Glaeßner, G.-J. and Wallace, I. (1992) *The German Revolution of 1989: Causes and Consequences*, Oxford: Berg (one of the standard works in English on the *Wende*).

Keithly, D. (1992) *The Collapse of East German Communism: The Year the Wall Came Down*, Westport, CT: Praeger (one of the standard American accounts of the *Wende*).

McFalls, L. (1995) *Communism's Collapse. Democracy's Demise? The Cultural Context and Consequences of the East German Revolution*, London: Macmillan (concentrates on the political background to the *Wende*).

PETER BARKER

Wendehals

The German word for the wryneck, a bird which has the capacity to turn its head 180 degrees, is also used to describe people who are able to adapt quickly to a new situation by changing direction completely. In the context of the GDR, and of post-unification Germany, it has in particular been applied to communists and others who were strongly identified with the regime of the GDR, but who adapted very quickly and opportunistically to the new political and economic environment of a united Germany.

See also: *Wende*

PETER BARKER

Wenders, Wim

b. 14 August 1945, Düsseldorf

Filmmaker and photographer

The most cosmopolitan and self-consciously 'American' director of the **New German Cinema**, whose road movies, genre films and collaborations with Austrian writer Peter **Handke** have earned him an international reputation.

Between 1967 and 1970, whilst studying at the Munich School for Television and Film, he directed a series of experimental short films establishing in miniature the motifs and obsessions which dominate his feature films – atmospheric cityscapes, Hollywood, the American dream, juke boxes and rock'n'roll. *Alabama: 2000 Light Years* (1969), a wonderfully moody mini-gangster-movie with an evocative music soundtrack, introduces his favourite character type – the rootless, lonely and taciturn outsider.

His first feature after graduating was an adaptation of Handke's novel *The Goalie's Fear of the Penalty* (*Die Angst des Tormanns beim Elfmeter*, 1972), a study in social and linguistic alienation, and in 1974 he achieved his breakthrough with one of his most intimate films, *Alice in the Cities* (*Alice in den Städten*), the story of a reserved young German – Rüdiger Vogler as the director's alter ego – who helps a girl find her grandmother in Germany after she is deserted by her mother in New York. Perceptive, witty and beautifully shot in black and white by Wenders's regular cameraman Robby Müller, it offers a revealing portrait of a fatherless generation in search of its identity. This theme is developed in *Kings of the Road* (*Im Lauf der Zeit*, 1975), an improvised road movie tracing the tentative steps towards friendship between two itinerant young men. It provided German cinema with the famous lament 'the Americans have colonized our subconscious'.

Wenders realized his long-cherished desire to escape to Hollywood in 1977. Protracted feuds over the biopic *Hammett* (1982), however, made his seven-year American sojourn a chastening experience, sardonically depicted in *The State of Things* (1981). It ended on a more positive note with a collaboration with Sam Shepherd on *Paris Texas* (1984). Starring Harry Dean Stanton and Nastassja

Kinski, this became one of his most popular films, partly due to an evocative soundtrack by Ry Cooder.

Wenders marked his return to Germany with a further Handke collaboration, *Wings of Desire* (*Der Himmel über Berlin*, 1987), an expansive, lyrical homage to the divided city, its history and the filmmaker's art. Like much of Wenders' subsequent work, including the sequel *Faraway, So Close* (*In weiter Ferne, so nah!*, 1993), it divided the critics: hailed by many as a poetic masterpiece, it also provoked accusations of misogyny and political naïvity. During the 1980s Wenders directed a number of diary films and published a striking book of photographs, rekindling debate as to whether he is an outstanding image-maker rather than a genuine storyteller.

See also: New German Cinema

Further reading

Grafe, F. *et al.* (eds) (1992) *Wim Wenders*, Munich and Vienna: Carl Hanser (a detailed survey with essays, an interview and extensive bibliography).

Kolker, P.K. and Beicken, P. (1993) *The Films of Wim Wenders: Cinema as Vision and Desire*, Cambridge: Cambridge University Press (a substantial and far-reaching biography).

MARTIN BRADY

Wenzel, Hans-Eckardt

b. 31 July 1955, Wittenberg

Poet, singer and clown

Wenzel established his reputation in the cabaret *Karls Enkel* (Karl's Grandchildren) during his years as a student in East Berlin, especially (from 1979 onwards) in joint performance with his close friend Steffen **Mensching**. They launched their popular alternative clown-show *Neues aus der Da Da eR* (News from the GDR/DADA-land) in 1982, regularly updating it until it became *Letztes aus der Da Da eR* (Final News from the GDR/DADA-land) in 1990, which was also made into a film. A first volume of his poems appeared in 1984, his first record-album in 1986.

DENNIS TATE

Weyrauch, Wolfgang

b. 15 October 1904, Königsberg; d. 7 November 1980, Darmstadt

Writer and newspaper editor

Influenced by his war experiences as a soldier and a prisoner in Russia, Weyrauch was an ardent pacifist and a committed humanist. He was a major proponent of experimental literary techniques, and an early member of the **Gruppe 47**; he coined the term **Kahlschlag** in the afterword to his prose anthology *Tausend Gramm* (Thousand Grams) (1949). Interested in radio plays (see also *Hörspiel: FRG*) from their earliest form, he wrote over forty.

MICHAEL RICHARDSON

Wicki, Bernhard

b. 28 October 1919, St Pölten (Austria)

Filmmaker and actor

Wicki trained as an actor in Berlin and Vienna and continued to appear in films after he took up filmmaking in 1958. His first feature, *The Bridge* (*Die Brücke*, 1959), is his most celebrated film: documentary in style, this powerful anti-war drama follows seven boys forced to defend a bridge at the end of WWII. After a short spell in Hollywood, he directed literary adaptations for both cinema and television, including *Das Spinnennetz* (The Spider's Web, 1989) based on the novel by Josef Roth.

See also: film: FRG

MARTIN BRADY

Wiener, Oswald

b. 5 October 1935, Vienna

Writer

Wiener organized the literary cabaret of the **Wiener Gruppe** in 1959; he had been a member of the group since 1953, but denounced his early participation later and destroyed his texts from that period. His collaboration with the Wiener Aktionisten in search of a more radical confrontation with a complacent Austrian audience resulted in temporary political exile in Germany following a tumultuous event at the University of Vienna in 1968. Wiener's 1967 linguistic experiment *die verbesserung von mitteleuropa* (the improvement of central europe) epitomizes his anarchistic demand for both theoretical and practical rupture and points to his ongoing interests in cybernetics, machines and cognitive science.

ANKE FINGER

Wiener Gruppe

Held together by ties of friendship rather than any theoretical programme, the Wiener Gruppe (Vienna Group) – Friedrich Achleitner, H.C. Artmann, Konrad Bayer, Gerhard Rühm and Oswald **Wiener** – emerged in Vienna in the early 1950s from a circle of avant-garde artists known as the 'Art-Club'. The Group's initial title, 'Exil', indicated the writers' view of their relationship to the official cultural scene of post-war Austria. The target of its anarchic activities was what the Vienna Group saw as an ossified cultural tradition and an entrenched provincialism, sustained by the *Restauration* politics of the Second Republic. The Group took its inspiration from those artists and writers whom Hitler had denounced and proscribed as 'degenerate': the German Expressionists, the Dadaists and the poets of surrealism. Extreme individualism and irrational spontaneity were set against both the traditional idea of the *Dichter* as poet-seer and the concept of high culture literature itself. Lacking conventional publishing outlets, the Group's work was disseminated in readings and unpredictable 'happenings' staged in bohemian cafés and small cellar theatres and, occasionally, on the streets of the capital.

The common denominator which links the Group's experimental work to **modernism** lies in its critical attitude to language. Fascinated by the language scepticism expressed at the turn of the century by Hugo von Hofmannsthal and philosophically explored by Ludwig **Wittgenstein**, the Group attempted to deconstruct the ways language shapes perception of the world and thus to reveal the ideological connection between linguistic conformity, as a product of historical determinants, and the social system that it helps to engineer. The hierarchical status of literature in this process was radically undermined by the exploitation of random forms of writing and utterance: puns, pointless (and sometimes tasteless) jokes, the jargon of bureaucracy, aleatory techniques and montage were all employed to reveal unexpectedly rich possibilities of expression which challenged establishment notions of culture and its normative role in society. The Group's primary concern with language as 'raw material', and especially Artmann's and Rühm's experiments with dialect poetry, can be linked to the work of Eugen **Gomringer** in Switzerland and the Noigandres Group in Brazil – an international phenomenon which became known as concrete poetry.

Loss of creative direction, and in the case of Bayer (who committed suicide in 1964) and Wiener, an increasing cultural pessimism, led to the dissolution of the Group in 1964. The Group's productions anticipated the growth of experimental writing in the FRG, especially the work of Helmut **Heißenbüttel**. In Austria, its influence can be detected both in the exuberant imagination of Ernst **Jandl** and the work of younger writers associated with the **Grazer Gruppe**.

See also: literature: Austria

Further reading

Butler, M. (1980) 'From the "Wiener Gruppe" to Ernst Jandl', in A. Best and H. Wolfschütz (eds), *Modern Austrian Writing. Literature and Society after 1945*, London: Oswald Wolff (survey article).

Rühm, G (ed.) (1967) *Die Wiener Gruppe. Achleitner, Artmann, Bayer, Rühm, Wiener. Texte, Gemeinschafts-*

arbeiten, Aktionen, Reinbek bei Hamburg: Rowohlt (brief history of the Group and representative selection of texts).

MICHAEL BUTLER

Wiener Zeitung

The *Wiener Zeitung*, the oldest Viennese daily paper and one of the oldest in the world, was first founded in 1703 as *Wiennerisches Diarium*, and sold to the state in 1857, gaining its present name in 1870. Under the Nazi regime (1938–45) it was banned for political reasons. Re-established in 1945, it is still owned by the Federal Republic of Austria. Apart from the usual reporting, official legal and administrative announcements, classified advertisements, and other official news are published in the main section of the paper as well as in a special supplement (the *Amtsblatt*). The government, however, does not interfere with editorial matters. With a print run of about 17,000 copies (1998) it is one of the smallest, but also one of the most respected papers in the country.

GEORG HELLMAYR

Wiens, Paul

b. 17 August 1922, Königsberg; d. 6 April 1982, (East) Berlin

Poet

Wiens began his career with poetry in the style of **socialist realism**, but his criticism of the Soviet Union in his 1958 volume entitled *Nachrichten aus der dritten Welt* (News from the Third World) stirred intense controversy. In the 1960s, he became a leading spokesmen for those authors in the GDR who believed in the social and cultural superiority of the socialist system, yet hoped for liberal reforms. Perhaps best known for his 1966 collection *Die neuen Harfenlieder von Oswald von Wolkenstein* (The New Songs for the Harp of Oswald von Wolkenstein), his lyrics are often witty and urbane but not especially passionate.

Further reading

Sax. B. (1987). *The Romantic Heritage of Marxism: A Study of East German Love Poetry*, New York: Peter Lang (contains a chapter on the poetry of Wiens and his relations with GDR cultural authorities).

BORIA SAX

Wiesenthal, Simon

b. 31 December 1908, Buchach (Galicia, now Ukraine)

Nazi-hunter

Captured by Nazis in 1941, Wiesenthal survived forced labour and concentration camps to become the world's most famous 'Nazi-hunter'. He chose not to return to architectural engineering, instead dedicating his life to tracking down those responsible for the 'final solution', the subject of his many successful books. He opened the Jewish Documentation Centre in Vienna in 1961, amid much publicity over his role in the capture of Adolf **Eichmann**. Subsequent revelations that he exaggerated his role in Eichmann's capture have damaged his reputation in Israel, but it remains untarnished in Germany, Austria and the United States (where a **Holocaust** Centre bears his name).

JOEL S.A. HAYWARD

Wilder, Billy

b. 22 June 1906, Vienna

Director, screenwriter and producer (real name Samuel Wilder)

Wilder studied law, then worked as a tabloid journalist in Vienna. Between 1929 and 1933 he wrote screenplays for notable German films in which he began to develop tightly woven, intricate narrative structures marked by incredible reversals, paradoxes and inversions that would characterize his best American work. He apprenticed under Ernst Lubitsch. Wilder directed *Emil und die Detektive* (1931), which utilized city streets as a psychological labyrinth and prefigured his complex use of physical settings in later films. In 1933 he became part of the large émigré influx to Hollywood. He received the Lifetime Achievement Award at the European Film Prize Ceremony in **Babelsberg** in 1992.

UTE LISCHKE-McNAB

wine

By the end of WWII, German vineyards were in a state of disrepair, with only a fraction of the total acres planted able to be harvested. Part of the disrepair stemmed from bombing and the lack of a labour force. Nevertheless, other factors contributed to the devastated wine trade of 1945. For example, by 1933, Nazi laws prohibited German Jewish wine merchants from doing business. Families who had specialized in wine trading for years, like the Loebs, the Sichels and the Hallgartens, all found themselves without recourse but to flee to Britain and the United States. Furthermore, the historic conflict over whether German land should be devoted to food production or to wine led easily to the Nazis' suggestion that cultivating wine was synonymous with the decadence of the aristocracy at the expense of the German *Volk*. This cultural conflict was exploited by the Nazi Reich Food Estate which reimagined the wine industry as an enterprise of 'the corrupt Jewish merchant'. In 1934, the Reich instituted legislation that prohibited new vineyard sites from being designated so that destroyed vineyards could not be replaced if the land was suitable for the production of corn. In this way, Nazi stewardship destroyed the wine industry, and by the war's end German winemaking desperately needed rehabilitation.

When Germans returned to making wine in 1950, they found themselves without a lot of the necessary elements for wine production. Britain, a perennial consumer of German *Hock*, as well as the American occupying forces, presented a potential market that encouraged winemakers and merchants to jumpstart the trade with an affordable product that could tap into the nostalgia for German wine prior to the war. They did not have to look far for a solution: since 1844, a generic table wine called *Liebfraumilch* had been reproduced cheaply from grapes harvested in northern Germany and Italy. The generic quality of the grapes and various methods of chaptalization allowed German winemakers to claim it as 'German table wine' without the amount of labour normally required. *Liebfraumilch* could thus be mass produced cheaply and marketed abroad successfully.

The necessary ingredient for making 'the new wine' became the varietal *Müller-Thurgau*, which replaced *Riesling* as the primary grape in the mass production of German wine because it yielded more grapes per acre and ripened several weeks earlier than the labour-intensive *Riesling*. In this way, *Müller-Thurgau* became known as the varietal of the **Economic Miracle** and the dominant grape in the making of *Liebfraumilch*.

By coming as it did at the historical crossroads between foreign occupation in Germany and a depressed wine industry, the popularity of *Liebfraumilch* helped to renew interest in German wines as a commodity. The sweeter table wines tended to be consumed outside of Germany because they came with an immediately recognizable and familiar taste: they were crafted to appeal to an Anglo-American market. Moreover, although *Liebfraumilch* is a key example, many others have reproduced other historic German wines, like *Piesporters* and *Niersteiners*, in similar ways. In fact, many consumers still believe 'the new German wines' to be indicative of – or at least related to – their vinological predecessors. Thus the transformation of *Liebfraumilch* is critical to understanding how a popular cultural narrative effected a reimagining of German wine history. Although the predecessor of the modern *Liebfraumilch*, *Liebfrauenmilch* of Worms, was known as an expensive cellaring wine and ultimately the property of the connoisseur, modern *Liebfraumilch* could be cheaply reproduced and could be owned by anyone willing to enter a supermarket. The case of the modern *Liebfraumilch* illustrates, furthermore, how the image and connotations of the modern wine's historic antecedent were cheaply copied and then deployed as 'the wine of the new Germany'.

Yet the cultural difference in the perception of these wines also suggests a conflict over the nature of wine: is it created for mass consumption or for the educated palate's appreciation? German winemakers themselves would answer yes to both queries. In fact, German wine categories reflect this tension over the cultural significance of wine, which derives from the initial conflict when wine was perceived as competing against agricultural crops. The problem of defining wine's status either as an object of consumerism or as an object requiring an educated palate is thus at the heart of understanding its cultural significance.

The four levels of quality for German wine, table wine (*Tafelwein*), regional wine (*Landwein*), quality wine from a specific growing region (*Qualitätswein eines bestimmten Anbaugebietes*), and quality wine with specific predicates or attributes (*Qualitätswein mit Prädikat*), represent as much how wine is perceived in German culture as how it is used by consumers. On the one hand, at the table wine and QbA levels, German wine does not warrant any recognition whatever of its structure or complexities. As a result, the wine's quality is really one-dimensional and often appears to be overly sweet. On the other hand, QmPs are the highest division in the categories of German wine and represent the greatest aesthetic achievements in German winemaking. The predicates are designated as *Kabinett, Spätlese, Auslese, Beerenauslese* and *Trockenbeerenauslese*. Although these categories existed historically in Germany, they were codified according to various stipulations of the highly complex 1971 Wine Legislation, with which German winemaking was co-ordinated as an industry rather than an inconsistent and haphazard field of production, so that some guarantee of quality could be offered both to the consumer and to the connoisseur.

For climatic reasons, wine-growing in Germany is confined largely to the southwestern and west-central parts of the country, which is where the eleven designated growing regions (*Anbaugebiete*) are found. These are the areas in which the consumption of wine (as opposed to **beer**) plays an important role in local culture. Frequently drunk on their own, rather than as an accompaniment to meals, German wines are predominantly white, the country's red wines accounting for only some 12 percent of overall production.

Wine in Austria

Austria's wine trade remains unknown for the large part in Anglo-American cultures because most of its small export production goes to Germany. However, Austria has always made fine wine: the first *Trockenbeerenauslese* was produced there in 1526. The wine culture in Austria is often seen in smaller villages where 'cellar houses' line the streets or in the taverns (*Heurige*) where winemakers sell their wines. Austria's main winemaking regions are the Burgenland, Lower Austria, Styria and the Vienna area.

Wine in Switzerland

Switzerland has four winemaking regions: Valais, East Switzerland, West Switzerland and the Ticino. The country's many microclimates permit winemakers to experiment with many kinds of red and white wine varietals.

Further reading

Hallgarten, S.F. (1981) *German Wines*, London: Publivin London.

Jamison, I. (1991) *German Wine*, London: Faber & Faber.

Jamison, I. and Johnson, H. (1986) *The Atlas of German Wines*, New York: Simon & Schuster.

Pigott, S. (1988) *Life Beyond Liebfraumilch*, London: Sidgwick & Jackson.

KITTY MILLET

Winkler, Angela

b. 22 January 1944, Templin (Brandenburg)

Actress

Winkler featured as a young star in Peter **Fleischmann**'s *Hunting Scenes From Lower Bavaria* (*Jagdszenen aus Niederbayern*, 1969) and was engaged by Peter **Stein** at the Berlin Schaubühne. She achieved international fame as Katharina **Blum** in the film by Volker **Schlöndorff** and Margarethe von **Trotta**, in which her frozen vulnerability betrays psychological anguish as she falters between passive self-restraint and passionate revolt. Principal roles in Schlöndorff's *The Tin Drum* (*Die Blechtrommel*, 1979) and von Trotta's *Friends and*

Husbands (*Heller Wahn*, 1982) confirmed her reputation for personifying quietly frenzied women.

See also: New German Cinema

HELEN HUGHES

Winter, Fritz

b. 22 September 1905, Altenbögge
  (Westphalia); d. 1 October 1976,
  Herrsching am Ammersee

Painter

A leading representative of post-war abstract art in West Germany, Winter is noted for the fact that both Nazi censorship and service in WWII did not significantly interrupt his artistic development. He deviated from the expressive and individualistic aims of much post-war abstraction; his art was instead founded on a meditative approach and strict conceptual ideas by which he hoped to convey a universal spirituality. Winter thus shared an idealistic belief in cosmic harmony with the artists of German romanticism and the Blue Rider group.

ALEX COOKE

Witt, Katarina

b. 3 December 1965, Staaken

Ice-skater

Witt started ice-skating at the age of five and was a victor at the children's and youth Spartakiad in 1975. Hailed as 'the beautiful face of communism', she enjoyed a high profile as one of the GDR's top sports 'ambassadors'. She was the Olympic gold medallist in figure-skating in 1984 and 1988 as well as world champion in 1984 and 1985. She turned professional in 1990. After her reinstatement as an amateur she was able to participate in the 1994 Olympics.

MIKE DENNIS

Wittgenstein, Ludwig

b. 26 April 1889, Vienna; d. 29 April
  1951, Cambridge

Philosopher

Ludwig Josef Johann Wittgenstein was the youngest of eight children born into one of the wealthiest families in Austria. The Wittgensteins, although prominent members of Viennese society, were not related to the German aristocratic family, the Seyn-Wittgensteins. Ludwig's paternal great grandfather, Moses Maier, adopted the Wittgenstein name after the Napoleonic decree of 1808 requiring Jews to adopt a surname.

Ludwig Wittgenstein came of age in *fin de siècle* Vienna. The Wittgenstein family entertained prominent Viennese intellectuals and artists at their family home in the Alleegasse. Johannes Brahms, Gustav Mahler, and Bruno Walter attended concerts at their home.

Wittgenstein's early education was guided by his older sister Margarete who introduced him to the writings of Karl Kraus, the editor of *Die Fackel*, and Otto Weininger, the author of the influential book entitled *Sex and Character*. After studying at Linz, Wittgenstein pursued mechanical engineering at the Technische Hochschule in Berlin. He left Germany to study in England where he earned his Ph.D. from Cambridge in 1929.

Wittgenstein's philosophical career is divided into two phases. His early period was influenced by the British mathematicians and philosophers A.N. Whitehead and Bertrand Russell. He also studied the *Grundgesetze der Arithmetik* by the German mathematician Gottlob Frege. Wittgenstein's *Tractatus Logico-Philosophicus* (1922) is indebted to the work of these men. The scientific implications of his early philosophical writings were recognized by the Vienna Circle.

The latter phase of Wittgenstein's philosophical thought departs from his earlier work. In the *Philosophical Investigations* (1953), it is the use of language in a social context that receives much attention. The meaning of words, for Wittgenstein, is determined by their use in a specific linguistic and social dynamic.

Many scholars consider Wittgenstein to be one of the greatest philosophical minds of the twentieth century. His legacy to German culture has been profound. With the recent emergence of **postmodernism** as a central philosophical and cultural concern, Wittgenstein's writings have achieved a renewed importance in academic circles. Contemporary continental philosophers view Wittgenstein's later philosophy as prefiguring postmodernism's focus on meaning and language within the social sphere. Many of the contributions made by postmodern studies were also prefigured by Wittgenstein's writings. During his final years, he wrote on a wide range of topics: colours, epistemology and culture. It is because of his understanding of the social dimension of language that Wittgenstein has become a central figure in contemporary continental philosophy.

While there is a renewed interest among academics in his philosophical writings, Wittgenstein was never comfortable with academia. He resigned his prestigious Professorship at Trinity College, Cambridge in 1947. He died of prostate cancer in Cambridge on 29 April 1951.

Further reading

Fann, K.T. (ed.) (1967) *Ludwig Wittgenstein: The Man and His Philosophy*, New York: Harvester.

Monk, R. (1990) *Ludwig Wittgenstein: The Duty of Genius*, New York: Macmillan.

Rhees, R. (1970) *Discussions of Wittgenstein*, London: Routledge.

VICTOR E. TAYLOR

Woche, Die

Established in 1993 by Hamburg publisher Thomas Ganske, the weekly *Die Woche* was conceived as a modern competitor to *Die* **Zeit**. At about 25 percent of *Die Zeit*'s page count, it is perhaps the most obvious example of a strong trend in modern newspapers to replace words by images, charts, diagrams and so on, in an attempt to fight the success of television by copying its means. With a circulation of 116,000 it seems doubtful whether this concept has succeeded in the case of *Die Woche*, in which the **Burda** group has had a 25 percent stake since 1995.

See also: journalism; newspapers

ROLF JUCKER

Wohmann, Gabriele

b. 21 May 1932, Darmstadt

Writer and critic

Author of short stories, novels and radio and television scripts, Wohmann is known for her critiques of West German society.

The daughter of a vicar, Wohmann began writing early and was one of the first members of the **Gruppe 47**. Her first stories, *Mit einem Messer* (With a Knife) (1958) convey cool glimpses of bourgeois life in West Germany and show some affinity with the style of Virginia Woolf and Katherine Mansfield. *Die Bütows* (The Bütows) (1967) contains a laconic and merciless portrayal of the fascist mentality; the world of children, deformed and terrorized by that of the adults, is described in *Ländliches Fest* (Country Idyll) (1968). Sometimes her work was misunderstood, as in *Paulinchen war allein zu Haus* (Little Pauline was Alone at Home) (1974), which contains satirical texts, and not, as some believed, an attack on progressive methods of upbringing. Wohmann was criticizing the extreme swing from reactionary behaviour to excessively 'free' attitudes in West Germany in the 1960s. Conflict between children and their parents is a central theme in her work. *Abschied für länger* (Leave-taking) (1965) portrays a woman's failure to leave her family. The novel *Ernste Absicht* (Serious Intention) (1970) examines, in language that is sometimes deliberately shocking, the failure of human relationships. The radio and television plays of the early 1970s deal with emotional deprivation, but in the mid-1970s her novel *Schönes Gehege* (Beautiful Cage) (1975) indicates a formal and thematic shift, a change in tempo. Within the biting criticism there is also a search for little pockets of happiness. *Ausflug mit der Mutter* (Outing with Mother) (1976) describes the wearisome struggle out of a failed mother–daughter relationship. *Frühherbst in Badenweiler* (Early Autumn in Badenweiler) (1978) is more realistic and contains more of Wohmann herself. It describes an individual's search for freedom. Strong sympathy for social problems is evident in the volume of poetry *Grund zur Aufregung* (Reason to be Upset) (1978), and the stories in *Paarlauf* (Couples) (1979) again treat problems in marriage but in more detail. In *Ach wie gut, daß niemand weiß* (What a Good Thing Nobody Knows) (1980) we see the cracks in the façade of middle-class prosperity: a psychologist has to face his own problems. *Das Glücksspiel* (The Gamble) (1981) features the neurosis of a piano teacher.

In 1981 Wohmann published seven novels, with five different publishers. She admitted to being obsessed with writing. She attempted all literary forms, even a play, although she does not think women are good at theatre. *Wanda Lords Gespenster* (Wanda Lord's Ghosts) (1980) was adapted from a radio play. She toured the country giving readings. She had become a kind of literary diva. Three more volumes of stories followed, depicting emotional deprivation amongst the middle classes: *Einsamkeit* (Loneliness) (1982), *Der kürzeste Tag des Jahres* (The Shortest Day of the Year) (1983) and *Der Irrgast* (The Wrong Guest) (1985). Like Christa **Wolf**, Wohmann produced a literary reaction to the Chernobyl disaster of 1986 in her novel *Der Flötenton* (The Sound of the Flute) (1987).

MARGARET VALLANCE

Wolf, Christa

b. 18 March 1929, Landsberg an der Warthe (now Gorzów, Poland)

Writer

The best known German woman writer of the twentieth century, certainly among English-language readers, Christa Wolf has been honoured with most of the major literary awards in both East and West Germany. Born to a middle-class family – her father was a grocer – in Landsberg an der Warthe, now Gorzów, Poland, she and her family were among the millions who fled west before the advancing Red Army in 1945. Wolf studied German literature at the universities of Jena and Leipzig, and her training is reflected in perceptive essays on authors such as the romantic writers

Bettina von Arnim and Karoline von Günderrode, as well as contemporaries she particularly admired, especially Anna **Seghers**, Ingeborg **Bachmann**, Max **Frisch**, and Maxie **Wander**. Upon completion of her studies in 1953 she was a researcher for the **Writers' Union of the GDR** and held various editorial positions in East Berlin publishing houses. While freelancing as an editor in Halle, where she lived from 1959 to 1962, Wolf also worked in a railway carriage factory, an experience mandated by the '*Bitterfelder Weg*' programme that charged intellectuals to involve themselves with the world of production and labour. After her first literary publication, *Moskauer Novelle* (Moscow Novella) (1961), a politically conformist text that she subsequently disavowed, won the literary prize of the city of Halle, Wolf returned to Berlin and embarked upon a full-time career as a writer, including occasional collaboration with the critic Gerhard Wolf, whom she had married in 1951.

Wolf's 1963 novel *Divided Heaven* (*Der geteilte Himmel*), for which she won the Heinrich Mann Prize of the GDR Academy of Arts and the National Prize for Art and Literature, reflects the Bitterfeld mandate in its depiction of a teacher trainee who spends her required period of practical experience in a train carriage factory. But, unlike most propagandistic factory novels (*Betriebsromane*) of the period, it is related from the young woman's perspective as she recovers in a sanatorium from an accident, possibly a suicide attempt, after the building of the Berlin Wall separates her permanently from her lover, who had fled to West Berlin out of frustrated scientific and personal ambition. Wolf also became a candidate member of the Central Committee of the **SED** in 1963, a status that was terminated in 1967 after she spoke out critically about cultural policy at the **Eleventh Plenum** in 1965. This was not the last time that her convictions would bring her into conflict with the party, despite her firm commitment to socialism over capitalism, a commitment that led her to oppose the movement towards German unification in 1989. Wolf's reaction to unification can be traced in the essays and speeches published in 1994 in *Parting from Phantoms* (*Auf dem Weg nach Tabou*). From 1955 until her protest against the **Biermann Affair** of 1976, Wolf was also a member of the executive committee of the Writers' Union of the

GDR. She thematized the harassment and surveillance to which a writer who thus challenged the state was subjected in a 1979 text, *What Remains* (*Was bleibt*), published (with some modifications) only after the end of the GDR. The delay resulted in a heated public debate, the so-called ***Literaturstreit***, about the writer and her loyalty to the state, a debate that was further fired by Wolf's belated admission that she served as a **Stasi** informer for a brief period between 1959 and 1962.

The Quest for Christa T. (*Nachdenken über Christa T.*), which appeared in a limited edition in 1968, marks a turning point in the GDR literary history, not only because of its rejection of the well-constructed fiction of **socialist realism** but also because of the intensely personal way in which the broken ideals of the past are confronted in the attempt to come to terms with the death of a young woman from leukemia or, as the text seems to suggest, alienation. The narrative principle of 'subjective authenticity' introduced in this novel was elaborated in Wolf's 'Selbstinterview' ('Interview with Myself') in her important first volume of essays, *The Reader and the Writer* (*Lesen und Schreiben*, 1972). The autobiographical dimension of this novel, set in the period from the end of the war to the narrator's present, is also evident in *Patterns of Childhood* (*Kindheitsmuster*, 1976), which explores the question of 'how we have become what we are today' by reconstructing the formative influence of a childhood under National Socialism. The autobiographical thread can also be traced in two shorter texts, *Accident/A Day's News* (*Störfall: Nachrichten eines Tages*), which exposes the simultaneous threat and promise of technology by juxtaposing radio reports of the Chernobyl nuclear disaster with the narrator's anxious telephoning about the progress of her brother's brain surgery, and *Sommerstück* (Summer Play) (1989), focused around an idyllic summer, their last together, spent by a group of friends in a Mecklenburg village outside Berlin.

Wolf has also reworked historical and mythological material in her fiction and often elucidated her concerns in related essays. This was the case, for example, in *No Place on Earth* (*Kein Ort. Nirgends.*) where a fictional encounter between the German romantic writers Heinrich von Kleist and Karoline von Günderrode becomes the device for reflecting upon troubled relationships between writers and society. *Cassandra* (*Kassandra*) and *Medea: A Modern Retelling* (*Medea Stimmen*) reach back to Greek mythology, the former employing the Cassandra legend to connect the terror of (nuclear) war with masculine aggression. *Cassandra* was published together with Wolf's lectures as holder of the prestigious Frankfurt University Chair in Poetics, where she elaborated her attempt to derive a 'feminine aesthetic' from female experience. *Medea* rewrites the encounter of that much maligned daughter of the king of Colchis, in the east, with Jason, the leader of the western Argonauts, depicting her as a victim of patriarchal violence, including the murder of her children. The novel, told from multiple narrative perspectives, has been read as Wolf's attempt to write in the 'new voice', appropriate to her new situation in unified Germany, towards which her controversial work *Was bleibt* seemed to be groping.

Major works

Wolf, C. (1961) *Moskauer Novelle*, Halle: Mitteldeutscher Verlag.
—— (1963) *Der geteilte Himmel*, Halle: Mitteldeutscher Verlag; trans. J. Becker, *Divided Heaven*, Berlin: Seven Seas, 1965.
—— (1968) *Nachdenken über Christa T.*, Halle: Mitteldeutscher Verlag; trans. C. Middleton, *The Quest for Christa T.*, New York: Farrar, Straus & Giroux, 1970.
—— (1972) *Lesen und Schreiben: Aufsätze und Betrachtungen*, Berlin: Aufbau; trans. J. Becker, *The Reader and the Writer: Essays, Sketches, Memories*, Berlin: Seven Seas, 1977.
—— (1972) *Till Eulenspiegel* (with Gerhard Wolf), Berlin: Aufbau.
—— (1974) *Unter den Linden: Drei unwahrscheinliche Geschichten*, Berlin: Aufbau.
—— (1976) *Kindheitsmuster*, Berlin: Aufbau; trans. U. Molinaro and H. Rappolt, *Patterns of Childhood*, New York: Farrar, Straus & Giroux, 1984.
—— (1979) *Fortgesetzter Versuch: Aufsätze, Gespräche, Essays*, Leipzig: Reclam.
—— (1979) *Kein Ort. Nirgends*, Berlin: Aufbau; trans. J. van Heurck, *No Place on Earth*, New York: Farrar, Straus & Giroux, 1982.
—— (1983) *Kassandra: Vier Vorlesungen und eine*

Erzählung, Berlin: Aufbau; trans. J. van Heurck, *Cassandra: A Novel and Four Essays*, New York: Farrar, Straus & Giroux, 1984.

—— (1986) *Die Dimension des Autors: Essays und Aufsätze, Reden und Gespräche 1959–1985*, Berlin: Aufbau; trans. H. Pilkington, *The Fourth Dimension: Interviews with Christa Wolf*, London: Verso, 1988; trans. J. van Heurck, *The Author's Dimension. Selected Essays*, ed. A. Stephan, New York: Farrar, Straus & Giroux, 1993.

—— (1987) *Störfall: Nachrichten eines Tages*, Berlin: Aufbau; trans. H. Schwarzbauer and R. Takvorian, *Accident/A Day's News*, New York: Farrar, Straus & Giroux, 1988.

—— (1989) *Sommerstück*, Berlin: Aufbau.

—— (1990) *Reden im Herbst*, Darmstadt and Neuwied: Luchterhand.

—— (1990) *Was bleibt*, Frankfurt am Main: Luchterhand; trans. H. Schwarzbauer and R. Takvorian, *What Remains and Other Stories*, New York: Farrar, Straus & Giroux, 1993.

—— (1994) *Auf dem Weg nach Tabou: Texte 1990–1994*, Cologne: Kiepenheuer & Witsch; trans. J. van Heurck, *Parting from Phantoms: Selected Writings 1990–1994*, Chicago, IL: University of Chicago Press, 1997.

—— (1996) *Medea: Stimmen*, Munich: Luchterhand.

—— and Wolf, G. (1985) *Ins Ungebundene gehet eine Sehnsucht: Gesprächsraum Romantik*, Berlin: Aufbau.

Further reading

Fries, M.S. (ed.) (1989) *Responses to Christa Wolf: Critical Essays*, Detroit, IL: Wayne State University Press.

Kuhn, A.K. (1988) *Christa Wolf's Utopian Vision: From Marxism to Feminism*, New York: Cambridge University Press.

Wallace, I. (ed.) (1994) *Christa Wolf in Perspective*, German Monitor 30, Amsterdam: Rodopi.

PATRICIA HERMINGHOUSE

Wolf, Konrad

b. 20 October 1925, Hechingen (Württemberg); d. 7 March 1982, (East) Berlin

Filmmaker

Internationally the most renowned GDR film director, Wolf's family background and personal development assured him the respect of the country's political establishment, his creative professionalism and personal integrity that of the film industry. As President of the East German Academy of Arts (since 1965) he appears to have been torn between his personal, liberal-humanist perception of the arts and the obligation to support official policies in the interest of party discipline. His death, shortly after his election to the Central Committee of the **SED** in 1981, was a blow for many who believed in the possibility of reforming doctrinaire socialism as practised in the GDR.

He was the son of the dramatist and writer Friedrich Wolf, a general practitioner of Jewish descent and a committed communist, who emigrated to Russia in 1934. Educated in Moscow at German and Russian schools, Wolf became a Soviet citizen in 1936. He joined the Red Army as a volunteer in 1942. Fighting against Nazi Germany, he received a number of decorations and rose to the rank of lieutenant. After the War, he worked as a journalist in the Soviet zone, enrolled at the Moscow Film Academy (1949), and was assistant to Joris Ivens and Kurt **Maetzig** before making his debut with the musical comedy *Einmal ist keinmal* (*Once Won't Hurt*) (1955). Wolf became a GDR citizen in 1952. The Babelsberg Film and Television Academy was named after him in 1985 in recognition of his achievements. He was the brother of Markus **Wolf**.

The subjects of Wolf's films are intricately linked with his biography. *Convalescence* (*Genesung*, 1955), *Lissy* (1957), *Stars* (*Sterne*, 1957), *People With Wings* (*Leute mit Flügeln*, 1960) and *Professor Mamlock* (1961, based on a play by his father) are anti-fascist films dealing with anti-Semitism, the rise of and resistance to National Socialism, and ***Vergangenheitsbewältigung***. *I Was Nineteen* (*Ich war neunzehn*, 1967, based on his diaries as a Russian soldier fighting against Germany) and *Mum, I'm Alive* (*Mama, ich lebe*, 1976, about

German PoWs who join the Russians in their fight against National Socialism) analyse German–Russian relationships and address questions of personal identity. Criticism by young people that these films only deal with problems of the past caused Wolf to make *Solo Sunny* (1979; script: Wolfgang **Kohlhaase**), his most popular film. Following the tradition of the 'Berlin Films', it relates the struggle of a pop singer to assert her individuality against pressures to conform to socialist society. Criticism levelled against *The Divided Heaven* (*Der geteilte Himmel*, 1964, based on Christa **Wolf**'s novel) and experiences with state interference and censorship while making *Sunseekers* (*Sonnensucher*, 1958, about the difficulties of building socialism in the GDR; shelved until 1972) inspired two films about the role of the artist in society. *Goya* (1971, a monumental two-part study of the Spanish painter) analyses the relationship between the artist and the ruling powers in an historical context, *The Naked Man on the Sportsground* (*Der nackte Mann auf dem Sportplatz*, 1973, a subtle comedy about a sculptor asked to design a statue for a football team) in a contemporary context.

See also: film: GDR

Further reading

Herlinghaus, H. (ed.) (1982) *Konrad Wolf. Sag' dein Wort! Dokumentation – eine Auswahl*, Potsdam-Babelsberg: Betriebsakademie des VEB DEFA-Studios (comprehensive collection of interviews with and articles by Wolf, relating to his life, films, cultural policies and GDR film).

HORST CLAUS

Wolf, Markus ('Mischa')

b. 19 January 1923, Hechingen (Württemberg)

Journalist and GDR functionary

The son of the communist writer, Friedrich Wolf, Markus returned from emigration in the Soviet Union in May 1945 and worked initially in Berlin as a radio journalist. From 1951 he worked in the Ministry for State Security of the GDR (**Stasi**) and was from 1958 to 1987 head of the *Hauptverwaltung*

Aufklärung (external espionage) and a Deputy Minister for State Security. He left the ministry 'at his own wish' in March 1987, and during the political changes in 1989 and 1990 attempted, without success, to enter the political arena as a reform communist. In 1993 he was sentenced to six years' imprisonment for treason, but the sentence was quashed in 1995.

PETER BARKER

Wollenberger, Vera

b. 4 May 1952, Sondershausen (Thuringia)

Political activist (née Lengsfeld)

A student of philosophy in the GDR in the 1970s, Wollenberger was expelled from the SED in 1983 because of her involvement in protests against the stationing of atomic weapons in the GDR. She was a founder member of the 'Church from Below' and active in several opposition groups in the 1980s. In January 1988 she was arrested at the official Rosa Luxemburg demonstration for displaying an unofficial banner and forced to leave the GDR. She returned in November 1989 and became a speaker for the Green party. In December 1990 she was elected to the Bundestag for Alliance 90/Greens and re-elected in October 1994. In December 1996 she left the Greens for the CDU because she feared that the Greens were prepared to cooperate with the **PDS**. Since the widely-publicized discovery that her husband Knud had been spying on her for the **Stasi**, she has divorced and is now known by her maiden name of Lengsfeld. In December 1996 she left the Greens for the CDU because she feared that the Greens were prepared to cooperate with the **PDS**.

See also: citizens' movements: GDR

PETER BARKER

Wollschläger, Hans

b. 17 March 1935, Minden

Writer and translator

Wollschläger is best known for his translation of

James Joyce's *Ulysses* (1975). He also translated Chandler, Hammett, Faulkner, Twain, Baldwin, and, in collaboration with his mentor Arno **Schmidt**, Poe. Wollschläger and Hermann Wiedenroth edited the critical edition of Karl May's collected works; he has long been active in the Karl May Society. He published one novel, *Herzgewächse* (Heart Growths) (1982), and many essays. Wollschläger knows twelve languages, has a degree in music, performs as an organ player, and works in psychoanalysis.

Further reading

Schweikert, R. (1995) *Hans Wollschläger*, Eggingen: Isele.

SABINE SCHMIDT

Womacka, Walter

b. 22 December 1925, Obergeorgenthal (Horní Jiřetín, Czechoslovakia)

Painter and graphic artist

The subjects of Womacka's figurative paintings and a number of his murals are closely related to the doctrines of **socialist realism**. Hence the depiction of workers, farmers and the production process in an uncritically optimistic manner. As Director of the Art school in Berlin-Weißensee from 1968 to 1990, and as long-standing Vice-President of the Artists' Association he had considerable influence on the realization of cultural policy in the visual arts of the GDR.

See also: cultural policy: GDR; painting

KERSTIN MEY

Wondratschek, Wolf

b. 14 August 1943, Rudolstadt (Thüringen)

Writer

Wondratschek began his writing career in 1967 by publishing poetry and short prose pieces. A successful writer of radio plays, he continues to

publish in journals and anthologies. He also writes film scripts and has worked on film, most notably with Werner **Schroeter** (Director) on *Im dunklen Herz des Nachmittags* (In the Dark Heart of the Afternoon) (1976) and Dieter Schidor (Director) on *Der Bauer von Babylon – Rainer Werner Fassbinder dreht 'Querelle'* (The Farmer from Babylon – Rainer Werner Fassbinder shoots *Querelle*) in 1982. Wondratschek lives in Munich and Hamburg and travels widely.

UTE LISCHKE-McNAB

Wortmann, Sönke

b. 25 August 1959, Marl

Filmmaker

Wortmann became Germany's most prominent director of popular films in the early 1990s, making a series of romantic comedies exploring the contemporary insecurities of young heterosexual males. In both his debut feature *Allein unter Frauen* (Alone Among Women) (1991) and his most commercially successful film *The Most Desired Man* (*Der bewegte Mann*, 1994), poverty, unemployment and homelessness necessitate humiliating flat-sharing arrangements for the macho protagonists (respectively, in a women's commune and with a gay man).

JONATHAN LEGG

Wotruba, Fritz

b. 23 April 1907, Vienna; d. 28 August 1975, Vienna

Sculptor

Wotruba's early work is situated within the European tradition of realistic sculpture. With maturity it developed a proximity to both archaic stylization and architecture. The human form was radically reduced to a sum of square stone blocks, yet the massive and static sculptural ensembles maintained rich anthropomorphic associations. His œuvre covers reliefs, statues and public monuments. He also worked extensively as a stage designer for the theatre.

Today he is regarded as one of the most important sculptors of the twentieth century.

See also: Hrdlicka, Alfred; sculpture

KERSTIN MEY

writers' congresses: GDR

The congresses of the **Writers' Union** were important events in the GDR, indicating trends in cultural policy and fluctuations in the relationship between authors and the SED leadership (see also **cultural policy: GDR**). Their agenda normally included keynote speeches by representatives of the Union's central executive, less formal workshop discussions, and the election of the new executive. The extent to which open debates occurred (and were published in the official protocol of each congress) was always taken as a yardstick of cultural vitality.

Ten congresses were held in the GDR's lifetime, if we include (as the Writers' Union did) the all-German congress of October 1947, organized by the **Kulturbund** and dominated by Cold War antagonisms, as the first. Despite the Union's claims that it was continuing to represent the interests of all German writers, the Second and Third Congresses, held in July 1950 and May 1952 respectively, were grimly parochial events, reflecting the SED's attempt to impose control over the newly created Writers' Union. The political context had changed decisively by the time the Fourth Congress took place, in January 1956: the eastern European process of liberalization known as the 'thaw' produced an unlikely alliance of writers and theorists (**Becher**, **Seghers**, **Brecht**, and the Hungarian guest-of-honour **Lukács**) supporting a radical break from the dogma of **socialist realism**. And even though their hopes had been frustrated by the repressive measures taken by the SED after the Hungarian uprising in the autumn of 1956, there were signs of renewed self-confidence when the Fifth Congress was held, in May 1961, with the rising star of West German literature, Günter **Grass**, as an outspoken invited guest.

The long gap before the Sixth Congress, in May 1969, was caused both by the general crisis following the building of the Berlin Wall and the specifically cultural aftermath of the **Eleventh Plenum** of 1965. The unresolved tensions were glaringly evident at that congress in the form of the attacks on Christa **Wolf**, whose novel *Christa T.* had just been published. The Seventh Congress, in November 1973, was a total contrast, the high point of writers' assertions of their autonomy as responsible socialists, in the wake of **Honecker**'s promise of 'no taboos', with Franz **Fühmann** and Volker **Braun** setting the tone. The pendulum had swung back again by May 1978, with the Eighth Congress marked by the absence of the key figures of 1973, who had subsequently become embroiled in the **Biermann Affair**. Neither on this occasion nor at the next congress, in June 1983, could the verbal acrobatics of the new president, Hermann **Kant**, conceal the mood of growing alienation. At the Tenth Congress, in November 1987, forthright attacks by Günter de **Bruyn** and Christoph **Hein** on censorship were tolerated, but produced only limited progress before the GDR finally collapsed.

Further reading

Jäger, M. (1995), *Kultur und Politik in der DDR*, Cologne: Verlag Wissenschaft und Politik (provides excerpts from congress speeches as part of a broader documentary history of GDR culture).

DENNIS TATE

Writers' Union of the GDR

The GDR Writers' Union came into existence, initially as a subsection of the *Kulturbund*, under confusing circumstances. It was given the misleading title '*German* Writers' Union' (Deutscher Schriftstellerverband, retained until 1973, when it became, more accurately, the Schriftstellerverband der DDR) as a means of underlining the newly created GDR's claim that it was more committed to fostering cultural unity than the FRG. It also emerged, in June 1950, during what was called the *Second* **Writers' Congress**, since the GDR preferred to think of the all-German Congress of

October 1947 as its own first one. The Union was then granted its formal autonomy at the Third Writers' Congress, two years later, in a move which also reflected the declining significance of the *Kulturbund* as an umbrella organization for cultural affairs.

The executive's choice of Anna **Seghers** as its first President (a position she was to hold unchallenged between 1952 and 1978) gave the Union a degree of respectability outside the GDR, although her room for manœuvre was restricted from the outset by the way the balance within the executive was tilted towards SED loyalists, as exemplified by its first secretary, the poet Kurt Barthel ('Kuba'). By the beginning of 1953 a new monthly journal, *Neue Deutsche Literatur*, had been founded as the organ of the Union.

Membership of the Union was structured on a regional basis: a branch was established in each of the GDR's administrative areas (see also **Bezirk (GDR)**), with its own executive and secretariat. Each branch thus had the power to determine which of its members attended each Writers' Congress as its delegates and thus became candidates for the central Union executive. The East Berlin branch attracted the largest and most sophisticated membership. It was also, as a result, the main forum for power struggles between critically-minded rank-and-file authors and the party bureaucracy.

Until the **Honecker** era conflicts within the Union tended to be resolved behind closed doors, for fear of giving ammunition to hostile West German media. The Basic Treaty signed between the two states in 1972 led, however, to a greater flow of information about its meetings, due both to the greater media access the Treaty permitted and to the greater willingness of writers to air their grievances in public, once the promises of cultural reform proved transitory. The mood of confrontation created by the **Biermann Affair** continued into the period of office of the Union's second President, Hermann **Kant** (from 1978–90), culminating in the meeting of the East Berlin branch in June 1979, when nine authors were expelled for their allegedly subversive activities. This action undermined the credibility of the Union as a body prepared to defend the interests of its members and led many of its best-known authors to boycott its activities thereafter, even though Kant maintained that he continued to mediate effectively on their behalf through the 1980s.

Further reading

Walther, J. (ed.) (1991) *Protokoll eines Tribunals: Die Ausschlüsse aus dem Schriftstellerverband 1979*, Reinbek bei Hamburg: Rowohlt (documentary record of the Writers' Union's darkest hour).

DENNIS TATE

Z

Zahl, Peter-Paul

b. 13 March 1944, Freiburg (Breisgau)

Writer and publisher

After an early printer's apprenticeship, in 1967 Zahl founded his own publishing house and printing studio in West Berlin. In 1974 Zahl was sentenced to prison for use of firearms; he was paroled in 1982. The episode formed the subject of a documentary report by Erich **Fried** and Helga M. **Novak** (see *Am Beispiel Peter-Paul Zahl: Eine Dokumentation*, 1976). He also worked in the theatre, and since 1985 has lived in Jamaica. He has written crime fiction including *Lauf um dein Leben* (Run for your Life) (1996), *Nichts wie weg* (Get Out as Fast as You Can) (1994) and *Der schöne Mann* (The Good-Looking Man) (1994).

JAMES KELLER

Zaisser, Wilhelm

b. 20 June 1893, Rotthausen (near Gelsenkirchen); d. 3 March 1958, (East) Berlin

GDR functionary

A political activist for the **KPD** in the 1920s and 1930s, Zaisser returned from Soviet emigration in 1947 and became head of the police force, and a year later Minister of the Interior, in Sachsen-Anhalt. In 1950 he became Minister for State Security in the GDR and a member of the **Politbüro**, but was removed from these posts in July 1953 after being accused, together with Rudolf **Herrnstadt**, of conspiring against the leadership of the **SED**. He was never rehabilitated.

PETER BARKER

ZDF

Zweites Deutsches Fernsehen (ZDF) (Second German Television) was the second terrestrial **television** service to be set up in the FRG. Unlike the 'first' television channel broadcast by the federally organized **ARD**, the ZDF is organized on a centralized basis, with its programmes being broadcast nationally from its headquarters in Mainz. True to its name, and in contrast to ARD, ZDF provides only a television service and no radio programmes.

The legal basis of ZDF is the ZDF Agreement of 31 August 1991, which was signed by united Germany's sixteen *Länder* and which stipulates that it is a self-governing, non-profit corporation under public law. However, it was created on 6 June 1961 by an inter-***Land*** treaty (*Staatsvertrag*) which was a direct result of a constitutional dispute between the federal government and the *Länder* over an attempt by Chancellor Konrad **Adenauer** to set up a Bonn-directed and commercial second national television channel. Four SPD-governed *Länder* took the federal government to the **Federal Constitutional Court**, which on 28 February 1961 gave its so-called 'First Television Ruling' ('*Erstes Fernsehurteil*'). According to this, the Adenauer government had offended against the constitutionally determined principle that cultural affairs, which included **broadcasting**, were the legislative competence of the *Länder* (a concept known as *Kulturhoheit*).

The new television service began transmissions on 1 April 1963. ZDF is now also a partner in two cable-distributed cultural satellite television channels, 3sat and ARTE, and in 1997 launched a children's channel with ARD. In the 1990s, ZDF (like ARD), saw its audience share reduced by competition with commercial channels (from 32.0 percent in 1989 to 14.7 percent in 1995).

The threefold supervisory and administrative structure of ZDF is based on federal and pluralistic principles and is similar to that found in other German public broadcasting stations. At the head is an *Intendant*, who is supervised and advised by the fourteen-member Administrative Council (*Verwaltungsrat*), which also oversees the station's financial affairs. The *Intendant*, like eight members of the Administrative Council, is elected by the seventy-seven members of the Television Council (Fernsehrat), the main role of which is to monitor programming. The membership of the two councils represents the interests of *Länder*, the federal government, and representatives of society ('socially relevant forces'). Council members are regularly subject to the influence and instructions of political parties and interest groups who meet regularly to discuss broadcasting policy.

For a long time, the ratio of ZDF's income from **advertising** and the licence fee was 40:60. This ratio changed significantly as a direct result of competition from commercial channels, and by 1997 it was 13:87. Cartoon figures known as '*Mainzelmännchen*' accompany ZDF's commercials and have become a popular symbol of the television station.

See also: constitution: FRG; federalism

Further reading

Humphreys, P.J. (1994) *Media and Media Policy in Germany. The Press and Broadcasting since 1945*, Oxford and Providence, RI: Berg (the most recent, English-language study examining ZDF within the broader media context).

Two of ZDF's own publications, *ZDF. German Television* (1994) and *ZDF. Zahlen Daten Fakten*

(1997), provide invaluable and accessible background information.

DAVID HEAD

Zeit, Die

Since 1947, this weekly journal of news and commentary, published in newspaper format, has occupied an important niche in the FRG. Situated on the liberal left, *Die Zeit* has maintained a cerebral tone that appeals primarily to intellectuals, professionals and the well-to-do. It played a prominent role in the ***Historikerstreit*** (historian's quarrel) of the late 1980s, publishing editorials and letters by Jürgen **Habermas** and his supporters. Published by Marion Gräfin **Dönhoff**, its editorial board includes former Chancellor Helmut **Schmidt**. More than any other West German journal, *Die Zeit* reported on the GDR prior to 1989. Its failure to establish a reliable readership in the new eastern states following unification, however, has led to a decline in market share.

See also: *Feuilleton*; newspapers

MICHAEL R. HAYSE

Zero Group

Activities of the Zero Group (1958–66) centred around Günther **Uecker**, Heinz **Mack** and Otto **Piene**, involving close collaboration with leading European artists like Yves Klein and Lucio Fontana. Coupling a keen sense of self-promotion through spectacular activities with a vision of art released into life, Zero introduced a radically enlarged conception of art to Germany. Reacting against the subjectivism of abstract expressionism, the Zero Group aimed for increased sensibility in human perception, working with monochrome or mechanically-structured surfaces, light and kineticism. Their projects and aesthetics were deeply affected by the technological optimism of the dawning space age, and moved, equally, by utopian visions and spiritual aspirations.

DANIEL KOEP

Ziewer, Christian

b. 1 April 1941, Danzig (now Gdańsk, Poland)

Filmmaker

Ziewer studied electrical engineering, social history and philosophy before making his first film in 1967. He was the leading feature filmmaker of the short-lived but hotly debated genre of politically engaged *Arbeiterfilme* ('worker films') in the FRG during the early 1970s. *Dear Mother, I'm Fine* (*Liebe Mutter, mir geht es gut*, 1971), *Snowdrops Bloom in September* (*Schneeglöckchen blühn im September*, 1974) and *Walking Tall* (*Der aufrechte Gang*, 1976), all funded by WDR (Westdeutscher Rundfunk), address the difficulties and benefits of solidarity amongst different groups of workers in a meticulously researched, naturalistic style.

See also: New German Cinema

MARTIN BRADY

Zimmermann, Bernd Alois

b. 20 March 1918, Bliesheim (near Cologne); d. 10 August 1970, Königs-dorf (near Cologne)

Composer

Though his studies in philology and music were interrupted by wartime military service, Zimmermann emerged in the late 1940s as a challenging and original figure. The hugely complex opera *Die Soldaten* (1958–64) best represents his pluralist philosophy of art in which the musics of all periods coexist within a simultaneous time-frame. The result can be a dazzling collage of quotation and original music, juxtaposing centuries with bewildering dexterity.

BEATRICE HARPER

Zinnemann, Fred

b. 29 April 1907, Vienna; d. 14 March 1997 London

Filmmaker

A consummate craftsman who endowed his work with meticulous attention to detail, Zinnemann possessed a penchant for realism and brilliant casting. He began his career in Germany as production assistant on *Menschen am Sonntag* (People on Sundays) (1929) and *Westfront 1918*. He was exiled to Hollywood in 1932. The Berlin Film Festival dedicated a retrospective to him in 1986, after he had directed twenty-two features, nineteen shorts and won three Oscars. *High Noon* (1952) was one of the first twenty-five American film classics chosen in 1989 for the National Film Registry. *From Here to Eternity* (1953) brought him his first Oscar for feature directing.

UTE LISCHKE-McNAB

zoological gardens

Although penned animal galleries and travelling menageries date back to ancient Asian, Greek and Roman times and the animal spectacles of renaissance fairs, Germany's largest zoos today, the Berlin Zoological Garden (1844), the Frankfurt Zoological Garden (1858), the Hellabrunn Zoo in Munich (1913), and Europe's oldest zoo, Schön-brunn Zoo in Vienna (1742), evolved from royal court menageries of the sixteenth and seventeenth centuries. While colonialist expansion and natural history broadened zoo collections to include a greater variety of exotic species and shifted their function from mere display to public education, German zoos today owe much of their recreative function to the Hagenbeck Zoo (1907) outside Hamburg, where Carl Hagenbeck introduced open animal parks, petting zoos, and landscaped panoramas.

See also: popular culture

Further reading

Ham, J. and Senior, M. (eds) (1997) *Animal Acts:*

Configuring the Human in Western History, New York: Routledge (a collection of essays on animality in western civilization).

JENNIFER HAM

Zuckmayer, Carl

b. 7 December 1896, Nackenheim (near Mainz); d. 18 January 1977, Visp (Switzerland)

Dramatist

Close to the anarchist expressionists in his opposition to WWI, Zuckmayer became well known as a dramatist in the 1920s. *Der Hauptmann von Köpenick* (The Captain of Köpenick) (1931), his classic satire on Prussian attitudes to authority, was filmed in 1932 and 1955. He worked for the theatre in Berlin with Max Reinhardt. In 1930 he wrote the screenplay for the film *The Blue Angel* based on the novel by Heinrich Mann. Banned by the Nazis he joined **Piscator** in his Dramatic Workshop in New York. His drama *The Devil's General* (*Des Teufels General*, 1946), examining ethical dilemmas confronting the military leadership in the Third Reich, was filmed in 1955. *Das kalte Licht* (The Cold Light) (1955) addressed the theme of atomic espionage.

MARGARET VALLANCE

Zweig, Arnold

b. 10 November 1887, Glogau (Silesia; now Głogow, Poland); d. 26 November 1968, (East) Berlin

Writer

Deeply influenced by the horrors of WWI, Zweig achieved world renown with his novel *Der Streit um den Sergeanten Grischa* (The Argument About Sergeant Grischa) (1927). The novels written during the 1930s depict the questioning of prevailing social values by artists and intellectuals. The anti-fascist 'social novel' was developed to its full potential in *Das Beil von Wandsbek* (The Axe of Wandsbeck) (1943). Zweig's post-war novels, *Die Feuerpause* (The Ceasefire) (1954) and *Die Zeit ist reif* (The Time is Ripe) (1957) depict the effects of war on the German middle classes.

MARGARET VALLANCE

Zwerenz, Gerhard

b. 3 June 1925, Gablenz bei Crim-mitschau (Saxony)

Writer

Zwerenz fought in WWII until he deserted to the Russians. He lived in the GDR until 1957 when his critical writing brought him into danger of being arrested, as was his friend Erich **Loest**, in the wake of the Hungarian Uprising. Author of over a hundred works, including the novel *Die Ehe der Maria Braun* (The Marriage of Maria Braun) (1979) (see also **Fassbinder, Rainer**), and a biography of Kurt Tucholsky, essays, political, erotic and humorous writings and poetry, Zwerenz continued to feel morally and intellectually involved with the GDR, though sceptical of all political ideology.

MARGARET VALLANCE

Index

Page numbers in **bold** indicate references for the main entry.